The Disability Studies Reader

D0224898

The Disability Studies Reader is the most comprehensive introduction to disability studies. Now in its third edition, it contains a wide range of seminal, cutting-edge, and classic articles in the field. The collection covers cultural studies, identity politics, literary criticism, sociology, philosophy, anthropology, the visual arts, gender, and race studies, as well as memoir, poetry, fiction, and prose non-fiction.

Lennard J. Davis is Distinguished Professor of Disability and Human Development, English, and Medical Education at the University of Illinois at Chicago. He is the author of, among other works, *Enforcing Normalcy: Disability, Deafness, and the Body; Bending Over Backwards: Disability, Dismodernism, and Other Difficult Positions; My Sense of Silence: Memoirs of a Childhood with Deafness;* and *Obsession: A History.*

ROUTLEDGE TITLES OF RELATED INTEREST

Reconstructing Motherhood and Disability in the Age of Perfect Babies by Gail Landsman

Feminist Theory Reader, Second Edition, edited by Carole McCann and Seung-kyung Kim

Global Gender Research, edited by Christine Bose and Minjeong Kim

Yes We Can?: White Racial Framing and the 2008 Presidential Campaign by Adia Harvey Wingfield and Joe R. Feagin

Racist America, Second Edition by Joe R. Feagin

Operation Gatekeeper and Beyond: The War On Illegals and the Remaking of the U.S.— Mexico Boundary by Joe Nevins

The Disability Studies Reader

Third Edition

**Edited by Lennard J. Davis
University of Illinois at Chicago**

Routledge
Taylor & Francis Group

NEW YORK AND LONDON

A Comprehensive set of test items for each reading is available to instructors
by e-mailing Routledge at saleshss@taylorandfrancis.com

First published 1997
by Routledge

Second edition published 2006
by Routledge

This edition published 2010
by Routledge
711 Third Avenue, 8th Floor,
New York, NY 10017, www.routledge.com

Simultaneously published in the UK
by Routledge
2 Park Square, Milton Park, Abingdon, Oxon OX14 4RN

Routledge is an imprint of the Taylor & Francis Group, an informa business

© 1997, 2006, 2010 Taylor & Francis

Typeset in Utopia by Swales & Willis Ltd, Exeter, Devon
Printed and bound in the United States of America on acid-free paper by Edwards Brothers, Inc.

Library of Congress Cataloging in Publication Data
The disability studies reader / edited by Lennard J. Davis.—3rd ed.
p. cm.
1. People with disabilities. 2. Sociology of disability. 3. Disability studies. I. Davis, Lennard J., 1949–
HV1568.D5696 2010
362.4—dc22
2009048680

ISBN 10: 0–415–87374–6 (hbk)
ISBN 10: 0–415–87376–2 (pbk)

ISBN 13: 978–0–415–87374–1 (hbk)
ISBN 13: 9780–415-87376–5 (pbk)

CONTENTS

PART III: STIGMA AND ILLNESS

PART IV: THEORIZING DISABILITY

PREFACE TO THE THIRD EDITION

Disability Studies is developing very rapidly as a discourse. In the first edition of this reader, I lamented the place of disability studies as the neglected category in the race, class, and gender mantra. In the second edition, I countermanded that assumption and said hopefully that I saw disability studies as on the rise. Now in the third edition, I can say that disability studies is definitely part of the academic world and civil society. When Barack Obama gave his acceptance speech to the throngs in Grant Park, we all duly noted his inclusion of people with disabilities as he said that his election was the answer to doubt about America's hope: "It's the answer spoken by young and old, rich and poor, Democrat and Republican, black, white, Latino, Asian, Native American, gay, straight, disabled and not disabled. . . ." In that last set of opposites, Obama echoed the new attention and concern for disability as an essential category—as essential as age, class, race, nationality, and sexual orientation.

The pace of disability scholarship and interest is picking up. There were ten years between the first and second edition of *The Disability Studies Reader*. Now, only four years have passed since the last edition hit the stands and already there are new areas that have been developing and in need of inclusion. This new edition will open up issues around globalization, postcoloniality, transgender, cognitive and affective disorders, identity politics, autism, cochlear implants, public art, visuality, music, and other areas of note. As an anthology, the book is a snapshot of a moment in a discourse that is getting more complex and more elaborated. Disability studies is at this moment on a par with women and gender studies, GLBT studies, and other area and identity studies. In that sense it is a vital part of our collective knowledge, and now we can say without exaggeration that to be ignorant of disability studies is simply to be ignorant.

I hope that this edition will be even more informative than the previous one. Routledge's market research has helped to determine which articles were being read and used the most and the least, and so, in reaction to that information I have tried to accentuate the positive and cull, where needed, to suit the needs of potential readers and users of this text. I do hope that when we decide on future editions of this text, some of the excellent scholars whose work had to be forgone this time will make repeat appearances.

I have tried to keep a balance between historically relevant works in disability studies and newer cutting-edge ones. It is important to hold onto the foundational texts of disability studies in the humanities, as well as to keep up with current trends. Some essays like Erving Goffman's on "stigma" have been cut, but I think it's important to recognize that when I included them in the first edition, they served to legitimize the fledgling field of disability studies. Goffman may have been influential in the early days of disability studies, but now disability scholars themselves are redefining stigma in ways uniquely suited to our own discussion.

One particular note of regret is that some readers had suggested, and I had hoped for, an electronic edition to make the book more accessible. It is an access issue and a civil rights issue when books are not made available in electronic form. We explored that option and Routledge agreed to put out such an edition, but as it turned out the price of electronic permission fees proved prohibitive when added to the normal print fees. It is relatively easy to produce an electronic version as long as the author or the press owns the copyright to the work. My two last books, for example, have print and electronic versions. But the problem comes in doing an anthology like this in which many of the classic disability works have necessarily been previously published by a wide variety of presses and require reprint permission and the accompanying fees, which are much higher for electronic rights than simply print rights. Many publishers charge double the reprint permission fee for these combined rights. I do deeply regret the unavailability of this option for this edition of *The Disability Studies Reader*. We all need to organize around the issue of how to encourage publishers to reduce their electronic permission fees, particularly for texts that have disability content and would tend to be used by disabled readers.

We've made the edition more teacher and classroom friendly by including brief descriptions of the essays in the Table of Contents and by providing a set of test or study questions for each essay. These questions can be used by teachers in preparing and administering their courses or can be provided to students as a means of giving them a better grasp of the issues and complexities of each essay. Instructors can obtain the questions by e-mailing Routledge at saleshss@taylorandfrancis.com.

This edition would have been utterly impossible to edit without the help of my research assistant Cynthia Barounis, who is so much more organized than I will ever be. Her assistance as well as counsel are reflected in this work. Steve Rutter of Routledge and his assistant Leah Babb-Rosenfeld were very good at keeping us on target while remaining flexible and supportive. I would also like to thank the instructors who reviewed the second edition of the book: Stacey Moran at UC Berkeley, Lisa Cunningham at St. John Fisher College, Lynn Rose at Truman State, Megan Conway at the University of Hawaii, Anna Kirkland at the University of Michigan, Elizabeth Wheeler at the University of Oregon, and Phillip Thurtle at the University of Washington. But most of all, I would like to thank the many members of the disability studies community who gave me suggestions and support; and very special thanks to the many scholars who sent me their work for consideration. Had I world and time enough (and funding) I would have included much more of what was sent me. The work that was not published this time around could easily have been assembled into an entirely other excellent reader. This efflorescence of productivity and quality is yet another sign of the ongoing burgeoning of disability studies.

PART I

*H*istorical Perspectives

CHAPTER 1

Constructing Normalcy

Lennard J. Davis

If such a thing as a psycho-analysis of today's prototypical culture were possible . . . such an investigation would needs show the sickness proper to the time to consist precisely in normality.
— Theodore Adorno, *Minima Moralia*

We live in a world of norms. Each of us endeavors to be normal or else deliberately tries to avoid that state. We consider what the average person does, thinks, earns, or consumes. We rank our intelligence, our cholesterol level, our weight, height, sex drive, bodily dimensions along some conceptual line from subnormal to above-average. We consume a minimum daily balance of vitamins and nutrients based on what an average human should consume. Our children are ranked in school and tested to determine where they fit into a normal curve of learning, of intelligence. Doctors measure and weigh them to see if they are above or below average on the height and weight curves. There is probably no area of contemporary life in which some idea of a norm, mean, or average has not been calculated.

To understand the disabled body, one must return to the concept of the norm, the normal body. So much of writing about disability has focused on the disabled person as the object of study, just as the study of race has focused on the person of color. But as with recent scholarship on race, which has turned its attention to whiteness, I would like to focus not so much on the construction of disability as on the construction of normalcy. I do this because the "problem" is not the person with disabilities; the problem is the way that normalcy is constructed to create the "problem" of the disabled person.

A common assumption would be that some concept of the norm must have always existed. After all, people seem to have an inherent desire to compare themselves to others. But the idea of a norm is less a condition of human nature than it is a feature of a certain kind of society. Recent work on the ancient Greeks, on preindustrial Europe, and on tribal peoples, for example, shows that disability was once regarded very differently from the way it is now. As we will see, the social process of disabling arrived with industrialization and with the set of practices and discourses that are linked to late eighteenth- and nineteenth-century notions of nationality, race, gender, criminality, sexual orientation, and so on.

I begin with the rather remarkable fact that the constellation of words describing this concept "normal," "normalcy," "normality," "norm," "average," "abnormal"— all entered the European languages rather late in human history. The word "normal" as "constituting, conforming to, not deviating or different from, the common type or standard, regular, usual" only enters the English language around 1840. (Previously, the word had meant "perpendicular"; the carpenter's square, called a "norm," provided the root meaning.) Likewise, the word "norm," in the modern sense, has only been in use since around 1855, and "normality" and "normalcy" appeared in 1849 and 1857, respectively. If the lexicographical information is relevant, it is possible to date the coming into consciousness in English of an idea of "the norm" over the period 1840–1860.

If we rethink our assumptions about the universality of the concept of the norm, what we might arrive at is the concept that preceded it: that of the "ideal," a word we find dating from the seventeenth century. Without making too simplistic a division in the historical chronotope, one can nevertheless try to imagine a world in which the hegemony of normalcy does not exist. Rather, what we have is the ideal body, as exemplified in the tradition of nude Venuses, for example. This idea presents a mytho-poetic body that is linked to that of the gods (in traditions in which the god's body is visualized). This divine body, then, this ideal body, is not attainable by a human. The notion of an ideal implies that, in this case, the human body as visualized in art or imagination must be composed from the ideal parts of living models. These models individually can never embody the ideal since an ideal, by definition, can never be found in this world. When ideal human bodies occur, they do so in mythology. So Venus or Helen of Troy, for example, would be the embodiment of female physical beauty.

The painting by François-André Vincent *Zeuxis Choosing as Models the Most Beautiful Girls of the Town of Crotona* (1789, Museum de Louvre, Paris) shows the Greek artist, as we are told by Pliny, lining up all the beautiful women of Crotona in order to select in each her ideal feature or body part and combine these into the ideal figure of Aphrodite, herself an ideal of beauty. One young woman provides a face and another her breasts. Classical painting and sculpture tend to idealize the body, evening out any particularity. The central point here is that in a culture with an ideal form of the body, all members of the population are below the ideal. No one young lady of Crotona can be the ideal. By definition, one can never have an ideal body. There is in such societies no demand that populations have bodies that conform to the ideal.

By contrast, the *grotesque* as a visual form was inversely related to the concept of the ideal and its corollary that all bodies are in some sense disabled. In that mode, the grotesque is a signifier of the people, of common life. As Bakhtin, Stallybrass and White, and others have shown, the use of the grotesque had a life-affirming transgressive quality in its inversion of the political hierarchy. However, the grotesque was not equivalent to the disabled, since, for example, it is impossible to think of people with disabilities now being used as architectural decorations as the grotesque were on the façades of cathedrals throughout Europe. The grotesque permeated culture and signified common humanity, whereas the disabled body, a later concept, was formulated as by definition excluded from culture, society, the norm.

If the concept of the norm or average enters European culture, or at least the European languages, only in the nineteenth century, one has to ask what is the cause of this conceptualization? One of the logical places to turn in trying to understand concepts like "norm" and "average" is that branch of knowledge known as statistics. Statistics begins in the early modern period as "political arithmetic"—a use of data for "promotion of sound, well-informed state policy" (Porter 1986, 18). The word *statistik* was first used in 1749 by Gottfried Achenwall, in the context of compiling information about the state. The concept migrated somewhat from the state to the body when Bisset Hawkins defined medical statistics in 1829 as "the application of numbers to illustrate the natural history of health and disease" (cited in Porter, 1986, 24). In France, statistics were mainly used in the area of public health in the early nineteenth century. The connection between the body and industry is tellingly revealed in the fact that the leading members of the first British statistical societies formed in the 1830s and 1840s were industrialists or had close ties to industry (ibid., 32).

It was the French statistician Adolphe Quetelet (1796–1847) who contributed the most to a generalized notion of the normal as an imperative. He noticed that the "law of error," used by astronomers to locate a star by plotting all the sightings and then averaging the errors, could be equally applied to the distribution of human features such as height and weight. He then took a further step of formulating the concept of "l'homme moyen" or the average man. Quetelet maintained that this abstract human was the average of all human attributes in a given country. For the average man, Quetelet wrote in 1835, "all things will occur in conformity with the mean results obtained for a society. If one seeks to establish, in some way, the basis of a social physics, it is he whom one should consider . . ." (cited in ibid., 53). Quetelet's average man was a combination of *l'homme moyen physique and l'homme moyen morale*, both a physically average and a morally average construct.

The social implications of this idea are central. In formulating the idea of *l'homme moyen*, Quetelet is also providing a justification for *les classes moyens*. With bourgeois hegemony comes scientific justification for moderation and middle-class

ideology. The average man, the body of the man in the middle, becomes the exemplar of the middle way of life. Quetelet was apparently influenced by the philosopher Victor Cousin in developing an analogy between the notion of an average man and the *juste milieu*. This term was associated with Louis Philippe's July monarchy—a concept that melded bourgeois hegemony with the constitutional monarchy and celebrated moderation and middleness (ibid., 101). In England too, the middle class as the middle way or mean had been searching for a scientific justification. The statement in *Robinson Crusoe* in which Robinson's father extols middle-class life as a kind of norm is a good example of this ideology:

> the middle Station had the fewest Disasters, and was not expos'd to so many Vicissitudes as the higher or lower Part of Mankind; nay, they were not subjected to so many Distempers and Uneasiness either of Body or Mind, as those were who, by vicious Living, Luxury and Extravagancies on one Hand, or by hard Labour, Want of Necessaries, and mean or insufficient Diet on the other Hand, bring Distempers upon themselves by the natural consequences of their Way of Living; That the middle Station of Life was calculated for all kinds of Vertues and all kinds of Enjoyments; that Peace and Plenty were the Hand-maids of a middle Fortune; that Temperance, Moderation, Quietness, Health, Society, all agreeable Diversions, and all desirable Pleasures, were the Blessings attending the middle Station of Life.
> (Defoe 1975, 6)

Statements of ideology of this kind saw the bourgeoisie as rationally placed in the mean position in the great order of things. This ideology can be seen as developing the kind of science that would then justify the notion of a norm.[1]

With such thinking, the average then becomes paradoxically a kind of ideal, a position devoutly to be wished. As Quetelet wrote, "an individual who epitomized in himself, at a given time, all the qualities of the average man, would represent at once all the greatness, beauty and goodness of that being" (cited in Porter 1986, 102). Such an average person might indeed be a literary character like Robinson Crusoe. Furthermore, one must observe that Quetelet meant this hegemony of the middle to apply not only to moral qualities but to the body as well. He wrote: "deviations more or less great from the mean have constituted [for artists] ugliness in body as well as vice in morals and a state of sickness with regard to the constitution" (ibid., 103). Here Zeuxis's notion of physical beauty as an exceptional ideal becomes transformed into beauty as the average.

Quetelet foresaw a kind of Utopia of the norm associated with progress, just as Marx foresaw a Utopia of the norm in so far as wealth and production is concerned.

> one of the principal acts of civilization is to compress more and more the limits within which the different elements relative to man oscillate. The more that enlightenment is propagated, the more will deviations from the mean diminish. . . . The perfectibility of the human species is derived as a necessary consequence of all our investigations. Defects and monstrosities disappear more and more from the body.
>
> (ibid., 104)

This concept of the average, as applied to the concept of the human, was used not only by statisticians but even by the likes of Marx. Marx actually cites Quetelet's notion of the average man in a discussion of the labor theory of value. We can see in retrospect that one of the most powerful ideas of Marx—the notion of labor value or average wages—in many ways is based on the idea of the worker constructed as an average worker. As Marx writes:

> Any average magnitude, however, is merely the average of a number of separate magnitudes all of one kind, but differing as to quantity. In every industry, each individual labourer, be he Peter or Paul, differs from the average labourer. These individual differences, or "errors" as they are called in mathematics, compensate one another and vanish, whenever a certain minimum number of workmen are employed together.
>
> (Marx 1970, 323)

So for Marx one can divide the collective work day of a large number of workers and come up with "one day of average social labor" (ibid., 323). As Quetelet had come up with an average man, so Marx postulates an average worker, and from that draws conclusions about the relationship between an average and the extremes of wealth and poverty that are found in society. Thus Marx develops his crucial concept of "abstract labor."

We tend not to thing of progressives like Marx as tied up with a movement led by businessmen, but it is equally true that Marx is unimaginable without a tendency to contemplate average humans and think about their abstract relation to work, wages, and so on. In this sense, Marx is very much in step with the movement of normalizing the body and the individual. In addition, Marxist thought encourages us toward an enforcing of normalcy in the sense that the deviations in society, in terms of the distribution of wealth for example, must be minimized.

The concept of a norm, unlike that of an ideal, implies that the majority of the population must or should somehow be part of the norm. The norm pins down that majority of the population that falls under the arch of the standard bell-shaped curve. This curve, the graph of an exponential function, that was known variously as the astronomer's "error law," the "normal distribution," the "Gaussian density function," or simply "the bell curve," became in its own way a symbol of the tyranny of the norm. Any bell curve will always have at its extremities those characteristics that deviate from the norm. So, with the concept of the norm comes the concept of deviations or extremes. When we think of bodies, in a society where the concept of the norm is operative, then people with disabilities will be thought of as deviants. This, as we have seen, is in contrast to societies with the concept of an ideal, in which all people have a non-ideal status.[2]

In England, there was an official and unofficial burst of interest in statistics during the 1830s. A statistical office was set up at the Board of Trade in 1832, and the General Register Office was created in 1837 to collect vital statistics. All of this interest in numbers concerning the state was a consequence of the Reform Act of 1832, the Factory Act of 1833, and the Poor Law of 1834. The country was being monitored and the poor were being surveiled. Private groups followed, and in 1833 a statistical section of the British Association for the Advancement of Science was formed in which Quetelet as well as Malthus participated. In the following year Malthus, Charles Babbage, and others founded the Statistical Society of London. The Royal London Statistical Society was founded in 1835.

The use of statistics began an important movement, and there is a telling connection for the purposes of this book between the founders of statistics and their larger intentions. The rather amazing fact is that almost all the early statisticians had one thing in common: they were eugenicists. The same is true of key figures in the movement: Sir Francis Galton, Karl Pearson, and R. A. Fisher.[3] While this coincidence seems almost too striking to be true, we must remember that there is a real connection between figuring the statistical measure of humans and then hoping to improve humans so that deviations from the norm diminish—as someone like Quetelet had suggested. Statistics is bound up with eugenics because the central insight of statistics is the idea that a population can be normed. An important consequence of the idea of the norm is that it divides the total population into standard and nonstandard subpopulations. The next step in conceiving of the population as norm and non-norm is for the state to attempt to norm the nonstandard—the aim of eugenics. Of course such an activity is profoundly paradoxical since the inviolable rule of statistics is that all phenomena will always conform to a bell curve. So norming the non-normal is an activity as problematic as untying the Gordian knot.

MacKenzie asserts that it is not so much that Galton's statistics made possible eugenics but rather that "the needs of eugenics in large part determined the content of Galton's statistical theory" (1981, 52). In any case, a symbiotic relationship exists between statistical science and eugenic concerns. Both bring into society the concept of a norm, particularly a normal body, and thus in effect create the concept of the disabled body.

It is also worth noting the interesting triangulation of eugenicist interests. On the one hand Sir Francis Galton was cousin to Charles Darwin, whose notion of the evolutionary advantage of the fittest lays the foundation for eugenics and also for the idea of a perfectible body undergoing progressive improvement. As one scholar has put it, "Eugenics was in reality applied biology based on the central biological theory of the day, namely the Darwinian theory of evolution" (Farrall 1985, 55). Darwin's ideas serve to place disabled people along the wayside as evolutionary defectives to be surpassed by natural selection. So, eugenics became obsessed with the elimination of "defectives," a category which included the "feebleminded," the deaf, the blind, the physically defective, and so on.

In a related discourse, Galton created the modern system of fingerprinting for personal identification. Galton's interest came out of a desire to show that certain physical traits could be inherited. As he wrote:

one of the inducements to making these inquiries into personal identification has been to discover independent features suitable for hereditary investigation. . . . it is not improbable, and worth taking pains to inquire whether each person may not carry visibly about his body undeniable evidence of his parentage and near kinships.

(cited in MacKenzie 1981, 65)

Fingerprinting was seen as a physical mark of parentage, a kind of serial number written on the body. But further, one can say that the notion of fingerprinting pushes forward the idea that the human body is standardized and contains a serial number, as it were, embedded in its corporeality. (Later technological innovations will reveal this fingerprint to be embedded at the genetic level.) Thus the body has an identity that coincides with its essence and cannot be altered by moral, artistic, or human will. This indelibility of corporeal identity only furthers the mark placed on the body by other physical qualities—intelligence, height, reaction time. By this logic, the person enters into an identical relationship with the body, the body forms the identity, and the identity is unchangeable and indelible as one's place on the normal curve. For our purposes, then, this fingerprinting of the body means that the marks of physical difference become synonymous with the identity of the person.

Finally, Galton is linked to that major figure connected with the discourse of disability in the nineteenth century—Alexander Graham Bell. In 1883, the same year that the term "eugenics" was coined by Galton, Bell delivered his eugenicist speech *Memoir upon the Formation of a Deaf Variety of the Human Race*, warning of the "tendency among deaf-mutes to select deaf-mutes as their partners in marriage" (1969, 19) with the dire consequence that a race of deaf people might be created. This echoing of Dr. Frankenstein's fear that his monster might mate and produce a race of monsters emphasizes the terror with which the "normal" beholds the differently abled.[4] Noting how the various interests come together in Galton, we can see evolution, fingerprinting, and the attempt to control the reproductive rights of the deaf as all pointing to a conception of the body as perfectible but only when subject to the necessary control of the eugenicists. The identity of people becomes defined by irrepressible identificatory physical qualities that can be measured. Deviance from the norm can be identified and indeed criminalized, particularly in the sense that fingerprints came to be associated with identifying deviants who wished to hide their identities.

Galton made significant changes in statistical theory that created the concept of the norm. He took what had been called "error theory," a technique by which astronomers attempted to show that one could locate a star by taking into account the variety of sightings. The sightings, all of which could not be correct, if plotted would fall into a bell curve, with most sightings falling into the center, that is to say, the correct location of the star. The errors would fall to the sides of the bell curve. Galton's contribution to statistics was to change the name of the curve from "the law of frequency of error" or "error curve," the term used by Quetelet, to the "normal distribution" curve.

The significance of these changes relates directly to Galton's eugenicist interests. In an "error curve" the extremes of the curve are the most mistaken in accuracy. But if one is looking at human traits, then the extremes, particularly what Galton saw as positive extremes—tallness, high intelligence, ambitiousness, strength, fertility—would have to be seen as errors. Rather than "errors" Galton wanted to think of the extremes as distributions of a trait. As MacKenzie notes:

Thus there was a gradual transition from use of the term "probable error" to the term "standard deviation" (which is free of the implication that a deviation is in any sense an error), and from the term "law of error" to the term "normal distribution."

(1981, 59)

But even without the idea of error, Galton still faced the problem that in a normal distribution curve that graphed height, for example, both tallness and shortness would be seen as extremes in a continuum where average stature would be the norm. The problem for Galton was that, given his desire to perfect the human race, or at least its British segment, tallness was preferable to shortness. How could both extremes be considered equally deviant from the norm? So Galton substituted the idea of ranking for the concept of averaging. That is, he changed the way one might look at the curve from one that used the mean to one that used the median—a significant change in thinking eugenically.

If a strait, say intelligence, is considered by its average, then the majority of people would determine what intelligence should be—and intelligence would be defined by the mediocre middle. Galton, wanting to avoid the middling of desired traits, would prefer to think of intelligence in ranked order. Although high intelligence in a normal distribution would simply be an extreme, under a ranked system it would become the highest ranked trait. Galton divided his curve into quartiles, so that he was able to emphasize ranked orders of intelligence, as we would say that someone was in the first quartile in intelligence (low intelligence) or the fourth quartile (high intelligence). Galton's work led directly to current "intelligence quotient" (IQ) and scholastic achievement tests. In fact, Galton revised Gauss's bell curve to show the superiority of the desired trait (for example, high intelligence). He created what he called an "ogive," which is arranged in quartiles with an ascending curve that features the desired trait as "higher" than the undesirable deviation. As Stigler notes:

> If a hundred individuals' talents were ordered, each could be assigned the numerical value corresponding to its percentile in the curve of "deviations from an average": the middlemost (or median) talent had value 0 (representing mediocrity), an individual at the upper quartile was assigned the value 1 (representing one probable error above mediocrity), and so on.
>
> (1986, 271)

What these revisions by Galton signify is an attempt to redefine the concept of the "ideal" in relation to the general population. First, the application of the idea of a norm to the human body creates the idea of deviance or a "deviant" body. Second, the idea of a norm pushes the normal variation of the body through a stricter template guiding the way the body "should" be. Third, the revision of the "normal curve of distribution" into quartiles, ranked in order, and so on, creates a new kind of "ideal." This statistical ideal is unlike the classical ideal which contains no imperative to be the ideal. The new ideal of ranked order is powered by the imperative of the norm, and then is supplemented by the notion of progress, human perfectibility, and the elimination of deviance, to create a dominating, hegemonic vision of what the human body should be.

While we tend to associate eugenics with a Nazi-like racial supremacy, it is important to realize that eugenics was not the trade of a fringe group of rightwing, fascist maniacs. Rather, it became the common practice of many, if not most, European and American citizens. When Marx used Quetelet's idea of the average in his formulation of average wage and abstract labor, socialists as well as others embraced eugenic claims, seeing in the perfectibility of the human body a Utopian hope for social improvement. Once people allowed that there were norms and ranks in human physiology, then the idea that we might want to, for example, increase the intelligence of humans, or decrease birth defects, did not seem so farfetched. These ideas were widely influential: in the ensuing years the leaders of the socialist Fabian Society, including Beatrice and Sidney Webb, George Bernard Shaw and H. G. Wells, were among the eugenicists (MacKenzie, 1981, 34). The influence of eugenicist ideas persisted well into the twentieth century, so that someone like Emma Goldman could write that unless birth control was encouraged, the state would "legally encourage the increase of paupers, syphilitics, epileptics, dipsomaniacs, cripples, criminals, and degenerates" (Kevles 1985, 90).

The problem for people with disabilities was that eugenicists tended to group together all allegedly "undesirable" traits. So, for example, criminals, the poor, and people with disabilities might be mentioned in the same breath. Take Karl Pearson, a leading figure in the eugenics movement, who defined the "unfit" as follows: "the habitual criminal, the professional tramp, the tuberculous, the insane, the mentally defective, the alcoholic, the diseased from birth or from excess" (cited in Kevles 1985, 33). In 1911, Pearson headed the Department of Applied Statistics, which included the Galton and Biometric Laboratories at University College in London. This department gathered eugenic information on the inheritance of physical and mental traits including "scientific, commercial, and legal ability, but also hermaphroditism, hemophilia, cleft palate, harelip, tuberculosis, diabetes, deaf-mutism, polydactyly (more than five fingers) or brachydactyly (stub fingers), insanity, and mental deficiency" (ibid., 38–9). Here again one sees a strange selection of disabilities merged with other types of human variations. All of these deviations from the norm were regarded in the long run as contributing to the disease of the nation. As one official in the Eugenics Record Office asserted:

the calculus of correlations is the sole rational and effective method for attacking . . . what makes for, and what mars national fitness. . . . The only way to keep a nation strong mentally and physically is to see that each new generation is derived chiefly from the fitter members of the generation before.

(ibid., 39–40)

The emphasis on nation and national fitness obviously plays into the metaphor of the body. If individual citizens are not fit, if they do not fit into the nation, then the national body will not be fit. Of course, such arguments are based on a false notion of the body politic—as if a hunchbacked citizenry would make a hunchbacked nation. Nevertheless, the eugenic notion that individual variations would accumulate into a composite national identity was a powerful one. This belief combined with an industrial mentality that saw workers as interchangeable and therefore sought to create a universal worker whose physical characteristics would be uniform, as would the result of their labors—a uniform product.

One of the central foci of eugenics was what was broadly called "feeble-mindedness."[5] This term included low intelligence, mental illness, and even "pauperism," since low income was equated with "relative inefficiency" (ibid., 46).[6] Likewise, certain ethnic groups were associated with feeble-mindedness and pauperism. Charles Davenport, an American eugenicist, thought that the influx of European immigrants would make the American population "darker in pigmentation, smaller in stature . . . more given to crimes of larceny, assault, murder, rape, and sex-immorality" (cited in ibid., 48). In his research, Davenport scrutinized the records of "prisons, hospitals, almshouses, and institutions for the mentally deficient, the deaf, the blind, and the insane" (ibid., 55).

The loose association between what we would now call disability and criminal activity, mental incompetence, sexual license, and so on established a legacy that people with disabilities are still having trouble living down. This equation was so strong that an American journalist writing in the early twentieth century could celebrate "the inspiring, the wonderful, message of the new heredity" as opposed to the sorrow of bearing children who were "diseased or crippled or depraved" (ibid., 67). The conflation of disability with depravity expressed itself in the formulation "defective class." As the president of the University of Wisconsin declared after World War One, "we know enough about eugenics so that if the knowledge were applied, the defective classes would disappear within a generation" (ibid., 68). And it must be reiterated that the eugenics movement was not stocked with eccentrics. Davenport was funded by Averell Harriman's sister Mary Harriman, as well as John D. Rockefeller, Prime Ministers A. J. Balfour, Neville Chamberlain, and Winston Churchill, President Theodore Roosevelt, H. G. Wells, John Maynard Keynes, and H. J. Laski, among many others, were members of eugenicist organizations. Francis Galton was knighted in 1909 for his work, and in 1910 he received the Copley Medal, the Royal Society's highest honor. A Galton Society met regularly in the American Museum of Natural History in New York City. In 1911 the Oxford University Union moved approval of the main principles behind eugenics by a vote of almost two to one. In Kansas, the 1920 state fair held a contest for "fitter families" based on their eugenic family histories, administered intelligence tests, medical examinations, and venereal disease tests. A brochure for the contest noted about the awards, "this trophy and medal are worth more than livestock sweepstakes. . . . For health is wealth and a sound mind in a sound body is the most priceless of human possessions" (ibid., 62).

In England, bills were introduced in Parliament to control mentally disabled people, and in 1933 the prestigious scientific magazine *Nature* approved the Nazis' proposal of a bill for "the avoidance of inherited diseases in posterity" by sterilizing the disabled. The magazine editorial said "the Bill, as it reads, will command the appreciative attention of all who are interested in the controlled and deliberate improvement of human stock." The list of disabilities for which sterilization would be appropriate were "congenital feeblemindedness, manic depressive insanity, schizophrenia, hereditary epilepsy, hereditary St. Vitus's dance, hereditary blindness and deafness, hereditary bodily malformation and habitual alcoholism" (cited in MacKenzie 1981, 44). We have largely forgotten that what Hitler did in developing a hideous policy of eugenics was just to implement the theories of the British and American eugenicists. Hitler's statement in *Mein Kampf* that "the struggle for the daily livelihood [between species] leaves behind, in the ruck, everything that is weak or diseased or wavering" (cited in Blacker 1952, 143) is not qualitatively different from any of the many similar statements we have seen before. And even the conclusions Hitler draws are not very different from those of the likes of Galton, Bell, and others.

> In this matter, the State must assert itself as the trustee of a millennial future. . . . In order to fulfill this duty in a practical manner, the State will have to avail itself of modern medical discoveries. It must proclaim as unfit for procreation all those who are afflicted with some visible hereditary disease or are the carriers of it; and practical measures must be adopted to have such people rendered sterile.
> (cited in Blacker 1952, 144)

One might want to add here a set of speculations about Sigmund Freud. His work was made especially possible by the idea of the normal. It shows us that sexuality, long relegated to the trash heap of human instincts, was in fact normal and that perversion was simply a displacement of "normal" sexual interest. Dreams which behave in a manner unknown or only exceptionally permissible in normal mental life" (Freud 1977, 297) are seen as actually normal and "the dreams of neurotics do not differ in any important respect from those of normal people" (ibid., 456). In fact, it is hard to imagine the existence of psychoanalysis without the concept of normalcy. Indeed, one of the core principles behind psychoanalysis was that we each start out with normal psychosexual development and neurotics become abnormal through a problem in that normal development. As Freud put it: "if the *vita sexualis* is normal, there can be no neurosis" (ibid., 386). Psychoanalysis can correct that mistake and bring patients back to their normal selves. Although I cannot go into a close analysis of Freud's work here, it is instructive to think of the ways in which Freud is producing a eugenics of the mind—creating the concepts of normal sexuality, normal function, and then contrasting them with the perverse, abnormal, pathological, and even criminal. Indeed, one of the major critiques of Freud's work now centers on his assumption about what constitutes normal sexuality and sexual development for women and men.

The first depiction in literature of an attempt to norm an individual member of the population occurred in the 1850s during the development of the idea of the normal body. In Flaubert's *Madame Bovary*, Charles Bovary is influenced by Homais, the self-serving pharmacist, and Emma to perform a trendy operation that would correct the club foot of Hippolyte, the stableboy of the local inn. This corrective operation is seen as "new" and related to "progress" (Flaubert 1965, 125). Hippolyte is assailed with reasons why he should alter his foot. He is told, it "must considerably interfere with the proper performance of your work" (ibid., 126). And in addition to redefining him in terms of his ability to carry out work, Homais adds: "Think what would have happened if you had been called into the 'army, and had to fight under our national banner!" (ibid., 126). So national interests and again productivity are emphasized. But Hippolyte has been doing fine in his job as stableboy; his disability has not interfered with his performance in the community under traditional standards. In fact, Hippolyte seems to use his club foot to his advantage, as the narrator notes:

> But on the equine foot, wide indeed as a horse's hoof, with is horny skin, and large toes, whose black nails resembled the nails of a horse shoe, the cripple ran about like a deer from morn till night. He was constantly to be seen on the Square, jumping round the carts, thrusting his limping foot forwards. He seemed even stronger on that leg than the other. By dint of hard service it had acquired, as it were, moral qualities of patience and energy; and when he was given some heavy work to do, he would support himself on it in preference to the sound one.
>
> (ibid., 126)

Hippolyte's disability is in fact an ability, one which he relies on, and from which he gets extra horsepower, as it were. But although Hippolyte is more than capable, the operation must be performed to bring him back to the human and away from the equine, which the first syllable of his name suggests. To have a disability is to be an animal, to be part of the Other.

A newspaper article appears after the operation's apparent initial success, praising the spirit of progress. The article envisages Hippolyte's welcome back into the human community.

> Everything tends to show that his convalescence will be brief; and who knows if, at our next village festivity we shall not see our good Hippolyte appear in the midst of a bacchic dance, surrounded by a group of gay companions . . .
>
> (ibid., 128)

The article goes on to proclaim, "Hasn't the time come to cry out that the blind shall see, the deaf hear, the lame walk?" The imperative is clear: science will eradicate disability. However, by a touch of Flaubertian irony, Hippolyte's leg becomes gangrenous and has to be amputated. The older doctor who performs the operation lectures Charles about his attempt to norm this individual.

> This is what you get from listening to the fads from Paris! . . . We are practitioners; we cure people, and we wouldn't dream of operating on someone who is in perfect health. Straighten club feet! As if one could straighten club feet indeed! It is as if one wished to make a hunchback straight!
>
> (ibid., 131)

While Flaubert's work illustrates some of the points I have been making, it is important that we do no simply think of the novel as merely an example of how an historical development lodges within a particular text. Rather, I think there is a larger claim to be made about novels and norms.

While Flaubert may parody current ideas about normalcy in medicine, there is another sense in which the novel as a form promotes and symbolically produces normative structures. Indeed, the whole focus of *Madame Bovary* is on Emma's abnormality and Flaubert's abhorrence of normal life. If we accept that novels are a social practice that arose as part of the project of middle-class hegemony,[7] then we can see that the plot and character development of novels tend to pull toward the normative. For example, most characters in nineteenth-century novels are somewhat ordinary people who are put in abnormal circumstances, as opposed to the heroic characters who represent the ideal in earlier forms such as the epic.

If disability appears in a novel, it is rarely centrally represented. It is unusual for a main character to be a person with disabilities, although minor characters, like Tiny Tim, can be deformed in ways that arouse pity. In the case of Esther Summerson, who is scarred by smallpox, her scars are made virtually to disappear through the agency of love. On the other hand, as sufficient research has shown, more often than not villains tend to be physically abnormal: scarred, deformed, or mutilated.[8]

I am not saying simply that novels embody the prejudices of society toward people with disabilities. That is clearly a truism. Rather, I am asserting that the very structures on which the novel rests tend to be normative, ideologically emphasizing the universal quality of the central character whose normativity encourages us to identify with him or her.[9] Furthermore, the novel's goal is to reproduce, on some level, the semiologically normative signs surrounding the reader, that paradoxically help the reader to read those signs in the world as well as the text. Thus the middleness of life, the middleness of the material world, the middleness of the normal body, the middleness of a sexually gendered, ethnically middle world is created in symbolic form and then reproduced symbolically. This normativity in narrative will by definition create the abnormal, the Other, the disabled, the native, the colonized subject, and so on.

Even on the level of plot, one can see the implication of eugenic notions of normativity. The parentage of characters in novels plays a crucial role. Rather than being self-creating beings, characters in novels have deep biological debts to their forebears, even if the characters are orphans—or perhaps especially if they are orphans. The great Heliodoric plots of romance, in which lower-class characters are found actually to be noble, take a new turn in the novel. While nobility may be less important, characters nevertheless inherit bourgeois respectability, moral rectitude, and eventually money and position through their genetic connection. In the novelistic world of nature versus nurture, nature almost always wins out. Thus Oliver Twist will naturally bear the banner of bourgeois morality and linguistic normativity, even though he grows up in the workhouse. Oliver will always be normal, even in abnormal circumstances.[10]

A further development in the novel can be seen in Zola's works. Before Zola, for example in the work of Balzac, the author attempted to show how the inherently good character of a protagonist was affected by the material world. Thus we read of the journey of the soul, of everyman or everywoman, through a trying and corrupting world. But Zola's theory of the novel depends on the idea of inherited traits and biological determinism. As Zola wrote in *The Experimental Novel*:

> Determinism dominates everything. It is scientific investigation, it is experimental reasoning, which combats one by one the hypotheses of the idealists, and which replaces purely imaginary novels by novels of observation and experimentation.
>
> (1964, 18)

In this view, the author is a kind of scientist watching how humans, with their naturally inherited dispositions, interact with each other. As Zola wrote, his intention in the Rougon-Macquart series was to show how heredity would influence a family "making superhuman efforts but always failing because of its own nature and the influences upon it" (Zola 1993, viii). This series would be a study of the "singular effect of heredity" (ibid.). Zola mentions the work of Darwin and links his own novels to notions of how inherited traits interact in particular environments over time and to generalizations about human behavior:

> And this is what constitutes the experimental novel: to possess a knowledge of the mechanism of the phenomena inherent in man, to show the machinery of his intellectual and sensory manifestations, under the influence of heredity and environment, such as physiology shall give them to us.
>
> (Zola 1964, 21)

Clearly stating his debt to science, Zola says that "the experimental novel is a consequence of the scientific evolution of the century" (ibid., 23). The older novel, according to Zola, is composed of imaginary adventures while the new novel is "a report, nothing more" (ibid., 124). In being a report, the new novel rejects idealized characters in favor of the norm.

> These young girls so pure, these young men so loyal, represented to us in certain novels, do not belong to the earth. . . . We tell everything, we do not make a choice, neither do we idealize.
>
> (ibid., 127)

Zola's characters belong to "the earth." This commitment constitutes Zola's new realism, one based on the norm, the average, the inherited.

My point is that a disabilities studies consciousness can alter the way we see not just novels that have main characters who are disabled but any novel. In thinking through the issue of disability, I have come to see that almost any literary work will have some reference to the abnormal, to disability, and so on. I would explain this phenomenon as a result of the hegemony of normalcy. This normalcy must constantly be enforced in public venues (like the novel), must always be creating and bolstering its image by processing, comparing, constructing, deconstructing images of normalcy and the abnormal. In fact, once one begins to notice, there really is a rare novel that does not have some characters with disabilities—characters who are lame, tubercular, dying of AIDS, chronically ill, depressed, mentally ill, and so on.

Let me take the example of some novels by Joseph Conrad. I pick Conrad not because he is especially representative, but just because I happen to be teaching a course on Conrad. Although he is not remembered in any sense as a writer on disability, Conrad is a good test case, as it turns out, because he wrote during a period when eugenics had permeated British society and when Freud had begun to write about normal and abnormal psychology. Conrad, too, was somewhat influenced by Zola, particularly in *The Secret Agent*.

The first thing I noticed about Conrad's work is that metaphors of disability abound. Each book has numerous instances of phrases like the following selections from *Lord Jim*:

> a dance of lame, blind, mute thoughts—a whirl of awful cripples.
> (Conrad 1986, 114)

> [he] comported himself in that clatter as though he had been stone-deaf.
> (ibid., 183)

> there was nothing of the cripple about him.
> (ibid., 234)

> Her broken figure hovered in crippled little jumps . . .
> (ibid., 263)

> he was made blind and deaf and without pity . . .
> (ibid., 300)

> a blind belief in the righteousness of his will against all mankind . . .
> (ibid., 317)

> They were erring men whom suffering had made blind to right and wrong.
> (ibid., 333)

> you dismal cripples, you . . .
> (ibid., 340)

> unmoved like a deaf man . . .
> (ibid., 319)

These references are almost like tics, appearing at regular intervals. They tend to focus on deafness, blindness, dumbness, and lameness, and they tend to use these metaphors to represent limitations on normal morals, ethics, and of course language. While it is entirely possible to maintain that these figures of speech are hardly more than mere linguistic convention, I would argue that the very regularity of these occurrences speaks to a reflexive patrolling function in which the author continuously checks and notes instances of normalcy and instances of disability—right down to the linguistic level.

Conrad's emphasis on exotic locations can also be seen as related to the issue of normalcy. Indeed the whole conception of imperialism on which writers like Conrad depend is largely based on notions of race and ethnicity that are intricately tied up with eugenics, statistical proofs of intelligence, ability, and so on. And these in turn are part of the hegemony of normalcy. Conrad's exotic settings are highlighted in his novels for their deviance from European conceptions. The protagonists are skewed from European standards of normal behavior specifically because they have traveled from Europe to, for example, the South Seas or the Belgian Congo. And Conrad focuses on those characters who, because they are influenced by these abnormal environments, lose their "singleness of purpose" (which he frequently defines as an English trait) and on those who do not.

The use of phrenology, too, is linked to the patrolling of normalcy, through the construction of character. So, in *Heart of Darkness* for example, when Marlow is about to leave for Africa a doctor measures the dimensions of his skull to enable him to discern if any quantitative changes subsequently occur as a result of the colonial encounter. So many of the characters in novels are formed from the ableist cultural repertoire of normalized head, face, and body features that characteristically signify personal qualities. Thus in *The Secret Agent*, the corpulent, lazy body of Verloc indicates his moral sleaziness, and Stevie's large ears and head shape are explicitly seen by

Ossipon as characteristic of degeneracy and criminality as described in the theories of the nineteenth-century eugenic phrenologist Cesare Lombroso.

Stevie Conrad's most obviously disabled character, is a kind of center or focus of *The Secret Agent*. In a Zolaesque moment of insight, Ossipon sees Stevie's degeneracy as linked to his sister Winnie:

> he gazed scientifically at that woman, the sister of a degenerate, a degenerate herself—of a murdering type. He gazed at her and invoked Lombroso. . . . He gazed scientifically. He gazed at her cheeks, at her nose, at her eyes, at her ears . . . Bad! . . . Fatal!
> (Conrad 1968, 269)

This eugenic gaze that scrutinizes Winnie and Stevie is really only a recapitulation of the novelistic gaze that sees meaning in normative and nonnormative features. In fact, every member of the Verloc family has something "wrong" with them, including Winnie's mother who has trouble walking on her edematous legs. The moral turpitude and physical grimness of London is embodied in Verloc's inner circle. Michaelis, too, is obese and "wheezed as if deadened and oppressed by the layer of fat on his chest" (ibid., 73). Karl Yundt is toothless, gouty, and walks with a cane. Ossipon is racially abnormal having "crinkly yellow hair . . . a flattened nose and prominent mouth cast in the rough mould of the Negro type . . . [and] almond-shaped eyes [that] leered languidly over high cheek-bones" (ibid., 75)—all features indicating African and Asian qualities, particularly the cunning, opiated glance.

Stevie, the metaphoric central figure and sacrificial victim of the novel, is mentally delayed. His mental slowness becomes a metaphor for his radical innocence and childlike revulsion from cruelty. He is also, in his endless drawing of circles, seen as invoking "the symbolism of a mad art attempting the inconceivable" (ibid., 76). In this sense, his vision of the world is allied with that of Conrad, who himself could easily be described as embarked on the same project. Stevie is literally taken apart, not only by Ossipon's gaze and by that of the novelist, but centrally by the bungled explosion. His fragmented body[11] becomes a kind of symbol of the fragmentation that Conrad emphasizes throughout his opus and that the Professor recommends in his high-tech view of anarchism as based on the power of explosion and conflagration. Stevie becomes sensitized to the exploitation of workers by his encountering a coachman with a prosthetic hook for an arm, whose whipping of his horse causes Stevie anguish. The prosthetic arm appears sinister at first, particularly as a metonymic agent of the action of whipping. But the one-armed man explains: "'This ain't an easy world . . . 'Ard on 'osses, but dam' sight 'arder on poor chaps like me,' he wheezed just audibly" (ibid., 165). Stevie's radical innocence is most fittingly convinced by the man's appeal to class solidarity, so Stevie ultimately is blown up for the sins of all.

In *Under Western Eyes*, the issue of normalcy is first signaled in the author's Introduction. Conrad apologizes for Razumov's being "slightly abnormal" and explains away this deviation by citing a kind of personal sensitivity as well as a Russian temperament. In addition, Conrad says that although his characters may seem odd, "nobody is exhibited as a monster here" (Conrad 1957, 51). The mention of exhibition of monsters immediately alerts us to the issue of nineteenth-century freak shows and raises the point that by depicting "abnormal" people, the author might see his own work as a kind of display of freaks.[12] Finally, Conrad makes the point that all these "abnormal" characters "are not the product of the exceptional but of the general—of the normality of their place, and time, and race" (ibid., 51). The conjunction of race and normality also alerts us to eugenic aims. What Conrad can be seen as apologizing for is the normalizing (and abnormalizing) role of the novel that must take a group of nationals (Russians) and make them into the abnormal, non-European, nonnormal Other. Interestingly, Conrad refers to anarchists and autocrats both as "imbecile." The use of this word made current by eugenic testing also shows us how pervasive is the hegemony of normalcy.

Razumov's abnormality is referred to by the narrator, at one point, as being seen by a man looking at a mirror "formulating to himself reassuring excuses for his appearance marked by the taint of some insidious hereditary disease" (ibid., 220). What makes Razumov into the cipher he is to all concerned is his lack of a recognizable identity aside from his being a Russian. So when he arrives in Geneva, Razumov says to Peter Ivanovitch, the radical political philosopher, that he will never be "a mere blind tool" simply to be used (ibid., 231). His refusal to be a "blind tool" ends up, ironically, in Razumov being made deaf by Necator, who deliberately bursts his eardrums with blows to the head. The world becomes for Razumov "perfectly silent—soundless as shadows" (ibid., 339) and "a world of mutes. Silent men, moving, unheard . . ." (ibid., 340). For both Conrad and Razumov, deafness is the end of language, the end of discourse, the ultimate punishment that makes all the rest of the characters appear as if their words were useless anyway. As Necator says, "He shall never be any use as spy on any one. He won't talk, because he will never hear anything in his life—not a thing" (ibid., 341). After Razumov walks into the street and is run over by a car, he is described as "a hopeless cripple, and stone deaf with that" (ibid., 343). He dies from his disabilities, as if life were in fact impossible to survive under those conditions. Miss Haldin, in contrast, gains her meaning in life from these events and says, "my eyes are open at last and my hands are free now" (ibid., 345). These sets of arrangements play

an intimate part in the novel and show that disability looms before the writer as a *memento mori*. Normality has to protect itself by looking into the maw of disability and then recovering from that glance.

I am not claiming that this reading of some texts by Conrad is brilliant or definitive. But I do want to show that even in texts that do not appear to be about disability, the issue of normalcy is fully deployed. One can find in almost any novel, I would argue, a kind of surveying of the terrain of the body, an attention to difference—physical, mental, and national. This activity of consolidating the hegemony of normalcy is one that needs more attention, in addition to the kinds of work that have been done in locating the thematics of disability in literature.

What I have tried to show here is that the very term that permeates our contemporary life—the normal—is a configuration that arises in a particular historical moment. It is part of a notion of progress, of industrialization, and of ideological consolidation of the power of the bourgeoisie. The implications of the hegemony of normalcy are profound and extend into the very heart of cultural production. The novel form, that proliferator of ideology, is intricately connected with concepts of the norm. From the typicality of the central character, to the normalizing devices of plot to bring deviant characters back into the norms of society, to the normalizing coda of endings, the nineteenth- and twentieth-century novel promulgates and disburses notions of normalcy and by extension makes of physical differences ideological differences. Characters with disabilities are always marked with ideological meaning, as are moments of disease or accident that transform such characters. One of the tasks for a developing consciousness of disability issues is the attempt, then, to reverse the hegemony of the normal and to institute alternative ways of thinking about the abnormal.

NOTES

1. This thinking obviously is still alive and well. During the U.S. Presidential election of 1994, Newt Gingrich accused President Clinton of being "the enemy of normal Americans." When asked at a later date to clarify what he meant, he said his meaning was that "normal" meant "middle class" (*New York Times*, November 14, 1994, A17).

2. One wants to make sure that Aristotle's idea of the mean is not confused with the norm. The Aristotelian mean is a kind of fictional construct. Aristotle advocates that in choosing between personal traits, one should tend to chose between the extremes. He does not however think of the population as falling generally into that mean. The mean, for Aristotle, is more of heuristic device to assist in moral and ethical choices. In the sense of being a middle term or a middle way, it carries more of a spacial sense than does the term "average" or "norm."

3. This rather remarkable confluence between eugenics and statistics has been pointed out by Donald A. MacKenzie, but I do not believe his observations have had the impact they should.

4. See my *Enforcing Disability* Chapter Six for more on the novel *Frankenstein* and its relation to notions of disability.

5. Many twentieth century prejudices against the learning disabled come from this period. The founder of the intelligence test still in use, Alfred Binet, was a Galton acolyte. The American psychologist Henry H. Goddard used Binet's tests in America and turned the numbers into categories—"idiots" being those whose mental age was one or two, "imbeciles" ranged in mental age from three to seven. Goddard invented the term "moron" (which he took from the Greek for "dull" or "stupid") for those between eight and twelve. Pejorative terms like "moron" or "retarded" have by now found their way into common usage. (Kevles, 78) And even the term "mongoloid idiot" to describe a person with Down's syndrome was used as recently as 1970s not as a pejorative term but in medical texts as a diagnosis. [See Michael Bérubé's fascinating article "Life As We Know It" for more on this phenomenon of labelling.]

6. If this argument sounds strangely familiar, it is being repeated and promulgated in the neo-conservative book *The Bell Curve* which claims that poverty and intelligence are linked through inherited characteristics.

7. This assumption is based on my previous works—*Factual Fictions: Origins of the English Novel and Resisting Novels: Fiction and Ideology*—as well as the cumulative body of writing about the relationship between capitalism, material life, culture, and fiction. The work of Raymond Wiliams, Terry Eagleton, Nancy Armstrong, Mary Poovey, John Bender, Michael McKeon, and others points in similar directions.

8. The issue of people with disabilities in literature is a well-documented one and is one I want generally to avoid in this work. Excellent books abound on the subject, including Alan Gartner and Tom Joe, eds., *Images of the Disabled, Disabling Images* (New York: Praeger, 1987) and the work of Deborah Kent including "In Search of a Heroine: Images of Women with Disabilities in Fiction and Drama" in Michelle Fine and Adrienne Asch, eds. *Women with Disabilities: Essays in Psychology, Culture, and Politics* (Philadelphia: Temple University Press, 1988).

9. And if the main character has a major disability, then we are encouraged to identify with that character's ability to overcome their disability.

10. The genealogical family line is both hereditary and financial in the bourgeois novel. The role of the family is defined by Jürgen Habermas thus: "as a genealogical link it [the family] guaranteed a continuity of personnel that consisted materially in the accumulation of capital and was anchored in the absence of legal restrictions concerning the inheritance of property" (47). The fact that the biological connectedness and the financial connectedness are conflated in the novel only furthers the point that normality is an enforced condition that upholds the totality of the bourgeois system.

11. I deal with the Lacanian idea of the *corps morcelé* in Chapter 6 of *Enforcing Normalcy*. In that section I show the relation between the fragmented body and the response to disability. Here, let me just say that Stevie's turning into a fragmented body makes sense given the fear "normal" observers have that if they allow a concept of disability to associate with their bodies, they will lose control of their normalcy and their bodies will fall apart.

12. See Chapter 4 of *Enforcing Normalcy* for more on the relation of freak shows to nationalism, colonialism, and disability. See also Rosemarie Garland-Thomson's *Freakery: Cultural Spectacles of the Extraordinary Body* (New York: NYU Press, 1996).

WORKS CITED

Bell, Alexander Graham. 1969. *Memoir upon the Formation of a Deaf Variety of the Human Race.* Washington, D.C.: Alexander Graham Bell Association for the Deaf.

Blacker, C. P. 1952. *Eugenics: Galton and After*. Cambridge, Mass.: Harvard University Press.

Conrad, Joseph. 1924. "An Outpost of Progress." In *Tales of Unrest*. Garden City: Doubleday, Page & Company.

——. 1924. *Youth*. Garden City: Doubleday, Page & Company.

——. 1986. *Lord Jim*. London: Penguin.

——. 1989. [1957]. *Under Western Eyes*. London: Penguin.

——. 1990 [1968]. *The Secret Agent*. London: Penguin.

Defoe, Daniel. 1975. *Robinson Crusoe*. New York: Norton.

Farrall, Lyndsay Andrew. 1985. *The Origin and Growth of the English Eugenics Movement 1865–1925*. New York: Garland.

Flaubert, Gustave. 1965. *Madam Bovary*. Trans. Paul de Man. New York: Norton.

Freud, Sigmund. 1977. *Introductory Lectures on Psychoanalysis*. Trans. James Strachey. New York: Norton.

Kevles, Daniel J. 1985. *In the Name of Eugenics: Genetics and the Uses of Human* Heredity. New York: Alfred A. Knopf.

MacKenzie, Donald A. 1981. *Statistics in Britain, 1865–1930*. Edinburgh: Edinburgh University Press.

Marx, Karl. 1970. *Capital*. Vol. 1. Trans. Samuel Moore and Edward Aveling. New York: International Publishers.

Porter, Theodore M. 1986. *The Rise of Statistical Thinking 1820–1900*. Princeton: Princeton University Press.

Stallybass, Peter and Allon White. 1987. *The Politics of Transgression*. Ithaca, N.Y.: Cornell University Press.

Stigler, Stephen M. 1986. *The History of Statistics: The Measurement of Uncertainty before 1900*. Cambridge, Mass.: Harvard University Press.

Zola, Emile. 1964. *The Experimental Novel and Other Essays*. Trans. Belle M. Sherman. New York: Haskel House.

——. 1993. *The Masterpiece*. Trans. Thomas Walton. London: Oxford University Press.

CHAPTER 2

A Brief History of Discrimination and Disabled People

Colin Barnes

To appreciate fully the extent and complexity of the discrimination experienced by disabled people in modern Britain an understanding of history is critical. Consequently the main objectives of this chapter are to draw attention to the philosophical and cultural foundations of discrimination; to outline briefly the discriminatory practices and policies of the past; and to show how they have influenced current British attitudes and institutions.

EARLY INFLUENCES

To pinpoint precisely the origins of society's attitudes toward disability and disabled people would be almost impossible. Among the many suggestions that have been made is the view that our perceptions of impairment and disability are coloured by a deep-rooted psychological fear of the unknown, the anomalous and the abnormal (Douglas, 1966). It is widely acknowledged, however, that our perceptions of normality are partly if not wholly determined by others through learning and the natural transmission of ideology and culture. Here ideology and culture both refer to a communally accepted set of values and beliefs which influences the perceptions of individuals. It provides in advance some basic categories and a set of rules in which ideas and values are formed. Above all, 'it has authority, since each is induced to assent because of the assent of others' (Douglas, 1966). While individual perceptions and ideas vary slightly, cultural concepts are usually more rigid.

Some writers have suggested that cultural intolerance of disability and disabled people can be explained by reference to the economy. For example, our distant ancestors lived in such a harsh environment that there was little opportunity to support individuals with impairments who could not take care of themselves (Thomas, 1982), but with the advent of relatively stable communities able to produce an economic surplus through the development of agriculture, such an analysis becomes difficult to sustain. Indeed there is sufficient historical and anthropological evidence to show that there is no universal approach to disability, either in the way disabled people are perceived or in the way societies respond to them (see Hanks and Hanks, 1980; Oliver, 1981, 1990). Consequently explanations which rely solely on the economy are untenable; cultural factors must be considered also.

In the cultural precursors to our own society, however, there is evidence of a consistent bias against disability and disabled people which has only recently been seriously challenged. Examples can be found in religion, Greek philosophy and European drama and art since well before the Renaissance.

In the Old Testament much of Leviticus is devoted to a reiteration of the physical and mental perfections deemed necessary for all aspects of religious ritual (Lev. 21.16–20). Indeed, only lately have people with learning difficulties been allowed to receive some sacraments in the Roman Catholic Church. Moreover, while the ancient Greeks and Romans placed a high priority upon the care of those injured and subsequently disabled in battle, they were enthusiastic advocates of infanticide for sickly or deformed children. In Sparta these policies were demanded by law (Tooley, 1983).

Throughout the Middle Ages disabled people were the subject of superstition, persecution and rejection. Haffter (1968) has pointed out that in medieval Europe disability was associated with evil and witchcraft. Deformed and disabled children were seen as 'changelings' or the Devil's substitutes for human children, the outcome of their parents' involvement with the black arts or sorcery. The *Malleus Maleficarum* of 1487 declared that these children were the product of the mothers' intercourse with Satan. The idea that any form of physical or mental impairment was the result of divine judgement for wrongdoing was pervasive throughout the British Isles in this period. And the association between disability and evil was not limited to the layman. Protestant reformer Martin Luther (1483–1546) proclaimed that he saw the Devil in a profoundly disabled child. If these children lived, Luther recommended killing them. They were the focus of a mixture of emotions which embodied guilt, fear and contempt.

William Shakespeare's *Richard III* illustrates clearly the attitudes that would be experienced by someone born into a world which placed a high premium upon physical normality:

Cheated of feature by dissembling nature,
Deformed, unfinished, sent before my time
Into this breathing world, scarce half made
up,
And that so lamely and unfashionable
The dogs bark at me as I halt by them.

Shakespeare portrays Richard as twisted in both body and mind. Since he cannot succeed as a lover because of his deformity he is determined to succeed as a villain. This essentially distorted and inherently negative view of disabled people is evident in a great deal of literature and art, both classical and popular, and continues to be produced today (see Gartner and Joe, 1987).

Mental and physical impairments were also primary targets for amusement and ridicule during the Middle Ages. And Thomas' (1977) analysis of the joke books of Tudor and Stuart England reveals the extent of this dimension of the discrimination encountered by disabled people. Besides references to the other so-called timeless universals of 'popular' humour such as foreigners, women, and the clergy, there are many jokes about impairment and disabled people:

> Every disability from idiocy to insanity to diabetes and bad breath was a welcome source of amusement, 'we jest at a man's body that is not well proportioned', said Thomas Wilson, 'and laugh at his countenance . . . if it be not comely by nature'. A typical Elizabethan joke book contains 'merry jests at fools' and merry jests at 'blind folk'. While some of the tricksters' pranks are brutal to the extreme. (Thomas, 1977, pp. 80–1)

Visits to Bedlam were also a common form of amusement for the socially well placed and the practice of keeping 'idiots' as objects of entertainment was prevalent among the aristocracy (Ryan and Thomas, 1980). As we shall see later, disabled people are still the focus for much of what passes as comedy.

Until the seventeenth century those disabled people who were rejected by their families, along with other disadvantaged groups such as the sick, the elderly and the poor, relied almost exclusively on the haphazard and often ineffectual tradition of Christian charity and alms-giving for subsistence. They were rarely gathered together under one roof, however. Despite disenfranchising them from religious ceremony, Christianity, in keeping with the other major western religions, has always acknowledged a responsibility for disabled people. Individuals with severe impairments were usually admitted to one of the very small medieval hospitals in which the sick and bedridden poor were gathered. But the ethos of these hospitals was ecclesiastical rather than medical; they were dedicated to 'care' rather than 'cure' (Scull, 1984).

During the sixteenth century the wealth and power of the Church was greatly reduced because of a series of unsuccessful political confrontations with the monarchy. There was also a steady growth in the numbers of people seeking alms. This was due to several factors, including a growth in the population after a period of stagnation and depletion due to plagues, the beginnings of the commercialisation of agriculture, successive poor harvests, and an influx of immigrants from Ireland and Wales (Stone, 1985). Hence the fear of 'bands of sturdy beggars' preyed on the minds of local magistrates, who demanded a response from the central authority, namely the Crown (Trevelyan, 1948). To secure their allegiance, the Tudor monarchs were forced to make economic provision for people dependent upon charity. Consequently the Poor Law of 1601 marks the first official recognition of the need for state intervention in the lives of disabled people.

A general suspicion of those claiming alms, however, had already been formally established with the statute of 1388 which mandated local officials to discriminate between the 'deserving' and 'undeserving' poor. But although people with impairments were among the 'deserving poor', there was little attempt to separate them from the rest of the community. On the contrary, every effort was made to keep them within the local environment.

Although there was some parochial variation in the actual level of benefit, there was a degree of uniformity in the way disabled people were treated. The lion's share of resources was directed toward domestic or 'household relief' for people who were regarded as unable to work and were confined to the home. Funds were frequently provided to individuals and families willing to accept responsibility for people considered to be incapable of looking after themselves. Major changes to this essentially non-segregationist policy did not begin to be discussed or implemented until the nineteenth century.

However, a clear insight into society's general attitude toward disabled people during this period can be gleaned from an essay written by William Hay in 1754. Born in 1695, Hay was a typical gentleman of the period, a country squire, a Justice of the Peace and a Member of Parliament. He wrote an autobiographical essay titled *Deformity* one year before his death, which is in essence a heartfelt philosophical analysis of disability: a subject of which he had personal experience.

Hay describes himself as barely 5 feet tall with a back 'bent in my mother's womb'. His essay is an outline of the socio-psychological difficulties he experienced because of his impairment. He believed it had caused him to be bashful, uneasy and unsure of himself. He was extremely conscious of his personal appearance and considered himself very fortunate to have been born into a social class where a high emphasis was placed on good manners and politeness. This prevented any 'gentleman' from making derogatory remarks concerning his stature. He noted, however, how the gentle 'friendly' teasing of his close friends contrasted sharply with the treatment of disabled people by society at large, 'where insolence grows in proportion as the man sinks in condition' (Hay, 1754, quoted in Thomas, 1982, p. 62).

INDUSTRIALISATION AND AFTER

Throughout the eighteenth and nineteenth centuries the policy of segregating severely disabled people into institutional settings slowly increased and was subsequently extended to other disadvantaged groups. Although the term 'institution' can be used to refer to a variety of social organisations ranging from the family to a university, it refers here to 'any long term provision of a highly organized kind on a residential basis with the expressed aims of "care", "treatment" or "custody"' (Jones and Fowles, 1984, p. 207). They include hospitals, asylums, workhouses and prisons.

One explanation for this important break with the past links it to the breakdown of early forms of state welfare in the face of large-scale urban industrialisation and the inevitable spread of poverty which followed (Mechanic, 1964). But the impetus to build institutions came before the growth of cities and was more pronounced in rural communities (Ingelby, 1983). A variation on this theme, however, suggests that the widespread incarceration of disabled people is directly attributable to the transition from agriculture and cottage-based industries to the large-scale factory-type system:

> The speed of factory work, the enforced discipline, the time keeping and production norms—all these were a highly unfavourable change from the slower, more self-determined and flexible methods of work into which many handicapped people had been integrated. (Ryan and Thomas, 1980, p. 101)

Although such arguments tend to play down the general antipathy which surrounded disability before the Industrial Revolution, it is clear that the economic and social conditions created by the new system compounded the difficulties faced by disabled people. First, a family dependent upon waged labour alone could not provide for its members during economic depression, so that large groups of dependents were created by industrialisation. Secondly, the system of Poor Law relief which had survived since Elizabethan times was directly at odds with the ascending free market economy. Waged labour made the distinction between the able-bodied and the non-able-bodied poor crucially important, since parochial relief to the able-bodied poor interfered with labour mobility.

Segregating the poor into institutions, on the other hand, had several advantages over domestic relief; it was efficient, it acted as a major deterrent to the able-bodied malingerer, and it could instil good work habits into the inmates (Ingelby, 1983). These conclusions are clearly reflected in the Report of the Poor Law Commission and the Poor Law Amendment Act of 1834. The 1834 reforms introduced three new principles for state welfare policy: national uniformity, denial of relief outside an institution, and deterrence as the basis for setting the levels of welfare benefits.

Uniformity of provision was considered important in order to discourage potential workers from moving from one parish to the next in search of better benefits. Moreover, since aid was set at subsistence level only, uniformity would encourage people to move where the work was in the search for a better standard of living. As early as 1722 Parliament had granted local authorities the right to refuse benefit or outdoor relief to anyone unwilling to enter a workhouse, but the 1834 Poor Law reforms expressly endorsed it, although this instruction was never fully implemented.

Deterrence was evident in the principle of 'least eligibility' whereby a pauper's situation should be less comfortable than that of an 'independent labourer of the lowest class' before benefits could be granted. The workhouse was intended to be as unpleasant as possible so that no-one would enter it willingly. Families were broken up, inmates were made to wear specific uniforms, there were no recreational facilities and socialising was strictly forbidden in working hours. Routines were rigidly enforced and food was limited to what was considered necessary for survival and work.

Besides the horrors of institutions, described so vividly in the novels of Charles Dickens, the nineteenth century was also significant for an upsurge of Christian morality and humanitarian values which were to have a profound effect upon the lives of disabled people. A mixture of religious altruism and conscience, this spirit of Victorian patronage put an end to the widespread practice of infanticide for disabled children, which had hitherto been the rule rather than the exception (Tooley, 1983). It also stimulated some Victorians to question seriously the harsh treatment meted out to people who were generally considered incapable of finding work. When combined with the institutionalised mistrust of people claiming charity, these philanthropic ideals set in motion a process of differentiation which not only separated disabled people from other disadvantaged sections of the community, but also divided them up into specific categories and groups, with differing treatment for each group. The legacy of this policy remains with us today.

From the outset the Poor Law Commission decreed that the workhouses should separate the incarcerated population into four different groupings, namely able-bodied males, able-bodied females, children, and the 'aged and infirm'. It was intended that the latter, or those perceived as the 'deserving poor', were to be housed in different buildings and accorded different treatment. In the following years these categories were refined still further. Aided by the burgeoning medical profession, Poor Law Officials developed four specific categories for dealing with the non-able-bodied poor. They were the 'sick', the 'insane', 'defectives', and the 'aged and infirm' (Stone, 1985).

The term 'sick' described people with acute, temporary or infectious diseases. This group often automatically qualified for outdoor relief if it was available. But where incarceration was deemed necessary, separate accommodation was usually provided, although the conditions in these facilities were rarely better than those in the workhouse. Illness and impairment could not be seen as a route to better treatment, or it would discourage the poor from making provision for the future, and thus undermine the prevailing philosophy of self-reliance.

The 'insane' were singled out for special treatment from the outset. Despite the difficulties of definition and diagnosis, there was already a universal recognition of the 'problem' posed by people with mental illness. There were two main strategies for dealing with it. People termed 'idiots', 'lunatics', 'mad', 'mentally infirm', or 'suffering from diseases of the brain' (Scull, 1978) were either admitted to an asylum or boarded out on contract to families willing to be held responsible for them.

Several private asylums had been established in the seventeenth century. But the public outcry over the atrocious conditions in many of these establishments, brought to light by Evangelical reformers, forced the Government into setting up a state-run system in 1845. It is important to note, however, that the cruelty accorded to people perceived as mentally ill inside institutions was often no worse than that which they encountered in the community at large (Roth and Kroll, 1986).

Until 1871 Poor Law officials had no right to detain citizens in an institution against their will, but this did not apply to people termed insane. Prior to the Lunacy Legislation of 1845, the certification of insanity was the responsibility of local lay officials. Following that date confirmation of mental illness was valid only if a doctor was involved. This change has been attributed to doctors' assertions that mental illness had physiological causes and was responsive to medical treatment, and their successful struggle for control within private and public institutions (Scull, 1984). Once defined as mentally ill an individual could be detained on a doctor's recommendation and moved from one institution to another against her/his will. Doctors still retain this power (DHSS, 1987). Hence, 1845 can be seen as the start of the medical profession's subsequent domination of all aspects of disability.

The term 'defectives' was used to describe people with sensory impairments such as blindness, deafness and the lack of speech. After 1903 people with epilepsy and children termed 'mentally subnormal' were also added to this category. Although members of this group were still liable to be put into an institution, and their treatment therein was no different from that of other inmates, they were frequently singled out for special attention by Victorian philanthropists and charities. Many of the charities which exist today were founded during this period. For example, the British and Foreign Association for Promoting the Education of the Blind (now known as the Royal National Institute for the Blind [RNIB]) was formed in 1863 (RNIB, 1990).

'Aged and infirm', the oldest of the four categories, referred to people with chronic illness and/or permanent impairments. While there was little official controversy over their eligibility for outdoor relief, more often than not they too were directed into an institutional setting.

Towards the end of the nineteenth century the pressures to incarcerate people classified as belonging to one of these categories increased dramatically. First, the transition from relatively light industries such as textiles to the much heavier capital goods industries like iron, steel and the railways, in what has been called the 'second phase of industrialization' (Hobsbawn, 1968), further emphasised the importance of physical fitness as a criterion for finding work among working people. Secondly, welfare policies, particularly with regard to outdoor relief, were severely tightened during the 1870s and 1880s due to escalating costs because of rising unemployment after a decade of economic depression which began with the severe winter of 1860/1. This put more pressure on local authorities to apply the 'workhouse test' to anyone seeking aid. Thirdly, there was a further expansion of segregated institutions for the non-able-bodied poor following another set of public scandals and government enquiries exposing the appalling conditions in workhouses (Stone, 1985). The number of disabled people consigned to these establishments rose accordingly, and did not begin to fall until the 1950s (Scull, 1984).

Ideological legitimacy for the intensified oppression of disabled people during the eighteenth and nineteenth centuries can be found in the ascendant egocentric philosophies of the period, which stressed the rights and privileges of the individual over and above those of the group or state, in relation to property rights, politics and culture (Macfarland, 1978). 'Scientific' authenticity was forthcoming in 1859 with the publication of Charles Darwin's *On the Origin of Species*.

Based on Darwin's observations during his voyages on the *Beagle*, this study outlines his monumental theory of evolution, which places great emphasis upon the process of natural selection, the survival of the fittest, the notion that evolution is progress, and that progress is inherently beneficial.

It had an understandable appeal to a society dominated by a relatively small elite of property-owning, self-interested, 'rational' individuals who welcomed any opportunity to justify their newly-acquired wealth, status and power. It was quickly adapted from the biological domain to apply to human societies (see Russell, 1948).

What later became known as 'Social Darwinism' dispelled and allayed the qualms of the rich about not helping the disadvantaged by assuring them that the latter's sufferings were the inevitable price of progress, which could only be resolved through the struggle for existence. Endorsed by a number of eminent intellectuals and academics of the period, these ideas were to have significant political and social repercussions throughout nineteenth- and twentieth-century Europe, and indeed the world.

Out of the general tendency to apply Darwin's theories to human affairs emerged the Eugenics movement. Concerned mainly with what they saw as racial degeneration through the birth of disabled children, the Eugenicists reiterated ancient fears that disabled people were a serious threat to British and European society. The work of Galton (1869), Dugdale (1910) and Goddard (1912) reinforced traditional myths that there were genetic links between physical and mental impairments, crime, unemployment and other social evils (see Sapsford, 1981). The stated aim of the Eugenicists was to improve the British race by preventing the reproduction of 'defectives' by means of sterilisation and segregation.

In 1896 the National Association for the Care and Control of the Feeble-Minded was set up as a pressure group for the lifetime segregation of disabled people. During the 1910 general election it campaigned vigorously on these issues. In the following two decades Eugenic fears were further endorsed by the invention and widespread use of Intelligence Quotient (IQ) tests in British schools. Their inventors, the French psychologists Binet and Simon, and principal advocates, notably the psychologist Cyril Burt, asserted confidently that intelligence is innate and that the majority of defectives were ineducable. Moreover, despite the fact that there are serious doubts about the validity of IQ-type tests as objective measures of intelligence (since they measure only a comparatively small range of human qualities, the nature of which is culturally determined [Tomlinson, 1981]) similar techniques are used today to separate the 'normal' from the 'subnormal'.

Eugenic fears were prevalent throughout the 1920s and 1930s. For example, the Report of the Departmental Committee on Sterilization chaired by Lord Brock recommended legislation to ensure the 'voluntary' sterilisation of 'mentally defective women' (Ryan and Thomas, 1980). Although such legislation was never actually passed in Britain (unlike America, where sterilisation became compulsory in a number of states), this has not prevented many such operations being carried out under various forms of coercion. Only recently a 36-year-old 'voluntary' patient in a mental hospital, who was described as 'mentally handicapped', was sterilised without her consent after she had developed a relationship with a male patient which 'probably' involved sexual intercourse or 'something close to it' (Morgan, 1989). The operation was justified on the grounds that the woman would be unable to cope with pregnancy or motherhood.

Eugenic ideals reached their logical conclusion during the 1939–45 war with the extermination of between 80,000 and 100,000 disabled people by the Nazis (Wolfensberger, 1980). But while the atrocities of the Nazi death camps put an end to the overt persecution of disabled people throughout Europe, there remains tacit support for comparable ideas among some sections of the British population, notably supporters of the National Front (Ryan and Thomas, 1980).

Moreover, research on human foetuses has recently been officially sanctioned by Parliament, partly on the basis that it might prevent the birth of disabled children (*Hansard*, 1990c). It is not uncommon, although rarely discussed openly, for some doctors with the compliance of parents to allow 'severely' impaired babies to die if the impairment is unexpected (Shearer, 1981). And it is considered socially acceptable for British women to have an abortion if there is any 'substantial risk' that the unborn child will be 'seriously handicapped' (HMSO, 1989), although 'seriously handicapped', is rarely defined. In addition, disabled children are more likely to be abandoned by their parents than their able-bodied peers, they have less chance of being adopted (Burrell, 1989), and they are more prone to physical and sexual abuse (Kennedy, 1989; Watson, 1989).

THE IMPACT OF THE WELFARE STATE

With the inception of the welfare state during the 1940s, official policy with regard to disabled people moved away from the extremes of earlier epochs in favour of a more overtly paternalistic approach. This can be explained with reference to a number of factors, including the humanitarian influence of the Victorian philanthropists, the general concern felt toward disabled ex-servicemen during and after the 1914–18 and 1939–45 wars, the changing political climate, and the prospect of a buoyant economy.

A number of welfare and training schemes had been set up for war casualties after the 1914–18 conflict. An expansion of these and similar facilities was recommended by the Tomlinson Report of 1941 (Schlesinger and Whelan, 1979). Moreover, the economic and social upheavals brought about by the depression of the 1930s, in conjunction with the need for national unity during and immediately after the 1939–45 war, stimulated among many politicians a concern for welfare programmes which had hitherto been absent (Doyal, 1980).

This resulted in a flurry of legislation which was to have a significant impact on the lives of disabled people. Indeed the first Act of Parliament to treat disabled people as a single group was the Disabled Persons (Employment) Act of 1944. As well as attempting to ensure that employers employed disabled people, this Act made provision for a variety of rehabilitation services and vocational training courses. The 1944 Education Act stated that every child should receive education suitable for her/his age, ability and aptitude, and obliged local education authorities to provide special educational treatment for those thought to need it. The National Health Service Act 1948 provided for the acute medical needs of disabled people, and made it possible for local authority health departments to provide any medical aids necessary to enable disabled people to live in their own homes. Finally, the National Assistance Act of 1948 made some provision for meeting the financial needs of disabled people, and mandated local authorities to provide residential facilities and services for people 'who are substantially and permanently handicapped by illness, injury or congenital deformity' (quoted in Oliver, 1983).

Since the late 1950s there has been a concerted attempt by successive governments to reduce the numbers of people living in segregated institutions by expanding community-based services. The origins of the use of the phrase 'community care' can be found in the Report of the Royal Commission on Mental Deficiency of 1954–7, which considered the problems arising from outdated mental hospitals and the stigma associated with in-patient treatment. Although there was no precise definition given, subsequent government statements and documents on services for disabled people have increasingly used the term. It should be noted, however, that the phrase has different meanings for different groups of people and is discussed in more detail in Chapter 6.

The shift toward community-based services took a more decisive turn in 1961 when the Government announced its decision to halve the number of beds in mental hospitals, a move which prompted a number of critics to argue that the motives behind this change in policy were economic rather than humanitarian. One commentator, Titmuss, challenged the Government to refute this allegation, but there was no official reply. In 1962 the Ministry of Health published *A Hospital Plan*. This was followed one year later by *Health and Welfare: The Development of Community Care*, generally referred to as *The Community Care Blue Book*.

These two documents provided a sketchy outline of plans for community-based services, including proposals for increases in the numbers of general practitioners, home helps, district nurses, health visitors, sheltered housing schemes and sheltered workshops. Provision was intended for four specific groups, namely mothers and children, the elderly, 'the mentally disordered' and the 'physically handicapped' (Jones *et al.*, 1983).

Around this time a number of critical investigations into institutional life by social scientists was published (see for example Barton, 1959; Goffman, 1961; Miller, and Gwynne, 1972; Townsend, 1967). In addition, there was a spate of sensational public expositions by the national press of the cruelty and harsh treatment manifest in institutions for 'the elderly' and 'the mentally ill'. All were subsequently investigated and in one particular case, the Ely enquiry, criminal proceedings were brought against hospital personnel (Jones *et al.*, 1983).

As a result of these enquiries, public and in some cases professional confidence in the services provided in long-stay hospitals and similar establishments was again seriously undermined. Local authority services, on the other hand, remained relatively unscathed and underdeveloped. Consequently the pressure to reduce the numbers of people in institutions run by the health service intensified while local authorities were encouraged to expand their facilities accordingly.

There was little agreement as to what services should be provided or where the money to fund the expansion should come from. Extensive variation characterised provision at the local level and budgets were already stretched due to two main factors. The first was the rising expectations of the general population after the setting up of the welfare state, and the second a steady increase in the numbers of 'dependent' people after the 1939–45 war. These included children, people over retirement age, and disabled people.

In an effort to develop and rationalise social service provision at the local level, the Government set up a commission of inquiry which published its findings in 1968. The Seebohm Report is generally considered a watershed in the development of community-based services for disabled people. Among its principal conclusions were the recommendations that local authorities should accumulate data relating to the nature and size of the problems associated with disability; and that they should develop and/or expand services in conjunction with those already provided by the health service and the voluntary sector. These recommendations were subsequently incorporated into the Local Authority Act 1970 and the Chronically Sick and Disabled Persons Act 1970. The establishment of social service departments in their present form quickly followed.

In conjunction with provision for the

other main dependent groups, the new departments were responsible for social services for disabled people. These included the provision of social workers, occupational therapists, residential and day centre facilities, holidays, meals on wheels, respite services, and disability aids and adaptations. This resulted in the situation where almost every aspect of life for a disabled person had its counterpart in a profession or voluntary organisation. Indeed one study estimated that there could be as many as twenty-three professional helpers involved in the life of one disabled person (Brechin and Liddiard, 1985).

Clearly the positive effects of this expansion are that the majority of disabled people now have more access to, relatively, more services and, on the whole, are less likely than, say, before the 1939–45 war to be consigned into a segregated residential setting. On the other hand, the organisation of these services risks their being sucked into a 'culture of dependence' which is predicated upon the assumption that individuals with impairments are people who are helpless and unable to make their own decisions and to choose for themselves the aids and services they need (Shearer, 1981). This is largely due to the fact that the majority of professionals and service-providers adhere either explicitly or implicitly to the traditional individualistic medically-influenced definitions of disability (Davis, 1986; Oliver, 1983; Sutherland, 1981).

From the late 1950s onwards there has been a general tendency by government agencies to reduce the various categories of disability into one all-embracing conceptual framework. This revision was more pronounced in the 1960s, when it became clear that there was insufficient data available to facilitate the proposed expansion of services and to cost the development of new social security benefits. Accordingly the Office of Population, Censuses and Surveys (OPCS) was contracted by the Government to undertake a national disability survey. Findings were published by Harris in 1971 (Harris, 1971).

Harris used functional assessments of disability based on a threefold distinction between impairment, disability and handicap. Similar work was completed by Wood in 1981 (Wood, 1981) for the World Health Organization (WHO). Known as the International Classification of Impairment, Disability and Handicap (ICIDH), Wood's model was used in the second OPCS disability survey carried out during the 1980s (Martin, Meltzer and Elliot, 1988).

This approach remains close to medical classifications of disease. It conserves the notion of impairment as abnormality in function, disability as not being able to perform an activity considered normal for a human being, and handicap as the inability to perform a 'normal' social role (Oliver, 1990). Clearly this model is based upon assumptions about mental and physical normality. It assumes that disability and handicap are caused by psychological or physiological abnormality or impairment, and therefore the impairment is the primary focus of attention.

The first major problem with this approach is that psychological and physical normality and subsequently impairments are not easily defined. Definitions are dependent upon temporal, cultural and situational factors. For example, although homosexuality was considered normal by the ancient Greeks, until very recently it was perceived as a mental illness in many western societies. A male adult less than 5 feet tall might be construed as having a physical impairment in modern Britain, although he might be physiologically healthy.

Secondly, the human being is perceived as flexible and alterable while the physical and social environments are assumed to be fixed and unalterable. This is clearly unrealistic since historically humans have always moulded the environment to suit their needs rather than the other way round.

Thirdly, since psychological and physical impairments are presented as the cause of disability and handicap, it follows that they should be cured by psychological or medical intervention. People with impairments become objects to be treated, changed, improved and made normal.

While medical intervention for treating illness and disease may be quite appropriate, from the perspective of the disabled person it is quite inappropriate for treating disability.

> In the past especially, doctors have been too willing to suggest medical treatment and hospitalization, even when this would not necessarily improve the quality of life for the person concerned. Indeed, questions about the quality of life have sometimes been portrayed as an intrusion upon the medical equation. (Brisenden, 1986, p. 176)

Fourthly, because it is assumed that disabled people must adapt to a hostile environment, they are subjected to all kinds of emotional pressure in the process of adaptation. Those who succeed are sanctified and held up as exemplars of individual will and effort, while the majority who do not are referred to as passive, apathetic or worse (Reiser and Mason, 1990). This has obvious negative psychological implications, which can and often do compound impairment.

Fifthly, these definitions tend to present impairment, disability and handicap as static states. Apart from being inaccurate (Oliver, 1990), this approach creates artificial distinctions and barriers between disabled people and the rest of society (Zola, 1981) which, at best, prolong ignorance and misunderstanding and, at worst, nourish and sustain ancient fears and prejudices.

In short, these definitions not only help to create and perpetuate discrimination in all its forms but also waste valuable resources, both human and financial, 'on a grand scale' (Davis, 1986). Indeed, the fact that disabled people were excluded from participating in a meaningful way from the process of constructing these schemes is an indication of institutional discrimination by professionals. Above all, it is a waste of the most valuable resource of all, namely the perceptions of people who experience disability every day of their lives. It is not surprising therefore that these models are being rejected by a growing number of disabled people and their organisations, including the British Council of Disabled People (BCODP) and Disabled People's International (DPI).

Finally, Oliver (1990) has demonstrated that there is a far more sinister dimension to these schemes. His comparison of two sets of questions relating to the same topics illustrates the point. The first is based on the official individualised definition of disability and was used in the recent OPCS surveys, while the second is constructed on the basis of a social definition.

What complaint causes your difficulty in holding, gripping or turning things?

Have you attended a special school because of a long-term health problem or disability?

Does your health problem/disability prevent you from going out as often or as far as you would like?

Does your health problem/disability affect your work in any way at present?

These questions effectively reduce the problems that people with impairments face in their daily lives to their own personal inadequacies or functional limitations, and could have been reformulated as follows:

What defects in the design of everyday equipment like jars, bottles and tins causes you difficulty in holding, gripping or turning them?

Have you attended a special school

because of your education authority's policy of sending people with your impairment to such places?

What are the environmental constraints which make it difficult for you to get about in your immediate neighbourhood?

Do you have problems at work because of the physical environment or the attitudes of others?

To understand why the first set of questions is intimidating for individual disabled people it is important to know something about the actual research process. In the OPCS surveys, for example, individuals with impairments were visited in their own home by official 'expert' researchers. They were asked a specified sequence of formal questions and there was no opportunity to clarify or discuss their answers. It is hardly surprising then that

> . . . . by the end of the interview, the disabled person has come to believe that his or her problems are caused by their own health disability problems rather than by the organization of society. It is in this sense that the process of the interview is oppressive, reinforcing onto isolated, individual disabled people the idea that the problems they experience in every day living are a direct result of their own inadequacies or functional limitations. (Oliver, 1990, p. 12)

CONCLUSION

It is plain from the above discussion that although economic factors are significant in explaining social responses to and the experience of disability, cultural considerations are equally important. It is also evident that the philosophical and ideological foundations upon which discrimination against disabled people is justified are well entrenched within the core institutions of society.

The data show that there was substantial discrimination against disabled people in Britain prior to industrialisation, but it was relatively fragmented and took many forms. The economic and social upheavals which accompanied industrial development, however, precipitated discrimination becoming institutionalised throughout society. Indeed, the growing importance of economic rationality, individualism and medical science during this period contributed to and compounded ancient fears and prejudices, and provided intellectual justification for relatively more extreme discriminatory practices, notably the systematic removal of disabled people from the mainstream of economic and social life.

Since the 1939–45 war, however, there has been a general 'softening' of attitudes and a definite attempt to reverse this policy and integrate people with impairments into the community. To facilitate this goal there has been a rapid expansion of community-based services in both the state and private sectors, and a subsequent proliferation of professional helpers. While the positive effects of these developments are not in doubt, it is clear that they rest upon basically traditional perceptions of impairment and disability. Discrimination has not disappeared; it has simply been transformed into more subtle and less obvious forms.

REFERENCES

Barton, W. R (1959) *Institutional Neurosis*, John Wright and Sons, Bristol.

Brechin, A. and Liddiard, P. (eds) (4th imp. 1985) *Look at it This Way*, Hodder and Stoughton in association with the Open University Press, Milton Keynes.

Brisenden, S. (1986) 'Independent Living and the Medical Model of Disability', *Disability, Handicap and Society*, 1, 2, pp. 173–179.

Burrell, E. (1989) 'Fostering Children with Disabilities: The Lessons of the Last Ten Years', *Foster Care*, Sept., 59, pp. 22–3.

Davis, K. (1986) *Developing our own Definitions*—Draft for Discussion, British Council of Organizations of Disabled People, London.

DHSS (1987) 'Mental Illness and Mental Handicap Hospitals and Units in England: Legal Status and

Statistics 1982–1985', *DHSS Statistical Bulletin* 2/87, HMSO, London.

Douglas, M. (1966) *Purity and Danger*, Routledge and Kegan Paul, London.

Doyal, L. (1980) *The Political Economy of Health*, Pluto Press, London.

Goffman, E. (1961) *Asylums*, Penguin, Harmondsworth.

Haffter, C. (1968) 'The Changeling; History and Psychodynamics of Attitudes to Handicapped Children in European Folklore', *Journal of the History of Behavioural Studies*, 4.

Hanks, J. and Hanks, L. (1980) 'The Physically Handicapped in Certain Non-Occidental Societies', in Philips, W. and Rosenberg, J. (eds), *Social Scientists and the Physically Handicapped*, Arno Press, London.

Hansard (1990c) 29 June.

Harris, A. (1971) *Handicapped and Impaired in Great Britain*, HMSO, London.

HMSO (1989) *Health and Personal Social Services Statistics for England 1989 Edition*, HMSO, London.

Hobsbawn, E. J. (1968) *Industry and Empire*, Penguin, Harmondsworth.

Ingelby, D. (1983) 'Mental Health and Social order', in Cohen, S. and Scull, A. (eds), *Social Control and the State*, Basil Blackwell, London.

Jones, K. *et al.* (1983) *Issues in Social Policy* (2nd edn), Routledge and Kegan Paul, London.

Jones, K. and Fowles, A. J. (1984) *Ideas on Institutions*, Routledge and Kegan Paul, London.

Kennedy, M. (1989) 'Child Abuse, Child Sexual Abuse', *Deafness*, 3, 2, p. 47.

Macfarland, A. (1978) *The Origins of English Individualism*, Basil Blackwell, Oxford.

Martin, J., Meltzer, H. and Elliot, D. (1988) *The Prevalence of Disability among Adults*, OPCS, London.

Mechanic, D. (1964) 'Mental Health and Social Policy', Prentice-Hall, Englewood Cliffs, New Jersey.

Miller, E. J. and Gwynne, G. V. (1972) *A Life Apart*, Tavistock, London.

Morgan, D. (1989) 'Sterilisation and Mental Incompetance', *Bulletin of Medical Ethics*, 53, Sep./Oct., pp. 18–23.

Oliver, M. (1981) Disablement in Society (Unit 2 of OU course; The Handicapped Person in the Community), Open University Press, Milton Keynes.

—— (1983) *Social Work with Disabled People*, Macmillan, Basingstoke.

—— (1990) *Disablement in Society: A Socio-Political Approach*, Thames Polytechnic, London.

Reiser, R. and Mason, M. (1990) *Disability Equality in the Class-room: A Human Rights Issue*, Inner London Education Authority, London.

RNIB (1990) *Thomas Rhodes Armitage—RNIB's Founder*, RNIB, London.

Roth, M. and Kroll, J. (1986) *The Reality of Mental Illness*, Cambridge University Press.

Russell, B. (1948) *History of Western Philosophy*, Geo. Allen and Unwin, London.

Ryan, J. and Thomas, F. (1980) *The Politics of Mental Handicap*, Penguin, Harmondsworth.

Sapsford, R. J. (1981) 'Individual Deviance; The Search for the Criminal Personality' in Fitzgerald, M., McLennan, G. and Pawson, J. (eds), *Crime and Society: Readings in History and Theory*, Open University Press, Milton Keynes.

Schlesinger, H. and Whelan, E. (1979) *Industry and Effort*, Spastics Society, London.

Scull, A. (1978) *Museums of Madness*, Allen Lane, London.

—— (1984) *Decarceration* (2nd edn), Polity Press, London.

Shearer, A. (1981) 'A Framework for Independent Living' in Walker, A. and Townsend, P. (eds), *Disability Rights in Britain*, Martin Robertson, Oxford.

Stone, D. A. (1985) *The Disabled State*, Macmillan, London.

Sutherland, A. T. (1981) *Disabled We Stand*, Souvenir Press. London.

Thomas, D. (1982) *The Experience of Handicap*, Methuen, London.

Thomas, K. (1977) 'The Place of Laughter in Tudor and Stuart England', *Times Literary Supplement*, 21 Jan., pp. 77–81.

Tomlinson, S. (1981) *Educational Subnormality: A Study in Decision Making*, Routledge and Kegan Paul, London.

Tooley, M. (1983) *Abortion and Infanticide*, Oxford University Press, New York.

Townsend, P. (1967) *The Last Refuge—A Survey of Residential Institutions and Homes for the Aged in England and Wales*, Routledge and Kegan Paul, London.

Trevelyan, G. M. (1948) *English Social History*, Longmans Green, London.

Watson, G. (1989) 'The Abuse of Disabled Children and Young People', in Stanton, W. *et al.* (eds), *Child Abuse and Neglect: Facing the Challenge*, Batsford, London.

Wolfensberger, W. (1980) 'The Extermination of Handicapped People in World War II', *American Journal on Mental Deficiency*, 19, 1.

Wood, P. (1981) 'International Classification of Impairments, Disabilities and Handicaps', World Health Organization (WHO), Geneva.

Zola, I. (1981) *Missing Pieces: A Chronicle of Living with a Disability*, Temple University Press, Philadelphia.

CHAPTER 3

"A Silent Exile on This Earth": The Metaphorical Construction of Deafness in the Nineteenth Century

Douglas Baynton

Deafness is a cultural construction as well as a physical phenomenon. The difference between the hearing and the deaf is typically construed as simply a matter of audiology. For most hearing people, this is the common sense of the matter—the difference between the deaf and the hearing is that the deaf cannot hear. The result is that the relationship between the deaf and the hearing appears solely as a natural one. The meanings of "hearing" and "deaf" are not transparent, however. As with gender, age, race, and other such categories, physical difference is involved, but physical differences do not carry inherent meanings. They must be interpreted and cannot be apprehended apart from a culturally created web of meaning. The meaning of deafness is contested, although most hearing and many deaf people are not aware that it is contested, and it changes over time. It has, that is to say, a history.[1]

The meaning of deafness changed during the course of the nineteenth century for educators of the deaf, and the kind of education deaf people received changed along with it. Until the 1860s, deafness was most often described as an affliction that isolated the individual from the Christian community. Its tragedy was that deaf people lived beyond the reach of the gospel. After the 1860s, deafness was redefined as a condition that isolated people from the national community. Deaf people were cut off from the English-speaking American culture, and *that* was the tragedy. The remedies proffered for each of these kinds of isolation were dramatically different. During the early and middle decades of the nineteenth century, sign language was a widely used and respected language among educators at schools for the deaf. By the end of the century it was widely condemned and banished from many classrooms. In short, sign language was compatible with the former construction of deafness, but not with the latter.

Schools for deaf people were first established in the United States by Evangelical Protestant reformers during the Second Great Awakening. They learned sign language, much as other missionaries of the time learned Native American or African languages, and organized schools where deaf people could be brought together and given a Christian education. The first school, the American Asylum for the Deaf and Dumb at Hartford, Connecticut, was founded in 1817 by the Reverend Thomas H. Gallaudet, with a young deaf man from Paris, Laurent Clerc, as his head teacher.

With the creation of this residential school, and the others which soon followed, the deaf in the United States may be said to have become the Deaf; that is, hearing-impaired individuals became a cultural and linguistic community.[2] To be sure, wherever sufficient numbers of deaf people have congregated, a distinctive community has come into existence—we know of one such community in eighteenth-century Paris.[3] These early schools, however, gathered together larger numbers of deaf people than ever before, most of them in adolescence, placed them in a communal living situation, and taught them formally not only about the world but also about themselves. Those from small towns and the countryside—the majority—met other deaf people for the first time and learned, also for the first time, how to communicate beyond the level of pantomime and gesture. They encountered the surprising knowledge that they had a history and an identity shared by many others. Embracing a common language and common experience, they began to create an American deaf community.[4]

Beginning in the 1860s and continuing into the twentieth century, another group of reformers sought to unmake that community and culture. Central to that project was a campaign to eliminate the use of sign language in the classroom (referred to in the nineteenth century as the philosophy of "manualism") and replace it with the *exclusive* use of lip-reading and speech (known as "oralism"). Residential schools for the deaf had been manualist from their beginnings, conducting their classes in sign language, finger-spelling, and written English. Lessons in speech and lip-reading were added to curriculums in most schools for the deaf by the latter decades of the century, but this was not the crux of the issue for those who called themselves oralists. They were opposed to the use of sign language in any form, for any purpose.[5]

Afraid that deaf people were isolated from the life of the nation, and comparing the deaf community to communities of immigrants, oralists charged that the use of sign language encouraged deaf people to associate principally with each other and to avoid the hard work of learning to communicate with people who were *speaking* English. All deaf people, they thought, should be able to learn to communicate orally. They believed that a purely oral education would lead to greater assimilation, which they believed to be a goal of the highest importance.

The larger goals of the oralist movement were not achieved—the deaf community was not unmade, and sign language continued to be used within it. Most deaf people rejected the oralist philosophy, and maintained an alternative vision of what being deaf meant for them. The deaf community did not, however, control the schools, and the campaign to eliminate sign language from the classroom was largely successful. By the turn of the century, nearly 40 percent of American deaf students were taught without the use of sign language, and over half were so taught in at least some of their classes.[6] The number of children taught entirely without sign language was nearly 80 percent by the end of World War I, and oralism remained orthodox until the 1970s.[7]

Why did educators of the deaf take this road? While this widespread and rapid shift away from the use of sign language has been well documented and described, it has yet to be adequately explained. Oralists at the turn of the century, looking back upon the ascendance of their cause and the demise of manualism, explained it in terms of the march of progress.[8] Improved techniques and knowledge made the use of sign language no longer necessary, they believed. This remained the dominant view in the field until the efficacy of purely oral education began to be questioned in the 1960s and 1970s. Since most recent research and practice supports an eclectic approach that includes the use of sign language—and since, as one recent writer said with only slight exaggeration, the "Old Orthodoxy of oral-or-nothing paternalism has died a richly deserved death"—the progress model has become rather less tenable.[9]

Most deaf adults and their organizations in the nineteenth century strenuously opposed the elimination of sign language from the classroom.[10] At the Convention of American Instructors of the Deaf in 1890, an angry deaf member pointed out that "Chinese women bind their babies' feet to make them small; the Flathead Indians bind their babies' heads to make them flat." Those who prohibit sign language in the schools, he declared, "are denying the deaf their free mental growth . . . and are in the same class of criminals."[11]

Scholars today in the new and still very small field of deaf history have, in general, agreed with this assessment, and have been uniformly critical of oralism. Oralists, it has been argued, were in many cases woefully ignorant of deafness. Their faith in oralism was based more upon wishful thinking than evidence, and they were often taken in by charlatans and quacks.[12] Others, such as Alexander Graham Bell, were more knowledgeable but motivated by eugenicist fears that intermarriage among the deaf, encouraged by separate schools and the use of sign language, would lead to the "formation of a deaf variety of the human race." Bell's prestige, leadership skills, and dedication to the cause gave a tremendous boost to oralism.[13] Opponents of sign language believed that its use discouraged the learning of oral communication skills; hearing parents, eager to believe their deaf children could learn to function like hearing people, supported its proscription. State legislators were persuaded by claims that oral education would be less expensive.[14] Finally, "on the face of it, people are quite afraid of human diversity. . . . [This] fear of diversity leads majorities to oppress minorities"; the suppression of sign language was one more example of the

suppression of a minority language by an intolerant majority.[15]

The question of why schools adopted and continued to practice manualism for over half a century has been given less attention. Manualism has seemed less in need of explanation than oralism; since it is closer to current practice, the manualist philosophy of the nineteenth century has simply come to seem more sensible. With oralism now widely rejected, the focus has been upon explaining how and why such a philosophy gained ascendance.[16] Why manualism took root so readily in the first half of the nineteenth century and why attempts to establish oral schools were unsuccessful until the decades after the Civil War are questions that have not been adequately addressed. Rather than treating manualism as merely sensible and oralism as an unfortunate aberration, seeing both as embedded in historically created constructions of deafness can illuminate them as well as the reform eras of which they were a part.

Manualism and oralism were expressions of two very different reform eras in American history. Manualism was a product of the Evangelical, romantic reform movements of the antebellum years, which emphasized moral regeneration and salvation. Reformers of this period usually traced social evils to the weaknesses of individuals and believed that the reformation of society would come about only through the moral reform of its members. The primary responsibility of the Evangelical reformer, then, was to educate and convert individuals. The Christian nation they sought, and the millennial hopes they nurtured, came with each success one step closer to fruition.

Oralism was the product of a much changed reform atmosphere after the Civil War. While Protestantism continued to be an important ingredient, the emphasis shifted from the reform of the individual to, among other things, the creation of national unity and social order through homogeneity of language and culture. Much reform of the time, oralism included, reflected widespread fears of unchecked immigration and expanding, multiethnic cities. Deaf people in both eras served as convenient, and not always willing, projection screens for the anxieties of their times. The history of deaf education is as much, or more, about concerns over national identity and selfhood as it is about pedagogical technique or theory.

Oralists and manualists have generally been portrayed as standing on opposite sides of an ideological fault line. While in many ways accurate, this formulation obscures fundamental similarities between them. Both created images of deaf people as outsiders. Implicit in these images was the message that deaf people depended upon hearing people to rescue them from their exile. And both based their methods of education upon the images they created. Where they differed was in their definition of the "outsider," and of what constituted "inside" and "outside." For the manualists, the Christian community was the measure, while for the oralists it was an American nation defined in the secular terms of language and culture. Deafness, constructed as a condition that excluded people from the community, was defined and redefined according to what their hearing educators saw as the essential community.

The manualist image of deafness can be seen in the pages of what was in 1847 a remarkable new journal. Published by the American Asylum for the Deaf and Dumb and proclaiming itself the first of its kind in the English language, the *American Annals of the Deaf and Dumb* was intended to be not only a journal of education but also a "treasury of information upon all questions and subjects related, either immediately or remotely, to the deaf and dumb." The editors noted that not only did "the deaf and dumb constitute a distinct and, in some respect, strongly marked class of human beings," they also "have a history peculiar to themselves . . . sustaining relations, of more or less interest, to the general history of the human race." The implication of this, and of the editors' suggestion of such topics for investigation as the "social and political condition in ancient times" of the deaf, and "a careful exposition of the philosophy of the language of signs," was that deaf people were not so much handicapped *individuals* as they were a collectivity, a people—albeit, as we shall see, an inferior one, and one in need of missionary guidance.[17]

In "The Natural Language of Signs," Gallaudet wrote that there was "scarcely a more interesting sight than a bright, cheerful deaf-mute, of one or two years of age" in the midst of its hearing family. "The strangeness of his condition, from the first moment of their discovering it, has attracted their curiosity. They wonder at it." Gallaudet and others of his generation also wondered at the deaf. The source of their wonderment, and of the "greatest delight" for the family, was the child's efforts "to convey his thoughts and emotions . . . by those various expressions of countenance, and descriptive signs and gestures, which his own spontaneous feelings lead him to employ." For Gallaudet, "substantial good has come out of apparent evil," for this family would now have the privilege of learning "a novel, highly poetical, and singular descriptive language, adapted as well to spiritual as to material objects."[18]

Gallaudet praised the beauty of sign language, the "picture-like delineation, pantomimic spirit, variety, and grace . . . the transparent beaming forth of the soul . . . that merely oral language does not possess." Not only should the language of signs not be denied to the deaf, but it should also be given as a gift to the hearing as well, in order to "supply the deficiencies of our oral intercourse [and] perfect the communion of one soul with another." Superior to spoken language in its beauty and emotional expressiveness, sign language brought "kindred souls into a much more close and conscious communion than . . . speech can possibly do."[19]

Such a language was ideal for alleviating what Gallaudet saw as the overriding problem facing deaf people: they lived beyond the reach of the gospel. They knew nothing of God and the promise of salvation, nor had they a firm basis for the development of a moral sense. An essential part of education was learning "the necessity and the mode of controlling, directing, and at times subduing" the passions. Gallaudet emphasized the need to develop the conscience, to explain vice and virtue, to employ both hope and fear and "the sanctions of religion" in order to create a moral human being.[20]

The "moral influence" with which Gallaudet was concerned, however, could not "be brought to bear . . . without language, and a language intelligible to such a mind." Learning to speak and read lips was a "long and laborious process, even in the comparatively few cases of complete success." Communication between student and teacher, furthermore, was not sufficient. A language was needed with which "the deaf-mute can intelligibly conduct his private devotions, and join in social religious exercises with his fellow pupils."[21]

For Gallaudet, then, to educate was to impart moral and religious knowledge. Such teaching was not primarily directed to the mind through abstractions—rather, "the heart is the principle thing which we must aim to reach"; oral language may better communicate abstraction, he believed, but "the heart claims as its peculiar and appropriate language that of the eye and countenance, of the attitudes, movements, and gestures of the body."[22] Gallaudet described the progress of the student with the use of sign language:

Every day he is improving in this language; and this medium of moral influence is rapidly enlarging. His mind becomes more and more enlightened; his conscience more and more easily addressed; his heart more and more prepared to be accessible to the simple truths and precepts of the Word of God.[23]

The interdependence of the mind, the heart, and the conscience, of both knowledge and morality, run through these teachers' writings. Morality, and the self-discipline it required, depended upon a knowledge of God's existence as well as a heartfelt conviction that the soul was immortal and that the promise of its salvation was real. What was more, the proper development of the moral nature not only depended upon knowledge but in its turn also stimulated the higher faculties to yet greater learning.[24]

As David Walker Howe has recently pointed out, achieving inner self-discipline was important for Evangelicals not just for the sake of self-control, but for the liberation of the self as well. Liberation and control were seen by antebellum Evangelicals as "two sides of the same redemptive process." Evangelicals, according to Howe, "were typically concerned to redeem people who were not functioning as free moral agents: slaves, criminals, the insane, alcoholics, children."[25] The contributors to the *Annals* in its first year clearly placed deaf people in this same category: outsiders to the Christian community. Teachers at the Asylum at Hartford, "preeminently a Christian institution" dedicated to teaching those "truths which are received in common by all evangelical denominations," bemoaned the fact that "in this Christian land" there were still deaf people living "in utter seclusion from the direct influences of the gospel."[26] These deaf people "might almost as well have been born in benighted Asia, as in this land of light," and were "little short of a community of heathen at our very doors."[27]

Throughout this first year of the journal, images of imprisonment, darkness, blankness, and isolation were repeatedly used to describe the condition of deaf people without education. These metaphors were interconnected, as was made plain by the descriptions of the uninstructed deaf by the Reverend Collins Stone, a teacher at the Hartford school: "scarcely a ray of intellectual or moral light ever dawns upon his solitude"; "his mind is a perfect blank"; if "he dies unblessed by education, he dies in this utter moral darkness"; we must "open the doors of his prison, and let in upon him the light of truth," for the terrible fact is that "even in the midst of Christian society, he must grope his way in darkness and gloom . . . unless some kind hand penetrates his solitude."[28]

The image of the animal appeared frequently as well. Stone wrote that the uneducated deaf were reduced "to the level of mere animal life" because the "great facts and truths relating to God and a future state" are unknown to them. What "makes us differ from the animals and things around us" is the possession of a soul and an understanding of what that possession means. Without this understanding, deaf people were capable of nothing higher than "mere animal enjoyment."[29] With the use of sign language, however, as J. A. Ayres believed, "it will be seen at once that the deaf-mute is restored to his position in the human family, from which his loss had well-nigh excluded him."[30]

Writer after writer used the same or similar metaphors, with the same emphasis upon the knowledge of God and the immortality of the soul as that which distinguishes the human from the nonhuman. The Reverend Luzerne Ray, speculating upon the "Thoughts of the deaf and Dumb before Instruction," asked the reader to imagine a child born with no senses, to imagine that "the animal life of this infant is preserved, and that he grows up to be, in outward appearance at least, a man." Ray asked, "can we properly say that here would be any mind at all? . . . [C]ould there be any conscious self-existence or self-activity of a soul imprisoned within such a body?" He concluded that to answer in the affirmative would be to succumb to "the lowest form of materialism." While no such person had ever existed, uneducated deaf people living "in a state of isolation the most complete that is ever seen among men" came close.[31] Henry B. Camp, writing on the "Claims of the Deaf and Dumb upon Public Sympathy and Aid," lamented the "darkness and solitude" of the person who lives in a "condition but little superior to that of the brute creation," with "no key to unlock the prison of his own mind."[32]

For the manualists, then, the "real calamity for the deaf-mute" was "not that his ear is closed to the cheerful tones of the human voice"; and it was "not that all the treasures of literature and science, of philosophy and history . . . are to him as though they were not"; the calamity was that "the light of divine truth never shines upon his path."[33] The darkness, the emptiness, the solitude, were all of a particular kind: uneducated deaf people were cut off from the Christian community and its message.

A peculiar duality that runs throughout their writings illuminates the meaning of deafness for these teachers. Deafness was an affliction, they believed, but they called it a blessing as well. One explained that the only unusual aspect of educating deaf people on moral and religious matters was that they had "a *simplicity* of mental character and an *ignorance* of the world, highly favorable to the entrance and dominion of this highest and best motive of action" (emphasis added). The properly educated deaf person, he believed, will exhibit "a pleasing combination of strength and simplicity." The strength would come from proper education, but the simplicity was inherent in the deafness; it "flows naturally from that comparative isolation of the mind which prevents its being formed too much on the model of others."[34]

Another writer touched on the same duality when explaining the "beautiful compensation" for deafness:

> Deprived of many blessings, he is also shut out from many temptations, and it is rare indeed that the claims of religion and the reasonings of morality fail to secure the ready assent both of his heart and his understanding.[35]

Deaf people were thought to have a great moral advantage in that they have been left relatively unscathed by a corrupt world. They are innocent, rather than living in darkness, and their deafness is an asylum rather than a prison. Deafness, then, confers both the benefit of innocence and the burden of ignorance: two sides of the same coin. It is a positive good if temporary and discovered by the right people but an evil if neglected and left uncultivated. The difference between virginity and barrenness (whether of women or of land) is analogous—the first is a blessed state, the second a calamity. The deaf are blessed if virginal, innocent, and fertile, but would be accursed if left forever in that state. They would then be barren. Innocence holds within it the germ of knowledge and salvation. Ignorance is only darkness.

The dark side was expressed in a poem by a former student at the Hartford school, published in the *Annals*:

> I moved—a silent exile on this earth;
> As in his dreary cell one doomed for life,
> My tongue is mute, and closed ear heedeth
>   not;
>
> Deep silence over all, and all seems lifeless;
> The orators exciting strains the crowd
> Enraptur'd hear, while meteor-like his wit
> Illuminates the dark abyss of mind—
> Alone, left in the dark—*I hear them not.*
>
> The balmy words of God's own messenger
> Excite to love, and troubled spirits sooth—
> Religion's dew-drops bright—*I feel them
>   not.*[36]

But some months later, a poem entitled "The Children of Silence" was published in response "to show that there are times and circumstances," in the editor's words, "when not to be able to hear must be accounted a blessing rather than a misfortune":

> Not for your ears the bitter word
> Escapes the lips once filled with love;
> The serpent speaking through the dove,
> Oh Blessed! ye have never heard.
> Your minds by mercy here are sealed
> From half the sin in man revealed.[37]

The use of "silent" and "silence" in these poems embodies the contradictions in the innocence and ignorance metaphor. It was (and is) a common description of the world of deafness, and at first glance would seem a common sense description as well. Deaf people use it as well as hearing people. In the nineteenth century, for example, journals by and for the deaf had such titles as the *Silent Worker* and *Silent World*. Today there are newspapers such as the *Silent News,* and clubs with such names as the Chicago Silent Dramatic Club.

"Silence" is not a straightforward or unproblematic description of the experience of a deaf person, however. First, few deaf people hear nothing. Most have hearing losses which are not uniform across the entire range of pitch—they will hear low sounds better than high ones, or vice versa. Sounds will often be quite distorted, but heard nevertheless. And second, for those who do not hear, what does the word silence signify? Unless they once heard and *became* deaf, the word is meaningless as a description of their experience. (Even for those who once heard, as the experience of sound recedes further into the past, so too does the significance of silence diminish.) Silence is experienced by the hearing as an absence of sound. For those who have never heard, deafness is not an absence. To be deaf is *not* to not hear for most profoundly deaf people, but a social relation—that is, a relation with other human beings, those called "hearing" and those called "deaf." What the deaf person sees in these other people is not the presence or absence of hearing, not their soundfulness or their silence, but their mode of communication—they sign, or they move their lips. That is why deaf people in the nineteenth century typically referred to themselves not as deaf people but as "mutes." That is why the sign still used today that is translated as "hearing person" is made next to the mouth, not the ear, and literally means "speaking person."

Silence is a metaphor rather than a simple description of the experience of most deaf people.[38] Deafness is a relationship, not a state, and the use of the "silence" metaphor is one indication of how the relationship is dominated by the hearing. Hearing is defined as the universal, and deafness, therefore, as an absence, as an emptiness. Silence can represent innocence and fertility, and silence can represent darkness and barrenness. In both cases it is empty. In both cases it needs to be filled. Images such as these—images of light and dark, of solitude and society, of animal and human—construct a world in which deaf people lack what hearing people alone can provide.

The absence which defined deaf people was framed as a place in which the deaf lived: a darkness within which they could not escape, a blankness and ignorance which denied them humanity. But of course the converse was also true: the problem was not only that the deaf could not see *out* but also that the hearing could not see *in*. The minds of deaf people represented impenetrable dark spaces within Christian society—or better, *without* Christian society—of which the hearing had little knowledge. Sign language was the light that could illuminate the darkness.

In 1899, the *Association Review* was established as the journal of the American Association to Promote the Teaching of Speech to the Deaf, the first president of which was Alexander Graham Bell. In the introduction to the first issue, the editor Frank Booth was able to state confidently that "the spirit prevalent in our schools is one entirely favorable to speech for the deaf, and to more and better speech teaching so soon as more favorable conditions may warrant and permit."[39] Indeed, with 55 percent of their teachers now speech teachers (as compared with 24 percent in 1886, the first year for which we have figures), the acquisition of speech was rapidly becoming the preeminent aim in the education of the deaf.[40]

The times were not only favorable to speech but quite hostile to sign language. Nearly 40 percent of American deaf students now sat in classrooms from which sign language had been banished. Within twenty years it would be 80 percent.[41] Deaf teachers were rarely hired by the schools anymore and made up less than 20 percent of the teaching corps, down from more than twice that number in the 1850s and 1860s.[42] Those who remained were increasingly confined to teaching industrial education courses, to which students who were "oral failures" were relegated. The new teacher training school established in 1891 at Gallaudet College, a liberal arts college primarily for deaf students, itself refused, as a matter of policy, to train deaf teachers.[43] Booth himself would forbid the use of sign language at the Nebraska school when he became its superintendent in 1911. "That language is not now used in the schoolroom," he wrote to Olaf Hanson, president of the National Association of the Deaf, "and I hope to do away with its use outside of the school-room."[44]

Booth was certainly correct that the "spirit now prevalent" was much changed. The *American Annals of the Deaf* at the turn of the century reflected the changed climate as well. Educational philosophy had shifted ground so dramatically that unabashed manualism had nearly disappeared from its pages, with the majority of opinion ranging between oralism and what was called the "combined system." The definition of the latter varied widely. In some cases it mean supplementing speech with fingerspelling but forbidding sign language; in others, speech alone was used in the classroom, with sign language permitted outside; in many cases it meant using speech with all young students and resorting later to sign language only with older "oral failures." To Edward M. Gallaudet, son of Thomas and first president of Gallaudet College, the combined system meant preserving sign language but using it in the classroom "as little as possible." He defended his tiny remnant of his father's world in an article bearing the plaintive title "Must the Sign-Language Go?"[45]

The new aversion to sign language had many causes, but a profound change in the images and meanings of deafness during the second half of the nineteenth century was fundamental. The opening article of the first issue of the *Association Review* is revealing. Reprinted from an address delivered before a meeting of the Association by John M. Tyler (president of Amherst College), "The Teacher and the State" was concerned with what teachers could do about two related national problems: the new immigration and the decline in law and order. There was a "struggle between rival civilizations" within America. "Shall her standards and aims, in one word her civilization, be those of old New England, or shall they be Canadian or Irish, or somewhat better or worse than any of these?" The burden rested upon the teachers, for "'Waterloo was won at Rugby' [and] it was the German schoolmaster who triumphed at Sedan." Furthermore, teachers could no longer focus on "purely intellectual training," for "[t]he material which we are trying to fashion has changed; the children are no longer of the former blood, stock, and

training." Teachers must make up for the new immigrants' deficiencies as parents, he warned: "the emergency remains and we must meet it as best we can." If they do not, the "uncontrolled child grows into the lawless youth and the anarchistic adult."[46]

Tyler's speech was not directly about deaf people, but it must have resonated with his audience of educators of the deaf. Metaphors of deafness by the turn of the century were no longer ones of spiritual darkness but instead conjured images of foreign enclaves within American society. Articles about deaf people in the *Association Review* might just as well have been about immigrant communities, with metaphors of foreignness at work on several levels. First there was the problem of what was not commonly referred to as "the foreign language of signs."[47] Educators worried that if deaf people "are to exercise intelligently the rights of citizenship, then they must be made people of our language."[48] They insisted that "the English language must be made the vernacular of the deaf if they are not to become a class unto themselves—foreigners among their own countrymen."[49] Oralism was about much more than just speech and lip-reading. It was part of a larger argument about language and the maintenance of a national community.

The image of foreignness was not confined to the pages of the *Association Review*. A parent wrote to the superintendent of the Illinois Institution in 1898, requesting information about methods of deaf education. The answer she received was that there were two: "the English language method," and the method in which "the English language is considered a foreign language," taught through "translation from the indefinite and crude sign language."[50]

"Sign language is an evil," avowed a teacher from the Pennsylvania Institution for Deaf-Mutes, one of the first state schools to adopt the oralist philosophy, in an 1892 article in the *Silent Educator*. The mastery of English was not, by itself, the point, he argued. Sign language made deaf people "a kind of foreigners in tongue," and this was so whether or not they also mastered English. Deaf people who signed could not be full members of the English-speaking American community; they were, instead, "a sign making people who have studied English so as to carry on business relations with those who do not understand signs." Using another language was the offense, for "English is a jealous mistress. She brooks no rival. She was born to conquer and to spread all over the world. She has no equal."[51]

This was an extreme example of a usually more subtle nationalism expressed by opponents of sign language. Most oralists did not exhibit open xenophobia, insist upon Anglo-Saxon superiority, nor advocate one worldwide language. Most emphasized their belief that sign language isolated deaf people and made the deaf person an outsider who was "not an Englishman, a German, a Frenchman, or a member of any other nationality, but, intellectually, a man without a country."[52] They were convinced and deeply troubled by the conviction that signing deaf people existed apart and isolated from the life of the nation. An earlier generation of educators had believed that sign language liberated deaf people from their confinement, but for oralists it was the instrument of their imprisonment.

Even some hearing educators who had long supported sign language had begun to criticize what they termed the "clannishness" of deaf people. In 1873, Edward M. Gallaudet had condemned the conventions, associations and newspapers of deaf people, as well as their intermarriage, for discouraging the intercourse of the deaf "with their race and the world." It was injurious to the best interests of the deaf when they came to consider themselves "members of society with interests apart from the mass, . . . a 'community,' with its leaders and rulers, its associations and organs, and its channels of communication." Gallaudet's concerns were similar to those of the oralists, except that sign language was, he thought, still necessary—a "necessary evil." It could not be relinquished, he argued, because few people profoundly deaf from an early age could become proficient enough at oral communication for a full education or participation in religious services.[53] Oralists escalated the charge of "clannishness" to "foreignness," however, a term with more ominous connotations.

This was a metaphor of great significance for Americans of the late nineteenth century. References to deaf people as foreigners coincided with the greatest influx of immigrants in U.S. history. The new immigrants were concentrated in urban areas, and no major city was without its quilt pattern of immigrant communities. Many came from eastern and southern Europe, bringing with them cultural beliefs and habits that native-born Americans often regarded as peculiar, inferior, or even dangerous. As Frederick E. Hoxie has noted in his study of the Indian Assimilation movement (a movement contemporaneous with and sharing many characteristics with the oralist movement), in the late nineteenth century "growing social diversity and shrinking social space threatened many Americans' sense of national identity."[54] Nativism, never far from the surface of American life, resurged with calls for immigration restriction, limits on the employment of foreigners, and the proscription of languages other than English in the schools. To say that sign language made deaf people appear foreign was to make a telling point for these educators. That foreignness should be avoided at all costs was generally expressed as a self-evident truth.

"Foreignness" had two related meanings. As with the manualists' metaphor of darkness, this was a metaphor with two centers. Looking from the outside in, the metaphor suggested a space within American society that was mysterious to outsiders, into which hearing Americans could see only obscurely if at all. As such it posed vague threats of deviance from the majority culture. Looking from the inside out—that is, empathizing with what the oralists imagined to be the experience of deaf people—it seemed a place in which deaf people became trapped, from which they could not escape without assistance. "Foreignness" was both a threat and a plight. The deaf community, as one of a host of insular and alien-appearing communities, was seen as harmful to both the well-being of the nation and to its own members.

For many hearing people, what they saw looking in from the outside was troubling. Journals and magazines such as the *Silent World* and the *Deaf-Mute Journal*, written and printed by deaf people for a deaf audience, were thriving in every state. Deaf adults across the country were actively involved in local clubs, school alumnae associations, and state and national organizations. They attended churches together where sign language was used. The great majority found both their friends and their spouses within the deaf community. According to the research of Bell, the rate of intermarriage was at least 80 percent, a fact that caused him great alarm.[55]

The two chief interests of Bell's life, eugenics and deaf education, came together over this issue. In a paper published by the National Academy of Sciences in 1884, Bell warned that a "great calamity" for the nation was imminent due to the high rate of intermarriage among the deaf: the "formation of a deaf variety of the human race." The proliferation of deaf clubs, associations, and periodicals, with their tendency to "foster class-feeling among the deaf," were ominous developments. Already, he warned, "a special language adapted for the use of such a race" was in existence, "a language as different from English as French or German or Russian."[56]

While other oralists would call for legislation to "prevent the marriage of persons who are liable to transmit defects to their offspring," Bell believed such legislation would be difficult to enforce.[57] His solution was this: *(1) Determine the causes that promote intermarriages among the deaf and dumb; and (2) remove them*" [emphasis his]. Bell identified two principal causes: "segregation for the purposes of education, and the use, as a means of communication, of a language which is different from that of the people." Indeed, he wrote, "if we desired to create a deaf variety of the race . . . we could not invent more complete or more efficient methods than those."[58]

Bell's fears were unfounded. His findings, published in the year of Gregor Mendel's death and before the latter's research on genetic transmission had become known, were based upon a faulty understanding of genetics. Others soon countered his empirical evidence as well; most deafness was not heritable, and marriages between deaf people produced on average no greater number of deaf offspring than mixed marriages of deaf and hearing partners.[59] But the image of an insular, inbred, and proliferating deaf community, with its own "foreign" language and culture, became a potent weapon for the oralist cause. Bell was to become one of the most prominent and effective crusaders against both residential schools and sign language.[60]

More often, oralists emphasized the empathetic side of the metaphor. They insisted that their intent was to rescue deaf people from their confinement, not to attack them. Deaf adults, however, actively defended the space from which they were urged to escape and from which deaf children were supposed to be rescued. But just as deaf people resisted the oralist conception of their needs, oralists likewise resisted the portrayal of themselves by deaf leaders as "enemies of the true welfare of the deaf."[61] As did the advocates of Indian and immigrant assimilation, they spoke of themselves as the "friends of the deaf." They tried to project themselves into that mysterious space they saw deaf people inhabiting and to empathize with the experience of deafness.

They were especially concerned that "because a child is deaf he is . . . considered peculiar, with all the unpleasant significance attached to the word."[62] The great failure of deaf education was that "in many cases, this opinion is justified by deaf children who are growing up without being helped . . . to acquire any use of language."[63] ("Language" was frequently used as a synonym for "spoken English.") Peculiarity was spoken of as part of the curse of foreignness, and "to go through life as one of a peculiar class . . . is the sum of human misery. No other human misfortune is comparable to this."[64] This peculiarity of deaf people was not unavoidable, but "solely the result of shutting up deaf children to be educated in sign schools, whence they emerge . . . aliens in their own country!"[65] Cease to educate deaf people with sign language, oralists believed, and they will "cease to be mysterious beings."[66]

Like their contemporaries in other fields of reform, oralists worried that the lives of people were diminished by being a part of such restricted communities as the deaf community; they would not, it was feared, fully share in the life of the nation. The deaf community, like ethnic communities, narrowed the minds and outlooks of its members. "The individual must be one with the race," one wrote in words that could have come from Jane Addams or John Dewey or any number of Progressive reformers, "or he is virtually annihilated"; the chief curse of deafness was "apartness from the life of the world," and it was just this that oralism was designed to remedy.[67] This was the darkness of the manualists redefined for a new world.

Oralists believed sign language was to blame for making deaf people seem foreign, peculiar, and isolated from the nation and claimed it was an inferior language that impoverished the minds of its users. This language of "beauty and grace," in the words of Thomas H. Gallaudet, now was called a wretched makeshift of the language."[68] It was "immeasurably inferior to English" and any "culture dependent upon it must be proportionately inferior."[69] The implication of foreignness, barbarism, was not left unspoken. As one opponent of sign language stated, "if speech is better for hearing people than barbaric signs, it is better for the deaf."[70] In an age when social scientists ranked cultures and languages on The evolutionary scale from savage to civilized, teachers of the deaf came to depict sign language as "characteristic of tribes low in the scale of development."[71] It was in fact identical to the gestures used by "a people of lowest type" found to exist "in the ends of the earth where no gleam of civilization had penetrated."[72] Like the races supposed to be lowest on the evolution scale, sign language was barely human.

For some it was not human at all. The metaphor of animality reappeared in different guise. Benjamin D. Pettingill, a teacher at the Pennsylvania School for the Deaf, noted as early as 1873 that sign language was being "decried, denounced, and ridiculed . . . as a set of monkey-like grimaces and antics."[73] Sarah Porter, a teacher at the Kendall School, in 1894 wrote that the common charge against the use of sign language—"You look like monkeys when you make signs"—would be "hardly worth noticing except for its . . . incessant repetition."[74] A teacher from Scotland complained in 1899 in the pages of the *American Annals of the Deaf* that it was wrong to "impress [deaf people] with the thought that it is apish to talk on the fingers."[75]

Lewis Dudley, a trustee of the first oral school in the nation, the Clarke Institution, implied in 1880 that deaf people who used sign language themselves felt less than human. When he visited a school in which sign language was used, the children looked at him.

> with a downcast pensive look which seemed to say, "Oh, you have come to see the unfortunate; you have come to see young creatures human in shape, but only half human in attributes; you have come here much as you would go to a menagerie to see something peculiar and strange."[76]

He contrasted the demeanor of these children with that of a young girl he had met who had recently learned to speak: "the radiant face and the beaming eye showed a consciousness of elevation in the scale of being. It was a real elevation."[77] The metaphors of the subhuman and the animal had been used by the manualists to signify ignorance of the soul. To the oralists they came to signify ignorance of spoken language.

Clearly the "real calamity of the deaf-mute" had been redefined. The 1819 annual report of the American Asylum did not ask if most Americans could understand signs, but "does God understand signs?"[78] To this they answered yes and were satisfied. At mid-century the calamity still was "not that his ear is closed to the cheerful tones of the human voice," but that the deaf person might be denied "the light of divine truth."[79] When the manualist generation had spoken of deaf people being "restored to society" and to "human brotherhood," membership in the Christian community was the measure of that restoration.[80] Sign language had made it possible. The isolation of the deaf was a problem that had been solved.

By the turn of the century, however, the problem had returned. Once again educators of the deaf spoke of rescuing the deaf from their "state of almost total isolation from society," "restoring" them to "their proper and rightful place in society,"[81] and once again deaf people lived "outside."

They were "outside" because "inside" had been redefined. Whereas manualists had believed that to teach their students "the gospel of Christ, and by it to save their souls, is our great duty," it was now the "grand aim of every teacher of the deaf . . . to put his pupils in possession of the spoken language of their country."[82] The relevant community was no longer the Christian community, but a national community defined in large part by language.

Both manualists and oralists understood deafness in the context of movements for national unity, and their metaphors came from those movements. Evangelical Protestantism brought together a nation no longer unified by the common experience of the Revolution, unsettled by rapid social and economic change, and worried about the effects of the opening of the West upon both the morality and the unity of the nation. In crafting that unity, by creating a common set of experiences for understanding of the world, Evangelicalism emphasized above any other kind of cultural or linguistic homogeneity a common spiritual understanding. When Evangelicals saw dangers in the immigration of the time, it was not foreignness *per se* that principally concerned them, but Catholicism.[83] That definition of unity was not necessarily more tolerant of difference in general, but it did mean that sign language and the deaf community were not seen as inimical to it.

The movement for national unity at the time of the rise of oralism had a different source. This time it was the multiplicity of immigrant communities crowded into burgeoning industrial cities that seemed to threaten the bonds of nationhood. Two streams converged to make sign language repugnant to many hearing Americans: at the same time that deaf people were creating a deaf community, with its own clubs, associations, and periodicals, American ethnic communities were doing the same to an extent alarming to the majority culture. At the same time that deaf children were attending separate schools in which deaf teachers taught them with both English and sign language, immigrant children were attending parochial schools in which immigrant teachers taught them in both English and their native languages.[84] The convergence was merely fortuitous, but it was not difficult to transfer anxieties from one to the other.

If the fragmentation of American society into distinct and unconnected groups was the fear that drove the oralists, the coalescence of a homogeneous society of equal individuals was the vision that drew them together. For the oralists, as for their contemporaries in other fields of reform—the assimilation of the Indian, the uplifting of the working class, the Americanization of the immigrant—equality was synonymous with sameness. The ideal was achieved when one could "walk into . . . our hearing schools and find the deaf boys working right along with their hearing brothers . . . [where] no difference is felt by the teacher."[85] Just as manualism arose within a larger Evangelical revival, so did oralism partake of the late nineteenth-century quest for national unity through the assimilation of ethnic cultures.[86]

Humans use metaphor and mental imagery to understand things of which they have no direct experience.[87] For people who are not deaf, then, the use of metaphor to understand deafness is inevitable: they can approach it no other way. The problem is that hearing people are in positions to make, on the basis of their metaphors— usually unaware that they *are* metaphors— decisions with profound and lasting effects upon the lives of deaf people. The most persistent images of deafness among hearing people have been ones of isolation and exclusion, and these are images that are consistently rejected by deaf people who see themselves as part of a deaf community and culture. Feelings of isolation may even

be less common for members of this tightly knit community than among the general population.[88] The metaphors of deafness— of isolation and foreignness, of animality, of darkness and silence—are projections reflecting the needs and standards of the dominant culture, not the experiences of most deaf people.

The oralists and the manualists appeared to be opposing forces—"old fashioned" manualists fought bitterly with "progressive" oralists. The deaf community saw a clear difference, siding with the manualists and resisting with all its resources the changes in educational practice that the oralists sought. One reason was that manual schools employed deaf teachers. Oral schools generally did not—deaf people could not teach speech.[89] Furthermore, oralists simply did not believe that the deaf should exist as a social group; to hire deaf teachers would imply that deaf people had something to teach each other, that there was a significant group experience. Manualists seem to have been more egalitarian for this reason. While deaf people taught in manualist schools, however, they generally found positions of authority closed to them. Few became principals or superintendents, and probably no deaf person ever sat on a school governing board.[90] One result was that when the hearing society refashioned its images of deafness and turned toward oralism, the deaf community had limited means of resistance.

Resist it did through that combination of open and subterranean means commonly resorted to by beleaguered minorities. From the beginnings of oralism until its demise in the 1970s, deaf people organized to lobby legislatures and school boards in support of sign language in the schools.[91] Deaf parents passed sign language on to their children, and those children who were deaf and attended schools where sign language was banned surreptitiously taught others. Those unable to learn sign language as children learned it as adults when they found themselves free to associate with whomever they pleased, however they pleased; over 90 percent continued to marry other deaf people and deaf clubs and associations continued to thrive.[92] But their means of resistance within the educational establishment were scant, a legacy at least in part of the paternalism of the manualist educators.

Manualists and oralists had paternalism in common, and much else. Both groups saw deafness through their own cultural biases and sought to reshape deaf people in accordance with them. Both used similar clusters of metaphors to forge images of deaf people as fundamentally flawed, incomplete, isolated and dependent. And both used that imagery to justify not only methods of education, but also the inherent authority of the hearing over the deaf. That did not change.

Still, deaf people sided with the manualists. We do not know exactly how deaf people responded to the images created by either manualists or oralists, to what extent they internalized them, rejected them, or used them for their own purposes. The creation of alternative meanings for deafness by the deaf community has a complex history all its own, one that is still largely unwritten.[93] But while the reception of the Evangelical *message* by deaf people during the manualist years is not yet clear, the Evangelical *medium*—sign language within a sign-using community—was clearly welcomed by most. And whether or not deaf adults accepted the oralist depiction of their community as "foreign" or akin to an immigrant community, most of them clearly rejected the oralist understanding of what those images meant.

Whatever metaphors of deafness manual*ists* may have used, manual*ism* allowed the possibility of alternative constructions of deafness by deaf people themselves. So long as deaf people had their own language and community, they possessed a cultural space in which to create alternative meanings for their lives. Within that space they could resist the meanings that hearing people attached to deafness, adopt them and put them to new uses, or create their own. Oralism, whose ideal was the thoroughly assimilated deaf person, would do away with that alternative. Oralism failed, finally, and sign language survived, because deaf people chose not to relinquish the autonomous cultural space their community gave them.

NOTES

1. For an example of a radically different construction of deafness than has been typical in the United States, see Nora Groce, *Everyone Here Spoke Sign Language: Hereditary Deafness on Martha's Vineyard* (Cambridge, Mass., 1985). From the sixteenth to the nineteenth century, an unusually high rate of inherited deafness on Martha's Vineyard combined with premodern village values to produce communities in which deafness was apparently not considered a significant difference at all. The hearing people in these communities were all bilingual in spoken English and a variety of British Sign Language. There were no apparent differences between the social, economic, or political lives of the hearing and the deaf, according to Groce.

2. Within forty years there would be twenty residential schools in the United States; by the turn of the century, more than fifty. See "Tabular Statement of Schools for the Deaf, 1897–98," *American Annals of the Deaf* 43 (Jan. 1898): 46–47 (hereafter cited as *Annals*).

   The use of "deaf" (with a lower case *d*) to refer primarily to an audiological condition of hearing loss, and "Deaf" (with an upper case *D*) to refer to a cultural identity (deaf people, that is, who use American Sign Language, share certain attitudes and beliefs about themselves and their relation to the hearing world, and self-consciously think of themselves as part of a separate Deaf culture) has become standard in the literature on Deaf culture. The distinction, while useful and important, is often difficult in practice to apply to individuals, especially when dealing with historical figures. I have not tried to make the distinction in this paper. See Carol Padden and Tom Humphries, *Deaf in America: Voices from a Culture* (Cambridge, Mass., 1988), 2–6.

3. Pierre Desloges, a deaf Parisian, wrote in 1779 that "matters are completely different for the deaf living in society in a great city like Paris. . . . In intercourse with his fellows he promptly acquires the supposedly difficult art of depicting and expressing all his thoughts. . . . No event— in Paris, in France, or in the four corners of the world—lies outside the scope of our discussion. We express ourselves on all subjects with as much order, precision, and rapidity as if we enjoyed the faculty of speech and hearing." Desloges's short book, *Observations d'un sourd et muet sur "Un Cours elementaire d'education des sourds et muets"* is translated in Harlan Lane, ed., *The Deaf Experience: Classics in Language and Education,* trans. Franklin Philip (Cambridge, 1984), 36.

4. The best account of the contemporary American Deaf community can be found in Padden and Humphries, *Deaf in America.* For anyone wishing to understand the world of deaf people, this small but rich and insightful book is a fine place to start. For a concise history of the formation of the deaf community in nineteenth-century United States, see John Vickrey Van Cleve and Barry Crouch, *A Place of Their Own: Creating the Deaf Community in America* (Washington, D. C., 1989); see also, Jack Gannon, *Deaf Heritage: A Narrative History of Deaf America* (Silver Spring, Md., 1981), a popular history that was written by a deaf man, published by the National Association of the Deaf, and created primarily for the deaf community.

5. I am using "sign language" here as a generic term referring to any complex means of manual communication. In the nineteenth century, as today, there were (to simplify) two forms of sign language in use: American Sign Language, a natural language that has evolved over the course of American history within the deaf community, having roots in French Sign Language, indigenous sign languages, and a variety of British Sign Language brought to Martha's Vineyard; and signed English (called "methodical signs" in the nineteenth century), of which several varieties exists. These latter are not true languages but manual codes invented for educational use to represent English manually. Manualists in the nineteenth century at different times used both, and oralists opposed both. See Joseph D. Stedt and Donald F. Moores, "Manual Codes on English and American Sign Language: Historical perspectives and Current Realities," in Harry Borstein, ed., *Manual Communication: Implications for Education* (Washington, D.C., 1990), 1–20; James Woodward, "Historical Bases of American Sign Language," in Patricia Siple,

ed., *Understanding Language Through Sign Language Research* (New York, 1978), 333–48.

6. According to Alexander Graham Bell, 23.7 percent "taught wholly by oral methods"; 14.7 percent "taught also by Manual Spelling (no Sign-language)"; 53.1 percent "with whom speech is used [in at least some classes] as a means of instruction." See "Address of the President," *Association Review* 1 (Oct. 1899), 78–79 (in 1910 renamed the *Volta Review*). Bell's figures differ somewhat from those provided by the *American Annals of the Deaf*—see, for example, Edward Allen Fay in "Progress of Speech-Teaching in the United States," *Annals* 60 (Jan. 1915): 115. Bell's method of counting, as he explains in the same issue, is more precise in that he distinguishes between those taught wholly by oral methods and those taught in part orally and in part manually.

7. "Statistics of Speech Teaching in American Schools for the Deaf," *Volta Review* 22 (June 1920): 372.

8. See, for example, J. C. Gordon, "Dr. Gordon's Report," *American Review* 1 (Dec. 1899): 213; Mary McCowen, "Educational and Social Work for the Deaf and Deafened in the Middle West," *Oralism and Auralism* 6 (Jan. 1927): 67.

9. Henry Kisor, *What's That Pig Outdoors? A Memoir of Deafness* (New York, 1990), 259; Kisor was orally educated, never learned sign language, and has been very successful communicating orally all his life. Nevertheless he condemns "the history of oralism, the unrelenting and largely unsuccessful attempt to teach *all* the deaf to speak and read lips without relying on sign language" (9).

The reintroduction of sign language into the classroom has been even more rapid than its banishment at the turn of the century; it occurred amidst widespread dissatisfaction with oralism—after a series of studies suggested that early use of sign language had no negative effect on speech skills and positive effects on English acquisition as well as social and intellectual development. See Donald F. Moores, *Educating the Deaf: Psychology, Principals and Practices* (Boston, 1987), 10–13. Julia M. Davis and Edward J. Hardick, *Rehabilitative Audiology for Children and Adults* (New York, 1981), 319–25; Mimi Whei Ping Lou, "The History of Language Use in the Education of the Deaf in the United States," in Michael Strong, ed., *Language Learning and Deafness* (Cambridge, 1988), 88–94; Leo M. Jacobs, *A Deaf Adult Speaks Out* (Washington, D. C., 1980), 26, 41–50.

10. Van Cleve and Crouch, *A Place of Their Own*, 128–41; Beryl Lieff Benderly, *Dancing Without Music:*

Deafness in America (Garden City, N.Y., 1980), 127–29; Harlan Lane, *When the Mind Hears: A History of the Deaf* (New York, 1984), 371–72; Padden and Humphries, *Deaf in America*, 110–12; Oliver Sacks, *Seeing Voices: A Journey into the World of the Deaf* (Berkeley, 1989), 25–28.

11. Quoted in Lane, *When the Mind Hears*. 371

12. Lane, *When the Mind Hears*, 301–2.

13. Richard Winefield, *Never the Twain Shall Meet: Bell, Gallaudet, and the Communications Debate* (Washington, D.C., 1987), 81–96; Van Cleve and Crouch, *A Place of Their Own*, 114–27; Lane, *When the Mind Hears*, 353–61.

14. Van Cleve and Crouch, *A Place of Their Own*, 106–7, 119, 126.

15. Lane, *When the Mind Hears*, xiii, 283–85.

16. Instruction in oral communication is still given in all educational programs for deaf and hearing-impaired children. "Oralism" as a philosophy of education does not mean simply oral instruction, but is rather a philosophy that maintains that all or most deaf children can be taught this way *exclusively*. The current philosophy, known as "Total Communication," and nineteenth-century manualism have in common the use of sign language. But American Sign Language was commonly used in the nineteenth century, while today some form of signed English delivered simultaneously with speech is most common. The integration of deaf pupils into the public schools, with the use of interpreters, is now the norm. The arguments today are not for the most part between oralists and manualists but between the advocates of signed English and American Sign Language, and between mainstreaming and separate residential schooling. See Moores, *Educating the Deaf*, 1–28.

17. Luzerne Ray, "Introductory," *Annals* 1 (Oct. 1847): 4.

18. Thomas H. Gallaudet, "The Natural Language of Signs," *Annals* 1 (Oct. 1847): 55–56.

19. Ibid., 56.

20. Thomas H. Gallaudet, "The Natural Language of Signs—II" *Annals* 1 (Jan. 1848): 82, 88.

21. Ibid., 82–85.

22. Ibid., 88–89. The emphasis on the heart rather than the intellect was of course a commonplace of Second great Awakening Evangelicalism. Reason and knowledge were not, however, seen as opposed to religion, and were also highly valued; see Jean V. Matthews, *Toward a New Society: American Thought and Culture*, 1800–1830 (Boston, 1991) 35.

23. Thomas H. Gallaudet, "The Natural Language of Signs—II," 86.

24. Lucius Woodruff, "The Motives to Intellectual

Effort on the part of the Young Deaf-Mute," *Annals* 1 (Apr. 1848): 163–65.

25. David Walker Howe, "The Evangelical Movement and Political Culture in the North during the Second Party System," *Journal of American History* 77 (Mar. 1991): 1220.

26. Collins Stone, "The Religious State and Instruction of the Deaf and Dumb," *Annals* 1 (Apr. 1848): 144.

27. Henry B. Camp, "Claims of the Deaf and Dumb Upon Public Sympathy and Aid," *Annals* 1 (July 1848): 213–14.

28. Stone, "The Religious State," 133–34, 137.

29. Ibid., 134–35, 138.

30. J. A. Ayres, "An Inquiry into the Extent to which the Misfortune of Deafness may be Alleviated," *Annals* 1 (July 1848): 223.

31. Luzerne Ray, "Thoughts of the Deaf and Dumb before Instruction," *Annals* 1 (Apr. 1848): 150–51.

32. Camp, "Claims of the Deaf," 210–15. See also Woodruff, "The Motives to Intellectual Effort," 163–65.

33. Stone, "The Religious State," 136–37.

34. Woodruff, "The Motives to Intellectual Effort," 165–66.

35. Ayres, "An Inquiry," 224.

36. John Carlin, "The Mute's Lament," *Annals* 1 (Oct. 1847): 15. Carlin, a successful artist, was well known for his expressions of what today might be termed "self hatred." He was a contradictory individual. Although he married a deaf woman, used sign language, and was an ardent supported of the establishment of Gallaudet College, he claimed to prefer the company of hearing people and expressed contempt for deaf people and sign language. While he did not speak or lip-read, he became one of the small minority of deaf adults who supported the oralist movement. Carlin derided proposals for a separatist community of deaf people on the grounds that "it is a well known fact that the majority of them [deaf people] show little decision of purpose in any enterprise whatever." *Annals* 10 (Apr. 1858): 89. See also Lane, *When the Mind Hears*, 245–46, 275–76, 325; Van Cleve and Crouch, *A Place of Their Own*, 66, 76–78.

37. Anon., *Annals* 1 (July 1848): 209.

38. Padden and Humphries identify the use of "silence" in reference to deaf people as metaphorical. They explain that sound (to greatly simplify their argument) directly and indirectly plays an important role in the lives of deaf people and has important meanings for them, albeit quite different ones than for the hearing; *Deaf in America*, 91–109.

39. Frank Booth, "The Association Magazine," *Association Review* 1 (Oct. 1899): 4.

40. Alexander Graham Bell, "Address of the President," *Association Review* 1 (Oct. 1899): 74–75, 85.

41. Bell, "Address of the President," 78–79 (see note 6). "Statistics of Speech Teaching in American Schools for the Deaf," 372.

42. Percentages of deaf teachers by year: 1852–38 percent; 1858–41 percent; 1870–41 percent; 1880–29 percent; 1892–24 percent; 1897–18 percent; 1915–15 percent, compiled from periodic reports of schools for the deaf, published in the *American Annals of the Deaf* during the years indicated, under the heading "Tabular Statement of American Schools for the Deaf."

43. Winefield, *Never the Twain Shall Meet*, 48.

44. John Van Cleve, "Nebraska's Oral Law of 1911 and the Deaf Community," *Nebraska History* 65 (Summer 1984): 208.

45. *Annals* 44 (June 1899): 221–29.

46. John M. Tyler, "The Teacher and the State," *Association Review* 1 (Oct. 1899): 9, 12–13.

47. Katherine T. Bingham, "All Along the Line, *Association Review* 2 (Feb. 1900): 27, 29.

48. Edward C. Rider, "The Annual Report of the Northern New York Institution for the Year Ending September 30, 1898," reprinted in the *Association Review* 1 (Dec. 1899): 214–15.

49. S. G. Davidson, "The Relation of Language to Mental Development and of Speech to Language Teaching," *Association Review* 1 (Dec. 1899), 132. See also, Alexander Graham Bell, *Proceedings of the Twelfth Convention of American Instructors of the Deaf* (New York, 1890), 181.

50. Joseph C. Gordon, *The Difference Between the Two Systems of Teaching Deaf-Mute Children the English Language: Extracts from a Letter to a Parent Requesting Information Relative to the Prevailing Methods of Teaching Language to Deaf-Mutes in America* (Washington, D. C., 1898), 1.

51. J. D. Kirkhuff, "The Sign System Arraigned," *Silent Educator* 3 (Jan. 1892): 88a.

52. S. G. Davidson, "The Relation of Language Teaching to Mental Development," *National Educational Association: Journal of Proceedings and Addresses of the Thirty-Seventh Annual Meeting* (Washington, D. C., 1898), 1044.

53. Edward M. Gallaudet, "'Deaf Mute' Conventions, Associations, and Newspapers," *Annals* 18 (July 1873): 200–206.

54. Frederick E. Hoxie, *A Final Promise: The Campaign to Assimilate the Indians, 1880–1920* (Lincoln, Neb., 1984), 12.

55. Alexander Graham Bell, *Memoir Upon the Formation of a Deaf Variety of the Human Race* (Washington, D. C., 1884), 194.

56. Bell, *Memoir*, 194, 217–18, 223.

57. Mary S. Garrett, "The State of the Case," *National Educational Association: Journal of Proceedings and Addresses of the Thirty-Ninth Annual Meeting* (Washington, D.C., 1900), 663; Bell, *Memoir*, 221–22.

58. Bell, *Memoir*, 217, 221–23.

59. Edward Allen Fay, "An Inquiry Concerning the Results of Marriages of the Deaf in America," *Annals* 42 (Feb. 1897): 100–102; see also the discussion of this issue in Van Cleve and Crouch, *A Place of Their Own*, 150–52.

60. On the influence of eugenics upon Bell's work in deaf education, see Winefield, *Never the Twain Shall Meet*, 82–96; Lane, *When the Mind Hears*, 353–61; Van Cleve and Crouch, *A Place of Their Own*, 145–52; for a more sympathetic view of Bell's eugenic concerns about deafness, see Robert V. Bruce, *Bell: Alexander Graham Bell and the Conquest of Solitude* (Ithaca, N. Y., 1973), 409–12.

61. Quoted in Padden and Humphries, *Deaf in America*, 36.

62. Helen Taylor, "The Importance of a Right Beginning," *Association Review* 1 (Dec. 1899): 159.

63. Ibid.

64. Bingham, "All Along the Line," 28–29.

65. Ibid. See also, J. C. Gordon, "Dr. Gordon's Report," *Association Review* 1 (Dec. 1899): 204.

66. Gordon, "Dr. Gordon's Report," 213.

67. Bingham, "All Along the Line," 29; see also Emma Garrett, "A Plea that the Deaf 'Mutes' of America May be Taught to Use Their Voices," *Annals* 28 (Jan. 1883): 18.

68. Thomas H. Gallaudet, "The Natural Language of Signs—II," 89; J. D. Kirkhuff, "The Sign System Arraigned," 88a.

69. Davidson, "The Relation of Language," 132.

70. Emma Garrett, "A Plea," 18.

71. Gordon, "Dr. Gordon's Report," 206.

72. Bingham, "All Along the Line," 22.

73. Benjamin D. Pettingill, "The Sign-Language," *Annals* 18 (Jan. 1873), 4.

74. Sara Harvey Porter, "The Suppression of Signs by Force," *Annals* 39 (June 1894): 171. Porter repeated this observation in 1913, when she stated that in the "old primitive fighting days the oralists cried to us, derisively: 'Your children, making signs, look like monkeys!" In the context it is not clear whether she believed those fighting days were over, or whether she was calling for their end; *Annals* 58 (May 1913): 284.

75. R. W. Dodds, "The Practical Benefits of Methods Compared," *Annals* 44 (Feb. 1899): 124.

76. Lewis J. Dudley, "Address of Mr. Dudley in 1880," *Fifteenth Annual Report of the Clarke Institution for Deaf-Mutes* (Northhampton, Mass., 1882), 7.

77. Ibid.
78. From extracts reprinted in Alexander Graham Bell, "Historical Notes Concerning the Teaching of Speech to the Deaf," *Association Review* (Apr. 1902): 151.
79. Stone, "On the Religious State," 137.
80. Camp, "Claims of the Deaf," 214.
81. Bingham, "All Along the Line," 28; Taylor, "The Importance of a Right Beginning," 158.
82. J. A. Jacobs, "To Save the Souls of His Pupils, the Great Duty of a Teacher of Deaf-Mutes," *Annals* 8 (July 1856): 211; Susanna E. Hull, "The Psychological Method of Teaching Language," *Annals* 43 (Apr. 1898): 190.
83. Donald G. Matthews, "The Second Great Awakening as an Organizing Process, 1780–1830; An Hypothesis," *American Quarterly* 21 (Spring 1969): 23–43; Richard Carwardine, "The Know-Nothing Party, the Protestant Evangelical Community and American National Identity," in *Religion and National Identity*, Stuart Mews, ed. (Oxford, 1982), 449–63.
84. Rivka Shpak Lissak, *Pluralism and Progressives: Hull House and the New Immigrants, 1890–1919* (Chicago, 1989): 50–55.
85. Taylor, "The Importance of a Right beginning," 158. The equation of equality with sameness was a staple of Progressive reform thought; see Lissak, *Pluralism and Progressives*, 153.
86. Lissak, *Pluralism and Progressives*; Hoxie, *A Final Promise*; Joshua A. Fishman, *Language Loyalty in the United States: The Maintenance and Perpetuation of Non-English Mother Tongues by American Ethnic and Religious Groups* (The Hague, 1966).
87. George Lakoff, *Women, Fire, and Dangerous Things: What Categories Reveal about the Mind* (Chicago, 1987), xiv.
88. Leo M. Jacobs, *A Deaf Adult Speaks Out* (Washington, D.C., 1980), 90–100; Jerome D. Schein, *At Home Among Strangers: Exploring the Deaf Community in the United States* (Washington, D. C., 1989), 130; Paul C. Higgins, *Outsiders in a Hearing World: A Sociology of Deafness* (Beverly Hills, 1980), 69–76; James Woodward, "How You Gonna Get to Heaven if You Can't Talk with Jesus: The Educational Establishment vs. the Deaf Community," in *How You Gonna Get to Heaven if You Can't Talk with Jesus: On Depathologizing Deafness* (Silver Spring, Md., 1982), 11.
89. In the first five years of Gallaudet College (1869 to 1874), a liberal arts college exclusively for deaf students, 75 percent of its graduates became teachers at schools for the deaf. From 1894 to 1899, fewer than a third did so. See Edward P. Clarke, "An Analysis of the Schools and Instructors of the Deaf in the United States," *American Annals of the Deaf* 45 (Apr. 1900): 229.
90. Van Cleve and Crouch, *A Place of Their Own*, 128.
91. See W. Earl Hall, "To Speak or Not to Speak: That is the Question Behind the Bitter Deaf-Teaching Battle," *Iowan* 4 (Feb.–Mar. 1956) for a brief description of a battle between the Iowa Association of the Deaf and the Iowa School for the Deaf in the 1950s over this issue. See also Van Cleve, "Nebraska's Oral Law," 195–220; Van Cleve and Crouch, *A Place of Their Own*, 128–41.
92. Padden and Humphries, *Deaf in America*, 5–6; Benderly, *Dancing Without Music*, 218–39; Schein, *At Home Among Strangers*, 72–105, 106, 120.
93. Padden and Humphries, *Deaf in America*, 26–38, 110–21, explore the alternative meanings of deafness created by the deaf community; their focus is on the present, but their brief forays into the historical roots of these meanings are suggestive and insightful.

CHAPTER 4

Disability and the Human Genome

James C. Wilson

If this is the Book of Life, we should not settle for a rough draft over the long term but should remain committed to producing a final, highly accurate version.
—Francis S. Collins, "Shattuck Lecture: Medical and Societal Consequences of the Human Genome Project"

So this book . . . maps its particular investigations along the double helix of a work's reception history and its production history. But the work of knowing demands that the map be followed into the textual field, where "the meaning of the texts" will appear as a set of concrete and always changing conditions; because the meaning is in the use, and textuality is a social condition of various times, places, and persons.
—Jerome J. McGann, *The Textual Condition*

When Francis S. Collins, the director of the National Human Genome Research Institute, delivered the 109th Shattuck Lecture at the 1999 meeting of the Massachusetts Medical Society, he likened the sequencing of the human genome to "the great expeditions—those of Lewis and Clark, Sir Edmund Hillary, and even Neil Armstrong." The search for what Collins called the "complete set of genetic instructions of the human being" was undertaken by scientists in order to "map the human genetic terrain, knowing it would lead them to

previously unimaginable insights, and from there to the common good" (28). It is this concept of the genetic body-text—and the implications of the resulting construction of disability as textual error—that I wish to examine.

First, a few definitions for those readers who are not immediately familiar with genetics. A genome refers to the complete DNA code of a particular organism or species. DNA molecules are found in the nucleus of every cell, carried on chemical structures known as chromosomes. Sequencing the human genome involves identifying its roughly three billion pairs of nucleotide bases and then storing this information in computer databases. Mapping involves location analysis meant to establish linkage. In one sense linkage refers to the location of a particular gene in relation to other genes, but it can also mean correlation with a phenotype (i.e., a gene "linked" to Parkinson's). Biotechnology and pharmaceutical companies hope to make billions of dollars as the function of more and more genes is established and feasible treatment options for harmful mutations within them are developed.[1]

The expedition to sequence and map the human genome has evolved into a two-way race between the Human Genome Project and Celera Genomics, a private biotechnology company located in Rockville, Maryland. The two competitors made a joint announcement in June 2000, issuing a joint report and releasing a "working draft" of the genome. Celera intends to finish its sequence of the human genome by December 2001 (or earlier) and then to patent sequences auspicious for therapeutic development.[2] To compete with Celera, the Human Genome Project will finish computing the entire sequence by the end of 2003. The Human Genome Project is an international consortium that includes the U.S. National Institutes of Health and Department of Energy, the Wellcome Trust of London, and ten pharmaceutical companies. In contrast to Celera's for-profit approach, the Human Genome Project has adopted a policy of releasing data every twenty-four hours to a free, publicly accessible database called GenBank.[3]

Sequencing the human genome was proclaimed to be "the single most important project in biology and the biomedical sciences—one that will permanently change biology and medicine" by members of the National Institutes of Health and Department of Energy planning groups in their "New Goals for the U.S. Human Genome Project: 1998–2003."[4] The transition to "sequence-based" biology, they announced, will aid in the development of "highly accurate DNA-based medical diagnostics and therapeutics" (Collins et al., 682). Francis S. Collins concluded his "Shattuck Lecture," subtitled "Medical and Societal Consequences of the Human Genome Project," by declaring that the project's goal was to "uncover the hereditary factors in virtually every disease" so as to make that information available for the prevention and cure of those diseases (36). Likewise, the Human Genome Project's Web page proclaims: "The ultimate goal is to use this information to develop new ways to treat, cure, or even prevent the thousands of diseases that afflict humankind." The dozens of news and research articles linked to the Human Genome Project's Web page contain repeated references to "defective genes" and "genetic mistakes."[5] Thus the stated purpose, the very promise of genome sequencing and mapping, is to "correct" errors in the genetic "instruction book" that result in disease and disability. Indeed, this promise of genetic-based medicine has enabled those involved in genetic research to successfully promote their work in the public arena and solicit enormous subsidies from the U.S. Congress (more on this later). The allied fields of genetics and molecular biology are therefore in the process of constructing a model of disability as flawed genetic text in need of rewriting.

In the remainder of this article I will argue that the concept of (re)writing the genetic body-text (in addition to being simplistic and misleading) reinforces our culture's negative constructions of disability and creates a "genetic Other." In contrast, I will suggest that a more realistic understanding of genetics as difference supports the model of disability theorized by disability studies.[6]

(RE)WRITING THE GENETIC BODY-TEXT

Genome sequencing—or genomics—has created the new scientific field of bioinformatics. Genomes are sequenced by high-speed robotic sequencing machines; the resulting information is transformed into an alphabetical pattern of symbols for DNA subunits called bases (C, T, A, G),[7] which are stored as digital information in computer databases. This digital information is accessible on the Internet (at sites like GenBank) to anyone who has a computer. Digitalization/alphabetization of the genetic body-text has fostered the much used analogy of DNA as a molecular language where the "letters" are bases, the "words" are genes, and the "book" is the complete genome.[8] Scientists, science writers, and science journalists frequently use this analogy to explain genomics to lay audiences. In this analogy genetics becomes textuality, and the human genome becomes the "Book of Life." Scientific journals, as well as the mass media, borrow the terminology of textual criticism, editing, and computer science as a way of making genetics comprehensible—to explain the mechanism by which DNA participates in the production of the proteins involved in all biological activities.[9]

Implicit in this textual analogy is the fiction of the standard(ized) body-text. Donna J. Haraway has referred to the sequencing of the human genome as an "act of canonization," the production of a "standard reference work . . . through which human diversity and its pathologies could be tamed in the exhaustive code kept by a national or international genetic bureau of standards" (215). The logic here suggests that any deviation from this authoritative genetic script results in a flawed and thus corrupted text. One recent example of this usage is "Repairing the Genome's Spelling Mistakes" by science writer Trisha Gura in *Science*. The article begins: "On the computer, correcting spelling errors takes nothing but a quick keystroke or two. Now, researchers are trying to harness the cell's own spell-check program—its DNA repair machinery—to tackle a much more difficult problem: fixing errors in the flawed genes that cause such hereditary diseases as sickle cell anemia and cystic fibrosis" (316). Thus disease/disability is cast as textual irregularity, and those in the biomedical community become editors who attempt to amend, delete, and correct the defective texts of disabled bodies.

However, the concept of a single, authoritative text—now mostly outdated in the humanities—poses as many problems for genome sequencers as it does for textual editors. To begin with, the Human Genome Project and Celera Genomics are both constructing a hypothetical DNA sequence by assembling multiple DNA fragments into a complete genome. This "consensus" DNA sequence (even if only a statistical generalization) will be, like all composites, a fiction. Partly in response to this issue, the Human Genome Diversity Project was formed in 1993 to "explore the full range of genome diversity within the human family," according to its Web page. Stressing the importance of understanding genetic diversity, the Human Genome Diversity Project warns: "Without this Project, science will characterize 'the' human genome, with its historical and medical implications, largely in terms of what is known from a small sample of people of European origin."[10] In actuality, there is no prototypical genetic script by which to measure or evaluate all others. The notion of the "correct" genetic text resembles that of the "unitary text of modern scholarship," which hypertext theorizer George P. Landow characterizes as a "bizarrely fictional idealization" (66).

Jerome J. McGann's work in textual criticism is relevant here and can help identify the problems inherent in creating a "correct" genetic text. McGann argues that "textuality is a social condition" (1991, 16), and thus the textual condition is one of indeterminacy. "Instability is an essential feature of the text in process" (94), McGann writes, arguing that "no single 'text' of a particular work . . . can be imagined or hypothesized as the 'correct' one" (62). Instead, texts are produced and reproduced in a process defined by multiplicity, that is, a process that results in different texts with different intentionalities that reflect particular social and institutional conditions. All texts, McGann explains, are social products, mediated by "determinate sociohistorical conditions" (9). And perhaps most important for the purposes of this article, the "meaning" of a text is in its use.

Like McGann's literary text and Landow's hypertext, no unitary genetic script exists that can be considered definitive. "The Human Genome Project is founded upon a fallacy," writes Matt Ridley in *Genome: The Autobiography of a Species in 23 Chapters.* "There is no such thing as 'the human genome.' Neither in space nor in time can such a definitive object be defined. . . . Variation is an inherent and integral part of the human—or indeed any—genome" (145). No two human genomes are or can ever be alike: all exhibit mutations, deletions, and other genetic variants (beyond having different alleles for the same gene). Not only is genetic variation (in the larger sense) the norm, these variations are never fixed, but always in the process of becoming. Genomes are dynamic, constantly evolving over time, shaped by both internal and external factors (such as infectious disease, which I will discuss later). Even when mutations occur, many of them are gradually purged by genetic drift, random change (Ridley). Thus, in the final analysis, arguments that posit a correct genetic script are ultimately teleological: they imply a kind of evolutionary "final intention" that recalls the concept of authorial final intention that has so troubled modern textual scholars. As McGann, and other textual critics, has shown, the theory (McGann calls it an "ideology") of "final intentions' is "a deeply problematic concept" (1983, 68).

Though molecular genetics continues to detect genome variations, writes Lois Wingerson in *Unnatural Selection: The Promise and the Power of Human Gene Research,* "it helps to remember that in many cases it is our environment and often simply our society that defines these variations as 'disorders' " (332). I am not denying, and neither is Wingerson, that some genetic mutations (for example) can be deleterious; clearly they can. Rather, my quarrel here is with the simplistic construction of normal versus abnormal genomes and the implica-

tion of that textual fiction for people with disabilities. The Human Genome Project's Web page illustrates this construction of normality. Here we find (a typical example) that DNA testing "involves comparing the sequence of DNA bases in a patient's gene to a normal version of the gene."[11] However, since genomes are constantly changing, a normal genome is an impossibility; that would be like saying that there is a normal course of evolution.

If the Human Genome Project does indeed have the potential to "permanently change biology and medicine," as Francis S. Collins and many others in the biomedical community have argued, it also has the potential to permanently stigmatize disability as the genetic Other. To understand this danger we need to recognize that the meaning of genetic medicine is constructed by the intersection of genetic codes and social codes.

GENOHYPE AND THE MYTH OF THE ALL-POWERFUL GENE

The Human Genome Project has engendered what Neil A. Holtzman, of Genetics and Public Policy Studies at Johns Hopkins Medical Institutions, calls "genohype." The genohype can at times obscure the fact that cultural meanings are automatically coded into words like "genes" and "inherited traits." Indeed, such terms, when manipulated and proliferated by the mass media, lead to the popular assumption that genetics represents the fundamental essence, the inescapable fate of a person. This ideological baggage, Celeste Michelle Condit argues, "encourage[s] an asocial biological determinism and discriminatory attitudes with regard to both class and disability" ("Character," 178). Condit and many other critics believe that this biological/genetic determinism is inaccurate and misleading.[12]

Here it might be helpful to take a closer look at the all-powerful gene. It is important to remember that genes are conceptual as well as physical, referring to functional segments of DNA. (Up to 90 percent of human DNA is—apparently—nonfunctional and therefore categorized as "junk" DNA.)[13] The DNA segments designated as genes are functional in that they participate in the manufacture of protein by coding the order of the amino acids used to assemble the proteins. Often, scientists as well as science writers and journalists will construct a hierarchical model of this process with the gene at the top and the many other factors involved at the bottom. The active verbs most often used to describe what genes do clearly reveal this bias: genes are said to "control," to "program," to "determine," to "encode" proteins. Consider this typical example from "Gene Therapy's Focus Shifts from Rare Illnesses" by *New York Times* science journalist Andrew Pollack: "The idea is simple and eloquent. Many inherited diseases are caused by a *faulty* gene, which makes the body unable to produce some essential protein or enzyme" (my italics). Or consider this variation that relies on the familiar but awkward trope of "genes gone bad" by Emma Ross of the Associated Press: "Genes can promote or cause disease when they don't work *properly.* Some illnesses linked to genes gone bad include cancer, arthritis, diabetes, high blood pressure, Alzheimer's and multiple sclerosis" (A11, my italics). Even the Human Genome Project's Web page states: "The successes of the Human Genome Project (HGP) have even enabled researchers to pinpoint errors in genes—the smallest units of heredity—that cause or contribute to disease."[14]

How does this hierarchical model of protein production serve the biomedical community? For one thing, it makes public relations, as well as lobbying and fund-raising, easier when scientists can point to a single gene as the culprit in the production of a certain protein, linked to diabetes or breast cancer, for example. With adequate funding, so the suggestion goes, biomedical editors can rewrite this and other flawed genes that produce disease and disability so as to produce a genetically altered—and approved—text.

In actuality, other factors participate in the formation of proteins, including ribosomes, messenger RNA (mRNA), transfer RNA (tRNA), and amino acids, as well as external factors such as environmental stresses like viruses or toxins.[15] Making the situation even more complicated, some traits are polygenic (that is, they involve multiple genes). Moreover, gene expression is dynamic (meaning that in a matter of minutes genes can be switched on and off).

"We must remember that genetic functions are embedded in complex networks of biological reactions and social and economic relationships," write Ruth Hubbard and Elijah Wald in *Exploding the Gene Myth* (12). Harvard biologist Richard Lewontin calls it "bad biology" to separate genes from their environment. In his recent *The Triple Helix: Gene, Organism, and Environment,* he argues: "If we had the complete DNA sequence of an organism and unlimited computational power, we could not compute the organism, because the organism does not compute itself from its genes." He goes on to explain that "the ontogeny of an organism is the consequence of a unique interaction between the genes it carries, the temporal sequence of external environments through which it passes during its life, and random events of molecular interactions within individual cells" (17–18).

Matt Ridley examines some of the environmental factors that have shaped (and continue to shape) the human genome, including infectious disease. The great epidemic diseases of the past (such as plague, measles, smallpox, typhoid, and malaria) all left their imprint on the human genome.[16] Mutations that granted resistance to these infectious diseases thrived but in turn created a susceptibility to other disorders (such as sickle cell anemia, for example). Ridley also discusses the emerging field of "psychoneuroimmunology," which studies the link between the mind, the body, the immune system, and the genome. "The mind drives the body, which drives the genome," Ridley writes (157). All of these factors prompt Ridley to conclude: "The genome that we decipher in this generation is but a snapshot of an ever-changing document. There is no definitive edition" (146).

The point here is that genes do not act alone but participate in an integrated network of systems: biological, social, psychological, environmental, etc. Though more accurate, the integrated network model of DNA transcription poses problems to science writers and journalists eager to employ pat phrases like "genes gone bad" to relay complex information to their audiences. The integrated network model also complicates fund-raising and public relations for the scientific community. As academics know all too well, it is not so easy to get multimillion-dollar grants to investigate environmental or social systems.

GENETICIZING DISABILITY

As I begin my final section, let me just say that I am not opposed to genetic medicine. It would be absurd for those of us in the disability community to argue against genetic research or medical technology. Indeed, many people who have experienced disability are alive today because of medical technology (myself included) and are understandably grateful for any research that promises to improve the lives of the disabled. My concern here is that genomics, as the field is currently constituted and presented to the public, reinforces the social stigma attached to disability.[17] Indeed, as we have seen, the genetic model of disability as defective or corrupted text

reduces people with disabilities to the level of spelling mistakes, typographical errors that need to be eliminated by genetic editors. Feminist philosopher of science Sandra Harding reminds us that science is not value-free and that its technologies participate in the "translation of social agendas into technological ones" (37). Unfortunately, many of the new technologies associated with genomics—such as genetic tests and genetic screening—raise the specter of an old social agenda that is still very much a part of medical science's professional and public discourse: eugenics.[18] In fact, philosopher Philip Kitcher has referred to genetic screening as "laissez-fair eugenics."

Underwriting the model of disability as flawed genetic text is the binary construction of normal versus abnormal. The tyranny of the norm goes back at least as far as Aristotle, whose taxonomies provide the foundation of Western intellectual tradition. Aristotle established binary opposites—normal versus abnormal—in discursive realms that encompassed poetics, rhetoric, ethics, politics, as well as the natural sciences.[19] In "Constructing Normalcy: The Bell Curve, the Novel, and the Invention of the Disabled Body in the Nineteenth Century," Lennard J. Davis traces the evolution of the norm from a concept to an ideology of human perfectibility, as measured and created by statistics, eugenics, the bell curve, and intelligence tests:

> The concept of a norm, unlike that of an ideal, implies that the majority of the population must or should somehow be part of the norm. The norm pins down that majority of the population that falls under the arch of the standard bell-shaped curve. This curve, the graph of an exponential function, that was known variously as the astronomer's "error law," the "normal distribution," the "Gaussian density function," or simply "the bell curve," became in its own way a symbol of the tyranny of the norm. Any bell curve

will always have at its extremities those characteristics that deviate from the norm. (13)

The binary construction of normal versus abnormal is equally prevalent in contemporary biomedical discourse (as we have seen previously in an example from the HGP Web page). Consider another recent example from *Science,* where Esmail D. Zanjani and W. French Anderson write in "Prospects for in Utero Human Gene Therapy": "For the neurologic genetic diseases (such as Tay-Sachs, Niemann-Pick, Lesch-Nyhan, Sandhoff, Leigh, many leukodystrophies, generalized gangliosidosis) that appear to produce irreversible damage during gestation, treatment before birth (perhaps early in pregnancy) may be required to allow the birth of a normal baby" (2084). The point here is that this binary construction masks a social hierarchy (with those who are "abnormal" at the bottom) and therefore reinforces the stigma attached to disability. Sometimes the language itself reinforces this social stigma, as in the case of science writer Trisha Gura's "Gene Defect Linked to Rett Syndrome," a report on the gene "at fault in Rett Syndrome, which afflicts at least one in 10,000 girls." "Exactly how the defect leads to the neurological decline of the afflicted girls has yet to be deciphered" (27), Gura admits, but her use of the word "afflicted," with its biblical implications of divine punishment for sin, suggests that those who have Rett syndrome are somehow deserving of their condition.[20] This newly defined category of genetically afflicted provides a clear example of the interconnection of medical and social codes, here equally complicit in stigmatizing disability.

The attempt to geneticize disability relates to what sociologist Troy Duster calls a "'drift' toward greater receptivity to genetic explanation for an increasing variety of human behaviors" (119). These behaviors include violence, homosexuality, alcoholism, criminality, polygamy, and other behaviors considered socially deviant by the dominant culture. The danger, of course, is that as more genes are mapped, sequenced, and patented, new variations in the genetic script will be identified that will stigmatize still other behaviors and conditions. As Hubbard and Wald remark, rather sarcastically, "As long as every deviation . . . is considered 'abnormal,' physicians, geneticists, and the biotechnology companies will not run out of customers" (71).

And, I might add, the Human Genome Project will not run out of funding. It is especially troubling to me that so much of the National Institutes of Health's research and development funding goes to genetic research and so little to directly help those who live with the diseases and impairments that the Human Genome Project claims to be attempting to remediate. For example, in 1996, the last year for which I have figures, the National Institutes of Health allocated $200 million to the Human Genome Project, while providing only $1,410,925 for AIDS research, $381,880 for breast cancer research, and $111,479 for schizophrenia research.[21] Admittedly, there are other sources of government funding for this research, such as the National Science Foundation. Nevertheless, the numbers speak for themselves about NIH priorities.

The biomedical community's success in fund-raising has come at the expense of people with disabilities in yet another way. Scientists actively participate in the creation of the "specter" of disability, which they then exploit for public relations purposes. This specter, which preys on the public's fear of disease and disability, allows scientists to justify their biomedical projects and generate research and development funding. In this bogeyman representation, disability becomes not only a personal tragedy but a public burden that costs taxpayers excessively. One sees the disability-as-burden rhetoric used repeatedly in scientific discourse and public relations materials. Consider a recent example from the *New England Journal of Medicine,* taken from a review article on "Neural-Tube Defects." The authors, all associated with the National Center for Environmental Health at the Centers for Disease Control and Prevention, review current strategies to prevent neural-tube defects such as spina bifida. In a section entitled "The Burden of Disease," the authors write:

> In addition to the emotional cost of spina bifida, the estimated monetary cost is staggering. In the United States alone, the total cost of spina bifida over a lifetime (the direct costs of medical, developmental, and educational services and the indirect costs associated with morbidity and mortality, in 1992 dollars) for affected infants born in 1988 was almost $500 million, or $294,000 for each infant.
>
> (Botto et al., 1511)

Once again, I am not arguing against research that might someday prevent at least some spina bifidas; rather, I am pointing out that the rhetoric employed by much of this literature casts people born with these conditions as "burdens." In fact, as the authors of this article admit, neural-tube defects have been recognized since antiquity and are quite common, occurring in 1 of every 1,000 pregnancies (1509). That is, neural-tube defects are (and have always been) a regularly occurring—yes, normal—part of human variation. Perhaps the focus should be not on how to eliminate, but instead on how to accommodate, variation. Rhetoric that casts disability as burden stigmatizes people with disabilities and makes this accommodation much more difficult.

Genomics has enormous potential to advance the understanding of human diversity. We need to remember that genetics *is* variation, and that variation is not only healthy but essential for the survival of a species. Indeed, evolution could not work without genetic diversity. Stephen Jay Gould's analysis of evolution, marked by what he calls "chaos and contingency," comes to mind. Webs of life and anatomical diversity "are so intricate, so imbued with random and chaotic elements, so unrepeatable in encompassing such a multitude of unique (and uniquely interacting) objects, that standard models of simple prediction and replication do not apply" (1994, 85).[22] Any standard biology textbook will instill in its readers an appreciation of the beauty of genetic diversity: the diversity of recombination, spontaneous mutation, speciation, gene expression, and so on. As Lois Wingerson concludes, "If genetics leads us anywhere, it leads us not toward purity but toward a new understanding of variation" (338). The reality is enormous genetic heterogeneity.

If genomics, both the science and the industry, were to more effectively emphasize the normality of variation, the fact that human variation is a continuous spectrum, then surely there would be a better understanding and acceptance of disability. In turn, this acceptance could result in a commitment to accommodation rather than erasure. With its vast resources the Human Genome Project has the potential—and, I would argue, the responsibility—to further this process. And yet, to date, the opposite has happened: the Human Genome Project has pathologized disability and created the genetic Other. Here it is important to note that geneticizing disability is hardly disinterested. Constructing disability as internal genetic mistakes (rather than lack of social accommodation, as disability studies argues) allows private biotechnology companies to develop genetic tests and medicines that turn disability into opportunities for private profit while at the same time limiting public discourse of social responsibility and accommodation.

As Sandra Harding points out, "the sciences generate information that is used to produce technologies and applications that are not morally and politically neutral" (37). Thus the technologies and applications produced by sequencing the human genome raise profound moral and political issues. We should understand that genomics involves more than just compiling databases; it stands to alter the material conditions and shape the lives of the disabled in countless, concrete ways.

NOTES

1. As early as 1995, over fifty biotechnology companies were developing or providing tests to diagnose genetic disorders or predict the risk of their occurrence. See Holtzman.
2. As of October 1999, Celera had filed for 6,500 provisional patents that would give it and its client drug companies—Amgen, Novartis, and Pharmacia & Upjohn—a year to decide which genes they would pursue in their search for genetic tests and genetic medicine.
3. At http://www.ncbi.nlm.nih.gov.
4. The planning groups included Francis S. Collins and Elke Jordan from the National Human Genome Research Institute and Ari Patrinos from the Office of Biological and Environmental Research at the Department of Energy.
5. At http://www.ornl.gov/TechResources/Human_Genome/resource/medicine.html.
6. The field of disability studies emerged in the early 1990s, drawing from other interdisciplinary studies (such as feminism and cultural studies) amid the interest in identity issues growing out of postmodern inquiries into subjectivity. Both a studies area and an approach, what Simi Linton calls "a location and a means to think critically about disability" (1), disability studies has developed a social theory of disability. Linton and others working in the field set aside the medical model of disability as disease or trauma and the "natural" view of it as deficit or defect. Instead, disability studies considers disability as socially constituted. How the disabled are—and historically have been—represented, situated, marginalized, educated, and employed, for example, yields a recognition that what it means to be disabled, indeed the very conditions of disability, are crucially determined by the social order in which one lives.
7. The letters represent the four bases in DNA: cytosine, thymine, adenine, and guanine.
8. An alternate but less popular analogy is the human genome as blueprint. For example, Barbara R. Jasny and Pamela J. Hines write in "Genome Prospecting" that "Much as an architect's blueprint forms the plan of a building, genomic sequence supplies the directions from which a living organism is constructed."
9. For example, consider these recent headlines from *Science*: "Faithful Translations" (September 10, 1999) and "Dirty Transcripts from Clean DNA" (April 2, 1999). Likewise, the original research articles published in *Science* make use of the same textual-editing language. For example, the authors of "A Molecular Pathway Revealing a Genetic Basis for Human Cardiac and Craniofacial Defects" claim to have discovered a gene that, when absent, triggers a common congenital heart defect associated with DiGeorge syndrome, second only to Down's syndrome in causing malformations of the heart. Ninety percent of people with DiGeorge syndrome are missing three megabases of DNA from chromosome 22, designated by the authors as a "DiGeorge deletion site" (Yamagishi et al., 1093). The first two sentences of the authors' abstract demonstrate the genetic-body-as-text model: "Microdeletions of chromosome 22q11 are the most common genetic defects associated with cardiac and craniofacial anomalies in humans. A screen for mouse genes dependent on dHAND, a transcription factor implicated in neural crest development, identified Ufd1, which maps to human 22q11 and encodes a protein involved in degradation of ubiquitinated proteins" (1158).
10. At http://www.stanford.edu/group/morrinst/hgdp/faq.html#Q1. The Human Genome Diversity Project, which is not officially connected to the Human Genome Project, has from its beginning in the early 1990s stressed the importance of understanding genetic variation and the meaning of diversity. Unfortunately, the Project has never been adequately funded and thus far has been powerless to do anything but call attention to the need to consider issues of diversity.
11. At http://www.ornl.gov/TechResources/Human_Genome/resource/medicine.html.
12. J. Weiner argues in *Time, Love, Memory: A Great Biologist and His Quest for the Origins of Behavior* that the popular construction of "a gene for _____" (fill in the blank) comes from the genetics of Thomas Hunt Morgan, an American biologist who won a 1933 Nobel prize for discoveries relating to the hereditary function of chromosomes.
13. By most estimates, there are some 30,000 to 100,000 genes in the human genome.

14. At http://www.ornl.gov/TechResources/Human_Genome/resource/medicine.html.

15. Ribosomes are tiny particles in the cell that bind to messenger RNA, which carries the genetic information needed for protein synthesis, as well as to transfer RNA, the kind of molecule that supplies the ribosome with amino acids, the building blocks of proteins. For more information, see Elizabeth Pennisi, "The Race to the Ribosome Structure."

16. According to Ridley, there are several thousand nearly complete viral genomes integrated into the human genome, most of them now inert and missing a crucial gene. For example, human endogenous retroviruses account for 1.3 percent of the human genome. Another related form, retrotransposons, account for 14.6 percent of the entire genome (125).

17. It can be argued that, curiously, genetic "causes" of disorders absolve disabled people of responsibility at the same time that they stigmatize those same people. For more on this, see Celeste M. Condit's *The Meanings of the Gene: Public Debates about Human Heredity.*

18. Coincidentally, the infamous Eugenics Record Office was located at Cold Spring Harbor, about an hour east of New York City on Long Island. Today the Cold Spring Harbor Laboratory is a major genetics research center.

19. For example, in *Generation of Animals,* his treatise on biology, Aristotle classifies both animals and humans. With humans, any physical difference that "departs from type" (the able-bodied male) becomes a "monstrosity" that, by its very essence, is less than human. The "first beginning of this deviation is when a female is formed instead of a male," Aristotle claims (IV.iii.767b). He goes on to say, "we should look upon the female state as being as it were a deformity" (IV.vi.775a). Among the most extreme cases of such "deformity" are children born with birth anomalies. "Sometimes," he writes, a child "has reached such a point that in the end it no longer has the appearance of a human being at all, but that of an animal only" (IV.iii.769b). In *Nicomachean Ethics* Aristotle takes his argument to its (il)logical conclusion, identifying the norm (or mean) with moral virtue and the abnormal with vice. Thus physical "deformity" becomes moral flaw, exposing Aristotle's binary configuration for what it really is—a social hierarchy.

20. For a discussion of how medical rhetoric constructs people with disease and/or disability as deserving of their conditions, see "Medical Discourse and Subjectivity," in G. Thomas Couser's *Recovering Bodies: Illness, Disability, and Life Writing;* and Scott L. Montgomery's "Illness and Image in Holistic Discourse: How Alternative Is 'Alternative'?" in *Cultural Critique.*

21. The numbers for HGP funding come from Ari Patrinos et al., "New Goals for the U.S. Human Genome Project: 1998–2003," *Science* 282, no. 5389 (1998): 682–89. The numbers for NIH funding of research on specific diseases come from Cary P. Gross et al., "The Relation between Funding by the National Institutes of Health and the Burden of Disease," *New England Journal of Medicine* 340, no. 24 (1999): 1881–87.

22. For a more complete discussion of evolution, see Gould's *Evolution and the History of Life.* See also *The Book of Life,* which Gould edited.

WORKS CITED

Aristotle. *Generation of Animals.* Trans. A. L. Peck. Cambridge: Harvard University Press, 1979.

——. *The Nicomachean Ethics.* Trans. H. Rackham. Cambridge: Harvard University Press, 1975.

Botto, Lorenzo D., Cynthia A. Moore, Muin J. Khoury, and J. David Erickson. "Neural-Tube Defects." *New England Journal of Medicine* 341, no. 20 (1999): 1509–19.

Collins, Francis S. "Shattuck Lecture: Medical and Societal Consequences of the Human Genome Project." *New England Journal of Medicine* 341, no. 1 (1999): 28–37.

Collins, Francis S., Ari Patrinos, et al. "New Goals for the U.S. Human Genome Project: 1998–2003." *Science* 282, no. 5389 (1998): 682–89.

Condit, Celeste Michelle. "The Character of 'History' in Rhetoric and Cultural Studies: Recoding Genetics." In *At the Intersection: Cultural Studies and Rhetorical Studies.* Ed. Thomas Rosteck, 168–85. New York: Guilford, 1999.

——. *The Meanings of the Gene: Public Debates about Human Heredity.* Madison: University of Wisconsin Press, 1999.

Couser, G. Thomas. *Recovering Bodies: Illness, Disability, and Life Writing.* Madison: University of Wisconsin Press, 1997.

Davis, Lennard J. "Constructing Normalcy: The Bell Curve, the Novel, and the Invention of the Disabled Body in the Nineteenth Century." In *The Disability Studies Reader.* New York: Routledge, 1997.

Duster, Troy. "The Prism of Heritability and the Sociology of Knowledge." In *Naked Science: Anthropological Inquiry into Boundaries, Power, and Knowledge.* Ed. Laura Nader. New York: Routledge, 1996. 119–30.

Gould, Stephen Jay. *Evolution and the History of Life.* New York: Basic, 2000.

———. "The Evolution of Life on the Earth." *Scientific American* (October 1994): 85–91.

———, ed. *The Book of Life*. New York: W.W. Norton, 1993.

Gura, Trisha. "Gene Defect Linked to Rett Syndrome." *Science* 286, no. 5437 (1999): 27.

———. "Repairing the Genome's Spelling Mistakes." *Science* 285, no. 5426 (1999): 316–18.

Haraway, Donna J. *Simians, Cyborgs, and Women: The Reinvention of Nature*. New York: Routledge, 1991.

Harding, Sandra. *Whose Science? Whose Knowledge?* Ithaca, N.Y.: Cornell University Press, 1991.

Holtzman, Neil A. "Are Genetic Tests Adequately Regulated?" *Science* 286, no. 5439 (1999): 409.

Hubbard, Ruth, and Elijah Wald. *Exploding the Gene Myth*. Boston: Beacon, 1997.

Jasny, Barbara R., and Pamela J. Hines. "Genome Prospecting." *Science* 286, no. 5439 (1999): 443.

Kitcher, Philip. *The Lives to Come*. New York: Simon and Schuster, 1996.

Landow, George P. *Hypertext 2.0: The Convergence of Contemporary Critical Theory and Technology*. Baltimore: Johns Hopkins University Press, 1997.

Lewontin, Richard. *The Triple Helix: Gene, Organism, and Environment*. Cambridge: Harvard University Press, 2000.

Linton, Simi. *Claiming Disability: Knowledge and Identity*. New York: New York University Press, 1998.

McGann, Jerome J. *The Textual Condition*. Princeton, N.J.: Princeton University Press, 1991.

———. *A Critique of Modern Textual Criticism*. Chicago: University of Chicago Press, 1983.

Montgomery, Scott L. "Illness and Image in Holistic Discourse: How Alternative Is 'Alternative'?" *Cultural Critique* 25 (1993): 65–89.

Pennisi, Elizabeth. "The Race to the Ribosome Structure." *Science* 285, no. 5436 (1999): 2048–51.

Pollack, Andrew. "Gene Therapy's Focus Shifts from Rare Illnesses." *New York Times on the Web*, August 4, 1998, http://www.nytimes.com.

Ridley, Matt. *Genome: The Autobiography of a Species in 23 Chapters*. New York: Harper Collins, 1999.

Ross, Emma. "Scientists Near Goal: DNA Code of Chromosome." *Cincinnati Enquirer*, October 22, 1999, A11.

Weiner, J. *Time, Love, Memory: A Great Biologist and His Quest for the Origins of Behavior*. New York: Knopf, 1999.

Wingerson, Lois. *Unnatural Selection: The Promise and the Power of Human Gene Research*. New York: Bantam, 1998.

Yamagishi, Hiroyuki, Vidu Garg, et al. "A Molecular Pathway Revealing a Genetic Basis for Human Cardiac and Craniofacial Defects." *Science* 283, no. 5405 (1999): 1158–61.

Zanjani, Esmail D., and W. French Anderson. "Prospects for In Utero Human Gene Therapy. *Science* 285, no. 5436 (1999): 2084–88.

CHAPTER 5

Medieval Constructions of Blindness in France and England

Edward Wheatley

This essay will explore some of the cultural forces in medieval England and France that gave varied meanings to blindness, both for blind people and for the societies in which they lived. While these two countries were united under the religious dominance of Catholicism, which brought with it certain ideas and attitudes toward blindness, differing social and political developments in each country resulted in different constructions of this disability. The contrast between France's multivalent engagement with blindness and England's relatively benign neglect of it provide a remarkable range of responses.

Integral to my discussion is the distinction often made in disability studies between impairment and disability: impairment is the particular physical condition (in this case, visual impairment), while disability is constituted by the restrictive social and political practices that construct the environment of a person with an impairment. Among disability theorists this distinction has received some criticism for being reductive, because impairments can create discomforts or limitations that are not purely socially constructed.[1] However, in her book *Disability in Medieval Europe: Thinking about Physical Impairment during the High Middle Ages, c. 1100–1400*, Irina Metzler offers a defense of these terms.

She writes, "It is . . . preferable to speak of 'impairment' during the medieval period rather than of 'disability,' which implies certain social and cultural connotations that medieval impaired persons may not have shared with modern impaired people."[2] The distinction is useful in this essay because many of the medieval constructions that gave blindness its meanings did not grow directly out of the impairment, and not only our historical distance from the Middle Ages but also our different constructions of blindness allow us to understand the constructed nature of the earlier ones more fully.

The two dominant models that have grown out of the modern field of disability studies, the medical model and the social model, require reexamination and some revision in relation to this pre-industrial period of history. The social model demands redefinition of "able-bodied" and "disabled" in such a way that society can acknowledge and include the full spectrum of physical types. Disability is no longer individualized as a condition "belonging" to a person but as one of a number of possible physical states in society. Thus the social model "refram[es] disability as a designation having primarily social and political significance."[3] Disability theorist Lennard Davis has modified this paradigm and called it the "constructionist model," thus highlighting the artificiality of the process through which people with impairments become disabled. He writes, "[T]he constructionist model sees disability as a social process in which no inherent meanings attach to physical difference other than those assigned by a community."[4]

In contrast to the social model, the medical model constructs disability as a deficit or a pathology that requires correction or cure. Simi Linton describes the medical model in its modern context but also in a way that will be helpful in relation to what I perceive as its analogue in the Middle Ages. In *Claiming Disability: Knowledge and Identity*, Linton writes:

> Briefly, the medicalization of disability casts human variation as deviance from the norm, as pathological condition, as deficit, and, significantly, as an individual burden and personal tragedy. Society, in agreeing to assign medical meaning to disability, colludes to keep the issue within the purview of the medical establishment, to keep it a personal matter and "treat" the condition and the person with the condition rather than "treating" the social processes and policies that constrict disabled people's lives.[5]

The medical model of disability obviously does not apply to the Middle Ages, when medicine had hardly begun to develop into the powerful institution that it is now; until the Renaissance it remained largely under the control of the church. But that very power dynamic, whereby the church was powerful enough to control not only medicine but also many other cultural practices, requires interrogation. I argue that the church actually maintained cultural control over disability in a manner somewhat analogous to the way modern medicine attempts to maintain control over it. I have chosen to call the medieval European construction of disability through the culturally dominant Catholic church the religious model.

The church's control of the discursive terrain of illness and disability grew out of the New Testament. Doctrinally the church's interest in the disabled was based on Jesus's role as miraculous healer and spiritual "physician." His most significant encounter with a blind person is described in John 9.

1. And Jesus passing by, saw a man, who was blind from his birth:
2. And his disciples asked him: Rabbi, who hath sinned, this man, or his parents, that he should be born blind.
3. Jesus answered: Neither hath this man sinned, nor his parents; but that the works of God should be made manifest in him.[6]

Jesus then goes on to cure the man. This passage alludes to the conception of blindness as punishment for sin, which is a pathological condition in Christian teaching, but Jesus negates that possibility, only to recast the impairment as a site of deficit ready for divine intervention and miraculous cure.

However, another miraculous cure from John problematizes the connection between disability and true Christian belief. Jesus's words to a man who had been lame for 38 years were quoted in the one of the widely reproduced canons of the influential Fourth Lateran Council of 1215, which regularized the practice of confession. The canon reads as follows:

> Since bodily infirmity is sometimes caused by sin, the Lord saying to the sick man whom he had healed: "Go and sin no more, lest some worse thing happen to thee" (John 5:14), we declare in the present decree and strictly command that when physicians of the body are called to the bedside of the sick, before all else they admonish them to call for the physician of souls, so that after spiritual health has been restored to them, the application of bodily medicine may be of greater benefit, for the cause being removed, the effect will pass away.[7]

Here the examination of spiritual health takes precedence over medical intervention as the church tried to circumscribe the nascent practice of medicine within the conventions of Christianity. It is surely not coincidental that this edict came out of the same council that required the annual confession of sins, which may be the restoration of spiritual health to which the passage refers.

Repeatedly in medieval literature, art, and religious teaching, disability in general and blindness in particular functioned in a way that was largely structured by Jesus' miracles. The disability was the site where a saint or holy figure was to prove his or her holiness, and the religious figures were aided in that effort if the person with a disability claimed to have unshakeable faith in the curer. Representations of moments of miraculous cure saturated all types of medieval visual art, and they were also performed frequently in the living art of drama. Aside from their importance in the Bible, such miracles filled what has been called "the only book more widely read than the Bible" in the late Middle Ages, Jacobus de Voragine's *Legenda Aurea* or *Golden Legend*, a lengthy compilation of saints' lives and other religious texts, written about 1260.[8] Of course proof that a potential saint had performed miracles while alive was integral to the canonization process, and paramount among those was the cure of disabilities.

The few medieval beliefs and practices outlined here hint at similarities between the discursive power of religion in the Middle Ages and that of medicine in the modern world. At its most restrictive, medicine tends to view a disability as an absence of full health that requires a cure; similarly, medieval Christianity sometimes constructed disability as a spiritually pathological site of absence of the divine where, as Jesus said, "the works of God [can] be made manifest." Modern medicine tends

to retain discursive control of disability by holding out the promise of cures that are already available or that might be developed through research; medieval Christianity held out the promise of cure through freedom from sin and increased personal faith, whether it came from within the person with the disability or was created by a miracle worker. And thus, to some extent in modern medicine and to a greater one in medieval Christianity, there is a tacit but implicit attitude that somehow the disabled person himself is to blame for resisting a cure. Lest we allow ourselves to think that the religious model is uniquely medieval, we should remind ourselves that it is alive and well at European holy sites such as Lourdes and Medjegorje, and in the United States it is exemplified in the faith healing of pentecostal preachers. It has also brought about legal intervention in some cases involving Christian Scientists, who abjure medicine in favor of prayer for cures of illnesses and disabilities.

The church also retained economic control over some disabled people through charity based on both alms-giving to individuals and institutional foundations for groups, practices.[9] The care of the ill and the disabled earned generous gifts and bequests for religious institutions, particularly monasteries and convents. Hospitals founded by kings, lords, merchants, guilds, and municipalities were generally under the control of religious orders, some of which were founded specifically to care for the infirm.[10] Treatises written by and for clerics practicing medicine abjured payment from the poor but encouraged acceptance of payment from the wealthy.[11] However, the role of Christian charity in the lives of medieval people with disabilities is sometimes overemphasized. Even if the majority of people with disabilities needed alms or institutional care, many others, living with and receiving care from their families, would have needed neither, and therefore charity would not have dominated their experience of disability. But more importantly, both those who wanted to receive charity and those who did not needed to internalize the discipline of the doctrines of the church, including penance, if they were to have any hope of miraculous cure. Therefore the aspects of the religious model described above take precedence over acts of charity: people with disabilities had to make themselves worthy to receive the benevolence of the church, whether economic or spiritual. Overemphasis on charity also deprives disabled people of agency. Some blind people worked in the Middle Ages, and the same would have been true of people with other disabilities; they were not all passive recipients of hand-outs, even though they might have been the objects of paternalistic attitudes.

The religious model of disability neither denies medicine its place in medieval society nor asserts that medieval people always viewed impairment as the result of sin. Metzler has helpfully outlined the ways in which modern historiography rather than medieval attitudes has created the monolithic view that in medieval Europe impairment was inevitably associated with sin.[12] Rather, the religious model as a *discursive* model was the most widely available construction in medieval European culture for recasting impairment as disability. Furthermore, while the medical model may have grown in acceptance in relation to certain kinds of impairments in the later Middle Ages, medicine had very little to offer people with visual impairments.

Up to this point my definition of the religious model has not consistently differentiated between blind people and people with other disabilities. However, within the larger framework sketched here, the blind and visually impaired were disadvantaged in a particular way by an important religious practice of the medieval church—in fact, perhaps its most important practice for lay people. From the twelfth century through the remainder of the Middle Ages, the laity generally partook of the eucharist through only their sense of sight. In its earliest form, the so-called "elevatio" involved the priest consecrating the eucharistic bread and then raising it to make it visible to the congregants. The synodal statues of Paris of 1205–1208 mandated that the "elevatio" take place only after the bread was consecrated, so that the viewers would be looking not at bread but at the actual body of Christ, and the synod instructed priests to be sure to raise the Host high enough for all of the faithful to see. According to Eamon Duffy, the "elevatio" became "the high point of the lay experience of the Mass,"[13] as witnessed not only in written texts but also the visual arts, in which representations of the Host generally showed it at the moment when the priest was raising it. After the Synod of Paris mentioned above, the practice of elevating the Host spread across Europe within a surprisingly short period of fifteen years,[14] and during the later Middle Ages it "almost completely replac[ed] sacramental communion."[15]

The "elevatio" became so popular that people sometimes walked from church to church to see the Host repeatedly. Christians under interdict for sinfulness were forbidden to enter any church building, but they were known to drill holes in the doors of churches in order to catch a glimpse of the "elevatio."[16] In some churches where wooden rood-screens blocked the view of the host, holes called "elevation squints" were bored through the wood at the eye level of the kneeling congregants.[17] The fervor to see the the Host at least partially contributed to the creation of Corpus Christi Day in 1264, the celebration of which sometimes involved taking the Host out of the church to be displayed in some type of public procession.[18]

Beliefs that came to be associated with the "elevatio" disavantaged the blind and visually impaired even further. People who could see the host derived spiritual benefits from this practice without having to confess their sins, whereas the taking of communion required confession. As G.J.C. Snoek says, "'communion with the eyes' implied no confession and no danger of receiving communion unworthily."[19] For the visually impaired, then, the spiritual renewal of this common form of quasi-communion was unavailable, and in a very real sense, this lack of availability would have rendered them less spiritually pure in the eyes of the sighted communities around them.

Texts from both sides of the channel attest to the significance of the "elevatio" and connect visual impairment to it. According to an anonymous Middle English chronicle written by a London author in the late 1460s,[20] a locksmith who had helped a heretical Lollard steal the Eucharist later went to mass to pray for forgiveness, where he was unable to see the Host any of the times that it should have been visible: "when the priest held up that holy sacrament to the time of elevation he might see nothing of that blessed body of Christ at any time during the Mass, not even during the Agnus Dei." Doubting his own sanity, the man drank an entire hod of ale and attended three more masses but experienced similar selective blindness. Then he and his accomplices were arrested, thrown in Newgate prison, and sentenced to death. On the day of his execution the locksmith confessed his sins and again went to mass, where now he could "see that blessed sacrament well enough." The chronicler closes the story by saying that he "truste[d] that their souls were saved."[21] The text thus equates sinfulness with the inability to see the elevation of the host, and spiritual rectitude with restored vision. The locksmith's relief at his reentry into the Christian fold hours before his death must have been akin to the relief of fourteenth-century French poet Gilles li Muisis when he reentered the community of the sighted after having his cataracts removed. In a poem thanking the Virgin Mary for the miracle of his restored vision, he mentions specifically his joy in being able to see the Savior at the altar ("Je voy me Sauveur al autel vrayement . . ."[22]). Seeing the Savior specifically at the altar when most churches have multiple images of him is almost certainly a reference to the "elevatio."

One last aspect of the religious construction of blindness requires a passing mention here. In Christian discourse, as elsewhere, terms for disabilities have a strong metaphorical dimension, and blindness as a spiritual condition has significant metaphorical connotations. But Simi Linton has correctly asserted that metaphors of disability are "powerful tools of persuasion," and metaphor and reality structure each other synergistically.[23] The metaphor of blindness in Christian discourse was used with great frequency as an epithet to apply to Jews for refusing to "see" the divinity of Jesus. This figurative association of blind people with Jews manifested itself in similar types of stereotyping, marginalization, and punishment for both groups.[24]

The medieval Christian religious model overlapped with the social model of disability in England and France, because a person's religious community was also his social community. However, in the social environment, additional practices structured the disability of blindness.

The implication that "uncured" disabilities somehow represented shameful incompleteness was an important aspect of what sociologist Erving Goffman called "stigmatization" in his book *Stigma: Notes on the Management of Spoiled Identity*. Goffman traces the term to the branding or scarring that identified Greek slaves, and he adds that in the Christian era it referred to "bodily signs of physical disorder." He continues, "Today, the term is widely used in something like the original literal sense, but is applied more to the disgrace itself than to the bodily evidence of it. Furthermore, shifts have occurred in the kind of disgrace that arouse concern."[25] Goffman wrote decades before the constructionist model of disability was delineated, but his ideas closely resemble it: the "disgrace" that attaches itself to a stigma is more powerful than the bodily evidence that gives rise to the stigma. In other words, the disgrace constructs the disability, regardless of the impairment, and the kind of disgrace caused by particular "bodily evidence" changes over time, as do the disabilities relating to a particular impairment.

Applied to the Christian Middle Ages, Goffman's ideas highlight the church's creation of a complex set of attitudes toward blind people which resulted in stigmatization. However, the stigma associated with spiritual "incompleteness" or sinfulness of blind people did not relate to religious discourse alone; in France, England, and elsewhere in Europe, disability could be read as a sign of sociopolitical sinfulness, which is to say criminality. Physical mutilation as punishment, particularly among the Normans and the French, seriously problematized the social meaning of several disabilities. At certain times and places in medieval Europe, people must have very consciously asked themselves questions about the type of stigma that certain disabilities represented. Was a man without a hand born that way, or did he lose it in an accident, or did he lose it as punishment for theft? Was a blind person's impairment caused by God for spiritual reasons or by the king for criminal ones? The use of blinding as punishment would have kept such questions alive until well into the Renaissance, particularly on the continent. Mutilation as punishment situates the social meaning of blindness in the Middle Ages ambiguously between the bodily marks of shame suffered by Greek slaves and Goffman's modern concept of stigma, due to the possibility that disability could have been a marked sign of a literal judgment of criminal activity rather than a unmarked impairment. Blinding as punishment in a sense criminalizes the impairment of blindness, thus constructing a kind of disability that no longer exists in the modern world.

The English and the French had very different attitudes toward mutilation as punishment in the Middle Ages. Historical evidence shows that blinding as punishment was used much more frequently by the French and the Normans than by the English, and when blinding was done on English soil, it was often done by the Norman colonizers. I have found only three episodes of punitive blinding in England before 1066. Anglo-Saxon law mentions this punishment only once as appropriate for serial criminals after they had been mutilated in other ways. Interestingly for my purposes here, this law came about not under an English king but a Danish one, Cnut, in 1035, but I have seen no evidence that it was ever enforced.[26]

After the Norman Conquest of England in 1066, records show that William the Conqueror used punitive blinding frequently, and extant evidence of blinding by Norman colonizers does not include undocumented examples of the enforcement of William's infamous poaching laws, whereby poachers of deer could be blinded as soon as they were apprehended.[27] The practice of blinding even spread to the Norman clergy. In the year of William's death, Archbishop Lanfranc ordered the blinding of citizens of Canterbury who protested the installation of a Norman abbot at St. Augustine's Abbey.[28] The latest example of punitive blinding that I have found was in 1223,[29] though the practice is mentioned as a possible punishment in the borough customs (i.e. local laws) of Portsmouth in 1272.[30] On the other hand, in the thirteenth century the forest laws associated with the Magna Carta did away with blinding for poachers, and in 1285, the Second Statutes of Westminster ruled that rape was to be punished by the execution of the rapist, whereas earlier, blinding and castration were evidently permissible (though unrecorded) in some boroughs.[31] So blinding was done to the English largely by the colonial powers, and therefore in the years immediately following the Conquest, being blinded as punishment could have been read by the English public as evidence of admirable political resistance rather than criminal activity.

The situation was very different in France, where the Norman practices were adopted by the French even before Normandy came under full French rule. The bloodiest episode occurred in 1210 at the hands of Simon de Montfort during the Albigensian Crusade against the Cathar heretics in the settlement of Bram, between Carcassonne and Castelnaudary. The events at Bram were a direct response to an enemy having blinded some of Simon's soldiers. Here is a description of chronicler Pierre de Vaux-de-Cernay, a supporter of de Montfort.

> They put out the eyes of the defenders [of Bram], over a hundred in number, and cut off their noses. One man was spared one eye so that, as a demonstration of our contempt for our enemies, he could lead the others to Cabaret. The Count [de Montfort] had this punishment carried out not because the mutilation gave him any pleasure but because his opponents had been the first to indulge in atrocities and, cruel executioners that they were, were given to butchering any of our men they might capture by dismembering them . . . The Count never took delight in cruelty or in the torture of his enemies.[32]

Pierre's self-conscious justification for de Montfort's cruelty gives added credence to this horrifying event.

Examples of blinding as punishment in France are unfortunately too numerous to list here, but the practice continued through the fourteenth and into the last quarter of the fifteenth century.[33]

The association of blindness and criminality apparently gave rise to a largely French set of stereotypes of the blind as untrustworthy criminals and agents of misrule. These stereotypes are available relatively early in such literature as a thirteenth-century farce *Le Garçon et l'Aveugle* (*The Boy and the Blind Man*), in which a blind beggar, who has been described as "drunk, gluttonous, coarse, cynical, and debauched,"[34] has amassed a small fortune from his begging. The boy of the title agrees to serve as the blind man's guide but then humiliates him and ultimately robs him of his money and his clothes, leaving him stripped and silent on stage. Although this play survives in only one manuscript, it contains additions and emendations that indicate its use as a perfomance text for two centuries.[35] Similar plots involving the humiliation of blind characters not only appear in other farces[36] but also provide comic interludes in lengthy plays based on stories from the Bible. For example, *Le Mystère de la Résurrection* from Angers, first performed in 1456, took three days to present, and each day features an appearance by a blind man, Galleboys, and his tricky guide Saudret, who both steals from and beats Galleboys in the course of the action.[37]

The distrust of blind people inherent in such texts is closely related to the medieval figure of the beggar who feigns disability. This figure loomed so large in the medieval imagination that it affected the treatment of the genuinely visually impaired. Politically it resulted in a number of laws limiting the movements of beggars to specified areas; such measures kept them in a community that knew whether they were actually disabled. The effect of anxiety about feigned beggars also resulted in the marking of people who were really visually impaired; some wore badges that identified them as residents of particular institutions, and others wore emblems that served as recognizable licenses to beg. A variety of textual evidence about feigned disabilities among beggars comes from both France and England. For example, in the fabliau *Les Trois Aveugles de Compiègne* (*The Three Blind Men of Compiègne*),[38] the plot is set in motion by a clerk who wants to test whether three men making their way along a road are pretending to be blind. In William Langland's *Piers Plowman*, the allegorical figure of Hunger "cures" beggars feigning disability by making them so hungry that they can no longer avoid working to earn their daily bread.[39]

During the centuries when blinding was used as punishment, an equally important and probably not unrelated historical development was occurring in France: the foundation of hospices for the blind. And perhaps not coincidentally, some of them were founded by William the Conqueror, who himself used blinding punitively. According to a medieval verse chronicle, William founded hospices either entirely or partially reserved for blind inhabitants in Cherbourg, Rouen, Bayeux, and Caen.[40] It is unclear whether these were founded before or after the Norman Conquest, but it is tempting to assert that William was trying to atone at home for the sins he had committed abroad. A pivotal event in the social history of blindness took place in Paris around 1258, when Louis IX, later Saint Louis, founded the Hospice des Quinze-Vingts ("Hospital of the Fifteen-Twenties," i.e. for three hundred residents). This institution, which still exists as the National Center for Ophthalmology, was the first of its kind not to be under church control, and the hospice's richly documented medieval history is full of conflicts with the bishops and clergy of Paris. The residents were not cloistered, but were encouraged to go out into the streets of Paris wearing special *fleur de lys* badges that identified

their affiliation, and they could beg or hold other jobs to earn money. They were actually licensed to beg at church doors anywhere in France, competitively close to the alms boxes that served the local poor, which further increased the tensions with the church.[41] Other "*aveugleries*" modeled on the same principles were founded elsewhere in France: l'Hospice des Six-Vingts in Chartres in 1291, and other such institutions in Tournai (now Belgium) in 1351, Meaux in the same year, Caen by 1364, Rouen in 1478, and Orléans by the end of the century.[42]

Louis's hospice and later ones modeled on it effected a significant rupture in the social construction of blindness: the royal protection of blind people must have improved their lives in certain ways, but it also created a higher public profile for them, evidently leading to envy, contempt, and what might now be called a backlash. In a poem by Rutebeuf the residents of the Quinze-Vingts became the objects of scorn within a few years of the institution's foundation, well before Louis's death.

> Li roi a mis en un repaire
> (Més je ne sai pas por qoi faire)
> Trois cens aveugles route a route.
> Parmi Paris en va trois paire;
> Tote jor ne finent de braire:
> "Aus trois cens qui ne voient goute!"
> Li uns sache, li autres boute,
> Si se donent mainte çacoute,
> Qu'il n'i a nul qui lor esclaire.
> Si feus i prent, ce n'est pas doute,
> L'ordre sera brullee toute,
> S'avra li rois plus a refaire.[43]

[The king has assembled in a residence (although I don't know what for) three hundred blind people, troop after troop. Across Paris they go three by three; all day long they do not stop braying, "Give to the three hundred who don't see anything." One pulls, another pushes, they often give each other jolts because there is no one to guide them. If the fire took it, there is no doubt that the house of their order would be entirely burnt down, and the king will again have more to do.]

Two centuries later, the poet François Villon reinforced this satirical view of the institution in his *Testament* (*Will*) by bequeathing his spectacles to the residents there.[44]

But what of England and its institutions for the blind? Evidently there were none founded solely for people with that impairment. It has been suggested that St Mary within Cripplegate, also called Elsingspital in honor of its founder William Elsing, was a hospital for the blind,[45] but Elsing's charter of 1331 stipulated that the institution give preference to blind or paralyzed priests; any remaining space in the hospital could be given to blind beggars.[46] So although Elsing had an interest in the blind, his generosity was first and foremost directed toward disabled priests who could no longer perform the mass. In contrast to the Quinze-Vingts, this hospital, which was always under religious control and was administered by Austin canons after 1340, had a relatively short history plagued with financial problems even before Elsing's death; it spawned no imitators and was closed in 1536.[47] The hospital of the Papey has also been labeled an institution specifically for the blind, but in fact it, too, was meant for infirm members of the clergy,[48] and thus it resembled Elsingspital in its primary clientele. These hospitals strongly reinforce the religious model not only because they were under church control[49] but also because they were actually ministering primarily to priests, who were likely to believe in some form of the religious model of disability.

While the religious model of blindness is similar in England and France, their social models are radically different. In French and Norman culture the more frequent use of blinding as punishment had some influence, as would the privileges afforded residents of royal hospices. These practices and institutions in France resulted in attitudes that to some extent commodified human sight and often resulted in inhumane satire against the blind in French literature, both secular and religious. In England, where blinding as punishment was rare except at the hands of colonizers and where there were no hospices solely for the blind, blindness existed as a relatively unmarked disability, and therefore the blind may have been singled out for ridicule less frequently in art and literature. Thus the basic difference in the construction of blindness in these two countries is that in France, where the blind were more socially visible due to highly visible practices and institutions, the social or constructionist model of disability tended to dominate, whereas in England, where the blind were in a sense less visible, the religious model tended to dominate. The commodification of sight in France represents a disturbing inversion of the social model of disability defined above, which states that disability should not "belong" to an individual but to a society. Blinding as punishment very concretely demonstrates that in medieval society, a person's *sight* did not entirely belong to him either.

The constructions and stereotypes of blindness sketched here were not all equally operative in all parts of England and France from the late eleventh through the fifteenth centuries. However, these constructions of blindness were woven together through such a complex set of beliefs and practices that none could be fully operative without one or more of the others. The evidence presented here demonstrates that the medieval social model of disability at its most benign is not "without ideology";[50] rather, it seems that the ideological stumbling blocks before blind people in the Middle Ages were so thoroughly internalized in medieval Christian society that they became utterly and invisibly normative.

NOTES

1. For a summary of these arguments, see Tom Shakespeare, "The Social Model of Disability: An Outdated Ideology?" in *Exploring Theories and Expanding Methodologies: Where We Are and Where We Need to Go*, eds. S N. Barnartt and B.M. Altman (Amsterdam: JAI, Elsevier Science, 2001), 11–20.

2. Irina Metzler, *Disability in Medieval Europe: Thinking about Physical Impairment during the High Middle Ages* (London and New York: Routledge, 2006), 2.

3. Simi Linton, *Claiming Disability: Knowledge and Identity* (New York: NYU Press, 1998), 2.

4. Davis, "Crips Strike Back: The Rise of Disability Studies," in *Bending Over Backwards: Disability, Dismodernism, and Other Difficult Positions* (New York: NYU Press, 2002), 41. Davis' essay provides a helpful, readable overview of some of the major issues in the evolution of disability studies.

5. New York: New York University Press, 1998, p. 11.

6. *Holy Bible* (Douay-Rheims Translation; Rockford, Illinois: Tan Books, 1899). Less socially and theologically complex episodes of Jesus curing blind men are recounted in Matthew 9:27–31 and 20:30–34, Mark 8:22–26 and 10:46–52. The blind are also mentioned in groups of people with a variety of disabilities whom Jesus cures; see, for example, Matthew 11:5 and 15:30 and Luke 7:21.

7. Qtd. in "The Medieval Catholic Tradition," Darrel W. Amundsen, pp. 88–89, in *Caring and Curing: Health and Medicine in the Western Religious Traditions*, ed. Ronald L. Numbers and Darrel W. Amundsen (New York: Macmillan, 1986).

8. The *Golden Legend* survives in about 1,000 manuscripts, and after 1450 numerous printed editions appeared in not only Latin but every Western European language. The book's availability in vernacular languages made it more accessible to medieval readers than the Bible, translation of which was limited by the church. See William Granger Ryan, intro., *The Golden Legend: Readings on the Saints* (Princeton, NJ: Princeton University Press, 1993), vol. 1, xiii.

9. These practices have been examined by Henri-Jacques Stiker in his 1982 book *The History of Disability* in his chapter on the Middle Ages entitled "The System(s) of Charity" (trans. William Sayers, Ann Arbor: University of Michigan Press, 1999: 73–74).

10. Amundsen, 86.

11. Ibid., 85

12. *Disability in Medieval Europe*, 11–13. For a consideration of this issue from a sociological perspective, see Nichola Hutchinson, "Disabling Beliefs? Impaired Embodiment in the Religious Tradition in the West," *Body and Society* 12 (4): 1–23.

13. Eamon Duffy, *The Stripping of the Altars* (New Haven: Yale University Press, 1992), 96.

14. G.J.C. Snoek, *Medieval Piety from Relics to the Eucharist* (Leiden: E.J. Brill, 1995), 56.

15. Ibid., 59.

16. Ibid., 60.

17. Duffy, 97. Duffy also includes photographs of squints that are still extant in churches in Ipswich and Lavenham (figs. 46 and 53).

18. Snoek, 59–61.

19. Ibid., 293.

20. Douglas Gray, *The Oxford Book of Late Medieval Verse and Prose* (Oxford: Clarendon, 1985), 418.

21. Ibid., 11–12; translations mine. Gray reproduces the text from J. Gairdner, *The Historical Collections of a London Citizen* (London: Camden Society, 1876), who took the narrative from MS BL Egerton 1995, f. 219. The story is quoted in less detail in Duffy, 101–102.

22. *Poésies de Gilles li Muisis*, ed. Kervyn de Lettenhove (Louvain: J. LeFever, 1882), vol. 2, p. 234.

23. *Claiming Disability: Knowledge and Identity* (New York: NYU Press, 1998), 125 ff. See also Susan Sontag, *Illness as Metaphor* (New York: Farrar, Straus, and Giroux, 1978).

24. See Edward Wheatley, "'Blind' Jews and Blind Christians: The Metaphorics of Marginalization in Medieval Europe," *Exemplaria: A Journal of Theory in Medieval and Renaissance Studies* 14.2 (October 2002), 351–82.

25. Goffman, *Stigma* (New York: Simon & Schuster, 1963, repr. 1986), 1–2.

26. Frederick Pollock and Edward Maitland, in their authoritative *History of English Law Before the Time of Edward I* (2nd ed.; Cambridge: Cambridge University Press, 1968), listed a number of forms of mutilation used as punishment in preconquest England (". . . loss of ears, nose, upper lip, hands, feet," as well as castration;" vol. 2, 452–53), but blindness is notably absent from their list.

27. David C. Douglas and George W. Greenaway, eds., *English Historical Documents, 1042–1189* (London: Eyre and Spottiswoode, 1953), 164.

28. J. Earle and C. Plumner, eds., *Two of the Anglo-Saxon Chronicles Parallel* (Oxford: 1892, 1899), 1: 287–92.

29. See the case of the attack of Thomas de Bestenoure, in which two of his attackers were sentenced to be blinded and castrated; *Curia Regis Rolls of the Reign of Henry III: 7 to 9 Henry III* (London: Her Majesty's Stationery Office, 1955), 219–20.

30. Mary Bateson, *Borough Customs* (London: Quaritch, 1904), vol. 1, 77.
31. These findings accord with Pollock and Maitland (see note 26), who in their *History of English Law* sketch a decline in mutilation as punishment for felons as it was replaced "very slowly" during the thirteenth century by the death penalty (vol. 2, 461).
32. Peter of les Vaux-de-Cernay, *The History of the Albigensian Crusade: Peter of les Vaux-de-Cernay's Historia Albigensis* (Woodbridge, Suffolk: Boydell, 1998), 79.
33. Nicole Gonthier, *Le châtiment du crime au Moyen Âge* (Rennes: Presses Universitaires de Rennes, 1998), 145–46.
34. Zina Weygand, *Vivre sans Voir: Les aveugles dans la société française du Moyen Age au siècle de Louis Braille* (Paris: Créaphis, 2003), 26.
35. Carol Symes, "*The Boy and the Blind Man*: A Medieval Play Script and Its Editors," in Siân Echard and Stephen Partridge, eds., *The Book Unbound: Editing and Reading Medieval Manuscripts and Texts* (Toronto: University of Toronto Press, 2004), 105–45.
36. See, for example, *La Farce du Goguelu*, in Gustave Cohen, ed., *Recueil de Farces Françaises Inédites du Xve Siècle* (Cambridge, MA: Medieval Academy of America, 1949), 357–67.
37. *Le Mystère de la Résurrection, Angers (1456)*, ed. Pierre Servet (Geneva: Droz, 1993). See also François Briand, *Quatre histoires par personnaiges sur quatre évangiles de l'advent à iouer par les petits enfants les quatre dimenches dudit advent*, ed. Henri Chardon (Paris: Champion, 1906).
38. Cortebarbe, *Les Trois Aveugles de Compiègne*, 109–20 in Philippe Ménard, ed., *Fabliaux français au Moyen Age*, vol. 1 (Geneva: Droz, 1979).
39. *Piers Plowman: The B Version*, rev. ed. Eds. George Kane and E. Talbot Donaldson. (London: Athlone, 1988), VI. 191–92.
40. Brigitte Gauthier, "Les 'aveugleries' médiévales (XIème-XVème siècles)," *Cahiers d'histoire* (Lyon) 29, 2–3 (1984): 99–100.
41. Louis Guillaumat and Jean-Pierre Bailliart, *Les Quinze-Vingts de Paris: Echos Historiques du XIIIe au XXe Siècle* [n.l.: Société Francophone d'Histoire de l'Opthalmologie, 1998], 39–40.
42. Ibid., 115–17.
43. Qtd. in *Le garçon et l'aveugle, jeu du XIIIe siècle*, ed. Mario Roques; intro. and trans. Jean Dufournet (Paris: Honoré Champion, 1989), 63.
44. François Villon, *Le Testament Villon*, ed. Jean Rychner and Albert Henry (Geneva: Droz, 1974), vol. 1, p. 132, lines 1728–35.
45. Nicholas Orme and Margaret Webster, *The English Hospital, 1070–1570* (New Haven: Yale University Press, 1995), 121.
46. *The Victoria History of the Counties of England: London* (London: Constable & Co., 1909), 535.
47. Ibid., 536.
48. Orme and Webster, *The English Hospital, 1070–1570*, 121.
49. In the case of Elsingspital, the institution's debts may have been caused by the church associated with it. A 1448 inventory shows that it possessed three relics, furniture, ornaments, and some fine vestments, and the building itself was so large that "after the Dissolution, when the principal aisle had been pulled down, the remaining part sufficed for a parish church." *The Victoria History of the Counties of England: London* (London: Constable & Co., 1909), 536.
50. Stiker, *A History of Disability*, 65.

PART II

*T*he Politics of Disability

CHAPTER 6

Construction of Deafness

Harlan Lane

SOCIAL PROBLEMS ARE CONSTRUCTED

It is obvious that our society is beset by numerous social problems. A brief historical perspective on four of them reveals something not so obvious: social problems are constructed in particular cultures, at particular times, in response to the efforts of interested parties.

The social problem of alcoholism evidently consists in this: there is a particular segment of the population that suffers from the use of alcohol; these sufferers need specially trained people to help them—for example alcoholism counselors, psychologists and psychiatrists; they need special facilities such as detoxification centers; and special organizations like AA. This understanding of alcoholism is less than fifty years old. Recall that the Temperance Movement of the last century viewed excessive drinking not as a disease but as an act of will; alcoholics victimized their families and imposed on the rest of society. The movement advocated not treatment but prohibition. Some groups favored prohibition and took the moral high ground; other groups felt justified in breaking the law. Special facilities existed then to house and treat many problem groups—mentally ill people, for example—but not people who

drank too much. Only recently has a consensus developed that excessive drinking "is" a disease—a matter of individual suffering more than a political dispute. With this shift in the construction of alcoholism and alcoholics—from victimizers to victims—the evident need was for medical research to alleviate suffering; vast sums of money are now devoted to research on alcoholism, and there is now a large treatment establishment with halfway houses, hospital wards, outpatient clinics, and specialized hospitals (Gusfield, 1982).

The discovery of child abuse dates from the 1950s. Radiologists and pediatricians first decried the evidence they were seeing of parents beating their children. The Children's Bureau and the media took up the cause (it is still very present in TV and the newspapers) and made the public aware of this social problem. In the decade that followed, the states passed laws requiring reports of child abuse and providing penalties. Of course, parents did not start beating their children only in the 1950s. Rather, a social consensus emerged in that decade that a problem existed requiring laws, special welfare workers, and special budgetary provisions. In the last century, the major problems associated with children concerned poverty and child labor—a rather different and much more political construction of the problem of improper treatment of children (Gusfield, 1989).

For a very long time, the dominant construction of homosexuality, like that of alcoholism, was a moral one: men and women were making sinful choices; the problem was "owned" by the church. Later psychiatry gave it a new construction: it "is" an illness they claimed that psychiatrists could treat (Conrad & Schneider, 1980). In the third phase, Gays and Lesbians were presented as a minority group; they ask for the same protection as all other groups that are discriminated against based on the circumstances of their birth, such as blacks and women.

Disability, too, has had moral, medical and now social constructions, as numerous articles in this journal have explicated. The Disability Rights Movement has shifted the construct of disability "off the body and into the interface between people with impairments and socially disabling conditions" (Hevey, 1993, p. 426).

Alcoholism has changed from a moral failure to a disease; child abuse from an economic problem to a criminal one; homosexuality from disease to personal constitution to human rights; disability from tragic flaw to social barriers. Social problems, it seems, are partly what we make of them; they are not just out there "lying in the road to be discovered by passers-by" (Gusfield, 1984, p. 38). The particular way in which society understands alcoholism, disability and so forth determines exactly what these labels mean, how large groups of people are treated, and the problems that they face. Deafness, too, has had many constructions; they differ with time and place. Where there were many deaf people in small communities in the last century, on Martha's Vineyard, for example, as in Henniker, New Hampshire, deafness was apparently not seen as a problem requiring special intervention. Most Americans had quite a different construction of deaf-

ness at that time, however: it was an individual affliction that befell family members and had to be accommodated within the family. The great challenge facing Thomas Gallaudet and Laurent Clerc in their efforts to create the first American school for the deaf was to persuade state legislatures and wealthy Americans of quite a different construction which they had learned in Europe: Deafness was not an individual but a social problem, deaf people had to be brought together for their instruction, special "asylums" were needed. Nowadays, two constructions of deafness in particular are dominant and compete for shaping deaf peoples' destinies. The one construes deaf as a category of disability; the other construes deaf as designating a member of a linguistic minority. There is a growing practice of capitalizing Deaf when referring specifically to its second construction, which I will follow hereafter.

DISABILITY VS. LINGUISTIC MINORITY

Numerous organizations are associated with each of the prominent constructions of deafness. In the U.S., National organizations primarily associated with deafness as disability include the A. G. Bell Association (4,500 members), the American Speech-Language-Hearing Association (40,000), the American Association of Late-Deafened Adults (1,300), Self-Help for the Hard of Hearing (13,000), the American Academy of Otolaryngology, Head and Neck Surgery (5,600), and the National Hearing Aid Society (4,000). National organizations associated primarily with the construction of Deaf as a linguistic minority include the National Association of the Deaf (20,000), the Registry of Interpreters for the Deaf (2,700), and the National Fraternal Society of the Deaf (13,000) (Van Cleve, 1987; Burek, 1993).

Each construction has a core client

group. No one disputes the claim of the hearing adult become deaf from illness or aging that he or she has a disability and is not a member of Deaf culture. Nor, on the other hand, has any one yet criticized Deaf parents for insisting that their Deaf child has a distinct linguistic and cultural heritage. The struggle between some of the groups adhering to the two constructions persists across the centuries (Lane, 1984) in part because there is no simple criterion for identifying most childhood candidates as clients of the one position or the other. More generally, we can observe that late deafening and moderate hearing loss tend to be associated with the disability construction of deafness while early and profound deafness involve an entire organization of the person's language, culture and thought around vision and tend to be associated with the linguistic minority construction.

In general, we identify children as members of a language minority when their native language is not the language of the majority. Ninety percent of Deaf children, however, have hearing parents who are unable to effectively model the spoken language for most of them. Advocates of the disability construction contend these are hearing-impaired children whose language and culture (though they may have acquired little of either) are in principle those of their parents; advocates of the linguistic minority construction contend that the children's native language, in the sense of primary language, must be manual language and that their life trajectory will bring them fully into the circle of Deaf culture. Two archetypes for these two constructions, disability and linguistic minority, were recently placed side by side before our eyes on the U.S. television program, *Sixty Minutes*. On the one hand, seven-year-old Caitlin Parton, representing the unreconstructed disability-as-impairment: presented as a victim of a personal tragedy,

utterly disabled in communication by her loss of hearing but enabled by technology, and dedicated professional efforts (yes, we meet the surgeon), to approach normal, for which she yearns, as she herself explains. On the other hand, Roslyn Rosen, then president of the National Association of the Deaf, from a large Deaf family, native speaker of ASL, proud of her status as a member of a linguistic minority, insistent that she experiences life and the world fully and has no desire to be any different (*Sixty Minutes*, 1992).

PROFESSIONAL INFLUENCE OVER CONSTRUCTIONS

Organizations espousing each construction of deafness compete to "own" the children and define their needs. Their very economic survival depends on their success in that competition. Which construction of a social problem prevails is thus no mere academic matter. There is a body of knowledge associated with construction A and a quite different body with construction B; the theories and facts associated with construction A have been studied by the professional people who grapple with the social problem; they are the basis of their specialized training and professional credentials and therefore contribute to their self-esteem; they are used to maintain respect from clients, to obtain federal and state funding, to insure one's standing in a fraternity of like professionals; they legitimate the professional person's daily activities. Professionals examine students on this body of knowledge, give certificates, and insert themselves into the legal and social norms based on their competence in that body of knowledge. Whoever says A is a mistaken construction is of course not welcome. More than that, whoever says A is a construction is not welcome, for that implies that there could be or is another construction, B, say, which is better. What the parties to each construction want is that their construction not be seen as a construction at all; rather, they insist, they merely reflect the way things are in the world (cf. Gusfield, 1984).

These "troubled-persons industries," in the words of sociologist Joseph Gusfield, "bestow benevolence on people defined as in need" (Gusfield, 1989, p. 432). These industries have grown astronomically in recent decades (Albrecht, 1992). The professional services fueled by the disability construction of deafness are provided by some administrators of schools and training programs, experts in counseling and rehabilitation, teachers, interpreters, audiologists, speech therapists, otologists, psychologists, psychiatrists, librarians, researchers, social workers, and hearing aid specialists. All these people and the facilities they command, their clinics, operating rooms, laboratories, classrooms, offices and shops, owe their livelihood or existence to deafness problems. Gusfield cites the story about American missionaries who settled in Hawaii. They went to do good. They stayed and did well (Gusfield, 1989).

The troubled-person professions serve not only their clientele but also themselves, and are actively involved in perpetuating and expanding their activities. Teachers of the Deaf, for example, seek fewer students per teacher and earlier intervention (Johnson *et al.*, 1989). American audiologists have formally proposed testing of the hearing of all American newborns without exception. The self-aggrandizement of the troubled-persons professions when it comes to Deaf people is guided by a genuine belief in their exclusive construction of the social problem and their ability to alleviate it. Some of their promotional methods are readily seen; for example, they employ lobbyists to encourage legislation that requires and pays for their services. Other measures are more subtle; for example, the

structural relation between the service provider and the client often has the effect of disempowering the client and maintaining dependency.

LESSONS FROM SERVICES FOR BLIND PEOPLE

The history of services to blind people illustrates some of the pitfalls of the professionalization of a social problem. Workshops for blind people have large budgets, provide good income for sighted managers, and have a national organization to lobby for their interest. Blind people, however, commonly view sheltered workshops as a dead end that involves permanent dependency. The editor of the journal *Braille Monitor* says that "professional" is a swear word among blind people, "a bitter term of mockery and disillusionment" (Vaughan, 1991). A light-house for the blind was raked over the coals in that journal for having one pay scale for blind employees and a higher one for sighted employees performing the same work; moreover, the blind employees were paid below minimum wage (Braille Monitor, 1989). The National Accreditation Council for Agencies Serving the Blind and visually Handicapped (NAC) was disowned by organizations of blind people for its efforts to keep blind people in custodial care, its refusal to hear blind witnesses, and its token representation of blind people on the board; the Council rebutted that it had to consider the needs of agencies and professionals and not just blind people. For decades blind people picketed the NAC annual meetings (Braille Monitor, 1973; Jernigan, 1973; Vaughan, 1991).

A conference convened to define the new specialization of mobility trainer for the blind concluded that it required graduate study to learn this art and that "the teaching of mobility is a task for the sighted rather than a blind individual" (quoted in Vaughan, 1991, p. 209). This approach was naturally challenged by blind consumers. At first, the American Association of Workers with the Blind required normal vision for certification; then this was seen as discriminatory, in violation of section 504 of the Rehabilitation Act of 1973. So the criteria were changed. To enter the training program, the student must be able to assess the collision path of a blind person with obstacles nearly a block away. As it turns out, the functions claimed to be essential to mobility teaching just happen to require normal vision. Needless to say, blind people have been teaching blind people how to get about for centuries (Olson, 1981).

Workers with blind people view blindness as a devastating personal tragedy although blind people themselves commonly do not. Said the president of the National Association of the Blind "We do not regard our lives . . . as tragic or disastrous and no amount of professional jargon or trumped up theory can made us do so" (Jernigan quoted in Olson, 1977, p. 408). As sociologist R. A. Scott explains in his classic monograph, *The Making of Blind Men,* the sighted professionals believe that the blind man's only hope for solving his problems is to submit to their long-term program of psychological services and training. To succeed, the blind man is told, he must change his beliefs about blindness, most of all, his belief that he is basically fine and only needs one or two services. The cooperative client is the one who welcomes all the services provided; the uncooperative client is the one who welcomes all the services provided; the uncooperative client is the one who fails to realize how many and great his needs are—who is in denial. The troubled-persons industries thus stand the normal relation between needs and services on its head: services do not evolve purely to meet needs; clients must recognize that they need the services provided by the professionals. Scott comments that it is easy to be deluded about the reality of these special needs. There are always a few blind clients who can be relied on to endorse these beliefs in the profound need for professional services. These blind individuals have been socialized, perhaps since childhood, to the professional construction of blindness. They confirm that blind people have the needs the agency says they have (Scott, 1981).

So it is with deafness. In much of the world, including the United States, deaf people are largely excluded from the ranks of professionals serving deaf children. In many communities it just happens that to be a teacher of deaf children you must first qualify as a teacher of hearing children, and deaf people are excluded as teachers of hearing children. In other communities, it just happens that to become a teacher of deaf children the candidate who is most capable of communicating with them is disbarred because he or she must pass an examination couched in high register English without an interpreter. And as with services for blind people, many of the professions associated with the disability construction of deafness insist that the plight of the deaf child is truly desperate—so desperate, in fact, that some professionals propose implant surgery followed by rigorous and prolonged speech and hearing therapy. The successful use of a cochlear implant in everyday communication calls on a prior knowledge of spoken language (Staller *et al.,* 1991) that only one child candidate in ten possesses (Allen *et al.,* 1994); this has not, however, deterred professionals from recruiting among the other ninety percent; it is doubtful that the cochlear-implant industry would survive, certainly not flourish, if it sold its services and equipment only to the core clientele for the disability construction.

As with service providers for blind people, the troubled-persons industry associated with deafness seeks total conformity of the client to the underlying construction of deafness as disability. In the words of an audiology textbook: "One is not simply dealing with a handicapped child, one is dealing with a family with a handicap" (Tucker & Nolan, 1984 quoted in Gregory & Hartley, 1991, p. 87). The text goes on to state: "This concept of 'total child' being child plus hearing aids is one which parents may need time to come to terms with and fully accept." The profession wants to intervene in that family's life as early as possible and seeks to provide "a saturation service" (Tucker & Nolan, 1984 quoted in Gregory & Hartley, 1991, p. 97).

The criteria for disability, presented as objective, in fact conform to the interests of the profession (Oliver, 1990). Audiologic criteria decide which children will receive special education, so the audiologist must be consulted. In most countries of the world, audiology and special education are intimately related; the role of special education is to achieve as far as possible what audiology and otology could not do—minimize the child's disability. Writes one audiologist: "Education cannot cure deafness; it can only alleviate its worst effects" (Lynas, 1986, quoted in Gregory & Hartley, 1991, p. 155). Parents generally have little say about the right educational placement for their child; neither are there any functional tests of what the child can understand in different kinds of classrooms. Instead, audiologic criteria prevail, even if they have little predictive value. For example, the academic achievement scores of children classified as severely hearing-impaired are scarcely different from those of children classified as profoundly hearing impaired (Allen, 1986). Research has shown that some children categorized as profoundly hearing impaired can understand words and sentences whereas others do not even detect sound (Osberger *et al.*, 1993). Likewise, Scott states that the official definition of blindness is "based upon a meaningless demarcation among those with severely impaired vision" (Scott, 1981, p. 42).

THE MAKING OF DEAF MEN

The family that has received "saturation services" from the deafness troubled-persons industry will participate in socializing the deaf child to adapt the child's needs to those of the industry. A recent handbook for parents with implanted children states: "Parents should accept a primary role in helping their child adjust to the implant. They must assume responsibility for maintaining the implant device, for ensuring that the child is wearing it properly, and assuring that the auditory speech stimulation occurs in both the home and school" (Tye-Murray, 1992, p. xvi). "The child should wear the implant during all waking hours" (Tye-Murray, 1992, p. 18). Ultimately, the child should see the implant as part of himself, like his ears or hands. The handbook recounts enthusiastically how one implanted schoolchild, told to draw a self portrait, included the speech processor and microphone/transmitter in great detail: "This self-portrait demonstrated the child's positive image of himself and the acceptance of his cochlear implant" (Tye-Murray, 1992, p. 20).

The construction of the deaf child as disabled is legitimized early on by the medical profession and later by the special education and welfare bureaucracy. When the child is sent to a special educational program and obliged to wear cumbersome hearing aids, his or her socialization into the role of disabled person is promoted. In face-to-face encounters with therapists and teachers the child learns to cooperate in promoting a view of himself or herself as disabled. Teachers label large numbers of these deaf children emotionally disturbed or learning disabled (Lane, 1992). Once labeled as "multiply handicapped" in this way, deaf children are treated differently— for example, placed in a less demanding academic program where they learn less, so the label is self-validating. In the end, the troubled-persons industry creates the disabled deaf person.

DEAF AS LINGUISTIC MINORITY

From the vantage point of Deaf culture, deafness is not a disability (Jones & Pullen, 1989). British Deaf leader Paddy Ladd put it this way: "We wish for the recognition of our right to exist as a linguistic minority group . . . Labeling us as disabled demonstrates a failure to understand that we are not disabled in any way within our own community" (Dant & Gregory, 1991, p. 14). U.S. Deaf scholar Tom Humphries concurs: "There is no room within the culture of Deaf people for an ideology that all Deaf people are deficient. It simple does not compute. There is no "handicap" to overcome . . . (Humphries, 1993, p. 14). American Deaf leader M.J. Bienvenu asks: "Who benefits when we attempt to work in coalition with disability groups? . . . How can we fight for official recognition of ASL and allow ourselves as "communication disordered" at the same time?" And she concludes: "We are proud of our language, culture and heritage. Disabled we are not!" (Bienvenu, 1989, p. 13).

Nevertheless, many in the disability rights movement, and even some Deaf leaders, have joined professionals in promoting the disability construction of all deafness. To defend this construction, one leading disability advocate, Vic Finkelstein, has advanced the following argument based on the views of the people directly concerned: Minorities that have been discriminated against, like blacks, would refuse an operation to eliminate what sets them apart, but this is not true for disabled people: "every (!) disabled person would welcome such an operation" (*Finkelstein's exclamation point*). And, from this perspective, Deaf people, he maintains, "have more in common with other disability groups than they do with groups based upon race and

gender" (Finkelstein, 1991, p. 265). However, in fact, American Deaf people are more like blacks in that most would refuse an operation to eliminate what sets them apart (as Dr. Rosen did on *Sixty Minutes*). One U.S. survey of Deaf adults asked if they would like an implant operation so they could hear; more than eight out of 10 declined (Evans, 1989). When the magazine *Deaf Life* queried its subscribers, 87 percent of respondents said that they did not consider themselves handicapped.

There are other indications that American Deaf culture simply does not have the ambivalence that, according to Abberley, is called for in disability: "Impairment must be identified as a bad thing, insofar as it is an undesirable consequence of a distorted social development, at the same time as it is held to be a positive attribute of the individual who is impaired" (Abberley, 1987, p. 9). American Deaf people (like their counterparts in many other nations) think cultural Deafness is a good thing and would like to see more of it. Expectant Deaf parents, like those in any other language minority, commonly hope to have Deaf children with whom they can share their language, culture and unique experiences. One Deaf mother from Los Angeles recounted to a researcher her reaction when she noticed that her baby did not react to Fourth of July fireworks: "I thought to myself, 'She must be deaf.' I wasn't disappointed; I thought, 'It will be all right. We are both deaf, so we will know what to do' (Becker, 1980, p. 55). Likewise an expectant Deaf mother in Boston told the *Globe*, "I want my daughters to be like me, to be deaf" (Saltus, 1989, p. 27). The Deaf community, writes Paddy Ladd, "regards the birth of each and every deaf child as a precious gift" (quoted in Oliver, 1989, p. 199). Deaf and hearing scholars expressed the same view in a 1991 report to the U.S. National Institutes of Health; research in genetics to improve deaf people's quality of life is certainly important, they said, but must not become, in the hands of hearing people, research on ways of reducing the deaf minority (Padden, 1990).

Finkelstein acknowledges that many Deaf people reject the label "disabled" but he attributes it to the desire of Deaf people to distance themselves from social discrimination. What is missing from the construction of deafness is what lies at the heart of the linguistic minority construction: Deaf culture. Since people with disabilities are themselves engaged in a struggle to change the construction of disability, they surely recognize that disabilities are not "lying there in the road" but are indeed socially constructed. Why is this not applied to Deaf people? Not surprisingly, deafness is constructed differently in Deaf cultures than it is in hearing cultures.

Advocates of the disability construction for all deaf people, use the term "deaf community" to refer to all people with significant hearing impairment, on the model of "the disability community." So the term seems to legitimate the acultural perspective on Deaf people. When Ladd (*supra*) and other advocates of the linguistic minority construction speak of the Deaf community, however, the term refers to a much smaller group with a distinct manual language, culture, and social organization.[1] It is instructive, as American Deaf leader Ben Bahan has suggested, to see how ASL speakers refer to their minority; one term can be glossed as DEAF-WORLD. The claim that one is in the DEAF-WORLD, or that someone else is, is not a claim about hearing status at all; it is an expression of that self-recognition or recognition of others that is defining for all ethnic collectivities (Johnson & Erting, 1989). It is predictive about social behavior (including attitudes, beliefs and values) and language, but not about hearing status. All degrees of hearing can be found among Deaf people (it is a matter of discussion whether some hearing people with Deaf parents are Deaf), and

most people who are hearing-impaired are not members of the DEAF-WORLD.

In ASL the sign whose semantic field most overlaps that of the English "disability" can be glossed in English LIMP-BLIND-ETC. I have asked numerous informants to give me examples from that category: they have responded by citing (in literal translation) people in wheelchairs, blind people, mentally retarded people, and people with cerebral palsy, but no informant has ever listed DEAF and all reject it when asked. Another term in use in the Boston area (and elsewhere), which began as a fingerspelled borrowing from English, can be glossed D–A. My informants agree that Deaf is not D–A. The sign M–H–C (roughly, "multiply-handicapped") also has some currency. When I have asked Deaf people here for examples of M–H–C, DEAF-BLIND has never been listed, and when I propose it, it is rejected.

Other important differences between culturally Deaf people and people with disabilities come to light when we consider these groups' priorities. Among the preconditions for equal participation in society by disabled persons, the U.N. *Standard Rules* (1994) list medical care, rehabilitation, and support services such as personal assistance. "Personal assistance services are the new top of the agenda issue for the disability rights movement," one chronicler reports (Shapiro, 1993, p. 251). From my observation, Deaf people do not attach particular importance to medical care, not place any special value on rehabilitation or personal assistance services,[2] not have any particular concern with autonomy and independent living. Instead, the preconditions for Deaf participation are more like those of other language minorities: culturally Deaf people campaign for acceptance of their language and its broader use in the schools, the workplace, and in public events.

Integration, in the classroom, the workforce and the community, "has become a primary goal of today's disability movement" (Shapiro, 1993, p. 144). School integration is anathema to the DEAF-WORLD. Because most Deaf children have hearing parents, they can only acquire full language and socialization in specialized schools, in particular the prized network of residential schools; Deaf children are drowning in the mainstream (Lane, 1992). While advocates for people with disabilities recoil in horror at segregated institutions, evoking images of Willowbrook and worse, the Deaf alumni of residential schools return to their alma mater repeatedly over the years, contribute to their support, send their Deaf children to them, and vigorously protest the efforts of well-meaning but grievously ill-informed members of the disability rights movement to close those schools. These advocates fail to take account of language and culture and therefore of the difference between imposed and elective segregation. Where people with disabilities cherish independence, culturally Deaf people cherish interdependence. People with disabilities may gather for political action; Deaf people traditionally gather primarily for socializing. Deaf people marry Deaf people 90 percent of the time in the U.S. (Schein, 1989).

With the shift in the construction of disability has come an emphasis on the bonds that unite people with disabilities to the rest of society with whom they generally share not only culture but also ranges of capacities and incapacities (cf. Barton, 1993). "We try to make disability fixed and dichotomous," writes Zola, "but it is fluid and continuous" (Zola, 1993, p. 24). More than 20 percent of the noninstitutionalized population of the U.S. has a disability, we are told, and over 7.7 million Americans report that hearing is their primary functional limitation (Dowler & Hirsch, 1994). This universalizing view, according to which most people have some disability at least some of the time, is strikingly at odds with the DEAF-WORLD, small, tightly knit, with its own language and culture, sharply demarcated from the rest of society: there is no slippery slope between Deaf and hearing. "Deaf people are foreigners," wrote an early president of the National Association of the Deaf, "[living] among a people whose language they can never learn" (Hanson, cited in Van Cleve & Crouch, 1989, p. ix).

It is significant that the four student leaders who led the uprising known as the Gallaudet Revolution, were Deaf children of Deaf parents, deeply imbued with a sense of DEAF-WORLD, and natively fluent in ASL. One of them explained to *USA Today* the significance of the Revolution as it relates to the construction of deafness: "Hearing people sometimes call us handicapped. But most—maybe all deaf people—feel that we're more of an ethnic group because we speak a different language . . . We also have our own culture . . . There's more of an ethnic difference than a handicap difference between us and hearing people" (Hlibok, 1988, p. 11a). The new Deaf president of Gallaudet sought to explain the difference in the underlying construction in these terms: "More people realize now that deafness is a difference, not a deficiency" (Jordan, quoted in Gannon, 1989, p. 173).

So there is no reason to think that Paddy Ladd, Tom Humphries and MJ Bienvenu are being insincere when they claim that Deaf people are not disabled. Quite the contrary: since all are leaders of Deaf communities and are steeped in deaf culture, they advance the construction of deafness that arises from their culture. Mr. Finkelstein could have been tipped off to this very different construction by observing how various groups choose to be labeled: disability groups may find labels such as "disabled" or "motorically-impaired" or "visually handicapped" distasteful and reserve for themselves the right to call someone a "crip," but Deaf culture embraces the label "Deaf" and asks that everyone use it, as in The National Association of the Deaf and The World

Federation of the Deaf. It seems right to speak of "the Deaf" as we speak of "The French" or "The British." It is alien to Deaf culture on two counts to speak of its members as "people with hearing-impairment." First, it is the troubled-persons industry for deafness that invented and promoted the label in English "hearing-impaired" (Ross & Calvert, 1967; Wilson *et al.*, 1974; Castle, 1990). Second, the "people with" construction implies that the trait is incidental rather than defining, but one's culture is never an incidental trait. It seems to be an error in ordinary language to say, "I happen to be Hispanic," or "I happen to be Deaf"; who would you be, after all, if you were you and yet not Hispanic, or not Deaf? But it is acceptable to say, "I happen to have a spinal cord injury."

Deaf cultures do not exist in a vacuum. Deaf Americans embrace many cultural values, attitudes, beliefs and behaviors that are part of the larger American culture and, in some instances, that are part of ethnic minority cultures such as African-American, Hispanic-American, etc. Because hearing people have obliged Deaf people to interact with the larger hearing society in terms of a disability model, that model has left its mark on Deaf culture. In particular, Deaf people frequently have found themselves recipients of unwanted special services provided by hearing people. "In terms of its economic, political and social relations to hearing society, the Deaf minority can be viewed as a colony" (Markowicz & Woodward, 1978, p. 33). As with colonized peoples, some Deaf people have internalized the "other's" (disability) construction of them alongside their own cultural construction (Lane, 1992). For example, they may be active in their Deaf club and yet denigrate skilled use of ASL as "low sign"; "high sign" is a contact variety of ASL that is closer to English-language word order. The Deaf person who uses a variety of ASL marked as English frequently has greater access to wider resources such as education and employment. Knowing when to use which variety is an important part of being Deaf (Johnson & Erting, 1989). Granted that culturally Deaf people must take account of the disability model of deafness, that they sometimes internalize it, and that it leaves its mark on their culture, all this does not legitimize that model—any more than granting that African-Americans had to take account of the construction of the slave as property, sometimes internalized that construction, and found their culture marked by it legitimizes that construction of their ethnic group.

Neither culturally Deaf people nor people with disabilities are a homogeneous group.[3] Many of the differences between the two that I have cited will not apply to particular subgroups or individuals; nevertheless, it should be clear that cultural Deafness involves a constellation of traits quite different from those of any disability group. Faced with these salient differences, those who would argue that Deaf people are "really" disabled, sometimes resort instead to arguing that they are "really not" like linguistic minorities (Fishman, 1982). Certainly there are differences. For example, Deaf people cannot learn English as a second language as easily as other minorities. Second and third generation Deaf children find learning English no easier than their forbears, but second and third generation immigrants to the U.S. frequently learn English before entering school. The language of the DEAF-WORLD is not usually passed on from generation to generation; instead, it is commonly transmitted by peers or associates. Normally, Deaf people are not proficient in this native language until they reach school age. Deaf people are more scattered geographically than many linguistic minorities. The availability of interpreters is even more vital for Deaf people than for many other linguistic minorities because there are so few Deaf lawyers, doctors and accountants, etc. Few Deaf people are in high-status public positions in our society (in contrast with, say, Hispanics), and this has hindered the legitimation of ASL use (Kyle, 1990, 1991; Parratt & Tipping, 1991). However, many, perhaps all, linguistic minorities have significant features that differentiate them: Members of the Chinese-American community are increasingly marrying outside their linguistic minority but this is rare for ASL speakers. Many Native American languages are dying out or have disappeared; this is not true of ASL which is unlikely ever to die out. Spanish-speaking Americans are so diverse a group that it may not be appropriate to speak of the Hispanic community in the U.S. (Wright, 1994). Neither the newer strategy of citing what is special about the ASL-speaking minority nor the older one of minimizing ASL itself hold much promise of discrediting the construction of deafness as linguistic minority.

It is undeniable that culturally Deaf people have great common cause with people with disabilities. Both pay the price of social stigma. Both struggle with the troubled-persons industries for control of their destiny. Both endeavor to promote their construction of their identity in competition with the interested (and generally better funded) efforts of professionals to promote *their* constructions. And Deaf people have special reasons for solidarity with people with hearing impairments; their combined numbers have created services, commissions and laws that the DEAF-WORLD alone probably could not have achieved. Solidarity, yes, but when culturally Deaf people allow their special identity to be subsumed under the construct of disability they set themselves up for wrong solutions and bitter disappointments.

It is because disability advocates think of Deaf children as disabled that they want to close the special schools and absurdly plunge Deaf children into hearing classrooms in a totally exclusionary program called inclusion. It is because government is allowed to proceed with a disability construction of cultural Deafness that the U.S. Office of Bilingual Education and Minority Language Affairs has refused for decades to provide special resources for schools with large numbers of ASL-using children although the law requires it to do so for children using any other non-English language. It is because of the disability construction that court rulings requiring that children who do not speak English receive instruction initially in their best language have not been applied to ASL-using children. It is because of the disability construction that the teachers most able to communicate with Britain's Deaf children are excluded from the profession on the pretext that they have a disqualifying disability. It is because lawmakers have been encouraged to believe by some disability advocates and prominent deaf figures that Deaf people are disabled that, in response to the Gallaudet Revolution, the U.S. Congress passed a law, not recognizing ASL or the DEAF-WORLD as a minority, but a law establishing another institute of *health*, The National Institute on Deafness and Other Communications Disorders [*sic*], operated by the deafness troubled persons industry, and sponsoring research to reduce hereditary deafness. It is because of the disability construction that organizations *for* the Deaf (e.g., the Royal National Institute for the Deaf) are vastly better funded by government that organizations *of* the Deaf (e.g., the British Deaf Association).

One would think that people with disabilities might be the first to grasp and sympathize with the claims of Deaf people that they are victims of a mistaken identity. People with disabilities should no more resist the self-construction of culturally Deaf people, than Deaf people should subscribe to a view of people with disabilities as tragic victims of an inherent flaw.

CHANGING TO THE LINGUISTIC MINORITY CONSTRUCTION

Suppose our society were generally to adopt a disability construction of deafness for most late-deafened children and adults and a linguistic minority construction of Deaf people for most others, how would things change? The admirable Open University course, *Issues in Deafness* (1991) prompted these speculations.

(1) Changing the construction changes the legitimate authority concerning the social problem. In many areas, such as schooling, the authority would become Deaf adults, linguists and sociologists, among others. There would be many more service providers from the minority: Deaf teachers, foster and adoptive parents, information officers, social workers, advocates. Non-Deaf service providers would be expected to know the language, history, and culture of the Deaf linguistic minority.

(2) Changing the construction changes how behavior is construed. Deaf people would be expected to use ASL (in the U.S.) and to have interpreters available; poor speech would be seen as inappropriate.

(3) Changing the construction may change the legal status of the social problem group. Most Deaf people would no longer claim disability benefits or services under the present legislation for disabled people. The services to which the Deaf linguistic minority has a right in order to obtain equal treatment under the law would be provided by other legislation and bureaucracies. Deaf people would receive greater protection against employment discrimination under civil rights laws and rulings. Where there are special provisions to assist the education of linguistic minority children, Deaf children would be eligible.

(4) Changing the construction changes the arena where identification and labeling take place. In the disability construction, deafness is medicalized and labeled in the audiologist's clinic. In the construction as linguistic minority, deafness is viewed as a social variety and would be labeled in the peer group.

(5) Changing the construction changes the kinds of intervention. The Deaf child would not be operated on for deafness but brought together with other Deaf children and adults. The disability construction orients hearing parents to the question, what can be done to mitigate my child's impairment? The linguistic minority construction presents them with the challenge of insuring that their child has language and role models from the minority (Hawcroft, 1991).

OBSTACLES TO CHANGE

The obstacles to replacing a disability construction of deafness for much of the concerned population with a linguistic minority construction are daunting. In the first place, people who have little familiarity with deafness find the disability construction self-evident and the minority construction elusive. As I argue in *The Mask of Benevolence* (Lane, 1992), hearing people led to reflect on deafness generally begin by imagining themselves without hearing—which is, of course, to have a disability but not to be Deaf. Legislators can easily grasp the disability construction, not so the linguistic minority construction. The same tendency to uncritically accept the disability model led *Sixty Minutes* to feature a child from among the nine percent of childhood implant candidates who were deafened after learning English rather than from the 91 percent who do not identify with the English-speaking majority (Allen *et al.*, 1994). Not only did the interviewer find the disability construction of deafness easier to grasp but no doubt the producers thought heir millions of viewers would do likewise. Social problems are a favorite theme of the media but they are almost always presented as private troubles—deafness is no exception—because it makes for more entertaining viewing.

The troubled-persons industry associated with deafness—the "audist establishment" (Lane, 1992)—vigorously resists efforts to replace their construction of deafness. Audist policy is that ASL is a kind of primitive prosthesis, a way around the communication impasse caused by deaf peoples' disability. The audists control teacher training programs, university research facilities, the process of peer review for federal grant monies, the presentations made at professional meetings, and publications in professional journals; they control promotion and through promotion, salary. They have privileged access to the media and to law-making bodies when deafness is at issue. Although they lack the credibility of Deaf people themselves, they have expert credentials and they are fluent in speaking and writing English so law and policy makers and the media find it easier to consult them.

When a troubled-persons industry recasts social problems as private troubles it can treat, it is protecting its construction by removing the appearance of a social issue on which there might be political disagreement. The World Health Organization, for example, has medicalized and individualized what is social; services are based on an individualized view of disability and are designed by professionals in the disability industry (Oliver, 1991). The U.S. National Institute on Deafness and Other Communications Disorders proclaims in its very title the disability construction of deafness that it seeks to promote. The American Speech-Language Hearing Association, for example, has the power of accrediting graduate programs for training professionals who work with Deaf people; a program that deviated too far from the disability construction could lose its accreditation; without accreditation its students would not be certified; without the promise of certification, no one would enter the training program.

Some of the gravest obstacles to broader acceptance of the linguistic minority model come from members of the minority itself. Many members of the minority were socialized in part by professionals (and parents) to adopt a disabled role. Some Deaf people openly embrace the disability construction and thus undercut the efforts of other Deaf people to discredit it. Worse yet, many opportunities are provided to Deaf people (e.g., access to interpreters) on the condition that they adopt the alien disability construction. This double blind—accept our construction of your life or give up your access to equal citizenship—is a powerful form of oppression. Thus, many members of the DEAF-WORLD endorsed the Americans with Disabilities Act with its provisions for deaf people, all the while believing they are not disabled but lending credence to the claim that they are. In a related double blind, Deaf adults who want to become part of the professions serving Deaf people, find that they must subscribe to audist views of rehabilitation, special education, etc.

Exponents of the linguistic minority construction are at a further disadvantage because there is little built-in cultural transmission of their beliefs. The most persuasive advocates for Deaf children, their parents, must be taught generation after generation the counter-intuitive linguistic minority construction because most are neither Deaf themselves nor did they have Deaf parents.

A further obstacle arising within the DEAF-WORLD to promoting the linguistic minority construction concerns, ironically, the form that much Deaf political activism takes. Ever since the first congresses of Deaf people organized in response to the

Congress of Milan in 1880, Deaf leaders have appeared before friendly Deaf audiences to express their outrage—to preach to the converted. Written documents—position papers, articles and proceedings—have similarly been addressed to and read by primarily the DEAF-WORLD. It is entirely natural to prefer audiences with whom one shares language and culture, the more so as Deaf people have rarely been permitted to address audiences comprised of hearing professionals. Admittedly, preaching to the converted has value—it may evoke fresh ideas and it builds solidarity and commitment. Advocates of the disability construction do the same; childhood implant conferences, for example, rigorously exclude the voices of the cautious or frankly opposed.

I hope it may be allowed, however, to someone who has been invited to address numerous Deaf audiences and is exasperated by the slow pace of reform to point out that too much of this is an obstacle to true reform because it requires effort, permits the illusion that significant action has been taken, and yet changes little since Deaf people themselves are not responsible for the spread of the disability construction and have little direct power to change its range of application. What part of the battle is won when a Deaf leader receives a standing ovation from a Deaf audience? In the tradition of Deaf activism during the International Congress on the Education of the Deaf in Manchester in 1985, and during the Gallaudet Revolution, the past year have seen a striking increase in Europe of Deaf groups turning outward and presenting their views to hearing people and the media uninvited, particularly in opposition to cochlear implant surgery on Deaf children (Lane, 1994).

PRODUCTION CHANGE

Despite all the obstacles, there are powerful social forces to assist the efforts of the DEAF-WORLD to promote the linguistic minority construction. The body of knowledge developed in linguistics, history, sociology, and anthropology (to mention just four disciplines) concerning Deaf communities has influenced Deaf leadership, bureaucratic decision-making, and legislation. The civil rights movement has given great impetus to the belief that minorities should define themselves and that minority leaders should have a significant say in the conduct of minority affairs. Moreover, the failure of the present predominant disability construction to deliver more able deaf children is a source of professional and public embarrassment and promotes change. Then, too, Deaf children of Deaf parents are frequently insulated against the disability construction to a degree by their early language and cultural acquisition within the DEAF-WORLD. These native ASL-users have important allies in the DEAF-WORLD, among hearing children of Deaf parents, and among disaffected hearing professionals. The Gallaudet Revolution did not change the disability construction on a large scale but it led to inroads against it. Growing numbers of schools, for example, are turning to the linguistic minority construction to guide their planning, curricula, teacher selection and training.

Numerous organizations have committed extensive effort and money to promoting the disability construction. What can the national associations of the Deaf do to promote the linguistic minority construction? Publications like the British Deaf Association *News* or the National Association of the Deaf *Deaf American* are an important step because they provide a forum for national political discussion. However, the discussion has lacked focus. In addition to a forum, such associations need an explicit political agenda and a plan for implementing it. Such an agenda might include, illustratively, building a greater awareness of the difference between hearing-impairment and cultural Deafness; greater acceptance of the national sign language; removal or reduction of language barriers; improving culturally sensitive health care. Nowhere I know of are such agendas made explicit—given priorities, implementation, a time plan. If these were published they could provide the needed focus for the debate. Commentary on the agenda and plan would be invited as well as rebuttals to the commentaries in subsequent issues. Such agendas, plans and debates are buttressed by scholarship. An important resource to develop is a graduate program in public administration or political science focused on the DEAF-WORLD and the promotion of the linguistic minority construction.

NOTES

I acknowledge gratefully helpful discussions with Ben Bahan, and Robert Hoffmeister, Boston University; Alma Bournazian, Northeastern University; Robert E. Johnson, Gallaudet University; Osamu Nagase, United Nations Program on Disability; M.J. Bienvenu, the Bicultural Center; and helpful criticism from two unidentified journal reviewers.

1. Padden (1980) makes a distinction between a deaf community, a group of Deaf and hearing individuals who work to achieve certain goals, and a Deaf culture, to which Deaf members of that community belong.

2. In an effort to retain the disability construction of deafness, it has been suggested that sign language interpreters should be viewed as personal assistants. However, the services of these highly trained professionals are frequently not personal but provided to large audiences and they "assist" hearing people as well as, and at the same time as, Deaf people. Nor is interpreting between any other two languages (for example, at the United Nations) considered personal assistance.

3. I am not contending that there is a unitary homogenous DEAF-WORLD. My claims about Deaf culture are best taken as hypotheses for further verification, all the more as I am not a member of the DEAF-WORLD. My means of arriving at cultural principles are the usual ones for an outsider: encounters, ASL language and literature (including stories, legends, anecdotes, poetry, plays, humor, rituals, sign play), magazines and newspaper stories, films, histories, informants, scholarly studies, and the search for principles of coherence. See Stokoe (1994) and Kyle (1990).

REFERENCES

Aberley, P. (1987) The concept of oppression and the development of a social theory of disability, *Disability, Handicap and Society,* 2, pp. 5–19.

Albrecht, G. L. (1992) *The Disability Business: Rehabilitation in America* (Newbury Park CA, Sage).

Allen, T. E. (1986) Patterns of academic achievement among hearing-impaired students: 1974 and 1983, in: A. N. Schildroth & M. A. Karchmer (Eds.) *Deaf Children in America* (San Diego, College-Hill).

Allen, T. E., Rawlings, B. W. & Remington, E. (1994) Demographic and audiologic profiles of deaf children in Texas with cochlear implants, A*merican Annals of the Deaf,* 138, pp. 260–266.

Barton, L. (1993) The struggle for citizenship: the case of disabled people, *Disability, Handicap and Society,* 8, pp. 235–248.

Becker, G. (1980) *Growing Old in Silence* (Berkeley, University of California Press).

Bienvenu, M. J. (1989) Disability, *The Bicultural Center News,* 13 (April), p. 1.

Braille Monitor (1973) NAC—unfair to the blind, *Braille Monitor,* 2, pp. 127–128.

Braille Monitor (1989) Blind workers claim wages exploitative, *Braille Monitor,* 6, p. 322.

Burek, D. M. (Ed.) (1993) *Encyclopedia of Associations* (Detroit, Gale Research).

Cant, T. & Gregory, S. (1991) Unit 8. The social construction of deafness, in: Open University (Eds.) *Issues in Deafness* (Milton Keynes, Open University).

Castle, D. (1990) Employment bridges cultures, *Deaf American,* 40, pp. 19–21.

Conrad, P. & Schneider, J. (1980) *Deviance and Medicalization: from Badness to Sickness* (Columbia, OH, Merrill).

Dowler, D. L. & Hirsh, A. (1994) Accommodations in the workplace for people who are deaf or hard of hearing, *Technology and Disability,* 3, pp. 15–25.

Evans, J. W. (1989) Thoughts on the psychosocial implications of cochlear implantation in children, in: E. Owens & D. Kessler (Eds.) *Cochlear Implants in Young Deaf Children* (Boston, Little, Brown).

Finkelstein, V. (1991) 'We' are not disabled, 'you' are, in: S. Gregory & G. M. Hartley (Eds.) *Constructing Deafness* (London, Pinter).

Fishman, J. (1982) A critique of six papers on the socialization of the deaf child, in: J. B. Christiansen (Ed.) *Conference highlights: National Research Conference on the Social Aspects of Deafness,* pp. 6–20 (Washington, DC, Gallaudet College).

Gannon, J. (1989) *The Week the World Heard Gallaudet* (Washington, DC, Gallaudet University Press).

Gregory, S. & Hartley, G. M. (Eds.) (1991) *Constructing Deafness* (London, Pinter).

Gusfield, J. (1982) Deviance in the welfare state: the alcoholism profession and the entitlements of stigma, in: M. Lewis (Ed.) *Research in Social Problems and Public Policy*, Vol. 2 (Greenwich, CT, JAI press).

Gusfield, J. (1984) On the side: practical action and social constructivism in social problems theory, in: J. Schneider & J. Kitsuse (Eds.) *Studies in the Sociology of Social Problems* (Rutgers, NJ, Ablex).

Gusfield, J. (1989) Constructing the ownership of social problems: fun and profit in the welfare state, *Social Problems*, 36, pp. 431–441.

Hawcroft, L. (1991) Block 2, unit 7. Whose welfare?, in: Open University (Eds.) *Issues in Deafness* (Milton Keynes, Open University).

Hevey, D. (1993) From self-love to the picket line: strategies for change in disability representation, *Disability, Handicap and Society*, 8, pp. 423–430.

Hlibok, G. (1988) Quoted in *USA Today*, 15 March, p. 11a.

Humphries, T. (1993) Deaf culture and cultures, in: K. M. Christensen & G. L. Delgado (Eds.) *Multicultural Issues in Deafness* (White Plains, NY, Longman).

Jernigan, K. (1973) Partial victory in the NAC battle—and the beat goes on, *Braille Monitor*, January, pp. 1–3.

Johnson, R. E. & Erting, C. (1989) Ethnicity and socialization in a classroom for deaf children, in: C. Lucas (Ed.) *The sociolinguistics of the Deaf Community*, pp. 41–84 (New York, Academic Press).

Johnson, R. E. Liddell, S. K. & Erting, C.J. (1989) Unlocking the curriculum: principles for achieving access in deaf education, *Gallaudet Research Institute Working Papers*, 89–3.

Jones, L. & Pullen, G. (1989) 'Inside we are all equal': a European social policy survey of people who are deaf, in: L. Barton (Ed.) *Disability and Dependency* (Bristol, PA, Taylor & Francis/Falmer Press).

Kyle, J. (1990) The Deaf community: culture, custom and tradition, in: S. Prillwitz & T. Vollhaber (Eds.) *Sign Language Research and Application* (Hamburg, Signum).

Kyle, J. (1991) Deaf people and minority groups in the UK, in: S. Gregory & G. M. Hartley (Eds.) *Constructing Deafness* (London, Pinter).

Lane, H. (1984) *When the Mind Hears: a history of the deaf* (New York, Random House).

Lane, H. (1992) *The Mask of Benevolence: disabling the deaf community* (New York, Alfred Knopf).

Lane, H. (1994) The cochlear implant controversy, *World Federation of the Deaf News*, 2–3, pp. 22–28.

Lynas, W. (1986) *Integrating the Handicapped into Ordinary Schools: a study of hearing-impaired pupils* (London, Croom Helm).

Markowicz, H. & Woodward, J. (1978) Language and the maintenance of ethnic boundaries in the deaf community, *Communication and Cognition*, 11, pp. 29–38.

Oliver, M. (1989) Disability and dependency: a creation of industrial societies, in: L. Barton (Ed.) *Disability and Dependency*, pp. 6–22 (Bristol, PA, Taylor & Francis/Falmer Press).

Oliver, M. (1990) *The Politics of Disablement* (New York, St. Martin's Press).

Oliver, M. (1991) Multispecialist and multidisciplinary—a recipe for confusion? 'Too many cooks spoil the broth', *Disability, Handicap & Society*, 6, pp. 65–68.

Olson, C. (1977) Blindness can be reduced to an inconvenience, *Journal of Visual Impairment and Blindness*, 11, pp. 408–409.

Olson, C. (1981) Paper barriers, *Journal of Visual Impairment and Blindness*, 15, pp. 337–339.

Open University (1991) *Issues in Deafness* (Milton Keynes, Open University).

Osberger, M. J., Maso, M. & Sam, L. K. (1993) Speech intelligibility of children with cochlear implants, tactile aids, or hearing aids, *Journal of Speech and Hearing Research*, 36, pp. 186–203.

Padden, C. (1980) The deaf community and the culture of deaf people, in: C. Baker & R. Battison (Eds.) *Sign Language and the Desf Community: essays in honor of William C. Stokoe*, pp. 89–103 (Silver Spring, MD, National Association of the Deaf).

Padden, C. (Ed.) (1990) *Report of the Working Group on Deaf Community Concerns* (Bethesda, MD, National Institute on Deafness and Other Communication Disorders).

Parratt, D. & Tipping, B. (1991) The state, social work and deafness, in: S. Gregory & G. M. Hartley (Eds.) *Constructing Deafness* (London, Pinter).

Ross, M. & Calvert, D. R. (1967) Semantics of deafness, *Volta Review*, 69, pp. 644–649.

Saltus, R. (1989) Returning to the world of sound, *Boston Globe*, 10 July, pp. 27, 29.

Schein, J. D. (1989) *At Home Among Strangers* (Washington, DC, Gallaudet University Press).

Schneider, J. & Kitsuse, J. (Eds.) (1989) *Studies in the Sociology of Social Problems* (Rutgers, NJ, Ablex).

Scott, R. A. (1981) *The Making of Blind Men* (New Brunswick, NJ, Transaction).

Shapiro, J. P. (1993) *No Pity: people with disabilities forging a new Civil Rights Movement* (New York: Times Books).

Sixty Minutes (1992) Caitlin's story, 8 November.

Staller, S. S., Better, A. L., Brimacombe, J. A., Mecklenburg, D. J. & Arndt, P. (1991) Pediatric performance with the Nucleus 22-channel cochlear implant system, *American Journal of Otology,* 12 (Suppl.), pp. 126–136.

Stokos, W. (1994) An SLS print symposium [on culture]: an introduction, *Sign Language Studies,* 83, pp. 97–102.

Tucker, I. & Nolan, M. (1984) *Educational Audiology* (London, Croom Helm).

Tye-Murray, N. (1992) *Cochlear Implants and Children: a handbook for parents, teachers and speech professionals* (Washington, DC, A. G. Bell Association).

United Nations (1994) *The Standard Rules on the Equalization of Opportunities for Persons with Disabilities* (New York, United Nations).

Van Cleve, J. (Ed.) (1987) *The Gallaudet Encyclopedia of Deaf People and Deafness* (New York, McGraw-Hill).

Vaughan, C. E. (1991) The social basis of conflict between blind people and agents of rehabilitation, *Disability, Handicap & Society,* 6, pp. 203–217.

Wilson, G. B., Ross, M. & Calvert, D. R. (1974) An experimental study of the semantics of deafness, *Volta Review,* 76, pp. 408–414.

Wright, L. (1994) Annals of politics: one drop of blood, *The New Yorker,* 25 July, pp. 46–55.

Zola, I. K. (1993) Disability statistics, what we count and what it tells us, *Journal of Disability Policy Studies,* 4, pp. 9–39.

CHAPTER 7

(Post)colonizing Disability

Mark Sherry

Disability and postcolonialism are two important, and inter-related, discourses in the social construction of the nation and of those bodies deemed worthy of citizenship rights. This paper acknowledges the material dimensions of disability, impairment—and postcolonialism and its associated inequalities—but it also highlights the rhetorical connections that are commonly made between elements of postcolonialism (exile, diaspora, apartheid, slavery, and so on) and experiences of disability (deafness, psychiatric illness, blindness, etc.). The paper argues that researchers need to be far more careful in their language around experiences of both disability and postcolonialism. Neither disability nor postcolonialism should be understood as simply a metaphor for the other experience; nor should they be rhetorically employed as a symbol of the oppression involved in a completely different experience. A central focus of this paper is the rhetorical connection commonly made between various elements of postcolonialism (colonization, exile, diaspora, apartheid, slavery, and so on) and experiences of disability. The paper also argues that researchers need to be far more thoughtful and careful in theorizing of this relationship. Postcolonialism should not be understood as simply a metaphor for the experience of disability; nor should the terms "colonialism" or "disability" be rhetorically employed as a symbol of the oppression involved in a completely different experience.

DEFINITIONS OF DISABILITY AND POSTCOLONIALISM

Before discussing the interconnectedness of these phenomena, it is useful to define the key terms, "disability" and "postcolonialism." In discussing "disability", the author adopts two definitions. The first, which is consistent with a social model of disability and particularly popular within disability studies involves making a heuristic distinction between disability and impairment—where impairment is defined as a form of biological, cognitive, sensory or psychiatric difference that is defined within a medical context, and disability is the negative social reaction to those differences. The rationale for this heuristic distinction is to separate the experience of biological difference from the prejudice, discrimination and other negative social consequences that many disabled people experience. The second definition of disability adopted in this paper is that of an identity. In this context, disability (like "race", gender or religion) is not necessarily regarded as a bad thing—it is an identity, with both social and personal dimensions, which may be associated with feelings of community, solidarity and pride, or conversely, with feelings of difference, exclusion and shame. A "disability" identity is not necessarily a medicalized identity—it could simply be an identity that is based on identifying someone who navigates the world in atypical ways, facing many attitudinal and physical barriers. Adopting two definitions of disability may seem cumbersome, and confusing, but it is important given the rise of identity politics associated with the disability movement.

The definition of "postcolonialism" adopted in this paper is that offered by Ashcroft, Griffiths and Tiffin (2003):

> We use the term 'post-colonial', however, to cover all the culture affected by the imperial process from the moment of colonization to the present day. This is because there is a continuity of preoccupations throughout the historical process initiated by European imperial aggression. We also suggest that it is the most appropriate as a term for the new cross-cultural criticism which has emerged in recent years and for the discourse through which this is constituted.
>
> (p. 2)

Unlike Ashcroft, Griffiths and Tiffin, however, this paper does not employ the hyphen between "post" and "colonial", since it is not being suggested that this era is coming after the moment of colonialism. The use of the term "post" within "postcolonialism" is not meant to imply that the contemporary world does not experience ongoing effects of the racism, genocide, violence and environmental abuse which has characterized contact between the First World and the majority world. Rather, it is intended to acknowledge the ongoing effects of such practices, as well as the changing forms of oppression embedded in contemporary international relations, following the national liberation movements of various majority world countries. As Loomba (2001) argues, postcolonialism is not a term that signifies the end of colonialism, but rather signifies new forms of contesting colonial domination and the legacies of colonialism. In this sense, postcolonial criticism is understood as examining the relations of domination between and within nations, "races", or cultures, recognizing the historical roots of such practices within colonialism (Moore-Gilbert, 1998).

UNPACKING THE CONNECTIONS

Postcolonial themes are commonly used metaphorically within disability studies. Metaphors have been a major element of traditional descriptions of pain, illness and disability; these metaphors have likened the relationship between disability, illness and the body to such diverse experiences as military operations, machinery, extraterrestrialism, sexuality, and colonialism (Lupton, 2003). So it probably should not be surprising that disability is often used as a metaphor for the problems experienced by a nation. However, the nature of those metaphors is particularly interesting, because the connections they make between quite disparate experiences evoke meanings that shape perception, identity and experience. As Susan Sontag (1989) has commented, "Of course, one cannot think without metaphors. But that does not mean there aren't some metaphors we might well abstain from or try to retire" (p. 5).

The metaphorical connections between disability and postcolonialism are so extensive that they cannot be fully summarized in one brief paper. Nevertheless, it may be sufficient to note that the failure to recognize American Sign Language as a distinct culture has been represented as a form of "colonialism" (Lane, 1993); contemporary interactions between patients and doctors have been characterized as a form of "medical colonialism" (Frank, 1997, 2002);

and the experiences of racism and disablism have been equated, as in the concept of "the cripple as Negro" (sic) (Kriegel, 1969, but see also Asch 2004 and Domurat Dreger 2004). Disability has also been compared to "exile" (e.g. Clare, 1999; Michalko, 1999), as well as "internal exile" (Ingram, 2003); it has been presented as a form of "apartheid" (Goggin and Newell, 2004; Wood, 1994); the treatment of people diagnosed as having psychiatric impairments has been presented as a form of "slavery" (Szasz, 2003); and disability has been positioned as a form of "diaspora" (Thrower, 2003). The quest to "cure" impairment in the majority world has been a major element of Orientalist discourse (Jarman, 2004). Unfortunately, superficial comparisons between experiences of disability and "race" have sometimes been made that suggest the two experiences are completely interchangeable. For instance, in *One of Us*, Alice Domurat Dredger (2004) suggests that her adopted African-American brother could be described as "disabled" simply on the basis of his ethnicity:

> . . . by virtue of being black in a place where to be black was abnormal, Paul might have counted as disabled according to the basic definition since provided by the Americans with Disabilities Act: people regarded him as having an anatomical impairment that substantially limited his major activities.
>
> (p. 15)

Such conflation of "race" and disability is not only factually inaccurate (her brother could not be regarded as "disabled" under the ADA) but offers a puerile conflation of fundamentally different social experiences.

Nevertheless, disability and postcolonial experiences are often conflated. For instance, in *The Mask of Benevolence*, Harlan Lane (1993) describes Deaf people as a linguistic minority who have experienced "colonialism".[1] Lane's arguments stemmed from his work in Burundi, which had made him realize that negative stereotypes of African people were often similar to the stereotypes about Deaf people. Lane positions colonialism as "the standard, as it were, against which other forms of cultural oppression can be scaled, involving as it did the physical subjugation of a disempowered people, the imposition of alien language and mores, and the regulation of education in behalf of the colonizer's goals" (p. 31). Lane argues that hearing people have acted as colonialists because their behaviors have been marked by paternalism, ethnocentrism, negative stereotypes, the artificial creation of dependence, and economic exploitation. He states

> Like the paternalism of the colonizers, hearing paternalism begins with defective perception, because it superimposes its image of the familiar world of hearing people on the unfamiliar world of deaf people. Hearing paternalism likewise sees its task as "civilizing" its charges: restoring deaf people to society. And hearing paternalism fails to understand the structure and values of deaf society. The hearing people who control the affairs of deaf children and adults commonly do not know deaf people and do not want to. Since they cannot see deaf people as they really are, they make up imaginary deaf people of their own, in accord with their own experiences and needs.
>
> (p. 37)

Lane does not examine what makes colonialism a unique form of power, nor does he clearly differentiate "colonialism" from various forms of power over bodies, which may fall under the category of "disability". Indeed, Lane's approach to Deafness as a unique culture means that he does not wish to engage in a dialogue about similarities between Deaf and disabled people, a task that would fall to other scholars—particularly those with a stronger interest in identity (for instance, Corker, 1999).

The rhetorical connections which Lane makes between disability and colonialism have also been observed by a number of other scholars. For instance, Arthur Frank (1997, p. 10) describes patient-doctor interactions as "medical colonization" which can continue for a lifetime. Frank (1997) argues, "Colonization was central to the achievement of modernist medicine" (p. 10). Discussing the work of the postcolonial theorist Gayatri Spivak, Frank (1997) argues that the medical encounter is not just analogous, but exactly the same:

> This is exactly the colonization that Spivak speaks of: the master text of the medical journal article needs the suffering person, but the individuality of that suffering cannot be acknowledged.
>
> (p. 12)

Frank (2002) continues to argue in his most recent work, "medicine tries to colonize your body" (p. 57). He argues that the process of becoming a patient means, "being colonized as medical territory and becoming a spectator to your own drama" which means that "you lose yourself" (p. 57).

Tom Shakespeare (2000), who explicitly engages with the work of postcolonial theorists such as Edward Said, Albert Memmi and Frantz Fanon, also compares the disability experience to that of colonialism and imperialism. Shakespeare engages with the feminist literature on care, and recognizes in passing that the majority of care is done by women, but does not sufficiently engage with the connections between "race", ethnicity, disability and care. Specifically, what is missing is an inclusion of the role of women of color in giving and receiving care, imbued with explicit acknowledgement and analysis of racial/ethnic difference. The inclusion of such an analysis would enable scholars to identify the cultural, social, historical, sexual and representational implications of such differences. Nevertheless, Shakespeare (2000, p. x) does not engage in such analysis and instead simply parallels disability and postcolonialism. He states

> I suggest that 'care' can operate as a kind of imperialism. In the early twentieth century, residential institutions were often actually called 'colonies'. Still today, people who receive welfare or medical help may be taken over, their homes or bodies invaded. In return for help, they have to give up control over their lives. The colonialism incipient in the caring relationship can mean that the power to define the problem, let alone the way that the problem should be solved, is removed from the person and monopolized by the helper. The help-receiver may be regarded as incapable, incompetent, sometimes even morally inferior—just like attitudes to 'natives' in the former colonies.
>
> (Memmi, 1990)

This technique of using postcolonial themes to describe disability is far more common than might be assumed. For instance, in his discussion of adventitious blindness, Michalko (1999) relies very heavily on the concept of "exile" and the work of Edward Said. Although Michalko recognizes that blind people are not usually "banished" from their homeland, and thus reduces the concept of exile to a metaphor, he maintains that this is a legitimate parallel because adventitiously blind people "remember the 'homeland' of the visual world in the way that the exile remembers the sweetness of home" (p. 97). Further, Michalko states:

> Like Said's exile, the blind person knows that in a world of contingency, homes are provisional. We can be sighted today and blind tomorrow. Like the exile's experience of crossing political and geographical boundaries, crossing the border from sightedness to blindness provides for the possibility of breaking the barriers of "thought and experience".
>
> (p. 107)

In the work of Richard Ingram (2003), the related concept of "internal exile" is used to describe the experience of psychiatric system survivors. However, Ingram does not simply wish to acknowledge similarities between the experiences of those in internal exile and psychiatric system survivors. He employs this rhetoric to suggest that psychiatric system survivors in fact experience far greater human rights violations than others in "internal exile":

> First, our encounter with psychiatry either begins with internment, or with becoming exposed to the threat of internment. Second, we are not just stripped of access to one or more languages, literatures, and cultures, but to language, literature, and culture per se. Third, the application of these techniques of isolation is wrapped in a discourse of benevolent care, and backed up with irresistible force. Once a psychiatrist has informed you that "you're not making sense," you no longer have any say in determining what is in your interest, and all rights vanish into air.
>
> (p. 8)

Unfortunately, Ingram's gender-blind approach fails to recognize the complexity, multiplicity and differentiation of those with experiences of psychiatric confinement and also those who have experiences of internal exile. This is important, because other studies have shown that men are more likely to be admitted to mental hospitals, but women are more likely to be labeled mentally ill based on their gender roles (Cockerham, 2003).

The well-known critic of psychiatry, Thomas Szasz (1977), has emphasized the similarities between colonialism and disability for many years. In his classic work, *Psychiatric Slavery*, Szasz acknowledged that psychiatric slavery was not chattel slavery, but argued that there were ideological, economic, political, linguistic and legal similarities between involuntary servitude and involuntary psychiatry. This is a theme that Szasz has continued in his recent work. In *Liberation by Oppression: A Comparative Study of Slavery and Psychiatry*, Szasz (2003) maintains that the nexus between diagnosis, treatment and incarceration lies at the core of psychiatric intolerance and coercion. Continuing the comparison between people diagnosed as having mental illnesses and what Szasz refers to as "the Negro" (sic), he labels laws concerning psychiatry as "psychiatric Jim Crow laws—'unequal and separate'" (p. 33). Again, however, there is no analysis of the differential impact of gender on the subjects of psychiatric incarceration; neither is there any mention of the sexual dynamics of slavery.

Unfortunately, the pattern of treating postcolonialism simply as a metaphor within disability studies has been matched by a similar pattern of treating disability as metaphor within postcolonial writing. For instance, the colonial experience has been characterized as a form of national disablement (Choi, 2001), colonialism in Africa has been presented as "disabling the colonized" (Quayson, 2002, p. 228), and colonial culture has been described as a form of "crippled minds" (Goonatilake, 1982). In Korea, Choi asserts, there was both a conscious and an unconscious re-imagining of the colonized nation as a disabled entity as a result of the pressures of colonization, capitalization, modernization and urbanization. Korean intellectuals sought to capture national aspirations and history through the trope of disability. Choi suggests that this is the reason why narratives from Korea in the colonial period tend to present the majority of the population as disabled or impaired. Choi identifies an "inseparable relationship between the literary imagination and the historical and political situation of Koreans as colonized subjects", suggesting that "the trope of disability surfaced largely within a sociopolitical perspective that emerged in response to a sense of national crisis" (p. 438). Choi's analysis suggests that Korea's experience of colonialism was understood through the metaphor of disability and illness in the national body.

Another important dimension of the relationship between disability and post-colonialism is that disability is sometimes presented as the symbol of the evils of colonialism. Imagery of disease and disability is often associated with concern for the social order and Sontag (1978) emphasizes the long history of using metaphors of illness to describe social corruption. Some disability studies scholars suggest that such metaphorical use of disability is not co-incidental. Mitchell and Snyder (2003) argue that disability pervades literature as "an opportunistic metaphorical device" (p. 47) which differentiates characters from normative categories. The use of disability metaphors, they suggest, has been a "crutch upon which literary narratives lean for the representational power, disruptive potentiality, and analytical insight" (p. 49).

Perhaps the best example of this tendency within postcolonial literature is Franz Fanon's (1963) classic, *The Wretched of the Earth*. Disability is central to Fanon's arguments: one of the main features of colonialism which he identifies is the creation of specific mental "pathologies" and "disorders" as a result of the colonial relationship. Not surprisingly, given that Fanon was a psychiatrist, he adopts a medical model of disability. In the medical model, the experts are doctors and allied health professionals, and the diagnostic process is often assumed to be a fairly unproblematic process of simply recognizing "objective" symptoms of a "disorder" and labeling it accordingly. Thus, Fanon believes that colonial wars create specific sorts of mental distress. While Fanon recognizes that the identities adopted in response to colonialist developments (such as those of the nationalist resistance movements) are thoroughly

social constructs, he seems to assume that the disability labels which he applies to people reflect objective mental states, rather than subjective interpretations of another person's reality. For instance, he describes an individual as experiencing "marked anxiety psychosis of the depersonalization type" (p. 261), another as "accusatory delirium and suicidal conduct disguised as 'terrorist activity'" (p. 273); and refers to women experiencing "puerperal disorders" associated with childbirth without questioning whether the process of diagnosing such "mental disorders" could be in anyway problematic. For Fanon, psychiatric impairments are a sign of the horrors of colonialism. Get rid of colonialism, and we will avoid many disability experiences, and that is unquestionably assumed to be a good thing.

Fanon (1963) not only assumes that medical diagnoses are objective and scientific, he further assumes that medical responses are unproblematically beneficial. For instance, he laments the fact that people who have been electrocuted often present with symptoms that make it "completely impossible" for doctors to suggest shock therapy (p. 283), ignoring the fact that such "treatments" cause brain injuries, may be fatal, and always have major negative consequences on patients.[2] Likewise, Fanon's "objective" descriptions of impairments—such as a case study of one man's "impotence" following the rape of his wife (which is described as "her dishonor" (p. 255)—actually mask wider power dynamics, such as sexism. But Fanon's implicit medical model of disability leads him to largely ignore the role of social factors other than colonialism in the creation of disability and impairment. This is deeply problematic, as postcolonial theorists have shown, because it reduces what Bhabha (1994) has called "the cultural and historical hybridity of the postcolonial world" (p. 21). Such an approach also forecloses examination of the cultural processes of ambivalence, distortion, repetition and slippage inherent in both colonial discourses of differentiation and in resistance to them (Bhabha 1994).

Fanon's masculinist approach to colonialism can be contrasted to Aretxaga's (2006) more complex (and more interesting) study of gender and colonialism in Northern Ireland between 1978 and 1981. During that time, male and female members of the Irish Republican Army and the Irish National Liberation Army participated in a "Dirty Protest" where they refused to leave their cells in order to wash or use the toilets, instead letting those cells fill up with dirt and body waste. Feces and menstrual blood became the symbols of political protest. Aretxaga interprets this as a highly gendered protest against British colonialism—transferring the issue of menstrual blood, for instance, from the bodies of women onto the body politics of colonialism. The interconnections between bodily pain, symbols of violence and sexual difference were central to this protest. Indeed, Aretxaga (2006) concludes that "political violence performed on and from the body cannot escape the meaning of sexual difference" (p. 307). Given that ethnic and political violence is implicated both in the discursive construction of sexual difference as well as ethnic identity, violence against women's bodies in the context of colonialism cannot be assumed to be a mirror image of violence against male bodies. However, Aretxaga's analysis is nevertheless limited by its failure to analyze the relationship between bodily pain, embodied protest and disability within this context. It could be argued that disability is actually central to the connections between pain, flesh, physical vulnerability and "leaky bodies" (to borrow a term from Shildrick, 1997). However, Aretxaga's account of the protest is somehow diminished because of the failure to make such connections.

An equally problematic response to the issues of postcolonialism and disability is to marginalize the issues as if they were of concern only to those people who identify both as disabled and members of a colonized group. The flaws with such an additive model of identity have been well established with regard to gender and ethnicity, but nevertheless remain present in some of the literature on disability and postcolonialism. One recent example of such an additive model of identity is the work of Lacom (2002), which suggests that disabled people within postcolonial contexts are "doubly colonized" because "the colonized subject who is Other in terms of body and voice is made doubly Other by means of her disability" (p. 138). Clearly, more sophisticated approaches to such questions are needed. This paper now highlights some of the efforts that have been made to develop a more complex theorization of the relationship between postcolonialism and disability.

MORE PRODUCTIVE APPROACHES TO THESE ISSUES

It is a truism to say that the historical legacy of colonialism is the poverty of the majority world, which has created large numbers of impairments. Abject poverty, starvation, and war cause impairments; these are undisputed facts. This poverty is a human rights issue, as is the social creation of impairment in this manner, as are the presence of disabling barriers in the social and physical environment (see Stone, 1999; Priestley, 2001). However, such a recognition is insufficient for developing a complex understanding of the relationship between disability and postcolonialism. Rather than simply bemoan disability as a symbol of the horrors of imperialism, a far more interesting approach is to unpack the power dynamics which link the two experiences, both in practice and in rhetoric.

For instance, an important element of the rhetorical connections between postcolonialism and disability has been the racist discourses about particular populations being associated with contamination and disease—a theme which is particularly evident in the AIDS literature (Farmer, 1993). Likewise, the discourse of AIDS and contagion is laden with gendered messages about reproduction, women's bodies, medical resources, and the role of bodies in an interpersonal and an international context (Lewin, 2006). In this way, postcolonialism intersects with disability and gender in order to construct what has been called "the geography of blame" (Farmer, 1993, p. 191). And yet the position of women, the role of gender more broadly, and the specific intersections of racism and sexism in the lives of black women in the production of such discourses are rarely acknowledged. As Ogundipe-Leslie (2001) comments "the black women's absence is ever central and taken for granted" (p. 135).

Racist themes of contamination (thoroughly interspersed with discourses about the creation of disability) have been attributed to particular ethnic populations over many centuries. Such ideas have actually been a mainstay of anti-Semitism for hundreds of years (Gilman, 1985). Racism and disablism were also combined in the exoticism and spectacle of the freak shows of the early 20th century (Bogdan, 1990). In the mid 20th century, the connections between disability and racism were particularly evident in eugenics, which was premised on a desire to eradicate both racial difference and impairment (Kerr and Shakespeare, 2002). Of course, the eugenic programs of Nazi Germany not only led to the mass genocide of millions of Jews in the Holocaust, they also resulted in the murder and involuntary sterilization of hundreds of thousands of disabled people. Eugenics had a particularly important sexual dimension. Barlow's (2005) study of

eugenic ideology suggests that women's sexual behavior was central to the eugenic themes of hygiene, racial vitality, and the production of the "fit" and the "unfit". Barlow argues that such gender dynamics are central, rather than peripheral to colonialism. In both national and international eugenic ideology, "these scientized, biologized, evolutionized identities of woman and man constitute core elements of colonial modernity" (p. 378). Likewise, Larson (1995) has highlighted the interconnections among racism, sexism and eugenics: in the face of racist fears and prejudices which created pressure to protect and purify the Caucasian race, eugenicists implemented marriage restrictions, sexual segregation, compulsory sterilization and immigration restrictions.

The combination of racism and disablism, as well as homophobia, was also apparent in the First World's response to AIDS, particularly in the accusations and blame directed towards Haitians. AIDS, in its early stages, was commonly associated with what was called "the Four-H Club": homosexuality, heroin addicts, hemophiliacs, and Haitians. The spurious connections made between Haitian voodoo and the transmission of the AIDS virus, which emerged early in the pandemic before any detailed epidemiological studies had been conducted, remain a powerful symbol of the intersection of discourses of disability and racism and reflect long-standing mythology around exoticism and sexual diseases. The notion that "disease-ridden" Haitians brought AIDS to the First World reproduced long-standing racist conspiracy theories about blackness, animals and sexually transmitted diseases (Farmer, 1993). As Sontag notes, (1989), "there is a link between imagining disease and imagining foreignness" (p. 48).

It is true, of course, that particular ethnic populations experience higher rates of certain impairments and diseases than others. The incidence of Tay-Sachs disease, for instance, is approximately a hundred times greater among Ashkenazi Jews than it is among the general population; malignant osteopetrosis is a high-frequency disease among people from Costa Rica; and higher rates of Thalassemia have been found among a number of populations, including South East Asians and Africans (Duster, 2003). However, it would be a mistake to simply note the presence of impairment in particular ethnic populations and to assume a direct unmediated relationship between impairment and disability experiences. Unfortunately, many epidemiological studies of the prevalence of disability in indigenous populations have made precisely this assumption, and have produced reports of disability which are largely inconsistent with the ways in which the populations being studied understand their own experiences (for instance, Thomson and Snow, 1994). In order to understand the social construction of disability in a particular socio-cultural context, it is necessary to examine the specific economic, ideological, institutional, political, military, ethnic, gender and age-related dynamics present in that society. These cannot simply be "read off" a list of the most common impairments in a region. Nevertheless, this has unfortunately been a common mistake—even within disability studies literature. Stone (1999), for instance, simply rattles off a list of impairments in "developing countries" (sic) as if the process of disablement were a natural and direct consequence of the incidence of impairment. The statistics which Stone quotes are undoubtedly powerful—for instance, she notes that over 100 million people have impairments stemming from malnutrition and a quarter of a million children go blind every year due to a lack of Vitamin A. However, Stone seems to assume that a linear connection exists between disability and impairment. This is a deeply problematic assumption from the perspective of many disability scholars. Tremain (2002) for instance has criticized the tendency of such work to assume that impairment is objective, transhistorical and transcultural.

One of the best illustrations of the need for a culturally-specific examination of disability and impairment is O'Nell's (1996) study of depression in a Native American community. Some Flathead Indian people suggested to O'Nell that between 70% and 80% of their community experienced depression. However, the incidence of depression was not generally connected to accounts of illness. Instead, a sense of suffering was regarded as a marker of maturity and Indian identity. For many people living on the Flathead Reservation, depression is the natural and esteemed condition of "real Indians", those who have "disciplined hearts", and who have used their sadness as a source of compassionate responsibility for others. The idea that most Flathead people are depressed makes sense when their narratives are understood in their cultural context, in which the narrators try to use their stories as a basis for an individual and collective charter for modern Indian life. In such narratives, a strong emphasis is placed on moral development, social relations, history and contemporary American Indian identity. O'Nell interprets loneliness and depression as a part of the political process of individual and collective demoralization and "remoralization" of the Flathead Indian people. Such a nuanced, culturally-specific understanding of depression is impossible under the medical model, which tends to assume that impairments such as mental illness are objective and ahistorical.

Both postcolonialism and disability studies also have a long way to go in exploring the racist creation of disability. For instance, in the United States, healthcare disparities in a range of areas continue to lead to higher morbidity and mortality rates for African-Americans and members of other ethnic minorities. There is significant evidence to show that disparities in coronary revascularization procedures are leading to higher mortality rates for African-Americans; there are also significant differences in the patterns of diagnostic tests, treatments and analgesics offered to African-Americans with cancer; African-Americans with HIV receive less antiretroviral therapy, prophylaxis for pneumocystic pneumonia, and protease inhibitors; and African-American patients are 3.6 times more likely to receive amputations than whites and 2.4 times more likely to receive bilateral orchietomy—the removal of both testicles due to cancer or fear of cancer (Sherry, 2004). All of these inequities can be investigated more by researchers working on the intersection of disability and postcolonialism.

Another important dimension of the relationship between postcolonialism and disability has been raised by Baynton (2001) whose investigation of immigration debates in America suggests that the absence of disability within ethnic minorities is rhetorically employed as a measure of worthiness to be a citizen. This argument is deeply problematic, particularly when one considers disability as an identity—the second definition offered in the introduction to this paper. In this context, strategic efforts by disabled activists to build disability pride and promote a culture of disability may be directly undermined by the engagement of immigrant groups in the politics of shame and stigma. Baynton's arguments are similar in some respects to another argument offered by Lacom, that colonized people often attempt to become liberated by creating a "new category of *monsters*—the disabled, the deformed, the mad" (p. 141). In this context, Lacom argues, disabled people are disavowed by both colonizers and colonized people.

There are, of course, major differences between the experiences of disability and the experience of postcolonialism which cannot simply be ignored. These also need to be incorporated into the discussions. As Shakespeare (1996) has noted, the vast majority of people in postcolonial contexts share ethnic identities with their family members, whereas the vast majority of disabled people are the only members of their families who have that identity, and they therefore lack role models within the family. The patterns of support and socialization for each group may therefore be significantly different. Researchers need to investigate such issues empirically.

At the level of theory, there are also significant differences between postcolonialism and disability studies. It seems that some postcolonial literature has a far more nuanced approach to identity issues than is evident within disability studies. For instance, a great deal of disability studies still reproduces the disabled/nondisabled divide (for example, Hughes, 2002; Barnes and Mercer, 2003; Longmore, 2003 and Tregaskis, 2004). However, postcolonial literature suggests such a binary and essentialist approach to identity is conceptually flawed, inconsistent and has undesirable moral and political consequences (see Smith, 1998 and Donaldson, 1992). This work would seem to suggest that in the same way that a black/white divide is theoretically inadequate for conceptualizing ethnicity, the disabled/non-disabled divide is also deeply problematic and conceptually limited. People often position themselves somewhere in-between or outside these binary categories, and this positioning is fluid and contextually dependent. Their ambiguities and contradictions may lead to hybrid identities, ambivalences, and forms of domination and resistance existing beyond the binary.

The issue of power, agency and resistance is indeed one which postcolonial authors such as Bhabha (1994) have examined far more carefully than disability scholars. Bhabha's examination of subtle forms of resistance, such as the displacement, distortion, dislocation and ambivalence generated by the process of colonial domination is far more complex than the simple models of unilateral "oppression" which can be found in many disability studies texts (e.g. Charlton, 2000; Priestley, 1999; Imrie, 1996). Rather than look for overt signs of protest and conflict around issues of "oppression", the implication of Bhabha's work is to study carefully the production of hybridity, mimicry, and "sly civility" as forms of ambivalence generated by dominating discourses of hierarchy, marginalization and normalization. Postcolonial scholars use such concepts in order to identify the nation as the symbol of the problematic boundaries of modernity—but disability studies may also find such a complex, and subtle, approach to power far more fruitful than to dismiss both the political effectiveness and the psychologically affective elements of dominant discourses. In exploring the cultural and political issues associated with the liminality of the nation-state, Bhabha stresses that it is important to identify those in-between moments that initiate new sites of identity, new collaborations, and new conflicts over identity. Again, this sophisticated approach to forms of domination and alterity is markedly different from the approach of disability scholars, who tend to favor simplistic models of oppression and uncritically regard minority discourse as signs of political strength and unity, rather than ambivalence (for instance, Charlton, 2000).

Although the discipline of disability studies can undoubtedly learn a great deal from the postcolonial literature on identity, it may have its own lessons to teach on the issue of embodiment. For instance, while there is a tendency within critical race theory to emphasize the socially constructed nature of our responses to human variation, both the biological and the social dimensions of embodiment receive a great deal of attention within disability studies. As Williams (2003) has argued, a sophisticated understanding of embodiment is absolutely necessary. Such an understanding should not conflate the epistemological and ontological nature of biology, but should also recognize that biology enables as well as constrains. It also needs to acknowledge the dynamic and developmental nature of biology—and to recognize that biology can expose social inequalities and oppression, rather than simply legitimate them. This is an issue which postcolonialism could certainly engage with in more detail.

CONCLUSION

This paper has attempted to illustrate the problematic approaches towards the intersection of disability and postcolonialism that underpins a great deal of the literature. It has stressed that disability should not be treated as a metaphor for postcolonialism, and that postcolonialism should not be treated as a metaphor for disability. Each experience may share some similarities, but they are also quite distinct. The paper has concluded by identifying more promising ways of unpacking this complex relationship. It has highlighted the rhetorical connections between disability and postcolonialism in racist and sexist discourses of contamination and disease, and has stressed the importance of further research into the racist creation of disability. The paper has also emphasized the importance of examining the interconnections of sexism, racism and disablism in postcolonialism and in the study of disability. It has highlighted the need for disability studies to examine the subtle forms of resistance that can be theorized in more complex ways than a simple model of uni-lateral oppression would suggest. Likewise, the paper has stressed the need for more attention to the issue of embodiment within postcolonial literature. All of these suggested changes would create a more theoretically rigorous approach to both the study of postcolonialism and disability.

NOTES

1. Although Lane uses the phrase "deaf" to describe this population, it is more accurate from a dis-ability and Deaf studies viewpoint to use the uppercase "Deaf" to describe a distinct linguistic minority, as opposed to people who simply have a hearing impairment. This is another interest-ing difference between disability as defined by the social model and from the perspective of identity politics.
2. Fanon's support for electroshock therapy con-trasts starkly with accounts written by psy-chiatric system survivors and their advocates. For a far more critical discussion of "brain damage as miracle therapy", see Whitaker 2003, pp. 106–13.

REFERENCES

Aretxaga, B. (1995). Dirty Protest: Symbolic Overdetermination and Gender in Northern Ireland Ethnic Violence. In Lewan, E. (Ed.), *Feminist Anthropology: A Reader* (pp. 295–310). Malden, MA: Blackwell Publishing.

Asch, A. (2004). Critical Race Theory, Feminism and Disability: Reflections on Social Justice and Personal Identity. In Smith, B. G. and Hutchison, B. (Eds), *Gendering Disability* (pp. 9–44). New Brunswick, NJ: Rutgers University Press.

Ashcroft, B., Griffiths, G. and Tiffin, H. (2003). *The Empire Writes Back* (2nd edn). London: Routledge.

Barlow, T. E. (2005). Eugenic Woman, Semicolonialism, and Colonial Modernity as Problems for Postcolonial Theory. In Loomba, A., Kaul, S., Bunzl, M. and Burton, A. (Eds), *Postcolonial Studies and Beyond* (pp. 359–384). Durham, NC: Duke University Press.

Barnes, C. and Mercer, G. (2003). *Disability*. London: Polity Press.

Baynton, D. (2001). Disability and the Justification of Inequality in American History. In Longmore, P. K. and Umansky, L. (Eds), *The New Disability History:*

American Perspectives (pp. 1–32). New York: New York University Press.

Bhabha, H. (1994). *The Location of Culture*. London: Routledge.

Bogdan, R. (1990). *Freak Show: Presenting Human Oddities for Amusement and for Profit*. Chicago, IL: University of Chicago Press.

Charlton, J. (2000). *Nothing About Us Without Us: Disability Oppression and Empowerment*. Berkeley, CA: University of California Press.

Choi, Kyeong-Hee. (2001). Impaired Body as Colonial Trope: Kang Kyong'ae's 'Underground Village'. *Public Culture*, 13(3), 431–458.

Clare, E. (1999). *Exile and Pride*. Cambridge, MA: South End Press.

Cockerham, W. C. (2003). *Sociology of Mental Disorder* (6th edn). Upper Saddle River, NJ: Prentice Hall.

Corker, M. (1999). *Deaf and Disabled, or Deafness Disabled?*. Buckingham: Open University Press.

Domurat Dreger, A. (2004). *One of Us: Conjoined Twins and the Future of Normal*. Cambridge, MA: Harvard University Press.

Donaldson, L. E. (1992). *Decolonizing Feminisms: Race, Gender and Empire Building*. Chapel Hill, NC: University of North Carolina Press.

Duster, T. (2003). *Backdoor to Eugenics* (2nd edn). New York: Routledge.

Fanon, F. (1963). *The Wretched of the Earth*. New York: Grove Press.

Farmer, P. (1993). *AIDS and Accusation: Haiti and the Geography of Blame*. Berkeley, CA: University of California Press.

Frank, A. (1997). *The Wounded Storyteller: Body, Illness and Ethics*. Chicago, IL: The University of Chicago Press.

Frank, A. (2002). *At the Will of the Body*. New York: Mariner Books.

Gilman, S. (1985). *Difference and Pathology: Stereotypes of Sexuality, Race and Madness*. Ithaca, NY: Cornell University Press.

Goggin, G. and Newell, C. (2004). *Disability in Australia: Exposing a Social Apartheid*. Sydney: University of New South Wales Press.

Goonatilake, S. (1982). *Crippled Minds: An Exploration into Colonial Culture*. New Delhi: Vikas.

Hughes, B. (2002). Disability and the Body. In Barnes, C., Oliver, M. and Barton, L. (Eds), *Disability Studies Today* (pp. 58–76). Cambridge: Polity Press.

Imrie, R. (1996). *Disability and the City: International Perspectives*. London: Paul Chapman.

Ingram, R. A. (2003). "You're Not Making Sense": Psychiatrization and Internal Exile. Paper pre-sented at the Inaugural Conference of the Disability Studies Association, University of Lancaster, UK; September 4–6, 2003. Retrieved May 13, 2007 from http://www.disabilitystudies.net/dsaconf2003/fullpapers/ingram.doc

Jarman, M. (2004). The Labor of Assimilation. Paper presented at Society for Disability Studies Conference, St Louis, MO, June 3–6, 2004.

Kerr, A. and Shakespeare, T. (2002). *Genetic Politics: From Eugenics to Genome*. Cheltenham: New Clarion Press.

Kriegel, L. (1969). Uncle Tom and Tiny Tim: Some Reflections on the Cripple as Negro. *The American Scholar*, 38(3), 412–430.

Lacom, C. (2002). Revising the Subject: Disability as "Third Dimension" in *Clear Light of Day* and *You Have Come Back*. *NWSA Journal*, 14(3), 138–154.

Lane, H. (1993). *The Mask of Benevolence: Disabling the Deaf Community*. New York: Vintage Books.

Larson, E. (1995). *Sex, Race, and Science: Eugenics in the Deep South*. Baltimore, MD: The Johns Hopkins University Press.

Lewin, E. (2006). "Introduction." In Lewan, E. (Ed.) *Feminist Anthropology: A Reader*, (pp. 1–38). Maden, MA: Blackwell Publishing.

Longmore, P. (2003). *Why I Burned My Book and Other Essays on Disability*. Philadelphia, PA: Temple University Press.

Loomba, A. (2001). *Colonialism/Postcolonialism*. London: Routledge.

Lupton, D. (2003). *Medicine as Culture* (2nd edn). London: Sage.

Michalko, R. (1999). *The Two-In-One: Walking with Smokie, Walking with Blindness*. Philadelphia, PA: Temple University Press.

Mitchell, D. and Snyder, S. (2003). *Narrative Prosthesis*. Ann Arbor, MI: The University of Michigan Press.

Moore-Gilbert, B. (1998). *Postcolonial Theory: Contexts, Practices, Politics*. London: Verso.

O'Nell, T. D. (1996). *Disciplined Hearts: History, Identity and Depression in an American Indian Community*. Berkeley, CA: University of California Press.

Ogundipe-Leslie, M. (2001). Moving the Mountains, Making the Links. In Bhavnani, K. (Ed.), *Feminism and 'Race'* (pp. 134–144). Oxford: Oxford University Press.

Priestley, M. (1999). *Disability Politics and Community Care*. London: Jessica Kingsley.

Priestley, M. (Ed.) (2001). *Disability and the Life Course: Global Perspectives*. Cambridge: Cambridge University Press.

Quayson, A. (2002). Looking Awry: Tropes of Disability in Postcolonial Writing. In Goldberg, D. T. and Quayson, A. (Eds), *Relocating Postcolonialism* (pp. 217–230). Oxford: Blackwell Publishers.

Shakespeare, T. (1996). Disability, Identity, Difference. In Barnes, C. and Mercer, G. (Eds), *Exploring the Divide* (pp. 94–113). Leeds: The Disability Press.

Shakespeare, T. (2000). *Help*. Birmingham, UK: Venture Press.

Sherry, M. (2004). Unequal Treatment. *Sociology of Health and Illness*, 26(4), 489–493.

Shildrick, M. (1997). *Leaky Bodies and Boundaries: Feminism, Postmodernism and (Bio)ethics*. New York: Routledge.

Smith, V. (1998). *Not Just Race, Not Just Gender: Black Feminist Readings*. London: Routledge.

Sontag, S. (1989). *AIDS and Its Metaphors*. New York: Farrar, Straus and Giroux.

Sontag, S. (1978). *Illness as Metaphor*. New York: Farrar, Straus and Giroux.

Stone, E. (1999). Disability and Development in the Majority World. In Stone, E. (Ed.), *Disability and Development: Learning from Action and Research on Disability in the Majority World* (pp. 1–18). Leeds: The Disability Press.

Szasz, T. (1977). *Psychiatric Slavery*. New York: The Free Press.

Szasz, T. (2003). *Liberation by Oppression: A Comparative Study of Slavery and Psychiatry*. New Brunswick, NJ: Transaction.

Thomson, N. and Snow, C. (1994). *Disability and Handicap among Aborigines of the Taree area of New South Wales*. Canberra: Australian Government Publishing Service.

Thrower, T. (2003). Finding Disability Identity in Diaspora and Cyborg Theory. Paper presented at Society for Disability Studies Conference, Bethesda, Maryland, June 11–15, 2003.

Tregaskis, C. (2004). *Constructions of Disability: Researching the Interface between Disabled and Non-Disabled People*. London: Routledge.

Tremain, S. (2001). On the Subject of Impairment. In Corker, M. and Shakespeare, T. (Eds), *Disability-Postmodernity: Embodying Disability Theory*. London: Continuum Press.

Whitaker, R. (2003). *Mad in America*. Cambridge, MA: Perseus Publishing.

Williams, S. (2003). *Medicine and the Body*. London: Sage.

Wood, R. (1994). Social, Cultural and Economic Rights—The Most Widespread Form of Oppression. *DPI European Union Committees' International Disability e-mail news service*, 24(94), November 9, 1994.

CHAPTER 8

Abortion and Disability: Who Should and Should Not Inhabit the World?

Ruth Hubbard

Political agitation and education during the past few decades have made most people aware of what constitutes discrimination against blacks and other racial and ethnic minorities and against women. And legal and social measures have been enacted to begin to counter such discrimination. Where people with disabilities are concerned, our level of awareness is low, and the measures that exist are enforced haphazardly. Yet people with disabilities and disability-rights advocates have stressed again and again that it is often far easier to cope with the physical aspects of a disability than with the discrimination and oppression they encounter because of it (Asch, 1988; Asch and Fine, 1988). People shun persons who have disabilities and isolate them so they will not have to see them. They fear them as though the disability were contagious. And it is, in the sense that it forces us to face our own vulnerability.

Most of us would be horrified if a scientist offered to develop a test to diagnose skin color prenatally so as to enable racially mixed people (which means essentially everyone who is considered black and many of those considered white in the Americas) to have light-skinned children. And if the scientist explained that because it is difficult to grow up black in America, he or she wanted to spare people suffering because of the color of their skin, we would counter that it is irresponsible to use scientific means to reinforce racial prejudices. Yet we see nothing wrong, and indeed hail as progress, tests that enable us to try to avoid having children who have disabilities or are said to have a tendency to acquire a specific disease or disability later in life.

The scientists and physicians who develop and implement these tests believe they are reducing human suffering. This justification seems more appropriate for speed limits, seat-belt laws, and laws to further occupational safety and health than for tests to avoid the existence of certain kinds of people. When it comes to women or to racial or ethnic groups, we insist that it is discriminatory to judge individuals on the basis of their group affiliation. But we lump people with disabilities as though all disabilities were the same and always devastating and as though all people who have one were alike.

Health and physical prowess are poor criteria of human worth. Many of us know people with a disease or disability whom we value highly and so-called healthy people whom we could readily do without. It is fortunate for human variety and variability that most of us are not called on to make such judgments, much less to implement them.

It is not new for people to view disability as a form of pollution, evidence of sin. Disability has been considered divine punishment or, alternatively, the result of witches' spells. In our scientific and medical era we look to heredity for explanations unless there is an obvious external cause, such as an accident or infectious disease. Nowadays, even if an infection can explain the disability, scientists have begun to suggest that our genes might have made us unusually susceptible to it.

In a sense, hereditary disabilities are contagious because they can be passed from one generation to the next. For this reason, well before there was a science of genetics, scientists proposed eugenic measures to stem the perpetuation of "defects."

THE RISE OF EUGENICS IN BRITAIN AND THE UNITED STATES

Eugenics met its apotheosis under the Nazis, which is why many Germans oppose genetic testing and gene therapy and their use is being hotly debated in the parliament. Germans tend to understand better than people in other countries what can happen when the concern that people with disabilities will become social and economic burdens or that they will lead to a deterioration of the race begins to dictate so-called preventive health policies. They are aware that scientists and physicians were the ones who developed the Nazi policies of "selection and eradication" (*Auslese und Ausmerze*) and who oversaw their execution. What happened under the Nazis has been largely misrepresented and misinterpreted in this country, as well as among Nazi apologists in Germany. To make what happened clearer, I shall briefly review the scientific underpinnings of the Nazi extermination program, which are obscured when these practices are treated as though they were incomprehensible aberrations without historical roots or meaning—a holocaust.

German eugenics, the attempt to improve the German race, or *Volk*, by ridding it of inferior and foreign elements, was based on arguments and policies developed largely in Great Britain and the United States during the latter part of the nineteenth and the beginning of the twentieth centuries. (In what follows I shall not translate the german word *Volk* because it has no English equivalent. The closest is "people," singular, used as a collective noun, as in "the German people *is* patriotic." But "people," singular, does not convey the collectivity of *Volk* because to us "people" means individuals. Therefore, we would ordinarily phrase my example, "the German people *are* patriotic.")

The term *eugenics* is derived from the Greek word for "well born." It was coined in 1883 by Francis Galton, cousin of Charles Darwin, as "a brief word to express the science of improving the stock, which is by no means confined to questions of judicious mating, but which, especially in the case of man [*sic*], takes cognizance of all the influences that tend in however remote a degree to give the more suitable races or strains of blood a better chance of prevailing speedily over the less suitable than they otherwise would have had" (pp. 24–25). Galton later helped found the English Eugenics Education Society and eventually became its honorary president.

British eugenics counted among its supporters many distinguished biologists and social scientists. Even as late as 1941, while the Nazis were implementing their eugenic extermination program, the distinguished biologist Julian Huxley (1941)—brother of Aldous—opened a semipopular article entitled "The Vital Importance of Eugenics" with the words: "Eugenics is running the usual course of many new ideas. It has ceased to be regarded as a fad, is now receiving serious study, and in the near future, will be regarded as an urgent practical problem." In the article, he argues that it is crucial for society "to ensure that mental defectives [*sic*] shall not have children" and defines as mentally defective "someone with such a feeble mind that he cannot support himself or look after himself unaided." (Notice the mix of eugenics and economics.) He says that he refuses to enter into the argument over whether such "racial degeneration" should be forestalled by "prohibition of marriage" or "segregation in institutions" combined with "sterilization for those who are at large." He states as fact that most "mental defects" are hereditary and suggests that it would therefore be better if one could "discover how to diagnose the carriers of the defect" who are "apparently normal." "If these could but be detected, and then discouraged *or prevented* from reproducing, mental defects could very speedily be reduced to negligible proportions among our population" (my emphasis). It is shocking that at a time when the Nazi program of eugenic sterilization and euthanasia was in full force across the Channel, Huxley expressed regret that it was "at the moment very difficult to envisage methods for putting even a limited constructive program [of eugenics] into effect" and complained that "that is due as much to difficulties in our present socio-economic organization as to our ignorance of human heredity, and most of all to the absence of a eugenic sense in the public at large."

The American eugenics movement built on Galton and attained its greatest influence between 1905 and 1935. An underlying concern of the eugenicists is expressed in a statement by Lewis Terman (1924), one of the chief engineers of I.Q. testing: "The fecundity of the family stocks from which our most gifted children come appears to be definitely on the wane. . . . It has been figured that if the present differential birth rate continues 1,000 Harvard graduates will, at the end of 200 years, have but 56 descendants, while in the same period, 1,000

S. Italians will have multiplied to 100,000." To cope with this dire eventuality, eugenics programs had two prongs: "positive eugenics"—encouraging the "fit" (read "well-to-do") to have lots of children—and "negative eugenics"—preventing the "unfit" (defined to include people suffering from so-called insanity, epilepsy, alcoholism, pauperism, criminality, sexual perversion, drug abuse, and especially feeble-mindedness) from having any.

Many distinguished American geneticists supported eugenics, but none was more active in promoting it than Charles Davenport, who, after holding faculty appointments at Harvard and the University of Chicago, in 1904 became director of the "station for the experimental study of evolution," which he persuaded the Carnegie Institution of Washington to set up in Cold Spring Harbor on Long Island. His goal was to collect large amounts of data on human inheritance and store them in a central office. In 1910, he managed to persuade the heiress to the Harriman railroad fortune to fund the Eugenics Record Office at Cold Spring Harbor, for which he got additional money from John D. Rockefeller, Jr. He appointed Harry W. Laughlin, a Princeton Ph.D., as superintendent and recruited a staff of young graduates from Radcliffe, Vassar, Cornell, Harvard, and other elite institutions as fieldworkers to accumulate interview data about a large number of so-called mental and social defectives. The office and its staff became major resources for promoting the two legislative programs that formed the backbone of U.S. eugenics: involuntary-sterilization laws and the Immigration Restriction Act of 1924.

The first sterilization law was enacted in Indiana in 1907, and by 1931 some thirty states had compulsory-sterilization laws on their books. Aimed in general at the insane and "feeble-minded" (broadly interpreted to include many recent immigrants and other people who did badly on

I.Q. tests because they were functionally illiterate or barely spoke English), these laws often extended to so-called sexual perverts, drug fiends, drunkards, epileptics, and "other diseased and degenerate persons" (Ludmerer, 1972). Although most of these laws were not enforced, by January 1935 some twenty thousand people in the United States had been forcibly sterilized, nearly half of them in California. Indeed, the California law was not repealed until 1980 and eugenic-sterilization laws are still on the books in about twenty states.

The eugenic intent of the Immigration Restriction Act of 1924 was equally explicit. It was designed to decrease the proportion of poor immigrants from southern and eastern Europe so as to give predominance to Americans of British and north European descent. This goal was accomplished by restricting the number of immigrants allowed into the United States from any one country in each calendar year to at most 2 percent of U.S. residents who had been born in that country as listed in the Census of 1890 (so, thirty-four years earlier). The date 1890 was chosen because it established as a baseline the ethnic composition of the U.S. population prior to the major immigrations from eastern and southern Europe, which began in the 1890s. Laughlin of the Eugenics Record Office was one of the most important lobbyists and witnesses at the Congressional hearings that preceded passage of the Immigration Restriction Act and was appointed "expert eugenical agent" of the House Committee on Immigration and Naturalization (Kevles, 1985).

RACIAL HYGIENE IN GERMANY

What was called eugenics in the United States and Britain came to be known as racial hygiene in Germany. It was the response to several related and widely held beliefs: (1) that humane care for people with disabilities would enfeeble the "race" because they would survive to pass their disabilities on to their children; (2) that not just mental and physical diseases and so-called defects, but also poverty, criminality, alcoholism, prostitution, and other social problems were based in biology and inherited; and (3) that genetically inferior people were reproducing faster than superior people and would eventually displace them. Although these beliefs were not based in fact, they fueled racist thinking and social programs in Britain and the United States as well as in Germany.

German racial hygiene was founded in 1895, some dozen years after Galton's eugenics, by a physician, Alfred Plötz, and was based on much the same analysis of social problems as the British and American eugenics movements were. In 1924, Plötz started the *Archive of Race- and Socio-biology (Archiv für Rassen- und Gesellschaftsbiologie)* and the next year helped found the Society for Racial Hygiene (Gesellschaft für Rassenhygiene). German racial hygiene initially did not concern itself with preventing the admixture of "inferior" races, such as Jews or gypsies, in contrast to the British and American movements where miscegenation with blacks, Asians, Native Americans, and immigrants of almost any sort was one of the major concerns. The recommended means for preventing racial degeneration in Germany, as elsewhere, was sterilization. Around 1930 even some German socialists and communists supported the eugenic sterilization of inmates of psychiatric institutions, although the main impetus came from the Nazis. The active melding of anti-Semitism and racial hygiene in Germany began during World War I and accelerated during the 1920s, partly in response to economic pressures and a scarcity of available positions, which resulted in severe competition for jobs and incomes among scientists and physicians, many of whom were Jews.

Racial hygiene was established as an academic discipline in 1923, when Fritz Lenz, a physician and geneticist, was appointed to the newly created Chair of Racial Hygiene at the University of Munich, a position he kept until 1933, when he moved to the Chair of Racial Hygiene at the University of Berlin. Lenz, Eugen Fischer, and Erwin Baer coauthored the most important textbook on genetics and racial hygiene in German. Published in 1921, it was hailed in a review in the *American Journal of Heredity* in 1928 as "the standard textbook of human genetics" in the world (quoted in Proctor, 1988, p. 58). In 1931, it was translated into English, and the translation was favorably reviewed in Britain and the United States despite its blatant racism, or perhaps because of it. By 1933, eugenics and racial hygiene were being taught in most medical schools in Germany.

Therefore the academic infrastructure was in place when the Nazis came to power and began to build a society that gave biologists, anthropologists, and physicians the opportunity to put their racist and eugenic theories into practice. Looking back on this period, Eugen Fischer, who directed the Kaiser Wilhelm Institute for Anthropology, Human Genetics, and Eugenics in Berlin from 1927 to 1942, wrote in a newspaper article in 1943: "It is special and rare good luck when research of an intrinsically theoretical nature falls into a time when the general world view appreciates and welcomes it and, what is more, when its practical results are immediately accepted as the basis for governmental procedures" (quoted in Müller-Hill, 1984, p. 64; my translation). It is not true, as has sometimes been claimed, that German scientists were perverted by Nazi racism. Robert Proctor (1988) points out that "it was largely medical scientists who *invented* racial hygiene in the first place" (p. 38; original emphasis).

A eugenic-sterilization law, drafted along the lines of a "Model Sterilization Law" published by Laughlin (the superintendent of Davenport's Eugenics Record Office at Cold Spring Harbor), was being considered in 1932 by the Weimar government. On July 14, 1933, barely six months after Hitler took over, the Nazi government passed its eugenic-sterilization law. This law established genetic health courts (*Erbgesundheitsgerichte*), presided over by a lawyer and two physicians, one of whom was to be an expert on "hereditary pathology" (*Erbpathologie*), whose rulings could be appealed to similarly constituted supreme genetic health courts. However, during the entire Nazi period only about 3 percent of lower-court decisions were reversed. The genetic health courts could order the sterilization of people on grounds that they had a "genetically determined" disease, such as "inborn feeble-mindedness, schizophrenia, manic-depressive insanity, hereditary epilepsy, Huntington's disease, hereditary blindness, hereditary deafness, severe physical malformations, and severe alcoholism" (Müller-Hill, 1984, p. 32; my translation). The law was probably written by Dr. Ernst Rüdin, professor of psychiatry and director of the Kaiser Wilhelm Institute for Genealogy and Demography of the German Research Institute for Psychiatry in Munich. The official commentary and interpretation of the law was published under his name and those of an official of the Ministry of the Interior, also a medical doctor, and of a representative of the Health Ministry in the Department of the Interior who was a doctor of laws. All practicing physicians were sent copies of the law and commentaries describing the acceptable procedures for sterilization and castration.

The intent of the law was eugenic, not punitive. Physicians were expected to report patients and their close relatives to the nearest local health court and were fined if they failed to report someone with a so-called hereditary disease. Although some physicians raised the objection that this requirement invaded the doctor-patient relationship, the health authorities argued that this obligation to notify then was no different from requirements that physicians report the incidence of specific infectious diseases or births and deaths. The eugenic measures were to be regarded as health measures pure and simple. And this is the crucial point: the people who designed these policies and the later policies of euthanasia and mass extermination as well as those who oversaw their execution looked on them as sanitary measures, required in this case to cure not individual patients but the collective—the *Volk*—of threats to its health (Lifton, 1987; Proctor, 1988).

As early as 1934, Professor Otmar von Verschuer, then dean of the University of Frankfurt and director of its Institute for Genetics and Racial Hygiene and later the successor of Fischer as director of the Kaiser Wilhelm Institute for Anthropology, Human Genetics, and Eugenics in Berlin, urged that patients should not be looked on, and treated, as individuals. Rather the patient is but "one part of a much larger whole or unity: of his family, his race, his *Volk*" (quoted in Proctor, 1988, p. 105). Minister of the Interior Wilhelm Frisch estimated that at least half a million Germans had genetic diseases, but some experts thought that the true figure was more like one in five, which would be equivalent to thirteen million. In any event, by 1939 some three to four hundred thousand people had been sterilized, with a mortality of about 0.5 percent (Proctor, 1988, pp. 108–109). After that there were few individual sterilizations. Later, large numbers of people were sterilized in the concentration camps, but that was done without benefit of health courts, as part of the program of human experimentation.

The eugenic-sterilization law of 1933 did not provide for sterilization on racial grounds. Nonetheless, in 1937 about five hundred racially mixed children were sterilized; the children had been fathered by black French colonial troops brought to Europe from Africa after World War I to occupy the Rhineland (the so-called Rheinlandbastarde).

The first racist eugenic measures were passed in 1935. They were the Nürnberg antimiscegenation, or blood-protection laws, which forbade intermarriage or sexual relations between Jews and non-Jews and forbade Jews from employing non-Jews in their homes. The Nürnberg laws also included a "Law for the Protection of the Genetic Health of the German People," which required premarital medical examinations to detect "racial damage" and required people who were judged "damaged" to marry only others like themselves, provided they first submitted to sterilization. The Nürnberg laws were considered health laws, and physicians were enlisted to enforce them. So-called positive eugenics was practiced by encouraging "genetically healthy" German women to have as many children as possible. They were persuaded to do so by means of propaganda, economic incentives, breeding camps, and strict enforcement of the law forbidding abortion except for eugenic reasons (Koonz, 1987).

The next stage in the campaign of "selection and eradication" was opened at the Nazi party congress in 1935, where plans were made for the "destruction of lives not worth living." The phrase was borrowed from the title of a book published much earlier, in 1920, by Alfred Hoche, professor of psychiatry and director of the Psychiatric Clinic at Freiburg, and Rudolf Binding, professor of jurisprudence at the University of Leipzig. In their book, entitled *The Release for Destruction of Lives Not Worth Living (Die Freigabe zur Vernichtung lebensunwerten Lebens)*, these professors argued for killing "worthless" people, whom they defined as those who are "mentally completely dead" and those who constitute "a foreign body in human society" (quoted in Chorover, 1979, p. 97). At the time the program was initiated, the arguments focused on the money wasted in keeping institutionalized (hence "worthless") people alive, for in the early stages the rationale of the euthanasia campaign was economic as much as eugenic. Therefore the extermination campaign was directed primarily at inmates of state psychiatric hospitals and children living in state institutions for the mentally and physically disabled. Jews were specifically excluded because they were not considered worthy of euthanasia. (Here, too, the Nazis were not alone. In 1942, as the last inmates of German mental hospitals were being finished off, Dr. Foster Kennedy, an American psychiatrist writing in the official publication of the American Psychiatric Association, advocated killing mentally retarded children of five and older (Proctor, 1988). The arguments were phrased in humane terms like these: "Parents who have seen the difficult life of a crippled or feebleminded child must be convinced that though they have the moral obligation to care for the unfortunate creatures, the wider public should not be obliged . . . to assume the enormous costs that long-term institutionalization might entail" (quoted in Proctor, 1988, p. 183). This argument calls to mind the statement by Bentley Glass (1971) about parents not having "a right to burden society with a malformed or a mentally incompetent child."

In Germany, the propaganda was subtle and widespread. For example, Proctor (1988, p. 184) cites practice problems in a high school mathematics text published for the school year 1935–36, in which students were asked to calculate the costs to the Reich of maintaining mentally ill people in various kinds of institutions for different lengths of time and to compare the costs of constructing insane asylums and housing units. How is that for relevance?

Although the euthanasia program was planned in the mid-1930s, it was not implemented until 1939, when wartime dislocation and secrecy made it relatively easy to institute such extreme measures. Two weeks before the invasion of Poland an advisory committee commissioned by Hitler issued a secret report recommending that children born with Down syndrome, microcephaly, and various deformities be registered with the Ministry of the Interior. Euthanasia, like sterilization, was to proceed with the trappings of selection. Therefore physicians were asked to fill out questionnaires about all children in their care up to age three who had any of these kinds of disabilities. The completed questionnaires were sent to three-man committees of medical experts charged with marking each form "plus" or "minus." Although none of these "experts" ever saw the children, those whose forms were marked "plus" were transferred to one of a number of institutions where they were killed. Some of the oldest and most respected hospitals in Germany served as such extermination centers. By 1941 the program was expanded to include older children with disabilities and by 1943, to include healthy Jewish children. Also in 1939, evaluation forms were sent to psychiatric institutions for adults for selection and so-called euthanasia.

By September 1941 over seventy thousand inmates had been killed at some of the most distinguished psychiatric hospitals in Germany, which had been equipped for this purpose with gas chambers, disguised as showers, and with crematoria (Lifton, 1986; Proctor, 1988). (When the mass extermination of Jews and other "undesirables" began shortly thereafter, these gas chambers were shipped east and installed at Auschwitz and other extermination camps.) Most patients were gassed or killed by injection with legal drugs, but a few physicians were reluctant to intervene so actively and let children die of slow starvation and the infectious diseases to which they became susceptible, referring to this as death from "natural" causes. Relatives were notified that their family member had died suddenly of one of a number of infectious diseases and that the body had been cremated for reasons of public health. Nevertheless, rumors began to circulate, and by 1941 hospital killings virtually ceased because of protests, especially from the Church.

There is a direct link between this campaign of "selection and eradication" and the subsequent genocide of Jews, gypsies, communists, homosexuals, and other "undesirables." Early on these people were described as "diseased" and their presence, as an infection or a cancer in the body of the *Volk*. Proctor (1988, p. 194) calls this rationalization "the medicalization of antisemitism." The point is that the Nazi leaders shouted anti-Semitic and racist propaganda from their platforms, but when it came to devising the measures for ridding the Thousand Year Reich of Jews, gypsies, and the other undesirables, the task was shouldered by the scientists and physicians who had earlier devised the sterilization and euthanasia programs for the mentally or physically disabled. Therefore, nothing came easier than a medical metaphor: Jews as cancer, Jews as disease. And so the Nazi extermination program was viewed by its perpetrators as a gigantic program in sanitation and public health. It started with quarantining the offending organisms in ghettoes and concentration camps and ended with the extermination of those who did not succumb to the "natural" consequences of the quarantine, such as the various epidemics and hunger.

Yet a measure of selection was practiced throughout the eradication process: It was still *Auslese* as well as *Ausmerze*. At every step choices were made of who could still be used and who had become "worthless." We have read the books and seen the films that show selections being made as the cattle cars emptied the victims into the concentration camps: to work or to die? That is where Joseph Mengele, an M.D./Ph.D., selected the twins and other unfortunates to use as subjects for his scientific experiments at Auschwitz, performed in collaboration with Professor von Verschuer, at that time director of the Kaiser Wilhelm Institute for Anthropology, Human Genetics, and Eugenics in Berlin. And von Verschuer was not the only distinguished scientist who gratefully accepted the human tissues and body fluids provided by Mengele. After the war it became fashionable to characterize the experiments as "bad science," but as Beno Müller-Hill (1984) emphasizes, nothing about them would be considered "bad" were they done with mice. What was "bad" was not their scientific content but the fact that they were being done with "disenfranchised human beings" (p. 97).

PRENATAL TESTING: WHO SHOULD INHABIT THE WORLD?

I want to come back to the present, but I needed to go over this history in order to put my misgivings and those of some of the Germans who are opposing genetic testing into the proper perspective. I can phrase the problem best by rephrasing a question Hannah Arendt asks in the epilogue of her commentary on the trial of Adolf Eichmann. Who has the "right to determine who should and who should not inhabit the world?" (1977). That's what it comes down to.

So let me be clear: I am not suggesting that prenatal diagnosis followed by abortion is similar to euthanasia. Fetuses are not people. And a woman must have the right to terminate her pregnancy, whatever her reasons. I am also not drawing an analogy between what the Nazis did and what we and others in many of the industrialized countries are doing now. Because the circumstances are different, different things are being done and for different reasons. But a similar eugenic ideology underlies what happened then and the techniques now being developed. So it is important that we understand how what happened then came about—and not in some faraway culture that is altogether different from ours but in the heart of Europe, in a country that has produced artists, writers, composers, philosophers, jurists, scientists, and physicians the equal of any in the Western world. Given that record, we cannot afford to be complacent.

Scientists and physicians in this and other countries are once more engaged in developing the means to decide what lives are worth living and who should and should not inhabit the world. Except that now they provide only the tools, while pregnant women themselves have to make the decisions, euphemistically called choices. No one is forced to do anything. A pregnant woman must merely "choose" whether to terminate a wanted pregnancy because she has been informed that her future child will have a disability (although, as I have said before, usually no one can tell her how severe the disability will be). If she "chooses" not to take the tests or not to terminate a pregnancy despite a positive result, she accepts responsibility for whatever the disability will mean to that child and to her and the rest of her family. In that case, her child, her family, and the rest of society can reproach her for having so-to-speak "caused" that human being's physical pain as well as the social pain he or she experiences because our society does not look kindly on people with disabilities.

There is something terribly wrong with this situation, and although it differs in many ways from what went wrong in Germany, at base are similar principles of selection and eradication. Lest this analogy seem too abstract, let me give a few examples of how the principle of selection and eradication now works in practice.

Think of people who have Huntington's disease; as you may remember they were on the list of people to be sterilized in Germany. Huntington's disease is a degenerative disease of the nervous system and is unusual among hereditary diseases in that it is inherited as what geneticists call a dominant trait. In other words, even people in whom only one of the pair of genes that is involved with regulating the relevant metabolic processes is affected manifest the disease. Most other gene-mediated diseases, such as Tay-Sachs disease or sickle-cell anemia, are so-called recessives: Only people in whom both members of the relevant pair of genes are affected manifest the disease. In the case of recessive diseases, people with only one affected gene are called carriers: They do not have the disease and usually do not even know that they carry a gene for it. To inherit a recessive disease such as sickle-cell anemia, a child must get an affected gene from each of its parents; to inherit a dominant disease, such as Huntington's disease, it is enough is she or he gets an affected gene from either parent.

The symptoms of Huntington's disease usually do not appear until people are in their thirties, forties, or fifties—in other words, after most people who want to have children have already had one or more. Woody Guthrie had Huntington's disease, but he did not become ill until after he had lived a varied and productive life, produced a large legacy of songs, and fathered his children. At present, there is no cure for Huntington's disease, although scientists have been working to find one. However, a test has been developed that makes it possible to establish with fair reliability whether a person or fetus carries the gene for Huntington's disease, provided a sufficient number of people in that family is willing to be tested.

The existence of this test puts people with a family history of Huntington's disease in an outrageous position: Although they themselves are healthy and do not know whether they will get the disease, they must decide whether to be tested, whether to persuade as many of their relatives as possible to do the same, and whether to test their future child prenatally so they can terminate the pregnancy if the test reveals that the fetus has the gene for Huntington's disease. If it does and they decide on abortion, they are as much as saying that a life lived in the knowledge that one will eventually die of Huntington's disease is not worth living. What does that say about their own life and the lives of their family members who now know that they have the gene for Huntington's disease? If the fetus has the gene and they do not abort, they are knowingly wishing a cruel, degenerative disease on their future child. And if they refuse the test, they can be accused of sticking their heads in the sand. This is an obscene "choice" for anyone to have to make!

Some other inherited diseases also do not become evident until later in life, such as retinitis pigmentosa, a degenerative eye disease. People with this disease are born with normal vision, but their eyesight deteriorates, although usually not until midlife, and they may eventually lose their sight. (People with this disease presumably also were slated for sterilization by the Nazis because it is a form of "hereditary blindness.") There are different patterns of inheritance of retinitis pigmentosa, and prenatal diagnosis is becoming available for one of these patterns and being sought for others. What are prospective parents to do when confronted with the "choice" of aborting a pregnancy because their future child may become blind at some time during its life?

Another, rather different, problem arises with regard to the so-called neural-tube defects (NTDs), a group of developmental disorders which, in fact, are not inherited. They include anencephaly (failure to develop a brain) and spina bifida (failure of the spinal column, and sometimes also the overlying tissues, to close properly) Babies with anencephaly die before birth or shortly thereafter. The severity of the health problems of children who have spina bifida depends on where along the spinal column the defect is located and can vary from life-threatening to relatively mild. The incidence of NTDs varies geographically and tends to be higher in industrialized than in nonindustrialized areas. Women who carry a fetus with a neural-tube defect have a grater than usual concentration of a specific substance, called alpha-feto-protein, in their blood. A blood test has been developed to detect NTDs prenatally, and California now requires that all pregnant women in the state be offered this test. The women are first counseled about NTDs and about the test and then have to sign a consent or refusal form. If they refuse, that is the end of it. If they consent, they can later refuse to abort the fetus even if the test is positive. This procedure sounds relatively unproblematical, although the requirement to sign a refusal form is coercive. (You cannot walk away; you must say no.) The trouble is that although the test detects virtually all fetuses who have NTDs, it yields a large number of false positive results that suggest that the fetus has a NTD although it does not.

Let us look at some numbers. In California there are about two hundred thousand births a year and the incidence of NTDs is about one per thousand. So, about 200 pregnant women a year carry fetuses with NTDs and 199,800 do not. However, about 5 percent of women test positive on a first test. In other words, if all pregnant women agreed to be tested, 10,000 women would have a positive test, 9,800 of which would be false positives. Those 10,000 women would then have to undergo the stress of worrying as well as further tests in order to determine who among them is in fact carrying a fetus with a NTD. And no test will tell the 200 women whose fetus, in fact, has a NTD how severe their child's health problem will be. All this testing with uncertain results must be offered at this time, when health dollars in California, as elsewhere, have been cut to the bone, and increasing numbers of pregnant women are coming to term with little or no prenatal services of any sort.

The reason I have spelled this problem out in such detail is to make it clear that in many of these situations parents have only the most tenuous basis for making their decisions. Because of the fear of raising a child with a serious disability, many women "choose" to abort a wanted pregnancy if they are told that there is any likelihood whatever that their future child may have a health problem. At times like that we seem to forget that we live in a society in which every day people of all ages are disabled by accidents—at work, on the street, or at home—many of which could be prevented if the necessary money were spent, the necessary precautions taken. What is more, because of the deteriorating economic conditions of poor people and especially women, increasing numbers of babies are born with disabilities that could easily be prevented and are prevented in most other industrialized nations. I question our excessive preoccupation with inherited diseases while callousness and economic mismanagement disable and kill increasing numbers of children and adults.

To say again, I am not arguing against a woman's right to abortion. Women must have that right because it involves a decision about our bodies and about the way we will spend the rest of our lives. But for scientists to argue that they are developing these tests out of concern for the "quality of life" of future children is like the arguments about "lives not worth living." No one can make that kind of decision about someone else. No one these days openly suggests that certain kinds of people be killed; they just should not be born. Yet that involves a process of selection and a decision about what kinds of people should and should not inhabit the world.

German women, who know the history of Nazi eugenics and how genetic counseling centers functioned during the Nazi period, have organized against the new genetic and reproductive technologies (Duelli Klein, Corea, and Hubbard, 1985). They are suspicious of prenatal testing and counseling centers because some of the scientists and physicians working in them are the same people who designed and implemented the eugenics program during the Nazi period. Others are former co-workers or students of these Nazi professors.

Our history is different, but not different enough. Eugenic thinking is part of our heritage and so are eugenic sterilizations. Here they were not carried over to mass exterminations because we live in a democracy with constitutional safeguards. But, as I mentioned before, even in recent times black, Hispanic, and Native-American women have been sterilized against their wills (Rodriguez-Trias, 1982). We do not exalt the body of the people, as a collective, over that of individuals, but we come dangerously close to doing so when we question the "right" of parents to bear a child who has a disability or when we draw unfavorable comparisons between the costs of care for children with disabilities and the costs of prenatal diagnosis and abortion. We come mighty close when we once again let scientists and physicians make judgments about who should and who should not inhabit the world and applaud them when they develop the technologies that let us implement such judgments. Is it in our interest to have to decide not just whether we want to bear a child but what kind of children to bear? If we try to do that we become entirely dependent on the decisions scientists and physicians make about what technologies to develop and what disabilities to "target." Those decisions are usually made on grounds of professional interest, technical feasibility, and economic and eugenic considerations, not out of a regard for the needs of women and children.

PROBLEMS WITH SELECTIVE ABORTION

I want to be explicit about how I think a woman's right to abortion fits into this analysis and about some of the connections I see between what the Nazis did and what is happening now. I repeat: A woman must have the right to abort a fetus, whatever her reasons, precisely because it is a decision about her body and about how she will live her life. But decisions about what kind of baby to bear inevitably are bedeviled by overt and unspoken judgments about which lives are "worth living."

Nazi eugenic practices were fairly coercive. The state decided who should not inhabit the world, and lawyers, physicians, and scientists provided the justifications and means to implement these decisions. In today's liberal democracies the situation is different. Eugenic principles are part of our largely unexamined and unspoken preconceptions about who should and who should not inhabit the world, and scientists and physicians provide the ways to put them into practice. Women are expected to implement the society's eugenic prejudices by "choosing" to have the appropriate tests and "electing" not to initiate or to terminate pregnancies if it looks as though the outcome will offend. And to a considerable extent not initiating or terminating these pregnancies may indeed be what women want to do. But one reason we want to is that society promises much grief to parents of children it deems unfit to inhabit the world. People with disabilities, like the rest of us, need opportunities to act in the world, and sometimes that means that they need special provisions and consideration.

So once more, yes, a woman must have the right to terminate a pregnancy, whatever her reasons, but she must also feel empowered not to terminate it, confident that the society will do what it can to enable here and her child to live fulfilling lives. To the extent that prenatal interventions implement social prejudices against people with disabilities they do not expand our reproductive rights. They constrict them.

Focusing the discussion on individualistic questions, such as every woman's right to bear healthy children (which in some people's minds quickly translates into her duty not to "burden society" with unhealthy ones) or the responsibility of scientists and physicians to develop techniques to make that possible, obscures crucial questions such as: How many women have economic access to these kinds of choices? How many have the educational and cultural background to evaluate the information they can get from physicians critically enough to make an informed choice? It also obscures questions about a humane society's responsibilities to satisfy the requirements of people with special needs and to offer them the opportunity to participate as full-fledged members in the culture.

Our present situation connects with the Nazi past in that once again scientists and physicians are making the decisions about what lives to "target" as not worth living by deciding which tests to develop. Yet if people are to have real choices, the decisions that determine the context within which we must choose must not be made in our absence—by professionals, research review panels, or funding organizations. And the situation is not improved by inserting a new group of professionals—bioethicists—between the technical professionals and the public. This public—the women and men who must live in the world that the scientific/medical/industrial complex constructs—must be able to take part in the process by which such decisions are made. Until mechanisms exist that give people a decisive voice in setting the relevant scientific and technical agendas and until scientists and physicians are made accountable to the people whose lives they change, technical innovations do not constitute new choices. They merely replace previous social constraints with new ones.

WORKS CITED

Arendt, Hannah. 1977. *Eichmann in Jerusalem: A Report on the Banality of Evil.* New York: Penguin.

Asch, Adrienne. 1988. "Reproductive Technology and Disability." In Sherrill Cohen and Nadine Taub, eds., *Reproductive Laws for the 1990s.* Clifton, N. J.: Humana Press.

Asch, Adrienne, and Michelle Fine. 1988. "Introduction: Beyond Pedestals." In Michelle Fine and Adrienne Asch, eds., *Women with Disabilities.* Philadelphia: Temple University Press.

Chrorover, Stephan L. 1979. *From Genesis to Genocide.* Cambridge, Mass.: MIT Press.

Duelli Klein, Renate, Gena Corea, and Ruth Hubbard. 1985. "German Women say No to Gene and Reproductive Technology: Reflections on a Conference in Bonn, West Germany, April 19–21, 1985." *Feminist Forum: Women's Studies International Forum* 9(3): I–IV.

Galton, Francis. 1883. *Inquiries into Human Faculty.* London: Macmillan.

Glass, Bentley. 1971. "Science: Endless Horizons or Golden Age?" *Science* 171: 23–29.

Kevles, Daniel J. 1985. *In the Name of Eugenics: Genetics and the Uses of Human Heredity.* New York: Knopf.

Koonz, Claudia. 1987. *Mothers in the Fatherland: Women, the Family and Nazi Politics.* New York: St. Martin's Press.

Lifton, Robert J. 1986. *The Nazi Doctors.* New York: Basic Books.

Ludmerer, Kenneth M. 1972. *Genetics and American Society.* Baltimore: Johns Hopkins University Press.

Müller-Hill, Benno. 1984. *Tödliche Wissenshaft.* Reinbek, West Germany: Rowohlt. (Translation 1988. *Murderous Science.* Oxford: Oxford University Press.)

Proctor, Robert N. 1988. *Racial Hygiene: Medicine and the Nazis.* Cambridge: Harvard University Press.

Rodriguez-Trias, Helen. 1982. *In Labor: Women and Power in the Birthplace.* New York: Norton.

Terman, Lewis M. 1924. "The Conservation of Talent." *School and Society* 19(483): 359–364.

CHAPTER 9

Disability Rights and Selective Abortion

Marsha Saxton

Disability rights activists are now articulating a critical view of the widespread practice of prenatal diagnosis with the intent to abort if the pregnancy might result in a child with a disability. Underlying this critique are historical factors behind a growing activism in the United States, Germany, Great Britain, and many other countries, an activism that confronts the social stigmatization of people with disabilities.

For disabled persons, women's consciousness-raising groups in the 1960s and 1970s offered a model for connecting with others in an "invisible" oppressed social group and confirming the experience of pervasive social oppression. ("That happened to you, too?") Participants in such groups began to challenge a basic tenet of disability oppression: that disability *causes* the low socioeconomic status of disabled persons. Collective consciousness-raising has made it clear that stigma is the cause.

Effective medical and rehabilitation resources since the 1950s have also contributed to activism. Antibiotics and improved surgical techniques have helped to alleviate previously fatal conditions. Consequently, disabled people are living longer and healthier lives, and the population of people with severely disabling conditions has increased. Motorized wheelchairs, lift-equipped wheelchair vans, mobile respirators, and computer and communication technologies have increased the mobility and access to education and employment for people previously ostracized because of their disabilities.

Effective community organizing by blind, deaf, and mobility-impaired citizen groups and disabled student groups flourished in the late 1960s and resulted in new legislation. In 1973 the Rehabilitation Act Amendments (Section 504) prohibited discrimination in federally funded programs. The Americans with Disabilities Act of 1990 (ADA) provides substantial civil rights protection and has helped bring about a profound change in the collective self-image of an estimated 45 million Americans. Today, many disabled people view themselves as part of a distinct minority and reject the pervasive stereotypes of disabled people as defective, burdensome, and unattractive.

It is ironic that just when disabled citizens have achieved so much, the new reproductive and genetic technologies are promising to eliminate births of disabled children—children with Down's syndrome, spina bifida, muscular dystrophy, sickle cell anemia, and hundreds of other conditions. The American public has apparently accepted these screening technologies based on the "commonsense" assumptions that prenatal screening and selective abortion can potentially reduce the incidence of disease and disability and thus improve the quality of life. A deeper look into the medical system's views of disability and the broader social factors contributing to disability discrimination challenges these assumptions.

REPRODUCTIVE RIGHTS IN A DISABILITY CONTEXT

There is a key difference between the goals of the reproductive rights movement and the disability rights movement regarding reproductive freedom: the reproductive rights movement emphasizes the right to have an abortion; the disability rights movement, the right *not to have to have* an abortion. Disability rights advocates believe that disabled women have the right to bear children and be mothers, and that all women have the right to resist pressure to abort when the fetus is identified as potentially having a disability.

Women with disabilities raised these issues at a conference on new reproductive technologies (NRTs) in Vancouver in 1994.[1] For many of the conference participants, we were an unsettling group: women in wheelchairs; blind women with guide dogs; deaf women who required a sign-language interpreter; women with scarring from burns or facial anomalies; women with missing limbs, crutches, or canes. I noticed there what we often experience from people who first encounter us: averted eyes or stolen glances, pinched smiles, awkward or overeager helpfulness—in other words, discomfort accompanied by the struggle to pretend there was none.

It was clear to me that this situation was constraining communication, and I decided to do something about it. I approached several of the nondisabled women, asking them how they felt about meeting such a diverse group of disabled women. Many of the women were honest when invited to be:

"I'm nervous. Am I going to say something offensive?" "I feel pretty awkward. Some of these women's bodies are so different!" One woman, herself disabled, said that she'd had a nightmare image of a disabled woman's very different body. One woman confessed: "I feel terrible for some of these unfortunate disabled women, but I know I'm not supposed to feel pity. That's awful of me, right?"

This awkwardness reveals how isolated the broader society and even progressive feminists are from people with disabilities. The dangerous void of information about disability is the *context* in which the public's attitudes about prenatal diagnosis and selective abortion are formed. In the United States this information void has yielded a number of unexamined assumptions, including the belief that the quality and enjoyment of life for disabled people is necessarily inferior, that raising a child with a disability is a wholly undesirable experience, that selective abortion will save mothers from the burdens of raising disabled children, and that ultimately we as a society have the means and the right to decide who is better off not being born.

What the women with disabilities were trying to do at the Vancouver conference, and what I wish to do in this essay, is explain how selective abortion or *eugenic abortion*, as some disability activists have called it, not only oppresses people with disabilities but also hurts all women.

EUGENICS AND THE BIRTH CONTROL MOVEMENT

The eugenic interest that stimulates reliance on prenatal screening and selective abortion today has had a central place in reproductive politics for more than half a century. In the nineteenth century, eugenicists believed that most traits, including such human "failings" as pauperism, alcoholism, and thievery, as well as such desired traits as intelligence, musical ability, and "good character," were hereditary. They sought to perfect the human race through controlled procreation, encouraging those from "healthy stock" to mate and discouraging reproduction of those eugenicists defined as socially "unfit," that is, with undesirable traits. Through a series of laws and court decisions American eugenicists mandated a program of social engineering. The most famous of these was the 1927 U.S. Supreme Court ruling in *Buck v. Bell*.[2]

Leaders in the early birth control movement in the United States, including Margaret Sanger, generally embraced a eugenic view, encouraging white Anglo-Saxon women to reproduce while discouraging reproduction among nonwhite, immigrant, and disabled people. Proponents of eugenics portrayed disabled women in particular as unfit for procreation and as incompetent mothers. In the 1920s Margaret Sanger's group, the American Birth Control League, allied itself with the director of the American Eugenics Society, Guy Irving Burch. The resulting coalition supported the forced sterilization of people with epilepsy, as well as those diagnosed as mentally retarded and mentally ill. By 1937, in the midst of the Great Depression, twenty-eight states had adopted eugenics sterilization laws aimed primarily at women for whom "procreation was deemed inadvisable." These laws sanctioned the sterilizations of over 200,000 women between the 1930s and the 1970s.[3]

While today's feminists are not responsible for the eugenic biases of their foremothers, some of these prejudices have persisted or gone unchallenged in the reproductive rights movement today.[4] Consequently, many women with disabilities feel alienated from this movement. On the other hand, some pro-choice feminists have felt so deeply alienated from the disability community that they have been willing to claim, "The right wing wants to force us to have defective babies."[5] Clearly, there is work to be done.

DISABILITY-POSITIVE IDENTITY VERSUS SELECTIVE ABORTION

It is clear that some medical professionals and public health officials are promoting prenatal diagnosis and abortion with the intention of eliminating categories of disabled people, people with Down's syndrome and my own disability, spina bifida, for example. For this reason and others, many disability activists and feminists regard selective abortion as "the new eugenics." These people resist the use of prenatal diagnosis and selective abortion.

The resistance to selective abortion in the disability activist community is ultimately related to how we define ourselves. As feminists have transformed women's sense of self, the disability community has reframed the experience of having a disability. In part, through developing a sense of community, we've come to realize that the stereotyped notions of the "tragedy" and "suffering" of "the disabled" result from the *isolation* of disabled people in society. Disabled people with no connections to others with disabilities in their communities are, indeed, afflicted with the social role assignment of a tragic, burdensome existence. It is true, most disabled people I know have told me with certainty, that the disability, the pain, the need for compensatory devices and assistance can produce considerable inconvenience. But the inconvenience becomes minimal once the disabled person makes the transition to a typical everyday life. It is discriminatory attitudes and thoughtless behaviors, and the ensuing ostracism and lack of accommodation, that make life difficult. That oppression is what's most disabling about disability.

Many disabled people have a growing but still precarious sense of pride in an identity as "people with disabilities." With decades of hard work, disability activists have fought institutionalization and challenged discrimination in employment, education, transportation, and housing. We have fought for rehabilitation and Independent Living programs, and we have proved that disabled people can participate in and contribute to society.

As a political movement, the disability rights community has conducted protests and effective civil disobedience to publicize our demand for full citizenship. Many of our tactics were inspired by the women's movement and the black civil rights movement in the 1960s. In the United States we fought for and won one of the most far-reaching pieces of civil rights legislation ever, the Americans with Disabilities Act. This piece of legislation is the envy of the international community of disability activists, most of whom live in countries where disabled people are viewed with pity and charity, and accorded low social and legal status. Disability activists have fought for mentor programs led by adults with disabilities. We see disabled children as "the youth" of the movement, the ones who offer hope that life will continue to improve for people with disabilities for generations to come.

In part because of our hopes for disabled children, the "Baby Doe" cases of the 1980s caught the attention of the growing disability rights movement. These cases revealed that "selective nontreatment" of disabled infants (leaving disabled infants to starve because the parents or doctors choose not to intervene with even routine treatments such as antibiotics) was not a thing of the past. In this same period, we also took note of the growing number of "wrongful birth" suits—medical malpractice suits brought against physicians, purportedly on behalf of disabled children, by parents who feel that the child's condition should have been identified prenatally.[6] These lawsuits claim that disabled babies, once born, are too great a burden, and that the doctors who failed to eliminate the "damaged" fetuses should be financially punished.

But many parents of disabled children have spoken up to validate the joys and satisfactions of raising a disabled child. The many books and articles by these parents confirm the view that discriminatory attitudes make raising a disabled child much more difficult than the actual logistics of care.[7] Having developed a disability-centered perspective on these cases, disabled adults have joined with many parents of disabled children in challenging the notion that raising a child with a disability is necessarily undesirable.

The attitudes that disabled people are frightening or inhuman result from lack of meaningful interaction with disabled people. Segregation in this case, as in all cases, allows stereotypes to abound. But beyond advocating contact with disabled people, disability rights proponents claim that it is crucial to challenge limiting definitions of "acceptably human." Many parents of children with Down's syndrome say that their children bring them joy. But among people with little exposure to disabled people, it is common to think that this is a romanticization or rationalization of someone stuck with the burden of a damaged child.

Many who resist selective abortion insist that there is something deeply valuable and profoundly human (though difficult to articulate in the sound bites of contemporary thought) in meeting and loving a child or adult with a severe disability. Thus, contributions of human beings cannot be judged by how we fit into the mold of normalcy, productivity, or cost-benefit. People who are different from us (whether in color, ability, age, or ethnic origin) have much to share about what it means to be human. We must not deny ourselves the opportunity for connection to basic humanness by dismissing the existence of people labeled "severely disabled."

MIXED FEELINGS: DISABLED PEOPLE RESPOND TO SELECTIVE ABORTION

The disability *activist* community has begun to challenge selective abortion. But among disabled people as a whole, there is no agreement about these issues. After all, the "disability community" is as diverse as any other broad constituency, like "the working class" or "women." Aspects of this issue can be perplexing to people with disabilities because of the nature of the prejudice we experience. For example, the culture typically invalidates our bodies, denying our sexuality and our potential as parents. These cultural impulses are complexly intertwined with the issue of prenatal testing. Since the early 1990s, disability rights activists have been exploring and debating our views on selective abortion in the disability community's literature.[8] In addition, just like the general population's attitudes about *abortion*, views held by people with disabilities about *selective abortion* relate to personal experience (in this case, personal history with disability) and to class, ethnic, and religious backgrounds.

People with different kinds of disabilities may have complex feelings about prenatal screening tests. While some disabled people regard the tests as a kind of genocide, others choose to use screening tests during their own pregnancies to avoid the birth of a disabled child. But disabled people may also use the tests differently from women who share the larger culture's anti-disability bias.

Many people with dwarfism, for example, are incensed by the idea that a woman or couple would choose to abort simply because the fetus would become a dwarf. When someone who carries the dwarfism trait mates with another with the same trait, there is a likelihood of each partner contributing one dominant dwarfism gene to the fetus. This results in a condition called "double dominance" for the offspring, which, in this "extra dose of the gene" form, is invariably accompanied by severe medical complications and early death. So prospective parents who are carriers of the dwarfism gene, or are themselves dwarfs, who would readily welcome a dwarf child, might still elect to use the screening test to avoid the birth of a fetus identified with "double dominance."

Deafness provides an entirely different example. There is as yet no prenatal test for deafness, but if, goes the ethical conundrum, a hearing couple could eliminate the fetus that would become a deaf child, why shouldn't deaf people, proud of their own distinct sign-language culture, elect for a deaf child and abort a fetus (that would become a hearing person) on a similar basis?

Those who challenge selective or eugenic abortion claim that people with disabilities are the ones who have the information about what having a disability is like. The medical system, unable to cure or fix us, exaggerates the suffering and burden of disability. The media, especially the movies, distort our lives by using disability as a metaphor for evil, impotence, eternal dependence, or tragedy—or coversely as a metaphor for courage, inspiration, or sainthood. Disabled people alone can speak to the women facing these tests. Only we can speak about our real lives, our ordinary lives, and the lives of disabled children.

"DID YOU GET YOUR AMNIO YET?": THE PRESSURE TO TEST AND ABORT

How do women decide about tests, and how do attitudes about disability affect women's choices? The reproductive technology market has, since the mid-1970s, gradually changed the experience of pregnancy. Some prenatal care facilities now present patients with their ultrasound photo in a pink or blue frame. Women are increasingly pressured to use prenatal testing under a cultural imperative claiming that this is the "responsible thing to do." Strangers in the supermarket, even characters in TV sit-coms, readily ask a woman with a pregnant belly, "Did you get your amnio yet?" While the ostensible justification is "reassurance that the baby is fine," the underlying communication is clear: screening out disabled fetuses is the right thing, "the healthy thing," to do. As feminist biologist Ruth Hubbard put it, "Women are expected to implement the society's eugenic prejudices by 'choosing' to have the appropriate tests and 'electing' not to initiate or to terminate pregnancies if it looks as though the outcome will offend."[9]

Often prospective parents have never considered the issue of disability until it is raised in relation to prenatal testing. What comes to the minds of parents at the mention of the term *birth defects?* Usually prospective parents summon up the most stereotyped visions of disabled people derived from telethons and checkout-counter charity displays. This is not to say that all women who elect selective abortion do so based on simple, mindless stereotypes. I have met women who have aborted on the basis of test results. Their stories and their difficult decisions were very moving. They made the decisions they felt were the only ones possible for them, given information they had been provided by doctors, counselors, and society.

Indeed, some doctors and counselors do make a good-faith effort to explore with prospective parents the point at which selective abortion may seem clearly "justifiable," with respect to the severity of the condition or the emotional or financial costs involved. These efforts are fraught with enormous social and ethical difficulty. Often, however, unacknowledged stereotypes prevail, as does a commitment to a libertarian view ("Let people do whatever they want!"). Together, these strains frequently push prospective parents to succumb to the medical control of birth, while passively colluding with pervasive disability discrimination.

Among the most common justifications of selective abortion is that it "ends suffering." Women as cultural nurturers and medical providers as official guardians of well-being are both vulnerable to this message. Health care providers are trying, despite the profit-based health care system, to improve life for people they serve. But the medical system takes a very narrow view of disease and "the alleviation of suffering." What is too often missed in medical training and treatment are the *social factors* that contribute to suffering. Physicians, by the very nature of their work, often have a distorted picture of the lives of disabled people. They encounter disabled persons having health problems, complicated by the stresses of a marginalized life, perhaps exacerbated by poverty and race or gender discrimination, but because of their training, the doctors tend to project the individual's overall struggle onto the disability as the "cause" of distress. Most doctors have few opportunities to see ordinary disabled individuals living in their communities among friends and family.

Conditions receiving priority attention for prenatal screening include Down's syndrome, spina bifida, cystic fibrosis, and fragile X, all of which are associated with mildly to moderately disabling clinical outcomes. Individuals with these conditions can live good lives. There are severe cases, but the medical system tends to underestimate the functional abilities and overestimate the "burden" and suffering of people with these conditions. Moreover, among the priority conditions for prenatal screening are diseases that occur very infrequently. Tay-Sachs disease, for example, a debilitating, fatal disease that affects primarily Jews of eastern European descent, is often cited as a condition that justifies prenatal screening. But as a rare disease, it's a poor basis for a treatment mandate.

Those who advocate selective abortion to alleviate the suffering of children may often raise that cornerstone of contemporary political rhetoric, *cost-benefit*. Of course, cost-benefit analysis is not woman-centered, yet women can be directly pressured or subtly intimidated by both arguments. It may be difficult for some to resist the argument that it is their duty to "save scarce health care dollars," by eliminating the expense of disabled children. But those who resist these arguments believe the value of a child's life cannot be measured in dollars. It is notable that families with disabled children who are familiar with the actual impact of the disabilities tend not to seek the tests for subsequent children.[10] The bottom line is that the cost-benefit argument disintegrates when the outlay of funds required to provide services for disabled persons is measured against the enormous resources expended to test for a few rare genetic disorders. In addition, it is important to recognize that promotion and funding of prenatal tests distract attention and resources from addressing possible environmental causes of disability and disease.

DISABLED PEOPLE AND THE FETUS

I mentioned to a friend, an experienced disability activist, that I planned to call a conference for disabled people and genetics professionals to discuss these controversial issues. She said, "I think the conference is important, but I have to tell you, I have trouble being in the same room with professionals who are trying to eliminate my people." I was struck by her identification with fetuses as "our people."

Are those in the disability rights movement who question or resist selective abortion trying to save the "endangered species" of disabled fetuses? When this metaphor first surfaced, I was shocked to think of disabled people as the target of intentional elimination, shocked to realize that I identified with the fetus as one of my "species" that I must try to protect.

When we refer to the fetus as a *disabled* (rather than defective) fetus, we *personify* the fetus via a term of pride in the disability community. The fetus is named as a member of our community. The connection disabled people feel with the "disabled fetus" may seem to be in conflict with the pro-choice stance that the fetus is only a part of the woman's body, with no independent human status.[11]

Many of us with disabilities might have been prenatally screened and aborted if tests had been available to our mothers. I've actually heard people say, "Too bad that baby with [*x* disease] didn't 'get caught' in prenatal screening." (This is the sentiment of "wrongful birth" suits.) It is important to make the distinction between a pregnant woman who chooses to terminate the pregnancy because she *doesn't want to be pregnant* as opposed to a pregnant woman who *wanted to be pregnant* but rejects a particular fetus, a particular potential child. Fetuses that are wanted are called "babies." Prenatal screening results can turn a "wanted baby" into an "unwanted fetus."

It is difficult to contemplate one's own hypothetical nonexistence. But I know several disabled teenagers, born in an era when they could have been "screened out," for whom this is not at all an abstraction. In biology class their teachers, believing themselves to be liberal, raised abortion issues. These teachers, however, were less than sensitive to the disabled students when they talked about "eliminating the burden of the disabled" through technological innovation.

In the context of screening tests, those of us with screenable conditions represent living adult fetuses that didn't get aborted. We are the constituency of the potentially aborted. Our resistance to the systematic abortion of "our young" is a challenge to the "nonhumanness," the nonstatus of the fetus. This issue of the humanness of the fetus is a tricky one for those of us who identify both as pro-choice feminists and as disability rights activists. Our dual perspective offers important insights for those who are debating the ethics of the new reproductive technologies.

DISENTANGLING PATRIARCHAL CONTROL AND EUGENICS FROM REPRODUCTIVE FREEDOM

The issue of selective abortion is not just about the rights or considerations of disabled people. Women's rights and the rights of all human beings are implicated here.

When disability rights activists challenge the practice of selective abortion, as we did in Vancouver, many feminists react with alarm. They feel "uncomfortable" with language that accords human status to the fetus. One woman said: "You can't talk about the fetus as an entity being supported by advocates. It's too 'right to life.'" Disabled women activists do not want to be associated with the violent anti-choice movement. In the disability community we make a clear distinction between our views and those of anti-abortion groups. There may have been efforts to court disabled people to support anti-abortion ideology, but anti-abortion groups have never taken up the issues of expanding resources for disabled people or parents of disabled children, never lobbied for disability legislation. They have shown no interest in disabled people after they are born.[12]

But a crucial issue compels some of us to risk making people uncomfortable by discussing the fetus: we must clarify the connection between control of "defective fetuses" and the control of women as vessels or producers of quality-controllable products. This continuum between control of women's bodies and control of the *products of women's bodies* must be examined and discussed if we are going to make headway in challenging the ways that new reproductive technologies can increasingly take control of reproduction away from women and place it within the commercial medical system.

A consideration of selective abortion as a control mechanism must include a view of the procedure as a wedge into the "quality control" of all humans. If a condition (like Down's syndrome) is unacceptable, how long will it be before experts use selective abortion to manipulate—eliminate or enhance—other (presumed genetic) socially charged characteristics: sexual orientation, race, attractiveness, height, intelligence? Pre-implantation diagnosis, now used with in vitro fertilization, offers the prospect of "admission standards" for all fetuses.

Some of the pro-screening arguments masquerade today as "feminist" when they are not. Selective abortion is promoted in many doctors' offices as a "reproductive option" and "personal choice." But as anthropologist Rayna Rapp notes, "Private choices always have public consequences."[13] When a woman's individual decision is the result of social pressure, it can have repercussions for all others in the society.

How is it possible to defend selective abortion on the basis of "a woman's right to choose" when this "choice" is so constrained by oppressive values and attitudes? Consider the use of selective abortion for sex selection. The feminist community generally regards the abortion of fetuses on the basis of gender—widely practiced in some countries to eliminate female fetuses—as furthering the devaluation of women. Yet women have been pressed to "choose" to perpetuate their own devaluation.[14] For those with "disability-positive" attitudes, the analogy with sex selection is obvious. Oppressive assumptions, not inherent characteristics, have devalued who this fetus will grow into.

Fetal anomaly has sometimes been used as a *justification* for legal abortion. This justification reinforces the idea that women are horribly oppressed by disabled children. When disability is sanctioned as a justification for legal abortion, then abortion for sex selection may be more easily sanctioned as well. If "choice" is made to mean choosing the "perfect child," or the child of the "right gender," then pregnancy is turned into a process and children are turned into products that are perfectible through technology. Those of us who believe that pregnancy and children must not be commodified believe that real "choice" must include the birth of a child with a disability.

To blame a woman's oppression on the characteristics of the fetus is to obscure and distract us from the core of the "choice" position: women's control over our own bodies and reproductive capacities. It also obscures the different access to "choice" of different groups of women. At conferences I've been asked, "Would I want to force a poor black woman to bear a disabled child?" That question reinforces what feminists of color have been saying, that the framework of "choice" trivializes the issues for nonprivileged women. It reveals distortions in the public's perception of users of prenatal screening; in fact, it is the middle and upper class who most often can purchase these "reproductive choices." It's not poor women, or families with problematic genetic traits, who are creating the market for tests. Women with aspirations for the "perfect baby" are establishing new "standards of care." Responding to the lure of consumerism, they are helping create a lucrative market that exploits the culture's fear of disability and makes huge profits for the biotech industry.

Some proponents argue that prenatal tests are feminist tools because they save women from the excessive burdens associated with raising disabled children.[15] This is like calling the washer-dryer a feminist tool; technological innovation may "save time," even allow women to work outside the home, but it has not changed who does the housework. Women still do the vast majority of child care, and child care is not valued as real work. Rather, raising children is regarded as women's "duty" and is not valued as "worth" paying mothers for (or worth paying teachers or day-care workers well). Selective abortion will not challenge the sexism of the family structure in which women provide most of the care for children, for elderly parents, and for those disabled in accidents or from nongenetic diseases. We are being sold an illusion that the "burden" and problems of motherhood are being alleviated by medical science. But using selective abortion to eliminate the "burden" of disabled children is like taking aspirin for an ulcer. It provides temporary relief that both masks and exacerbates the underlying problems.

The job of helping disabled people must not be confused with the traditional devaluing of women in the caregiver role. Indeed, women can be overwhelmed and oppressed by their work of caring for disabled family members. But this is *not caused by the disabilities per se.* It is caused by lack of community services and inaccessibility, and greatly exacerbated by the sexism that isolates and overworks women caregivers. Almost any kind of work with people, if sufficiently shared and validated, can be meaningful, important, joyful, and productive.

I believe that at this point in history the decision to abort a fetus with a disability even because it "just seems too difficult" must be respected. A woman who makes this decision is best suited to assess her own resources. But it is important for her to realize this "choice" is actually made under duress. Our society profoundly limits the "choice" to love and care for a baby with a disability. This failure of society should not be projected onto the disabled fetus or child. No child is "defective." A child's disability doesn't ruin a woman's dream of motherhood. Our society's inability to appreciate and support people is what threatens our dreams.

In our struggle to lead our individual lives, we all fall short of adhering to our own highest values. We forget to recycle. We ride in cars that pollute the planet. We buy sneakers from "developing countries" that exploit workers and perpetuate the distortions in world economic power. Every day we have to make judgment calls as we assess our ability to live well and right, and it is always difficult, especially in relation to raising our own children—perhaps in this era more so than ever—to include a vision of social change in our personal decisions.

Women sometimes conclude, "I'm not saintly or brave enough to raise a disabled child." This objectifies and distorts the experience of mothers of disabled children. They're not saints; they're ordinary women, as are the women who care for spouses or their own parents who become disabled. It doesn't take a "special woman" to mother a disabled child. It takes a caring parent to raise any child. If her child became disabled, any mother would do the best job she could caring for that child. It is everyday life that trains people to do the right thing, sometimes to be leaders.

DISABLED WOMEN HAVE A LEGITIMATE VOICE IN THE ABORTION DEBATE!

Unfortunately, I've heard some ethicists and pro-choice advocates say that disabled people should not be allowed a voice in the selective abortion debate because "they make women feel guilty." The problem with this perspective is evident when one considers that there is no meaningful distinction between "disabled people" and "women." Fifty percent of adults with disabilities are women, and up to 20 percent of the female population have disabilities. The many prospective mothers who have disabilities or who are carriers of genetic traits for disabling conditions may have particular interests either in challenging or in utilizing reproductive technologies, *and* these women have key perspectives to contribute.

Why should hearing the perspectives of disabled people "make women feel guilty"? The unhappy truth is that so many decisions that women make about procreation are fraught with guilt and anxiety because sexism makes women feel guilty about their decisions. One might ask whether white people feel guilty when people of color challenge them about racism. And if so, doesn't that ultimately benefit everyone?

Do I think a woman who has utilized selective abortion intended to oppress *me* or wishes I were not born? Of course not. No more than any woman who has had an abortion means to eliminate the human race. Surely one must never condemn a woman for making the best choice she can with the information and resources available to her in the crisis of decision. In resisting prenatal testing, we do not aim to blame any individual woman or compromise her individual control over her own life or body. We *do* mean to offer information to empower her and to raise her awareness of the stakes involved for her as a woman and member of the community of all women.

A PROPOSAL FOR THE REPRODUCTIVE RIGHTS MOVEMENT

The feminist community is making some headway in demanding that women's perspectives be included in formulating policies and practices for new reproductive technologies, but the disability-centered aspects of prenatal diagnosis remain marginalized. Because the technologies have emerged in a society with entrenched attitudes about disability and illness, the tests have become embedded in medical "standards of care." They have also become an integral part of the biotech industry, a new "bright hope" of capitalist health care and the national economy. The challenge is great, the odds discouraging.

Our tasks are to gain clarity about prenatal diagnosis, challenge eugenic uses of reproductive technologies, and support the rights of all women to maintain control over reproduction. Here are some suggestions for action:

- We must actively pursue close connections between reproductive rights groups and disabled women's groups with the long-range goal of uniting our communities, as we intend to do with all other marginalized groups.
- We must make the issue of selective abortion a high priority in our movements' agendas, pushing women's groups and disability and parent groups to take a stand in the debate on selective abortion, instead of evading the issue.
- We must recognize disability as a feminist issue. All females (including teenagers and girls) will benefit from information and discussion about disability *before* they consider pregnancy, so they can avoid poorly informed decisions.
- Inclusion of people with disabilities must be part of the planning and outreach of reproductive rights organizations. Inclusion involves not only use of appropriate language and terminology for disability issues but also *involvement of disabled people* as resources. Women's organizations must learn about and comply with the Americans with Disabilities Act (or

related laws in other countries). If we are going to promote far-reaching radical feminist programs for justice and equality, we must surely comply with minimal standards set by the U.S. Congress.
- We must support family initiatives— such as parental leave for mothers and fathers, flex- and part-time work, child care resources, programs for low-income families, and comprehensive health care programs—that help *all* parents and thus make parenting children with disabilities more feasible.
- We must convince legislatures, the courts, and our communities that fetal anomaly must never be used again as a justification or a defense for safe and legal abortion. This is a disservice to the disability community and an insupportable argument for abortion rights.
- We must make the case that "wrongful life" suits should be eliminated. "Wrongful birth" suits (that seek damages for the cost of caring for a disabled child) should be carefully controlled only to protect against medical malpractice, not to punish medical practitioners for not complying with eugenic policy.
- We must break the *taboo* in the feminist movement against discussing the fetus. Getting "uncomfortable" will move us toward clarity, deepening the discussion about women's control of our bodies and reproduction.
- In response to the imperative from medical providers to utilize reproductive technologies, we can create programs to train "NRT peer counselors" to help women to learn more about new reproductive technologies, become truly informed consumers, and avoid being pressured to undergo unwanted tests. *People with disabilities must be included as NRT peer counselors.*
- We can help ourselves and each other gain clarity regarding the decision to abort a fetus with a disability. To begin

with, we can encourage women to examine their motivations for having children, ideally before becoming pregnant. We can ask ourselves and each other: What needs are we trying to satisfy in becoming a mother? How will the characteristics of the potential child figure into these motivations? What opportunities might there be for welcoming a child who does not meet our ideals of motherhood? What are the benefits of taking on the expectations and prejudices of family and friends? Have we met and interacted meaningfully with children and adults with disabilities? Do we have sufficient knowledge about disability, and sufficient awareness of our own feelings about disabled people, for our choices to be based on real information, not stereotypes?

Taking these steps and responding to these questions will be a start toward increasing our clarity about selective abortion.

CARING ABOUT OURSELVES AND EACH OTHER

Here are some things I have learned while working to educate others on this issue. I try to be patient with potential allies, to take time to explain my feelings. I try to take nothing for granted, try not to get defensive when people show their confusion or disagreement. I must remember that these issues are hard to understand; they run contrary to common and pervasive assumptions about people and life. I have to remember that it took me a long time to begin to understand disability stereotyping myself. At the same time, I have very high expectations for people. I believe it is possible to be pushy but patient and loving at the same time.

To feminist organizations attempting to include disabled women in discussions of abortion and other feminist issues: for-

give us for our occasional impatience. To disabled people: forgive potential allies for their ignorance and awkwardness. At meetings we disabled people hope to be heard, but we also perceive the "discomfort" that nondisabled people reveal, based on lack of real information about who we are. *There is no way around this awkward phase.* Better to reveal ignorance than to pretend and thereby preclude getting to know each other as people. Ask questions; make mistakes!

I sometimes remember that not only have I taken on this cutting-edge work for future generations, but I'm doing this *for myself now.* The message at the heart of widespread selective abortion on the basis of prenatal diagnosis is the greatest insult: some of us are "too flawed" in our very DNA to exist; we are unworthy of being born. This message is painful to confront. It seems tempting to take on easier battles, or even just to give in. But fighting for this issue, our right and worthiness to be born, is the fundamental challenge to disability oppression; it underpins our most basic claim to justice and equality—we are indeed worthy of being born, worth the help and expense, and we know it! The great opportunity with this issue is to think and act and take leadership in the place where feminism, disability rights, and human liberation meet.

NOTES

1. *New reproductive technologies* is the term often used to describe procreative medical technologies, including such prenatal diagnostic tests as ultrasound, alpha fetal protein (AFP) blood screening, amniocentesis, chorionic villi screening (CVS, a sampling of a segment of the amniotic sac), and the whole host of other screening tests for fetal anomalies. NRTs also include in vitro fertilization and related fertility-enhancing technologies. The conference, "New Reproductive Technologies: The Contradictions of Choice; the Common Ground between Disability Rights and Feminist Analysis," held in Vancouver, No-

vember 1994, was sponsored by the DisAbled Women's Network (DAWN), and the National Action Council on the Status of Women (NAC).

2. David J. Kevles, *In the Name of Eugenics* (New York: Knopf, 1985).

3. Not long after eugenics became a respectable science in the United States, Nazi leaders modeled state policies on their brutal reading of U.S. laws and practices. After their rise to power in 1933 the Nazis began their "therapeutic elimination" of people with mental disabilities, and they killed 120,000 people with disabilities during the Holocaust. See Robert J. Lifton, *The Nazi Doctors: Medical Killing and the Psychology of Genocide* (New York: Basic Books, 1986).

4. Marlene Fried, ed., *From Abortion to Reproductive Freedom: Transforming a Movement* (Boston: South End Press, 1990), 159.

5. Michelle Fine and Adrienne Asch, "The Question of Disability: No Easy Answers for the Women's Movement," *Reproductive Rights Newsletter* 4, no. 3 (Fall 1982). See also Rita Arditti, Renate Duelli Klein, and Shelley Minden, *Test-Tube Women: What Future for Motherhood?* (London: Routledge and Kegan Paul, 1984); Adrienne Asch, "The Human Genome and Disability Rights," *Disability Rag and Resource*, February 1994, 12–13; Adrienne Asch and Michelle Fine, "Shared Dreams: A Left Perspective on Disability Rights and Reproductive Rights," in *From Abortion to Reproductive Freedom*, ed. Fried; Lisa Blumberg, "The Politics of Prenatal Testing and Selective Abortion," in *Women with Disabilities: Reproduction and Motherhood*, special issue of *Sexuality and Disability Journal* 12, no. 2 (Summer 1994); Michelle Fine and Adrienne Asch, *Women with Disabilities: Essays in Psychology, Culture, and Politics* (Philadelphia: Temple University Press, 1988); Laura Hershey, "Choosing Disability," *Ms.*, July/August 1994; Ruth Hubbard and Elijah Wald, *Exploding the Gene Myth: How Genetic Information Is Produced and Manipulated by Scientists, Physicians, Employers, Insurance Companies, Educators and Law Enforcers* (Boston: Beacon Press, 1993); Marsha Saxton, "The Politics of Genetics," *Women's Review of Books* 9, no. 10–11 (July 1994); Marsha Saxton, "Prenatal Screening and Discriminatory Attitudes about Disability, in *Embryos, Ethics and Women's Rights: Exploring the New Reproductive Technologies*, ed. Elaine Hoffman Baruch, Amadeo F. D'Adamo, and Joni Seager (New York: Haworth Press, 1988); Marsha Saxton and Florence Howe, eds., *With Wings: An Anthology by and about Women with Disabilities* (New York: Feminist Press, 1987).

6. Adrienne Asch, "Reproductive Technology and Disability," in *Reproductive Laws for the 1990s: A Briefing Handbook*, ed. Nadine Taub and Sherrill Cohen (New Brunswick, N.J.: Rutgers University Press, 1989).

7. Helen Featherstone, *A Difference in the Family: Life with a Disabled Child* (New York: Basic Books, 1980).

8. To my knowledge, Anne Finger was the first disability activist to raise this issue in the U.S. women's literature. In her book *Past Due: Disability, Pregnancy, and Birth* (Seattle: Seal Press, 1990), which includes references to her earlier writings, Finger describes a small conference where feminists and disability activists discussed this topic. German and British disability activists and feminists pioneered this issue.

9. Ruth Hubbard, *The Politics of Women's Biology* (New Brunswick, N.J.: Rutgers University Press, 1990), 197.

10. Dorothy Wertz, "Attitudes toward Abortion among Parents of Children with Cystic Fibrosis," *American Journal of Public Health* 81, no. 8 (1991).

11. This view must be reevaluated in the era of in vitro fertilization (IVF), where the embryo or a genetically prescreened embryo (following "pre-implantation diagnosis") can be fertilized outside the woman's body and frozen or can be implanted in another woman. Such a fetus has come to have legal status apart from the mother's body: for example, in divorce cases where the fate of these fetuses is decided by the courts.

12. Many "pro-life" groups support abortion for "defective fetuses." Most state laws, even conservative ones, allow later-stage abortions when the fetus is "defective."

13. Rayna Rapp, "Accounting for Amniocentesis," in *Knowledge, Power, and Practice: The Anthropology of Medicine in Everyday Life*, ed. Shirley Lindenbaum and Margaret Lock (Berkeley: University of California Press, 1993).

14. Suneri Thobani, "From Reproduction to Mal[e] Production: Women and Sex Selection Technology," in *Misconceptions: The Social Construction of Choice and the New Reproductive Technologies*, vol. I, ed. Gwynne Basen, Margaret Eichler, and Abby Lippman (Quebec: Voyager Publishing, 1994).

15. Dorothy C. Wertz and John C. Fletcher, "A Critique of Some Feminist Challenges to Prenatal Diagnosis," *Journal of Women's Health* 2 (1993).

CHAPTER 10

Universal Design: The Work of Disability in an Age of Globalization

Michael Davidson

"Today, something we do will touch your life."

(Union Carbide advertisement)

GLOBAL BODIES

My title refers to the architectural design that provides access to the built environment for all people, disabled or not. The phrase takes on more insidious implications in a globalized environment where structural adjustment politics (SAPs) instituted during the worldwide debt crises of the 1970s and 1980s protected global finance from default by allowing debtor nations to continue making interest payments on foreign loans at the expense of social programs, education, and healthcare in countries that had incurred such debts. In this sense, universal design refers to the global aspirations of wealthy countries in configuring development around growth rather than social improvement. For persons with disabilities, universal design poses the conundrum that increased access promised by the internationalization of social services, healthcare, and technology is thwarted by limiting the meaning of access to new markets and economic opportunities.

A global perspective on disability must begin with some incontrovertible facts.

There are more than a half billion disabled people in the world today. One in ten persons lives with a cognitive or physical disability, and according to UN estimates, 80 percent live in developing countries.[1] More than 50 percent of the people in the world's forty-six poorest countries are without access to modern healthcare. Approximately three billion people in developing countries do not have access to sanitation facilities, and one billion in those countries lack safe drinking water. The developing world carries 90 percent of the disease burden, yet these countries have access to 10 percent of world health resources.[2] As Paul Farmer Points out, "HIV has become the world's leading infectious cause of adult deaths . . . [but most] of the 42 million people now infected, most live in the developing world and cannot afford the drugs that might extend their lives."[3] In Africa, governments transfer to northern creditors four times more in debt payments than they spend on the health and education of their citizens. In Nicaragua, where three fourths of the population live below the poverty line, debt repayments exceed the total social-sector budget. In Bolivia, where 80 percent of the highland population lives in poverty, debt repayments for 1997 accounted for three times the spending allocated for rural poverty reduction.[4] Although the United

States has pledged two-hundred million dollars to the UN Global Aids fund, it receives two-hundred million dollars *weekly* from debt repayments.[5] There are more than one-hundred-ten million land mines in sixty-four countries. There are one and a half mines per person in Angola, where one-hundred-twenty people per month become amputees. There are twelve million land mines in Afghanistan, one for every two people. It seems hardly necessary to add that land mines are created not to kill but to disable, thereby maximizing the impact of bodily damage on the extended family and community.[6]

How might the incorporation of such facts into disability studies modify or even challenge some of its primary concerns? What might a critical disability studies perspective bring to the globalization debate? To some extent, the two terms—disability and globalization—are linked in much earlier forms of internationalization and consolidation. U.S. Immigration laws in the nineteenth century, for example, were often written around bodies deemed "unhealthy" or "diseased" and therefore unfit for national citizenship. New racial panics about immigrants and miscegenation were often framed by narratives of bodily deformity and weakness. Nayan Shah has shown how Chinese migrant laborers in the latter nineteenth century were marginalized during the immigration process, their bodies examined and regulated according to perceived epidemiological hazards that they posed to white America.[7] The same could be said for international labor history which is a story of workplace impairments, chronic lung disease, repetitive stress disorders and psychological damage caused by "fordist" modes of production and "taylorized" efficiency. And as industrial societies created new forms of disability, so they developed a health and rehabilitation service industry which they exported to developing countries."[8] Such examples

suggest that many aspects of what we call international modernity are founded upon the unequal valuation of some bodies over others.

At another level, linking disability and globalization serves to direct the focus of economic stabilization onto the physical bodies in whose name those strategies are often legitimated. We understand the ways that political violence and civil conflict create disability through warfare, landmines, and displacement, but we need to remember the structural violence that maintains disability through seemingly innocuous economic systems and political consensus.[9] Union Carbide's buoyant motto that I use for my epigraph, "Today, something we do will touch your life," means something very different for the three-hundred-thousand residents of Bhopal, India "touched" by that company in 1984.[10] The ways that global capital "touches" the body allow us to rethink the separation of bodies and public spaces, of bodies without organs and organizations without bodies. Just as national borders are being redrawn around new corporate trading zones and partnerships, so the borders of the body are being rethought in an age of neo-natal screening, genetic engineering, and body modification. Disability studies has monitored such remappings as they impact social attitudes about nontraditional bodies, but it has not paid adequate attention to the political economy of the global body. As a result, disability studies risks remaining a vestige of an earlier identity politics rather than a critical intervention into social justice at large.

A common refrain in disability studies is that disability is the one identity category that, if we live long enough, everyone will inhabit. White people will not become black, and men will not become women, but most people will become disabled. This has led some disability scholars to posit disability as a kind of *ur*-identity that, by virtue of its ubiquitousness and fluidity, its crossing of racial, sexual, gendered categories, challenges the integrity of identity politics altogether.[11] While it is true that many of us will become disabled, it is just as certain that those who become disabled earlier in life, who have the least access to medical insurance and healthcare, who suffer longer and die younger, who have the least legal redress are poor and live in an underdeveloped country. Malnutrition may not be on the minority world agenda of disability issues, but in the majority world defined by the World Health Organization, it is on the front line. Hence the first challenge that globalization poses for disability studies is a consideration of class and the unequal distribution of wealth.

When we consider disability as a global phenomenon we are forced to reevaluate some of the keywords of disability studies—stigma, normalcy, ableism, bodily difference—from a comparative cultural perspective.[12] We must ask to what extent the discourse of "disability" is underwritten by a Western, state-centered model that assumes values of individual rights and equality guaranteed by legal contract. The Americans with Disabilities Act (ADA) recognizes both the material and social meanings of disability, but its ability to mitigate issues of access and employment discrimination presumes a level of economic prosperity and political stability that does not easily translate. What is considered a disability in the first world may be a physical advantage or blessing in another: "[the] disfiguring scar in Dallas becomes an honorific mark in Dahomey."[13] And when U.S. policy makers attempt to intervene in global health crises in developing countries, they often bring Western assumptions about social normalization that undermine the goodwill gesture. The 1984 Reagan administration's executive order banning U.S. government financial support for U.S. and foreign family plan-

ning agencies that provided information about abortion—the so-called "Mexico City Policy"—is typical of this gesture. Thus the attempt to study disability through the social model as a set of discourses about a hypothetical, normal body, must be situated within individual cultural landscapes.

And it is landscape that motivates the theoretical armature of my paper. Arjun Appadurai describes the cultural logic of globalization as a series of "imaginary landscapes"—ethnoscapes, mediascapes, technoscapes, financescapes, and ideoscapes —that define "historically situated imaginations of person and groups spread around the globe."[14] Appadurai's theory of "scapes" is particularly useful for explaining the multiple, overlapping sites in which disability is produced and perpetuated. If we imagine that disability is something that bodies "have" or display, then we restrict the meaning of the term to a medical definition of that impairment. But if we imagine that disability as defined within regimes of pharmaceutical exchange, labor migration, ethnic displacement, epidemiology, genomic research, and trade wars, then the question must be asked differently: does disability exist in a cell, a body, a building, a race, a DNA molecule, a set of residential schools, a special education curriculum, a sweatshop, a rural clinic? The implications of seeing disability spatially force us to re-think the embodied character of impairment and disease.[15]

When we consider the *place* of disability, we begin to see the extent to which physical and cognitive impairment is directly related to material conditions and structures of power. The increased presence of depression among female *maquiladora* workers along the Mexico/U.S. border or cancers among agricultural workers in the California Central Valley must be linked to labor and migration in export processing zones following the passage of NAFTA.[16] Harlan Lane's description of Deaf persons as a colonial regime invokes the rhetoric of postcoloniality and imperialism to describe a physical condition (deafness) as well as a set of cultural practices relating to the use of manual signing that have little to do with an ability to hear and everything to do with community and culture. Keith Wailoo's work on sickle cell anemia in Memphis shows how a disease found predominantly among persons of African descent and characterized by acute physical pain became visible as a disease when changes in civil rights laws began to recognize the historic pain of black people.[17] The global market in body parts is inextricable from what Appadurai calls the "ethnoscape"—contexts of labor migration, sexual tourism, and ethnic conflicts through which this market does its business. In such cases, does disability rest with the person with kidney disease or with the so-called "donor" who sells the kidney, with the wealthy recipient whose life is sustained by an operation or the immigrant whose health is drastically compromised as a result of it? Obviously phrased in this way, disability is as much about national and cultural power differentials as it is a matter of medicine and bodies.

DISABILITY STUDIES IN A GLOBAL PERSPECTIVE

The salient feature of U.S., Canadian, and British work in disability studies in the past ten years is a shift from a medical to a social model of impairment. The medical definition of disability locates impairment in the individual as someone who lacks the full complement of physical and cognitive elements of true personhood and who must be cured or rehabilitated. The social model locates disability not in the individual's impairment but in the environment—in social attitudes, institutional structures, and physical or communicational barriers that prevent full participation as citizen subject. Much of this work is reinforced

by language in the Americans with Disabilities Act (1990) that recognizes that a person in a wheelchair becomes disabled when he or she encounters a building without elevators or when a sight impaired person tries to use an ATM machine without Braille signage. It also recognizes that one may be equally disabled by social stigma. Phrases like "wheelchair bound," "retarded," or "deaf and dumb" are no less oppressive than lack of physical access since they mark how certain bodies are interpreted and read.

In the humanities, this social model has been accompanied by a disability hermeneutics that looks critically at the ways disabled characters in literature have been seen as sites of moral failing, pity, or sexual panic. David Mitchell and Sharon Snyder have seen this analogical treatment of disability as a "narrative prosthesis" by which a disabled character serves as a crutch to shore up normalcy somewhere else.[18] The disabled character is prosthetic in the sense that he or she provides an illusion of bodily wholeness upon which the novel erects its formal claims to totality, in which ethical or moral failings in one sphere are signified through physical limitations in another. In Richard Wright's *Native Son*, Mrs. Dalton's blindness could be read as a sign of the moral limits of white liberal attitudes that mask racism. Wright is less interested in blindness itself than the way it enables a story about racial violence and liberal guilt. In *A Christmas Carol* Charles Dickens does not use Tiny Tim to condemn the treatment of crippled children in Victorian society but to finesse Scrooge's awakening to charity and human kindness towards others. By regarding disability as a "narrative prosthesis," Mitchell and Snyder underscore the ways that the material bodies of blind or crippled persons are deflected onto an able bodied normalcy that the story must reinforce. Indeed, narrative's claim to formal coherence is underwritten by that which it cannot contain, as evidenced by the carnival grotesques, madwomen in attics, blind prophets, and mute soothsayers that underwrite much narrative theory.

Despite Mitchell and Snyder's important warnings about the dangers of analogical treatments of disability, there are cases in which a prosthesis is *still* a prosthesis. The first world texts that have been the site of most work in disability studies may very well have narrative closure as their telos, but regarded in a more globalized environment, the social meaning of both disability and narrative may have to be expanded. In Mohsen Makhmalbaf's 2001 film, *Kandahar*, the main character, a female journalist, Nafas (Niloufar Pazira) is traveling from the Iranian border to Kandahar in Afghanistan to save her sister from what appears to be an immanent suicide attempt. The film is set during the Taliban regime, and Nafas wears a *burqa* while traveling, her clothing serving as a metaphor for the limits to female agency but also providing a degree of protection from threatening forces she encounters along the way. In one scene, Nafas observes a group of amputated Afghani men on crutches lurching across the desert to retrieve prosthetic legs that have been parachuted out of a Red Cross airplane. The image of prosthetic legs falling gracefully to earth is a powerful, if bizarre, image of post-colonial disruptions.

It would be tempting to regard the prostheses as representing the unreality of everyday life under the Taliban or as surrogates for the *burqa*, metaphors for gendered and sexual limits within religious fundamentalism. But at another level, the prosthetic appendages testify to the pervasiveness of historical impairments caused by thousands of land mines left by both Soviets and mujahadin after the war. Here disability is not a metaphor but a lived reality for tens of thousands of people who have endured the ravages of post-colonial wars and factionalist struggles. In Ato

Quayson's terms, "to have full disclosure about the social and political grounds of an impairment is perforce to go beyond the impairment and to engage the social, political, and cultural forces that produce disability."[19] "Full disclosure" in the case of *Kandahar* is located not merely in the explosion that led to amputation but in the long history of colonization, political occupation, and nationalisms that mark both landscape and landmine.

Just as "prosthesis" within a global disability perspective must be looked at historically, so must the term "narrative." It is impossible to consider cultural forms in Africa without mentioning the role of AIDS activism and especially the Treatment Action Campaign (TAC) that has legislated for increased access to antiretroviral drugs. Here, representations of disability and social action converge in performances designed to educate and entertain. Moreover, due to the informational nature of this performance—what some call "edutainment"—issues of readability mean something very different from what they do in Western narrative theory. Within Theatre for Development performances around HIV/AIDS, the stage may be an open clearing or flatbed truck, a movable stage or community center where performances occur. The audience is encouraged to participate in the performance, often taking on roles themselves or shouting encouragement to the actors. Traditional oral and folkloric materials may be fused with references to proper nutrition and safe sex; street protests merge with street theater; popular culture (comics, hip hop) combines with classic theater. The work of art in an age of globalization may be a tape cassette about the need to wear a condom.

If disability studies has been reticent on the subject of globalization, recent literature on globalization has been silent about disability. Such work often mentions the ill effects of multinational corporations and structural adjustment policies on health-care systems, but they devote scant attention to disability as a cultural problem.[20] Where disability studies has focused much of its attention on the role of stigma and social marginalization, anti-globalist theory tends to treat disabled persons as victims of economic processes rather than subjects. Often themes of powerlessness and dependency are filtered through the rhetoric of disability, as in Gillian Hart's important book on South Africa, *Disabling Globalization* which, despite its title, never mentions AIDS or the country's active disability rights movement.[21] Richard Wolff's essay, "World Bank/Class Blindness" excoriates development theorists who ignore class issues in formulating economic policy, using the word "blindness" throughout the essay to describe ignorance and obtuseness.[22] I do not mean to dismiss globalization theory by focusing on ableist rhetoric, but such usage underscores how easily a critique of class blindness may dismiss blindness itself.

What if we submitted Wolff's appeal for a reading of class as a contributor to the production of surplus to specific disabled] people's lives? Two examples come to mind. In 1983, the Centers for Disease Control (CDC) observed that pooled blood products (rather than the life-styles of gay men) were responsible for AIDS among hemophilia patients. In 1984, the Bayer unit of Cutter Biological sold millions of dollars worth of its blood-clotting factor for hemophiliacs to Asia and Latin America when it discovered that the company had large stores of product that were now unsaleable in the United States and Europe. Instead of destroying the tainted product and alerting distributors abroad, Bayer continued to sell factor in Malaysia, Singapore, Indonesia, Japan, and Argentina where thousands of hemophiliacs and other patients needing transfusions became infected with HIV. These events were occurring despite the fact that the company had developed a safer, heat-treated product that it was selling in the United States and Europe. In a statement to the *New York Times*, Bayer officials claimed that they had "behaved responsibly, ethically and humanely" in continuing to sell the old product in these parts of the world.[23] Not only did Bayer continue to sell infected product, it continued to *make* the old type of factor in order to fill orders from several large fixed-price contracts. The result was a worldwide HIV infection rate of 90% among severe hemophiliacs and a four million dollar profit for Bayer. Although similar scandals erupted within the United States Canada, Japan, and France, the practice of transnational corporations selling unwanted products to developing countries in order to maintain the bottom line at home is the specter haunting a globalized economy.[24] Supporters of a global marketplace will argue that despite local inequities, a free market will ultimately benefit those most in need, but this assumption obviously depends on what one means by "free." When HIV infected recipients of blood transfusions become "collateral damage" in a worldwide trade war, one wonders who is being served by open markets.

My second example concerns the definitions that the World Bank uses for persons with disabilities in order to calculate cost effective interventions in health policy. In its 1993 World Development Report, "Investing in Health," the World Bank applied the concept of the Disability Adjusted Life Years (DALY) as an indicator of the "time lived with a disability and the time lost due to premature mortality."[25] The language of the report is full of references to "global burdens" and the "cost effectiveness of different interventions at reducing the disease burdens due to a particular condition."[26] Obviously the World Bank is trying to do the right thing by assessing priorities for intervention in health matters, but by defining individuals by lost productivity instead of medical need, the bank imposes an actuarial value on its largesse. Those deemed least useful in certain cultures—women, children, aged, and disabled persons will, as Nirmala Erevelles says, "have little or no entitlement to health services at public expense."[27]

In both of these examples, the lack of monitoring or quality control on pharmaceutical products, the application of cost-benefit analysis to matters of health and mortality, and the ability of transnational corporations like Bayer to control worldwide distribution and prevent competition are only the most obvious ways that internationalization of healthcare creates—rather than eliminates—disability and calls into question the degree to which markets can ever achieve the kind of equality that free market economists advocate.

DEVELOPMENT, DEVALUATION, AND DISABILITY

I want now to provide several cultural examples that read the scapes of globalization through a disability optic. My ocular metaphor calls attention to the importance of performance in all of my examples, but it also reinforces the ways that disability focalizes the inherently unrepresentable quality of global economic processes. As critics have pointed out, the homogenization of commodities, signage, and technology that we associate with globalization creates a placelessness for which mimetic criteria seem inadequate. In Raymond Williams's terms, globalization could be seen as a "structure of feeling" that cannot be contained in a single image or narrative.[28] We could imagine this structure of feeling around globalization as a kind of phantom limb phenomenon that registers a phantasmatic "whole body" that can no longer be constituted by an appeal to national origins or cultural integrity.

The films of Jibril Diop Mambety, Senegal's best known film maker, are often based on traditional folk tales, yet their retellings of the trickster, Yadikoon, or the animal fables of rabbit and hyena, are placed in contemporary settings. As the title to his incomplete final trilogy indicates, he tells the story of "les petites gens," the "little people," marginalized by devaluations, both human and economic. In addition to being poor, Mambety's characters are often disabled, played by nonprofessional, disabled actors who, far from serving as metaphors for an Africa "crippled" by debt are often the moral centers of each tale. Disability in these films is used to frame the burdens produced in the social and political infrastructure of Senegal following the 1994 devaluation of the West African Franc (CFA) by European and American financial institutions.[29] Almost overnight, the value of domestic products was cut in half, the price of a sack of rice doubled, export prices plummeted. In Mambety's films, the financescape of devaluation is manifest in the various ways that the market is depicted—from the lottery ticket seller of *Le franc*, who embodies the economic world of poor Africans after devaluation to the dusty, bustling marketplace of Dakar in *La petite vendeuse de* Soleil to the hardscrabble country store that is the centerpiece of *Hyenas.* Framing these local economic sites stand the anonymous corporate buildings of Dakar, looming over the "little" dramas of Mambety's characters. This financescape is combined with both mediascape and ethnoscape through which global information (newspapers, radio) is passed and communal identities (religious institutions, family units) interrupted. In *Le Franc*, the Muslim call to prayer comes via the same public address system that broadcasts the winning lottery ticket numbers. Religious and economic rituals vie for a common electronic voice in the marketplace. By situating each of his disabled characters in relation to a massive economic shift in west African finance, Mambety studies the impact of devaluation and development on those most affected.

Mambety's last film, *La petite vendeuse de* soleil (*The Little Girl Who Sold* The Sun), tells of a twelve year old paraplegic girl, Sili Laam, who begs for money in the crowded market of Dakar with her blind grandmother. Seeing that boys make more money by selling the local paper, *Soleil*, she tries her entrepreneurial hand as a news vendor. Her resilience and toughness carry her through the crowded, competitive world of the market where street vendors vie for the smallest share and where corrupt police lurk at the edges. Sili's paraplegia, possibly due to polio, suggests the condition of all bodies kept in poverty by structural adjustment, but she is not reduced to being a "cripple." We see her moving forcefully through the crowd, getting a ride to Dakar in a horse cart, dancing in a yellow dress with other girls, defending herself against threatening police and predatory gangs, giving her earnings to beggars in the market. The theme of structural adjustment is manifest through references to the devaluation of the CFA in the headlines that Lili shouts. Lili's market is dominated by a combination of individual initiative and corruption, not the blessings of free trade. However flawed, it is also a market in which mixtures of people and products converge—a place where disabled citizens mutually support each other and where exchange of products coincides with sharing of opinions and ideas.[30]

Throughout the film, Lili establishes a friendship with a young boy, Babou Seck, who protects her from a gang of threatening news vendors. In this last scene of the film, Lili and Babou are selling papers whose headlines read "Afrique quitte le franc zone" (Africa has left the franc zone), announcing a future, as yet unrealized francophone Africa that has severed its dependence on the French franc and must adapt to a world economy. Lili is set upon by a gang of boys who knock her down and steal her crutch. Babou tries unsuccessfully to retrieve it. "What do we do now?" Babou asks to which Lili responds, "We continue." He hoists her onto his back and carries her through a crowded arcade of the market. The other vendors fade back into the stalls, leaving only the sound of Babou's footsteps echoing through the hall. The moral of the story—perhaps too bluntly stated—is that in a society damaged by fluctuating, international markets and plagued by local corruption, the salvific value is mutual aid and support, not dependence or victimization. In short, Mambety allows us to witness an alternative form of development, one based on self-reliance rather than ruthless competition.

Mambety is constantly aware of the relationship between disability and market driven poverty, a connection made concrete in a scene that takes place at a ferry dock called "Goree," a reference to the infamous Goree Island slave port in West Africa from which slaves were sent to the new world. Lili is often viewed by a young man in a wheelchair who cradles a large boombox in his arms and who, for a few coins, plays music. He functions as a kind of silent chorus, his music providing entertainment and perhaps a site of resistance (he plays songs celebrating African freedom fighters), his disabled perspective becomes the viewer's vantage from which we too see Lili. Finally, Lili must negotiate a literally rocky terrain—streets with potholes and puddles of water, garbage strewn about, making the term "access" seem laughable. Clearly, a country that must divert all of its resources to settling its international debts cannot be bothered with providing better infrastructure and curb cuts. At the end of the film, Mambety provides a voice over moral in a male voice: "This tale is thrown to the sea," suggesting that it is up to the audience to uncork the bottle and read its meanings into the future. But Lili delivers the last words by saying, "The first to breathe it will go to heaven," providing a redemptive parable of emancipation through mutual (not foreign) aid.

My second example concerns a number of recent films, plays, and novels that deal with the international organ trade in which the body quite literally becomes a commodity, its components exchanged in a worldwide market that mirrors the structural inequality between wealth and poverty. Nancy Scheper-Hughes points out that organ transplantation "now takes place in a trans-national space with both donors and recipients following the paths of capital and technology in the global economy."[31] Nor is "space" a metaphor. Lawrence Cohen describes what he calls the "kidneyvakkam" of India where many poor residents have undergone kidney operations and where the day's buying and selling prices of organs are publicly posted.[32] Transplantation narratives reinforce the links between the space of the body and the global space of capital, between a body regarded as a totality of parts and a communicational and media space in which those parts are sold, packaged in ice chests, and shipped around the world. And organ trafficking is a discursive matter. Rumors of children stolen, soldiers's bodies "looted," and hospital patients misdiagnosed for their organs add a Gothic element to the organ sale narrative, a literary-subgenre that Scheper-Hughes calls "neo-cannibalism."[33]

We could divide transplantation narratives into two forms. The first, typified by films like *Dirty Pretty Things* and *Central Station*, might be called "organ diaspora stories." These situate the context of body part trafficking within an ethnoscape of transnational labor flows, black market crime, and moral panic. In Walter Salles' 1998 movie, *Central Station*, a young orphaned boy is rescued by a woman who writes letters for poor, illiterate city dwellers in her Rio de Janeiro stall. Her decision to save the boy is motivated by fears that he will become a victim of unscrupulous body part salesmen in a country where everyone at birth is declared a universal organ donor. In Stephen Frears' *Dirty Pretty Things*, organ sales occur within a the migrant worker population in London—from the sleazy black market broker, Senor Juan, to the Somalian man who has had his kidney removed to Okwe, who, as both illegal immigrant and doctor, is constantly tempted to use his medical skills illegally to alleviate economic problems. The second form of transplantation narrative is a more futuristic one that imagines a world in which the ideal of replacing an aging or disabled body with new parts retrofits a nineteenth-century eugenics story in a globalized environment. In Manjula Padmanabhan's *Harvest* the play's characters are divided up into "Donors," poor, Bombay city dwellers, and "Receivers" wealthy, first world customers for body parts.[34] In Andrew Niccol's *Gattaca*, a man with congenital heart disease purchases "pure" DNA stock from a paraplegic but otherwise eugenically perfect male in order to participate in a space program. Such science fiction fantasies are, of course, present day potentialities, and one of the cultural functions that such representations serves is to bring into visibility the links between medical technology, racialist science, infomatics, and global economy.

Dirty Pretty Things (2003) depicts a modern London in which the entire population comes from elsewhere, employed as service workers, hotel clerks, prostitutes, cab drivers, and hospital orderlies. The film concerns a Nigerian immigrant, Okwe (Chiwte Ejiofor) who had been a doctor in his native country but who now works illegally in London as a desk clerk at a hotel. What little sleep he gets he obtains on the couch of a fellow immigrant, Senay (Audrey

Tautou), a young Turkish Muslim woman who works clandestinely as a maid in the same hotel. While checking on a room whose toilet is overflowing, Okwe discovers a human heart stuck in the plumbing, and after checking with his friend at the hospital, realizes that the manager of the hotel, Senor Juan, has been conducting a black market business in organ sales. Because Okwe is illegally in the country and needs his job, he cannot go to the police, and the hotel manager threatens to turn him in to immigration authorities if he pursues the matter. Just as the clandestine organ trade is part of an invisible global economy, so its actors must remain invisible to the "normal" functioning of touristic London.

The dirty and pretty things that maintain the hotel's functioning also support the marginal existence of the vast immigrant labor force. The oxymoronic blazon of the film—a heart in a toilet bowl—defines the existence of individuals whose lifeblood is wasted in repetitive, unremunerative labor under constant surveillance, whose bodies are literally waste products. Whatever romance Okwe and Senay might share is thwarted by the constant presence of immigration police and the possibility of deportation. Forced to flee her hotel job and a second job in a sweatshop, Senay turns to the only option available to her—to offer her own kidney to Senor Juan—for a passport and passage out of the country. Okwe realizes what she is about to do and offers the manager to do the operation himself so that it will be hygienic. He prepares the hotel room with proper surgical equipment but ends up drugging Senor Juan instead and substituting him as the kidney patient. Okwe completes the operation, with the help of Senay and other friends, and delivers the organ to the broker. When the broker sees Okwe and his subaltern assistants, he says "I've never seen you before," and Okwe responds, "Oh yes you have. We're the ones who drive your cars,

clean your rooms and suck your cocks."[35] This is a particularly vivid representation of the status of immigrant labor in a globalized economy. This necessary but invisible laboring body is metonymized in a kidney exchanged with a wealthy client whose life is prolonged while that of the immigrant donor is compromised.

At one point in *Dirty Pretty Things* Senay asks Okwe why he came to London. He replies, "It's an African story." He is speaking about the post-colonial diaspora of Africans throughout the Western world, but he could equally be speaking about the diaspora of HIV/AIDS within Africa. There is a relationship between the two African stories insofar as poverty and transnational labor movements drive both. What form does this "African Story" take? Can Western theories of textuality and aesthetic coherence account for the story of post-Apartheid Africa, especially when it concerns disability and development? Most importantly, how does the context of AIDS challenge the division between art and politics, cultural forms and social movements? These questions emerge forcefully in Theater for Development projects in which performance has become central to pedagogical efforts to explain government policies or health issues.[36] Although activists are sometimes skeptical about Theater for Development as a tool of state interests, there is a growing acceptance of its importance in addressing HIV/AIDS. Theater for Development is reminiscent of other forms of activist theater—Luis Valdez's "Actos" or the militant theater of the U.S. Black Nationalism—that combine pedagogy and audience participation. As "edutainment," these new cultural forms challenge formalist aesthetics, their sometimes didactic message and instrumental character elaborated through popular genres involving puppetry, dance, hiphop music, comics, posters, and mime.

In speaking of *Kandahar* I referred to Nafas' use of a tape cassette to record her difficult desert journey; I now want to conclude with reference to another tape cassette, forged in the Theater for Development arena, whose function, far from representing an outlawed interiority, establishes an imagined community among travelers. "Yiriba" is a thirty-minute tape cassette developed by several local NGO's and CIDA (the Canadian Agency for International Development) designed to be distributed among long-distance truck drivers who cover routes in West Africa's "AIDS" corridor.[37] This hugely popular tape features the voices of two well known Malian griots, Djeli Daouda Dembele and his wife Hawa Dembele, who warn truck drivers of the dangers of sexually transmitted diseases, using traditional oral tales and musical accompaniment. Daouda tells the story of a truck driver, Yiriba, who is approached by a good looking woman, Korotouma, at a truck stop, who asks for a lift to the next town. They end up at a hotel and begin to engage in sexual activity. When Yiriba produces a condom, Korotouma chastizes him for thinking she might be a prostitute. Yiriba delivers a speech about the need for prudence—"Both of us travel a lot, and we meet many people every day. This condom will protect you and me. I must say we hardly know one another." Korotouma, insulted, leaves and takes up with another driver, Seydou. The same scenario occurs, but Seydou does not use a condom and, as a result, becomes infected with HIV. When Yiriba visits his now ailing friend, he learns that Seydou has infected other women as well as his wife, causing her to become infertile. Finally, because of his illness, Seydou has entrusted his truck to his apprentice who promptly steals it, leaving him without a means of livelihood. Throughout the tale, Hawa Dembele sings a refrain: "I have traveled to the East, to the West, to the North, and to the South. I have never encountered a similar fever, Father of the griots."

There are several stylistic features of the tape that link the tape to traditional story telling traditions and that make this more than a simple cautionary tale. The griot poses as the "great bard of truck drivers" and urges solidarity with each other during the long night drives. The Dembeles act both as story tellers and actors who take on various roles. Daoda also praises the AIDS doctors of West Africa and mentions truck stops, cities and health centers that drivers are likely to encounter. Most significantly, he praises rig owners "who help their drivers when these latter fall ill."[38]

"Yiriba" raises provocative questions about the work of art in an age of globalization. The cassette exists in a liminal space between several cultural forms, some archaic (the griot tale) and some modern (truck routes, tape recorders). It is, in James Clifford's terms, a form of "traveling culture," crossing national, ethnic, and linguistic boundaries, linking truck drivers from different areas who share the same routes and the same potential for HIV infection.[39] Daouda and Hawa can count on their fame as storytellers among their listeners to validate their message—and along the way, to legitimate the NGO's that sponsor the tape. Thus the cautionary story of "Yiriba," simple though it may seem on the surface, brings the AIDS story and the African story together.

THE WORK OF THE ADA IN AN AGE OF GLOBALIZATION

Thus far I have stressed the ways in which disability—like the aesthetic—challenges ideas of bodily and cognitive normalcy. Cultural forms such as the ones I have briefly mentioned permit us to examine globalization through what I have been calling a disability optic, one that like the camera obscura permits us to see the familiar upside down. In the United States we benefit from legal statutes like the ADA—as well as section 504 of the 1973 Rehabilitation Act and the 1975 Individuals with Disabilities Education Act—that provide a safety net for those who otherwise would fall through the cracks. This safety net is a privilege that a wealthy country can—and should—afford, but as a result, "universal design" remains largely a first world concept rather than a global reality. And like all legal protections, the ADA is vulnerable to change. In recent years, there have been several major challenges to the ADA, and in the current business-friendly administration more are likely to appear. The Rehnquist Court overturned cases on appeal that would expand the class of persons protected, especially plaintiffs with correctable disabilities (high blood pressure, nearsightedness) or cases that would contradict existing state statutes. A more ominous fact is that of the numerous claims made under ADA protection, 95 percent are decided in favor of employers, leading many in the disability rights movement to conclude that legal arguments for limiting the class and kinds of cases applicable under federal protection are often based on cost-accounting rather than the welfare of the plaintiffs. In an era of increasingly privatized healthcare, restrictions on Medicare, and the possible evacuation of Social Security, the ADA may become more of a symbolic document than a map for redress.[40]

In my introduction I described disability as a series of sites that include the spaces of the body but that extend into a more public arena of communities and institutions. If we think of disability as located in societal barriers, not in individuals, then disability must be seen as a matter of social justice. The remedy for social justice as Nancy Fraser points out, involves synthesizing a politics of recognition and a politics of redistribution, a theory of justice based on cultural identities and one based on the reorganization of material resources around those identities.[41] Disability would seem to be the test cast for such a synthesis since any recognition of, say, children with developmental disabilities, will require, as Michael Berubé says, access to "a free and appropriate public education in the least restrictive environment."[42] Recognition of disability as a civil right entails making sure that a person with a disability has access to the buildings, classrooms, and courts where those rights are learned and adjudicated. As Berubé says, if the ADA "were understood as broad civil rights law . . . [pertaining] to the entire population of the country, then maybe disability law would be understood not as fringe addition to civil rights law but as its very fulfillment."[43]

Adapting these remarks, I would suggest that if disability were considered as a matter of global human rights rather than as a "healthcare problem," perhaps the ADA could serve as a roadmap for universal design in its best estate. Rather than seeing globalization narrowly as providing greater access to computer chips, phone lines, raw materials, and cheap labor, it could be seen as something relating to all of us who have bodies, the spirit of inclusion promised by the ADA might extend beyond its current national jurisdiction. This would entail a recognition on the part of wealthier nations that access to public spaces, healthcare, social justice cannot be made contingent on private sector interests or moral/ideological restrictions. Such recognition is not likely to come soon, and so we must look to the fruitful alliances among local community organizations, church groups, NGO's, health centers, and political action campaigns that have formed a vital global disability rights movement. Under the motto, "Nothing About Us Without Us," this network of nonaligned organizations is providing both access and knowledge across—and in some cases against—the economic landscape that often confuses "development" with "growth."

NOTES

1. James I. Charlton, *Nothing About Us Without Us: Disability, Oppression and Empowerment.* (Berkeley: U of California Press, 2000), p. 8. See also Lennard Davis, *Enforcing Normalcy: Disability, Deafness, and the Body* (London: Verso, 1995), p. 7.

2. World Health figures quoted in *Dying for Growth: Global Inequality and the Health of the Poor,* ed. Jim Young Kim et al, (Monroe, Maine: Common Courage Press, 2000), p. 4.

3. Paul Farmer, "Introduction." *Global AIDS: Myths and Facts.*(Cambridge: South End Press, 2003), p. xvii.

4. *Dying for Growth,* p. 25.

5. Louise Bourgault, *Playing for Life: Performance in Africa in the Age of AIDS.* (Durham: Carolina Academic Press, 2003), p. 261.

6. James Charlton, "The Disability Rights Movement as a Counter-Hegemonic Popular Social Movement." Unpublished MS, p. 5. See also David Levi Strauss, "Broken Wings," in *Between the Eyes: Essays on Photography and Politics* (New York: Aperture, 2003), pp. 56–64.

7. Nayan Shah, *Contagious Divides: Epidemics and Race in San Francisco's Chinatown* (Berkeley: U of California Press, 2001).

8. Chris Holden and Peter Beresford, "Globalization and Disability," *Disability Studies Today,* ed. Colin Barnes, Mike Oliver, and Len Barton (London: Polity Press, 2002), p. 194.

9. On "structural violence," see Johan Galtung, "Violence, Peace and Peace Research." *Journal of Peace Research* 3 (1969), p. 171. See also *Dying for Growth* (pp. 102–4) and Paul Farmer, *Pathologies of Power: Health, Human Rights, and the New War on the Poor* (Berkeley: U of California Press, 2003), pp. 29–50.

10. This ad appeared in *Scientific American* 231:1 (July 1974), p. 9.

11. See, for example, Lennard Davis, *Bending Over Backwards: Disability, Dismodernism and Other Difficult Positions* (New York: New York U Press, 2002), p. 25.

12. For discussions of global disability from a social science perspective see the following: Brigitte Holzer, Arthur Vreede, Gabriele Weight, ed. *Disability in Different Cultures: Reflections on Local Concepts* (New Brunswick: Transaction Publishers, 1999); Benedicte Ingstad and Susan Reynolds Whyte, ed. *Disability and Culture* (Berkeley:

U of California Press, 1995); Mark Priestley, ed. *Disability and the Life Course: Global Perspectives* (Cambridge: Cambridge U Press, 2001).

13. J. Hanks quoted in Colin Barnes and Geof Mercer, *Disability* (London: Polity Press, 2003), p. 135.

14. Arjun Appadurai, *Modernity at Large: Cultural Dimensions of Globalization* (Minneapolis: U of Minnesota Press 1996), p. 33.

15. Keith Wailoo, *Dying in the City of the Blues: Sickle Cell Anemia and the Politics of Race and Health* (Chapel Hill: U of North Carolina Press, 2001), p. 6. On the "space" of disease, see Keith Wailoo, "Inventing the Heterozygote: Molecular Biology, Racial Identity, and the Narratives of Sickle Cell Disease, Tay-Sachs, and Cystic Fibrosis." *Race, Nature, and the Politics of Difference,* ed. Donald S. Moore, Jake Kosek, and Anand Pandian (Durham: Duke U Press, 2004), pp. 236–53. Charles Rosenberg and Janet Golden, eds. *Framing Disease: Studies in Cultural History* (New Brunswick: Rutgers U Press, 1992).

16. Howard Frumkin, Mauricio Hernandez-Avila, Felipe Espinsoa Torres, "Maquiladoras: A Case Study of Free Trade Zones." *Occupational and Environmental Health* 1.2 (April/June, 1995): 96-109. See also Joel Brenner, Jennifer Ross, Janie Simmons, and Sarah Zaidi, "Neoliberal Trade and Investment and the Health of *Maquiladora* Workers on the U.S.-Mexico Border." *Dying for Growth,* pp. 261–90.

17. Keith Wailoo, *Dying in the City of the Blues,* 10–11.

18. David T. Mitchell and Sharon L. Snyder, *Narrative Prosthesis: Disability and the Dependencies of Discourse* (Ann Arbor: U of Michigan Press, 2001).

19. Ato Quayson, *Calibrations,* p. 117.

20. See, for example, David Held and Anthony McGrew, ed. *The Global Transformations Reader: An Introduction to the Globalization Debate* (Cambridge: Polity, 2000); Jim Young Kim, et al, *Dying for Growth*; Rob Wilson and Wimal Dissanayake, ed. *Global/Local: Cultural Production and the Transnational Imaginary* (Durham: Duke U Press, 1996; Amitava Kumar, ed. *World Bank Literature* (Minneapolis: U of Minnesota Press, 2003); Fredric Jameson and Masao Miyoshi, ed. *The Cultures of Globalization* (Durham: Duke U Press, 1999; Joseph E. Stiglitz, *Globalization and its Discontents* (New York: Norton, 2003).

21. Gillian Hart, *Disabling Globalization: Places of Power in Post-Apartheid South Africa* (Berkeley: U of California Press, 2002).

22. Richard Wolff, "World Bank/Class Blindness," *World Bank Literature,* ed. Amitava Kumar

(Minneapolis: U of Minnesota Press, 2003), pp. 174–83.

23. Walt Bogdanich and Eric Koli, "2 Paths of Bayer Drug in 80's: Riskier Type Went Overseas." *New York Times* (May 22, 2003), C5.

24. In contrast, Cuba initiated an HIV screening program early, once it was suspected that HIV was blood borne. According to Paul Farmer, in 1983 Cuba "banned the importation of factor VIII and other hemo-derivatives, and the Ministry of Public Health ordered the destruction of twenty thousand units of blood product." These actions have resulted in Cuba's having one of the lowest incidence of HIV infection in the western hemisphere. Farmer, *Pathologies of Power*, 70.

25. Nuria Homedes, "The Disability-Adjusted Life Year (DALY) Definition, Measurement and Potential Use." Human Capital Development and Operations Policy Working Papers available at http://www.worldbank.org/html/extdr/hnp/hddflash/workp/wp_00068.html, 3. See also David Wasserman et al. eds. *Quality of Life and Human Difference* (Cambridge: Cambridge U Press, 2005).

26. Homedes, 8.

27. Nirmala Erevelles, "Disability in the New World Order: The Political Economy of World Bank Intervention in (Post/Neo)colonial Context." (Unpublished manuscript, p. 5)

28. This aspect of globalization is developed in Lisa Lowe, "The Metaphoricity of Globalization." Unpublished MS, p. 3. I am grateful to Professor Lowe for allowing me to see this unpublished manuscript.

29. On the 1994 devaluation, see Manthia Diawara, "Toward a Regional Imaginary in Africa." *World Bank Literature*, p. 65.

30. On the cultural function of West African markets, see Diawara, pp. 73–80.

31. Nancy Sheper-Hughes, "The End of the Body: The Global Traffic in Organs for Transplant Surgery," available at http://www.sunsite.berkeley.edu/biotech/organsswatch/pages/cadraft.html

32. Lawrence Cohen, "Where it Hurts: Indian Material for an Ethics of Organ Transplantation." *Daedalus* 128:4 (Fall, 1999), pp. 4–5.

33. On rumor and organ trafficking see Scheper-Hughes, "Theft of Life: The Globalization of Organ Stealing Rumours." *Anthropology Today*, vol. 12, no. 3 (June, 1996), pp. 3–11; Claudia Castaneda, *Figurations: Child, Bodies, Worlds* (Durham: Duke U Press, 2002).

34. Manjula Padmanabhan, *Harvest. Postcolonial Plays: An Anthology*, Ed. Helen Gilbert (London: Routledge, 2001), pp. 214–49.

35. Stephen Frears, *Dirty Pretty Things* (Miramax and BBC Films, 2003).

36. On Theatre for Development, see *African Theatre in Development*, ed. Martin Banham, James Gibbs, Femi Osofisan, ed.(Bloomington, U of Indiana Press, 1999); *Politics and Performance: Theatre, Poetry and Song in Southern Africa*, ed. Liz Gunner (Johannesburg: Witwatersrand U Press, 2001); Louise M. Bourgault, *Playing for Life: Performance in Africa in the Age of AIDS* (Durham: Caroline Academic Press, 2003).

37. "Yiriba" is discussed in Louise Bourgault, *Playing for Life: Performance in Africa in the Age of AIDS*, pp. 132–38. A CD-ROM accompanies the book that includes clips of plays, dances, songs, and "edutainment" performances.

38. Bourgault, p. 137.

39. James Clifford, *Routes: Travel and Translation in the Late Twentieth-Century* (Cambridge: Harvard U Press, 1997).

40. Documentation of judicial responses to the ADA can be seen in *Backlash Against the ADA: Reinterpreting Disability Rights*, Linda Hamilton Kriger, ed. (Ann Arbor: U of Michigan Press, 2003).

41. Nancy Fraser, *Justice Interruptus: Critical Reflections on the 'Postsocialist' Condition* (New York: Routledge, 1997), p. 12.

42. Michael Berube, "Citizenship and Disability." *Dissent* (Spring, 2003), p. 3.

43. Berube, p. 3.

CHAPTER 11

The Dimensions of Disability Oppression

James Charlton

The vast majority of people with disabilities have always been poor, powerless, and degraded. Disability oppression is a product of both the past and the present. Some aspects of disability oppression are remnants of ancien régimes of politics and economics, customs and beliefs, and others can be traced to more recent developments. To understand the consequences and implications for people with disabilities an analysis is called for which considers how the overarching structures of society influence this trend. This is especially relevant in light of the United Nations' contention that their condition is worsening: "Handicapped people remain *outcasts* around the world, living in shame and squalor among populations lacking not only in resources to help them but also in understanding. And with their numbers growing rapidly, their plight is getting worse. . . . The normal perception is that nothing can be done for disabled children. This has to do with prejudice and old-fashioned thinking that this punishment comes from God, some evil spirits or magic. . . . We have a catastrophic human rights situation. . . . They [disabled persons] are a group without power."[1]

There is a great deal to say about disability oppression, not only because it is complex and multifaceted but also because we have so little experience conceptualizing its phenomenology and logic. Until very recently most analyses of why people with disabilities have been and continue to be poor, powerless, and degraded have been mired in an anachronistic academic tradition that understands the "status" of people with disabilities in terms of deviance and stigma. This has been compounded by the lack of participation by people with disabilities in these analyses. Fortunately, this has begun to change. Disability rights activists have recently undertaken important and fruitful efforts to frame disability oppression. These projects, however insightful, have been limited by their scope and inability to account for the systemic nature of disability oppression. For example, in the article "Malcolm Teaches Us, Too," in the *Disability Rag*, Marta Russell writes,

> Malcolm's most important message was to love blackness, to love black culture. Malcolm insisted that loving blackness itself was an act of resistance in a white dominated society. By exposing the internalized racial self-hatred that deeply penetrated the psyches of U.S. colonized black people, Malcolm taught that blacks could decolonize their minds by coming to blackness to be spiritually renewed, transformed. He believed that, only then, could blacks unite to gain the equality they rightfully deserved. . . . It is equally important for disabled persons to recognize

what it means to live as a disabled person in a physicalist society—that is, one which places its value on physical agility. When our bodies do not work like able-bodied person's bodies, we're disvalued. Our oppression by able-bodied persons is rife with the message: There is something wrong, something "defective" with us—because we have a disability. . . . We must identify with ourselves and others like us. Like Malcolm sought for his race, disabled persons must build a culture which will unify us and enable us to gain our human rights.

(1994: 11–12)

There is much of value for the DRM in what Russell says. She is patently correct, for instance, to point people with disabilities toward Malcolm X in terms of recognition and identity, self-hatred and self-respect. But she, like Malcolm X, is wrong on the question of where the basis of oppression lies. Both identify oppression with the Other, a view that is quite prevalent among disability rights activists. For Russell, the Other is able-bodied people; for Malcolm, it was white people (although he began to change this view shortly before his assassination). Both situate oppression in the realm of the ideas of others and not in systems or structures that marginalize people for political-economic and sociocultural reasons. As the great Mexican novelist Julio Cortazar writes in *Hopscotch*, "Nothing can be denounced if the denouncing is done within the system that belongs to the thing denounced" ([1966]1987: chap. 99). My project then is as much a polemic directed at the disability rights movement as at a more general public. My point to other activists is that the logic of disability oppression closely parallels the oppression of other groups. It is a logic bound up with political-economic needs and belief systems of domination. From these priorities and values has evolved a world system dominated by the laws of capital and profit and the ethos of individualism and image

worship. This point is just as important as my call to the general public, especially the international community, to recognize and respond to an extraordinary human rights tragedy, what former UN Secretary General Javier Perez de Cuellar once called "the silent emergency."

POLITICAL ECONOMY AND THE WORLD SYSTEM

Political economy is crucial in constructing a theory of disability oppression because poverty and powerlessness are cornerstones of the dependency people with disabilities experience. As the social science of how politics and economics influence and limit everyday life, political economy is primarily concerned with issues of class because class positions groups of people in relation to economic production and exchange, political power and privilege. Today, class not only structures the political and economic relationships between the worker, peasant, farmer, intellectual, small-scale entrepreneur, government bureaucrat, army general, banker, and industrialist, it mediates family and community life insofar as relationships exist in these which affect people's economic viability.[2] In political-economic terms, everyday life is informed by where and how individuals, families, and communities are incorporated into a world system dominated by the few who control the means of production and force. This has been the case for a long time. The logic of this system regulates and explains who survives and prospers, who controls and who is controlled, and, not simply metaphorically, who is on the inside and who is on the outside (of power).

Perhaps the most fitting characterization of the socioeconomic condition of people with disabilities is that they are outcasts. This is how they are portrayed in the UN report cited at the beginning of this chapter. It was also repeated by many of the disability rights activists I interviewed. It seems reasonable to ask, why is this depiction so common? The answer is two-sided, sociocultural and political-economic. On one side are the panoply of reactionary and iconoclastic attitudes about disability. These are addressed briefly in the next section and in depth in chapter 4. On the other side stands a political-economic formation that does not need and in fact cannot accommodate a vast group of people in its production, exchange, and reproduction. Put differently, people with disabilities, like many others, are preponderantly part of a worldwide phenomenon that James O'Connor called "surplus population" (1973: 161)[3] and Istvan Meszaros called "superfluous people" (1995: 702).

The extent and implications of this phenomenon are experienced differently. For example, it is readily apparent that people, even those with disabilities, living in the more economically developed regions of the world have higher "standards of living" than their counterparts in the Third World. The United States and Europe have safety nets that catch "outcasts" before their very livelihoods are called into question. This is not necessarily the case in the Third World.

The 300 million to 400 million people with disabilities who live in the periphery, like the vast majority of people in those regions, exist in abject poverty, but I would go further and argue that, for social and cultural reasons, their lives are even more difficult. These are the poorest and most powerless people on earth.

As the global economy developed, it created more than just the wandering gypsies of southern Europe and the *posseiros* (squatters) of South America. It created an enormous number of outcasts who must be set apart from what Karl Marx called the "reserve army of labor"—a resource to be tapped in times of economic expansion (although Marx uses them interchangeably

in *Grundrisse* [1973: 491]). For hundreds of millions of outcasts—beggars and others who depend on charity for survival; prostitutes, drug dealers, and others who survive through criminal activities; the homeless, refugees, and others forced to live somewhere besides their home or homeland;[4] and many others—will seldom, if ever, under ordinary circumstances be used in the production, exchange, and distribution of political and economic goods and services. They are essentially declassed. So many people fall into this category that U.S. economists have created the category "underclass" to refer to them. The UN has even created the preposterous category "admissible levels of poverty" to describe the condition of the best-off among these people.

People with disabilities, at least as a group, may have been the first to join the ranks of the underclass. Since feudalism and even earlier, they have lived outside the economy and political process.[5] It should be noted, of course, that few people with physical disabilities survived for very long in precapitalist economies.

The emergence and development of capitalism had an extraordinarily profound and positive impact on people with disabilities. For the first time, probably in the mid-1700s in parts of Europe, people living outside the spheres of production and exchange, the "surplus people," could rely on others to survive. Family members and friends who could accumulate more than the barest minimum necessary for survival had the "luxury" of being able to care for others. A century later the political-economic conditions were such that charities, which supported a large number of people, were established. Those who were cared for by these charities most often were the mentally ill, the blind, the alcoholic, the chronically ill. My analysis throughout this book centers on the political-economic and sociocultural relationships born out of these times and how they have developed differently in different economic zones and in different cultures. Essentially, I will argue, as Audre Lorde does in *Sister Outsider*, that these formations now not only stand as barriers to progress but also are the basis for peoples' oppression: "Institutionalized rejection of *difference* is an absolute necessity in a profit economy which needs outsiders as surplus people. As members of such an economy, we have *all* been programmed to respond to the human differences between us with fear and loathing and to handle that difference in one of three ways: ignore it, and if that is not possible, copy it if we think it is dominant, or destroy it if we think it is subordinate. But we have no patterns for relating across our human differences as equals. As a result, those differences have been misnamed and misused in the service of separation and confusion" (1984: 77).

CULTURE(S) AND BELIEF SYSTEMS

The modern world is composed of thousands of cultures, each with its own ways of thinking about other people, nature, family and community, social phenomena, and so on. Culture is sustained through customs, rituals, mythology, signs and symbols, and institutions such as religion and the mass media. Each of these informs the beliefs and attitudes that contribute to disability oppression. These attitudes are almost universally pejorative. They hold that people with disabilities are pitiful and that disability itself is abnormal. This is one of the social norms used to separate people with disabilities through classification systems that encompass education, housing, transportation, health care, and family life.

For early anthropologists, "culture" meant how values were attached to belief systems (Kroeber and Kluckhorn 1952: 180–182). Since then the meaning of the term "culture" has become so contested

that some have argued for its abandonment. Others consider it simply a "lived experience" or "lived antagonistic experiences." For Clifford Geertz, one of anthropology's preeminent theorists, the "culture concept . . . denotes a historically transmitted pattern of meanings embodied in symbols, a system of inherited conceptions expressed in symbolic forms by means of which men communicate, perpetuate, and develop their knowledge and attitudes toward life" (1973: 89). Geertz's theory has many adherents, but it has also garnered its share of criticism, most commonly that it neglects the influence of politics and power. In *Ideology and Modern Culture*, John Thompson postulates a more reasonable position. Thompson's formulation is that the study of symbols as a way to interpret cultures must be done contextually, by recognizing that power relations order the experiences of everyday life in which these signs and symbols are produced, transmitted, and received:

> The symbolic conception is a suitable starting point for the development of a constructive approach to the study of cultural phenomena. But the weakness of this conception—in the form it appears, for instance, in the writings of Geertz—is that it gives insufficient attention to the structured social relations within which symbols and symbolic actions are always embedded. Hence, I formulate what I call the structural conception of culture. Cultural phenomena, according to this conception, may be understood as symbolic forms in structured contexts, and cultural analysis may be construed as the study of the meaningful constitution and social contextualization of symbolic forms.
>
> (1990: 123)

My notion of culture(s) is similar to Thompson's. Contrary to many traditions in anthropology, cultures are not independent or static formations. They interface and interact in the everyday world with history, politics and power, economic conditions and institutions, and nature. To neglect these important influences seems to miss important interstices where culture happens, is expressed, and, most important, is experienced. The point is not that one culture makes people do or think this and another that but that ideas and beliefs are informed by and in cultures and that cultures are partial expressions of a world in which the dualities of domination/subordination, superiority/inferiority, normality/abnormality are relentlessly reinforced and legitimized. Anthropologists may be able to find obscure cultures in which these dualities are not determinant, but this does not minimize their overarching influence.

The essential problem of recent anthropological work on culture and disability is that it perpetuates outmoded beliefs and continues to distance research from lived oppression. Contributors to Benedicte Ingstad and Susan Reynolds Whyte's *Disability and Culture* seem to be oblivious to the extraordinary poverty and degradation of people with disabilities. The book does add to our understanding of how the conceptualization and symbolization of disability takes place, but its language and perspective are still lodged in the past. In the first forty pages alone we find the words *suffering, lameness, interest group, incapacitated, handicapped, deformities.* Notions of oppression, dominant culture, justice, human rights, political movement, and self-determination are conspicuously absent. We can read hundreds of pages without even contemplating degradation. Unlike these anthropologists and of course many others, my thesis is that backward attitudes about disability are not the basis for disability oppression, disability oppression is the basis for backward attitudes.

(FALSE) CONSCIOUSNESS AND ALIENATION

The third component of disability oppression is its psychological internalization.

This creates a (false) consciousness and alienation that divides people and isolates individuals. Most people with disabilities actually come to believe they are less normal, less capable than others. Self-pity, self-hate, shame, and other manifestations of this process are devastating for they prevent people with disabilities from knowing their real selves, their real needs, and their real capabilities and from recognizing the options they in fact have. False consciousness and alienation also obscure the source of their oppression. They cannot recognize that their self-perceived pitiful lives are simply a perverse mirroring of a pitiful world order. In this regard people with disabilities have much in common with others who also have internalized their own oppression. Marx called this "the self-annihilation of the worker" and Frantz Fanon "the psychic alienation of the colonized." In *Femininity and Domination*, Sandra Lee Bartky exposes the roles of alienation, narcissism, and shame in the oppression of women. Each of these examples highlights the centrality of consciousness to any discussion of oppression. Consciousness, like culture, means different things to different people. Carl Jung said it is "everything that is not unconscious." Sartre said "consciousness is being" or "being-in-itself." For the Egyptian novelist Naguib Moufouz, it is "an awareness of the concealed side." Recently there have been attempts to develop a neurobiological theory of consciousness, the best known of which is Gerald Edelman's *The Remembered Present* (1989).

Whole philosophical systems and schools of psychology are built on the concept of consciousness. Appropriately, most postulate stages or types, even archetypes of consciousness. For Jung, everything important was interior, was "thought." The highest consciousness was individuation, or self-realization (the "summit"). This required gaining command of all four thought functions: sensation, feeling, thinking, and intuition. When one arrives at the intersection of these functions, "one opens one's eyes" (Campbell 1988: xxvi–xxx).

Marxism typically understood consciousness as metaphorical spirals of practice (experience) and theory (thought) intertwined. These spirals move incrementally, quantitatively. Consciousness, however, is not a linear progression. At points this quantitative buildup congeals into a "rupture," or a qualitative or transformational leap to another stage of consciousness where another spiral-like phenomenon begins. Consciousness can leap from being-in-itself (existence as is) to being-for-itself (consciously desiring change), Marx's equivalent of a leap in self-realization. While Jung's and, before him, Freud's great contribution to modern psychology was the discovery of the importance of the unconscious, their systems excluded political and social conditions. They were asocial and apolitical. This is where idealism (e.g., Jung, Hegel) and materialism (e.g., Marx, Sartre) split most dramatically. Sartre's withering critique of psychology began with this difference. According to Sartre, "the Ego is not in consciousness, which is utterly translucent, but in the world" (Sartre [1943] 1957: xii). For Sartre, consciousness has three stages, being-in-itself, being-for-itself, and being-for-others, which reflects a growing awareness. He argues that consciousness is intentional, it has a direction. In his attack on traditional psychology, Sartre is saying one must step back and ponder reality (there is a "power of withdrawal") because reality has a thoroughgoing impact on consciousness.

Consciousness is an awareness of oneself and the world. Furthermore, consciousness has depth, and as one moves through this space one's perception of oneself and the world changes. This does not automatically entail greater self-clarity. Movement through this "space-depth" is contingent on factors such as intelligence, curiosity, character, personality, experience, and chance; political-economic and cultural structures (class, race, gender, disability, age, sexual preference); and social institutions.

Evolution of consciousness depends on how one perceives and what questions one asks. What one concludes from the thousands of impulses and impressions one receives throughout life depends on, following Albert Einstein, where the observer is and how he or she observes. Take sunsets as an example. We "see" sunsets. But how we see a sunset depends on the weather (e.g., clouds), who we are with and our state of mind at the time, the vantage point (boat, beach, high-rise building), and so on. How we see a sunset is dependent on what we think a sunset is. For many, it is the descent of the sun below the perceived horizon. I can confirm this personally, having watched tourists jump into their tour bus immediately after the sun disappears. For others, the sunset continues until the sun's rays shine back against the darkening sky and produce a sublime radiance.

The point is that consciousness cannot be separated from the real world, from politics and culture. There is an important relationship between being and consciousness.[6] Social being informs consciousness, and consciousness informs being. There is a mutual interplay. Consciousness is not a container that ideas and experiences are poured into. Consciousness is a process of awareness that is influenced by social conditions, chance, and innate cognition.

People are sometimes described as not having consciousness. This is not so. Everyone has consciousness; it is just that for some, probably most, that consciousness is partially false. From childhood, people are constantly bombarded with the values of the dominant culture. These values reflect the "naturalness" of superiority and inferiority, dominance and subordination.

POWER AND IDEOLOGY

The greatest challenge in conceptualizing oppression of any kind is understanding how it is organized and how it is reproduced. It is relatively easy to outline general characteristics such as poverty, degradation, exclusion, and so on. But to answer these questions, we must examine the diffuse circuitry of power and ideology. This exercise is particularly difficult because power and ideology not only organize the way in which individuals experience politics, economics, and culture, they contradictorily obscure or illuminate why and how the dimensions of (disability) oppression are reproduced.

Oppression is a phenomenon of power in which relations between people and between groups are experienced in terms of domination and subordination, superiority and inferiority. At the center of this phenomenon is control. Those with power control; those without power lack control. Power presupposes political, economic, and social hierarchies, structured relations of groups of people, and a system or regime of power. This system, the existing power structure, encompasses the thousands of ways some groups and individuals impose control over others.

Power is diffuse, ambiguous, and complicated: "Power is more general and operates in a wider space than force; it includes much more, but is less dynamic. It is more ceremonious and even has a certain measure of patience. . . . [S]pace, hope, watchfulness and destructive intent, can be called the actual body of power, or, more simply, power itself" (Canetti [1962] 1984: 281). It is not simply a system of oppressors and oppressed. There are many kinds and experiences of power: employer/employee, men/women, dominant race/subordinated race, parent/child, principal/teacher, teacher/student, doctor/patient, to name some. Power more accurately should be considered power(s). These power relations are irreducible products of history. These histories of power(s) collectively make up the regime of power informing the manner and method of governing.

Power should not be confused with rule, however. A ruling class, historically forged by political and economic factors, governs. But other privileged groups and individuals have and exercise power. In the obscure vernacular of French philosophy, the relationship of power between those who are privileged and those who are not is *overdetermined* by class rule.[7]

There are many ways for significantly empowered classes and groups to exercise and maintain power. All regimes, regardless of political philosophy, have ruled through a combination of force and coercion, legitimation and consent. In the Western democracies and parts of the Third World, consent is prevalent and force seldom used. In many parts of the Third World, though, state-sponsored repression is common. The repressive practices of Third World dictatorships are well known and documented. In these countries there exists a pathology between military control and consent. People fear the government and the military because these institutions promote fear through constant harassment and repression.

The primary method through which power relations are reproduced is not physical—military force and state coercion—but metaphysical—people's consent to the existing power structure. This is certainly the case for the hundreds of millions of people with disabilities throughout the world. In chapter 5, I analyze the passive acquiescence of people with disabilities, individually and collectively, in the face of extraordinary lived oppression.

The passive acquiescence to oppression is partially based in what the British cultural historian Raymond Williams has called the "spiritual character" of power:

"In particular, ideology needs to be studied to find out how it justifies and boosts the economic activities of particular classes; that is, the study of ideology enables us to study the intention of the articulate classes and the spiritual character of a particular class's rule" (1973: 6). Williams is suggesting that the dominant classes and culture constantly and everywhere impress on people the naturalness or normality of their power and privilege. Williams, following Antonio Gramsci, called this process *hegemony*.[8] Hegemony is projected multidimensionally and multidirectionally. It is not projected like a motion picture projects images. The impulses and impressions, beliefs and values, standards and manners are projected more like sunlight. Hegemony is diffuse and appears everywhere as natural. It (re)enforces domination not only through the (armed) state but also throughout society: in families, churches, schools, the workplace, legal institutions, bureaucracy, and culture.

Schooling is a particularly notable example of this process because it cuts across so many boundaries and affects so many, including people with disabilities. If, as we are led to believe, the mission of schooling is teaching and learning, then the logical questions are, who gets to teach? what is taught? how do students learn? and, most important, why? First, let me suggest that schooling has two principal "political" functions. Its narrow purpose is to teach acquiescence to power structures operating in the educational arena. Its broad purpose is to teach acquiescence to the larger status quo, especially the discipline of its workforce.

How does this work? First teachers are trained. Then their training (knowledge) is certified and licensed. Education is "professionalized." Teachers become educational experts. Students sit in rows, all pointing toward this repository of knowledge. The teacher pours his or her knowledge into the students' "empty" heads didactically. There is little sharing of knowledge between the teacher and the student,[9] for the teacher has learned that the process is unidirectional. The curriculum itself is standardized and licensed by state education officials, often the same body that licenses teachers. Moreover, administrators are far removed from the classroom, their only regular contact with students being discipline. They allow little innovation and flexibility. Many administrators continue the same rules and programs for decades. Power comes from above. Everyone and everything in the schooling process is authorized. Students are, in Jürgen Habermas's term, *steered*. Numerous studies have shown that girls are treated differently from boys regardless of the teacher's gender. Students from some families are encouraged and others discouraged. Some, for example, students with disabilities, are segregated in different schools or classrooms.[10]

The latter point is particularly important for understanding the fundamental connections between ideology and power as they relate to disability. Students with disabilities, as soon as their disability is recognized by school officials, are placed on a separate track. They are immediately labeled by authorized (credentialed) professionals (who never themselves have experienced these labels) as LD, ED EMH, and so on. The meaning and definition of the labels differ, but they all signify inferiority on their face. Furthermore, these students are constantly told what they can (potentially/expect to) do and what they cannot do from the very date of their labeling. This happens as a natural matter of course in the classroom.

All activists I interviewed who had a disability in grade school or high school told similar kinds of horror stories—detention and retention, threats and insults, physical and emotional abuse. In Chicago, I have colleagues and friends who were told they could not become teachers because they used wheelchairs; colleagues and friends who are deaf and went through twelve years of school without a single teacher who was proficient in sign language (they were told it was good for them because they should learn to read lips). I have visited segregated schools that required its personnel to wear white lab coats (to impress on the disabled students that they were first and foremost sickly). I know of a student art exhibition that was canceled because some drawings portrayed the students growing up to be doctors and other "unrealistic vocations."

It is possible to identify numerous ways that students with disabilities are controlled and taught their place: (1) labeling; (2) symbols (e.g., white lab coats, "Handicapped Room" signs); (3) structure (pull-out programs, segregated classrooms, "special" schools, inaccessible areas); (4) curricula especially designed for students with disabilities (behavior modification for emotionally disturbed kids, training skills without knowledge instruction for significantly mentally retarded students and students with autistic behavior) or having significant implications for these students; (5) testing and evaluation biased toward the functional needs of the dominant culture (Stanford-Binet and Wexler tests); (6) body language and disposition of school culture (teachers almost never look into the eyes of students with disabilities and practice even greater patterns of superiority and paternalism than they do with other students); and (7) discipline (physical restraints, isolation/time-out rooms with locked doors, use of Haldol and other sedatives).[11]

Special Education, like so many other reforms won by the popular struggle, has been transformed from a way to increase the probability that students with disabilities will get some kind of an education into a badge of inferiority and a rule-bound, bureaucratic process of separating and then warehousing millions of young people that the dominant culture has no need for. While this process is uneven, with a minority benefiting from true inclusionary practices, the overarching influences of race and class preclude any significant and meaningful equalization of educational opportunities.[12]

The sociopolitical implications of this process are clear to many disability rights activists.

Danilo Delfin: "Disability rights advocacy in Southeast Asia is very hard. Children are taught never to argue with their teacher. It is a long socialization process."

The Chicago educators and disability rights activists Carol Gill and Larry Voss interviewed twenty-one people who went through Special Education. Their survey respondents indicated that they believed that Special Education made them more passive and convinced them of their lot in life.[13]

We can begin to see the similarities between power and hegemony. Power, as Elias Canetti reminds us, is "more general and operates in a wider space than force," and hegemony, according to Raymond Williams, is "a whole body of practices and expectations, over the whole of living: our senses and assignments of energy, our shaping perceptions of ourselves and our world. It is a lived system of meaning and values . . . but a culture which has also to be seen as the lived dominance and subordination of particular classes" (Eagleton 1989: 110). The meanings and values of society are defined by the powerful. Hegemony is omnipresent. It is embedded in the social fabric of life.

One of the ironies of hegemony is that the dominant culture's success in inculcating its contrived value system is contingent on the extent to which that worldview makes sense. On one level, and I will consider this in greater detail later, the legitimation of the dominant culture, marked by acquiescence and consent, is founded on real-world experiences. This is what Ellen Meiksins Wood means when she writes in *The Retreat from Class,*

> What gives this political form its peculiar hegemonic power . . . is that the consent it commands from the dominated classes does not simply rest on their submission to an acknowledged ruling class or their acceptance of its right to rule. The parliamentary democratic state is a unique form of class rule because it casts doubt on the very existence of a ruling class. It does not achieve this by pure mystification. As always hegemony has two sides. It is not possible unless it is plausible.
>
> (1986: 149)

We can recognize this clearly when it comes to disability. People with disabilities are usually seen as sick and pitiful, and in fact many became disabled through disease and most live in pitiful conditions. Furthermore, most people with disabilities are only noticed when they are being lifted up steps, or walk into an obstacle, or are being assisted across a street. Historically, most people with disabilities live apart from the rest of society. Most people do not regularly interact with people with disabilities in the classroom, at work, at the movies, and so on. Instead of curing the social conditions that cause disease and desperation, or removing the steps that necessitate assistance, the dominant culture explains the pitiful conditions people are forced to live in by creating a stratum or group of "naturally" pitiful individuals to conceal its pitiful status quo. The dominant culture turns reality on its head.

Today the mass media play the greatest role in what Noam Chomsky and Edward Herman (1988) called "manufacturing consent" through the use of filters that select and shape information. Indeed, its role in creating and promoting images has grown exponentially in recent times as its capacity to project images has grown. The philosopher Roger Gottlieb links the mass media's role in maintaining order to creating an "authorized reality." He echoes Wood's earlier point that this created truth must actually reflect certain aspects of reality:

> In this complex sense, the media, like the state and the doctor, serve as authority figures. Their authority is derived from the compelling power of the images they produce—just as the authority of the medieval church derived from the size of its cathedrals. . . . And it is not foolishness or stupidity that leads us to take these images so seriously. It is the fact that real needs are manipulated into false hopes. Our needs for sexuality, love, community, an interesting life, family respect, and self-respect are transformed by the ubiquitous images of an unattainable reality into the sense that our sexuality, family, and personal lives are unreal. And it is this mechanism that sustains social authorities no longer believed to be legitimate.
>
> (1987: 156, 159)

What images of disability are most prevalent in the mass media? Television shows depicting the helpless and angry cripple as a counterpoint to a poignant story about love or redemption. Tragic news stories about how drugs or violence have "ruined" someone's life by causing him or her to become disabled, or even worse, stories of the heroic person with a disability who has "miraculously," against all odds, become a successful person (whatever that means) and actually inched very close to being "normal" or at least to living a "normal" life. Most despicable are the telethons "for" *crippled* people, especially, poor, pathetic, crippled children. These telethons parade young children in front of the camera while celebrities like Jerry Lewis pander to people's goodwill and pity to get their money. In the United States surveys have shown that more people form attitudes about disabilities from telethons than from any other source.[14]

These images merge nicely with the language used to describe people with disabilities.[15] Consider, for example, "cripple," "invalid," "retard." In Zimbabwe, the term is *chirema*, which literally translates as "useless." In Brazil, the term is *pena*, which is slang for an affliction that comes as punishment. These terms are evidence of how people with disabilities are dehumanized. The process of assigning "meaning" through language, signs, and symbols is relentless and takes place most significantly in families, religious institutions, communities, and schools.

The dehumanization of people with disabilities through language (as just one obvious example) has a profound influence on consciousness. They, like other oppressed peoples, are constantly told by the dominant culture what they cannot do and what their place is in society. The fact that most oppressed people accept their place (read: oppression) is not hard to comprehend when we consider all the ideological powers at work. Their false consciousness has little to do with intelligence. It does have to do with two interactive and mutually dependent sources. The first is the capacity of ruling regimes to instill its values in the mass of people through double-speak, misdirection (blame the victim), naturalized inferiority, and legitimated authority. This is *hegemony*. The second is the psychological devastation people experience which creates self-pity and self-annihilation and makes self-awareness, awareness of peers, and awareness of their own humanity extremely difficult. This is *alienation*. Hegemony and alienation are two sides of the same phenomenon—ideological domination.[16]

In the case of disability, domination is organized and reproduced principally by a circuitry of power and ideology that constantly amplifies the normality of domination and compresses difference into classification norms (through symbols and categories) of superiority and normality against inferiority and abnormality.

NOTES

1. Einar Helander, at a press conference on the release of the United Nations Report *Human Rights and Disabled Persons* (*Chicago Tribune*, December 5, 1993). Herlander has written a number of reports for the UN, including Prejudice and Dignity and, with Padmani Mendis, Gunnel Nelson, and Ann Goerdt, Training in the Disabled Community.

2. For example, unpaid domestic labor contributes to the socially necessary sustenance and nurturance of paid nondomestic labor, and the people, prominently women, involved in this work should be considered part of the laboring class. See Ferguson 1989.

3. O'Connor does not mean to imply that people defined as surplus are unnecessary. He means they are irrelevant to the present political-economic system. The notion of surplus people was explicitly developed to account for the treatment of people with mental retardation in Farber 1968.

4. To a great extent, exiles have avoided this "declassing." They have, at least in many cases, become incorporated into new economic milieus subsequent to their forced expulsion from their homeland.

5. Much has been written about precapitalist economic formations. There have been a number of efforts to refine the classification of their primitive, feudal, or semifeudal characteristics: "archaic" (Polanyi 1944); "tributary" (Amin 1990); "precapitalist" (Dobb 1946). Many have simply used the term "traditional."

6. This is in sharp distinction not only to psychology, as discussed earlier, but also to the German idealist philosophy of Kant, Hegel, and Schopenhauer. For these people separated society and being from consciousness and thought. For example, in *The Phenomenology of Mind* Hegel extinguishes any social relationship to truth or any civil or state (government) relationship to justice. Later, in *The Science of Logic*, he merged the two. Thought *is* being, and there is a distinction between reality and actuality.

7. Overdetermination is a theory associated primarily with Louis Althusser. Trying to avoid orthodox Marxism's theory that economic relations determine all social relations, he conceived the notion that the "superstructures" (language, law,

custom, religion, etc.) have their own "specific effectivity." But Althusser argues that these distinct realities are subject to the "determination in the last instance by the [economic] mode of production," although there is "the relative autonomy of the superstructures and their specific effectivity" (1964: 111). This is overdetermination. While I do not subscribe to Althusser's idea that superstructures (his structuralism), I do believe that overdetermination is an insightful way of thinking about relationships. In this case, while powers have their own specific effectivity, they are ordered by class rule. Once the ensemble of power relationships is configured or ordered, these relationships evolve primarily from their internal dynamics.

8. The theory of hegemony is one of the great contributions of the Italian communist Antonio Gramsci, who insisted that the principal way power was projected by the capitalist ruling class (Italy in the 1920s) was through hegemony or ideological domination. In his *The Two Revolutions* Carl Boggs argues that Gramsci's theory of hegemony penetrated the realm of power where ideology (most notably culture) and political economy met: "For Gramsci ideas, beliefs, cultural preferences, and even myths and superstitions possessed a certain material reality of their own since in their power to inspire people towards action, they interact with economic conditions, which other wise would be nothing more than empty abstractions" (1984: 158).

9. See Paulo Friere's "banking theory" in *The Pedagogy of the Oppressed* (1973)

10. Freire is probably the best-known theorist of hegemonic practices of schooling. He has been influential in developing counterhegemonic education. He is associated with literacy campaigns in Cuba, Guinea-Bissau, Nicaragua, and Brazil. In *Ideology, Culture, and the Process of Schooling*, the critical theorist and educator Henry Giroux writes, "According to Freire, it is the cultural institutions of the dominant elite that play a major role in inculcating the oppressed with myths and beliefs that later become anchored in their psyches and character structure. To the degree that repressive institutions are successful in universalizing the belief system of the oppressor class, people will consent to their own exploitation and powerlessness" (1988: 134).

Samuel Bowles and Herbert Gintis (1976), Michael Apple (1979), Henry Giroux (1988), Paulo Freire (1968, 1973, 1987), and Michel Focault (1980) successfully demonstrate the role of schooling in the production of a monoculture and the reproduction of existing power relations.

It is ironic that while the literature theorizing the hegemonic practices of schooling has burgeoned in recent years, the voices of radical educators, especially those critical theorists who have promoted such views, have been silent on disability, inclusion, and special education, where the oppression and control of students has been the greatest. While this omission of radical pedagogy does not compare to the common outrageous treatment of students with disabilities, it is just as telling of the status of students with disabilities.

11. Joseph Tropea's article, "Bureaucratic Order and Special Children," is useful because of its focus on the historical socioeconomic necessities that framed early attempts to warehouse "incorrigible, backward and otherwise defective pupils" (1987: 32)

12. The same regulations that are being used to provide students with access are also being implemented in such a way that many students are being inappropriately removed from regular education, resulting in questionable educational benefit and possible harm (Gartner and Lipsky 1987). This is particularly true in the area of high-incidence mild disabilities, the so-called educable mentally handicapped, learning disabled, and behaviorally/emotionally disordered. Special education is increasingly used to segregate students labeled "mildly handicapped"—students whom schools have difficulty serving or whom they choose not to serve. These programs often have a disproportionate enrollment of racial minority students. For instance, though African-American students make up 16 percent of the public school population, they represent 35 percent of those labeled educable mentally handicapped.

13. An unpublished paper that Gill and Voss developed at the Chicago Institute of Disability Research: "Inclusion Beyond the Classroom: Asking Persons with Disabilities About Education."

14. In 1993 the magazine Vanity Fair ran a series on telethons. Most of the commentary centered on the "worth" of a life with disability. This brought Paul Longmore's work to the fore. Longmore, a leading disability rights academic then at Stanford University, had decisively shown elsewhere that telethons promoting charities are the principal ideological mediums transmitting and inculcating attitudes about disability in the United States. Longmore writes that the four major telethons—Easter Seals, Arthritis Foundation, United Cerebral Palsy, and Muscular Dystrophy Association—reach a combined audience of 250 million people and their message "is hegemonic

in creating attitudes and ideas about disability" (Longmore, quoted in Bennets 1993: 2.

15. For the purposes of this book, I use the term "language" as it is commonly understood. I recognize that Ferdinand de Saussure in his Course in General Linguistics distinguished "language" from "speech" to argue that language is unable to be transformed, that it is an unconscious code. Emile Durkheim argued that this "split" was the basis of society. In this sense I am most often exploring speech, although I make the point numerous times that language, as it is used, is interiorized and its meaning inculcated.

16. Some people argue that ideology is partisan in that it is inherently at the service of the dominant culture; others argue that it is neutral and a contested terrain of ideas. Just before he died, Sartre defined ideology in the former terms: ""Ideology . . . is an ensemble of ideas which underlies alienated acts and reflects them. . . . Ideologies represent powers and are active. Philosophies are formed in opposition to ideologies, although they reflect them to a certain extent while at the same time criticizing them and going beyond them" (Schilpp 1991: 20). Sartre sees ideology as always partisan. Slavoj Zizek, editor of *Mapping Ideology*, thinks ideology is more limited and more neutral: "Ideology either exerts an influence that is crucial but constrained to some narrow social stratum, or its role in social reproduction is marginal" (1994: 14). For the purposes of this book it is most useful to think of ideology as a system of ideas and beliefs that are projected.

WORKS CITED

Althusser, Louis. 1964. *For Marx.* London: Verso.

Amin, Samir. 1990. *Maldevelopment: Anatomy of Global Failure.* London: Zed Press.

——, Arrighi, Giovanni; Gunder, Frank Andre; and Wallerstein, Immanuel. 1990. *Transforming the Revolution: Social Movements in the World System.* New York: Monthly Review Press.

Apple, Michael. 1979. *Ideology and Curriculum.* London: Routledge and Kegan Paul.

Bennets, L. 1993. "Letter from Las Vegas." *Vanity Fair* (September). 82–96

Boggs, Carl. 1984. *The Two Revolutions: Gramsci and the Dilemmas of Western Marxism.* Boston: South End Press.

Bowles, Samuel and Gintis, Herbert. 1976. *Schooling in Capitalist America.* New York: Basic Books.

Maurice, Dobb. 1946. *Studies in the Development of Capitalism.* London: Oxford University Press.

Farber, B. 1968. *Mental Retardation: Its Social Context and Social Consequences.* Boston: Houghton Mifflin.

Ferguson, Ann. 1989. *Blood at the Root.* London: Pandora.

Freire, P. 1987. *Education for Critical Consciousness.* New York: Continuum.

——. 1973. *The Pedagogy of the Oppressed.* New York: Seabury Press.

——. 1968. *Cultural Action for Freedom.* Cambridge, Mass: Center for the Study of Change.

Gartner, Alan, and Kerzner Lipsky, Dorothy. 1987. "Beyond Special Education:Toward a Quality System for All Students." *Harvard Educational Review* 57 (4): 367–396.

Giroux, Henry A. 1988. *Ideology, Culture, and the Process of Schooling.* Philadelphia: Temple University Press.

Polanyi, Karl. 1944. *The Great Transformation.* New York: Rinehart.

Schlipp, Paul Arthur, ed. 1991. *The Philosophy of Jean-Paul Sartre.* Lasalle, Ill: Open Court.

Tropea, Joseph. 1987. "Bureaucratic Order and Special Children: Urban Schools 1890s–1940s." *History of Education Quarterly* 27 (1): 29–52.

Zizek, Slavoj, ed. 1994. *Mapping Ideology.* London: Verso.

CHAPTER 12

A Mad Fight: Psychiatry and Disability Activism

Bradley Lewis

In the late summer of 2003, six people gathered at a small building in Pasadena, California and starved themselves for twenty-two days. The small group of hunger strikers were later joined by over a dozen "solidarity strikers" around the world. Their strike was about "human rights in mental health" and, in particular, it sought to protest the "international domination" of biological approaches to psychiatry and the ever-increasing and widespread use of prescription drugs to treat "mental and emotional crises" (Mindfreedom, July 28, 2003).

The hunger strike caught the attention of the *LA Times*, *The Washington Post* and, most important for those involved, the attention of the American Psychiatric Association (APA). One of the central aims of the strike was to challenge the main institutions in psychiatry—namely the American Psychiatric Association, the National Alliance of the Mentally Ill (NAMI) and the U.S. Surgeon General—and to rouse them into providing "evidence that clearly establishes the validity of 'schizophrenia,' 'depression' or other 'major mental illnesses' as biologically-based brain diseases" (Mindfreedom, July 28, 2003). The fasters demanded evidence that mental and emotional distress results from "chemical imbalances" in the brain; a view that underpins the biopsychiatric medical model and which currently dominates mental health treatment in the West.

In demanding this evidence, the strikers were taking a risk. Using a hunger strike to challenge psychiatry and its scientific findings (which are now almost ubiquitously accepted throughout the medical world and wider culture), the protestors faced the possibility of being labeled "mad"—after all, isn't psychiatry a science? Shouldn't scientific questions be decided in laboratories and in peer-reviewed articles filled with graphs and statistical analysis? What sense does it make to hold a hunger strike to challenge contemporary scientific beliefs?

The hunger strikers took the risk because, indeed, they are mad. They are all members of a psychiatry disability activist group known among their friends and allies as "Mad Pride." This activist group is an international coalition devoted to resisting and critiquing clinician-centered psychiatric systems, finding alternative and peer-run approaches to mental health recovery, and helping those who wish to do so minimize their involvement with current psychiatric institutions. They affectionately call themselves "Mad Pride" because they believe mainstream psychiatry over exaggerates psychic pathology and over enforces psychic conformity in the guise of diagnostic labeling and treatment—which all too often comes in the form of forced or manipulated hospitalizations, restraints, seclusions, and medications. Like the celebratory and reappropriative uses of the terms "Crip," "Queer," and "Black Pride," the term "Mad Pride" overturns traditional distinctions and hierarchies. It signifies a reversal of standard pathological connotations of "madness." Rather than pathologizing mental difference, Mad Pride signifies a stance of respect, appreciation, and affirmation.

In this chapter, I discuss the relation of Mad Pride to disability studies, review the history the movement, and work through its contemporary struggles with psychiatry. Throughout the discussion, I highlight the importance of Mad Pride's efforts to go beyond "politics-as-usual." Mad Pride, like other forms of "biocultural" activisms (such as Women's Health Movement and AIDS Coalition to Unleash Power), is located at the interface of bioscience and politics. As such, Mad Pride continuously struggles with epistemological issues along with more typical political issues. In short, the people in Mad Pride struggle over *both* truth and values.

This commingling of politics, power, and truth is familiar ground for disability studies. Similar to Mad Pride, disability studies unpacks and undermines stereotyped representations of disability in science and popular culture to understand and intervene in how "representation attaches meanings to bodies" (Garland-Thomson 1997, 5). Michael Oliver gives a good sense of these stereotyped disability representations by dividing them into key themes of "individualism," "medicalization," and "normality" (Oliver 1990, 56, 58). *Individualism* refers to the perspective that disability is a "personal tragedy." This frame undergirds a "hegemony of disability" which views disability as "pathological and problem-oriented" (Oliver 1996, 129).

It leads to a ubiquitous *medicalization* that legitimizes the medical infrastructure for acquiring knowledge about the disabled individual. The logic of this medical infrastructure rests on notions *normality* and the dichotomy between normal and pathological. The able-bodied and the disabled, the valued and the devalued, become co-constituted cultural divisions which structure medical and cultural preoccupations (Davis 1995). One side of the binary defines the other and both operate together as "opposing twin figures that legitimate a system of social, economic, and political empowerment justified by physiological differences" (Garland-Thomson 1997, 8).

Together, these stereotyped disability representations direct the health care industry toward a near exclusive focus on individual biomedical cures. Rather than adjust social environments to meet differing bodily needs, medical interventions seek to cure the individual "abnormal" body. Disability activists resist these individualizing and medicalizing approaches by reframing disability as a social restriction and oppression rather than simply a medical problem. Emphasizing a social model rather than a medical model they call attention to the fact that much of the suffering of different bodies comes from social exclusion, isolation, and lack of opportunity, along with the often pernicious side effects of a medical industry bent on aggressive intervention to achieve "normal" bodies.[1]

The task of undermining stereotyped representations of individualism, medicalization, and normality are also central to the Mad Pride movement. Individualistic approaches to mental difference and distress blame and punish the victim for structural problems that are often better understood as located in families, communities, and society. Medicalization, or psychiatrization, legitimizes the medical community's expert authority over the domain of mental difference. And the binary between normal and abnormal shores up this psychiatrization by providing tremendous social and psychological pressure to stay on the side of normality, or sanity. Disability studies scholars refer to social stigma and oppression against the physically different as "ableism"; those in Mad Pride refer to social stigma and oppression against mental difference as "mentalism" or "sanism" (Chamberlin 1977, 219; Perlin 2000, 21).

Despite these similarities, disability activists and Mad Pride members have had difficulty forming a sustained coalition. Part of this difficulty involves the simple fact that two groups are composed of different subcultures—with different histories, different cultural artifacts, and different networks of association. But, beyond this, there are other, deeper reasons. Some disability advocates continue to harbor sanist style associations toward mental difference and do not wish to be associated or "tarnished" by Mad Pride. Likewise, many in Mad Pride (like many in the Deaf community) express discomfort with the "disability" label. They do not see their mental difference as a disability, but rather as a valued capacity. In addition, many in Mad Pride feel that disability struggles are separate from their concerns because physical disability does not involve the same level of state coercion. People with physical differences are often inappropriately confined (through limited choices and multiple manipulations), but Mad Pride activists must deal with an additional layer of state sponsored coercion in the forms of involuntary commitment and forced medication laws.[2]

Like many in both movements, however, I believe it is wise to foreground the similarities between disability activism and Mad Pride. Clearly, all of the new social movements, in one way or another, have to struggle with both truth and values—largely because biomedical science has been used to justify such a broad range of subordination practices. But, more than most, Mad Pride and disability activism face a combined political and epistemological struggle. The very heart of these activisms begins with expressly biomedical assignments of impairment. This comes not in the form of a general pronouncement of inferiority, but in a direct and specific diagnosis and treatment process. Because of this, Mad Pride and disability activist efforts to reduce individualization, medicalization, and ableism require a dual struggle that goes beyond politics-as-usual. The challenge of this dual epistemological and political struggle requires all the allies you can get. When disability activist and Mad Pride work together, they can form a formidable coalition.

THE BIRTH OF MAD PRIDE MOVEMENT

Mad Pride activists have had extensive experience going beyond politics-as-usual. Their lesson of dual engagement goes back to the nineteenth century efforts of Mrs. Elizabeth Ware Packard, an early precursor to today's Mad Pride movement. In 1886, Packard, a former mental hospital patient and founder of the Anti-Insane Asylum Society, began publishing a series of books and pamphlets critical of psychiatry. Packard's writings challenged the subordination of women to their husbands and the remarkable complicity of the political and psychiatric establishment to this subordination (Packard 1868, 1874). As Gerald Grob explains, "When Packard refused to play the role of obedient [minister's] wife and expressed religious ideas bordering on mysticism, her husband had her committed in 1860 to the Illinois State Hospital for the Insane" (Grob 1994, 84). Packard remained incarcerated for three years and only won her freedom by going to court to challenge her confinement. The trial received national publicity and eventually led to Packard being declared sane by the court and released from the asylum. She spent the next twenty years campaigning for personal liberty laws that would protect individuals from wrongful commitment and retention in the asylums.

Even in this early precursor to today's movement, the issues of epistemological struggle and political struggle are inseparably intertwined. Packard challenged pathologizing diagnostic practices that would treat people as insane "simply for the expression of opinions, no matter how absurd these opinions may appear for others" (quoted in Geller and Harris 1994, 66). And she challenged the political abuses that occurred once the insanity diagnosis had been made. Lunatic asylums, she argued, too often left people at the complete mercy of hospital despotism where they were treated worse than convicts or criminals. Packard's dual stress on both the "facts" of insanity and the inhumane treatment of those considered to be insane reverberate into today's resistance to psychiatry.

The more proximate antecedents to today's Mad Pride movement began in the 1970's. Mad Pride activists, during these years, gained momentum from the black civil rights movement, the women's movement, and from the early stages of lesbian and gay movement and the disability movement. Like Elizabeth Packard almost a century before, the key experience that motivated Mad Pride activists was their negative treatment within the psychiatric system. Early founders of the movement shared common experiences of being treated with disrespect, disregard, and discrimination at the hands of psychiatry. Many also suffered from unjustified confinement, verbal and physical abuse, and exclusion from treatment planning.

The testimony of Leonard Roy Frank, cofounder of the Network Against Psychiatric Assault (1972), provides a helpful glimpse into the experiences of many. After graduating from Wharton, Frank moved to San Francisco to sell commercial real estate. He was in his own words "an extraordinarily conventional person" (Farber 1993, 191). Gradually, during his late twenties, he started discovering a new world within himself and began going through an "obvious clash between . . . my emerging self and that of my old self" (191). He later thought of this as a "spiritual transformation." But, at the time, he responded by doing serious reading and reflection on his emerging insights. He ended up rethinking everything in his life: "what was happening to me was that I was busy being born" (191).

A key text for Frank during his transformation was Mohandas Gandhi's autobiography. Frank took seriously Gandhi's message that one's inner life and outer life should interact and compliment each other. Reading Gandhi opened his eyes to the violence of political injustice and to the power of non-violent resistance. It also raised his awareness that animals had feelings and could suffer. The more Frank thought about Gandhi's writings on meat-eating, the more he concluded it was inescapably cruel to both animals and to humans: "We can't avoid harming ourselves when we harm other beings, whether human or animal. Meat-eating was an excellent example of how this principle played out in real life . . . Because it was inherently cruel to animals and morally wrong, it affected the wrong doers by causing them to become sick and cutting short their lives" (206). This combination of insights made it difficult for Frank to continue his previous lifestyle and his work selling commercial real estate; he soon lost his job, grew a beard, became vegetarian, and devoted himself to full time spiritual exploration.

Frank was exhilarated by the process, but his parents were deeply concerned. Seeing Frank's transition through the stereotyped frames of individualization, psychiatrization, and sanism, they thought he was having a "breakdown." They tried to persuade him to see a psychiatrist, but Frank resisted. They responded by arranging an involuntary commitment. The hospital records show that Frank's psychiatrists document symptoms of "not working, withdrawal, growing a beard, becoming a vegetarian, bizarre behavior, negativism, strong beliefs, piercing eyes, and religious preoccupations" (193). The psychiatrists diagnosed him as "paranoid schizophrenia," and they started a sustained course of court authorized insulin-electroshock treatments that lasted nine months and included fifty insulin comas and thirty-five electroshocks.

When the psychiatrists were not giving him shock treatments, their "therapeutic" interactions with Frank revolved around his behavior: particularly his refusal to shave or eat meat. There was never any discussion of his emerging beliefs or his spirituality. Instead, Frank's psychiatrists focused on changing overt signs of "abnormality." They even went so far as to shave his beard while he was unconscious from an insulin treatment. Frank eventually came to realize that his hospital resistance was futile, and, with the ever increasing numbers of shock treatments, he also came to fear he was in a "life or death" situation: "These so-called [shock] treatments literally wiped out all my memory for the [previous] two-year period . . . I realized that my high-school and college were all but gone; educationally, I was at about the eighth-grade level" (196).

Rather than risk more "treatments," Frank surrendered. He played the psychiatrists' game and did what they wanted: "I shaved voluntarily, ate some non vegetarian foods like clam chowder and eggs, was somewhat sociable, and smiled 'appropriately' at my jailers" (196). After his release, it took six years to recover from his treatment. But, throughout it all, he never gave up on his beliefs, and he never saw another psychiatrist for treatment. He went on to become a major figure in early Mad Pride activism.

During the early 1970's, people like Frank began to recognize they were not alone and started organizing local consciousness-raising groups. In the United States this includes such organization as the Insane Liberation Front in Portland Oregon (1970), the Mental Patient's Liberation Project in New York City (1971), and the Mental Patients' Liberation Front in Boston (1971). These groups built support programs, advocated for hospitalized patients, lobbied for changes in the laws, and educated the public through guest lectures and newsletters. In addition, they began the process of developing alternative, creative, and artistic ways of dealing with emotional suffering and psychological difference outside the medical models of psychiatry. The publication of Mad Pride activist Judi Chamberlin's book *On Our Own* (1977) in the mainstream press was a milestone in the development of peer run alternatives (Van Tosh & del Vecchio 2000, 9). Chamberlin used the book to expose her own abuse at the hands of psychiatry and to give a detailed account of burgeoning consumer run alternatives. The eloquence, optimism, and timing of the book was a critical catalyst for many in the movement. As ex-patient Mary O'Hagan puts it: "When my mood swings died away I was angry and amazed at how the mental health system could be so ineffective. There had to be a better way. I searched the library not quite knowing what I was looking for. And there it was, a book called *On Our Own* by Judi Chamberlin. It was all about ex-patients who set up their own alternatives to the mental health system and it set me on my journey in to the psychiatric survivor movement" (quoted in Chamberlin, 1977, back cover).

The newly formed local Mad Pride groups also organized an annual Conference on Human Rights and Psychiatric Oppression to help connect local members with the wider movement. At these meetings, activists from across the country gathered to socialize, strategize, and share experiences. They gained solidarity and increasing momentum from the experience of being with like minded activists. Between meetings local groups communicated through a newspaper forum. The San Francisco local newsletter, *Madness Network News*, evolved into a newspaper format which covered ex-patient activities across North America and around the world. This publication became the major voice of the movement, with each issue containing a rich selection of personal memoirs, creative writing, cartoons, humor, art, political commentary, and factual reporting—all from the ex-patient point of view (Hirsch 1974; Chamberlin 1990, 327).

This early period of the Mad Pride movement was also the most radical in its epistemological critique. Early leaders of the movement drew philosophical support from high-profile critical writers that, as a group, came to be known as "anti-psychiatry." Writers such as Erving Goffman (1961), R. D. Laing (1967), Thomas Scheff (1966), and Thomas Szasz (1961) may have differed widely in their philosophies, but collectively their main tenets were clear. Mental illness is not an objective medical reality but rather either a negative label or a strategy for coping in a mad world. As Laing put it, "the apparent irrationality of the single 'psychotic' individual" may often be understood "within the context of the family." And, in turn, the irrationality of the family can be understood if it is placed "within the context of yet larger organizations and institutions" (Laing 1968, 15). Put in context in this way, madness has a legitimacy of its own which is erased by medical-model approaches that can only pathologize it. For many anti-psychiatry writers, mental suffering can be the beginning of a healing process and should not be suppressed through aggressive behavioral or biological interventions.

The most epistemologically radical of the anti-psychiatry writers, Thomas Szasz, had the most influence on U.S. activists. Szasz, a dissident psychiatrist, was shunned within his own field, but his prolific writings (over twenty-five books) and forceful prose gave him tremendous influence outside psychiatry (Leifer 1997). Throughout his work, Szasz's argument was always two-fold: (1) mental illness is a myth and (2) there should be complete separation between psychiatry and the state. As Szasz put it in a summary statement, "Involuntary mental hospitalization is imprisonment under the guise of treatment; it is a covert form of social control that subverts the rule of law. No one ought to be deprived of liberty except for a criminal offense, after a trial by jury guided by legal rules of evidence. No one ought to be detained against their will in a building called 'hospital,' or any other medical institution, on the basis of expert opinion" (Szasz 1998).

Consistent with others in the Mad Pride movement, Szasz combined his epistemology and his politics. Szasz's insistence on the autonomy of mental health clients rested directly on his epistemology, which he based on a strong positivist philosophy of science that emphasized a sharp demarcation between observation and conjecture. For Szasz, *physical illness* was real because it was based on actual observation, but *mental illness* was at best a metaphor. A broken leg is real because you can see the x-ray, but a "broken brain" is a myth because there is no x-ray that will show it. For Szasz, to see mental illness as "real" rather than as a metaphor was to make a serious category mistake. "Mental illness" is not objectively observable; it is a myth.

MAD PRIDE TODAY

During the last thirty years of their struggle, Mad Pride has increasingly infiltrated the mental health system rather than simply criticizing it from outside. Despite the fact that institutional psychiatry continues to ignore and denigrate their efforts, important government agencies involved in mental health policy have begun to pay attention. Mad Pride activists have been particularly successful in increasing consumer participation in treatment planning and facility governance. In addition, they have gained increasing respect for the work developing peer run treatment alternatives.

The most important agency to pay attention to Mad Pride perspectives has been the national Center for Mental Health Services (CMHS). This little known public agency is "charged with leading the national system that delivers mental health services" (Center for Mental Health Services 2002). Following on the success of Chamberlin's *On Our Own*, the agency worked with a local California peer group to publish *Reaching Across: Mental Health Clients Helping Each Other*, a "how to" manual for peer run services (Zinnman, Harp, and Budd 1987). For too long, CMHS explains, "decisions about mental health policies and services were made without any input from people who have mental illnesses or their families. As a result, some policies and programs failed to meet the needs of the people they were intended to serve" (Center for Mental Health Services 2004) CMHS worked to change this by sponsoring peer-run research, training, and technical assistance centers, and producing federally mandated documents encouraging states to include consumer-operated alternatives to traditional treatment programs. Since 1985, CMHS has also sponsored an annual, national level, Alternatives Conference that brings together consumers and ex-patients to network and to share the results of their scholarship and program development.

These political successes have gradually necessitated a change in Mad Pride's epistemological critique. Szasz's strong epistemological critique of psychiatry was useful in the early days of the movement, but it became less so as Mad Pride shifted into its more contemporary formations. The early anti-psychiatry literature set up an either/or relation between consumers and providers. People had to either be with psychiatry or against it. Szasz's rigid positivist epistemology left little room for contradiction and coalition politics. As sociologist and Mad Pride activist Linda Morrison points out, with increasing infiltration of the mental health system, many members no longer took a hard-line approach to psychiatry. These members identified themselves more as "consumers" than "survivors" or "ex-patients." Consumers, by definition, were critical of aspects of psychiatry but were willing to legitimize and participate in other aspects (Morrison 2005). Mad Pride needed to embrace these contradictions and adopt coalition politics to avoid losing these members.

Contemporary Mad Pride members have made just this kind of epistemological shift. Though activists still reference Szasz favorably, they now draw more on his political values (of autonomy and separation of psychiatry and state) than on his epistemology. Mad Pride members mark this shifting epistemology by referring to themselves as "consumer/survivor/ex-patient" groups. This hyphenated designation, usually shortened to "c/s/x" or "consumer/survivors," highlights that today's Mad Pride is a coalition of critical activists—some whom have a more radical epistemological critique than others (Morrison 2005).

This shift has set the stage for additional coalitional possibilities between Mad Pride and critical psychiatrists. Increasingly, critical psychiatrists are moving beyond the narrow approaches of their training and drawing from interdisciplinary theory in science studies, disability studies, and the humanities. Like Mad Pride, they are developing alternative perspectives on psychiatry that emphasizes the importance of social models and of democratic research and treatment. In Britain, an influential Critical Psychiatry Network (www.critpsynet.freeuk.com/critpsynet.htm) has recently formed, bringing together a coalition of critical providers and consumer/survivors (Double 2002).[3]

Contemporary Mad Pride's political success at getting a seat at the table of mental health policy has also necessitated a change in the more radical infrastructure of the movement. The Conference on Human Rights and Psychiatric Oppression no longer meets and has now been replaced by the Alternatives Conference sponsored by CMHS. The different name of the conference is consistent with a shift in emphasis from psychiatric oppression to peer-run support and service involvement. The change is subtle as both oppression and support remain paramount for Mad Pride, but the change does mark a shift of the emphasis within the movement.

In addition, the newspaper *Madness Network News* is no longer being published. Today's Mad Pride connects its members largely through the activities of the Support Coalitions International (SCI) which brings together one hundred international local groups. Under the leadership of David Oaks, SCI has become "the epicenter of the Mad Movement" ("Windows into madness," 2002). It runs a Web site (www.mindfreedom.com), an e-mail list, a magazine (*Mindfreedom Journal*), and an online "Mad Market" (where interested parties can find "a little library of dangerous books"). Much of the success of the center comes from Oaks' capacity to build a coalition of consumers, survivors, and ex-patients. Like Packard, Frank, and

Chamberlin before him, Oaks' motivation for mental health activism comes from his experiences of psychiatric abuse: including forced hospitalization and forced treatment. Like so many others, he has taken those experiences and turned them into political action.

RECENT STRUGGLES WITH PSYCHIATRY

Despite the successes Mad Pride has had within the mental health system, their epistemological and political struggle with psychiatry continues. These struggles are often complicated, and they require impressive political savvy. In this section, I work through some examples of these struggles to give a sense of the political terrain and the critical importance of today's consumer/survivor activism. The 2003 hunger strike is a good example of Mad Pride's contemporary epistemological battles. To understand the context of the strike, it is important to note that during the same time Mad Pride has complicated its epistemology, psychiatry has gone in the exact opposite direction. The last thirty years have seen a "scientific revolution" in psychiatry that primarily values quantitative, positivistic protocols for research (Lewis, 2006). The emphasis on "objective" data has created a preference for neuroscience and genetics at the expense of an array of cultural and humanistic styles of inquiry. This new scientific psychiatry, working in tandem with pharmaceutical funding, has gone on to create today's dominant clinical model of psychiatry, "biopsychiatry"—whose emphasis is almost exclusively biomedical style diagnoses and pharmacological treatments.

The blockbuster medication, Prozac, gives a window into biopsychiatry's dominance. Between 1987 and 2002 (the year Prozac came off patent), over 27 million new prescriptions for the drug were written. Combined with the multiple "me too" drugs it inspired—the class of anti-depressants known as "selective serotonin inhibitors" (SSRI)—that total reached 67.5 million in the United States alone (Aldred 2004). That means almost one in every four people in the United States were started on a Prozac-type drug between 1987 and 2002. These same one in four people were dealing with sufficient emotional issues that someone thought they needed help.

For some of these people, the SSRIs may have been the best choice. But was it the best choice for 67.5 million people? Psychiatry's professional literature, its patient hand-outs, and the popular press all tell us "yes." They tout "scientific progress in the treatment of depression" as the main reason for the SSRIs extensive use (Gardner 2003; Lewis 2006; Metzl 2003). But, if we scratch the surface, we find that the SSRIs are highly controversial, and researchers have not been able to agree on even simple questions like: Do the drugs work? Or, are they safe? The *Handbook of Psychiatric Drug Therapy*, typical of most clinical reviews, claims with great authority that the SSRIs are highly effective and that they have a mild side effect profile (Arana and Rosenbaum 2000, 57, 76). But critical analysts conclude just the opposite: that the SSRIs are not much better than sugar pills and that they have major side effects—including sexual dysfunction, suicidality, and even violence (Breggin 1994, 65; Fisher and Fisher 1996; Glenmullen 2000; Healy 2004; Kirsch and Sapirstein 1998). Going further, scientific opinion is also at odds regarding the question of explanation. Some argue that the SSRIs have effects because they treat biological disease. But others argue these drugs are simply stimulants like cocaine and amphetamines. These researchers conclude that SSRIs are mood brighteners and psychic energizers because they work on the same neurotrans-

mitters as other stimulants (Breggin 1994; Glenmullen 2000).

When we take these controversies surrounding the Prozac-type drugs into account, it seems highly questionable that the SSRIs were the best choice for 67.5 million people. For most of these people, alternatives like psychotherapy, peer-support, and personal and political activism would have likely been better options than taking drugs that are expensive, are possibly no better than placebo, have multiple side effects, and may be little more than a dressed up version speed. But, because of the hype of biopsychiatry, these controversies are not well known and alternatives are not given a chance. The SSRIs are seen as quick and easy solutions backed by advances in psychiatric science and individual medical recommendations. For most people thrown in that situation, they are seen as the only viable option.

Mad Pride's hunger strike was directed squarely at this so-called "biological revolution" in psychiatry. The fasters, organized by David Oaks and Support Coalition International, demanded evidence that emotional and mental distress can be deemed "biologically-based" brain diseases, and also evidence that psychopharmaceutical treatments can correct those "chemical imbalances" attributed to a psychiatric diagnoses (MindFreedom, July 28, 2003).

The strikers were not trying to show that the biopsychiatric model of mental illness is myth, and they were not touting another model of mental distress as better or more accurate. The protestors stated from the outset that they were aware that psychopharmaceuticals work for some people, and that they were not judging individuals who choose to employ biopsychiatric approaches in an effort to seek relief. For Oaks and his fellow protestors, there are "many ways to help people experiencing severe mental and emotional crises . . .

We respect the right of people to choose the option of prescribed psychiatric drugs. Many of us have made this personal choice. . . . However, choice in the mental health field is severely limited. One approach dominates, and that is a belief in chemical imbalances, genetic determinism and psychiatric drugs as the treatment of choice. Far too often this limited choice has been exceedingly harmful to both the body and the spirit" (MindFreedom, July 28, 2003). In demanding evidence, the strikers hoped to show that the "chemical imbalance" theory of mental distress is not watertight, and to therefore challenge the overinvestment in this "biopsychiatric approach" by the mental health institutions.

In the early days of the strike, the APA brushed off the strikers demands for evidence and told them to consult introductory textbooks on psychiatry. The strikers responded by persisting in their demands and by sending a letter to the APA written by a panel of fourteen critical scholars. The letter showed that within the very textbooks that the APA had recommended there were numerous statements that invalidated the notion that mental illnesses have specific biological bases (MindFreedom, August 22, 2003). Using psychiatry's own knowledge against itself, the hunger strikers prompted the APA to respond more fully, and a follow up communiqué from APA finally conceded that "brain science has not advanced to the point where scientists or clinicians can point to readily discernible pathological lesions or genetic abnormalities that in and of themselves serve as a reliable or predictive biomarkers of a given mental disorder" (APA 2003). This reluctant admission from the APA marked an important epistemological victory for Mad Pride. In an interview, Oaks said: "They acknowledged that they didn't have the biological evidence [of mental illness], so that's on the record" (Davis 2003). The hunger strike vividly demonstrated how problematic it is to accept without question the "truths" of biopsychiatry.[4]

Despite this small success, Mad Pride's epistemological struggle continues to be a tough one. They are battling against a veritable superpower whose main ally is the hugely profitable and very influential pharmaceutical industry. As David Davis reports in his *LA Times* article on the hunger strike, Mad Pride is up against both an American Psychiatric Association, whose conventions bustle with "brightly colored" booths of the drug companies, and a booming pharmaceutical industry whose "sales of psychotherapeutics reached $21 billion in 2002, almost double the $11 billion in sales in 1998" (Davis 2003).[5]

Because of the influence and clout of biopsychiatry, Mad Pride knows all too well that skirmishes over epistemology are only part of the struggle. While it is vital to strike at the heart of mainstream psychiatry's "knowledge" and "truths," it is just as vital to realize that the epistemology game is hard to win. Science studies scholar Bruno Latour explains that dissenters of science can only go so far by using scientific literature against itself. For alternative perspectives to successfully join in the process of science (and truth) in the making, they must build their own "counter-laboratories," which of course requires tremendous resources (Latour 1987, 79). Mad Pride clearly does not have the resources to compete laboratory for laboratory with the institutions of psychiatry and their pharmaceutical supporters. Thus, while Mad Pride continues to play the game of epistemology, and continues to have some successes destabilizing psychiatry's biomedical model, it also struggles with psychiatry on the more typically political and economic terrain.

This was particularly evident in 2002 when President George W. Bush's administration initiated what David Oaks dubbed "the Bush triple play," which prompted

Mad Pride to mobilize swiftly and energetically to fight on the political front (Oaks 2002–2003). The triple play included:

1. The planned appointment of a controversial conservative psychiatrist, Dr. Sally Satel, to the important National Advisory Council for Mental Health.
2. The announcement of budget cuts to key government sponsored consumer/survivor technical support centers.
3. The creation of a New Freedom Commission to study U.S. mental health services.

All aspects of this triple play posed direct threats to Mad Pride and to the consumer/survivor movement, and they threatened the freedoms and rights of those suffering mental and emotional crises.

The first part of the triple play began with a White House leak, with word coming out that Dr. Sally Satel was being selected by the Bush administration for a position on the advisory council for the CMHS (the very organization which has been most receptive to consumer/survivor initiatives). Dr. Satel—a fellow at the American Enterprise Institute (a conservative political think tank)—is the author of the controversial book *P. C., M.D.: How Political Correctness is Corrupting Medicine*. She is not only a vociferous advocate of the biopsychiatric model of mental illness, she is also an outspoken critic of the consumer survivor movement, and an insistent lobbyist for involuntary commitment and treatment laws. In *P.C., M.D.,* under a chapter titled "Inmates Take Over the Asylum," Satel names the leaders of the Mad Pride movement and attacks their hard fought efforts to increase peer run services and reduce involuntary treatments. She denigrates mental health administrators who have taken Mad Pride seriously: "Tragically, they [mental health administrators] seem to be willing to sacrifice the needs of those with the most severe illnesses to political correctness and to the expediency of placating the vocal and annoying consumer/survivor lobby" (76). And she even goes so far as to describe the Alternatives Conference as the "guinea pig rebellion" (50).

For Mad Pride, Satel's appointment and her public vilification of consumer-run organizations signaled an overall Bush administration strategy to aggressively push a controversial biopsychiatry paradigm, to abandon consumer run self-help and peer support programs, and to increase forced psychiatric medication.

These concerns were reinforced by the second part of the Bush triple play. Soon after the leak about Dr. Satel, the Bush administration announced budget cuts for CMHS sponsored consumer/survivor technical assistance centers. Although the cuts totaled only $2 million out of the total CMHS budget, they were targeted directly at consumer/survivors. Three out of five of these centers were consumer run, which represented a clear about face for CMHS. Joseph Rogers, director of one of the programs to be cut, the National Mental Health Consumer Self-Help Clearinghouse, commented that "We had no warning. The cuts just came out of the blue, and we've had no explanation since that makes any sense" (Mulligan 2002).

The third part of the Bush triple play was the creation of a New Freedom Commission on mental health. Bush hailed the commission as a major step toward improving mental health services, and he charged it with the ambitious goals of reviewing the quality of mental health services, identifying innovative programs, and formulating federal, state, and local level policy options. The administration stipulated that the commission be composed of fifteen members and that these members be selected from a range of stakeholder groups: including providers, payers, administrators, consumers, and family members (Bush 2002).

Although all of this sounded laudable enough, but true to Mad Pride concerns, when the New Freedom Commission's fifteen members were made public, only one person self-identified as having personally experienced the mental health system or as involved in the consumer/survivor movement. The New Freedom Commission's choice of members appeared not to be about true stakeholder inclusion, but only a crude form of tokenism.

For many consumer/survivors, the Bush triple play was not only an outrage, it was a serious danger. These three deft moves threatened to undo all the gains consumer/survivors had made over the past thirty years. Oaks put it this way: "Mental health consumers and psychiatric survivors have experienced fierce repression. But to have a well-funded think tank unite with a Presidential administration to openly attack our movement in such a way is unprecedented. As the enormity of the attacks set in, several activists said they were numb with disbelief" (Oaks 2002–2003).

Mad Pride activists could have reasonably given up at this juncture. Instead, they held a strategy meeting with colleagues from the international movement, and they decided to directly oppose each part of the Bush triple play. Opposition to Dr. Satel's appointment and the cuts to CHMS programs took the form of a blitz of emails to consumer/survivor list-servs, active lobbying of mental health administrators, and a barrage of critical faxes to Secretary Tommy Thompson of the U.S. Dept. of Health & Human Services. And, rather than being dismayed by the non-democratic message of the New Freedom Commission's selection process, consumer/survivors took full advantage of the Commission's plan to hold public hearings on psychiatric services. Four days before the first scheduled hearing, consumer/survivors gathered for an emergency meeting with a network of physical disability activists. Judi Chamberlin, who has been a long-time advocate of disability and Mad Pride coalitions, explained the rationale for involving the larger disability movement, "When a wolf wants to target a whole flock, it looks for the most vulnerable lamb. The Bush administration is targeting psychiatric survivors today, but the whole disability movement is the target tomorrow" (Oaks 2002–2003).

The meeting turned out to be a major inspiration for consumer/survivors. The first speaker that night was Justin Dart, who many call the "Martin Luther King" of the disability movement. Dart, struggling with the last stages of terminal illness (he died just eight days later), gave a rousing speech which set the tone for the meeting. Dart proposed that,

> . . . we in the disability communities must unite with all who love justice to lead a revolution of empowerment. A revolution, to create a culture that will empower every single individual including all people with psychiatric disabilities, to live his or her God given potential for self determination, productivity and quality of life.
>
> Empowerment means choices—individual choices about where we live, how we live, where we work, choices about health care. We have a right to complete quality health care of our own choosing.
>
> NO FORCED TREATMENT EVER.
> We choose our own doctors and medication. We choose the places of care. No denial of treatment ever.
>
> NO FORCED TREATMENT EVER. (Oaks 2002)

The combined presence of Dart and several other disability representatives created the strategic capacity to get the word out and rally support and resistance far beyond the usual consumer/survivor community. It also further advanced a cross-disability activist connection between the disability movement and consumer/survivors.

On the day of the New Freedom Commission's first public meeting, consumer/

survivor activists and their disability activist comrades, made their presence known. Not only did they hand out their own press release and talk individually to members of the Bush Commission, they also made public announcements. Judi Chamberlin's testimony was typical. Announcing that she was a "psychiatric survivor" and "an advocate" on consumer/survivor issues for more than thirty years," she pointed out:

> A basic premise of the disability rights movement is simply this: Nothing About Us Without Us. The makeup of the Commission violates this basic principle. Just as women would not accept the legitimacy of a commission of "expert" men to define women's needs, or ethnic and racial minorities would not accept a panel of "expert" white people to define their needs, we similarly see the Commission as basically irrelevant to our struggle to define our own needs.
>
> (Chamberlin 2002)

Chamberlin argued that the New Freedom Commission lacked the "expertise on the consumer/survivor experience" as well as the "expertise of disability rights activists, those knowledgeable about the legal and civil rights of people diagnosed with mental illness, and experts in community integration." And she went on to detail how that expertise could be provided.

Unlike the results of the hunger strike, however, the results of Mad Pride's efforts to resist the Bush triple play can only be described as mixed. With regard to part one of the triple play, Mad Pride was unable to stop Sally Satel's appointment to the advisory board. Once on the board, she predictably advocated for more forced treatment and for discontinuation of consumer-run programs. But part two of the triple play, the planned budget cuts to peer support programs, never materialized. The three technical centers sponsored by CMHS continued to be funded.

The New Freedom Commission results were also contradictory. On the one hand, the commission was quite responsive to Mad Pride concerns. It agreed with Mad Pride that the mental health system is fundamentally broken, that it needs extensive overhaul (not just piecemeal reform), that mental health services must consumer and family centered, that modern psychiatry over emphasizes reductionist biomedical approaches, and that consumers must be protected from unjust incarceration and the use of seclusion and restraints. Together these recommendations signified an impressive success for Mad Pride's (and their disability allies) efforts to reach the commission and have their voices included in the report.

But, on the other hand, all was not rosy with the commission's report. In addition to the above recommendations, the New Freedom Commission also recommended nationwide mental health screenings in schools, primary care offices, prisons, and the welfare system. The ominous dimension of this plan was pointed out the *British Medical Journal* (*BMJ*) in an exposé titled "Bush plans to screen whole US population for mental illness." The *BMJ* explained that the New Freedom Commission recommendation for nationwide screening was linked to their recommendation for "evidence-based" treatment protocols. In psychiatry, these protocols are code words for the Texas Medication Algorithm Project (TMAP). TMAP was started in 1995 as an alliance between the pharmaceutical industry, the University of Texas, and the mental health system to set up expert guidelines for psychiatric practices. But a whistle blower at TMAP, Allen Jones, revealed that key officials received money and perks from the drug companies to unnecessarily promote expensive on-patent drugs. As Jones explained, "the same political/pharmaceutical alliance" behind TMAP are also behind the New Freedom Commission.

This alliance is "poised to consolidate the TMAP effort into a comprehensive national policy" of over-treating mental illness with expensive medications (Lenzer 2004). When you add to this state of affairs the recent National Institute of Health conclusion that half of all Americans will meet the criteria for a *DSM-IV* disorder some time in their life, the profiteering possibilities of the New Freedom Commission's political/pharmaceutical alliance is easy to imagine (Kessler 2005).

Of course, none of this screening will go forward without resistance. In quick response to the *BMJ* exposé, Mindfreedom sent out a news release "What You Gonna Do When They Screen For You" and set up a section of its Web site titled "President Bush and the Shrinking of the USA" (see http://www.mindfreedom.org/mindfreedom/bush_psychiatry.shtml). This news board gives access to breaking stories and commentary, plus it provides answers to frequently asked questions concerning the controversy. In addition, the Mad Pride advocacy group, Alliance for Human Research Protection (AHRP), has begun to monitor closely the outcomes of the New Freedom Commission (see http://www.ahrp.org/about/about.php). At the time of this writing, AHRP reports that lawsuits are already being filed in Indiana to resist the effects of "TeenScreen Depression"—a program funded partly with new federal grants initiated by the New Freedom Commission.[6]

CONCLUSION

These recent conflicts with psychiatry provide an important window into Mad Pride's ongoing epistemological and political struggles. Against tremendous odds, the movement has worked impressively to expose psychiatry as a limited field of inquiry, to open up its clinical services to more peer-run alternatives, and to reduce coercive connections between psychiatry and the state. Their fight to reduce individualization, psychiatrization, and sanist approaches to psychic life is arduous, and at times a little "mad." But the stakes are high and the struggle must continue. With the increasing coalition with the broader disability movement and the emergence of a critical psychiatry network, the fight is becoming more and more mainstream. Soon the battle will be one about which we all know and in which we can all participate. Active biocultural citizenship regarding mental difference and distress requires nothing less.

As the editors of *Adbusters* sum up in their issue on Mad Pride, in a culture of hardening isolation, status, materialism, and environmental degradation, "Mad Pride can be a broad embrace. It is a signal that we will allow ourselves our deep sorrow, our manic hope, or fierce anxiety, our imperfect rage. These will be our feedback into the system. We reserve the right to seek relief from both our most troubling symptoms and from society's most punitive norms. The sickness runs deep; without madness, there is no hope of cure" ("Deep sadness, manic hope," 2002).

NOTES

1. Public health scholar Barbara Starfield estimates that the combined effect of medical adverse effects in the United States are as follows:

   - 12,000 deaths/year from unnecessary surgery
   - 7,000 deaths/year from medication errors in hospitals
   - 20,000 deaths/year from other errors in hospitals
   - 80,000 deaths/year from nosocomial infections in hospitals
   - 106,000 deaths/year from nonerror, adverse effects of medications

   That comes to a total to 225,000 deaths per year from iatrogenic causes—which constitutes the third leading cause of death in the United States.

Just after heart disease and cancer (Starfield 2000, 484).

2. For an extended discussion of confinement and disability see the "Confinement" entry in the *Encyclopedia of Disability Studies* (Lewis 2005).

3. The Critical Psychiatry Network organizes its members less under the banner of "anti-psychiatry" and more under the banner of "post-psychiatry" (Thomas and Bracken 2004). The epistemological underpinning of post-psychiatry avoids the either/or problems of anti-psychiatry. Relying on the philosophy of Michel Foucault, a post-psychiatric perspective blurs the binary between truth and myth as all forms of human knowledge making are understand to be both material and semantic (Bracken and Thomas 2001; Foucault 1965 and 2003; Lewis 2006). This shift moves the legitimacy question of psychiatric knowledge from "truth" to "consequences." The issue is not whether psychiatric knowledge magically mirrors the world, but who is allowed to participate in making the knowledge? What kinds of consequences (and for whom) will follow from the knowledge?

4. For an extended analysis of the exchange between Mad Pride and the APA see critical psychiatrists Duncan Double's review: "Biomedical Bias of the American Psychiatric Association" (Double 2004).

5. See former editor-in-chief of the *New England Journal of Medicine* Marcia Angell's book, *The Truth about Drug Companies: How They Deceive Us and What to do About It* (2004), for an extended discussion of the influence of the pharmaceuticals on medical research and practice. Also see Pulitzer Prize finalist Robert Whitaker's book, *Mad in America: Bad Science, Bad Medicine, and the Enduring Mistreatment of the Mentally Ill* (2002) for an historical perspective specific to psychiatry.

6. Theresa and Michael Rhoades, who filed the first suit, claim that TeenScreen sent their daughter home from school telling her she had been diagnosed with obsessive compulsive disorder and social anxiety disorder. The Rhoades "claim that the survey was erroneous, improper, and done with reckless disregard for their daughter's welfare and that they did not give the school permission to give the test" (Pringle 2005). High profile attorney John Whitehead calls the situation an "Orwellian Nightmare" and has agreed to take on the Rhoades case. However, "because of the financial backing of pharmaceutical companies and the Bush administration's support through the New Freedom Commission," even Whitehead is concerned and considers his opposition to be formidable foes (Alliance for Human Research Protection 2005).

REFERENCES

Aldred, G. (2004). "An Analysis of the Use of Prozac, Paxil, and Zoloft in USA 1988–2002." Retrieved on June 2, 2005 from the Alliance for Research Protection, http://www.ahrp.org/risks/usSSRIuse0604.pdf.

Alliance for Human Research Protection (2005). "The Rutherford Institute takes on TeenScreen case in Indiana." Retrieved on July 25 from http://www.ahrp.org/infomail/05/06/13.php.

American Psychiatric Association (2003). *Statement on Diagnosis and Treatment of Mental Disorders.* Release no. 03-39, September 25, 2003. Retrieved on July 15, 2005 from http://www.psych.org/news_room/press_releases/mentaldisorders0339.pdf.

Angell, M. (2004). *The truth about drug companies: How they deceive us and what to do about it.* New York: Random House.

Arana, G., and Rosenbaum, J. (2000). *Handbook of psychiatric drug therapy,* 4th ed. Philadelphia: Lippincott Williams and Wilkins.

Braken, P., and Thomas, P. (2001). Postpsychiatry: a new direction for mental health. *British Medical Journal* 322:724–727.

Breggin, P. (1994). *Talking back to Prozac: What doctors aren't telling you about today's most controversial drugs.* New York: St. Martins Press.

Bush, G. W. (2002). "President's New Freedom Commission on Mental Health: Executive Order." The White House. President George W. Bush On line. Released on April, 29, 2002. Retrieved on June 17, 2005 from http://www.whitehouse.gov/news/releases/2002/04/20020429-2.html.

Center for Mental Health Services (2002). "About CMHS." Retrieved on July 20, 2005 from http://www.mentalhealth.samhsa.gov/cmhs/about.asp.

Center for Mental Health Services (2004). "Consumer affairs program." Retrieved on July 20, 2005 from http://www.mentalhealth.samhsa.gov/consumersurvivor/about.asp.

Chamberlin, J. (1977). *On our own: Patient-controlled alternatives to the mental health system.* Lawrence, MA: National Empowerment Center, Inc.

Chamberlin, J. (1990). The ex-patients' movement: Where we've been and where we are going. *Journal of Mind and Behavior* 11 (3&4): 323–336.

Chamberlin, J. (2002). "Testimony of Judi Chamberlin." American Association of People with Disabilities On line. Retrieved on June 17, 2005 from http://www.aapd-dc.org/News/disability/testjudichamberlin.html.

Davis, D. (2003). David Oaks and others in the "Mad Pride" movement believe drugs are being overused in treating mental illness, and they want the abuse stopped. *L.A. Times Magazine*, Sunday, October 23, 2003 .Retrieved on July 20, 2005 from http://www.latimes.com.

Davis, L. (1995). *Enforcing normalcy: Disability, deafness, and the body*. London: Verso.

"Deep sadness, manic hope: A movement for liberty, and the pursuit of madness." (2002). *Adbusters* (10) 3.

Double, D (2002).The limits of psychiatry. *British Medical Journal* 324: 900-904.

Double, D. (2004). "Biomedical bias of the American Psychiatric Association." Critical Psychiatry Web site. Retrieved on June 22, 2005 from http://www.critpsynet.freeuk.com/biomedicalbias.htm.

Farber, S. (1993). From victim to revolutionary: An interview with Lennard Frank. In *Madness, heresy, and the rumor of angels: The revolt against the mental health system*. Chicago: Open Court.

Fisher, R., and Fisher, S., (1996). Antidepressants for children: Is scientific support necessary? *Journal of nervous and mental disease* 184: 99–102.

Foucault, M. (1965). *Madness and civilization: A history of insanity in the age of reason*. New York: Vintage Books.

Foucault, M. (2003). *Abnormal: Lectures at the College of France 1974–1975*. New York: Picador.

Gardner, P. (2003). Distorted packaging: Marketing depression as illness, drugs as cures. *Journal of medical humanities* 24 (1/2): 105–130.

Garland-Thomson, R. (1997). *Extraordinary bodies: figuring physical disability in American culture and literature*. New York: Columbia University Press.

Geller, J., and Harris, M. (1994). *Women of asylum: Voices from behind the walls 1840–1945*. New York: Doubleday.

Glenmullen, J. (2000). *Prozac backlash: Overcoming the dangers of Prozac, Zoloft, Paxil, and other antidepressants with save, effective alternatives*. New York: Touchstone.

Goffman, E. (1961). *Asylums: Essays on the social situation of mental patients and other inmates*. New York: Doubleday.

Grob, G. (1994). *The mad among us: A history of the care of America's mentally ill*. Cambridge, MA: Harvard University Press.

Healy, D. (2004). *Let them eat Prozac: The unhealthy relationship between the pharmaceutical industry and depression*. New York: New York University Press.

Hirsch, S. (Ed.) (1974) *Madness Network News Reader*. San Francisco: Glide Publications.

Hogan, M. (2003) "Cover letter: Presidents New Freedom Commission on Mental Health." Retrieved on June 17, 2005 from http://www.mentalhealthcommission.gov/reports/Final Report/CoverLetter.htm.

Kessler, R. et al. (2005). Lifetime prevalence and age-of-onset distributions of *DSM-IV* disorders in the national comorbidity survey replication. *Archives of General Psychiatry*Vol. 62. Retrieved on July 25, 2005 from http://www.archgenpsychiatry.com.

Kirsch, I., and Sapirstein, G. (1998). Listening to Prozac but hearing placebo: A meta-analysis of antidepressant medications. *Prevention and treatment*. Retrieved on July 25, 2005 from http://journals.apa.org/prevention/volume1.

Laing, R. (1967). *The politics of experience*. New York: Ballantine.

Laing, R.D. (1968) "The obvious." In D. Cooper (Ed.). *The dialectics of liberation*. Harmondsworth: Penguin.

Latour, B. (1987). *Science in action*. Cambridge, MA: Harvard University Press.

Leifer, R. (1997). The psychiatric repression of Dr. Thomas Szasz: Its social and political significance. *Review of Existential Psychology and Psychiatry* XXIII (1, 2 & 3): 85 –107.

Lenzer, J. (2004) "Bush plans to screen whole US population for mental illness." *British Medical Journal*. Vol 328. June 19, 2004. Retrieved on August 10, 2004 from http://www.bmj.com.

Lewis, B. (2005). "Confinement." In G. Albrect (Ed.). *The encyclopedia of disability*. Thousand Oaks, CA: Sage Publications.

Lewis, B. (2006). *Moving beyond Prozac, DSM, and the new psychiatry: The birth of postpsychiatry*. Ann Arbor: University of Michigan Press.

Metzl, J. (2003). Selling sanity through gender: The psychodynamics of psychotropic advertising. *Journal of Medical Humanities* 24 (1/2): 79–105.

MindFreedom (July 28, 2003). "Original statement by the Fast for Freedom in Mental Health to the American Psychiatric Association, National Alliance for the Mentally Ill, and the US Office of the Surgeon General." Retrieved on July 10, 2005 from http://www.mindfreedom.org/mindfreedom/hungerstrike1.shtml#original.

Morrison, L. (2005). *Talking back to psychiatry: The consumer/surivor/ex-patient movement*. New York. Routledge.

Mulligan, K. (2002). CMHS budget cuts harm consumer involvement. *Psychiatric News* 37(6): 17.

Oaks, D. (2002). "From patients to passion: A call for nonviolent revolution in the mental health system. Plenary Address Alternatives 2002 Convention. Retrieved on March 3, 2003 from http://www.mindfreedom.org/mindfreedom/conference.shtml.

Oaks, D. (2002–2003). "President Bush's position on people with psychiatric labels." *Mindfreedom Journal* (Winter): 4–6.

Oliver, M. (1990). *The politics of disablement: A sociological approach*. New York: St. Martin's Press.

Oliver, M. (1996). *Understanding disability: From theory to practice*. London: Macmillan.

Packard, E. (1868). *The prisoner's hidden life, or insane asylums unveiled: As demonstrated by the report of the investigating committee of the legislature of Illinois*. Chicago: Published by the Author, A.B. Case.

Packard, E. (1874). *Modern persecutions, or married woman's liabilities*. Hartford, CT: Case, Lockwood and Brainard.

Perlin, M. (2000). *The hidden prejudice: Mental disability on trial*. Washington, DC: American Psychological Association.

President's New Freedom Commission (2003). "Executive Summary." Retrieved on June 17, 2005 from http://www.mentalhealthcommission.gov/reports/FinalReport/FullReport.htm.

Pringle, E. (2005). TeenScreen: The lawsuits begin. *CounterPunch*. June 13, 2005. Retrieved July 25, 2005 from http://www.counterpunch.org/pringle06132005.html.

Richman, S. (2004) "Bush's brave new world." *The Washington Times*. October 17, 2004. Retrieved on July 25, 2005 from http://www.washingtontimes.com/commentary/20041016-115126-9840r.htm.

Satel, S. (2000). *P.C., M.D.: How political correctness is corrupting medicine*. New York: Basic Books.

Scheff, T. (1966). *Being mentally ill*. Chicago: Aldine.

Starfield, B. 2000. Is US health really the best in the world? *Journal of the American Medical Association* 284 (4): 483–485.

Support Coalition News (May 15, 2002). "Stop the appointment of extremist psychiatrist Sally Satel!" Retrieved on June 15, 2005 from http://www.mindfreedom.org/mindfreedom/satel_f.shtml.

Szasz, T. (1961). *The myth of mental illness: Foundations of a theory of personal conduct*. New York: Hoeber-Harper.

Szasz, T. (1998). "Thomas Szasz's summary statement and manifesto." Retrieved on July 20, 2005 from http://www.szasz.com/manifesto.html.

Thomas, P., and Bracken, P. (2004). Critical psychiatry in practice. *Advances in Psychiatric Treatment* 10: 361–370.

Van Tosh, L., and del Vecchio, P. (2000). *Consumer-operated and self-help programs: A technical report*. Rockville, MD: U.S. Center for Mental Health Services.

Whitaker, R. (2002). *Mad in America: Bad science, bad medicine, and the enduring mistreatment of the mentally ill*. Cambridge, MA: Perseus Publishing.

"Windows into madness" (2002). *Adbusters* (10) 3.

Zinnman, S., Howie the Harp, and Budd, S. (Eds.) (1987). *Reaching across: Mental health clients helping each other*. Sacramento, CA: California Network of Mental Health Clients.

PART III

Stigma and Illness

CHAPTER 13

Stigma: An Enigma Demystified

Lerita M. Coleman Brown

Nature caused us all to be born equal; if fate is pleased to disturb this plan of the general law, it is our responsibility to correct its caprice, and to repair by our attention the usurpations of the stronger.

—Maurice Blanchot

What is stigma and why does stigma remain? Because stigmas mirror culture and society, they are in constant flux, and therefore the answers to these two questions continue to elude social scientists. Viewing stigma from multiple perspectives exposes its intricate nature and helps us to disentangle its web of complexities and paradoxes. Stigma represents a view of life; a set of personal and social constructs; a set of social relations and social relationships; a form of social reality. Stigma has been a difficult concept to conceptualize because it reflects a property, a process, a form of social categorization, and an affective state.

Two primary questions, then, that we as social scientists have addressed are how and why during certain historical periods, in specific cultures or within particular social groups, some human differences are valued and desired, and other human differences are devalued, feared, or stigmatized. In attempting to answer these questions, I propose another view of stigma, one that takes into account its behavioral, cognitive, and affective components and reveals that stigma is a response to the dilemma of difference.

THE DILEMMA

No two human beings are exactly alike: there are countless ways to differ. Shape, size, skin color, gender, age, cultural background, personality, and years of formal education are just a few of the infinite number of ways in which people can vary. Perceptually, and in actuality, there is greater variation on some of these dimensions than on others. Age and gender, for example, are dimensions with limited and quantifiable ranges; yet they interact exponentially with other physical or social characteristics that have larger continua (e.g., body shape, income, cultural background) to create a vast number of human differences. Goffman states, though, that "stigma is equivalent to an undesired differentness" (see Stafford & Scott). The infinite variety of human attributes suggests that what is undesired or stigmatized is heavily dependent on the social context and to some extent arbitrarily defined. The large number of stigmatizable attributes and several taxonomies of stigmas in the literature offer further evidence of how arbitrary the selection of undesired differences may be (see Ainlay & Crosby; Becker & Arnold; Solomon; Stafford & Scott).

What is most poignant about Goffman's description of stigma is that it suggests that all human differences are potentially stigmatizable. As we move out of one social context where a difference is desired into another context where the difference is undesired, we begin to feel the effects of stigma. This conceptualization of stigma also indicates that those possessing power, the dominant group, can determine which human differences are desired and undesired. In part, stigmas reflect the value judgments of a dominant group.

Many people, however, especially those who have some role in determining the desired and undesired differences of the zeitgeist, often think of stigma only as a property of individuals. They operate under the illusion that stigma exists only for certain segments of the population. But the truth is that any "nonstigmatized" person can easily become "stigmatized." "Nearly everyone at some point in life will experience stigma either temporarily or permanently. . . . Why do we persist in this denial?" (Zola, 1979, p. 454). Given that human differences serve as the basis for stigmas, being or feeling stigmatized is virtually an inescapable fate. Because stigmas differ depending upon the culture and the historical period. It becomes evident that it is mere chance whether a person is born into a nonstigmatized or severely stigmatized group.

Because stigmatization often occurs within the confines of a psychologically constructed or actual social relationship, the experience itself reflects relative comparisons, the contrasting of desired and undesired differences. Assuming that flawless people do not exist, relative comparisons give rise to a feeling of superiority in some contexts (where one possesses a desired trait that another person is lacking) but perhaps a feeling of inferiority in other contexts (where one lacks a desired trait that another person possesses). It is also important to note that it is only when we make comparisons that we can feel different. Stigmatization or feeling stigmatized is a consequence of social comparison. For this reason, stigma represents a continuum of undesired differences that depend upon many factors (e.g., geographical location, culture, life cycle stage) (see Becker & Arnold).

Although some stigmatized conditions appear escapable or may be temporary, some undesired traits have graver social consequences than others. Being a medical resident, being a new professor, being 7 feet tall, having cancer, being black, or being physically disfigured or mentally retarded can all lead to feelings of stigmatization (feeling discredited or devalued in a particular role), but obviously these are not equally stigmatizing conditions. The degree of stigmatization might depend on how undesired the difference is in a particular social group.

Physical abnormalities, for example, may be the most severely stigmatized differences because they are physically salient, represent some deficiency or distortion in the bodily form, and in most cases are unalterable. Other physically salient differences, such as skin color or nationality, are considered very stigmatizing because they also are permanent conditions and cannot be changed. Yet the stigmatization that one feels as a result of being black or Jewish or Japanese depends on the social context, specifically social contexts in which one's skin color or nationality is not a desired one. A white American could feel temporarily stigmatized when visiting Japan due to a difference in height. A black student could feel stigmatized in a predominantly white university because the majority of the students are white and white skin is a desired trait. But a black student in a predominantly black university is not likely to feel the effects of stigma. Thus, the sense of being stigmatized or having a stigma is inextricably tied to social context. Of equal importance are the norms in that context that determine which are desirable and undesirable attributes. Moving from one social or cultural context to another can change both the definitions and the consequences of stigma.

Stigma often results in a special kind of downward mobility. Part of the power of stigmatization lies in the realization that people who are stigmatized or acquire a stigma lose their place in the social hierarchy. Consequently, most people want to ensure that they are counted in the nonstigmatized "majority." This, of course, leads to more stigmatization.

Stigma, then, is also a term that connotes a relationship. It seems that this relationship is vital to understanding the stigmatizing process. Stigma allows some individuals to feel superior to others. Superiority and inferiority, however, are two sides of the same coin. In order for one person to feel superior, there must be another person who is perceived to be or who actually feels inferior. Stigmatized people are needed in order for the many nonstigmatized people to feel good about themselves.

On the other hand, there are many stigmatized people who feel inferior and concede that other persons are superior because they possess certain attributes. In order for the process to occur (for one person to stigmatize another and have the stigmatized person feel the effects of stigma), there must be some agreement that the differentness is inherently undesirable. Moreover, even among stigmatized people, relative comparisons are made, and people are reassured by the fact that there is someone else who is worse off. The dilemma of difference, therefore, affects both stigmatized and nonstigmatized people.

Some might contend that this is the very old scapegoat argument, and there is some truth to that contention. But the issues here are more finely intertwined. If stigma is a social construct, constructed by cultures, by social groups, and by individuals to designate some human differences as discrediting, then the stigmatization process is indeed a powerful and pernicious social tool. The inferiority/superiority issue is a most interesting way of understanding how and why people continue to stigmatize.

Some stigmas are more physically salient than others, and some people are more capable of concealing their stigmas or escaping from the negative social consequences of being stigmatized. The ideal prototype (e.g., young, white, tall, married, male, with a recent record in sports) that Stafford cites may actually possess traits that would be the source of much scorn and derision in another social context. Yet, by insulating himself in his own community, a man like the one described in the example can ensure that his "differentness" will receive approbation rather than rejection, and he will not be subject to constant and severe stigmatization. This is a common response to stigma among people with some social influence (e.g., artists, academics, millionaires). Often, attributes or behaviors that might otherwise be considered "abnormal" or stigmatized are labeled as "eccentric" among persons of power or influence. The fact that what is perceived as the "ideal" person varies from one social context to another, however, is tied to Martin's notion that people learn ways to stigmatize in each new situation.

In contrast, some categories of stigmatized people (e.g., the physically disabled, members of ethnic groups, poor people) cannot alter their stigmas nor easily disguise them. People, then, feel permanently stigmatized in contexts where their differentness is undesired and in social environments that they cannot easily escape. Hence, power, social influence, and social control play a major role in the stigmatization process.

In summary, stigma stems from differences. By focusing on differences we actively create stigmas because any attribute or difference is potentially stigmatizable. Often we attend to a single different attribute rather than to the large number of similar attributes that any two individuals share. Why people focus on differences and denigrate people on the basis of them is important to understanding how some stigmas originate and persist. By reexamining the historical origins of stigma and the way children develop the propensity to stigmatize, we can see how some differences evolve into stigmas and how the process is linked to the behavioral (social control), affective (fear, dislike), and cognitive (perception of differences, social categorization) components of stigma.

THE ORIGINS OF STIGMA

The phrase *to stigmatize* originally referred to the branding or marking of certain people (e.g., criminals, prostitutes) in order to make them appear different and separate from others (Goffman, 1963). The act of marking people in this way resulted in exile or avoidance. In most cultures, physical marking or branding has declined, but a more cognitive manifestation of stigmatization—social marking—has increased and has become the basis for most stigmas (Jones *et al.*, 1984). Goffman points out, though, that stigma has retained much of its original connotation. People use differences to exile or avoid others. In addition, what is most intriguing about the ontogenesis of the stigma concept is the broadening of its predominant affective responses such as dislike and disgust to include the emotional reaction of fear. Presently, *fear* may be instrumental in the perpetuation of stigma and in maintaining its original social functions. Yet as the developmental literature reveals, fear is not a natural but an acquired response to differences of stigmas.

Sigelman and Singleton offer a number of insightful observations about how children learn to stigmatize. Children develop a natural wariness of strangers as their ability to differentiate familiar from novel objects increases (Sroufe, 1977). Developmental psychologists note that stranger anxiety is a universal phenomenon in infants and appears around the age of seven months. This reaction to differences (e.g., women versus men, children versus adults, blacks versus whites) is an interesting one and, as Sigelman and Singleton point out, may serve as a prototype for stigmatizing. Many children respond in a positive (friendly) or negative (fearful, apprehensive) manner to strangers. Strangers often arouse the interest (Brooks & Lewis, 1976) of children but elicit negative reactions if they intrude on their personal space (Sroufe, 1977). Stranger anxiety tends to fade with age, but when coupled with self-referencing it may create the conditions for a child to learn how to respond to human differences or how to stigmatize.

Self-referencing, or the use of another's interpretation of a situation to form one's own understanding of it, commonly occurs in young children. Infants often look toward caregivers when encountering something different, such as a novel object, person, or event (Feinman, 1982). The response to novel stimuli in an ambiguous situation may depend on the emotional displays of the caregiver; young children have been known to respond positively to situations if their mothers respond reassuringly (Feinman, 1982). Self-referencing is instrumental to understanding the development of stigmatization because it may be through this process that caregivers shape young children's responses to people, especially those who possess physically salient differences (Klinnert, Campos, Sorce, Emde, & Svejda, 1983). We may continue to learn about how to stigmatize from other important figures (e.g., mentors, role models) as we progress through the life cycle. Powerful authority figures may serve as the source of self-referencing behavior in new social contexts (Martin).

Sigelman and Singleton also point out that preschoolers notice differences and tend to establish preferences but do not necessarily stigmatize. Even on meeting other children with physical disabilities, children do not automatically eschew them but may respond to actual physical and behavioral similarities and differences. There is evidence, moreover, indicating that young children are curious about human differences and often stare at novel stimuli (Brooks & Lewis, 1976). Children frequently inquire of their parents or of stigmatized persons about their distinctive physical attributes. In many cases, the affective response of young children is interest rather than fear.

Barbarin offers a poignant example of the difference between interest and fear in his vignette about Myra, a child with cancer. She talks about young children who are honest and direct about her illness, an attitude that does not cause her consternation. What does disturb her, though, are parents who will not permit her to baby-sit with their children for *fear* that she might give them cancer. Thus, interest and curiosity about stigma or human differences may be natural for children, but they must *learn* fear and avoidance as well as which categories or attributes to dislike, *fear*, or stigmatize. Children may learn to stigmatize without ever grasping "why" they do so (Martin), just as adults have beliefs about members of stigmatized groups without ever having met any individuals from the group (Crocker & Lutsky). The predisposition to stigmatize is passed from one generation to the next through social learning (Martin) or socialization (Crocker & Lutsky; Stafford & Scott).

Sigelman and Singleton agree with Martin that social norms subtly impinge upon the information-processing capacities of young children so that negative responses to stigma later become automatic. At some point, the development of social cognition must intersect with the affective responses that parents or adults display toward stigmatized people. Certain negative emotions become attached to social categories (e.g., *all* ex-mental patients are dangerous, *all* blacks are angry or harmful). Although the attitudes (cognitions) about stigma assessed in paper-and-pencil tasks may change in the direction of what is socially acceptable, the affect and behavior of elementary- and secondary-school children as well as adults reflect the early negative affective associations with stigma. The norms about stigma, though, are ambiguous and confusing. They teach young children to avoid or dislike stigmatized people, even though similar behavior in adults is considered socially unacceptable.

STIGMA AS A FORM OF COGNITIVE PROCESSING

The perceptual processing of human differences appears to be universal. Ainlay and Crosby suggest that differences arouse us; they can please or distress us. From a phenomenological perspective, we carry around "recipes" and "typifications" as structures for categorizing and ordering stimuli. Similarly, social psychologists speak of our need to categorize social stimuli in such terms as *schemas* and *stereotypes* (Crocker & Lutsky). These approaches to the perception of human differences indirectly posit that stigmatizing is a natural response, a way to maintain order in a potentially chaotic world of social stimuli. People want to believe that the world is ordered.

Although various approaches to social categorization may explain how people stereotype on the basis of a specific attribute (e.g., skin color, religious beliefs, deafness), they do not explain the next step—the negative imputations. Traditional approaches to sociocognitive processing also do not offer ideas about how people can perceptually move beyond the stereotype, the typification, or stigma to perceive an individual. Studies of stereotyping and stigma regularly reveal that beliefs about the inferiority of a person predominate in the thoughts of the perceiver (Crocker & Lutsky).

Stigma appears to be a special and insidious kind of social categorization or, as Martin explains, a process of generalizing from a single experience. People are treated categorically rather than individually, and in the process are devalued (Ainlay & Crosby; Barbarin; Crocker & Lutsky; Stafford & Scott). In addition, as Crocker and Lutsky point out, coding people in terms of categories (e.g., "X is a redhead") instead of specific attributes ("X has red hair") allows people to feel that stigmatized persons are fundamentally different and establishes greater psychological and social distance.

A discussion of the perceptual basis of stigma inevitably leads back to the notion of master status (Goffman, 1963). Perceptually, stigma becomes the master status, the attribute that colors the perception of the entire person. All other aspects of the person are ignored except those that fit the stereotype associated with the stigma (Kanter, 1979). Stigma as a form of negative stereotyping has a way of neutralizing positive qualities and undermining the identity of stigmatized individuals (Barbarin). This kind of social categorization has also been described by one sociologist as a "discordance with personal attributes" (Davis, 1964). Thus, many stigmatized people are not expected to be intelligent, attractive, or upper class.

Another important issue in the perception of human differences or social cognition is the relative comparisons that are made between and within stigmatized and nonstigmatized groups. Several authors discuss the need for people to accentuate between-group differences and minimize within-group differences as a requisite for group identity (Ainlay & Crosby; Crocker & Lutsky; Sigelman & Singleton). Yet these authors do not explore in depth the reasons for denigrating the attributes of the out-group members and elevating the attributes of one's own group, unless there is some feeling that the out-group could threaten the balance of power. Crocker and Lutsky note, however, that stereotyping is frequently tied to the need for self-enhancement. People with low self-esteem are more likely to identify and maintain negative stereotypes about members of stigmatized groups; such people are more negative in general. This line of reasoning takes us back to viewing stigma as a means of maintaining the status quo through social control. Could it be that stigma as a perceptual tool helps to reinforce the differentiation of the population that in earlier times was deliberately designated by marking? One explanation offered by many theorists is that stereotypes about stigmatized groups help to maintain the exploitation of such groups and preserve the existing societal structure.

Are there special arrangements or special circumstance, Ainlay and Crosby ask, that allow people to notice differences but not denigrate those who have them? On occasion, nonstigmatized people are able to "break through" and to see a stigmatized person as a real, whole person with a variety of attributes, some similar traits and some different from their own (Davis, 1964). Just how frequently and in what ways does this happen?

Ainlay and Crosby suggest that we begin to note differences within a type when we *need* to do so. The example they give about telephones is a good one. We learn differences among types of telephones, appliances, schools, or even groups of people when we need to. Hence stereotyping or stigmatizing is not necessarily automatic; when we want to perceive differences we perceive them, just as we perceive similarities when we *want* to. In some historical instances, society appears to have recognized full human potential when it was required, while ignoring certain devalued traits. When women were needed to occupy traditionally male occupations in the United States during World War II, gender differences were ignored as they have been ignored in other societies when women were needed for combat. Similarly, the U. S. armed forces became racially integrated when there was a need for more soldiers to fight in World War II (Terry, 1984).

Thus, schemas or stereotypes about stigmatized individuals can be modified but only under specific conditions. When stigmatized people have essential information or possess needed expertise, we discover that some of their attributes are not so different, or that they are more similar to us than different. "Cooperative interdependence" stemming from shared goals may change the nature of perceptions and the nature of relationships (Crocker & Lutsky). Future research on stigma and on social perception might continue to investigate the conditions under which people are less likely to stereotype and more likely to respond to individuals rather than categories (cf., Locksley, Borgida, Brekke, & Hepburn, 1980; Locksley, Hepburn & Ortiz, 1982).

THE MEANING OF STIGMA FOR SOCIAL RELATIONS

I have intimated that "stigmatized" and "nonstigmatized" people are tied together in a perpetual inferior/superior relationship. This relationship is key to understanding the meaning of stigma. To conceptualize stigma as a social relationship raises some vital questions about stigma. These questions include (a) when

and under what conditions does an attribute become a stigmatized one? (b) can a person experience stigmatization without knowing that a trait is devalued in a specific social context? (c) does a person feel stigmatized even though in a particular social context the attribute is not stigmatized or the stigma is not physically or behaviorally apparent? (d) can a person refuse to be stigmatized or destigmatize an attribute by ignoring the prevailing norms that define it as a stigma?

These questions lead to another one: Would stigma persist if stigmatized people did not feel stigmatized or inferior? Certainly, a national pride did not lessen the persecution of the Jews, nor does it provide freedom for blacks in South Africa. These two examples illustrate how pervasive and powerful the social control aspects of stigma are, empowering the stigmatizer and stripping the stigmatized of power. Yet a personal awakening, a discover that the responsibility for being stigmatized does not lie with oneself, is important. Understanding that the rationale for discrimination and segregation based on stigma lies in the mind of the stigmatizer has led people like Mahatma Gandhi and civil rights activist Rosa Parks to rise above the feeling of stigmatization, to ignore the norms, and to disobey the exiting laws based on stigma. There have been women, elderly adults, gays, disabled people, and many others who at some point realized that their fundamental similarities outweighed and outnumbered their differences. It becomes clear that, in most oppressive situations the primary problem lies with the stigmatizer and not with the stigmatized (Sartre, 1948; Schur, 1980, 1983). Many stigmatized people also begin to understand that the stigmatizer, having established a position of false superiority and consequently the need to maintain it, is enslaved to the concept that stigmatized people are fundamentally inferior. In fact, some stigmatized individuals question the norms about stigma and attempt to change the social environments for their peers.

In contrast, there are some stigmatized persons who accept their devalued status as legitimate. Attempting to "pass" and derogating others like themselves are two ways in which stigmatized people effectively accept the society's negative perceptions of their stigma (Goffman, cited in Gibbons). It is clear, especially from accounts of those who move from a nonstigmatized to a stigmatized role, that stigmatization is difficult to resist if everyone begins to reinforce the inferior status with their behavior. Two of the most common ways in which nonstigmatized people convey a sense of fundamental inferiority to stigmatized people are social rejection or social isolation and lowered expectations.

There are many ways in which people communicate social rejection such as speech, eye contact, and interpersonal distance. The stigmatized role, as conceptualized by the symbolic interactionism approach, is similar to any other role (e.g., professor, doctor) in which we behave according to the role expectations of others and change our identity to be congruent with them. Thus, in the case of stigma, role expectations are often the same as the stereotypes. Some stigmatized people become dependent, passive, helpless, and childlike because that is what is expected of them.

Social rejection or avoidance affects not only the stigmatized individual but everyone who is socially involved, such as family, friends, and relatives (Barbarin). This permanent form of social quarantine forces people to limit their relationships to other stigmatized people and to those for whom the social bond outweighs the stigma, such as family members. In this way, avoidance or social rejection also acts as a form of social control or containment (Edgerton, 1967; Goffman, 1963; Schur, 1983; Scott, 1969). Social rejection is perhaps most difficult for younger children who are banned from most social activities of their peers.

Social exile conveys another message about expectations. Many stigmatized people are not encouraged to develop or grow, to have aspirations or to be successful. Barbarin reports that children with cancer lose friendships and receive special, lenient treatment from teachers. They are not expected to achieve in the same manner as other children. Parents, too, sometimes allow stigmatized children to behave in ways that "normal" children in the same family are not permitted to do. Social exclusion as well as overprotection can lead to decreased performance. Lowered expectations also lead to decreased self-esteem.

The negative identity that ensues becomes a pervasive personality trait and inhibits the stigmatized person from developing other parts of the self. Another detrimental aspect of stigmatization is the practice of treating people, such as the ex-con and ex-mental patient who are attempting to reintegrate themselves into society, as if they still had the stigma. Even the terms we use to describer such persons suggest that role expectations remain the same despite the stigmatized person's efforts to relinquish them. It seems that the paradoxical societal norms that establish a subordinate and dependent position for stigmatized people while ostracizing them for it may stem from the need of nonstigmatized people to maintain a sense of superiority. Their position is supported and reinforced by their perceptions that stigmatized people are fundamentally inferior, passive, helpless, and childlike.

The most pernicious consequence of bearing a stigma is that stigmatized people may develop the same perceptual problems that nonstigmatized people have. They begin to see themselves and their lives through the stigma, or as Sartre (1948) writes about the Jews, they "allow themselves to be poisoned by the stereotype and live in fear that they will correspond to it" (p. 95). As Gibbons observes, stigmatized individuals sometimes blame their difficulties on the stigmatized trait, rather than confronting the root of their personal difficulties. Thus, normal issues that one encounters in life often act as a barrier to growth for stigmatized people because of the attributional process involved.

The need to maintain one's identity manifests itself in a number of ways, such as the mischievous behavior of the adolescent boy with cancer cited in Barbarin's chapter. "Attaining normalcy within the limits of stigma" (Tracy & Gussow, 1978) seems to be another way of describing the need to establish or recapture one's identity (Weiner, 1975).

Stigma uniquely alters perceptions in other ways, especially with respect to the notion of "normality", and raises other questions about the dilemma of difference. Most people do not want to be perceived as different or "abnormal." Becker and Arnold and Gibbons discuss normalization as attempts to be "not different" and to appear "normal." Such strategies include "passing" or disguising the stigma and acting "normal" by "covering up"—keeping up with the pace of nonstigmatized individuals (Davis, 1964; Gibbons; Goffman, 1963; Weiner, 1975). For stigmatized people, the idea of normality takes on an exaggerated importance. Normality becomes the supreme goal for many stigmatized individuals until they realize that there is no precise definition of normality except what they would be without their stigma. Given the dilemma of difference that stigma reflects, it is not clear whether anyone can ever feel "normal."

Out of this state of social isolation and lowered expectations, though, can arise some positive consequences. Although the process can be fraught with pain and difficulty, stigmatized people who manage to reject the perceptions of themselves as inferior often come away with greater inner strength (Jones *et al.*, 1984). They learn to depend on their own resources and, like the earlier examples of Mahatma Gandhi and Rosa Parks, they begin to question the bases for defining normality. Many stigmatized people regain their identity through redefining normality and realizing that it is acceptable to be who they are (Ablon, 1981; Barbarin; Becker, 1980; Becker & Arnold).

FEAR AND STIGMA

Fear is important to a discussion of how and why stigma persists. In many cultures that do not use the term *stigma*, there is some emotional reaction beyond interest or curiosity to differences such as children who are born with birthmarks, epilepsy, or a caul. Certain physical characteristics or illnesses elicit fear because the etiology of the attribute or disease is unknown, unpredictable, and unexpected (Sontag, 1979). People even have fears about the sexuality of certain stigmatized groups such as persons who are mentally retarded, feeling that if they are allowed to reproduce they will have retarded offspring (Gibbons). It seems that what gives stigma its intensity and reality is fear.

The nature of the fear appears to vary with the type of stigma. For most stigmas stemming from physical or mental problems, including cancer, people experience fear of contagion even though they know that the stigma cannot be developed through contact (see Barbarin). This fear usually stems from not knowing about the etiology of a condition, its predictability, and its course.

The stigmatization of certain racial, ethnic, and gender categories may also be based on fear. This fear, though, cannot stem from contagion because attributes (of skin color, ethnic background, and gender) cannot possibly be transmitted to nonstigmatized people. One explanation for the fear is that people want to avoid "courtesy stigmas" or stigmatization by association (Goffman, 1963). Another explanation underlying this type of fear may be the notion of scarce resources. This is the perception that if certain groups of people are allowed to have a share in all resources, there will not be enough: not enough jobs, not enough land, not enough water, or not enough food. Similar explanations from the deviance literature suggest that people who stigmatize feel threatened and collectively feel that their position of social, economic, and political dominance will be dismantled by members of stigmatized groups (Schur, 1980, 1983). A related explanation is provided by Hughes, who states, "that it may be that those whose positions are insecure and whose hopes for the higher goals are already fading express more violent hostility to new people" (1945, p. 356). This attitude may account for the increased aggression toward members of stigmatized groups during dire economic periods.

Fear affects not only nonstigmatized but stigmatized individuals as well. Many stigmatized people (e.g., ex-cons, mentally retarded adults) who are attempting to "pass" live in fear that their stigmatized attribute will be discovered (Gibbons). These fears are grounded in a realistic assessment of the negative social consequences of stigmatization and reflect the long-term social and psychological damage to individuals resulting from stigma.

At some level, therefore, most people are concerned with stigma because they are fearful of its unpredictable and uncontrollable nature. Stigmatization appears uncontrollable because human differences serve as the basis for stigmas. Therefore, *any* attribute can become a stigma. No one really ever knows when or if he or she will acquire a stigma or when societal norms might change to stigmatize a trait he or she already possesses. To deny this truth by attempting to isolate stigmatized people or escape from stigma is a manifestation of the underlying fear.

The unpredictability of stigma is similar to the unpredictability of death. Both Gibbons and Barbarin note that the development of a stigmatized condition in a loved one or in oneself represents a major breach of trust—a destruction of the belief that life is predictable. In a sense, stigma represents a kind of death—a social death. Nonstigmatized people, through avoidance and social rejection, often treat stigmatized people as if they were invisible, nonexistent, or dead. Many stigmas, in particular childhood cancer, remove the usual disguises of mortality. Such stigmas can act as a symbolic reminder of everyone's inevitable death (see Barbarin's discussion of Ernest Becker's (1973) *The Denial of Death*). These same fears can be applied to the acquisition of other stigmas (e.g., mental illness, physical disabilities) and help to intensify and perpetuate the negative responses to most stigmatized categories. Thus, irrational fears may help stigmatization to be self-perpetuating with little encouragement needed in the form of forced segregation from the political and social structure.

The ultimate answers about why stigma persists may lie in an examination of why people fear differences, fear the future, fear the unknown, and therefore stigmatize that which is different and unknown. An equally important issue to investigate is how stigmatization may be linked to the fear of being different.

CONCLUSION

Stigma is clearly a very complex multidisciplinary issue, with each additional perspective containing another piece of this enigma. A multidisciplinary approach allowed us as social scientists to perceive stigma as a whole; to see from within it rather than to look down upon it. Our joint perspectives have also demonstrated that there are many shared ideas across disciplines, and in many cases only the terminology is different.

Three important aspects of stigma emerge from this multidisciplinary examination and may forecast its future. They are fear, stigma's primary affective component; stereotyping, its primary cognitive component; and social control, its primary behavioral component. The study of the relationship of stigma to fear, stereotyping, and social control may elucidate our understanding of the paradoxes that a multidisciplinary perspective reveals. It may also bring us closer to understanding what stigma really is—not primarily a property of individuals as many have conceptualized it to be but a humanly constructed perception, constantly in flux and legitimizing our negative responses to human differences (Ainlay & Crosby). To further clarify the definition of stigma, one must differentiate between an "undesired differentness" that is likely to lead to feelings of stigmatization and actual forms of stigmatization. *It appears that stigmatization occurs only when the social control component is imposed, or when the undesired differentness leads to some restriction in physical and social mobility and access to opportunities that allow an individual to develop his or her potential. This definition combines the original meaning of stigma with more contemporary connotations and uses.*

In another vein, stigma is a statement about personal and social responsibility. People irrationally feel that, by separating themselves from stigmatized individuals, they may reduce their own risk of acquiring the stigma (Barbarin). By isolating individuals, people feel they can also isolate the problem. If stigma is ignored, the responsibility for its existence and perpetuation can be shifted elsewhere. Making stigmatized people feel responsible for their own stigma allows nonstigmatized people to

relinquish the onus for creating or perpetuating the conditions that surround it.

Changing political and economic climates are also important to the stigmatization and destigmatization process. What is economically feasible or politically enhancing for a group in power will partially determine what attributes are stigmatized, or at least how they are stigmatized. As many sociologists have suggested, some people are stigmatized for violating norms, whereas others are stigmatized for being of little economic or political value (Birenbaum & Sagarin, 1976, cited in Stafford & Scott). We should admit that stigma persists as a social problem because it continues to have some of its original social utility as a means of controlling certain segments of the population and ensuring that power is not easily exchanged. Stigma helps to maintain the existing social hierarchy.

One might then ask if there will ever be societies or historical periods without stigma. Some authors hold a positive vision of the future. Gibbons, for example, suggests that as traditionally stigmatized groups become more integrated into the general population, stigmatizing attributes will lose some of their onus. But historical analysis would suggest that new stigmas will replace old ones. Educational programs are probably of only limited help, as learning to stigmatize is a part of early social learning experiences (Martin; Sigelman & Singleton). The social learning of stigma is indeed very different from learning about the concept abstractly in a classroom. School experiences sometimes merely reinforce what children learn about stigmatization from parents and significant others.

From a sociological perspective, the economic, psychological and social benefits of stigma sustain it. Stigmas will disappear when we no longer need to legitimize social exclusion and segregation (Zola, 1979). From the perspective of cognitive psychology, when people find it necessary or beneficial to perceive the fundamental similarities they share with stigmatized people rather than the differences, we will see the beginnings of a real elimination of stigma. This process may have already occurred during some particular historical period or within particular societies. It is certainly an important area for historians, anthropologists, and psychologists to explore.

Although it would seem that the core of the problem lies with the nonstigmatized individuals, stigmatized people also play an important role in the destigmatization process. Stigma contests, or the struggles to determine which attributes are devalued and to what extent they are devalued, involve stigmatized and nonstigmatized individuals alike (Schur, 1980). Stigmatized people, too, have choices as to whether to accept their stigmatized condition and the negative social consequences or continue to fight for more integration into nonstigmatized communities. Their cognitive and affective attitudes toward themselves as individuals and as a group are no small element in shaping societal responses to them. As long as they continue to focus on the negative, affective components of stigma, such as low self-esteem, it is not likely that their devalued status will change. Self-help groups may play an important role in countering this tendency.

There is volition or personal choice. Each stigmatized or nonstigmatized individual can choose to feel superior or inferior, and each individual can make choices about social control and about fear. Sartre (1948) views this as the choice between authenticity or authentic freedom, and inauthenticity or fear of being oneself. Each individual can choose to ignore social norms regarding stigma. Personal beliefs about a situation or circumstance often differ from norms, but people usually follow the social norms anyway, fearing to step beyond conformity to exercise their own personal

beliefs about stigma (see Ainlay & Crosby and Stafford & Scott, discussions of personal versus socially shared forms of stigma). Changing human behavior is not as simple as encouraging people to exercise their personal beliefs. As social scientists, we know a number of issues may be involved in the way personal volition interacts with social norms and personal values.

The multidisciplinary approach could be used in a variety of creative ways to study stigma and other social problems. Different models of how stigma has evolved and is perpetuated could be subject to test by a number of social scientists. They could combine their efforts to examine whether stigma evolves in a similar manner in different cultures, or among children of different cultural and social backgrounds, or during different historical periods. The study of stigma encompasses as many factors and dimensions as are represented in a multidisciplinary approach. All of the elements are interactive and in constant flux. The effective, cognitive, and behavioral dimensions are subject to the current cultural, historical, political, and economic climates, which are in turn linked to the norms and laws. We know that the responses of stigmatized and nonstigmatized individuals may at times appear to be separate, but that they are also interconnected and may produce other responses when considered together. This graphic portrayal of the issues vital to the study of stigma is neither exhaustive nor definitive. It does suggest, however, that a multidimensional model of stigma is needed to understand how these factors, dimensions, and responses co-vary.

We need more cross-disciplinary research from researchers who do not commonly study stigma. For example, a joint project among historians, psychologists, economists, and political scientists might examine the relationship between economic climate, perceptions of scarcity, and stigmatization. Other joint ventures by anthropologists and economists could design research on how much income is lost over a lifetime by members of a stigmatized category (e.g., blind, deaf, overweight), and how this loss adversely affects the GNP and the overall economy. Another example would be work by political scientists and historians or anthropologists to understand the links between the stigmatization of specific attributes and the maintenance of social control and power by certain political groups. Psychologists might team up with novelists or anthropologists to use case studies to understand individual differences or to examine how some stigmatized persons overcome their discredited status. Other studies of the positive consequences of stigma might include a joint investigation by anthropologists and psychologists of cultures that successfully integrate stigmatized individuals into nonstigmatized communities and utilize whatever resources or talents a stigmatized person has to offer (as the shaman is used in many societies) (Halifax, 1979, 1982).

The study of stigma by developmental and social psychologists, sociologists, anthropologists, economists, and historians may also offer new insights into the evolution of sex roles and sex role identity across the life cycle and during changing economic climates. Indeed, linguists, psychologists, and sociologists may be able to chronicle the changes in identity and self-concept of stigmatized and nonstigmatized alike, by studying the way people describe themselves and the language they use in their interactions with stigmatized and nonstigmatized others (Coleman, 1985; Edelsky & Rosengrant, 1981).

The real challenge for social scientists will be to better understand the need to stigmatize; the need for people to reject rather than accept others; the need for people to denigrate rather than uplift others. We need to know more about the relationship between stigma and perceived threat, and how stigma may represent "the kinds of deviance that it seeks out" (Schur, 1980, p. 22). Finally, social scientists need to concentrate on designing an optimal system in which every member of society is permitted to develop one's talents and experience one's full potential regardless of any particular attribute. If such a society were to come about, then perhaps some positive consequences would arise from the dilemma of difference.

REFERENCES

Ablon, J. 1981. "Stigmatized health conditions." *Social Science and Medicine*, 15: 5–9.

Ainlay, S. and F. Cosby. 1986. "Stigma, justice and the dilemma of difference." In S. Ainlay, G. Becker, and L. M. Coleman, eds., *The Dilemma of Difference: A Multicultural View of Stigma*, 17–38. New York: Plenum.

Barbarin, O. 1986. "Family experience of stigma in childhood cancer." In S. Ainlay, G. Becker, and L. M. Coleman, eds., *The Dilemma of Difference: A Multicultural View of Stigma*. New York: Plenum, 163–184.

Becker, G. 1980. *Growing Old in Silence*. Berkeley: University of California Press.

Becker, G. and R. Arnold. 1986. "Stigma as social and cultural construct." In S. Ainlay, G. Becker, and L. M. Coleman, eds., *The Dilemma of Difference: A Multicultural View of Stigma*. New York. Plenum, 39–58.

Brooks, J. and Lewis, M. 1976. "Infants' responses to strangers: Midget, adult, and child." *Child Development* 47: 323–332.

Coleman, L. 1985. "Language and the evolution of identity and self-concept." In F. Kessel, ed., *The development of language and language researchers: Essays in honor of Roger Brown*. Hillsdale, N. J.: Erlbaum.

Crocker, J. and N. Lutsky. 1986. "Stigma and the dynamics of social cognition." In S. Ainlay, G. Becker, and L. M. Coleman, eds., *The Dilemma of Difference: A Multicultural View of Stigma* New York. Plenum, 95–122.

Davis, F. 1964. "Deviance disavowal: The management of strained interaction by the visibly handicapped." In H. Becker, ed., *The Other Side*. New York: Free Press, 119–138.

Edelsky, C. and Rosengrant, T. 1981. "Interactions with handicapped children: Who's handicapped?" *Sociolinguistic Working Paper 92*. Austin, TX: Southwest Educational Development Laboratory.

192 | LERITA M. COLEMAN BROWN

Edgerton, R. G. 1967. *The Cloak of Competence: Stigma in the Lives of the Mentally Retarded.* Berkeley: University of California Press.

Feinman, S. 1982. "Social referencing in infancy." *Merrill-Palmer Quarterly* 28: 445–70.

Gibbons, F. X. 1986. "Stigma and Interpersonal Relations." In S. C. Ainsley, G. Becker, and L. M. Coleman, eds., *The Dilemma of Difference: A Multidisciplinary View of Stigma.* New York. Plenum. 95–122.

Goffman, E. 1963. *Stigma: Notes on the Management of Spoiled Identity.* Englewood Cliffs, N.J.: Prentice Hall.

Hallifax, J. 1979. *Shamanic Voices: A Survey of Visionary Narratives.* New York: Dutton.

——. 1982. *Shaman: The Wounded Healer.* London: Thames and Hudson.

Jones. E. E., A. Farina, A. H. Hastof, H. Markus, D. T. Miller, and R. A. Scott, 1984. *Social Stigma: The Psychology of Marked Relationships.* New York: Freeman.

Kanter, R. M. 1979. *Men and Women of the Corporation.* New York: Basic Books.

Klinnert, M. D., J. J. Campos, J. F. Sorce, R. Emde and M. Svejda. 1983. "Emotions as behavior regulators: Social referencing in infancy." In R. Plutchik and H. Kellerman, eds. *Emotion Theory, Research, and Experience. Vol. II. Emotions in Early Development.* New York: Academic Press, 57–88.

Locksley, A., E. Borgida, N. Brekke, and C. Hepburn. 1980. "Sexual stereotypes and social judgment." *Journal of Personality and Social Psychology,* 39: 821–31.

Locksley, A., C. Hepburn, and V. Ortiz. 1982. "Social stereotypes and judgments of individuals: An instance of the base-rate fallacy." *Journal of Experimental Social Psychology.* 18: 23–42.

Martin, L. G. 1986. "Stigma: A social learning perspective." In S. Ainlay, G. Becker, and L. M. Coleman, eds., *The Dilemma of Difference: A Multicultural View of Stigma.* New York. Plenum, 1–16.

Sartre, J. 1948. *Anti-Semite and Jew.* New York: Schocken Books.

Schur, E. 1980. *The Politics Of Deviance: A Sociological Introduction.* Englewood Cliffs, N. J.: Prentice Hall.

——. 1983. *Labeling Women Deviant: Gender, Stigma, and Social Control.* Philadelphia: Temple University Press.

Scott, R., 1969. *The Making of Blind Men.* New York: Russel Sage Foundation.

Sigelman, C. and L. C. Singleton. 1986. "Stigmatization in childhood: A survey of developmental trends and issues." In S. Ainlay, G. Becker, and L. M. Coleman, eds., *The Dilemma of Difference: A Multicultural View of Stigma.* New York. Plenum. 185–210.

Solomon, Howard M. 1986. "Stigma and Western culture: A historical approach." In S. Ainlay, G. Becker, and L. M. Coleman, eds., *The Dilemma of Difference: A Multicultural View of Stigma.* New York: Plenum, 59–76.

Sontag, S. 1979. *Illness as Metaphor.* New York: Random House.

Sroufe, L. A. 1977. "Wariness of strangers and the study of infant development." *Child Development,* 48: 731–46.

Stafford, M and R. Scott. 1986. "Stigma, deviance and social control: Some conceptual issues." In S. Ainlay, G. Becker, and L. M. Coleman, eds., *The Dilemma of Difference: A Multicultural View of Stigma.* New York. Plenum, 77–94.

Terry, W. 1984. *Bloods: An Oral History of the Vietnam War by Black Veterans.* New York: Random House.

Tracy, G. S., and Gussow, Z. 1978. "Self-help health groups: A grass-roots response to a need for services." *Journal of Applied Behavioral Science:* 81–396.

Weiner, C. L., 1975. "The burden of rheumatoid arthritis: Tolerating the uncertainty." *Social Science and Medicine:* 99, 97–104.

Zola, I. Z. 1979. "Helping one another: A speculative history of the self-help movement. *Archive of Physical Medicine and Rehabilitation:* 60, 452.

CHAPTER 14

AIDS and Its Metaphors

Susan Sontag

Because of countless metaphoric flour-ishes that have made cancer synonymous with evil, having cancer has been expe-rienced by many as shameful, therefore something to conceal, and also unjust, a betrayal by one's body. Why me? the can-cer patient exclaims bitterly. With AIDS, the shame is linked to an imputation of guilt; and the scandal is not at all obscure. Few wonder, Why me? Most people outside of Sub-Saharan Africa who have AIDS know (or think they know) how they got it. It is not a mysterious affliction that seems to strike at random. Indeed, to get AIDS is precisely to be revealed, in the majority of cases so far, as a member of a certain "risk group," a community of pariahs. The illness flushes out an identity that might have remained hidden from neighbors, job-mates, family, friends. It also confirms an identity and, among the risk group in the United States most affected in the beginning, homosex-ual men, has been a creator of community as well as an experience that isolates the ill and exposes them to harassment and per-secution.

Getting cancer, too, is sometimes un-derstood as the fault of someone who has indulged in "unsafe" behavior—the alco-holic with cancer of the esophagus, the smoker with lung cancer: punishment for living unhealthy lives. (In contrast to those obliged to perform unsafe occupations, like the worker in a petrochemical factory who gets bladder cancer.) More and more link-ages are sought between primary organs or systems and specific practices that people are invited to repudiate, as in recent specu-lation associating colon cancer and breast cancer with diets rich in animal fats. But the unsafe habits associated with cancer, among other illnesses—even heart disease, hitherto little culpabilized, is now largely viewed as the price one pays for excesses of diet and "life-style"—are the result of a weakness of the will or a lack of prudence, or of addiction to legal (albeit very danger-ous) chemicals. The unsafe behavior that produces AIDS is judged to be more than just weakness. It is indulgence, delinquen-cy—addictions to chemicals that are illegal and to sex regarded as deviant.

The sexual transmission of this illness, considered by most people as a calam-ity one brings on oneself, is judged more harshly than other means—especially since AIDS is understood as a disease not only of sexual excess but of perversity. (I am think-ing, of course, of the United States, where people are currently being told that het-erosexual transmission is extremely rare, and unlikely—as if Africa did not exist.) An infectious disease whose principal means of transmission is sexual necessarily puts at greater risk those who are sexually more active—and is easy to view as a punishment for that activity. True of syphilis, this is even truer of AIDS, since not just promiscuity but a specific sexual "practice" regarded as unnatural is named as more endangering. Getting the disease through a sexual practice is thought to be more willful, therefore deserves more blame. Addicts who get the illness by sharing contaminated needles are seen as committing (or completing) a kind of inadvertent suicide. Promiscuous homosexual men practicing their vehement sexual customs under the illusory conviction, fostered by medical ideology with its cure-all antibiotics, of the relative innocuousness of all sexually transmitted diseases, could be viewed as dedicated hedonists—though it's now clear that their behavior was no less suicidal. Those like hemophiliacs and blood-transfusion recipients, who cannot by any stretch of the blaming faculty be considered responsible for their illness, may be as ruth-lessly ostracized by frightened people, and potentially represent a greater threat because, unlike the already stigmatized, they are not as easy to identify.

Infectious disease to which sexual fault is attached always inspire fears of easy contagion and bizarre fantasies of transmission by nonvenereal means in public places. The removal of doorknobs and the installation of swinging doors on U.S. Navy ships and the disappearance of the metal drinking cups affixed to public water fountains in the United States in the first decades of the century were early consequences of the "discovery" of syphilis's "innocently transmitted infection"; and the warning to generations of middle-class children always to interpose paper between bare bottom and the public toilet seat is another trace of the horror stories about the germs of syphilis being passed to the innocent by the dirty that were rife once and are still widely believed. Every feared epidemic disease, but especially those associated with sexual license, generates a preoccupying distinction between the disease's putative carriers (which usually means just the poor and, in this part of the world, people with darker skins) and those defined—health professionals and other bureaucrats do the defining—as "the general population." AIDS has revived similar phobias and fears of contamination among *this* disease's version of "the general population": white heterosexuals who do not inject themselves with drugs or have sexual relations with those who do. Like syphilis a disease of, or contracted from, dangerous others, AIDS is perceived as afflicting, in greater proportions than syphilis ever did, the already stigmatized. But syphilis was not identified with certain death, death that follows a protracted agony, as cancer was once imagined and AIDS is now held to be.

That AIDS is not a single illness but a syndrome, consisting of a seemingly open-ended list of contributing or "presenting" illnesses which constitute (that is, qualify the patient as having) the disease, makes it more a product of definition or construction than even a very complex, multiform illness like cancer. Indeed, the contention that AIDS is invariably fatal depends partly on what doctors decided to define as AIDS—and keep in reserve as distinct earlier stages of the disease. And this decision rests on a notion no less primitively metaphorical than that of a "full-blown" (or "full-fledged") disease.[1] "Full-blown is the form in which the disease is inevitably fatal. As what is immature is destined to become mature, what buds to become full-blown (fledglings to become full-fledged)—the doctors' botanical or zoological metaphor makes development or evolution into AIDS the norm, the rule. I am not saying that the metaphor creates the clinical conception, but I am arguing that it does much more than just ratify it. It lends support to an interpretation of the clinical evidence which is far from proved or, yet, provable. It is simply too early to conclude, of a disease identified only seven years ago, that infection will always produce something to die from, or even that everybody who has what is defined as AIDS will die of it. (As some medical writers have speculated, the appalling mortality rates could be registering the early, mostly rapid deaths of those most vulnerable to the virus—because of diminished immune competence, because of genetic predisposition, among other possible co-factors—not the ravages of a uniformly fatal infection.) Construing the disease as divided into distinct stages was the necessary way of implementing the metaphor of "full-blown disease." But it also slightly weakened the notion of inevitability suggested by the metaphor. Those sensibly interested in hedging their bets about how uniformly lethal infection would prove could use the standard three-tier classification—HIV infection, AIDS-related complex (ARC), and AIDS—to entertain either of two possibilities or both: the less catastrophic one, that *not* everybody infected would "advance" or "graduate" from HIV infection, and the more catastrophic one, that everybody would.

It is more catastrophic reading of the evidence that for some time has dominated debate about the disease, which means that a change in nomenclature is under way. Influential administrators of the way the disease is understood have decided that there should be no more of the false reassurance that might be had from the use of different acronyms for different stages of the disease. (It could never have been more than minimally reassuring.) Recent proposals for redoing terminology—for instance, to phase out the category of ARC—do not challenge the construction of the disease in stages, but do place additional stress on the *continuity* of the disease process. "Full-blown disease" is viewed as more inevitable now, and that strengthens the fatalism already in place.[2]

From the beginning the construction of the illness had depended on notions that separated one group of people from another—the sick from the well, people with ARC from people with AIDS, them and us—while implying the imminent dissolution of these distinctions. However hedged, the predictions always sounded fatalistic. Thus, the frequent pronouncements by AIDS specialists and public health officials on the chances of those infected with the virus coming down with "full-blown" disease have seemed mostly an exercise in the management of public opinion, dosing out the harrowing news in several steps. Estimates of the percentage expected to show symptoms classifying them as having AIDS within five years, which may be too low—at the time of this writing, the figure is 30 to 35 percent—are invariably followed by the assertion that "most," after which comes "probably all," those infected will eventually become ill. The critical number, then, is not the percentage of people likely to develop AIDS within a relatively short time but the *maximum* interval that could elapse between infection with HIV (described as lifelong and irreversible) and appearance of the first symptoms. As the years add up in which the illness has been tracked, so does the possible number of years between infection and becoming ill, now estimated, seven years into the epidemic, at between ten and fifteen years. This figure, which will presumably continue to be revised upward, does much to maintain the definition of AIDS as an inexorable, invariably fatal disease.

The obvious consequence of believing that all those who "harbor" the virus will eventually come down with the illness is that those who test positive for it are regarded as people-with-AIDS, who just don't have it...yet. It is only a matter of time, like any death sentence. Less obviously, such people are often regarded as if they *do* have it. Testing positive for HIV (which usually means having been tested for the presence not of the virus but of antibodies to the virus) is increasingly equated with being ill. Infected *means* ill, from that point forward. "Infected but not ill," that invaluable notion of clinical medicine (the body "harbors" many infections), is being superseded by biomedical concepts which, whatever their scientific justification, amount to reviving the antiscientific logic of defilement, and make infected-but-healthy a contradiction in terms. Being ill in this new sense can have many practical consequences. People are losing their jobs when it is learned that they are HIV-positive (though it is not legal in the United States to fire someone for that reason) and the temptation to conceal a positive finding must be immense. The consequences of testing HIV-positive are even more punitive for those selected populations—there will be more—upon which the government has already made testing mandatory. The U.S. Department of Defense has announced that military personnel discovered to be HIV-positive are being removed "from sensitive, stressful jobs," because of evidence indicating that mere infection with the virus, in the absence of any other symptoms, produces subtle changes in mental abilities in a significant minority of virus carriers. (The evidence cited: lower scores on certain neurological tests given to some who had tested positive, which could reflect mental impairment caused by exposure to the virus, though most doctors think this extremely improbably, or could be caused—as officially acknowledged under questioning—by "the anger, depression, fear, and panic" of people who have just learned that they are HIV-positive.) And, of course, testing positive now makes one ineligible to immigrate everywhere.

In every previous epidemic of an infectious nature, the epidemic is equivalent to the number of tabulated cases. This epidemic is regarded as consisting *now of* that figure plus a calculation about a much larger number of people apparently in good health (seemingly healthy, but doomed) who are infected. The calculations are being made and remade all the time, and pressure is building to identify these people, and to tag them. With the most up-to-date biomedical testing, it is possible to create a new class of lifetime pariahs, the future ill. But the result of this radical expansion of the notion of illness created by the triumph of modern medical scrutiny also seems a throwback to the past, before the era of medical triumphalism, when illnesses were innumerable, mysterious, and the progression from being seriously ill to dying was something normal (not, as now, medicine's lapse or failure, destined to be corrected). AIDS, in which people are understood as ill before they are ill; which produces a seemingly innumerable array of symptom-illnesses; for which there are only palliatives; and which brings to many a social death the precedes the physical one—AIDS reinstates something like a premodern experience of illness, as described in Donne's *Devotions*, in which "every thing that disorders a faculty and the function of that is a sicknesse," which starts when we

> are preafflicted, super-afflicted with these jealousies and suspitions, and apprehensions of Sicknes, before we can call it a sicknes; we are not sure we are ill; one hand askes the other by the pulse, and our eye asks our own urine, how we do. . . . we are tormented with sicknes, and cannot stay till the torment come. . . .

whose agonizing outreach to every part of the body makes a real cure chimerical, since what "is but an accident, but a symptom of the main disease, is so violent, that the Physician must attend the cure of that" rather than "the cure of the disease it self," and whose consequence is abandonment:

> As Sicknesse is the greatest misery, so the greatest misery of sicknes is solitude; when

the infectiousness of the disease deterrs them who should assist, from coming; even the Physician dares scarce come. . . . it is an Outlawry, an Excommunication upon the patient. . . .

In premodern medicine, illness is described as it is experienced intuitively, as a relation of outside and inside: an interior sensation or something to be discerned on the body's surface, by sight (or just below, by listening, palpating), which is confirmed when the interior is opened to viewing (in surgery, in autopsy). Modern—that is, effective—medicine is characterized by far more complex notions of what is to be observed inside the body: not just the disease's results (damaged organs) but its cause (microorganisms), and by a far more intricate typology of illness.

In the older era of artisanal diagnoses, being examined produced an immediate verdict, immediate as the physician's willingness to speak. Now an examination means tests. And being tested introduces a time lapse that, given the unavoidably industrial character of competent medical testing, can stretch out for weeks: an agonizing delay for those who think they are awaiting a death sentence or an acquittal. Many are reluctant to be tested out of dread of the verdict, out of fear of being put on a list that could bring future discrimination or worse, and out of fatalism (what good would it do?). The usefulness of self-examination for the early detection of certain common cancers, much less likely to be fatal if treated before they are very advanced, is now widely understood. Early detection of an illness thought to be inexorable and incurable cannot seem to bring any advantage.

Like other diseases that arouse feelings of shame, AIDS is often a secret, but not from the patient. A cancer diagnosis was frequently concealed from patients by their families; an AIDS diagnosis is at least as often concealed from their families by patients. And as with other grave illnesses regarded as more than just illnesses, many people with AIDS are drawn to whole-body rather than illness-specific treatments, which are thought to be either ineffectual or dangerous. (The disparagement of effective, scientific medicine for offering treatments that are *merely* illness-specific, and likely to be toxic, is a recurrent misconjecture of opinion that regards itself as enlightened.) This disastrous choice is still being made by some people with cancer, an illness that surgery and drugs can often cure. And a predictable mix of superstition and resignation is leading some people with AIDS to refuse antiviral chemotherapy, which, even in the absence of a cure, has proved of some effectiveness (in slowing down the syndrome's progress and in staving off some common presenting illnesses), and instead to seek to heal themselves, often under the auspices of some "alternative medicine" guru. But subjecting an emaciated body to the purification of a macrobiotic diet is about as helpful in treating AIDS as having oneself bled, the "holistic" medical treatment of choice in the era of Donne.

NOTES

1. The standard definition distinguishes between people with the disease or syndrome "fulfilling the criteria for the surveillance definition of AIDS" from a larger number infected with HIV and symptomatic "who do not fulfill the empiric criteria for the full-blown disease. This constellation of signs and symptoms in the context of HIV infection has been termed the AIDS-related complex (ARC)." Then follows the obligatory percentage. "It is estimated that approximately 25 percent of patients with ARC will develop full-blown disease within 3 years." Harrison's *Principles of Internal Medicine*, 11th edition (1987), p. 1394.

The first major illness known by an acronym, the condition called AIDS does not have, as it were, natural borders. It is an illness whose identity is designed for purposes of investigation and with tabulation and surveillance by medical and other bureaucracies in view. Hence, the unselfconscious equating in the medical text-book of what is empirical with what pertains to surveillance, two notions deriving from quite different models of understanding. (AIDS is what fulfills that which is referred to as either the "criteria for the surveillance definition" or the "empiric criteria": HIV infection plus the presence of one or more diseases included on the roster drown up by the disease's principal administrator of definition in the United States, the federal Centers for Disease Control in Atlanta.) This completely stipulative definition with its metaphor of maturing disease decisively influences how the illness is understood.

2. The 1988 Presidential Commission on the epidemic recommended "de-emphasizing" the use of the term ARC because it "tends to obscure the life-threatening aspects of this stage of illness."

There is some pressure to drop the term AIDS, too. The report by the President Commission pointedly used the acronym HIV for the epidemic itself, as part of a recommended shift from "monitoring disease" to "monitoring infection." Again, one of the reasons given is that the present terminology masks the true gravity of the menace. ("This longstanding concentration on the clinical manifestations of AIDS rather than on all stages of HIV infection [i.e., from initial infection to seroconversion, to an antibody-positive asymptomatic stage, to full-blown AIDS] has had the unintended effect of misleading the public as to the extent of infection in the population. . . .") It does seem likely that the disease will, eventually, be renamed. *This* change in nomenclature would justify officially the policy of including the infected but asymptomatic among the ill.

CHAPTER 15

Beholding

Rosemarie Garland-Thomson

It's not that I'm ugly. It's more that most people don't know
how to look at me.
—Harriet McBryde Johnson in *New York Times Magazine*, February 16, 2003

AN ETHICS OF LOOKING

We all stare. Sights that stimulate our eyes—the magic show extravaganza, the burning Towers, the twisted cars on the freeway—lead to wonder, horror, or just thrills. When we stare at one another, as we have seen, things get more complicated. We are all potential starees as well as starers, and between people, staring is a communicative gesture. Between strangers, staring is uncomfortable, especially the intense, prohibited, baroque staring that does not disguise itself. That discomfort can be positive, however, rather than oppressive. A stare is a response to someone's distinctiveness, and a staring exchange can thus beget mutual recognition, however fleeting. In this way, how we look at one another can be a productive aspect of our interpersonal, even our political, lives. If all this is so, then the question for starers is not whether we *should* stare, but rather *how* we should stare. The question for starees is not whether we *will* be stared at, but rather *how* we will be stared at. As a productive, albeit volatile social relationship, staring necessarily brings with it these ethical dilemmas.

The cultural critic Susan Sontag (2003) takes up the question of whether and how we should stare in her last book, *Regarding the Pain of Others*.[1] The book considers the ethics of looking at photographs of suffering, hurt, or dead bodies. For Sontag, staring is a one-way dynamic, in part because she is considering photographs rather than lived interactions but also because she is concerned about the ethics of looking rather than the ethics of being looked at. She evaluates whether we ought to be looking at what she broadly takes to be other people's suffering and ponders how we should respond when we do look.

What Sontag considers these "repulsive attractions," of course, are exactly sights that most attract stares (96). The intense attraction to such scenes, the compelling human impulse to stare at them, is for Sontag an "unworthy desire," which she condemns (96). Her thinking is in line with the familiar American disapproval of staring as inappropriate looking—as visual intrusion, a surrender to the sensational, or unconstrained, voyeurism. Sontag sees "the attraction of mutilated bodies" both in lived experience and in photographic images as unseemly. Viewing human pain, she insists, particularly from the distance that images and anonymity involve, is "a prurient interest" that should be in all of us a "despised impulse" (95, 97). Staring is an ethical violation, Sontag concludes, because it is motivated by "curiosity," which is only worthy if tempered by "reason" that quashes any "voyeuristic lure" (96, 97, 99).

Even though Sontag maintains that the urge to stare at human pain, death, and disability is a "despised impulse," she nonetheless claims that staring can be redeemed by a proper response. Accordingly, she lays out a model of good and bad staring—in other words, of how and when we should stare. Bad staring satisfies supposedly salacious curiosity and leads to the ethical dead end of *schaudenfreude*, of taking satisfaction in someone else's misfortune. For Sontag, looking at photographs of human pain is bad if our interest in them affirms that "This is not happening to *me*" (99). This response kindles indifference and complacency born of feeling secure and produces an unethical "passivity." Bad staring, in short, is inadequate identification between starer and staree. Rather than responding with this-could-be-me, a bad starer concludes this-cannot-be-me. Bad staring fails to make the leap from a place of discomfort, shock, or fear toward empathic identification. This unethical stare, in other words, is looking without recognizing, a separated stare that refuses to move toward one's fellow human.[2] To use Martin Buber's (1958) language, bad staring is all I and no Thou.

Good staring, Sontag suggests, reaches out. So the "unworthy desire" to look hard at "repulsive attractions" can be transformed into an ethical relation if it is mobilized into political action. If starers can identify with starees enough to jumpstart a sympathetic response that is then "translated into action," staring turns the corner toward the ethical (101). It would be unethical, then, to gawk in the checkout line at shocking pictures of human mutilation and grotesqueness on the cover of the *National Inquirer*. Yet the same pictures in the *New York Times*, at a thoughtful art exhibition, or in a documentary film—contexts that ask for political engagement—could produce good staring. The shocking pictures from Sierra Leone of amputated hands that appear in the *Washington Post*, the stark photos in a medical textbook, or the amputee beggar on the street corner may rivet eyes equally. But only one that has the capacity to move us to volunteer our time or to petition Congress rather than recoiling and forgetting is ethical. The stareable sight is the same; the response, however, is different. Ethical action is the provenance of starers in Sontag's account of separated and engaged staring encounters.

But what of living and breathing starees? In *On Beauty and Being Just*, Elaine Scarry (1999) augments Sontag's ethics of looking by realizing the object of stares have an active role in an encounter. Intense looking, Scarry claims, initiates an interactional "compact" between a perceiver and a perceived object of beauty (90). Whereas Sontag contemplates what horrifying images do to starers, Scarry ponders how beautiful objects affect them. For Scarry, beauty, like the "repulsive attractions" Sontag contemplates, is a stareable sight that attracts attention and demands engagement. It is not that beauty attracts us per se but rather that by attracting us something becomes beauty.

Scarry's compact between starer and staree is not static but collaborative. Beauty is what beauty does. Staring at beauty, according to Scarry, generates social justice.[3] Beauty is a perceptual process and a transitive action: it catches interest, prompts judgment, encourages scrutiny, creates knowledge. Being seized by beauty conveys "a sense of the newness of the entire world" (22). Even though a thing of beauty might be mundane in another context, its reception renders it extraordinary. In other words, beauty is novelty at work. Scarry's theory of beauty's work also inadvertently helps us understand how baroque engaged staring might work. Beauty, she says, catches you unprepared and provokes unexpected wonder, a reverential awe lost from our modern, disenchanted world.[4] An encounter with beauty is epiphanic, drenched in knowledge-producing narrative drama. Openness to beauty, she concludes, "is the basic impulse underlying education" (7). Looking at beauty generates social justice, Scarry argues, through moving its perceivers toward active "stewardship" of everyone's opportunity for access to beauty. Staring at beauty animates people to extend equity to fellow humans. This is exactly the "action" Sontag expects from good staring at bad pictures. One might say that such staring works to preserve the distinctiveness, the novelty, that animates the staring encounter.

Although Sontag discusses looking at "repulsive attractions" and Scarry at "beauty," together they offer a model with which to consider staring encounters. Scarry's concept of beauty is capacious; a sight becomes beautiful by doing the work of beauty. This understanding suggests that the unbeautiful is the unremarkable, the unnoticeable. We can conclude, then, that the capacity of both "beautiful" and "repulsive" attractions to make us look is similar and has comparable ethical potential. We become ethical starers by being conscious in the presence of something that compels our intense attention. What gives such attractions power in these formulations is their capacity to vivify human empathy through bearing visual witness. In other words, Sontag's and Scarry's accounts suggest that the impulse to stare at novel sights, whether we understand them as conventionally beautiful or repulsive, can move us toward recognizing a "newness" that can be transformative. These stareable sights disturb not just the visual status quo but the ethical status quo as well. Crucial to these interactions, this book asserts, is the role of the staree in the encounter.

SEEING RARE BEAUTY

Many starees we have considered find themselves in the uncomfortable position in a staring encounter of being someone's idea of what Sontag calls a "repulsive attraction." As we have seen, they have developed in response a range of strategies for directing staring interactions. The late disability rights lawyer, activist, and storyteller Harriet McBryde Johnson used media and public appearances to coach the public eye to see her distinctiveness according to her own story rather than the one they may have learned about people who look like her.

"Its not that I'm ugly," Johnson begins in the February 16, 2003, cover story of the *New York Times Magazine*, "It's more that most people don't know how to look at me" (52). With this edgy, yet understated flourish, Johnson begins a story of looking that illustrates how an ethics of staring might work. The photograph of Johnson on the cover shows her seated in her wheelchair, a surprising pose for a cover girl. Boldly beneath her picture sits the unsettling question that Johnson herself poses for many readers: "Should I Have Been Killed at Birth?" The inexplicable combination of this picture, this venue, and this question is startling. With the *New York Times* as her stage, Johnson gathers up starers and proceeds to show them "how to look."

The sight of me is routinely discombobulating. The power wheelchair is enough to inspire gawking, but that's the least of it. Much more impressive is the impact on my body of more than four decades of a muscle-wasting disease. At this stage of my life, I'm Karen Carpenter thin, flesh mostly vanished, a jumble of bones in a floppy bag of skin. At 15, I threw away the back brace and let my spine reshape itself into a deep twisty S-curve. Now my right side is two deep canyons. To keep myself upright, I lean forward, rest my rib cage on my lap, plant my elbows beside my knees. Since my backbone found its own natural shape, I've been entirely comfortable in my skin. (52)

In this description, Johnson takes charge of the staring encounter that began with her cover photo. She accounts for her unusual body, casually, even chirpily, letting us know what "happened" to her. The seeming contradiction between "four decades of a muscle-wasting disease" and the fact that she is "entirely comfortable in [her own] skin" (52) already disturbs our shared understandings of what it means to inhabit a body. Her compelling what-happened-to-you story makes what most of us would consider harrowing into an ordinary experience:

> I am in the first generation to survive to such decrepitude. Because antibiotics were available, we didn't die from the childhood pneumonias that often come with weakened respiratory systems. I guess it is natural enough that most people don't know what to make of us . . . Two or three times in my life . . . I have been looked at as a rare kind of beauty . . . some people call me Good Luck Lady. (52)

In this passage, Johnson continues to undermine complacent understandings by advancing yet another set of contradictions. Following the unlikely partnership of "disease" and "comfortable," comes "decrepitude" and "beauty." This "beauty," however, is not ordinary but "rare" in several ways. First, it is a beauty seldom recognized, only "two or three times in [her] life." Second, it is fragile and infrequent; she is one of the few survivors, not only of "childhood pneumonia" but potentially from the threat of being "killed at birth." Finally, this "rare beauty," this not-ugly, is distinct from typical beauty; it has a form and logic of its own, much like the unconventional beauty

Doug Auld's portraits of burn survivors presents.

In showing us how to look at her, Johnson retells our shared story about beauty. This is a novel beauty made of an elegant "twisty S-curve," of "deep canyons" in unexpected places. Hers is baroque beauty: irregular, exaggerated, and peculiar. Such "rare beauty" is hard to see, both difficult to look at and to appreciate. Like Sontag's pictures of pain, it is hard not to read Johnson's looks as an image of suffering or an occasion for pity or horror. Johnson's picture is hard to see as well because most of us lack the skills to properly appreciate the way she looks without her guidance. If we learn from her how to look, we may come away knowing how to recognize "rare beauty" when we see it again. If Johnson's story succeeds, the wide audience of *The New York Times* may be moved toward a kind of conservation campaign to value and save from extinction the "rare beauty" Johnson has showed them how to appreciate.

The possibilities for misrecognition, of seeing "ugly" where there is "beauty," are perpetual. When strangers catch sight of her, "most often" she reports, "the reactions are decidedly negative" (52):

> Strangers on the street are moved to comment:
> *I admire you for being out; most people would give up.*
> *God bless you! I'll pray for you.*
> *You don't let the pain hold you back, do you?*
> *If I had to live like you, I think I'd kill myself.* (52)

What people usually see, Johnson suggests, is unbearable pain, insurmountable adversity, a diminished life, and a fervent desire for a cured body. Johnson's starers bring with them these usual kinds of stories when they encounter the unusual sight of someone like her. Similarly to the way she showed her starers how to look at her, she proceeds next to show them how to imagine her life:

I used to try to explain that in fact I enjoy my life, that it's a great sensual pleasure to zoom by power chair on these delicious muggy streets, that I have no more reason to kill myself than most people. But it gets tedious. . . . they don't want to know. They think they know everything there is to know, just by looking at me. That's how stereotypes work. They don't know that they're confused, that they're really expressing the discombobulation that comes in my wake. (52)

What makes people who see Johnson "confused" and "discombobulated" is perhaps not so much how she looks but instead how she ended up on the cover of the *New York Times Magazine* rather than on a telethon, a medical textbook, or begging on the street corner. How could she say, "I enjoy my life"? This is not a life most people would claim to enjoy.[5] Johnson has the kind of body and the kind of life that people have learned is a sentence of suffering. She is the kind of person that genetic or prenatal tests screen out for elimination, whose feeding tube gets removed, or mostly who no one wants to become. And yet, with a closer look at her picture, you see fondly plaited long hair in a lovely, dark rope that winds across her slender shoulder. She wears those chic Chinese Mary Janes on feet that will never touch pavement. She is dressed in a flowing, gypsy outfit that hints at an artistic, sensual soul. She looks pretty hip, in her own way. This shot, upon closer look, feels much like the usual fashionable photos on the cover of magazines. In fact, with help from her story, a scene may begin to emerge of her enjoying "great sensual pleasure" zooming around "delicious muggy streets." The power wheelchair in which she seems so comfortably settled perhaps enables rather than confines. Maybe she does not have any reason to kill herself, after all.[6]

Johnson's tutorial on looking is no etiquette lesson about not staring at people with disabilities. Instead, she puts forward an invitation to stare and skillfully crafts its effect, much like other starees we have seen in this book who with great skill show their starers how to look at them. By confronting the readers of the *New York Times* with what they have learned to see as an unlivable life, she tells the story of a livable life—indeed, an enjoyable life of rare beauty.[7] She moves her audience from what they do not expect to see to perhaps expecting to see people like her again. In other words, she gets them accustomed to looking at her by making herself more familiar than strange, by bringing her life story closer to their own. By getting them to see her as unremarkable in her distinctiveness, she makes it possible to identify with her own aliveness, which as she tells it, seems pretty much like theirs. By both showing and telling her experience as if it were ordinary, Johnson reaches toward the work of Scarry's beauty and Sontag's good staring. If Johnson's approach succeeds, the staring encounter she stages will shift her audience from curiosity to knowledge. She will turn them away from arrested stares and set them on a path toward empathetic identification. To use Sontag's and Scarry's terms, she will rescue them from the "repulsive attraction" of bad staring and offer them an opportunity to enact social justice.

By staging strategic staring encounters that teach her audience a new way to look at her, she enables them to recognize her full humanity, to stare without stigmatizing. Understanding that people with stareable bodies can have livable lives contributes to a larger ethical goal of accepting and accommodating devalued human differences. Intolerance for human variation, Michael Ignatieff argues, is an unintended consequence of the "liberal experiment," which fostered sameness as a measure of equality (1997, 66). To counter this intolerance Ignatieff calls for "a polity based on equal rights with the full incorporation of all available human differences" (69). By putting forward what in political terms might be termed her minority embodiment, Johnson asks for recognition of her "differences," her rareness, as distinctive beauty rather than damning deviation. By looking at her closely, they can know her life as she knows it, not as they have learned to imagine it. In showing her audiences that she is not really "ugly," she undertakes the social justice work of "beauty," so that they might recognize "the newness of the entire world" (Scarry 1999, 22). This is her modest offering, then, to making ours a more equitable and inclusive world.

Johnson forges her particular contribution to social justice by using the expertise she has gained as a lifetime staree. One story she tells suggests how she, together with her family, developed staring management techniques. Here for example she describes learning to turn away unwanted stares and to meet them with wry humor:

> In public places, I am stared at so routinely that I typically don't notice it. . . . I do notice when it goes from staring to gawking or more active interaction. A gawking experience I remember as being particularly egregious was when I was 18, going through a crowded museum with my mother. In front of me was a girl, maybe 9 years old, who was actually walking backwards to gawk at me. My mother spoke to the parents: "Your daughter thinks my daughter is the most interesting thing in the museum." The parents grabbed her by the arm, "Come on Gayle, don't stare!" She turned, but 3 seconds later she was gawking again. The parents hollered "Come on Gayle," a couple more times, but then gave up. The aisles were too narrow for us to put space between us (my mother was behind me, pushing my chair), so we had to go through the whole exhibit with this backwards-walking child. It became a family saying for a while, whenever a child was staring: "Gayle's here." (2006 interview)

The skill set Johnson developed learning to manage the many "Gayles" in her life gives her a deep understanding of the way staring works and what it might accomplish. Johnson brings that expertise to her staring project in the *New York Times.* Like a fading language with only a few native speakers remaining, this knowledge is endangered. The picture Johnson presents of herself recommends that we conserve such rare beauty. Deeply settled in her wheelchair, charismatic rather than cute, ironic rather than pathetic, self-assured rather than suffering, Johnson answers the cover's provocative question: "Should I Have Been Killed at Birth?" This is what a life worth living looks like.

VISUAL ACTIVISM

By putting themselves in the public eye, saying "look at me" instead of "don't stare," people such as Matuschka and Johnson practice what might be called visual activism. In 1993 Matuschka exposed her scars and commanded "You Can't Look Away Anymore" to make the public accountable for knowing the reality of her body. Ten years later Johnson presented herself on the same *New York Times Magazine* cover to make the public accountable for knowing that people like her can flourish in their own distinctive way. In doing so, these twin cover girls put to work a three step process of visual activism: look, think, act. First, they use the human urge to look at new things to make people look at them. Second, they use the way they look, the way we look at them, and what they say about it to ask the public to think differently about people like them. The last step depends on their starers' receptiveness. If their visual politics of deliberatively structured self-disclosure succeeds, it can create a sense of obligation that primes people to act in new ways: to vote differently, to spend money differently, to build the world differently, to treat people differently, and to look at people differently.

The risk of all activism is that it will not make this last leap from intent to effect. The intense attentiveness of staring, however, might be particularly supple and effective raw material stareable people can invoke to influence others. To do their work, Matuschka and Johnson appropriate the model of lived face-to-face visual interactions between starers and starees. In other words, the women take what they know from life about how people look at them and go public with it on the pages of *The New York Times Magazine*. They draw on the can't-take-your-eyes-off-it quality of visual engagement, or what we have called baroque staring, that drives starers to keep looking and stay interested. Using a picture and story, they freeze the spontaneous face-to-face relation, expand it to a wide audience, and deliberately direct their starers' responses.

In contrast, lived staring encounters are pliable interventions that respond to the immediate needs and aims of both starers and starees. Stares can be broken off, turned away, continued, softened, or hardened as the participants move through the encounter. An experienced staree, as we have seen, often can take the lead, but a starer must be willing to follow, to stay with the staree if the interaction is to generate any mutual recognition. Because staring strives toward knowing by reducing unfamiliarity, if it is not short-circuited, it can be coaxed toward transformative interaction through the kind of deft management Johnson demonstrates so clearly in her staged staring encounter and starees often practice in their day-to-day lives. The cultural critic bell hooks describes the potential of intense visual interpersonal interaction as a conduit to relations of mutual equality. According to hooks, "eye-to-eye contact, the direct unmediated gaze of recognition . . . affirms subjectivity" (1992, 129-30).[8] To use the language of political philosophy put forward in chapter

10, "the look of recognition" hooks calls for constitutes us as equal citizens and equally legitimate reciprocal participants in the public sphere. To be shut away through segregation or to cover up devalued human differences thwarts opportunities for this recognition. To be recognized, one needs literally to be seen.

In other words, what begins as simple staring, a visual groping toward a new and stimulating sight, has the potential to enact something akin to what psychologist D.W. Winnicott (1965) calls the holding function.[9] To be held in the visual regard of another enables humans to flourish and forge a sturdy sense of self. Being seen by another person is key to our psychological well-being, then, as well as our civil recognition. Staring's pattern of interest, attention, and engagement, the mobilization of its essential curiosity, might be understood as a potential act of be-holding, of holding the being of another particular individual in the eye of the beholder. Staring as beholding is a way to bring visual presence to another person, to recognize fully their "distinctive characteristics" (Fraser 2003, 29). The affirmative recognition visual activists stage is the ethical looking Sontag (2003) calls for and what Martin Buber (1958) describes in theological terms as the face of God in the face of the other. The work of a beholding encounter would be to create a sense of beholdenness, of human obligation that inheres in the productive discomfort mutual visual presence can generate. The radical besiegement of both starer and staree in such an intense visual interaction holds an unexpected opportunity for generating mutual new knowledge and potential social justice. This is an act of generosity, of political and interpersonal leadership, that starees offer starers.

This kind of visual engagement that stays steady when the sight gets uncomfortable is an often deliberate and sometimes inadvertent activist strategy Johnson and many other stareable people invoke every day in order simply to go about their lives with dignity.[10] Starees such as David Roche, Lori and Reba Schappell, Theresia Degener, Lezlie Frye, Mary Duffy, Cheryl Marie Wade, Brittany and Abigail Hensel, Tekki Lomnicki and many others teach starers how to look at them. Often without intention, stareable people, whether performing or just out on the street, reduce the unfamiliarity that the segregation of people with visually significant disabilities like theirs has created in the general public. Now that civil rights legislation has removed many barriers to equal access, people with disabilities are entering and being seen everywhere, from transportation, commercial spaces, employment to the political arena. The public venues for the very stareable have expanded from sideshows to all parts of public life. In contrast to the early decades in the twentieth century when the sight of President Franklin Delano Roosevelt in the wheelchair he used every day was hidden from stares, the sight of public figures who are openly disabled has changed the visual landscape of the public sphere. We now see and recognize as people with disabilities, for example, political figures such as Senator Max Cleland, the late Congresswoman Barbara Jordan, Congressman Jim Langevin, past EEO Commissioner Paul Steven Miller, and New York governor David A. Paterson. Celebrities such as the late actor Christopher Reeve; actors Michael J. Fox, Chris Burke, Peter Dinklage, Marlee Matlin, and Emmanuelle Laborit; journalist John Hockenberry; artist Chuck Close; violinist Itzak Perlman; supermodel Aimee Mullins; and landmine activist Heather Mills claim disability as part of their public persona. The public presence of people with disabilities stretches our shared understanding of the human variations we value and appreciate and invites us to accommodate them.

Positioning oneself in the public eye can be a strategy to "claim disability," explains visual activist and arts consultant Simi Linton. In her memoir *My Body Politic* (2005) Linton, who uses a wheelchair, writes about negotiating a new body and a new visibility after becoming disabled.[11] Linton's is not the expected story about tragedy, loss, or suffering but instead about a "robust and excitable" young woman's transition from "the walking world" into the unfamiliar world of disability and her sudden forfiture of civil inattention. Linton re-enters the world via her wheelchair with the support of peers from the disability community. With verve and wonder, she discovers her new body's new pleasures, hungers, surprises, hurts, strengths, limits, and uses. In "absorb[ing] disability," she also learns that her young body draws attention in a completely new way. Newly stareable, she is seen differently by people. Other disabled people teach her how to be stareable out in the world, how not to hide or cover, and what access routes she can take—from accessible buses, disability rights protests, to college degrees. The circle of collaborators who ease the way as she learns to be "a substantial person" also show her how to flaunt the visible marks of her disability and engage stares. "This new cadre of disabled people," she writes, "has come out of those special rooms set aside just for us. Casting off our drab institutional garb, we now don garments tailored for work and play, love and sport. Indeed, as an indicator of our new social standing, the high-toned among us even appear in television commercials wearing such finery. . . . [W]e wield that white cane or ride that wheelchair or limp that limp" (Linton 1998, 108). Here Linton captures the *relish* with which many practiced starees present themselves to the startled eyes of a public made insensate to the spectacular range of human variation by the social pressure toward visual conformity. The starees we have looked at together in this book show us how to look by showing us how they look. It is all a fine spectacle to behold.

NOTES

1. Sontag's 1977 book *On Photography* might have been titled *Against Photography*, according to W. J. T. Mitchell in *What Do Pictures Want?* (2005). Sontag's later work *Regarding the Pain of Others* (2003) reconsiders her arguments about the power of photography.

2. This kind of bad staring is particular to modernity, Sontag (2003) suggests. The kind of premodern staring at images of human suffering codified in Christian icons such as Saint Sebastian pierced by arrows from head to toe depicts suffering as "a kind of transfiguration," which "links pain to sacrifice," Sontag approves (99). I would continue her analysis by adding that the rhetorical purpose of such premodern sights of suffering and mutilation as the Crucifixion—the central image of Western religious culture (which Sontag surprisingly does not mention)—is to inspire the kind of identification good staring requires. But the intent of this identification is quite distinct from the modern dynamic of good staring at suffering Sontag calls for. The ubiquitous representation of the mutilated, dead, suffering body of the crucified Jesus in western iconography does not command us to work toward the social justice that will eliminate such suffering. In fact, this scene of suffering asks us to accept and transcend human pain, to endure rather than fix it, even to celebrate it. Sontag rightly observes that such depictions "could not be more alien to a modern sensibility, which regards suffering as something that is a mistake or an accident or a crime. Something to be fixed. Something to be refused. Something that makes one feel powerless" (99). Thomas Haskell (1985) has elaborated this same point more fully if less eloquently in his historical analysis of the relationship between the tandem rise of capitalism and benevolence in the nineteenth-century West.

3. Scarry (1999) does not use the word *staring* specifically as the perceptual means of apprehending beauty. However, beauty is available primarily through the visible register. The intensity and unexpectedness of the perception is what characterizes an encounter with beauty for Scarry. In this sense, apprehending beauty is a similar process to staring as I have elaborated it here.

4. See Horkheimer and Adorno (1987) and Campbell (1999).

5. The longer part of Johnson's story recounts her debate with Princeton philosopher and ethicist Peter Singer, who advocates euthanizing significantly disabled newborns. For Singer's argument, see his book, co-authored with Helga Kuhse (1985). Also see Harriet McBryde Johnson, "Not Dead At All" (2005).

6. Social psychologists Ellen Langer et al. (1976) find that people with disabilities are avoided, but discovers that such a response is not aversion, fear, disgust, or perhaps even prejudice but rather this avoidance is about staring. Avoiding or being uncomfortable around people with disabilities is a response caused by conflict between the desire to stare and the social injunction against staring at people. The evidence suggests that when the "stimuli" of difference becomes routine, avoidance and discomfort diminish.

7. For discussion of discrediting supposedly unlivable lives, see Butler (2004); for an examination of what might constitute a livable life, see Nussbaum and Sen (1993).

8. See especially chapter 7, "The Oppositional Gaze: Black Female Spectators."

9. See especially Winnicott (1965, 37–55). For Winnicott, the holding function is performed both by the mother's mirroring gaze and her literal holding of the infant close to her body.

10. Sociologist Fred Davis (1961) described this process as "deviance disavowal." While the stigma management techniques Davis describes are parallel to the performances of the visual activists discussed here and also to the strategies used by many of the informants here, the language of deviance disavowal does not address the full scope in the sociopolitical world of these social interactions.

11. See both of Linton's books: *My Body Politic* (2005) and *Claiming Disability* (1998).

REFERENCES

Butler, Judith. *Precarious Life*. New York: Verso, 2004.

Campbell, Mary B. *Wonder & Science: Imagining Worlds in Early Modern Europe*. Ithaca, N.Y.: Cornell University Press, 1999.

Davis, Fred. "Deviance Disavowal: The Management of Strained Interaction by the Visibly Handicapped." *Social Problems* 9 (1961): 120–32.

Garland-Thomson, Rosemarie. *Extraordinary Bodies: Figuring Physical Disability in American Culture and Literature*. New York: Columbia University Press, 1997.

Goffman, Erving. *Stigma: Notes on the Management*

of Spoiled Identity. New York: Simon & Schuster, 1986.

Haskell, Thomas L. "Capitalism and the Origins of the Humanitarian Sensibility, Part I." *American History Review* 90, no. 2 (1985): 339–61.

——. "Capitalism and the Origins of the Humanitarian Sensibility, Part 2." *American History Review* 90, no. 3 (1985): 547–66.

Horkheimer, Max, and Theodor W. Adorno. *Dialectic of Enlightenment*. New York: Continuum, 1987.

Johnson, Harriet McBryde. "Not Dead at All: Why Congress Was Right to Stick up for Terri Schiavo." *Slate Magazine,* 23 March 2005. http://slate.msn.com/id/2115208/ (accessed 30 August 2006).

Langer, Ellen J., et al. "Stigma, Staring, and Discomfort: A Novel-Stimulus Hypothesis." *Journal of Experimental Social Psychology* 12 (1976): 451–63.

Linton, Simi. *Claiming Disability: Knowledge and Identity.* New York: New York University Press, 1998.

——. *My Body Politic: A Memoir.* Ann Arbor: University of Michigan Press, 2005.

Mitchell, W. J. T. *What Do Pictures Want? The Lives and Loves of Images.* Chicago: University of Chicago Press, 2005.

Nussbaum, Martha, and Amartya Sen, eds. *The Quality of Life.* New York: Oxford University Press, 1993.

Scarry, Elaine. *On Beauty and Being Just.* Princeton, N.J.: Princeton University Press, 1999.

Singer, Peter, and Helga Kuhse. *Should the Baby Live? The Problems of Handicapped Infants.* New York: Oxford University Press, 1985.

Sontag, Susan. *On Photography.* New York: Farrar, Straus and Giroux, 1977.

——. *Regarding the Pain of Others.* New York: Farrar, Straus and Giroux/Picador, 2003.

Winnicott, D. W. *The Maturational Processes and the Facilitating Environment: Studies in the Theory of Emotional Development.* New York: International Universities Press, 1965.

CHAPTER 16

On (Almost) Passing

Brenda Brueggemann

3. REASONS YOU CANNOT BE DEAF

You don't sound funny.
You don't talk too loud.
You have such a nice voice.
You're so normal.
You can wear hearing aids.
You can turn up your hearing aids.
You can try harder.
You don't have any trouble hearing me.
You can do better if you try.
You can hear anything you want to hear.
You can try harder.
You can never really learn sign language.
You didn't grow up deaf.
You didn't go to a deaf school.
You tried to pass as hearing.
You try to pass as hearing.
You don't fit in.
You don't get the jokes.
You don't understand the language.
You don't understand the language.
You just don't understand
the language.
Reasons you can't be hearing:
You can't hear.

—Ilene C. Caroom, *"Like Love,*
This Choice of a Language"

It is much easier to pass as hearing than it is to feign deafness. To be hearing, you can try hard and harder, sound a little funny, talk a little too loud (and often, and fast), wear hearing aids (and hide them)—and you will, for the most part, pass well enough. I should know; I've done it all my life. If I were to write it, my brief biography would read much like Ilene Caroom's, the author of my epigraph: "Although she has a progressive hearing loss, Ilene C. Caroom was raised hearing, with hearing aids, and taught to lipread. She has a B.A. in English from Hollins College and a J.D. from the University of Maryland Law School."[1] While some particulars part us, the sum of our experience looks much the same: to hide my deafness, to pass as hearing, I've tried hard and done quite well. The reasons, as Caroom herself outlines them and unreasonable as they may seem to the hearing world, abound for why I cannot be d/Deaf.

It was not until I had embarked on my "coming out" as a deaf person that I considered my rites of passage and dwelled on my acts, both deliberate and unconscious, both past and present, of passing. Because my coming out was a midlife event, I had much to reflect back on and much to illuminate ahead of me. This passing through an identity crisis, and the rites of passage involved in uncovering the paths of my lifelong passing as "hearing," took place in a hall of mirrors. Later I would come to know this place as the art and act of rhetoric.

I think I first saw myself mirrored in several students I met at Gallaudet University.

I was thirty-two and finishing my Ph.D., writing a dissertation—that quintessential act of literate passing. What's more, I was finishing it by doing an ethnographic sort of study on deaf student writers at Gallaudet University; thus, I was using the guise of an academic grant and a Ph.D.—producing project as a professional foil to make a personal journey to the center of Deaf culture.

I was always good at finding a way to pass into places I shouldn't "normally" be.

So, there I was, doing time as a teacher and researcher at Gallaudet, collecting data for my study, taking a sign language class, living with a d/Deaf woman and faculty member at Gallaudet, going to Deaf gatherings, tutoring some of the students. Mostly, I was just trying to pass in ways that were both familiar and unfamiliar to me: to pass (unfamiliarly) as d/Deaf—and doing a lousy job of it—and to pass (more familiarly) as h/Hearing and thereby pass through this last of major academic hoops.

In this passing, I spent a good deal of time watching—an act for which I had, as a hard-of-hearing person, lifelong experience and impeccable credentials—watching myself, watching the students I was doing case studies of, watching everything in the ethnographic scene of Gallaudet Deaf culture before me. I kept seeing myself in and through many of the students I worked with in the "basic English" classrooms. They were the mirror in my ears. These students often had volatile, if not violent, histories of passing—especially academically. Most of them, by virtue of finding themselves "stuck" (there is a powerful sign for that—two fingers jammed into the throat, a desperate look on the face) in English 050, were still floundering mightily, struggling violently, to pass at basic English literacy. Having negotiated that passage rather adeptly I now, oddly enough, found myself struggling to squeeze through another doorway as I was myself engaged in a mighty, violent struggle to pass in basic d/Deaf literacy.

I don't think I ever got it right. Almost, but not quite. I couldn't be deaf any more than I could be hearing. I was hard-of-hearing; and therein I was as confused and displaced, in either Deaf or Hearing culture, as this multiply-hyphenated term indicates.

The mirror in my ears threw back odd images—distorted, illuminating, disturbing, fantastic, funny—but all somehow reflecting parts of me. It put my passing in various perspectives: perspectives of tense and time (past, present, future); perspectives of repeated situations and relationships in my personal and academic life; and perspectives about the ways that stories are told, identities forged, arguments made. These are but some of the things I saw as I passed through, by, on.

* * *

For some twenty-five years of my life, from age five on, I went to the movies. And while I think I always more or less got the plot, I missed everything in the dialogue. For twenty-five years I sat, passing time with a Three Musketeers candy bar, some popcorn, a Coke. I sat with my sisters as a grade school child on weeknights when my Mom had to work and my Dad was running the film from up in the little booth (both my parents had two jobs). To be sure, we often didn't sit so much as we crawled the aisles, playing hide-and-seek quietly in an always near-empty theater. Sometimes, more sensibly, I went to the lobby to do some homework. Through some films, though—the Disney classics and the cartoons that opened and closed each feature film—I did try to sit, to listen and watch. I don't think I had a conscious knowledge of it then, but now I know that I heard nothing, that I was a pro at passing even back then.

I got better, too, with age and the requisite social agility that becomes most junior high and high school girls. On weekends in my very small, very rural western Kansas town, the theater was the only place to go, the only thing to do. Past the Friday night football or basketball game, the movies beckoned; we'd often go to the same film both Saturday and Sunday night. Going to the movies was the only date possible in Tribune, Kansas.

I dated. They took me to countless movies, and I never heard a word. What's more, in the dark of the movie theater, with no hope of reading my date's lips as he struck up conversations with me, I nodded and feigned attention, agreement, acceptance all the more.

It now all seems so ludicrous, if not painful. For years I have listened to my friends—especially my academic friends—rave about movies, past and present. For years I have shifted back and forth on my feet at parties, smiling, nodding, looking genuinely interested in the discussion of this film or that. Not that I felt left out of their discussions. I just felt somehow disoriented, out of step—not quite passing. Like many deaf people, I not only saw films but enjoyed them. What I didn't know in all those years of adolescent pretense, but know so well now, is that I tend to enjoy films differently than hearing spectators do. I came to know that while they were concentrating on clues to solve the mystery, say, in the dialogue between characters, my eyes, a little more attuned to detail than theirs, would see in the background the weapon of death or notice the facial tension and odd mannerisms of the guilty party.

Take one example: in my early years of graduate school, one of the last years I still let dates take me to movies, I saw David Lynch's *Blue Velvet*. Just recently I had a conversation with my husband about that movie; it was a conversation based on memory, and on memory in different contexts since we had not seen the film together or even remotely in the same place. What

I remembered, what I talked about, were vivid visual details of the movie: the ear lying in the grass that opens the movie, the color of Isabella Rossellini's lips and the way they pouted and quivered, the tenseness in her body, the vivid surreal scenes splashed like canvases in a museum of modern art. And while he himself pointed out how visual the movie was (as indeed most movies are), what my husband remembered most clearly were the conversations. He knew that the severed ear in the grass belonged to Rossellini's husband, that the husband had been kidnapped, and that her actions throughout the movie were done as ransom to keep her husband alive (plenty of reason for body tension and quivering lips). My husband knew this, of course, because they talk about it in the movie.

But I didn't know this. I thought the ear was a symbol of all the scenes of eavesdropping that appear in the film, nothing more, nothing less. I thought the severed ear and the blue velvet forged some artistic link to van Gogh and to Picasso's blue period. This was the sense I made with one sense missing.

So, when the pieces began to fit together and I began, late in my twenties, to understand that I understood precious little of movies beyond the roar of the dinosaurs in *Jurassic Park* or the catchy little tunes of the latest animated Disney "classic," I just stopped going. I had better things to do with my time than hog down a Three Musketeers and bad popcorn. There were other options for dates—especially since my dates now preferred to actually talk about the movie after it was over with, trying out their latest readings in critical theory on the poor, defenseless film over coffee, a drink, dessert. I couldn't hold up my end of the conversation, so I let it stop before it could begin.

I could not always stop conversations before they began, though. (If a genie were ever to grant me three wishes, this would definitely be one of them.) And more times than enough, I found myself pressured into passing and then greatly pressured by my passing. Some days, you see, I could pass; some days I could *almost* pass; some other days the rug almost got yanked out from under me.

My first high school sweetheart was, now that I look back, a real sweetheart; when he could have yanked, he didn't. He let me pass, and he let me do so with grace, saving my hidden deaf face, as it were.

What first attracted me to him was his gentle manner, his quiet, soft-spoken demeanor. It was that demeanor, of course, that doomed our relationship. He was a senior, I only a sophomore—and although I felt enormously comfortable around him (maybe because he didn't talk much, so I didn't have to listen much?), I wanted greatly to impress him. Apparently I did so, because a short month after dating several times, we were cruising main (the only option in Tribune besides "parking"—which only bad girls or longtime steadies did—or going to the movies) and Steve asked me to go steady with him, to wear his gigantic senior class ring. Actually, he asked three times. I didn't hear a one of them. But by the third time—even across the cavernous distance of his big Buick's front seat in the dark of a December night—I could *see* that he was saying something, trying *hard* to say something.

So I said the words that are surely the most common in my vocabulary: "What? Hmmmmm? Pardon me?" (I don't recall exactly which variation it was.)

Now Steve could have been mighty frustrated, out-and-out angry (and I would have not been surprised, since this response is all too common when we are asked to repeat something)—but instead he smiled in his gentle way, the way that had attracted me to him in the first place. He pulled the car over to the curb on main street right then and there, and he shut it off. He turned to face me directly and I could read his lips then. "I said," he still barely whispered, "would you wear my class ring?"

It was a bitter cold, blustery, snowy December night on the western Kansas plains. But I was hot, my face burning. Shamed. And shamed not so much at having not heard the question the first three times, but also in having myself, my deafness, so thoroughly unmasked. It felt as if someone were holding a mirror up to the sun with the reflected sunlight piercing through me. The mirror in my ears hurt. And it hurt even more because in that one fleeting instant in that big Buick at the age of fifteen, I realized, too, how DEAF I was. And I knew I would have to say "no" to soft-spoken Steve, his gentle ways, his giant class ring. I was not hearing enough; he was not deaf enough. And although I couldn't voice it at the time, I knew even then that this was more than just a sheet of glass between us, more than a barrier we could "talk" to each other through.

And I think—in fact, I'm sure—that he knew this, too. But still, instead of saying "never mind" or "oh, nothing" to my "What?" (the other most frequent responses) he let the moment play through, let me have the benefit of the words I had missed. He let me play at passing, let me play it as if it could really be, our going steady, our promise as a couple. He could have ridiculed me with taunts of "Gee, you just don't hear *anything*," or worse, in its "innocent" ignorance, "What's wrong, are you DEAF?" Those, too, are all-too-common responses to my requests that statements be repeated.

So, the moment passed. Steve and I didn't go steady. Nearly a decade later, when he and I were both married (to different persons, of course) we recounted this scene for our spouses; we laughed, they laughed. For a moment, Steve and I locked eyes— and I read it all there: he had known then, as he knew now, that I was indeed deaf. But neither he nor I, then nor at the present moment, would say the word. We let it pass. The conversation went on elsewhere.

* * *

When I began talking and working with deaf students at Gallaudet University as part of my dissertation research project, however, the conversation always went there directly: how I, how they, how we, coped with our deafness in personal relationships, especially with lovers and other significant others. We were trying out our mirrors on each other, trying to see if these multiple mirrors would help us negotiate the difficult passages we always encountered in relationships.

One student, David, an older nontraditional student, had mentioned several times in the course of his interview with me that his wife was far more deaf (in strict audiological terms) than he. It came up most strongly when I asked him directly about how much time he spent with hearing people and in "Hearing culture" as opposed to with deaf people and in "Deaf culture." His answer hinged on his relationship with his wife: "I have a little bit of a struggle with my wife over this issue. She isn't comfortable socializing with hearing people she doesn't know or with my hearing friends who don't sign. So I would end up having to interpret for her or stay right with her to keep her company. So I would either go alone, or go with her with a group of deaf people. I didn't have problems with either group [deaf or hearing], but she did have a problem with the hearing group." I mentioned, smiling, that were he asked, my husband might say some of the same things. We left the issue at that, and I went on to other questions. But at the end of the interview, when the videotape was off and the interpreter we used had left the room, David turned directly to me and in both spoken English and sign language, asked, "I'm curious. You said that

you and your husband have similar communication problems in hearing situations since you are hard-of-hearing and he isn't. How," David paused, with genuine pain on his face, "do you work around this?" I could see that this was a sore spot, a blemish on both our mirrors. And unfortunately, I didn't have any particularly inspiring answers—no secret passageways to divulge and to help us both thereby solve this mystery more neatly, more quickly. We were (and are) both just stumbling and groping, looking for light switches in the often dark hallways of our deafness within relationships.

In the past, too, I had looked to others, more deaf than I, to help illuminate my way through the relationship with my new husband. When I first came to Gallaudet in 1991, I became good friends with a woman some ten years older than I. She had become late-deafened; her gradual deafness was probably genetic and the result of auditory nerve degeneration; her intellect, acumen, wit, and passion amazed me; she liked simple food and good beer and wine; she was the heroic single mother of four teenagers; and she enjoyed the company of men thoroughly. In the fantasizing way, I think, of adopted children who often feel as if they never quite fit with their own parents, and in this time of substantial identity shifting for myself (I was, you see, trying to come out in my deafness), I fantasized her as potential role model, a mentor, a long-lost mother—or maybe sister—of sorts. I held up the mirror to myself and saw her in it; I held up the mirror to her and saw myself in it.

What I watched most carefully in that mirror was my own just-married relationship with a hearing man and the various reflections of my newfound friend, whom I'll call Lynn, in her relationships with men, both deaf and hearing, past and present. It was not always a pretty sight—on either side of the mirror. What I saw in watching

Lynn and in sharing many conversations with her about the dilemmas of life with a hearing man or life with a deaf man was as inspiring as often as it was scary. Either way, the specter of dependence, never really tangible in that mirror, always lurked: to marry a deaf man meant she (we) would be the one(s) that might be most depended on (especially because as late-deafened and exquisitely literate persons we had skills and experience well worth depending on)—and this, then, would leave us little room for the sometimes necessary dependence of our own; but on the flip side (the magnified side of that mirror?), marrying a hearing man might well mean we would come to be too dependent and would, therefore, put at risk our ability to pass on our own, as our own.

When the woman is deaf, in a culture in which the woman is still seen as typically more "dependent" in a male–female relationship, her further dependence on a hearing partner can dangerously diminish her autonomy. Yet at the same time men typically depend on women in certain specialized areas; as Bonnie Tucker has written in *The Feel of Silence,* her controversial autobiography about her deafness, men expect their female partners to carry out an array of social functions that demand precisely the kind of communicative competence that is challenging for the deaf. Women generally mediate between the home and the world in arranging the social obligations and daily domestic duties of (heterosexual) coupled and family life. This calls for speaking with many people, a high proportion of them strangers, both in person and by telephone (in stores, offices, schools . . .), in contexts in which the conversations can't be carefully anticipated or controlled. Discussing her own earlier marriage to a hearing man, Tucker sees the disruption of these cultural norms in the social parameters of male–female relationships as largely responsible for the fact that

successful relationships between hearing men and deaf women are few and far between.

Within Deaf culture, there is more at stake than the bounds of the intimate relationship: to marry either deaf or hearing marks one, proffers one a pass, in the eyes of Deaf culture. Often immediately after the initial identity-confronting question that greets one—"Are you deaf or hearing?"—comes the next test: "Is your spouse deaf or hearing?" In the strictest of cultural terms, to marry deaf is to be Deaf; to marry hearing is to be Hearing. Of course, these strict terms constitute far more an ideal than a reality. Many deaf—and even Deaf—persons I know have nondeaf partners. Still, according to surveys conducted by Jerome Schein and Marcus Delk, over 68 percent of deaf people marry endogamously, with 86 percent expressing a desire to do so.[2]

To marry one or the other, then, is to pass as one or the other. Yet another reason why I have *almost,* but not quite, passed: when Deaf culture seeks to identify me, it holds up the mirror and sees my husband, a hearing man. He is a gentle man, a generally soft-spoken man—like the Steve I didn't go steady with. And yes, I must often depend on him in ways I'd much rather not—asking him to make phone calls for me, asking him to interpret or relay bits of conversation I've missed in social settings, asking him to repeat what one of my own children has said, asking him to help me bow out of uncomfortable social situations, asking him to order for me at restaurants, asking him to pronounce with exaggeration words I'm not sure of, and often, most difficult of all, asking him to just intuitively know when I want to pass on my own and when I want to depend upon him.

It isn't easy. Sometimes I feel like shattering the mirror: it shows me as "crippled," as "disabled" in my dependence.

* * *

It was a young woman, a new and very much struggling student, that I met at Gallaudet when I first went there and was so engrossed in my own coming out, so obsessed with my own identity, who first showed me and let me feel the shards of that mirror. She had been a student in the English 50 class I was a teaching assistant in; I had also tutored her individually and she had served as one of my in-depth case studies, meeting with me weekly for interviews and videotapes of her in the process of writing. We had come to know each other well. And although she looked, figuratively or literally, nothing like Lynn, the older deaf woman I now know I fetishized, I think the mirror drew us to each other—in the way most of us can hardly resist glimpsing ourselves, can hardly resist turning to stare at ourselves, when we pass by any reflective glass. This younger woman (whom, interestingly or conveniently enough, I had assigned the pseudonym "Lynne") turned to me as her model and mentor—me the mainstreamed, academically and somewhat socially successful woman, who had married a hearing man and got along, so it seemed, rather well in the Hearing world.

I hadn't realized how much she had turned to see me in her mirror (and I, in that way that we do when the mirror flatters us, not only had let her but had probably encouraged her)—I hadn't realized until toward the end of the semester I received several desperate long-distance phone calls from her mother in Nebraska. Lynne was not doing well at Gallaudet. It wasn't just her grades, although those were bad enough, to be sure. (Lynne was one of those lifelong products of mainstreaming—now found in abundance at Gallaudet—who arrived as a college freshman with little sign language skills and found herself immersed, even drowning, in Deaf culture and the precedence of sign language—yet another language now, in addition to English, that she didn't quite get.) Lynne was

failing miserably in the Gallaudet social arena: she was lonely, depressed, even cast out. She just didn't fit. And her mother suffered for her, with her.

Back home, it turns out, Lynne had a hearing boyfriend. In righteous anger, her mother wanted her out of the "meanness" of Gallaudet, and so she had begun contacting me to seek my counsel on both the meanness and on getting Lynne out. Essentially, she wanted me to talk to Lynne and encourage her to abandon her long dream of studying at Gallaudet. Lynn's mother, understandably, wanted her back in the hearing world. It was mean there, too—but I think her mother had forgotten about that for the moment. What's more, she wanted Lynne married to a hearing man.

In a bit of conversation that jarred my very bones, her mother asked me if I was married. "Yes," I replied tentatively, not sure why this question had come up.

"Is he hearing?" she probed further. And then I knew just why the question had come up and where it was headed.

"Yes, he is," I confirmed.

"Are you happy—married to him?"

I sputtered a little, I remember, not quite comfortable with the suddenly personal tack that this conversation with a stranger some thousand miles away had taken. But I didn't know how to turn either back or away (mirrors are like this). "Yes," I answered simply.

"Well, good—then there's hope for Lynne, too. Would you tell her that? Could you tell her that she could be married—and happy—with a hearing man?"

I don't know what I said then. Stories and memories are selective, and, as Benedict Anderson has written, "all profound changes in consciousness, by their very nature, bring with them characteristic amnesias";[3] mirrors simply cannot say and show it all. But I do know that I felt deeply the pain of a shattered mirror—the pain of trying to be Lynne's inspiration, her role model, her fetish, her whatever. I could barely get it right for myself, could barely pass either as clearly and securely "d/Deaf" or as "h/Hearing"—how could I ever show someone like Lynne which, if any of those, to be?

I felt very much nailed to the threshold with several tons of doors, from both sides, closing on me.

*   *   *

When I get to feeling this way—trapped, nailed, stuck in between overwhelming options—I tend to get frantic, nervously energized, even mean. And my will to pass, to get through and beyond at all costs, kicks in ferociously. Some animals freeze in fear, shut down in fright; I run—harder, faster, longer. I run until I pass—until I pass on, or out.

And that running always seems to lead me to stories. I have always been a storyteller, a writer, a talker. These "talents" pass me off as "hearing" even as they connect me to "the Deaf way." "The Deaf way" revolves around narrative, around sharing stories— and the narration itself is, in Deaf culture, far more than incidental to the experience. Using sign language, Deaf culture prides itself on its "oral" and "narrative" nature. And for Deaf people, *who* tells the story and *how* they tell it is every bit as important as *what* the story is. The narrator, then, is in control of the experience instead of vice versa.

I tend to control conversations. This is not always a truth I am proud of, but it is the experience I present, the face I show in the mirror. I can talk a lot. I ramble, I chatter—especially on the phone and in one-on-one conversations. It is safer this way: if I don't shut up, if I keep talking, then voilà, I don't have to listen. And if I don't have to listen, I don't have to struggle, don't have to ask for repeats, don't have to assume any of the various appearances that I and other deaf/hard-of-hearing people often appear as—stupid, aloof, disapproving, suspicious. If I keep talking, I pass. I thrive and survive in perpetual animation.

But in situations in which animation affords me no control—in social settings with more than two in the conversation, for example, or as a student in the classroom—I resort quite rhetorically to another strategy: I disappear to what my mother and sisters called "Brenda's La-La Land." I just fade away, withdraw from the conversation. Here it is safer not to speak at all. For if I do, I am sure to be off-topic, three steps behind, completely out of sync with the others. Or even worse, if I speak, someone might ask me a question—a question I would struggle to hear, would have to ask to be repeated (probably more than once), would fail then to answer with wit, intelligence, clarity, quickness. Passing is treacherous going here, so I usually choose not to even venture out, not to cross over the mythical yellow line that marks the divide between d/Deaf and h/Hearing.

When I do venture out or across, I've been trapped more than once—have talked myself right back into the deaf corner. You see, when I talk, people sometimes wonder. "Where are you from? You have quite an accent," I have heard times too innumerable to count—and usually from near strangers. The question is, I suppose, innocent enough. But my answer apparently isn't. For many years I used to pass myself off as German; it was easy enough since my grandparents were quite German and I, as the child of an army family in the 1950s, was born in Germany. Of course, having grandparents who once spoke the language and having lived there, attached to the U.S. Army, for only the first four years of my life didn't really qualify me as a native speaker, complete with an accent. But my interlocutors didn't need to know any of that; when I said "German," they were satisfied. "Oh yes," they nodded, completely in understanding.

But some years ago, as another act of coming out, I stopped answering "German." First I tried out a simple, direct, "I'm deaf." But the result was too startling—it rendered my audience deaf and dumb. They sputtered, they stared at me speechlessly, they went away—fast. It quite unhinged them.

So I have softened the blow a bit and begun to respond, "I'm quite hard-of-hearing." To this I get a split response, which probably fits those multiple hyphens in my identity—they will both smile and nod an affirmative, "Oh yes, I understand now" (although I know that they really *don't* understand the connections between hearing loss and having an "accent"), and they will also back away rather quickly, still reluctant to continue a conversation under these circumstances.

I didn't like passing as German, but I'm never sure I like their response to my real answer any better. When I see the fright in their eyes, the "oh-my-god-what-should-I-say-now?" look that freezes their face into that patronizing smile, I feel cornered again. I feel scared, too, for the way it reflects back on the way I saw myself for many years. I wish I had just stayed mute.

For all that it frightens me, though, when I get cornered and I see my scared, caught-between-the-hyphens, hard-of-hearing face in the mirror, something comes of it. This happened to me first, and I think most significantly, at my first successful academic conference. I had just finished my first year of graduate school and had journeyed to give a paper at the Wyoming Conference on English. I had attended the conference the summer before as well, but I had been in my silently passing mode. This year, however, I was animated by everything from a very positive response to my own paper on the first day, to the glitter of the featured speakers, to a headful of theory-stuff mixed near explosively with my first year of teaching college freshman in a university principally composed of minority and Appalachian, first-generation college students. I was primed. I was talking a lot.

On the third day of the conference we were having a picnic lunch up in the mountains; at a table with one of the conference's biggest stars, I was feeling lit up, I guess by the glitter he was sprinkling on me by showing genuine interest in my own projects and things I had said in earlier sessions. I was telling stories about growing up in western Kansas. Everyone was listening, engaged, laughing.

Then a woman across the table, slightly to the left of me, wearing a tag from some small place in Louisiana, I remember, asked me, point-blank, "So, how long have you been DEAF?" (And that word, especially, went echoing off the mountain walls, I swear.) The question did not fall on deaf ears. The table, full of some sixteen people, went silent—awfully, awesomely silent. They waited.

"A-a-all my life." Silence again. Eons of silence. Echoes of silence.

"Wow," said the star, and he touched my arm—a genuine touch, a caring touch, a you-don't-have-to-feel-bad touch.

But I felt plenty bad. I excused myself under pretense of wanting some more potato salad. Instead I went behind a giant pine tree on the other side of the chow table and tried to breathe, tried to think of how I could make it past those people, to my car, out of here, out of here, out of here.

I know that in this telling the incident may all sound quite melodramatic. But in that moment, I learned, if nothing else and quite melodramatically, that I am the narrator of my experience. I learned that there was a price for passing, that the ticket cost more than just a pretty penny, that the fear of always, at any moment, being "found out" was far worse than just telling at the outset. (Like telling a lie and having to remember who you told it to, who you didn't.)

And what was I so afraid of in the first place?

That moment in Wyoming, at the dawn of my academic career, shortly before I entered my thirties, was the first time I think I asked myself that question. And when I began asking it, I also began taking care and charge of narrating my own experience and identity. I began coming out. At the age of thirty, I took my first sign language class. And I cried mightily on the first night at the sheer thrill of not having to sit in the chair at the front and center of the classroom so I could "hear" the instructor—cried for the simple freedom of choosing my own seat. I also dreamed up a dissertation project, rhetorician that I was, that would take me into "deafness"—my own and others—and to Gallaudet University, to the "heart" of Deaf culture.

If nothing else, I could always write about it, read about it. I had been doing literacy, and doing it well, all my life as yet another supremely successful act of passing. In all those classrooms I disappeared from as I drifted off, when my ability to attend carefully was used up and I wafted away to Brenda's La-La Land, I made up my absence by reading and writing on my own. If nothing else, I could always write about it, read about it.

> At Grandma's family gatherings for the holidays, Brenda was always in the other room, away from the crowds, reading. Nine times out of ten, when Brenda's high school friends went out for lunch and to quickly cruise main, Brenda went to the high school library and read (or wrote one of her crummy poems). The summer before she was to start college, Brenda spent her lifeguard breaks at the noisy pool in the corner of the office, plowing through a used introduction to psychology textbook she'd gotten from another older friend who was already at college. As it turns out, this plowing was what saved her when that fall she found herself in the cavernous intro to psych lecture hall with some three hundred other students—thankful that her name alphabetically allowed her to sit near the front, but still yearning to be an A so she could optimize the lecture from the choicest chair.

And she read. She bought or checked out a dozen more texts on psychology, biology, the skills of writing an essay. She took copious notes from each of them, recorded and memorized key vocabulary from them, read over those notes and her own in-class lecture notes (which she didn't trust) carefully each week, adding notes on top of those notes.

She spent most of her freshman year in the all-girl dorm holed up in her room, writing, reading, taking notes, passing. She went swimming—a silent, individual sport—for a "social" life. After that first frightful year of college it got better. The initial panic of failing, of being found out, subsided. She even skipped class now and then, forgot to study scrupulously for each and every test. She still passed quite well. She took a job—a safe one—lifeguarding in a tall, antisocial chair at the university pool on nights and weekends. She kept writing and reading, but now found her interests were far beyond ingesting college textbooks and taking careful notes; outside of her homework, she started working her way through Russian literature (don't ask me why) and writing short stories.

She avoided bars and parties—sooner or later a young man would come slosh a beer on her, ask her something, and not having heard him, but not wanting to appear any of those dreaded things, she would just nod "yes." It was not always the answer she meant to give.

Books were far easier to control. When she didn't understand a text, it didn't seem to mind her asking for a repeat. She could stare hard, be aloof, acquiesce without embarrassing consequences, speak out of turn, and question a book again and again. It didn't seem to mind. She wasn't deaf when she was reading or writing. In fact, she came to realize that we are all quite deaf when we read or write—engaged in a signing system that is not oral/aural and is removed from the present.

How many times must she have written—to herself or to someone else—"it's easier for me to write this than it is to say it; I find the words easier on paper." On paper she didn't sound deaf, she could be someone other than herself—an artificer (thus fulfilling Plato's worst nightmare about the rhetorical potential in writing). On paper she passed.

* * *

Through the years, although I've become more confident in public speaking and far more willing to unmask myself, my deafness, before others have a chance to, I've always been better at writing and reading than I have at speaking. In graduate school, I was given a prestigious fellowship—principally for my writing skills—and thus my colleagues, both the faculty and other graduate students, expected me, I think, to be a class leader, to speak often and well. I didn't. In fact, I later came to know that many interpreted my silence in the classroom as negligence about the reading, or just arrogant indifference. Negligence about reading was never a crime I was guilty of, although I might own up to some indifference. How could it be otherwise, when only two of my graduate school professors spoke loudly and clearly enough for me to understand more than half of their mumbled, head-down, lifeless, eyes-stuck-on-the-page lectures?

Mostly I was still afraid of myself—still scared of what I saw when I stood in front of the mirror and spoke. As long as I had a written text—something I had worked on and rehearsed in order to smooth out my odd "accent," my tendency for fast talk and illogical progression, and my tonal infelicities—I could be comfortable speaking from and through it. But just to speak well extemporaneously—this was risking breaking the mirror, seven years' bad luck. Writing smoothed the blemishes, softened the sharp edges.

Even when I teach, I teach from and with writing, thereby maintaining control. I avoid, at all costs, leading large group discussions that involve the whole class, discussions in which students might speak from the back of the room—from the places where even my hearing aids on the highest setting won't go. I put them in small groups for discussion and then I walk around, lean over their shoulders, sit down with a small group for a short time. Then I bring one group to the front of the class to help me lead the whole class through discussion, branching out from what they were talking about in their smaller groups. In this way, the students take charge of receiving the questions and become interpreters for me and each other. I like to argue that in this process they gain a new kind of responsibility and learning that they might not have had before; but I know, truth be told, that it's mostly just a matter of getting *me* past some of the more difficult parts of teaching.

My premier pedagogy for passing is, of course, writing. My students, even in the more literature-based classes, write a lot. They always keep journals; they always write too many papers (or so it seems when I'm reading and responding to all of them). And my students, for sixteen years now, are always amazed at how much I write in responding to their journals and papers. For here is a place where I can have a conversation, unthreatened and unstressed by my listening limitations. They write, and I write back.

Writing is my passageway; writing is my pass; through writing, I pass.

NOTES

1. Ilene Caroom's poem and her brief biography appear in Garretson, *Deafness*, p. 8.
2. These figures, to be sure, are likely somewhat outdated; see Schein and Delk, *Deaf Population of the United States*, pp. 15–34.
3. Anderson, *Imagined Communities*, p. 204.

PART IV

*T*heorizing Disability

CHAPTER 17

Reassigning Meaning

Simi Linton

The present examination of disability has no need for the medical language of symptoms and diagnostic categories. Disability studies looks to different kinds of signifiers and the identification of different kinds of syndromes for its material. The elements of interest here are the linguistic conventions that structure the meanings assigned to disability and the patterns of response to disability that emanate from, or are attendant upon, those meanings.

The medical meaning-making was negotiated among interested parties who packaged their version of disability in ways that increased the ideas' potency and marketability. The disability community has attempted to wrest control of the language from the previous owners, and reassign meaning to the terminology used to describe disability and disabled people. This new language conveys different meanings, and, significantly, the shifts serve as meta-communications about the social, political, intellectual, and ideological transformations that have taken place over the past two decades.

NAMING OPPRESSION

It has been particularly important to bring to light language that reinforces the dominant culture's views of disability. A useful step in that process has been the construction of the terms *ableist* and *ableism*, which can be used to organize ideas about the centering and domination of the nondisabled experience and point of view. *Ableism* has recently landed in the *Reader's Digest Oxford Wordfinder* (Tulloch 1993), where it is defined as "discrimination in favor of the able-bodied." I would add, extrapolating from the definitions of *racism* and *sexism*, that *ableism* also includes the idea that a person's abilities or characteristics are determined by disability or that people with disabilities as a group are inferior to nondisabled people. Although there is probably greater consensus among the general public on what could be labeled racist or sexist language than there is on what might be considered ableist, that may be because the nature of the oppression of disabled people is not yet as widely understood.

NAMING THE GROUP

Across the world and throughout history various terminologies and meanings are ascribed to the types of human variations known in contemporary Westernized countries as disabilities. Over the past century the term *disabled* and others, such as *handicapped* and the less inclusive term *crippled*, have emerged as collective nouns that convey the idea that there is something that links this disparate group of people. The terms have been used to arrange people in ways that are socially and economically convenient to the society.

There are various consequences of the chosen terminology and variation in the degree of control that the named group has over the labeling process. The terms *disability* and *disabled people* are the most commonly used by disability rights activists, and recently policy makers and health care professionals have begun to use these terms more consistently. Although there is some agreement on terminology, there are disagreements about what it is that unites disabled people and whether disabled people should have control over the naming of their experience.

The term *disability*, as it has been used in general parlance, appears to signify something material and concrete, a physical or psychological condition considered to have predominantly medical significance. Yet it is an arbitrary designation, used erratically both by professionals who lay claim to naming such phenomena and by confused citizens. A project of disability studies scholars and the disability rights movement has been to bring into sharp relief the processes by which *disability* has been imbued with the meaning(s) it has and to reassign a meaning that is consistent with a sociopolitical analysis of disability. Divesting it of its current meaning is no small feat. As typically used, the term *disability* is a linchpin in a complex web of social ideals, institutional structures, and government policies. As a result, many people have a vested interest in keeping a tenacious hold on the current meaning because it is consistent with the practices and policies that are central to their livelihood or their ideologies. People may not be driven as much by economic imperatives as by a personal investment in their own beliefs and practices, in metaphors they hold dear,

or in their own professional roles. Further, underlying this tangled web of needs and beliefs, and central to the arguments presented in this book is an epistemological structure that both generates and reflects current interpretations.[1]

A glance through a few dictionaries will reveal definitions of disability that include incapacity, a disadvantage, deficiency, especially a physical or mental impairment that restricts normal achievement; something that hinders or incapacitates, something that incapacitates or disqualifies. Legal definitions include legal incapacity or disqualification. *Stedman's Medical Dictionary* (1976) identifies *disability* as a "medicolegal term signifying loss of function and earning power," whereas *disablement* is a "medicolegal term signifying loss of function without loss of earning power" (400). These definitions are understood by the general public and by many in the academic community to be useful ones. *Disability* so defined is a medically derived term that assigns predominantly medical significance and meaning to certain types of human variation.

The decision to assign medical meanings to *disability* has had many and varied consequences for disabled people. One clear benefit has been the medical treatments that have increased the well-being and vitality of many disabled people, indeed have saved people's lives. Ongoing attention by the medical profession to the health and well-being of people with disabilities and to prevention of disease and impairments is critical. Yet, along with these benefits, there are enormous negative consequences that will take a large part of this book to list and explain. Briefly, the medicalization of disability casts human variation as deviance from the norm, as pathological condition, as deficit, and, significantly, as an individual burden and personal tragedy. Society, in agreeing to assign medical meaning to *disability*, colludes to keep the issue within the purview of the medical establishment, to keep it a personal matter and "treat" the condition and the person with the condition rather than "treating" the social processes and policies that constrict disabled people's lives. The disability studies' and disability rights movement's position is critical of the domination of the medical definition and views it as a major stumbling block to the reinterpretation of *disability* as a political category and to the social changes that could follow such a shift.

While retaining the term *disability*, despite its medical origins, a premise of most of the literature in disability studies is that *disability* is best understood as a marker of identity. As such, it has been used to build a coalition of people with significant impairments, people with behavioral or anatomical characteristics marked as deviant, and people who have or are suspected of having conditions, such as AIDS or emotional illness, that make them targets of discrimination.[2] As rendered in disability studies scholarship, disability has become a more capacious category, incorporating people with a range of physical, emotional, sensory, and cognitive conditions. Although the category is broad, the term is used to designate a specific minority group. When medical definitions of *disability* are dominant, it is logical to separate people according to biomedical condition through the use of diagnostic categories and to forefront medical perspectives on human variation. When disability is redefined as a social/political category, people with a variety of conditions are identified as *people with disabilities* or *disabled people*, a group bound by common social and political experience. These designations, as reclaimed by the community, are used to identify us as a constituency, to serve our needs for unity and identity, and to function as a basis for political activism.

The question of who "qualifies" as disabled is as answerable or as confounding as questions about any identity status. One simple response might be that you are disabled if you say you are. Although that declaration won't satisfy a worker's compensation board, it has a certain credibility with the disabled community. The degree and significance of an individual's impairment is often less of an issue than the degree to which someone identifies as disabled. Another way to answer the question is to say that disability "is mostly a social distinction . . . a marginalized status" and the status is assigned by "the majority culture tribunal" (Gill 1994, 44). But the problem gets stickier when the distinction between disabled and nondisabled is challenged by people who say, "Actually, we're all disabled in some way, aren't we?" (46). Gill says the answer is no to those whose difference "does *not* significantly affect daily life and the person does not [with some consistency] present himself/herself to the world at large as a disabled person" (46). I concur with Gill; I am not willing or interested in erasing the line between disabled and nondisabled people, as long as disabled people are devalued and discriminated against, and as long as naming the category serves to call attention to that treatment.

Over the past twenty years, disabled people have gained greater control over these definitional issues. *The disabled or the handicapped* was replaced in the mid-70s by *people with disabilities* to maintain disability as a characteristic of the individual, as opposed to the defining variable. At the time, some people would purposefully say *women and men with disabilities* to provide an extra dimension to the people being described and to deneuter the way *the disabled* were traditionally described. Beginning in the early 90s *disabled people* has been increasingly used in disability studies and disability rights circles when referring to the constituency group. Rather than maintaining disability as a secondary characteristic, *disabled* has become a marker of the identity that the individual and group wish to highlight and call attention to.

In this book, the terms *disabled and nondisabled* are used frequently to designate membership within or outside the community. Disabled is centered, and nondisabled is placed in the peripheral position in order to look at the world from the inside out, to expose the perspective and expertise that is silenced. Occasionally, *people with disabilities* is used as a variant of *disabled people*. The use of *nondisabled* is strategic: to center disability. Its inclusion in this chapter is also to set the stage for postulating about the nondisabled position in society and in scholarship in later chapters. This action is similar to the strategy of marking and articulating "whiteness." The assumed position in scholarship has always been the male, white, nondisabled scholar; it is the default category. As recent scholarship has shown, these positions are not only presumptively hegemonic because they are the assumed universal stance, as well as the presumed neutral or objective stance, but also undertheorized. The nondisabled stance, like the white stance, is veiled. "*White* cannot be said quite out loud, or it loses its crucial position as a precondition of vision and becomes the object of scrutiny" (Haraway 1989, 152). Therefore, centering the disabled position and labeling its opposite nondisabled focuses attention on both the structure of knowledge and the structure of society.

NICE WORDS

Terms such as *physically challenged*, the *able disabled, handicapable*, and *special people/children* surface at different times and places. They are rarely used by disabled activists and scholars (except with palpable irony). Although they may be considered well-meaning attempts to inflate the value of people with disabilities, they convey the boosterism and do-gooder mentality endemic to the paternalistic agencies that control many disabled people's lives.

Physically challenged is the only term that seems to have caught on. Nondisabled people use it in conversation around disabled people with no hint of anxiety, suggesting that they believe it is a positive term. This phrase does not make much sense to me. To say that I am physically challenged is to state that the obstacles to my participation are physical, not social, and that the barrier is my own disability. Further, it separates those of us with mobility impairments from other disabled people, not a valid or useful partition for those interested in coalition building and social change. Various derivatives of the term *challenged* have been adopted as a description used in jokes. For instance, "vertically challenged" is considered a humorous way to say short, and "calorically challenged" to say fat. A review of the Broadway musical *Big* in the *New Yorker* said that the score is "melodically challenged."

I observed a unique use of *challenged* in the local Barnes and Nobles superstore. The children's department has a section for books on "Children with Special Needs." There are shelves labeled "Epilepsy" and "Down Syndrome." A separate shelf at the bottom is labeled "Misc. Challenges," indicating that it is now used as an organizing category.

The term *able disabled* and *handicapable* have had a fairly short shelf life. They are used, it seems, to refute common stereotypes of incompetence. They are, though, defensive and reactive terms rather than terms that advance a new agenda.

A number of professions are built around the word *special*. A huge infrastructure rests on the idea that *special children* and *special education* are valid and useful structuring ideas. Although dictionaries insist that *special* be reserved for things that surpass what is common, are distinct among others of their kind, are peculiar to a specific person, have a limited or specific function, are arranged for a particular purpose, or are arranged for a particular occasion, experience teaches us that *special* when applied to education or to children means something different.

The naming of disabled children and the education that "is designed for students whose learning needs cannot be met by a standard school curriculum" (*American Heritage Dictionary* 1992) as *special* can be understood only as a euphemistic formulation, obscuring the reality that neither the children nor the education are considered desirable and that they are not thought to "surpass what is common."

Labeling the education and its recipients special may have been a deliberate attempt to confer legitimacy on the educational practice and to prop up a discarded group. It is also important to consider the unconscious feelings such a strategy may mask. It is my feeling that the nation in general responds to disabled people with great ambivalence. Whatever antipathy and disdain is felt is in competition with feelings of empathy, guilt, and identification. The term *special* may be evidence not of a deliberate maneuver but of a collective "reaction formation," Freud's term for the unconscious defense mechanism in which an individual adopts attitudes and behaviors that are opposite to his or her own true feelings, in order to protect the ego from the anxiety felt from experiencing the real feelings.

The ironic character of the word *special* has been captured in the routine on *Saturday Night Live*, where the character called the "Church Lady" declares when she encounters something distasteful or morally repugnant, "Isn't that special!"

NASTY WORDS

Some of the less subtle or more idiomatic terms for disabled people such as: *cripple,* *vegetable, dumb, deformed, retard,* and *gimp* have generally been expunged from public conversation but emerge in various types of discourse. Although they are understood to be offensive or hurtful, they are still used in jokes and in informal conversation.

Cripple as a descriptor of disabled people is considered impolite, but the word has retained its metaphoric vitality, as in "the exposé in the newspaper crippled the politician's campaign." The term is also used occasionally for its evocative power. A recent example appeared in *Lingua Franca* in a report on research on the behaviors of German academics. The article states that a professor had "documented the postwar careers of psychiatrists and geneticists involved in gassing thousands of cripples and schizophrenics" (Allen 1996, 37). *Cripple* is used rather loosely here to describe people with a broad range of disabilities. The victims of Nazi slaughter were people with mental illness, epilepsy, chronic illness, and mental retardation, as well as people with physical disabilities. Yet *cripple* is defined as "one that is partially disabled or unable to use a limb or limbs" (*American Heritage Dictionary* 1992) and is usually used only to refer to people with mobility impairments. Because *cripple* inadequately and inaccurately describes the group, the author of the report is likely to have chosen this term for its effect.

Cripple has also been revived by some in the disability community who refer to each other as "crips" or "cripples." A performance group with disabled actors call themselves the "Wry Crips." "In reclaiming 'cripple,' disabled people are taking the thing in their identity that scares the outside world the most and making it a cause to revel in with militant self-pride" (Shapiro 1993, 34).

A recent personal ad in the *Village Voice* shows how "out" the term is:

TWISTED CRIP: Very sexy, full-figured disabled BiWF artist sks fearless, fun, oral BiWF for hot, no-strings nights. Wheelchair, tattoo, dom. Shaved a + N/S No men/sleep-overs.

Cripple, gimp and freak as used by the disability community have transgressive potential. They are personally and politically useful as a means to comment on oppression because they assert our right to name experience.

SPEAKING ABOUT OVERCOMING AND PASSING

The popular phrase *overcoming a disability* is used most often to describe someone with a disability who seems competent and successful in some way, in a sentence something like "She has overcome her disability and is a great success." One interpretation of the phrase might be that the individual's disability no longer limits her or him, that sheer strength or willpower has brought the person to the point where the disability is no longer a hindrance. Another implication of the phrase may be that the person has risen above society's expectation for someone with those characteristics. Because it is physically impossible to *overcome* a disability, it seems that what is *overcome* is the social stigma of having a disability. This idea is reinforced by the equally confounding statement "I never think of you as disabled." An implication of these statements is that the other members of the group from which the individual has supposedly moved beyond are not as brave, strong, or extraordinary as the person who has *overcome* that designation.

The expression is similar in tone to the phrase that was once more commonly used to describe an African American who was considered exceptional in some way: "He/she is a credit to his/her race." The implication of this phrase is that the "race" is somehow discredited and needs people

with extraordinary talent to give the group the credibility that it otherwise lacks. In either case, talking about the person who is African American or talking about the person with a disability, these phrases are often said with the intention of complimenting someone. The compliment has a double edge. To accept it, one must accept the implication that the group is inferior and that the individual is unlike others in that group.

The ideas imbedded in the *overcoming* rhetoric are of personal triumph over a personal condition. The idea that someone can *overcome* a disability has not been generated within the community; it is a wish fulfillment generated from the outside. It is a demand that you be plucky and resolute, and not let the obstacles get in your way. If there are no curb cuts at the corner of the street so that people who use wheelchairs can get across, then you should learn to do wheelies and jump the curbs. If there are no sign language interpreters for deaf students at the high school, then you should study harder, read lips, and stay up late copying notes from a classmate. When disabled people internalize the demand to "overcome" rather than demand social change, they shoulder same kind of exhausting and self-defeating "Super Mom" burden that feminists have analyzed.

The phrase *overcome a disability* may also be a shorthand version of saying "someone with a disability overcame many obstacles." Tremblay (1996) uses that phrase when describing behaviors of disabled World War II veterans upon returning to the community: "[T]heir main strategies were to develop individualized strategies to overcome the obstacles they found in the community" (165). She introduces this idea as a means to describe how the vets relied on their own ingenuity to manage an inaccessible environment rather than demand that the community change to include them.

In both uses of *overcome*, the individual's responsibility for her or his own success is paramount. If we, as a society, place the onus on individuals with disabilities to work harder to "compensate" for their disabilities or to "overcome" their condition or the barriers in the environment, we have no need for civil rights legislation or affirmative action.

Lest I be misunderstood, I don't see working hard, doing well, or striving for health, fitness, and well-being as contradictory to the aims of the disability rights movement. Indeed, the movement's goal is to provide greater opportunity to pursue these activities. However, we shouldn't be impelled to do these because we have a disability, to prove to some social overseer that we can perform, but we should pursue them because they deliver their own rewards and satisfactions.

A related concept, familiar in African American culture as well as in lesbian and gay culture, is that of *passing*. African Americans who pass for white and lesbians and gays who pass for straight do so for a variety of personal, social, and often economic reasons. Disabled people, if they are able to conceal their impairment or confine their activities to those that do not reveal their disability, have been known to pass. For a member of any of these groups, passing may be a deliberate effort to avoid discrimination or ostracism, or it may be an almost unconscious, Herculean effort to deny to oneself the reality of one's racial history, sexual feelings, or bodily state. The attempt may be a deliberate act to protect oneself from the loathing of society or may be an unchecked impulse spurred by an internalized self-loathing. It is likely that often the reasons entail an admixture of any of these various parts.

Henry Louis Gates, Jr. (1996) spoke of the various reasons for passing in an essay on the literary critic Anatole Broyard. Broyard was born in New Orleans to a family that identified as "Negro." His skin was so light that for his entire career as "one of literary America's foremost gatekeepers" (66) the majority of people who knew him did not know this. His children, by then adults, learned of his racial history shortly before he died. Sandy Broyard, Anatole's wife, remarked that she thought that "his own personal history continued to be painful to him. . . . In passing, you cause your family great anguish, but I also think conversely, do we look at the anguish it causes the person who is passing? Or the anguish that it was born out of?" (75).

When disabled people are able to pass for nondisabled, and do, the emotional toll it takes is enormous. I have heard people talk about hiding a hearing impairment to classmates or colleagues for years, or others who manage to conceal parts of their body, or to hide a prosthesis. These actions, though, may not result in a family's anguish; they may, in fact, be behaviors that the family insists upon, reinforces, or otherwise shames the individual into. Some disabled people describe how they were subjected to numerous painful surgeries and medical procedures when they were young not so much, they believe, to increase their comfort and ease of mobility as to fulfill their families' wish to make them appear "more normal."

Even when a disability is obvious and impossible to hide on an ongoing basis, families sometimes create minifictions that disabled people are forced to play along with. Many people have told me that when family pictures were taken as they were growing up, they were removed from their wheelchairs, or they were shown only from the waist up, or they were excluded from pictures altogether. The messages are that this part of you, your disability or the symbol of disability, your wheelchair, is unacceptable, or, in the last case, you are not an acceptable member of the family.

I was recently in an elementary school

when class pictures were taken, and I learned that it is the custom for all the children who use wheelchairs to be removed from their chairs and carried up a few steps to the auditorium stage and placed on folding chairs. I spoke with people at the school who said they have thought about raising money to build a ramp to the stage, but in the meantime this was the solution. I wondered, of course, why they have to take pictures on the stage when it is inaccessible. The families of these children or the school personnel might even persist with this plan, believing that these actions have a positive effect on children, that they demonstrate that the disabled child is "just like everybody else." But these fictions are based more clearly on the projections of the adults than on the unadulterated feelings of the child. The message that I read in this action: You are like everyone else, but only as long as you hide or minimize your disability.

Both passing and overcoming take their toll. The loss of community, the anxiety, and the self-doubt that inevitably accompany this ambiguous social position and the ambivalent personal state are the enormous cost of declaring disability unacceptable. It is not surprising that disabled people also speak of "coming out" in the same way that members of the lesbian and gay community do. A woman I met at a disability studies conference not long ago said to me in the course of a conversation about personal experience: "I'm five years old." She went on to say that despite being significantly disabled for many years, she had really only recently discovered the disabled community and allied with it. For her, "coming out" was a process that began when she recognized how her effort to "be like everyone else" was not satisfying her own needs and wishes. She discovered other disabled people and began to identify clearly as disabled, and then purchased a motorized scooter, which meant she didn't have

to expend enormous energy walking. She told this tale with gusto, obviously pleased with the psychic and physical energy she had gained. Stories such as hers provide evidence of the personal burdens many disabled people live with. Shame and fear are personal burdens, but if these tales are told, we can demonstrate how the personal is indeed the political. And further, that the unexamined connections between the personal and political are the curricular.

NORMAL/ABNORMAL

Normal and *abnormal* are convenient but problematic terms used to describe a person or group of people. These terms are often used to distinguish between people with and without disabilities. In various academic disciplines and in common usage, *normal* and *abnormal* assume different meanings. In psychometrics, *norm* or *normal* are terms describing individuals or characteristics that fall within the center of the normal distribution on whatever variable is being measured. However, as the notion of *normal* is applied in social science contexts and certainly in general parlance, it implies its obverse—*abnormal*—and they both become value laden. Often, those who are not deemed normal are devalued and considered a burden or problem, or are highly valued and regarded as a potential resource. Two examples are the variables of height and intelligence. Short stature and low measured intelligence are devalued and labeled abnormal, and people with those characteristics are considered disabled. Tall people (particularly males) and high scores on IQ tests are valued, and, although not normal in the statistical sense, are not labeled abnormal or considered disabled.[3]

Davis (1995) describes the historical specificity of the use of *normal* and thereby calls attention to the social structures that are dependent on its use. "[T]he very term that permeates our contemporary life—the normal—is a configuration that arises in a particular historical moment. It is part of a notion of progress, of industrialization, and of ideological consolidation of the power of the bourgeoisie. The implications of the hegemony of normalcy are profound and extend into the very heart of cultural production" (49).

The use of the terms *abnormal* and *normal* also moves discourse to a high level of abstraction, thereby avoiding concrete discussion of specific characteristics and increasing ambiguity in communication. In interactions, there is an assumed agreement between speaker and audience of what is normal that sets up an aura of empathy and "us-ness." This process "enhances social unity among those who feel they are normal" (Freilich, Raybeck, and Savishinsky 1991, 22), necessarily excluding the other or abnormal group.

These dynamics often emerge in discussions about disabled people when comparisons are made, for instance, between "the normal" and "the hearing impaired," or "the normal children" and "the handicapped children." The first example contrasts two groups of people; one defined by an abstract and evaluative term (the normal), the other by a more specific, concrete, and nonevaluative term (the hearing impaired). In the second comparison, the "handicapped children" are labeled abnormal by default. Setting up these dichotomies avoids concrete discussion of the ways the two groups of children actually differ, devalues the children with disabilities, and forces an "us and them" division of the population.

The absolute categories *normal* and *abnormal* depend on each other for their existence and depend on the maintenance of the opposition for their meaning. Sedgwick (1990), in *Epistemology of the Closet*, comments on a similar pattern in the forced choice categories homosexual and heterosexual:

[C]ategories presented in a culture as symmetrical binary oppositions—heterosexual/homosexual, in this case—actually subsist in a more unsettled and dynamic tacit relation according to which, first, term B is not symmetrical with but subordinated to term A; but, second, the ontologically valorized term A actually depends for its meaning on the simultaneous subsumption and exclusion of term B; hence, third, the question of priority between the supposed central and the supposed marginal category of each dyad is irresolvably unstable, an instability caused by the fact that term B is constituted as at once internal and external to term A. (9–10)

Despite the instability and the relational nature of the designations *normal* and *abnormal*, they are used as absolute categories. They have achieved their certainty by association with empiricism, and they suffer from empiricism's reductive and simplifying tendencies. Their power and reach are enormous. They affect individuals' most private deliberations about their worth and acceptability, and they determine social position and societal response to behavior. The relationship between abnormality and disability accords to the nondisabled the legitimacy and potency denied to disabled people. And, central to our concerns here, the reification of *normal* and *abnormal* structures curriculum. Courses with titles such as "Abnormal Psychology," "Sociology of Deviance," "Special Education," and "Psychopathology" assume the internal consistency of a curriculum focused on "the abnormal" and depend on the curriculum of the "normal" being taught elsewhere. In fact, this organization of knowledge implicitly suggests that the rest of the curriculum is "normal."

Rosemarie Garland-Thomson (1997) has coined the term *the normate*, which, like *nondisabled*, is useful for marking the unexamined center. "This neologism names the veiled subject position of cultural self, the figure outlined by the array of deviant others whose marked bodies shore up the normate's boundaries. The term *normate* usefully designates the social figure through which people can represent themselves as definitive human beings" (8). By meeting *normal* on some of its own terms, *normate* inflects its root, and challenges the validity, indeed the possibility, of normal. At the same time, its ironic twist gives a more flavorful reading of the idea of normal.

PASSIVITY VERSUS CONTROL

Language that conveys passivity and victimization reinforces certain stereotypes when applied to disabled people. Some of the stereotypes that are particularly entrenched are that people with disabilities are more dependent, childlike, passive, sensitive, and miserable and are less competent than people who do not have disabilities. Much of the language used to depict disabled people relates the lack of control to the perceived incapacities, and implies that sadness and misery are the product of the disabling condition.

These deterministic and essentialist perspectives flourish in the absence of contradictory information. Historically, disabled people have had few opportunities to be active in society, and various social and political forces often undermine the capacity for self-determination. In addition, disabled people are rarely depicted on television, in films, or in fiction as being in control of their own lives—in charge or actively seeking out and obtaining what they want and need. More often, disabled people are depicted as pained by their fate or, if happy, it is through personal triumph over their adversity. The adversity is not depicted as lack of opportunity, discrimination, institutionalization, and ostracism; it is the personal burden of their own body or means of functioning.

Phrases such as *the woman is a victim of cerebral palsy* implies an active agent

(cerebral palsy) perpetrating an aggressive act on a vulnerable, helpless "victim." The use of the term *victim*, a word typically used in the context of criminal acts, evokes the relationship between perpetrator and victim. Using this language attributes life, power, and intention to the condition and disempowers the person with the disability, rendering him or her helpless and passive. Instead, if there is a particular need to note what an individual's disability is, saying *the woman has cerebral palsy* describes solely the characteristic of importance to the situation, without imposing extraneous meaning.

Grover (1987) analyzes the word *victim* as used to describe people with AIDS. She notes that the term implies fatalism, and therefore "enable[s] the passive spectator or the AIDS 'spectacle' to remain passive." Use of the term may also express the unconscious wish that the people with AIDS may have been "complicit with, to have courted, their fate" (29), in which case the individual would be seen as a *victim* of her or his own drives. This is particularly apparent when the phrase *innocent victim* is used to distinguish those who acquire HIV from blood transfusions or other medical procedures from those who contract HIV from sexual contact or shared needles. This analysis is also pertinent to people with other disabilities because a number of belief systems consider disability, or some disabilities, as punishment for sin in this or a former life.

Disabled people are frequently described as *suffering from* or *afflicted with* certain conditions. Saying that someone is *suffering from* a condition implies that there is a perpetual state of suffering, uninterrupted by pleasurable moments or satisfactions. *Afflicted* carries similar assumptions. The verb *afflict* shares with *agonize, excruciate, rack, torment,* and *torture* the central meaning "to bring great harm or suffering to someone" (*American Heritage Dictionary* 1992,

30). Although some people may experience their disability this way, these terms are not used as descriptors of a verified experience but are projected onto disability. Rather than assume suffering in the description of the situation, it is more accurate and less histrionic to say simply that a person *has a disability*. Then, wherever it is relevant, describe the nature and extent of the difficulty experienced. My argument here isn't to eliminate descriptions of suffering but to be accurate in their appointment. It is interesting that AIDS activists intentionally use the phrase *living with AIDS* rather than *dying from AIDS*, not to deny the reality of AIDS but to emphasize that people are often actively engaged in living even in the face of a serious illness.

The ascription of passivity can be seen in language used to describe the relationship between disabled people and their wheelchairs. The phrases *wheelchair bound* or *confined to a wheelchair* are frequently seen in newspapers and magazines, and heard in conversation. A more puzzling variant was spotted in *Lingua Franca*, which described the former governor of Alabama, George Wallace, as the "slumped, wheelchair-ridden 'Guv'nah'" (Zalewski 1995, 19). The choice here was to paint the wheelchair user as *ridden*, meaning "dominated, harassed, or obsessed by" (*American Heritage Dictionary* 1992), rather than the rider in the wheelchair. The various terms imply that a wheelchair restricts the individual, holds a person prisoner. Disabled people are more likely to say that someone *uses a wheelchair*. The latter phrase not only indicates the active nature of the user and the positive way that wheelchairs increase mobility and activity but recognizes that people get in and out of wheelchairs for different activities: driving a car, going swimming, sitting on the couch, or, occasionally, for making love.

A recent oral history conducted with disabled Canadian World War II veterans and other disabled people who are contemporaries of the vets recounts their memories of the transition from hospital-style wicker wheelchairs used to transport patients to self-propelled, lighter-weight, folding chairs that were provided to disabled people, mostly to veterans, in the years following the war. Prior to the new chairs, one man recalls that "one was often confined to bed for long periods of time. . . . There were a few cerebral palsy chaps there. . . . If they transgressed any rule . . . they'd take their wheelchairs away from them and leave them in bed for two weeks" (Tremblay 1996, 153). In this and other interviews the value of wheelchairs is revealed. A vet described how the medical staff's efforts were geared toward getting veterans to walk with crutches, but when the vets discovered the self-propelled chairs they realized "it didn't make much sense spending all that energy covering a short distance [on crutches] . . . when you could do it quickly and easily with a wheelchair. . . . It didn't take long for people to get over the idea that walking was that essential" (158–59). Another veteran recalled how the staff's emphasis on getting the men to walk "delayed our rehabilitation for months and months" (159). The staff obviously understood the value of the wheelchair to disabled people; otherwise they would not have used it as a means of control, yet they resisted purchasing the new self-push chairs for some time after they were made available. It is that type of manipulation and control, along with architectural and attitudinal barriers, that confine people. It is not wheelchairs.

MULTIPLE MEANINGS

Are *invalid*, with the emphasis on the first syllable, and *invalid*, with the emphasis on the second, synonyms or homonyms? Does the identical housing of *patient*, the adjective, and *patient*, the noun, conflate the two meanings? Did their conceptual relationship initially determine their uniform casing?

For instance, *invalid* is a designation used to identify some disabled people. The term is seen most prominently on the sides of vans used to transport people with mobility impairments. Disabled people, desperate for accessible transportation, must use vans with the dubious appellation *"Invalid Coach"* printed in bold letters on the side. Aside from this being a fertile source of jokes about the aptness of these notoriously bad transportation services being identified as "not factually or legally valid; falsely based or reasoned; faulty" (*American Heritage Dictionary* 1992), those on the inside of the bus suffer the humiliation of being written off so summarily. Both *invalids* share the Latin root *invalidus*, which means weak. It could be argued that some disabilities do result in weakening of the body, or, more likely, parts of the body, but the totalizing noun, *invalid*, does not confine the weakness to the specific bodily functions; it is more encompassing.

The homonymic *patient/patient*, is, I think, not coincidental or irrelevant. The noun *patient* is a role designation that is always relational. A patient is understood to belong to a doctor or other health care professional, or more generally to an institution. As a noun, *patient* is a neutral description of the role of "one who receives medical attention, care, or treatment" (*American Heritage Dictionary* 1992). The adjective *patient* moves beyond the noun's neutral designation to describe a person who is capable of "bearing or enduring pain, difficulty, provocation, or annoyance with calmness" as well as "tolerant . . . persevering . . . constant . . . not hasty" (*American Heritage Dictionary* 1992). The "good" patient is one who does not challenge the authority of the practitioner or institution and who complies with the regimen set out by the expert, in other words a patient. Disabled people, who have often spent a great deal of time as patients, discuss the ways that we have been socialized in the medical culture to be compliant, and that has often undermined our ability to challenge authority or to function autonomously. Further, the description of disabled people as patients in situations where we are not, reinforces these ideas.[4]

REFLECTIONS ON THE *DIS* IN DISABILITY

Before discussing the prefix *dis*, let's examine a similar bound morpheme that conveys meaning and significantly modifies the words it is attached to. The suffix *ette*, when appended to nouns, forms words meaning small or diminutive, as in *kitchenette;* female, as in *usherette;* or imitation or inferior kind, as in *leatherette* (*American Heritage Dictionary* 1992). These various meanings of *ette* slip around in our minds to influence how we interpret other words with the same suffix. So, for instance, although the word *leatherette* is used to tell us it is not the real thing and an inferior version of leather, *usherette* becomes, by association, not only the female version of usher but denotes a poor imitation. *Usherette* becomes, like *kitchenette*, the diminutive version. These various meanings tumble into one another, propagating new meanings, unintended and imprecise. I recently met a woman who told me that she had been a Rockette at Radio City Music Hall in Rockefeller Center for twenty years. I realized that this string of high-kicking, synchronized dancing women are perpetually cast as the smaller, imitation, inferior and female counterparts of the great male barons, the Rockefellers.

The prefix *dis*, like the suffix *ette*, has similarly unchecked impulses. Although *ette* qualifies its base and reduces it to the more diminutive and less valid version, a relationship is maintained between the base and its amended version. However, the prefix *dis* connotes separation, taking apart, sundering in two. The prefix has various meanings such as not, as in *dissimilar*; absence of, as in *disinterest*; opposite of, as in *disfavor*; undo, do the opposite of, as in *disarrange*; and deprive of, as in *disfranchise*. The Latin root *dis* means apart, asunder. Therefore, to use the verb *disable*, means, in part, to deprive of capability or effectiveness. The prefix creates a barrier, cleaving in two ability and its absence, its opposite. Disability is the "not" condition, the repudiation of ability.

Canguilhem (1991), in his explorations of the normal and the pathological, recognizes the way that prefixes signal their relationship to the words they modify. He asserts that

> the pathological phenomena found in living organisms are nothing more than quantitative variations, greater or lesser according to corresponding physiological phenomena. Semantically, the pathological is designated as departing from the normal not so much by *a-* or *dys-* as by *hyper-* or *hypo-*. . . . [T]his approach is far from considering health and sickness as qualitatively opposed, or as forces joined in battle." (42)

Ette, hyper and *hypo*, and *dis* have semantic consequences, but, moreover, each recapitulates a particular social arrangement. The suffix *ette* not only qualifies the meaning of the root word it is attached to but speaks of the unequal yet dynamic relationship between women and men, in which "woman was, as we see in the profoundly influential works of Aristotle, not the equal opposite of man but a failed version of the supposedly defining type" (Minnich 1990, 54). The medical prefixes *hyper* and *hypo* are typically attached to medical conditions that are temporary or circumscribed. People with those conditions are not socially marked and separated as are those with the more pronounced, and long standing conditions known as disabilities. With *hyper* and *hypo* conditions, there is less semantic and social disjuncture. However, the construction of *dis/ability* does not imply the continuum approach Canguilhem finds in diagnostic categories. *Dis* is the semantic reincarnation of the split between disabled and nondisabled people in society.

Yet *women and men with disabilities, disabled people*, and the *disability community* are terms of choice for the group. We have decided to reassign meaning rather than choose a new name. In retaining *disability* we run the risk of preserving the medicalized ideas attendant upon it in most people's idea of disability. What I think will help us out of the dilemma is the naming of the political category in which *disability* belongs. Women is a category of *gender*, and black or Latino/a are categories of *race/ethnicity*, and it is the recognition of those categories that has fostered understanding of the political meaning of *women* and *black*. Although *race* and *gender* are not perfect terms because they retain biological meanings in many quarters, the categories are increasingly understood as axes of oppression; axes along which power and resources are distributed. Although those of us within the disability community recognize that power is distributed along disability lines, the naming and recognition of the axis will be a significant step in gaining broader recognition of the issues. Further, it will enrich the discussion of the intersections of the axes of class, race, gender and sexual orientation, and disability.

Constructing the axis on which disabled and nondisabled fall will be a critical step in marking all points along it. Currently, there is increased attention to the privileged points on the continua of race, gender, and sexual orientation. There is growing recognition that the white, the male, and the heterosexual positions need to be noted and theorized. Similarly, it is important to examine the nondisabled position and its privilege and power. It is not the neutral, universal position from which disabled people deviate, rather, it is a category of people whose power and cultural capital keep them at the center.

In this book, though, disabled people's perspectives are kept central and are made explicit, partly to comment on how marginal and obscure they typically are, and partly to suggest the disciplinary and intellectual transformation consequent on putting disability studies at the center.

NOTES

1. Various authors have discussed issues related to definitions of *disability*. See Wendell (1996), Longmore (1985b, 1987), and Hahn (1987), and also the June Isaacson Kailes (1995) monograph *Language Is More Than a Trivial Concern!* which is available from the Institute on Disability Culture, 2260 Sunrise Point Road, Las Cruces, New Mexico 88011.

2. The definition of *disability* under the Americans with Disabilities Act is consistent with the sociopolitical model employed in disability studies. A person is considered to have a disability if he or she:

   - has a physical or mental impairment that substantially limits one or more of his or her major life activities;
   - has a record of such an impairment; or
   - is regarded as having such an impairment.

   The last two parts of this definition acknowledge that even in the absence of a substantially limiting impairment, people can be discriminated against. For instance, this may occur because someone has a facial disfigurement or has, or is suspected of having, HIV or mental illness. The ADA recognizes that social forces, such as myths and fears regarding disability, function to substantially limit opportunity.

3. I am indebted to my colleague John O'Neill for his input on these ideas about the use of the term *normal*.

4. See June Isaacson Kailes's (1995), *Language Is More Than a Trivial Concern!* for a discussion on language use.

WORKS CITED

Allen, A. 1996. Open secret: A German academic hides his past—in plain sight. *Lingua Franca* 6 (3): 28–41.

American Heritage Dictionary. 1992. 3rd ed. Boston: Houghton Mifflin.

Cangiulhem, G. 1991. *The normal and the pathological.* New York: Zone Books.

Davis, L. J. 1995. *Enforcing normalcy: Disability, deafness, and the body.* London: Verso.

Freilich, M., Raybeck, D., and Savishinsky, J. 1991. *Deviance: Anthropological perspectives.* New York: Bergin and Garvey.

Garland-Thomson, R. (1997) Extraordinary bodies: *Figuring physical disability in American culture and literature.* New York: Columbia UP.

Gates, H. L., Jr. 1996. White like me. *New Yorker* 72 (16): 66–81.

Gill, C. J. 1994. Questioning continuum. In B. Shaw, ed., *The ragged edge: The disability experience from the pages of the first fifteen years of "The Disability Rag,"* 42–49. Louisville, Ky.: Advocado Press.

Grover, J.Z. 1987. AIDS: Keywords. In Douglas Crimp, ed., *AIDS: Cultural analysis,* 17–30. Cambridge: MIT Press.

Hahn, H. 1987. Disability and capitalism: Advertising the acceptably employable image. *Policy Studies Journal* 15 (3): 551–70.

Haraway, D. 1989. *Primate visions: Gender, race, and nature in the world of modern science.* New York: Routledge.

Kailes, J. I. 1995. *Language is more than a trivial concern!* (Available from June Isaacson Kailes, Disability Policy Consultant, 6201 Ocean Front Walk, Suite 2, Plaza del Rey, California 90293–7556).

Longmore, P. K. 1985. The life of Randolph Bourne and the need for a history of disabled people. *Reviews in American History* 586 (December) 581–587.

———. 1987. Uncovering the hidden history of people with disabilities. *Reviews in American History* 15 (3) (September): 355–364.

Minnick, E. K. 1990. *Transforming knowledge.* Philadelphia: Temple UP.

Sedgwick, E. K. 1990. *Epistemology of the closet.* Berkeley: U of California P.

Shapiro, J. P. 1993. *No pity: People with disabilities forging a new civil rights movement.* New York: Times Books.

Steadman's Medical Dictionary. 1976. 23d ed. Baltimore: Williams and Wilkins.

Tremblay, M. 1996. Going back to civvy street: A historical account of the Everest and Jennings wheelchair for Canadian World War II veterans with spinal cord injury. *Disability and Society* 11(2): 146–169.

Tulloch, S., ed. 1993. *The Reader's Digest Oxford wordfinder.* Oxford, Eng.: Clarendon Press.

Wendell, S. 1996. *The rejected body: Feminist philosophical reflections on disability.* New York: Routledge.

CHAPTER 18

Enabling Disability: Rewriting Kinship, Reimagining Citizenship

Faye Ginsburg and Rayna Rapp

In trying to portray my son in the literary model known as a novel, I have passed through . . . stages. In the case of a person like him with a mental disability, it isn't the individual himself but rather his family that has to pass from the "shock phase" to the "acceptance phase." In a sense, my work on this theme has mirrored that process. I have had to learn through concrete experience to answer such questions as how a handicapped person and his family can survive the shock, denial, and confusion phases and learn to live with each of those particular kinds of pain. I then had to find out how we could move beyond this to a more positive adjustment, before finally reaching our own "acceptance phase"—*in effect coming to accept ourselves as handicapped, as the family of a handicapped person.* And it was only then that I felt the development of my work itself was at last complete.

(Oe 1995: 46, emphasis added)

In 1963, when the Japanese novelist Kenzaburo Oe's son Hikari was born with a dangerous brain tumor, Oe and his wife chose to have it removed, a process that, along with a range of other kinds of supports, enabled the infant Hikari to survive, but with a profound disability. Since then, the family has had to re-create itself and its narrative. In his book, *A Healing Family*, Oe describes his family's capacity to embrace Hikari.

Healing is used here in two senses that draw our interest as researchers. The word's immediate referent would seem to be the capacity of parents and siblings to help heal the wound of difference for the affected boy. But Oe also emphasizes the work the family has undertaken to heal the wound of difference dealt to its own kinship narrative and practice. Oe, who won the Nobel Prize in literature in 1994, has written several other books chronicling the transformations in their familial universe inaugurated by the birth of Hikari. His works have helped his family and, at a remove, his readers, to imagine an unanticipated cultural future that could give meaning and possibility to the reshaped habitus of daily life with a disabled family member.[1] Oe's compassionate and frank story of how his family came to embrace "being handicapped" is representative of a kind of shift in consciousness— disability consciousness—suggestive of a more expansive sense of kinship across embodied difference that, we argue, is essential to the growing public presence of disability in contemporary postindustrial democracies.

The proliferation of publicly circulating representations of disability as a form of diversity we all eventually share—through our own bodies or attachments to others —offers potential sites of identification and even kinship that extend beyond the biological family. In the United States in particular, such public representations of the connections (and disconnections) of disabled people and their families across embodied difference have helped to introduce a sense of public intimacy that, we argue, is crucial to redeeming the ADA promissory note of a polity "beyond ramps" (Russell 1998). The simultaneous emergence of the U.S. disability rights movement along with the escalation of reproductive and neonatal technologies has intensified cultural awareness of a range of broader issues. These increasingly both shape and destabilize contemporary kinship practices as well as debates among disability rights activists, feminists, bioethicists, and health service providers.

Such concerns engage questions about medical ethics and the complexities of reproductive choice; concrete dilemmas about how to organize the practical logistics of care for disabled children; political and distributive queries about what citizens are owed; and conceptual questions about how disability is figured discursively. While such issues are often made the subject of public policy debate, they come already anchored in the daily and intimate practices of embracing or rejecting kinship with disabled fetuses, newborns, and young children. We suggest, then, that disability criticism should encompass not only the public arenas of law, medicine, and education, or the phenomenology of embodiment. It also needs to engage the intimate arena of kinship as a site where contemporary social dramas around changing understandings and practices of reproduction and disability are often first played out. Although the term *kinship* is conventionally associated with the private or domestic sphere, we stress the cultural work performed by the circulation of kinship narratives through various public media as an essential element in the

refiguring of the body politic as envisioned by advocates of both disability and reproductive rights.

The efforts of families to "rewrite" kinship are crucial to creating a new cultural terrain in which disability is not just begrudgingly accommodated under the mandates of expanded post-1970s civil rights legislation, but is positively incorporated into the social body. Likewise, rejection of the disabled from the familial and social body continues to occur, occasionally played out in the public media as scandals of exclusion[2] and in more intimate arenas as the conventional limits of kinship are sustained rather than transcended.

When we began to explore the world of disability—both as parents of disabled children and as anthropologists interested in reproduction, kinship, and social activism—we were struck by narratives like Oe's and their proliferation in a world in which constructions of the body and identity are increasingly mediated by biomedical technologies.[3] We were particularly interested in contradictions between, on the one hand, burgeoning genetic knowledge and the neoeugenic practices it has fostered; and, on the other, the expansion of more inclusive democratic discourses—in particular, that of disability rights. To explore this tension, in this essay we foreground the domains of kinship and reproduction as key social sites at which many disabilities are initially assigned cultural meaning in the United States. We focus in particular on contemporary dilemmas surrounding pregnancy and the care of newborns and children with disabilities, which in turn underscore questions concerning the social location of caretaking and its political economy.

We locate our work at this nexus not only because reproductive choices—and the role played in them by the possibility of disability—are increasingly implicated in the new genetic knowledge, but also because the parent-child relationship is a nexus at which dramatic alternatives are articulated: dependency versus autonomy; intimacy versus authority; the acceptance of caretaking versus its rejection; normative cultural scripts versus alternative, more inclusive "rewritings." Clearly, the "passions and interests" (cf. Hirschman 1977) at work here can divide the points of view of children and parents. These potential divisions can be particularly acute in the case of children with disabilities, whose bodily and sensory (and, eventually, social and political) experiences may be profoundly different from those of their parents. Recent debates about cochlear implants for deaf children or facial surgery for children with Down syndrome highlight divisions over the value of mainstreaming technologies. Such issues divide families who differ over what constitutes "the best interests of their children." Although conflicts between the perspectives of parents and children are typically associated with the separation and self-definition that intensify at adolescence, we focus here on dilemmas that emerge much earlier—indeed, from the embryonic stage or before.

REWRITING KINSHIP

The birth of a child who is, in one sense, profoundly different from other family members can pose an immediate crisis to the nuclear and extended family. In addition to providing medical support for the affected child, families face the task of incorporating unexpected differences into a comprehensible narrative of kinship (Landsman 1999, 2000; Layne 1996). The birth of anomalous children is an occasion for meaning-making, whether through the acceptance of "God's special angels" or the infanticide of offspring deemed unacceptable. And in millennial America, new technologies have made the domain of kinship and reproduction— the locus classicus of

anthropology—particularly charged with cultural contradictions surrounding questions of bodily difference.

A wide variety of contemporary cultural productions testify to this intensification. It is our argument that such public storytelling—whether in family narratives, memoirs, television talk shows and sitcoms, movies, or, most recently, through Web sites and Internet discussion groups—is crucial to expanding what we call the social fund of knowledge about disability. In opening up the experiential epistemology of disability, as shaped by and shaping the intimate world of nonnormative family life, such forms of public culture widen the space of possibility in which relationships can be imagined and resources claimed. We underscore the significance of this burgeoning public circulation of intimate disability stories, expanding the arguments of others regarding the place of intimacy in constituting subjectivities of all sorts. As Lauren Berlant writes in her introduction to the special issue of *Critical Inquiry* on intimacy,

> Rethinking intimacy calls out not only for redescription but for transformative analyses of the rhetorical and material conditions that enable hegemonic fantasies to thrive in the minds and on the bodies of subjects while, at the same time, attachments are developing that might redirect the different routes taken by history and biography. To rethink intimacy is to appraise how we have been and how we live and how we might imagine lives that make more sense than the ones so many are living. (Berlant 1998: 286)

In the expanded domain of "public intimacy" linked to disability, different forms of embodiment are represented within the context of domestic routines and subjectivity. If this is true of information-sharing magazines such as *Exceptional Parent* and the slick and upbeat activist publication and Web site *WeMedia*, it is no less characteristic of academic writings by scholars who may themselves be disabled (Asch 1989; Charlton 1998; Fries 1997; Handler 1998; Hockenberry 1995; Kuusisto 1998; Linton 1998; Mairs 1996), or caring for disabled family members (Beck 1999; Bérubé 1996; Featherstone 1980; Finger 1990; Jablow 1982; Kittay 1999; Seligman and Darling 1989). We suggest that such representations—what we call disability narratives—are foundational to the integration of disability into everyday life in the United States, a process that is in turn essential to the more capacious notions of citizenship championed by the disability rights movement. As authored by disabled people and/or their family members, these narratives offer revised, phenomenologically based understandings that at times also anchor substantial analyses of the social, cultural, and political construction of disability. The dissemination of such intimate insights among a broader public has helped to mobilize an extraordinary and rapid transformation since the 1970s in the way such notions as rights, entitlement, and citizenship are conceived—a transformation that is shaping public policy in areas such as health care, education, transportation, and access to built, aural, and visual environments.

Of course, not all disability narratives are so inclusive. A very different discourse about disability has emerged around the proliferation of reproductive technologies, in particular prenatal testing for detectable fetal anomalies. Certain assumptions are foundational to these processes. While U.S. genetic counselors are trained to express neutrality about the choices a pregnant woman and her partner may make around amniocentesis testing, the very existence of such a technology and the offer of such tests under the terms of consumer choice are premised on the desire for normalcy and fear of unknown abnormalities (Parens and Asch 2000). As anthropologists, our task is to understand how these neoeugenic technologies come to make cultural sense despite the emergence of more inclusive discourses of disability in other cultural domains. Prenatal screening, for example, is attractive to cost-accounting health care bureaucracies in which market forces increasingly stratify the "choices" made available to different constituencies as medical care becomes subject to the spreading hegemony of neo-liberal practices and ideologies. The attractiveness of prenatal screening to cost-conscious health bureaucracies is a case in point: with the administration of medical care increasingly under the sway of hegemonic neoliberalism, market forces come to dictate what choices are available to different constituencies.

In the United States, and increasingly throughout the postindustrial world, the anxieties that accompany pregnancy are, we argue, exacerbated by the individualized and privatized nature of medical decision-making. When it comes to information about the forms of medical and community support that might be available to the family of a child with a stigmatized difference, the access of prospective parents is limited. They are often unaware of the social fund of knowledge that would help them make a more knowledgeable choice (Ginsburg and Rapp 1999). This de facto segregation is apparent in narratives elicited by researchers from pregnant women and their supporters about their attitudes and aspirations regarding prenatal testing (Browner 1996; Kolker and Burke 1993; Press and Browner 1995; Rapp 1999; Rothman 1986). Unlike the stories discussed earlier, few encounters with prenatal testing are rendered as public narrations. While the social science literature suggests that awaiting the results of an amniocentesis is quite stressful, the stress turns out to be ephemeral for those who receive normal diagnoses of their fetuses.

They retrospectively experience the test as a nonevent; amniocentesis is quickly subsumed within the schedule of now-routine health procedures whose presumed outcome is a "normal" baby. By contrast, most of those whose diagnosis is positive choose to end the pregnancy. Such events generally pass unmarked, as is the case with most abortions in the West (for the counterexample of Japan, see Hardacre 1997). Writing about abortion, especially under circumstances such as these, when the pregnancy was initially desired, is fraught with personal and political risk. Those few pregnant women who have breached the veil of privacy surrounding prenatal testing and abortion tend to circulate their stories only in specialized medical contexts (Green 1992; Brewster 1984; but cf. Rapp 1999). In describing their decision-making processes, they tend to emphasize the limits of caretaking within an available family structure and concern for a child's potential suffering.

> Some people say that abortion is hate. I say my abortion was an act of love. I've got three kids. I was forty-three when we accidentally got pregnant again. We decided that there was enough love in our family to handle it, even though finances would be tight. But we also decided to have the test. A kid with a serious problem was more than we could handle. And when we got the bad news, I knew immediately what I had to do. At forty-three, you think about your own death. It would have been tough now, but think what would have happened to my other kids, especially my daughter. Oh, the boys, Tommy and Alex, would have done okay. But Laura would have been the one who got stuck. It's always the girls. It would have been me, and then, after I'm gone, it would have been the big sister that took care of that child. Saving Laura from that burden was an act of love. (Rapp 1999: 247)

Such stories provide an illuminating, if stark, comparison to the more established and more acceptable genre of disability narratives. The themes shaping these different genres of narratives about disability reveal the crucial role that kinship plays in social exclusion, on the one hand, and as a site for the transformative cultural work that can help resituate disability in contemporary American social life, on the other. Clearly, disability stories are complex and variable. The parenting literature, for example, is fraught with the tensions between efforts to normalize the experience of disability and the need for advocacy and special resources to accommodate those who cannot enter mainstream American society through the same pathways or trajectories as most others.

These tensions are themselves a reflection of the way that consumer capitalism is shaping the experience of reproduction in the United States. Perhaps the starkest examples are provided by the contemporary trend of increasingly aggressive medical intervention, with the new reproductive technology of prenatal testing conjuring up a familiar specter from dystopian science fiction: that of designer babies for the market (McGee 1997). At the same time, large numbers of compromised babies are able to survive thanks to advances in medicine and in therapeutic regimens such as occupational therapy and infant stimulation programs (Landsman 1999, 2000). These diverging sociomedical practices, which are increasingly part of normal obstetric and neonatal medicine, embody a doubled telos of modernity and technology. The practices of genetic testing, and other genetic research, seem to promise perfectibility for those who choose and can afford cutting-edge interventions (although what "perfectibility" might mean in practice is highly contested, as we discuss below). Concomitantly, other new technologies, medical and otherwise, offer another promise of expansive democratic inclusion and improved quality of life for those marked by difference from a hegemonic norm of embodiment (Blair 2000).

Suppressed in these narratives of modernity, which stress individual choice and achievement, is the crucial place of kinship and gender in structuring these possibilities. Specifically, this double telos places pregnant women under the very American pressure of "choice." Many women, and especially women with first pregnancies, imagine themselves entering the workplace of contemporary mothering in one of two ways. Most plan to control the balance between participation in wage labor and the domestic economy. They use prenatal testing hoping never to face a pregnancy whose outcome would demand more caretaking than they feel they could provide; selective abortion haunts this dilemma. This model of rationality fits easily with the one that has emerged with genetic counseling, which assumes the power of individuals, no matter how constrained, to make rational choices that will "improve the quality" of their lives. A minority of women approach these tests differently, without intent to abort. They view the test as a technology for appropriate preparation should they need to provide specialized support for the birth of a child with a serious disability. In both cases, the assumption endures that infant and child care are primarily the responsibility of the individual mother, with support from other kin and recourse to the marketplace, if finances permit.

The caretaking of a disabled infant requires different and expanded resources than can be provided by most kin groups without additional forms of support. The complexities of mobilizing the necessary medical, therapeutic, and social support reveal the limits of kinship within a gendered nuclear family structure. It is through this revelation, we suggest, that some begin to reimagine the boundaries and capacities of kinship and to recognize the necessity of broader support for caretaking. On

occasion, they are motivated to rewrite kinship in ways that circulate within larger discursive fields of representation and activism.

THE LIMITS OF KINSHIP

Despite a quarter century of activism, policy innovation, and the substantial provision of public services, in the United States, the securing of care for disabled members rests with the family. A vast gap remains between the rhetoric of public inclusion that mandates everything from universal design to inclusive classrooms and the battles that still have to be fought on a daily basis to ensure their availability—battles which not everyone can or will fight. As the mother and the aunt of a child with significant disabilities point out in the article "Uncommon Children":

> Laws attempt to provide parity in society for disabled individuals, but do they go far enough? Underfunded and understaffed public schools may be hard-pressed to meet sophisticated or extensive needs. Parents of "special ed" children become angry at the lack of responsiveness while parents of typical children grow resentful of monies seemingly diverted from regular ed. The very people who need to work together to meet these complex challenges are often pitted against each other.
>
> We expect parents of children with disabilities to "rise to the occasion," but some don't or can't. As a nation we were recently horrified by the Kelsos, who left their profoundly disabled ten-year-old at a Delaware hospital with a note saying they could no longer care for him. Certainly, they did the wrong thing. But their desperate act should not be dismissed lightly as simply aberrant. (O'Connell and Foster 2000: 18)

When we step back from this impassioned description of a grim social landscape, we recognize this narrative as grounded in a potentially productive tension between a capacious view of liberal democracy, in which law and social services are expanding to accommodate the needs of people with disabilities, and the reality of the daily tasks of caretaking, which remain in the household, dependent on family— and overwhelmingly female—labor. At the same time, biomedical technology holds out utopian promises that elide the dilemmas of caretaking while raising others about perfectibility, exemplified in a variety of sometimes controversial supports to people with disabilities, from cochlear implants for the hearing-impaired to computer resources for "fast-forwarding" learning-disabled students. Technology has also delivered a rapidly expanding panoply of reproductive choices. Reliable and inexpensive birth control, infertility treatments, and safe and legal abortion have greatly enhanced women's ability to control the circumstances of mothering. The prenatal diagnosis of disabling conditions in fetuses is surely part of this technological modernity. The common choice to abort based on such diagnoses suggests the limits of the expansion described above and the implicit recognition that much of the labor of caretaking, especially in infancy and childhood, still falls on mothers.[4] In a sense, technologies such as amniocentesis are allowing pregnant women and their partners to construct the limits of kinship on their own terms, however constrained. Realistically, many fear that the social support that they would need for a disabled child might be difficult to obtain. This was true in many of the narratives of working-class women who chose amniocentesis, who had vivid images of what a chronically ill child might do to their lives. One woman explained her decision to have prenatal testing this way:

With my other two, Lionel worked nights, I'm on days, we managed with a little help from my mother. When Eliza was three, my mother passed on, then my sister, she helped me out as much as she could. With this one, we're planning to ask for help from a neighbor who takes in a few kids. I couldn't keep a baby with health problems. Who would baby-sit? (Rapp 1999: 145)

Such stories poignantly illustrate how close to the edge many parents feel when they imagine the juggling of work and family obligations should disability enter an already tight domestic economy. Such stories can also mask deep-seated prejudices against the imagined "courtesy stigma" incurred by those close to people with "spoiled identities" (Goffman 1963). Yet it is important to highlight the material pressures under which many families with two working parents find themselves and that serve as the matrix in which the decision to use prenatal testing is made.

As we noted above, some have argued that in an upper-middle-class environment where children are increasingly regarded as commodities, genetic testing raises expectations among parents that they can "choose" to have a "perfect" baby (Browner and Press 1996; Press and Browner 1995; Corea 1985; Rothman 1986). A more complex scenario emerges when women of diverse class, racial, religious, and national backgrounds who were offered prenatal testing were interviewed (Rapp 1999). Whatever their cultural background, most pregnant women and their supporters are concerned not so much with perfection, but seek basic health and "normalcy," recognizing the limits of the material circumstances within which they undertake mothering. Indeed, some were willing to live with a range of disabling conditions if they could manage it practically and if the child could enjoy life. Nonetheless, most were frightened by the stigmatizing conditions that the test might predict, about which they knew almost nothing, and whose consequences they could only imagine (Rapp 1999). Such conflicted responses are not surprising, given that the survival of disabled infants has escalated dramatically thanks to improvements in infant surgery, antibiotics, and life-support technologies. At the same time, the knowledge of what is entailed in caring for such children remains absent from mainstream discourse, underscoring a sense of social segregation and stigma. On the genetic frontier, where the use of prenatal diagnostic technologies is rapidly becoming routine, a gap exists between the medical diagnosis of a fetal anomaly and social knowledge about life with a child who bears that condition. In this gap, the use of amniocentesis and selective abortion becomes perfectly rational. This tendency to marginalize and segregate disability issues will continue, legal progress and expanded public consciousness notwithstanding, until the conditions of care are less privatized and the social fund of knowledge is increased. It is this disjunction, then, between neighboring fields of social knowledge that animates the narrative urgency of those compelled to tell what might be termed their *un-natural histories*, as they struggle to represent the difference that disability makes in the domain of kinship.

CHANGING CULTURAL SCRIPTS

The cultural dialectic between perfectibility and inclusion has often animated the work of the activist individuals, families, and groups who are the crucial link between the intimate domain of kinship and the broader public sphere. The utopian promise of perfectible children has had a long-standing hold on the American cultural imagination and is particularly powerful under current techno-scientific regimes. At the same time, the ideal of equality has been the touchstone of a range of social movements that demand inclusion for those excluded on the basis of differences coded as biological deficiencies. Over the last twenty-five years, they have helped to catalyze policy initiatives that offer a potentially radical challenge to the boundaries of citizenship and the relations of obligation between (temporarily) able-bodied and dependent people across the life cycle. The IDEA, or Individuals with Disabilities Education Act (1975), followed by the ADA, or Americans with Disabilities Act (1990), are the two key pieces of postwar federal legislation that have established the framework for the civil rights for Americans with disabilities. These accomplishments have dramatically transformed both the institutional and intimate frameworks within which American families operate.

The responses of what Oe calls "disabled families" have shaped and been shaped by these historically shifting conditions. In the 1950s and 1960s, for example, many middle-class parents were commonly advised to institutionalize "non-normal" children whose survival rate was rising due to aggressive medical innovations, erasing their presence from the household and muffling their voices in family stories. Since the 1970s, however, deinstitutionalization and early-intervention programs have increasingly supported families in keeping disabled children at home. Responding to these changed circumstances, some families have begun to articulate new and public versions of domestic life with disabled children in an effort to reconfigure the discursive space defining these social fields. At the same time, a combination of forces—the *Roe v. Wade* decision legalizing abortion in 1973; the international development of prenatal genetic testing; and the rise of second-wave feminism, with its advocacy of broad-based options for women's public and private lives—increasingly medicalized and individualized the cultural salience of reproductive choice. Twenty years on, the dilemmas of such "choices" have become a staple of public debate, as powerful medical, genetic, and prosthetic technologies extend and enable fragile lives even as prenatal screening technologies give prospective parents the option to terminate an anomalous pregnancy. Citizens of this "republic of choice" (after Friedman 1990) face contradictory options that exceed the extant frameworks for ethical deliberation. In the contemporary scenario, it is women in particular who have thus been cast as moral pioneers. These anxiety-provoking circumstances generate and are reflected in contemporary public testimony about disability, whether in the work of accomplished writers such as the Nobel Prize-winning Oe or in less prominent forms of cultural production. Such narrative engagements with unanticipated difference within the intimate culture of the family can be understood as interventions into the public sphere. They work to subvert the hegemonic discourse of perfectibility disseminated by such sites as obstetric medicine, middle-class parenting literature, and, more generally, contemporary U.S. models of personhood that valorize celebrity and individual will.

The cultural activity of rewriting life stories and kinship narratives around the fact of disability, whether in memoir, film, or everyday storytelling, enables families to comprehend (in both senses) this anomalous experience, not only because of the capacity of stories to make meaning, but also because of their dialogical relationship with larger social arenas. Indeed, the transformation of both emotional and technical knowledge developed in kin groups with disabled family members can foster networks of support from which activism may emerge. In other words, the way that family members articulate changing experiences and awareness of disability in the domain of kinship not only provides a model for the body politic as a whole, but also helps to constitute a broader

understanding of citizenship in which disability rights are understood as civil rights (Asch 1989; Bérubé and Lyon 1998; Kittay 1999; Linton 1998).

MEDIATING DISABILITY

The creation of kinship ties between non-disabled and disabled people requires the imagining, for many families, of an unanticipated social landscape. This sense of reorientation to a place of possibility, as opposed to disappointment, is evident in the text of a flyer posted prominently in many American pediatric wards. It offers families of chronically ill and disabled children a parable of an unexpected journey to an unknown world, a counternarrative of hope in the face of the sense of crisis experienced by many families with hospitalized offspring:

> *Welcome to Holland*
> Imagine you have planned a vacation to Italy, to see the rose gardens of Florence. You are totally excited, you have read all the guide books, your suitcases are packed, and off you go. As the plane lands, the pilot announces, "Sorry, ladies and gentlemen, but this flight has been rerouted to the Netherlands." At first you are very upset: the vacation you dreamed about has been canceled. But you get off the plane, determined to make the best of it. And you gradually discover that the blue tulips of Holland are every bit as pretty as the red roses you had hoped to see in Florence. They may not be as famous, but they are every bit as wonderful. You didn't get a red rose. But you got a blue tulip, and that's quite special, too.[5]

The almost invisible yet widespread circulation of this endlessly photocopied document joins a range of popular imagery in which people with disabling conditions are becoming ever more visible in the public sphere. There is indeed often a direct relationship between the initial efforts of families to reimagine their narratives and the more public actions they undertake to help rescript narratives of inclusion at a broader cultural level. But the call to rethink kinship enacted in the posting of the Blue Tulips flyer is relatively recent and very much the product of the activism of families who have struggled against the categories imposed by medical and bureaucratic regimes.

The example of Down syndrome can illustrate the negotiation of such a category. Until the 1970s, many U.S. doctors would not treat the esophageal and heart problems for which newborns with DS are at increased risk, although the procedures for repair were increasingly well known. Parents of such children were encouraged to "let go," and often had no source of knowledge with which to dispute medical experts. The result was passive infanticide, or what medical historian Martin Pernick (1996) has called the "Black Stork." For children who survived, institutionalization was common; removal from their families was considered the responsible action to take for their care. Children with DS were regarded as incapable of emotional attachment or education. It is only since the 1970s that the conjunction of the deinstitutionalization movement, the creation of early-intervention programs for developmentally delayed infants and toddlers, and the passage of federal and state laws protecting the civil rights of the disabled have provided a social environment in which most families of DS children are now able to take them home at birth. This remarkable shift in biomedical, legal, and familial discourse and practice can be attributed in part to the direct activism of parents' groups such as the Association for Retarded Children (now the Arc) as well as to the indirect impact of writings by the kin of DS people—and eventually by affected individuals themselves—particularly in the form of memoir. Such rescriptings present an alternative

world of kinship based on a shared difference, a phenomenon common to many disability support networks (Rapp, Heath, and Taussig 2001). The following quote from two authors who recently became disability activists on behalf of their child clearly acknowledges an indebtedness to those whose narratives have created a sense of kinship that spans generations and crosses biological family lines:

> Like all parents of children with Down syndrome, we owe a great deal to the authors of books like *Count Us In*—themselves young men with Down's syndrome—and their families for having transformed the social meaning of Down's syndrome by helping to develop what's now called "early intervention for infants with disabilities." But we also find ourselves the unwitting heirs of people and movements *we never knew we were related to.* We saunter with our Jamie publicly largely thanks to Dale Evans who, in 1953, wrote *Angel Unaware*, a best selling memoir of her daughter Robin who was born with Down's syndrome and died at age two. (Bérubé and Lyon 1998: 274, emphasis added)

Despite the progress that has been made since the publication *of Angel Unaware*, bringing a child with DS home is still an act of personal assertion in the United States; in New York state and many other places, the mother of a newborn diagnosed in the hospital is always offered fosterage or adoption placement. Although this practice is shockingly offensive to many new mothers, we should point out that it developed with "the best interests of the child" in mind. Hospital personnel know that disabled babies are at high risk of being abandoned; as they grow older and more difficult to care for, they also grow harder to place in a good home. As newborns are the easiest babies to place, social workers offer information on adoption right away. But the practice has an unintended consequence. The task of composing a normalizing narrative that can create a space of inclusion for the DS child within the family circle is immediately thrust upon the mother, who has to justify to medical personnel the otherwise unproblematic action of taking her newborn home with her.

Constructing such a normalizing narrative is an ongoing process. Down syndrome affects the full spectrum of class and ethnic differences in the United States, and parents of DS children pursue a correspondingly wide variety of strategies for expanding the reach and support of their children's lives. The established script of Down syndrome is being rewritten across a range of sites in a way that opens up a supportive universe for disabled people and their kin. The Special Olympics; infant stimulation programs; consciousness-raising and other sorts of events organized by the disability rights community; and Internet chat groups are all examples of sites that can help reconfigure community for dubious family members.

These forms of positive public mediation of disabled people play an important role in refiguring the cultural landscape for new generations of families engaging with the social fact of disability. The activism of one parent, Emily Kingsley, a scriptwriter for the children's television program *Sesame Street*, is exemplary of this process. Kingsley was told that her son "would never have a single meaningful thought" when Jason was born and diagnosed with Down syndrome. She was counseled to institutionalize Jason immediately and to "try again" (Kingsley and Levitz 1994: 3). Instead, she wrote him into the script of *Sesame Street*, where he appeared throughout his childhood. Contrary to the dire predictions for his intelligence, at age six he was "counting in Spanish for the cameras" (1994: 4). The Kingsleys' cultural activism opened the door for people with other disabilities—people using wheelchairs, braces, and seeing-eye dogs—to appear as part of the quotidian world of mass media that is now an integral part of the public sphere of most postindustrial countries. Jason himself went on to coauthor the aforementioned book, *Count Us In*, with his friend Mitchell Levitz, who also has DS. Later, his mother scripted a prime-time docudrama based on her family's experiences, entitled *Kids Like These* (CBS, 1991). Of course, this ability to work in (and have access to) such media venues is not simply a matter of individual achievement, but also of the cultural capital of activist families. As Bérubé and Lyon (1998: 282) point out: "Their fame . . . depends on their good fortune: not only were they born into extremely supportive families that contested the medical wisdom of their day, but they were born into families well-positioned for activism." Another mother, Gail Williamson, whose son Blair has DS and has also appeared on television, was moved to establish Hollywood's first talent agency for disabled actors in the entertainment industry (Gray 1999).

Many Americans met their first person with Down syndrome in the late 1980s through the virtual presence in their living rooms of Chris Burke, who became a teen star in ABC's *Life Goes On*. Introduced by cast members singing the Beatles' popular song, "Ob-La-Di, Ob-La-Da, Life Goes On," the show provided a realistic depiction of disability as part of everyday family life, while indexing, as the theme song's lyrics do, an optimistic message of possibility. But Chris's story is not only about his heroic triumph over adversity as an individual (Burke and McDaniel 1991). It is imbricated in the complex nexus of changing contexts sketched above that have radically altered the biomedical, familial, practical, and legal narratives structuring disability in America over the last three decades.

Inevitably, the advertising industry was quick to follow the lead of *Life Goes On*, recognizing the potential for growth, not only in direct sales to market niches ranging from psychotropic pharmaceuticals to adaptive technologies, but also in a more indirect appeal to the loyalty of families with disabled members, through the inclusion of DS kids and teens in commercials for McDonald's, Benetton, and even in popular advertising circulars. Such efforts have been subject to criticism from some activists for reducing issues of citizenship to consumption. Yet the presence of people with visible disabilities in the landscape of popular and commercial culture has been embraced enthusiastically by many families as a sign of the growing public incorporation of this historically stigmatized difference. It speaks as well to the erasure of disabled characters that continues to prevail in the popular media since the appearance of such figures, even in advertising, is still regarded as exceptional.

"WHAT ARE YOU STARING AT?"

Whatever progress has been made, there are still relatively few televisual spaces for children that regularly feature kids with disabilities talking about their own lives (as opposed to what some disabled children refer to as "models in wheelchairs"). The shows discussed above are salient exceptions, as is the Nickelodeon children's cable network's magazine program, *Nick News*. "What Are You Staring At?" was an innovative special produced by *Nick News* that aired repeatedly during 1999. The half-hour program featured a group of kids and teens with a range of disabilities—DS, hearing and visual impairments, cerebral palsy, polio, burn injuries—talking about their lives with celebrity crips, journalist John Hockenberry and actor Christopher Reeve. The anecdote that follows, an account of one youngster's experience of this show, may be read as an illustration of the way that such public interventions can help to create an alternative horizon of kinship extending beyond the nuclear family.

In the summer of 1999 in New York City, ten-year-old Samantha Myers surfed onto "What Are You Staring At?" and was riveted. When the final credits ended, she announced to her mother that she wanted to talk about her disability on television. Samantha's disorder, Familial Dysautonomia (FD),[6] is an extremely rare condition of the involuntary nervous system that affects all forms of body regulation, including temperature, blood pressure, swallowing, and respiration. With some adult assistance, she found the Web site for the Make-A-Wish Foundation, a group that grants "wishes" to children with life-threatening diseases. She e-mailed them, explaining that her wish was to go on *Nick News* and talk about her life with FD. Within two weeks, she was working with a friend and a Make-A-Wish volunteer, making a pitch book with color photos and handwritten text about her life and disability. Sam's inventory of her life included police-style pictures she took of all her medical equipment, as well as photos of her dog, friends, and relatives.

By her eleventh birthday, she was working with a producer from *Nick News* to make a five-minute segment that she narrated, replete with footage of her school, doctor, friends, and some whimsical computer animation to make it kid-friendly. In late April 2000, the show was broadcast; as a result, over the next few months, Sam was invited to show her tape and talk to a number of groups. Of greatest significance to Sam was that so many FD kids were able to see another child like them on television. She was deluged with e-mail from families with FD children around the country who were thrilled to see an image and story that for once included their experience. Many, like Sam, went on to use copies of the tape to help teachers and classmates understand the particular issues that kids with FD face on a daily basis.

MEDIATED KINSHIP

The media world into which Sam surfed at the end of the twentieth century is evidence of a transforming public culture in which disability is becoming a more visible presence in daily life. This anecdotal evidence—Sam's immediate sense of kinship with the disabled kids she saw and heard on television and her desire to join that process—suggests how significant such imagery can be to those who do not see themselves regularly in dominant forms of representation. Indeed, much of the early writing in disability studies focused not only on the need for changes in civil rights legislation, but also on the absence of disabled people from literature and popular media—or, where present, the negativity of their portrayal, citing the legacy of freak shows, circuses, and asylums (Bogdan 1988; Thomson 1997). Others were working actively to alter the media landscape itself. Along with parent-activists who worked in the mainstream media, such as Emily Kingsley, there were people like Mary Johnson and Cass Irvin, who in 1980 founded the alternative journal *The Disability Rag* (Shaw 1994). Nowadays, the work of activists in visual media is increasingly evident in the plethora of photography shows and film and video festivals devoted in part or entirely to the topic of disability. And, of course, the Web sites, e-lists, and chat groups of the Internet have dramatically expanded the range of sites at which images of disability are being negotiated.

The circulatory reach of electronic media is the key factor in the creation of what we call *mediated kinship*. Emerging as a neighboring—and sometimes overlapping—field to the formal, institutionalized discourse of disability rights, mediated kinship offers a critique of normative American family life that is embedded within everyday cultural practice. Across many genres,

a common theme is an implicit rejection of the pressure to produce "perfect families through the incorporation of difference under the sign of love and intimacy in the domain of kinship relations. We suggest that these mediated spaces of public intimacy—talk shows, on-line disability support groups, Web sites, and so on—are crucial for building a social fund of knowledge more inclusive of the fact of disability. These media practices provide a counterdiscourse to the naturalized stratification of family membership that for so long has marginalized, in particular, those disabled from birth. It is not only the acceptance of difference within families, but also the embrace of relatedness that such models of inclusion present to the body politic that makes these spaces potentially radical in their implications. As sites of information and free play of imagination, these cultural forms help to create a new social landscape.

The struggle to form inclusive familial units takes place within an increasingly complex discursive world, a terrain in which the so-called genetic revolution—and the part played within it by prenatal testing—cannot be ignored. One suggestive source of images by which that revolution is imagined is via a classic trope of science fiction: the neoeugenic dystopia, as portrayed in books such as *The Handmaid's Tale* (Atwood 1986) and in films such as *Gattaca* (Andrew Niccol, 1997); these are stories of monstrous kinship. But a more common discursive field is the science or business page of the newspaper, where advances in scientific knowledge, especially genetic technologies, are regularly reported, yet the social dilemmas they index go largely undiscussed.

These dilemmas beg questions about who is entitled to make interventions into reproduction, the capacity of kinship to encompass difference, and the social location of care. Although these are experienced as private, family matters, they cannot be contained within domestic domains. Caretaking is perhaps the most naturalized of these, conventionally attached to the unpaid labor of women in the home. Yet, in the United States, it is rapidly becoming a politicized arena in a privatizing economy in which families are expected to be "always on call," as Carol Levine argues in her book of that title, to care for disabled kin (Levine 2000; see also Nussbaum 2001). If paid, the labor of family caregivers would cost about $200 billion a year (Langone 2000). Nevertheless, while health insurance increasingly covers the routinization of new reproductive technologies (NRTs) and the costs of neonatal intensive care units (NICUs), most home-based personal assistance—a need estimated at 21 billion hours yearly—goes unpaid by public funds, despite the demonstrable bodily, emotional, and economic benefits of deinstitutionalizing support (Johnson 2000: 14; Linton 1998; Russell 1998). This is a skeletal sketch of the political economy of health care and assisted living "choices" that affects all Americans. Yet it is a barely visible landscape to most people unless and until their own or a family member's disability reveals its limitations on a practical, daily level.[7]

These revelations of the limits of kinship-based caretaking and the need for broader social recognition and resources for people with disabilities fuel the narrative urgency we have described throughout, beginning with Oe's compelling story of a "healing family," offering stories of familial inclusion that can serve as models of social inclusion as well. Additionally, progress in legal arenas has problematized the presumption of American citizenship as the exclusive entitlement of a normative, able-bodied, non-dependent, wage-earning individual. At best, this model of personhood describes only a portion of the normal human life cycle. At worst, it systematically erases the rights of the disabled and their caretakers to have their fundamental needs addressed in the public arena.

Although we have focused here on the nexus of disability rights and reproductive decision-making as highlighted in the parent-child relationship, kinship and disability—as instantiated by congenital difference, accident, illness, infancy, or old age—remain entwined throughout the life cycle. Thus, the disjunction between the aspiration for democratic inclusion and the fantasy of bodily perfectibility through technological intervention has energized much popular cultural expression, creating a growing sense of public intimacy with experiences of disability. In this gap, disability narratives offer what we have called *unnatural histories*, visions of lives lived against the grain of normalcy. It is here, we have argued, that the relations of kinship have the capacity to enable disability, giving narrative shape and cultural imagination to efforts to form a more perfect union.

NOTES

We have many people to thank, first and foremost our children, who have opened our eyes to worlds more exotic than we ever imagined we would encounter as anthropologists. We thank Carol A. Breckenridge, Candace Vogler, and the editorial board of *Public Culture* for helpful comments, and Barbara Abrash and Simi Linton for their constructive engagement with the final draft.

1. Oe's writings point to the impossibility of individual solutions—even at the level of narrative—to what are cultural and social dilemmas. In a kind of parallel process, Oe has also written movingly on the aftermath of Hiroshima, an assignment he began the same year Hikari was born. This project enabled him to cope with the incomprehensibility of his son's condition by placing it in an even more inexplicable context of social suffering.

2. For example, national attention was riveted on the upper-middle-class Kelso family of suburban Philadelphia in December 1999, when they abandoned their ten-year-old son, Steven, with his diapers, medications, toys, and medical records at the Du Pont Hospital for Children in Wilmington, Delaware. Their nursing schedule

had fallen apart over the holidays, and the parents claimed they could no longer cope with the intensity of their child's needs. While stories of abandonment are not uncommon, this one made public headlines in part because the mother had been a prominent volunteer on the Pennsylvania Developmental Disabilities Council.

3. The recent explosion of U.S. writing on disability, building on the groundbreaking work of scholars/activists who have been writing since the 1970s, is reflected in such developments as the dramatic growth of the Society for Disability Studies, the launching of book series such as Corporealities: Discourses of Disability (edited by David T. Mitchell and Sharon L. Snyder for the University of Michigan Press), and the creation of university-based disabilities studies programs, such as the one at the University of Illinois at Chicago. All are founded on a commitment to the centrality of disabled people both as researchers and subjects (see e.g., Charlton 1998, *Nothing about Us without Us).* In anthropology, the efforts of pioneers such as Robert Edgerton (1993, first published 1967) and Henri-Jacques Stiker (1999, first published 1982) ave been joined by an emerging scholarship focusing on issues ranging from stigma (Ingstad and Whyte 1995), to cultural communities of difference (Groce 1985), to the phenomenology of differently abled bodies (Frank 2000; Murphy 1987).

4. Of course, fathers have frequently been deeply involved and committed to this kind of labor and have played exemplary public roles as well (e.g., Oe 1995; Bérubé 1996). However, the high divorce rates in families with disabled children is one indication that such fathers might be more the exception than the rule. We also note the gendered nature of caretaking and the professions associated with it, such as nursing, home health care, special education, and occupational and physical therapy.

5. Rayna Rapp first heard this parable, attributed to Emily Kingsley, at a Down syndrome parents' support group in 1985. It was plastered on the walls of the pediatric ward Faye Ginsburg occupied with her daughter for most of 1989. More elaborate versions have since appeared in print, at sites as diverse as the Brooklyn waiting room of a school board Committee on Special Education and the back of a newsletter for parents of disabled children.

6. Information on FD is readily accessible at two Web sites: www.FamilialDysautonomia.org and www.FDVillage.org.

7. In the United States and throughout much of the world, the tasks of caretaking continue to be naturalized in the domain of unpaid domestic labor. Increasingly, however, challenges to this situation are emerging as a result of the expanding needs of caretaking over the life cycle. The increased rate of survival among such formerly high-risk groups as low-birth-weight babies, the chronically ill, and the elderly make claims on public resources, usually mediated through their kin. Advocacy groups such as the growing movement for Independent Living seek public support for personal assistance, a policy that, they argue, "would relieve an enormous amount of stress on families and, over time . . . would begin to alter the public perception toward significantly disabled people and the people who relate to them" (Marca Bistro, head of the National Council on Disability, quoted in Johnson 2000: 14).

REFERENCES

Asch, Adrienne. 1989. Reproductive technology and disability. In *Reproductive laws for the 1990's,* edited by Sherrill Cohen and Nadine Taub. Clifton, N.J.: Humana.

Atwood, Margaret. 1986. *The handmaid's tale.* Boston: Houghton-Mifflin.

Beck, Martha N. 1999. *Expecting Adam: A true story of birth, rebirth, and everyday magic.* New York: Times Books.

Berlant, Lauren. 1998. Intimacy: A special issue. *Critical Inquiry* 24: 281–88.

Bérubé, Michael. 1996. *Life as we know it: A father, a family, and an exceptional child.* New York: Pantheon.

Bérubé, Michael, and Janet Lyon. 1998. Living on disability: Language and social policy in the wake of the ADA. In *The visible woman: Imaging technologies, gender, and science,* edited by Paula. A. Treichler, Lisa Cartwright, and Constance Penley. New York: New York University Press.

Blair, John. 2000. Online deliveries lighten burden for the disabled. *New York Times,* 5 September, B1, 5.

Blumberg, Lisa. 1998. The bad baby blues: Reproductive technology and the threat to diversity. *The Ragged Edge,* July/August, 12–14, 16.

Bogdan, Robert. 1988. *Freak show: Presenting human oddities for amusement and profit.* Chicago: University of Chicago Press.

Brewster, Arlene. 1984. After hours: A patient's reaction to amniocentesis. *Obstetrics and Gynecology* 67: 443–44.

Browner, Carol H., and Nancy Ann Press. 1996. The production of authoritative knowledge in American prenatal care. *Medical Anthropology Quarterly* 10: 141–56.

Burke, Chris, and Jo Beth McDaniel. 1991. *A special kind of hero: Chris Burke's own story*. New York: Doubleday.

Charlton, James. 1998. *Nothing about us without us: Disability oppression and empowerment*. Berkeley: University of California Press.

Corea, Gena. 1985. *The mother machine: Reproductive technologies from artificial insemination to artificial wombs*. New York: Harper and Row.

Edgerton, Robert B. 1993. *The cloak of competence: Stigma in the lives of the mentally retarded*. 1967. Reprint, Berkeley: University of California Press.

Evans, Dale. 1953. *Angel unaware*. Westwood, N.J.: Revell.

Featherstone, Helen. 1980. *A difference in the family: Life with a disabled child*. New York: Basic Books.

Finger, Anne. 1990. *Past due: A story of disability, pregnancy, and birth*. Seattle: Seal.

Frank, Gelya. 2000. *Venus on wheels: Two decades of dialogue on disability, biography, and being female in America*. Berkeley: University of California Press.

Friedman, Lawrence. 1990. *Republic of choice: Law, authority and culture*. Cambridge: Harvard University Press.

Fries, Kenny, ed. 1997. *Staring back: The disability experience from the inside out*. New York: Plume.

Ginsburg, Faye, and Rayna Rapp. 1999. Fetal reflections: Confessions of two feminist anthropologists as mutual informants. In *Fetal subject, feminist positions*, edited by Lynn M. Morgan and Meredith W. Michaels. Philadelphia: University of Pennsylvania Press.

Goffman, Erving. 1963. *Stigma: Notes on the management of spoiled identity*. Englewood Cliffs, N.J.: Prentice-Hall.

Gray, Barbara. 1999. They're her all-star kids. *Family Circle*, 13 July, 15–18.

Green, Rose. 1992. Letter to a genetic counselor. *Journal of Genetic Counseling* 1: 55–70.

Groce, Nora. 1985. *Everyone here spoke sign language: Hereditary deafness on Martha's Vineyard*. Cambridge: Harvard University Press.

Handler, Lowell. 1998. *Twitch and shout: A Tourreter's tale*. New York: Dutton.

Hardacre, Helen. 1997. *Marketing the menacing fetus in Japan*. Berkeley: University of California Press.

Hirschman, Albert O. 1977. *The passions and the interests: Political arguments for capitalism before its triumph*. Princeton, N.J.: Princeton University Press.

Hockenberry, John. 1995. *Moving violations: War zones, wheelchairs, and declarations of independence*. New York: Hyperion.

Ingstad, Benedicte, and Susanne Reynolds Whyte, eds. 1995. *Disability and culture*. Berkeley: University of California Press.

Jablow, Martha Moraghan. 1982. *Cara: Growing with a retarded child*. Philadelphia: Temple University Press.

Johnson, Mary. 2000. The "care" juggernaut. *The Ragged Edge*, November/December: 10–12, 14.

Kingsley, Jason, and Mitchell Levitz. 1994. *Count us in: Growing up with Down syndrome*. New York: Harcourt Brace.

Kittay, Eva Feder. 1999. *Love's labor: Essays on women, equality, and dependency*. New York: Routledge.

Kolker, Aliza, and Meredith Burke. 1993. Grieving the wanted child. *Health Care for Women International* 14: 513–26.

Kuusisto, Stephen. 1998. *Planet of the blind: A memoir*. New York: Delta.

Landsman, Gail. 1999. Does God give special kids to special parents? Personhood and the child with disabilities as gift and as giver. In *Transformative motherhood: On giving and getting in a consumer culture*, edited by Linda L. Layne. New York: New York University Press.

———. 2000. "Real motherhood": Class and children with disabilities. In *Ideologies and technologies of motherhood: Race, class, sexuality, nationalism*, edited by France Winddance Twine and Heléna Ragoné. New Brunswick, N.J.: Rutgers University Press.

Langone, John. 2000. When friends and family fill most of a patient's medical needs. *New York Times*, 12 October, F6.

Layne, Linda. 1996. "How's the baby doing?": Struggling with narratives of progress in a neonatal intensive care unit. *Medical Anthropological Quarterly* 10: 624–56.

Levine, Carol, ed. 2000. *Always on call: When illness turns families into caregivers*. New York: United Hospital Fund of New York.

Linton, Simi. 1998. *Claiming disability: Knowledge and identity*. New York: New York University Press.

Mairs, Nancy. 1996. *Waist-high in the world: A life among the non-disabled*. Boston: Beacon.

McGee, Glenn. 1997. *The perfect baby: A pragmatic approach to genetics*. Lanham, Md.: Rowman and Littlefield.

Murphy, Robert. 1987. *The body silent*. New York: Henry Holt.

Nussbaum, Martha. 2001. Disabled lives: Who cares? *New York Review of Books* 48: 34–37.

O'Connell, Linda G., and Lisa G. Foster. 2000. Uncommon children. *Mt. Holyoke Alumnae Quarterly*, spring, 13–18.

Oe, Kenzaburo. 1995. *A healing family*, edited by S. Shaw and translated by Stephen Snyder. Tokyo: Kodansha International.

Parens, Erik, and Adrienne Asch, eds. 2000. *Prenatal testing and disability rights*. Washington, D.C.: Georgetown University Press.

Pernick, Martin S. 1996. *The black stork: Eugenics and the death of "defective" babies in American medicine and motion pictures since 1915*. New York: Oxford University Press.

Press, Nancy Ann, and Carol H. Browner. 1995. The normalization of prenatal diagnostic screening. In *Conceiving the new world order: The global politics of reproduction*, edited by Faye D. Ginsburg and Rayna Rapp. Berkeley: University of California Press.

Rapp, Rayna. 1999. *Testing women, testing the fetus: The social impact of amniocentesis in America*. New York: Routledge.

Rapp, Rayna, Deborah Heath, and Karen Sue Taussig. 2001. Genealogical disease: Where hereditary abnormality, biomedical explanation, and family responsibility meet. In *Relative matters: New directions in the study of kinship*, edited by Sarah Franklin and Susan MacKinnon. Durham, N.C.: Duke University Press.

Rothman, Barbara Katz. 1986. *The tentative pregnancy: Prenatal diagnosis and the future of motherhood*. New York: W. W. Norton.

Russell, Marta. 1998. *Beyond ramps: Disability at the end of the social contract: A warning from an uppity crip*. Monroe, Maine: Common Courage.

Seligman, Milton, and Rosalyn Benjamin Darling. 1989. *Ordinary families, special children: A systems approach to childhood disability*. New York: Guilford.

Shaw, Barrett. 1994. *The ragged edge: The disability experience from the pages of the first fifteen years of* The Disability Rag. Louisville, Ky.: Advocado.

Stiker, Henri-Jacques. 1999. *A history of disability*, translated by William Sayers. Ann Arbor: University of Michigan Press.

Thomson, Rosemarie Garland. 1997. *Extraordinary bodies: Figuring physical disability in American culture and literature*. New York: Columbia University Press.

CHAPTER 19

Aesthetic Nervousness

Ato Quayson

WHAT IS AESTHETIC NERVOUSNESS?

Let me begin formulaically: Aesthetic nervousness is seen when the dominant protocols of representation within the literary text are short-circuited in relation to disability. The primary level in which it may be discerned is in the interaction between a disabled and nondisabled character, where a variety of tensions may be identified. However, in most texts aesthetic nervousness is hardly ever limited to this primary level, but is augmented by tensions refracted across other levels of the text such as the disposition of symbols and motifs, the overall narrative or dramatic perspective, the constitution and reversals of plot structure, and so on. The final dimension of aesthetic nervousness is that between the reader and the text. The reader's status within a given text is a function of the several interacting elements such as the identification with the vicissitudes of the life of a particular character, or the alignment between the reader and the shifting positions of the narrator, or the necessary reformulations of the reader's perspective enjoined by the modulations of various plot elements and so on. As I shall show throughout this study, in works where disability plays a prominent role, the reader's perspective is also affected by the short-circuiting of the dominant protocols governing the text—a short-circuit triggered by the representation of disability. For the reader, aesthetic nervousness overlaps social attitudes to disability that themselves often remain unexamined in their prejudices and biases. The reader in this account is predominantly a nondisabled reader, but the insights about aesthetic nervousness are also pertinent to readers with disabilities, since it is the construction of a universe of apparent corporeal normativity both within the literary text and outside it whose basis requires examination and challenge that is generally at issue in this study. The various dimensions of aesthetic nervousness will be dealt with both individually and as parts of larger textual configurations in the works of Samuel Beckett, Toni Morrison, Wole Soyinka, and J. M. Coetzee. The final chapter, on the history of disability on Robben Island in South Africa, will be used to refocus attention from the literary-aesthetic domain to that of the historical intersection between disability, colonialism, and apartheid. This will help us see what extensions might be possible for the concept of aesthetic nervousness beyond the literary-aesthetic field.

There are two main sources for the notion of aesthetic nervousness that I want to elaborate here. One is Rosemarie Garland

Thomson's highly suggestive concept of the normate, which we have already touched on briefly, and the other is drawn from Lennard Davis's and Mitchell and Snyder's reformulations of literary history from a disability studies perspective. As Thomson (1997) argues in a stimulating extension of some of Erving Goffman's (1959) insights about stigma, first-time social encounters between the nondisabled and people with disabilities are often short-circuited by the ways in which impairments are interpreted. She puts the matter in this way:

> In a first encounter with another person, a tremendous amount of information must be organized and interpreted simultaneously: each participant probes the explicit for the implicit, determines what is significant for particular purposes, and prepares a response that is guided by many cues, both subtle and obvious. When one person has a visible disability, however, it almost always dominates and skews the normate's process of sorting out perceptions and forming a reaction. The interaction is usually strained because the nondisabled person may feel fear, pity, fascination, repulsion, or merely surprise, none of which is expressible according to social protocol. Besides the discomforting dissonance between experienced and expressed reaction, a nondisabled person often does not know how to act toward a disabled person: how or whether to offer assistance; whether to acknowledge the disability; what words, gestures, or expectations to use or avoid. Perhaps most destructive to the potential for continuing relations is the normate's frequent assumption that a disability cancels out other qualities, reducing the complex person to a single attribute.
>
> (Thomson 1997, 12)

To this we should quickly recall Mitchell and Snyder's remark concerning the degree to which Brueghel's paintings succeeded in disrupting and variegating the visual encounter between bodies in painting. Clearly, disruption and variegation are also features of real-world encounters between the nondisabled and persons with disabilities. Thomson proposes the notion of the "normate" to explicate the cluster of attitudes that govern the nondisabled's perception of themselves and their relations to the various "others" of corporeal normativity. As she persuasively shows, there are complex processes by which forms of corporeal diversity acquire cultural meanings that in their turn undergird a perceived hierarchy of bodily traits determining the distribution of privilege, status, and power. In other words, corporeal difference is part of a structure of power, and its meanings are governed by the unmarked regularities of the normate. However, as the paragraph quoted above shows, there are various elements of this complex relationship that do not disclose themselves as elements of power as such, but rather as forms of anxiety, dissonance, and disorder. The common impulse toward categorization in interpersonal encounters is itself part of an ideal of order that is assumed as implicit in the universe, making the probing of the explicit for the implicit part of the quest for an order that is thought to lie elsewhere. It is this, as we noted in the previous section, that persistently leads to the idea that the disabled body is somehow a cipher of metaphysical or divine significance. Yet the impairment is often taken to be the physical manifestation of the exact opposite of order, thus forcing a revaluation of that impulse, and indeed, of what it means to be human in a world governed by a radical contingency. The causes of impairment can never be fully anticipated or indeed prepared for. Every/body is subject to chance and contingent events. The recognition of this radical contingency produces features of a primal scene of extreme anxiety whose roots lie in barely acknowledged vertiginous fears of loss of control over the body itself (Grosz 1996; Wasserman 2001; Lacan 1948, 1949).[1] The corporeal body, to echo the sonnet

"Death Be Not Proud" by John Donne, is victim to "Fate, chance, kings, and desperate men" and subject to "poison, warre, and sicknesse" as well. The dissonance and anxiety that cannot be properly articulated via available social protocols then define the affective and emotional economy of the recognition of contingency. In other words, the sudden recognition of contingency is not solely a philosophical one—in fact, it hardly ever is at the moment of the social encounter itself—but is also and perhaps primarily an emotional and affective one. The usefulness of the social model of disability is precisely the fact that it now forces the subliminal cultural assumptions about the disabled out into the open for examination, thus holding out the possibility that the nondisabled may ultimately be brought to recognize the sources of the constructedness of the normate and the prejudices that flow from it.

Since the world is structured with a particular notion of unmarked normativity in mind, people with disabilities themselves also have to confront some of these ideas about contingency in trying to articulate their own deeply felt sense of being (Murphy 1990, 96–115). At a practical and material level, there are also the problems of adjustment to a largely indifferent world. As Wood and Bradley (1978, 149) put it: "On a material plane the disabled individual is . . . less able to adapt to the demands of his environment: he has reduced power to insulate himself from the assaults of an essentially hostile milieu. However, the disadvantage he experiences is likely to differ in relation to the nature of the society in which he finds himself." Contradictory emotions arise precisely because the disabled are continually located within multiple and contradictory frames of significance within which they, on the one hand, are materially disadvantaged, and, on the other, have to cope with the culturally regulated gaze of the normate. My use of the word "frames"

in this context is not idle. Going back to the Scope poster, it is useful to think of such frames in the light of physical coordinates, as if thinking of a picture frame. The frames within which the disabled are continually placed by the normate are ones in which a variety of concepts of wholeness, beauty, and economic competitiveness structure persons with disability and place them at the center of a peculiar conjuncture of conceptions.

Thomson's notion of the relations between the normate and the disabled derives ultimately from a symbolic interactionism model. To put it simply, a symbolic interactionism model of interpretation operates on the assumption that "people do not respond to the world directly, but instead place social meanings on it, organize it, and respond to it on the basis of these meanings" (Albrecht 2002, 27). The idea of symbolic interactionism is pertinent to the discussion of literary texts that will follow because not only do the characters organize their perceptions of one another on the basis of given symbolic assumptions, but as fictional characters they are themselves also woven out of a network of symbols and interact through a symbolic relay of signs. Furthermore, as I shall show incrementally in different chapters and in a more situated form in the chapter on J.M. Coetzee (chapter 6 [original volume]), symbolic interactionism also implies the presence of an implied interlocutor with whom the character or indeed real-life person enters into a series of dialogical relationships, thus helping to shape a horizon of expectations against which versions of the self are rehearsed. Following Thomson's lead, the first aspect of aesthetic nervousness that I want to specify is that it is triggered by the implicit disruption of the frames within which the disabled are located as subjects of symbolic notions of wholeness and normativity. Disability returns the aesthetic domain to an active ethical core that serves to disrupt the surface of representation. Read from a perspective of disability studies, this active ethical core becomes manifest because the disability representation is seen as having a direct effect on social views of people with disability in a way that representations of other literary details, tropes, and motifs do not offer. In other words, the representation of disability has an efficaciousness that ultimately transcends the literary domain and refuses to be assimilated to it. This does not mean that disability in literature can be read solely via an instrumentalist dimension of interpretation; any intervention that might be adduced for it is not inserted into an inert and stable disability "reality" that lies out there. For, as we have noted, disability in the real world already incites interpretation in and of itself. Nevertheless, an instrumentalist dimension cannot be easily suspended either. To put the matter somewhat formulaically: the representation of disability oscillates uneasily between the aesthetic and the ethical domains, in such a way as to force a reading of the aesthetic fields in which the disabled are represented as always having an ethical dimension that cannot be easily subsumed under the aesthetic structure. Ultimately, aesthetic nervousness has to be seen as coextensive with the nervousness regarding the disabled in the real world. The embarrassment, fear, and confusion that attend the disabled in their everyday reality is translated in literature and the aesthetic field into a series of structural devices that betray themselves when the disability representation is seen predominantly from the perspective of the disabled rather than from the normative position of the nondisabled.

In his essay entitled "Who Put the *The* in The Novel?" Lennard Davis (2002) explores the links that have largely been taken for granted in literary history between the novel form, an *English* nation, and the various destabilizations of the social status of character that help to define the essential structure of the novel in the eighteenth and nineteenth centuries. The realist novels of the two centuries were based on the construction of the "average" citizen. This average citizen was nonheroic and middle class. But the average citizen was also linked to the concept of "virtue." As Davis notes, "Virtue implied that there was a specific and knowable moral path and stance that a character could and should take. In other words, a normative set of behaviours was demanded of characters in novels" (94). Entangled with these dual notions of the average citizen and of virtue were implicit ideas of wholeness, with no major protagonist in the entire period marked by a physical disability. Undergirding the novel's rise then is a binary opposition between normal/abnormal, with this binary generating a series of plots. Essentially, the key element of such plots is the initial destabilization of the character's social circumstances, followed by their efforts to rectify their loss and return, perhaps chastened, to their former position. Crucially, however, as the nineteenth century progresses the negative or immoral gets somatized and represented as a disability (95–98). One of the conclusions Davis draws from his discussion is that plot functions in the eighteenth and nineteenth centuries "by temporarily deforming or disabling the fantasy of nation, social class, and gender behaviors that are constructed norms" (97).

In taking forward Davis's argument, there are a number of qualifications I want to register. Distinctive in his account is the link he persuasively establishes between nation, the average citizen, virtue, and specific forms of novelistic emplotment. That cannot be questioned. However, it is not entirely accurate that the binary of normal/abnormal starts with the eighteenth- and nineteenth-century novels or indeed that they inaugurate the plots of the deformation of social status. On the contrary, as can be shown from an examination of folktales from all over the world, the plot of physical and/or social deformation is actually one of the commonest starting points of most story plots (see Propp 1958; Zipes 1979), so much so that it is almost as if the deformation of physical and/or social status becomes the universal starting point for the generation of narrative emplotment as such. As Davis points out, in agreement with established scholarship on the novel, the crucial term that is introduced in the eighteenth and nineteenth century is "realism," the notion that somehow the novelistic form refracts a verisimilar world outside of its framework. But realism is itself a cultural construction, since for the Greeks their myths were also a form of realism. What needs to be taken from Davis's account is the effect that the collocation of the social imaginary of the nation and the production of a specific form of bodily and sexual realism had on the way the novel was taken to represent reality. In each instance, the assumed representation of reality depended upon unacknowledged views of social order deriving not just from an understanding of class relations but from an implicit hierarchization of corporeal differences. Even though Davis is not the only one to have noted the peculiar place of the disabled in the eighteenth- and nineteenth-century novel (see Holmes 2000, for example), it is in clarifying the status of the disabled body as *structurally constitutive* to the maintenance of the novel's realism that he makes a distinctive contribution to literary history.

However, in trying to extend the significance of the constitutive function of deformation from the novel to other literary forms, we also have to note that "deformation" can no longer be limited solely to that of social or class position, as Davis suggests in his discussion. From the novels of the early twentieth century onward, the deformations emerge from the intersection of a variety of vectors including gender, ethnicity, sexuality, urban identity, and particularly disability, these providing a variety of *constitutive points for the process of emplotment*. Indeed, Davis himself notes in another context the reiteration of disability in the works of Conrad. A similar view can be expressed of the work of Joyce (*Ulysses, Finnegans Wake*), Virginia Woolf (*Mrs. Dalloway*), Thomas Mann (*The Magic Mountain*), and T. S. Eliot's "The Waste Land," among others. I choose the phrase "constitutive points" as opposed to "starting points" to signal the fact that the social deformation does not always show itself at the beginning of the plot. In much of the work we will look at, from Beckett and Soyinka through Morrison and Coetzee, there are various articulations of a sense of social deformation. However, the deformation is not always necessarily revealed as inaugural or indeed placed at the starting point of the action or narrative as such. It is often revealed progressively or in fragments in the minds of the characters, or even as flashbacks that serve to reorder the salience of events within the plot. The varied disclosures of social deformation are also ultimately linked to the status of disability as a trigger or mechanism for such plot review and disclosure. In that sense, the range of literary texts we shall be exploring is not undergirded exclusively by the binary opposition of normal/abnormal, but by the *dialectical interplay* between unacknowledged social assumptions and the reminders of contingency as reflected in the body of the person with disability.

The notion of dialectical interplay is crucial to my model of interpretation, because one of the points I will repeat throughout the study is that a dialectical interplay can be shown to affect all levels of the literary text, from the perspectival modulations of the narrator (whether first or third person) and the characters to the temporal sequencing and ordering of leitmotifs and symbolic discourses that come together to structure the plotlines. Even though, as Davis rightly notes, the plots of social deformation dominated the eighteenth- and nineteenth-century novel, this view cannot be limited solely to novelistic discourse. Following the point I made a moment ago about the near universality of such plots, I want to suggest that we consider the plot of social deformation as it is tied to some form of physical or mental deformation to be relevant for the discussion of *all* literary texts. This is a potentially controversial point, but given the ubiquity of the role of the disabled in texts from a range of cultures and periods it is difficult to shake off the view that disability is a marker of the aesthetic field as such. Disability teases us out of thought, to echo Keats, not because it resists representation, but because in being represented it automatically restores an ethical core to the literary-aesthetic domain while also invoking the boundary between the real and the metaphysical or otherworldly. Along with the category of the sublime, it inaugurates and constitutes the aesthetic field as such. And like the sublime, disability elicits language and narrativity even while resisting or frustrating complete comprehension and representation and placing itself on the boundary between the real and the metaphysical. When I state that disability "inaugurates" the aesthetic domain, it is not to privilege the "firstness" or "primariness" of first-time encounters between the disabled and nondisabled characters, even though this has been implied in my reliance on Thomson. Rather, I intend the term "inaugurate" in the sense of the setting of the contours of the interlocking vectors of representation, particularly in narrative and drama, which are the two literary forms that will feature mainly in this study. My position overlaps with

Davis's but extends his insights to accommodate a more variegated methodology for understanding the status of disability in literary writing.

The analogy between the inaugural status of the sublime and of disability serves to open up a number of ways in which the structurally constitutive function of disability to literary form might be explored. In the *Critique of Judgment*, Kant follows his discussion of the beautiful and its relation to purposelessness or autonomy with the discussion of the sublime and its inherent link to the principle of disorder. For Kant, "*Beauty* is an object's form of purposiveness insofar as it is perceived in the object *without the presentation of purpose*" (1987, 31), the idea here being that only the lack of a determinate or instrumental end allows the subjective feeling of beauty to occur. The sublime, on the other hand, is an aspect of understanding in confrontation with something ineffable that appears to resist delimitation or organization. It exposes the struggle between Imagination and Reason: "[What happens is that] our imagination strives to progress toward infinity, while our reason demands absolute totality as a real idea, and so [the imagination,] our power of estimating the magnitude of things in the world of sense, is inadequate to that idea. Yet this inadequacy itself is the arousal in us of the feeling that we have within us a supersensible power" (108; translator's brackets). Even while generative of representation, the sublime transcends the imaginative capacity to represent it. As Crockett (2001, 75) notes in glossing the nature of this struggle, "the sublime is contra-purposive, because it conflicts with one's purposeful ability to represent it." The implicit dichotomy in the *Critique of Judgment* between the sublime and the beautiful has been explored in different directions by scholars in the intervening three hundred and fifty years since its formulation, but what has generally been agreed upon is the idea of the resistance of the sublime to complete representation, even if this resistance is then incorporated into a motivation for representation as such.[2] What the representation of disability suggests, which both overlaps and distinguishes itself from the sublime as a conceptual category, is that even while also producing a contradictory semiotics of inarticulacy and articulation, it is quite directly and specifically tied to forms of social hierarchization. For disability, the semiotics of articulation/inarticulation that may be perceived within the literary domain reflect difficulties regarding its salience for the nondisabled world. This, as can be gleaned from the Whyte and Ingstad collection already referred to, cuts across cultures. Thus even if the ambivalent status of disability for literary representation is likened to that of the sublime, it must always be remembered that, unlike the effects of the sublime on literary discourse, disability's ambivalence manifests itself within the real world in socially mediated forms of closure. We might then say that disability is an analogue of the sublime in literary-aesthetic representation (ineffability/articulation) yet engenders attempts at social hierarchization and closure within the real world.

Disability might also be productively thought of as being on a continuum with the sublime in terms of its oscillation between a pure abstraction and a set of material circumstances and conditions. Considered in this way, we can think of the sublime as occupying one end of the spectrum (being a pure abstraction despite generating certain psychological effects of judgment and the impulse to represent it in material forms) and disability occupying the other end and being defined by a different kind of oscillation between the abstract and the material. For unlike the sublime, disability oscillates between a pure process of abstraction (via a series of discursive framings,

metaphysical transpositions, and socially constituted modalities of [non]response, and so forth) and a set of material conditions (such as impairment, accessibility and mobility difficulties, and economic considerations). It is not to be discounted also that many impairments also involve living with different levels of pain, such that the categories of pain and disability not infrequently imply each other. It is disability's rapid oscillation between a pure process of abstraction and a set of material conditions that ensures that the ethical core of its representation is never allowed to be completely assimilated to the literary-aesthetic domain as such. Disability serves then to close the gap between representation and ethics, making visible the aesthetic field's relationship to the social situation of persons with disability in the real world. This does not necessarily mean that we must always read the literary representation in a directly instrumental way. As noted earlier, the intervention of the literary representation is an intervention into a world that already situates disability within insistent framings and interpretations. The literary domain rather helps us to understand the complex *processes* of such framings and the ethical implications that derive from such processes.

Finally, it is to Mitchell and Snyder's book *Narrative Prosthesis* (2003) that I wish to turn in elaborating what I mean by aesthetic nervousness. Mitchell and Snyder follow David Wills (1995) in trying to define literary discourse as essentially performing certain prosthetic functions. Among these prosthetic functions are the obvious ones of using the disabled as a signal of moral disorder such that the nondisabled may glean an ethical value from their encounter with persons with disabilities. Since Mitchell and Snyder are also keen to situate narrative prosthesis as having significance for the lived experience of disability, they also assign an inherently pragmatic orientation to what they describe as textual prosthesis: "Whereas an actual prosthesis is always somewhat discomforting, a textual prosthesis alleviates discomfort by removing the unsightly from view. . . . [T]he erasure of disability via a "quick fix" of an impaired physicality or intellect removes an audience's need for concern or continuing vigilance" (8). They make these particular remarks in the context of films and narratives in which persons with disabilities somehow manage to overcome their difficulties and live a happy life within the realm of art. In such instances, the representation of disability serves a pragmatic/cathartic function for the audience and the reader. More significantly, however, they also note that even while disability recurs in various works as a potent force to challenge cultural ideas about the normal and the whole, it also *operates as the textual obstacle that causes the literary operation of open-endedness to close down or stumble*" (50).

This last observation brings their discussion of narrative prosthesis very close to my own notion of aesthetic nervousness, except that they proceed to expound upon this blocking function in what can only be nonaesthetic terms. This is how they put it:

> This "closing down" of an otherwise permeable and dynamic narrative form demonstrates the historical conundrum of disability. [Various disabled characters from literature] provide powerful counterpoints to their respective cultures' normalizing Truths about the construction of deviance in particular, and the fixity of knowledge systems in general. Yet each of these characterizations also evidences that the artifice of disability binds disabled characters to a programmatic (even deterministic) identity.
>
> (Mitchell and Snyder 2003, 50)

Thus Mitchell and Snyder's idea of the shutting down or stumbling of the literary operation is extrinsic to the literary field itself and is to be determined by setting the literary representations of disability against socio-cultural understandings. While agreeing with them that the ultimate test of the salience of a disability representation are the various social and cultural contexts within which they might be thought to have an effect, I want to focus my attention on the devices of aesthetic collapse that occur *within* the literary frameworks themselves. Also, I would like to disagree with them on their view of the programmatic identity assigned to the disabled, because, as I will try to show by reading the disabled character within the wider discursive structure of relations among different levels of the text, we find that even if programmatic roles were originally assigned, these roles can shift quite suddenly, thus leading to the "stumbling" they speak of. I choose to elaborate the textual "stumbling" in terms of aesthetic nervousness.

When it comes to their specific style of reading, Mitchell and Snyder are inspired by Wills to elaborate the following provisional typology:

> Our notion of narrative prosthesis evolves out of this specific recognition: a narrative issues to resolve or correct—to "prostheticize" in David Wills's sense of the term—a deviance marked as improper to a social context. A simple schematic of narrative structure might run thus: first, a deviance or marked difference is exposed to the reader; second, a narrative consolidates the need for its own existence by calling for an explanation of the deviation's origins and formative consequences; third, the deviance is brought from the periphery of concerns to the center of the story to come; and fourth, the remainder of the story rehabilitates or fixes the deviance in some manner. The fourth step of the repair of the deviance may involve an obliteration of the difference through a "cure," the rescue of the despised object from social censure, the extermination of the deviant as a purification of the social body, or the revaluation of an alternative mode of being.

. . . Narratives turn signs of cultural deviance into textually marked bodies.

(53–54)

Again, their method is defined by an assumption of narrative pragmatism or instrumentalism; that is to say, the literary text aims solely to resolve or correct a deviance that is thought to be improper to a social context. Unlike them, I will be trying to show that this prostheticizing function is bound to fail, not because of the difficulties in erasing the effects of disability in the real world, but because the aesthetic domain itself is short-circuited upon the encounter with disability. As mentioned earlier, disability joins the sublime as marking the constitutive points of aesthetic representation. Aesthetic nervousness is what ensues and can be discerned in the suspension, collapse, or general short-circuiting of the hitherto dominant protocols of representation that may have governed the text. To my mind, in this paragraph Mitchell and Snyder are attempting to define processes of representation that may occur separately (i.e., across individual and distinguishable texts) as well as serialized within a particular text. One of my central points is precisely the fact that even when the disabled character appears to be represented programmatically, the restless dialectic of representation may unmoor her from the programmatic location and place her elsewhere as the dominant aesthetic protocols governing the representation are short-circuited.

To establish the central parameters of aesthetic nervousness, then, a number of things have to be kept in mind. First is that in literature, the disabled are fictional characters created out of language. This point is not made in order to sidestep the responsibility to acknowledge language's social efficaciousness. Rather, I want to stress that as linguistic creations, the disabled in literature may trade a series of features with the nondisabled, thus transferring some of their significations to the nondisabled and vice versa. Furthermore, I want to suggest that when the various references to disability and to disability representation are seen within the broad range of an individual writer's work, it helps to foreground hitherto unacknowledged dimensions of their writing and, in certain cases, this can even lead to a complete revaluation of critical emphasis. Consider in this regard Shakespeare's *Richard III*, for instance, which is of course very widely discussed in disability studies. However, in Shakespeare disability also acts as a metaphor to mark anomalous social states such as those involving half-brothers and bastards. Indeed, there is a studied pattern in Shakespeare where bastards are considered to be internally deformed and villainous, their bastardy being directly correlated to a presumed moral deficit. And so we have the elemental and almost homicidal competition between half-brothers that reappears in conflicts between Robert Falconbridge and his bastard brother Philip in *King John*, between Don John and Don Pedro in *Much Ado About Nothing*, between Edmund and Edgar in *King Lear*, and between Richard III and Edward in *Richard III*. This last play is of course grounded on the resonance of jealousy and brotherhood, as well as on the Machiavellianism of a deformed protagonist. There the disability is placed at the foreground of the action from the beginning and brings together various threads that serve to focalize the question of whether Richard's deformity is an insignia of or indeed the cause of his villainy.[3] Thus to understand Richard III properly, we would have to attend equally to his disability and his bastardy in the wider scheme of Shakespeare's work. Once this is done, we find that our interpretation of the character has to be more complicated than just recognizing his villainy, which of course is the dominant invitation proffered by the play.

The choice of Beckett, Soyinka, Morrison, and Coetzee is partly meant to serve this function of establishing the interrelations between disability and other vectors of representation among the wide oeuvre of each writer. However, comparisons and contrasts within the work of individual writers or indeed between them will not be made chronologically or with the suggestion of evolution and change in the representation of disability. Rather, I shall be focusing on thematic clusterings and on making links between apparently unrelated characters and scenes across the various texts to show how the parameters of aesthetic nervousness operate within individual texts as well as across various representations. Also, the writers will be used as nodal points from which to make connections to the work of other writers. Thus each chapter, though focusing predominantly on the individual writer in question, will also provide a gateway for connecting these writers to various others that have had something to say about disability. Each chapter is conceived of as comparative both in terms of the relations among the works of the main writers in the study and between these and the many other representations of disability that will be touched upon over the course of the discussions.

I want to emphasize my view that to properly establish the contours of aesthetic nervousness, we have to understand disability's resonance on a multiplicity of levels simultaneously; disability acts as a threshold or focal point from which various vectors of the text may be examined. Thus, as we shall see with respect to Toni Morrison, though her physically disabled female characters seem to be strong and empowered, there is often a contradiction between the levels of narratorial perspective, symbolic implication, and the determinants of the interactions among the characters themselves that ends up unsettling the unquestioned sense of strength that we might get from just focusing on what the disabled women in her texts do or do not do. With Beckett, on the other hand, we find that as he proliferates devices by which to undermine the stability of ontological categories, he ends up also undermining the means by which the many disabilities that he frequently represents in his texts may be interpreted. As can be seen from the vast scholarship on Beckett, it is very rare that his impaired characters are read as disabled, even though their disabilities are blatant and should be impossible to ignore. Rather, the characters are routinely assimilated by critics to philosophical categories and read off as such. This is due to the peculiarly self-undermining structures of his works, both the novels and the plays. Beckett is also unusual among the writers in this study in that he seems to fulfill a central feature of what Sandblom (1997) describes as the inextricable link between disease and creativity. Pertinent to the discussion of Beckett's work is that he himself suffered endless illnesses ranging from an arrhythmic heartbeat and night sweats to cysts and abscesses on his fingers, the palm of his left hand, the top of his palate, his scrotum and, most painfully later in life, his left lung. Often these cysts and abscesses had to be lanced or operated upon, leading to great and regular discomfort. It is not for nothing then that the deteriorating and impaired body held a special fascination for him. He used the disabled, maimed, and decaying body as a multiple referent for a variety of ideas that seem to have been at least partially triggered by encounters with others and his own personal experience of pain and temporary disability. This is something that has passed largely unremarked in the critical writings on Beckett, and I propose to center on it to discuss the peculiar status he assigns to disability and pain in works such as *Endgame* and *Molloy*, both of which should to all intents and purposes be "painfull" but are not.

In a way, Wole Soyinka's work is quite different from that of the other three in the study. His writing focuses more securely on a set of ritual dispositions drawn from a traditional Yoruba and African cultural sensibility. This sensibility is then combined with an intense political consciousness, such that each of his plays may be read as partial allegories of the Nigerian and African postcolonial condition. The combination of the ritualistic with the political is something for which Soyinka has become notably famous. What I shall show with regard to his work are the ways in which disability acts as a marker of both ritual and the political, but in ways that interrupt the two domains and force us to rethink the conceptual movement between the two. The final chapter, on Robben Island, will be used to bring to conclusion a particular vector of interpretation that will have been suggested in the chapter on Beckett, given further elaboration in the discussions of Morrison and Soyinka, and picked up and intensified in the one on Coetzee. I shall discuss this in various guises, but they will all come together under the conceptual rubric of the *structure of skeptical interlocution.* In essence, the idea derives from Bakhtin's proposition of the inherent dialogism of speech acts, that anticipation of an interlocutor even when the context of communication does not seem to explicitly denominate one. The choice of the plays of Beckett and Soyinka allows a certain salience to the idea of the (skeptical) interlocutor, since as dramatic texts they incorporate dialogue as an explicit feature of dialogism. But what I have in mind in relation to the structure of skeptical interlocution is a little bit more complicated than can be captured solely in dramatic texts. Rather, I mean to suggest that there is always an anticipation of doubt within the perceptual and imagined horizon of the disabled character in literature, and that this doubt is incorporated into their rep-

resentation. This is so whether the character is represented in the first person, as we see in Beckett's Molloy, or in the third person, as we see in Coetzee's *Life and Times of Michael K.* The chapter on Coetzee will be used to focus on the difference between speech and the elective silence of autistic characters and on the ways in which these raise peculiar problems for the status of the skeptical interlocutor in literary writing. Autism features in that chapter not just as a dimension of disability but as a theoretical paradigm for raising questions about narrativity as such. However, it is when we come to the chapter on Robben Island that the structure of skeptical interlocution will be allowed to take life (literally and metaphorically, as will be demonstrated). The structure of interlocution with regard to the history of Robben Island will help to shed light on how aesthetic nervousness might be extended from discussions of the literary-aesthetic domain to an analysis of historical personages and real-life events.

I should like to address a point of potential confusion that may have arisen in this introduction. So far I have proceeded as though the literary representation of disabled persons and the aesthetic nervousness that attends such representation can be taken as an analogue to the real-life responses toward people with disabilities by society at large. This fusion of levels is only partially intended. For, as I noted earlier, there is no doubt that literary representation of disability somewhat subtends real-life treatment of disabled people in a variety of ways. However, I also want to note that the aesthetic nervousness of the literary-aesthetic domain cannot by any means be said to be equivalent to the responses to disabled persons in reality. To say that the literary model provides an analogue to reality does not mean that it is the same as that reality. The epistemological effect of representation is quite different from the emotional effects of misunderstanding and stereotyping in the real world. Thus the first may be used to illuminate aspects of the second but must not be taken to have exhausted or replaced it. Our commitment must ultimately be to changing the world and not merely reading and commenting on it.

It is important also to state at the outset that central to the ways in which I propose to establish the parameters of aesthetic nervousness is the device of close reading. This seems to me necessary in order to be able to do full justice to the subtle cues by which the literary text "stumbles" (to return to Mitchell and Snyder) and by which the literary representation reveals the parameters of aesthetic nervousness. Apart from Morrison, none of the writers in this study has previously been read from the perspective of disability studies. Part of my task will involve the rather boring process of taxonomizing the disability representations we find in the works in question. This will be done to provide a map of the varied uses to which the writers put the disabled in order to allow us to discern patterns that are elaborated upon or repeated across the works. It is a happy coincidence that all four writers are Nobel Prize winners and thus likely to be widely taken up in literary curricula. My choice of them was not informed by this fact, however (in fact, Coetzee was part of my study long before his Nobel Prize). I settle on them because of my years of teaching and thinking about their work in different contexts and the fact that they enable us to see a full range of discourses regarding disability and other details of literary representation. I wish to see students and other readers being able to pay close attention to all the subtle details of literary representation well beyond the focus on disability, even if that is their starting point. The focus on disability is thus meant to achieve two related effects: One is to make more prominent the active ethical core that is necessarily related to disability and that hopefully helps to restore a fully ethical reading to literature. The other is that from using disability to open up the possibility of close reading, I hope to encourage us to lift our eyes from the reading of literature to attend more closely to the implications of the social universe around us.

NOTES

1. On first considering this point about the vertiginous fears of the nondisabled regarding disability I focused primarily on Lacan's discussion of the mirror phase and his exploration of the *imagos* of dismemberment that come up for people under psychic stress. From this, I elaborated what I termed the primal scene of the encounter between the disabled and the nondisabled, which, as I argued, was riven by constitutive emotional ambiguities. Even though I still find that perspective persuasive, in the current discussion I want to leave the contours of the psychoanalytic interpretation to one side and instead invoke the work of philosophers and disability writers who have thought and written about this matter. For my earlier argument, see "Disability and Contingency" in *Calibrations: Reading for the Social* (2003). At any rate, though I didn't know it then, the argument about Lacan and the primal scene of disability had already been quite persuasively put by Lennard Davis (1995, 140–142) and so will not be reprised here.

2. For the discussions of the sublime and the beautiful that I have drawn upon, see Allison (2001), Crockett (2001), Ashfield and de Bolla (1996), Caruth (1988), and de Man (1990). The issue of whether the sublime triggers an ethical recognition or not is a contentious one and not yet settled on either side, but Ashfield and de Bolla provide a good account of how the ethical debates on the sublime have unfolded in British literary history from the eighteenth century onward.

3. For particularly insightful readings of *Richard III* from a disability studies perspective, see Mitchell and Snyder (2000, 95–118) and Lennard Davis.

CHAPTER 20

The Social Model of Disability

Tom Shakespeare

INTRODUCTION

In many countries of the world, disabled people and their allies have organised over the last three decades to challenge the historical oppression and exclusion of disabled people (Driedger, 1989; Campbell and Oliver, 1996; Charlton, 1998). Key to these struggles has been the challenge to over-medicalized and individualist accounts of disability. While the problems of disabled people have been explained historically in terms of divine punishment, karma or moral failing, and post-Enlightenment in terms of biological deficit, the disability movement has focused attention onto social oppression, cultural discourse, and environmental barriers.

The global politics of disability rights and deinstitutionalisation has launched a family of social explanations of disability. In North America, these have usually been framed using the terminology of minority groups and civil rights (Hahn, 1988). In the Nordic countries, the dominant conceptualisation has been the relational model (Gustavsson et al., 2005). In many countries, the idea of normalisation and social role valorisation has been inspirational, particularly amongst those working with people with learning difficulties (Wolfensburger, 1972). In Britain, it has been the

social model of disability which has provided the structural analysis of disabled people's social exclusion (Hasler, 1993).

The social model emerged from the intellectual and political arguments of the *Union of Physically Impaired Against Segregation* (UPIAS). This network had been formed after Paul Hunt, a former resident of the Lee Court Cheshire Home, wrote to *The Guardian* newspaper in 1971, proposing the creation of a consumer group of disabled residents of institutions. In forming the organization and developing its ideology, Hunt worked closely with Vic Finkelstein, a South African psychologist, who had come to Britain in 1968 after being expelled for his anti-apartheid activities. UPIAS was a small, hardcore group of disabled people, inspired by Marxism, who rejected the liberal and reformist campaigns of more mainstream disability organisations such as the Disablement Income Group and the Disability Alliance. According to their policy statement (adopted December 1974), the aim of UPIAS was to replace segregated facilities with opportunities for people with impairments to participate fully in society, to live independently, to undertake productive work and to have full control over their own lives. The policy statement defined disabled people as an oppressed group and highlighted barriers:

We find ourselves isolated and excluded by such things as flights of steps, inadequate public and personal transport, unsuitable housing, rigid work routines in factories and offices, and a lack of up-to-date aids and equipment.

(UPIAS Aims paragraph 1)

Even in Britain, the social model of disability was not the only political ideology on offer to the first generation of activists (Campbell and Oliver, 1996). Other disabled-led activist groups had emerged, including the Liberation Network of People with Disabilities. Their draft Liberation Policy, published in 1981, argued that while the basis of social divisions in society was economic, these divisions were sustained by psychological beliefs in inherent superiority or inferiority. Crucially, the Liberation Network argued that people with disabilities, unlike other groups, suffered inherent problems because of their disabilities. Their strategy for liberation included: developing connections with other disabled people and creating an inclusive disability community for mutual support; exploring social conditioning and positive self-awareness; the abolition of all segregation; seeking control over media representation; working out a just economic policy; encouraging the formation of groups of people with disabilities.

However, the organization which dominated and set the tone for the subsequent development of the British disability movement, and of disability studies in Britain, was UPIAS. Where the Liberation Network was dialogic, inclusive and feminist, UPIAS was hard-line, male-dominated, and determined. The British Council of Organisations of Disabled People, set up as a coalition of disabled-led groups in 1981, adopted the UPIAS approach to disability. Vic Finkelstein and the other BCODP delegates to the first Disabled People's International World Congress in Singapore later that year, worked hard to have their definitions of disability adopted on the global stage (Driedger, 1989). At the same time, Vic Finkelstein, John Swain and others were working with the Open University to create an academic course which would promote and develop disability politics (Finkelstein, 1998). Joining the team was Mike Oliver, who quickly adopted the structural approach to understanding disability, and was to coin the term "social model of disability" in 1983.

WHAT IS THE SOCIAL MODEL OF DISABILITY?

While the first UPIAS Statement of Aims had talked of social problems as an added burden faced by people with impairment, the Fundamental Principles of Disability discussion document, recording their disagreements with the reformist Disability Alliance, went further:

> In our view, it is society which disables physically impaired people. Disability is something imposed on top of our impairments, by the way we are unnecessarily isolated and excluded from full participation in society. Disabled people are therefore an oppressed group in society.
>
> (UPIAS, 1975)

Here and in the later development of UPIAS thinking are the key elements of the social model: the distinction between disability (social exclusion) and impairment (physical limitation) and the claim that disabled people are an oppressed group. Disability is now defined, not in functional terms, but as

> the disadvantage or restriction of activity caused by a contemporary social organisation which takes little or no account of people who have physical impairments and thus excludes them from participation in the mainstream of social activities.
>
> (UPIAS, 1975)

This redefinition of disability itself is what sets the British social model apart from all other socio-political approaches to disability, and what paradoxically gives the social model both its strengths and its weaknesses.

Key to social model thinking is a series of dichotomies:

1. Impairment is distinguished from disability. The former is individual and private, the latter is structural and public. While doctors and professions allied to medicine seek to remedy impairment, the real priority is to accept impairment and to remove disability. Here there is an analogy with feminism, and the distinction between biological sex (male and female) and social gender (masculine and feminine) (Oakley, 1972). Like gender, disability is a culturally and historically specific phenomenon, not a universal and unchanging essence.

2. The social model is distinguished from the medical or individual model. Whereas the former defines disability as a social creation—a relationship between people with impairment and a disabling society—the latter defines disability in terms of individual deficit. Mike Oliver writes:

> Models are ways of translating ideas into practice and the idea underpinning the individual model was that of personal tragedy, while the idea underpinning the social model was that of externally imposed restriction.
> (Oliver, 2004, 19)

Medical model thinking is enshrined in the liberal term "people with disabilities," and in approaches that seek to count the numbers of people with impairment, or to reduce the complex problems of disabled people to issues of medical prevention, cure or rehabilitation. Social model thinking mandates barrier removal, anti-discrimination legislation, independent living and other responses to social oppression. From a disability rights perspective, social model approaches are progressive, medical model approaches are reactionary.

3. Disabled people are distinguished from non-disabled people. Disabled people are an oppressed group, and often non-disabled people and organisations—such as professionals and charities—are the causes or contributors to that oppression. Civil rights, rather than charity or pity, are the way to solve the disability problem. Organisations and services controlled and run by disabled people provide the most appropriate solutions. Research accountable to, and preferably done by, disabled people offers the best insights.

For more than ten years, a debate has raged in Britain about the value and applicability of the social model (Morris, 1991; Crow, 1992; French, 1993; Williams, 1999; Shakespeare and Watson, 2002). In response to critiques, academics and activists maintain that the social model has been misunderstood, misapplied, or even wrongly viewed as a social theory. Many leading advocates of the social model approach maintain that the essential insights developed by UPIAS in the 1970s still remain accurate and valid three decades later.

STRENGTHS OF THE SOCIAL MODEL

As demonstrated internationally, disability activism and civil rights are possible without adopting social model ideology. Yet the British social model is arguably the most powerful form which social approaches to disability have taken. The social model is simple, memorable, and effective, each of which is a key requirement of a political slogan or ideology. The benefits of the social model have been shown in three main areas.

First, the social model, called "the big idea" of the British disability movement (Hasler, 1993), has been effective *politically* in building the social movement of disabled people. It is easily explained and understood, and it generates a clear agenda for social change. The social model offers a straightforward way of distinguishing allies from enemies. At its most basic, this reduces to the terminology people use: "disabled people" signals a social model approach, whereas "people with disabilities" signals a mainstream approach.

Second, by identifying social barriers to be removed, the social model has been effective *instrumentally* in the liberation of disabled people. Michael Oliver argues that the social model is a "practical tool, not a theory, an idea or a concept" (2004, 30). The social model demonstrates that the problems disabled people face are the result of social oppression and exclusion, not their individual deficits. This places the moral responsibility on society to remove the burdens which have been imposed, and to enable disabled people to participate. In Britain, campaigners used the social model philosophy to name the various forms of discrimination which disabled people (Barnes, 1991), and used this evidence as the argument by which to achieve the 1995 Disability Discrimination Act. In the subsequent decade, services, buildings and public transport have been required to be accessible to disabled people, and most statutory and voluntary organizations have adopted the social model approach.

Third, the social model has been effective *psychologically* in improving the self-esteem of disabled people and building a positive sense of collective identity. In traditional accounts of disability, people with impairments feel that they are at fault. Language such as "invalid" reinforce a sense of personal deficit and failure. The focus is on the individual, and on her limitations of body and brain. Lack of self-esteem and self-confidence is a major obstacle to disabled people participating in society. The social model has the power to change the perception of disabled people. The problem of disability is relocated from the individual, to the barriers and attitudes which disable her. It is not the disabled person who is to blame, but society. She does not have to change, society does. Rather than feeling self-pity, she can feel anger and pride.

WEAKNESSES OF THE SOCIAL MODEL

The simplicity which is the hallmark of the social model is also its fatal flaw. The social model's benefits as a slogan and political ideology are its drawbacks as an academic account of disability. Another problem is its authorship by a small group of activists, the majority of whom had spinal injury or other physical impairments and were white heterosexual men. Arguably, had UPIAS included people with learning difficulties, mental health problems, or with more complex physical impairments, or more representative of different experiences, it could not have produced such a narrow understanding of disability.

Among the weaknesses of the social model are:

1. The neglect of impairment as an important aspect of many disabled people's lives. Feminists Jenny Morris (1991), Sally French (1993), and Liz Crow (1992) were pioneers in this criticism of the social model neglect of individual experience of impairment:

> As individuals, most of us simply cannot pretend with any conviction that our impairments are irrelevant because they influence every aspect of our lives. We must find a way to integrate them into our whole experience and identity for the sake of our physical and emotional well-being, and, subsequently, for our capacity to work against Disability.
> (Crow, 1992, 7)

The social model so strongly disowns individual and medical approaches, that it risks implying that impairment is not a problem. Whereas other socio-political accounts of disability have developed the important insight that people with impaired are disabled by society as well as by their bodies, the social model suggests that people are disabled by society not by their bodies. Rather than simply opposing medicalization, it can be interpreted as rejecting medical prevention, rehabilitation or cure of impairment, even if this is not what either UPIAS, Finkelstein, Oliver, or Barnes intended. For individuals with static impairments, which do not degenerate or cause medical complications, it may be possible to regard disability as entirely socially created. For those who have degenerative conditions which may cause premature death, or which any condition which involves pain and discomfort, it is harder to ignore the negative aspects of impairment. As Simon Williams has argued,

> . . . endorsement of disability solely as social oppression is really only an option, and an erroneous one at that, for those spared the ravages of chronic illness.
>
> (Williams, 1999, 812)

Carol Thomas (1999) has tried to develop the social model to include what she calls "impairment effects," in order to account for the limitations and difficulties of medical conditions. Subsequently, she subsequently suggested that a relational interpretation of the social model enables disabling aspects to be attributed to impairment, as well as social oppression:

> once the term "disability" is ring-fenced to mean forms of oppressive social reactions visited upon people with impairments, there is no need to deny that impairment and illness cause some restrictions of activity, or that in many situations both disability and impairment effects interact to place limits on activity.
>
> (2004, 29)

One curious consequence of the ingenious reformulation is that only people with impairment who face oppression can be called disabled people. This relates to another problem:

2. The social model assumes what it needs to prove: that disabled people are oppressed. The sex/gender distinction defines gender as a social dimension, not as oppression. Feminists claimed that gender relations *involved* oppression, but did not define gender relations *as* oppression. However, the social model defines disability as oppression. In other words, the question is not whether disabled people are oppressed in a particular situation, but only the extent to which they are oppressed. A circularity enters into disability research: it is logically impossible for a qualitative researcher to find disabled people who are not oppressed.

3. The analogy with feminist debates about sex and gender highlights another problem: the crude distinction between impairment (medical) and disability (social). Any researcher who does qualitative research with disabled people immediately discovers that in everyday life it is very hard to distinguish clearly between the impact of impairment, and the impact of social barriers (see Watson, 2002; Sherry, 2002). In practice, it is the interaction of individual bodies and social environments which produces disability. For example, steps only become an obstacle if someone has a mobility impairment: each element is necessary but not sufficient for the individual to be disabled. If a person with multiple sclerosis is depressed, how easy is it to make a causal separation between the effect of the impairment itself; her reaction to having an impairment; her reaction to being oppressed and excluded on the basis of having an impairment; other, unrelated reasons for her to be depressed? In practice, social and individual aspects are almost inextricable in the complexity of the lived experience of disability.

Moreover, feminists have now abandoned the sex/gender distinction, because it implies that sex is not a social concept. Judith Butler (1990) and others show that what we think of as sexual difference is always viewed through the lens of gender. Shelley Tremain (2002) has claimed similarly that the social model treats impairment as an unsocialized and universal concept, whereas, like sex, impairment is always already social.

4. The concept of the barrier-free utopia. The idea of the enabling environment, in which all socially imposed barriers are removed, is usually implicit rather than explicit in social model thinking, although it does form the title of a major academic collection (Swain et al., 1993). Vic Finkelstein (1981) also wrote a simple parable of a village designed for wheelchair users to illustrate the way that social model thinking turned the problem of disability on its head. Yet despite the value of approaches such as Universal Design, the concept of a world in which people with impairments were free of environmental barriers is hard to operationalize.

For example, numerous parts of the natural world will remain inaccessible to many disabled people: mountains, bogs, beaches are almost impossible for wheelchair users to traverse, while sunsets, birdsong, and other aspects of nature are difficult for those lacking sight or hearing to experience. In urban settings, many barriers can be mitigated, although historic buildings often cannot easily be adapted. However, accommodations are sometimes incompatible because people with different impairments may require different solutions: blind people prefer steps and defined curbs and indented paving, while wheelchair users need ramps, dropped curbs, and smooth surfaces. Sometimes, people with the same impairment require different solutions: some visually impaired people access text in Braille, others in large

print, audio tape or electronic files. Practicality and resource constraints make it unfeasible to overcome every barrier: for example, the New York subway and London Underground systems would require huge investments to make every line and station accessible to wheelchair users. A copyright library of five million books could never afford to provide all these texts in all the different formats that visually impaired users might potentially require. In these situations, it seems more practical to make other arrangements to overcome the problems: for example, Transport for London have an almost totally accessible fleet of buses, to compensate those who cannot use the tube, while libraries increasingly have arrangements to make particular books accessible on demand, given notice.

Moreover, physical and sensory impairments are in many senses the easiest to accommodate. What would it mean to create a barrier free utopia for people with learning difficulties? Reading and writing and other cognitive abilities are required for full participation in many areas of contemporary life in developed nations. What about people on the autistic spectrum, who may find social contact difficult to cope with: a barrier free utopia might be a place where they did not have to meet, communicate with, or have to interpret other people. With many solutions to the disability problem, the concept of addressing special needs seems more coherent than the concept of the barrier free utopia. Barrier free enclaves are possible, but not a barrier free world.

While environments and services can and should be adapted wherever possible, there remains disadvantage associated with having many impairments which no amount of environmental change could entirely eliminate. People who rely on wheelchairs, or personal assistance, or other provision are more vulnerable and have fewer choices than the majority of able-bodied people. When Michael Oliver claims that

> An aeroplane is a mobility aid for non-flyers in exactly the same way as a wheelchair is a mobility aid for non-walkers.
>
> (Oliver, 1996, 108)

his suggestion is amusing and thought provoking, but cannot be taken seriously. As Michael Bury has argued,

> It is difficult to imagine any modern industrial society (however organised) in which, for example, a severe loss of mobility or dexterity, or sensory impairments, would not be 'disabling' in the sense of restricting activity to some degree. The reduction of barriers to participation does not amount to abolishing disability as a whole.
>
> (Bury, 1997, 137)

Drawing together these weaknesses, a final and important distinction needs to be made. The disability movement has often drawn analogies with other forms of identity politics, as I have done in this chapter. The disability rights struggle has even been called the "Last Liberation Movement" (Driedger, 1989). Yet while disabled people do face discrimination and prejudice, like women, gay and lesbian people, and minority ethnic communities, and while the disability rights movement does resemble in its forms and activities many of these other movements, there is a central and important difference. There is nothing intrinsically problematic about being female or having a different sexual orientation, or a different skin pigmentation or body shape. These other experiences are about wrongful limitation of negative freedom. Remove the social discrimination, and women and people of color and gay and lesbian people will be able to flourish and participate. But disabled people face both discrimination and intrinsic limitations. This claim has three implications. First, even if social barriers are removed as far as practically

possible, it will remain disadvantageous to have many forms of impairment. Second, it is harder to celebrate disability than it is to celebrate Blackness, or Gay Pride, or being a woman. "Disability pride" is problematic, because disability is difficult to recuperate as a concept, as it refers either to limitation and incapacity, or else to oppression and exclusion, or else to both dimensions. Third, if disabled people are to be emancipated, then society will have to provide extra resources to meet the needs and overcome the disadvantage which arises from impairment, not just work to minimize discrimination (Bickenbach et al., 1999).

BEYOND THE SOCIAL MODEL?

In this chapter, I have tried to offer a balanced assessment of the strengths and weaknesses of the British social model of disability. While acknowledging the benefits of the social model in launching the disability movement, promoting a positive disability identity, and mandating civil rights legislation and barrier removal, it is my belief that the social model has now become a barrier to further progress.

As a researcher, I find the social model unhelpful in understanding the complex interplay of individual and environmental factors in the lives of disabled people. In policy terms, it seems to me that the social model is a blunt instrument for explaining and combating the social exclusion that disabled people face, and the complexity of our needs. Politically, the social model has generated a form of identity politics which has become inward looking and separatist.

A social approach to disability is indispensable. The medicalization of disability is inappropriate and an obstacle to effective analysis and policy. But the social model is only one of the available options for theorizing disability. More sophisticated and complex approaches are needed, perhaps building on the WHO initiative to create the

International Classification of Functioning, Disability and Health. One strength of this approach is the recognition that disability is a complex phenomenon, requiring different levels of analysis and intervention, ranging from the medical to the socio-political. Another is the insight that disability is not a minority issue, affecting only those people defined as disabled people. As Irving Zola (1989) maintained, disability is a universal experience of humanity.

BIBLIOGRAPHY

Barnes, C. (1991). *Disabled People in Britain and Discrimination.* London: Hurst and Co.

Bickenbach, J. E., Chatterji, S., Badley, E. M., and Ustun, T. B. (1999). "Models of Disablement, Universalism and the International Classification of Impairments, Disabilities and Handicaps." *Social Science and Medicine,* 48: 1173–1187.

Bury, M. (1997). *Health and Illness in a Changing Society.* London: Routledge.

Butler, J (1990). *Gender Trouble: Feminism and the Subversion of Identity.* New York: Routledge.

Campbell, J. and Oliver, M. (1996). *Disability Politics: Understanding Our Past, Changing Our Future.* London: Routledge.

Charlton J (1998). *Nothing About Us Without Us: Disability, Oppression and Empowerment.* Berkeley: University of California Press.

Crow, L. (1992). "Renewing the Social Model of Disability." *Coalition,* July: 5–9.

Dreidger, D. (1989). *The Last Civil Rights Movement.* London: Hurst.

Finkelstein, V. (1981). "To Deny or Not to Deny Disability." In *Handicap in a Social World,* edited by A Brehin et al. Sevenoaks: OUP/Hodder and Stoughton.

Finkelstein, V. (1998). "Emancipating disability studies." In *The Disability Reader: Social Science Perspectives,* edited by T. Shakespeare. London: Cassell.

French, S. (1993). "Disability, Impairment or Something in Between." In *Disabling Barriers, Enabling Environments,* edited by J. Swain, S. French, C. Barnes, C. Thomas. London: Sage, 17–25.

Gustavsson, A., Sandvin, J., Traustadóttir, R. and Tossebrø, J (2005). *Resistance, Reflection and Change: Nordic disability Research.* Lund, Sweden: Studentlitteratur.

Hahn, H. (1988). "The Politics of Physical Differences: Disability and Discrimination." *Journal of Social Issues,* 44 (1) 39–47.

Hasler, F. (1993). "Developments in the Disabled People's Movement." In *Disabling Barriers, Enabling Environments,* edited by J. Swain, S. French, C. Barnes, C. Thomas et al. London: Sage.

Morris, J. (1991). *Pride Against Prejudice.* London: Women's Press.

Oakley, A. (1972). *Sex, Gender and Society.* London: Maurice Temple Smith.

Oliver, M. (1996). *Understanding Disability: From Theory to Practice.* Basingstoke: Macmillan.

Oliver, M. (2004). "The Social Model in Action: If I Had a Hammer." In *Implementing the Social Model of Disability: Theory and Research,* edited by C. Barnes and G. Merce.: Leeds: The Disability Press.

Shakespeare, T. and Watson, N. (2001). "The Social Model of Disability: An Outdated ideology?" In *Exploring Theories and Expanding Methodologies: Where Are We and Where Do We Need to Go? Research in Social Science and Disability volume 2,* edited by S. Barnartt and B. M. Altman. Amsterdam: JAI.

Sherry, M. (2002). "If Only I Had a Brain." Unpublished PhD dissertation, University of Queensland.

Swain, J., Finkelstein, V., French, S. and Oliver, M. eds. (1993). *Disabling Barriers, Enabling Environments.* London: OUP/Sage.

Thomas, C. (1999). *Female Forms.* Buckingham: Open University Press.

Thomas, C. (2004). "Developing the Social Relational in the Social Model of Disability: A Theoretical Agenda." In *Implementing the Social Model of Disability: Theory and Rresearch,* edited by C. Barnes and G. Mercer. Leeds: The Disability Press.

Tremain, S. (2002). "On the Subject of Impairment." In *Disability/Postmodernity: Embodying Disability Theory,* edited by M. Corker and T. Shakespeare, pp. 32–47. London: Continuum.

Union of the Physically Impaired Against Segregation (1974/5). Policy Statement, available at http://www.leeds.ac.uk/disability-studies/archiveuk/archframe.htm; accessed August 10, 2005.

Union of the Physically Impaired Against Segregation (1975). Fundamental Principles, available at http://www.leeds.ac.uk/disability-studies/archiveuk/archframe.htm; accessed August 10, 2005.

Watson, N. (2002). "Well, I Know This Is Going to Sound Very Strange to You, But I Don't See Myself as a Disabled Person: Identity and Disability." *Disability and Society,* 17, 5: 509–528.

Williams, S. J. (1999). "Is Anybody There? Critical Realism, Chronic Illness, and the Disability Debate." *Sociology of Health and Illness,* 21, 6: 797–819.

Wolfensberger, W. (1972). *The Principle of Normalization in Human Services.* Toronto: National Institute on Mental Retardation.

Zola, I. K. (1989). "Towards the Necessary Universalizing of a Disability Policy." *The Milbank Quarterly,* 67, suppl.2, Pt. 2: 401–428.

CHAPTER 21

Narrative Prosthesis

David Mitchell and Sharon Snyder

LITERATURE AND THE UNDISCIPLINED BODY OF DISABILITY

This chapter prefaces the close readings to come [in *Narrative Prosthesis*] by deepening our theory of narrative prosthesis as shared characteristics in the literary representation of disability. We demonstrate one of a variety of approaches in disability studies to the "problem" that disability and disabled populations pose to all cultures. Nearly every culture views disability as a problem in need of a solution, and this belief establishes one of the major modes of historical address directed toward people with disabilities. The necessity for developing various kinds of cultural accommodations to handle the "problem" of corporeal difference (through charitable organizations, modifications of physical architecture, welfare doles, quarantine, genocide, euthanasia programs, etc.) situates people with disabilities in a profoundly ambivalent relationship to the cultures and stories they inhabit. The perception of a "crisis" or a "special situation" has made disabled people the subject of not only governmental policies and social programs but also a primary object of literary representation.

Our thesis centers not simply upon the fact that people with disabilities have been the object of representational treatments, but rather that their function in literary discourse is primarily twofold: disability pervades literary narrative, first, as a stock feature of characterization and, second, as an opportunistic metaphorical device. We term this perpetual discursive dependency upon disability *narrative prosthesis*. Disability lends a distinctive idiosyncrasy to any character that differentiates the character from the anonymous background of the "norm." To exemplify this phenomenon, the opening half of this chapter analyzes the Victorian children's story *The Steadfast Tin Soldier* in order to demonstrate that disability serves as a primary impetus of the storyteller's efforts. In the second instance, disability also serves as a metaphorical signifier of social and individual collapse. Physical and cognitive anomalies promise to lend a "tangible" body to textual abstractions; we term this metaphorical use of disability the *materiality of metaphor* and analyze its workings as narrative prosthesis in our concluding discussion of Sophocles' drama *Oedipus the King*. We contend that disability's centrality to these two principal representational strategies establishes a conundrum: while stories rely upon the potency of disability as a symbolic figure, they rarely take up disability as an experience of social or political dimensions.

While each of the chapters that follow [in *Narrative Prosthesis*] set out some of the key cultural components and specific historical contexts that inform this history of disabled representations, our main objective addresses the development of a representational or "literary" history. By "literary" we mean to suggest a form of writing that explicitly values the production of what narrative theorists such as Barthes, Blanchot, and Chambers have referred to as "open-ended" narrative.[1] The identification of the open-ended narrative differentiates a distinctively "literary" component of particular kinds of storytelling: those texts that not only deploy but explicitly foreground the "play" of multiple meanings as a facet of their discursive production. While this definition does not overlook the fact that all texts are inherently "open" to a multiplicity of interpretations, our notion of literary narrative identifies works that *stage* the arbitrariness of linguistic sign systems as a characterizing feature of their plots and commentaries. Not only do the artistic and philosophical works under discussion here present themselves as available to a multiplicity of readings, they openly perform their textual *inexhaustibility*. Each shares a literary objective of destabilizing sedimented cultural meanings that accrue around ideas of bodily "deviance." Thus, we approach the writings of Montaigne, Nietzsche, Shakespeare, Melville, Anderson, Dunn, and an array of post-1945 American authors as writers who interrogate the objectives of narrative in general and the corporeal body in particular as discursive products. Their narratives all share a self-reflexive mode of address about their own textual production of disabled bodies.

This textual performance of ever-shifting and unstable meanings is critical in our interpretive approach to the representation of disability. The close readings that follow hinge upon the identification of disability as an ambivalent and mutable category of cultural and literary investment. Within literary narratives, disability serves as an interruptive force that confronts cultural truisms. The inherent vulnerability and variability of bodies serves literary narratives as a metonym for that which refuses to conform to the mind's desire for order and rationality. Within this schema, disability acts as a metaphor and fleshly example of the body's unruly resistance to the cultural desire to "enforce normalcy."[2] The literary narratives we discuss all deploy the mutable or "deviant" body as an "unbearable weight" (to use Susan Bordo's phrase) in order to counterbalance the "meaning-laden" and ethereal projections of the mind. The body's weighty materiality functions as a textual and cultural other—an object with its own undisciplined language that exceeds the text's ability to control it.

As many theorists have pointed out, this representational split between body and mind/text has been inherited from Descartes (although we demonstrate that disability has been entrenched in these assumptions throughout history). Keeping in mind that the perception of disability shifts from one epoch to another, and sometimes within decades and years, we want to argue that the disabled body has consistently held down a "privileged" position with respect to thematic variations on the mind/body split. Whether a culture approaches the body's materiality as a denigrated symbol of earthly contamination (such as in early Christian cultures), or as a perfectible *technē* of the self (as in ancient Athenian culture), or as an object of medical interpretation (as in Victorian culture), or as specular commodity in the age of electronic media (as is the case in postmodernism), disability perpetually serves as the symbolical symptom to be interpreted by discourses on the body. Whereas the "able" body has no definitional core (it poses as transparently "average" or "normal"), the disabled body surfaces as any body capable of being narrated as "outside the norm." Within such a representational schema, literary narratives revisit disabled bodies as a reminder of the "real" physical limits that "weigh down" transcendent ideals of the mind and knowledge-producing disciplines. In this sense, disability serves as the *hard kernel* or recalcitrant corporeal matter that cannot be deconstructed away by the textual operations of even the most canny narratives or philosophical idealisms.[3]

For our purposes in [*Narrative Prosthesis]*, the representation of disability has both allowed an interrogation of static beliefs about the body and also erupted as the unseemly *matter* of narrative that cannot be textually undone. We therefore forward readings of disability as a narrative device upon which the literary writer of "open-ended" narratives depends for his or her disruptive punch. Our phrase *narrative prosthesis* is meant to indicate that disability has been used throughout history as a crutch upon which literary narratives lean for their representational power, disruptive potentiality, and analytical insight. Bodies show up in stories as dynamic entities that resist or refuse the cultural scripts assigned to them. While we do not simply extol these literary approaches to the representation of the body (particularly in relation to recurring tropes of disability), we want to demonstrate that the disabled body represents a potent symbolic site of literary investment.

The reasons for this dependency upon disability as a device of characterization and interrogation are many, and our concept of narrative prosthesis establishes a variety of motivations that ground the narrative deployment of the "deviant" body. However, what surfaces as a theme throughout these chapters is the paradoxical impetus that makes disability into both a destabilizing sign of cultural prescrip-

tions about the body *and* a deterministic vehicle of characterization for characters constructed as disabled. Thus, in works as artistically varied and culturally distinct as Shakespeare's *Richard III*, Montaigne's "Of Cripples," Melville's *Moby-Dick*, Nietzsche's *Thus Spoke Zarathustra*, Anderson's *Winesburg, Ohio*, Faulkner's *The Sound and the Fury*, Salinger's *The Catcher in the Rye*, Lee's *To Kill a Mockingbird*, Kesey's *One Flew Over the Cuckoo's Nest*, Dunn's *Geek Love*, Powers's *Operation Wandering Soul*, and Egoyan's *The Sweet Hereafter*, the meaning of the relationship between having a physical disability and the nature of a character's identity comes under scrutiny. Disability recurs in these works as a potent force that challenges cultural ideals of the "normal" or "whole" body. *At the same time, disability also operates as the textual obstacle that causes the literary operation of open-endedness to close down or stumble.*

This "closing down" of an otherwise permeable and dynamic narrative form demonstrates the historical conundrum of disability. Characters such as Montaigne's "les boiteux," Shakespeare's "hunchback'd king," Melville's "crippled" captain, Nietzsche's interlocutory "throng of cripples," Anderson's storied "grotesques," Faulkner's "tale told by an idiot," Salinger's fantasized commune of deaf-mutes, Lee's racial and cognitive outsiders, Kesey's ward of acutes and chronics, Dunn's chemically altered freaks, and Power's postapocalyptic wandering children provide powerful counterpoints to their respective cultures' normalizing Truths about the construction of deviance in particular, and the fixity of knowledge systems in general. Yet each of these characterizations also evidences that the artifice of disability binds disabled characters to a programmatic (even deterministic) identity. Disability may provide an explanation for the origins of a character's identity, but its deployment usually proves either too programmatic or unerringly "deep" and mysterious. In each work analyzed in [*Narrative Prosthesis*], disability is used to underscore, in the words of Richard Powers, adapting the theories of Lacan, that the body functions "like a language" as a dynamic network of misfirings and arbitrary adaptations (*Goldbug* 545). Yet, this defining corporeal unruliness consistently produces characters who are indentured to their biological programming in the most essentializing manner. Their disabilities surface to explain everything or nothing with respect to their portraits as embodied beings.

All of the above examples help to demonstrate one of the central assumptions undergirding [*Narrative Prosthesis*]: *disability is foundational to both cultural definition and to the literary narratives that challenge normalizing prescriptive ideals.* By contrasting and comparing the depiction of disability across cultures and histories, one realizes that disability provides an important barometer by which to assess shifting values and norms imposed upon the body. Our approach in the chapters that follow [in ibid.] is to treat disability as a narrative device—an artistic prosthesis—that reveals the pervasive dependency of artistic, cultural, and philosophical discourses upon the powerful alterity assigned to people with disabilities. In short, disability characterization can be understood as a prosthetic contrivance upon which so many of our cultural and literary narratives rely.

THE (IN)VISIBILITY OF PROSTHESIS

The hypothesis of this *discursive dependency* upon disability strikes most scholars and readers at first glance as relatively insubstantial. During a recent conference of the Herman Melville Society in Volos, Greece, we met a scholar from Japan interested in representations of disability in American literature. When asked if Japanese literature made use of disabled characters to the same extent as American and European literatures, he honestly replied that he had never encountered any. Upon further reflection, he listed several examples and laughingly added that of course the Nobel Prize winner Kenzaburo Oë wrote almost exclusively about the subject. This "surprise" about the pervasive nature of disabled images in national literatures catches even the most knowledgeable scholars unaware. Without developed models for analyzing the purpose and function of representational strategies of disability, readers tend to filter a multitude of disability figures absently through their imaginations.

For film scholarship, Paul Longmore has perceptively formulated this paradox, asking why we screen so many images of disability and simultaneously screen them out of our minds. In television and film portraits of disability, Longmore argues, this screening out occurs because we are trained to compartmentalize impairment as an isolated and individual condition of existence. Consequently, we rarely connect together stories of people with disabilities as evidence of a wider systemic predicament. This same phenomenon can be applied to other representational discourses.

As we discussed in our introduction to *The Body and Physical Difference*, our current models of minority representations tend to formulate this problem of literary/critical neglect in the obverse manner (5). One might expect to find the argument in the pages to come that disability is an ignored, overlooked, or marginal experience in literary narrative, that its absence marks an ominous silence in the literary repertoire of human experiences. In pursuing such an argument one could rightly redress, castigate, or bemoan the neglect of this essential life experience within discourses that might have seen fit to take up the important task of exploring disability in serious terms. Within such an approach, disability would prove to be an unarticulated subject whose real-life counterparts could then charge that their own social marginality was the result of an attendant representational erasure outside of medical discourses. Such a methodology would theorize that disability's absence proves evidence of a profound cultural repression to escape the reality of biological and cognitive differences.

However, what we hope to demonstrate in [*Narrative Prosthesis*] is that disability has an unusual literary history. Between the social marginality of people with disabilities and their corresponding representational milieus, disability undergoes a different representational fate. While racial, sexual, and ethnic criticisms have often founded their critiques upon a pervasive absence of their images in the dominant culture's literature, we argue that images of disabled people abound in history.[4] Even if we disregard the fact that entire fields of study have been devoted to the assessment, cataloging, taxonomization, pathologization, objectification, and rehabilitation of disabled people, one is struck by disability's prevalence in discourses outside of medicine and the hard sciences. Once a reader begins to seek out representations of disability in our literatures, it is difficult to avoid their proliferation in texts with which one believed oneself to be utterly familiar. Consequently, as in the discussion of images of disability in Japanese literature mentioned above, the representational prevalence of people with disabilities is far from absent or tangential. As we discussed in *Narrative Prosthesis,* scholarship in the humanities study of disability has sought to pursue previously unexplored questions of the utility of disability to numerous discursive modes, including literature. Our hypothesis in *Narrative Prosthesis* is a paradoxical one: disabled peoples' social invisibility has occurred in the wake of their perpetual circulation throughout print history. This question is not simply a matter of stereotypes or "bad objects," to borrow Naomi Schor's phrase.[5] Rather, the interpretation of representations of disability strikes at the very core of cultural definitions and values. What is the significance of the fact that the earliest known cuneiform tablets catalog 120 omens interpreted from the "deformities" of Sumerian fetuses and irregularly shaped sheep's and calf's livers? How does one explain the disabled gods, such as the blind Hod, the one-eyed Odin, the one-armed Tyr, who are central to Norse myths, or Hephaestus, the "crook-footed god," in Greek literature? What do these modes of representation reveal about cultures as they forward or suppress physical differences? Why does the "visual" spectacle of so many disabilities become a predominating trope in the nonvisual textual mediums of literary narratives?

SUPPLEMENTING THE VOID

What calls stories into being, and what does disability have to do with this most basic preoccupation of narrative? Narrative prosthesis (or the dependency of literary narratives upon disability) forwards the notion that all narratives operate out of a desire to compensate for a limitation or to reign in excess. This narrative approach to difference identifies the literary object par excellence as that which has become extraordinary—a deviation from a widely accepted norm. Literary narratives begin a process of explanatory compensation wherein perceived "aberrancies" can be rescued from ignorance, neglect, or misunderstanding for their readerships. As Michel de Certeau explains in his well-known essay "The Savage 'I,'" the new world travel narrative in the fifteenth and sixteenth centuries provides a model for thinking about the movement of all narrative. A narrative is inaugurated "by the search for the strange, which is presumed different from the place assigned it in the beginning by the discourse of the culture" from which it originates (69). The very need for a story is called into being when something has gone amiss with the known world, and, thus, the language of a tale seeks to comprehend that which has stepped out of line. In this sense, stories compensate for an unknown or unnatural deviance that begs an explanation.

Our notion of narrative prosthesis evolves out of this specific recognition: a narrative issues to resolve or correct—to "prostheticize" in David Wills's sense of the term—a deviance marked as improper to a social context. A simple schematic of narrative structure might run thus: first, a deviance or marked difference is exposed to a reader; second, a narrative consolidates the need for its own existence by calling for an explanation of the deviation's origins and formative consequences; third, the deviance is brought from the periphery of concerns to the center of the story to come; and fourth, the remainder of the story rehabilitates or fixes the deviance in some manner. This fourth step of the repair of deviance may involve an obliteration of the difference through a "cure," the rescue of the despised object from social censure, the extermination of the deviant as a purification of the social body, or the revaluation of an alternative mode of being. Since what we now call disability has been historically narrated as that which characterizes a body as deviant from shared norms of bodily appearance and ability, disability has functioned throughout history as one of the most marked and remarked upon differences that originates the act of storytelling. Narratives turn signs of cultural deviance into textually marked bodies.

In one of our six-year-old son's books entitled *The Steadfast Tin Soldier*, this prosthetic relation of narrative to physical difference is exemplified. The story opens with a child receiving a box of tin soldiers as a birthday gift. The twenty-five soldiers stand erect and uniform in every way, for they "had all been made from the same tin spoon" (Campbell 1). Each of the soldiers comes equipped with a rifle and bayonet, a blue and red outfit signifying membership in the same regiment, black boots, and a stern military visage. The limited omniscient narrator inaugurates the conflict that will propel the story by pointing out a lack in one soldier that mars the uniformity of the gift: "All of the soldiers were exactly alike, with the exception of one, who differed from the rest in having only one leg" (2). This unfortunate blemish, which mars the otherwise flawless ideal of the soldiers standing in unison, becomes the springboard for the story that ensues. The incomplete leg becomes a locus for attention, and from this imperfection a story issues forth. The twenty-four perfect soldiers are quickly left behind in the box for the reason of their very perfection and uniformity—the "ideal" or "intended" soldier's form promises no story. As Barbara Maria Stafford points out, "there [is] only a single way of being healthy and lovely, but an infinity of ways of being sick and wretched" (284). This infinity of ways helps to explain the pervasive dependency of literary narratives upon the trope of disability. Narrative interest solidifies only in the identification and pursuit of an anomaly that inaugurates the exceptional tale or the tale of exception.

The story of *The Steadfast Tin Soldier* stands in a prosthetic relation to the missing leg of the titular protagonist. The narrative in question (and narrative in a general sense) rehabilitates or compensates for its "lesser" subject by demonstrating that the outward flaw "attracts" the storyteller's—and by extension the reader's—interest. The act of characterization is such that narrative must establish the exceptionality of its subject matter to justify the telling of a story. A subject demands a story only in relation to the degree that it can establish its own extra-ordinary circumstances.[6] The normal, routine, average, and familiar (by definition) fail to mobilize the storytelling effort because they fall short of the litmus test of exceptionality. The anonymity of normalcy is no story at all. Deviance serves as the basis and common denominator of all narrative. In this sense, the missing leg presents the aberrant soldier as the story's focus, for his physical difference exiles him from the rank and file of the uniform and physically undifferentiated troop. Whereas a sociality might reject, isolate, institutionalize, reprimand, or obliterate this liability of a single leg, narrative embraces the opportunity that such a "lack" provides—in fact, wills it into existence—as the impetus that calls a story into being. Such a paradox underscores the ironic promise of disability to all narrative.

Display demands difference. The arrival of a narrative must be attended by the "unsightly" eruption of the anomalous (often physical in nature) within the social field of vision. The (re)mark upon disability begins with a stare, a gesture of disgust, a slander or derisive comment upon bodily ignominy, a note of gossip about a rare or unsightly presence, a comment upon the unsuitability of deformity for the appetites of polite society, or a sentiment about the unfortunate circumstances that bring disabilities into being. This ruling out-of-bounds of the socially anomalous subject engenders an act of violence that stories seek to 'rescue' or "reclaim" as worthy of narrative attention. Stories always perform a compensatory function in their efforts to renew interest in a previously denigrated object. While there exist myriad inroads to the identification of the anomalous—femininity, race, class, sexuality—disability services this narrative appetite for difference as often as any other constructed category of deviance.

The politics of this recourse to disability as a device of narrative characterization demonstrates the importance of disability to storytelling itself. Literary narratives support our appetites for the exotic by posing disability as an "alien" terrain that promises the revelation of a previously uncomprehended experience. Literature borrows the potency of the lure of difference that a socially stigmatized condition provides. Yet the reliance upon disability in narrative rarely develops into a means of identifying people with disabilities as a disenfranchised cultural constituency. The ascription of absolute singularity to disability performs a contradictory operation: a character "stands out" as a result of an attributed blemish, but this exceptionality divorces him or her from a shared social identity. As in the story of *The Steadfast Tin Soldier*, a narrative disability establishes the uniqueness of an individual character and is quickly left behind as a purely biological fact. Disability marks a character as "unlike" the rest of a fiction's cast, and once singled out, the character becomes a case of special interest who retains originality to the detriment of all other characteristics. Disability cannot be accommodated within the ranks of the norm(als), and, thus, the options for dealing with the difference that drives the story's plot is twofold: a disability is either left behind or punished for its lack of conformity.

In the story of *The Steadfast Tin Soldier* we witness the exercise of both operations on the visible difference that the protagonist's disability poses. Once the soldier's incomplete leg is identified, its difference is quickly nullified. Nowhere in the story does the narrator call attention to a difficult negotiation that must be attempted as a result of the missing appendage. In fact, like the adventurer of de Certeau's paradigmatic travel narrative, the tin figure undergoes a series of epic encounters without further reference to his limitation: after he falls out of a window, his bayonet gets stuck in a crack; a storm rages over him later that night; two boys find the figure, place him into a newspaper boat, and sail him down the gutter into a street drain; he is accosted by a street rat who poses as gatekeeper to the underworld; the newspaper boat sinks in a canal where the soldier is swallowed by a large fish; and finally he is returned to his home of origin when the family purchases the fish for dinner and discovers the one-legged figure in the belly. The series of dangerous encounters recalls the epic adventure of the physically able Odysseus on his way home from Troy; likewise, the tin soldier endures the physically taxing experience without further remark upon the incomplete leg in the course of the tale. The journey and ultimate return home embody the cyclical nature of all narrative (and the story of disability in particular)—the deficiency inaugurates the need for a story but is quickly forgotten once the difference is established.

However, a marred appearance cannot ultimately be allowed to return home unscathed. Near the end of the story the significance of the missing leg returns when the tin soldier is reintroduced to his love—the paper maiden who pirouettes upon one leg. Because the soldier mistakes the dancer as possessing only one leg like himself, the story's conclusion hinges upon the irony of an argument about human attraction based upon shared likeness. If the maiden shares the fate of one-leggedness, then, the soldier reasons, she must be meant for him. However, in a narrative twist of deus ex machina the blemished soldier is inexplicably thrown into the fire by a boy right at the moment of his imagined reconciliation with the "one-legged" maiden. One can read this ending as a punishment for his willingness to desire someone physically perfect and therefore unlike himself. Shelley's story of Frankenstein (discussed in chapter 5 [of *Narrative Prosthesis*]) ends in the monster's anticipated obliteration on his own funeral pyre in the wake of his misinterpretation as monstrous, and the tin soldier's fable reaches its conclusion in a similar manner. Disability inaugurates narrative, but narrative inevitably punishes its own prurient interests by overseeing the extermination of the object of its fascination.

THE PHYSIOGNOMY OF DISABILITY

What is the significance of disability as a pervasive category of narrative interest? Why do the convolutions, distortions, and ruptures that mark the disabled body's surface prove seductive to literary representation? What is the relationship of the external evidence of disability's perceived deviances and the core of the disabled subject's being? The disabled body occupies a crossroads in the age-old literary debate about the relationship of form to content. Whereas the "unmarred" surface enjoys its cultural anonymity and promises little more than a confirmation of the adage of a "healthy" mind in a "healthy" body, disability signifies a more variegated and sordid series of assumptions and experiences. Its unruliness must be tamed by multiple mappings of the surface. If form leads to content or "embodies" meaning, then disability's disruption of acculturated bodily norms also suggests a corresponding misalignment of subjectivity itself.

In *Volatile Bodies* Elizabeth Grosz argues that philosophy has often reduced the body to a "fundamental continuity with brute, inorganic matter" (8). Instead of this reductive tendency, Grosz calls for a more complex engagement with our theorizations of the body: "the body provides a point of mediation between what is perceived as purely internal and accessible only to the subject and what is external and publicly observable, a point from which to rethink the opposition between the inside and the outside" (20). Approaching the body as a mediating force between the outside world and internal subjectivity would allow a more thoroughgoing theory of subjectivity's relationship to materiality. In this way, Grosz argues that the body should not be understood as a receptacle or package for the contents of subjectivity, but rather plays an important role in the formation of psychic identity itself.

Disability will play a crucial role in the reformulation of the opposition between interior and exterior because physical differences have so often served as an example of bodily form following function or vice versa. The mutability of bodies causes them to change over time (both individually and historically), and yet the disabled body is sedimented within an ongoing narrative of breakdown and abnormality. However, while we situate our argument in opposition to reading physical disability as a one-to-one correspondence with subjecthood, we do not deny its role as a foundational aspect of identity. The disabled subject's navigation of social attitudes toward people with disabilities, medical pathologies, the management of embodiment itself, and daily encounters with "perfected" physicalities in the media demonstrates that the disabled body has a substantial impact upon subjectivity as a whole. The study of disability must understand the impact of the experience of disability upon subjectivity *without simultaneously situating the internal and external body within a strict mirroring relationship to one another.*

In literature this mediating role of the external body with respect to internal subjectivity is often represented as a relation of strict correspondence. Either the "deviant" body deforms subjectivity, or "deviant" subjectivity violently erupts upon the surface of its bodily container. In either instance the corporeal body of disability is represented as manifesting its own internal symptoms. Such an approach places the body in an automatic physiognomic relation to the subjectivity it harbors. As Barbara Maria Stafford has demonstrated, practices of interpreting the significance of bodily appearances since the eighteenth century have depended upon variations of the physiognomic method.

> Physiognomics was body criticism. As corporeal connoisseurship, it diagnosed unseen spiritual qualities by scrutinizing visible traits. Since its adherents claimed privileged powers of detection, it was a somewhat sinister capability. . . . The master eighteenth-century physiognomist, Lavater, noted that men formed conjectures "by reasoning from the exterior to the interior." He continued: "What is universal nature but physiognomy. Is not everything surface and contents? Body and soul? External effect and internal faculty? Invisible principle and visible end?" (84)

For cultures that operated upon models of bodily interpretation prior to the development of internal imaging techniques, the corporeal surface was freighted with significance. Physiognomy became a paradigm of access to the ephemeral and intangible workings of the interior body. Speculative qualities such as moral integrity, honesty, trustworthiness, criminality, fortitude, cynicism, sanity, and so forth, suddenly became available for scrutiny by virtue of the "irregularities" of the body that enveloped them. For the physiognomist, the body allowed meaning to be inferred from the outside in; such a speculative practice resulted in the ability to anticipate intangible qualities of one's personhood without having to await the "proof" of actions or the intimacy of a relationship developed over time. By "reasoning from the exterior to the interior," the trained physiognomist extracted the meaning of the soul without the permission or participation of the interpreted.

If the "external effect" led directly to a knowledge of the "internal faculty," then those who inhabited bodies deemed "outside the norm" proved most ripe for a scrutiny of their moral or intellectual content. Since disabled people by definition embodied a form that was identified as "outside" the normal or permissible, their visages and bodily outlines became the physiognomist's (and later the pathologist's) object par excellence. Yet, the "sinister capability" of physiognomy proves more complex than just the exclusivity of interpretive authority that Stafford suggests. If the body would offer a surface manifestation of internal symptomatology, then disability and deformity automatically preface an equally irregular subjectivity. Physiognomy proves a deadly practice to a population already existing on the fringes of social interaction and "humanity." While the "authorized" physiognomist was officially sanctioned to interpret the symbology of the bodily surface, the disabled person became every person's Rorschach test. While physiognomists discerned the nuances of facial countenances and phrenologists surveyed protuberances of the skull, the extreme examples offered by those with physical disabilities and deformities invited the armchair psychology of the literary practitioner to participate in the symbolic manipulation of bodily exteriors.

Novelists, dramatists, philosophers, poets, essayists, painters, and moralists all flocked to the site of a physiognomic circus from the eighteenth century on. "Irregular" bodies became a fertile field for symbolists of all stripes. Disability and deformity retained their fascination for would-be interpreters because their "despoiled" visages commanded a rationale that narrative (textual or visual) promised to decipher. Because disability represents that which goes awry in the normalizing bodily schema, narratives sought to unravel the riddle of anomaly's origins. Such a riddle

was inherently social in its making. The physiognomic corollary seemed to provide a way in to the secrets of identity itself. The chapters that follow demonstrate that the problem of the representation of disability is not the search for a more "positive" story of disability, as it has often been formulated in disability studies, *but rather a thoroughgoing challenge to the undergirding authorization to interpret that disability invites.* There is a politics at stake in the fact that disability inaugurates an explanatory need that the unmarked body eludes by virtue of its physical anonymity. To participate in an ideological system of bodily norms that promotes some kinds of bodies while devaluing others is to ignore the malleability of bodies and their definitively mutant natures.

Stafford's argument notwithstanding, the body's manipulation by physiognomic practices did not develop as an exclusively eighteenth-century phenomenon. Our own research demonstrates that while physiognomics came to be consolidated as a scientific ideology in the eighteenth and nineteenth centuries, people with disabilities and deformities have always been subject to varieties of this interpretive practice. Elizabeth Cornelia Evans argues that physiognomic beliefs can be traced back as far as ancient Greece. She cites Aristotle as promoting physiognomic reasoning when he proclaims,

> It is possible to infer character from physique, if it is granted that body and soul change together in all natural affections . . . For if a peculiar affection applies to any individual class, e.g., courage to lions, there must be some corresponding sign for it; for it has been assumed that body and soul are affected together (7).

In fact, one might argue that physiognomics came to be consolidated out of a general historical practice applied to the bodies of disabled peoples. If the extreme evidence of marked physical differences provided a catalog of reliable signs, then perhaps more minute bodily differentiations could also be cataloged and interpreted. In this sense, people with disabilities ironically served as the historical locus for the invention of physiognomy.

As we pointed out earlier, the oldest surviving tablets found along the Tigris River in Mesopotamia and dated from 3000 to 2000 B.C. deployed a physiognomic method to prognosticate from deformed fetuses and irregular animal livers. The evidence of bodily anomalies allowed royalty and high priests to forecast harvest cycles, geographic conditions, the outcomes of impending wars, and the future of city-states. The symbolic prediction of larger cultural conditions from physical differences suggests one of the primary differences between the ancient and modern periods: physical anomalies metamorphosed from a symbolic interpretation of worldly meanings to a primarily individualized locus of information. The movement of disability from a macro to a micro level of prediction underscores our point that disability has served as a foundational category of cultural interpretation. The long-standing practice of physiognomic readings demonstrates that disability and deformity serve as the impetus to analyze an otherwise obscured meaning or pattern at the individual level. In either case the overdetermined symbolism ascribed to disabled bodies obscured the more complex and banal reality of those who inhabited them.

THE MATERIALITY OF METAPHOR

Like Oedipus (another renowned disabled fictional creation), cultures thrive upon solving the riddle of disability's rhyme and reason. When the limping Greek protagonist overcomes the Sphinx by answering "man who walks with a cane" as the concluding answer to her three-part query,

we must assume that his own disability served as an experiential source for this insight. The master riddle solver in effect trumps the Sphinx's feminine otherness with knowledge gleaned from his own experience of inhabiting an alien body. In doing so, Oedipus taps into the cultural reservoir of disability's myriad symbolic associations as an interpretive source for his own riddle-solving methodology. Whereas disability usually provides the riddle in need of a narrative solution, in this instance the experience of disability momentarily serves as the source of Oedipus's interpretive mastery. Yet, Sophocles' willingness to represent disability as a mode of experience-based knowledge proves a rare literary occasion and a fleeting moment in the play's dramatic structure.

While Oedipus solves the Sphinx's riddle in the wake of his own physical experience as a lame interpreter and an interpreter of lameness, his disability remains inconsequential to the myth's plot. Oedipus's disability—the result of Laius's pinning of his infant son's ankles as he sends him off to die of exposure—"marks" his character as distinctive and worthy of the exceptional tale. Beyond this physical fact, Sophocles neglects to explore the relationship of the body's mediating function with respect to Oedipus's kingly subjectivity. Either his "crippling" results in an insignificant physical difference, or the detailing of his difference can be understood to embody a vaguely remembered history of childhood violence enacted against him by his father. The disability remains a physical fact of his character that the text literally overlooks once this difference is established as a remnant of his repressed childhood. Perhaps those who share the stage with Oedipus either have learned to look away from his disability or have imbibed the injunction of polite society to refuse commentary upon the existence of the protagonist's physical difference.

However, without the pinning of Oedipus's ankles and his resulting lameness two important aspects of the plot would be compromised. First, Oedipus might have faltered at the riddle of the Sphinx like others before him and fallen prey to the voracious appetite of the she-beast; second, Sophocles' protagonist would lose the physical sign that literally connects him to an otherwise inscrutable past. In this sense, Oedipus's physical difference secures key components of the plot that allow the riddle of his identity to be unraveled. At the same time, his disability serves as the source of little substantive commentary in the course of the drama itself. Oedipus as a "lame interpreter" establishes the literal source of his ability to solve the baffling riddle and allows the dramatist to metaphorize humanity's incapacity to fathom the dictums of the gods. This movement exemplifies the literary oscillation between micro and macro levels of metaphorical meaning supplied by disability. Sophocles later moves to Oedipus's self-blinding as a further example of how the physical body provides a corporeal correlative to the ability of dramatic myth to bridge personal and public symbology.

What is of interest for us in this ancient text is the way in which one can read its representational strategy as a paradigm for literary approaches to disability. The ability of disabled characters to allow authors the metaphorical "play" between macro and micro registers of meaning-making establishes the role of the body in literature as a liminal point in the representational process. In his study of editorial cartoonings and caricatures of the body leading up to the French Revolution, Antoine de Baecque argues that the corporeal metaphor provided a means of giving the abstractions of political ideals an "embodied" power. To "know oneself" and provide a visual correlative to a political commentary,

French cartoonists and essayists deployed the body as a metaphor because the body "succeeds in *connecting* narrative and knowledge, meaning and knowing" most viscerally (5). This form of textual embodiment concretizes an otherwise ephemeral concept within a corporeal essence. To give an abstraction a body allows the idea to simulate a foothold in the material world that it would otherwise fail to procure.

Whereas an ideal such as democracy imparts a weak and abstracted notion of governmental and economic reform, for example, the embodied caricature of a hunchbacked monarch overshadowed by a physically superior democratic citizen proved more powerful than any ideological argument. Instead of political harangue, the body offers an illusion of fixity to a textual effect:

> [Body] metaphors were able simultaneously to describe the event and to make the description attain the level of the imaginary. The deployment of these bodily *topoi*—the degeneracy of the nobility, the impotence of the king, the herculean strength of the citizenry, the goddesses of politics appearing naked like Truth, the congenital deformity of the aristocrats, the bleeding wound of the martyrs—allowed political society to represent itself at a pivotal moment of its history. . . . One must pass through the [bodily] forms of a narrative in order to reach knowledge. (De Baecque 4–5)

Such a process of giving body to belief exemplifies the corporeal seduction of the body to textual mediums. The desire to access the seeming solidity of the body's materiality offers representational literatures a way of grasping that which is most unavailable to them. For de Baecque, representing a body in its specificity as the bearer of an otherwise intangible concept grounds the reality of an ideological meaning. The passage through a bodily form helps secure a knowledge that would otherwise drift away of its own insubstantiality. The corporeal metaphor offers narrative the one thing it cannot possess—an anchor in materiality. Such a process embodies the materiality of metaphor; and literature is the writing that aims to concretize theory through its ability to provide an embodied account of physical, sensory life.

While de Baecque's theory of the material metaphor argues that the attempt to harness the body to a specific ideological program provides the text with an illusory opportunity to embody Truth, he overlooks the fact that the same process embeds the body within a limiting array of symbolic meanings: crippling conditions equate with monarchical immobility, corpulence evidences tyrannical greed, deformity represents malevolent motivation, and so on. Delineating his corporeal catalog, the historian bestows upon the body an elusive, general character while depending for his readings almost exclusively upon the potent symbolism of disabled bodies in particular. Visible degeneracy, impotency, congenital deformity, festering ulcerations, and bleeding wounds in the passage previously quoted provide the contrastive bodily coordinates to the muscular, aesthetic, and symmetrical bodies of the healthy citizenry. One cannot narrate the story of a healthy body or national reform movement without the contrastive device of disability to bear out the symbolic potency of the message. The materiality of metaphor via disabled bodies gives all bodies a tangible essence in that the "healthy" corporeal surface fails to achieve its symbolic effect without its disabled counterpart.

As Georges Canguilhem has pointed out, the body only calls attention to itself in the midst of its breakdown or disrepair (209). The representation of the process of breakdown or incapacity is fraught with political and ideological significance. To make the body speak essential truths, one must give a language to it. Elaine Scarry argues that

"there is ordinarily no language for [the body in] pain" (13). However, we would argue that the body itself has no language, since language is something foreign to its nonlinguistic materiality. It must be spoken for if its meanings are to prove narratable. The narration of the disabled body allows a textual body to *mean* through its long-standing historical representation as an overdetermined symbolic surface; the disabled body also offers narrative the illusion of grounding abstract knowledge within a bodily materiality. *If the body is the Other of text, then textual representation seeks access to that which it is least able to grasp.* If the nondysfunctional body proves too uninteresting to narrate, the disabled body becomes a paramount device of characterization. Narrative prosthesis, or the dependency upon the disabled body, proves essential to (even the essence of) the stories analyzed in the chapters to come.

NOTES

1. Many critics have designated a distinctive space for "the literary" by identifying those works whose meaning is inherently elastic and multiple. Maurice Blanchot identifies literary narrative as that which refuses closure and readerly mastery—"to write [literature] is to surrender to the interminable" (27). In his study of Balzac's *Sarrasine*, Roland Barthes characterizes the "plural text" as that which is allied with a literary value whose "networks are many and interact, without any one of them being able to surpass the rest; the text is a galaxy of signifiers, not a structure of signifieds; it has no beginning; it is reversible; we gain access to it by several entrances, none of which can be authoritatively declared to be the main one" (5). Ross Chambers's analysis of oppositionality argues that literature strategically deploys the "play" or "leeway" in discursive systems as a means of disturbing the restrictive prescriptions of authoritative regimes (iv). As our study develops, we demonstrate that the strategic "open-endedness" of literary narrative is paralleled by the multiplicity of meanings bequeathed to people with disabilities in history. In doing so, we argue not only that the open-endedness of literature challenges sedimented historical truths,

but that disability has been one of the primary weapons in literature's disruptive agenda.

2. In his important study *Enforcing Normalcy*, Lennard Davis theorizes the "normal" body as an ideological construct that tyrannizes over those bodies that fail to conform. Accordingly, while all bodies feel insubstantial when compared to our abstract ideals of the body, disabled people experience a form of subjugation or oppression as a result of this phenomenon. Within such a system, we will argue in tandem with Davis that disability provides the contrastive term against which the concepts health, beauty, and ability are determined: "Just as the conceptualization of race, class, and gender shapes the lives of those who are not black, poor, or female, so the concept of disability regulates the bodies of those who are 'normal.' In fact, the very concept of normalcy by which most people (by definition) shape their existence is in fact tied inexorably to the concept of disability, or rather, the concept of disability is a function of a concept of normalcy. Normalcy and disability are part of the same system" (2).

3. Following the theories of Lacan, Slavoj Zizek in *The Sublime Object of Ideology* extracts the notion of the "hard kernel" of ideology. For Zizek, it represents the underlying core of belief that refuses to be deconstructed away by even the most radical operations of political critique. More than merely a rational component of ideological identification, the "hard kernel" represents the irrationality behind belief that secures the interpellated subject's "illogical" participation in a linguistically permeable system.

4. There is an equivalent problem to the representation of disability in literary narratives within our own critical rubrics of the body. The disabled body continues to fall outside of critical categories that identify bodies as the product of cultural constructions. While challenging a generic notion of white, male body as ideological proves desirable in our own moment within trhe realms of race, gender, sexuality, and class, there has been a more pernicious history of literary and critical approaches to the disabled body. In our introduction to *The Body and Physical Difference*, we argue that minority discourses in the humanities tend to deploy the evidence of "corporeal aberrancy" as a means of identifying the invention of an ideologically encoded body: "While physical aberrancy is often recognized as constructed and historically variable it is rarely remarked upon as its own legitimized or politically fraught identity" (5).

5. For Naomi Schor the phrase "bad objects" implies a discursive object that has been ruled out of bounds by the prevailing academic politics of the day, or one that represents a "critical perversion" (xv). Our use of the phrase implies both of these definitions in relation to disability. The literary object of disability has been almost entirely neglected by literary criticism in general until the past few years, when disability studies in the humanites have developed; and "disability" as a topic of investigation still strikes many as a "perverse" interest for academic contemplation. To these two definitions we would also add that the labeling of disability as a "bad object" nonetheless overlooks the fact that disabilities fill the pages of literary interest. The reasons for overabundance of images of disability in literature is the subject [*Narrative Prosthesis*].

6. The title of Thomson's *Extraordinary Bodies: Figuring Disabiltiy in American Culture and Literature* forwards the term extraordinary in order to play off of its multiple nuances. It can suggest the powerful sentimentality of overcoming narratives so often attached to stories about disabled people. It can also suggest those whose bodies are the products of overdetermined social meaning that exaggerate physical differences or perform them as a way of enhancing their exoticness. In addition, we share with Thomson the belief that disabled bodies prove extraordinary in the ways in which they expose the variety and mutable nature of physicality itself.

WORKS CITED

Blanchot, Maurice. *The Space of Literature*. 1955. Trans. Ann Smock. Lincoln: U of Nebraska P, 1982.

Campbell, Katie. *The Steadfast Tin Soldier*. Morris Plains, NJ: Unicorn, 1990.

Chambers, Ross. *Room For Maneuver: Reading the Oppositional in Narrative*. Chicago: U of Chicago P, 1991.

Davis, Lennard. *Enforcing Normalcy: Disability, Deafness, and the Body*. New York: Verso, 1995.

Mitchell, David and Snyder, Susan (eds.) *The Body and Physical Difference: Discourses of Disability*. Ann Arbor: U of Michigan P, 1997.

Schor, Naomi. *Bad Objects: Essays Popular and Unpopular*. Durham, NC: Duke UP, 1995.

Stafford, Barbara Maria. *Body Criticism: Imaging the Unseen in Enlightenment Art and Medicine*. Cambridge, MA: MIT Press, 1994.

Thomson, Rosemarie Garland. *Extraordinary Bodies: Figuring Disability in American Culture and Literature*. New York: Columbia UP, 1997.

Zizek, Slavoj. *The Sublime Object of Ideology*. New York: Verso, 1999.

CHAPTER 22

The Unexceptional Schizophrenic: A Post-Postmodern Introduction

Catherine Prendergast

Postmodern theory has been indispensable to disability studies because it has challenged normativity and destabilized narratives of national progress, social order, and identity. The essay nevertheless contends that crucial texts of postmodern theory have only achieved such destabilizations by holding one identity stable: that of the schizophrenic. These texts base their understanding of schizophrenia (and, by extension, the postmodern condition) on the writing of a few, distinctly exceptional, schizophrenics. An explosion of civic writing in the mid-1990s by writers who mark themselves specifically as non-exceptional schizophrenics, however, interrogates the desire for the stable schizophrenic, easy to recognize and therefore incarcerate, or celebrate, as the occasion demands. Attention to such writing reveals schizophrenics to be an active and growing constituency arguing for their rights in the public sphere. The essay concludes that recognition of this constituency and the multitude of voices it represents could greatly inform future theoretical programs that invoke "the schizophrenic."

Wasn't it because they didn't go far enough in listening to the insane that the great observers who drew up the first classifications impoverished the material they were given—to such an extent it appeared problematic and fragmentary to them?

(Jacques Lacan)

Postmodern theory owes a great debt to schizophrenics—and to cyborgs, border-crossers, and other figures culturally designated as hybrid. But most belatedly, and most significantly to disability studies, the debt is owed to schizophrenics, those people who bear the diagnosis of schizophrenia, along with its legal, social, and rhetorical consequences. Without schizophrenics, postmodernity would struggle to limn its boundaries, for the schizophrenic in postmodern theory marks the point of departure from the modern, the Oedipal, the referential, the old. Postmodern theory has been indispensable to disability studies because it has allowed not only for a challenge to normativity, but also for the destabilizing of narratives of national progress, social order, and identity (Corker and Shakespeare). However crucial texts of postmodern theory have only achieved these destabilizations by holding one identity stable: that of the schizophrenic.

"Someone asked us if we had seen a schizophrenic—no, no, we have never seen one," Deleuze and Guattari assert in the final pages of *Anti-Oedipus: Capitalism* and *Schizophrenia* (380). While this claim, on its face, is somewhat unlikely for at least Guattari, the more immediate question is, how do they know? The schizophrenic is imagined here to be immediately recognizable with a disorder visible, and yet, because not seen, at the same time invisible and outside the social order. So distanced from the public domain, the schizophrenic is ripe for appropriation by Deleuze and Guattari who find in this figure their anti-Oedipus. It's a peculiarly honorary position the schizophrenic seems to hold: "The schizophrenic is closest to the beating heart of reality" (87), "the possessor of the most touchingly meager capital" (12). Rosi Braidotti, writing for *The Deleuze Dictionary*, aptly summarizes the importance of the schizophrenic to the anti-Oedipal project: "[T]he image of thought implied by liberal individualism and classical humanism is disrupted in favour of a multi-layered dynamic subject. On this level schizophrenia acts as an alternative to how the art of thinking can be practiced" (239). And yet this dynamic subject, always seemingly in motion, ever demonstrating this new mode of thinking, is nonetheless in Deleuze and Guattari's work to be sharply differentiated from "the schizo," reduced by hospitalization, "deaf, dumb and blind," cut off from reality, "occupying the void" (88). By *A Thousand Plateaus*, the schizophrenic has disappeared almost entirely, metaphorically consumed by the rhizome.

It is probable, that when Deleuze and Guattari proclaimed that "no, no," they had never seen a schizophrenic, they were not expecting to be taken literally. As active readers we might try a thought experiment of our own and replace "schizophrenic" in that phrase with "woman," or the designation for an individual of any racialized group. Such a statement would be so much less likely, because at the time *Anti-Oedipus* was published (originally in 1972, in French), the civil rights movement and the burgeoning women's rights movements would have drained the resulting expression of any ironic value. In the wake of a formerly disadvantaged group's clear entrée into the civic sphere, no purchase can be gained through claiming—even facetiously—never to have met a member of that group. That Deleuze and Guattari can make the claim to mediate schizophrenic experience while never having met a schizophrenic says a great deal about the lack of self-identifying schizophrenics in the public sphere one generation ago.

Deleuze and Guattari are hardly the only postmodern theorists to ground their analysis of the late capitalist order in a stereotypical portrayal of the schizophrenic. Fredric Jameson also delineates the position of the schizophrenic, analogizing the postmodern condition to the breakdown of the signifying chain that characterizes schizophrenic thought: "[T]he schizophrenic is reduced to an experience of pure material signifiers, or, in other words, a series of pure and unrelated presents in time" (27). Jean Baudrillard, similarly, analogizes the experience of postmodern reality to the experience of schizophrenia, correcting modernist notions of the schizophrenic as he does so: "The schizophrenic is not, as generally claimed, characterized by his loss of touch with reality, but by the absolute proximity to and total instantaneousness with things, this overexposure to the transparency of the world" (27). Reality is thus accessible to postmodern theory through the thought patterns of the schizophrenic. What is common in these moments of access is the certitude with which schizophrenics are discussed; the schizophrenic is allowed no change in position or in thinking, and no agenda of her or his own. In the wake of this certainty regarding how schizophrenics think and how they act, Petra Kuppers's comment on her viewing of the work of artist and schizophrenic Martin Ramírez is very refreshing: "I can't know Ramírez—that is the only firm knowledge I can take away from the images and their history of making, storing, display, and criticism" (189).

Postmodern theory has many roots, and in discussing Jameson, Baudrillard, and Deleuze and Guattari, those who have specifically drawn upon schizophrenia to elucidate postmodernity, I am not limiting postmodernism to those entities. Nor do I find reason to challenge the central insights of postmodern theory and their utility to much of disability studies. I do, however, believe that it is productive to consider postmodern attempts to ground the shared postmodern condition in the unshared position of the schizophrenic, and interrogate those attempts within the context of the disability rights and specifically mental disability rights movements. My examination of how one theoretical program can propose to liberate at the same time as it (certainly unwittingly) casts certain identities outside the social order—whether in celebratory fashion, as in Deleuze and Guattari or Jameson, or in pathologizing fashion, as in Baudrillard—draws inspiration from David T. Mitchell and Sharon L. Snyder's recollection in *Narrative Prosthesis* that the identity work conducted by race and sexuality studies historically involved distancing people of color and women from the "real" abnormalities with which they had long been metaphorically associated:

> As feminist, race, and sexuality studies sought to unmoor their identities from debilitating physical and cognitive associations, they inevitably positioned disability as the "real" limitation from which they must escape. . . . Formerly denigrated identities are "rescued" by understanding gendered, racial, and sexual differences as textually produced, distancing them from the "real" of physical

or cognitive aberrancy projected onto their figures. (2–3)

Following Mitchell and Snyder, it is interesting to note that Deleuze and Guattari, to launch their critique of late capitalism, have to distance schizoanalysis from the "real" schizo, stuck in the void. This central displacement is necessary to allow for the metaphorizing of schizophrenia along the exclusively positive channels Deleuze and Guattari allow. However positive, this metaphorizing enacts what Susan Sontag would call a "rhetorical ownership" over schizophrenia. Sontag suggests that the "metaphorical trappings" that attach to diagnoses have very real consequences, in terms of how people seek treatment, or don't, including what kind of treatment they seek. She writes: "it is highly desirable for a specific dreaded illness to come to be seen as ordinary. . . . Much in the way of individual experience and social policy depends on the struggle for rhetorical ownership of the illness: how it is possessed, assimilated in argument and in cliché" (93–94).

Clichés are, by definition, metaphors that have become too stable. The appropriation of the schizophrenic by postmodern theory is a cliché, one that posits continually the rhetorical exceptionalism of schizophrenics. This stability mirrors the medicalized investment, which, as Snyder and Mitchell have observed in "Disability Haunting in American Poetics," finds disability to be "an organic predicament based on the common sense notion that disability status cannot be altered" (2). As a result of this common sense notion, Snyder and Mitchell argue, the disabled are not allowed to enter the history of U.S. social conflict as an active constituency arguing for their rights within the public sphere. Postmodern theory values schizophrenics precisely because it imagines them insulated from civic life. They are to remain the "exceptional, private citizenry" that Snyder and Mitchell identify as typical of the role given to the disabled. There is, however, an increasingly public citizenry of schizophrenics who claim the following: to speak publicly, particularly on issues that affect their lives; to self-identify as schizophrenic without having to embrace the stigma associated with the term nor undersign any medicalized investment; to found and use their own press organs to further their causes (in this way, very much the "bodies with organs"); to be considered in public addresses, and finally, to enjoy a rhetorical position and a life that is not predicated on complete absence of impairment. In short, they claim the right to unexceptional instability, which is not something postmodern theory has readily granted them.

THE MODEL SCHIZOPHRENIC

It is not surprising that the postmodern theory I have reviewed should hold the identity of schizophrenics so constant, because much of it is based on a few, rather exceptional schizophrenics. The history of perhaps the most exceptional I will turn to here: Judge Daniel Paul Schreber. As Rosemary Dinnage observes, Schreber's 1903 *Memoirs of My Nervous Illness*, something of a self-report, is "the most written-about document in all psychiatric literature. . . . Everyone has had something to say about Schreber" (xi). Schreber's writings cannot help but come to us as metaphor, saturated with the resonances of his commentators: Freud, Jung, Lacan, and Deleuze and Guattari, chief among them. Equally exceptional as the reception of his work were Schreber's life and the course of his illness. A prominent German judge, Schreber was the son of Moritz Schreber, an immensely influential though controversial German authority on child-rearing. That Moritz Schreber's

systems for parenting stressed nearly sadistic obedience and control is a fact about which analyzers of Daniel Schreber's pathology make some hay.[1] Also well-noted is that Schreber's schizophrenia did not manifest until he was in his forties in the midst of his career.[2] He recovered from his first breakdown only to be incarcerated for nearly a decade when he was in his fifties. While in the asylum, he recorded his observations of his body and his religious conceptions including those supernatural matters "which cannot be expressed in human language; they exceed human understanding" (Schreber 16). Schreber was keen to publish his manuscript (his family, fearing embarrassment, not so very keen), however, inmates of asylums were not permitted by law to publish their work. In 1902, after a protracted legal battle, Schreber secured his release entering into the public sphere physically, and soon after, rhetorically. His *Memoirs*, published the following year, were quickly recognized as a critical account of psychosis. He had become fully exceptional. Lacan, who analyzed Schreber through his *Memoirs* wrote: "That Schreber was *exceptionally gifted*, as he himself puts it, at observing phenomena of which he is the center and at searching for their truth, makes his testimony incomparably valuable" (233, emphasis Lacan's).

Undeniably, however, what made Judge Schreber most exceptional to modern commentators including Lacan was Freud's 1911 analysis of the Schreber case. Schreber might at first seem an unusual subject for Freud to analyze given that Freud considered schizophrenics unfit subjects for the talking cure. Colin McCabe records, "Any psychotic patient that presented him or herself in Freud's consulting rooms would, by the very nature of their condition, swiftly either refuse treatment or be referred on to a hospital" (ix). McCabe puzzles why Freud did not read Schreber's *Memoirs* until seven years after its publication, even though it had been a topic of great discussion in psychiatric circles. That Freud did eventually turn his attention to the Schreber case McCabe credits to Freud's fear that psychoanalysis, particularly its tenets grounding the relationship between the unconscious and the conscious in sexuality, faced threats from competing biological and social theories of the psyche. Schreber, to Freud, then, was also exceptional; Freud's location of Schreber's psychosis in repressed homosexuality was to be the exception that proved his rule of neurosis.

Freud's defensive and unconvincing analysis of Schreber through the *Memoirs*, ("very unsatisfactory" Jung would deem it),[3] made Schreber the perfect platform from which Deleuze and Guattari could launch their assault on psychoanalytic theory's complicity with the capitalist order. Judge Schreber, along with the also exceptional Antonin Artaud, became their model schizophrenics. But it was Schreber who allowed for the most direct attack on Freud. Deleuze and Guattari declared that Freud had done Schreber a great disservice in his reading of *Memoirs*, cutting off Schreber rhetorically at the kneecaps. "Not one word is retained," they complained, of Schreber's original work in Freud's treatment. Schreber, they wryly remarked, was not only sodomized by rays from heaven (as Schreber in his *Memoirs* describes), but was "posthumously oedipalized by Freud," who, they point out, never met his "patient" *in vivo* (57).

The concern Deleuze and Guattari have for Schreber seems to be one of recuperating his rhetorical position; Schreber, thus rhetorically enabled, can become the agent who can trick Freud in the session that never occurred, breaking through "the simplistic terms and functions of the Oedipal triangle" (14). However, Deleuze and Guattari themselves evince less than total confidence in Schreber's self-account. Their remark, "if we are to believe Judge Schreber's

doctrine" (19) suggests that Schreber occupies only a qualified rhetorical position in *Anti-Oedipus*, one that is valuable, but provisional, even on the subject of Schreber's own experience. Deleuze and Guattari find in Schreber's memoirs the seeds of the break from representation, but they can only access it through an act of representation, one that grants Schreber no firmer rhetorical ground than he enjoyed through Freud's text.

Where Deleuze and Guattari find Schreber through Freud, Jameson finds him through Lacan: "I have found Lacan's account of schizophrenia useful here not because I have any way of knowing whether it has clinical accuracy but chiefly because—as description rather than diagnosis—it seems to me to offer a suggestive aesthetic model" (26). Through Jameson's formulation of Schreber's condition, we can understand schizophrenia as that state which enacts disruptions of temporality. Jameson cites as further examples of such disruption the work of John Cage and Samuel Beckett, neither of whom were diagnosed schizophrenics. Cage and Beckett quickly, however, become metaphors of schizophrenia through Jameson's analysis. In the end Jameson leaves us with an aestheticization of the schizophrenic experience. Schizophrenia is always/already artistic, always/already literary, always/already metaphorical. What might usefully rescue schizophrenia from these metaphoric entrapments is a shift in focus toward a rhetorical exploration, one that examines the circumstances of publication of schizophrenic writing, situating that writing within, as Snyder and Mitchell have suggested, histories of conflict over who may take up space in the public sphere.

NEWS FROM THE VOID

Two publications by schizophrenics entering the public sphere in 1995 form an interesting juxtaposition in this regard. One will be familiar and widely recognizable as exceptional: the publication of Ted Kaczynski's "Industrial Society and its Future" [commonly known as the "Unabomber manifesto"] in *The New York Times*, a 36,000 word rant against modernity Kaczynski would go so far as to kill to see published. The other publication is much less well known. In 1995 Editor-in-Chief Ken Steele released the inaugural edition of *New York City Voices: A Consumer Journal for Mental Health.* To appreciate the profundity of this publication, a short biography of Steele is appropriate. Steele began hearing voices in 1962 when he was fourteen years old. The voices urged him repeatedly to kill himself. After a few failed attempts to follow their orders, Steele ran away from home, and was shortly afterward diagnosed with schizophrenia by a physician. At age seventeen he took off for New York City and was quickly ushered into the world of male hustling. Over the next thirty years he would be homeless, raped, shuttled between several psychiatric hospitals, and he would attempt to end his life several more times. In 1995, then under treatment with a new medication, Ken Steele's voices stopped. Five years later, Steele died of a heart attack, possibly related to obesity that has since been identified as a common side effect of the medication he had been taking.

Significantly, Steele had actually begun engaging in advocacy slightly before the end of his voices. In order to fulfill the mandated "structured activity" as part of his care, he decided to found a voter registration project for the mentally ill. He had become alarmed at growing threats to Social Security Disability and proposed cutbacks to a range of other services the mentally ill rely on: housing, mental health clinics, and research. While he was still coping with his voices, he took a folding table and voter registration cards to homeless shelters and mental health clinics to register mentally ill voters of any party. After his voices stopped, however, he decided not only to help the mentally ill enter the polity via the vote, but also to use rhetoric as a tool to increase their civic presence. He founded *New York City Voices* primarily as a journal to inform about legislative issues, but writing the journal itself served its own enfranchising purposes.

A typical example of a story from *New York City Voices*, written by Steele himself in the July/August 1999 issue, is not rhetorically exceptional in any of the ways postmodern theorists might expect:

> Did you know that only one-half of one percent of those Americans with disabilities presently receiving Social Security Disability Insurance (SSDI) or Supplemental Security Income (SSI) are employed? How many more of us do you think would like to work but cannot, because we would lose cash benefits if we earn over $500 a month and Medicare and Medicaid health coverage if we work more than three years?

What follows is a plea to support the Ticket to Work and Self-Sufficiency Program. There is nothing distinctly disorganized about this opening of rhetorical questions, which lays out the false choice Steele sees between accepting work and accepting health coverage. I would even venture to say that were it not for Steele's self-identification as mentally ill throughout the article (and his invocation of an audience of the mentally ill), there would be nothing to mark Steele as schizophrenic.

Another writer for the journal, Lisa Gibson, in an article advocating for insurance parity in the Jan/Feb 2000 issue, writes that her manic depression has been the most crucial element of her life, exceeding the force of other social categories to which she also belongs. She begins by describing the importance of narrative in self-identification:

Charles Dickens began his book David Copperfield with the words "I am born." If I were to write an autobiography, I would begin with the words "I am born with manic-depression," for this illness has been the single most defining factor of my life and my personality. No other factor—being female, being southern, being the middle child—has had such an impact on me as this disease.

As Steele notes in *The Day the Voices Stopped*:

> Most striking about *New York City Voices* has been the inclusion of personal stories by people with mental illness, written in our own words and under our own bylines (often accompanied by a photograph of the contributor). A bold but necessary move, self-disclosure is a first step toward successfully addressing the stigma associated with being mentally ill. (221)

This self-disclosure is a defining feature of a rhetoric self-conscious of the usual position of the schizophrenic rhetor; typically schizophrenics are considered beings with speech, but speech that is generally treated as an index of sanity or insanity, with referentiality only to diagnostic criteria, and without referentiality to the civic world. Self-disclosure is thus a necessary component of civic rhetoric for these authors, involving the investiture of the previously stigmatizing moniker *schizophrenic* with new meaning. These writers appropriate the term *schizophrenic* in much the same way as the gay community successfully appropriated the previously denigrating term *queer*.

Snyder and Mitchell have identified the 1970s as the moment disability memoirs began to be published *en masse*: "These first person stories interrupted several hundred years of inaccurate disability representation by interested professionals in medicine, rehabilitation, and other caring professions" (9). When we look back at the mid-1990s from a vantage point thirty years hence, we will see it as the moment mental disability narratives began appearing *en masse*—which explains why the most blatant appropriations of the schizophrenic seem to end in the late 1980s. There is little getting around the fact that the explosion of civic rhetoric by schizophrenics corresponds with the advent of atypical antipsychotic medications in the 1990s. The first mass-market magazine authored primarily by schizophrenics, *Schizophrenia Digest*, began in 1994, for example, and continues to this day to chronicle schizophrenics' struggles with social discrimination, limited treatment options, and those medications that may have allowed for certain forms of expression, but with troubling and sometimes life-threatening side-effects. Within the *Digest*'s pages, schizophrenics write of the need to speak in order to break through the assumption of the normative audience that informs most published material. As Vicky Yeung writes of her experience reading personal finance books written from a normative perspective:

> [T]he author assumes I'm not limited by my mind's matter as to how much money I conceivably can make. These writers give tips that are unhelpful for me, like increasing my income through investing in mutual funds, working at several jobs, etc., as if I could do any of those things. Really, they're writing for the "normal healthy mind" audience. (47)

In this passage Yeung elucidates her exclusion from the normative processes of late capitalism, incapable as those processes are of incorporating a non-incarcerated, non-revenue producing, non-exceptional subject. Her quotation marks around "normal healthy mind" indicate that she does not consider herself "exceptional," except that normativity makes her so.

As Daniel Frey, successor to Steele as Editor-in-Chief of *New York City*

Voices has observed of the erasure of this non-exceptional subject through the exceptionalizing of schizophrenics:

> The extremes of schizophrenia get the most publicity, like the genius John Nash on the one hand and the subway killer Gary Goldstein on the other. Every day people like me get overlooked even though we compose the vast majority of schizophrenics. The mental health consumer movement is the last great civil rights movement in this country.

Frey asks here for a move away from both pathologized and vaunted genius/artist versions of schizophrenics; he suggests movement toward the vast middle ground of schizophrenics who hold unexceptional jobs, or move through multiple hospitalizations without either killing anyone or winning Nobel prizes. Frey's speech does not ask for leaps of interpretation, does not mark itself as any more "everyday" than he marks himself. He simply heralds the end of the exemplar schizophrenic. He asks that schizophrenics be able to participate in, as well as critique, late capitalism; one wonders what Deleuze and Guattari would have made of schizophrenic Bill MacPhee, publisher of *Schizophrenia Digest* in which Vicky Yeung's critique of capitalism appears, who affirmed that his life was changed in 1994 by the book "101 Ways to Start a Business with Little or No Capital." His business? A magazine for schizophrenics.

To see the "ordinary" schizophrenic is, in short, to give up the stable schizophrenic. The identity of being a schizophrenic, because it is tied to a history of having been diagnosed with the condition, may remain constant, but impairments fluctuate in time. As Kuppers notes, "Mental health is a contested terrain: on the one hand, mental normalcy is a problematic concept given the malleability and changing nature of human mental and emotional states. On the other hand, certain permutations of mentality are severely policed and bracketed off into deviancy" (59). The public seemingly only desires the stable schizophrenic, easy to incarcerate, or easy to celebrate as the occasion requires. The public does not want to allow for fluctuation between states, and even less for the possibility that both states exist at once. A genuinely postmodern perspective would not insist that schizophrenic rhetoric be fixed, but rather would allow for Bill MacPhee, Lisa Gibson, Vicki Yeung, and Daniel Frey to continue to engage in civic rhetoric, while being schizophrenic. It would allow them to occupy the contested public sphere, bringing to it the force of their narratives.

The narrative power of fluctuations between mental states is perhaps best captured by Richard MacLean's memoir *Recovered, not Cured*. MacLean begins the work on a past moment of impairment, set off in space and time:

> Another World, August 1994. I am crouching in an alleyway. They can't see me here, so for a moment I am safe. There must be hundreds of loudspeakers projecting secret messages, and umpteen video cameras tracking every move I make (xi).

The book ends in "The Present":

> Nowadays, I say that I am recovered, not cured. I have a job as a graphic designer and illustrator, I have a band in which I do vocals and guitar, I have my friends and my family. I pay my taxes and do the dishes; I'm independent. I have achieved a sense of normality and live with the knowledge that a couple of pills a day will keep me slightly lethargic yet "sane" at the same time. I can live with that. (174)

The actual structure of MacLean's text belies the sense of progression that these two time points imply. Interspersed through MacLean's narrative are his own illustrations, many created "years ago," as well as numerous emails from schizophrenics he has received since beginning a life of public advocacy. This structure enacts a merging of all states in the present, a time when "sane" appears only in quotation marks. MacLean acknowledges in a section entitled "A Kind of Closure":

> If I had my way, of course, all this would never have happened. However, I hoped that by writing about it I might be able to seal off all the chaos I had experienced; seal it up with sealing wax, put it in a cupboard or throw it to the sea. It hasn't worked out quite so simply. To this day, although my illness is at a manageable level, I am residually delusional and sometimes read odd meanings into things. (172)

There is, MacLean asserts, no definitive closure for him.

I would like to return, in only provisional closing then, to the quote from Lacan I selected for the epigraph, a reflection on schizophrenic voice: "Wasn't it because they didn't go far enough in listening to the insane that the great observers who drew up the first classifications impoverished the material they were given—to such an extent it appeared problematic and fragmentary to them?" Lacan suggests that schizophrenics had not been listened to except metaphorically. The problem according to Lacan is that these great observers thought that what schizophrenics were saying could not really be what they were actually saying. It would have to be something else. Lacan was, ironically, talking about the much-observed Schreber, who died in an asylum four years after the publication of the *Memoirs*. Let us change Lacan's "it," though, so it no longer stands simply for the utterances of one schizophrenic at one moment in time. Let us have "it" stand in for all schizophrenic utterances at all points in time. That "it"

should appear problematic. It should appear fragmentary. But it should appear, and once appearing, be considered unexceptional.[4]

NOTES

1. See, for example, *Soul Murder* by Schatzman.
2. Schreber was not diagnosed schizophrenic during his life (the diagnosis not then being in use), however, Deleuze and Guattari, typical of his modern commentators, ascribe him that condition.
3. Jung's response quoted in Dinnage, and further elaborated in McCabe.
4. Many thanks to the JLD reviewers for their invaluable comments on an earlier version of this essay.

WORKS CITED

Baudrillard, Jean. *The Ecstasy of Communication*. Trans. Bernard Schutze and Caroline Schutze. New York: Semiotext(e), 1988.

Braidotti, Rose. "Schizophrenia." *The Deleuze Dictionary*. Ed. Adrian Parr. New York: Columbia UP, 2005, 237–40.

Corker, Mairian and Tom Shakespeare, ed. *Disability/Postmodernity: Embodying Disability Theory*. New York: Continuum, 2002.

Deleuze, Gilles and Félix Guattari. *A Thousand Plateaus: Capitalism and Schizophrenia*. Trans. Brian Massumi. Minneapolis: U of Minnesota P, 1987.

——. *Anti-Oedipus: Capitalism and Schizophrenia*. Trans. Robert Hurley, Mark Seem, and Helen R. Lane. Minneapolis: U of Minnesota P, 2000.

Dinnage, Rosemary. Introduction. In *Memoirs of My Nervous Illness by Daniel Paul Schreber*, eds. Ida Macalpine and Richard A. Hunter, xi–xxiv. New York: New York Review of Books, 2000.

Freud, Sigmund. *The Schreber Case*. Trans. Andrew Webber. New York: Penguin, 2002.

Frey, Daniel. "First Break: Three Years Later." *New York City Voices*, www.nycvoices.org, posted 2002.

Gibson, Lisa. "Parity Matters to Me." *New York City Voices*, www.nyvoices.org, posted 2000.

Jameson, Frederic. *Postmodernism, or, the Cultural Logic of Late Capitalism*. Durham: Duke UP, 1992.

Kuppers, Petra. *The Scar of Visibility: Medical Performance and Contemporary Art*. Minneapolis: U of Minnesota P, 2007.

Lacan, Jacques. *The Seminar of Jacques Lacan Book III: The Psychoses 1955–1956*. Trans. Russell

Grigg. Ed. Jacques-Alain Miller. New York: Norton, 1997.

MacLean, Richard. *Recovered, Not Cured: A Journey through Schizophrenia*. Crows Nest, Australia: Allen & Unwin, 2003.

McCabe, Colin. Introduction. *The Schreber Case*. By Sigmund Freud, trans. Andrew Webber, vi–xxii. New York: Penguin, 2002.

Mitchell, David T. and Sharon L. Snyder. *Narrative Prosthesis: Disability and the Dependencies of Discourse*. Ann Arbor: U of Michigan P, 2001.

Schatzman, Morton. *Soul Murder: Persecution in the Family*. New York: Random House, 1973.

Schreber, Daniel Paul. *Memoirs of My Nervous Illness*. Trans. Ida Macalpine and Richard A. Hunter. New York: New York Review of Books, 2000.

Snyder, Sharon L. and David T. Mitchell. "Disability Haunting in American Poetics." *Journal of Literary Disability* 1.1 (2007): 1–12.

Sontag, Susan. *Aids and Its Metaphors*. New York: Farrar, Straus, and Giroux, 1988.

——. *Illness as Metaphor*. New York: Farrar, Straus and Giroux, 1978.

Steele, Ken and Claire Berman. *The Day the Voices Stopped*. New York: Basic Books, 2002.

Yeung, Vicky. "Born with a Gift and a Purpose." *Schizophrenia Digest* 5.3 (2007): 47.

PART V

*I*dentities and Intersectionalities

CHAPTER 23

The End of Identity Politics: On Disability as an Unstable Category

Lennard J. Davis

There are times when the black man is locked into his body. Now, "for a being who has acquired consciousness of himself and of his body, who has attained the dialectic of subject and object, the body is no longer a cause of the structure of consciousness, it has become an object of consciousness."
—Frantz Fanon, citing Merleau-Ponty,
Black Skin, White Masks

At times we might look back nostalgically to the moment when identity was relatively simple, when it was possible to say that one *was* black or white, male or female, "Indian" or not. It might once have been possible to answer the question that James Weldon Johnson's narrator in *The Autobiography of an Ex-Colored Man* asks his mother "Are you white?" with her clear reply, "No, I am not white . . ." (8). But the issue of identity by race, gender, or sexual orientation, particularly in America, has become more clouded, fuzzier, grainier than it used to be. And so, the issue of a disability identity has begun to enter murkier grounds.

When I discussed the idea of clouding the issue of disability identity, a prominent disability scholar advised me not to pursue this line of thinking. "We're not ready to dissolve disability identity. We're just beginning to form it." While I agree that there is a strategic kind of identity politics one might want to pursue, especially early on in an academic or political movement, I also think that ignoring the current seismic shifts in identity politics would be equally disastrous and could lead to major instability in the near future. If disability studies were to ignore the current intellectual moment and plow ahead using increasingly antiquated models, the very basis for the study of the subject could be harmed by making its premises seem irrelevant, shoddily thought through, and so on.

In effect, we do have to acknowledge that, unlike race, class, gender, sexual preference, and the like, disability is a relatively new category. Although the category has existed for a long time, its present form as a political and cultural formation has only been around since the 1970s, and has come into some kind of greater visibility since the late 1980s. The political and academic movement around disability is at best a first- or second-wave enterprise. The first wave of any struggle involves the establishment of the identity against the societal definitions that were formed largely by oppression. In this first phase, the identity—be it blackness, or gayness, or Deafness—is hypostasized, normalized, turned positive against the negative descriptions used by the oppressive regime. Thus "Black is Beautiful," "Gay Pride," and "Deaf Power" might be seen as mere reappropriations of a formerly derogatory discourse. The first phase also implies a pulling together of forces, an agreement to agree for political ends and group solidarity, along with the tacit approval of an agenda for the establishment of basic rights and prohibitions against various kinds of discrimination and ostracism.

In a second wave, a newer generation of people within the identity group, ones who have grown up with the libratory models well in place, begin to redefine the struggle and the subject of study. They no longer seek group solidarity since they have a firm sense of identity. In a second wave, the principals are comfortable about self-examining, finding diversity within the group, and struggling to redefine the identity in somewhat more nuanced and complex ways. Often this phase will produce conflict within a group rather than unity. We've seen this most dramatically in the feminist movement when second-wave thinkers like Judith Butler have critiqued earlier essentialist notions that pulled the movement together initially. The conflict can come from differences that have been suppressed for the sake of maintaining a unified front so that the group could emerge in the first place and resist the formerly oppressive categorization and treatment.

Disability studies is, as I have said, a relatively new field of study. Its earliest proponents were writing in the 1970s and 1980s. The second wave of disability writing can be seen as emerging in the 1990s. Both the first and second waves have had a strong interest in preserving the notion of a distinct and clear entity known variously as "people with disabilities" (PWDs) or "Deaf people." In the case of PWDs, the interest has been in creating a collectivity where before there had been disunity. In the past, people with disabilities did not identify as such. Medical definitions of impairments were developed with no need to create unity among diverse patient groups. Wheelchair users saw no commonality with people with chronic fatigue syndrome or Deaf people. Given the American ethic of individuality and personal achievement, there would have been little incentive for PWDs to identify with the "handicaps" of other people. Rather, the emphasis would have been on personal growth, or overcoming the disability, and normalization through cure, prosthesis, or medical interventions. With the return of veterans from the Vietnam war, a movement grew up around civil rights for people with disabilities, which culminated in the Americans with Disabilities Act of 1990. By the beginning of the millennium disability activism, consciousness, and disability studies is well established, although many areas of the ADA are being rolled back in the courts and in the legislature.[1]

To begin with, one might want to point out the obvious point that history repeats itself. As Marx wrote about the failed revolution in France, people tend to model political movements on those of the past. For people with disabilities the civil rights model was seen as more progressive and better than the earlier charity and medical models. In the earlier versions, people with disabilities were seen variously as poor, destitute creatures in need of the help of the church or as helpless victims of disease in need of the correction offered by modern medical procedures. The civil rights model, based on the struggles of African Americans in the United States, seemed to offer a better paradigm. Not plagued by God nor beset by disease, people with disabilities were seen as minority citizens deprived of their rights by a dominant ableist majority.

Along with this model went the social model, which saw disability as a constructed category, not one bred into the bone. This social model is in dialogue with what is often referred to as the British model, which sees a distinction between impairment and disability. Impairment is the physical fact of lacking an arm or a leg. Disability is the social process that turns an impairment into a negative by creating barriers to access. The clearest example of this distinction is seen in the case of wheelchair users. They have impairments that limit mobility, but are not disabled unless they are in environments without ramps, lifts, and automatic doors. So, as long as the minority and/or social model held fast, this model seems to have worked pretty well, or at least as well as the civil rights model itself worked.

Enter postmodernity. The postmodern critique is one that destabilizes grand, unifying theories, that renders problematic desires to unify, to create wholes, to establish foundations. One could fill archives with what has been said or written about the culture wars, the science wars, and whatever other wars. In terms of identity, there has been an interesting and puzzling result. The one area that remained relatively unchallenged despite the postmodern deconstructionist assault was the notion of group identity. Indeed, the postmodern period is the one that saw the proliferation of multiculturality. One could attack the shibboleths of almost any ground of knowledge, but one could never attack the notion of being, for example, African American, a woman, or gay. To do so would be tantamount to being part of the oppressive system that created categories of oppressed others. One could interrogate the unity of the novel, science, even physics, but one could not interrogate one's right to be female, of color, or queer. Given this resistant notion of identity, the disability movement quite rightly desired to include disability as part of the multicultural quilt. If all the identities were under the same tent, then disability wanted to be part of the academic and cultural solidarity that being of a particular, oppressed minority represented.

Yet, within that strong notion of identity and identity politics, a deconstructive worm of thought began its own parasitic life. That worm targeted "essentialism." Just as no one wants to be a vulgar Marxist, no one wanted to be an essentialist. Essentialists—and there were fewer and fewer of them very soon after we began to hear the word—were putatively accused of claiming in a rather simple-minded way that being a woman or an ethnic minority was somehow rooted in the body. That identity was tied to the body, written on the body. Rather, the way out of this reductionist mode was to say that the body and identities around the body were socially constructed and performative. So while postmodernism eschewed the whole, it could accept that the sum of the parts made up the whole in the form of the multicultural, rainbow quilt of identities.[2] Social constructionism and performativity seemed to offer the way out of the problem caused by the worm of essentialism, but it also created severe problems in shaping notions of identity.[3] If all identities are socially constructed or performative, is there a core identity there? Is there a there?

Disability offers us a way to rethink some of these dilemmas, but in order to do so, I think we need to reexamine the identity of disability, and to do so without flinching, without hesitating because we may be undoing a way of knowing. As with race, gender, and sexual orientation, we are in the midst of a grand reexamination. Disability, as the most recent identity group on the block, offers us the one that is perhaps least resistant to change or changing thoughts about identity. And, most importantly, as I will argue, disability may turn out to be the identity that links other identities, replacing the notion of postmodernism with something I want to call "dismodernism."

I am arguing that disability can be seen as the postmodern subject position for several reasons. But the one I want to focus on now is that these other discourses of race, gender, and sexuality began in the mid-nineteenth century, and they did so because that is when the scientific study of humans began. The key connecting point for all these studies was the development of eugenics.[4] Eugenics saw the possible improvement of the race as being accomplished by diminishing problematic peoples and their problematic behaviors—these peoples were clearly delineated under the rubric of feeble-mindedness and degeneration as women, people of color, homosexuals, the working classes, and so on. All these were considered to be categories of disability, although we do not think of them as connected in this way today. Indeed, one could argue that categories of oppression were given scientific license through these medicalized, scientificized discourses, and that, in many cases, the specific categories were established through these studies.

Postmodernity along with science now offers us the solvent to dissolve many of these categories. In the area of race, we now know, for example, that there is no genetic basis to the idea that race, in its eugenic sense, exists. Thus far, no one has been able to identify a person as belonging to a specific "race" through DNA analysis. In fact, DNA analysis lets us understand that the category of race does not exist in physiological terms. Further, DNA analysis tells us that there is more genetic variation within a group we have called a race than within the entire human gene pool. Indeed, no one is even able to tell us how many races there are, and fine distinctions between phenotypes tend to dissolve the notion of categorical racial identities even further. The Human Genome Project offered up the possibility of mapping with certainty the complete sequence of approximately 3.2 billion pairs of nucleotides that make

us human. But the project has left us with more questions than it has answered. For example, scientists are puzzling over the relatively low count of genes in the human genome. It had been estimated that humans would have approximately 100,000 genes, but the study yielded a mere 30,000, putting Homo sapiens on par with the mustard cress plant (25,000 genes) in terms of genetic complexity.[5] More annoying and less known is the fact that the two groups who analyzed the genome, the privately owned Celera group and the government-financed consortium of academic centers, have come up with only 15,000 that they jointly agree on. Fifteen thousand more genes do not overlap in either analysis.[6] Considerable doubt exists as to whether these genes are "real."

More to the point, there is considerable confusion over race in relation to genetics. On the one hand, we are told that the mapped human genome, taken from the DNA of one or two individuals, is the same for all humans. We are further informed that there is relatively little diversity in our genetic makeup. But we are also told that various "races" and ethnic groups have differing genetic markers for disability, defect, and disease. The contradiction is one that has been little explored, and those who have pursued the point have come under criticism for racializing genetics.[7] Central to the confusion is the category of race itself. If we say, on the one hand, that there is no genetic way to ascertain race, and we also say that we have examined certain racial groups and discovered a greater chance of finding a particular gene, then we have indeed mixed our scientific categories.[8]

If we step back from the genetic level, we might want to investigate identity questions at the cellular level. Here, tellingly, we could investigate the HeLa cells widely used in laboratories and schools in what is called an "immortal cell line," much like the lines developed currently for stem-cell research. These cells all derive from an African American woman named Henrietta Lacks who died in 1951 of cervical cancer. The cells were taken without the permission of Ms. Lacks, and became so widespread as to be ubiquitous. For the point of view of this discussion, the cells were presumed to be universal until 1967, when a geneticist named Stanley Gartler announced that at least eighteen other cell lines had been contaminated by the HeLa cells. He determined this by insisting that the presence of G6PD (glucose-6-phosphate dehydrogenase), an enzyme which is a factor in red blood cell production, had been a marker in all these lines and that this type of enzyme "has been found only in Negroes" (61).[9] Thus, during the early period of genetic research previously universal cells were racialized at the cellular level. But the appearance of race at the cellular level is no longer possible or relevant. The markers thought to be of a specific racial group have no validity for that identificatory purpose.

The issue of race is also complicated by the use of in vitro fertilization in a recent case of "scrambled eggs," in which a fertility doctor implanted in a woman's womb not only her own fertilized embryo but that of another couple as well. The resulting birth was of fraternal twins, one white and the other black.[10] Such complications of reproductive technologies will certainly lead to other kinds of choices being made by parents and physicians, intentional as well as unintentional, with the effect of rendering even more complex racial or even gender identity.[11] Finally, the patrolled area of "mixed race" is being interrogated. The fact that multiracial identifications have been prohibited on national censuses is now being challenged. The reasons for keeping single-race checkoff boxes is itself a highly politicized and tactical arena in which, understandably, oppressed groups have gained redress and power by creating a unified subject. Where censuses allow a mixed-race checkoff, the statistical stronghold of race may well become weakened with questionable results.

In the area of gender, we are also seeing confusions in otherwise fixed categories. A culture of transgendered peoples is now being more widely permitted and the right to be transgendered is being actively fought for. The neat binaries of male and female are being complicated by volition, surgery, and the use of pharmaceuticals. Intersexuals, formerly known as hermaphrodites, were routinely operated upon at birth to assign them a specific gender. That move is now being contested by groups of adult intersexuals. Some feel they were assigned the wrong gender, and others feel that they would have liked to remain indeterminate. Transsexuals now routinely occupy various locations along a gender continuum, demarcating their place by clothing and other style-related choices, surgical corrections, and hormonal therapy. Even on the genetic level, females who are genetically male and males who are genetically female are a naturally occurring phenomenon. The gender determination is suppressed or enhanced in these cases of "Turner Syndrome" or "Klinefelter Syndrome," so that the genetic markers do not express the expected sexual phenotypes.[12]

Likewise, ethnicity is increasingly seen as problematic. Indeed, writers like Benedict Anderson have shown us that the idea of the nation is formed out of the suppression of ethnicities, although those ethnicities can end up forming new national consciousnesses. Steven Steinberg asserts that ethnicity is only one generation deep, and that all citizens become Americans after that generation, with only a thin veneer of food choices or other accoutrements of their ethnic origin to hold onto.[13]

Sexual orientation, which in the heyday of identity politics had a fairly definitive hold on defining a self, is now being questioned by many under the rubric of "queer studies." Whereas once the choice of sexual partner indicated who one was—gay, lesbian, heterosexual, or bisexual—now, in an era of dissolving boundaries, sexual orientation has become strangely unhinged, especially with the advent of transgender politics. When a male-to-female transsexual marries a person who defines herself as a woman, should that relationship be called lesbian? If an intersexual person chooses a person of either gender, or another intersexual, how do we define the relationship? In such cases, sexual orientation becomes the only option that does not define the person in all ways as fitting into a discrete category. The change from the expression "sexual preference" to "sexual orientation" serves to indicate something hardwired into a person's identity.

There has been some suggestion that there exists a "gay" gene, which, if it could be found definitively, would somehow settle the issue of gayness. But what we are seeing in the development of the Human Genome Project is that genetics is not the court of last resort in the story of life. No one gene determines the course of a human life. At this moment, while much good science has gone into the project of genetics, there is still no gene therapy that works. In addition, the low number of genes in the recent mapping indicates that genes alone will not tell the story. Further, even where genes are shown to contribute to disease, as in for example the case of Jewish women of Eastern European origin who carry a marker for a type of breast cancer, there is no good explanation for why only one-third of all such women will eventually develop breast cancer. If genes were the uncomplicated set of instructions that we are told they are, in a process of scientific grandiosity sometimes referred to as "geno-hype," there would be a one-for-one correspondence between the incidence of markers and the occurrence of disease.

Ultimately, if the grounds for an essentialist view of the human body are being challenged, so are the notions that identity is socially constructed. Most coherent of these critiques is Ian Hacking's *The Social Construction of What?* Hacking shows, to my satisfaction at least, that the idea of social constructionism, while very useful in many regards, is itself tremendously underdeveloped theoretically and methodologically. And it has reached the end of its shelf life. Once shocking and daring, now it has simply become a way of saying that objects in the world have a history of shifting feelings, concepts, and durations. In addition, Walter Benn Michaels has recently said at a public presentation at the University of Illinois at Chicago in March 2001, that if we agree that there is no biological basis for race, then how does it make sense to say there is a social construction of it? Michaels gives the example that if we agree there is no scientific basis for the existence of unicorns, does it make sense to say let's talk about the social construction of the unicorn?

So, if we follow this line of thinking, joining forces with the major critique of identity, we find ourselves in a morass in terms of identity politics and studies. There are various tactics one can take in the face of this conceptual dead end. One can object vehemently that X does indeed exist, that people have suffered for being X, and still do. Therefore, while there may be no basis in theory for being X, large numbers of people are nevertheless X and suffer even now for being so. Or one can claim that although no one has been able to prove the biological existence of X, they will be able to do so someday. In the gap between then and now, we should hold onto the idea of being X. Or one could say that despite the fact that there is no proof of the existence of X, one wants to hold to that identity because it is, after all, one's identity. Finally, we can say that we know X isn't really a biologically valid identity, but we should act strategically to keep the category so that we can pass laws to benefit groups who have been discriminated against because of the pseudo-existence of this category.

All these positions have merit, but are probably indefensible rationally. The idea of maintaining a category of being just because oppressive people in the past created it so they could exploit a segment of the population, does not make sense. To say that one wants to memorialize that category based on the suffering of people who occupy it makes some sense, but does the memorialization have to take the form of continuing the identity?[14] Even attempts to remake the identity will inevitably end up relying on the categories first used to create the oppression. Finally, strategic essentialism, as it is called, is based on several flawed premises, most notably the idea that we can keep secret our doubts so that legislators and the general public won't catch on. This Emperor's New Clothes approach is condescending to all parties, including the proponents of it.

Let us pause for a moment here to take into consideration the concept of disability as a state of injury, to use Wendy Brown's term. One of the central motivations for the Human Genome Project is the elimination of "genetic defects." The argument is based on a vision of the "correct" or "real" genome being one without errors or mistakes. Somewhere, in some empyrean there exists the platonic human genome. This genome is a book or text made up of letters sequenced in the right order without "mistakes." As such, it is in fact a sacred text and our correct reading of it is not unlike the vision that the fundamentalist has that his or her sacred text is infallible. However, the problem is that, as it stands now, the human genome is in need of fixing to make it perfect. Errors of transcription have ruined the primal perfection of the text. The problem is related to exegesis and amanuensis.

Thus, people with genetic diseases have "birth defects" and are "defective."

This explanation, like most, is partial and error-laden. It is based on a pre-postmodern definition of human subjects as whole, complete, perfect, self-sustaining. This is the neoclassical model of Pico della Mirandola, Descartes, Locke, Hume, Kant, and so on. But if we think of cystic fibrosis or sickle cell anemia as "defects" in an otherwise perfect and whole human subject, are we making a grand mistake? Clearly, the people who have such genetic conditions are in grave peril. Few, if any, will live to a ripe old age. Each will have health issues. It would be in the interest of both those people and their physicians to heal their illnesses. Since there is no cure for these diseases at the present time, it seems reasonable to think that we can eliminate the defect by means of genetic medicine. So the idea that one would want to fix these genetic defects seems more than logical.

Yet the model involved in the idea of birth "defect" comes to us direct and unaltered from a eugenic model of the human body. Words like "fit," "normal," "degenerate," "feeble," "defect," and "defective" are all interlaced. Their roots lie directly in the "scientific" study of humans that reached its liminal threshold in the middle of the nineteenth century. We now openly repudiate eugenics, mainly because of the Nazis' use of "negative eugenics," that is, the direct elimination of "defectives" from the human race. This seems so horrendous to us that the term is no longer used. But organizations in the United States and England have simply morphed their names into ones that use the term "genetics," preserving the Latin linguistic root in both eugenic and genetic. Now eugenics (or genetics) is carried out through two avenues—prenatal screening, which works some of the time, and genetic engineering, which has not worked on humans so far. In both cases, the aim is to improve the human stock and to remove genetic defects. With the advent of the Human Genome and genetic sequencing projects, the illusion is that single genes will be discovered that can be "fixed" with an improved consequence. There is, of course, the problem of the "single gene" hypothesis, now being hotly debated in the context of the latest claim that there is a single gene for speech.[15]

Many would claim that for behaviors like speech, sexual orientation, or intelligence, there can be no single gene or genetic causality. So the premise that we can fix a single gene is itself a problem. Further, the idea of a "mistake" is also problematic. Take the examples I have given of sickle-cell anemia and cystic fibrosis. The genetic markers for both these are recessive, which means that a great number of the population will have genetic information (or misinformation) for these diseases. It turns out that people who carry the trait are resistant to malaria (in the case of sickle-cell anemia) and cholera (in the case of cystic fibrosis). If we posit that other "defects" are also protective against pandemic diseases, we can see that the simple elimination of such defects might be a complicated process with a possibly dubious result. What we are discussing is an algorithm of collective protectivity through genetic diversity versus harm to select individuals. I'm not arguing for a trade-off, but I think evolution has made that trade-off and our genes contain the history of humans and pandemics.

The use of genetic testing to avoid giving birth to children with genetic defects is itself problematic. On a simple statistical level, it can probably only be done in relatively wealthy countries and among middle- and upper-class people. Paradoxically, the effect of doing so may actually serve to increase the incidence of the condition because each time a person is born with the disease, two of the inherited traits end with the person upon his or her death. By bypassing this draconian form of genetic regulation, we may actually be contributing to the increased distribution of the trait in the gene pool, particularly in developing countries. The effect shows us that the simple answer of fixing the defect itself is not simple. Further, we may be tampering with the ability of humans to survive pandemics that we know about and others that we don't know about. How many people, for example, are now protected against developing active AIDS because they carry a trait for a "defect"?

Another aspect of this "defect" scenario is that a new issue is beginning to arise in the courts—the right not to be born. French courts upheld this idea in regard to women who did not receive genetic testing and who gave birth to children who were, for example, born without an arm. The courts endorsed compensatory payments to such children who had the right to not be born and whose parents were not able to exercise that right because of lack of information. The legislature in a subsequent act voided the court's ruling. Nevertheless, here indeed is a slippery slope, which many people with disabilities have regarded with suspicion. They rightly claim that their parents might have aborted them had they known of their upcoming impairment as children. On the other side of the disability divide, Deaf parents and parents of small stature have the ability to screen for the birth of a hearing child or a normal-sized child and to abort. And, of course, in countries like India and China, genetic testing is used to abort female fetuses. In the United States, the American Society for Reproductive Medicine, which sets the standards for most fertility clinics, officially stated that it is sometimes acceptable for couples to choose the sex of their children by selecting either male or female embryos and discarding the rest.[16] These cases begin to blur the notion of what a "defect" is and is not. Designer babies, as foreseen in the film *Gattaca*, can begin to be seen as those who will not contain, for example, genes for breast cancer or high blood pressure. The possibilities are limitless.

Some of the issues I've outlined here are the result of a destabilization of the categories we have known concerning the body. The body is never a single physical thing so much as a series of attitudes toward it. The grand categories of the body were established during the Renaissance and the Enlightenment, and then refined through the use of science and eugenics. Postmodernism along with science has assaulted many of these categories of self and identity. What we need now is a new ethics of the body that acknowledges the advances of science but also acknowledges that we can't simply go back to a relatively simple notion of identity. Genetics offers the way back, without, thus far, being able to deliver on that promise.

What I would like to propose is that this new ethics of the body begin with disability rather than end with it. To do so, I want to make clear that disability is itself an unstable category. I think it would be a major error for disability scholars and advocates to define the category in the by-now very problematic and depleted guise of one among many identities. In fact I argue that disability can capitalize on its rather different set of definitions from other current and known identities. To do this, it must not ignore the instability of its self-definitions but acknowledge that their instability allows disability to transcend the problems of identity politics. In setting up this model we must also acknowledge that not only is disability an unstable category but so is its doppelgänger—impairment.

In the social model, disability is presented as a social and political problem that turns an impairment into an oppression either by erecting barriers or by refusing to create barrier-free environments (where barrier is used in a very general and metaphoric sense). But impairment is not a neutral and easily understood term. It relies heavily on a medical model for the diagnosis of the impairment. For example, is Asperger's Syndrome or hysteria an impairment or the creation of the *folie à deux* of the observing physician and the cooperating patient?[17] Is anorexia or ADD an impairment or a disability? Particularly with illnesses that did not exist in the past, the plethora of syndromes and conditions that have sprouted in the hearts and minds of physicians and patients—conditions like attention deficit disorder, fugue states, pseudoneurotic schizophrenia, or borderline psychosis—we have to question the clear line drawn between the socially constructed "disability" and the preexistent and somatic "impairment." Ian Hacking, in *Mad Travelers: Reflections on the Reality of Transient Mental Illnesses*, points out that fidgety children were not considered to have impairments until ADD began. Is the impairment bred into the bone, or can it be a creation of a medical—technological—pharmaceutical complex?

Further, it is hard if not impossible to make the case that the actual category of disability really has internal coherence. It includes, according to the Americans with Disabilities Act of 1990, conditions like obesity, attention deficit disorder, diabetes, back pain, carpal tunnel syndrome, severe facial scarring, chronic fatigue syndrome, skin conditions, and hundreds of other conditions. Further, the law specifies that if one is "regarded" as having these impairments, one is part of the protected class.

The perceived legal problem is that the protected class is too large, and that is one of the reasons there is a perceived backlash in the United States against the ADA. In response to initial concerns that too many people with minor conditions were qualifying as disabled, the federal courts have issued very narrow interpretations of disability.[18] While we must deplore the fact that approximately 95 percent of cases brought before the courts are currently decided in favor of employers, we may also understand that some of this backlash is generated by a fear of creating a protected class that is too large. As with affirmative action, there is also general resentment among the populace that certain minority groups have special rights and privileges with regard to college admissions, job hiring, and so on. I want to be clear that I am not arguing against the protection of historically oppressed groups, as I will explain further. But I am calling attention to the increasingly ineffective means of achieving a goal of equality and equity in housing, jobs, and public accommodations.

Indeed, the protected class will only become larger as the general population ages. With the graying of the baby boomers, we will see a major increase in the sheer numbers of people with disabilities. As noted in the Introduction, the World Health Organization (WHO) predicts that by the year 2020, there will be more than 690 million people over the age of sixty-five, in contrast with today's 380 million. Two-thirds of the elderly will be in developing and under-developed nations. The increase in the elderly population will cause a major change in the disease patterns of these countries. There will be increasing rates of cancer, kidney failure, eye disease, diabetes, mental illness, and other chronic, degenerative illnesses such as cardiovascular disease. Although we may want to call all these senior citizens people with disabilities, what will that mean? Will we have to start making decisions about who is disabled and who is not? What Occam's razor will we use to hone the definition then? And how will this majority of older people redefine disability, since they did not grow up with a disability or acquire one early in life? Who will get to claim the definition of disability or the lack of one?

Complicating the issue of disability identity is the notion of cure. Just as people can slip into disability in the blink of an eye or the swerve of a wheel, so too can people be cured. Indeed, although we don't expect this in the near future, it is possible to imagine a world in which disability decreases from 15 to 20 percent of the population to just 2 or 3 percent. Just as we saw a major reduction in infectious diseases in the West over the previous century, so too may we see a decrease in disabilities. Gene therapy, colossally unsuccessful up until this point, could have a major although unlikely breakthrough and become the treatment of choice for many illnesses. Stem cell research could lead to the regeneration of many tissues that are the cause of degenerative and traumatic diseases and conditions. And technological fixes may become much more sophisticated, so that, for example, cochlear implants, now very problematic even if you believe in the concept, could become foolproof. Indeed, this specter is rather terrifying and offensive to many Deaf people, and with good reason. Advances in biotechnology could create natural and effective gaits for paraplegics or useful prostheses that might be virtually indistinguishable from human limbs. Indeed, political issues aside, the possibility does exist of cures for many impairments that now define a group we call "people with disabilities." We must recall though, that cures will of course only be available to people with means in wealthy countries.

What we are discussing is the instability of the category of disability as a subset of the instability of identity in a postmodern era. It would be understandable if one responded to what I've suggested by saying that, notwithstanding this instability, the category must be left alone. It must be maintained for all the reasons I had suggested earlier. Or, as one of my students responded, "What will happen to the handicapped parking space, if what you advocated happens?" True, but I want to propose that the very rationale for disability activism and study is good enough, indeed better than good enough, rationale for many people—people other than those we now call People with Disabilities. Rather than ignore the unstable nature of disability, rather than try to fix it, we should amplify that quality to distinguish it from other identity groups that have, as I have indicated, reached the limits of their own projects. Indeed, instability spells the end of many identity groups; in fact it can create a dismodernist approach to disability as a neoidentity.

What characterizes the limitations of the identity group model is its exclusivity (which contains the seeds of its own dissolution through the paradox of the proliferation of identity groups). Indeed, you have to be pretty *unidentified* in this day and age to be without an identity. So the very criticism of the category of disability as being too large, as containing too big a protected class, is actually a *fait accompli* with the notion of identity in general. We should not go on record as saying that disability is a fixed identity, when the power behind the concept is that disability presents us with a malleable view of the human body and identity.

Enlightenment thought would have it that the human is a measurable quantity, that all men are created equal, and that each individual is paradoxically both the same and different. Or perhaps, as Kierkegaard put it, "the single individual is the particular that has its *telos* in the universal."[19] In the past much of the paradoxical attitude toward citizens with disabilities arose from the conflict between notions of the equality of universal rights and the inequality of particular bodies.[20]

For all the hype of postmodern and deconstructive theory, these intellectual attempts made little or no impression on identity politics. Rather, those who pushed identity had very strong Enlightenment notions of the universal and the individual.

The universal subject of postmodernism may be pierced and narrative-resistant but that subject was still whole, independent, unified, self-making, and capable. The dismodern era ushers in the concept that difference is what all of us have in common. That identity is not fixed but malleable. That technology is not separate but part of the body. That dependence, not individual independence, is the rule. There is no single clockmaker who made the uniform clock of the human body. The watchword of dismodernism could be: Form follows dysfunction.

What dismodernism signals is a new kind of universalism and cosmopolitanism that is reacting to the localization of identity. It reflects a global view of the world. To accomplish a dismodernist view of the body, we need to consider a new ethics of the body. We may take Kierkegaard's by-now naïve belief in the universal and transform it, knowing that this new universalism cannot be a return to Enlightenment values. Rather it must be a corrective to the myths not only of the Enlightenment but of postmodernism as well.

A new ethics of the dismodernist body consists of three areas: The first concerns the official stance—care *of* the body is now a requirement for existence in a consumer society. We are encouraged and beseeched to engage in this care; indeed, it is seen as a requirement of citizenship. This care of the body involves the purchase of a vast number of products for personal care and grooming, products necessary to having a body in our society. Although we are seen as self-completing, the contemporary body can only be completed by means of consumption. This is the official stance: that the contemporary human body is incomplete without deodorant, hair gel, sanitary products, lotions, perfumes, shaving creams, toothpastes, and so on.[21] In addition, the body is increasingly becoming a module onto which various technological additions can be attached. The by-now routine glasses, contact lenses, and hearing aids are supplemented by birth-control implants, breast implants, penile implants, pacemakers, insulin regulators, monitors, and the like. Further work will also intimately link us to more sophisticated cybertechnology. All this contributes to what Zygmund Bauman calls "the privatization of the body," which he sees as the "primal scene of postmodern ambivalence." The aim and goal, above all, is to make this industrial-modeled, consumer-designed body appear "normal." And even people with disabilities have to subscribe to this model and join the ranks of consumers.[22]

Another official area pertains to care *for* the body, an area that also links the economy with the body. Here we must confront an entire industry devoted to caring for the human body. We are discussing the health-care industry and the dependent care industry. Included here are physicians' private practices, clinics, medical insurance companies, medical laboratories, hospitals, extended-care facilities, hospitals, hospices, nursing homes, in-home caregivers, pharmacies, manufacturers of assistive devices, and organizations that promote the research, development, and care of certain kinds of illnesses and conditions. In most countries, this industry makes up the largest sector of the economy. There are obviously huge economic advantages to the creation and maintenance of the disability industry. It is important to recall that since huge financial commitments are being made to the abnormal body, the ethics involved in the distribution of resources and the shaping of this industry is a major part of our approach to an ethical society. By and large, this industry is controlled and dominated by people who are not people with disabilities.

Finally, to secure a dismodernist ethics, in opposition or in some cases in alliance with the official stance, we need to discuss caring *about* the body. This is the area I would most like to emphasize. If we care about the body, that is to say care about the issues I have raised, we finally begin to open up and develop a dismodernist discourse of the body and the uses of bodies. This area begins with attention paid to human rights and civil rights that have to be achieved to bring people with disabilities to the awareness of other identity groups. Here we must discuss the oppression of so-called abnormal bodies, and the treatment of the poor with disabilities. Class again becomes an issue in identity. We must focus on the poor, since by all estimates the majority of people with disability are poor, unemployed, and undereducated. In the United States, only one-third of people with disabilities are employed, versus upward of 70 percent of "normal" workers. Indeed, many people with disabilities end up in prisons—particularly those with cognitive and affective disabilities. A *New York Times* article (August 7, 2000) pointed out that one in ten death row inmates are mentally retarded. Since the majority of people in the United States become quadriplegic or paraplegic from gunshot wounds, a disproportionate number of African American males are so impaired. And therefore a large number of these males with disabilities are also in prisons, often without adequate accommodations.

On an international level, land mines create impairments on a daily basis, and this fact combined with other technologies of war and extremely poor working conditions in sweatshop environments creates a level of disability in so-called developing countries that requires attention and thought. The treatment of women and female babies—including the abortion of female fetuses, the use of clitorectomies, the oppression of gay, lesbian, bisexual, and transgendered people—often intersects in familiar and unfamiliar ways with the mechanisms of disablement. It can be said that the most oppressed person in the world is a disabled female, Third World, homosexual, woman of color. In addition, the absence of adequate wheelchairs in poor countries, along with inadequate street and public accommodation facilities create a virtually inaccessible world for people with mobility impairments.

My point is that with a dismodernist ethic, you realize that caring *about* the body subsumes and analyzes care *of* and care *for* the body. The latter two produce oppressive subjection, while the former gives us an ethic of liberation. And the former always involves the use of culture and symbolic production in either furthering the liberation or the oppression of people with disabilities.

An ethics of the body provides us with a special insight into the complex and by now dead end of identity politics. The problem presented to us by identity politics is the emphasis on an exclusivity surrounding a specific so-called identity. Writers like Kenneth Warren, K. Anthony Appiah, Paul Gilroy, Wendy Brown, Walter Benn Michaels, Thomas Holt, and others are now critiquing the notion of a politics based on specific identities and on victim status. Disability studies can provide a critique of and a politics to discuss how all groups, based on physical traits or markings, are selected for disablement by a larger system of regulation and signification. So it is paradoxically the most marginalized group—people with disabilities—who can provide the broadest way of understanding contemporary systems of oppression.

This new way of thinking, which I am calling dismodernism, rests on the operative notion that postmodernism is still based on a humanistic model. Politics have been directed toward making all identities equal under a model of the rights of the dominant, often white, male, "normal" subject. In a dismodernist mode, the ideal is not a hypostatization of the normal (that

is, dominant) subject, but aims to create a new category based on the partial, incomplete subject whose realization is not autonomy and independence but dependency and interdependence. This is a very different notion from subjectivity organized around wounded identities; rather, *all* humans are seen as wounded. Wounds are not the result of oppression, but rather the other way around. Protections are not inherent, endowed by the creator, but created by society at large and administered to all. The idea of a protected class in law now becomes less necessary since the protections offered to that class are offered to all. Thus, to belatedly answer my student, normal parking becomes a subset of handicapped parking.

The dismodernist subject is in fact disabled, only completed by technology and by interventions. Rather than the idea of the complete, independent subject, endowed with rights (which are in actuality conferred by privilege), the dismodernist subject sees that metanarratives are only "socially created" and accepts them as that, gaining help and relying on legislation, law, and technology. It acknowledges the social and technological to arrive at functionality. As the quadriplegic is incomplete without the motorized wheelchair and the controls manipulated by the mouth or tongue, so the citizen is incomplete without information technology, protective legislation, and globalized forms of securing order and peace. The fracturing of identities based on somatic markers will eventually be seen as a device to distract us from the unity of new ways of regarding humans and their bodies to further social justice and freedom.

We can thus better understand how the by now outdated postmodern subject is a ruse to disguise the hegemony of normalcy. Foucault is our best example. His work is, as Edward Said has noted, in *Power, Politics and Culture: Interview with Edward W. Said*, a homage to power, not an undermining of it. Said calls Foucault a "scribe" of power because of his fascination with the subject. For Foucault the state is power and citizens are docile bodies. This overtly sadomasochistic model is one that is part of a will-to-power, a fantasy of utter power and utter subjection. That model appeared to be postmodern, but was in fact the nineteenth century of Freud, Sacher-Masoch, and imperialism writ large. Instead, dismodernism doesn't require the abjection of wounds or docility to describe the populace, or the identity groups within. Rather it replaces the binary of docility and power with another—impairment and normalcy. Impairment is the rule, and normalcy is the fantasy. Dependence is the reality, and independence grandiose thinking. Barrier-free access is the goal, and the right to pursue happiness the false consciousness that obscures it. Universal design becomes the template for social and political designs.

The rhizomatic vision of Deleuze's solution to the postmodernist quandary presented by power, with its decentered, deracinated notion of action, along with the neorationalist denial of universals, leaves us with a temporary, contingent way of thinking about agency and change. The dismodernist vision allows for a clearer, more concrete mode of action—a clear notion of expanding the protected class to the entire population; a commitment to removing barriers and creating access for all. This includes removing the veil of ideology from the concept of the normal, and denying the locality of identity. This new ethic permits, indeed encourages, cosmopolitanism, a new kind of empire, to rephrase Hardt and Negri, that relies on the electronic senses as well as the neoclassical five. It moves beyond the fixity of the body to a literally constructed body, which can then be reconstructed with all the above goals in mind.

Clearly, what I am describing is the beginning of a long process. It began with the efforts of various identities to escape oppression based on their category of oppression. That struggle is not over and must continue. While there is no race, there is still racism. But dismodernism argues for a commonality of bodies within the notion of difference. It is too easy to say, "We're all disabled." But it is possible to say that we are all disabled by injustice and oppression of various kinds. We are all nonstandard, and it is under that standard that we should be able to found the dismodernist ethic.

What is universal in life, if there are universals, is the experience of the limitations of the body. Yet the fantasy of culture, democracy, capitalism, sexism, and racism, to name only a few ideologies, is the perfection of the body and its activities. As Paul Gilroy writes, "The reoccurrence of pain, disease, humiliation, grief, and care for those one loves can all contribute to an abstract sense of human similarity powerful enough to make solidarities based on cultural particularity appear suddenly trivial."[23] It is this aspect of experience, a dismodern view, that seems suddenly to be, at the beginning of the twenty-first century, about the only one we can justify.

NOTES

1. For more on this, see a special issue of the *Berkeley Journal of Employment and Labor Law* 22:1 (2000), and also Leslie Francis and Anita Silvers, eds., *Americans with Disabilities: Exploring Implications of the Law for Individuals and Institutions* (New York: Routledge, 2000).

2. I have written more about this aspect of identity and disability in chapter 5 of *Bending Over Backwards: Disability, Dismodernism and Other Difficult Positions* (New York: New York University Press, 2002).

3. See Ian Hacking, *The Social Construction of What?* (Cambridge: Harvard UP, 1999; rpt. 2001).

4. I have made this point elsewhere. See Lennard J. Davis, *Enforcing Normalcy: Disability, Deafness, and the Body* (London: Verso, 1995) for greater exposition.

5. Let us not even consider the further problem that in order to locate a gene, we have to cordon off "good DNA" from "junk" DNA may have a role to play in "influencing" the good DNA. Thus the exact science of genetics begins to resemble other explanatory systems requiring influence based on humors, astrological causes, and so on. Indeed, many human traits are polygenic, involving several different genes working in coordination with each other and with other processes.

6. Raymond Bonniet and Sarah Rimer, *New York Times* (August 24, 2001), A13

7. See Steve Olsen, "The Genetic Archeology of Race," *Atlantic Monthly* (April 2001).

8. See works like Tukufu Zuberi, *Thicker than Blood: An Essay on How Racial Statistics Lie* (Minneapolis: University of Minnesota Press, 2001).

9. For the most complete discussion of HeLa cells in regard to racial politics, see Hannah Landecker, "Immortality, In Vitro: A History of the HeLa Cell Line," in *Biotechnology and Culture: Bodies, Anxieties, Ethics*, ed. Paul E. Brodwin (Bloomington: Indiana UP, 2000), 53-72.

10. Dwight Garner, *New York Times Sunday Magazine* (March 25, 2001).

11. Although, as Dorothy Roberts has pointed out, prenatal technology is still very much a site of racial discrimination. See her "Race and the New Reproduction," *Hastings Law Journal* 47: 4 (1996).

12. For more on this subject, see Leslie Feinberg, *Transgender Warriors: Making History from Joan of Arc to Dennis Rodman* (Boston: Beacon Press, 1996). Also see Bob Beale, "New Insights into the X and Y Chromosomes," *The Scientist* (July 23, 2001) 15 (15): 18.

13. Steven Steinberg, *The Ethnic Myth* (Boston: Beacon Press, 2001).

14. See Wendy Brown, *States of Injury: Power and Freedom in Late Modernity* (Princeton: Princeton UP, 1995).

15. Nicholas Wade, *New York Times* (October 4, 2001

16. Gina Kolata, *New York Times* (September 28, 2001), A14.

17. See Ian Hacking's discussion of transient mental illnesses in *Mad Travelers: Reflections on the Reality of Transient Mental Illnesses* (Charlottesville: University of Virginia, 1998).

18. For an extensive discussion of the legal issues around disability, see a special issue of the *Berkeley Journal of Employment and Labor Law* 21: 1 (2000). For background on many of these issues, see Ruth O'Brien, *Crippled Justice: The History of Modern Disabiltiy Policy in the Workplace* (Chicago: U of Chicago P, 2001).

19. Soren Kierkegaard, *Fear and Trembling*, trans. Alastair Hanney (London: Penguin, 1985), 83

20. See my chapter, "Constructing Normalcy: The Bell Curve, the Novel, and the Invention of the Disabled Body in the Nineteenth Century," in this volume.

21. As an assignment, I ask my students to tally up the cost of all the products they buy for their bodies. The annual cost is astounding.

22. Magazines like *We* and *Poz* generate income by selling trendy and sexy wheelchairs and other equipment for people with disabilities. Of course, the routine body care products are called for here as well.

23. Paul Gilroy, *Against Race: Imagining Political Culture beyond the Color Line* (Cambridge: Harvard UP, 2000), 17.

CHAPTER 24

Disability and the Theory of Complex Embodiment—For Identity Politics in a New Register

Tobin Siebers

THE IDEOLOGY OF ABILITY

We seem caught as persons living finite lives between two sets of contradictory ideas about our status as human beings. The first contradiction targets our understanding of the body itself. On the one hand, bodies do not seem to matter to who we are. They contain or dress up the spirit, the soul, the mind, the self. I am, as Descartes explained, the thinking part. At best, the body is a vehicle, the means by which we convey who we are from place to place. At worst, the body is a fashion accessory. We are all playing at Dorian Gray, so confident that the self can be freed from the dead weight of the body, but we have forgotten somehow to read to the end of the novel. On the other hand, modern culture feels the urgent need to perfect the body. Whether medical scientists are working on a cure for the common cold or the elimination of all disease, a cure for cancer or the banishment of death, a cure for HIV/AIDS or control of the genetic code, their preposterous and yet rarely questioned goal is to give everyone a perfect body. We hardly ever consider how incongruous is this understanding of the body—that the body seems both inconsequential and perfectible.

A second but related contradiction targets the understanding of the human being in time. The briefest look at history reveals that human beings are fragile. Human life confronts the overwhelming reality of sickness, injury, disfigurement, enfeeblement, old age, and death. Natural disasters, accidents, warfare and violence, starvation, disease, and pollution of the natural environment attack human life on all fronts, and there are no survivors. This is not to say that life on this earth is wretched and happiness nonexistent. The point is simply that history reveals one unavoidable truth about human beings—whatever our destiny as a species, we are as individuals feeble and finite. And yet the vision of the future to which we often hold promises an existence that bears little or no resemblance to our history. The future obeys an entirely different imperative, one that commands our triumph over death and contradicts everything that history tells us about our lot in life. Many religions instruct that human beings will someday win eternal life. Science fiction fantasizes about aliens who have left behind their mortal sheath; they are superior to us, but we are evolving in their direction. Cybernetics treats human intelligence as software that can be moved from machine to machine. It promises a future where human beings might be downloaded into new hardware whenever their old hardware wears out. The reason given for exploring human cloning is to defeat disease and aging. Apparently, in some future epoch, a quick trip to the spare-parts depot will cure what ails us; people will look better, feel healthier, and live three times longer. Finally, the human genome project, like eugenics before it, places its faith in a future understanding of human genetics that will perfect human characteristics and extend human life indefinitely.

However stark these contradictions, however false in their extremes, they seem credible in relation to each other. We are capable of believing at once that the body does not matter and that it should be perfected. We believe at once that history charts the radical finitude of human life but that the future promises radical infinitude. That we embrace these contradictions without interrogating them reveals that our thinking is steeped in ideology. Ideology does not permit the thought of contradiction necessary to question it; it sutures together opposites, turning them into apparent complements of each other, smoothing over contradictions, and making almost unrecognizable any perspective that would offer a critique of it. In fact, some cultural theorists claim to believe that ideology is as impenetrable as the Freudian unconscious—that there is no outside to ideology, that it can contain any negative, and that it sprouts contradictions without suffering them (see Goodheart 1996; Siebers 1999). I argue another position: ideology creates, by virtue of its exclusionary nature, social locations outside of itself and therefore capable of making epistemological claims about it. The arguments that follow here are based on the contention that oppressed social locations create identities and perspectives, embodiments and feelings, histories and experiences that stand outside of and offer valuable knowledge about the powerful ideologies that seem to enclose us.

This book pursues a critique of one of these powerful ideologies—one I call the ideology of ability. The ideology of ability is at its simplest the preference for able-bodiedness. At its most radical, it defines the baseline by which humanness is determined, setting the measure of body and mind that gives or denies human status to individual persons. It affects nearly all of our judgments, definitions, and values about human beings, but because it is discriminatory and exclusionary, it creates social locations outside of and critical of its purview, most notably in this case, the perspective of disability. Disability defines the invisible center around which our contradictory ideology about human ability revolves. For the ideology of ability makes us fear disability, requiring that we imagine our bodies are of no consequence while dreaming at the same time that we might perfect them. It describes disability as what we flee in the past and hope to defeat in the future. Disability identity stands in uneasy relationship to the ideology of ability, presenting a critical framework that disturbs and critiques it.

One project of this book is to define the ideology of ability and to make its workings legible and familiar, despite how imbricated it may be in our thinking and practices, and despite how little we notice its patterns, authority, contradictions, and influence as a result. A second and more important project is to bring disability out of the shadow of the ideology of ability, to increase awareness about disability, and to illuminate its kinds, values, and realities. Disability creates theories of embodiment more complex than the ideology of ability allows, and these many embodiments are each crucial to the understanding of humanity and its variations, whether physical, mental, social, or historical. These two projects unfold slowly over the course of my argument for the simple reason that both involve dramatic changes in thinking.

The level of literacy about disability is so low as to be nonexistent, and the ideology of ability is so much a part of every action, thought, judgment, and intention that its hold on us is difficult to root out. The sharp difference between disability and ability may be grasped superficially in the idea that disability is essentially a "medical matter," while ability concerns natural gifts, talents, intelligence, creativity, physical prowess, imagination, dedication, the eagerness to strive, including the capacity and desire to strive—in brief, the essence of the human spirit. It is easy to write a short list about disability, but the list concerning ability goes on and on, almost without end, revealing the fact that we are always dreaming about it but rarely thinking critically about why and how we are dreaming.

I resort at the outset to the modern convention of the bullet point to introduce the ideology of ability as simply as possible. The bullet points follow without the thought of being exhaustive or avoiding contradiction and without the full commentary that they deserve. Some of the bullets are intended to look like definitions; others describe ability or disability as operators; others still gather stereotypes and prejudices. The point is to begin the accumulation of ideas, narratives, myths, and stereotypes about disability whose theory this book seeks to advance, to provide a few small descriptions on which to build further discussion of ability as an ideology, and to start readers questioning their own feelings about ability and disability:

- Ability is the ideological baseline by which humanness is determined. The lesser the ability, the lesser the human being.
- The ideology of ability simultaneously banishes disability and turns it into a principle of exclusion.
- Ability is the supreme indicator of value when judging human actions, conditions, thoughts, goals, intentions, and desires.
- If one is able-bodied, one is not really aware of the body. One feels the body only when something goes wrong with it.
- The able body has a great capacity for self-transformation. It can be trained to do almost anything; it adjusts to new situations. The disabled body is limited in what it can do and what it can be trained to do. It experiences new situations as obstacles.
- Disability is always individual, a property of one body, not a feature common to all human beings, while ability defines a feature essential to the human species.
- Disability can be overcome through will power or acts of the imagination. It is not real but imaginary.
- "Disability's no big deal," as Mark O'Brien writes in his poem, "Walkers" (1997, 36).
- It is better to be dead than disabled.
- Nondisabled people have the right to choose when to be able-bodied. Disabled people must try to be as able-bodied as possible all the time.
- Overcoming a disability is an event to be celebrated. It is an ability in itself to be able to overcome disability.
- The value of a human life arises as a question only when a person is disabled. Disabled people are worth less than nondisabled people, and the difference is counted in dollars and cents.
- Disabilities are the gateway to special abilities. Turn disability to an advantage.
- Loss of ability translates into loss of sociability. People with disabilities are bitter, angry, self-pitying, or selfish. Because they cannot see beyond their own pain, they lose the ability to consider the feelings of other people. Disability makes narcissists of us all.
- People who wish to identify as disabled are psychologically damaged. If they could think of themselves as able-bodied, they would be healthier and happier.

To reverse the negative connotations of disability apparent in this list, it will be necessary to claim the value and variety of disability in ways that may seem strange to readers who have little experience with disability studies. But it is vital to show to what extent the ideology of ability collapses once we "claim disability" as a positive identity (Linton 1998). It is equally vital to understand that claiming disability, while a significant political act, is not only political but also a practice that improves quality of life for disabled people. As documented in the case of other minority identities, individuals who identify positively rather than negatively with their disability status lead more productive and happier lives. Feminism, the black and red power movements, as well as gay and disability pride—to name only a few positive identity formations—win tangible benefits for their members, freeing them not only from the violence, hatred, and prejudice directed toward them but also providing them with both shared experiences to guide life choices and a community in which to prosper.

Some readers with a heightened sense of paradox may object that claiming disability as a positive identity merely turns disability into ability and so remains within its ideological horizon. But disability identity does not flounder on this paradox. Rather, the paradox demonstrates how difficult it is to think beyond the ideological horizon of ability and how crucial it is to make the attempt. For thinking of disability as ability, we will see, changes the meaning and usage of ability.

MINORITY IDENTITY AS THEORY

Identity is out of fashion as a category in critical and cultural theory. While it has been associated by the Right and Left with self-victimization, group think, and political correctness, these associations are not the real reason for its fall from grace. The real reason is that identity is seen as a crutch for the person who needs extra help, who is in pain, who cannot think independently. I use the word "crutch" on purpose because the attack on identity is best understood in the context of disability.

According to Linda Martin Alcoff's extensive and persuasive analysis in *Visible Identities*, the current rejection of identity has a particular philosophical lineage, one driven, I believe, by the ideology of ability (2006, 47–83). The line of descent begins with the Enlightenment theory of rational autonomy, which represents the inability to reason as the sign of inbuilt inferiority. Usually, the defense of reason attacked non-Europeans as intellectually defective, but because these racist theories relied on the idea of biological inferiority, they necessarily based themselves from the start on the exclusion of disability. "The norm of rational maturity," Alcoff makes clear, "required a core self stripped of its identity. Groups too immature to practice this kind of abstract thought or to transcend their ascribed cultural identities were deemed incapable of full autonomy, and their lack of maturity was often 'explained' via racist theories of the innate inferiority of non-European peoples" (2006, 22). The Enlightenment view then descends to two modern theories, each of which sees dependence on others as a form of weakness that leads to oppressive rather than cooperative behavior. The first theory belongs to Freud, for whom strong identity attachments relate to pathological psychology and figure as symptoms of ego dysfunction. In psychoanalysis, in effect, a lack lies at the heart of identity (2006, 74), and those unable to overcome this lack fall into patterns of dependence and aggression. Second, in Sartre's existential ontology, identity is alienated from the real self. Identity represents for Sartre a social role, linked to bad faith and motivated by moral failing and intellectual weakness, that tempts the self with inauthentic existence, that is, an existence insufficiently free from the influence of others (2006, 68).

Dossier No. 1 *The Nation* November 6, 2006

Show Him the Money

By Katha Pollitt

I wanted to admire *The Trouble with Diversity*, Walter Benn Michaels's much-discussed polemic against identity politics and economic inequality. Like him, I'm bothered by the extent to which symbolic politics has replaced class grievances on campus, and off it too: the obsessive cultivation of one's roots, the fetishizing of difference, the nitpicky moral one-upmanship over language. Call an argument "lame" on one academic-feminist list I'm on and you'll get—still!—an electronic earful about your insensitivity to the disabled . . . .

These two strains of thinking, despite their differences, support the contemporary distrust of identity. Thus, for Michel Foucault and Judith Butler—to name two of the most influential theorists on the scene today—identity represents a "social necessity that is also a social pathology" (Alcoff 2006, 66); there supposedly exists no form of identity not linked ultimately to subjugation by others. In short, contemporary theorists banish identity when they associate it with lack, pathology, dependence, and intellectual weakness. Identity in their eyes is not merely a liability but a disability.

Notice, however, that identity is thought defective only in the case of minorities, whereas it plays no role in the critique of majority identifications, even among theorists who assail them. For example, no one attacks Americanness specifically because it is an identity. It may be criticized as an example of nationalism, but identity receives little or no mention in the critique. Identity is attacked most frequently in the analysis of minority identity—only people of color, Jews, Muslims, gay, lesbian, bisexual, and transgendered people, women, and people with disabilities seem to possess unhealthy identities. It is as if identity itself occupied a minority position in present critical and cultural theory—for those who reject identity appear to do so only because of its minority status, a status linked again and again to disability.

Moreover, the rejection of minority identity repeats in nearly every case the same psychological scenario. The minority identity, a product of damage inflicted systematically on a people by a dominant culture, is rearticulated by the suffering group as self-affirming, but because the identity was born of suffering, it is supposedly unable to shed its pain, and this pain soon comes to justify feelings of selfishness, resentment, bitterness, and self-pity—all of which combine to justify the oppression of other people. Thus, J. C. Lester (2006) complains that "the disabled are in danger of being changed," because of disability studies, "from the proper object of decent voluntary help, where there is genuine need, into a privileged and growing interest group of oppressors of more ordinary people." Nancy Fraser also points out that identity politics "encourages the reification of group identities" and promotes "conformism, intolerance, and patriarchalism" (2000, 113, 112). Even if this tired scenario were credible—and it is not because it derives from false ideas about disability—it is amazing that so-called politically minded people are worried that a few minority groups might somehow, some day, gain the power to retaliate for injustice, when the wealthy, powerful, and wicked are actively plundering the globe in every conceivable manner: the decimation of nonindustrial countries by the industrial nations, arms-trafficking, enforcement of poverty to maintain the circuit between cheap labor and robust consumerism, global warming, sexual trafficking of women, industrial pollution by the chemical and oil companies, inflation of costs for drugs necessary to fight epidemics, and the cynical failure by the wealthiest nations to feed their own poor, not to mention starving people outside their borders.

My argument here takes issue with those who believe that identity politics either springs from disability or disables people for viable political action. I offer a defense of identity politics and a counterargument to the idea, embraced by the Right and Left, that identity politics cannot be justified because it is linked to pain and suffering. The idea that suffering produces weak identities both enforces the ideology of ability and demonstrates a profound misunderstanding of disability: disability is not a pathological condition, only analyzable via individual psychology, but a social location complexly embodied. Identities, narratives, and experiences based on disability have the status of theory because they represent locations and forms of embodiment from which the dominant ideologies of society become visible and open to criticism. One of my specific tactics throughout this book is to tap this theoretical power by juxtaposing my argument with dossier entries detailing disability identities, narratives, images, and experiences. The dossier is compiled for the most part from news stories of the kind that appear in major newspapers across the country every day, although I have avoided the feel-good human-interest stories dominating the news that recount how their disabled protagonists overcome their disabilities to lead "normal" lives. Rather, the dossier tends to contain testimony about the oppression of disabled people, sometimes framed in their own language, sometimes framed in the language of their oppressors. At first, the dossier entries may have no particular meaning to those untutored in disability studies, but my hope is

that they will grow stranger and stranger as the reader progresses, until they begin to invoke feelings of horror and disgust at the blatant and persistent prejudices directed against disabled people. The dossier represents a deliberate act of identity politics, and I offer no apology for it because identity politics remains in my view the most practical course of action by which to address social injustices against minority peoples and to apply the new ideas, narratives, and experiences discovered by them to the future of progressive, democratic society.

Identity is neither a liability nor a disability. Nor is it an ontological property or a state of being. Identity is, properly defined, an epistemological construction that contains a broad array of theories about navigating social environments. Manuel Castells calls identity a collective meaning, necessarily internalized by individuals for the purpose of social action (1997, 7), while Charles Taylor argues, "My identity is defined by the commitments and identifications which provide the frame or horizon within which I can try to determine from case to case what is good, or valuable, or what ought to be done, or what I endorse or oppose" (1987, 27). Alcoff explains that "identity is not merely that which is given to an individual or group, but is also a way of inhabiting, interpreting, and working through, both collectively and individually, an objective social location and group history" (2006, 42). We do well to follow these writers and to consider identity a theory-laden construction, rather than a mere social construction, in which knowledge for social living adheres—though not always and necessarily the best knowledge. Thus, identity is not the structure that creates a person's pristine individuality or inner essence but the structure by which that person identifies and becomes identified with a set of social narratives, ideas, myths, values, and types of knowledge of varying reliability, usefulness, and verifiability. It represents the means by which the person, qua individual, comes to join a particular social body. It also represents the capacity to belong to a collective on the basis not merely of biological tendencies but symbolic ones—the very capacity that distinguishes human beings from other animals.

While all identities contain social knowledge, mainstream identities are less critical, though not less effective for being so, because they are normative. Minority identities acquire the ability to make epistemological claims about the society in which they hold liminal positions, owing precisely to their liminality. The early work of Abdul JanMohamed and David Lloyd, for example, privileges the power of the minor as critique: "The study—and production—of minority discourse requires, as an inevitable consequence of its mode of existence, the transgression of the very disciplinary boundaries by which culture appears as a sublimated form with universal validity. This makes it virtually *the* privileged domain of cultural critique" (1987, 9). The critique offered by minority identity is necessarily historical because it relies on the temporal contingency of its marginal position. Different groups occupy minority positions at different times, but this does not mean that their social location is any less objective relative to their times. Nor does it suggest that structures of oppression differ in the case of every minority identity. If history has taught us anything, it is that those in power have the ability to manipulate the same oppressive structures, dependent upon the same prejudicial representations, for the exclusion of different groups. The experiences of contemporary minority people, once brought to light, resound backward in history, like a reverse echo effect, to comment on the experiences of past minority peoples, while at the same time these past experiences contribute,

one hopes, to an accumulation of knowledge about how oppression works.

Minority identity discovers its theoretical force by representing the experiences of oppression and struggle lived by minority peoples separately but also precisely as minorities, for attention to the similarities between different minority identities exposes their relation to oppression as well as increases the chance of political solidarity. According to the definition of Gary and Rosalind Dworkin, minority identity has recognizable features that repeat across the spectrum of oppressed people. "We propose," Dworkin and Dworkin write, "that a minority group is a group characterized by four qualities: identifiability, differential power, differential and pejorative treatment, and group awareness" (1976, 17). These four features form the basis of my argument about minority identity as well, with one notable addition—that minority status also meet an ethical test judged both relative to society and universally. These features require, each one in turn, a brief discussion to grasp their collective simplicity and power and to arrive at a precise and universal definition of minority identity on which to base the elaboration of disability identity, to describe its relation to minority identity in general, and to defend identity politics as crucial to the future of minority peoples and their quest for social justice and inclusion.

1. Identifiability as a quality exists at the heart of identity itself because we must be able to distinguish a group before we can begin to imagine an identity. Often we conceive of identifiability as involving visible differences connected to the body, such as skin color, gender traits, gestures, affect, voice, and body shapes. These physical traits, however, are not universal with respect to different cultures, and there may be actions or cultural differences that also figure as the basis of identifiability. Note as well that identifiability exists in time,

and time shifts its meaning. As a group is identified, it acquires certain representations, and the growth of representations connected to the group may then change how identifiability works. For example, the existence of a group called disabled people produces a general idea of the people in the group—although the existence of the group does not depend on every disabled person fitting into it—and it then becomes easier, first, to identify people with it and, second, to shift the meaning of the group definition. Fat people are not generally considered disabled at this moment, but there are signs that they may be in the not too distant future (Kirkland 2006). Deaf and intersex people have resisted being described as disabled; their future relation to the identity of disabled people is not clear.

Two other obvious characteristics of identifiability need to be stressed. First, identifiability is tied powerfully to the representation of difference. In cases where an existing minority group is not easily identified and those in power want to isolate the group, techniques will be used to produce identifiability. For example, the Nazis required that Jews wear yellow armbands because they were not, despite Nazi racist mythology, identifiably different from Germans. Second, identity is social, and so is the quality of identifiability. There are many physical differences among human beings that simply do not count for identifiability. It is not the fact of physical difference that matters, then, but the representation attached to difference—what makes the difference identifiable. Representation is the difference that makes a difference. We might contend that there is no such thing as private identity in the same way that Wittgenstein claimed that private language does not exist. Identity must be representable and communicable to qualify as identifiable. Identity serves social purposes, and a form of identity not representable

in society would be incomprehensible and ineffective for these purposes.

Of course, people may identify themselves. Especially in societies where groups are identified for differential and pejorative treatment, individuals belonging to these groups may internalize prejudices against themselves and do on their own the work of making themselves identifiable. Jim Crow laws in the American South counted on people policing themselves—not drinking at a white water fountain if they were black, for example. But the way in which individuals claim identifiability also changes as the history of the group changes. A group may be singled out for persecution, but as it grows more rebellious, it may work to preserve its identity, while transforming simultaneously the political values attached to it. The American military's policy, "Don't ask, don't tell" in the case of gay soldiers, tries to stymie the tendency of individuals to claim a positive minority identity for political reasons.

2. Differential power is a strong indicator of the difference between majority and minority identity; in fact, it may be the most important indicator because minority status relies on differential power rather than on numbers. The numerical majority is not necessarily the most powerful group. There are more women than men, and men hold more political power and have higher salaries for the same jobs. Numerical advantage is significant, but a better indicator is the presence of social power in one group over another. Dworkin and Dworkin mention the American South in the 1950s and South Africa under apartheid as good examples of differential power located in a nonnumerical majority (12). Minorities hold less power than majority groups.

3. A central question is whether the existence of differential treatment already implies pejorative treatment. Allowing that differential treatment may exist for legitimate reasons—and it is not at all certain

that we should make this allowance—the addition of pejorative treatment as a quality of minority identity stresses the defining connection between oppression and minority status. Differential and pejorative treatment is what minority group members experience as a consequence of their minority position. It affects their economic standing, cultural prestige, educational opportunities, and civil rights, among other things. Discrimination as pejorative treatment often becomes the focus of identity politics, those concerted attempts by minorities to protest their inferior and unjust status by forming political action groups.

The emergence of identity politics, then, relies on a new epistemological claim. While it is not necessarily the case that a group will protest against discrimination, since there is a history of groups that accept inferior status and even fight to maintain it, the shift to a protest stance must involve claims different from those supporting the discriminatory behavior. A sense of inequity comes to pervade the consciousness of the minority identity, and individuals can find no reasonable justification for their differential treatment. Individuals in protest against unjust treatment begin to develop theories that oppose majority opinion not only about themselves but about the nature of the society that supports the pejorative behavior. They develop ways to represent the actions used to perpetuate the injustice against them, attacking stereotypes, use of violence and physical attack, and discrimination. Individuals begin to constitute themselves as a minority identity, moving from the form of consciousness called internal colonization to one characterized by a new group awareness.

4. Group awareness does not refer to group identifiability but to the perception of common goals pursued through cooperation, to the realization that differential and pejorative treatment is not justified by actual qualities of the minority group, and to the conviction that majority society is a disabling environment that must be transformed by recourse to social justice. In other words, awareness is not merely self-consciousness but an epistemology that adheres in group identity status. It is the identity that brings down injustice initially on the individual's head. This identity is constructed in such a way that it can be supported only by certain false claims and stereotypes. Resistance to these false claims is pursued and shared by members of the minority identity through counterarguments about, and criticism of, the existing state of knowledge. Thus, minority identity linked to group awareness achieves the status of a theoretical claim in itself, one in conflict with the mainstream and a valuable source of meaningful diversity. Opponents of identity politics often argue that identity politics preserves the identities created by oppression: these identities are born of suffering, and embracing them supposedly represents a form of self-victimization. This argument does not understand that new epistemological claims are central to identity politics. For example, societies that oppress women often assert that they are irrational, morally depraved, and physically weak. The minority identity "woman," embraced by feminist identity politics, disputes these assertions and presents alternative, positive theories about women. Identity politics do not preserve the persecuted identities created by oppressors because the knowledge claims adhering in the new identities are completely different from those embraced by the persecuting groups.

Opponents of identity politics are not wrong, however, when they associate minority identity with suffering. They are wrong because they do not accept that pain and suffering may sometimes be resources for the epistemological insights of minority identity. This issue will arise whenever we consider disability identity, since it is the identity most associated with pain, and a great deal of discrimination against people with disabilities derives from the irrational fear of pain. It is not uncommon for disabled people to be told by complete strangers that they would kill themselves if they had such a disability. Doctors often withhold treatment of minor illnesses from disabled people because they believe they are better off dead—the doctors want to end the suffering of their patients, but these disabled people do not necessarily think of themselves as in pain, although they must suffer discriminatory attitudes (Gill 2000; Longmore 2003, 149–203). Nevertheless, people with disabilities are not the only people who suffer from prejudice. The epistemological claims of minority identity in general are often based on feelings of injustice that are painful. Wounds received in physical attacks may pale against the suffering experienced in the idea that one is being attacked because one is unjustly thought inferior—and yet suffering may have theoretical value for the person in pain. While there is a long history of describing pain and suffering as leading to egotism and narcissism—a metapsychology that plays, I argue in chapter 2, an ancillary role in the evolution of the ideology of ability—we might consider that the strong focus given to the self in pain has epistemological value.[1] Suffering is a signal to the self at risk, and this signal applies equally to physical and social situations. The body signals with pain when a person is engaged in an activity that may do that person physical harm. Similarly, consciousness feels pain when the individual is in social danger. Suffering has a theoretical component because it draws attention to situations that jeopardize the future of the individual, and when individuals who suffer from oppression gather together to share their experiences, this theoretical component may be directed toward political ends.

By suggesting that suffering is theory-laden—that is, a sensation evaluative of states of reality—I am trying to track how and why minority identity makes epistemological claims about society. All identity is social theory. Identities are the theories that we use to fit into and travel through the social world. Our identities have a content that makes knowledge claims about the society in which they have evolved, and we adjust our identities, when we can, to different situations to improve our chances of success. But because mainstream identities so robustly mimic existing social norms, it is difficult to abstract their claims about society. Identities in conflict with society, however, have the ability to expose its norms. Minority identity gains the status of social critique once its content has been sufficiently developed by groups that unite to protest their unjust treatment by the society in which they live.

5. In addition to the four qualities proposed by Dworkin and Dworkin, groups claiming minority identity need to meet an ethical test. Minority identities make epistemological claims about the societies in which they hold liminal positions, but not all theories are equal in ethical content, especially relative to minority identity, since it begins as a product of oppression and acquires the status of social critique. While matters ethical are notoriously difficult to sort out, it is nevertheless worth pausing briefly over how ethics relates to minority identity because ethical content may serve to check fraudulent claims of minority status. For example, in South Africa of recent date, the ideology of apartheid represented the majority position because it held power, identified the nature of minority identity, and dictated differential and pejorative treatment of those in the minority. Today in South Africa, however, the apartheidists are no longer in the majority. Applying the theory of Dworkin and Dworkin, they might be construed as

having a minority identity: they are identifiable, they have differential power, they are treated pejoratively, and they possess group awareness—that is, they present a set of claims that actively and consciously criticize majority society. They also believe themselves to be persecuted, and no doubt they feel suffering about their marginal position.

Why are the apartheidists not deserving of minority status? The answer is that the theories contained in apartheidist identity do not pass an ethical test. The contrast between its ethical claims and those of the majority are sufficiently striking to recognize. The apartheidists propose a racist society as the norm to which all South African citizens should adhere. Relative to South African social beliefs and those of many other countries, apartheid ideology is unacceptable on ethical grounds because it is biased, violent, and oppressive. Consequently, the apartheidists fail to persuade us with their claims, and we judge them not a minority group subject to oppression but a fringe group trying to gain unlawful advantage over others.

To summarize, the definition embraced here—and used to theorize disability identity—does not understand minority identity as statistical, fixed in time, or exclusively biological but as a politicized identity possessing the ability to offer social critiques. There are those who attack minority identities precisely because they are politicized, as if only minorities made political arguments based on identity and politicized identity in itself were a species of defective attachment. But many other examples of politicized identity exist on the current scene—Democrats, Republicans, Socialists, the Christian Coalition, the American Nazi Party, and so on. In fact, any group that forms a coalition to make arguments on its own behalf and on the behalf of others in the public forum takes on a politicized identity. Arguments to out-law minority political action groups merely because they encourage politicized identities would have to abolish other political groups as well.

DISABILITY AND THE THEORY OF COMPLEX EMBODIMENT

Feminist philosophers have long argued that all knowledge is situated, that it adheres in social locations, that it is embodied, with the consequence that they have been able to claim that people in marginal social positions enjoy an epistemological privilege that allows them to theorize society differently from those in dominant social locations (Haraway 1991, 183–201; Harding 1986). Knowledge is situated, first of all, because it is based on perspective. There is a difference between the knowledge present in a view of the earth from the moon and a view of the earth from the perspective of an ant. We speak blandly of finding different perspectives on things, but different perspectives do in fact give varying conceptions of objects, especially social objects. Nevertheless, situated knowledge does not rely only on changing perspectives. Situated knowledge adheres in embodiment. The disposition of the body determines perspectives, but it also spices these perspectives with phenomenological knowledge—lifeworld experience—that affects the interpretation of perspective. To take a famous example from Iris Young, the fact that many women "throw like a girl" is not based on a physical difference. The female arm is as capable of throwing a baseball as the male arm. It is the representation of femininity in a given society that disables women, pressuring them to move their bodies in certain, similar ways, and once they become accustomed to moving in these certain, similar ways, it is difficult to retrain the body. "Women in sexist society are physically handicapped," Young explains. "Insofar as we learn to live out our existence in accordance with the definition that patriarchal culture assigns to us, we are physically inhibited, confined, positioned, and objectified" (2005, 171). It is possible to read the differential and pejorative treatment of women, as if it were a disability, on the surface of their skin, in muscle mass, in corporeal agility. This form of embodiment is also, however, a form of situated knowledge about the claims being made about and by women in a given society. To consider some positive examples, the particular embodiment of a woman means that she might, after experiencing childbirth, have a new and useful perception of physical pain. Women may also have, because of menstruation, a different knowledge of blood. Female gender identity is differently embodied because of women's role in reproductive labor. The presence of the body does not boil down only to perspective but to profound ideas and significant theories about the world.

Embodiment is, of course, central to the field of disability studies. In fact, a focus on disability makes it easier to understand that embodiment and social location are one and the same. Arguments for the specificity of disability identity tend to stress the critical nature of embodiment, and the tacit or embodied knowledge associated with particular disabilities often justifies their value to larger society. For example, George Lane's body, we will see in chapter 6, incorporates a set of theoretical claims about architecture that the Supreme Court interprets in its ruling against the State of Tennessee, finding that Lane's inability to enter the Polk County Courthouse reveals a pattern of discrimination against people with disabilities found throughout the American court system. Chapter 5 explores disability passing not as avoidance of social responsibility or manipulation for selfish interests but as a form of embodied knowledge—forced into usage by prejudices against disability—about the relationship between the social environment and human ability. The young deaf woman who tries to pass for hearing will succeed only if she possesses significant knowledge about the informational potential, manners, physical gestures, conversational rituals, and cultural activities that define hearing in her society. Disabled people who pass for able-bodied are neither cowards, cheats, nor con artists but skillful interpreters of the world from whom we all might learn.

Dossier No. 2 *New York Times Online*
November 15, 2006

Officials Clash over Mentally Ill in Florida Jails

By Abby Goodnough

MIAMI, Nov. 14—For years, circuit judges here have ordered state officials to obey Florida law and promptly transfer severely mentally ill inmates from jails to state hospitals. But with few hospital beds available, Gov. Jeb Bush's administration began flouting those court orders in August. . . .

"This type of arrogant activity cannot be tolerated in an orderly society," Judge Crockett Farnell of Pinellas-Pasco Circuit Court wrote in an Oct. 11 ruling.

State law requires that inmates found incompetent to stand trial be moved from county jails to psychiatric hospitals within 15 days of the state's receiving the commitment orders. Florida has broken that law for years, provoking some public defenders to seek court orders forcing swift compliance. . . .

Two mentally ill inmates in the Escambia County Jail in Pensacola died over the last year and a half after being subdued by guards, according to news reports. And in the Pinellas County Jail in Clearwater, a schizophrenic inmate gouged out his eye after waiting weeks for a hospital bed, his lawyer said. . . .

The problem is not unique to Florida, although it is especially severe in Miami-Dade County, which has one of the nation's largest percentages of mentally ill residents, according to the National Alliance for the Mentally Ill, an advocacy group. . . .

In Miami, an average of 25 to 40 acutely psychotic people live in a unit of the main county jail that a lawyer for Human Rights Watch, Jennifer Daskal, described as squalid after visiting last month. . . . Ms. Daskal said that some of the unit's 14 "suicide cells"— dim, bare and designed for one inmate—were holding two or three at a time, and that the inmates were kept in their cells 24 hours a day except to shower. . . .

But embodiment also appears as a bone of contention in disability studies because it seems caught between competing models of disability. Briefly, the medical model defines disability as a property of the individual body that requires medical intervention. The medical model has a biological orientation, focusing almost exclusively on disability as embodiment. The social model opposes the medical model by defining disability relative to the social and built environment, arguing that disabling environments produce disability in bodies and require interventions at the level of social justice. Some scholars complain that the medical model pays too much attention to embodiment, while the social model leaves it out of the picture. Without returning to a medical model, which labels individuals as defective, the next step for disability studies is to develop a theory of complex embodiment that values disability as a form of human variation.

The theory of complex embodiment raises awareness of the effects of disabling environments on people's lived experience of the body, but it emphasizes as well that some factors affecting disability, such as chronic pain, secondary health effects, and aging, derive from the body. These last disabilities are neither less significant than disabilities caused by the environment nor to be considered defects or deviations merely because they are resistant to change. Rather, they belong to the spectrum of human variation, conceived both as variability between individuals and as variability within an individual's life cycle,

and they need to be considered in tandem with social forces affecting disability.[2] The theory of complex embodiment views the economy between social representations and the body not as unidirectional as in the social model, or nonexistent as in the medical model, but as reciprocal. Complex embodiment theorizes the body and its representations as mutually transformative. Social representations obviously affect the experience of the body, as Young makes clear in her seminal essay, but the body possesses the ability to determine its social representation as well, and some situations exist where representation exerts no control over the life of the body.

As a living entity, the body is vital and chaotic, possessing complexity in equal share to that claimed today by critical and cultural theorists for linguistic systems. The association of the body with human mortality and fragility, however, forces a general distrust of the knowledge embodied in it. It is easier to imagine the body as a garment, vehicle, or burden than as a complex system that defines our humanity, any knowledge that we might possess, and our individual and collective futures. Disability gives even greater urgency to the fears and limitations associated with the body, tempting us to believe that the body can be changed as easily as changing clothes. The ideology of ability stands ready to attack any desire to know and to accept the disabled body in its current state. The more likely response to disability is to try to erase any signs of change, to wish to return the body magically to a past era of supposed perfection, to insist that the body has no value as human variation if it is not flawless.

Ideology and prejudice, of course, abound in all circles of human existence, labeling some groups and individuals as inferior or less than human: people of color, women, the poor, people with different sexual orientations, and the disabled confront the intolerance of society on a daily basis. In nearly no other sphere of existence, however, do people risk waking up one morning having become the persons whom they hated the day before. Imagine the white racist suddenly transformed into a black man, the anti-Semite into a Jew, the misogynist into a woman, and one might begin to approach the change in mental landscape demanded by the onset of disability. We require the stuff of science fiction to describe these scenarios, most often for comic effect or paltry moralizing. But no recourse to fiction is required to imagine an able-bodied person becoming disabled. It happens every minute of every day.

The young soldier who loses his arm on an Iraqi battlefield wakes up in bed having become the kind of person whom he has always feared and whom society names as contemptible (Corbett 2004). Given these circumstances, how might we expect him to embrace and to value his new identity? He is living his worst nightmare. He cannot sleep. He hates what he has become. He distances himself from his wife and family. He begins to drink too much. He tries to use a functional prosthetic, but he loathes being seen with a hook. The natural prosthetic offered to him by Army doctors does not really work, and he prefers to master tasks with his one good arm. He cannot stand the stares of those around him, the looks of pity and contempt as he tries to perform simple tasks in public, and he begins to look upon himself with disdain.

The soldier has little chance, despite the promise of prosthetic science, to return to his former state. What he is going through is completely understandable, but he needs to come to a different conception of himself, one based not on the past but on the present and the future. His body will continue to change with age, and he may have greater disabling conditions in the future. He is no different in this regard from any other human being. Some disabilities can be approached by demanding changes in how people with disabilities are perceived, others-by changes in the built environment. Some can be treated through medical care. Other disabilities cannot be approached by changes in either the environment or the body. In almost every case, however, people with disabilities have a better chance of future happiness and health if they accept their disability as a positive identity and benefit from the knowledge embodied in it. The value of people with disabilities to themselves does not lie in finding a way to return through medical intervention to a former physical perfection, since that perfection is a myth, nor in trying to conceal from others and themselves that they are disabled. Rather, embodiment seen complexly understands disability as an epistemology that rejects the temptation to value the body as anything other than what it was and that embraces what the body has become and will become relative to the demands on it, whether environmental, representational, or corporeal.

INTERSECTIONAL IDENTITY COMPLEXLY EMBODIED

The ultimate purpose of complex embodiment as theory is to give disabled people greater knowledge of and control over their bodies in situations where increased knowledge and control are possible. But the theory has side benefits for at least two crucial debates raging on the current scene as well. First, complex embodiment makes a contribution to influential arguments about intersectionality—the idea that analyses of social oppression take account of overlapping identities based on race, gender, sexuality, class, and disability.[3] While theorists of intersectionality have never argued for a simple additive model in which oppressed identities are stacked one upon another, a notion of disability embodiment helps to resist the temptation of seeing some identities as more pathological than others, and it offers valuable advice about how to conceive the standpoint of others for the purpose of understanding the prejudices against them. This is not to suggest that the intersection of various identities produces the same results for all oppressed groups, since differences in the hierarchical organization of race, gender, sexuality, class, and disability do exist (Collins 2003, 212). Rather, it is to emphasize, first, that intersectionality as a theory references the tendency of identities to construct one another reciprocally (Collins 2003, 208); second, that identities are not merely standpoints where one may stand or try to stand but also complex embodiments; and, third, that the ideology of ability uses the language of pathology to justify labeling some identities as inferior to others.[4]

For example, theorists of intersectional identity might find useful the arguments in disability studies against disability simulation because they offer a view of complex embodiment that enlarges standpoint theory. The applied fields of occupational therapy and rehabilitation science sometimes recommend the use of disability simulations to raise the consciousness of therapists who treat people with disabilities. Instructors ask students to spend a day in a wheelchair or to try navigating classroom buildings blindfolded to get a better sense of the challenges faced by their patients. The idea is that students may stand for a time in the places occupied by disabled people and come to grasp their perspectives. Disability theorists have attacked the use of simulations for a variety of reasons, the most important being that they fail to give the student pretenders a sense of the embodied knowledge contained in disability identities. Disability simulations of this kind fail because they place students in a time-one position of disability, before knowledge about disability is acquired,

usually resulting in emotions of loss, shock, and pity at how dreadful it is to be disabled. Students experience their body relative to their usual embodiment, and they become so preoccupied with sensations of bodily inadequacy that they cannot perceive the extent to which their "disability" results from social rather than physical causes. Notice that such games focus almost entirely on the phenomenology of the individual body. The pretender asks how his or her body would be changed, how his or her personhood would be changed, by disability. It is an act of individual imagination, then, not an act of cultural imagination. Moreover, simulations tempt students to play the game of "What is Worse?" as they experiment with different simulations. Is it worse to be blind or deaf, worse to lose a leg or an arm, worse to be paralyzed or deaf, mute, and blind? The result is a thoroughly negative and unrealistic impression of disability.

The critique of disability simulation has applications in several areas of intersectional theory. First, the practice of peeling off minority identities from people to determine their place in the hierarchy of oppression is revealed to degrade all minority identities by giving a one-dimensional view of them. It also fails to understand the ways in which different identities constitute one another. Identities may trump one another in the hierarchy of oppression, but intersectional identity, because embodied complexly, produces not competition between minority identities but "outsider" theories about the lived experience of oppression (see Collins 1998). Additionally, coming to an understanding of intersecting minority identities demands that one imagine social location not only as perspective but also as complex embodiment, and complex embodiment combines social and corporeal factors. Rather than blindfolding students for an hour, then, it is preferable to send them off wearing sunglasses and carrying a white cane, in the company of a friend, to restaurants and department stores, where they may observe firsthand the spectacle of discrimination against blind people as passersby avoid and gawk at them, clerks refuse to wait on them or condescend to ask the friend what the student is looking for, and waiters request, usually at the top of their lungs and very slowly (since blind people must also be deaf and cognitively disabled), what the student would like to eat.[5]

It is crucial to resist playing the game of "What Is Worse?" when conceiving of intersectional identity, just as it is when imagining different disabilities. Asking whether it is worse to be a woman or a Latina, worse to be black or blind, worse to be gay or poor registers each identity as a form of ability that has greater or lesser powers to overcome social intolerance and prejudice. Although one may try to keep the focus on society and the question of whether it oppresses one identity more than another, the debate devolves all too soon and often to discussions of the comparative costs of changing society and making accommodations, comparisons about quality of life, and speculations about whether social disadvantages are intrinsic or extrinsic to the group. The compelling issue for minority identity does not turn on the question of whether one group has the more arduous existence but on the fact that every minority group faces social discrimination, violence, and intolerance that exert toxic and unfair influence on the ability to live life to the fullest (see Asch 2001, 406–7).

SOCIAL CONSTRUCTION COMPLEXLY EMBODIED

Second, the theory of complex embodiment makes it possible to move forward arguments raging currently about social construction, identity, and the body. Aside from proposing a theory better suited to the experiences of disabled people, the goal is to advance questions in identity and body theory unresponsive to the social construction model. Chapters 3, 4, and 6 [original volume] make an explicit adjustment in social construction theory by focusing on the realism of identities and bodies. By "realism" I understand neither a positivistic claim about reality unmediated by social representations, nor a linguistic claim about reality unmediated by objects of representation, but a theory that describes reality as a mediation, no less real for being such, between representation and its social objects.[6] Rather than viewing representation as a pale shadow of the world or the world as a shadow world of representation, my claim is that both sides push back in the construction of reality. The hope is to advance discourse theory to the next stage by defining construction in a radical way, one that reveals constructions as possessing both social and physical form. While identities are socially constructed, they are nevertheless meaningful and real precisely because they are complexly embodied. The complex embodiment apparent in disability is an especially strong example to contemplate because the disabled body compels one to give concrete form to the theory of social construction and to take its metaphors literally.

Consider an introductory example of the way in which disability complexly embodied extends the social construction argument in the direction of realism. In August 2000 a controversy about access at the Galehead hut in the Appalachian Mountains came to a climax (Goldberg 2000). The Appalachian Mountain Club of New Hampshire had just constructed a rustic thirty-eight bed lodge at an elevation of thirty-eight hundred feet. The United States Forest Service required that the hut comply with the Americans with Disabilities Act (ADA) and be accessible to people with disabilities, that it have a wheelchair ramp and grab bars in larger toilet stalls. The Appalachian Mountain Club had to pay an extra $30,000 to $50,000 for a building already costing $400,000 because the accessible features were late design changes. Its members ridiculed the idea that the building, which could be reached only by a super-rugged 4.6 mile trail, would ever be visited by wheelchair users, and the media tended to take their side.

At this point a group from Northeast Passage, a program at the University of New Hampshire that works with people with disabilities, decided to make a visit to the Galehead hut. Jill Gravink, the director of Northeast Passage, led a group of three hikers in wheelchairs and two on crutches on a twelve-hour climb to the lodge, at the end of which they rolled happily up the ramp to its front door. A local television reporter on the scene asked why, if people in wheelchairs could drag themselves up the trail, they could not drag themselves up the steps into the hut, implying that the ramp was a waste of money. Gravink responded, "Why bother putting steps on the hut at all? Why not drag yourself in through a window?"

The design environment, Gravink suggests pointedly, determines who is able-bodied at the Galehead lodge. The distinction between the disabled and non-disabled is socially constructed, and it is a rather fine distinction at that. Those who are willing and able to climb stairs are considered able-bodied, while those who are not willing and able to climb stairs are disabled. However, those who do climb stairs but are not willing and able to enter the building through a window are not considered disabled. It is taken for granted that nondisabled people may choose when to be able-bodied. In fact, the built environment is full of technologies that make life easier for those people who possess the physical power to perform tasks without these technologies. Stairs, elevators, escalators, washing machines, leaf and snow blowers, eggbeaters, chainsaws, and other tools help to relax physical standards for performing certain tasks. These tools are nevertheless viewed as natural extensions of the body, and no one thinks twice about using them. The moment that individuals are marked as disabled or diseased, however, the expectation is that they will maintain the maximum standard of physical performance at every moment, and the technologies designed to make their life easier are viewed as expensive additions, unnecessary accommodations, and a burden on society.

The example of the Galehead hut exposes the ideology of ability—the ideology that uses ability to determine human status, demands that people with disabilities always present as able-bodied as possible, and measures the value of disabled people in dollars and cents. It reveals how constructed are our attitudes about identity and the body. This is a familiar point, and usually social analysis comes to a conclusion here, no doubt because the idea of construction is more metaphorical than real. The implication seems to be that knowledge of an object as socially constructed is sufficient to undo any of its negative effects. How many books and essays have been written in the last ten years, whose authors are content with the conclusion that x, y, or z is socially constructed, as if the conclusion itself were a victory over oppression?

Far from being satisfied with this conclusion, my analysis here will always take it as a point of departure from which to move directly to the elucidation of embodied causes and effects. Oppression is driven not by individual, unconscious syndromes but by social ideologies that are embodied, and precisely because ideologies are embodied, their effects are readable, and must be read, in the construction and history of societies. When a Down syndrome citizen tries to enter a polling place and is turned away, a social construction is revealed and must be read. When wheelchair users are called selfish if they complain about the inaccessibility of public toilets, a social construction is revealed and must be read (Shapiro 1994, 126–27). When handicapped entrances to buildings are located in the rear, next to garbage cans, a social construction is revealed and must be read. When a cosmetic surgeon removes the thumb on a little boy's right hand because he was born with no thumb on his left hand, a social construction is revealed and must be read (Marks 1999, 67). What if we were to embrace the metaphor implied by social construction, if we required that the "construction" in social construction be understood as a building, as the Galehead hut for example, and that its blueprint be made available? Not only would this requirement stipulate that we elaborate claims about social construction in concrete terms, it would insist that we locate the construction in time and place as a form of complex embodiment.

Whenever anyone mentions the idea of social construction, we should ask on principle to see the blueprint—not to challenge the value of the idea but to put it to practical use—to map as many details about the construction as possible and to track its political, epistemological, and real effects in the world of human beings. To encourage this new requirement, I cite three familiar ideas about social construction, as currently theorized, from which flow—or at least should—three methodological principles. These three principles underlie the arguments to follow, suggesting how to look for blueprints and how to begin reading them:

- Knowledge is socially situated—which means that knowledge has an objective and verifiable relation to its social location.
- Identities are socially constructed—which means that identities contain complex theories about social reality.
- Some bodies are excluded by dominant social ideologies—which means that these bodies display the workings of ideology and expose it to critique and the demand for political change.

NOTES

1. The nature of pain and the methodology of its study are diverse because they involve the definition of emotion and consciousness. Aydede collects a strong sampling of contemporary views about pain; one of which, the perceptual theory, appeals to the idea that pain has the capacity to signal changes in states of reality (59–98).

2. Snyder and Mitchell express this view powerfully throughout *Cultural Locations of Disability*. For example: "As Darwin insisted in *On the Origin of Species*, variation serves the good of the species. The more variable a species is, the more flexible it is with respect to shifting environmental forces. Within this formulation, one that is central to disability studies, variations are features of biological elasticity rather than a discordant expression of a 'natural' process gone awry" (2006, 70).

3. The literature on intersectionality is now vast. Some key texts relating to disability include Barbee and Little; Beale; Butler and Parr; Fawcett; Hayman and Levit; Ikemoto; Jackson-Braboy and Williams; Martin; O'Toole (2004); and Tyjewski.

4. While not aware of disability studies per se, Johnny Williams provides an excellent intersectional analysis of stereotypical conflations of race and class, arguing that American society explains the social and economic failures of minority groups in terms of personal "inabilities," while maintaining the belief that "social arrangements are fundamentally just" (221).

5. Catherine Kudlick proposed, on the DS-HUM listserve, an exercise similar to this one to replace traditional and biased disability simulations often used by classroom instructors. I am indebted to her discussion.

6. Philosophical realism has a number of varieties. The particular lineage of interest to me focuses on Hilary Putnam in philosophy and Richard Boyd in the philosophy of science. Satya P. Mohanty imports Boyd's ideas into the humanities in general and critical theory in particular, putting the concept of realism in the service of minority studies in novel and convincing ways. Other important figures in philosophical realism working in the humanities include Linda Martin Alcoff, Michael Hames-Garcia, Paula M. L. Moya, and Sean Teuton.

REFERENCES

Alcoff, Linda Martin. *Real Knowing: New Versions of Coherence Theory.* Ithaca, N.Y.: Cornell University Press, 1996.

——. "Who's Afraid of Identity Politics?" *Reclaiming Identity: Realist Theory and the Predicament of Postmodernism.* Ed. Paula M. L. Moya and Michael R. Hames-Garcia. Berkeley and Los Angeles: University of California Press, 2000. Pp. 312–44.

——. *Visible Identities: Race, Gender and the Self.* New York: Oxford University Press, 2006.

Alcoff, Linda Martin, Michael Hames-Garcia, Satya P. Mohanty, and Paula M. L. Moya, eds. *Identity Politics Reconsidered.* New York: Palgrave Macmillan, 2006.

Asch, Adrienne, and Harilyn Rousso. "Therapists with Disabilities: Theoretical and Clinical Issues." *Psychiatry* 48 (1985): 1–12.

Asch, Adrienne, and Michelle Fine. *Women with Disabilities: Essays in Psychology, Culture, and Politics.* Philadelphia: Temple University Press, 1988.

Asch, Adrienne. "Critical Race Theory, Feminism, and Disability: Reflections on Social Justice and Personal Identity." *Ohio State Law Journal* 62.1 (2001): 391–423.

Castells, Manuel. *The Power of Identity.* 2nd ed. Oxford: Blackwell, 1997 (2004).

Collins, Patricia Hill. "Some Group Matters: Intersectionality, Situated Standpoints, and Black Feminist Thought." *A Companion to African-American Philosophy.* Ed. Tommy L. Lott and John P. Pittman. Malden: Blackwell, 2003. Pp. 205–29.

——. "Learning from the Outsider within Revisited." *Fighting Words: Black Women and the Search for Justice.* Minneapolis: University of Minnesota Press, 1998. Pp. 3–10.

Corbett Sara. "The Permanent Scars of Iraq." *New York Times Magazine,* 15 February 2004: 34–41, 58, 60, 66.

Dworkin, Anthony Gary, and Rosalind J. Dworkin, eds. *The Minority Report: An Introduction to Racial, Ethnic, and Gender Relations.* New York: Praeger, 1976.

Fraser, Nancy. "Rethinking Recognition." *New Left Review* 3 (May–June 2000): 107–20.

Gill, Carol J. "Health Professionals, Disability, and Assisted Suicide: An Examination of Relevant Empirical Evidence and Reply to Batavia." *Psychology, Public Policy, and Law* 6.2 (2000): 526–45.

Goldberg, Carey. "For These Trailblazers, Wheelchairs Matter. *New York Times Online,* August 17, 2000. Available at http://query.nytimes.com/gst/fullpage.html.res9EoCE3DA173EF934A2575BCoA9669C8B63&sec=health&spon=&pagewanted=all (accessed December 22, 2006).

Goodheart, Eugene. *The Reign of Ideology.* New York: Columbia University Press, 1996.

Haraway, Donna J. *Simians, Cyborgs, and Women: The Reinvention of Nature.* New York: Routledge, 1991.

Harding, Sandra. *The Science Question in Feminism.* Ithaca, N.Y.: Cornell University Press, 1986.

JanMohamed, Abdul, and David Lloyd. "Introduction: Minority Discourse—What Is to Be Done?" *Cultural Critique* 7 (1987): 5–17.

Kirkland, Anna. "What's at Stake in Fatness as a Disability?" *Disability Studies Quarterly* 26.1, (2006). Available at www.dsq-sds.org/_articles_htmlJ2006/winter/kirkland.asp (accessed November 17, 2006).

Lester, J. C. "The Disability Studies Industry." *Libertarian Alliance,* September 26, 2002. Available at www.la-articles.org.uk/dsi.htm (accessed November 11, 2006).

Linton, Simi. *Claiming Disability: Knowledge and Identity.* New York: New York University Press, 1998.

Linton, Simi, Susan Mello, and John O'Neill. "Disability Studies: Expanding the Parameters of Diversity." *Radical Teacher* 47 (1995): 4–10.

Longmore, Paul. *Why I Burned My Book and Other Essays on Disability.* Philadelphia: Temple University Press, 2003.

Marks, Deborah. *Disability: Controversial Debates and Psychosocial Perspectives.* London: Routledge, 1999.

O'Brien, Mark. "On Seeing a Sex Surrogate." *The Sun* 174 (May), 1990. Available at www.pacificnews.org/marko/sex-surrogate.html (accessed April 29, 2005).

——. *The Man in the Iron Lung.* Berkeley, Calif.: Lemonade Factory, 1997.

——. N.d. "Questions I Feared the Journalist Would Ask." Mark O'Brien Papers, BANC MSS 99/247 c. Bancroft Library, University of California, Berkeley.

O'Brien, Mark, with Gillian Kendall. *How I Became a Human Being: A Disabled Man's Quest for Independence.* Madison: University of Wisconsin Press, 2003.

Shapiro, Joseph. *No Pity: People with Disabilities Forging a New Civil Rights Movement.* New York: Three Rivers Press, 1993.

——. "Disability Policy and the Media: A Stealth Civil Rights Movement Bypasses the Press and Defies Conventional Wisdom." *Policy Studies Journal* 22.1 (1994): 123–32.

Siebers, Tobin. *Morals and Stories.* New York: Columbia University Press, 1992.

——. "Kant and the Politics of Beauty." *Philosophy and Literature* 22.1 (1998): 31–50.

——. "My Withered Limb." *Michigan Quarterly Review* 37.2 (1998):196–205.

——. *The Subject and Other Subjects: On Ethical, Aesthetic, and Political Identity.* Ann Arbor: University of Michigan Press, 1998.

——. "*The Reign of Ideology* by Eugene Goodheart." *Modern Philology* 96.4 (1999): 560–63.

——. *The Mirror of Medusa.* Rev. ed. Christchurch, New Zealand: Cybereditions, 2000.

——. "What Can Disability Studies Learn from the Culture Wars?" *Cultural Critique* 55 (2003): 182–216.

Taylor, Charles. *Sources of the Self: The Making of Modern Identity.* Cambridge, Mass.: Harvard University Press, 1987.

Young, Iris. *On Female Body Experience: "Throwing Like a Girl" and Other Essays.* Cambridge, Mass.: Oxford University Press, 2005.

CHAPTER 25

Toward a Feminist Theory of Disability

Susan Wendell

In 1985, I fell ill overnight with what turned out to be a disabling chronic disease. In the long struggle to come to terms with it, I had to learn to live with a body that felt entirely different to me—weak, tired, painful, nauseated, dizzy, unpredictable. I learned at first by listening to other people with chronic illness or disabilities; suddenly able-bodied people seem to me profoundly ignorant of everything I most needed to know. Although doctors told me there was a good chance I would eventually recover completely, I realized after a year that waiting to get well, hoping to recovery my healthy body, was a dangerous strategy. I began slowly to identify with my new, disabled body and to learn to work with it. As I moved back into the world, I also began to experience the world as structure for people who have no weaknesses.[1] The process of encountering the able-bodied world led me gradually to identify myself as a disabled person, and to reflect on the nature of disability.

Some time ago, I decided to delve into what I assumed would be a substantial philosophical literature in medical ethics on the nature and experience of disability. I consulted *The Philosopher's Index*, looking under "Disability," "Handicap," "Illness," and "Disease." This was a depressing experience. At least 90 percent of philosophical articles on these topics are concerned with two questions: Under what conditions is it morally permissible/right to kill/let die a disabled person and how potentially disabled does a fetus have to be before it is permissible/right to prevent its being born? Thus, what I have to say here about disability is not a response to philosophical literature on the subject. Instead, it reflects what I have learned from the writings of other disabled people (especially disabled women), from talking with disabled people who have shared their insights and experiences with me, and from my own experience of disability. It also reflects my commitment to feminist theory, which offers perspectives and categories of analysis that help to illuminate the personal and social realities of disability, and which would, in turn, be enriched by a greater understanding of disability.

We need a theory of disability. It should be a social and political theory, because disability is largely socially constructed, but it has to be more than that; any deep understanding of disability must include thinking about the ethical, psychological and epistemic issues of living with disability. This theory should be feminist, because more than half of disabled people are women and approximately 16 percent of women are disabled (Fine and Asch

1988), and because feminist thinkers have raised the most radical issues bout cultural attitudes to the body. Some of the same attitudes about the body which contribute to women's oppression generally also contribute to the social and psychological disablement of people who have physical disabilities. In addition, feminists are grappling with issues that disabled people also face in a different context: Whether to stress sameness or difference in relation to the dominant group and in relation to each other; whether to place great value on independence from the help of other people, as the dominant culture does, or to question a value-system which distrusts and devalues dependence on other people and vulnerability in general; whether to take full integration into male dominated/able-bodied society as the goal, seeking equal power with men/able-bodied people in that society, or whether to preserve some degree of separate culture, in which the abilities, knowledge and values of women/the disabled are specifically honoured and developed.[2]

Disabled women struggle with both the oppressions of being women in male-dominated societies and the oppressions of being disabled in societies dominated by the able-bodied. They are bringing the knowledge and concerns of women with disabilities into feminism and feminist perspectives into the disability rights movement. To build a feminist theory of disability that takes adequate account of our differences, we will need to know how experiences of disability and the social oppression of the disabled interact with sexism, racism and class oppression. Michelle Fine and Adrienne Asch and the contributors to their 1988 volume, *Women and Disabilities*, have made a major contribution to our understanding of the complex interactions of gender and disability. Barbara Hillyer Davis has written in depth about the issue of dependency/independence as

it relates to disability and feminism (Davis 1984). Other important contributions to theory are scattered throughout the extensive, primarily experiential, writing by disabled women;[3] this work offers vital insights into the nature of embodiment and the experience of oppression.

Unfortunately, feminist perspectives on disability are not yet widely discussed in feminist theory, nor have the insights offered by women writing about disability been integrated into feminist theorizing about the body. My purpose in writing this essay is to persuade feminist theorists, especially feminist philosophers, to turn more attention to constructing a theory of disability and to integrating the experiences and knowledge of disabled people into feminist theory as a whole. Toward this end I will discuss physical disability[4] from a theoretical perspective, including: some problems of defining it (here I will criticize the most widely used definitions—those of the United Nations); the social construction of disability from biological reality on analogy with the social construction of gender; cultural attitudes toward the body which oppress disabled people while also alienating the able-bodied from their own experiences of embodiment; the "otherness" of disabled people; the knowledge that disabled people could contribute to culture from our diverse experiences and some of the ways this knowledge is silenced and invalidated. Along the way, I will describe briefly three issues discussed in disability theory that have been taken up in different contexts by feminist theory: sameness vs. difference, independence vs. dependency and integration vs. separatism.

I do not presume to speak for disabled women. Like everyone who is disabled, I have a particular standpoint determined in part by both my physical condition and my social situation. My own disability may be temporary; it could get better or worse. My disability is usually invisible (except when I use a walking stick). I am a white university professor who has adequate medical and long-term disability insurance; that makes me very privileged among the disabled. I write what I can see from my standpoint. Because I do not want simply to describe my own experience but to understand it in a much larger context, I must venture beyond what I know first-hand. I rely on others to correct my mistakes and fill in those parts of the picture I cannot see.

WHO IS PHYSICALLY DISABLED?

The United Nations offers the following definitions of and distinctions among impairment, disability and handicap:

> "*Impairment*: Any loss or abnormality of psychological, physiological, or anatomical structure or function. *Disability*: Any restriction or lack (resulting from an impairment) of ability to perform an activity in the manner or within the range considered normal for a human being. *Handicap*: A disadvantage for a given individual, resulting from an impairment or disability, that limits or prevents the fulfillment of a role that is normal, depending on age, sex, social and cultural factors, for that individual."
>
> Handicap is therefore a function of the relationship between disabled persons and their environment. It occurs when they encounter cultural, physical or social barriers which prevent their access to the various systems of society that are available to other citizens. Thus, handicap is the loss or limitation of opportunities to take part in the life of the community on an equal level with others.
>
> (U.N. 1983: 1.c. 6–7)

These definitions may be good enough for the political purposes of the U.N. They have two advantages: First, they clearly include many conditions that are not always recognized by the general public as disabling, for example, debilitating chronic illnesses that limit people's facilities but do not necessarily cause any visible disability, such as Crohn's Disease. Second, the definition of "handicap" explicitly recognizes the possibility that the primary cause of a disabled person's inability to do certain things may be social—denial of opportunities, lack of accessibility, lack of services, poverty, discrimination—which it often is.

However, by trying to define "impairment" and "disability" in physical terms and "handicap" in cultural, physical and social terms, the U.N. document appears to be making a shaky distinction between the physical and the social aspects of disability. Not only the "normal" roles for one's age, sex, society, and culture, but also "normal" structure and function, and "normal" ability to perform an activity, depend on the society in which the standards of normality are generated. Paradigms of health and ideas about appropriate kinds and levels of performance are culturally dependent. In addition, within each society there is much variation from the norm of any ability; at what point does this variation become disability? The answer depends on such factors as what activities a society values and how it distributes labour and resources. The idea that there is some universal, perhaps biologically or medically describable paradigm of human physical ability is an illusion. Therefore, I prefer to use a single term, "disability," and to emphasize that disability is socially constructed from biological reality.

Another objection I have to the U.N. definitions is that they imply that women can be disabled, but not handicapped, by being unable to do things which are not considered part of the normal role for their sex. For example, if a society does not consider it essential to a woman's normal role that she be able to read, then a blind woman who is not provided with education in Braille is not handicapped, according to these definitions.

In addition, these definitions suggest that we can be disabled, but not handicapped, by the normal process of aging, since although we may lose some ability, we are not handicapped unless we cannot fulfill roles that are normal *for our age*. Yet a society which provides few resources to allow disabled people to participate in it will be likely to marginalize *all* the disabled, including the old, and to define the appropriate roles of old people as very limited, thus handicapping them. Aging is disabling. Recognizing this helps us to see that disabled people are not "other," that they are really "us." Unless we die suddenly, we are all disabled eventually. Most of us will live part of our lives with bodies that hurt, that move with difficulty or not at all, that deprive us of activities we once took for granted or that others take for granted, bodies that make daily life a physical struggle. We need an understanding of disability that does not support a paradigm of humanity as young and healthy. Encouraging everyone to acknowledge, accommodate and identify with a wide range of physical conditions is ultimately the road to self-acceptance as well as the road to liberating those who are disabled now.

Ultimately, we might eliminate the category of "the disabled" altogether, and simply talk about individuals' physical abilities in their social context. For the present, although "the disabled" is a category of "the other" to the able-bodied, and for that very reason it is also a politically useful and socially meaningful category to those who are in it. Disabled people share forms of social oppression, and the most important measures to relieve that oppression have been initiated by disabled people themselves. Social oppression may be the only thing the disabled have in common;[5] our struggles with our bodies are extremely diverse.

Finally, in thinking about disability we have to keep in mind that a society's labels do not always fit the people to whom they are applied. Thus, some people are perceived as disabled who do not experience themselves as disabled. Although they have physical conditions that disable other people, because of their opportunities and the context of their lives, they do not feel significantly limited in their activities (see Sacks 1988); these people may be surprised or resentful that they are considered disabled. On the other hand, many people whose bodies cause them great physical, psychological and economic struggles are not considered disabled because the public and/or the medical profession do not recognize their disabling conditions. These people often long to be perceived as disabled, because society stubbornly continues to expect them to perform as healthy people when they cannot and refuses to acknowledge and support their struggles.[6] Of course, no one wants the social stigma associated with disability, but social recognition of disability determines the practical help a person receives from doctors, government agencies, insurance companies, charity organizations, and often from family and friends. Thus, how a society defines disability and whom it recognizes as disabled are of enormous psychological, economic and social importance, both to people who are experiencing themselves as disabled and to those who are not but are nevertheless given the label.

There is no definitive answer to the question: Who is physically disabled? Disability has social, experiential and biological components, present and recognized in different measures for different people. Whether a particular physical condition is disabling changes with time and place, depending on such factors as social expectations, the state of technology and its availability to people in that condition, the educational system, architecture, attitudes towards physical appearance, and the pace of life. (If, for example, the pace of life increases without changes in other factors, more people become disabled simply because fewer people can keep up the "normal" pace.)

THE SOCIAL CONSTRUCTION OF DISABILITY

If we ask the questions: Why are so many disabled people unemployed or under-employed, impoverished, lonely, isolated; why do so many find it difficult or impossible to get an education (Davis and Marshall 1987; Fine and Asch 1988, 10–11); why are they victims of violence and coercion; why do able-bodied people ridicule, avoid, pity, stereotype and patronize them?, we may be tempted to see the disabled as victims of nature or accident. Feminists should be, and many are, profoundly suspicious of this answer. We are used to countering claims that insofar as women are oppressed they are oppressed by nature, which puts them at a disadvantage in the competition for power and resources. We know that if being biologically female is a disadvantage, it is because a social context makes it a disadvantage. From the standpoint of a disabled person, one can see how society could minimize the disadvantages of most disabilities, and, in some instances, turn them into advantages.

Consider an extreme case: the situation of physicist Stephen Hawking, who has had Amyotrophic Lateral Sclerosis (Lou Gehrig's Disease) for more than 26 years. Professor Hawking can no longer speak and is capable of only the smallest muscle movements. Yet, in his context of social and technological support, he is able to function as a professor of physics at Cambridge University; indeed he says his disability has given him the *advantage* of having more time to think, and he is one of the foremost theoretical physicists of our time. He is a courageous and talented man, but he is able to live the creative life he has only because of the help of his family, three nurses, a graduate student who travels with him to maintain his computer-communications systems, and the fact that his talent had been developed and recognized before he fell seriously ill (*Newsweek* 1988).

Many people consider providing resources for disabled people a form of charity, superogatory in part because the disabled are perceived as unproductive members of society. Yet most disabled people are placed in a double-bind: they have access to inadequate resources because they are unemployed or underemployed, and they are unemployed or underemployed because they lack the resources that would enable them to make their full contribution to society (Matthews 1983; Hannaford 1985). Often governments and charity organizations will spend far more money to keep disabled people in institutions where they have no chance to be productive than they will spend to enable the same people to live independently and productively. In addition, many of the "special" resources the disabled need merely compensate for bad social planning that is based on the illusion that everyone is young, strong, healthy (and, often, male).

Disability is also frequently regarded as a personal or family problem rather than a matter for social responsibility. Disabled people are often expected to overcome obstacles to participation by their own extraordinary efforts, or their families are expected to provide what they need (sometimes at great personal sacrifice). Helping in personal or family matters is seen as superogatory for people who are not members of the family.

Many factors contribute to determining whether providing a particular resource is regarded as a social or a personal (or family) responsibility.[7] One such factor is whether the majority can identify with people who need the resource. Most North Americans feel that society should be organized to provide short-term medical care made necessary by illness or accident, I think because they can imagine themselves needing it. Relatively few people can identify with those who cannot be "repaired" by medical intervention. Sue Halpern makes the following observation:

> Physical health is contingent and often short-lived. But this truth eludes us as long as we are able to walk by simply putting one foot in front of the other. As a consequence, empathy for the disabled is unavailable to most able-bodied persons. Sympathy, yes, empathy, no, for every attempt to project oneself into that condition, to feel what it is like not to be ambulatory, for instance, is mediated by an ability to walk.
>
> (Halpern 1988, 3)

If the able-bodied saw the disabled as potentially themselves or as their future selves, they would be more inclined to feel that society should be organized to provide the resources that would make disabled people fully integrated and contributing members. They would feel that "charity" is as inappropriate a way of thinking about resources for disabled people as it is about emergency medical care of education.

Careful study of the lives of disabled people will reveal how artificial the line is that we draw between the biological and the social. Feminists have already challenged this line in part by showing how processes such as childbirth, menstruation and menopause, which may be presented, treated, and therefore experienced as illnesses or disabilities, are socially constructed from biological reality (Rich 1976; Ehrenreich and English 1979). Disabled people's relations to our bodies involve elements of struggle which perhaps cannot be eliminated, perhaps not even mitigated, by social arrangements. *But* much of what is *disabling* about our physical conditions is also a consequence of social arrangements (Finger 1983; Fine and Asch 1988) which could, but do not, either compensate for our physical conditions, or accommodate them so that we can participate fully, or support our struggles and integrate us into the community *and our struggles into the cultural concept of life as it is ordinarily lived.*

Feminists have shown that the world has been designed for men. In North America at least, life and work have been structured as though no one of any importance in the public world, and certainly no one who works outside the home for wages, has to breast-feed a baby or look after a sick child. Common colds can be acknowledged publicly, and allowances made for them, but menstruation cannot. Much of the world is also structured as though everyone is physically strong, as though all bodies are "ideally shaped," as though everyone can walk, hear and see well, as though everyone can work and play at a pace that is not compatible with any kind of illness or pain, as though no one is ever dizzy or incontinent or simply needs to sit or lie down. (For instance, where could you sit down in a supermarket if you needed to?) Not only the architecture, but the entire physical and social organization of life, assumes that we are either strong and healthy and able to do what the average able-bodied person can do, or that we are completely disabled, unable to participate in life.

In the split between the public and the private worlds, women (and children) have been relegated to the private, and so have the disabled, the sick and the old (and mostly women take care of them). The public world is the world of strength, the positive (valued) body, performance and production, the able-bodied and youth. Weakness, illness, rest and recovery, pain, death and the negative (de-valued) body are private, generally hidden, and often neglected. Coming into the public world with illness, pain or a de-valued body, we encounter resistance to mixing the two worlds; the split is vividly revealed. Much of our experience goes underground, because there is no socially acceptable way of expressing it and having our physical and psychological experience acknowledged and shared. A few close friends may share it, but there is a strong impulse to protect them from it too, because it seems so private, so unacceptable. I found that, after a couple of years of illness, even answering the question, "How are you?" became a difficult, conflict-ridden business. I don't want to alienate my friends from my experience, but I don't want to risk their discomfort and rejection by telling them what they don't want to know.[8]

Disabled people learn that many, perhaps most, able-bodied people do not want to know about suffering caused by the body. Visibly disabled women report that curiosity about medical diagnoses, physical appearance and the sexual and other intimate aspects of disability is more common than willingness to listen and try to understand the experience of disability (Matthews 1983). It is not unusual for people with invisible disabilities to keep them entirely secret from everyone but their closest friends.

Contrary to what Sue Halpern says, it is not simply because they are in able bodies that the able-bodied fail to identify with the disabled. Able-bodied people can often make the imaginative leap into the skins of people physically unlike themselves; women can identify with a male protagonist in a story, for example, and adults can identify with children or with people much older than themselves. Something more powerful than being in a different body is at work. Suffering caused by the body, and the inability to control the body, are despised, pitied, and above all, feared. This fear, experienced individually, is also deeply embedded in our culture.

THE OPPRESSION OF DISABLED PEOPLE IS THE OPPRESSION OF EVERYONE'S REAL BODY

Our real human bodies are exceedingly diverse—in size, shape, colour, texture, structure, function, range and habits of movements, and development—and they are constantly changing. Yet we do not absorb or reflect this simple fact in our culture. Instead, we idealize the human body. Our physical ideals change from time to time, but we always have ideals. These ideals are not just about appearance; they are also ideals of strength and energy and proper control of the body. We are perpetually bombarded with images of these ideals, demands for them, and offers of consumer products and services to help us achieve them.[9] Idealizing the body prevents everyone, able-bodied and disabled, from identifying with and loving her/his real body. Some people can have the illusion of acceptance that comes from believing that their bodies are "close enough" to the ideal, but this illusion only draws them deeper into identifying with the ideal and into the endless task of reconciling the reality with it. Sooner or later they must fail.

Before I became disabled, I was one of those people who felt "close enough" to cultural ideals to be reasonably accepting of my body. Like most feminists I know, I was aware of some alienation from it, and I worked at liking my body better. Nevertheless, I knew in my heart that too much of my liking still depended on being "close enough." When I was disabled by illness, I experienced a much more profound alienation from my body. After a year spent mostly in bed, I could barely identify my body as my own. I felt that "it" was torturing "me," trapping me in exhaustion, pain and inability to do many of the simplest things I did when I was healthy. The shock of this experience and the effort to identify with a new, disabled body, made me realize I had been living a luxury of the able-bodied. The able-bodied can postpone the luxury of identifying with their *real* bodies. The disabled don't have the luxury of demanding that their bodies fit the physical ideals of their culture. As Barbara Hillyer

Davis says: "For all of us the difficult work of finding (one's) self includes the body, but people who live with disability in a society that glorifies fitness and physical conformity are forced to understand more fully what bodily integrity means" (Davis 1984, 3).

In a society which idealizes the body, the physically disabled are marginalized. People learn to identify with their own strengths (by cultural standards) and to hate, fear and neglect their own weaknesses. The disabled are not only de-valued for their de-valued bodies (Hannaford 1985), they are constant reminders to the able-bodied of the negative body—of what the able-bodied are trying to avoid, forget and ignore (Lessing 1981). For example, if someone tells me she is in pain, she reminds me of the existence of pain, the imperfection and fragility of the body, the possibility of my own pain, the *inevitability* of it. The less willing I am to accept all these, the less I want to know about her pain; if I cannot avoid it in her presence, I will avoid her. I may even blame her for it. I may tell myself that she *could have* avoided it, in order to go on believing that I *can* avoid it. I want to believe I am not like her; I cling to the differences. Gradually, I make her "other" because I don't want to confront my real body, which I fear and cannot accept.[10]

Disabled people can participate in marginalizing ourselves. We can wish for bodies we do not have, with frustration, shame, self-hatred. We can feel trapped in the negative body; it is our internalized oppression to feel this. Every (visibly or invisibly) disabled person I have talked to or read has felt this; some never stop feeling it. In addition, disabled women suffer more than disabled men from the demand that people have "ideal" bodies, because in patriarchal culture people judge women more by their bodies than they do men. Disabled women often do not feel seen (because they are often not seen) by others as whole people,

especially not as sexual people (Campling 1981; Matthews 1983; Hannaford 1985; Fine and Asch 1988). Thus, part of their struggle against oppression is a much harder version of the struggle able-bodied women have for a realistic *and positive* self-image (Bogle and Shaul 1981). On the other hand, disabled people who cannot hope to meet the physical ideals of a culture can help reveal that those ideals are not "natural" or "normal" but artificial social creations that oppress everyone.

Feminist theorists have probed the causes of our patriarchal culture's desire for control of the body—fear of death, fear of the strong impulses and feelings the body give us, fear of nature, fear and resentment of the mother's power over the infant (de Beauvoir 1949; Dinnerstein 1976; Griffin 1981). Idealizing the body and wanting to control it go hand-in-hand; it is impossible to say whether one causes the other. A physical ideal gives us the goal of our efforts to control the body, and the myth that total control is possible deceives us into striving for the ideal. The consequences for women have been widely discussed in the literature of feminism. The consequences for disabled people are less often recognized. In a culture which loves the idea that the body can be controlled, those who cannot control their bodies are seen (and may see themselves) as failures.

When you listen to this culture in a disabled body, you hear how often health and physical vigour are talked about as if they were moral virtues. People constantly praise others for their "energy," their stamina, their ability to work long hours. Of course, acting on behalf of one's health can be a virtue, and undermining one's health can be a vice, but "success" at being healthy, like beauty, is always partly a matter of luck and therefore beyond our control. When health is spoken of as a virtue, people who lack it are made to feel inadequate. I am not suggesting that it is always wrong to praise people's physical strength or accomplishments, any more than it is always wrong to praise their physical beauty. But just as treating cultural standards of beauty as essential virtues for women harms most women, treating health and vigour as moral virtues for everyone harms people with disabilities and illnesses.

The myth that the body can be controlled is not easily dispelled, because it is not very vulnerable to evidence against it. When I became ill, several people wanted to discuss with me what I thought I had done to "make myself" ill or "allow myself" to become sick. At first I fell in with this, generating theories about what I had done wrong; even though I had always taken good care of my health, I was able to find some (rather far-fetched) accounts of my responsibility for my illness. When a few close friends offered hypotheses as to how *they* might be responsible for my being ill, I began to suspect that something was wrong. Gradually, I realized that we were all trying to believe that nothing this important is beyond our control.

Of course, there are sometimes controllable social and psychological forces at work in creating ill health and disability (Kleinman 1988). Nevertheless our cultural insistence on controlling the body blames the victims of disability for failing and burdens them with self-doubt and self-blame. The search for psychological, moral and spiritual causes of illness, accident and disability is often a harmful expression of this insistence on control (see Sontag 1977).

Modern Western medicine plays into and conforms to our cultural myth that the body can be controlled. Collectively, doctors and medical researchers exhibit very little modesty about their knowledge. They focus their (and our) attention on cures and imminent cures, on successful medical interventions. Research, funding and medical care are more directed toward life-threatening conditions than toward chronic illnesses and disabilities. Even pain was relatively neglected as a medical problem until the second half of this century. Surgery and saving lives bolster the illusion of control much better than does the long, patient process of rehabilitation or the management of long-term illness. These latter, less visible functions of medicine tend to be performed by nurses, physiotherapists and other low-prestige members of the profession. Doctors are trained to do something to control the body, to "make it better" (Kleinman 1988); they are the heroes of medicine. They may like being in the role of hero, but we also like them in that role and try to keep them there, because *we* want to believe that someone can always "make it better."[11] As long as we cling to this belief, the patients who cannot be "repaired"—the chronically ill, the disabled and the dying—will symbolize the failure of medicine and more, the failure of the Western scientific project to control nature. They will carry this stigma in medicine and in the culture as a whole.

When philosophers of medical ethics confine themselves to discussing life-and-death issues of medicine, they help perpetuate the idea that the main purpose of medicine is to control the body. Life-and-death interventions are the ultimate exercise of control. If medical ethicists looked more closely at who needs and who receives medical help, they would discover a host of issues concerning how medicine and society understand, mediate, assist with and integrate experiences of illness, injury and disability.

Because of the heroic approach to medicine, and because disabled people's experience is not integrated into the culture, most people know little or nothing about how to live with long-term or life-threatening illness, how to communicate with doctors and nurses and medical bureaucrats about these matters, how to live with limitation, uncertainty, pain, nausea, and other symptoms when doctors cannot make them go away. Recently, patients' support groups have arisen to fill this gap for people with nearly every type of illness and disability. They are vitally important sources of knowledge and encouragement for many of us, but they do not fill the cultural gulf between the able-bodied and the disabled. The problems of living with a disability are not private problems, separable from the rest of life and the rest of society. They are problems which can and should be shared throughout the culture as much as we share the problems of love, work and family life.

Consider the example of pain. It is difficult for most people who have not lived with prolonged or recurring pain to understand the benefits of accepting it. Yet some people who live with chronic pain speak of "making friends" with it as the road to feeling better and enjoying life. How do they picture their pain and think about it; what kind of attention do they give it and when; how do they live around and through it, and what do they learn from it? We all need to know this as part of our education. Some of the fear of experiencing pain is a consequence of ignorance and lack of guidance. The effort to avoid pain contributes to such widespread problems as drug and alcohol addiction, eating disorders, and sedentary lives. People with painful disabilities can teach us about pain, because they *can't* avoid it and have had to learn how to face it and live with it. The pernicious myth that it is possible to avoid almost all pain by controlling the body gives the fear of pain greater power than it should have and blames the victims of unavoidable pain. The fear of pain is also expressed or displaced as a fear of people in pain, which often isolates those with painful disabilities. All this is unnecessary. People *in* pain and knowledge *of* pain could be fully integrated into our culture, to everyone's benefit.

If we knew more about pain, about physical limitation, about loss of abilities, about what it is like to be "too far" from the cultural ideal of the body, perhaps we would have less fear of the negative body, less fear of our own weaknesses and "imperfections," of our inevitable deterioration and death. Perhaps we could give up our idealizations and relax our desire for control of the body; until we do, we maintain them at the expense of disabled people and at the expense of our ability to accept and love our own real bodies.

DISABLED PEOPLE AS "OTHER"

When we make people "other," we group them together as the objects of *our* experience instead of regarding them as fellow *subjects* of experience with whom we might identify. If you are "other" to me, I see you primarily as symbolic of something else— usually, but not always, something I reject and fear and that I project onto you. We can all do this to each other, but very often the process is not symmetrical, because one group of people may have more power to call itself the paradigm of humanity and to make the world suit its own needs and validate its own experiences.[12] Disabled people are "other" to able-bodied people, and (as I have tried to show) the consequences are socially, economically and psychologically oppressive to the disabled and psychologically oppressive to the able-bodied. Able-bodied people may be "other" to disabled people, but the consequences of this for the able-bodied are minor (most able-bodied people can afford not to notice it). There are, however, several political and philosophical issues that being "other" to a more powerful group raises for disabled people.

I have said that for the able-bodied, the disabled often symbolize failure to control the body and the failure of science and medicine to protect us all. However, some disabled people also become symbols of heroic control against all odds; these are the "disabled heroes," who are comforting to the able-bodied because they reaffirm the possibility of overcoming the body. Disabled heroes are people with visible disabilities who receive public attention because they accomplish things that are unusual even for the able-bodied. It is revealing that, with few exceptions (Helen Keller and, very recently, Stephen Hawking are among them), disabled heroes are recognized for performing feats of physical strength and endurance. While disabled heroes can be inspiring and heartening to the disabled, they may give the able-bodied the false impression that anyone can "overcome" a disability. Disabled heroes usually have extraordinary social, economic and physical resources that are not available to most people with those disabilities. In addition, many disabled people are not capable of performing physical heroics, because many (perhaps most) disabilities reduce or consume the energy and stamina of people who have them and do not just limit them in some particular kind of physical activity. Amputee and wheelchair athletes are exceptional, not because of their ambition, discipline and hard work, but because they are in better health than most disabled people can be. Arthritis, Parkinsonism and stroke cause severe disability in far more people than do spinal cord injuries and amputations (Bury 1979). The image of the disabled hero may reduce the "otherness" of a few disabled people, but because it creates an ideal which most disabled people cannot meet, it *increases* the "otherness" of the majority of disabled people.

One recent attempt to reduce the "otherness" of disabled people is the introduction of the term, "differently-abled." I assume the point of using this term is to suggest that there is nothing *wrong* with being the way we are, just different. Yet to call someone "differently-abled" is much like calling her "differently-coloured" or "differently-gendered." It says: "This person is not the norm or paradigm of humanity." If anything, it increases the "otherness" of disabled people, because it reinforces the paradigm of humanity as young, strong and healthy, with all body parts working "perfectly," from which this person is "different." Using the term "differently-abled" also suggests a (polite? patronizing? protective? self-protective?) disregard of the special difficulties, struggles and suffering disabled people face. We are *dis-abled*. We live with particular social and physical struggles that are partly consequences of the conditions of our bodies and partly consequences of the structures and expectations of our societies, but they are struggles which only people with bodies like ours experience.

The positive side of the term "differently-abled" is that it might remind the able bodied that to be disabled in some respects is not to be disabled in all respects. It also suggests that a disabled person may have abilities that the able-bodied lack in virtue of being able-bodied. Nevertheless, on the whole, the term "differently-abled" should be abandoned, because it reinforces the able-bodied paradigm of humanity and fails to acknowledge the struggles disabled people face.

The problems of being "the other" to a dominant group are always politically complex. Our solution is to emphasize similarities to the dominant group in the hope that they will identify with the oppressed, recognize their rights, gradually give them equal opportunities, and eventually assimilate them. Many disabled people are tired of being symbols to the able-bodied, visible only or primarily for their disabilities, and they want nothing more than to be seen as individuals rather than as members of the group, "the disabled." Emphasizing similarities to the able-bodied, making their disabilities unnoticeable in comparison to their other human qualities may bring about assimilation one-by-one. It does not directly challenge the able-bodied paradigm of humanity, just as women moving into traditionally male arenas of both may produce a gradual change in the paradigms. In addition, assimilation may be very difficult for the disabled to achieve. Although the able-bodied like disabled tokens who do not seem very different from themselves, they may *need* someone to carry the burden of the negative body as long as they continue to idealize and try to control the body. They may therefore resist the assimilation of most disabled people.

The reasons in favour of the alternative solution to "otherness"—*emphasizing differences* from the able-bodied—are also reasons for emphasizing similarities among the disabled, especially social and political similarities. Disabled people share positions of social oppression that separate us from the able-bodied, and we share physical, psychological and social experiences of disability. Emphasizing differences from the able-bodied demands that those differences be acknowledged and respected and fosters solidarity among the disabled. It challenges the able-bodied paradigm of humanity and creates the possibility of a deeper challenge to the idealization of the body and the demand for its control. Invisibly disabled people tend to be drawn to solutions that emphasize difference, because our need to have our struggles acknowledged is great, and we have far less experience than those who are visibly disabled of being symbolic to the able-bodied.

Whether one wants to emphasize sameness or difference in dealing with the problem of being "the other" depends in part on how radically one wants to challenge the value-structure of the dominant group. A very important issue in this category for both women and disabled people is the value of independence from the help of others, so highly esteemed in our patri-archal culture and now being questioned in feminist ethics (see, for example, Sherwin 1984, 1987; Kittay and Meyers 1987) and discussed in the writings of disabled women (see, for example, Fisher and Galler 1981; Davis 1984; Frank 1988). Many disabled people who can see the possibility of living as independently as any able-bodied person, or who have achieved this goal after long struggle, value their independence above everything. Dependence on the help of others is humiliating in a society which prizes independence. In addition, this issue holds special complications for disabled women; reading the stories of women who became disabled as adults, I was struck by their struggle with shame and loss of self-esteem at being transformed from people who took physical care of others (husbands and children) to people who were physically dependent. All this suggests that disabled people need every bit of independence we can get. Yet there are disabled people who will always need a lot of help from other individuals just to survive (those who have very little control of movement, for example), and to the extent that everyone considers independence necessary to respect and self-esteem, those people will be condemned to be de-valued. In addition, some disabled people spend tremendous energy being independent in ways that might be considered trivial in a culture less insistent on self-reliance; if our culture valued *interdependence* more highly, they could use that energy for more satisfying activities.

In her excellent discussion of the issue of dependency and independence, Barbara Hillyer Davis argues that women with disabilities and those who care for them can work out a model of *reciprocity* for all of us, if we are willing to learn from them. "Reciprocity involves the difficulty of recognizing each other's needs, relying on the other, asking and receiving help, delegating responsibility, giving and receiving empathy, respecting boundaries" (Davis 1984,

4). I hope that disabled and able-bodied feminists will join in questioning our cultural obsession with independence and ultimately replacing it with such a model of reciprocity. If *all* the disabled are to be fully integrated into society without symbolizing failure, then we have to change social values to recognize the value of depending on other and being depended upon. This would also reduce the fear and shame associated with dependency in old age—a condition most of us will reach.

Whether one wants to emphasize sameness or difference in dealing with the problems of being "other" is also related to whether one sees anything valuable to be preserved by maintaining, either temporarily or in the long-run, some separateness of the oppressed group. Is there a special culture of the oppressed group or the seeds of a special culture which could be developed in a supportive context of solidarity? Do members of the oppressed group have accumulated knowledge or ways of knowing which might be lost if assimilation takes place without the dominant culture being transformed?

It would be hard to claim that disabled people as a whole have an alternative culture or even the seeds of one. One subgroup, the deaf, has a separate culture from the hearing, and they are fighting for its recognition and preservation, as well as for their right to continue making their own culture (Sacks 1988). Disabled people do have both knowledge and ways of knowing that are not available to the able-bodied. Although ultimately I hope that disabled people's knowledge will be integrated into the culture as a whole, I suspect that a culture which fears and denigrates the real body would rather silence this knowledge than make the changes necessary to absorb it. It may have to be nurtured and cultivated separately while the able-bodied culture is transformed enough to receive and integrate it.

THE KNOWLEDGE OF DISABLED PEOPLE AND HOW IT IS SILENCED

In my second year of illness, I was reading an article about the psychological and philosophical relationship of mind to body. When the author painted a rosy picture of the experience of being embodied, I was outraged at the presumption of the writer to speak for everyone from a healthy body. I decided I didn't want to hear *anything* about the body from anyone who was not physically disabled. Before that moment, it had not occurred to me that there was a world of experience from which I was shut out while I was able-bodied.

Not only do physically disabled people have experiences which are not available to the able-bodied, they are in a better position to transcend cultural mythologies about the body, because they *cannot* do things that the able-bodied fell they *must* do in order to be happy, "normal" and sane. For example, paraplegics and quadriplegics have revolutionary things to teach about the possibilities of sexuality which contradict patriarchal culture's obsession with the genitals (Bullard and Knight 1981). Some people can have orgasms in any part of their bodies where they feel touch. One man said he never knew how good sex could be until he lost the feeling in his genitals. Few able-bodied people know these things, and, to my knowledge, no one has explored their implications for the able-bodied.

If disabled people were truly heard, an explosion of knowledge of the human body and psyche would take place. We have access to realms of experience that our culture has not tapped (even for medical science, which takes relatively little interest in people's *experience* of their bodies). Like women's particular knowledge, which comes from access to experiences most men do not have, disabled people's knowledge is dismissed as trivial, complaining, mundane (or bizarre), *less than* that of the dominant group.

The cognitive authority (Addelson 1983) of medicine plays an important role in distorting and silencing the knowledge of the disabled. Medical professionals have been given the power to describe and validate everyone's experience of the body. If you go to doctors with symptoms they cannot observe directly or verify independently of what you tell them, such as pain or weakness or numbness or dizziness or difficulty concentrating, and if they cannot find an objectively observable cause of those symptoms, you are likely to be told that there is "nothing wrong with you," no matter how you feel. Unless you are very lucky in your doctors, no matter how trustworthy and responsible you were considered to be *before* you started saying you were ill, your experience will be invalidated.[13] *Other* people are the authorities on the reality of the experiences of your body.

When you are very ill, you desperately need medical validation of your experience, not only for economic reasons (insurance claims, pensions, welfare and disability benefits all depend upon official diagnosis), but also for social and psychological reasons. People with unrecognized illnesses are often abandoned by their friends and families.[14] Because almost everyone accepts the cognitive authority of medicine, the person whose bodily experience is radically different from medical descriptions of her/his condition is invalidated as a knower. Either you decide to hide your experience, or you are socially isolated with it by being labelled mentally ill[15] or dishonest. In both cases you are silenced.

Even when your experience is recognized by medicine, it is often re-described in ways that are inaccurate from your standpoint. The objectively observable condition of your body may be used to determine the severity of your pain, for instance, regardless of your own reports of it. For example, until recently, relatively few doctors were willing to acknowledge that severe phantom limb pain can persist for months or even years after an amputation. The accumulated experience of doctors who were themselves amputees has begun to legitimize the other patients' reports (Madruga 1979).

When you are forced to realize that other people have more social authority than you do to describe your experience of your own body, your confidence in yourself and your relationship to reality is radically undermined. What can you know if you cannot know that you are experiencing suffering or joy; what can you communicate to people who don't believe you know even this?[16] Most people will censor what they tell or say nothing rather than expose themselves repeatedly to such deeply felt invalidation. They are silenced by fear and confusion. The process is familiar from our understanding of how women are silenced in and by patriarchal culture.

One final caution: As with women's "special knowledge," there is a danger of sentimentalizing disabled people's knowledge and abilities and keeping us "other" by doing so. We need to bring this knowledge into the culture and to transform the culture and society so that everyone can receive and make use of it, so that it can be fully integrated, along with disabled people, into a shared social life.

CONCLUSION

I have tried to introduce the reader to the rich variety of intellectual and political issues that are raised by experiences of physical disability. Confronting these issues has increased my appreciation of the insights that feminist theory already offers into cultural attitudes about the body and the many form of social oppression. Feminists have been challenging medicine's authority for many years now, but not, I think, as radically as we would if we knew what disabled people have to tell. I look forward to the development of a full feminist theory of disability.[17] We need a theory of disability for the liberation of both disabled and able-bodied people, since the theory of disability is also the theory of the oppression of the body by a society and its culture.

NOTES

Many thanks to Kathy Gose, Joyce Frazee, Mary Barnes, Barbara Beach, Elliot Gose and Gordon Renwick for helping me to think about these questions, and to Maureen Ashfield for helping me to research them. Thanks also to the editors of the issue of *Hypatia* in which this article was originally published, Virginia Warren, and two anonymous reviewers for their work on editing an earlier version of the paper.

1. Itzhak Perlman, when asked in a recent CBC interview about the problems of the disabled, said disabled people have two problems: the fact that the world is not made for people with any weaknesses but for supermen and the attitudes of able-bodied people.

2. An excellent description of this last issue as it confronts the deaf is found in Sacks 1988.

3. See Matthews 1983; Hannaford 1985; Rooney and Israel (eds.) 1985, esp. the articles by Jill Weiss, Charlynn Toews, Myra Rosenfield, and Susan Russell; and, for a doctor's theories, Kleinman 1988.

4. We also need a feminist theory of mental disability, but I will not be discussing mental disability in this essay.

5. In a recent article in *Signs*, Linda Alcoff argues that we should define "woman" thus: "woman is a position from which a feminist politics can emerge rather than a set of attributes that are 'objectively identifiable.'" (Alcoff 1988, 435). I think a similar approach may be the best one for defining "disability."

6. For example, Pelvic Inflammatory Disease causes severe prolonged disability in some women. These women often have to endure medical diagnoses of psychological illness and the skepticism of family and friends, in addition to having to live with chronic severe pain. See Moore 1985.

7. Feminism has challenged the distribution of responsibility for providing such resources as childcare and protection from family violence. Increasingly many people who once thought of these as family or personal concerns now think of them as social responsibilities.

8. Some people save me that trouble by *telling me* I am fine and walking away. Of course, people also encounter difficulties with answering "How are you?" during and after crises, such as separation from a partner, death of a loved one, or a nervous breakdown. There is a temporary alienation from what is considered ordinary shared experience. In disability, the alienation lasts longer, often for a lifetime, and, in my experience, is more profound.

9. The idealization of the body is clearly related in complex ways to the economic processes of a consumer society. Since it pre-dated capitalism, we know that capitalism did not cause it, but it is undeniable that idealization now generates tremendous profits and that the quest for profit demands the reinforcement of idealization and the constant development of new ideals.

10. Susan Griffin, in a characteristically honest and insightful passage, describes an encounter with the fear that makes it hard to identify with disabled people. See Griffin 1982, 648–649.

11. Thanks to Joyce Frazee for pointing this out to me.

12. When Simone de Beauvoir uses this term to elucidate men's view of women (and women's view of ourselves), she emphasizes that Man is considered essential, Woman inessential; Man is the Subject, Woman the Other (de Beauvoir 1952, xvi). Susan Griffin expands upon this idea by showing how we project rejected aspects of ourselves onto groups of people who are designated the Other (Griffin 1981).

13. Many women with M.S. have lived through this nightmare in the early stages of their illness. Although this happens to men too, women's experience of the body, like women's experience generally, is more likely to be invalidated (Hannaford 1985).

14. Accounts of the experience of relatively unknown, newly discovered, or hard-to-diagnose diseases and conditions confirm this. See, for example, Jeffreys 1982, for the story of an experience of Chronic Fatigue Syndrome, which is more common in women than in men.

15. Frequently people with undiagnosed illnesses are sent by their doctors to psychiatrists, who cannot help and may send them back to their doctors saying they must be physically ill. This can leave patients in a dangerous medical and social limbo. Sometimes they commit suicide because of it (Ramsay 1986). Psychiatrists who know enough about living with physical illness or disability to help someone cope with it are rare.

16. For more discussion of his subject, see Zaner 1983 and Rawlinson 1983.

17. At this stage of the disability rights movement, it is impossible to anticipate everything that a full feminist theory will include, just as it would have been impossible to predict in 1970 the present state of feminist theory of mothering. Nevertheless, we can see that besides dealing more fully with the issues I have raised here, an adequate feminist theory of disability will examine all the ways in which disability is socially constructed; it will explain the interaction of disability with gender, race and class position; it will examine every aspect of the cognitive authority of medicine and science over our experiences of our bodies; it will discuss the relationship of technology to disability; it will question the belief that disabled lives are not worth living or preserving when it is implied in our theorizing about abortion and euthanasia; it will give us a detailed vision of the full integration of disabled people in society, and it will propose practical political strategies for the liberation of disabled people and the liberation of the able-bodied from the social oppression of their bodies.

REFERENCES

Addelson, Kathryn P. 1983. The man of professional wisdom. In *Discovering reality*. Sandra Harding and Merrill B. Hintikka, eds. Boston: D. Reidel.

Alcoff, Linda. 1988. Cultural feminism versus post-structuralism: The identity crisis in feminist theory. *Signs: Journal of Women in Culture and Society* 13(3): 405–436.

Bullard, David G. and Susan E. Knight, eds. 1981. *Sexuality and physical disability*. St. Louis: C. V. Mosby.

Bury, M. R. 1979. Disablement in society: Towards an integrated perspective. *International Journal of Rehabilitation Research* 2(1): 33–40.

Beauvoir, Simone de. 1952. *The second sex*. New York: Alfred A. Knopf.

Campling, Jo, ed. 1981. *Images of ourselves—women with disabilities talking*. London: Routledge and Kegan Paul.

Davis, Barbara Hillyer. 1984. Women, disability and feminism: Notes toward a new theory. *Frontiers: A Journal of Women Studies* VIII(1): 1–5.

Davis, Melanie and Catherine Marshall. 1987. Female and disabled: Challenged women in education. *National Women's Studies Association Perspectives* 5: 39–41.

Dinnerstein, Dorothy. 1976. *The mermaid and the minotaur: Sexual arrangements and human malaise*. New York: Harper and Row.

Ehrenreich, Barbara and Dierdre English. 1979. *For her own good: 150 years of the experts' advice to women*. New York: Anchor.

Fine, Michelle and Adrienne Asch, eds. 1988. *Women with disabilities: Essays in psychology, culture and politics*. Philadelphia: Temple University Press.

Finger, Anne. 1983. Disability and reproductive rights. *off our backs* 13(9): 18–19.

Fisher, Bernice and Robert Galler. 1981. Conversation between two friends about feminism and disability. *off our backs* 11(5): 14–15.

Frank, Gelya. 1988. On embodiment: A case study of congenital limb deficiency in American culture. In *Women with disabilities*. Michelle Fine and Adrienne Asch, eds. Philadelphia: Temple University Press.

Griffin, Susan. 1981. *Pornography and silence: Culture's revenge against nature*. New York: Harper and Row.

Halpern, Sue M. 1988. Portrait of the artist. Review of *Under the eye of the clock* by Christopher Nolan. *The New York Times Review of Books*, June 30: 3–4.

Hannaford, Susan. 1985. *Living outside inside. A disabled woman's experience. Towards a social and political perspective*. Berkeley: Canterbury Press.

Jeffreys, Toni. 1982. *The mile-high staircase*. Sydney: Hodder and Stoughton Ltd.

Kittay, Eva Feder and Diana T. Meyers, eds. 1987. *Women and moral theory*. Totowa, NJ: Rowman and Littlefield.

Kleinman, Arthur. 1988. *The illness narratives: Suffering, healing, and the human condition*. New York: Basic Books.

Lessing, Jill. 1981. Denial and disability. *off our backs* 11(5): 21.

Madruga, Lenor. 1979. One *step at a time*. Toronto: McGraw-Hill.

Matthews, Gwyneth Ferguson. 1983. *Voices from the shadows: Women with disabilities speak out*. Toronto: Women's Educational Press.

Moore, Maureen. 1985. Coping with pelvic inflammatory disease. In *Women and Disability*. Frances Rooney and Pat Israel, eds. *Resources for Feminist Research* 14(1).

Newsweek. 1988. Reading God's mind. June 13. 56–59.

Ramsay, A. Melvin. 1986. *Postviral fatigue syndrome, the saga of Royal Free disease*. London: Gower Medical Publishing.

Rawlinson, Mary. 1983. The facticity of illness and the appropriation of health. In *Phenomenology in a pluralistic context*. William L. McBride and Calvin O. Schrag, eds. Albany: SUNY Press.

Rich, Adrienne. 1976. *Of woman born: Motherhood as experience and institution*. New York: W. W. Norton.

Rooney, Frances and Pat Israel, eds. 1985. *Women and disability. Resources for Feminist Research* 14(1).

Sacks, Oliver. 1988. The revolution of the deaf. *The New York Review of Books*, June 2, 23–28.

Shaul, Susan L. and Jane Elder Bogle. 1981. Body image and the woman with a disability. In *Sexuality and physical disability*. David G. Bullard and Susan E. Knight, eds. St. Louis: C. V. Mosby.

Sherwin. Susan. 1984–85. A feminist approach to ethics. *Dalhousie Review* 64(4): 704–713.

Sherwin, Susan. 1987. Feminist ethics and in vitro fertilization. In *Science, morality and feminist theory*. Marsha Hanen and Kai Nielsen, eds. Calgary: The University of Calgary Press.

Sontag, Susan. 1977. *Illness as metaphor*. New York: Random House.

U.N. Decade of Disabled Persons 1983–1992. 1983. *World programme of action concerning disabled persons*. New York: United Nations.

Whitbeck, Caroline. Afterword to the maternal instinct. In *Mothering: Essays in feminist theory*. Joyce Trebilcot, ed. Totowa: Rowman and Allanheld.

Zaner, Richard M. 1983. Flirtations or engagement? Prolegomenon to a philosophy of medicine. In *Phenomenology in a pluralistic context*. Wilharn L. McBride and Calvin O. Schrag, eds. Albany: SUNY Press.

CHAPTER 26

Integrating Disability, Transforming Feminist Theory

Rosemarie Garland-Thomson

DISABILITY STUDIES AND FEMINIST STUDIES

Over the last several years, disability studies has moved out of the applied fields of medicine, social work, and rehabilitation to become a vibrant new field of inquiry within the critical genre of identity studies that has developed so productively in the humanities over the last twenty or so years. Charged with the residual fervor of the civil rights movement, women's studies and race studies established a model in the academy for identity-based critical enterprises that followed, such as gender studies, queer studies, disability studies, and a proliferation of ethnic studies, all of which have enriched and complicated our understandings of social justice, subject formation, subjugated knowledges, and collective action.

Even though disability studies is now flourishing in disciplines such as history, literature, religion, theater, and philosophy in precisely the same way feminist studies did twenty-five years ago, many of its practitioners do not recognize that disability studies is part of this larger undertaking that can be called identity studies. Indeed, I must wearily conclude that much of current disability studies does a great deal of wheel reinventing. This is largely due to the fact that many disability studies scholars simply don't know either feminist theory or the institutional history of women's studies. All too often the pronouncements in disability studies of what we need to start addressing are precisely issues that feminist theory has been grappling with for years. This is not to say that feminist theory can be transferred wholly and in tact over to the study of disability studies, but it is to suggest that feminist theory can offer profound insights, methods, and perspectives that would deepen disability studies.

Conversely, feminist theories all too often do not recognize disability in their litanies of identities that inflect the category of woman. Repeatedly, feminist issues that are intricately entangled with disability—such as reproductive technology, the place of bodily differences, the particularities of oppression, the ethics of care, the construction of the subject—are discussed without any reference to disability. Like disability studies practitioners unaware of feminism, feminist scholars are often simply unacquainted with disability studies perspectives. The most sophisticated and nuanced analyses of disability, in my view, come from scholars conversant with feminist theory. And the most compelling and complex analyses of gender intersectionality take into consideration what I call the ability/disability system—along with race, ethnicity, sexuality, and class.

I want to give the omissions I am describing here the most generous interpretation I can. The archive, Foucault has shown us, determines what we can know. There has been no archive, no template for understanding disability as a category of analysis and knowledge, as a cultural trope and an historical community. So just as the now widely recognized centrality of gender and race analyses to all knowledge was unthinkable thirty years ago, disability is still not an icon on many critical desktops now. I think, however, that feminist theory's omission of disability differs from disability studies' ignorance of feminist theory. I find feminist theory and those familiar with it quick to grasp the broad outlines of disability theory and eager to consider its implications. This, of course, is because feminist theory itself has undertaken internal critiques and proved to be porous and flexible. Disability studies is news, but feminist theory is not. Nevertheless, feminist theory is still resisted for exactly the same reasons that scholars might resist disability studies: the assumption that it is narrow, particular, and has little to do with the mainstream of academic practice and knowledge (or with themselves). This reductive notion that identity studies are intellectual ghettos limited to a narrow constituency demanding special pleading is the persistent obstacle that both feminist theory and disability studies must surmount.

Disability studies can benefit from feminist theory and feminist theory can benefit from disability studies. Both feminism and disability studies are comparative and concurrent academic enterprises. Just as feminism has expanded the lexicon of what we imagine as womanly, has sought to understand and destigmatize what we call the subject position of woman, so has disability studies examined the identity disability in the service of integrating disabled people more fully into our society. As such, both are insurgencies that are becoming institutionalized underpinning inquiries outside and inside the academy. A feminist disability theory builds on the strengths of both.

FEMINIST DISABILITY THEORY

My title here, "Integrating Disability, Transforming Feminist Theory," invokes and links two notions, integration and transformation, both of which are fundamental to the feminist project and to the larger civil rights movement that informed it. Integration suggests achieving parity by fully including that which has been excluded and subordinated. Transformation suggests reimagining established knowledge and the order of things. By alluding to integration and transformation, I set my own modest project of integrating disability into feminist theory in the politicized context of the civil rights movement in order to gesture toward the explicit relation that feminism supposes between intellectual work and a commitment to creating a more just, equitable, and integrated society.

This essay aims to amplify feminist theory by articulating and fostering feminist disability theory. In naming feminist disability studies here as an academic field of inquiry, I am sometimes describing work that is already underway, some of which explicitly addresses disability and some which gestures implicitly to the topic. At other times, I am calling for study that needs to be done to better illuminate feminist thought. In other words, this essay in part sets an agenda for future work in feminist disability theory. Most fundamentally, though, the goal of feminist disability theory, as I lay it out in this essay, is to augment the terms and confront the limits of the ways we understand human diversity, the materiality of the body, multiculturalism, and the social formations that interpret bodily differences. The fundamental point

I will make here is that integrating disability as a category of analysis and a system of representation deepens, expands, and challenges feminist theory.

Academic feminism is a complex and contradictory matrix of theories, strategies, pedagogies and practices. One way to think about feminist theory is to say that it investigates how culture saturates the particularities of bodies with meanings and probes the consequences of those meanings. Feminist theory is a collaborative, interdisciplinary inquiry and a self-conscious cultural critique that interrogates how subjects are multiply interpellated: in other words, how the representational systems of gender, race, ethnicity, ability, sexuality, and class mutually produce, inflect, and contradict one another. These systems intersect to produce and sustain ascribed, achieved, and acquired identities, both those that claim us and those that we claim for ourselves. A feminist disability theory introduces the ability/disability system as a category of analysis into this diverse and diffuse enterprise. It aims to extend current notions of cultural diversity and to more fully integrate the academy and the larger world it helps shape.

A feminist disability approach fosters more complex understandings of the cultural history of the body. By considering the ability/disability system, feminist disability theory goes beyond explicit disability topics such as illness, health, beauty, genetics, eugenics, aging, reproductive technologies, prosthetics, and access issues. Feminist disability theory addresses such broad feminist concerns as the unity of the category "woman," the status of the lived body, the politics of appearance, the medicalization of the body, the privilege of normalcy, multiculturalism, sexuality, the social construction of identity, and the commitment to integration. To borrow Toni Morrison's notion that blackness is an idea that permeates American culture, disability too is a pervasive, often unarticulated, ideology informing our cultural notions of self and other (Playing in the Dark 19). Disability—like gender—is a concept that pervades all aspects of culture: its structuring institutions, social identities, cultural practices, political positions, historical communities, and the shared human experience of embodiment.

Integrating disability into feminist theory is generative, broadening our collective inquires, questioning our assumptions, and contributing to feminism's multiculturalism. Introducing a disability analysis does not narrow the inquiry, limit the focus to only women with disabilities, or preclude engaging other manifestations of feminisms. Indeed, the multiplicity of foci we now call feminisms is not a group of fragmented, competing subfields, but rather a vibrant, complex conversation. In talking about "feminist disability theory," I am not proposing yet another discrete "feminism," but suggesting instead some ways that thinking about disability transforms feminist theory. Integrating disability does not obscure our critical focus on the registers of race, sexuality, ethnicity, or gender, nor is it additive (to use Gerda Lerner's famous idea). Rather, considering disability shifts the conceptual framework to strengthen our understanding of how these multiple systems intertwine, redefine, and mutually constitute one another. Integrating disability clarifies how this aggregate of systems operate together, yet distinctly, to support an imaginary norm and structure the relations that grant power, privilege, and status to that norm. Indeed, the cultural function of the disabled figure is to act as a synecdoche for all forms that culture deems non-normative.

We need to study disability in a feminist context to direct our highly honed critical skills toward the dual scholarly tasks of unmasking and reimagining disability, not only for people with disabilities but for everyone. As Simi Linton puts it, studying disability is "a prism through which one can gain a broader understanding of society and human experience" (1998, 118). It deepens the understanding of gender and sexuality, individualism and equality, minority group definitions, autonomy, wholeness, independence, dependence, health, physical appearance, aesthetics, the integrity of the body, community, and ideas of progress and perfection in every aspect of culture. A feminist disability theory introduces what Eve Sedgwick has called a "universalizing view" of disability that will replace an often persisting "minoritizing view." Such a view will cast disability as "an issue of continuing, determinative importance in the lives of people across the spectrum" (1990, 1). In other words, understanding how disability operates as an identity category and cultural concept will enhance how we understand what it is to be human, our relationships with one another, and the experience of embodiment. The constituency for a feminist disability theory is all of us, not only women with disabilities: disability is the most human of experiences, touching every family and—if we live long enough—touching us all.

THE ABILITY/DISABILITY SYSTEM

Feminist disability theory's radical critique hinges on a broad understanding of disability as a pervasive cultural system that stigmatizes certain kinds of bodily variations. At the same time, this system has the potential to incite a critical politics. The informing premise of feminist disability theory is that disability, like femaleness, is not a natural state of corporeal inferiority, inadequacy, excess, or a stroke of misfortune. Rather, disability is a culturally fabricated narrative of the body, similar to what we understand as the fictions of race and gender. The disability/ability system produces subjects by differentiating and marking bodies. Although this comparison of bodies is ideological rather than biological, it nevertheless penetrates into the formation of culture, legitimating an unequal distribution of resources, status, and power within a biased social and architectural environment. As such, disability has four aspects: first, it is a system for interpreting and disciplining bodily variations; second, it is a relationship between bodies and their environments; third, it is a set of practices that produce both the able-bodied and the disabled; fourth, it is a way of describing the inherent instability of the embodied self. The disability system excludes the kinds of bodily forms, functions, impairments, changes, or ambiguities that call into question our cultural fantasy of the body as a neutral, compliant instrument of some transcendent will. Moreover, disability is a broad term within which cluster ideological categories as varied as sick, deformed, abnormal, crazy, ugly, old, feebleminded, maimed, afflicted, mad, or debilitated—all of which disadvantage people by devaluing bodies that do not conform to cultural standards. Thus the disability system functions to preserve and validate such privileged designations as beautiful, healthy, normal, fit, competent, intelligent—all of which provide cultural capital to those who can claim such status, who can reside within these subject positions. It is, then, the various interactions between bodies and world that materialize disability from the stuff of human variation and precariousness.

A feminist disability theory denaturalizes disability by unseating the dominant assumption that disability is something that is wrong with someone. By this I mean, of course, that it mobilizes feminism's highly developed and complex critique of gender, class, race, ethnicity, and sexuality as exclusionary and oppressive systems rather than as the natural and appropriate order of things. To do this, feminist disability theory engages several of the fundamental premises of critical theory: 1) that representation structures reality; 2) that the margins define the center; 3) that gender (or disability) is a way of signifying relationships of power; 4) that human identity is multiple and unstable; 5) that all analysis and evaluation have political implications.

In order to elaborate on these premises, I discuss here four fundamental and interpenetrating domains of feminist theory and suggest some of the kinds of critical inquiries that considering disability can generate within these theoretical arenas. These domains are: 1) representation; 2) the body; 3) identity; 4) activism. While I have disentangled these domains here for the purposes of setting up a schematic organization for my analysis, these domains are, of course, not discrete in either concept or practice, but rather tend to be synchronous.

REPRESENTATION

The first domain of feminist theory that can be deepened by a disability analysis is representation. Western thought has long conflated femaleness and disability, understanding both as defective departures from a valued standard. Aristotle, for example, defined women as "mutilated males." Women, for Aristotle, have "improper form;" we are "monstrosit[ies]" (1944, 27–8; 8–9). As what Nancy Tuana calls "misbegotten men," women thus become the primal freaks in western history, envisioned as what we might now call congenitally deformed as a result of their what we might now term a genetic disability (1993, 18). More recently, feminist theorists have argued that female embodiment is a disabling condition in sexist culture. Iris Marion Young, for instance, examines how enforced feminine comportment delimits women's sense of embodied agency, restricting them to "throwing like a girl" (1990b, 141). Young asserts that, "Women

in a sexist society are physically handicapped" (1990b, 153). Even the general American public associates femininity and disability. A recent study on stereotyping showed that housewives, disabled people, blind people, so-called retarded people, and the elderly were judged as being similarly incompetent. Such a study suggests that intensely normatively feminine positions—such as a housewife—are aligned with negative attitudes about people with disabilities (Fiske 2001).[11]

Recognizing how the concept of disability has been used to cast the form and functioning of female bodies as non-normative can extend feminist critiques. Take, for example, the exploitation of Saartje Bartmann, the African woman exhibited as a freak in nineteenth-century Europe (Fausto Sterling 1995; Gilman 1985). Known as the Hottentot Venus, Bartmann's treatment has come to represent the most egregious form of racial and gendered degradation. What goes unremarked in studies of Bartmann's display, however, is the ways that the language and assumptions of the ability/disability system were implemented to pathologize and exoticize Bartmann. Her display invoked disability by presenting as deformities or abnormalities the characteristics that marked her as raced and gendered. I am not suggesting that Bartmann was disabled, but rather that the concepts of disability discourse framed her presentation to the western eye. Using disability as a category of analysis allows us to see that what was normative embodiment in her native context became abnormal to the western mind. More important, rather than simply supposing that being labeled as a freak is a slander, a disability analysis presses our critique further by challenging the premise that unusual embodiment is inherently inferior. The feminist interrogation of gender since Simone de Beauvoir has revealed how women are assigned a cluster of ascriptions, like Aristotle's, that mark us as Other. What is less widely recognized, however, is that this collection of interrelated characterizations is precisely the same set of supposed attributes affixed to people with disabilities.

The gender, race, and ability systems intertwine further in representing subjugated people as being pure body, unredeemed by mind or spirit. This sentence of embodiment is conceived of as either a lack or an excess. Women, for example, are considered castrated,—or to use Marge Piercy's wonderful term—"penis-poor" (1969). They are thought to be hysterical, or to have overactive hormones. Women have been cast as alternately having insatiable appetite in some eras and as pathologically self-denying in other times. Similarly, disabled people supposedly have extra chromosomes or limb deficiencies. The differences of disability are cast as atrophy, meaning degeneration, a hypertrophy, meaning enlargement. People with disabilities are described as having aplasia, meaning absence or failure of formation, or hypoplasia, meaning underdevelopment. All these terms police variation and reference a hidden norm from which the bodies of people with disabilities and women are imagined to depart.

Female, disabled, and dark bodies are supposed to be dependent, incomplete, vulnerable, and incompetent bodies. Femininity and race are the performance of disability. Women and the disabled are portrayed as helpless, dependent, weak, vulnerable, and incapable bodies. Women, the disabled, and people of color are always ready occasions for the aggrandizement of benevolent rescuers, whether strong males, distinguished doctors, abolitionists, or Jerry Lewis hosting his Telethons. For example, an 1885 medical illustration of a pathologically "love deficient" woman who fits the cultural stereotype of the ugly woman or perhaps the lesbian suggests how sexuality and appearance slide into the terms of disability. This illustration shows that the language of deficiency and abnormality used to simultaneously devalue women who depart from the mandates of femininity by equating them with disabled bodies. Such an interpretive move economically invokes the subjugating effect of one oppressive system to deprecate people marked by another system of representation.

Subjugated bodies are pictured as either deficient or as profligate. For instance, what Susan Bordo describes as the too-muchness of women also haunts disability and racial discourses, marking subjugated bodies as ungovernable, intemperate, or threatening (1993). The historical figure of the monster, as well, invokes disability, often to serve racism and sexism. Although the term has expanded to encompass all forms of social and corporeal aberration, monster originally described people with congenital impairments. As departures from the normatively human, monsters were seen as category violations or grotesque hybrids. The semantics of monstrosity are recruited to explain gender violations such as Julia Pastrana, for example, the Mexican Indian "bearded woman," whose body was displayed in nineteenth-century freak shows both during her lifetime and after her death. Pastrana's live and later embalmed body spectacularly confused and transgressed established cultural categories. Race, gender, disability, and sexuality augmented one another in Pastrana's display to produce a spectacle of embodied otherness that is simultaneously sensational, sentimental, and pathological (Thomson 1999). Furthermore much current feminist work theorizes figures of hybridity and excess such as monsters, grotesques, and cyborgs to suggest their transgressive potential for a feminist politics (Haraway 1991; Braidotti 1994; Russo 1994). However, this metaphorical invocation seldom acknowledges that these figures often refer to the actual bodies of people with disabilities.

Erasing real disabled bodies from the history of these terms compromises the very critique they intend to launch and misses an opportunity to use disability as a feminist critical category.

Such representations ultimately portray subjugated bodies not only as inadequate or unrestrained but at the same time as redundant and expendable. Bodies marked and selected by such systems are targeted for elimination by varying historical and cross-cultural practices. Women, people with disabilities or appearance impairments, ethnic others, gays and lesbians, and people of color are variously the objects of infanticide, selective abortion, eugenic programs, hate crimes, mercy killing, assisted suicide, lynching, bride burning, honor killings, forced conversion, coercive rehabilitation, domestic violence, genocide, normalizing surgical procedures, racial profiling, and neglect. All these discriminatory practices are legitimated by systems of representation, by collective cultural stories that shape the material world, underwrite exclusionary attitudes, inform human relations, and mold our senses of who we are. Understanding how disability functions along with other systems of representation clarifies how all the systems intersect and mutually constitute one another.

THE BODY

The second domain of feminist theory that a disability analysis can illuminate is the investigation of the body: its materiality, its politics, its lived experience, and its relation to subjectivity and identity. Confronting issues of representation is certainly crucial to the cultural critique of feminist disability theory. But we should not focus exclusively on the discursive realm. What distinguishes a feminist disability theory from other critical paradigms is that it scrutinizes a wide range of material practices involving the lived body. Perhaps because women and the disabled are cultural signifiers for the body, their actual bodies have been subjected relentlessly to what Michel Foucault calls "discipline" (1979). Together, the gender, race, ethnicity, sexuality, class, and ability systems exert tremendous social pressures to shape, regulate, and normalize subjugated bodies. Such disciplining is enacted primarily through the two interrelated cultural discourses of medicine and appearance.

Feminist disability theory offers a particularly trenchant analysis of the ways that the female body has been medicalized in modernity. As I have already suggested, both women and the disabled have been imagined as medically abnormal—as the quintessential "sick" ones. Sickness is gendered feminine. This gendering of illness has entailed distinct consequences in everything from epidemiology and diagnosis to prophylaxis and therapeutics.

Perhaps feminist disability theory's most incisive critique is revealing the intersections between the politics of appearance and the medicalization of subjugated bodies. Appearance norms have a long history in western culture, as is witnessed by the anthropometric composite figures of ideal male and female bodies made by Dudley Sargent in 1893. The classical ideal was to be worshiped rather than imitated, but increasingly in modernity the ideal has migrated to become the paradigm which is to be attained. As many feminist critics have pointed out, the standardization of the female body that the beauty system mandates has become a goal to be achieved through self-regulation and consumerism (Wolf 1991; Haiken 1997). Feminist disability theory suggests that appearance and health norms often have similar disciplinary goals. For example, the body braces developed in the 1930s to "correct" scoliosis, discipline the body to conform to the dictates of both the gender and the ability systems by enforcing standardized female form similarly to the nineteenth-century corset, which, ironically, often disabled female bodies. Although both devices normalize bodies, the brace is part of medical discourse while the corset is cast as a fashion practice.

Similarly, a feminist disability theory calls into question the separation of reconstructive and cosmetic surgery, recognizing their essentially normalizing function as what Sander L. Gilman calls "aesthetic surgery" (1998). Cosmetic surgery, driven by gender ideology and market forces, now enforces feminine body standards and standardizes female bodies toward what I have called the "normate"—the corporeal incarnation of culture's collective, unmarked, normative characteristics (1997, 8). Cosmetic surgery's twin, reconstructive surgery, eliminates disability and enforces the ideals of what might be thought of as the normalcy system. Both cosmetic and reconstructive procedures commodify the body and parade mutilations as enhancements that correct flaws so as to improve the psychological well being of the patient. The conception of the body as what Susan Bordo terms "cultural plastic" increasingly through surgical and medical interventions pressures people with disabilities or appearance impairments to become what Michel Foucault calls "docile bodies." (1993, 246; 1979, 135). The twin ideologies of normalcy and beauty posit female and disabled bodies, particularly, as not only spectacles to be looked at, but as pliable bodies to be shaped infinitely so as to conform to a set of standards called "normal" and "beautiful."

Normal has inflected beautiful in modernity. What is imagined as excess body fat, the effects of aging, marks of ethnicity such as "jewish" noses, bodily particularities thought of as blemishes or deformities, and marks of history such as scarring and impairments are now expected to be surgically erased to produce an unmarked body. This visually unobtrusive body may then pass unnoticed within the milieu of anonymity that is the hallmark of social relations beyond the personal in modernity. The point of aesthetic surgery, as well as the costuming of power, is not to appear unique—or to "be yourself," as the ads endlessly promise—but rather not to be conspicuous, not to look different. This flight from the nonconforming body translates into individual efforts to look normal, neutral, unmarked, to *not* look disabled, queer, ugly, fat, ethnic, or raced. For example, beauty is set out comparatively and supposedly self-evidently in an 1889 treatise called *The New Physiogomy* which juxtaposed a white, upper-class English face called "Princess Alexandra" with a stereotypical face of an Irish immigrant, called "Sally Muggins" in a class and ethnic-based binary of apparently self-evident beauty and ugliness. Beauty, then, dictates corporeal standards that create not distinction but utter conformity to a bland look that is at the same time unachievable so as to leash us to consumer practices that promise to deliver such sameness. In the language of contemporary cosmetic surgery, the unreconstructed female body is persistently cast as having abnormalities that can be corrected by surgical procedures which supposedly improve one's appearance by producing ostensibly natural looking noses, thighs, breasts, chins, and so on. Thus, our unmodified bodies are presented as unnatural and abnormal while the surgically altered bodies are portrayed as normal and natural. The beautiful woman of the twenty-first century is sculpted surgically from top to bottom, generically neutral, all irregularities regularized, all particularities expunged. She is thus non-disabled, deracialized, and de-ethnicized.

In addition, the politics of prosthetics enters the purview of feminism when we consider the contested use of breast implants and prostheses for breast cancer survivors. The famous 1993 *New York Times* cover photo of the fashion model, Matushka, baring her mastectomy scar or Audre Lorde's account of breast cancer in *The Cancer Journals* challenge the sexist assumption that the amputated breast must always pass for the normative, sexualized one either through concealment or prosthetics (1980). A vibrant feminist conversation has emerged about the politics of the surgically altered, the disabled, breast. Diane Price Herndl challenges Audre Lorde's refusal of a breast prosthesis after mastectomy and Iris Marion Young's classic essay "Breasted Experience" queries the cultural meanings of breasts under the knife (2002; 1990a).

Another entanglement of appearance and medicine involves the spectacle of the female breast, both normative and disabled. In January 2000, the San Francisco-based Breast Cancer Fund mounted "Obsessed with Breasts," a public awareness poster campaign showing women boldly displaying mastectomy scars. The posters parodied familiar commercial media sites—a Calvin Klein perfume ad, a Cosmopolitan magazine cover, and a Victoria Secret catalog cover—that routinely parade women's breasts as upscale soft porn. The posters replace the now unremarkable eroticized breast with the forbidden image of the amputated breast. In doing so, they disrupt the visual convention of the female breast as sexualized object for male appropriation and pleasure. The posters thus produce a powerful visual violation by exchanging the spectacle of the eroticized breast, which has been desensationalized by its endless circulation, with the medicalized image of the scarred breast, which has been concealed from public view. The Breast Cancer Fund used these remarkable images to challenge both sexism in medical research and treatment for breast cancer as well as the oppressive representational practices that make everyday erotic spectacles of women's breasts while erasing the fact of the amputated breast.

Feminist disability theory can press far its critique of the pervasive will-to-normalize the non-standard body. Take two related examples: first, the surgical separation of conjoined twins and, second, the surgical assignment of gender for the intersexed, people with ambiguous genitalia and gender characteristics. Both these forms of embodiment are regularly—if infrequently—occurring, congenital bodily variations that spectacularly violate sacred ideologies of western culture. Conjoined twins contradict our notion of the individual as discrete and autonomous—actually, quite similarly to the way pregnancy does. Intersexed infants challenge our insistence that biological gender is unequivocally binary. So threatening to the order of things is the natural embodiment of conjoined twins and intersexed people that they are almost always surgically normalized through amputation and mutilation immediately after birth (Clark and Myser 1996; Dreger 1998a; Kessler 1990; Fausto-Sterling 2000). Not infrequently, one conjoined twin is sacrificed to save the other from the supposed abnormality of their embodiment. Such mutilations are justified as preventing suffering and creating well adjusted individuals. So intolerable is their insult to dominant ideologies about who patriarchal culture insists that we are that the testimonies of adults with these forms of embodiment who say that they do not want to be separated is routinely ignored in establishing the rationale for "medical treatment." (Dreger 1998b). In truth, these procedures benefit not the affected individuals, but rather they expunge the kinds of corporeal human variations that contradict the ideologies the dominant order depends upon to anchor truths it insists are unequivocally encoded in bodies.

I do not want to oversimplify here by suggesting that women and disabled people should not use modern medicine to improve their lives or help their bodies function more fully. But the critical issues are complex and provocative. A feminist disability theory should illuminate and explain, not become ideological policing or set orthodoxy. The kinds of critical analyses I'm discussing here offer a counter logic to the overdetermined cultural mandates to comply with normal and beautiful at any cost. The medical commitment to healing, when coupled with modernity's faith in technology and interventions that control outcomes, has increasingly shifted toward an aggressive intent to fix, regulate, or eradicate ostensibly deviant bodies. Such a program of elimination has often been at the expense of creating a more accessible environment or providing better support services for people with disabilities. The privileging of medical technology over less ambitious programs such as rehabilitation has encouraged the cultural conviction that disability can be extirpated, inviting the belief that life with a disability is intolerable. As charity campaigns and telethons repeatedly affirm, cure rather than adjustment or accommodation is the overdetermined cultural response to disability (Longmore 1997). For instance, a 1949 March of Dimes poster shows an appealing little girl stepping out of her wheelchair into the supposed redemption of walking: "Look, I Can Walk Again!" the text proclaims while at once charging the viewers with the responsibility of assuring her future ambulation. Nowhere do we find posters suggesting that life as a wheelchair user might be full and satisfying, as many people who actually use them find their lives to be. This ideology of cure is not isolated in medical texts or charity campaigns, but in fact permeates the entire cultural conversation about disability and illness. Take, for example, the discourse of cure in get well cards. A 1950 card, for instance, urges its recipient to "snap out of it." Fusing racist, sexist, and ablist discourses, the card recruits the Mammy figure to insist on cure. The stereotypical racist figure asks, " Is you sick, Honey?" and then exhorts the recipient of her care to "jes hoodoo all dat illness out o you."

The ideology of cure directed at disabled people focuses on changing bodies imagined as abnormal and dysfunctional rather than on exclusionary attitudinal, environmental and economic barriers. The emphasis on cure reduces the cultural tolerance for human variation and vulnerability by locating disability in bodies imagined as flawed rather than social systems in need of fixing. A feminist disability studies would draw an important distinction between prevention and elimination. Preventing illness, suffering, and injury is a humane social objective. Eliminating the range of unacceptable and devalued bodily forms and functions the dominant order calls disability is, on the other hand, a eugenic undertaking. The ostensibly progressive socio-medical project of eradicating disability all too often is enacted as a program to eliminate people with disabilities through such practices as forced sterilization, so-called physician-assisted suicide and mercy killing, selective abortion, institutionization, and segregation policies.

A feminist disability theory extends its critique of the normalization of bodies and the medicalization of appearance to challenge some widely held assumptions about reproductive issues as well. The cultural mandate to eliminate the variations in form and function that we think of as disabilities has undergirded the reproductive practices of genetic testing and selective abortion (Saxton 1998; Parens and Asch 2000; Rapp 1999). Some disability activists argue that the "choice" to abort fetuses with disabilities is a coercive form of genocide against the disabled (Hubbard

1990). A more nuanced argument against selective abortion comes from Adrienne Asch and Gail Geller, who wish to preserve a woman's right choose whether to bear a child, but who at the same time objects to the ethics of selectively aborting a wanted fetus because it will become a person with a disability (1996). Asch and Geller counter the quality-of-life and prevention-of-suffering arguments so readily invoked to justify selective abortion, as well as physician-assisted suicide, by pointing out that we cannot predict or—more precisely—control in advance such equivocal human states as happiness, suffering, or success. Neither is any amount of prenatal engineering going to produce the life that any of us desire and value. Indeed, both hubris and a lack of imagination characterize the prejudicial and reductive assumption that having a disability ruins lives. A vague notion of suffering and its potential deterrence drives much of the logic of elimination that rationalizes selective abortion (Kittay 2000). Life chances and quality are simply far too contingent to justify prenatal prediction.

Similarly, genetic testing and applications of the Human Genome Project as the key to expunging disability are often critiqued as enactments of eugenic ideology, what the feminist biologist Evelyn Fox Keller calls a "eugenics of normalcy" (1992). The popular utopian notion that all forms of disability can be eliminated through prophylactic manipulation of genetics will only serve to intensify the prejudice against those who inevitably will acquire disabilities through aging and encounters with the environment. In the popular celebrations of the Human Genome Project as the quixotic pinnacle of technological progress, seldom do we hear a cautionary logic about the eugenic implications of this drive toward what Priscilla Wald calls "Future Perfect" (2000, 1). Disability scholars have entered the debate over so-called

physician-assisted suicide, as well, by arguing that oppressive attitudes toward disability distort the possibility of unbiased free choice (Battin et al. 1998). The practices of genetic and prenatal testing as well as physician-administered euthanasia, then, become potentially eugenic practices within the context of a culture deeply intolerant of disability. Both the rhetoric and the enactment of this kind of disability discrimination create a hostile and exclusionary environment for people with disabilities that perhaps exceeds the less virulent architectural barriers that keep them out of the workforce and the public sphere.

Integrating disability into feminism's conversation about the place of the body in the equality and difference debates produces fresh insights as well. Whereas liberal feminism emphasizes sameness, choice, and autonomy, cultural feminism critiques the premises of liberalism. Out of cultural feminism's insistence on difference and its positive interpretation of feminine culture comes the affirmation of a feminist ethic of care. This ethic of care contends that care giving is a moral benefit for its practitioners and for humankind. A feminist disability studies complicates both the feminist ethic of care and liberal feminism in regard to the politics of care and dependency.

A disability perspective nuances feminist theory's consideration of the ethics of care by examining the power relations between the givers and receivers of care. Anita Silvers has argued strongly that being the object of care precludes the equality that a liberal democracy depends upon and undermines the claim to justice as equality that undergirds a civil rights approach used to counter discrimination (1995). Eva Kittay, on the other hand, formulates a "dependency critique of equality" (1999, 4), which asserts that the ideal of equality under liberalism repudiates the fact of human dependency, the need for mutual care, and the asymmetries of care relations. Similarly, Barbara Hillyer has called attention to dependency in order to critique a liberal tendency in the rhetoric of disability rights (1993). Disability itself demands that human interdependence and the universal need for assistance be figured into our dialogues about rights and subjectivity.

IDENTITY

The third domain of feminist theory that a disability analysis complicates is identity. Feminist theory has productively and rigorously critiqued the identity category of woman, on which the entire feminist enterprise seemed to rest. Feminism increasingly recognizes that no woman is ever *only* a woman, that she occupies multiple subject positions and is claimed by several cultural identity categories (Spelman 1988). This complication of *woman* compelled feminist theory to turn from an exclusively male/female focus to look more fully at the exclusionary, essentialist, oppressive, and binary aspects of the category woman itself. Disability is one such identity vector that disrupts the unity of the classification woman and challenges the primacy of gender as a monolithic category.

Disabled women are, of course, a marked and excluded—albeit quite varied—group within the larger social class of women. The relative privileges of normative femininity are often denied to disabled women (Fine and Asch 1988). Cultural stereotypes imagine disabled women as asexual, unfit to reproduce, overly dependent, unattractive—as generally removed from the sphere of true womanhood and feminine beauty. Woman with disabilities often must often struggle to have their sexuality and rights to bear children recognized (Finger 1990). Disability thus both intensifies and attenuates the cultural scripts of femininity. Aging is a form of disablement that disqualifies older women from the limited power allotted females who are young and meet the criteria for attracting men. Depression, anorexia, and agoraphobia are female-dominant, psycho-physical disabilities that exaggerate normative gendered roles. Feminine cultural practices such as foot binding, clitorectomies, and corsetting, as well as their less hyperbolic costuming rituals such as stiletto high heels, girdles, and chastity belts—impair women's bodies and restrict their physical agency, imposing disability on them.

Banishment from femininity can be both a liability and a benefit. Let me offer—with some irony- an instructive example from popular culture. Barbie, that cultural icon of femininity, offers a disability analysis that clarifies both how multiple identity and diversity is commodified and how the commercial realm might offers politically useful feminist counterimages. Perhaps the measure of a group's arrival into the mainstream of multiculturalism is to be represented in the Barbie pantheon. While Barbie herself still identifies as able-bodied—despite her severely deformed body—we now have several incarnations of Barbie's "friend," Share-A-Smile Becky. One Becky uses a cool hot pink wheelchair; another is Paralympic Champion Becky, brought out for the 2000 Sydney Olympics in a chic red-white-and-blue warm-up suit with matching chair. Most interesting however is Becky, the school photographer, clad in a preppy outfit, complete with camera and red high-top sneakers. As she perkily gazes at an alluring Barbie in her camera's viewfinder, this Becky may be the incarnation of what one scholar has called "Barbie's queer assessories" (Rand 1995).

A disabled, queer Becky is certainly a provocative and subversive fusion of stigmatized identities, but more important is that Becky challenges notions of normalcy in feminist ways. The disabled Becky, for example, wears comfortable clothes: pants with elastic-waists no doubt, sensible shoes, and roomy shirts. Becky is also one of the few dolls who has flat feet and legs that bend at the knee. The disabled Becky is dressed and poised for agency, action, and creative engagement with the world. In contrast, the prototypical Barbie performs excessive femininity in her restrictive sequined gowns, crowns, and push-up bras. So while Becky implies on the one hand that disabled girls are purged from the feminine economy, on the other hand Becky also suggests that disabled girls might be liberated from those oppressive and debilitating scripts. The last word on Barbies comes from a disability activist who quipped that he'd like to outfit a disabled doll with a power wheelchair chair and a briefcase to make her a civil rights lawyer who enforces the Americans with Disabilities Act. He wants to call her "Sue-Your-Ass-Becky."[22] I think she'd make a very good role model.

The paradox of Barbie and Becky, of course, is that the ultra-feminized Barbie is a target for sexual appropriation both by men and beauty practices while the disabled Becky escapes such sexual objectification at the potential cost of losing her sense of identity as a feminine sexual being. Some disabled women negotiate this possible identity crisis by developing alternate sexualities, such as lesbianism (Brownsworth and Raffo 1999). However, what Harlan Hahn calls the "asexual objectification" of people with disabilities complicates the feminist critique of normative sexual objectification (1988). Consider the 1987 *Playboy* magazine photos of the paraplegic actress Ellen Stohl. After becoming disabled, Stohl wrote to editor Hugh Hefner that she wanted to pose nude for *Playboy* because "sexuality is the hardest thing for disabled persons to hold onto." ("Meet Ellen Stohl," 68.) For Stohl, it would seem that the performance of excessive feminine sexuality was necessary to counter the social interpretation that disability cancels

out sexuality. This confirmation of normative heterosexuality was then for Stohl no Butlerian parody, but rather was the affirmation she needed as a disabled woman to be sexual at all.

Ellen Stohl's presentation by way of the sexist conventions of the porn magazine illuminates the relation between identity and the body, an aspect of subject formation that disability analysis can offer. Although binary identities are conferred from outside through social relations, these identities are nevertheless inscribed on the body as either manifest or incipient visual traces. Identity's social meaning turns on this play of visibility. The photos of Stohl in *Playboy* both refuse and insist on marking her impairment. The centerfold spread—so to speak—of Stohl nude and masturbating erases her impairment to conform to the sexualized conventions of the centerfold. This photo expunges her wheelchair and any other visual clues to her impairment. In other words, to avoid the cultural contradiction of a sexual disabled woman, the pornographic photos must offer up Stohl as visually nondisabled. But to appeal to the cultural narrative of overcoming disability that sells so well, seems novel, and capitalizes on sentimental interest, Stohl must be visually dramatized as disabled at the same time. So *Playboy* includes several shots of Stohl that mark her as disabled by picturing her in her wheelchair, entirely without the typical porn conventions. In fact, the photos of her using her wheelchair invoke the asexual poster child. Thus, the affirmation of Stohl's sexuality she sought by posing nude in the porn magazine came at the expense of denying through the powerful visual register her identity as a woman with a disability, even while she attempted to claim that identity textually.

Another aspect of subject formation that disability confirms is that identity is always in transition. Disability reminds us that the body is, as Denise Riley asserts, "an unsteady mark, scarred in its long decay" (Riley 1999, 224). As Caroline Walker Bynum's intriguing work on werewolf narratives suggests, the body is in a perpetual state of transformation (1999). Caring for her father for over twenty years of Alzheimer's disease prompted Bynum to investigate how we can understand individual identity as continuous even though both body and mind can and do change dramatically, certainly over a lifetime and sometimes quite suddenly. Disability invites us to query what the continuity of the self might depend upon if the body perpetually metamorphoses. We envision our racial, gender, or ethnic identities as tethered to bodily traits that are relatively secure. Disability and sexual identity, however, seem more fluid, although sexual mutability is imagined as elective where disability is seldom conceived of as a choice. Disability is an identity category that anyone can enter at any time, and we will all join it if we live long enough. As such, disability reveals the essential dynamism of identity. Thus, disability attenuates the cherished cultural belief that the body is the unchanging anchor of identity. Moreover, it undermines our fantasies of stable, enduring identities in ways that may illuminate the fluidity of all identity.

Disability's clarification of the body's corporeal truths suggests as well that the body/self materializes—in Judith Butler's sense—not so much through discourse, but through history (1993). The self materializes in response to an embodied engagement with its environment, both social and concrete. The disabled body is a body whose variations or transformations have rendered it out of sync with its environment, both the physical and the attitudinal environments. In other words, the body becomes disabled when it is incongruent both in space and the milieu of expectations. Furthermore, a feminist disability theory presses us to ask what kinds of knowledge might be produced through having a body radically marked by its own particularity, a body that materializes at the ends of the curve of human variation. For example, an alternative epistemology that emerges from the lived experience of disability is nicely summed up in Nancy Mairs' book title, *Waist High in the World*, which she irreverently considered calling "cock high in the world." What perspectives or politics arise from encountering the world from such an atypical position? Perhaps Mairs' epistemology can offer us a critical positionality called sitpoint theory, a neologism I can offer that interrogates the ableist assumptions underlying the notion of standpoint theory (Harstock 1983).

Our collective cultural consciousness emphatically denies the knowledge of bodily vulnerability, contingency, and mortality. Disability insists otherwise, contradicting such phallic ideology. I would argue that disability is perhaps the essential characteristic of being human. The body is dynamic, constantly interactive with history and environment. We evolve into disability. Our bodies need care; we all need assistance to live. An equality model of feminist theory sometimes prizes individualistic autonomy as the key to women's liberation. A feminist disability theory, however, suggests that we are better off learning to individually and collectively accommodate the body's limits and evolutions than trying to eliminate or deny them.

Identity formation is at the center of feminist theory. Disability can complicate feminist theory often quite succinctly by invoking established theoretical paradigms. This kind of theoretical intertextuality inflects familiar feminist concepts with new resonance. Let me offer several examples: the idea of "compulsory ablebodiedness," which Robert McRuer has coined, extends Adrienne Rich's famous analysis of "compulsory heterosexuality" (2001, 1986). Joan

Wallach Scott's germinal work on gender is recruited when we discuss disability as "a useful category of analysis" (1988, 1). The feminist elaboration of the gender system informs my use of the disability system. Lennard Davis suggests that the term *normalcy studies* supplant the name *disability studies*, in the way that *gender studies* sometimes succeeds *feminism* (1995). The oft invoked distinction between sex and gender clarifies a differentiation between impairment and disability, even though both binaries are fraught. The concept of performing disability, cites (as it were) Judith Butler's vigorous critique of essentialism (1990). Reading disabled bodies as exemplary instances of "docile bodies" invokes Foucault (1979). To suggest that identity is lodged in the body, I propose that the body haunts the subject, alluding to Susan Bordo's notion regarding masculinity that "the penis haunts the phallus" (1994, 1). My own work has complicated the familiar discourse of the gaze to theorize what I call the stare, which I argue produces disability identity. Such theoretical shorthand impels us to reconsider the ways that identity categories cut across and redefine one another, pressuring both the terms *woman* and *disabled.*

A feminist disability theory can also highlight intersections and convergences with other identity-based critical perspectives such as queer and ethnic studies. Disability coming-out stories, for example, borrow from gay and lesbian identity narratives to expose what previously was hidden, privatized, medicalized in order to enter into a political community. The politicized sphere into which many scholars come out is feminist disability studies, which enables critique, claims disability identity, and creates affirming counter narratives. Disability coming-out narratives raise questions about the body's role in identity by asking how markers so conspicuous as crutches, wheelchairs, hearing

aides, guide dogs, white canes, or empty sleeves could ever have been closeted.

Passing as nondisabled complicates ethnic and queer studies' analyses of how this seductive but psychically estranging access to privilege operates. Some of my friends, for example, have measured their regard for me by saying, "But I don't think of you as disabled." What they point to in such a compliment is the contradiction they find between their perception of me as a valuable, capable, lovable person and the cultural figure of the disabled person whom they take to be precisely my opposite: worthless, incapable, and unlovable. People with disabilities themselves routinely announce that they don't consider themselves as disabled. Although they are often repudiating the literal meaning of the word *disabled*, their words nevertheless serve to disassociate them from the identity group of the disabled. Our culture offers profound disincentives and few rewards to identifying as disabled. The trouble, of course, with such statements is that they leave intact without challenge the oppressive stereotypes that permit, among other things, the unexamined use of disability terms such as *crippled, lame, dumb, idiot, moron* as verbal gestures of derision. The refusal to claim disability identity is in part due to a lack of ways to understand or talk about disability that are not oppressive. People with disabilities and those who care about them flee from the language of *crippled* or *deformed* and have no other alternatives. Yet, the civil rights movement and the accompanying Black-is-beautiful identity politics have generally shown white culture what is problematic with saying to Black friends, "I don't think of you as Black." Nonetheless, by disavowing disability identity, many of us learned to save ourselves from devaluation by a complicity that perpetuates oppressive notions about ostensibly "real" disabled people. Thus, together we help make the alternately menacing and pathetic cultural figures who rattle tin cups or rave on street corners, ones we with impairments often flee from more surely than those who imagine themselves as nondisabled.

ACTIVISM

The final domain of feminist theory that a disability analysis expands is activism. There are many arenas of what can be seen as feminist disability activism: marches, protests, the Breast Cancer Fund poster campaign I discussed above, action groups such as the Intersex Society of North America (ISNA), and Not Dead Yet, who oppose physician-assisted suicide, or the American Disabled for Accessible Public Transit (ADAPT). What counts as activism cuts a wide swath through U.S. society and the academy. I want to suggest here two unlikely, even quirky, cultural practices that function in activist ways but are seldom considered as potentially transformative. One practice is disabled fashion modeling and the other is academic tolerance. Both are different genres of activism from the more traditional marching-on-Washington or chaining-yourself-to-a-bus modes. Both are less theatrical, but perhaps fresher and more interestingly controversial ways to change the social landscape and to promote equality, which I take to be the goal of activism.

The theologian and sociologist, Nancy Eiesland, has argued that in addition to legislative, economic, and social changes, achieving equality for people with disabilities depends upon cultural "resymbolization" (1994, 98). Eiesland asserts that the way we imagine disability and disabled people must shift in order for real social change to occur. Whereas Eiesland's work resymbolizes our conceptions of disability in religious iconography, my own examinations of disabled fashion models do similar cultural work in the popular sphere, introducing some interesting complications into her notion of resymbolization.

Images of disabled fashion models in the media can shake up established categories and expectations. Because commercial visual media are the most widespread and commanding source of images in modern, image-saturated culture, they have great potential for shaping public consciousness–as feminist cultural critics are well aware. Fashion imagery is the visual distillation of the normative, gilded with the chic and the luxurious to render it desirable. The commercial sphere is completely amoral, driven as it is by the single logic of the bottom line. As we know, it sweeps through culture seizing with alarming neutrality anything it senses will sell. This value-free aspect of advertising produces a kind of pliable potency that sometimes can yield unexpected results.

Take, for example, a shot from the monthly fashion feature in *WE Magazine*, a *Cosmopolitan* knock-off targeted toward the disabled consumer market. In this conventional, stylized, high fashion shot, a typical female model—slender, white, blond, clad in a black evening gown—is accompanied by her service dog. My argument is that public images such as this are radical because they fuse two previously antithetical visual discourses—the chic high fashion shot and the earnest charity campaign. Public representations of disability have traditionally been contained within the conventions of sentimental charity images, exotic freak show portraits, medical illustrations, or sensational and forbidden pictures. Indeed, people with disabilities have been excluded most fully from the dominant, public world of the marketplace. Before the civil rights initiatives of the mid-twentieth century began to transform the public architectural and institutional environment, disabled people were segregated to the private and the medical spheres.

Until recently, the only available public image of a woman with a service dog that shaped the public imagination was street-corner beggar or a charity poster. By juxtaposing the elite body of a visually normative fashion model with the mark of disability, this image shakes up our assumptions about the normal and the abnormal, the public and the private, the chic and the desolate, the compelling and the repelling. Introducing a service dog—a standard prop of indigents and poster children—into the conventional composition of an upscale fashion photo forces the viewer to reconfigure assumptions about what constitutes the attractive and the desirable.

I am arguing that the emergence of disabled fashion models is inadvertent activism without any legitimate agent for positive social change. Their appearance is simply a result of market forces. This both troubling and empowering form of entry into democratic capitalism produces a kind of instrumental form of equality: the freedom to be appropriated by consumer culture. In a democracy, to reject this paradoxical liberty is one thing; not to be granted it is another. Ever straining for novelty and capitalizing on titillation, the fashion advertising world promptly appropriated the power of disabled figures to provoke responses. Diversity appeals to an upscale liberal sensibility these days, making consumers feel good about buying from companies that are charitable toward the traditionally disadvantaged. More important, the disability market is burgeoning. At 54 million people and growing fast as the baby boomers age, their spending power was estimated to have reached the trillion-dollar mark in 2000 (Williams 1999).

For the most part, commercial advertising that features disabled models are presented the same as nondisabled models, simply because all models look essentially the same. The physical markings of gender, race, ethnicity, and disability are muted to the level of gesture, subordinated to the overall normativity of the models' appearance. Thus, commercial visual media cast disabled consumers as simply one of many variations that compose the market to which they appeal. Such routinization of disability imagery—however stylized and unrealistic it may be—nevertheless brings disability as a human experience out of the closet and into the normative public sphere. Images of disabled fashion models enable people with disabilities, especially those who acquire impairments as adults, to imagine themselves as a part of the ordinary, albeit consumerist, world rather than as in a special class of excluded untouchables and unviewables. Images of impairment as a familiar, even mundane, experience in the lives of seemingly successful, happy, well-adjusted people can reduce the identifying against oneself that is the overwhelming effect of oppressive and discriminatory attitudes toward people with disabilities. Such images, then, are at once liberatory and oppressive. They do the cultural work of integrating a previously excluded group into the dominant order—for better or worse—much like the inclusion of women in the military.

This form of popular resymbolization produces counterimages that have activist potential. A clearer example of disability activism might be Aimee Mullins, who is a fashion model, celebrity, champion runner, a Georgetown University student, and double amputee. Mullins was also one of *People Magazine*'s 50 Most Beautiful people of 1999. An icon of disability pride and equality, Mullins exposes—in fact calls attention to—the mark of her disability in most photos, refusing to normalize or hide her disability in order to pass for nondisabled. Indeed, her public version of her career is that her disability has been a benefit: she has several sets of legs, both cosmetic and functional, and so is able to choose how tall she wants to be. Photographed in her prosthetic legs, she embodies the sexualized jock look that demands women be both slender and fit. In her cosmetic legs, she captures the look of the high fashion beauty in the controversial shoot by Nick Knight called "Accessible," showcasing outfits created by designers such as Alexander McQueen. But this is high fashion with a difference. In the jock shot her functional legs are brazenly displayed, and even in the voguishly costumed shot, the knee joints of her artificial legs are exposed. Never is there an attempt to disguise her prosthetic legs; rather the entire photos thematically echo her prostheses and render the whole image chic. Mullins' prosthetic legs—whether cosmetic or functional—parody, indeed proudly mock, the fantasy of the perfect body that is the mark of fashion, even while the rest of her body conforms precisely to fashion's impossible standards. So rather than concealing, normalizing, or erasing disability, these photos use the hyperbole and stigmata traditionally associated with disability to quench postmodernity's perpetual search for the new and arresting image. Such a narrative of advantage works against oppressive narratives and practices usually invoked about disabilities. First, Mullins counters the insistent narrative that one must overcome an impairment rather than incorporating it into one's life and self, even perhaps as a benefit. Second, Mullins counters the practice of passing for non-disabled that people with disabilities are often obliged to enact in the public sphere. So Mullins uses her conformity with beauty standards to assert her disability's violation of those very standards. As legless and beautiful, she is an embodied paradox, asserting an inherently disruptive potential.

What my analysis of these images reveals is that feminist cultural critiques are complex. On the one hand, feminists have rightly unmasked consumer capitalism's appropriation of women as sexual objects for male gratification. On the other hand, these images imply that the same capitalist system in its drive to harvest new markets can produce politically progressive counter images and counternarratives, however fraught they may be in their entanglement with consumer culture. Images of disabled fashion models are both complicit and critical of the beauty system that oppresses all women. Nevertheless, they suggest that consumer culture can provide the raw material for its own critique.

The concluding version of activism I offer is less controversial and more subtle than glitzy fashion spreads. It is what I call academic activism—the activism of integrating education—in the very broadest sense of that term. The academy is no ivory tower but rather it is the grass roots of the educational enterprise. Scholars and teachers shape the communal knowledge and the archive that is disseminated from kindergarten to the university. Academic activism is most self-consciously vibrant in the aggregate of interdisciplinary identity studies—of which women's studies is exemplary—that strive to expose the workings of oppression, examine subject formation, and offer counter-narratives for subjugated groups. Their cultural work is building an archive through historical and textual retrieval, canon reformation, role modeling, mentoring, curricular reform, and course and program development.

A specific form of feminist academic activism I elaborate here can be deepened through the complication of a disability analysis. I call it the methodology of intellectual tolerance. By this I don't mean tolerance in the more usual sense of tolerating each other—although that would be useful as well. What I mean is the intellectual position of tolerating what has previously been thought of as incoherence. As feminism has embraced the paradoxes that have emerged from its challenge to the gender system, it has not collapsed into chaos, but rather it developed a methodology that tolerates internal conflict and contradiction. This method asks difficult questions, but accepts provisional answers. This method recognizes the power of identity at the same time that it reveals identity as a fiction. This method both seeks equality, and it claims difference. This method allows us to teach with authority at the same time that we reject notions of pedagogical mastery. This method establishes institutional presences even while it acknowledges the limitations of institutions. This method validates the personal but implements disinterested inquiry. This method both writes new stories and recovers traditional ones. Considering disability as a vector of identity that intersects gender is one more internal challenge that threatens the coherence of woman, of course. But feminism can accommodate such complication and the contradictions it cultivates. Indeed the intellectual tolerance I am arguing for espouses the partial, the provisional, the particular. Such an intellectual habit can be informed by disability experience and acceptance. To embrace the supposedly flawed body of disability is to critique the normalizing, phallic fantasies of wholeness, unity, coherence, and completeness. The disabled body is contradiction, ambiguity, and partiality incarnate.

My claim here has been that integrating disability as a category of analysis, a historical community, a set of material practices, a social identity, a political position, and a representational system into the content of feminist—indeed into all—inquiry can strengthen the critique that is feminism. Disability, like gender and race, is everywhere, once we know how to look for it. Integrating disability analyses will enrich and deepen all our teaching and scholarship. Moreover, such critical intellectual work facilitates a fuller integration of the sociopolitical world—for the benefit of everyone. As with gender, race,

sexuality, and class: to understand how disability operates is to understand what it is to be fully human.

NOTES

1. Interestingly, in Fiske's study, feminists, businesswomen, Asians, Northerners, and Black professionals were stereotyped as highly competent, thus envied. In addition to having very low competence, housewives, disabled people, blind people, so-called retarded people, and the elderly were rated as warm, thus pitied.
2. Personal conversation with Paul Longmore, San Francisco, CA, June 2000.

WORKS CITED

Americans with Disabilities Act of 1990. Retrieved 15 August 2002, from http://www.usdoj.gov/crt/ada/pubs/ada.txt.
Aristotle. 1944. *Generation of Animals.* Trans. A.L. Peck. Cambridge: Harvard UP.
Asch, Adrienne, and Gail Geller. 1996. "Feminism, Bioethics and Genetics." In *Feminism, Bioethics: Beyond Reproduction*, ed. S.M. Wolf, 318–50. Oxford: Oxford UP.
Battin, Margaret P., Rosamond Rhodes, and Anita Silvers, eds. 1998. *Physician Assisted Suicide: Expanding the Debate.* New York: Routledge.
Bordo, Susan. 1994. "Reading the Male Body." In *The Male Body*, ed. Laurence Goldstein, 265–306. Ann Arbor: U of Michigan P.
———. 1993. *Unbearable Weight: Feminism, Western Culture and the Body.* Berkeley: U of California P.
Braidotti, Rosi. 1994. *Nomadic Subjects: Embodiment and Sexual Difference in Contemporary Feminist Thought.* New York: Columbia UP.
Brownsworth, Victoria A., and Susan Raffo, eds. 1999. *Restricted Access: Lesbians on Disability.* Seattle: Seal Press.
Butler, Judith. 1993. *Bodies that Matter.* New York: Routledge.
———. 1990. *Gender Trouble.* New York: Routledge.
Bynum, Caroline Walker. 1999. "Shape and Story: Metamorphosis in the Western Tradition." Paper presented at NEH Jefferson Lecture. 22 March, at Washington, DC.
Clark, David L., and Catherine Myser. 1996. "Being Humaned: Medical Documentaries and the Hyperrealization of Conjoined Twins." In *Freakery: Cultural Spectacles of the Extraordinary Body*, ed. Rosemarie Garland Thomson, 338-55. New York: New York UP.

Davis, Lennard. 1995. *Enforcing Normalcy: Disability, Deafness, and the Body*. New York: Verso.

De Beauvoir, Simone. (1952) 1974. *The Second Sex*. Trans. H.M. Parshley. New York: Vintage Press.

Dreger, Alice Domurat. 1998a. *Hermaphrodites and the Medical Invention of Sex*. Cambridge: Harvard UP.

——. 1998b. "The Limits of the Individuality: Ritual and Sacrifice in the Lives and Medical Treatment of Conjoined Twins." In *Freakery: Cultural Spectacles of the Extraordinary Body*, ed. Rosemarie Garland–Thomson, 338–55. New York: New York UP.

Eiesland, Nancy. 1994. *The Disabled God: Toward a Liberatory Theology of Disability*. Nahsville: Abingdon Press.

Fausto-Sterling, Anne. 2000. *Sexing the Body: Gender Politics and the Construction of Sexuality*. New York: Basic Books.

——. 1995. "Gender, Race, and Nation: The Comparative Anatomy of Hottentot Women in Europe, 1815–1817." In *Deviant Bodies: Cultural Perspectives in Science and Popular Culture*, eds. Jennifer Terry and Jacqueline Urla, 19–48. Bloomington: Indiana UP.

Fine, Michelle, and Adrienne Asch, eds. 1988. *Women with Disabilities: Essays in Psychology, Culture, and Politics*. Philadelphia: Temple UP.

Finger, Anne. 1990. *Past Due: A Story of Disability, Pregnancy, and Birth*. Seattle: Seal Press.

Fiske, Susan T., Amy J. C. Cuddy, and Peter Glick. 2001. "A Model of (Often Mixed) Stereotype Content: Competence and Warmth Respectively Follow from Perceived Status and Competition." Unpublished study.

Foucault, Michel. 1979. *Discipline and Punish: The Birth of the Prison*. Trans. Alan M. Sheridan-Smith. New York: Vintage Books.

Garland–Thomson, Rosemarie. 1999. "Narratives of Deviance and Delight: Staring at Julia Pastrana, 'The Extraordinary Lady.'" In *Beyond the Binary*, ed. Timothy Powell, 81–106. New Brunswick: Rutgers UP.

Gilman, Sander L. 1999. *Making the Body Beautiful*. Princeton: Princeton UP.

——. 1998. *Creating Beauty to Cure the Soul*. Durham: Duke UP.

——. 1985. *Difference and Pathology: Stereotypes of Sexuality, Race, and Madness*. Ithaca: Cornell UP.

Hahn, Harlan. 1988. "Can Disability Be Beautiful?" *Social Policy* 18 (Winter): 26–31.

Haiken, Elizabeth. 1997. *Venus Envy: A History of Cosmetic Surgery*. Baltimore: Johns Hopkins UP.

Haraway, Donna. 1991. *Simians, Cyborgs, and Women*. New York: Routledge.

Harstock, Nancy. 1983. "The Feminist Standpoint: Developing the Ground for a Specifically Feminist Historical Materialism." In *Discovering Reality*, eds. Sandra Harding and Merrell Hintikka, 283–305. Dortrecht, Holland: Reidel Publishing.

Herndl, Diane Price. 2002. "Reconstructing the Posthuman Feminist Body: Twenty Years after Audre Lorde's *Cancer Journals*." In *Disability Studies: Enabling the Humanities*, eds. Sharon Snyder, Brenda Brueggemann, and Rosemarie Garland-Thomson, 144–55. New York: MLA Press.

Hillyer, Barbara. 1993. *Feminism and Disability*. Norman: U of Oklahoma P.

Hubbard, Ruth. 1990. "Who Should and Who Should Not Inhabit the World?" In *The Politics of Women's Biology*, 179–98. New Brunswick: Rutgers UP.

Keller, Evelyn Fox. 1992. "Nature, Nurture and the Human Genome Project." In *The Code of Codes: Scientific and Social Issues in the Human Genome Project*, eds. Daniel J. Kevles and Leroy Hood, 281–99. Cambridge: Harvard UP.

Kessler, Suzanne J. 1990. *Lessons from the Intersexed*. New Brunswick: Rutgers UP.

Kittay, Eva Feder. 1999. *Love's Labor: Essays on Women, Equality, and Dependency*. New York: Routledge.

Kittay, Eva, with Leo Kittay. 2000. "On the Expressivity and Ethics of Selective Abortion for Disability: Conversations with My Son." In *Prenatal Testing and Disability Rights*, eds. Erik Parens and Adrienne Asch, 165–95. Georgetown: Georgetown UP.

Linton, Simi. 1998. *Claiming Disability: Knowledge and Identity*. New York: New York UP.

Longmore, Paul K. 1997. "Conspicuous Contribution and American Cultural Dilemmas: Telethon Rituals of Cleansing and Renewal." In *The Body and Physical Difference: Discourses of Disability*, eds. David Mitchell and Sharon Snyder, 134–58. Ann Arbor: U of Michigan P.

Lorde, Audre. 1980. *The Cancer Journals*. San Francisco: Spinsters Ink.

Mairs, Nancy. 1996. *Waist High in the World: A Life Among the Disabled*. Boston: Beacon Press.

McRuer, Robert. 1999. "Compulsory Able-Bodiedness and Queer/Disabled Existence." Paper presented at MLA Convention, 28 December, at Chicago, IL.

"Meet Ellen Stohl." 1987. *Playboy*. July: 68–74

Morrison, Toni. 1992. *Playing in the Dark: Whiteness and the Literary Imagination*. Cambridge: Harvard UP.

Parens, Erik, and Adrienne Asch. 2000. *Prenatal Testing and Disability Rights*. Georgetown: Georgetown UP.

Piercy, Marge. 1969. "Unlearning Not to Speak." In *Circles on Water*, 97. New York: Doubleday.

Rand, Erica. 1995. *Barbie's Queer Accessories*. Durham: Duke UP.

Rapp, Rayna. 1999. *Testing Women, Testing the Fetus:*

The Social Impact of Amniocentesis in America. New York: Routledge.

Rich, Adrienne. 1986. "Compulsory Heterosexuality and Lesbian Existence." In *Blood, Bread, and Poetry*, 23–75. New York: Norton.

Riley, Denise. 1999. "Bodies, Identities, Feminisms." In *Feminist Theory and the Body: A Reader*, eds. Janet Price and Margrit Shildrick, 220–6. Edinburgh, Scotland: Edinburgh UP.

Russo, Mary. 1994. *The Female Grotesque: Risk, Excess, and Modernity.* New York: Routledge.

Saxton, Marsha. 1998. "Disability Rights and Selective Abortion." In *Abortion Wars: A Half Century of Struggle (1950-2000)*, ed. Ricky Solinger, 374–93. Berkeley: U of California P.

Scott, Joan Wallach. 1988. "Gender as Useful Category of Analysis." In *Gender and the Politics of History*, 29–50. New York: Columbia UP.

Sedgwick, Eve Kosofsky. 1990. *Epistemology of the Closet.* Berkeley: U of California P.

Silvers, Anita. 1995. "Reconciling Equality to Difference: Caring (f)or Justice for People with Disabilities." *Hypatia* 10(1): 30–55.

Spelman, Elizabeth, V. 1988. *Inessential Woman: Problems of Exclusion in Feminist Thought.* Boston: Beacon Press.

——. 1997. *Extraordinary Bodies: Figuring Physical Disability in American Culture and Literature.* New York: Columbia UP.

Tuana, Nancy. 1993. *The Less Noble Sex: Scientific, Religious and Philosophical Conceptions of Woman's Nature.* Indianapolis: Indiana UP.

Wald, Priscilla. 2000. "Future Perfect: Grammar, Genes, and Geography." *New Literary History* 31(4): 681–708.

Williams, John M. 1999. "And Here's the Pitch: Madison Avenue Discovers the 'Invisible Consumer.'" *WE Magazine*, July/August: 28–31.

Wolf, Naomi. 1991. *The Beauty Myth: How Images of Beauty Are Used Against Women.* New York: William Morrow and Co.

Young, Iris Marion. 1990a. "Breasted Experience." In *Throwing Like a Girl and Other Essays in Feminist Philosophy and Social Theory*, 189–209. Bloomington: Indiana UP.

——. 1990b. "Throwing Like a Girl." In *Throwing Like a Girl and Other Essays in Feminist Philosophy and Social Theory*, 141–59. Bloomington: Indiana UP.

CHAPTER 27

Is Disability Studies Actually White Disability Studies?

Chris Bell

My modest proposal is inspired by a popular television program airing on the Chicago PBS affiliate. "Check, Please!" gathers three "ordinary" residents who, after selecting their favorite restaurant, anonymously dine at all three establishments, then gather in a studio to debate the relative merits and shortfalls of each culinary venue. During one episode, the trio included a self-styled *bon vivant* whom I will call Dorian Gray. Dorian, while sharing his observations about a Chinese restaurant in a south Chicago suburb, expressed his unadulterated amazement at the composition of one particular entrée. "The shrimp were *artificial*!" he bemoaned, dread contorting his facial features into an expression of unrecoverable distress. The individual selecting said restaurant as his favorite—I'll call him Bubba Gump—blinked nary an eye at this revelation. Instead, Bubba stoically intoned, "If it looks like a shrimp, and it smells and tastes like a shrimp, it's a shrimp."

Bubba Gump's matter-of-fact rejoinder to Dorian Gray is, I think, indicative of the whiteness of Disability Studies in its present incarnation. The fact that Disability Studies is marketed as such when it is in actuality an artificial (read: limited and limiting) version of the field does nothing to prevent it from being understood as Disability Studies, which is what Bubba, by

extension, apprised Dorian of. I contend that it is disingenuous to keep up the pretense that the field is an inclusive one when it is not. On that score, I would like to concede the failure of Disability Studies to engage issues of race and ethnicity in a substantive capacity, thereby entrenching whiteness as its constitutive underpinning. In short, I want to call a shrimp a shrimp and acknowledge Disability Studies for what it is, White Disability Studies.

In contradistinction to Disability Studies, White Disability Studies recognizes its tendency to whitewash disability history, ontology and phenomenology. White Disability Studies, while not wholeheartedly excluding people of color from its critique,[1] by and large focuses on the work of white individuals and is itself largely produced by a corps of white scholars and activists. White Disability Studies envisions nothing ill-advised with this leaning because it is innocently done and far too difficult to remedy. A synoptic review of some of the literature and related aspects of Disability Studies bears this out.

"VITAL SIGNS: CRIP CULTURE TALKS BACK"

This documentary was filmed during a conference on Disability and the Arts on the campus of the University of Michigan. The film is distressing because of its absence of non-white individuals. Given the absence of people of color, I suggest that a significant number of myths and misconceptions about who/what is constitutive of disability or "crip" culture are bolstered and reinforced in the film.

NO PITY: PEOPLE WITH DISABILITIES FORGING A NEW CIVIL RIGHTS MOVEMENT

In his introduction, author Joseph Shapiro refers to the disabled community as the largest minority community in the United States, with more members than communities tallied by race, ethnicity, or sexual orientation amongst other socially-constructed identity categories (7). What interests me is Shapiro's obfuscation of divisions within this ostensibly-largest minority community and his insinuation that the disabled community is a monolithic one, struggling against the same oppressors, striving for identical degrees of dignity, recognition and cultural representation. Such a characterization is a limited one that does not consider or address the rich diversity within disability communities—racial and ethnic diversity, for example.

A MATTER OF DIGNITY: CHANGING THE LIVES OF THE DISABLED

Comprised of a series of interviews with disabled people from various life strata, the dearth of people of color in the text is as undeniable as it is flagrant. In order to prevent this text from surprising the unexpecting reader, it might be a good idea to acknowledge that whiteness is positioned as its center. Doing so would make for a much more accurate description of who/what is represented.

CLAIMING DISABILITY: KNOWLEDGE AND IDENTITY

In her well-known text, Simi Linton describes Disability Studies by stating, "The field explores the critical divisions our society makes in creating the normal versus the pathological, the insider versus the outsider, or the competent citizen versus the ward of the state" (2). The reader should recognize the dichotomous line of thought here, the binary fashion with which Linton makes her critique. At the very least, it should be understood that many white disabled people have cultural capital by virtue of their race and are, therefore, more on the inside than they are on the outside. As an insider, Linton appears unaware of her positioning, and it is that unawareness that is one of the hallmarks of White Disability Studies.

ENFORCING NORMALCY: DISABILITY, DEAFNESS AND THE BODY

Throughout this text, Davis takes whiteness as a norm. From his discussion of the desirability of the Venus de Milo to his examination of the protagonist in "Born on the Fourth of July," Davis's emphasis on whiteness is undeniable. There is, to be sure, nothing wrong with this focus (aside from being egregiously misleading with regard to which communities and subjectivities are constitutive of "disability"). I only wish Davis had broadened his source materials, or at the very least opted for a more accurate title e.g., *Enforcing Normalcy: Disability, Deafness and the White Body*. Moreover, it matters that an excerpt from this text is reprinted in *The Norton Anthology of Literary Criticism*, the ostensible Bible of literary studies. Those readers coming across this excerpt will necessarily receive a distorted view of Disability Studies as a result of Davis's focus on whiteness.

QUEER DISABILITY CONFERENCE

Near the conclusion of the first day of this conference that convened in San Francisco in June 2002, I met with approximately thirteen other self-identified queer and disabled people of color during a caucus session. Our conversation focused on our individual and collective sense of exclusion based on race and ethnicity.[2] We could not fathom how the conference organizers—every one of them a white person—could publicize this conference in numerous international contexts and venues—drawing participants from Finland, Australia, and the United Kingdom among other nations—but fail to devise and implement an outreach plan that would attract people of color and other marginalized groups within the queer and disabled communities in the local Bay Area. We also could not understand the overarching mentality of many of the attendees, perhaps best expressed by a remark made in a breakout session: "Being disabled is just like being black, so society should stop hating us and give us our rights."

SOCIETY FOR DISABILITY STUDIES ANNUAL CONFERENCE, 2005

During the business meeting at the conference's conclusion, the people of color caucus presented a list of action items to the membership in an effort to shore up the marginal presence race and ethnicity had at the conference (despite the fact that the conference was themed "Conversations and Connections Across Race and Disability"). Although the hour-long conversation that ensued was collegial and productive, I cannot help wondering, drawing on my experience at the Queer Disability Conference,[3] how many times these questions of inclusion and exclusion have to be raised by people of color to white individuals? As I averred during the business meeting, "I'm tired of being one of the few to point out what should be obvious."

MODERN LANGUAGE ASSOCIATION (MLA) CONFERENCE ON DISABILITY STUDIES AND THE UNIVERSITY

Convened on the campus of Emory University March 5–7, 2004, the conference is notable at the outset for the sheer whiteness of those who presented. A quick glance down the list of presenters (as published in *PMLA* in 2005)[4] bears this out. An additional concern is the content of what was shared during this conference.

In his address, "Disability: The Next Wave or Twilight of the Gods?," Lennard Davis, thankfully, speaks to the white nature of Disability Studies: "Disability studies has by and large been carried out by white people" (530). He is grossly incorrect, however, in the follow-up assertion that the field will benefit from "the disability studies book about the African American experience of disability" (ibid). To be sure, there is no singular, structuralist African American experience of disability and it is imprudent to advocate for one. Davis is further incorrect when he insists that said text must incorporate the recent "post-race" debate. Placing strictures on a text is foolish, especially when the strictures themselves lack intellectual value and integrity.[5]

In "What Is Disability Studies?," Simi Linton includes an instructive albeit telling example to illustrate the difficulty of answering the titular question:

> A few years ago, a controversy about the golfer Casey Martin and the golf cart captured a great deal of attention. Martin petitioned the PGA—the Professional Golfers' Association—for permission to ride a golf cart in pro tournaments as an accommodation for a mobility impairment. When the PGA turned him down, Martin took the case to court. It was eventually deliberated in the Supreme Court, where Martin prevailed. The most

significant outcome of the debate, I think, is that the discussion came down to the question, What *is* the game of golf? Some people said, If he rides a cart, that's not golf. I'd like to know, then, what golf is and who has decided. (519)

As I mentioned, the example is instructive, but also rather telling: GOLF?! Come on! I challenge the reader to name one non-white golfer . . . Okay, now name one non-white golfer *besides* Tiger and Vijay.

On a more serious note, as I read through the collection of essays and presentations from the Emory conference I am concerned with how often each scholar cites the other, revealing an uncomfortable incestuousness about Disability Studies. These individuals seem unwilling to step aside even briefly and let someone else have the (proverbial) microphone for a moment. Granted, if the MLA calls, there is appeal in the form of professional legitimacy. But I also suggest that there is appeal in giving someone else a chance to speak to the issues embedded in and examined by Disability Studies, in asking who will be there and figuring out who *should* be there, as well as who has not been asked and why. The failure to do so practically ensures that the silences, namely those concerning race and ethnicity, will not be addressed and will continue.

*　*　*　*　*

If Disability Studies as a field had taken a reflexive look at itself at some point, particularly with regard to its failings in examining issues of race and ethnicity, there might not be such a glaring dearth of disability-related scholarship by and about disabled people of color. As it stands, Disability Studies has a tenuous relationship with race and ethnicity: while the field readily acknowledges its debt to and inspiration by inquiries such as Black Studies, its efforts at addressing intersections between disability, race, and ethnicity are, at best, wanting. Disability Studies claims to examine the experiences of a vast number of disabled people, yet the form that representation takes is, far too often, a white one. This is by no means a sporadic occurrence. Quite the contrary, the slights occur habitually and, as the preceding examples prove, in various contexts, from published works to conferences. I think it is essential to illuminate the fragile relationship between disability, race, and ethnicity in extant Disability Studies, arguing not so much for a sea-change in this formulation, rather for a more definitive and accurate identification of the happening.

What follows then is my ten-point scheme (*pace*, Mr. Letterman) on how to keep White Disability Studies in vogue and instantiated as disability praxis. Given the fact that well-intentioned individuals are inclined to ask what can be done to "make things more diverse," I have purposely crafted the following as a series of "do nots." By doing so, I hope to shore up how presumptuous it is to position the subaltern as the all-knowing savant insofar as issues of diversity; requesting definitive answers from that person when the answers might best come from within, following an extended period of rumination.

10. **Do not change a thing.** Let's keep doing what we're doing. Let's remain firmly rooted in *this* wave of disability, consciously opting not to move to the next. Let's continue to acknowledge white individuals as the Disability Studies core constituency.[6] Do not outreach to communities of color or participate in their events when the opportunity to forge connections arises. Do not solicit for a themed issue of *Disability Studies Quarterly* on race, ethnicity and disability[7] and if by chance said issue should be produced, make sure that it

occurs only once; that there are no efforts to ensure that these intersections are spoken to throughout future iterations of the journal in a non-"special issue" context. In sum, do not change a thing. Continue to fetishize and exoticize people of color as subalterns by constantly focusing on *their* race and ethnicity, but not that of the white subject.

9. **Do not address ethnicity, rather continually focus on race.** Many Disability Studies scholars—and people in general—are unwilling or unable to pick up on the cultural significance of ethnicity in contraposition to what some are (erroneously) convinced is the biological foundation of race. Regardless of where the two concepts spring from, the fact is that they are distinct. It becomes problematic then when all that comprises ethnicity gets collapsed under the umbrella term of race. As a field White Disability Studies has no stake in this process and therefore should do nothing to address it.

8. **Do not consider that, as Stuart Hall has explained, "Cultural identity is not an essence but a positioning"** (229). Generally speaking, the same people who hold power in the community of scholars known as Disability Studies are a mimetic rendering of those holding power in non-disabled communities: white people. Despite the fact that people of color outnumber white people in the world, white people harbor hegemony and cultural capital. Whether or not disabled people of color outnumber disabled white individuals—or whether people of color interested in Disability Studies outnumber whites interested in the same—the fact is Disability Studies is conceived of as a white field (recall Davis's comments from the Emory conference). White Disability Studies should pay no attention to this,

doing nothing to change this conception, this positioning. It does not matter that whiteness is not an essentialist prerequisite for a disability identity. We can just pretend that it is.

7. **Pay no attention to Ann duCille's recognition that "[O]ne of the dangers of standing at an intersection . . . is the likelihood of being run over"** (593). When you come across a non-white disabled person, focus on the disability, eliding the race and ethnicity, letting them be run over, forgotten. Do not consider how the intersection in which this subject lives influences her actions and the way she is seen. Choose not to see that intersection and quickly move on down the road of disability, away from the "perpendicular" roads of race and ethnicity. The fact that the intersection exists is not your fault. It is a prime example of poor engineering.

6. **Disregard Evelynn Hammonds's idea that "visibility in and of itself does not erase a history of silence nor does it challenge the structure of power and domination, symbolic and material, that determines what can and cannot be seen"** (141). Do not forgot to revel in the idea that as more and more disabled people enter the mainstream, all disabled people, irrespective of their racial and ethnic subjectivity, occupy the same place at the table. Equate visibility with inclusivity. Sit back and be satisfied, and do not allow yourself to be troubled by those who carp about their invisibility within disability communities.

5. **Ignore Horkheimer and Adorno's augury that failure to conform to the culture industry results in the individual being "left behind"** (37). The two theorists warn of the perils of living in a culture industry whereby one must subscribe to the right magazines and watch the correct films in order

to be accepted in the culture. White Disability Studies is nothing like this; there is nothing even remotely similar to a "disability industry." Thus, it is not true that if you make a film about "crip culture" and you populate that film with only white people, you will be left behind. Quite the contrary, you will receive awards and plaudits, kudos and huzzahs, for this. It is not true that if you enter a room that purports to gather together those interested and engaged in Disability Studies and see not a single person of color present, those people have been left behind or otherwise disinvited. Be still; speak not. Do not draw attention to their absence. Let them be remaindered out. They always have been, and besides, they have probably chosen not to enter the space.

4. **Make no allowances for liminality and hybridity.** Instead, continue the pretence of normality, the idea that everything's just fine and that the disability community is one happy family with no diversity, no multivalence, only a collective sameness. Do not conceive of the silences that are imbricated in extant Disability Studies. Likewise, do not conceive of the concerted efforts to counter those silences, to advocate for liminality and hybridity, as described, in a different context, in Abena Busia's "Silencing Sycorax: On African Colonial Discourse and the Unvoiced Female":

The systematic refusal to hear our [African American females] speech is not the same thing as our silence. That we have hitherto been spoken of as absent of silenced does not mean we have been so . . . The systematic refusal to hear our speech which colonial literature mirrors, though it has historically removed us from the nexus of certain kinds of power, does not and never actually could render us silent. In unmasking the dispossessions of the silences of fiction and the fictions of silence, we (re)construct

self-understanding. Furthermore, for women, "Narrative" is not always and only, or even necessarily a speech act. We women signify: we have many modes of (re)dress. (103–4)

Do not consider how minority discourse from within a minority discourse is in and of itself counter-hegemonic. Do not encourage the proliferation of that discourse even though it is resistive and liberating. As we all know, the presence of too many voices results in senseless cacophony and what good is that?

3. **Do whatever you can *not* to discuss those texts rife with possibilities insofar as parsing out intersections between disability, race, and ethnicity, namely:**

The Souls of Black Folk

In 1903, W.E.B. DuBois introduced his concept of double consciousness that speaks to the black American's irreconcilable sense of self as "an African" and "an American." Since there is nothing to be gained by applying this theory to black disabled subjects (triple consciousness?), it is best not to consider this text as having any bearing on Disability Studies.

Up From Slavery

Published around the same time as DuBois's text, *Up From Slavery* is frequently taught alongside *The Souls of Black Folk*. Washington takes a much more assimilationist approach to black subjectivity in contraposition to DuBois. Perhaps a Disability Studies scholar might draw parallels between the Washington/DuBois ideas of black subjectivity and the difference between those disabled subjects who want to advocate for peaceful resistance and mainstreaming in juxtaposition to those who take a more activist, resistant stance. But then again, that would be an utter waste of the scholar's time.

Invisible Man

> I am an invisible man . . . I am invisible, understand, simply because people refuse to see me. (3)

The first lines of Ellison's text speak to the difficulty of black ontology in the United States. Ellison's protagonist, of course, is not speaking of a literal invisibility so much as he is drawing light to how it is that others (read: whites with hegemonic power) choose not to see him in totality. If this characterization does not seem applicable to Disability Studies—wherein the racialized subaltern is remembered and considered solely as a matter of convenience more often than not—I don't know what would be. Yet it would be foolish to illuminate this text's applicability to Disability Studies, or, furthermore, to consider the prophetic final lines of the novel—"who know but that, on the lower frequencies, I speak for you?" (581)—wherein the protagonist considers the complexities of representing and/or embodying communal univocality. I do not recommend examining this.

Roots

A Disability Studies scholar might examine aspects of disability throughout the text, namely those that are linked to racial positioning (e.g., the causes and effects of Kunta Kinte's "crippling"). Then again, she might not.

Beauty: When the Other Dancer Is the Self

This widely-anthologized personal narrative describes Alice Walker's sense of self as a disabled subject after she is blinded as a child. "I didn't pray for sight," she writes, "I prayed for beauty." Any Disability Studies scholar worth her salt should immediately discern the implications of this statement, but that does not mean that she must act upon it in her scholarship. Likewise, the scholar might pay attention to Walker's intentional use of language, e.g., the allusion to Stevie Wonder towards the end of the narrative. Alas, she might pay attention to it, but there is absolutely nothing to be gained from explicating it.

The Cure

Ginu Kamani's short story is set in contemporary India. The protagonist must deal with living in a culture that has deemed her "too-tall." What is interesting is that the reader never learns just how tall she is, evidentiary of a societal code that is unspoken and yet accepted. Unfortunately, since the story is set in India, where whites are the minority, it cannot be of interest to a Disability Studies scholar.

"The Adventures of Felix"

Race is usually considered a black and white issue. This film complicates that assessment. The protagonist, the titular Felix, is a multiracial French gay man with HIV who sets out to find the father he never knew. Although many critics and individuals familiar with AIDS narratives herald the film for its portrayal of a person with AIDS who is effortlessly "handling" his disease, a disability theorist might pay particular attention to how easily AIDS is removed from the narrative in favor of other concerns. But I doubt that would ever happen.

"Birth of a Nation, or The Clansman"

Long before "Triumph of the Will" was unleashed on the populace, this legendary slice of propaganda was released and heralded. The issues of performativity at play here are rife for discussion, as are their implications insofar as who gets to represent race and/or disability. A Disability Studies scholar might link the use of blackface in this film with the use of nondisabled actors to play disabled figures in contemporary films. But, again, I doubt that would ever happen.

In sum, continue thinking that these texts are too long (e.g., *Invisible Man*) and that the disability perspective is too tangential (e.g., "The Adventures of Felix") to warrant devoting time to. Do not select key scenes to analyze and discuss. Ignore the texts altogether. Continue to herald the overt elisions and missed opportunities.

2. **Do not note how odd "White Disability Studies" looks on this page,** how much effort it requires (or does it?) to contort one's tongue in order to articulate it. Do not take into account how foreign a phrase it seems (although just because something is foreign doesn't necessarily mean that it is incomprehensible . . .).

1. **Do not change a thing.** Keep doing what *you're* doing. Do so because what you're doing is fine, more than enough to keep White Disability Studies firmly instantiated as the norm. Make no effort to be more inclusive in your scholarship. Do not start today, do not start tomorrow. Wait for someone else to do inclusive work. Wait for however long it takes.

*   *   *   *   *

By way of conclusion, I want to stress that Disability Studies is not the only field of inquiry wherein individuals of color are treated as second-class citizens. If anything, Disability Studies is merely aping the ideology of the vast majority of academic disciplines and ways of thinking that preceded it and which it now sits alongside of. While I could have devoted this modest proposal to advocating for a more hybrid Disability Studies, a liminal version, the fact is I am not certain that advocating for such an idea is a worthwhile undertaking. I deem it far more instructive to acknowledge that we are positioned in the realm of "White Disability Studies" and continue along with the truth of this positioning in mind.

Moreover, offering White Disability Studies, even in the form of a tongue-in-cheek modest proposal, is bound to unnerve many of the individuals who consider themselves engaged in Disability Studies. White Disability Studies will most likely strike these individuals as a hyperbolic and counterintuitive claim. Perhaps my actions might be deemed impolitic and offensive. That is the point. I think it is tactless to dismiss a message solely because of its ostensible unpopularity or because the individual bearing the message seems undesirable. Such a process is itself counterintuitive, intended to draw attention away from a message that, while perhaps unpopular, might contain more than a modicum of validity. Because Disability Studies in its current incarnation *is* White Disability Studies, proposing we honor that creates no crisis of conscience for me. If anything, I take heart in remembering what Bubba Gump declared to Dorian Gray on "Check, Please!": "If it looks like a shrimp, and it smells and tastes like a shrimp, it's a shrimp."

NOTES

1. Far from excluding people of color, White Disability Studies treats people of color as if they were white people; as if there are no critical exigencies involved in being people of color that might necessitate these individuals understanding and negotiating disability in a different way from their white counterparts.

2. Reader: If you think it odd that our feelings of solidarity were premised on disinvitation,

realize that this is a reality of many people of color engaged in White Disability Studies.

3. Coincidentally, the people of color caucuses at both conferences presented their list of action items in the exact same space, the Mary Ward Hall at San Francisco State University.

4. The pagination to follow is from this issue of *PMLA*.

5. Briefly, the "post-race debate" argues that race is no longer a valid social construct or marker. By that light, the culture as a whole should move on and focus on other, purportedly more pressing issues e.g., class. I can deconstruct the entire post-race argument by simply pointing out that in a culture where racism exists and is pervasive, the casual dismissal of race is specious.

6. I offer AIDS as a precedent here. From the early 1980s until fairly recently, the conception of the AIDS afflicted subject was a gay white man. Indeed, the legacy still retains purchase on mainstream cultural consciousness. Of course, if there were only a few overtures to assess how the disease was impacting women and people of color—and when you think about the history of AIDS, you realize that up until quite recently this was the case—then it becomes obvious how gay white men became equated with AIDS. It is difficult to offer a counternarrative when the structures of power determining which identities comprise a subject are unyielding in their conception.

7. A cursory glance of the past few years of *DSQ*'s topical issues is rather enlightening in this regard. There is an abundance of special topics, none of which verge on what is, to me, one of the more obvious absences in the discourse.

WORKS CITED

The Adventures of Felix. Dir. Olivier Ducastel and Jacques Martineau. DVD. Perf. Sami Bouajila. Fox Lorber, 2000.

Birth of a Nation, or The Clansman. Dir. D.W. Griffiths. 1915. DVD. Perf. Lillian Gish. Image Entertainment, 2002.

Busia, Abena P. A. "Silencing Sycorax: On African Colonial Discourse and the Unvoiced Female." *Cultural Critique* 14 (Winter 1989–90): 81–104.

DuBois, W.E.B. *The Souls of Black Folk*. 1903. New York: Penguin, 1996.

duCille, Ann. "The Occult of True Black Womanhood: Critical Demeanor and Black Feminist Studies." *Signs* 19, 3 (Spring 1994): 591–629.

Davis, Lennard. "Disability: The Next Wave or Twilight of the Gods?" Conference on Disability Studies and the University. *PMLA* 120, 2 (March/April 2005): 527–532.

——. *Enforcing Disability: Disability, Deafness and the Body*. London: Verso, 1995.

Ellison, Ralph. *Invisible Man*. New York: Random House, 1952.

Haley, Alex. *Roots*. New York: Doubleday, 1976.

Hall, Stuart. "Cultural Studies and Its Theoretical Legacies." In *Cultural Studies*, edited by Lawrence Grossberg, Cary Nelson, and Paula Treichler et al., 227–234. New York: Routledge, 1992.

Hammonds, Evelynn. "Black (W)holes and the Geometry of Black Female Sexuality." *differences* 6, 2–3 (1994): 126–145.

Horkheimer, Max, and Theodor Adorno. "The Culture Industry: Enlightenment as Mass Deception." *The Dialectic of Enlightenment* (originally published as Dialektik der Aufklarung, 1944). New York: Continuum, 1993.

Kamani, Ginu. "The Cure." *Junglee Girl*. San Francisco: Aunt Lute, 1995.

Leitch, Vincent et al. *The Norton Anthology of Theory and Criticism*. New York: W.W. Norton and Company, 2001.

Linton, Simi. *Claiming Disability: Knowledge and Identity*. New York: NYU Press, 1998.

——. "What Is Disability Studies?" Conference on Disability Studies and the University. *PMLA*. 120, 2 (March/April 2005): 518–522.

Potok, Andrew. *A Matter of Dignity: Changing the Lives of the Disabled*. New York: Bantam, 2003.

Shapiro, Joseph. *No Pity: People with Disabilities Forging a New Civil Rights Movement*. New York: Times Books, 1993.

Vital Signs: Crip Culture Talks Back. Dir. David Mitchell and Sharon Snyder. DVD. Brace Yourselves Productions, 1996.

Walker, Alice. "Beauty: When the Other Dancer Is the Self." *In Search of Our Mother's Gardens: Womanist Prose*, 361–370. New York: Harcourt, Brace and Jovanovich, 1983.

Washington, Booker T. *Up From Slavery*. 1900. New York: Dover, 1995.

CHAPTER 28

Compulsory Able-Bodiedness and Queer/Disabled Existence

Robert McRuer

CONTEXTUALIZING DISABILITY

In her famous critique of compulsory het-erosexuality Adrienne Rich opens with the suggestion that lesbian existence has often been "simply rendered invisible" (178), but the bulk of her analysis belies that render-ing. In fact, throughout "Compulsory Het-erosexuality and Lesbian Existence," one of Rich's points seems to be that compulsory heterosexuality depends as much on the ways in which lesbian identities are made visible (or, we might say, comprehensible) as on the ways in which they are made in-visible or incomprehensible. She writes:

> Any theory of cultural/political creation that treats lesbian existence as a marginal or less "natural" phenomenon, as mere "sexual preference," or as the mirror image of either heterosexual or male homosexual relations is profoundly weakened thereby, whatever its other contributions. Feminist theory can no longer afford merely to voice a toleration of "lesbianism" as an "alternative life-style," or make token allusion to lesbians. A femi-nist critique of compulsory heterosexual ori-entation for women is long overdue. (178)

The critique that Rich calls for proceeds not through a simple recognition or even valuation of "lesbian existence" but rather through an interrogation of how the system of compulsory heterosexuality utilizes that

existence. Indeed, I would extract from her suspicion of mere "toleration" confirmation for the idea that one of the ways in which heterosexuality is currently constituted or founded, established as the foundational sexual identity for women, is precisely through the deployment of lesbian exis-tence as always and everywhere supple-mentary—the margin to heterosexuality's center, the mere reflection of (straight and gay) patriarchal realities. Compulsory het-erosexuality's casting of some identities as alternatives ironically buttresses the ideo-logical notion that dominant identities are not really alternatives but rather the natu-ral order of things.[1]

More than twenty years after it was ini-tially published, Rich's critique of com-pulsory heterosexuality is indispensable, the criticisms of her ahistorical notion of a "lesbian continuum" notwithstanding.[2] Despite its continued relevance, however, the realm of compulsory heterosexuality might seem to be an unlikely place to begin contextualizing disability.[3] I want to chal-lenge that by considering what might be gained by understanding "compulsory het-erosexuality" as a key concept in disability studies. Through a reading of compulsory heterosexuality, I want to put forward a theory of what I call compulsory able-bod-iedness. The Latin root for *contextualize* denotes the act of weaving together, inter-weaving, joining together, or composing. This chapter thus contextualizes disability in the root sense of the word, because I argue that the system of compulsory able-bodied-ness that produces disability is thoroughly interwoven with the system of compulsory heterosexuality that produces queerness, that—in fact—compulsory heterosexuality is contingent on compulsory able-bodied-ness and vice versa. And, although I reiterate it in my conclusion, I want to make it clear at the outset that this particular con-textualizing of disability is offered as part of a much larger and collective project of un-raveling and decomposing both systems.[4]

The idea of imbricated systems is, of course, not new—Rich's own analysis re-peatedly stresses the imbrication of com-pulsory heterosexuality and patriarchy. I would argue, however, as others have, that feminist and queer theories (and cultural theories generally) are not yet accustomed to figuring ability/disability into the equa-tion, and thus this theory of compulsory able-bodiedness is offered as a preliminary contribution to that much-needed conver-sation.[5]

ABLE-BODIED HETEROSEXUALITY

In his introduction to *Keywords: A Vocabu-lary of Culture and Society*, Raymond Wil-liams describes his project as

> the record of an inquiry into a *vocabulary*: a shared body of words and meanings in our most general discussions, in English, of the practices and institutions which we group as *culture* and *society*. Every word which I have included has at some time, in the course of some argument, virtually forced itself on my attention because the problems of its mean-ing seemed to me inextricably bound up with the problems it was being used to dis-cuss. (15)

Although Williams is not particularly con-cerned in *Keywords* with feminism or gay and lesbian liberation, the processes he de-scribes should be recognizable to feminists and queer theorists, as well as to scholars and activists in other contemporary move-ments, such as African American studies or critical race theory. As these movements have developed, increasing numbers of words have indeed forced themselves on our attention, so that an inquiry into not just the marginalized identity but also the dominant identity has become necessary. The problem of the meaning of masculinity (or even maleness), of whiteness, of hetero-sexuality has increasingly been understood as inextricably bound up with the problems the term is being used to discuss.

One need go no further than the *Oxford English Dictionary* to locate problems with the meaning of heterosexuality. In 1971 the *OED Supplement* defined *heterosexual* as "pertaining to or characterized by the normal relations of the sexes; opp. to *ho-mosexual*." At this point, of course, a few decades of critical work by feminists and queer theorists have made it possible to acknowledge quite readily that heterosex-ual and homosexual are in fact not equal and opposite identities. Rather, the ongo-ing subordination of homosexuality (and bisexuality) to heterosexuality allows for heterosexuality to be institutionalized as "the normal relations of the sexes," while the institutionalization of heterosexuality as the "normal relations of the sexes" al-lows for homosexuality (and bisexuality) to be subordinated. And, as queer theory con-tinues to demonstrate, it is precisely the introduction of normalcy into the system that introduces compulsion: "Nearly every-one," Michael Warner writes in *The Trouble with Normal: Sex, Politics, and the Ethics of Queer Life*, "wants to be normal. And who can blame them, if the alternative is be-ing abnormal, or deviant, or not being one of the rest of us? Put in those terms, there doesn't seem to be a choice at all. Especially in America where [being] normal probably outranks all other social aspirations" (53). Compulsion is here produced and covered over, with the appearance of choice (sexual preference) mystifying a system in which there actually is no choice.

A critique of normalcy has similarly been central to the disability rights movement and to disability studies, with—for example—Lennard Davis's overview and critique of the historical emergence of normalcy or Rosemarie Garland-Thomson's introduction of the concept of the "normate" (Davis, 23–49; Thomson, 8–9). Such scholarly and activist work positions us to locate the problems of able-bodied identity, to see the problem of the meaning of able-bodiedness as bound up with the problems it is being used to discuss. Arguably, able-bodied identity is at this juncture even more naturalized than heterosexual identity. At the very least, many people not sympathetic to queer theory will concede that ways of being heterosexual are culturally produced and culturally variable, even if and even as they understood heterosexual identity itself to be entirely natural. The same cannot be said, on the whole, for able-bodied identity. An extreme example that nonetheless encapsulates currently hegemonic thought on ability and disability is a notorious *Salon* article by Norah Vincent attacking disability studies that appeared online in the summer of 1999. Vincent writes, "It's hard to deny that something called normalcy exists. The human body is a machine, after all—one that has evolved functional parts: lungs for breathing, legs for walking, eyes for seeing, ears for hearing, a tongue for speaking and most crucially for all the academics concerned, a brain for thinking. This is science, not culture."[6] In a nutshell, you either have an able body, or you don't.

Yet the desire for definitional clarity might unleash more problems than it contains; if it's hard to deny that something called normalcy exists, it's even harder to pinpoint what that something is. The

OED defines *able-bodied* redundantly and negatively as "having an able body, i.e. one free from physical disability, and capable of the physical exertions required of it; in bodily health; robust." Able-bodiedness, in turn, is defined vaguely as "soundness of health; ability to work; robustness." The parallel structure of the definitions of ability and sexuality is quite striking: first, to be able-bodied is to be "free from physical disability," just as to be heterosexual is to be "the opposite of homosexual." Second, even though the language of "the normal relations" expected of human beings is not present in the definition of able-bodied, the sense of "normal relations" is, especially with the emphasis on work: being able-bodied means being capable of the normal physical exertions required in a particular system of labor. It is here, in fact, that both able-bodied identity and the *Oxford English Dictionary* betray their origins in the nineteenth century and the rise of industrial capitalism. It is here as well that we can begin to understand the compulsory nature of able-bodiedness: in the emergent industrial capitalist system, free to sell one's labor but not free to do anything else effectively meant free to have an able body but not particularly free to have anything else.

Like compulsory heterosexuality, then, compulsory able-bodiedness functions by covering over, with the appearance of choice, a system in which there actually is no choice. I would not locate this compulsion, moreover, solely in the past, with the rise of industrial capitalism. Just as the origins of heterosexual/homosexual identity are now obscured for most people so that compulsory heterosexuality functions as a disciplinary formation seemingly emanating from everywhere and nowhere, so too are the origins of able-bodied/disabled identity obscured, allowing what Susan Wendell calls "the disciplines of normality" (87) to cohere in a system of compulsory able-bodiedness that similarly emanates from everywhere and nowhere. Able-bodied dilutions and misunderstandings of the minority thesis put forward in the disability rights movement and disability studies have even, in some ways, strengthened the system: the dutiful (or docile) able-bodied subject now recognizes that some groups of people have chosen to adjust to or even take pride in their "condition," but that recognition, and the tolerance that undergirds it, covers over the compulsory nature of the able-bodied subject's own identity.[7]

Michael Bérubé's memoir about his son Jamie, who has Down syndrome, helps exemplify some of the ideological demands currently sustaining compulsory able-bodiedness. Bérubé writes of how he "sometimes feel[s] cornered by talking about Jamie's intelligence, as if the burden of proof is on me, official spokesman on his behalf." The subtext of these encounters always seems to be the same: "*In the end, aren't you disappointed to have a retarded child?* [. . .] *Do we really have to give this person our full attention?*" (180). Bérubé's excavation of this subtext pinpoints an important common experience that links all people with disabilities under a system of compulsory able-bodiedness—the experience of the able-bodied need for an agreed-on common ground. I can imagine that answers might be incredibly varied to similar questions—"In the end, wouldn't you rather be hearing?" and "In the end, wouldn't you rather not be HIV positive?" would seem, after all, to be very different questions, the first (with its thinly veiled desire for Deafness not to exist) more obviously genocidal than the second. But they are not really different questions, in that their constant repetition (or their presence as ongoing subtexts) reveals more about the able-bodied culture doing the asking than about the bodies being interrogated. The culture asking such questions assumes in advance that we all agree: able-bodied identities, able-bodied perspectives are preferable and what we all, collectively, are aiming for. A system of compulsory able-bodiedness repeatedly demands that people with disabilities embody for others an affirmative answer to the unspoken question, Yes, but in the end, wouldn't you rather be more like me?

It is with this repetition that we can begin to locate both the ways in which compulsory able-bodiedness and compulsory heterosexuality are interwoven and the ways in which they might be contested. In queer theory, Judith Butler is most famous for identifying the repetitions required to maintain heterosexual hegemony:

> The "reality" of heterosexual identities is performatively constituted through an imitation that sets itself up as the origin and the ground of all imitations. In other words, heterosexuality is always in the process of imitating and approximating its own phantasmatic idealization of itself—*and failing.* Precisely because it is bound to fail, and yet endeavors to succeed, the project of heterosexual identity is propelled into an endless repetition of itself. ("Imitation," 21)

If anything, the emphasis on identities that are constituted through repetitive performances is even more central to compulsory able-bodiedness—think, after all, of how many institutions in our culture are showcases for able-bodied performance. Moreover, as with heterosexuality, this repetition is bound to fail, as the ideal able-bodied identity can never, once and for all, be achieved. Able-bodied identity and heterosexual identity are linked in their mutual impossibility and in their mutual incomprehensibility—they are incomprehensible in that each is an identity that is simultaneously the ground on which all identities supposedly rest and an impressive achievement that is always deferred and thus never really guaranteed. Hence Butler's queer theories of gender performativity could be easily extended to disability studies, as this slightly paraphrased excerpt from *Gender Trouble* might suggest (I substitute, by bracketing, terms having to do literally with embodiment for Butler's terms of gender and sexuality):

> [Able-bodiedness] offers normative . . . positions that are intrinsically impossible to embody, and the persistent failure to identify fully and without incoherence with these positions reveals [able-bodiedness] itself not only as a compulsory law, but as an inevitable comedy. Indeed, I would offer this insight into [able-bodied identity] as both a compulsory system and an intrinsic comedy, a constant parody of itself, as an alternative [disabled] perspective. (122)

In short, Butler's theory of gender trouble might be resignified in the context of queer/disability studies to highlight what we could call "ability trouble"—meaning not the so-called problem of disability but the inevitable impossibility, even as it is made compulsory, of an able-bodied identity.

QUEER/DISABLED EXISTENCE

The cultural management of the endemic crises surrounding the performance of heterosexual and able-bodied identity effects a panicked consolidation of hegemonic identities. The most successful heterosexual subject is the one whose sexuality is not compromised by disability (metaphorized as queerness); the most successful able-bodied subject is the one whose ability is not compromised by queerness (metaphorized as disability). This consolidation occurs through complex processes of conflation and stereotype: people with disabilities are often understood as somehow queer (as paradoxical stereotypes of the asexual or oversexual person with disabilities would suggest), while queers are often understood as somehow disabled (as

ongoing medicalization of identity, similar to what people with disabilities more generally encounter, would suggest). Once these conflations are available in the popular imagination, queer/disabled figures can be tolerated and, in fact, utilized in order to maintain the fiction that able-bodied heterosexuality is not in crisis. As lesbian existence is deployed, in Rich's analysis, to reflect back heterosexual and patriarchal "realities," queer/disabled existence can be deployed to buttress compulsory able-bodiedness. Since queerness and disability both have the potential to disrupt the performance of able-bodied heterosexuality, both must be safely contained—embodied—in such figures.

In the 1997 film *As Good As It Gets*, for example, although Melvin Udall (Jack Nicholson), who is diagnosed in the film as obsessive-compulsive, is represented visually in many ways that initally position him in what Martin F. Norden calls "the cinema of isolation" (i.e., Melvin is represented in ways that link him to other representations of people with disabilities), the trajectory of the film is toward able-bodied heterosexuality. To effect the consolidation of heterosexual and able-bodied norms, disability and queerness in the film are visibly located elsewhere, in the gay character Simon Bishop (Greg Kinnear). Over the course of the film, Melvin progressively sheds his own sense of inhabiting an anomalous body, and disability is firmly located in the non-heterosexual character, who is initially represented as able-bodied, but who ends up, after he is attacked and beaten by a group of burglars, using a wheelchair and cane for most of the film. More important, the disabled/queer figure, as in many other contemporary cultural representations, facilitates the heterosexual romance: Melvin first learns to accept the differences Simon comes to embody, and Simon then encourages Melvin to reconcile with his girlfriend, Carol Connelly (Helen Hunt).

Having served their purpose, Simon, disability, and queerness are all hustled offstage together. The film concludes with a fairly traditional romantic reunion between the (able-bodied) male and female leads.[8]

CRITICALLY QUEER, SEVERELY DISABLED

The crisis surrounding heterosexual identity and able-bodied identity does not automatically lead to their undoing. Indeed, as this brief consideration of *As Good As It Gets* should suggest, this crisis and the anxieties that accompany it can be invoked in a wide range of cultural texts precisely to be (temporarily) resolved or alleviated. Neither gender trouble nor ability trouble is sufficient in and of itself to unravel compulsory heterosexuality or compulsory able-bodiedness. Butler acknowledges this problem: "This failure to approximate the norm [. . .] is not the same as the subversion of the norm. There is no promise that subversion will follow from the reiteration of constitutive norms; there is no guarantee that exposing the naturalized status of heterosexuality will lead to its subversion" ("Critically Queer," 22; quoted in Warner, "Normal and Normaller" 168–169, n. 87). For Warner, this acknowledgment in Butler locates a potential gap in her theory, "let us say, between virtually queer and critically queer" (Warner, "Normal and Normaller," 168–169, n. 87). In contrast to a virtually queer identity, which would be experienced by anyone who failed to perform heterosexuality without contradiction and incoherence (i.e., everyone), a critically queer perspective could presumably mobilize the inevitable failure to approximate the norm, collectively "working the weakness in the norm," to use Butler's phrase ("Critically Queer," 26).[9]

A similar gap could be located if we appropriate Butler's theories for disability studies. Everyone is virtually disabled, both in the sense that able-bodied norms are "intrinsically impossible to embody" fully, and in the sense that able-bodied status is always temporary, disability being the one identity category that all people will embody if they live long enough. What we might call a critically disabled position, however, would differ from such a virtually disabled position; it would call attention to the ways in which the disability rights movement and disability studies have resisted the demands of compulsory able-bodiedness and have demanded access to a newly imagined and newly configured public sphere where full participation is not contingent on an able body.

We might, in fact, extend the concept and see such a perspective not as critically disabled but rather as severely disabled, with *severe* performing work similar to the critically queer work of *fabulous*. Tony Kushner writes:

> *Fabulous* became a popular word in the queer community—well, it was never *un*popular, but for a while it became a battle cry of a new queer politics, carnival and camp, aggressively fruity, celebratory and tough like a streetwise drag queen: *"FAAAAABULOUS!"* [. . .] *Fabulous* is one of those words that provide a measure of the degree to which a person or event manifests a particular, usually oppressed, subculture's most distinctive, invigorating features. (vii)

Severe, though less common than *fabulous*, has a similar queer history: a severe critique is a fierce critique, a defiant critique, one that thoroughly and carefully reads a situation—and I mean reading in the street sense of loudly calling out the inadequacies of a given situation, person, text, or ideology. "Severely disabled," according to such a queer conception, would reverse the able-bodied understanding of severely disabled bodies as the most marginalized, the most excluded from a privileged and always elusive normalcy, and would instead suggest that it is precisely those bodies that are best positioned to refuse "mere toleration" and to call out the inadequacies of compulsory able-bodiedness. Whether it is the "army of one-breasted women" Audre Lorde imagines descending on the Capitol; the Rolling Quads, whose resistance sparked the independent living movement in Berkeley, California; Deaf students shutting down Gallaudet University in the Deaf President Now action; or ACT UP storming the National Institutes of Health or the Food and Drug Administration, severely disabled/critically queer bodies have already generated ability trouble that remaps the public sphere and reimagines and reshapes the limited forms of embodiment and desire proffered by the systems that would contain us all.[10]

Compulsory heterosexuality is intertwined with compulsory able-bodiedness; both systems work to (re)produce the able body and heterosexuality. But precisely because these systems depend on a queer/disabled existence that can never quite be contained, able-bodied heterosexuality's hegemony is always in danger of being disrupted. I draw attention to critically queer, severely disabled possibilities to further an incorporation of the two fields, queer theory and disability studies, in the hope that such a collaboration (which in some cases is already occurring, even when it is not acknowledged or explicitly named as such) will exacerbate, in more productive ways, the crisis of authority that currently besets heterosexual/able-bodied norms. Instead of invoking the crisis in order to resolve it (as in a film like *As Good As It Gets*), I would argue that a queer/disability studies (in productive conversations with disabled/queer movements outside the academy) can continuously invoke, in order to further the crisis, the inadequate resolutions that compulsory heterosexuality and compulsory able-bodiedness offer us.

And in contrast to an able-bodied culture that holds out the promise of a substantive (but paradoxically always elusive) ideal, a queer/disabled perspective would resist delimiting the kinds of bodies and abilities that are acceptable or that will bring about change. Ideally, a queer/disability studies—like the term *queer* itself—might function "oppositionally and relationally but not necessarily substantively, not as a positivity but as a positionality, not as a thing, but as a resistance to the norm" (Halperin, 66). Of course, in calling for a queer/disability studies without a necessary substance, I hope it is clear that I do not mean to deny the materiality of queer/disabled bodies, as it is precisely those material bodies that have populated the movements and brought about the changes detailed above. Rather, I mean to argue that critical queerness and severe disability are about collectively transforming (in ways that cannot necessarily be predicted in advance) the substantive uses to which queer/disabled existence has been put by a system of compulsory able-bodiedness, about insisting that such a system is never as good as it gets, and about imagining bodies and desires otherwise.

NOTES

1. In 1976, the Brussels Tribunal on Crimes against Women identified "compulsory heterosexuality" as one such crime (Katz, 26). A year earlier, in her important article "The Traffic in Women: Notes on the 'Political Economy' of Sex," Gayle Rubin examined the ways in which "obligatory heterosexuality" and "compulsory heterosexuality" function in what she theorized as a larger sex/gender system (179, 198; cited in Katz, 132). Rich's 1980 article, which has been widely cited and reproduced since its initial publication, was one of the most extensive analyses of compulsory heterosexuality in feminism. I agree with Jonathan Ned Katz's insistence that the concept is redundant because "any society split between heterosexual and homosexual is compulsory" (164), but I also acknowledge the historical and critical usefulness of the phrase. It is easier to

understand the ways in which a society split between heterosexual and homosexual is compulsory precisely because of feminist deployments of the redundancy of compulsory heterosexuality. I would also suggest that popular queer theorizing outside of the academy (from drag performances to activist street theater) has often employed redundancy performatively to make a critical point.

2. In an effort to forge a political connection between all women, Rich uses the terms "lesbian" and "lesbian continuum" to describe a vast array of sexual and affectional connections throughout history, many of which emerge from historical and cultural conditions quite different from those that have made possible the identity of lesbian (192–199). Moreover, by using "lesbian continuum" to affirm the connection between lesbian and heterosexual women, Rich effaces the cultural and sexual specificity of contemporary lesbian existence.

3. The incorporation of queer theory and disability studies that I argue for here is still in its infancy. It is in cultural activism and cultural theory about AIDS (such as John Nguyet Erni's *Unstable Frontiers* or Cindy Patton's *Fatal Advice*) that a collaboration between queer theory and disability studies is already proceeding and has been for some time, even though it is not yet acknowledged or explicitly named as such. Michael Davidson's "Strange Blood: Hemophobia and the Unexplored Boundaries of Queer Nation" is one of the finest analyses to date of the connections between disability studies and queer theory.

4. The collective projects that I refer to are, of course, the projects of gay liberation and queer studies in the academy and the disability rights movement and disability studies in the academy. This chapter is part of my own contribution to these projects and is part of my longer work in progress, titled *Crip Theory: Cultural Signs of Queerness and Disability.*

5. David Mitchell and Sharon Snyder are in line with many scholars working in disability studies when they point out the "ominous silence in the humanities" on the subject of disability (1). See, for other examples, Simi Linton's discussion of the "divided curriculum" (71–116), and assertions by Rosemarie Garland-Thomson and by Lennard Davis about the necessity of examining disability alongside other categories of difference such as race, class, gender, and sexuality (Garland-Thomson, 5; Davis, xi).

6. Disability studies is not the only field Vincent has attacked in the mainstream media; see her article "The Future of Queer: Wedded to Orthodoxy," which mocks academic queer theory. Neither being disabled nor being gay or lesbian in and of itself guarantees the critical consciousness generated in the disability rights or queer movements, or in queer theory or disability studies: Vincent herself is a lesbian journalist, but her writing clearly supports both able-bodied and heterosexual norms. Instead of a stigmaphilic response to queer/disabled existence, finding "a commonality with those who suffer from stigma, and in this alternative realm [learning] to value the very things the rest of the world despises" (Warner, *Trouble*, 43), Vincent reproduces the dominant culture's stigmaphobic response. See Warner's discussion of Erving Goffman's concepts of stigmaphobe and stigmaphile (41–45).

7. Michel Foucault's discussion of "docile bodies" and his theories of disciplinary practices are in the background of much of my analysis here (135–169).

8. The consolidation of able-bodied and heterosexuality identity is probably most common in mainstream films and television movies about AIDS, even—or perhaps especially—when those films are marketed as new and daring." The 1997 Christopher Reeve-directed HBO film *In the Gloaming* is an example. In the film, the disabled/queer character (yet again, in a tradition that reaches back to *An Early Frost* [1985]), is eliminated at the end but not before effecting a healing of the heteronormative family. As Simon Watney writes about *An Early Frost*, "The closing shot [. . .] shows a 'family album' picture. [. . .] A traumatic episode is over. The family closes ranks, with the problem son conveniently dispatched, and life getting back to normal" (114). I am focusing on a non-AIDS-related film about disability and homosexuality, because I think the processes I theorize here have a much wider currency and can be found in many cultural texts that attempt to represent queerness or disability. There is not space here to analyze *As Good As It Gets* fully; for a more comprehensive close reading of how heterosexual/able-bodied consolidation works in the film and other cultural texts, see my article "As Good As It Gets: Queer Theory and Critical Disability." I do not, incidentally, think that these processes are unique to fictional texts: the MLA's annual *Job Information List*, for instance, provides evidence of other locations where heterosexual and able-bodied norms support each other while ostensibly allowing for tolerance of queerness and disability. The recent high visibility of queer studies and disability studies on university press lists, conference

proceedings, and even syllabi has not necessarily translated into more jobs for disabled/queer scholars.

9. See my discussion of Butler, Gloria Anzaldua, and critical queerness in *The Queer Renaissance: Contemporary American Literature and the Reinvention of Lesbian and Gay Identities* (149–153).

10. On the history of the AIDS Coalition to Unleash Power (ACT UP), see Douglas Crimp and Adam Rolston's *AIDS DemoGraphics*. Lorde recounts her experiences with breast cancer and imagines a movement of one-breasted women in *The Cancer Journals*. Joseph P. Shapiro recounts both the history of the Rolling Quads and the Independent Living Movement and the Deaf President Now action in *No Pity: People with Disabilities Forging a New Civil Rights Movement* (41–58; 74–85). Deaf activists have insisted for some time that deafness should not be understood as a disability and that people living with deafness, instead, should be seen as having a distinct language and culture. As the disability rights movement has matured, however, some Deaf activists and scholars in Deaf studies have rethought this position and have claimed disability (that is, disability revalued by a disability rights movement and disability studies) in an attempt to affirm a coalition with other people with disabilities. It is precisely such a reclaiming of disability that I want to stress here with my emphasis on severe disability.

WORKS CITED

As Good As It Gets. Dir. James L. Brooks. Perf. Jack Nicholson, Helen Hunt, and Greg Kinnear. TriStar, 1997.

Berube, Michael. *Life As We Know It: A Father, a Family, and an Exceptional Child*. New York: Vintage-Random House, 1996.

Butler, Judith. "Critically Queer." *GLQ: A Journal of Lesbian and Gay Studies* 1.1 (1993): 17–32

———. *Gender Trouble: Feminism and the Subversion of Identity*. New York: Routledge, 1990.

———. "Imitation and Gender Insubordination." In *Inside/Out: Lesbian Theories, Gay Theories*, edited by Diana Fuss, (13–31). New York: Routledge, 1991.

Crimp, Douglas, and Adam Rolston. *AIDS Demo-Graphics*. Seattle: Bay Press, 1990.

Davidson, Michael. "Strange Blood: Hemophobia and the Unexplored Boundaries of Queer Nation." In *Beyond the Binary: Reconstructing Cultural Identity in a Multicultural Context*, edited by

Timothy Powell (39–60). New Brunswick: Rutgers UP, 1999.

Davis, Lennard J. *Enforcing Normalcy: Disability, Deafness, and the Body*. London: Verso, 1995.

Erni, John Nguyet. *Unstable Frontiers: Technomedicine and the Cultural Politics of "Curing" AIDS*. Minneapolis: U of Minnesota P, 1994.

In the Gloaming. Dir. Christopher Reeve. Perf. Glenn Close, Robert Sean Leonard, and David Strathairn. HBO, 1997.

Foucault, Michel. *Discipline and Punish: The Birth of the Prison*. Translated by Alan Sheridan. New York: Vintage-Random House, 1977.

Garland-Thomson, Rosemarie. *Extraordinary Bodies: Figuring Physical Disability in American Culture and Literature*. New York: Columbia UP, 1997.

Halperin, David, *Saint Foucault: Toward a Gay Historiography*, Oxford: Oxford UP, 1995.

Katz, Jonathan Ned. *The Invention of Heterosexuality*. New York: Dutton, 1995.

Kushner, Tony. "Foreword: Notes Toward a Theater of the Fabulous." In *Staging Lives: An Anthology of Contemporary Gay Theater*, edited by John M. Clum, vii–ix. Boulder: Westview Press, 1996.

Linton, Simi. *Claiming Disability: Knowledge and Identity*. New York: NYU Press, 1998.

Lorde, Audre. *The Cancer Journals*. San Francisco: Aunt Lute Books, 1980.

McRuer, Robert. "As Good As It Gets: Queer Theory and Critical Disability." *GLQ: A Journal of Lesbian and Gay Studies* 9.1–2 (2003): 79–105.

———. *Crip Theory: Cultural Signs of Queerness and Disability*. New York: NYU Press, 2006.

———. *The Queer Renaissance: Contemporary American Literature and the Reinvention of Lesbian and Gay Identities*. New York: NYU Press, 1997.

Mitchell, David T., and Sharon L. Snyder. "Introduction: Disability Studies and the Double Bind of Representation." In *The Body and Physical Difference: Discourses of Disability*, edited by Mitchell and Snyder, 1–31. Ann Arbor: U of Michigan P, 1997.

Norden, Martin F. *The Cinema of Isolation: A History of Physical Disability in the Movies*. New Brunswick: Rutgers UP, 1994.

Patton, Cindy. *Fatal Advice: How Safe-Sex Education Went Wrong*. Durham: Duke UP, 1997.

Rich, Adrienne. "Compulsory Heterosexuality and Lesbian Existence." In *Powers of Desire: The Politics of Sexuality*, edited by Ann Snitow, Christine Stansell, and Sharon Thompson, 177–205. New York: Monthly Review Press, 1983.

Rubin, Gayle. "The Traffic in Women: Notes on the 'Political Economy' of Sex." In *Toward an Anthropology of Women*, edited by Rayna R. Reiter, 157–210. New York: Monthly Review Press, 1975. .

Shapiro, Joseph P. *No Pity: People with Disabilities Forging a New Civil Rights Movement.* New York: Times Books-Random House, 1993.

Vincent, Norah. "Enabling Disabled Scholarship." *Salon.* Aug. 18, 1999. Available at http://www.salon.com/books/it/1999/08/18/disability

———. "The Future of Queer: Wedded to Orthodoxy." *The Village Voice* 22 Feb. 2000: 16.

Warner, Michael. "Normal and Normaller: Beyond Gay Marriage." *GLQ: A Journal of Lesbian and Gay Studies* 5.2 (1999): 119–171.

———. *The Trouble with Normal: Sex, Politics, and the Ethics of Queer Life.* New York: The Free Press, 1999.

Watney, Simon. *Policing Desire: Pornography, AIDS, and the Media.* 2nd ed. Minneapolis: U of Minnesota P, 1989.

Wendell, Susan. *The Rejected Body: Feminist Philosophical Reflections on Disability.* New York: Routledge, 1996.

Williams, Raymond. *Keywords: A Vocabulary of Culture and Society.* Rev. ed. New York: Oxford UP, 1983.

CHAPTER 29

Deaf People: A Different Center

Carol Padden and Tom Humphries

Our friend Howard said "I never knew I was deaf until I went to school." Howard's statement shows that the meanings of DEAF and "deaf" are, at the very least, not the same. DEAF is a means of identifying the group and one's connection to it, and "deaf" is a means of commenting on one's inability to speak and hear. During a conversation with another friend, we began to understand that behind the two supposedly straightforward terms "deaf" and DEAF lie worlds of meaning that are rarely described.

The subject was whether a mutual acquaintance could use the telephone. She couldn't use the phone, our friend told us, because she was only "A-LITTLE HARD-OF-HEARING." We understood this to mean that the woman could hear only a little, not well enough to use the telephone.

On another occasion, another Deaf friend brought up the name of a woman we did not know, and explained that she had many of the recognizable characteristics of a person who could hear well, because she was VERY HARD-OF-HEARING. Our friend added that this woman regularly used the telephone to conduct business.

At the time, we did not recognize the conversations as strange; we did not think about the fact that these ASL terms, if translated literally into English, would mean the opposite of what they mean in English. Instead of using A-LITTLE HARD-OF-HEARING to mean someone whose hearing is only slightly impaired, and VERY HARD-OF-HEARING to mean someone who doesn't hear well, we and our friends used the signs to express exactly the opposite of their English meanings.

It was not until much later, when an older member of our community, Dan, asked if we realized that the signs A-LITTLE HARD-OF-HEARING and VERY HARD-OF-HEARING were being used incorrectly by some Deaf people, that we began to understand. Dan offered an explanation for these "errors": he said they were the kinds of mistakes Deaf people are inclined to make because they lack skill in the English language. We were not surprised by the explanation; at one time it would probably have occurred to us to say the same thing. Deaf people cannot hear English, so they learn it imperfectly. In this case, it was simply a matter of getting the meanings backward. Deaf people ought to be made aware of these kinds of incorrect uses of signs, Dan told us.

But if they were mistakes, we wondered, why did so many Deaf people, including those fluent in English, use them in this way? Perhaps these were not errors at all, but simply a different set of meanings.

Signs from ASL are often thought to be direct representations of spoken words, but in fact they are independent of English. Although signs and their translations may have overlapping meanings, signs are not simply codes for English words. We told Dan he should describe signs in terms independent of the English words used to translate them.

But Dan was ready with his next argument. Surely we had noticed that not all Deaf people use the terms in the "wrong" way. Some, in fact many, Deaf people use the signed phrase A-LITTLE HARD-OF-HEARING to mean a person who can hear quite well and VERY HARD-OF-HEARING for someone who cannot hear well at all. What explanation did we have for that? We had to agree that these terms were also being used according to the "correct" English definitions.

Faced with two opposite sets of meanings, Dan decided that the way to resolve the contradiction was to assign a "correct" definition for HARD-OF-HEARING, and for that he chose the one that conformed to the English meaning. The other use of the term was simply incorrect in his eyes, and no amount of arguing could sway him. There must be one official definition, and any others must be simply wrong.

Our first clue to an explanation for these backward definitions came from a story another friend told us. At a football game between two Deaf schools, he saw members of the home team refer to the opposing team as HEARING. Even though the name of the opponents' school was prominently displayed on the scoreboard, the home team had strangely "forgotten" that the opponents were also Deaf. We exchanged laughs. But it occurred to us that this "error" brought out a key concept in defining HEARING: HEARING means the opposite of what we are.

The sign HEARING has an official English translation, "can hear," but in ASL HEAR-ING is aligned in interesting ways with respect to DEAF and HARD-OF-HEARING. In ASL, as in English, HARD-OF-HEARING represents a deviation of some kind. Someone who is A-LITTLE HARD-OF-HEARING has a smaller deviation than someone who is VERY HARD-OF-HEARING. In this way, ASL and English are similar—and yet the terms have opposite meanings in the two languages. The reason for this is clear: for Deaf people, the greatest deviation is HEARING.

This is the crucial element in understanding these "backward" definitions: there is a different center, a different point from which one deviates. In this case, DEAF, not HEARING, is taken as the central point of reference. A-LITTLE HARD-OF-HEARING is a small deviation from DEAF, and thus is used for someone who is only slightly hearing. VERY HARD-OF-HEARING is someone who departs from the center greatly, thus someone who can hear quite well.

Once we had noticed the different meanings, we began to watch how these terms were used. Many of our friends, like us, did not use one definition exclusively, but often switched meanings according to context and situation. The switching never seemed awkward or confusing, but was normal and expected; the shifts were unconscious. Until our friend brought them to our attention, we had never thought about how we used the terms.

These definitions of DEAF and HARD-OF-HEARING are not remarkable and isolated examples, but are indications of a larger world of meaning where there are conventions for describing relationships between conditions and identities. Within this world of meaning—compared to that of English and the world of others—there is a different alignment, toward a different center.

We knew from our conversations with friends and colleagues that these labels and definitions and many more that Deaf people give themselves and others would compose a rich area of study, one often overlooked in favor of "official" or literal English meanings. When we began writing this book, people often asked us about whose lives we would describe. One friend asked if we would only write about our professional friends, or if we would also include "the average Deaf person." He reminded us that there were a lot of "average Deaf people" out there and we couldn't write only about "exceptional" Deaf people. Not all Deaf people were like us, and he wanted us to be sure to address the problems of those victimized by poor education.

Another friend, testing us, asked if we planned to write about "peddlers," the itinerant vendors who make a living by selling tokens and alphabet cards in exchange for donations. Would our book be about only the "hard-working, honest Deaf person," he asked with a hint of irony, or about all Deaf people, including the seamier types? Other friends suggested we write a book that would set "a good example" to the "hearing world" by focusing on "the intelligent Deaf."

Each recommendation, each label, points to a group within the central category of DEAF, but more clearly to us, the recommendations taken together reveal a rarely described world of meaning used by people who refer to themselves as DEAF. As we began to sort out the different categories, we focused not so much on who was in each category as on how each category was used as a way of talking about the self and about relationships with other people.

Some of the labels we came across are not used to establish commonality, but are used to label certain people as having lesser status—to marginalize them. To ignore the ways that Deaf people use a variety of labels, those which mock and tease as well as those which praise and respect, not only would paint an overly romantic picture but would make our description less rich. Each

label, however petty or harsh some might seem, in its own way helps us to understand the group's deep beliefs and fears.

We started with what seemed to be the most straightforward distinction, that between DEAF and HEARING. What is DEAF? DEAF is first and foremost the group's official name for itself. Deaf organizations take care to specify "of the Deaf" in their names, as in the American Athletic Association of the Deaf, the National Fraternal Society of the Deaf, and the National Association of the Deaf (NAD). These official names contrast with that of an organization recently founded to meet the needs of adults who have lost their hearing at later ages: Self-Help for the Hard of Hearing (SHHH). Although this group's membership includes people who are deaf, its social and political agenda is distinctly different from those of the other organizations. A look at the programs for recent national conventions makes the differences clear. The NAD regularly features workshops on sign language, on improving the image of Deaf people in the media, and on how to lobby for local social service agencies "of, by and for the deaf." In contrast, SHHH offers workshops on promising new medical treatments for hearing impairment, on improving lip-reading skills, and on how to use assistive devices such as amplifiers. Although in recent years the term "hearing impaired" has been proposed by many in an attempt to include both Deaf people and other people who do not hear, Deaf people still refer to themselves as DEAF.

A chance meeting with a Deaf acquaintance on the San Francisco subway (the BART) told us something about what DEAF is not. After the usual greetings, we began to make conversation: Did he work in San Francisco? Did he enjoy riding the subway? He did, and he told us he always rode the Bart because he could take advantage of a "handicapped" discount that made the subway much cheaper than driving to work. But then, quickly, he added, "I don't like using this disabled discount." We nodded sympathetically, and he continued, "But, hey, they offered it to me anyway, and look at how much money I'm saving." We congratulated him on his effective use of public funds. But we took note of his uneasiness and understood that for him the term "disabled" describes those who are blind or physically handicapped, not Deaf people.

"Disabled" is a label that historically has not belonged to Deaf people. It suggests political self-representations and goals unfamiliar to the group. When Deaf people discuss their deafness, they use terms deeply related to their language, their past, and their community. Their enduring concerns have been the preservation of their language, policies for educating deaf children, and maintenance of their social and political organizations. The modern language of "access" and "civil rights," as unfamiliar as it is to Deaf people, has been used by Deaf leaders because the public understands these concerns more readily than ones specific to the Deaf community. Knowing well the special benefits, economic and otherwise, of calling themselves disabled, Deaf people have a history, albeit an uneasy one, of alignment with other disabled groups. But as our friend on the subway reminded us, "disabled" is not a primary term of self-identification, indeed it is one that requires a disclaimer.

*   *   *

Our friend's uneasiness brought us back to an earlier debate among Deaf people about how they should represent themselves to others. Beginning during World War II, Deaf organizations and political leaders began to complain of an alarming increase in the number of deaf peddlers who were soliciting donations from the public. Although deaf peddlers have existed at least since biblical times, these organizations made it clear that peddling by these "able-bodied louts" would no longer be tolerated by "honest and hard-working" Deaf people.

An older member of the community used the sign BEGGING when he talked about peddlers, but technically, to avoid vagrancy laws, peddlers do not beg but sell inexpensive tokens in exchange for "contributions." After the war years, they sold packets of adhesive bandages with small cards explaining that they were deaf and had trouble finding jobs and feeding themselves and their families. The backs of the cards characteristically had an illustration of the manual alphabet with a short note: "Learn to Communicate with the Deaf!" After the war, railroad stations and downtown bars were favorite places for peddlers. A dime or a quarter was the usual contribution; on a good day, a peddler could make between $25 and $30. Peddlers still make their rounds today, but popular wisdom has it that they are "heavily into drugs." Their places of operation have been upgraded to airports and shopping malls, and they sell not bandages but combs, pens, scissors, or religious bookmarks.

The debate about peddlers probably reached its highest and most emotional point after the war. Along with the subject of sign language, a frequent topic in columns and letters to the editor in popular Deaf newsmagazines was the "problem" of peddlers. Arthur L. Roberts, the president of the National Fraternal Society of the Deaf ("The Frat"), wrote relentlessly against peddlers in the organization's publication. In one editorial he wrote: "Tell citizens they should refuse to contribute a cent to these able-bodied louts who ride around the country in good automobiles, stay at good hotels, 'work' only a few hours daily, and ridicule the gullibility of the public which supports them with their ill-gotten means of livelihood" (Roberts 1948). Roberts also made attempts to confront peddlers personally, including posting a list of names of alleged peddlers in the local Deaf club hall. The hearing son of a reputed "king" peddler, an attorney, threatened to sue him for libel and the list was removed.

The NAD established a Committee for the Suppression of Peddling, and in its official publication, the *Silent Worker*, invited readers to offer suggestions for "wiping out peddlers." Occasionally a minority voice was printed, decrying the leaders for their vicious campaigns:

> How I wish Mr. [Arnold] Daulton and his committee for the suppression of peddling could come down to Arkansas and get a glimpse of the number of unemployed here—men with mouths to feed and no money to feed them with. I just don't have it in my heart to condemn these men when, after months of struggling with their conscience, they take to peddling. I have been loud in my protests against peddling, but I know that to solve a problem you must get to the root of it. Get our Arkansas peddlers jobs! I'll bet my last nickel there wouldn't be any peddling in our town then. (Collums 1950).

The Frat and the NAD, with their new leaders, wanted a visible social and political agenda, and a crackdown on peddling was consistent with their beliefs about how to improve the lives of Deaf people. They believed that Deaf people's economic difficulties stemmed from a public image of them as lazy and ineffective. Each Deaf person was individually responsible for maintaining an appropriate image to the public. Roberts firmly believed that eliminating peddlers would also eliminate the larger society's perception that Deaf people were beggars.

A play set in a fictitious Deaf club, *Tales from a Clubroom* (Bragg and Bergman 1981), brings to the surface the tensions revealed by the controversy about peddling. The club's members snipe about a "flashy well-dressed" peddler who comes to their socials and acts as if he is one of them. But the peddler has a ready answer for those who accuse him of not getting a job and of stealing from the "hearies": "You accuse me of stealing money? Who, me? No, you're wrong. I'm only taking back what hearing people took from me because I'm deaf" (Bragg and Bergman 1981: 113). Whatever the justification raised for peddling, it is counter to the way most Deaf people see themselves or want others to see them.

* * *

Peddlers are drawn from the ranks of what is often referred to as "the average deaf person." Leo Jacobs, in *A Deaf Adult Speaks Out* (1974), identifies nine categories of deaf people: the average deaf adult, prelingually deaf adults who come from deaf families, other prelingually deaf adults, low-verbal deaf adults, uneducated deaf adults, products of oral programs, products of public schools, deafened adults, and hard-of-hearing adults.

The first category is an important one for Jacobs. In English one might say "I'm just your average American," but in ASL the phrase "average deaf person" does not have the same quality of normality; instead it suggests someone "simple" or lacking in knowledge of the world. Deaf people who are competent in the English language and have a reasonably good knowledge of others' world are not "average" but "educated." Jacobs rails against the victimization of Deaf people that has resulted in a large group of those called "average," those who suffer because of ignorance, poor education, or poor childrearing practices. The term acknowledges the common belief that the average deaf person is more likely than not to have been victimized in this way.

The label L-V ("low-verbal") is used for educational unfortunates, but often also as a blanket term for low-income ethnic minorities. A common alternative term for

L-V is "not smart." Jacobs describes these people as having "missed for various reasons a great deal of education that they should have received," so that they are almost illiterate. When we once inquired about attending a Deaf club in an urban area, we were told that we would not find it useful to go because members of the club were mostly L-V. Carol was told as a child that many Deaf peddlers were L-V, manipulated into working for unscrupulous king peddlers. More informal terms include, loosely translated, "those out of it," "locals," and "those who do drugs." Again, although these distinctions primarily refer to educational features, they are ways of labeling the uneducated, the working poor, and the chronically unemployed.

With his use of the term "prelingually," Jacobs acknowledges the official distinctions others use for the Deaf population. Those who "lost their hearing before the acquisition of language" are called "prelingually" Deaf, while "postlingually" Deaf is used for those who lost their hearing after having acquired "language." "Language" in this sense, of course, is used to mean English, not sign language. The distinction ignores those who have learned sign language as a first language, and who hence are native users of a human language, like those who are "postlingually deaf." The terms, as would be expected within an official frame with HEARING at the center, emphasize the role of onset of hearing loss and the presence of English, rather than the age at which any human language, including ASL, is acquired.

But Jacobs modifies this distinction and incorporates another; working around the official frame, he adds a new category: "prelingually deaf adults who come from deaf families." He writes that members of this category are "more outgoing and at ease with other deaf persons" and are less likely to have feelings of inferiority. "Other prelingually deaf adults," that is, those who do not have deaf families, form "the bulk of the deaf community," and "come from hearing families who have had trouble communicating with them when they were little." Jacobs adds the unfair generalization that "they are for the most part less aggressive and confident" than those "prelingually deaf adults who come from deaf families" (1974: 56–57).

* * *

Deaf children of Deaf parents may have a respected status among Deaf people because they display effortless facility in the language of the group. But like all the distinctions we have been discussing, this one is not simple. For one thing, outside the group, the notion that parents knowingly gave birth to children when there was a good possibility that the children might be deaf is not an acceptable one. This opinion of others has insidiously affected the way Deaf people view their own Deaf children. On the one hand they are respected and on the other stigmatized.

Out of this deep contradiction, the two groups, Deaf children of Deaf families and Deaf children of hearing families, play out their public images and respond to this tension in different ways. The husband of a Deaf couple told us that for a long time he harbored feelings of superiority over his wife when he introduced himself as having lost his hearing in childhood. His wife, on the other hand, introduced herself as having Deaf parents. By explaining that he had lost his hearing, he could avoid the silent condemnation he believed hearing people directed toward his wife, who had inherited her deafness. He himself could not be held responsible for his condition because he had become deaf "by accident," that is, through illness.

Stories we have heard about hearing children born to Deaf families also involve conflicting sentiments that reveal the complexity of the rules for categorization and identity. For example, a friend told us about a recent dispute at a local Deaf basketball club over a hearing son of Deaf parents who wanted to play for the club. Because this young man could hear, he would have been automatically barred from playing in any games sanctioned by the American Athletic Association of the Deaf (AAAD). Sports organizations like these are one of the few places where Deaf people exercise almost total control over their own affairs, from deciding their own rules to determining who qualifies as a member. And one of the inviolable rules is that hearing players cannot play, on grounds of "unfair" competition. But in this particular case, the club's officers wavered and delayed action that would have removed the player. When the officers of the regional organization learned that the club had a player who was not "legally" Deaf, they pressed the club to act. Recognizing that the hearing player was in all other respects a member of the group, behaved as a Deaf person, and was virtually indistinguishable from his teammates, the club tried labeling him HARD-OF-HEARING. When the regional officers insisted on an audiological test, the club's officers knew they had played their last card and regretfully asked him to leave the team.

The club probably would not have tried to violate the rules if the hearing player had not had Deaf parents. There would have been no question of his being allowed to play. Despite the national organization's watchfulness, there are stories of other basketball clubs where "arrangements" are made allowing hearing children of Deaf parents to play, either "illegally" or at non-AAAD-sanctioned games. No such allowance is ever made for genuine outsiders.

Hearing children of Deaf parents represent a special problem. They have blood ties to Deaf people as well as knowledge of the customs and language of the group. The club officials knew their efforts to keep the player would be supported by the members, and their attempt to label him HARD-OF-HEARING was a desperate but not impossible move to keep him within the category of DEAF. When that move failed, they had no choice but to remove him. In matters where these labels count, such as competing fairly for a prize, the boundaries between DEAF and HEARING are firm.

* * *

Real HARD-OF-HEARING people walk a thin line between being Deaf people who can be like hearing people and Deaf people who are too much like hearing people. They can be admired for their ability to seem like others for specific purposes, but they are viewed with suspicion when they begin to display behaviors of the others when there is no apparent need to, such as when there are no hearing people present. A friend who uses the telephone "without effort" confided that in the presence of new Deaf acquaintances she finds herself feigning difficulty on the telephone to avoid being categorized toward the hearing end of the HARD-OF-HEARING continuum. Another Deaf woman whose Deaf parents and friends call her HARD-OF-HEARING remembers that in her adolescence her parents showed surprise and disbelief when she described having problems communicating with her hearing co-workers. "But you can hear and talk," they told her. Since she was more like hearing people, she was not entitled to make the kinds of complaints Deaf people use about the difficulty of communicating with hearing people.

A hard-of-hearing friend who successfully walks this line was described as "DEAF but really HARD-OF-HEARING," an acknowledgment of his ability to use his skills selectively. HARD-OF-HEARING people can also be DEAF, but there is an imaginary asterisk by their label, qualifying them from time to time.

The label HARD-OF-HEARING involves discussion about having characteristics like hearing people, but being called ORAL is a stronger accusation. A Deaf man reported that though he had no hearing and his voice was barely intelligible, he had become used to being called HARD-OF-HEARING because his mouthing behavior was very "hearing-like." He had lost his hearing at six years of age and did not mind being called "deafened," but he drew the line at being called ORAL. Because ORAL represents a misaligned center, the results of having made wrong choices in life, it is an unacceptable insinuation to someone who considers himself DEAF.

The sign ORAL incorporates a long social and political history of the role of the school in the community. "Oral" schools promote ideologies counter to those of Deaf people; "manual" schools, which allow use of signed language in the schools, are ideologically appealing to Deaf people. Although the term "oral" is slowly losing its traditional context—many schools are no longer represented as either "oral" or "manual," the labels having been replaced by newer terms such as "total communication"—it is still used to represent an ever-present threat, the malevolent opposition.

At a conference for teachers of ASL, a woman stood before her peers and warned that while teachers squabble among themselves about signed language and the different "sign systems," there are "oralists" out there hatching new plots to remove signed language from the education of Deaf children. Let us not forget our true enemy, she proclaimed.

ORAL recalls many extreme stereotypes; our friends gave us two: MIND RICH and ALWAYS PLAN. ORAL individuals are stereotypically represented as members of the establishment, as coming from hearing families that are inflexible about their children's behavior. As the belief goes, the richer the family, the more likely the family will embrace oralism (MIND RICH). The second stereotype portrays a typical ORAL person as one who actively tries to pass as hearing, and must be alert to every possible situation in order to pass successfully (ALWAYS PLAN). In its strongest connotations, ORAL means one who "cozies up to the opposition" and uncritically embraces the world of others.

ORA FAIL ("oral failure") is a term used for those who are products of oppressive educational programs. Deaf teachers talk of having to take in "oral failures" in their "manual" classrooms, of having to take care of others' "rejects." One example appears in *A Deaf Adult Speaks Out*:

> The deaf pupils were only allowed to change to "manual classes" when they proved to be failures in the oral method, usually during their adolescence. These older pupils were generally considered to be brain damaged, aphasic or "slow" by their teachers. Thus many bright and capable youngsters were labeled failures in everything else. Thus incalculable damage was done not only to their self-image but also to their capabilities for optimum achievement toward desirable careers. (Jacobs 1974: 34)

"Oral failures" are, like ORALS, those who pay the price for wrong life choices, but they can be redeemed and become #EX ORAL. (The symbol # is a convention used to represent vocabulary borrowed from fingerspelling.) Jacobs recounts stories of "oral failures" who recover from the damage done to them in their early years and, with the help of instruction in signed language, regain their hidden abilities: "Ted found himself when he discovered manual communication, and was soon making astonishing progress. He caught up with his age level, and displayed an extraordinary bent for mathematics. His language developed at such a rate that he was writing fairly adequate English at the time of his graduation from the school" (p. 36).

In *Tales from a Clubroom,* members of the club charitably call their resident oralist, Spencer Collins, an #EX ORAL because he has repented and joined their ranks. But his slow, lumbering manner remains a comfortable symbol to the others of his past and their own good luck in not being ORAL themselves.

Stories about people like Collins are popular. They are defectors from others' world, those oralists who, when they come of age and are free to make their own choices, join the world of Deaf people as adults and learn signed language. Carol remembers as a child attending an evening at a local Deaf bowling league where a friend pointed out a woman several alleys down. This woman's father was a prominent leader of oral education, the friend said, and yet here she was, mixing and signing with us like a regular. She had rebelled against her father and married a Deaf man! The defection was as significant as that of a daughter of a prominent Soviet party official. All it takes, Carol's friend explained, is a taste of our world and they want to leave the old one behind.

In fantasy storytelling, an ORAL is a powerful symbol of one in need of being rescued. At a party, a man told a variation on a Cinderella story with an impoverished ORAL girl. The simple structure of the fairy tale highlighted the idealized difference between those who are ORAL and those who are DEAF. This deaf Cinderella is given a pair of glass gloves by her fairy godmother, allowing her to sign effortlessly and gracefully. Her ragged clothing disappears under her godmother's wand, and she finds herself wearing jewelry made by Deaf artists. She goes to the Deaf club and falls in love with the son of the club president. With her glass gloves, she captivates the "prince" of the club. At midnight, true to the original story, she flees, leaving behind one of the glass gloves. The story ends as predicted: the "prince" finds the girl of his dreams, and she becomes his "princess," her magic gloves allowing her to erase her many years as an ORAL person and gain the difficult but admired skill of signing like a native.

A trendier accusation that one Deaf person can make of another, one some older members of the community find confusing, is THINK-HEARING. Its literal meaning is "to think and act like a hearing person," but a more accurate translation is "to embrace uncritically the ideology of others." The term's range of meaning is similar to that of ORAL, except that the accusation can be made against any Deaf person, including those who are not ORAL, that is, not orally trained.

THINK-HEARING illustrates the present generation's sophistication with sign structure (which we describe in Chapter 5). Instead of an adaptation of an existing sign, as with ORAL which also means SPEECH or MOVING-LIPS, THINK-HEARING is a novel creation formed by combining selected elements from the two signs THINK and HEARING. THINK-HEARING goes beyond ORAL to include other unacceptable choices such as voicing opposition to ASL, or insisting that signers should use among themselves invented sign vocabulary developed for teaching English to deaf children. Older members of the community, more comfortable with the distinction between "oral" and "manual," or between not signing and signing, find accusations based on what kind of signing one uses unfamiliar. THINK-HEARING, through its self-conscious analysis of signs, emphasizes a modern realignment of the center.

* * *

As we have said, to understand how these categorizations and labels work one must begin from a different center. Deaf people work around different assumptions about deafness and hearing from those of hearing people. The condition of not hearing, or of being hard of hearing, cannot be described apart from its placement in the context of categories of cultural meaning. Names applied to one another are labels that define relationships. The relationships Deaf people have defined include their struggles with those who are more powerful than they, such as hearing others.

A person who is "DEAF but really HARD-OF-HEARING" has skillfully managed his relationships across groups. Deaf people may use a politically advantageous label such as "disabled," but they must apologize for it among themselves. Jacobs borrows the supposedly scientific distinction between "prelingually deaf" and "postlingually deaf" and adds modifiers that readjust the relationships in ways that are more compatible with group knowledge. All of these adjustments indicate how well the center accommodates and, at the same time, how tightly it holds.

WORKS CITED

Bragg, Bernard. *Lessons in Laughter: The Autobiography of a Deaf Actor.* Bernard Bragg as signed to Eugene Bergman. Washington, D.C.: Gallaudet UP, 1989.

Collums, C. 1950. "Letter to the Open Forum." *Silent Worker* 2:31.

Jacobs, Leo. *A Deaf Adult Speaks Out.* Washington, D.C.: Gallaudet College Press, 1974.

CHAPTER 30

"Hearing Aids Are Not Deaf": A Historical Perspective on Technology in the Deaf World

R. A. R. Edwards

Class was coming to an end. With an equally mixed deaf-hearing student body, our discussion about cochlear implants had been intense, engaging, thoughtful, and passionate. Now, a hearing student raised a hand. "Okay," he began. "I understand now why Deaf people are so opposed to cochlear implants. But then, why are hearing aids acceptable?" I looked around the room. A goodly number of students in this American Deaf History class were wearing digital hearing aids, after all. Slowly, the Deafest student in the room raised her hand. She was Deaf of Deaf of Deaf, with a Deaf family that went back several generations. Her opinion would therefore be taken with great seriousness. All eyes in the room fixed on her and we all waited. Finally she began. "Hearing aids," she signed deliberately, with an edge of contempt, but a bit reluctantly, as if she knew she had to make this announcement from the cultural heartland, with the knowledge that not everyone in the room would be comfortable with her coming declaration. "Hearing aids," she repeated. "Hearing aids are not Deaf."

The pronouncement left the class stunned. The hearing students were surprised by this sudden and, from their point of view, unexpected correlation of two technologies. Most of the Deaf students in

the class came from hearing families. They also tended to view the two technologies quite differently. Their thinking went like this: I might wear hearing aids, but at least I don't have an implant. I know where the line is! But this Deaf student, from a Deaf family, with neither aids nor implants, refused to admit the existence of the line. She adamantly insisted that the two technologies rested instead along a continuum. They could not be so neatly divided.

As it turns out, her cultural knowledge, handed down to her through her Deaf family, mirrors the historical record. In fact, the Deaf community's reaction to the emergence of hearing aids in the 1950s very much prefigures the debate over cochlear implants that followed in the 1990s. That is, historically, the Deaf community's response to technology has been quite consistent. The Deaf community is quite technologically sophisticated; in fact, it is the overwhelming use of personal electronic devices among deaf people that gives Washington, D.C., the distinction of having the highest usage of cell power in the country. (And, yes, this was a surprise to hearing business executives who commissioned the study to find out which American city needed more service.) It is decidedly not a Deaf Luddism which drives opposition to implants. Rather, the community embraces or rejects technologies based on their intent. When the Deaf community turns to technology, it seeks technology to enable the living of a richer Deaf life. But when hearing people offer technologies to deaf people, they have generally promoted medical technologies to eliminate deaf life. Unsurprisingly, the Deaf community rejected these technologies, first hearing aids, and then cochlear implants.

The first electronic amplifying device was developed by Ferdinand Alt in Vienna in 1900. Max Goldstein, an American otologist, impressed with the work of the medical community in Vienna, introduced a group hearing aid into classrooms for the deaf in the 1920s. By the early 1940s, small, individual hearing aids had finally started to appear on the market in larger numbers. Many hearing observers and educators celebrated the influx of hearing aids into deaf classrooms, believing they would enable the deaf to be integrated into hearing society.[1]

Those classrooms were oral in pedagogy. While nineteenth-century deaf education had been manual, that is, deaf children were educated with the use of American Sign Language, twentieth-century deaf education was oral. Signed communication of any sort was generally forbidden. Deaf children, regardless of their audiological status, were expected to learn how to speak and lipread to communicate as hearing people did. The goal of oral education was to make deaf people over in a hearing image, so that they would integrate perfectly into hearing society. It was assumed that both the sign language and the Deaf community would be eliminated as a result. They would not be needed if all deaf children could be made culturally hearing. In this way, oralism became deeply entwined with eugenics.

Indeed, the leading oralist of his generation, Alexander Graham Bell, was also an avowed eugenicist. He yoked the two causes together in his 1883 speech, "Memoir Upon the Formation of a Deaf Variety of the Human Race," in which he wished that it were possible to pass legislation forbidding deaf people from marrying, in order to prevent them from spreading their inferior deaf genes into the next generation. Conceding that the passage of such laws was impracticable, Bell argued instead that the field of deaf education would have to rely on oralist means to achieve eugenic ends. If deaf children could be made to speak, they would seek out hearing partners and live in the hearing world. The threat of the rise of a deaf variety of the human race would fade accordingly.

The Deaf community had organized itself at this same time, in part to fight against the oralism and eugenicism which threatened the community's very survival. The National Association of the Deaf was founded in 1880. It aggressively fought back against the oral method, attacking both its pedagogy and its negative portrayal of deafness. It defended the sign language vigorously, producing a series of films to try to capture the power of the language and share it with wider audiences. Unlike oralist educators, the NAD viewed the move of this new assistive hearing technology into classrooms with suspicion. This was surely just another way of trying to turn deaf children into hearing children, now perhaps literally.

By the 1950s, as the average price of an individual hearing aid dropped, the technology came within reach of more individuals and, as a result, hearing aid usage grew. As a result, the National Association of the Deaf determined that it needed to do more to counter the appeal of hearing aids in the hearing public and offer a Deaf critique of this technology. The NAD took on the hearing aid industry by launching a campaign to combat what it called misleading, and derogatory, hearing aid advertising claims.[2]

The NAD began its campaign in 1950 by writing to the American Bureau of Public Relations, charging that the use of the word deaf in advertising copy was misleading, as "hearing aids are useful only to the hard of hearing." One company, Paravox, agreed to eliminate the use of the word deafness from all its advertising in the future.[3] The NAD certainly appreciated the fact that Paravox acknowledged that the use of 'deaf' in advertising copy was "improper if it offended the deaf."[4] Not all companies were as accommodating to the NAD's point of view. NAD president Byron B. Burnes complained that "Acoustican, for instance, insisted that the advertising was approved by a panel of highly skilled and highly paid advisers to make sure it didn't offend anybody. We pointed out that it was offensive to us but the fact didn't register at all."[5]

Faced with an industry so willing to ignore the Deaf perspective, Burnes suggested a writing campaign, but he "urged the deaf to be fair." As he put it, "Don't write to any company unless it emphasizes the word deaf in its advertising. Let the companies which confine their advertising to the hard of hearing strictly alone. Don't bother Paravox, for instance. But give the others both barrels, beginning now. They deserve it."[6]

Hearing aid advertisements explicitly called hearing aids a cure for deafness. One Acousticon ad promised, "If you act today you may stop being deaf! For only $69.50, full price."[7] Such claims, the NAD complained, only raised false hopes for hearing parents of deaf children and misled the public into thinking that medical science could cure deafness. Marcus Kenner, a businessman who served as NAD president from 1934 to 1940, complained bitterly about this language. Citing the Beltone Hearing Aid Company's advertisement copy, "Don't be deaf!," he wrote sarcastically, "(It) would be just as logical for opticians to advertise: 'Don't be BLIND—use our spectacles.' "[8]

Soon other deaf papers, like *The Silent Cavalier*, joined in the NAD campaign.[9] Not content to pursue the issue only in the silent press, the NAD also turned to the mainstream press for support. Burnes enlisted the Chicago *Tribune*, which called upon advertisers to tone down their rhetoric. The *Tribune* agreed with the NAD's position that "the hearing public already is woefully ignorant of the nature of deafness and will harbor even greater misconceptions because of the barrage of hearing aid advertisements."[10]

To the NAD, this was the crux of the issue. As Burnes explained, "Our handicap is not in the fact that we are deaf, but in the fact that the public is not acquainted with us."[11] The advertising industry and the high-pressure tactics of hearing aid salesmen combined to create a negative public image of deaf people, as pitiful and morose, waiting for medical technology to rescue them from their silent world. The advertisements traded in stereotypes.[12] The NAD took these advertisements seriously precisely because they slandered a minority group. Other Deaf Americans beyond the NAD leadership took up the cause. Elmer Long wrote columns blasting what he called "the hearing aid racket."[13] He also urged other Deaf people to speak out on issues important to the community. "Yes, we are a minority group," he declared, "but we need not be voiceless!"[14]

Hearing aids were also disturbing to the Deaf community because they were clearly yoked to oral education. This was a technology laden with oralist hopes. Roger M. Falberg presented his own version of the schoolchild's encounter with oralism and hearing aids in a column for *The Silent Worker* in 1957.[15] He wrote:

> You see, I wasn't in a day school class with other deaf and hard-of-hearing children. I was the "great experiment," the deaf child "restored" to the hearing world attending

public schools . . . My lip-reading teacher taught day-school classes during the day, and twice a week I'd go to her home and recite after her the words I read on her lips. She really laid it on thick, that woman did. She never tired of telling me and my parents how wonderful it was for me to be doing so well in school. I'll give her credit–she meant well, and thought she was doing the right thing. But nobody ever asked me what *I* wanted. And what I wanted, more than anything else in the world, was a friend I could trust! . . . Dad died when I was 15 and in my first year of high school. Mother had to go to work in a clothing factory. She scraped together her pennies and bought me a hearing aid–about $200 gone out the window. That salesman even kidded me into thinking the aid was helping me! I junked it during my first year at Gally [Gallaudet University] and never wore it since. I'm certainly no paragon of virtue even now, but I'm very, very happy to be working and living with the people I understand and who understand me—the deaf. . . . I'm casting my bread upon the waters in the sincere hope that this story will result in just *one* parent waking up to the light and sending just *one* child to a residential school for the deaf where he belongs–to bring the truth and the sign language into just *one* young life before it is too late! Amen.[16]

This simple story makes a complex challenge to both oralism and hearing aids. Falberg acknowledged and rejected oralist talk of restoring the deaf to society. He knew this was what his hearing parents wanted for him, but he also knew that throwing him into a classroom of hearing people hardly restored him to anyone's society. Oral deaf education, with its use of hearing aids, served his parent's needs to have a "normal" child more than his own.[17] Again, no one ever asked him what he needed, and what he needed was to stop being a deaf person and become a Deaf person. He finally achieved this transformation by attending Gallaudet College, the world's only liberal arts college for the deaf, making Deaf friends, learning sign language, and

junking his hearing aid. As a deaf person who had to struggle to claim his Deafness, he urged other hearing parents of deaf children to make the path smoother, by exposing their children to sign language and the Deaf community early on.

In addition, the quest to claim one's Deafness was increasingly informed by the emergence of the civil rights movement. Casting Deafness in a positive light, much like framing black as beautiful, threw hearing aids into a new, and far more political, light. For instance, Mary Jane Rhodes, a hearing mother of a deaf son, recalled sending her son away for summer camp. "Just before Ronnie left for camp," she remembered, "I was teasing him about never using his hearing aid. He is deaf but can hear some sounds with amplification. I asked him if he would like to take the hearing aid to camp. He looked me straight in the eye and said, 'I want to be an original deaf person–not an artificial deaf person.' I have given much thought to his reply." Rhodes linked her son's rejection of hearing aids to what she called a growing Deaf Pride movement. "During the past couple of years, deaf adults around the country have told me that they don't want to be hearing people . . . but they are tired of being looked down because they use methods of manual communication. They are losing respect and patience with hearing people who insist that our deaf citizen's goal should be that of imitating the hearing world."[18]

This antipathy toward hearing aids continued for the rest of the twentieth century. As Harlan Lane argues, the hearing aid is a "symbolic object" and the Deaf community both understands and rejects the meaning of that symbol.[19] Deaf artists like Betty Miller began to incorporate a Deaf view of hearing aids in their art, attacking both the technology itself and its oralist implications.[20] A 1989 *Deaf Life* reader's poll asked, "Should Deaf children be forced to wear hearing aids?" An overwhelming

73 percent of readers responded no.[21] And in a powerful moment at the opening ceremony of the International Conference on Sign Language in July 1990, French Deaf leader Jean-Francois Mercurio smashed a hearing aid with a sledgehammer.[22]

But despite the Deaf community's long-standing rejection of hearing aids, hearing aids became more and more common, especially among deaf schoolchildren, as the twentieth century progressed. Why? Lane attributes the success of the hearing aid industry to what he calls "audism." Audism, in his view, refers to the host of attitudes that result in the medicalization of the cultural condition of deafness. In this way, theories of audism parallel ongoing efforts in the disability studies community to interrogate what is termed the medical model, that is, the view of disability through a medicalizing, and usually pathologizing, lens. As Lane argues, "audism is the hearing way of dominating, restructuring, and exercising authority over the deaf community." Oral education was only one expression of this domination. Medicine is another. Having conceptualized deafness as a medical problem, audism assumes the need for medical technologies and cures, and persons to administer such interventions to a now subject population. Audists include hearing administrators of schools for the deaf, audiologists, speech therapists, vocation rehabilitation specialists, social workers, and hearing aid specialists.[23]

H. Dirksen Bauman similarly advances his own theory of audism, writing that audist practices "enforc(e) a normalcy that privileges speech over sign and hearing over deafness." He critiques the power of audism in deaf education, arguing that oral education, in particular, engages in the practice of "disciplining Deaf bodies into becoming closer to normal hearing bodies."[24] Deaf bodies are literally disciplined through speech, as deaf people are schooled in a pedagogy that controls their very breath in an effort to ensure that they communicate like hearing people.[25]

The attempt to make deaf bodies come "closer to normal human bodies" underscores both the logic of oral education and of medical technology, and that technology includes both hearing aids and cochlear implants. Cochlear implants hold out the same promise as this earlier technology, to make the deaf body hear, to make Deaf people into hearing people. Given the Deaf community's response to hearing aids, it should come as no surprise that Deaf people would react strongly to this new technology. To them, cochlear implants attacked both deafness and Deafness, and therefore served an oralist agenda.

Cochlear implants were first developed in France in the 1950s, though the work progressed slowly. By the mid-1970s, French otologist Claude-Henri Chouard implanted on average only one deaf patient per month.[26] But the French Deaf community increasingly raised protests against the procedure. "For example, in December 1977, in France, a number of deaf people suggested that cochlear implants were not needed since they were perfectly happy the way they were. Moreover, many deaf people did not appreciate the suggestion that they needed to be able to hear and speak to lead productive lives."[27] Another French Deaf leader, D. Albinhac, pointedly asked in 1978, "Why not bleach the blacks . . .? When are they going to stop, once and for all, using us as guinea pigs?"[28]

Opposition in the 1970s also emerged in Australia, where one of the leading researchers into implants, Dr. Graeme Clark, was based. Clark expressed some surprise that Deaf Australians "did not appreciate what they perceived to be the negative image of deaf people that was conveyed in some of the fund-raising telethons" he held with his colleagues during the decade.[29] Opposition in the international Deaf community continued to spread over the next two decades. In March 1993, Swiss Deaf people staged a demonstration against pediatric implants, and a few months later, a crowd of 800 French Deaf gathered in Lyons for a similar demonstration. Canadian Deaf protested in Ontario in January 1994.[30]

In the United States, clinical trials of cochlear implants began in 1985. The device was approved for commercial distribution for use in postlingually deafened adults only. Manufacturers sought approval for use in children as well, and the Food and Drug Administration (FDA) approved the device for use in patients as young as two years of age in June 1990.[31] By the year 2000, over 35,000 people around the world had received implants and about half of that number were children under the age of 18.[32]

The websites of cochlear implant manufacturers serve as advertisements for their products. These sites employ many of the same arguments and stereotypes that the NAD fought during its campaign against hearing aid advertisements. Unsurprisingly, Deaf people have also reacted quite negatively to this new technology. The community's anger "comes . . . from the tendency of many medical personnel . . ., the media, and hearing parents to focus on the cochlear implant as a way to enhance the quality of life, as if deaf people's lives were inherently lacking and unfulfilled without the implant."[33]

Cochlear implant manufacturers routinely invoke such images of deaf life. Advanced Bionics, for instance, declares that people get cochlear implants for the following reasons: "They want to be included instead of left out. They want to be more independent. They want to be more peaceful and relaxed."[34] A San Francisco implant center assures visitors that implant users can "learn a foreign language, enjoy the movies, enjoy the theatre, participate in social activities."[35] The implication, of course, is that without the implant deaf adults cannot do any of these things.

Marilyn Howe, former vice-president of the Association of Late-Deafened Adults, called these "untruths in advertising." She wrote, "The implication . . . of the ads is, 'Gee, why be deaf and miserable when you can be hearing and happy again?' " She further charged that, while cochlear implant manufacturers are likely to strike this tone, "the hearing aid industry is often as guilty. There is more than one corporation that tells us this little device will perform miracles in our ear."[36] The Greater Los Angeles Council on Deafness (GLAD), in its position paper on implants, tried to explain that "the view that hearing, no matter now much (or how little) has the power to change social, political, economic, or psychological conditions for the individual is simplistic."[37]

Many in the Deaf community have vigorously objected to this hearing characterization of their lives. Kathryn Woodcock writes that many Deaf people believe that cochlear implants prove "that hearing people want to eradicate deafness and, by implication, wish that they—Deaf people—didn't exist. That's a pretty difficult message to accept equably."[38] Richard Eckert complained, "I surely get annoyed when CI advocates ascribe onto me a stigmatization that I am somehow defective and in need of repair. I don't need to be fixed. I am not broken!"[39] *DeafNation* columnist Mark Drolsbaugh was "chagrined" to discover that a hearing relative had gone to a cochlear implant informational session behind his back to find out if he was a potential candidate for the procedure. She was dismayed to learn he was not. "Okay, okay, I know she does it out of love," he wrote, "(and) in her own way, she does what she thinks is best for me. Yet it still pains me to see that to her, I will never be the successful Deaf adult that I am. To her, I will always be the hearing impaired person in the family . . . the man who needs to be repaired."[40]

The oralist assumptions of cochlear implant manufacturers, doctors, and hearing parents also outrage the Deaf community. Spoken language acquisition is the stated goal of the procedure. To be a candidate for the procedure, Advanced Bionics recommends the child live "in a positive learning environment where speaking and listening are encouraged."[41] Similarly the Cochlear Corporation recommends that patients secure "placement in an educational program that emphasizes development of auditory skills after the implant has been fitted."[42] The websites of both manufacturers and implant centers overwhelmingly emphasize speech and listening as the goals of implant surgery.[43] Hearing parents generally support this goal. A major survey of parents of implanted children conducted in the summer of 1999 found that 52 percent cited "ease in development and use of oral spoken language" as the main reason they had their child implanted.[44]

The Deaf community fears that the growing trend to implant deaf children heralds an increasing emphasis on oral education for deaf children. *Salon* magazine has reported that "more than a dozen new oralist schools have started in the past three years to educate implanted kids."[45] Public officials, like North Carolina Department of Health and Human Services Secretary David Bruton, increasingly speak of the need for early diagnosis and intervention, and of a corresponding need to emphasize oral education at the expense of sign language. Reflecting on a trip to Germany, one of the birthplaces of the oral method, he told a crowd in 1999, "Every one of those German children talked to me in English. They had learned to hear with their eyes and talk with their vocal cords and mouths. Our children—wonderful, bright people sentenced by us to silence—can only talk by signaling somebody who can read their sign language and talk for them. Now, I'm not going to be a part of that kind of child abuse."[46]

The potential return of oral education, with its oppression of Deaf ways and language, strikes fear in the Deaf community. This fear drew the NAD into the fray. The NAD took a strong position against implanting deaf children in its first position paper on cochlear implants, released in 1991.[47] The paper began, "The NAD deplores the decision of the Food and Drug Administration, which was unsound scientifically, procedurally, and ethically," and then continued on to outline the specific errors the NAD believed had occurred. The NAD charged that there was "no evidence that early-implanted children will do better at acquiring English than they would with noninvasive aids or with no aids whatsoever."[48] To the NAD, there was also "no evidence that early-implanted children will have greater educational success than is currently experienced by children of similar circumstances who do not undergo this invasive surgical procedure." For these reasons, the NAD concluded, "implantation of cochlear prostheses in early-deafened children remains highly experimental." Experimenting on children, the statement added, "is ethically offensive."

The NAD also blasted the FDA for its failure to consult with anyone from the Deaf community as it made its decision.

Otologists, speech, and hearing scientists, manufacturers, parents, and members of the FDA staff were all consulted formally by the FDA in arriving at its decision. FDA's failure to consult with deaf spokespersons represents, if an oversight, gross ignorance concerning growing up deaf in America, or, if willful, an offensive against fundamental American values of individual liberties, cultural diversity, and consumer rights.

In its attack on cochlear implants, the NAD characterized the technology as an assault on a cultural minority group, as a medical device that would undermine America's much celebrated cultural diversity. With this line of argument, the NAD hoped to appeal to a wider audience than its own constituency. It hoped to explain that Deafness was a culture worth fighting for, not against.

The NAD could make such an argument in 1991 because, ironically, the Deaf community was perhaps at its strongest point in American history just as cochlear implants appeared on the scene. Implants were approved just as Deaf culture and ASL were becoming more visible on the American cultural landscape. The Deaf President Now (DPN) strike in March 1988, which culminated in the installation of the first Deaf president in Gallaudet University's history, had suddenly thrust Deaf concerns onto the national news.[49]

Deaf people, and their language, were suddenly visible, on the streets of Washington, on the national news, on the Capitol steps. As they marched on the Capitol, they carried a huge banner that read "We Still Have a Dream!," effectively linking their cause with that of the civil rights movement. Politicians and the media quickly accepted the argument that DPN represented a new civil rights struggle. A political cartoon appeared in the *Denver Post* showing a Deaf man signing "We Shall Overcome". A march on the Capitol on Friday, 11 March 1988, found the crowd greeted by Rep. Steve Gunderson, who welcomed them saying, "If this is your march on Selma, I want to congratulate you on your successful arrival."[50]

Strike chroniclers John Christiansen and Sharon Barnartt argue that the success of DPN, and the extensive, and overwhelmingly positive, media coverage, helped speed the passage of the Americans with Disabilities Act (ADA) two years later. DPN, in their view, reframed the way that Americans perceived the issue of disability rights, by opening a new perspective, one

that "viewed persons with disabilities as a minority group, whose members experience discrimination."[51] Deaf people led the way in this new civil rights battle, and in turn, this battle re-energized the Deaf community.

The early 1990s therefore saw the juxtaposition of the renaissance of Deaf culture and the rise of cochlear implants. Books about Deaf culture exploded on the scene. ASL poetry came into its own, developing strongly after the first sign poetry workshop held at the National Technical Institute for the Deaf in 1984. Both Clayton Valli and Ella Mae Lentz released videos of their ASL poems in 1995. In poll after readers' poll, the Deaf community affirmed the values of Deaf culture: most Deaf people would refuse a pill that would make them instantly hearing; most believed that the best method for teaching deaf children was to use ASL; most thought the best educational setting for a deaf children was a residential school for the deaf; most rejected the idea that deafness is a handicap.[52]

This Deaf renaissance seemed even to force medical ethicists to rethink implants by the mid-1990s. Robert Crouch argued that medical doctors should not be so quick to recommend implantation for young deaf children and should instead consider "letting the deaf be Deaf."[53] Crouch was disturbed by the limited benefits that the first wave of long-term studies of implants seemed to reveal. These concerns seemed validated by the National Institutes of Health, which admitted in a 1995 position paper on implants that studies showed that cochlear implants were most effective for postlingually deafened adults. The NIH advised doctors to be aware that "oral language development in deaf children, including those with cochlear implants, remains a slow, training-intensive process, and results will typically be delayed in comparison with normal hearing peers." While the NIH recommended that the implantation of young deaf children continue, it urged doctors, parents of implanted children, and patients to understand that implants do not restore normal hearing, and that auditory and speech outcomes are both highly variable and completely unpredictable.[54]

For Crouch and others, this was precisely why the deaf were better off Deaf. If the technology was so unpredictable, why favor it over Deafness? For Deaf activists, of course, questions of effectiveness were wholly irrelevant. Even a perfect implant would be rejected. Deaf radical M.J. Bienvenu compared implant surgeons to Nazis. Deaf writer Ben Bahan made a link between deaf and hearing histories, declaring, "Bell and Hitler both wanted to wipe out what they considered 'defective.' "[55] The Deaf community, having had experience with earlier eugenic assaults on their bodies, could not help but interpret implants as another such assault on Deafness. To them, cochlear implants brought the specter of a potential genocide.

These Deaf cultural issues began to reach a hearing audience in the 1990s as well. The *New York Times Magazine* and *The Atlantic Monthly* each published cover stories about Deaf culture, in 1994 and 1993 respectively.[56] Both articles tried to introduce readers to Deaf culture and both discussed cochlear implants from a Deaf point of view. In his *New York Times xx Magazine* article, Andrew Solomon acknowledged that hearing people seem mystified by this Deaf rejection of an apparent cure, but pointed out that Americans had encountered similar arguments about the appropriateness of cures in the recent past. "Twenty-five years ago," he reminded readers,

before the principle of gay rights had been broadly articulated, few people questioned that it was right and fit to try to cure homosexuality . . . Twenty-five years ago, the

arguments for curing gayness seemed as unarguable as the arguments for curing the Deaf seem to be now. When and how did the shift from the pathological to the cultural view of gayness take place?[57]

Solomon asked readers to consider the possibility that if such a shift had taken place for gayness, a similar shift might be both possible and appropriate for deafness as well.

Edward Dolnick's article was reprinted in *Deaf Life*. *Deaf Life* also printed letters that *The Atlantic* received in response to the article. But while Dolnick had treated "Deafness as Culture," these letter writers were largely unsympathetic to that claim. Writers made reference to "deafism cultists" and the "deaf isolationists." One writer called deaf culture a "trendy self-segregation movement," arguing that "proponents of Deaf Culture have misappropriated the terminology of the civil rights movement." Another predicted that "the cochlear prosthesis . . . will lead inevitably to the extinction of the alternative culture of the Deaf, probably within a decade."[58]

In presenting the letters *Deaf Life* editorialized, "Is the Deaf community doomed? Are cochlear implants going to become routinely prescribed for deaf babies, as commonplace and inevitable as childhood vaccinations? Are we fighting a losing battle? The answers are yes, yes, and yes—if we continue sleeping, if we don't wake up, if we don't mobilize ourselves."[59] Even in the midst of a Deaf cultural renaissance, implant technology gained ground. It is no wonder that a 1997 *Deaf Life* survey found readers in a fearful mood. When asked "Is the cochlear implant destroying the future of the deaf culture?", an overwhelming 79 percent said yes.[60]

A random survey of Gallaudet students, alumni, and faculty and staff produced similar results in the summer of 2000. While at first blush, it appeared that

51 percent of respondents agreed with the statement that one "could have a CI and be Deaf," the numbers, when broken down further, revealed something quite different. 39 percent of deaf responders disagreed, whereas 81 percent of the hearing agreed and 71 percent of those who identified themselves as hard of hearing agreed. The statement that the "deaf community will eventually disappear in American because of cochlear implanted children," produced a similar split. 58 percent overall disagreed, but over 70 percent of both hard of hearing and hearing disagreed, while 34 percent of deaf agreed. And when confronted with the statement, "Hearing parents should be permitted to get a cochlear implant for their child under 5 if they study the issue carefully," 56 percent disagreed overall, but an overwhelming 72 percent of deaf responders disagreed, while 78 percent of hearing agreed and 53 percent of hard of hearing agreed.[61] How one viewed the issues depended very much on whether or not the respondent was deaf or hearing.

The fact that so much of one's reaction to cochlear implants apparently depends on one's audiological status suggests that the turn from the pathological to the cultural that Solomon looked for in 1994 has not yet occurred. The Deaf view of deafness remains most persuasive only to Deaf people, and has not yet convinced many hearing people. As one *Salon* reader complained, "Anti-implant deaf people . . . don't want to be seen as disabled or defective or whatever. Too bad! They can't hear!"[62]

It is true that deaf people cannot hear. But, while the letter writer assumes there is only one possible cultural meaning to being unable to hear, Deaf people have attempted to attach a different set of meanings to deafness. They have asked their fellow Americans to value, rather than denigrate, their difference. The history of the twentieth-century Deaf experience, especially their encounters

with technology, suggests that this request has not been affirmatively answered. Though Deaf people value their deafness as well as their Deafness, and have been saying so for over one hundred years in the United States, the hearing community largely has yet to hear them.

This case study has also tried to address the larger questions of disability studies as historian Catherine Kudlick has presented them. She states that disability studies goes to the heart of "the overarching questions central to our mission as scholars and teachers in a humanistic discipline: what does it mean to be human? How can we respond ethically to difference? What is the value of a human life? Who decides these questions, and what do the answers reveal?"[63]

These are the questions the historical actors in this case study understood well and sought to answer. But the result, perhaps, is a cautionary tale. Even as the Deaf activists recounted here skillfully attacked the medical model and demonstrated its weaknesses, biases, and limitations, hearing people nonetheless remained far more interested in pursuing medical technologies to eliminate deafness than in celebrating deafness as another valuable culture in the American melting pot. In this history of the Deaf community's encounter with assistive technologies, it is, in the end, hearing people who have largely determined the answers to these questions. It is hearing people who have yet to understand that hearing aids, and cochlear implants, are not Deaf. And they have yet to understand why it even matters.

This, then, is the challenge for both the new disability history and deaf history. Deaf history has been praised as having the best potential to "help scholars move from thinking about disability as an individual's pathological characteristic to considering it as a social category."[64] How can the insights of these fields be brought to a wider public?

How can the lessons of this history be brought to bear on our present? How can our students meet across their differences and learn from one another? And who will take up the challenge of helping them to do so?

NOTES

1. Hearing aid history found in Bender, *The Conquest of Deafness*, 171–81.
2. A brief discussion of the campaign may be found in Gannon, *Deaf Heritage*, ed. Butler and Gilbert, 263–264.
3. "Hearing Aid Firm Agrees to Truthful Advertising," *Silent Worker*, 3 (Nov. 1950), 2.
4. "NAD Fight Fruitful, Chi.Trib. Bars 'Deaf' in Hearing Aid Ads," *Cavalier* 11 (March 1951), 1.
5. Ibid.
6. Ibid.
7. As cited in "Chicago Tribune Endorses Stand on Hearing Aids," 14.
8. Marcus L. Kenner, "Ken's Korner," *Silent Worker* 10 (June 1958), 11.
9. All information on *The Cavalier* from Gannon, *Deaf Heritage*, ed. Butler and Gilbert, 244–246. Originally founded as a monthly magazine of the Virginia Association of the Deaf, in 1943, the paper moved to Washington, D.C., dropped the *Silent* from its title, and began to grow into a paper with a national reach. At the height of its circulation, it had over 4,000 paid subscribers across the country. In this campaign, it found itself in the unusual position of supporting the NAD; *The Cavalier* was typically highly critical of the NAD for not being more active in its leadership of the national Deaf community.
10. "Chicago Tribune Endorses Stand on Hearing Aids," 14.
11. Burnes as quoted in Elmer Long, "The Long View: Let's Use Our Voice," *Silent Worker* 3 (March 1951), 15.
12. For more on the kinds of stereotypes hearing aid ads relied on, including a consideration of gender, see Hillel Schwartz, "Hearing Aids: Sweet Nothings, or An Ear for and Ear," in *The Gendered Object*, ed. Pat Kirkham (New York, 1996).
13. Elmer Long, "The Long View: The Hearing Aid Racket," *Silent Worker* 3 (April 1951), 18.
14. Elmer Long, "The Long View: Let's Use Our Voice," 15.
15. *The Silent Worker* was founded in New Jersey around the turn of the twentieth century by George Porter and Weston Jenkins. It grew to become arguably the premier magazine for deaf readers in the country. When Porter retired in 1928, the magazine did not long survive him. It folded in June 1929. In 1948, the National Association of the Deaf revived it, with the help of a handful of the original staffers. In 1964, owing to Cold War sensibilities, the name was changed to *The Deaf American*. For more, see Gannon, *Deaf Heritage*, ed. Butler and Gilbert, 240–242, 246–247.
16. Roger Falberg, "Sifting the Sands . . .," *Silent Worker* 9 (February 1957), 19. Italics in original.
17. For more on the question of normality in deaf history, see Baynton, *Forbidden Signs*, esp. chap. 6. For more theoretical treatments, see Davis, *Enforcing Normalcy*, and Harlan Lane, *The Mask of Benevolence: Disabling the Deaf Community* (New York, 1992).
18. Mary Jane Rhodes, "From a Parent's Point of View," *Deaf American* 22 (Sept. 1969), 29. Emphasis in original. Rhodes became well-known as an activist parent of a deaf child. Her *Deaf American* columns from February 1967 to June 1974 were collected and published in a single volume, *Thank God for My Deaf Child!* (Northridge, 1975).
19. Lane, *Mask of Benevolence*, 81.
20. For more on Betty Miller, see Gannon, *Deaf Heritage*, ed. Butler and Gilbert, 129–132. For more on Deaf art, see Deborah Sonnenstrahl, *Deaf Artists in America: Colonial to Contemporary* (San Diego, 2003).
21. "Readers' Viewpoint: Should deaf children be forced to wear hearing aids?", *Deaf Life* 1 (March 1989), 31. The poll does not indicate how many readers responded to the question. Interestingly, the column published the response of an audiologist who voted no, saying, "I am an audiologist and I know what hearing aids can and cannot do. They cannot make a deaf person hearing, just as glasses don't make a blind person seeing!"
22. Lane, *Mask of Benevolence*, 81.
23. By the Deaf community, Lane means those who are deaf from birth or from an early age, those, in other words, who have no useful experience with hearing and for whom deafness is their natural state. He does not mean people who lose their hearing over time, like so many elderly Americans. These are clearly deafened hearing people and aids are appropriate for them, and the audiologists who are providing that service would not fit Lane's definition of an audist. For more on audism, see Lane, *Mask of Benevolence*, esp. 43.
24. H-Dirksen L. Bauman, "Audism: Exploring the Metaphysics of Oppression," *Journal of*

Deaf Studies and Deaf Education 9 (Spring 2004), 245.

25. In "My Third Eye," the first original work of the National Theater of the Deaf, cast members wrote and performed biographical remembrances. Bernard Bragg recalled a story of going to an oral school. "Spontaneous outbursts of laughter in the classroom were often stilled by scornful reprimands from our fifth-grade teacher not so much because they . . . erupted at inappropriate times as because he said they sounded disgustedly unpleasant or irritating—even animalistic. Young and uncomprehending as we were, we were given long lectures on the importance of being consistently aware of what our laughter sounded like to those who could hear. From that time on, we were forced to undergo various [breathing] exercises . . . Compliments were often lavished upon those who came up with forced, but perfectly controlled laughter—and glares were given to those who . . . didn't sound like a 'normal' person. Some of us have since forgotten how to laugh the way we had been taught. And there are two or three from our group, who have chosen to laugh silently for the rest of their lives." As quoted in Gannon, *Deaf Heritage*, ed. Gilbert and Butler, 355–356).

26. John B. Christiansen and Irene W. Leigh, *Cochlear Implants in Children: Ethics and Choices* (Washington, 2002), 18.

27. Ibid., 24.

28. As quoted in Christiansen and Leigh, Ibid., 24.

29. Ibid., 24–25. For more on opposition to telethons from other disabled activists see Paul Longmore, "Conspicuous Contribution and American Cultural Dilemmas: Telethon Rituals of Cleansing and Renewal," in *The Body and Physical Difference: Discourses of Disability*, ed. David T. Mitchell and Sharon L. Snyder (Ann Arbor, 1997), 134–158.

30. Lane, Hoffmeister, and Bahan, *A Journey into the DEAF-WORLD*, 389.

31. Lane, *Mask of Benevolence*, 240.

32. Christiansen and Leigh, *Cochlear Implants in Children*, 35.

33. Ibid., 258.

34. This list of reasons appears on the first page of the Bionic Ear overview section of the Advanced Bionic website at <http://www.bionicear.com/tour/default.asp> (April 12, 2005).

35. The UCSF Douglas Grant Cochlear Implant Center, University of California, San Francisco, <http://www.ucsf.edu/implant/benefits.html> (Aug. 2, 2004).

36. Marilyn Howe, "Untruths in Advertising," *A Deaf American Monograph: Viewpoints on*

Deafness, ed. Mervin Garretson (Silver Spring, 1992), 67.

37. Carol Padden, "GLAD Publishes a Position Paper on Cochlear Implants," in *Deaf World*, ed. Lois Bragg (New York, 2001), 311. Originally published in *GLAD News* (summer 1985).

38. Kathryn Woodcock, "Cochlear Implants vs. Deaf Culture?," in *Deaf World*, ed. Bragg, 327. Article originally published in 1992.

39. Richard Eckert, "Unwired from Noise," *DeafNation* 4 (May 1999), 4.

40. Mark Drolsbaugh, "The Impossible Ideal," *DeafNation* 4 (Nov. 1998), 14.

41. Advanced Bionic pamphlet, "Cochlear Implants for Kids," printed January 1999.

42. Ibid., 3.

43. While this is admittedly not a comprehensive search of all cochlear implant centers in the United States, it is a sampling of centers from different regions of the country and the advice on all is remarkably consistent. All emphasize speech, hearing, lipreading, and listening training. All recommend that the implanted child enroll in an educational program that utilizes speech and language therapy. None mention sign language. See, for instance, websites for implant centers in Iowa <http://www.uihealthcare.com/depts/med/otolaryngoglogy/iacic/index.html>, San Francisco http://www.ucsf.edu/implant, New York City <http://www.med.nyu.edu/cochlear>, Michigan <http://www.med.umich.edu/oto/ci/childrensprogram.htm>, South Carolina <http://www.muschealth.com/medical_services/speciality_listing/spec_otolaryngoglogy/cochlear.htm>, and Massachusetts <http://www.umassmemorial.org/ummhc/hospitals/med_center/services/cochlear/cochlear_children.cfm>.

44. Figure in Christiansen and Leigh, *Cochlear Implants in Children*, 108. The survey was a 12-page questionnaire sent to parents of children with pediatric implants. It was sent to parents of 1,739 implanted children; parents of 439, a 24 percent return rate, completed the survey. 25 percent chose "environment awareness/child's safety" as the main reason for implanting, with "to gain hearing," "child's desire for an implant," "convenience in daily activities," "better future with more opportunities," and "concern for child's self-image" rounding out the list.

45. Arthur Allen, "Sound and Fury," *Salon*, posted May 24, 2000. Available on-line at <http://dir.salon.com/health/feature/2000/05/24/cochlear/index.html?pn=1>.

46. As quoted in Patricia S. Stivland, "A Rally in North

Carolina," *NAD Broadcaster* 21 (July/August 1999), 2. There comments directly echo those of nineteenth-century oralist Horace Mann. Mann was the first American educator to advocate a switch from manual education to oralism in 1844, also after a trip to Germany where little German schoolchildren spoke to him. In spite of the fact that Mann himself spoke no German, he was singularly impressed with their skill. At least Bruton was in a position to judge their English.

47. The NAD has since revised this position paper. The revised paper, released in 2000, takes a more conciliatory stance and welcomes implanted children and their parents into the Deaf community. It asks parents to remember that since cochlear implants are not a cure for deafness, their children are still deaf and will need the support of Deaf adults in their lives. It also asks parents to introduce their children to sign language, since the children are still primarily visual, as Deaf people, in their orientation. The new position paper has been hailed as "more balanced" in numerous reviews and articles. See National Association of the Deaf, "Cochlear Implants in Children: Position Paper of the National Association of the Deaf," *The NAD Broadcaster* (March 1991), 1. See National Association of the Deaf, "NAD Position Statement on Cochlear Implants," *The NAD Broadcaster* (January 2001), 14–15. The revised statement is also available on the NAD website, <http://www.nad.org> (April 12, 2005).

48. The NAD may have been right in its skepticism. A 1994 study assessed speech intelligibility scores of CI children who had used them for at least two years and found an average rate of intelligibility of 48 percent; ratings ranged from a low of 14 percent to a high of 93 percent. See M. Osberger, A. Robbins, S. Todd, and A. Riley, "Speech Intelligibility of Children with Cochlear Implants," *Volta Review* 96 (1994), 169–180. More recent research indicates that "the performance of children with implants rarely reaches the average range expected for hearing children of the same age" (Christiansen and Leigh, 230, 231). Patricia Spencer concludes that, "Despite the benefits provided to many children, cochlear implants do not provide a 'quick fix' for the language development challenges faced by deaf children and their parents. Although cochlear implants seem to help very profoundly deaf children, on average, function more like hard-of-hearing children, the results are highly variable. Some children show no discernable benefits, whereas others come to function almost like hearing children" (see ibid., 248).

49. For more on DPN, see John B. Christiansen and Sharon N. Barnartt, *Deaf President Now!: The 1988 Revolution at Gallaudet University* (Washington, 1995).

50. As quoted in Christiansen and Barnartt, *Deaf President Now!*, 153.

51. Ibid., 215.

52. See Padden and Humphries, *Deaf in America*; Wilcox, ed., *American Deaf Culture*; Leah Hagar Cohen, *Train Go Sorry: Inside a Deaf World* (New York, 1994); Oliver Sacks, *Seeing Voices: A Journey Into the World of the Deaf* (Berkeley, 1989). All the readers' polls mentioned here can be found in *Deaf Life*. The mainstreaming poll was taken in February 1992 and results were 85 percent opposed to 15 percent in favor. The language of instruction poll was taken twice, once in July 1992 and again in July 1996. Results were the same both times; 88 percent were in favor of ASL. The 1996 poll had tremendous interest; 632 readers responded, 72 percent of those were deaf and 28 percent were hearing. Interestingly, only 3 percent of respondents favored signed English, which finished behind oralism, which drew 9 percent of voters. 87 percent of readers rejected the label "handicapped." The 13 percent who accepted it seemed mostly to be late-deafened people, one of whom wrote, "Yes, I have a terrible handicap–and so do all of you, whether you know it or not." See "Readers' Responses: Should mainstreaming be the preferred choice for the majority of deaf children?", *Deaf Life* 4 (Feb. 1992), 29–30; "Readers' Responses: Most teachers of the deaf used a form of signed English to teach written English. Should they use ASL to teach English?", *Deaf Life* 5 (July 1992), 30. "Readers' Responses: Which method is best for teaching English to profoundly deaf children?", *Deaf Life* 9 (July 1996), 34. And the original 1855 proposal by John J. Flournoy was to found a Deaf state in the West. For more on Flournoy and his plan, see Christopher Krentz, ed., *A Mighty Change: An Anthology of Deaf American Writing, 1816–1864* (Washington, 2000), 161–211, and Hannah Joyner, *From Pity to Pride: Growing Up Deaf in the Old South* (Washington, 2004), 107–119. Flournoy would surely be delighted to find that 75 percent of readers thought a variation on this idea, a Deaf city, was still a good idea in 1996. See "Readers' Responses: Should we establsh a 'deaf village,' town, or colony?," *Deaf Life* 9 (Sept. 1996), 34. Apparently, many Deaf people still think this is a good idea. There is a proposal for a deaf town to be founded in South Dakota and named Laurent, in honor of Laurent Clerc. See Monica Davey, "As Town for the Deaf

Takes Shape, Debate on Isolation Re-Emerges," *New York Times*, March 21, 2005 http://www.nytimes.com/2005/03/21/national/21deaf.html. National Public Radio also produced a story on Laurent, "Building a Town on Sign Language," broadcast on *All Things Considered* on June 21, 2004. Audio transcript available online at http://www.npr.org/templates/story/story.php?storyId=1967748.

53. Robert Crouch, "Letting the deaf be Deaf: Reconsidering the Use of Cochlear Implants in Prelingually Deaf Children," *Hastings Center Report* 27 (July–August 1997), 14–21.

54. The 1995 NIH Consensus Statement on cochlear implants remains the most recent. It can be found at <http://consensus.nih.gov>, and it is entitled "Cochlear Implants in Adults and Children. NIH Consensus Statement Online, 1995 May 15–17."

55. Bienvenu as quoted in Andrew Solomon, "Defiantly Deaf," *New York Times Magazine* (Aug. 28, 1994), 65. Bahan in "What if . . . Alexander Graham Bell Had Gotten His Way?," in *American Deaf Culture*, ed. Wilcox, 86.

56. Edward Dolnick, "Deafness as Culture," *Atlantic Monthly* (Sept. 1993), 37–53; Andrew Solomon, "Defiantly Deaf," *New York Times Magazine* (Aug. 28, 1994), 38–45, 62, 65–68.

57. Solomon, "Defiantly Deaf," 67.

58. "*Atlantic Monthly* readers respond: a special letters feature," *Deaf Life* 6 (Dec. 1993), 26–33. See "The shame of the 'deafism cultists'," 26; "The 'deaf isolationists' and their 'one-size-fits all' philosophy/culture," 27–29, esp. 27; "Deaf Culture: a 'trendy self-segregation movement'," 30; "A doomed 'ghetto culture'," 33.

59. Ibid., 26.

60. "Readers' Responses: Is the cochlear implant destroying the future of the deaf culture?", *Deaf Life* 10 (Sept. 1997), 30. Of 458 readers who responded, 21 percent said no. No one was unsure about this one.

61. Numbers reported in Christiansen and Leigh, *Cochlear Implants in Children*, 282–284. This was a random sample mailed out in the summer of 2000, with 138 respondents, a 37 percent response rate.

62. Matthew Rosenberg, "Letter to the Editor," *Salon* <http://dir.salon.com/letters/daily/2000/05/30/cochlear/index.html> (April 12, 2005).

63. Kudlick, "Disability History," 764.

64. Kudlick, "Disability History," 781.

CHAPTER 31

Minority Politics in Korea: Disability, Interraciality, and Gender

Eunjung Kim

This essay examines the conflictual sites of different minority groups in South Korea and the effects on intersectional subjectivities provisionally formed in between identity categories. The emergence of disabled women in between disability rights movements and women's movements is one strong example of an intersectional identity position. Disabled women's new activism challenges previous activism's prioritized identities such as gender *or* disability. However, the legal framework to safeguard disabled women from sexual violence considers disability identity as qualification for eligibility but defines disability as the complete lack of capability. In order to interrogate the judicial and governmental categorical constructions, I trace the historical interconnection of stigma between interraciality and disability. The contemporary politics of the international marriage business between South Korean disabled men and Vietnamese women illustrates conflicts and exploitation as well as intersections of minority groups in Korea. I argue for a theory of multiple consciousness[1] about systems of oppressions—a theory that imagines new subject positions erased by dominant identities and that examines both the privileged and marginalized positions produced by classification of bodies.

DISABLED WOMEN OR FEMALE DISABLED PERSONS

The exploration of a space in between categories and the need for a new framework that grasps liminal experiences offer useful insights for articulating the difficult processes of disabled women's subject-making in South Korea. For example, when the disabled women's movement emerged, two different words were used by activists to name themselves because no category existed previously to label their "new" position. One is a combination of the words women and disabled people, *ysng-chan-gae-in* (women-disability-person), which means "female disabled persons"; the other word uses disability in its adjectival form to modify women, *changae-ysng* (disability-women), which means "disabled women." These neologisms demonstrate both the difficulty of escaping established categories and the interstitial politics of disabled women. The debate over the two terms was never settled, and both words are currently used by the media interchangeably without invoking a sense of political incorrectness. Nevertheless, various organizations in the disabled women's movement apply the two usages differently depending on whether they wish to give political emphasis to the female identity of disabled women or accent women as a subcategory of disabled people.[2] While it is evident that disabled women's positions are formed by the categories of "disability" and "female gender," the question remains which category represents the more determining identity. In terms of social classifications, which identity names the common denominator and which identity becomes the qualifying adjective?[3] Is there an essential disability experience not determined by gendered norms? Is there a female experience that is not enforced by the "ability/disability system" of a society (Garland-Thomson 2002)? These are questions about classification that touch upon both minority identity politics and the intersection of subject positions.

Ella Shohat envisions intersectionality as crossings between class, racial, national, sexual, and gender-based struggles, describing them as "axes of stratification" (1998: 1).[4] In my speculation, linear axes may cross from time to time, creating multiple intersections between separate trajectories of oppressions. Separate constructions of individual forms of oppression, even if they intersect at numerous points for people who belong to multiple categories, do not negate the existence of the nonintersecting essence of each trajectory unmediated by other identities. On the contrary, people with single minority identity markers of gender or race are not free from the influence of other privileged identities that are disguised as nonidentities (McRuer 2003). Thus, the identities of these people should be understood in relation to nonidentity and its effect on identity category making. Intersectionality, when based on linear axes, can leave essentialism unchallenged because, in that framework, each oppression is assumed to have an essence that does not intersect with that of other identities.[5]

Because many nondisabled people consider disabled people an internally undifferentiated group, recognizing the gender of disabled people raises concerns about dividing and weakening the power of the disability rights movement in general. For example, Disabled People International included the statement "disabled women are not a group separate from disabled people" in a discussion paper on the integration of women's issues at a UN convention (Arnade and Häfner 2005). The question of whether "disabled women" is a defining category has not been fully accepted by the disability community in general. The problem is that the two groups, women and disabled people, are frequently set against each other in cultural and political representations—a conflict that further silences disabled women. Consider that the remarks "disabled men are feminized" or "pregnant women are disabled people" are perceived as discriminatory because of stigmas attached to femininity or disability constructed prior to the alienation of disabled men or pregnant women. Rosemarie Garland-Thomson (2002) addresses this tension between femininity and disability. The language of deficiency and abnormality, according to her, is used to devalue women who are already seen as inferior to men. As a result, women have been associated historically with disability in Western culture. Such an interpretive move efficiently invokes one oppressive system to deprecate people marked by another system of representation (Garland-Thomson 2002: 8). This representational process has obscured the experience of disabled women because when femaleness registers as disability, hierarchies based on ability and disability status among women are trivialized. Furthermore, when anti-stigma movements try to emphasize women's competency as the basis of equality by saying "women are not disabled" or "disabled men are not feminine," the stigma attached to femininity or disability remains intact or is strengthened because the hierarchies between disability and able-bodiedness as well as femininity and masculinity remain unquestioned. Caught in between, disabled women find it difficult to combat their devaluation in these mutual negations. When one minority group tries to seek equality by breaking away from the stigma produced by association with another group, the claim of equality can further naturalize the other minority group's alienation.

Although the remarkable emergence of the disabled women's movement indicates a new challenge to both mainstream Korean society and the disabled people's movement, the legislative grouping of disabled women does not always provide an effective position for forwarding critiques of social hierarchies. The attention to disabled women can also be bound by essentialist thinking about which aspects of oppression are based on identity either as women or as disabled persons. Research projects addressing the experience and oppression of disabled women were conducted as a result of the emergence of the disabled women's movement in the late 1990s and its entrance into the international arena after the Fourth Beijing World Conference on Women in 1995. Researchers employed the strategy of identifying the reality of disabled women based on mathematical formulations by using the terms "double oppression" or "triple oppression" (Oh and Kim 2000).[6] Disabled women are understood in this framework as a group produced by combining two existing social groups (or three, including lower class). Disabled women experience discrimination as disabled people in the area of education, employment, and accessibility of the built environment; and discrimination as women in the area of reproduction, sexual violence, marriage, and domestic roles (Oh and Kim 2000). Oh and Kim largely define disability discrimination within the public sphere but formulate gender dis-

crimination within the domestic sphere. However, the binary of public versus private proves to be problematic in theorizing disabled women's everyday experiences. When public transport is made physically accessible, resolving disability discrimination, disabled women still experience frequent harassment by men and women when they use public transport. Disabled women are hired in irregular, low wage, and traditionally feminized positions, such as phone operators, more than disabled men. Such complicated workings of sexism and ableism often blur the public/private binary.

Sexual violence has been identified as the most urgent matter that has to be addressed for disabled women. Disability rights activists supported creating special consideration for victims with a disability in the Special Act on Sexual Violence of 1994 (Sngp'okryk T'ukbylbop). As a result, a provision was included in 1994 regulating a harsher sentence for raping disabled women. However, because the provision only included "physical disability" as a victim's identity for the law to be applied, cases against women with cognitive or mental disabilities were often dismissed. Later in 1997, disability activists were successful in their efforts to amend the law in order to include the rape cases of women with cognitive disabilities; the 1997 amendment includes "mental disability" in order to address nonphysical disabilities. Provision 8 of the Special Act on Sexual Violence on disabled people reads: "a person who has sexual intercourse with a woman or assaults a person using the status of incapability of defense caused by physical or mental disability should be convicted on the basis of the Criminal Code 297 (rape) or 298 (forceful assault)." In other words, the law defines sexual intercourse (kanm) as rape when it occurs not by using physical force but by taking advantage of a disabled victim's vulnerability. The provision poses two problems: the definition of disability as incapability of defense and the definition of rape as the use of force not by lack of consent. Violated persons often have to prove the presence of force by reporting defensive wounds on their bodies. If the violated person has a disability (or is considered to have one under provision 8), inability to defend oneself because of disability has to be proven for the code to be applied. Therefore, if a woman does not have the physical and mental ability to defend herself against force, she cannot presumably exercise her right to consent to sexual relations. Consequently, the burden of proof weighs on disabled women to demonstrate the preexistence of total defenselessness caused by disability. Alternatively, if a woman does not have a disability, the ability to defend is assumed automatically; to establish rape, she must show with her body signs of the violence that overpowered her resistance. The legislative system forces sexual violence victims either to be identified as disabled, which equates complete incapability of defense with disability, or to be identified as nondisabled and have physical wounds to prove that they tried to defend themselves.

The preemptive indistinctness between rape and sexual intercourse encourages legal action to dismiss rape cases by casting in doubt the existence of the victim's disability. Thus, despite concerned professionals' initial reaction that the legislation could be overprotective and violate disabled women's freedom to have sexual relations, the legislation does not function as a protective tool. On April 20, 2005, Pusan (Busan) Higher Court exonerated the defendant Kim who allegedly raped a woman with cognitive disability, because even though the victim had a cognitive disability according to professionals, the court found that she was not disabled. During the trial period, the victim had to go through intellectual ability tests to prove

her disability, and the tests determined that she had in fact the ability to defend herself, thus negating her disability status. The Sexual Violence Counseling Center for Disabled Women released a statement criticizing the court's decision, arguing that Kim's acquittal proved that the human rights of disabled women are not protected in Korea, because the identification of disability is dependent upon the power of the court and appointed professionals to define women as either disabled or nondisabled, no matter how the women identify themselves (Changaeysng Sngp'okryk Sangdamso 2005).

The example of sexual violence shows the inadequacy of identity based on legislation for ensuring human rights. Here disability identity functions merely as a screening condition for the legislation to be applied. The special legislation fails to address the vulnerabilities of disabled women that are created by society. Rather, due to the assumed lack of physical and cognitive ability to defend oneself, the legislation situates vulnerability within disabled women's bodies. Although disabled women's new subject positions articulate their unique identity and experiences, legislation that relies on the false separation between disabled and nondisabled persons assumes disability as well as gender identification as stable, measurable, and absolute. Thus, this legislation and its narrow interpretation fails to address rape as an action conditioned by the social tolerance of gendered violence and not by a victim's particular characteristics. In this scheme, disabled women are characterized as completely powerless victims and nondisabled women are thought able to defend themselves against rape if they do not consent. Both presumptions derive from a misogynous attitude that denies the existence of rape and places the blame on women's actions. The case of Kim was reconsidered in the Supreme Court of Korea revoking the previous ruling in July 2007. The Supreme Court states that the definition of disability has to be understood broadly considering not only the degree of disability but also social relationships, power dynamics, and contexts. This ruling addresses some of the problems raised in defining disability and hierarchy involved in sexual violence, although the problem of the term "defenselessness" as a basis of protection remains. It is important to think about how to eschew essentialist distinctions between disabled and nondisabled women and men and how to arrive at noncoercive and nonexclusionary conceptions of disability and gender identity that do not deny either individual agency or the spectrum of different abilities and genders.

INTERRACIAL BODIES, DISABILITY, AND NATIONALITY

To understand how a minority subject is interpolated by the state and subjected to control or protection, it is crucial to engage in a genealogical exploration of the political relationship among many identities. Disability, femininity, sexuality, and race—particularly in post-war South Korea demarcate the interlocking construction of problematized bodies managed together with nationality. Intersectionality here represents the organically interdependent construction of categories that need one another, rather than depending on the image of multiple, separate axes. My goal in this section is to provide a brief examination of such interdependent categories. In 1954, South Korea's Ministry of Health and Social Affairs started issuing annual statistical reports on populations that were considered to need the state's protection and surveillance. The first report included "leprosy patients, mixed-blood children, widows, drug addicts, patients with infectious diseases, and prostitutes" (Ministry of Health and Social Affairs 1954). A year

later the categories of people with disabilities ("physically handicapped") and disabled veterans ("disabled soldiers") joined the catalog (1955). Whereas disability, interraciality, prostitution, and diseases were juxtaposed for the purpose of public health surveillance in the 1955 report, the first nationwide census of "handicapped" children conducted in 1961 by the Korean Child Welfare Committee classified interraciality and diseases under the category of "handicaps" (1962).[7] The children of mixed races were listed alongside children with various physical and sensory impairments, classified according to physical, mental, and social handicaps: "children with limb handicaps; audio-visual; mental; speech impediments; miscellaneous deformities; social handicaps (children of mixed racial parentage)" (ibid.: 86). Although there was a distinction made among physical, mental, and social conditions, disability in general was not understood as solely an individual body's functional difference but rather as connected to the presence of external prejudice and stigma related to differentness.

Nonetheless, the stigma of interraciality was specifically constructed through its association with female gender and the lack of authentic Koreanness. The survey defined interracial children as "those children born of Korean *mothers* and foreigners" and excluded Chinese and Japanese (Korea Child Welfare Committee 1962: 91; emphasis added). By eliminating other East Asian ethnicities, the screening focused on the visibility of non-East Asian characteristics.[8] The survey was therefore designed specifically to count only children of Korean women and American military service men who had been born outside of marriage. The children were further classified into "white," "black," and "others," according to identifiable skin color, immediately reducing interracial children's race to that of the fathers and denying the heritage of Korean mothers. The survey also noted that interracial children who were born through legitimate marriages should be excluded from the definition of "handicap." After World War II and the Korean War, being labeled as interracial (*t'uigi* in the derogatory Korean vernacular term) referred to children born to Korean prostitutes and American soldiers. Women who worked in the U.S. camp town (*kijich'on*) were often called pejoratively "*yanggongju*" (Yankee princess or Western princess), with the connotation of being "vulgar, low, dirty, and socially shameful," but also called "patriots" who contributed to Korean economy and U.S.-South Korean security alliance by servicing American soldiers (Kim, H. 1997: 180). In postwar Korea, the term, *yanggongju* has expanded to include "GI Brides," or Korean women in interracial marriages with soldiers (ibid.: 178).

Until the end of the twentieth century, the popular term for interracial people was *honhyla*, meaning "*children* with mixed blood," implying figuratively that all interracial people have been infantilized, alienated, and marginalized in Korea and literally that most of them were presumably exiled from Korea before they grew up (National Human Rights Commission 2003: 6–7). The Korean Nationality Act defined nationality based on patrilineal heritage, granting nationality to people born to Korean fathers until the 1997 amendment. The focus on patrilineal heritage is more than just a sexist policy; it reflects how gender and reproduction were viewed in modern Korea. According to its hegemonic ideology, Korean nationality was made of one ethnicity (*minjok*),[9] and when a Korean woman gave birth after having a relationship with a foreign man without legally marrying him, that woman's body was considered to be violated or contaminated. To protect the symbolic and biological status of nationality from contamination, interracial people could not achieve Korean citizenship while growing up in Korea during the 1960s and 1970s.[10] Consequently, the newly emergent population of interracial people after the war—later called "Amerasians" was stigmatized because the mothers supposedly prostituted themselves to Western foreigners.

The article by Anne Davidson in the 1961 survey report explains the reason why only certain interracial children were considered disabled. "Most of the mixed racial children in Korea," she writes, "are illegitimate because their mothers are casual or regular prostitutes of foreign servicemen" (Davidson 1962: 73). According to Davidson, the prostitutes' status depends on American men and socially acceptable marriage:

> If a western marriage is registered, the Korean community accepts it, but if the eastern custom is followed in a mixed marriage, the western country may not recognize it legally. When there is a marriage by Korean custom, as long as her "husband" remains in Korea, she is a respectable member of society, but when her "husband" leaves and returns to his own country, leaving her behind, everyone feels that he is a deserter. She is then thrust back into the community as an outcast and joins the group of cast-off wives, and other rejected people. Her chances of rehabilitation become very small.
>
> (Davidson 1962: 71)

The stigma of interracial children is not mainly associated with their bodily characteristics but from their family arrangement and the lack of social sanction, the absence of a patriarch, and their mothers' prostitution, which causes disease and "feeble-mindedness" (Davidson 1962: 74). Davidson links prostitution, disability, and interracial reproduction directly. Davidson's description also suggests a hierarchy between Western and Korean culture. Of sole importance is the recognition of marriage by the husband's family, even if the wife's family has accepted the marriage.

Based on patrilineal ideology, governmental policies considered interracial people who were fathered by Americans to be Americans, thus construing them as national others. Therefore, a major policy of the government was to send interracial children "back" to the U.S. by migration or adoption. In the 1960s, those children were placed in segregated special schools and began to learn English as part of their curriculum in primary school in order to prepare for emigration (National Human Rights Commission 2003: 31–32). By 1968, 7,164 interracial children were adopted by U.S. citizens (Ministry of Health and Social Affairs 1968). In 1974, the category of "mixed blood" had disappeared from the annual statistical reports on public health and also from the disability category without a clear explanation. I speculate that the removal of the category does not necessarily reflect an actual decline in the number of interracial people. When forcing them to migrate was the primary goal, tracking their existence and integrating them into Korean society may have become insignificant. The comprehensive report on the lives of interracial people by the National Human Rights Commission states that the social integration of interracial people almost disappeared as an issue after 1982 from the media (2003).[11]

The removal of the interracial category from public health reports also reflects the transition of public health policy toward more medically configured disability and disease management divorced from the role of social stigma. Interracial people's lives in Korea were marked by rejection, exclusion, institutionalization, lack of education and employment, and poverty—all of which characterize life with disability in many aspects, including that of interracial people with physical and cognitive disabilities. This history of the construction of interraciality during the U.S. military occupation and afterwards, provides evidence that stigmatizing the body requires an association with the already devalued characteristics of other identities. The flexibility of disability as a category, one including interraciality in Korean history, cements a radical solidarity between the seemingly separate categories of disability and race. Furthermore, this solidarity allows us to recognize the positions of interracial people with disabilities as well as interracial sex workers who do not distance themselves from the stigma of prostitution.

However, in the discourse of contemporary minority activism, the human rights of interracial people often fails to mention the connection to other stigmatized groups, such as prostituted mothers and disabled people. Rather, human rights discourse often breaks away from other associated, stigmatized identities and attempts to valorize itself through qualifications of belonging to the dominant society, such as citizenship. In 2004, in order to generate awareness of interracial people's human rights, the National Human Rights Commission started broadcasting a television announcement. The announcement shows a series of still headshots of six people, one woman and five men, taken by the photographer Yi Jae Gap. Accompanied by inspirational music, the camera slowly zooms in on each photo to capture in-depth the gaze of the person. Each individual has an expressionless face looking back at the camera. These images compel viewers to meet the gaze of the person in the photo and to confront the long-avoided reality of interracial people's alienation. Following the photo of one person, the image of a Korean Resident Registration Card is given with the name of the birthplace in Korea. The ID card demonstrates the fact that these people are not foreigners but Koreans. Accompanying the photos, a man narrates the following: "My name is Bae Gi Cheol. I am Korean. Only because of different skin color, people say that I am different from them." The slow narration with pauses in between words demonstrates effectively that he speaks Korean as his mother tongue. At the end of the announcement, an official female voice addresses the audience with corresponding subtitles, "If you accept difference, you will see the world without discrimination."

Arguably, this television campaign is an attempt by the government to change the public understanding of "Koreanness" as not limited to Korean ethnicity. Meanwhile, it frames Koreanness as the ground of equality and human rights in specific ways, for example, speaking Korean, having a Korean name and official documentation, and being born in Korea. In fact, the announcement does not address interracial people's nationality based on their Korean heritage. The announcement presents an interesting contrast to the media frenzy about the American football player, Hines Ward, accepted as Korean in 2006. Because his mother is a Korean who was married to American G.I. and later emigrated to the U.S., he was claimed as one of "us" and awarded honorary Korean nationality. In the television announcement, however, the possibility that the interracial subjects may have one Korean parent is not included as evidence of their Koreanness. The audience is not informed whether they are descendants of foreigners or interracial people with Korean heritage. This absence is an attempt to dissociate the widely held stigma that interracial people are "tainted" children of prostitutes. Moreover, this formulaic remaking of interracial people as Koreans ignores the human rights of many illegal immigrant laborers, while appealing to a liberal sentiment about diversity and who belongs to the nation. The employment of Korean nationality as the basis of social acceptance poses a significant problem because the act of claiming human rights reinforces other privileges of nationality.

If the contemporary anti-stigma minority movement does not recognize its organic connection to other related stigmatized groups, it often ends up reinforcing and justifying the oppression of other groups. The danger in claiming minoritized others as one of "us" is that it ignores connections between minoritized people and creates further minority factionalism.

INTERNATIONAL MARRIAGE ENTERPRISE

The limitations of human rights grounded on nationality and citizenship, exemplified in the national human rights promotion for interracial people, become more evident if we take into account the impact of the international marriage trade on Korean minority men. The international marriage business targeting Korean men with intellectual or physical disabilities has become more visible since 2002 as a major consumer market. More and more billboards and banners about international marriage have appeared nationwide with the phrase "Marry a Vietnamese Virgin." In smaller font, most of the billboards say "For older, disabled people, first-time or second time marriage."[12] Given that culturally and legally sanctioned marriage is heterosexual in present-day Korea, "people" here means "men" because the word "virgin" (ch'ny) largely designates females (Kim and Chivers 2005). The number of agencies that promote Vietnamese brides for "second rate" Korean men, including disabled, rural, older, or divorced men, has increased, and with them, new advertisements with new phrases appear in many regions throughout the country. Some billboards include the disturbing phrase, "they never run away" in order to appease potential customers' fears about images of immigrant brides from China who "defraud" their Korean husbands and run away.[13] Other signs state that no payment is due until the marriage actually occurs. These statements reflect the view that these women are commodities (Kim and Chivers 2005).

More detailed advertising flyers distributed in the streets and subway stations in Seoul describe Vietnamese women as best suited for marriage with marginalized Korean men because these women admire Korean culture and men as affluent and caring. Such perceptions seemingly develop because of popular Korean television shows and films consumed in Vietnam. The flyers describe Vietnamese women as submissive, subservient, sacrificial, chaste, smart, possessing "beautiful faces, bodies, and similar ethnic origin to Koreans," and willing to "serve the parents-in-law and never divorce due to their traditional beliefs." The disparity between the economic situations and cultural enterprise of Vietnam and Korea allows for an intercultural hierarchy that supposedly compensates for disabled men's marginal status in South Korea.[14] The promotion emphasizes the invisibility of interracial characteristics of the second generation because Vietnamese presumably look similar to Koreans.

The association between disability and the bride business evolved before the international marriage trade between Korean men and foreign brides became popular. On the second of August 1990, *Kungmin Ilbo* (*Citizens Daily*) sensationally described Korean women in the marriage business as victims of trafficking. The article claimed that five Korean women were sent to marry "mentally retarded" men in Japan by a bride business agency ("Japan-Korea" 1990). This description sets up the disability of a husband as a horrifying condition that the Korean women are forced to accept. In the past, Korea was one of the countries from which women migrated to get jobs overseas or for a better life through marriage. While many Korean women migrate to other countries imagin-

ing better lives, the increasing rate of international marriage between foreign women and Korean men reflects Korea's transition from sending women away to bringing foreign women. Countries of origin of the women who come to Korea through marriage arrangement now include China, Vietnam, the Philippines, Mongolia, Thailand, and Cambodia (Kang 2005).[15]

The commercial penchant for treating women as commodities, in addition to the racism displayed in the advertisements, invokes concerns about immigrant women's human rights. In fact, the overwhelming number of advertisements about tourism to Vietnam sponsored by the bride business has disturbed many people, including Vietnamese university students in Korea. Human rights activists have started demanding legislation that bans the commercial advertisement of women (Cho 2007). The media, concerned about human rights violations in these marriages, often portray one side as the victim while ignoring the other side's marginality. The media tell horror stories about domestic abuses against immigrant women. These abuses include mental and physical disabilities resulting from the marriages but also note that the women are abused by concealment of their husband's disability status prior to the marriage (Im 2004; C. H. Kim 2007). The media also portray disabled men as victims of women who run away from marriages after they have achieved legal status in Korea (Chong 2000; C. Yu 2006). Sensational depictions of each party's victimizations reflect the marginal status of disabled men and immigrant women in marriage arrangements. Men's privilege, based on gender and nationality, and women's ablebodiedness form the ground on which both groups exploit each other.

The international marriage business illustrates the politics involved when multiple groups, marginalized on the basis of class, age, disability status, gender, and nationality, seek normalized lives. The mutual exploitation between groups can be tracked in marriage, caring labor, sexuality, reproduction, and cultural norms— all of which undergird the fantasy of the sanctioned heterosexual family. The discourse of one group's exploitation, i.e, Korean disabled men or nondisabled immigrant women as abused and defrauded by the other party, encourages the public to uphold the image of extreme vulnerability and pity for minority life. Inevitably, without understanding the system of marriage, which includes increased global migration, limited employment, and poverty, injustice can be easily blamed on another party.

How might we understand the alienation in marriage arrangements sought as a solution to marginalization? It is important to consider individuals' everyday life situations by giving attention to multiple systems of oppression. For example, the marriage transaction involves the devaluation of disability and unmarried life, the language and cultural differences of the spouses, legal naturalization of immigrants, and public attitudes about domestic violence. All of these factors help to construct the vulnerability of marginalized lives that exist under complicated circumstances leading individuals to choose the purchased marriage as an option, but rarely a viable one. The solution to isolation and limited social interactions, resources, and employment of disabled men cannot be easily provided by women from "lesser" cultures.

If an identity-based approach to human rights does not examine the "constitutive historicity" of categories and the erasure of differences, the liberation of one group will not necessarily bring about democratic changes in the social structure (Butler 1993). While the demands of Korean disabled men and their families for marriage as a solution to personal care, reproduction, and sexual fulfillment created a new international marriage market, disabled women did not invite social attention on similar terms. Rather, the disabled women's movement stresses the dangers that disabled women face in marriage; disabled women confront in their marriages unique problems of violence, economic dependence, and reproductive risk often not addressed by nondisabled women's movements (T'a-Ri 2003). Heavily gendered aspects of marriage, reproduction, and family life create an overly conflicted space for disabled women simply to demand access. Furthermore, when immigrant brides have a disability, they are considered undesirable or sent back to their home countries (Kim 2003; Yu 2003). If we are to decouple the identities used by oppressive formations, whether disability-maleness-heterosexuality or femaleness-heteronationality-ablebodiedness, it is important to pay attention to the perspectives of the erased groups lost in between minority groups because they represent the multiple structures involved—in this case, the perspectives of Korean and Vietnamese disabled women toward the cultural imperialism and discrimination that they experience in the marriage market and family life.

CONCLUDING REMARKS: INTERSECTIONALITY AND INTERMINORITY CONSCIOUSNESS

As feminism and disability studies faces the challenge of incorporating race, sexuality, class, gender, disability, age, religion, and nationality, many new provisional subject positions can be formed. These positions aim at eradicating multiple forms of subordination and generating a transnational democratic citizenship. Presumed impermeability between separate identity categories represses the voices of multiply identified people and standardizes intragroup differences. It also produces distance and tension between different groups on the margins (Crenshaw 1997a). For this reason, communication is often more complicated between two oppressed groups than between the dominant group and an oppressed group. Multiple identities for women of color based on their gender, race, ethnicity, disability, sexuality, class, nationality, and other differences are possible; however, these identities often lie in contradiction, for the act of claiming one identity requires the reservation of one and distance from another. Trina Grillo addresses this conflict by warning against the very use of multiple identities. "We speak with multiple voices," she states, "only because we have categories that describe these voices as separate from one another" (1995: 17). Moreover, many discussions of intersectionality recognize that political identities are grounded in categories enforced by the dominant culture. Donna Haraway speaks to this point: "Gender, race, or class consciousness is an achievement forced on us by the terrible historical experience of the contradictory social realities of patriarchy, colonialism, and capitalism. . . . Which identities are available to ground such a potent political myth called "us," and what could motivate enlistment in this collectivity?" (Haraway 1991: 155).

Although acts of reappropriating dominant cultural denominations as self-claimed identities may empower certain groups, people who are not called upon as primary subjects in identity politics do not automatically benefit from such empowerment. Silenced by external oppressions, internal hierarchy, and a sense of loyalty to an oppressed community, marginal people with multiple markers struggle against the fragmentation of their experiences by uneasy identity politics connected to dominant cultures and political activism alike. As the construction of South Korean minority categories shows, modern forms of subjugation often arrange gender, disability, race, class, nationality, and sexuality as interdependent coordinates of marginalization.

In *Looking White People in the Eye* (1998), Sherene Razack addresses the importance of examining the analytical tools of racism, sexism, and subcategories of women. She argues: "Analytical tools that consist of looking at how systems of oppression interlock, differ in emphasis from those that stress intersectionality. Interlocking systems need one another, and in tracing the complex ways in which they help to secure one another, we learn how women are produced into positions that exist symbiotically but hierarchically" (Razack 1998: 13).[16] Understanding symbiotic relationships in the construction of marginality demands attention to the fact that the body cannot be divided into countable marginalized identities when one marginalization is enabled by another identity. The imposition of stigma upon a certain unfamiliar body relies on existing stigmas, building an association between the established stigmas of one group and those of the unfamiliar group. For example, newly emergent interracial populations in South Korea were immediately associated with the stigma of prostitution, and simultaneously, the livelihood of mothers accused of prostitution were affected by the birth of interracial children. Reasserting the humanity of stigmatized groups by applying other identity qualifications, such as nationality, masculinity, or sanctioned family, presents a challenge to multiply identified minorities striving toward shared equality. Disability studies has criticized political theories including feminism and anti-racism for distancing themselves from disability and not recognizing their naturalization of disability stigma. Mitchell and Snyder, for example, argue, "Race, feminist, and queer studies have all participated to one degree or another in a philosophical lineage that seeks to distance those social categories from more 'real' biological incapacities" (1997: 6, cited in Snyder and Mitchell 2006: 17). Moreover, they propose that claims to equality often rely on the exclusion of disability: "Thus, in order to counteract charges of deviance historically assigned to blackness, femininity, or homosexuality, these political discourses have tended to reify disability as 'true' insufficiency, thereby extricating their own populations from equations of inferiority" (Snyder and Mitchell 2006: 17). In parallel, the disability rights movement and disability studies also need to develop multiple consciousness about transnational contexts beyond Western cultures, including a recognition that gender, race, sexuality, age, class, religion, nationality and other differences constitute hierarchies within the broad category of disability. Multiple consciousness about systems of oppressions, achieved by reconsidering parallel and interdependent categories, is imperative to fight the forces that create inequality among people.

NOTES

My work on this chapter is deeply indebted to a number of scholars whose ideas are incorporated here. I express my gratitude to Tobin Siebers whose feedback was vital to improving this chapter. I also thank Kyeonghee Choi, Sally Chivers, Mark Sherry, Michael Gill, Michelle Jarman, David Mitchell, Katrin Schultheiss, and Sharon Snyder who encouraged me to work on this issue and provided an enormous amount of help and discussion along the way. I am also indebted to many activists involved in the disabled women's movement in Seoul. I also thank the editors of the volume and the anonymous reviewers who provided great help.

1. In her influential essay "Multiple Jeopardy and Multiple Consciousness: The Context of A Black Feminist Ideology" Deborah King calls for multiple consciousness to address black women's situations in the U.S. and explains, "Although the complexities and ambiguities that merge a consciousness of race, class, and gender oppressions make the emergence and praxis of a multivalent ideology problematical, they also make such a task more necessary if we are to work toward our liberation as blacks, as the economically exploited, and as women" (312).

2. Changaeysng Konggam (Women with Disabilities Empathy) is one of the few organizations including the term "disabled women" in their Korean name. I was one of the advocates of the term "disabled women," arguing that "women" and "people" are redundant, as in "female disabled people," for designating personhood and that gender should not be treated as an additive feature. My argument was that disability should be treated as a changeable trait by social standards as well as gender. Now I am open to both terms because I do not think that one identity should be prioritized over the other and because gender is also a flexible trait.

3. I focus on identity as a social classification rather than an individual psychological and cultural identification, although the two are interrelated. Legal and political categories of minority groups and identifiability are a more important point of inquiry in this essay. Whether or not a disabled woman chooses to identify as a disabled person or a woman primarily is also influenced by social interactions and the political system.

4. Feminist legal theorist, Kimberlé Crenshaw suggests the notion of political intersectionality, along with structural and representational intersectionality (1997b), seeking to explain the systems of privilege and the problem of monolithic identity politics on which anti-discrimination legislation is based in the U.S.

5. Trina Grillo explains the relationship between essentialism and identity: "Essentialism is the notion that there is a single woman's, or Black person's, or any other group's experience that can be described independently from other aspects of the person—that there is an essence to that experience" (Grillo 1995: 20). Kimberle Crenshaw distinguishes intersectionality from anti-essentialism (1997a).

6. Similarly, Western scholars such as Michelle Fine and Adrienne Asch use of the term "double oppression," albeit in a scare quote, in their classic book *Women with Disabilities* (1988). Accordingly, they highlight the core of disabled women's experience as rolelessness, which makes disabled women a kind of "social nomad."

7. The survey was conducted by trained local agents from all precincts, who visited each household

and recorded the number of children and the characteristics of their bodily conditions in order to identify the welfare needs of "handicapped" children nationwide. The survey was funded by various North American organizations, including the U.S. Army, Pearl Buck, and Christian missionaries in Korea. This explains the survey's particular focus on interracial children and the U.S. adoption policy.

8. Although racialization and discrimination existed against Japanese and Chinese immigrants, there was a significant number of unmarked interethnic descendants in Korea.

9. *Minjok* refers to people who belong to a common ethnic group, such that all Koreans are assumed to constitute one homogenous Self. Invocation of this national self affirms a unified identity, based on an unchangeable essence that is transmitted through blood and homogeneous culture (Yang, H. 1997:128).

10. There was some exceptional application of the territorial principle *(jus soli)* for abandoned babies, whose father's nationality could not be identified and who were born in Korea. The government has allowed Amerasian children to be registered under the mother's name since 1980 without any information about the father (National Human Rights Commission 2003: 20). An amendment was made in 1997 to give nationality to people if either one of their parents is Korean.

11. In 1982, the U.S. legislated the Amerasian Act, which provided full and automatic citizenship for certain Amerasians migrating to the U.S. It states: "in order to qualify for benefits under this law, an alien must have been born in Cambodia, Korea, Laos, Thailand, or Vietnam after December 31, 1950, and before October 22, 1982, and have been fathered by a U.S. citizen" (U.S. Public Law 97–359). Migration provided only a partial "solution" to the marginalization of interracial people in Korea. Given that the U.S. army had been stationed in Korea since 1945, the window of birth years between 1951 and 1982 was not inclusive enough for many people born before 1951. When the legislation was enacted, many interracial adults in their thirties found it hardly viable to enter the U.S. through adoption (National Human Rights Commission 2003).

12. On February 22, 2007, *The New York Times* reported this phenomenon under the title, "Betrothed at First Sight: A Korean-Vietnamese Courtship" (Onishi). The article explains the reasons for the increase in Korean-Vietnamese marriages with two factors, rising social status of women and sex-screening technology, i.e. female fetus abortion that causes a surplus of unmarried men.

13. mong many newspaper articles reporting marriage fraud cases for Korean Chinese brides, *Seoul Sinmun (Seoul Newspaper)* reported the danger of an increasing number of scammed marriages by brides who used marriage as a way to migrate to South Korea, took money from the husband's family, and ran away (Pak 1996).

14. International or interracial marriage has not been a very popular phenomenon but has been traditionally considered taboo. Commercialized interracial and international marriage practices have emerged in Korean public culture since the 1980s. In the late 1980s, rural areas were being depopulated at a high rate. The difficulty that men in agricultural areas had in getting married emerged as a social issue. Urban women were depicted in the media as not wanting to marry rural men, to work in agriculture, or to accept traditional extended family living with parents-in-law. Unmarried males were considered more problematic than unattached females. In 1990, regional offices and agricultural associations began to promote international marriage between Korean men and Korean-Chinese women, even though the illegitimate trafficking in foreign brides already existed (2005).

15. In 2005, 27.4 percent of men in the agricultural and fishing industries married foreign women (Kang 2005).

16. Patricia Hill Collins also carefully distinguishes her theoretical concept, the "matrix of domination," from intersectionality (2000: 18). In 1978, the Combahee River Collective used the term "interlocking systems of oppressions" to describe the importance of collective political solidarity. See the group's essay in the edited volume by Hull et al. (1982).

BIBLIOGRAPHY

Amerasian Act. (1982) U.S. Public Law 97–359.1

Arnade, S. and Häfner S. (2005) "Towards Visibility of Women with Disabilities in the UN Convention," Disabled Peoples' International (ed.), a paper presented at Comprehensive and Integral International Convention on the Protection of the Rights and Dignity of Persons with Disabilities in Berlin, July 2005. Online. Available HTIP: http://v1.dpi.org/lang-en/resources/details.php?page=278 (accessed 26 September 2006).

Butler, J. (1993) *Bodies that Matter: On the Discursive Limit of "Sex,"* New York: Routledge.

Changaeysng Sngp'okryk Sangdamso [Sexual Violence Counseling Center for Disabled Women] (2005) "Official Announcement on Busan Court's Ruling Acquittal in the Case of the Woman with Cognitive Disability." Online. Available. HTTP: <http://www.was.or.kr> (accessed 5 January 2006).

Cho, H. (2007) "Vietnamese Virgin Billboards Will Disappear." *Han'gyre Sinmun* [Han'gyre Newspaper], 30 January.

Chong, H. (2000) "Marriage Scam of Mongolian Women." *Munhwa Ilbo*, 27 March.

Coleman, L. M. (2006) "Stigma: An Enigma Demystified," in L. Davis (ed.) *Disability Studies Reader*, 2nd edn, New York: Routledge.

Collins, P. H. (2000) *Black Feminist Thought: Knowledge, Consciousness and the Politics of Empowerment*, 2nd edn., New York: Routledge.

Crenshaw, K. (1997a) "Intersectionality and Identity Politics: Learning from Violence against Women of Color," in Wendy K. Kolmar and Frances Bartkowski (eds) *Feminist Theory*, 2nd edn, [2003], Boston: McGraw-Hill College.

Crenshaw, K. (1997b) "Beyond Racism and Misogyny: Black Feminism and 2 Live Crew," in Diana Tietjens Meyers (ed.) *Feminist Social Thought: A Reader*, New York: Routledge.

Davidson, A. (1962). "The Mixed Racial Child," in Korean Child Welfare Committee (ed.) *Handicapped Children's Survey Report*, Seoul: Korean Child Welfare Committee.

Fine, M. and Asch, A. (eds) (1988) *Women with Disabilities: Essays in Psychology, Culture and Politics*, Philadelphia, PA: Temple University Press.

Garland-Thomson, R. (2002) "Integrating Disability, Transforming Feminist Theory," *NWSA*, 14(3): 1–32.

Grillo, T. (1995) "Anti-Essentialism and Intersectionality: Tools to Dismantle the Master's House," *Berkeley Women's Law Journal*, 10: 17–30.

Haraway, D. (1991) "A Cyborg Manifesto: Science, Technology, and Socialist Feminism in the Late Twentieth Century," *Simians, Cyborgs and Women: The Reinvention of Nature*, New York: Routledge.

Hull, G., Scott, P. B., and Smith, B. (eds) (1982) *All the Women Are White, All the Blacks Are Men, but Some of Us Are Brave: Black Women's Studies*, Old Westbury, NY: Feminist Press.

Im, Y. (2004) "Immigrant Women, Vulnerable to Trafficking and Violence." *Ysng Sinmun* [Women's Newspaper], 10 December.

Kang, C. (2005) "One out of Four Rural Bachelors Marry Foreign Women." *Kynghang Sinmun* [Tendency Newspaper], 28 June.

Kim, C. H. (2007) "Does Paying Money Make Beating Okay?: International Marriage, Bruised by Verbal, Physical, and Sexual Violence." *Kungmin Ilbo* [Citizens Daily], 2 February.

Kim, E. and Chivers, S. (2005) "Trafficking Care: Race and Gender in In-Home Care Program," paper presented at Hidden Cost, Invisible Contribution Symposium at Trent University in Peterborough, Canada, 8–10 June.

Kim, H. S. (1997) "Yanggongju as an Allegory of the Nation: Images of Working-Class Women in Popular and Radical Texts," in E.H. Kim and C. Choi (eds) *Dangerous Women: Gender and Korean Nationalism*, New York: Routledge.

Kim, S. (2003) "Marriage Scam, Nat'asha and I," *Han'gyre* 21 450, 13 March. Online. Available HTTP:<http://www.hani.co.kr/section-021003000/2003/03/021003000200303130450014.html> (accessed 20 Mar 2006).

King, D. (1995) "Multiple Jeopardy, Multiple Consciousness: The Context of Black Feminist Ideology," in Beverly Guy-Sheftall (ed) *Words of Fire: An Anthology of African American Feminist Thought*. W.W. Norton.

Korean Child Welfare Committee ([1961] 1962) *Handicapped Children's Survey Report*, Seoul: Korean Child Welfare Committee.

Kungmin Ilbo [Citizens Daily] (1990) "Japan-Korea Matchmaking Scam. Five Korean Virgins Were Sent to Marry Japanese Disabled Person", 2 August.

Lloyd, M. (2005) *Beyond Identity Politics: Feminism, Power and Politics*, London: Sage.

McRuer, R. (2003) ''As Good As It Gets: Queer Theory and Critical Disability," *GLQ: A Journal of Lesbian and Gay Studies*, 9(1–2): 79–105.

Ministry of Health and Social Affairs (1954–1999) *Pogn Sahoi T'ongye Ynbo [Annual Statistics on Public Health and Social Affairs]*, Seoul: Ministry of Health and Social Affairs.

National Human Rights Commission (2003) *Kijich'on Honhylin ln'gwn Silt'ae Chosa [Army Base Mixed Blood People Human Rights Reality Survey]*. Online. Available HTTP: <http://www.human-rights.go.kr/> (accessed 2 April 2005).

National Human Rights Commission (2004) "Public Announcement." Video file. Online. Available. HTIP:<http://www.humanrights.go.kr/> (accessed 23 May 2005).

O, T'aejin (2005) "Imported Brides," *Chosun Ilbo*, 27 June.

Oh, H. G. and Kim, C. A. (2000) *Ysng Changaein-gwa Ijungch'abyl [Women with Disabilities and Double Discrimination]*, Seoul: Hakchisa.

Onishi, N. (2007) "Betrothed at First Sight: A Korean-Vietnamese Courtship," *The New York Times*, 22 February.

Pak, H. (1996) "Scam Marriage of Korean Chinese is

a Problem," *Seoul Sinmun [Seoul Newspaper]*, 4 March.

Razack, S. H. (1998) *Looking White People in the Eye: Gender, Race and Culture in Courtrooms and Classrooms*, Toronto: University of Toronto Press.

Shohat, E. (ed.) (1998) "Introduction," *TalkingVisions: Multicultural Feminism in a Transnational Age*, New York: New Museum of Contemporary Art.

Snyder, S. L. and Mitchell, D. T. (2006) *Cultural Locations of Disability*, Chicago, IL: University of Chicago Press.

T'a-Ri (2003) "'Yjnhi Nae Sarmn Kodan Hada': Changaeysng-gwa Kylhon" ["My Life is Still Tiring": Disabled Women and Marriage], *Konggam [Empathy]* ,6: 38–43.

Yang,H. (1997) "Remembering the Korean Military Comfort Women: Nationalism, Sexuality, and Silencing" in E.H. Kim and C. Choi (eds) *Dangerous Women: Gender and Korean Nationalism*. New York: Routledge.

Yu, C. (2006) "Old Bachelors with Disability Cried Twice," *Kangwn Ilbo [Kangwon Daily]*, 9 January. Online. Available. HTIP:<http://www.kwnews.co.kr/sub/searchldefault.asp?p=%CO%E5%BE%D6%CO%CE%B3%EB%C3%D1%BO%A2> (accessed 12 Feb 2007).

Yu, H. (2003) "Marriage or Dangerous Shopping," *Han'gyre* 21 450. 13 March./20 March. Online. Available. HTIP: <http://www.hani.co.kr/section-021003000/2003/03/021003000200303130450023.html> (accessed 20March 2006).

CHAPTER 32

This Is What We Think

Daniel Docherty, Richard Hughes, Patricia Phillips,
David Corbett, Brendan Regan, Andrew Barber, Michael Adams,
Kathy Boxall, Ian Kaplan, and Shayma Izzidien

INTRODUCTION

This article has been written by all of us. Some of us know what it is like to be learning disabled; others are university researchers who don't know what it is like. We had lots of meetings about writing the article and we used a tape recorder to make tapes of what we said at the meetings.

The university researchers asked questions during the meetings to make sure that they had understood what people were saying. They also listened to all of the tapes and changed them into writing. In our article, we mostly used the words that the learning disabled writers said on the tape without changing them. We also used large print and put in some pictures. The order was then changed around so that the article would be easier to follow and each section of the article was read out loud week by week, checked and changed, if necessary, by members of the group.

One of the first things we did was talk about the words we would use to write about people in our article. The learning disabled writers said people should be called *learning disabled*. 'Learning disabled' is the name we have chosen for ourselves, it widens it more than us, to other disabled people. Disabled means the same, whatever disability you've got. 'Learning

disabled' is the words we would use, not being told to or given by professionals. We don't like the old words that people used to use ages ago. We won't use words like that in our article.

We talked about whether we would have two parts to our article; one part for the learning disabled writers and a 'professional side' for the university researchers. In the end we decided that if we did two separate sections we wouldn't learn from each other; it would be like 'them' and 'us'. It's better all in one together with everybody helping and learning from each other, so the two groups have worked in partnership writing this article together. But really there haven't been two groups because *all* of us are researchers and we have supported *each other* in writing the article. The university researchers, who don't know what it is like to be learning disabled, have supported the learning disabled researchers to write the article and they have learnt from the knowledge of the learning disabled researchers.

WHY THE LEARNING DISABLED RESEARCHERS ARE WRITING THIS ARTICLE

We wanted to write an article in our own words. We think it's important that people get learning disabled people's point of view instead of listening to the lies from people in day services and places like that. We wanted to do an article like this, putting stuff down in writing about what we feel like, about what it's like for people who are learning disabled, what it's like to get bullied time and time again. Bullying can happen anywhere, even in People First groups sometimes.

Things have changed; the world has turned now. It's time to stop it always being the professionals doing everything. We want people to listen to us; listen to us and learn from us. We've seen tons and tons of reports about learning disability and they've all been done by people from organisations like BILD (British Institute of Learning Disabilities). There's lots of articles too, but most of the articles are written by professionals who think they know all about learning disability—people like Wolf Wolfensberger and John O'Brien. There's a lot of things that are misunderstood or mis-quoted about learning disability and it's time they included what we've got to say and what other learning disabled people have got to say, not just the professionals' and experts' views.

Other disabled people are doing research and writing as well—that's good but only if they don't use big words. There's a lot of disabled writers and researchers like Mike Higgins from BCODP (British Council of Disabled People) and Mike Oliver but there's not a lot of writing from learning disabled people.

PEER REVIEW

Peer review is when people double check an article to see if it's good enough. We don't think university people should double check this article. No disrespect to university people, but they don't know what it's like to be learning disabled, they don't have the knowledge. If you get university people

double checking this article, they won't be able to say if it's good enough or if it's not good enough. We think our article should be double checked by another group of learning disabled people. And they would get the opportunity to know what we are doing too. The more learning disabled people who get involved in this article the better.

Some of us work with other disabled people who aren't learning disabled. They generally have the same views on what we're saying, so maybe it wouldn't need to be another group of learning disabled people that checked our article, maybe it could be another group of disabled people, it would be better than professionals or university people checking it.

THE MEDICAL MODEL

Something we're concerned about is that we need to be sensitive to people's feelings in this article, people who have been in institutions. A bit of the past needs to go in the article, not a lot. People need to learn from the past, so we only need to touch on it then put something positive in as well. We need to tell people what's come out of all the hurt and pain and the nightmare but we don't want to be reminded of it every day. We need to go about it in a more positive way because if we go about it in a negative way it's not going to do anybody any good at all.

No doctor can diagnose a person and get it right for their whole life. They get it wrong. They did that with two of us. Both of us got told that we would be a 'cabbage'. How pathetic is that?! How wrong is that?!

In one of our meetings we watched the video *The Lying Doctors* (Portway Players 1998). It was a very upsetting video. Not everyone could watch it. We put it in our article because it's part of life.

The Lying Doctors
They write things down before you've even
  opened your mouth

They make their own minds up
They think they know about you without listening
They've all got their own ideas about you
They make your decisions for you

(Portway Players 1998)

Doctors put learning disabled people in hospitals and institutions; because we're not 'the norm' they wanted to hide us way. If people spend so long in hospital they get to feel, 'It's my fault'.

In the video *Perfect People* (Mencap 2001), Kevin Chettle goes back to Balderton Hospital (which is closed down now) and talks about what it was like when he was sent there:

The way you treated me was bad. All the patients what was here. All my friends was here—who died in the place. You have brought bad feelings to me. Goodbye, goodbye, goodbye forever! I have got a new life now.

(Kevin Chettle, in Mencap 2001)

Sending people away still goes on now. In the White Paper (DH 2001) it talks about making village communities. If we do that, we're really going backwards, making a village just for learning disabled people and making institutions instead of trying to include people like ourselves in society. It's like making a village just for Black people or a village just for gay and lesbian people. We want to be equal. We don't want to be segregated.

We should be looking forwards, not backwards. It's a bad idea going backwards. When are people going to learn that people like us have been to hell and back, been shut away because of other people's embarrassment?

Sometimes we just feel like packing our bags and running off somewhere

(Patricia Phillips, in Mencap 2001).

They don't want us to exist, but they don't realise the things that we can give to society.

(Di Lofthouse, in Mencap 2001)

They even want to wipe out disability.

I find it offensive that people are trying to wipe out disability. That's a way of people not being educated. People are not God. God is up there. Everybody's different. If everybody was the all the same, then there'd be a problem.

(Daniel Docherty, in Mencap 2001)

THE SOCIAL MODEL

Anne Louise Chappell (1998) says that learning disabled people are left out of the social model of disability. The social model of disability is in writing so that professionals can look at it. It's not accessible to learning disabled people. We might want to study the social model ourselves but we can't because it isn't accessible. It should be in pictures and large print.

If you look at the photograph on the front of Michael Oliver's (1990) book there's a wheelchair user, who is trying to get into a Polling Station to go and vote but he can't get in the building because of the steps (barriers) that are in the way.

Barriers make us disabled as well:

- **Information which isn't accessible**

  Anything that's been printed isn't accessible if people don't read. The things that they've got out now, texting and the web and things, they don't make them accessible. That's a barrier. There's no-one who's got the time to sit and teach us about websites, email and texting. They don't think that we can learn so we'd just be a waste of space, so what's the point in teaching us how to use a web page or text or email? They don't even want to take the time to teach us to read and write.

Some learning disabled people wouldn't know how to learn about email and web pages and they can't because they'd need support and they don't want to do it because if they try and go down that road people would say: 'You're worthless. Why are you doing this? You should be where you belong in an institution or in a day centre. You should be learning to use these web pages in a day service.'

- **Jargon and Offensive Terminology**

The services' language, like 'handicapped' and 'retardation', the jargon words they use, they're not the choices of the learning disabled people themselves. Their jargon is a way of the professionals and others keeping us out. Last night (5th February 2003) they used 'mental handicap' on the television news. It's all medical model, it's not social model. 'Handicapped' and 'retardation' are all medical, not what we would use and they're offensive. They shouldn't have said that about us. It may have slipped out though because they do know, but they tend to forget. Some of us were volunteers for the Commonwealth Games in Manchester. We did a lot of work and the BBC television people came down and took films of us while we were working. The BBC asked if it was all right to use 'disabled' and we said it was. We said, 'Don't use words like 'handicapped.'' and they said, 'All right, we won't.' That was when they came to film us at the Commonwealth Games.

People sometimes say things to us like, 'Are you being a good boy?' You say that to an animal, not to us. Even now people still call us horrible names like 'idiot', 'fool', 'thick', stupid' and 'dumb'. And they still call us 'chaps' and 'gents' when they're talking about us, like they did in the institutions. That's not how you should talk to a person. Gent's toilets, that's what it sounds like. You weren't a name in the institution, you were just a number and if somebody passed on, you got their number—so people had a dead person's number.

Mencap used to have a logo, 'Little Stephen' (a drawing of a little boy who was crying). It wasn't very nice and they had to scrap it because people complained about it being negative and Stephen would be about 35 now anyway!

- **People's Negative Attitudes**

The professionals, care managers, day centre staff, and parents and Joe Public judge us—all of them judge us—and they're frightened of change. A lot of learning disabled adults are in a rubber-band system. They say, 'You can go as far as that.' But if they see us progressing too far forward they say, 'Oh come back!' and pull us back. It isn't an equal society when you're in a day service.

People say, '*You can't!*' all the time.

> You can't get a job.
> You can't get married.
> You can't have a baby.
> You can't have your own house.
> You can't go out unless you're with someone else.
> You can't get on a university course.
> You can't have a normal life.

But now *we can* and people need to learn that we can. Other learning disabled people can do these things too—if they have support.

We're not first class citizens; we're second class citizens. People stop us from being first class citizens. It's like Wolfensberger (1998) said, people think that we're 'forever children' because we don't have the intelligence of a 'normal' adult. To us it's a put down, they put us down.

- **People Not Listening to Us**

People don't listen to us. Some people keep talking about the same thing. They don't let us say anything. They don't let us change the subject.

Other people who don't listen say, 'There, there, it doesn't matter'.

Social services are starting to listen to us now, because they have to, but it's a way of humouring us, they're not taking us seriously, they're listening because they have to.

WE ARE HERE AND WE'RE GOING TO STAY. WE WANT TO BE LISTENED TO AND WE'RE NOT GOING TO GO AWAY

- **People Being Patronising**

Sometimes people do listen to us but you know they're thinking, 'Oh let him go on for a little while, he'll be alright, he'll go away in a minute'.

- **People Who Don't Want to Know and Just Walk Away**

Some people just walk away from us.

- **People Who Want to Know You but Just Drop You Afterwards**

People sometimes use you. They only use you when they want you; then they just drop you and say 'Goodbye' afterwards.

WHY DO PEOPLE HAVE NEGATIVE ATTITUDES?

People have negative attitudes because they don't think we're the same as them, they don't think we can keep up with them. It goes back to when people were locked up in institutions and were experimented on. People's opinions and assumptions about people who were learning disabled were, 'They're slow on the uptake'. People assume and see us *not* as humans, but as zombies or as creatures from a different planet. It's the rest of society that should be educated, we should be educating society. They should be learning from the mistakes that happened in the past. Young people are not as bad as some of the older people who were educated when the institutions were around.

It does go back, if you look at history, but it's not just about being in an institution, it's here now and it's there. It's about people calling us, we get it when we go on buses, we get it when we go on the streets, in the pubs, cinemas and restaurants, in the shops, from work colleagues.

We get it from our parents sometimes, or foster parents, or our brothers or our sisters or relations, or at school. It's the way they were taught. If society doesn't learn from past mistakes we'll go full circle again. There are things happening now that are like eugenics. Learning disabled women want to have babies but people want to stop them having babies, stop them having *disabled* babies.

> I understood that they didn't want me to have a baby and said because I wouldn't be able to look after it. But I was also told at that same time that if I had a child, especially with the partner I was with at the time, it would be born with severe learning disabilities. But I've found out since then that that was an untruth.
>
> (Di Lofthouse, in Mencap 2001)

We know learning disabled people who have got babies and there's nothing wrong with them, they're not disabled. It'll go back to where they want people to be in institutions if the White Paper (DH 2001) doesn't work. Or, instead of institutions they've got a replacement, they've got eugenics, they can sterilise learning disabled adults like they used to. Society should learn and listen to the mistakes that were made in the past, if you don't, it's all going to happen again.

When you say we can't do this, we can't get a job, we can't get a house, we can't have a baby, it makes our self esteem go down, our morale go down. It makes you feel like you're worthless. It makes you feel sick. It's a type of bullying. And you get it drummed and drummed in all the time; that you're stupid, you can't get a job, you won't have a relationship or a house. Once people have told you that, that's how it looks and feels.

WHAT WOULD IT BE LIKE IF WE COULD TAKE AWAY ALL THESE BARRIERS?

Disabled for us means information problems but when we're talking about the social model, if information was accessible, then we wouldn't be disabled. There's a website with sound on that's actually run by disabled people, but lots of people who are learning disabled don't know about it, or have access to computers and speakers that would play the sound out.

Another thing about what disabled means, if somebody is helped to be a lot more independent, a lot more *enabled*, then they're not so disabled.

If we could get rid of all the negative ideas that other people have and think of the positive ideas, that would help. Everything would be a whole lot easier and a whole lot better.

People should just talk to the learning disabled people and ask what they want, not *assume* what they want. If you do talk to learning disabled people they want to dream what anybody would want to dream—they want to live on their own, get married—but it all comes down to the word 'money'.

Services make the decisions and there's a lot of broken promises. If learning disabled people want a baby, it's not just about how they would manage with a baby, it's about what it would cost, that's how they decide. They say 'Oh we can't afford this, we can't afford that. How can we afford that sort of 24 hour service?' But we're people, we're not a bank statement. The services make excuses and put barriers in the way of everything. It's OK for them to have a life; it should be OK for us to get a life too.

A rubber band is a barrier for somebody who is chained to the system, they can't get away from the system, they can't take the chain away. For example, when one of us left residential care they broke away from the chain of the residential care system but they're still going back to the system because they still get care from a carer coming to the house. And they've got a care manager so they're still chained to the system.

We get day care, we get day services, we get health care for learning disabled people but we should be like everybody else, choose what services we have instead of being pinned to a system we've got to put up with. A lot of people wouldn't want to be in learning disability services if they could choose.

It's all right for non-disabled people to make a fuss or complain about things or swear at the driver if they can't get their pram on the bus but if one of us swore on a bus or when we were complaining about services, they would just say, 'Oh he's got challenging behaviour'. It should be OK for us to complain loudly as well. You've got to shout or make a noise to be heard sometimes.

Another thing is people go too quickly, we've got to try and slow things down. We shouldn't have to rush but we have to.

THE DISABLED PEOPLE'S MOVEMENT

If you look at disability, there's like a chart of different kinds of disability. At the top you've got physical impairment and sensory impairment, we come with mental health right at the bottom, so we're like the doormat of disability. The higher you come in disability the better services you get. The lower you come, the more you're ignored. But everybody should be seen as the same, all disabled people coming together. It's not right to be split up into different groups, it's better to be all together, better than being on your own.

When disabled people come together, we're stronger. When we're with other disabled people we're not so disabled—we may have impairments but it's the world outside that makes us disabled. Being with other disabled people is better than being on your own but then again we want to try and get into ordinary education and housing and things like that. Everyone wants a normal life but sometimes it's a good idea to come together with other disabled people because you don't feel so disabled.

The government has put learning disabled people under Mental Health. We've been separated out from other disabled people. All disabled people should be together in one block. If we're all going in the same direction about disability we should be all together, not Down's syndrome down this way, people with visual impairment down that way. We all want the same things: equality, independence and human rights. All disabled people should be pulling together.

If the government put us all as one, it would be better; all the money together in one pot for all disabled people. We shouldn't argue among ourselves, the government has put us into boxes to make us fight among ourselves instead of working as one unit. What we should be doing is all fighting together for the same goal.

WHAT WE ARE DOING TO TRY AND CHANGE THINGS

All of the learning disabled researchers are members of local People First groups. A People First group is a group of learning disabled people who run their own organisation. We have our own committees and do things like training and organising conferences. Members of People First also go on Partnership Boards with health and social services and go to other groups and committees.

Manchester People First was started in 1992. Bury People First started about three years ago. Tameside People First started six years ago. People from Manchester People First helped train committee members for Bury People First and Tameside People First when they were setting up. We've also done training for committee members for Mencap.

The learning disabled researchers are all members of the Steering Group for a university course in Learning Disability Studies. The Steering Group has been going for two years now. We wanted to be involved 100% from the start to the end. We looked at the structure of the Steering Group, how it would work, what support would be needed for members of the group. We thought about how we could get people involved and we set ground rules. In the meetings we talk about what students should be learning on the course. If you want to bring in changes for learning disabled people, training students is a good place to start because they're the ones who are going to go and work in the services in the future.

We also do teaching and training about disabled people's rights. We come to the University and do training for the students, giving them our views and opinions about what we think about the White Paper (DH 2001). Some of us think the White Paper is quite good but some of us think it isn't very good.

Two of us did some training for the Greater Manchester Passenger Transport Executive (GMPTE). We told them what we thought would help and we asked questions. One of us is on the GMPTE Board now.

Some of us offered to do induction training for new Social Services staff about three months ago but Social Services haven't got back to us yet. If we come up with a good idea Social Services don't like it. They like to come up with the good ideas.

Some of the meetings we go to are a bit longwinded and some things aren't going very well. The Partnership Board is meant to be all the health and social services coming together and working together but it isn't going very well. Two of us do the Roadshows for the Partnership Board. We go out to all the day services and tell them what the Partnership Board is. We tell them who's on it and how to complain.

Person Centred Planning isn't going very well either. The Social Services aren't very clear about what they are doing. A person centred plan is supposed to be planned with the person, around the person, not around the service. It's supposed to be what the person wants in their life. Some of us have done person centred plans for our lives but we know that it's not going to happen, so what's the point? Social Services provide what they want, not what we want. There's too many ifs and buts about what we want.

BULLYING WORKSHOPS

Manchester People First came up with the idea of having some Bullying Workshops and then a Bullying Conference. People from other People First groups came to the workshops which were in February and March 2003. One workshop was about Public Transport, another was about Human Rights, another one was about Out and About. At the workshops we did things like:

- how to act if someone starts bullying you on the bus;
- how to complain to the driver;
- what to do if the driver doesn't want to do anything.

The big Bullying Conference was on the 27th March 2003. Altogether 71 people came—people from the Health Service; Patient Advice and Liaison Services (PALS); Victim Support; Stagecoach (a bus company) and others. We were hoping the Police would come so that so we could give them our suggestions and our ideas about what should be done, but they were too busy doing police stuff and they didn't have time for us.

The Bullying Conference was a complete success. We had question and answer sessions and we put the people who came on the spot and asked them what they were going to do about bullying. People from Stagecoach and the others didn't know what they'd let themselves in for, they were speechless about some of the things. At the end they said they that they would have learning disabled people on their committees and they wanted us to do training for their staff.

CONCLUSION

Now you have read our article, we hope you understand what we think, what we feel, what we need and what should be done to make things better for learning disabled people. If you had negative ideas about learning disabled people before you read this article, we hope you think more positively about learning disabled people now.

NOTE

This is an edited (slightly shortened) version of our original paper (Docherty and others 2005), published by Garant.

REFERENCES

Books

Chappell, A.L. (1998) Still Out in the Cold: People with learning difficulties and the social model of disability, in Shakespeare, T. (Ed) *The Disability Reader*, London, Cassell, pp. 211–220.

DH (2001) *Valuing People: A New Strategy for Learning Disability for the 21st Century*, London, Department of Health (http://www.dh.gov.uk/en/SocialCare/Deliveringadultsocialcare/Learningdisabilities/DH_4032080)

Docherty, D., Hughes, R., Phillips, P., Corbett, D., Regan, B., Barber, A., Adams, M., Boxall, K., Kaplan, I., Izzidien, S. (2005) 'This is What We Think', in Dan Goodley and Geert Van Hove, G. (Eds) *Another Disability Reader? Including people with learning difficulties*, Antwerp, Garant Publishers, pp. 29–49.

Oliver, M. (1990) *The Politics of Disablement*, Basingstoke, Macmillan.

Wolfensberger, W. (1998) *A Brief Introduction to Social Role Valorization*, Syracuse, NY, Training Institute for Human Services, Syracuse University.

Videos

Mencap (2001) *Perfect People*, London, Mencap National Centre (http://www.mencap.org.uk/).

Portway Players (1998) *The Lying Doctors*, Bristol, Art+Power (http://www.artandpower.com).

PART VI

*D*isability and Culture

Cripping Heterosexuality, Queering Able-Bodiedness: *Murderball, Brokeback Mountain* and the Contested Masculine Body

Cynthia Barounis

INTRODUCTION

At the 2006 Academy Awards, *Brokeback Mountain* took home three Oscars and the independent film *Murderball*, which chronicled the lives of a group of quadriplegic rugby players, was nominated for best documentary feature. The aesthetic elevation of these two particular films reveals much about how contemporary cultural anxieties regarding queerness and physical disability are negotiated through visual culture. It's not uncommon, of course, to see films that deal with disability and homosexuality at the Oscars. What was out of the ordinary, however, was the extent to which *Murderball* and *Brokeback Mountain* each harnessed the normalizing powers of masculinity, presenting a narrative of gender that helped to generate mainstream appeal in the box office and, more importantly, mainstream approval of a stigmatized social identity. In these narratives, disability and queer sexuality are not just shown to be compatible with masculinity; they are, more fundamentally, celebrated as the logical extension of masculinity's excess. But the emphasis on masculinity that these two films share is also the source of their antagonism. Indeed, a close reading of these two films exposes masculinity as the visual mechanism through which

disability and homosexuality distance themselves from one another, each identity to some extent disciplining the other. Such mutual regulation, however, is not arbitrary and I will argue that it is precisely the various historical linkages between queerness and disability—their continual status as uneasy bedfellows—that bring us to this reactionary cultural moment where able-bodiedness is queered and heterosexuality is defiantly "cripped."

Recently, critics have begun to explore the ways in which a queer theoretical approach might deepen our engagement with disability studies.[1] Robert McRuer's recent book *Crip Theory: Cultural Signs of Queerness and Disability* opens up some exciting possibilities for this dialogue. McRuer examines queerness and disability as parallel sites of oppression; the homosexual body and the disabled body are each regulated by a system of compulsory identity that privilege, respectively, heterosexuality and able-bodiedness. Thus disability studies, McRuer suggests, has much to gain by borrowing from the vocabulary and framework of queer theory. "Cripping" a text, for example, may begin to serve the same function for disability studies that "queering" did for gay and lesbian studies. McRuer makes clear, however, that systems of heterosexual and able-bodied privilege share more than just a family resemblance; not merely parallel, they are deeply intertwined. Thus "compulsory heterosexuality" and "compulsory able-bodiedness" are often wedded together in a mutual effort to both conflate and regulate disability and homosexuality. McRuer's analyses proceed from this assumption, and through a set of diverse cultural readings, he locates the places where able-bodied and heterosexual privilege join forces. While McRuer details several rich sites of cultural resistance, most of his mainstream examples suggest that "heteronormative epiphanies are repeatedly, and often necessarily, able-bodied ones" (McRuer, 2006: 13).[2] What such epiphanic moments of able-bodied heteronormativity require, he suggests, are bodies that are flexible enough to make it through a crisis. And more often than not, it's the heterosexual and able body that is brought out of this crisis, usually at the expense of a disabled character who has been queered or a queer character who has been "cripped."

In what follows, I will explore how the terms of this struggle have—in a short time—become radically reversed. In *Brokeback Mountain* and *Murderball*, systems of heterosexuality and able-bodiedness do not combine in order to produce a stigmatized disabled/queer subjectivity. Instead, these two films set up a world where the mainstreaming of homosexuality stigmatizes disability and where claiming an in-your-face crip subjectivity relies on successful heterosexual conquest. It is a universe where heteromasculine epiphanies are never able-bodied ones, and a queer male subjectivity forms in fundamental opposition to disability. Here, bodies are not flexible, but resolute and resistant to change. It is the very stubbornness of these bodies—their resistance to a traditional narrative arc of character growth—that enables the visual rhetoric of masculinity to do the work that it does in

both films, carrying the characters through an apparent transition that turns out to be no transition at all.

If these films turn McRuer's formulation inside out, however, it is only because they are reacting against the representational history that he has so thoroughly exposed—one in which queerness and disability are made to appear as two components of the same identity. Cinematic history had been permeated with such figures: medicalized images of the homosexual who is either psychologically or physically diseased, spiritualized idealizations of the desexualized disabled person, and nightmares of the injured heterosexual man whose acquired disability castrates him. Thus it is films like *Born on the Fourth of July* and *Philadelphia* that constitute the cultural unconscious of both films. This is the representational history that both films attempt to disavow, even as they structure themselves around it. But there may be a folly in too quickly dismissing those histories in which queerness and disability were intertwined. Confronting and critically showcasing that past, I'd like to propose, may ultimately be what offers us our most effective strategies for cultural critique.

REHABILITATING HETEROMASCULINITY

To suggest that *Murderball* (2005), a recent documentary chronicling the lives of a set of quadriplegic wheelchair rugby athletes, is invested in heteromasculinity more than likely states the obvious to anyone who has seen the film. The key players featured throughout are rugged, athletic—and occasionally tattooed—trash-talking men whose ultimate goal is to crush the competition and come home from the Paralympics with a gold medal. The documentary eschews sentimentality in favor of a more hard-edged realism that foregrounds its subjects as ordinary specimens of a male sports world. When they're not giving (or getting) a beating on the court, they're drinking and having sex with women, or bragging about drinking and having sex with women. Indeed, the film's emphasis on the heterosexual potency of quadriplegic men is one of its most provocative features, and one that has received widespread praise from reviewers.[3]

On a basic level, then, the film's popularity can be considered a success for disability cultural activism. It is an authentic portrayal of a disabled subculture that avoids the traditional narrative traps of many mainstream disability films.[4] The viewer is immediately directed to check his or her well-intentioned sympathies at the door, along with any preconceived notions about the fragility of the disabled body. And disabled sexuality, a taboo and uncomfortable territory for many non-disabled viewers, is reclaimed with a vengeance.[5] Indeed, one of the difficulties in analyzing *Murderball* is that its most radical features are simultaneously its most conventional. Thus, while non-disabled viewers may find their assumptions and stereotypes challenged by the masculine sexual bravado of *Murderball*'s quadriplegic rugby players, there may be a simultaneous sense of relief at ironclad endurance of male heterosexual privilege. Heterosexuality no longer functions as evidence that a disabled masculinity has finally been "cured"; instead, it's the masculinization of disability that holds the power to rehabilitate heteronormativity from its own gender trouble.

Far from the typical narrative arc of a heteromasculinity lost through injury and reclaimed through rehabilitation, the documentary figures disability as not only reflecting but, in fact, amplifying a deeply constant heterosexual masculine selfhood. Revisiting the night of his injury, for example, Mark Zupan explains doing "shots with the girls" at a local bar to celebrate a soccer win before passing out in the back of his best friend's truck; his friend, unaware of Zupan's presence in the vehicle, drove home drunk and had an accident in which Zupan was thrown into nearby canal where he held onto a branch for fourteen hours before anyone discovered him. It's a story that mixes ordinary masculinity with extraordinary toughness and endurance. Explaining the origins of their disabilities, the rugby players relate similar tales of risky behavior associated with conventions of "tough guy," "daredevil," or even just normative "frat boy" modes of masculinity. Scott Hogsett was thrown off of a balcony during a fistfight; Keith Cavill was injured while attempting a set of dangerous motorcycle stunts; and while Bob Lubjano explains that his amputated limbs are the effect of a "rare blood disease," the back of the DVD release puts on a slightly different spin, characterizing his impairment as the result of an encounter with "rogue bacteria." This act of anthropomorphosis endows the simple act of getting sick with a quality of combat, aggressivity, and risk and is characteristic of much of the rhetoric surrounding the film and the sport in general.[6]

This is not the first time that the language of combat has been used to redescribe disability through a lens of masculinity. In "Fighting Polio Like a Man," Daniel Wilson analyzes a set of interviews that were done with male polio survivors during the Cold War Era. Their narratives of rehabilitation were highly gendered:

Ironically, the very cultural values that initially emasculated the paralyzed polio survivor also provided the means by which a young male could construct a sense of masculinity consistent with society's values and expectations . . . Recovery from polio could be easily construed as a battle or contest against the virus, against the doctors and therapists, even against one's damaged body and sense of self . . . This new sense of manhood was constructed, or reconstructed, not on school athletic fields or on fields of battle but in the rehabilitation facilities.

(Wilson, 2004: 121)

In this narrative, the illness provides the opportunity for the reassertion of masculinity, but only insofar as illness is made into the obstacle which the subject must overcome in order to access normative categories of gender and sexuality. But while these earlier accounts framed disability as the foe to be vanquished, *Murderball* to the contrary claims disability as a weapon to be wielded *against* one's foe. While Wilson observes that the polio survivor's narratives "perform masculinity by demonstrating how these men . . . became men by the way they fought polio," (Wilson, 2004: 131), we find here that the *Murderball* athletes became men not by fighting their injuries but, to the contrary, by acquiring an injury that enabled them to fight.

Indeed, if honorable combat is positioned as that which put the players in the wheelchair, then it's the chair itself that that opens up larger, more mythic opportunities to accumulate battle scars. One reviewer admires the fact the rugby chairs resemble "chariots of war"—a point that is in no subtle way driven home by one interviewee who explains how the chairs are made: "What we do is we take these wheelchairs and turn them into a gladiator, a battling machine, a *Mad Max* wheelchair that can stand knocking the living daylights out of each other." In this respect, the film's opening sequence, characterized by Zupan himself as "preparing for battle," is worth examining. As the film begins, an uncomfortable silence accompanies our only glimpse of Zupan's vulnerability as he slowly and painstakingly pulls his pants down and off of his immobile legs. The camera sweeps erotically across his bare chest and limbs, eventually settling on the black tattoo that takes up the greater part of his shin. Zupan pulls on a pair of work-

out shorts, removes his shirt, and wheels out of the room. In the DVD director commentary that accompanies this moment, Rubin and Shapiro discuss the "Clark Kent" logic underlying the scene: "He's about to transform into the rugby guy. There will be the phone booth moment coming—you'll see when the garage door opens." But while Clark Kent's transformation always seemed to involve a stripping down—his nylon suit showing through his bourgeois dress shirt, his glasses always a discardable accessory—Zupan's transformation is shown as a welding on of new parts.[7]

The moment that the camera zooms in on Zupan's tattoo is the moment that the man becomes more than mere flesh. And it is precisely at that point that the intimacy and vulnerability of the scene's opening is eclipsed by a prosthetic remaking of the body—an elaborate new technology of gender.[8] We hear and see the rip of duct tape, the whirring of the wheel, and the clanging of metal. Later, we will watch an animated clip in which metal screws are incorporated into the skeletal drawing of a spine; the image gradually fades into a shot of the actual scars that mark one players neck. Thus both man and chair are visually constructed as the product of custom-built state-of-the-art manufacturing. If, according to the logic of the film, it was the amplification of ordinary masculinity that led to Zupan's injury, then this extraordinarily refashioned machinic masculinity is nothing less than mythic.

In a recent issue of *Narrative*, Rosemarie Garland-Thomson has described the players featured in *Murderball* as "[c]yborgs composed of steel fused with flesh," arguing that that, in the documentary, "[d]isability provides an unanticipated opportunity for boys to come into themselves as athletes and men" (Garland-Thomson, 2007: 115).[9] Garland-Thomson generously concludes, however, that rather than reconstructing heteronormative masculinity, *Murderball* provides us with "what Judith Halberstam calls an alternative masculinity," one which is "non-phallic" (Garland-Thomson, 2007: 116). But to redefine disability through masculinity, as the documentary certainly does, is not necessarily to redefine masculinity itself. Though the film does present us with multiple images of the male cyborg, these images seem to fall short of approximating Haraway's feminist technoscience or Halberstam's technotopic body.[10] Indeed, Haraway's cyborg myth contests both the legitimacy of the masculinist cyborg and the overall male monopoly on technoculture. Repudiating narratives of origin, cyborgs and technotopic bodies are not aimed at helping "boys to come into themselves as athletes and as men" but, rather, at creating alternative queer temporalities in which boys sometimes become something other than men, and girls sometimes become something other than women.

Additionally, Garland-Thomson's claim that *Murderball* creates an "innovative, non-phallic, alternative sexuality," (Garland-Thomson, 2007: 116) focuses on a single reference to cunnilingus while overlooking the dynamic staging that privileges heterosexual phallic penetration as the measurement of the players' masculinity. While Mark Zupan certainly mentions that most wheelchair athletes "like to eat pussy," it is important to point out that this comment is embedded within a sentence that begins with Zupan gesturing downwards and reassuring the viewer, "that still works." In another scene, the ability to have an erection is somewhat taken for granted as an essential feature of quadriplegia. After reassuring an attractive able-bodied woman that the three players sitting at the table are all fully functional, Scott Hogsett relates the following story:

When I first got injured, I was in intensive care, and, uh, everyone was curious how I was gonna be, how much function I was gonna have when I came out of my coma that I was in, and I was about ready to wake up, and the nurses decided to give me a bed-bath in the bed, and the one nurse got so excited that I got a woody, she ran outside and got my mom and showed her my, uh, erection.

What is significant about this exchange is the swiftness with which the image of the impotent quadriplegic is replaced by the image of the quadriplegic whose erection is being celebrated by the community of women surrounding him. While the woman's question might well have opened up a conversation about alternative sexual practices that don't privilege phallic potency, the response ultimately ends up both creating a heteronormatively functional elite among the disabled while simultaneously generalizing the situation of that elite to the entire quadriplegic community.

There is, however, at least one "alternative masculinity" present in *Murderball*. Following an exchange in which an American player accuses former U.S. Coach Joe Soares of "betray[ing] his country" by leaving to coach team Canada, the camera cuts to an evening scene in the hotel room where all four of the featured U.S. players, along with two or three others, play a game of modified poker. The circular movement of the camera and its various close-ups on individual players' faces as they banter back and forth creates a tightly sealed homosocial space within which this "alternative masculinity" is rigidly disciplined. Within the confusion of a lively dialogue, we witness a lanky, long-haired teammate named Sam defend Soares's decision to coach the Canadian team. The dialogue runs as follows:

Sam: On a professional level, I don't think there's anything wrong with it.
Andy: That's number two on the list of most stupid things I've ever heard

at this camp. I heard Sam say that he doesn't like big tits and he'd dump a girl with big tits, if everything was perfect—but, if she has big tits, [imitating Sam] "it's over, they get in the way"

Sam: I like athletic girls. That's what I said all along that night when they asked me.

Zupan: You knew you weren't going to live that one down.

Sam: I'm okay with my sexuality. I can say that. I don't like big tits.

Zupan: You like shoes though.

Sam: I do like shoes.

At this point, everyone laughs and the camera pans to the mechanical card shuffler that happens to be in motion. This is one of the most revealing scenes in the film because it invokes multiple vectors of the gender trouble that the film is careful to guard against. On the one hand, it immediately solidifies the link between heteromasculinity and patriotism. As I have argued, physical disability has been positioned within the film as the manly consequence of both heteromasculinity and honorable combat. This is why Sam's moral defense of a known "traitor" leads the players to move abruptly into an interrogation of Sam's heteronormativity. Though there's nothing homosexual about a man who "like[s] athletic girls," there is something queer, according the film's logic, about a man who lacks desire for the appropriate object choice—in this case, "a girl with big tits." "Big tits" are, of course, functioning here as a metonym of idealized femininity, with all of its attendant associations of passivity, nurturance and non-athleticism.[11] Sam's interest in "athletic girls" thus feminizes (and arguably queers) him to the extent that it's framed as a desire for masculinity (albeit a masculinity that is attached to a female body).[12] While this sequence opens up some fascinating tensions, the soft roar of the mechanical card shuffler has the

last word, and Sam—along with his antinormative desires—are silenced for the remainder of the film.

I have thus far suggested that in both the film and its reception, excessive heteromasculinity is celebrated as the originary moment out of which disability is generated as the inevitable consequence. But where does this leave disabled women, and the ideological status of femininity more generally? By coding disability as a property of heterosexual masculinity, *Murderball* simultaneously codes able-bodiedness as a property of heterosexual femininity. Within the logic of the film, it's the gender-normative able-bodied woman who reinforces heteromasculine potency.[13] Such women, in fact, are central to the film's network of associations, serving a specific and limited purpose—to humanize the disabled players by occupying their traditional role in the narrative of heterosexual conquest. Thus we see women in various contexts, but they are always feminine, always heterosexual, and always engaging in activities that support and reinforce the heterosexual masculinity of the players. They are featured as friendly nurses, cheering sections at games, concerned mothers, and most importantly, proof that whatever other effects the injury has had on their body, the men's ability to engage in heterosexual, penetrative sex is not compromised.[14]

But because the film has polarized disability as a property of athletic heteromasculinity and able-bodiedness as a property of heterosexual, non-athletic femininity, there is no longer a viable space for the physically disabled athletic woman; her body is not only rendered unintelligible but becomes a palpable threat to the narrative glue that holds masculinity, disability, and heteronormativity firmly together. Wendy Seymour has suggested that the same logic that masculinizes the quadriplegic or paraplegic man also functions to both masculinize and desexualize the quadriplegic or paraplegic woman (Seymour, 1998: 120). This brings up a set of thorny issues involving whether or not disabled women's exclusion from the structures of conventional heterosexual femininity can open up other liberatory possibilities, even as such exclusions simultaneously police and regulate their sexuality.[15] While a thorough negotiation of these issues is beyond the scope of this paper, the fact remains that *Murderball* explores neither side of the debate. Disabled women, and particularly disabled female athletes, are not celebrated as having been liberated from oppressive conventions of gender. Nor are they given access to normative femininity; visually, they are never made into objects of the voyeuristic male gaze that, after Laura Mulvey's classic 1975 article, has become common currency in discussions of cinematic spectatorship. Neither, interestingly, are they victims of "the stare," a visual dynamic coined by Garland-Thomson to encapsulate the revulsion of the able-bodied viewer whose lengthy hostile gaze at a "freakishly" embodied other is emptied of sexual desire (Garland-Thomson, 1997: 26). Indeed the few images of disabled women that the documentary presents function more as a set of fleeting and brief snapshots that, while easy to miss, do momentarily interrupt the temporal, and often verbal, logic through which these "boys" become "men." These more or less static images haunt the film's perimeter, a subtle threat to the coherence of a narrative that celebrates quadriplegia as the natural outcome of the hypermasculine male body.

Indeed, even the most attentive viewer might, on a first viewing, miss the few glimpses that are to be had of disabled female athletics. The first opportunity isn't until just before the final dramatic showdown between the U.S. and Canada at the 2004 Paralympics. In a brief montage that showcases a variety of Paralympic sports, there is a two-second clip of female leg amputees playing volleyball. Significantly, they are all low to the ground, and filmed (perhaps unavoidably) from above. Not only does the angle diminish their size and power, but also they are absent of any type of prosthesis or equipment and none of them are using wheelchairs. Given that prosthetics and wheelchair technology have earlier in the film been powerfully deployed to signify and naturalize disabled masculinity, and given that this clip is sandwiched between clips of Paralympic male sports (all of them requiring varying levels of prosthesis), it may be plausible to argue that the framing of these female athletes functions to neutralize any threat to disabled masculinity that their presence might pose.

The only other scene in which disabled women are presented in an athletic capacity is during the documentary's final scene, as the players teach a group of newly disabled Iraq War veterans the how to play the game. Between clips, we see two young women, though very briefly and in a limited context. Early in the scene, the camera abruptly cuts to a young woman standing with a basketball under one arm—her other arm visibly absent. The shot—lasting for no more than two seconds—catches her from the neck down; in fact we are only able to identify her as female because her white sports bra is visible underneath her white t-shirt. Because she is decapitated by the frame, we are unable to establish any filmic identification with her. Simultaneously, her disability and her desexualized wardrobe prevent the viewer from establishing her as an object of desire via conventional modes of cinematic spectatorship. Unlike the able-bodied girlfriends of the quad rugby players, or even the Paralympic volleyball players, this female body becomes visually unintelligible within the logic of the film.[16]

Later in the scene, the camera pans upwards from the feet of an individual wearing one prosthetic leg. As the frame reaches her chest, and then her face, we realize that it is a young, female veteran. Her shirt showcases the American flag and her gaze is intently fixed on something the viewer can't see. She's attractive and her demeanor exudes fortitude. In a sense, we have finally met the "athletic girl" whose specter was both invoked and repressed during the earlier poker scene.[17] This one, however, is not quite so quick to be dispelled. The camera quickly cuts to two male amputees who are wearing similar leg prostheses. While the purpose of this moment was no doubt to establish the effect that the Iraq War continues to have on American bodies, it serves simultaneously to establish a solid identification between the disabled woman and her male counterparts. The entire progression lasts only eight seconds, so it's easy to miss. But, I want to suggest, these eight seconds are what the rest of the documentary labors to repress. While most of the documentary features women only in conventional, able-bodied roles that reify masculinity by performing its opposite, this moment confronts the viewer with an unapologetic assertion of another type of "alternative masculinity," one that is attached to a female body.

But, although this moment lasts longer than any other depiction of a disabled woman in the film, it too is quickly redirected and contained by the dominant narrative of male heteromasculinity at work in the film. From here, the film dives quickly into the central tension of the scene. Masculine athleticism has once more found its proper object as a young man in a wheelchair expresses doubt in his ability to throw the ball. This first throw fails to reach its intended target, but after some hearty encouragement from the old pros, his second attempt is a success. The girl we have just seen is cut sporadically into this narrative, and in these brief half-second clips she appears to be actively involved in (and indeed taking delight from) a game of

quad rugby. But interestingly, the chair that she's using, though present by implication, is rendered invisible in these clips—we see her only from the elbows up. If the logic of the film has transformed the rugby chair into a metonym for a heteronormative masculinity that is reserved only for male bodies, then her temporary use of it becomes an appropriation that cannot be accommodated by the documentary's visual economy. The deconstructive potential of her participation is ultimately contained as the scene's primary drama resumes. The young male veteran finally throws a successful pass, establishing that masculinity has ultimately been returned to a male body. But while most of the documentary functions to contain the presence of the disabled female athlete, the film's epilogue ultimately lays bare some of this tension when it features Bob Lubjano kissing (albeit chastely) his girlfriend, who is identified as a Paralympic swimmer. We would do well to take this moment, as well as the others that preceded it, as an opportunity to reflect on and draw out the gender trouble that complicates not only the film, but also the cultural past that has conflated queerness and disability.

"GETTIN' OUT WHILE I STILL CAN WALK"

In some ways, the only thing that *Murderball* (2005) and *Brokeback Mountain* (2005) have in common is their release date. *Murderball* is about traveling the world to represent one's country; *Brokeback Mountain* is about spending a lifetime *in* the country. *Murderball* embraces the urban technologized body; *Brokeback Mountain*'s rural naturalism makes even the telephone look like technological excess. What the films do share, however, is a strategic deployment of masculinity that normalizes a historically marginalized population. But if *Murderball*'s celebration of quadriplegia is rooted in a narrative of heteronormative masculinity that disciplines and represses queerness, then *Brokeback Mountain* is conversely invested in particularly able-bodied masculinity that normalizes homosexuality by simultaneously disciplining disability.

It would be difficult to dispute the fact that Jack and Ennis emblematize a particular brand of frontier masculinity, one that has been until now historically off-limits in mainstream cinematic representations of homosexuality. But what *Brokeback Mountain* did was more than simply suggest that cowboys can be gay too; it implied that cowboys are gay precisely *because* they're cowboys.[18] Gay male sexuality in the film seems to spring directly from an inborn aggression and competitive instinct. It is figured as a natural corollary to male horseplay—the violent, almost primitive, crashing together of two male bodies. And above all else, it is organic.[19] Thus in the original story, we find Ennis in his first sexual encounter with Jack drawing upon what appears to be a physically innate drive: this was "nothing he'd done before, but no instruction manual needed" (Proulx, 1999: 259). Unlike the machinic heteromasculinity glorified in *Murderball*, this homosexual manliness is born directly out of the earth.

This organicism partially explains the able-bodied ideologies that underpin Jack and Ennis's masculinity. The stubbornness of their genders becomes to some extent the stubbornness of their physical bodies themselves. The Darwinian logic of the traditional frontier narrative places the male body in harsh conditions; it is the fittest who survive, the ablest bodies that endure. Thus the same excessive masculinity that *Murderball* celebrates as the cause of disability becomes, in *Brokeback Mountain*, the skill for keeping one's spine intact. Upon their first trip back to the mountain, the first thing that Jack and Ennis do is

strip off their clothes and jump from a peak into the stream below. But on Brokeback Mountain, the water is never too shallow and getting thrown from a horse leaves only some minor bruising.[20]

Part of Jack and Ennis's talent for remaining able-bodied, however, is tied directly to gay male sexuality. In several scenes, Ennis is presented with what ultimately becomes a choice between either facing harsh (and potentially debilitating) natural conditions or putting himself in a position that could lead to a homosexual encounter. Indeed on several occasions, the desire to remain able-bodied sends Ennis directly into Jack's arms. Thus the first sex scene unfolds out of Jack's concern for Ennis's health. Having had too much to drink, Ennis decides to sleep outdoors despite Jack's warning, "Freeze your ass off when that fire dies down. Better off sleepin' in the tent." But it is only when Jack's prediction comes true and Ennis seems on the verge of frostbite that he finally acquiesces; the two men share a blanket and their physical proximity quickly leads to their first sexual encounter. On another occasion, a storm breaks out, and Jack and Ennis can be observed shouting to one another in the entry flap of the tent. "Them sheep will drift if I don't get back up there tonight!" yells Ennis. Jack replies, "You'll get pitched off your mount in a storm like this. You'll wish you hadn't tried it! It's too cold! Close it up!" Thus Ennis's masculinity lies in his frontier brand of self-discipline, expressed through his avoidance of unnecessary risk and his knowledge of his own limitations in the face of nature. If his masculinity is of the earth, then his respect for natural law is what causes him ultimately to listen to Jack's advice. Having decided to keep Ennis's body out of danger, the two men close the tent flap, and presumably spend the night having sex. Thus the rugged homosexual masculinity of the expansive outdoors appears to carry sort of curative power that keeps male bodily integrity firmly intact.

But while Jack and Ennis constantly encounter and avoid threats from the wilderness they spend the summer inhabiting, the real threat of sickness, contamination, and disability comes from the world of heterosexual domesticity that lies below the mountain. Thus Joe Aguirre travels up the mountain to deliver news of Jack's sick uncle down below, on his deathbed as a result of pneumonia. "Bad news," Jack replies, "There ain't nothin' I can do about it up here, I guess." Aguirre responds, "There's not much you can do about it down there, neither. Not unless you can cure pneumonia." Aguirre's reply is no doubt designed to emphasize Aguirre's position as an unsympathetic boss and foreground Jack's exploitation as a working-class laborer. But it simultaneously emphasizes the contagion that spreads "down there" in the realm of rural domesticity, and the exposure to illness that Jack and Ennis avoid in the able-bodied "up here" of male homosexual freedom.

Thus the progression that starts off Jack and Ennis's descent from the mountain evokes multiple images of Jack and Ennis's newly vulnerable bodies. Jack mentions the possibility that the draft will prevent him from working on the mountain the following summer. The expansive sky that seemed unlimited on the mountain peak is claustrophobically framed by the walls of the alley where Ennis doubles over, retching in grief at his separation from Jack. Ennis's married life consists of a domestic routine that involves caring for his daughters' runny noses and coughs. In an effort to convince Ennis to move the family to more densely populated area of the town, Ennis's wife Alma argues "I'm scared for Jenny, scared if she has another one of 'em bad asthma spells." To top it off, Ennis's coworker delivers a monologue in which he explains, "My old lady's tryin' to get me

to quit this job. She says I'm gettin' too old to be breakin' my back shovelin' asphalt." Thus, the "up here" that Jack refers to in his conversation with Aguirre is the place where stubborn gay male bodies contend with the elements and, thanks to the balm of same-sex desire, emerge from this face-off intact. "Down there" is the heterosexual domestic space where male bodies are subject to pneumonia, vulnerable to the Vietnam draft, stricken with attacks of debilitating grief, responsible for asthmatic children, and exposed to literally "back-breaking" labor. Indeed, it becomes impossible to find an able-bodied domesticity anywhere in the film.[21] While domesticity is certainly framed as heterosexual, it is also a site that is implicated in the production of both disability and femininity (Ennis and his wife produce only daughters) and is thus no place for the able body of hypermasculine gay cowboy.

It should, of course, be pointed out that the acts of caring for asthmatic children, hearing about sick uncles, and working in physically taxing occupations never actually threaten to render Ennis literally disabled, and neither would any of the women who inhabit Ennis's heteronormative working class household identify themselves as a person with a disability. Indeed, by invoking these images of sickness and injury, I am gesturing less towards the presence of a concrete disabled identity within the film and more towards Jack and Ennis's construction as able-bodied subjects who are haunted by specters of corporeal fragility, specters that originate from the outside—and in their case, the heterosexual landscape. In this sense, I am actively following McRuer's suggestion that we "attempt to crip disability studies, which entails taking seriously the critique of identity that has animated other progressive theoretical projects, notably queer theory" (McRuer, 2006: 35). McRuer suggests that, like the "gender trouble" that underlies heterosexuality, we might similarly understand "ability trouble" as "not so much the problem of disability but the inevitable impossibility, even as it is made compulsory, of an able-bodied identity" (McRuer, 2006: 10). Just as my previous reading of *Murderball* suggested that it was not homosexuality but rather the heterosexual Sam and the disabled female athlete who held the power to queer the film's heteromasculine narrative, so too in *Brokeback Mountain* it is not disability *per se* but a set of failed performances of health and physical integrity that mark the heterodomestic sphere as a threatening site of "ability trouble."

The threat that heterosexual domesticity levels against masculine able-bodiedness is perhaps most explicit in Jack and Ennis's first conversation after having reunited following a four year separation. After having sex at a motel, they discuss their new roles as husbands and fathers. Jack explains, "Went down to Texas for rodeoin'. That's how I met Lureen." When Ennis asks, "Army didn't get you?" Jack replies "No, too busted up. And rodeoin' ain't what it was in my daddy's day. Got out while I could still walk." This process of getting "busted up" receives an even more elaborate treatment in the original story. In the same scene, when Ennis asks if the "army got [Jack]," Proulx has Jack reply:

> They can't get no use out a me. Got some crushed vertebrates. And a stress fracture, the arm bone here, you know how bullridin you're always levern it off your thigh?—she give a little ever time you do it. Even if you tape it good you break it a little goddamn bit at a time. Tell you what, hurts like a bitch afterwards. Had a busted leg. Busted in three places . . . Bunch a other things, fuckin busted ribs, sprains and pains, torn ligaments . . . I'm gettin out while I still can walk.
>
> (Proulx, 1999: 266)

When making argument about a film, it can be risky to draw evidence from the literary text upon which the film is based. However, because of the film's uncommon faithfulness to the short story—almost all of the dialogue in the film is taken word-for-word from the story and there's barely a single scene left out—such analysis seem justified. In a film that runs over two hours, it makes sense that the screenwriters might have cut some of the dialogue that merely extends a point that could be made more concisely. Thus what becomes clear when we trace this conversation back to the original source is the extreme threat that heterosexual domesticity poses to the able body of the gay cowboy. The rodeo to some extent functions as an extension of heterosexuality. It's where Jack met his wife, and it is, at the beginning at least, the way he has been financially supporting his family. But it also might break his back. The stakes are raised when Jack, explaining that he "don't got the bones a keep getting wrecked," proposes that he and Ennis settle down "in a little ranch together" (Proulx, 1999: 268). Indeed, this is where the short story sets up an ultimatum much like the ones I outlined earlier; a choice must be made between a future of disabled heterosexuality or a future of able-bodied homosexuality.

At the same time, however, Jack's sexuality occasionally complicates the able-bodied queer masculinity that the film attempts to naturalize. In particular, when Jack travels south of the border to engage in what one might consider "risky" anonymous sex with a male prostitute, the viewer might be reminded of one association that the film labors to repress—the historical connections between gay culture and the AIDS epidemic.[22] It is worth noting here that AIDS has been culturally constructed as a disease originating not only from homosexual men, but also as an "immigrant infection" that, originating from the outside, threatens to infiltrate and contaminate the United States population.

Subjected to mandatory HIV testing during the Regan era, immigrants joined gay men as one of the largest projected menaces to public health. This scapegoating of immigrants and queers functioned to externalize the threat of HIV infection, making it easy for officials to ignore the more important issues of prevention, treatment, and anti-discrimination (Brier, 2001: 253–270). While Jack's illicit encounter with the Mexican prostitute takes place before the start of the AIDS epidemic, and while the prostitute himself is not attempting to emigrate to the United States, the scene on some level still resonates with the cultural meanings that have conflated the tightly sealed national body with the healthy body—a seal that Jack breaks when he crosses back and forth over the border.[23] If we are to read this encounter with racial otherness as meta-phoric of the "infected" national body, then this becomes a moment when the narrative becomes haunted by its own future. And it is is a future in which the representational linkage between male homosexuality and AIDS—a linkage, in other words, between queerness and disability—will loom large.

In this context, it's worth noting the Brokeback Mountain has been repeatedly hailed as the first "mainstream gay movie from Hollywood" since Brian Demme's 1992 film Philadelphia and in numerous reviews the film's detachment from AIDS discourse is celebrated (Ehrenstein, 2006: 41). Thus Brokeback emerges from a queer filmic tradition in which the associations between homosexuality and AIDS have been largely figured and can, in this context, be read as participating in a representational backlash against homosexuality's place in the AIDS narrative.[24] The film escapes these associations by a feat of geographical and temporal disloca-tion, as the narrative ends just before the AIDS outbreak in the United States. In this context, barebacking loses its association with threats to public health, transformed instead into a life-affirming practice struc-tured around a principle of rural able-bod-ied masculinity. But because Brokeback seems so powerfully invested in disavow-ing the political legacy of AIDS activism, along with the historical process by which the epidemic has imprinted the queer community with the stigma of disability, some of those repressed elements do sur-face from time to time within the narrative, particularly through Jack in the moments I have just discussed.

I'd like to conclude this section by ten-tatively pointing to a verbal/visual divide similar to the one that I referenced in my discussion of Murderball's narrative per-formances of heteromasculinity and the static images of the disabled female body that momentarily stall those narratives. Though I have largely relied on verbal examples to describe the strategies thor-ough which the film constructs its ethos of able-bodiedness, the moments that most powerfully "crip" that narrative are gener-ally mute, relying instead on the transmis-sion of visual cues. When Jack visits Mexico, his encounter with the prostitute is mark-edly silent; and while Lureen's monotone rehearsal of the official narrative of Jack's death accompanies Ennis's entirely differ-ent visual reconstruction of the scene, the images of hate crime violence that confront the viewer in this clip are entirely absent of sound, and differently filmed, playing like a grainy home video without audio. The intrusion of these brief images gestures toward a queer-crip cultural past that can-not, ultimately, be spoken.

But why not take such moments as opportunities to critically consider, and perhaps occasionally even claim, those histories, both representational and mate-rial, in which queerness and disability are brought into uneasy proximity? What, ulti-mately, is to be gained by the current cul-tural impulse to dissolve this complicated, though albeit troubled, partnership? While critics of both films are certainly justified in celebrating the strategies through which newer films are defiantly cutting the ties that have historically bound queerness to disability, I want to suggest that we remain wary of accepting discourses that celebrate one marginal identity at the expense of another, and that we continue to ask who gets left out of this framework completely. While male homosexuality and male disability may be regulating one another in these films, what is perhaps most perplexing is that it is not the able-bodied gay man whose existence is disavowed *Murderball* but the physically disabled woman. And it is not entirely the heterosexual man who is linked to a disabling domesticity in *Brokeback Mountain*, but primarily the heterosexual woman. Transgender identity is meanwhile rendered unthinkable and race is dealt with problematically, at best. Of course, there is undoubtedly something productive happening when mainstream films begin to challenge the stereotype of the feminized or asexual male quadriplegic, or when those same films acknowledge that male homosexuality is not intrinsically bound up in illness. But these liberatory representations are accompanied by a set of political limitations that demand greater scrutiny. Rather than replace one regime of normalcy with another, we would do well to transform this uncomfortable representational history into an opportunity for continuing the difficult work of coalition building. Only then can we really achieve the cyborg myth of breaking with our origins to fashion new and unthinkable futures.

NOTES

My thanks to Lennard Davis for his feedback on as well as support for this essay.

1. While the relationship between disability and gender has often been theorized, many of these accounts have grown out of a feminist concern for the representations of disabled women and the linkages between femininity and illness. Indeed, many of the early canonical texts of feminist literary criticism focus on relationship between femininity, authorship and mental health, Sandra Gilbert and Susan Gubar's *The Mad Woman in the Attic* being perhaps the most well-known example. More recently, however, scholars like Rosemarie Garland-Thomson have prioritized the physical disability, as opposed to mental illness, in their analysis as well and brought race to bear on these issues in important ways.

2. McRuer does, however, provide a notable counterexample in his observations regarding ableist rhetoric in the popular television show *Queer Eye For the Straight Guy*.

3. Matthew Leyland, for example, offers the following praise in *Sight and Sound*: "Dispelling misconceptions in an unfussy fashion, Shapiro and Rubin . . . venture into taboo territory with an X-rated debate about quad sex. As well as answering questions most disability movies are afraid to ask, the sequence is very funny. 'The more pitiful I am, the more [women] like me,' one wheelchair user chirps unapologetically'" (Leyland, 2005: 70).

4. In *The Cinema of Isolation*, Martin Norden identifies one such narrative trap as the tendency for Hollywood to put well-known, able-bodied actors in disabled roles. Like a straight-identified actor playing a gay role, the casting of able-bodied stars in disabled roles become an opportunity for the able-bodied actor to demonstrate superior Oscar-quality acting skills by successfully impersonating what the public would view as extreme difference or otherness (Norden, 1994: 2).

5. In his comparative reading of the armless Venus de Milo and a quadriplegic woman, Pam Herbert, Lennard Davis draws our attention to the able-bodied assumptions underlying Western standards of physical beauty. Thus Davis explores "how people with disabilities are seen and why, by and large, they are de-eroticized" (Davis, 1995: 128). The film's intense eroticization of quadriplegic men can then be read as a radical reclaiming of that which has long been denied to disabled people; that this is accomplished through heteronormative masculinization and at the expense of the disabled whom are further "queered" by the logic of the film, however, is a tension that this section explores in greater detail.

6. In her magazine piece "Seat of Power," Melissa Davis Haller quotes James Gumbert (the coach

for Team USA) as pointing out that "Most of these guys didn't get into their chairs because they were timid . . . They were daredevils." The player featured in the piece agrees: " 'We're true athletes,' he says. 'We have the same rivalries and passion about our sport as anyone'" (Haller, 2005: 22).

7. The celebration of the prosthetic dimensions of Zupan's masculinity also constitutes a subversion of previous stereotypes. Norden points out the common villainization of disabled male figures who are "aided by . . . high tech prostheses" and "whose many battle injuries have transformed him into a walking wonderland of bionic effects . . . more machine than man" (Norden, 1994: 293).

8. Perhaps picking up on the prosthetic dimensions of the sport equipment, one reviewer has remarked upon a quad rugby who "handles the ball as if it were a part of his body" (Bennett, 2000: 60).

9. My thanks to Megan V. Davis for this reference.

10. Examining the work of three different visual artists, Halberstam defines this technotopic body as "a body situated in an immediate and visceral relation to technologies—guns, scalpel, cars, paintbrushes—that have marked, hurt, changed, imprinted, and brutally reconstructed it" and notes that "in all three instances, the impact of technological intervention is to disrupt gender stability . . . [suggesting that] we should locate femaleness not as the material with which we begin nor as the end product of medical engineering but as a stage and indeed as fleshly place of production" (Halberstam, 2005: 116–117). The men of *Murderball* are certainly "situated in an immediate and visceral relation to technologies that have marked" each of them. But while for Halberstam the technotopic body "disrupts gender stability" and showcases anatomical sex as neither the "material with which we begin nor as the end product of medical engineering," the technologized masculinity of the quad rugby athletes is visually framed within a narrative of continuity that privileges the anatomical origin of maleness and the technologically enhanced final product of heteronormative masculinity. What might have become a radical celebration of technology's roles in producing alternative or queer modes of embodiment here collapses into a reification of gender difference.

11. In *The Gender of Desire*, Michael Kimmel has argued that hegemonic masculinity is fundamentally rooted in a homophobic impulse to simultaneously deny and desire the feminine. If a boy is to access patriarchy, his successful identification with his father must be accompanied by a disavowal of the feminine within himself, a punishment of effeminacy in other men, and a willingness to turn his mother into an object of desire. (Kimmel, 2005: 34) If *Murderball* follows the traditional narrative of masculinity that Kimmel has outlined, the players' masculinity ultimately depends on the sexual acquisition of the girl whose "big tits" prove that she's everything that he's not.

12. Interestingly, the player commentary not only conflates Sam's queer object choice with feminization but also with a lack of sexual potency, and a general inability to engage in phallocentric penetrative sex. While watching the poker scene with the commentary function turned on, one hears the players add: "We tried to get Sammy laid the whole year, but he's just not a closer. He's had some opportunities but Sammy cuddles." Sam's decision to not be a "closer" simultaneously resists the narrative *closure* that protectively bounds heteromasculine sexuality in the film.

13. This argument is not an entirely new one; in the context of disabled veteran films, Martin Norden argues that "Movies continue to depend heavily on the idea of women acting as remasculinizing agents to facilitate the protagonists' Oedipal adventures, particularly those featuring embittered veterans" (322). Other films didn't necessarily rely on woman per se, but resolved similar tensions by situating the character among "advancements in science and technology in the form of highly potent prosthesis" (322). Both features, however, appear to be at play in *Murderball*.

14. To this effect, one reviewer celebrates the "lusty montage" which illuminates the "intriguing reasons why some women are particularly attracted to quadriplegic men." In another scene, the viewer is able to appreciate—and perhaps envy—Zupan's ability to attract an able-bodied, conventionally feminine woman who is featured in a black bikini on the side of a pool. Her interview portions in the film mainly function to emphasize the ways in which partnership with a quadriplegic man brings out the "mothering instinct" in women, a quality that she suggests could be what "attracts a lot of girls to quadriplegics." Cut alongside of a clip that features her tying Zupan's shoes, the implication is clear.

15. For a more thorough analysis of these issues, see Rosemarie Garland-Thomson's "Integrating Disability, Transforming Feminist Theory."

16. One analysis that I am omitting here, which is

beyond the scope of this paper, is the similarly problematic image of the disabled black man who shares the frame with this woman. While the frame catches her from the neck down, it simultaneously catches only the top right quadrant of his face in the bottom left corner of the frame. The only other exposure that the viewer has to African-American disabled masculinity are two entirely out-of-context interviews in which a disabled black man (whose name, team affiliation, and general relationship to the sport we never learn) describes some of the tensions he encounters when trying to pick up girls and elaborates upon the "modified doggy-style" that he has perfected during sex. The relative absence of African-American male quadriplegics from the film suggests that the players' disabled masculinity is not only invested in heterosexuality but in whiteness. The brief airtime given to African-American masculinity functions only to rhetorically infuse the sexuality of the featured (white) quadriplegic men with the primitive potency stereotypically projected onto African-American masculinity. That this particular African-American man happens to be describing the "doggy-style" position only exaggerates and exploits the dangerous cultural stereotypes that link African-American sexuality to animalism and aggressivity. Thus, while this moment might be read as a sensitive inclusion of a non-white voice in dialogue about male quadriplegia and sexuality, I would argue that it ulitmately collapses into merely another rhetorical building block in the construction and maintenance of the white heteromasculinity.

17. To this effect, it is striking how quickly the players, while appearing on Larry King Live, pass over the related inquiry of a female caller. While all of the other calls lasted several minutes, this particular seemed over as soon as it began. The entire dialogue runs as follows:

Woman: "Being from Alaska, where is [sic] the closest teams and how many are there, and is [sic] there any female teams?"

Bob: "There are women that play rugby, it's a co-ed sport."

Larry King: "And so women can be on *your* team?"

Mark: "Yeah, it's a co-ed sport."

Larry King: "Any in Alaska?"

Scott: "No, the closest team I'd say is in Seattle."

Larry King: "So you have to go to Seattle."

18. In this article, my use of the term "gay" should be read as a shorthand for male same-sex desire and homosexual erotic expression. By employing it in this context, I am by no means making an identity claim about Jack and Ennis—indeed, in both the film and the short story, both men make it clear that they don't self-identify as "queer." It is important, however, to acknowledge the impact that this film has had on members of the gay community, many of whom have identified with and claimed the characters, as well the effect it has had on mainstream understandings of the gay community. Thus by referring to "gay" masculinity or "gay" sexuality, I am referring to the representation of a behavior that has had a significant impact on the cultural understandings of a constructed identity category and the communities that have been formed around that category.

19. If *Murderball* follows a Freudian narrative in which a disavowal of the feminine in the self entails the transformation of women into objects of desire, then in *Brokeback Mountain*, the disavowal of the feminine in the self involves no such transformation; in *Brokeback Mountain*, to embody frontier masculinity is to disavow the feminine, period. Reviewer Constantine Hoffman puts it well when he points out that "*Brokeback* forced us to face the fact that the more 'manly' a man is the more he will enjoy the company of other manly men" (Hoffman, 2006: 26). Indeed, if twenty-five years ago, Adrienne Rich argued that lesbianism was the natural feminine state—a state from which women were coercively exiled by a system of "compulsory heterosexuality"—then *Brokeback Mountain* applies the same logic male same-sex desire. For a feminist disability critique of Rich's article, see Alison Kafer's "Compulsory Bodies: Reflections on Heterosexuality and Able-Bodiedness."

20. While the rodeo, which I will later discuss in more depth, is linked to both heterosexuality and disability, the scene where Ennis is thrown from his horse functions as its able-bodied queer counterpoint: Ennis is barely injured by the incident, able even to immediately chase the horse and mules who have run off. Additionally, upon their first trip back to the mountain after their long separation, the first thing we see Jack and Ennis do is strip off their clothes and jump from a tall cliff into the water below. We might productively compare this scene to the Spanish film *The Sea Inside* where a similar jump off of a similar cliff results in extreme quadriplegic impairment.

21. Robert McRuer's arguments about hetero-sexuality and able-bodied domesticity seem worth addressing in this context. McRuer argues that "[t]he ideological reconsolidation of the home as a site of intimacy and heterosexuality was also the reconsolidation of the home as a site for the redevelopment of able-bodied identities, practices, and relations." Thus an "inability to imagine a queer domesticity" becomes also the "inability to imagine a disabled domesticity" (McRuer, 2006: 89). While McRuer's argument is entirely valid within the context of his examples, *Brokeback Mountain* appears to signal a drastic resignification of these concepts, forcefully undoing the associational link between heterosexual domesticity and able-bodied ideologies.

22. Interestingly, in this respect, Jack emblematizes both the "cult of ability" that McRuer has identified as "the Good Gays who are capable of sustaining a marriage, who are not stigmatized by AIDS, and who went to Washington in 2000 for the Millennium March" and the "cultures of disability" that are made up of participants in "AIDS activism and the lesbian feminist traditions of health care activism that preceded it" (McRuer, 2006: 86).

23. We might consider this moment alongside of the scene that occurs directly after Jack convinces Ennis to spend the night with him in the tent during the hailstorm. What appears to be a decision on the side of able-bodied homo-sexuality turns out to result in another racial contamination—without Ennis there to shepherd them, Aguirre's flock has gotten mixed together with a flock of South American sheep. It is, of course, not at all my intention here to conflate Mexico and South America. However, their geographical proximity and their relationship to Hispanic racial identity does function to link them within the logic of the film.

24. Ironically, these associations were often accompanied by a different understanding of queer masculinity, one that, according to Tim Edwards, saw gay public sex cultures not only as a site of contamination but also as outgrowth of an aggressive and "unnatural" hypermasculine sex drive. If the urban manifestations of gay sexuality appeared to many to link hypermasculinity to sexual excess, indulgence, and disease then Ennis's rural brand of stoic masculinity, founded on an ethic of discipline and restraint, invests his homosexuality with the virtues of health, organicism, and able-bodiedness.

25. For a thorough treatment of cultural understandings of barebacking, see Gregory Tomso's "But Chasing, Barebacking, and the Risks of Care." Of course, on another level, the film might be said to constitute the realistic portrait of queer rural masculinities between 1960 and 1980. By no means is my intention to consolidate a grand narrative that privileges urban queer cultures at the exclusion of rural queer manifestations. The film does indeed help us to revise our assumptions about the proper "time and place" for queer sexualities (Halberstam, 2005). I would suggest, however, that in its intense disavowal of all things urban and disabled, *Brokeback Mountain* in fact lends remarkable authority to those representational histories that tied queerness to urban sex cultures and disability.

WORKS CITED

Bennett, R. (2000) "Rugby", *WeMedia* 4(5): pp. 60.

Brier, J. (2001) "The Immigrant Infection: Images of Race, Nation and Contagion in Public Debates on AIDS and Immigration." *Modern American Queer History*. Edited by Allida M. Black. Philadelphia: Temple University Press.

Davis, L. J. (1995) *Enforcing Normalcy: Disability, Deafness, and the Body*. New York: Verso Books.

Edwards, T. (1994) *Erotics & Politics: Gay Male Sexuality, Masculinity, and Feminism*. London: Routledge.

Ehrenstein, D. (2006) "Fun with Harv and George?", *Advocate*, February, p. 41.

Garland-Thomson, R. (1997) *Extraordinary Bodies: Figuring Physical Disability in American Culture and Literature*. New York: Columbia University Press.

Garland-Thomson, R. (2004) "Integrating Disability, Transforming Feminist Theory", in B.G. Smith and B. Hutchison (eds) *Gendering Disability*, pp. 73–104. New Brunswick, NJ: Rutgers University Press.

Garland-Thomson, R. (2007) "Shape Structures Story: Fresh and Feisty Stories about Disability", *Narrative*, 15(1): pp. 113–123.

Gilbert, S. and Gubar, S. (1979) *The Mad Woman in the Attic: The Woman Writer and the Nineteenth Century Literary Imagination*. New Haven, CT: Yale University Press.

Halberstam, J. (2005) *In a Queer Time and Place: Transgender Bodies, Subcultural Lives*. New York: New York University Press.

Haller, M.D. (2005) "Seat of Power", *Cincinnati Magazine*, October, 39(1): pp. 20, 22.

Haraway, D. (1991) *Simians, Cyborgs and Women: The Reinvention of Nature*. New York: Routledge.

Hoffman, C. (2006) "Memo From the Front: It's Just a Manly Thing", *Brandweek*, May, 47(18): p. 26.

Kafer, A. (2003) "Compulsory Bodies: Reflections on Heterosexuality and Able-Bodiedness", *Journal of Women's History*, 15(3): pp. 77–89.

Kimmel, M. S. (2005) *The Gender of Desire: Essays on Male Sexuality*. New York: State University of New York Press.

Lee, A. (2006) *Brokeback Mountain*. Universal Studios.

Leyland, M. (2005) "Murderball", *Sight and Sound*, 15(11): pp. 70–71.

McRuer, R. (2006) *Crip Theory: Cultural Signs of Queerness and Disability: Cultural Signs of Queerness and Disability*. New York: New York University Press.

Mulvey, L. (1975) "Visual Pleasure and Narrative Cinema", *Screen* 16(3): pp. 6–18.

Norden, M. F. (1994) *The Cinema of Isolation: A History of Physical Disability in the Movies*. New Brunswick, NJ: Rutgers University Press.

Proulx, A. (1999) *Close Range: Wyoming Stories*. New York: Scribners.

Seymour, W. (1998) *Remaking the Body: Rehabilitation and Change*. London: Routledge.

Shapiro, D. A., Mandel, J. and Rubin, H. A. (2005) *Murderball*. THINKFilm and MTV Films.

Tomso, G. (2004) "But Chasing, Barebacking, and the Risks of Care", *Literature and Medicine*, 23(1): pp. 88–111.

Wilson, D. J. (2004) "Fighting Polio Like a Man: Intersections of Masculinity, Disability and Aging", in B. G. Smith and B. Hutchison (eds) *Gendering Disability*, pp. 119–133. New Brunswick, NJ: Rutgers University Press.

CHAPTER 34

The Vulnerable Articulate: James Gillingham, Aimee Mullins, and Matthew Barney[1]

Marquard Smith

PROSTHETICS, AESTHETICS, EROTICS

This chapter circles around a particular question: what kinds of erotic fantasies are being played out across medical, commercial, and later avant-garde images of the body of the female amputee in our Western visual culture? In attending to this question, my aim is to consider how and why these images articulate *the subject of prosthesis* in academic discourse with regards to what Vivian Sobchack has called "a tropological currency for describing a vague and shifting constellation of relationships between bodies, technologies, and subjectivities."[2] Although these images that point towards the confluence of prosthetics, aesthetics, and erotics are often problematic in the extreme, and the arguments that fasten themselves to and emanate from them are similarly somewhat awkward, it is my hope that asking this question will make certain previously unthinkable possibilities available.

FLIRTING WITH TECHNO-FETISHISM[3]

I have of late been flirting with techno-fetishism. By techno-fetishism I refer simply to that well-known and wide spread series of cultural practices acted out by academics, writers, artists, and others who fetishize technology in their writings and art-making both within the confines of their intellectual communities and in everyday life. From the start, I'm happy to acknowledge that techno-fetishism is a practice of a "perverse" kind.[4] Fetishes always are in the West, seeing as how, since at least the late nineteenth-century's epistemological explosion of perversions, the presence of fetishistic practices and objects marks the distinction between the "normal" and the "abnormal," the normative and the pathological, the well hinged and the unhinged, the "straight" and the "perverse." We will remember that for Michel Foucault in volume 1 of *The History of Sexuality* fetishism was the "master perversion."[5]

This chapter is well disposed toward perverse, fetishistic practices and objects in general. But it is wary of the idea of techno-fetishism, a pernicious notion whose cause for concern is its dangerously implicit metaphorical opportunism. Philosophers of technology are prone to take advantage of metaphorical *opportunities* that are made available by thinking and writing about technology, and about the technologization of being. They tend to indulge in a metaphorical poetics of technologization at the expense of the more mundane reality of material lives that are lived through technology and the body *as it is experienced* through the technology that it must employ—to the extent, for instance, that the figure of the disabled body has for them become a living, shining embodiment of post-human existence in prosthetic times.[6] Even so, or perhaps because of this, this chapter must become intimate with techno-fetishism to gauge its impact on the constellation of bodies, technologies, and subjectivities—without ever losing sight of its potential dangers or my complicity with it.

Maintaining this fraught dialectic between material and the metaphorical, the literal and the figural, flesh and poetics, is the most productive way of engaging with the central concerns of this essay, the "constellation . . . of bodies, technologies, and subjectivities" in all of their real and phantasmatic, grounded and *un*grounded possibilities. Maintaining this dialectic becomes so pressing because it is only in attending to both the literal, material, and fleshy nature of things *and* flirting with techno-fetishism as a practice that involves an aestheticization, a poeticization, and a metaphorization of "the prosthetic"—as what Sobchack calls an "unfleshed" out catchword—that one can make use of such possibilities without becoming unduly sympathetic towards the very things one admonishes.

To this end, the following speculations are staged in two parts. Part 1 considers the role that "passing" plays in the discourse of prosthesis, and how the challenge that the amputee faces in trying to "pass" for something that they are not turns on questions of visibility and invisibility. To demonstrate this I draw on photographs from the early twentieth century that both follow a precedent set in medical imagery in the nineteenth century and pursue commercial ends that they offer us ways to take in the intermittent oscillation between the visible and the invisible that engenders a fetishistic eroticization of the female amputees represented in the images. Part 2 focuses on the American double amputee paralympian athlete Aimee Mullins. Mullins appeared provocatively in a Nick Knight photo shoot for an issue of the fashion magazine *Dazed and Confused,* guest edited by fashion designer Alexander McQueen in 1998; adorned the catwalk, Barbie doll-like on a revolving pedestal in McQueen's 1999 Spring-Summer Collection in London; and sprinted through the desert landscape of a television advertisement for the British Internet service provider Freeserve in 2000 on her carbon-graphite "cheetah" legs designed by Van Phillips. Here I shall be concentrating on Mullins in a more recent fine art context—the latest episode of American artist and filmmaker Matthew Barney's *Cremaster* cycle released in 2002—in order to consider how she is drawn on here to both re-affirm the mechanisms and the fantasies of techno-fetishism and at the same time offer some other nicely surprising possibilities.

Overall, then, I look to account for how these two historically distinct yet conceptually linked visual renderings of the confluences of bodies, technologies, and subjectivities as they are spun through the prism of prosthetics, aesthetics, and erotics makes it possible for us to begin to articulate something neglected and thus worthy of note in the etymology of perversion. This is to say that an etymology of perversion makes it possible to acknowledge, open up, and seek to separate the more obvious perverse practices of techno-fetishism as practices of an erotic kind from a far more fascinating thread of the genealogy of perversion—that is already apparent in Haverlock Ellis's sexology, Max Nordau's studies in degeneration, and Sigmund Freud's psychoanalysis—in which the matter of sexuality is but one part of perversion's desire to, in fact, mimic a "turning away" from such sexuality.[7]

The reason to insist upon the prospect of this separation—between the feat of perverting itself and perversions of a sexual kind—is founded on the need to preserve the promise of the former and to be wary of the sleight of hand of the latter. That is, to be wary of perversion's fetishizing in general, its fetishizing of technology in particular, its techno-fetishism, its ability to make things disappear, its imperative to loss. To put it another way, my endeavor here is to trace and rub up against the points of articulation between fetishistic practices, fetishistic objects, and perversion itself. To do so is to question some of the ways that—following the three primary models of fetishism; the anthropological, the Marxian, and the Freudian—the matter of fetishism and its supplementary nature turns on or hints at a disavowal, a displacement, a replacement of or a compensation for *something else*, a substitute or surrogate for *other things*, now lost, that are magical, mysterious, horrific. Although I am deeply suspicious of fetishism's role in the patterning of human sexuality and subjectivity, what interests me is the prospect of the perverting (but nonsexualizing) thread of the etymology of this genealogy of perversion in which it becomes possible to begin to understand the implications of how, as Emily Apter has put it so succinctly, fetishism necessitates "*inanimate* or *nonhuman objects*, [and] living part[s] of the body [that are] treated as dead or partial objects substituted for the whole" and how these inanimate, non-human, or partial objects are surinvested [or overvalued] to the exclusion of all other targets of desire" [emphasis mine].[8] To put it more simply, what fascinates me is a decision to "turn away" from perverse and fetishistic practices as being exclusively sexual and to turn toward the way in which fetishistic objects, including the possibility of animat*ed* and animat*ing* objects as replacing our phantasmatic desire for the human body as a totalized union and instead lead us into a malignant, which is to say enduring investment in things that are not wholly human. For Apter, following Jacques Lacan, a body is thus "composed of prosthetic parts . . . rather than [being] at risk of . . . loss."

I believe, then, that certain discourses on prosthesis have something provocative to tell us about the nature of fetishistic practices and fetishistic objects—especially given the *supplementary* nature of these fetishistic objects, that, for Freud at any rate, are only ever body parts or inanimate objects substituted inappropriately for the sexual object proper, ultimately taking its place and thereby encouraging us further to abandon this so called "proper" sexual aim. Since this is in essence the definition of perversion, *so by extension* the discourse on prosthesis also has the chance to tell us something unexpected about perversion—the very pathology *spawning* fetishistic practices. For me, something in the *material* and *metaphorical* articulations of the body and its prosthetic technologies is mirrored in the historical, theoretical, and morphological structure that we see unfolding in questions of fetishism and perversion, and as a consequence questions of the emergence of sexuality and eroticism.

PART 1

Passing: Commercial Photography And "Evidence of a New Invisibility"

I really cannot tell you what my friends thought of your work, I believe there was only one word and that was "marvellous," and when I had the leg on and began to walk about, *I don't think they fully realised it was me*, after walking with a crutch all these years.

I must tell you I had a good deal of practice while at home, I had a mile walk two days after I left you and I did not feel any inconvenience after and on Sunday I had the leg on nearly all day, and I only had the backache' a little. [emphasis mine]

This letter dated July 19, 1907 is one of a number of such patient testimonies that can be found in the Osteogenesis Collection at the Science Museum, London. It is attached to an archive of photographs of products manufactured by James Gillingham of Chard, a maker of artificial limbs since around 1866. These testimonies and images draw attention to the fact that at the heart of the modern discourse of prosthesis is the realization that the joining together of bodies and machines is not just a manufacturing process, or even just an art and a craft. An ethic is in play here that seeks to answer a challenge of presentation and utility: how an item of prosthetic technology is fashioned industrially, and also how this piece of machinery is experienced. At stake, then, is how a particular prosthesis is sculpted and utilized, how it looks and how it works, and how its aesthetic success and its practical success affect the ontology of its wearer, the body's experience of itself. These are matters of aesthetics, ergonomics, and sentience.

Most interesting for my purposes is the quality of *in*visibility that circles around the presence of the prosthesis in the late nineteenth and early twentieth centuries: as the patient says, *when they put on their leg and began to walk about, they didn't think their friends fully realised who they were*. Like an uncanny inversion of the phenomenon of the spectral phantom limb which is experienced by many amputees, here the identity of the patient has been disguised by the prosthetic device, and at the same time has transformed the patient into someone else by its material existence. This is a perfect instance of the history of the development of prosthetic technology as it stands, and falls, on its ability to play hide-and-seek with the truth. This is simultaneously a humanitarian success story and a story of inevitable failure. One story is about curative therapeutics, a pragmatic episteme of how medicine and technology come together with a shared compassion for the integrity of the human being to begin a process of reparation, to turn the *dis*abled into the *able*-bodied. Another story is about an ever more frantic effort to seek to conceal missing body parts, loss itself, by replacing them with artificial substitutes or surrogates, to replicate or imitate that lost object, an irreconcilable quest, to make the human body whole again, a will to verisimilitude that, in the end, simply draws attention to its own inability to approximate the real.[9]

In this patient testimony, then, success and failure turn on the edge between invisibility and visibility. Success is gauged in terms of invisibility, in terms of *not* being able to see the prosthetic device or its consequences. Given this, it is ironic that the success story of prosthesis is legitimated by its adherence to the truth of reparation when it is in fact determined by *hiding* the truth, making *invisible* the body's "disability" and the very thing that makes it "able-bodied" again. This sleight of hand allows the prosthetic wearer to carry out a so-called normal life safe in the knowledge that the rest of the world is unaware of their disability. But of course, the point is that as effective as evidence of this new invisibility might be in principle and *from a distance*, much like aesthetic surgery, so it is for prosthetic technology. In practice, our eyes can be deceiving. Once you get closer, intimate, there is always a small scar tucked away behind the ear or under the breast, or, in the case of prosthetic technology, a slightly irregular gait, or, as the letter indicates, a little bit of backache suffered by the patient, that evokes a memory, sometimes visible sometimes invisible, that is both a reminder of success and an admission of the failure to hide this truth.

This discourse of prosthesis as one of invisibility and visibility, success and failure, reparation and imitation, deceit and display, can be located in debates around aesthetic and cosmetic surgery especially towards the end of the nineteenth century, although its genealogy goes back much further than this, and in particular within the deeply ideological subject of "passing." While "passing" has been discussed recently by Judith Butler and Judith Halberstam in relation to questions of gender identity, performativity, and queer sexual practices, it is a topic that has also been revitalized by Sander L. Gilman in his cultural history of aesthetic surgery.[10] In *Making the Body Beautiful: A Cultural History of Aesthetic Surgery*, Gilman explores "passing," an aesthetic and, as I have already suggested, ideological undertaking, emerging directly out of the racialization of nineteenth-century culture, as a challenge by which an individual seeks to "pass" for something that they are not. This "passing" has historically assumed a variety of forms as an individual employs all kinds of aesthetic and medical deceits to become something other than what we are. This is not just a question of masquerading, then, but rather of actually *becoming* something other than what we are, looking to pass *as*, or pass *from*, say, being a man to being a woman, or vice versa, from being straight to being gay, or vice versa, from being black to being white, or vice versa, and so on. (One can see why theorists of gender subversion such as Butler and Halberstam would find this trope so productive.) Through this operation of passing, the individual passes from one category to another, for the most part moving in a not unexpected direction: from a category of exclusion to a community of inclusion, from being an abject pariah to an object of desire, from being anomalous to being something else more enviable.[11] And while it must be kept in mind that "passing" is inherently conservative because, as Gilman reminds us, unlike reconstructive surgery it is premised on a purely physical

metamorphosis in which signs of physical difference, so called pathological signs, are camouflaged through modification, the *consequences* are none the less very real.[12] As Gilman makes clear, such acts of "passing" do have a profound effect on the correlation between an individual's desire to overcome their physical stigmatization and their psychological unhappiness, or, to put it differently, the *visible* efforts at redesign will have a direct impact on an individual's *invisible* interior emotional architecture.

Much like Gilman's account of aesthetic surgery in which "techniques must constantly evolve so as to perfect the illusion that the boundary between the patient and the group [that they wish to join] never existed,"[13] developments in prosthetic technology, as I have already indicated, are *in principle* committed to the same evolutionary imperative: working seamlessly in such a way as to make themselves invisible. Similar to the narrative that takes place in the discourse of aesthetic surgery,[14] an account of the development of prosthetic technology is caught up in ideological concerns that are similar to those embedded in "passing" and thus might be characterized, as does Gilman for aesthetic surgery, as "evidence of a new invisibility."[15]

Given the importance of this evidence of the new invisibility, that the truth and success of the discourse of prosthesis are premised on hiding the presence of the amputee's disability, their physical otherness, and that visibility makes failure all too evident, it is ironic that the photographs of female amputees produced by James Gillingham do the exact opposite. They *reveal* their prosthetic devices to show the virtuosity of their maker, the triumph of the technology itself, the possibility of their machinic articulations, and the impact that they will have on their user, the purchaser. Let us not forget that the photographs are serving a commercial purpose. Because of this, the wearer, the patient, the model is obliged to display, at the expense of their refusal to disclose, the technology in such a way as to draw attention to the very disability that the technology has been developed to disguise. While male amputees are often presented utilizing their prosthetic limbs as model examples of the enhancing potential of human-machine synergy, and are shown fully integrated in the world of both work and leisure activity, letters in the archives of the Science Museum and elsewhere from *female* amputees emphasize a need for continued disguise, and a pleasure in such disguise, a pleasure in modestly and discreetly being able to pass for something other than dis-abled, in this case to be able to pass for being able-bodied.[16]

This is why the *exposure* of James Gillingham's patients in his catalogues is particularly troubling. In playing this game of hide and seek, the models, the photographer, the photographs themselves, the people using the ads to select prosthetic machinery for themselves, and we viewers as competent interpreters of images are obviously aware of this pivot between invisibility and visibility, hiding and revealing, concealment and revelation, and the assault to modesty that this exposure entails. This play between concealing and disclosure, secrets and their confession, also of course lies at the heart of debates in the discourse of fetishism, and it is writ large here, literally, in the complex way in which the revealing of the fetishistic substitute, the artificial limb, acts as both a desire to overcome loss and a exposure of that very loss itself. It is no wonder, then, that a consequent sexualization of the figure of the female amputee ensues. It is also worthwhile pointing out that because these photographs are images of female amputees displaying their wares for commercial purposes, this display, this exhibition, is a dual seduction that is at once commercial and erotic. Certainly one needs to keep in mind that these images are ads, the purpose of which is to sell Gillingham's products. But at the same time, the interior setting, the studio, the lighting, the painted backdrops, the props, the drapery, the staged quality of the images, and the carefully posed figures of the women themselves, certainly imply that an effort has been made to employ the accoutrements of portraiture—as commercial imperatives themselves maybe—to both humanize and individualize. Perhaps these very aspects of portraiture, coupled with the "theatricized or narritivized tableaux" further eroticises.[17] Some of these women have been invited to lift up their shirts, others to remove their overgarments, so that a potential customer might see more precisely the quality of the products crafted by Gillingham. In giving in to this request to disrobe, the amputees assist in the selling of the calipers, body supports with underarm stirrups, leather bodices, corsetry, and artificial limbs that are Gillingham's speciality. In so doing, they expose their arms, the napes of their neck, the tops of their thighs, the shadow effected by the point at which the tops of their thighs and buttocks meet, revealing skin that has been trussed up by the confines of straps, (garter) belts, and buckles. Skin is squeezed and molded by the bondaged tautness of its restricted lacing, the back-straightening contraptions have a sadistic edge, and the hints of undergarment betray a less than prudent photographer inviting our voyeuristic gaze. With a twist of the hips, the women turn away from the camera, to obscure their faces, to remain anonymous and disguised, to keep their modesty intact and their identity a secret. By averting their gazes, they also endeavor to frustrate the attention that we might lavish on them, which could, in turn, distract our eye from more properly consumerist desires.

PART 2

Matthew Barney's Aimee Mullins: Intimacy, Between Me and the Ground There Was Nothing

Aimee Mullins appears very differently in the final installment of American artist and filmmaker Matthew Barney's five-part *Cremaster* Cycle, begun in 1994. In this most recent episode that opened in 2002, unlike for Nick Knight, *Dazed and Confused*, Alexander McQueen, or Freeserve, Mullins is no longer the generic if individualized figure of sexual athleticism, the cyborgian sex kitten, or the eroticized amputee. Well, she is still all of these things, and explicitly so, but she is also somehow more. This may have something to do with the numerous guises that she slips into in Barney's *Cremaster 3*, the fictional parts that she takes on. These include: the character of Oonagh, the wife of the Irish giant Fionn MacCumhail; the role of Moll to Matthew Barney's Entered Apprentice; a unnamed woman sitting in a white room in the Cloud Club bar cutting potatoes with a device attached to the sole of her prosthetic legs; a figure known as Entered Novitiate, who quickly morphs into a cheetah divinity, languid one moment and fierce the next; and finally, at the very end of *Cremaster 3*, a dying, bleeding, blindfolded Madonna with a noose around her neck—which may or may not indicate sexual asphyxiation—who is sitting astride a flexi-glass sled tethered to five lambs and wearing clear prosthetic legs that end in man-o'-war tentacles. (And I shall return to this final image in a moment.)

To engage with these current incarnations of Aimee Mullins, and to distinguish them from her earlier phantasmatic, fetishized, and narcissistic manifestations, it is worthwhile focusing on the line of reasoning proposed by Nancy Spector, the curator of the Matthew Barney exhibition that toured the Museum Ludwig, Cologne; the

Museum of Modern Art of the City of Paris; and the Solomon R. Guggenheim Museum, New York. As the first, and as far as I can tell the only person so far to discuss, to any great extent, Mullins in the context of Barney's artwork, Spector gives us a way into the figures of Aimee Mullins in her extended catalogue essay "Only the Perverse Fantasy Can Still Save Us."[18] For Spector, the whole of Barney's five-part *Cremaster* film cycle has developed as a project that is, as she says, "a self-enclosed aesthetic system" in which the body "with its psychic drives and physical thresholds—symbolizes the potential of sheer creative force." For Spector, Barney's "perverse imagination" takes us on a journey, a rite of passage, through his physical, psychological, and geographical landscape of "digestion, repression, and morphing," a landscape that emerges from and is carved out of the psychosexual and the libidinal, and is for her narcissistic, anally sadistic, and at one and the same time a masturbatory machine—much like Marcel Duchamp's *Bride Stripped Bare by her Bachelors, Even* (1934) to which she refers.[19] Always meticulous, Barney's *Cremaster* cycle has for Spector "an attention to detail that can only be described as fetishistic"[20] while overall its "creative potential of perversion pervades [its] very genetic code."[21] It is clear that for Spector to be in Matthew Barney's *Cremaster* cycle is to be enveloped in the perverse and fetishistic folds of psychoanalysis.

There is much to debate and much to disagree with in Spector's catalogue essay as well as in the exhibition itself. Nonetheless, for my purposes, the most straightforward way to engage with the roles of Aimee Mullins in *Cremaster 3* is to pit Spector's essay with and against another part of her catalogue entitled "Personal Perspectives" in which a number of the individuals involved in Barney's *Cremaster* cycle—including Gabe Bartalos, the prosthetic makeup and special effects expert;[22] Norman Mailer, a protagonist in *Cremaster 2*; Richard Serra, a character in *Cremaster 3*; Ursula Andress, a star of *Cremaster 5*; and Aimee Mullins herself—are given a chance to speak about their pleasures of working on it.

Having already appeared in a number of early scenes in various guises, Mullins's central performance is at the heart of *Cremaster 3* in a section of the film entitled "The Order" which 'rehearses the secret initiation rites of the Masonic fraternity.'[23] This section is made up of five scenes or degrees as they are called in the film, and each scene reveals Matthew Barney's character, a modification of his earlier incarnation, the Entered Apprentice, as a cross between Odysseus, Lara Croft, and Donkey Kong, facing a challenge. This challenge is played out as a semi-comedic journey in which he scales the interior walls of the Guggenheim Museum, encountering combative obstacles as he progresses first up and then down the interior levels of the building's spiraling architecture. Each of the five Degrees of "The Order" is representative of one of the five episodes of the *Cremaster* cycle. Aimee Mullins comes into view in the third degree of "The Order," and thus personifies the third episode of the *Cremaster* cycle, *Cremaster 3* itself. She is a personification of the very film in which she acts, of which she is a part, and is thus for Spector the "narcissistic center of the cycle." Positioning Mullins in this way licenses Spector to claim that Mullins, as a character known as Entered Novitiate, a "couture model dressed in white gown with crystal legs," although I have always felt that her outfit is more naughty nurses uniform that couture, will mutate into "a hybrid Egyptian warrior whose lower body is that of a cheetah." For Spector, in this key role at the center of *Cremaster 3* Mullins "is, in essence, the Apprentice's [that is, Barney's] alter ego." Thus when Mullins and Barney confront one another face to face, Spector says that he is "facing himself in all his guises." She continues:

Looking into the mirror of his own soul, he is transformed into an apparition of his female element. They embrace each other with the FIVE Points of Fellowship in a moment of exquisite oneness, and the model whispers the divine words *Maha byn*[24] into his ear. But she then abruptly transmutes into the cheetah and attacks. An intense struggle ensues, which continues intermittently throughout the Order, until the Apprentice uses the stonemason's tools to slay the hybrid creature; with a blow to the plumb of her temple, she drops to one knee; hit with the level in the other, she drops to both knees; and struck in the forehead with the maul, she falls dead. Having ceremonially killed off his own reflection, the Apprentice achieves the level of Master Mason . . .[25]

At the end of *Cremaster 3*, we are given a final image of Aimee Mullins, presented to us by Nancy Spector thus:

The final image of the Order shows Mullins seated on a sleigh drawn by five baby lambs. She is dressed in the costume of the First Degree Masonic initiate. Blindfolded, she wears a noose around her neck. Blood spills from her temple and forehead, where she had endured the fatal wounds of the Mason's tools.[26]

I am less concerned than Spector is with Mullins as the narcissistic center of the cycle, as the Apprentice's/Barney's alter ego, the mirror of his soul, his feminine element, another wise, dead woman whose passing confirms the ascension of Barney's character to greatness. What interests me more is what Mullins has to say about this final scene in her "Personal Perspectives" section of Spector's catalogue. Mullins is well versed in the acknowledged and regulative symbolism of the *Cremaster* cycle. But while she is all too aware, confirming Spector's analysis, that her character is "essentially a reflection of Matthew's character,"[27] she also gives two alternative insights, political and personal, into this specific scene, neither of which is readily available in either Spector's text or Barney's *Cremaster 3*. The political insight is that when Barney "first told [her] about the Entered Novitiate character dressed as a candidate with the Masonic First Degree—with the left pant leg and right sleeve rolled up, the left breast exposed, blindfolded and wearing a noose— [she] thought, "I can't do that," [She] remember[s] thinking how many disability-rights activists were going to be calling [her], outraged."[28] The personal insight is even more telling:

> The clear legs ending in man-of-war tentacles worn by the Entered Novitiate [in this final scene] evolved as a compromise. Originally Matthew had wanted me to do that scene without prosthetics. He saw this as a way to express the Masonic theory that you have to lose your lower self in order to reach a higher level. I guess the literal representation of that would have been for me to sit on the sled without any limbs below the knee, but that would have been difficult for me because it's very, very intimate. We had a long dialogue about what we could do instead, and Matthew came up with the idea of making the legs appear like jellyfish tentacles because they're not a human form and they're clear. It worked for me because I don't feel so bare where there's something between me and the ground.[29]

I'm certainly not accusing Barney of being an amputee devotee. His desire to strip Mullins of her prosthetic legs so that he can make some spurious symbolic point is an act that on first viewing strikes me as *far more* disingenuous and boorish than that. In a sense, stripping her of her literal legs so that she can be seen to rise to a higher level replicates some of the most careless and ill-thought-through philosophies of disembodied techno-fetishism in which discussions of *post*-humanism are really little more than celebrations of *de*-humanization. This is what I earlier referred to as metaphorical opportunism. But if we put Barney's Masonic foolishness to one side, and listen carefully to what Mullins has to say, something quite surprising emerges. Hearing her say that to be without one's prosthetic limbs is to be exposed, to be laid bare, and that these prosthetic limbs are an emotional crutch as well as a corporeal support is not surprising. But learning that they are *a guard against intimacy* is unexpected. Or, rather, she tells us that it would have been too, too intimate to have appeared in *Cremaster 3 without* some kind of prosthetic machinery, even if the prosthetic takes the non-human anthropomorphic form of the tentacles of a large coelenterate hydrozoan, and even if it would not permit her to stand by herself, let alone to walk on her own. Anything, as long as there is something to stop her feeling the bareness between her self and the ground, to make sure that there is something, even if it is impossibly shaky and unstable, and makes you all the more vulnerable.

Although unrealized, in hoping to have Aimee Mullins appearing without her legs, her "cheetah legs," her "pretty legs," or even her man-of-war legs, Barney provides us with the chance to make out something very intimate, *too* intimate about the subject of prosthesis. And if you watch Mullins, you realize that there are, in fact, numerous moments of awkwardness throughout *Cremaster 3* in which we see her staggering around the set with her transparent legs, wobbly on her feet, walking backwards unsteadily, often on the brink of toppling over, holding onto the balustrade of the Guggenheim Museum for support, always trying to keep her balance on the oblique angle of the museum's run-way.

These uncomfortable movements, along with the far too intimate image of Mullins without her prosthetic legs, are redolent with a vulnerability that is not a ready part of the discourse of prosthesis with its overwhelming imperatives of rehabilitation, empowering, and resolute unshakability.

And yet, here we have many scenes in which Mullins is truly perverse, but in a properly etymological sense of that word. She "twists" and "turns the wrong way" which is to say away from her figuration as a perverse erotic fetishistic object and towards an almost desperate celebration of the relative failure of movement wherein her prosthetic legs are not a *metaphor* of lack, but a *metonymy* of movement, a substitute for nothing, for the space between her self and the ground, that otherwise unbridgeable gap between immobility and touching the ground, undoubtedly an incitement to movement.[30]

*   *   *

In this chapter I have tried to say something about the tensions and contradictions between stillness and movement, between the stillness of photographic stills and the movement of moving image culture. Many of the questions that make up a provocative engagement with the discourse of prosthesis lie in the variegated gaps *between* stillness and movement, the hinge between the inanimate and the animate, the so called disabled body that is rendered somewhat inoperative and the ways in which that body is jump-started into all kinds of mobile modifications, however unstable some of these experiences might be. This is very much the position that Aimee Mullins finds herself in, in Matthew Barney's *Cremaster 3*. So while I am all too aware of some of the naïve assumptions I am making about differently-abled bodies in our visual culture, I am more acutely aware that it is necessary to be attentive to the danger that the stillness of images can cause to bodies already often either rendered immobile or overly technologized by metaphorical opportunism. For it is this stillness, such an integral part of the fixity of the process of stereotyping, eroticizing, and objectifying that has played such a destructive part in the history of disability and in the discourse

of fetishism. It seems to me, at least in a provisional way, that fetishism, the practice of making an object a fixture, a mark of the recognition of disavowal, an inflexible substitute, a replacement for other things that have moved on for one reason or another, might be affected by the moving part of moving image culture. And at the same time, the discourse of *prosthesis* might wish to focus on the grey area between the inanimate and the animate, on the brink of articulation, which is precisely where we can best attend to the point of convergence between the metaphorization of the prosthetic body *and* its materiality; its moving flesh, as well as its wood, plastic, leather, metal, and hydraulic systems, because it is well worth remembering that the prostheticization of the human body does not mean a necessary material displacement of that body.[31]

While attending to this hinge between stillness and movement, between inanimate and animate, and to its effect on our understanding of both the material and metaphorical prosthetic body, I planned to move backward and forward across the question with which I began this essay: what kinds of erotic fantasies are being played out across medical, commercial, and avant-garde of the body of the female amputee in Western visual culture? In so doing, I did my best to keep two ideas in mind. The first idea was a need to be attentive to how two domains of visual imagery—medical/commercial photography and moving image culture—over the period of almost a hundred years offer almost identical instances of techno-fetishism. Having said that, I hope I have also begun to draw out some of the ways that these two instances of metaphorical opportunism are trying, intentionally or otherwise, to propose an alternative to such techno-fetishism, even if more often than not they fail to deliver in the end. (It is hard to envisage thinking fetishism through the movements of metonymy rather than through its structuring metaphorical dynamics.) The second idea was to consider how the discourse of prosthesis in its facility to articulate the confluence of bodies, technologies, and subjectivities, draws attention both to the role that perversion and fetishism play in the eroticization of visual imagery and some of the reasons why this might be so, and to the ways that we might be able to begin to think about perversion and fetishism, perverse practices and fetishistic objects, in ways that are resoundingly not sexual at all. In the end, I hope to have intimated that the discourse of prosthesis in fact makes it possible for us to begin to speak of fetishism and perversion in a way that is stripped of sexuality and eroticism, that exists beyond an economy of lack and, that endures in other kinds of productive practices, if one can imagine such a thing.

NOTES

1. The word "articulate" is being used here to mean "having joints" rather than "to be able to speak fluently and coherently." (*Oxford English Dictionary*.) A longer version of this chapter appeared as Marquard Smith, "The Vulnerable Articulate: James Gillingham, Aimee Mullins, and Matthew Barney," in *The Prosthetic Impulse: From a Posthuman Present to a Biocultural Future*, ed. Marquard Smith and Joanne Morra, Cambridge, MA: The MIT Press, 2005. Earlier versions of this chapter were presented at the Courtauld Institute of Art in October 2002 at the invitation of Caroline Arscott and Gavin Parkinson, and at the Association of Art Historians annual conference at UCL/Birkbeck College in April 2003 at the invitation of John Wood, Aura Satz, and Helen Weston. Thanks to them for the invitations, and to the many interesting questions thrown from the floor during both events. Thanks also to Tim Boon and Craig Brierly at the Science Museum, London, and special thanks to Jean-Baptiste Decavèle, Vivian Rehberg, and, of course, to Joanne Morra.

2. See Vivian Sobchack, "A Leg to Stand On: Prosthetics, Metaphor, and Materiality," in Marquard Smith and Joanne Morra, eds., *The Prosthetic Impulse: From a Posthuman Present to a Biocultural Future*, Cambridge: MA, The MIT Press, 2005. For a background to the kinds of discussions developed in my essay see also: Katherine Ott, David Serlin, and Stephen Mihm, eds., *Artificial Parts, Practical Lives: Modern Histories of Prosthetics* (New York: New York University Press, 2002); David T. Mitchell and Sharon L. Snyder, *Narrative Prosthesis: Disability and the Dependencies of Discourse* (Ann Arbor: The University of Michigan Press, 2000); David Wills, *Prosthesis* (Stanford: Stanford University Press, 1995); Jacques Derrida, passim; Marquard Smith, "The Uncertainty of Placing: Prosthetic Bodies, Sculptural Design, and Unhomely Dwelling in Marc Quinn, James Gillingham, and Sigmund Freud," *New Formations*, vol. 46, (Summer 2002), 85–102; Marquard Smith and Joanne Morra, *The Prosthetic Aesthetic*, themed issue of *New Formations*, 46, Summer 2002; Allucquère Roseanne Stone, *The War of Desire and Technology at the Close of the Mechanical Age* (Cambridge, MA: The MIT Press, 1995).

3. This chaptr is in certain ways a kind of flirtatious "thinking through," an effort to be curious, skeptical, and hesitant, to display a certain lack of commitment to certain ideas in order to sustain their speculative promise. To avoid making categorical judgments. Here I follow Adam Phillips' book *On Flirtation*, in which he notes, following George Simmel's essay "Flirtation," that "every conclusive decision brings flirtation to an end." See Adam Phillips, *On Flirtation* (London: Faber and Faber, 1994), xxi.

4. See Sigmund Freud, *Three Essays on the Theory of Sexuality* (Harmondsworth: Penguin Books, 1977). For Freud perversions are largely (so called) "non-productive" sexual practices that *deviate* for goal-directed sexual practices. Instances of this might involve an individual being interested in extended fore-pleasure or the deferral of coitus. The nineteenth century largely reserves perversion for men, women are rarely perverse, and are defined as anything other than perverse; hysterical, frigid, narcissistic, melancholic, psychotic, and so forth.

5. Michel Foucault, *The History of Sexuality, Volume I, An Introduction*, trans. Robert Hurley, (New York: Vintage/Random House, 1980). See also Robert A. Nye, "Medical origins of Sexual Fetishism," in *Fetishism as Cultural Discourse*, eds., Emily Apter and William Pietz (Ithaca: Cornell University Press, 1993), 13–30, 19. Apter and Pietz's collection is still the most engaging edited volume on fetishism available.

6. In addition to Sobchack's essay, for other

criticisms of this state of affairs see: Sarah S. Jain, "The Prosthetic Imagination: Enabling and Disabling the Prosthesis Trope," *Science, Technology, & Human Values*, vol 24, no. 1 (Winter 1999), 31–54; Rosemarie Garland-Thomson, *Extraordinary Bodies: Figuring Physical Disability in American Culture and Literature* (New York: Columbia University Press, 1997); David T. Mitchell and Sharon L. Snyder, "Introduction: Disability Studies and the Double Bind of Representation," in *The Body and Physical Difference: Discourses of Disability*, eds., Mitchell and Snyder, (Ann Arbor, MI: The University of Michigan Press, 1997), 1–31, 7, ftnt. 32. Mitchell and Snyder's "Introduction" includes a very useful overview of many of the issues at stake in techno-fetishism, ranging from a critique of Paul Virilio's writing on the subject to an embrace of N. Catherine Hayles's thought.

7. The Latin etymology of perversion, *pervertere*, means "to twist," "to turn the wrong way." This non-sexual etymology will have a profound impact on my later engagement with the art of Matthew Barney, and Aimee Mullins's place in it.

8. See Emily Apter, "Perversion," *Feminism and Psychoanalysis: A Critical Dictionary*, ed. Elizabeth Wright (Oxford: Blackwell, 1992), 311–314. As Apter goes on to say: "The dismantled, disembodied body (Lacan's *corps morcelé*) is preferred to the integral or totalised corpus because it presents, as it were, a body composed of prosthetic parts (already split or symbolically castrated) rather than a body at risk of phallic loss. In each of these instances the choice of love-object is neither arbitrary nor convertible. Functioning as an ambient fetish or prosthesis, figured as an *idée fixe*, this object-type both motivates the fantasm and directs the questing of the subject of perversion" (312).

9. One needs to keep in mind the importance of the ideological differences between the discourses of reconstructive surgery (utility, rehabilitation, empowerment) and aesthetic/cosmetic surgery (beauty, passing).

10. Sander L. Gilman, *Making the Body Beautiful: A Cultural History of Aesthetic Surgery* (Princeton, NJ: Princeton University Press, 1999), esp. 21–42.

11. And of course, as Gilman makes clear, historically, there is a direct correlation between an individual's physical stigmatization and their psychological unhappiness. As successful aesthetic surgery after successful aesthetic surgery has shown, the removal of said stigma brings about psychological happiness.

12. For Gilman, this dialectical (or rather binary) process of passing is inherently debilitating because it is premised on the fact that passing is a purely, *and need only be a purely* physical metamorphosis in which signs of physical difference, so called pathological signs, are disguised through modification. (This is, of course, why "passing" is so important an idea for Gilman, because the desire to "pass" is the very foundation upon which aesthetic surgery is built, is the way in which purely cosmetic [which is to say deeply ideological] aesthetic surgery is distinguished from the necessary, utilitarian practice of reconstructive surgery.)

13. Ibid., 37.

14. This narrative is best exemplified in the "before and after" photographs that began (as an initiative, although not directly in relation to aesthetic surgery) in the 1840s and reached their point of saturation in the decades to come, notably, in images of the rebuilt faces of Civil War soldiers in the 1860s.

15. Ibid., 39.

16. As Katherine Ott has said on these matters more generally, "[c]onventions of female modesty, as well as ignorance about and public reluctance to discuss female anatomy" accounts for the relative scarcity of disabled female bodies appearing in medical textbooks at this time. See Katherine Ott, David Serlin and Stephen Mihm, eds., *Artificial Parts, Practical Lives* (New York: New York University Press, 2002), 11. A need for modesty and anonymity may have something to do with why all of the figures of female amputees are turned away, while the majority of the photographs of male amputees are not.

17. This phrase is used by Abigail Solomon-Godeau in "The Legs of the Countess," reprinted in Apter and Pietz, eds. *Fetishism*, 274, originally published in *October*, 39 (Winter 1986), 65–108.

18. Nancy Spector, *Matthew Barney: The Cremaster Cycle* (New York: Guggenheim Museum Publications, 2002).

19. Ibid., 25.

20. Ibid., xii.

21. Ibid., 25.

22. Of working with Bartalos, Mullins says: "It was fascinating working with Gabe because his whole world is the aesthetic prosthetic realm and mine is the mechanics of prosthetics," in *Matthew Barney: The Cremaster Cycle* (New York: Guggenheim Museum Publications, 2002).

23. Spector, *Matthew Barney*, 53

24. Earlier Spector says that *Maha byn* is "an untranslatable term that stands as a surrogate for the words of divine knowledge lost in Abiff's [the architect, played by Richard Serra] death, much as the Hebrew word "Jahweh" is a surrogate for the name of God" (ibid., 44).

25. Ibid., 57.
26. Ibid.
27. Mullins, "Personal Perspective," in *Matthew Barney: The Cremaster Cycle* (New York: Guggenheim Museum Publications, 2002), 492–493.
28. Ibid., 493.
29. Ibid, 493.
30. At its most basic, and most significant, the point here is that as a metaphor, prosthesis is simply a symbol of something else—whether castration, emasculation, nationhood, body-machine interfaces, and so on. Spoken of as a metaphor—and this is an argument made well by Ott in her introduction to *Artificial Parts, Practical Lives,* and by Jain, and Sobchack—the discourse of prosthesis misses the fact that prosthesis is something incredibly complex in itself.
31. This is not about the autonomy or independent life of the fetishstic object—something both Freud and Marx comment upon.

CHAPTER 35

Sculpting Body Ideals: *Alison Lapper Pregnant* and the Public Display of Disability

Ann Millett-Gallant

In 2005, artist Alison Lapper was thrust into fame when her 11.5 foot tall, 13 ton sculptural portrait, *Alison Lapper Pregnant*, was unveiled on the fourth plinth of Trafalgar Square [see cover image]. Lapper agreed to being cast in the nude by British artist Marc Quinn when she was 7 months pregnant and to be placed on public display; many have called the piece a collaboration. The controversial sculpture has brought widespread attention to the model's body and her life story. Lapper, born without arms and with shortened legs, is an alumnus of British institutions for disabled children and programs for disabled artists, a now single mother, and an artist who makes work about her embodied experiences as a disabled woman. Carved from precious Italian marble and placed on a pedestal among statues of naval captains, Lapper has been called a contemporary heroine of cultural diversity, while the work has also been regarded as a tasteless publicity stunt for Quinn. The exposure of Lapper's body transcends the fact that she is nude, for Lapper grew up in insolated environments of public intuitions and had limited interactions with public life; for Lapper, the work is a true coming out. *Alison Lapper Pregnant* makes a public statement about this disabled woman's right to be represented as a productive social subject *and* a reproductive sexual being and her right to represent others.

This essay will interrogate the sculpture's representation of disability within the contexts of Trafalgar Square, the genre of Public Art, as well as in comparisons with Quinn's previous series of sculptural amputees, *The Complete Marbles* (2002), and, foremost, with Lapper's self-representations. I will argue that *Alison Lapper Pregnant* significantly responds to, as well as transforms, the history of its particular space and interacts with the populations who inhabit that space. Rather than displaying trite political correctness or simple shock value, as much of its criticism wages, the work plays monumental roles in the histories of both disability representation and art. As a public spectacle, it recycles, and I will argue contemporizes, the representation of disability as both heroic and freakish. Further, Lapper's photography and her recently published memoir are key components of such discussions, as they provide perspectives by and a voice to the disabled subject on display. By weaving together these contexts of and reactions to Quinn's and Lapper's works, this essay underscores the necessity of placing the works of disabled and non-disabled artists in dialogues with one another and with larger histories of visual culture.

Public art raises issues of social and artistic representation and the visibility and invisibility of certain members of society. Public space and its monuments have been gendered male and raced white traditionally, and public space is largely ableist in attitude, not to mention accessibility (or lack thereof). Public art, when the most effective, creates dialogues about the role of art in society and whom is included and excluded in the notion of the "public." By honoring individuals marginalized and erased by dominant values and the structures which personify them, many more contemporary public art projects have explicitly protested the status quo. These public art forms, in which I contextualize *Alison Lapper Pregnant*, embody cultural battles for and of representation.

The sculpture produces Lapper as a representative of the historically under-represented. Lapper has positioned the work at the forefront of such initiatives, stating: 'I regard it as a modern tribute to femininity, disability and motherhood . . . The sculpture makes the ultimate statement about disability—that it can be as beautiful and valid a form of being as any other." She acknowledges how her body becomes a monument to bodies and identities that have been socially devalued, shamed, and excluded from public life historically. Lapper goes on to note: "It is so rare to see disability in everyday life—let alone naked, pregnant and proud. The sculpture makes the ultimate statement about disability—that it can be as beautiful and valid a form of being as any other."[1] Here, she characterizes her body as a form of anti-monument, for it represents the "other" to traditional subjects of public monuments, as well as an anti-ideal. Positive feedback about the sculpture also champions it as a liberating anti-ideal.[2] The work may function to force the viewer to question their perceptions of the "ideal," while also questioning whose ideals Lapper is purported to represent.

The work functions visually on confusions between the ideal and anti-ideal. Quinn's work is specifically a quotation of 18th- and 19th-century Neoclassicism. Neoclassical figurative painting, sculpture, and architectural programs taught lessons on heroism and moral virtue, often by depicting the deeds of great and powerful men.[3] In Western culture from the Renaissance to today, this Neoclassical form is characteristically employed for public statues of religious and political heroes. Neoclassicism and its Classical heritage communicate philosophical and political ideals through mathematically constructed aesthetics, specifically, in "whole" bodies.

Quinn subverts the signification of Neoclassical form as the ideal "whole" in *Alison Lapper Pregnant* (2005) and in his series of life size, marble sculptures of amputees, *The Complete Marbles* (2002), which adopt particularly Roman qualities of portrait likeness. By using many high profile disabled models, such as artist Peter Hull and the confrontational "freak" performer and punk rock musician, Matt Fraser, Quinn produces depictions of recognizable subjects and celebrities. Titled with the subjects' proper names, these works challenge how the viewer perceives the body in art, as well as in everyday life, as whole and/or broken.[4] Quinn titled this series *The Complete Marbles* strategically. *The Elgin Marbles* are precious Classical sculptures appropriated from the Parthenon in Greece (produced c. 438–423 BCE). *The Elgin Marbles*, many broken and missing limbs and heads, were amputated from their architectural base (the Parthenon); they are fragments of profoundly aesthetic "wholes," for the Parthenon remains a cultural icon today for its integrated, carefully orchestrated balance and proportion and its intense, methodical control of aesthetics. Extracted from the Temple to Athena, the marbles both fragment and "stand" (or symbolize) one of the greatest symbols of power and wealth in Western history—specifically one famous for its ideal wholeness. Quinn's title for the series, *The Complete Marbles*, places contemporary disabled bodies in these historical legacies, and they are designated as "whole" by their own counter-conventional body standards and disarming beauty.

Quinn's artistic procedures and materials are central to the significances of his works. Like all of the pieces in *The Complete Marbles*, *Alison Lapper Pregnant* was sculpted in Quinn's studio in Pietrasenta, Italy, the center for Carrara marble—the same marble sought by Michelangelo and many Neoclassical sculptors. *Alison Lapper Pregnant* took 10 months to craft from the stubborn substance, which contains exalted histories and symbolic significances. Quinn is quite particular about the material, as he literally goes out of his way to use it, and he prefers this marble for its "intrinsic and metaphoric content."[5] Carrara marble provides a luminosity that makes his amputees shine and radiate, like works from the Greek Hellenistic period.

Many critics deem Quinn's art historical references as subversive, specifically because he focuses on disabled bodies. For example, art writer for the *Sunday Times*, Waldemar Januszczak, states the following about *Allison Lapper Pregnant*:

By carving Allison Lapper out of pristine marble, Quinn is *taking on* the Greeks; he is *disputing* with Phidias, with Michelangelo, with Sir Joshua Reynolds, with every authoritarian with imagination that has ever insisted upon a standard shape for the human in art; he is contradicting 2,000 years of creative *misrepresentation* of what being human means; and he is giving Allison Lapper the same amount of artistic attention that Canova gave the Empress Josephine. As if that were not enough, Quinn is also cheekily rhyming his sculptures with the broken remnants of classical art—the armless Venus, the legless Apollo—that are the staple diet of all collections of the antique. These are serious achievements.[6] (emphasis mine)

My italics here underscore how Januszczak describes Quinn's use of amputees in art historical, specifically Classical and Neoclassical images, as confrontational and revisionist, as if the works are affronts to these traditions because of the amputees featured. This comment suggests that certain social prejudices against amputees function in critical interpretations of Quinn's work. The form of the Lapper sculpture has been the target of much criticism; however, criticisms against the artistic value of *Alison Lapper Pregnant* (the work) may suggest simultaneous rejection of Alison Lapper pregnant (as an embodiment and social subject). Many have charged Quinn with capitalizing on the shock value and taboo nature of disabled bodies in public spaces.[7] The work functions to make such stereotypes visible and open to public debate.

On the other hand (or stump), positive evaluations of the *Alison Lapper Pregnant* further complicate how the sculpture represents disability in the public eye, as they purport Lapper to be a hero. This idea recalls the stereotype of a disabled hero that is premised on sentimentalization of and low expectations for disabled people in society. What kind of hero is Lapper in these descriptions, one who dismantles notions of appropriate versus shocking bodies? Or one who rehashes the stereotype of "overcoming," which functions to ignore social constructs of disability and is based on the problematic notion of disability as an individual "problem"? Framed as the representation of a hero, the sculpture celebrates Lapper's impairments and perhaps also de-politicizes, or literally aestheticizes disability, as a marginalizing social construct, for the public. Or perhaps it redefines our ideas about heroism and makes a disabled figure a role model, in a positive light.

Lapper's heroism may also be problematically tied to her pregnancy, such that motherhood becomes a means for Lapper to "overcome" disability by conforming to standards for women's roles in society, a point which Kim Q. Hall has interrogated. Hall quotes Quinn: "For me, *Alison Lapper Pregnant* is a monument to the future possibilities of the human race as well as the resilience of the human spirit."[8] Hall frames this comment within political propaganda that has imposed the duty upon women historically to reproduce the nation; such dogma is similar to that expressed throughout Trafalgar Square by the national heroes depicted. Hall argues that the sculpture is championed by Quinn and many others because it confounds the taboo nature of disabled bodies in public spaces, as well as patriarchal and heterosexual values that assert that reproduction validates women. Yet, Hall's persuasive arguments reframe how Lapper's presence in the square plays upon traditional gender roles and disability stereotypes only tangentially, for the sculpture's and Lapper's own consistent divergence from convention affirms the work's adamant non-conformity to "family values." Mainstream discourses that breed women for motherhood suggest that a productive female member of the society is a *reproductive* one, specifically within the institution of marriage. Far from glorifying a nuclear family, Lapper was born to a single, working class mother and is herself an unmarried mother, who has benefited from public programs for disabled artists. Many may view Lapper's choices as amoral and her subsistence as a public burden, therefore she hardly acts in the legacy of national heroes.

Lapper's maternal situation defies ideals of both society and of art for women's bodies. Pregnant bodies, seen most often in art history as fertility figures and virginal Madonnas, occupy a liminal status, as both an ideal state of the female motherhood, yet one that contrasts with the conventions for the sexualized nude, particularly for 21st-century eyes. Popular representations have tended to idealize pregnancy socially, yet they also veil the pregnant female body, reinstating its preferred existence within the proverbial home. Pregnancy is glorified and yet stigmatized and indeed often considered a disability. However, images of pregnant women have become trendy lately, particularly among the elite, with the celebrity "baby boom" displayed in the aesthetic "bumps" on otherwise perfect bodies and within the romanticized unions of the Brangelinas and Tom-Kats of the world; Demi Moore, Melania Trump, and most recently, Britney Spears have been featured by mainstream women's magazines as so-called liberated covergirls and centerfolds, revealing their scantily clad and fashionable pregnant bodies. Again, these pregnant bodies are framed specifically within dominant social ideals and values (with perhaps the exception of Spears and the notorious "Fed-Ex"), values to which Alison Lapper could never conform. *Alison Lapper Pregnant* confuses perceptions of the body in art history and popular culture, ultimately because, for many, the work assertively provokes the fear that the disabled body will reproduce another "damaged" child—from a "broken" body and a "broken" home. The work advocates controversial reproductive rights for disabled women and for single women more broadly. Further, any attempt on Lapper's part to fulfill her role to reproduce the next generation may produce a disabled one, which remains a horror rather than a triumph, according to mainstream values and exclusive social standards for quality of life. Lapper's maternal "acts" poignantly fail to service social ideals, as the sculpture becomes pregnant with ambivalent meanings.

Viewers' reactions to the work as shocking and/or inspiring seem polarized, and yet both connote, to varying degrees, the desire to make a lesson out of the disabled body, in order to justify its display. Many who critique the work and Quinn's *The Complete Marbles* series demand explanation about the cause of the models' impairments and the usefulness of such displays to society. Januszczak has also stated: "With a subject as serious as the loss of human limbs, or the birth of a child to a deformed mother, it is absolutely incumbent upon the gallery to cease playing aesthetic games and to make clearer the artist's intentions."[9] This quote expresses viewers' desire for medical diagnosis to make the works more palatable and less sensationalistic. However, the sculpture also provokes some viewers to question their own desires to know "what happened" to the body and assumptions that the disabled body necessarily connotes accident or victimization.

The notion of making the disabled body into a lesson is relevant to the realm of public art specifically, within which the body becomes a monument to instruct, for public art has a duty, in the eyes of many, to educate and inform. The origin of the word "monument" derives from Latin *monere*, meaning "to remind," "to admonish," "warn," "advise," and "instruct."[10] Poignantly, this word origin emerges also in the word "monster," as scholars of the freak show have pointed out, explaining how the disabled body has historically been seen as an indicator of either supernatural foreshadowing or scientific mistake. The use of the disabled body as a lesson has included public exploitation of so-called medical anomalies, practices which have reinforced medical models, crossed genres into freak shows, and staged the disabled body as an instructional object for the non-disabled viewers. The 19th- and early 20th-century freak show entertained and affirmed middle class spectators' senses of "normalcy," which was constructed specifically in binary opposition to the strikingly "abnormal" spectacle.

The freak show is another relevant comparison for considering the role of Lapper's body in a public space, particularly one that serves as a tourist attraction[11]: "She is presented "like some 19th-century fairground exhibit," one critic stated.[12] In the freak show, the disabled and other extraordinary (exotic, minority) bodies were eroticized; the nudity of the sculpture, to which some take offense, is intrinsic to its unashamed display of the pregnant disabled body and its Neoclassical form; it places the work in a both a history of art and a history of displaying the body as spectacle, in the freak show, pornography, and other voyeuristic venues. This context raises a key question: does the sculpture exploit Alison Lapper?

Lapper is benefiting from the attention the work has drawn to her own art and her life, as she recently published a memoir (2005). In it, she relates Quinn's sculpture to her own self-portrait nude photography, with which she expresses comfort in her own skin and challenges her personal history of being considered physically defective and sexually unattractive. Addressing the controversy regarding the nudity of the statue, Lapper has written:

> In most societies, even in Britain today, pregnant women are not considered to have a beautiful shape. On top of that, short people, who are missing both arms, are generally considered even less beautiful. I was someone who currently combined both disadvantages. How could Marc possibly think I was a suitable subject for a sculpture that people would want to look at? Statues are created and exhibited to give pleasure, to be admired. Would anybody be able to admire the statue of a naked, pregnant, disabled woman?[13]

She attributes the controversy of the sculpture to a society that is prudish to nudity in general, as well as to pregnancy and to disability specifically. Many may deem the work amoral, and therefore in direct opposition to Neoclassical, moralistic traditions, and yet, as Lapper articulates, moral judgments are subjective to the eyes of the beholders.

Lapper does not express feeling exploited. Describing her decision to pose, Lapper writes:

> It was January 1999 when I received a phone call from an artist called Marc Quinn. . . . I was extremely suspicious. I thought he might be just another one in the long line of people who have exploited disability and used it for its curiosity and value. However, when we talked, I realized Marc wasn't interested in disability in the way most people wanted to depict it. He wasn't pitying or moralising—I knew it wasn't a freak show or some kind of weird sexual focus that he was aiming at.[14]

Lapper here recognizes the problematic tropes of representing disabled bodies as sentimentalized heroes or freakish spectacles, both of which make the disabled body into a symbol and lesson to be learned by the so-called normal. Poignantly, she ties these tropes together. Yet by collaborating with Quinn, Lapper makes a statement about the need for public education and exposure of/to disability in contemporary society in order to overturn the stereotypes and the status quo.

Trafalgar Square is an ideal place to raise and interrogate these issues. The modern city, and public squares like Trafalgar especially, were built for tourist gazing, urban surveillance, and commercial spectatorship.[15] Trafalgar Square, designed by John Nash and built by Sir Charles Barry in the 1820s and 30s to commemorate British naval captain and famous imperialist Admiral Horatio Nelson (1758–1805), was named after the Spanish Cape Trafalgar where Nelson's last battle was won. Characteristic of 19th-century Roman revival in Britain, the square's architecture and statuary is specifically Neoclassical to portray political ideals. A monument to Lord Nelson became the central vision of the square. This Neoclassical likeness of Nelson stands on a 185 foot tall column, overseeing the public—a tradition which continues today. Nelson's monument, modeled after the triumphant Roman Column of Trajan, and its surroundings place modern Britain in the traditions of Roman imperialism. Surrounding Nelson are other monuments to British military heroes, represented in idealizing Neoclassical forms.[16] Like the design of the square, the Neoclassical monuments display a particular side of British history and society, one whose power depends on the subordination of those rendered invisible.

With her marble, feminine curves and serene posture, *Alison Lapper Pregnant* would seem out of place in such a paternalistic environment[17]—the freakish anti-hero. And yet others see the sculpture as right at home with the other monuments. She has been compared symbolically and corporeally with Admiral Nelson himself, as the work reinterprets notions of disabled and non-disabled heroes and spectacles. For examples, in letters to the editor, Michael Gallagher calls Lapper: "A great Briton in the truest sense of the word. I am sure that Nelson would have recognised her as a kindred spirit," and Jeanette Hart notes: ". . . Nelson only had one arm, and was blind in one eye, and he was just known as a great man; no one labelled him."[18] Nelson was indeed blinded in one eye during the capture of Corsica from French troops in 1794 and lost his arm in a 1797 capture of the Canary Islands. He continued to lead troops with these impairments until his death at the Battle of Trafalgar in 1805, an act which has augmented his status as a national hero. The column is topped by a statue of Nelson posed with his uniform coat sleeve draped along his chest and tucked into his suitcoat, in a conventional pose for leaders, yet his sleeve is empty. This view is not perceptible for the viewer below. Quinn's public display of Alison Lapper and its comparisons to Nelson's Column have illuminated for some that the disabled body is always already present in an existing vision of heroism. Viewing Lapper as a hero reinterprets or expands the image of a heroic body, and perhaps this designation does not simply rehash stereotypes of overcoming, but rather describes the meaning of her body as a public image within a specific location and historical context.

Alison Lapper Pregnant follows in multiple histories of public art that are celebratory of or in protest to their context—a simultaneous monument and anti-monument. All of the submissions for the Fourth Plinth project competition since 1990 have been consciously critical of the square's aristocratic, nationalistic, and paternalistic traditions, both in content and form. As art critic Paul Usherwood describes it, Lapper carries on this contemporary trend of mocking the square's: "macho triumphalism and formality."[19] Lapper's Neo- or post-Classical form embodies also a breaching of boundaries between convention and subversion. And by embodying contradictions, Lapper once again fits right into Trafalgar Square and translates its history to contemporary debates over civil and human rights. The controversial debates surrounding the work continue a longstanding history of Trafalgar Square, which has been wrought with conflict historically (as evidenced by the background stories on the lives of the men honored there). Trafalgar Square has served as the city's most popular rallying point and the site of: political, economic, and religious protests; interventions of military law; class battles; protests for freedom of speech and rights to assemble, for women's suffrage, and for civil rights, liberties, and decolonization; and pro and anti-war, pro and anti-Fascism and Semitism, and pro and anti- communism rallies.[20] Poignantly, all these displays

of activism represent multiple and opposing sides of social and political issues since the 19th-century, and, significant, most of these demonstrations have centered on the base of Nelson's column, because of its physical prominence and its symbolic significance. The monuments of Nelson and Lapper both embody multiple significances contextually and over time and have been witnesses to multiplicities of perspectives. Both Nelson's and Lapper's bodies in Trafalgar Square pay tribute to the necessity of public debate.

The sculpture of Alison Lapper and its social and symbolic meanings must be considered within its specific context. The work embodies, transforms, and contemporizes the history of its space. *Alison Lapper Pregnant* carries on the square's traditions by provoking debate and dissent. The controversy and many opposing opinions expressed publicly about the sculpture enact its social work. Lapper's body on display has provoked constructive investigation about the role of art in society and the roles of disabled bodies as heroes and spectacles. It asks us to interrogate our assumptions about what forms of bodies should or should not appear in public spaces and how. The dubious representations of disability the work evokes are both liberating and stereotypical, which is necessary to provoke debate. That Lapper herself has been so vocal in the discussions is key, for her collaboration with Quinn and her public mediation of the work shows how perspectives *of* disability, not just *about* them, are necessary for any productive dialogue.

Comparisons of Quinn's work with Lapper's own body art, which self-narrates her experiences as a disabled woman artist, provide significant dialogues about disability and visual representation. Born in 1965, Lapper grew up in institutional settings and art schools. Although she was always skilled at making art, Lapper remarks on having to prove herself repeatedly to non-disabled people, intellectually, artistically, and sexually, due to assumptions about her so-called "lacking" anatomy. She moved to London at age 19, where she lived independently for the first time, and later attended the University of Brighton, graduated with a degree in fine art at age 28, purchased a home in Southwick, near Brighton, and began her work as an artist. Lapper has been the focus of the BBC1 series *Child of Our Time* program, to which she has returned for annual appearances, and an hour-long documentary by Milton Media for Denmark's TV2, titled *Alison's Baby*, which has been broadcast in many countries and won the Prix Italia and the Prix Leonardo. In 2003, Lapper won the MBE award for service to the arts. Since graduation from Brighton, she has worked fulltime for the Mouth and Foot Painting Artists' Association of England (MFPA). Funding for this program comes from the artists' production of decorative images for card designs, marketed by the MFAP, and Lapper writes that she still enjoys producing such genre scenes and landscapes, along with her self-portrait work.

Lapper's self-portrait body art, in the forms of photography, sculpture, and installation, marks a continuous process of self discovery. At the University of Brighton, an opinionated viewer challenged the nature of Lapper's figurative work of non-disabled bodies, by suggesting that perhaps Lapper had not fully accepted her own body. This moment became a turning point for Lapper, as she began envisioning her own body as a work of art. Inspired by a photograph of the armless or "broken" Greek statue, the *Venus de Milo*, in which she saw her own likeness, Lapper began casting her body in plaster and photographing herself in Venus-like poses. Like arm-free performance artist Mary Duffy, who delivers impassioned speech about her experiences of being medically and socially objectified, while posing in the nude, Lapper adopted the Venus de Milo as her body image. Lapper's graduation exhibit featured an installation the viewer had to enter on hands and knees, at the height of Lapper herself, in order to see photographs and sculpted casts of her full body and body parts. This installation created an environment that removed the viewer from their own comfort zone physically and perceptually. Other disabled artists also employ their embodied perspectives in their work, such as little person Ricardo Gil. Gil photographs his wife and daughter, both little people, from the perspectives at which he views them—literally, in terms of his height, and figuratively, as intimate close-ups that establish affectionate, familial relationships between the subject and the camera's gaze. In *Johann's Kiss*, 1999, Gil features his smiling wife centered in the frame, embraced by an average-sized, kneeling man, whose head is cropped at the top of the photograph. Figures in the background are cut off at mid torso; however, these are not mistakes of an amateur. Here, "normal" size people don't fit in the little woman's privileged, compositional space or in Gil's proud gaze. Lapper's installation, like Gil's photographs, explored the relationships between the viewer's versus the artist's own acts of looking at, judging, and experiencing the disabled body.[21]

Lapper's self-portrait work and her personifications specifically of the armless Venus de Milo (a cultural icon of artistic and feminine beauty), like Duffy's, explore the complicated interactions of disability and sexuality, particularly for women. Lapper's shameless public exposure in a public art display (*Alison Lapper Pregnant*) takes root in a longer artistic and personal process of "coming out" as a sexual, and indeed reproductive woman. In contrast with the mainstream vision of Lapper's often assumed a-sexuality, a bold and seductive body image emerges in Lapper's work. Lapper's

Untitled (2000) features three views of her nude body in Venus-like, s-curve poses. The photographic media articulates her musculature, flesh, and curve of the breast, while aestheticizing equally her upper-arm "stumps." The strong contrasts of the black background with the marble whiteness of her skin create a photographic sculpture in the round. The photograph, like Duffy's performance and Quinn's *The Complete Marbles* series, plays with the viewer's recognition of Classical statuary (particularly a goddess of love and fertility) and the disabled flesh, as well as perceptions of "whole" versus "deficient" bodies. Carving a sculpture "in the round" refers specifically to Classical and Neoclassical methods of producing balanced, proportional "wholes." This symbolic practice was quoted also by feminist performance artist Eleanor Antin in *Carving: A Traditional Sculpture* (July 15, 1972–August 21, 1972), in which Antin documented her body from all sides daily, as it gradually reduced during a crash diet. Antin's photographs are formally clinical in their starkness, referring to the "before" and "after" photographs quite familiar in our makeover-obsessed contemporary culture, while her body becomes a piece of sculpture in characteristic practices of performance art. Particularly to 21st-century eyes, the Antin's images refer to eating disorders and the extents to which women will go to "perfect" their bodies, according to increasingly narrow and impossible social standards for beauty. Lapper's and Antin's photographic sculptures in the round, like Quinn's sculptures, expose the notion of the "ideal" as fabricated. Lapper's work especially presents a certain disruption between artistic and social visions of the ideal and anti-ideal female body.

Art has provided a means for Lapper to interrogate others' and her own images of her body and to reinvent her image in the public eye. These themes continued in a 2000 exhibit at the Fabrica Gallery in Brighton, featuring sculptural works and photographs of Lapper from childhood to adulthood. The photographic collection intentionally crossed genres, by including artistic self-portraits, snapshots taken by friends at key moments in Lapper's life, and early childhood medical photographs, which questioned viewers' assumptions about seeing her body in different visual contexts. The inclusion of medical photographs in particular was meant to disarm the viewer and incorporate, as well as intervene on, Lapper's experiences of feeling like a medical spectacle and specimen. Indeed, Lapper's unique medical history, chronicled in her memoir as a series of objectifying and shameful displays of her body by doctors to "instruct" their peers on deformity and anomaly, connects intimately in the process of her work; Lapper remarks on her extensive history of being measured and cast in plaster particularly, in both medical and artistic contexts. Other works in the show featured Lapper's face in the vintage black-and-white style of classic Hollywood photographs. These images were strategically placed in a frame on the floor and covered in salt crystals. The viewer had to kneel down and brush aside the crystals to see Lapper's face, portrayed in a photographic softness reminiscent of glamour shots and intended to offset the hard-edge format of the medical images. The demand for viewer interaction with these works, as well at their themes of veiling, revealing, and concealing the body, make them performative—another public display of the disabled body.

Lapper strives in this work to showcase the disabled body as artistic and worthy of aestheticized display. She also makes photographic collages with elements such as flowers and angel wings to symbolize her biographical and artistic journeys. In *Angel* (1999), Lapper's head and nude torso, shot in black and white film, project from the right edge of the painted frame. She bears wings and her body thrusts upward, soaring, like the winged messenger god, Hermes, or the confident, yet tragic Icarus, to unforeseen heights of knowledge and to personal vistas. Winged figures, from Classical mythology to contemporary fantasy, transverse the heavens and the earth—the realms of the gods and mortals; they are figures with extraordinary bodies and supernatural abilities for travel. Lapper here incarnates goddess imagery, enacting a re-vision of art history and resurgence of the disabled body in shameless, empowered self display. She appropriates allegorical bodies to present her own body image. In this frame, *Angel* invokes also the winged Nike, the mythical personification of victory, who is sometimes depicted bearing wings in the place of arms (as in the monumental, *Nike of Samothrace*, c.190 CE). Believed to once stand at the helm of a ship, the headless and armless Greek Hellenistic Nike is now a grand attraction at the Louvre Museum in Paris and a relic of Western culture. The Nike form is poignantly a derivative of Athena, the goddess known for her protection of the city of Athens and who is venerated still today at the Parthenon, the original home of the *Elgin Marbles*. Athena, or Minerva as she was known by the Romans, was a single mother and the goddess of wisdom, women's deeds, and the arts—a quite fitting allegory for Lapper to embody. Further, as Marina Warner (1985) describes, Athena shape-shifted to a number of personas and bodies in order to invoke powers and enact deeds. These performative masquerades of the goddess included her strategic exposure and concealment of her body and identity. Like Athena's performances, Lapper's self-portrait works reveal and conceal her body in multiplying references and significances; similarly to *Alison Lapper Pregnant*, Lapper's body work is pregnant with meaning.

Lapper's works, like Quinn's, juxtapose the portrayal of the body as symbolic allegory and as a portrait subject. As an allegorical figure, *Alison Lapper Pregnant* follows in a tradition of staging the female body particularly as a symbol of heroic, virtuous, and largely patriarchal social values. Justice, Prudence, Fortitude, and Temperance, for examples, are values embodied by the female allegory of British history, Britannia, a Neoclassical figure derived from the Roman Minerva (Athena) and featured most prominently in Neoclassical design on Roman-inspired British coins. Classical Roman revival in Britain, which inspired the architecture and figurative program of Trafalgar Square, appealed to traditions of piety, austerity, and humility in British society, social ideals upheld still today across much of Britain's political landscape. *Alison Lapper Pregnant*, as a Neoclassical sculpture in the round, brings to life the corporeal reality of metaphysical, bodily allegories. Lapper's arch defiance of such longstanding conservative ideals, however, radiates from the sparkling surface of her body and tells "other" stories of British citizenship. She both conforms to and reforms stereotypes of disability, as well as of the British "public." Lapper's self-portrait photographs present additionally graphic portrayals of her particularized experiences, while co-opting the powers of infamous female beings. Britannia follows in the legacy of Minerva as the civic goddess and as a symbol of law abiding chastity; as a reincarnation of these goddesses, Lapper gives birth to new histories of the square and the British nation, both by posing for the statue and by producing self-representations.

Lapper's role in the mediation of *Alison Lapper Pregnant* has brought a voice to its depiction of a pregnant amputee woman, as well as of a contemporary artist; Lapper's own work, which has experienced more attention, albeit slowly, contributes to significant dialogues and representations of disability in visual culture, both today and historically. Quinn's and Lapper's images cause the viewer to do a double-take and to perceive bodies on display in different lights and with frameworks outside of the strict conventions of social ideals. These artists call into question the integrity of Neoclassicism and other idealizing and/or disfiguring traditions for displaying the body in art, as well as in everyday life. These juxtapositions also emphasize the necessity of placing the works of disabled and non-disabled artists in dialogues with each other and with larger visual contexts, in order to see art through new eyes and from the perspective *of* disability. In collaboration, such dialogues can forge fresh, multidimensional images of disability in the public eye, and potentially, can sculpt new, liberating body ideals for the public.

NOTES

1. Alison Lapper (with Guy Feldman), *My Life in My Hands* (London; New York: Simon & Schuster UK, Ltd., 2005), 236.
2. For example, Bert Massie, the chairman of the commission, was quoted in *The Guardian* newspaper as stating: "Congratulations to Marc for realising that disabled bodies have a power and beauty rarely recognised in an age where youth and 'perfection' are idolised." This article also states that the Disability Rights Commission welcomed the statue as a source of pride and a blow against the cult of perfection that effectively disables bodies who don't conform to the norm. Others have suggested, like Lapper, that the work's depiction of a specific embodiment largely under-represented in visual life, at least in a positive way, broadens and humanizes notions of beauty, as well as humanizes certain socially stigmatized individuals. For example, see: Adrian Searle, "Arresting, strange and beautiful," *The Guardian* (Friday September 16, 2005).
3. Some of the better known artists of this style are the French painter Jacques-Louis David, as well as British painters Joshua Reynolds and Benjamin West, and the sculptors Antonio Canova and Bertel Thorvaldson. By reviving Classical figures, Neoclassical artists sought to portray eternal beauty and cultural idealism, in balanced, symmetrical, and "able," or extra-able bodies. In Classical traditions, on which Neoclassicism was based, figures were composed from the most idyllic features of different individuals and mathematically derived proportions in order to create a composite "whole" body ideal.
4. One the few works in *The Complete Marbles* that is not titled with the models' names, *Kiss*, 2002, refers specifically to Impressionist sculptor Auguste Rodin's canonical work *The Kiss*. Quinn's *Kiss* features two life-size amputees cast from live models, standing on one leg and leaning against one another (rather than seated, as in Rodin's original), to embrace passionately. Quinn here showcases a disabled couple in an allegory of romantic love and as contemporary sexual beings, which challenges popular stereotypes of disability as sexually undesirable. *Kiss* and other works in *The Complete Marbles* series are portraits that call for re-visions of art history and social ideals.
5. Preece.
6. Waldemar Januszczak, *The Sunday Times*, "Matter of life and death—Art-Profile—Marc Quinn," Dec. 10, 2000.
7. Quinn has a certain reputation as a "bad boy" among art critics, exacerbated by inclusion in the controversial exhibit of 1991, in which he debuted one of his most famous pieces, *Self* (1991), a self-portrait bust made from 9 pints of Quinn's blood frozen. Some have connected *Alison Lapper Pregnant* with a longer interest in birth in Quinn's work, as exemplified by *Birth* or *Lucas* (2001), a frozen representation of his son Lucas' head made from real placenta, three days old. His work has many bodily and biological themes; has worked with DNA imaging (*DNA Garden* (2002), grid of 77 Petri dishes), test tubes, and silicon preservation. Examples of Quinn's other works that use body fluids and forms are: *Yellow Cut Nervous Breakdown, Invisible Man, No Invisible Means of Escape XI* (formed from cast white rubber resembling flesh), *The Great Escape* (a cast of his body inside pod), *Continuous Present* (2000) (which features a skull that rotates around a reflective cylinder), *Shit Paintings* and *Shit Head* (1997), *Incarnate* (a boiled sausage form with his blood), *Eternal Spring* I and II (1998) (a series featuring Calla lilies suspended in water), and *Garden* (2000) (a glass walled installation of flora and fauna that was deceptively composed of frozen units of silicon). As exemplified by these examples, Quinn's work has repeatedly used blood, placenta, excrement, ice, and flowers. He chooses materials are chosen because of their corporeality and symbolic connotations.
8. Kim Q. Hall, "Pregnancy, Disability and Gendered Embodiment: Rethinking Alison Lapper

Pregnant," lecture delivered at the Society for Disability Studies Conference, Bethesda, MD, June 17, 2006.

9. Januszczak.

10. Charles L. Griswold, "The Vietnam Veterans Memorial and the Washington Mall: Philosophical Thoughts on Political Iconography," in *Critical Issues in Public Art: Content, Context, and Controversy*, Harriet F. Seine and Sally Webster, eds., 71–100 (Washington and London: Smithsonian Institute Press, 1992), 74.

11. Trafalgar Square is a center of tourist and civil exchange. It sits on a tourist path from the Houses of Parliament and Westminster Abbey and at the top of The Mall, which leads to Buckingham Palace. The National Gallery, the Admiralty, and the church of St. Martin in the Fields are also on the square.

12. Alice Thomson of the *Daily Telegraph* was quoted in Cederwell.

13. Lapper, 236.

14. Lapper, 234.

15. Miles.

16. At the south end of the square is an equestrian statue of Charles I in a conventional pose suggesting royalty and conquest, which is based on a famous Roman statue of Marcus Aurelius and was also the favored position of Louis XV and Napoleon to emphasize their military strength and leadership (for example in David's triumphant, Neoclassical portrait *Napoleon Crossing the Alps* (1801), which served as Imperial propaganda). On both sides of Nelson's Column are the bronze statues of Sir Henry Havelock and Sir Charles James Napier, and fronting the north wall of Trafalgar Square are busts of Generals Beatty, Jellicoe, and Cunningham, all famous military leaders. All of the "heroes" are significantly honored for their participation in the colonization of India, Egypt, and the Caribbean, and were known as brutal leaders of mutinous soldiers who were often of the nationality of the countries the generals fought to dominate.

17. This opinion was expressed, for example, in the following newspaper quote: "Roy Hattersley, in the Daily Mail, agreed that while the sculpture was 'a celebration of both courage and motherhood', it was nevertheless 'the wrong statue in the wrong place.' The Trafalgar Square plinth is crying out for 'individual examples of national achievement and British greatness,' he said. Hattersley drew up his own shortlist of likely greats, including Shakespeare, Milton, Elgar, Newton and Wren. 'Most of us will share the view that Lapper is someone to admire . . . but the simple truth is that Trafalgar Square is meant for something else.' Quoted from Cederwell.

18. Jeanette Hart, Letter to the editor, *The Guardian* (Wednesday September 21, 2005).

19. Paul Usherwood, "The Battle of Trafalgar Square," *Art Monthly* 2. no. 4 (March 2004), 43.

20. Rodney Mace, *Trafalgar Square: Emblem of Empire* (Southampton, UK: The Camelot Press, Ltd., 1976).

21. For more on Gil, see Ann Millett-Gallant, "Little Displays: The Photography of Ricardo Gil," in *The Review of Disability Studies: An International Journal* Issue 2, v.4 (June 2009).

SELECTED BIBLIOGRAPHY

Cederwell, William. "What they said about . . . the fourth plinth," *The Guardian*, Thursday March 18, 2004. Fourth Plinth Project website: http://www.fourthplinth.co.uk/

Gisbourne, Mark. "The Self and Others" in *Contemporary (U.K.)* no. 2 (Feb. 2002): 52–7.

Hall, Kim Q. "Pregnancy, Disability and Gendered Embodiment: Rethinking Alison Lapper Pregnant," lecture delivered at the Society for Disability Studies Conference, Bethesda, MD, June 17, 2006.

Hutchinson, Ray, editor. *Constructions of Urban Space*. Stamford, CT: Jai Press, Inc., 2000.

Januszczak, Waldemar. *The Sunday Times*, "Matter of life and death—Art-Profile—Marc Quinn," Dec. 10, 2000.

Jones, Jonathan. "Bold, graphic, subversive—but bad art," *The Guardian* (Tuesday March 16, 2004).

Kemp, M. and M. Wallace. *Spectacular Bodies: The Art and Science of the Human Body from Leonardo to Now*. London, Hayward Gallery; Los Angeles: University of California Press, 2000.

Kennedy, Maev. "Pregnant and proud: statue of artist wins place in Trafalgar Square," *The Guardian* (Tuesday March 16, 2004).

Lacy, Suzanne, editor. *Mapping the Terrain: New Genre Public Art*. Seattle: Bay Press, Inc., 1995.

Lapper, Alison. *My Life in My Hands*. London; New York: Simon & Schuster UK, Ltd., 2005.

Mace, Rodney. *Trafalgar Square: Emblem of Empire*. Southampton, UK: The Camelot Press, Ltd., 1976.

Miles, Malcolm. *Art, Space, and the City: Public Art and Urban Futures*. London and New York: Routledge, 1997.

Mitchell, David T. and Snyder, Sharon L. *Narrative Prosthesis: Disability and the Dependencies of Discourse*. Ann Arbor: University of Michigan Press, 2001.

Preece, Robert. "Just a Load of Shock? An Interview

with Marc Quinn," *Sculpture* 19, no. 8 (Oct. 2000): 14–19.

Seine, H.F. and Webster, S. editors. *Critical Issues in Public Art: Content, Context, and Controversy.* Washington and London: Smithsonian Institute Press, 1992.

Selwood, Sara. *The Benefits of Public Art: The Polemics of Public Places.* Poole, Dorset UK: Policy Studies Institute Publications, 1995.

Usherwood, Paul. "The Battle of Trafalgar Square," *Art Monthly* 2. no. 4 (March 2004), 43.

Warner, Marina. *Monuments and Maidens: The Allegory of the Female Form.* New York: Atheneum, 1985.

CHAPTER 36

"When *Black* Women Start Going on Prozac. . . .": The Politics of Race, Gender, and Emotional Distress in Meri Nana-Ama Danquah's *Willow Weep for Me*

Anna Mollow

INTRODUCTION: DISABILITY ESSENTIALISM; OR, WHAT COUNTS?

Meri Nana-Ama Danquah's *Willow Weep for Me: A Black Woman's Journey Through Depression* is a first-person narrative by an author who, without identifying as "disabled" or signaling any alliance with the disability rights movement, instead describes the "suffering" her "illness" caused and recounts her "triumph" over it, an overcoming achieved through a combination of "courage," "resilience," prescription drugs, and other medical interventions (237; 18; 262). As such, Danquah's memoir is precisely the kind of text that much disability scholarship in the humanities has taught us to critique. Foundational work in this field has stressed the formation and assertion of positive disability identities. It has also underscored the distinction between illness and disability, describing disability in terms of visible bodily difference rather than sickness or suffering. Moreover, disability scholars have criticized personal narratives that highlight disabled people's courage or show them "overcoming" their impairments; framing disability in terms of an individual's struggle against adversity, they have argued, deflects attention from the political realities of disability oppression.[1] These arguments have

enormous importance. They form the basis of a scholarship that has redefined disability, demonstrating that it is best understood not as a biological given, but rather as a social process requiring sustained intellectual and political attention.

Yet Danquah's memoir, in its deep engagement with the politics of race, gender, class, and mental illness, forces a reconsideration of several of these tenets of disability studies. Most important, *Willow Weep for Me* makes it clear that disability studies, which has tended to define disability as a visual, objectively observable phenomenon, must also carefully attend to the phenomenological aspects of impairment, particularly those that involve suffering and illness. Such attention will necessitate developing more nuanced ways of describing intersections of multiple forms of oppression than have predominated in the most influential disability scholarship. Examining such intersectionality in Danquah's memoir complicates aspects of some disabled people's critiques of the medical or psychiatric model of mental illness; for many Black women with depression, lack of access to health care, rather than involuntary administration of it, is the most oppressive aspect of the contemporary politics of mental illness.[2] Danquah's memoir may also be the basis for a critique of a tendency, within much disability scholarship, to avoid representing impairments in terms of sickness or suffering. The social model's impairment-disability binary, which has often lead to a de-politicization of impairments, cannot be upheld in *Willow Weep for Me*, which illuminates both the suffering that impairments can cause and the role of politics in producing them. But on the other hand, Danquah's narrative also complicates some disability theorists' deconstructions of the impairment-disability distinction. These postmodern analyses of impairment tend to see individuals' reliance upon impairment categories as invariably serving to buttress hegemonic constructions of disability; but Danquah's autopathography demonstrates that such categories can be mobilized in ways that are politically resistant. Finally, *Willow Weep for Me* presents challenges to disability studies' critique of "stories of overcoming"; by highlighting individuals' power in relation to oppressive political and economic structures, Danquah's narrative offers a powerful antidote to despair.

In order apprehend the significance of *Willow Weep for Me*, a critical method that can account for intersections of multiple forms of oppression is crucial. "I am black; I am female; I am an immigrant," Danquah writes. "Every one of these labels plays an equally significant part in my perception of myself and the world around me" (225).[3] Unfortunately, disability studies has been slow to theorize such intersectionality, particularly when it comes to race. While works like Bonnie G. Smith and Beth Hutchinson's 2004 anthology, *Gendering Disability*, testify to a growing interest in exploring connections between gender and disability, many of the most foundational works in disability studies have analyzed race and disability, not in tandem, but in opposition to each other.[4] In their efforts to stake out a claim for disability as worthy of intellectual and political attention, disability scholars

often represent the relationship between people with disabilities and other political minorities in hierarchical terms.[5] In a more subtle way, the frequent use of "like race" analogies in disability scholarship may also have the effect of opposing the interests of disabled people and people of color. When Rosemarie Garland-Thomson characterizes disability as a "form of ethnicity," or when Lennard J. Davis compares "the disabled figure" to "the body marked as differently pigmented," it's clear that neither intends to place race or ethnicity in opposition to disability; rather, they each seek to establish a likeness between two categories, and thus to gain recognition of disabled people as members of a political minority (Garland-Thomson, 6; Davis, EN, 80). But as Trina Grillo and Stephanie M. Wildman have argued, "like race" analogies often have the effect of "obscuring the importance of race," enabling the group making the analogy to take "center stage from people of color" (621). Moreover, such analogies assume a false separation between the forms of oppression being compared. As Grillo and Wildman point out in their discussion of analogies between race and gender, "[a]nalogizing sex discrimination to race discrimination makes it seem that all the women are white and all the men are African-American"; thus, they observe, "the experience of women of color . . . is rendered invisible" (623). The dangers of "like race" analogies in disability studies are similar: if race and disability are conceived of as discrete categories to be compared, contrasted, or arranged in order of priority, it becomes impossible to think through complex intersections of racism and ableism in the lives of disabled people of color.[6] This is not, of course, to deny that analogies can be useful; I share Ellen Samuels's sense that rather than attempting "somehow to escape from analogy," we might "seek to employ it more critically than in the past" (4).

These intersections must be understood in ways that are more than merely additive, as Angela P. Harris argues in her critique of "gender essentialism—the notion that a unitary, 'essential' women's experience can be isolated and described independently of race, class, sexual orientation, and other realities of experience" (585). According to an additive model of multiple oppressions, Harris argues, "black women will never be anything more than a crossroads between two kinds of domination, or at the bottom of a hierarchy of oppressions" (589).[7] I would therefore suggest that, in examining intersections of forms of oppression, we guard against the dangers of a "disability essentialism," in which the experiences, needs, desires, and aims of all disabled people are assumed to be the same and those with "different" experiences are accommodated only if they do not make claims that undermine the movement's foundational arguments. Many of these arguments have been developed primarily with physical disability in mind. Cognitive and psychiatric impairments, although they are gaining more attention, nonetheless remain marginalized, both within disability studies and in the broader culture. I was recently reminded of the extent of this marginalization when I mentioned to a colleague that I was writing an essay on Black women and depression; she responded by asking, "Does depression count as a disability?" Her question is crucial. "The short answer," I told my colleague, "is 'yes'." The longer answer would have involved a discussion of the ways in which truly "counting" the experiences of people with mental illness might necessitate revising some of disability studies' most frequently cited claims.

While the necessity of such revisions becomes particularly evident when the politics of race, gender, and mental illness are analyzed together, the arguments that follow should not be taken as part of an unitary account of such intersections: I wish to be clear that I am not suggesting any intrinsic relationship among Blackness, femininity, and mental illness; nor do I propose to read Danquah's memoir as representative of a monolithic "Black women's perspective on depression."[8] I do hope to show, however, that examining the converging effects of multiple forms of oppression can have profound implications for disability studies. Reading *Willow Weep for Me* with such effects in mind will require the rethinking of some of the field's most central tenets: its reluctance to understand disability in terms of sickness or suffering, its tendency to define disability in visual terms, and its resistance to stories of overcoming. If we avoid this critical reevaluation, we risk misreading as naïve or politically disengaged the work of Danquah and others whose perspectives diverge from disability studies' entrenched ideas.

GOING ON PROZAC

Among people with depression, the politics of mental illness are complex and highly contested. In particular, much controversy surrounds questions about whether people who experience emotional distress are sick. Throughout her memoir, Danquah emphasizes that her depression is an "illness"; by doing so, she adopts a strategy that diverges from that of the psychiatric survivor movement (18). Members of this movement define themselves as "survivors," not of mental illness, but rather of institutionalization in psychiatric hospitals.[9] Indeed, they often reject the very category of "mental illness," which they view as a largely meaningless invention of modern psychiatry that serves to enforce conformity to social norms and to derive money and power for mental health "experts." Protesting doctors' excessive control over the lives of people we diagnose as "mentally ill," psychiatric survivors describe incarceration in mental institutions that are often run like prisons, as well as nonconsensual administration of "therapies" that resemble punishments or even torture.[10] Moreover, they note that psychiatrists themselves are unable to define mental illness; that no biological or genetic cause of any putative mental disorder has ever been demonstrated; and that the most common treatments—psychoactive medications, electroconvulsive therapy (ECT), seclusion, and physical restraints—have no proven benefits and cause debilitating side effects, including brain damage.[11] Survivors' testimonies demonstrate the appalling extent to which the label of "mental illness" has been used to deprive people of autonomy, respect, and human rights.[12]

What, then, do we make of Danquah's definition of her depression as a "mental illness" (20)? In what context do we understand her emphasis upon the necessity of taking antidepressant medication? "I have tried to deny my need for medication and stopped taking it," Danquah explains. "Each time, at the slightest provocation, I have fallen, fast and hard, deeper into the depression" (220; 258). However, Danquah does not regard depression as purely a medical phenomenon. "The illness exists somewhere in that ghost space between consciousness and chemistry," she writes (257–58). She takes her Paxil "reluctantly," observing that "there is something that seems really wrong with the fact that Prozac is one of the most prescribed drugs in this country" (258).[13]

But for Danquah, in contrast to members of the psychiatric survivor movement, lack of access to health care, rather than involuntary imposition of it, is the most salient aspect of her interactions with the medical profession. Danquah sees adequate medical treatment for her depression as a necessity, to which poverty, racism, and gender bias have created almost insurmountable barriers. Her obstetrician dismisses one of her first episodes of severe depression as

the effect of "hormones" (36). Years later, she seeks treatment but has great difficulty locating a mental health clinic she can afford. Danquah is able to pay for only one of the medications she is prescribed, Zoloft, an antidepressant. Anxiety is a side effect of Zoloft, so her doctor writes her a prescription for BuSpar, an anxiety controllant. This drug, however, is prohibitively expensive, so Danquah resorts to alcohol to manage the side effects of her antidepressant. Indeed, the Zoloft seems to cause an insatiable craving for alcohol, which disappears when she discontinues the medication (221). Danquah is forced to figure most of this out without any medical supervision. Most of the practitioners at the mental health clinic she goes to are therapists-in-training, and hers leaves abruptly once she has completed her certification process. Rather than being "reassigned" at random to another therapist, Danquah suspends psychotherapy (208).

In addition to economic obstacles, Danquah faces cultural barriers to appropriate health care. Her psychiatrist, Dr. Fitzgerald, is a white man who describes at length his inability to "even fathom" the racism with which she routinely copes (224). Experiences like this are commonplace for African American women seeking mental health care. Julia A. Boyd, an African American psychotherapist, observes that many white mental health practitioners "remain in a passive state of denial concerning the therapeutic needs of black women" ("Ethnic," 232). In addition, people of color, especially African Americans, are less likely to be diagnosed with depression or prescribed medication when they report their symptoms to a doctor; even in studies controlling for income level and health insurance status, the disparities are great.[14]

The contrast between Danquah's experience and that of many members of the psychiatric survivor movement highlights a conundrum facing people with depression or other mental illnesses. The enormous power that the psychiatric profession wields in modern Western societies creates a double bind, in which both diagnosis with a mental illness or, alternatively, the lack of such a diagnosis, brings with it serious negative social consequences for people experiencing emotional distress.[15] Being diagnosed with a mental illness means risking social stigmatization, involuntary institutionalization, and treatment with dangerous medications. On the other hand, those who are not deemed truly mentally ill are often regarded as merely malingering. Depression, Danquah observes, is "not looked upon as a legitimate illness. Most employers really don't give a damn if you're depressed, and neither do landlords or bill collectors" (144).

This lack of social validation and support is exacerbated by racism. The symptoms of depression, Boyd points out, often "mirror the stereotypes that have been projected onto Black women"; before she was diagnosed with the disorder herself, Boyd thought that "being depressed meant that you were crazy, lazy, unmotivated" (8; 15). Moreover, as Danquah notes, depression is "still viewed as a predominantly 'white' illness"; when Black people become depressed, the symptoms and coping strategies usually go unrecognized (184).[16] Pervasive social denial and lack of access to necessary medical care are the political realities that Danquah highlights in her account of her struggles with depression. While these realities are inextricable from the politics of race, I do not wish to suggest that all Black women with depression share Danquah's perspective on the medicalization of emotional distress.[17]

In addition, it is important to remember that the other aspect of the double bind I have described—i.e., diagnosis of a mental illness as the justification for involuntary confinement and forcible "treatment"—also carries additional risks for Black people. While white people are more often diagnosed with depression and prescribed antidepressants, African Americans are diagnosed with schizophrenia at much higher rates and are also given antipsychotic medications more frequently and in higher doses. They are also more often institutionalized involuntarily, in part because racial stereotypes affect psychiatrists' assessments of their "dangerousness."[18] The pathologization of Black people is also built into what Danquah terms "the oppressive nature of the existing language surrounding depression," the commonplace metaphors of depression as darkness and blackness (21–22).[19]

Danquah's critique of the politics of race and mental illness exposes and protests linguistic, social, cultural, and economic barriers that impede Black women with depression from accessing health care. In contrast to the psychiatric survivor movement, her primary focus is on this lack of access, rather than the effects of involuntary treatment. But she shares with psychiatric survivors a profound sense of the importance of self-determination and control over one's own medical treatment. Danquah begins to see significant improvement in her depression when, as she puts it, "I took control of my own healing" (225). Recognizing that her own role in her treatment is more important than that of her psychiatrist, she realizes, "it did not make that much of a difference to me if Dr. Fitzgerald was listening or not, if he cared or not, if he understood or not. *I* was listening. *I* was hearing. *I* was understanding. *I* cared" (225–26).

DISABILITY OR IMPAIRMENT?: DEPRESSION AND THE SOCIAL MODEL

Danquah's understanding of her depression as a "disease" not only adds another dimension to the psychiatric survivor movement's critique of the mental health profession, but also complicates what has come to be known as the "social model" of disability. The social model was developed in Britain in the 1970s; a key moment in its emergence occurred in 1976, when the Union of the Physically Impaired Against Segregation (UPIAS) published its *Fundamental Principles of Disability*. Perhaps the most important of these "fundamental principles" was the crucial distinction the document made between "impairment" and "disability":

> In our view it is society which disables physically impaired people. Disability is something imposed on top of our impairments, by the way we are unnecessarily isolated and excluded from full participation in society . . . (3)

UPIAS's differentiation between the bodily (impairment) and the social (disability) formed the basis of what Mike Oliver subsequently presented as the "social model of disability."[20] The social model, like the minority group model that emerged in the United States, has enabled major transformations in the conceptualization of disability; rather than accepting traditional definitions of disability as a personal misfortune, this new paradigm frames disability in terms of social oppression.

What the social model may sacrifice, however, is a way of thinking in political terms about the suffering that some impairments cause. As Liz Crow points out, the social model sometimes has the effect of obscuring the reality that "[P]ain, fatigue, depression and chronic illness are constant facts of life" for many people with disabilities (58). This problem is pervasive not only in applications of Britain's social model, but also in disability studies in the United States, where the "critique of the medical model" is a fundamental principle. Critiquing the medical model does not necessarily preclude recognition of

chronic and terminal illnesses as disabling forms of impairment. However, in practice this critique often functions to differentiate people with disabilities from those who are ill.[21] Arguing for greater inclusion of people with chronic illness in the disability community, Susan Wendell takes issue with Eli Clare's contention that people with disabilities should not be regarded as "sick, diseased, ill people" hoping to be cured (Wendell 18; Clare 105). As Wendell points out, "some people with disabilities *are* sick, diseased, and ill"; moreover, she observes, some disabled people "very much want" to be cured (18). Danquah expresses this wish at the end of her memoir: "I choose to believe that somewhere, somehow, there is a cure for depression" (257).

If the experiences of those who define themselves as ill and hope to be cured are elided in much disability scholarship, this may be due in part to the field's emphasis on visible aspects of disability. Garland-Thomson's definition of disability as a process that emerges through "a complex relation between seer and seen" is of great value in thinking about the "extraordinary bodies" she discusses, but the framing of disability in terms of outward appearance is less useful for analyzing depression and other invisible impairments, particularly those that involve sickness and suffering (136). Similarly, Harlan Hahn's positing of a "correlation between the visibility of disabilities and the amount of discrimination which they might elicit" has little to do with Danquah' experience."[22] Danquah loses friends and jobs precisely because her disability is *not* visible and therefore is not recognized as a "legitimate illness" (144; 30).

Indeed, disability studies' emphasis upon observable manifestations of impairments makes it difficult to know how to begin thinking about a condition like depression, which is primarily a subjective experience. Moreover, it is an experience characterized by suffering: "Suffering . . .

was what depression was all about," Danquah reflects (237).[23] The issue of suffering has been vexed within disability studies. As Bill Hughes and Kevin Paterson observe, "Disabled people . . . feel uncomfortable with the concept of suffering because . . . it seems inextricably bound to a personal tragedy model of disability" (336). As Oliver states, "the social model is not about the personal experience of impairment but the collective experience of disablement" ("Social," 22). However, the strategy of maintaining a focus on social oppression rather than personal suffering—or on "disability" as opposed to "impairment"—risks reifying a dichotomy that does not easily apply to disorders like depression. While impairments ranging from cerebral palsy to blindness, spinal cord injury, or autism do not always cause suffering in and of themselves, it makes little sense for a person to say she is clinically depressed but does not suffer. And whereas it's illuminating, when discussing the politics surrounding mobility impairments, to observe that disability results from inaccessible architectural structures rather than from bodily deficiency, it's difficult to use this paradigm to understand depression. It is true that, to a certain extent, one could apply the impairment-disability distinction to Danquah's experience. Arguably, Danquah's impairment, depression, becomes disabling because of a societal unwillingness to accommodate it: "I lost my job because the temp agencies where I was registered could no longer tolerate my lengthy absences," she recounts (30). "I lost my friends. Most of them found it too troublesome to deal with my sudden moodiness and passivity" (30). These social pressures correspond to UPIAS's definition of "disability" as "something imposed on top of our impairments" (3).

But an analysis of Danquah's text that privileges "the collective experience" of disability over "the personal experience" of impairment would greatly distort her account of her struggles with depression (Oliver, UD, 12). A lack of social validation or understanding, although a persistent facet of her experience, seems to recede into the background of the intense and prolonged suffering in which her depression immerses her. Throughout *Willow Weep for Me*, Danquah describes this suffering in vivid and often metaphorical language, which contrasts with her matter-of-fact reports of lost friends and career opportunities. She writes that her life "disintegrated; first, into a strange and terrifying space of sadness and then, into a cobweb of fatigue" (27). She describes "nails of despair . . . digging . . . deeply into my skin" and "a dense cloud of melancholy [that] hung over my head" (30). As her depression worsens, she writes, "It seemed as if the world was closing in on me, squeezing me dry" (32). She remembers "absolute terror" and "despair [that] cut so deeply, I thought it would slice me in half" (42; 106). As such stark descriptions of suffering make clear, relegating "impairment" to a secondary status within an impairment-disability binary elides the phenomenological aspects of depression as a state of suffering.

Moreover, analyses that privilege disability over impairment deflect attention from the political nature of impairment itself. In Danquah's narrative, the social environment is important less for its imposition of an additional burden "on top of" a pre-existing impairment than for its role in producing her depression (UPIAS, 3). When Danquah is a child, her schoolmates ostracize her, mocking her accent and calling her "the African Monkey" (104). She recalls that the "host of . . . horrid epithets" to which she was subjected "shattered any personal pride I felt and replaced it with uncertainty and self-hatred" (105). When her father abandons the family, Danquah begins to think of herself as "the ugly little girl, the 'monkey,' the fatherless child" (109). In junior high, she is raped by a recent high school graduate she has a crush on (120). When she confides in her stepfather about the incident, he rapes her, too; the sexual abuse continues throughout her adolescence (124). As a young adult, undiagnosed postpartum depression coupled with physical abuse by the father of her child contribute to an episode of serious depression. A subsequent episode is triggered by the "not guilty" verdict in the Rodney King trial: "We, all black people, had just been told that our lives were of no value," Danquah remembers (42).

DISTRESS OR DISEASE?: DECONSTRUCTING THE SOCIAL MODEL

As Danquah's story illustrates, the oppression of disabled people is not merely "something imposed on top of" a pre-existing impairment; rather, the production of some impairments is itself a political process (UPIAS, 3). Therefore, *Willow Weep for Me* might at first seem to accord with the arguments of some disability scholars who, deconstructing the impairment-disability binary, claim that impairment is a discursive production.[24] Shelley Tremain argues that a Foucaultian analysis will reveal "that impairment and its materiality are naturalized *effects* of disciplinary knowledge/power" (SI, 34). Locating the origins of modern-day categorizations of bodies as normal or impaired in the nineteenth-century bio-medical discourses whose genealogies Foucault traces, Tremain observes that impairment is neither a "'prediscursive' antecedent" nor a set of "essential, biological characteristics of a 'real' body" (SI, 42).

Indeed, Tremain's theorization of impairment is *à propos* to any discussion of depression, whose constructedness as a disease entity is easily apparent. While the term "melancholy" is as old as ancient Greek medicine, its defining features have been broad and shifting, never corresponding to the present-day disease category of "clinical depression." The instability of depression as a discrete medical phenomenon is further evident in the extent to which those who wish to establish it as such must continually define it by differentiating it from ordinary states of sadness. "Depression isn't the same as ordinary sadness, it is hell," Danquah's friend Scott says (260). Or, as Danquah explains, "We have all, to some degree, experienced days of depression . . . But for some, such as myself, the depression doesn't lift at the end of the day . . . And when depression reaches clinical proportions, it *is* truly an illness" (18).[25]

Moreover, whereas most people in our culture would not question the validity of diseases like diabetes, cancer, or rheumatoid arthritis, skeptics abound when it comes to depression. Eboni, one of several African American woman with whom Boyd engages in a dialogue about depression, says, "look at what our mothers and grandmothers went through in their lives and we don't hear them whining about depression" (CI, 21). Eboni's comments not only underscore the constructedness of depression as a clinical entity, but also raise another set of questions. While it's relatively easy to observe that depression cannot be regarded as a prediscursive bodily or mental "given," what remains unclear are the possible effects of the processes by which it is currently being consolidated as a definable and describable disease. For example, does the construction of depression as an illness enable a potentially emancipatory reinterpretation of behaviors traditionally regarded as moral weakness, such as the "whining" that Eboni dismisses? It is in part to distinguish depression from "a character flaw" that Danquah insists that depression "*is* truly an illness" (18). But Tremain's analysis of the constructedness of impairments raises the possibility that Danquah's self-construction as a "depressive" might have "insidious" effects (Danquah, 18; Tremain, SI, 37). Reliance on biomedicine's constructions of bodily and mental difference, Tremain argues, may only further consolidate the pervasive power of disciplinary regimes (SI, 42).

Tremain's characterization of impairments as discursively produced is cogent and insightful. However, as I will argue, *Willow Weep for Me* demonstrates that impairment categories can be cited in ways that, rather than merely "meet[ing] requirements of contemporary political arrangements," instead also serve to undermine them (Tremain, SI, 42; FG, 10). To elucidate this process, it will be helpful to reflect upon the epistemic shift that Foucault and other historians have documented in late eighteenth- and early nineteenth-century medicine. With the rise of clinical medicine in the nineteenth century, the physical examination and the dissection of corpses supplanted patients' stories as the privileged modes of generating medical knowledge.[26] The dominant medical epistemology became visual rather than narrative: the patient came to be seen as a passive body, manifesting visible signs of disease which could be interpreted by the doctor's detached "gaze."[27] These visible "signs," or objective manifestations of disease, were privileged over "symptoms," which referred to subjective sensations the patient reported (Porter, 313). The sign-symptom binary remains a centerpiece of contemporary medical epistemology, and its continued importance helps explain why depression has not been regarded as a "real" disease in the same way as illnesses such as arthritis or multiple sclerosis, which can be visualized on X-rays or MRIs. Whereas the careful observation of bodily changes, the dissection of cadavers, and eventually the emerging science of bacteriology enabled nineteenth-century physicians to define diseases like tuberculosis as distinct clinical entities, the same cannot

be said of depression. Indeed, the project of solidifying depression as a bona fide medical condition is grounded in the expectation that it will one day be possible to identify specific biological markers of the disorder and thus to demonstrate that depression is an organic disease of the brain.

Because such signs remain elusive, the construction of depression as a disease is presently occurring in ways that differ significantly from the discursive materialization of most of the impairments that receive attention in disability studies; that is, from most visible impairments.[28] Western medicine has obtained significant knowledge about impairments such as cataracts, colitis, and heart disease, all of which manifest visible signs, without much active participation on the part of the patient; but a depressed person, to be understood as such, must be a subject who communicates.[29] Moreover, he or she must have a degree of psychological depth that a patient being examined for signs of a physical ailment need not be recognized as possessing. Instead of simply reporting a pain or displaying a rash, a fever, or a tremor, the depressed patient is most often subjectivized as such through the production of a narrative.[30] It is perhaps for this reason that, as Danquah observes, our culture is so reluctant to recognize depression in Black women. It is "hard," she remarks, "for black women to be seen as . . . emotionally complex" (21).

Yet it would certainly be a mistake to romanticize medicine's inclusion of subjects' accounts of their distress in its process of consolidating depression as a disease entity. The incorporation of patients' stories into medical discourses on depression or other forms of "mental illness" is shaped by a profound power imbalance between doctors and patients. While a diagnosis of depression is rarely made without the participation of the patient as a speaking subject, once one is labeled "mentally ill," one is often treated as less than a full subject, denied the right to choose a course of treatment or decline medical intervention altogether.[31] Moreover, as Anne Wilson and Peter Beresford point out, patients defined as "mentally ill" have little control over the ways in which their words are presented and interpreted in their medical records. Wilson and Beresford, who are themselves psychiatric system survivors, recall that "it can feel as if everything you say or do is being taken down and recorded to be used in evidence against you" (148). In addition, they point out, "as medical records are ineradicable, they also serve to make permanent and immutable the ostensible psychopathological difference or 'disorder' of those diagnosed 'mentally ill'" (149).

This power imbalance between doctors and "mentally ill" subjects exerts itself in more subtle ways as well. Wilson and Beresford relate that "it can be difficult even to begin to make sense of our experience outside of frameworks provided by 'experts,' whose theories and powers may extend to every aspect of our lives, not least our identity as 'mentally ill' (non-)persons" (145). This observation seems to illustrate Foucault's claim that the "individual is an effect of power" (TL, 98). And indeed, Foucault's arguments about subject formation raise questions about the relation of Danquah's narrative to dominant psychiatric discourses. Does Danquah, by defining herself as a "depressive," merely reinscribe the dictates of psychiatric medicine (18)? According to Tremain, "a Foucauldian approach to disability" shows that "the category of impairment . . . in part persists in order to legitimize the disciplinary regime that generated it" (FG,11; SI, 43). Tremain does not explore the possibility, however, that the production of specific impairment categories might have multiple, competing effects, including, paradoxically, the contestation of the assumptions on which these categories are based.

Such a contestation takes shape in Danquah's autopathography, which depends upon biomedicine's construction of depression as a disease entity but at the same time resists the normalizing effects of this construction. Danquah articulates her resistance to the disciplinary uses of depression as a medical category in ways that Foucault's concept of a "reverse discourse" can illuminate. Foucault argues that the nineteenth-century emergence of psychiatric and other discourses that brought into being "the homosexual"as a "species" had the effect, not only of enabling "a strong advance of social controls into this area of 'perversity,'" but also of making "possible the formation of a 'reverse' discourse: homosexuality began to speak on its own behalf, to demand that its legitimacy . . . be acknowledged, often in the same vocabulary, using the same categories by which it was medically disqualified" (HS, 101–02). Danquah's narrative might be understood as participating in a "reverse discourse" regarding depression. As we have seen, it employs the categories of psychiatric medicine in order to demand that depression's "legitimacy . . . be acknowledged" (HS, 101). Depression, Danquah maintains, is "a legitimate illness"; she is not "a flake or a fraud" (144).[32]

Additionally, at the same time that she emphasizes that depression is an authentic medical condition, Danquah also subverts some of psychiatry's most fundamental assumptions about what it means to be mentally ill. If today's "depressive" is "disqualified" in ways analogous to the disqualification of Foucault's nineteenth-century "homosexual," Danquah's narrative perhaps mobilizes a reverse discourse that resists this disqualification while nonetheless retaining the vocabulary and diagnostic categories that enable it. This can be seen in Danquah's emphasis on the imbrication of her illness with political oppression. A common mode of discrediting people with depression effects a discursive separation of symptoms from politics: depression is said to arise from feelings, beliefs, and attitudes which are disproportionately "negative" in relation to the afflicted person's actual circumstances.[33] Indeed, this is Eboni's critique of psychiatric constructions of depression: "I didn't hear where any of those big-time researchers were lookin' at things like racism or sexism," she points out (21). But this, of course, is exactly what Danquah does look at. By showing how the convergence of racism, sexual violence, and poverty literally made her ill, Danquah insists upon the validity of depression as a diagnostic category while at the same time contesting hegemonic accounts of its etiology.

Moreover, even as Danquah accepts the designation of her emotional distress as a "disease," she also undermines one of psychiatric medicine's most fundamental claims (18). As Wilson and Beresford point out, psychiatry's justification as an institution relies in large part upon "its construction of users of mental health services as Other—a separate and distinct group" (144). Interestingly, however, Danquah's gradual process of accepting that she is ill and needs medical treatment paradoxically culminates in her deconstruction of the normal/mentally ill binary upon which psychiatry's authority depends:

> I had always only thought of therapy in stark, clinical terms: an old bespectacled grey-haired white man with a couch in his office listening to the confessions of crazies. . . . What if, I asked myself, those "crazies" are no different than me? What if they are like me, ordinary people leading ordinary lives who woke up one day and discovered they couldn't get out of bed, no matter how much they wanted to or how hard they tried? (167–68)

Danquah decides to enter psychotherapy, then, not because she comes to define herself as "Other," but because she is able to imagine the dissolution of what Wilson and Beresford call psychiatry's "opposition between 'the mad' and 'the not-mad'" (154). Indeed, her sense that the depressive is not a distinct species, but rather a member of a community of "ordinary people," finds echo in Wilson and Beresford's assertion that "the world does not consist of 'normals' and 'the mentally ill'; it consists of *people*" (Danquah 167–68; Beresford and Wilson, 144).

Like the arguments of critics who use Foucaultian paradigms to analyze disability, Danquah's work demands a deconstruction of the impairment-disability distinction, forcing a theorization of impairment as itself a social process. Yet Danquah nonetheless accepts the category of mental illness and makes it integral to her self-conception. For this reason, an application of Tremain's or Wilson and Beresford's analyses of the constructedness of impairment categories might seem to authorize a reading of Danquah's narrative as "naïve," unaware of how the category of impairment operates within what Tremain, following Foucault, calls the "insidious" production of "an ever-expanding and increasingly totalizing web of social control" (SI, 34; 37; FG, 6).[34] But as we have seen, Foucault's understanding of power is more flexible than Tremain's characterization of it here suggests.[35] Rather than "a general system of domination" whose "effects . . . pervade the entire social body," Foucault describes a "multiple and mobile field of force relations, wherein far-reaching, but *never completely stable* effects of domination are produced" (HS, 92; 101–02; emphasis mine). "Discourse," he explains, "reinforces" power "but also undermines and exposes it" (HS, 101).

Foucault's conception of discourse as reversible points to the possibility that individuals might invoke discursive constructions such as "depression" so as to do more than merely, as Tremain puts it, "identify themselves in ways that make them governable" (SI, 37; FG, 6). It is true that, as David Halperin remarks, Foucault is critical "of discursive reversal . . . as a political strategy" in contemporary Western societies (58). Nevertheless, for Foucault a "reverse discourse" can constitute "a significant act of political resistance"; it is by no means "one and the same as the discourse it reverses" (Halperin, 59). Foucault explains that although reverse discourses and other forms of resistance cannot be delployed "outside" of power, "this does not mean that they are only a reaction or rebound . . . doomed to perpetual defeat" (HS, 95; 96).

Tremain accurately observes that the institutionalization of reverse discourses as identity politics movements poses significant dangers.[36] However, I wish to challenge what seems in her argument to be a global suspicion of any and all processes of "iteration and reiteration of regulatory norms and ideals about human function and structure, competency, intelligence and ability" (SI, 42). This suspicion seems to derive in part from Tremain's mapping of Judith Butler's deconstruction of the sex-gender binary onto the social model's distinction between impairment and disability (SI, 38–41). But the "reiteration" that Tremain regards as functioning to "sustain, and even augment, current social arrangements," is precisely the process in which Butler finds potential for revision of cultural norms and identity categories (SI, 42). Butler argues that "'sex'" is materialized "through a forcible reiteration" of "regulatory norms"; however, this process produces "instabilities" and "possibilities for rematerialization," in which "the force of the regulatory law can be turned against itself" (4). This turning of the regulatory law against itself, Butler suggests, might be achieved through what she calls a "citational politics," which entails a "reworking of abjection into political agency" (21).

Butler's discussion of "citational politics" focuses primarily upon instances in which "the public assertion of queerness" has the effect of "resignifying the abjection of homosexuality into defiance and legitimacy" (21). Although Danquah does not treat race, gender, or mental illness in ways that correspond exactly to Butler's description of queerness as performativity, one can nonetheless discern in *Willow Weep for Me* a "reworking of abjection into political agency" (Butler, 21).[37] Throughout her memoir, Danquah foregrounds abjection in the form of "weakness" (20). She observes that although mental illness is often regarded as a sign of "genius" in white men, of hysteria in white women, and of pathology in Black men, "when a black woman suffers from a mental disorder, the overwhelming opinion is that she is weak. And weakness in black women is intolerable" (20).

It is perhaps also unthinkable: "Clinical depression simply did not exist . . . within the realm of possibilities for any of the black women in my world," Danquah explains (18–19). "Emotional hardship is *supposed* to be built into the structure of our lives" (19). Indeed, when Danquah tells a white woman she meets at a dinner party that she's writing a book on Black women and depression, the woman responds sarcastically: "*Black* women and depression? Isn't that kinda redundant? . . . [W]hen *black* women start going on Prozac, you know the whole world is falling apart" (19–20). The foreclosure of depression as a possible diagnosis for Black women, Danquah argues, derives from the "myth" of Black women's "supposed birthright to strength" (19). "Black women are *supposed* to be strong—caretakers, nurturers, healers of other people—any of the twelve dozen variations of Mammy (19).[38]

By linking the image of the strong Black woman to the stereotype of the "mammy," Danquah points to the history of slavery in the United States as one of its possible origins. As Patricia Hill Collins observes, the figure of the "mammy," or the "faithful, obedient domestic servant," was invented in order to "justify the economic exploitation of house slaves" (71). Danquah's contestation of the ideal of an inherently strong Black womanhood thus resists the social demand that Black women deny their own emotional and material needs in order to attend to those of others.[39] As Evelyn C. White writes, "the vulnerability exposed in *Willow Weep for Me* . . . will do much to transform society's image of Black women as sturdy bridges to everyone's healing except their own" (Danquah NP).

Paradoxically, while the notion that Black women are uniquely equipped to endure hardship has historically served as a justification for their oppression, it may also have enabled their survival. "Given the history of black women in this country," Danquah argues, "one can easily understand how this pretense of strength was at one time necessary for survival" (NP). The belief that strength is a legacy of slavery persists in Black communities, Danquah remarks, pointing out that it is not only white people who dismiss Black women's depression. "If our people could make it through slavery, we can make it through anything," Black men and women have told Danquah (21). But what this "stereotypic image of strength . . . requires" of Black women, Danquah emphasizes, "is not really strength at all. It is stoicism. It is denial. It is a complete negation of their pain" (NP).[40]

Because Black women's emotional suffering is generally regarded as normative and unproblematic—"part of the package," as Danquah puts it—rather than symptomatic of a condition in need of a remedy, Danquah's pathologization of her distress cannot be seen as merely an accession to the social norms upon which the category of "mental illness" depends; rather, by defining her suffering as sickness, Danquah

transgresses the expectation that when Black women suffer, they do so silently and stoically (19). Refusing any denial of her pain, Danquah unflinchingly describes the shame and self-loathing that are both symptoms and sources of her depression. She relates that amid a severe episode of depression she stopped bathing and cleaning her house, leaving "a trail of undergarments and other articles of clothing" on the floor, "dishes with decaying food" on "every counter and tabletop" (28). She recalls feeling "truly pitiful," "hating myself so much I wanted to die" (219; 106). "Something had gone wrong with me," she realizes (29).

This conclusion may seem at odds with one of the central messages of the disability rights movement. Oliver's critique of the medical model on the grounds that it "tends to regard disabled people as 'having something wrong with them' and hence [being] the source of the problem" is a tenet of disability studies ("Social," 20). And while I certainly do not wish to reinstall hegemonic constructions of disability as a form of individual weakness or inferiority, I would suggest that in Danquah's narrative it's more complicated than a simple opposition between an individual and a social problem. Rather than imagining a wall of immunity between self and society, Danquah dramatizes the impossibility of ever remaining untouched by all that is wrong in the world (29). And her recognition that something has "gone wrong" with her is neither an indictment of herself as "the source of the problem" nor a cause of shame; instead, it is the impetus for her decision to make "a commitment to being alive" (Oliver, 20; Danquah, 230).

This commitment requires a valuing of herself that contrasts sharply with the "stereotypic image of strength" with which "African American women who are battling depression must, unfortunately, contend" (Danquah NP). The strength that Danquah displays—and it would be impossible to come away from her book without feeling the magnitude of that strength—is neither endurance nor self-sacrifice; rather, it is what Danquah describes as a readiness "to claim the life that I want" (266).

SHALL WE OVERCOME?

Danquah's memoir about depression ends on a hopeful note. "Having lived with the pain," she writes, "I know now that when you pass through it, there is beauty on the other side" (266). Indeed, as her book's subtitle indicates, hers is a "Black woman's journey *through* depression" (emphasis mine). As such, *Willow Weep for Me* could be read as a story of overcoming. The blurb on the back cover of the paperback edition promises "an inspirational story of healing," and Danquah herself employs many of the linguistic conventions associated with overcoming narratives. It takes "courage, devotion, and resilience" to "contend with depression" and to "triumph" over the illness, she writes (262). Such an emphasis on individual strength is at the crux of what many disability scholars critique in narratives of overcoming. As Simi Linton argues, "the ideas embedded in the *overcoming* rhetoric are of personal triumph over a personal condition," rather than a collective demand for "social change" (18). There is enormous value in this observation, and I wholeheartedly concur with Linton's objections to representations of disability that make "the individual's responsibility for her or his own success . . . paramount" (19). But as we have seen, the opposition between disability as personal misfortune and as social problem is not tenable in Danquah's autopathography, which understands depression as inextricably both of these things. And if despair is both a cause and a symptom of depression, then perhaps part of its solution is a hope that is both personal and political.[41] As Danquah explains, "The social and

economic realities of women, blacks, single parents, or any combination of the three" make "my chances for a life that is free of depression appear to be slim . . . While I recognize the importance of such information, I regard most of the data as blather and refuse to embrace it" (257). This refusal is not a denial of political realities; rather, it is an unwillingness to accept defeat, an assertion of personal strength amid overwhelming social oppression. As Danquah puts it, it is a "standing up in defiance of those things which had kept me silent and suffering to say that I, an African American woman, have made this journey through depression" (NP).

NOTES

I would like to thank Richard Ingram, Robert McRuer, and Sue Schweik for their feedback on earlier versions of this essay.

1. See Garland-Thomson 135–37; Linton 17–19; and Mitchell and Snyder 9–11. See also note 21 below.
2. Lack of access to health care is tied to the politics of both race and class. Cultural, linguistic, and geographical barriers, as well as racist stereotypes, present specific impediments for African American, Latino/a, Asian American, and Native American people seeking medical treatment for depression, regardless of income level and health insurance status ("Mental"). Access to health care has received less attention in disability studies than in the disability rights movement, where it has often been the focus of organizing.
3. Born in Ghana, Danquah emigrates to the United States when she is six years old (103). Although being an immigrant is of great importance to Danquah's self-definition, this aspect of her identity receives far less attention in her memoir than race, gender, class, or mental illness.
4. A special issue of *GLQ, Desiring Disability: Queer Theory Meets Disability Studies* (2003), edited by Robert McRuer and Abby Wilkerson, is devoted to the topic of queerness and disability.
5. In the introduction to *The Body and Physical Difference*, David T. Mitchell and Sharon L. Snyder write that "while literary and cultural studies have resurrected social identities such as gender, sexuality, class, and race from . . . obscurity and neglect . . . disability has suffered a distinctly

different disciplinary fate" (1–2). Barnes and Mercer draw a "sharp contrast" between the reception of disability studies in academia and that of "radical analyses of racism and sexism that quickly won favor" (IS, 4). Recently, leading disability scholars and activists have made similar comparisons between race and disability in their discussions of Clint Eastwood's 2005 film, *Million Dollar Baby* (Drake and Johnson, 1; Davis "Why," 2). And the chairman of Britain's Disability Rights Commission, Bert Massie, recently stated that "neglect and institutionalized exclusion" of disabled people is "more profound" than that of Black people ("Massie," 1).

6. Samuels's suggestion is part of her extended analysis of the dynamics of "passing" and "coming out" for queer people, racial minorities, and people with disabilities. For critiques of the "like race" analogy in queer theory and activism, see Janet E. Halley and Janet R. Jakobsen.

7. For critiques of additive models of racism and sexism, see Barbara Smith and Elizabeth Spelman. An example of an additive representation of intersectionality in disability studies is Davis's assertion that "the most oppressed person in the world is a disabled female, Third World, homosexual, woman of color" (BOB, 29). This formulation, while a useful beginning, leaves untheorized the specific ways in which various forms of oppression come together in individual lives.

8. The Surgeon General reports that "the prevalence of mental disorders for racial and ethnic minorities in the United States is similar to that for whites." These statistics, however, apply only to those "living in the community"; people who are "homeless, incarcerated, or institutionalized" have higher rates of all forms of mental illness ("Mental" 1). According to the American Psychological Association, women are twice as likely as men to suffer from depression; the reasons for this discrepancy remain controversial ("New," 1).

9. Information about the psychiatric survivor movement can be found at the Mind Freedom Support Coalition International Web site: http://www.mindfreedom.org/

10. Courts have long recognized that patients with physical illnesses or disabilities have the right to refuse medical treatment. This constitutional protection, however, has often been denied to people diagnosed with mental illness, who can be committed to mental institutions and treated involuntarily with toxic drugs and other potentially harmful therapies. In many states, involuntary outpatient treatment is also authorized by the courts. For more on this, see Jackson and Winick.

11. The side effects of ECT can be severe and permanent, as can those of neuroleptics, the medications most commonly prescribed for schizophrenia and other "psychotic" illnesses. The chemical effects of neuroleptic drugs are similar to those produced by lobotomies (Breggin, TP, 68–91).

12. Jeanine Grobe aptly compares the most common modern-day psychiatric practices to medieval treatments for "insanity": "[M]ore often than not, [contemporary psychiatric] "medicine" is a complete atrocity—comparable only to the history out of which it grew: is four-point restraint—being tied down at the wrists and ankles—an improvement over being bound with chains? Is the cage inhumane whereas the seclusion room is not? Are the deaths that result from the use of neuroleptic drugs better than the deaths that resulted from bloodletting? Is the terror inspired by the passing of electric current through the brain an improvement over the shock of being submerged in ice water?" (103).

13. The back of *Willow Weep for Me* includes the transcript of an interview of Danquah by Dr. Freda C. Lewis-Hall, director of the Lilly Center for Women's Health, which is part of Eli Lilly, the pharmaceutical company that manufactures Prozac. Danquah has also given book tours in conjunction with the National Mental Health Association's Campaign on Clinical Depression, which is funded by Eli Lilly (http://www.psych.org/pnews/98-05-15/nmha.html). This may raise concerns about bias in Danquah's representations of the benefits of psychoactive medications. However, *Willow Weep for Me* can hardly be said to read like an advertisement for antidepressants. As noted, Danquah expresses concern about their widespread use. In addition, she details the debilitating side effects she experienced from taking Zoloft. Most important, Danquah's memoir certainly does not understand depression as simply a biological illness that can be cured with drug therapy. If, as she claims, depression "exists somewhere in that ghost space between consciousness and chemistry," her interest in the former greatly exceeds her attention to the latter; describing only briefly her experiences with various medications, Danquah foregrounds her personal struggles and the political contexts in which they take place. I would like to thank Jonathan Metzl for bringing Danquah's relationship with Eli Lilly to my attention.

14. A 2001 Surgeon General's report on these disparities indicates that "racial and ethnic minorities" in the U.S. receive "less care and poorer

quality of care" than white people ("Mental"). And a 2000 study of the treatment of people already diagnosed with depression—controlled for age, gender, health insurance status, and other factors—found a striking disparity: 44 percent of white patients and 27.8 percent of Black patients were given antidepressant medication (UT, 70).

15. Anne Wilson and Peter Beresford describe this double bind as an "increasing polarization of madness and distress into two categories—of the 'threateningly mad' and the 'worried well'" (153). Reflecting psychiatry's distinction between "psychoses" and "neuroses," these categories "serve both to dismiss and to devalue the experience and distress of those of us not seen as 'ill' enough to require public resources for support, and to reinforce assumptions about a discrete and separate group of mad people that constitutes a threat to the rest of society" (154; 153).

16. For discussions of the misperception of depression as an illness affecting only white people, see Boyd (5–7) and Marano (2).

17. In Rhonda Collins's documentary film, *We Don't Live under Normal Conditions*, people of various races and ethnicities discuss what it means to them to be depressed; most, but not all, see the origins of their distress as primarily social. Most of the depression memoirs published in the last decade in the United States are authored by white people, many of whom describe the benefits of antidepressants. See Styron, Wurtzel, Solomon, and Jamison.

18. See *Unequal Treatment* 611–21. These discrepancies are well documented and alarming. For example, a 1993 study "found that 79 percent of African Americans in a public-sector hospital were diagnosed with schizophrenia, compared with 43 percent of whites" (613). In another study, "28 percent of African Americans in a university hospital emergency room were given such a diagnosis, compared with 20 percent of whites." A 1996 study found that "African American patients seen in an emergency room received 50 percent higher doses of antipsychotic medications than patients of other ethnic groups, while their doctors devoted less time to assessing them" (613). In a 1998 study, researchers asked psychiatrists to provide diagnoses of patients based upon written case histories. The psychiatrists each reviewed identical case histories, but their diagnoses varied widely, depending on what they were told the patients' race and gender were. The diagnosis of "paranoid schizophrenic disorder," which, the authors of the study note, is associated with "violence, suspiciousness, and dangerousness," was applied to patients believed to be Black men at a rate of 43 percent, compared with 6 percent for white men, 10 percent for white women, and 12 percent for Black women (615).

19. An awareness of the medical profession's pathologizing attitudes toward Black people deters many African Americans from seeking health care, especially for symptoms of mental illness. Psychological studies in reputable journals in the 1950s compared average Africans to "the white mental patient," "the lobotomized West European," and the "traditional psychopath" (L.R.C. Haward and W.A. Roland, "Some intercultural differences on the Draw-A-Person Test: Part I, Goodenough scores," *Man* 54 [1954], p. 87, qtd. in Bulhan, 83–84; J.C. Carothers, "The African mind in health and disease," Geneva, World Health Organization, 1953, qtd. in Bulhan, 84). The 1965 Moynihan Report claimed that African American families were disintegrating because of their putatively "matriarchal" structure (Boyd, "Ethnic," 230). In the 1960s and 1970s, respected neurosurgeons and psychiatrists publishing in venues such as the *Journal of the American Medical Association* advocated psychosurgery to treat the "brain disease" they claimed caused "riots and urban violence" (Breggin, WA, 117). In the early 1990s, Frederick Goodwin, the chief scientist at the National Institute of Mental Health, proposed a "violence initiative," which would identify among "inner-city" adolescents—whom Goodwin compared to monkeys in a jungle— those with a genetic predisposition to violence and then subject them to psychiatric interventions (Breggin, WA 8).

20. See Barnes and Mercer (IS, 2) and Oliver (PD, 11). Although the social model's authors intended it to serve primarily as a "heuristic device," rather than a comprehensive theory of disability, its distinction between impairment and disability remains fundamental to disability scholarship in both the UK and the United States (Barnes and Mercer, IS, 3).

21. The concluding chapter of Garland-Thomson's *Extraordinary Bodies* calls for a shift in understanding disability, "From Pathology to Identity." Steven Taylor argues that "a Disability Studies perspective questions the medical model and challenges" the equation of disability with "sickness and pathology" ("Guidelines," 4). Steven E. Brown states that "a person with a disability is not sick" (11). Barnes and Mercer criticize representations of people with disabilities as "sick" or "suffering" (*Disability*, 9; 10). And Simon Brisenden urges a differentiation "between a disability and a disease" (25). Asserting that "disability is not illness," Anita Silvers acknowledges that

chronic illnesses can be disabling but insists that "persons with paradigmatic disabilities—paraplegia, blindness, deafness, and others" must be distinguished from "people suffering from illness" (77). David Pfeiffer also emphasizes that "disability is not sickness" and claims that "for a half to three quarters of the disability community there is no present sickness which disables them" (6). Pfeiffer doesn't make clear, in his estimate of the statistical prevalence of illness among people with disabilities, how he defines the "disability community."

22. See Harlan Hahn, *The Issue of Equality: European Perceptions of Employment Policy for Disabled Persons* [New York: World Rehabilitation Fund, 1984], 14, qtd. in Hahn, "Advertising," 175.

23. This is not to suggest that suffering is the most important aspect of depression for everyone who experiences it. Jane Phillips describes her depression as a "dark and dangerous illness," but also as an experience that "seemed to serve a function," facilitating her emergence "into an utterly new spring" (140–41). I am grateful to Richard Ingram for bringing this passage to my attention.

24. Deconstructions of the social model share similarities with "universalizing" approaches to disability in the United States, which, rather than conceiving of people with disabilities as members of a distinct minority group, instead highlight the fluidity of disability as an identity category and describe bodily difference as existing on a continuum of human variation.

25. Danquah's assertion is tautological (illnesses, by definition, are conditions that "reach clinical proportions"); however, I am concerned here, not with establishing the "truth" or "falsity" of the claim that depression is an illness, but rather with delineating the tactical and strategic uses to which its construction as such is put. I would like to thank Richard Ingram for pointing out to me the tautological nature of Danquah's statement.

26. In the eighteenth century the physical examination was regarded as so unimportant that doctors often practiced medicine by mail, relying on patients' lengthy narratives to make diagnoses (Reiser, 5–6).

27. For detailed accounts of the history of clinical medicine, see Foucault (BC), Ackernecht, and Jewson.

28. There are exceptions to this trend, most of which are also invisible disabilities: "mental illnesses"; some cognitive disabilities; and physical conditions such as chronic fatigue syndrome, repetitive strain injury, Environmental Illness, and fibromyalgia, which don't produce objectively observable bodily changes. But most of these conditions, like depression, are "controversial"; they will be defined as "syndromes" rather than actual "diseases" until they can be correlated with measurable physiological abnormalities.

29. Disorders such as these illustrate the impossibility of any absolute binary between "visible" and "invisible" disabilities. These conditions may often be invisible to the casual observer, but their signs can be seen on medical tests. Notwithstanding medical technologies that rely on senses other than sight, the visual bias of modern medical epistemology is pronounced; it can be discerned even the word "stethoscope," which combines the Greek words for "chest" and "I view" (Reiser, 25).

30. Nonverbal people with disabilities can also be diagnosed with depression, but the formation of depression as an impairment category has depended in large part upon patients' verbal articulations of their distress.

31. I would like to thank Richard Ingram for pointing this out to me.

32. My comparison between Danquah's political strategy and that of the nineteenth-century "homosexual" Foucault describes illustrates the limits of analogies between different subject positions. Despite the similarities I will discuss, Danquah's desire to be cured contrasts with the nineteenth-century "homosexual"'s demands to be accepted as such. I would like to thank Sue Schweik for pointing this difference out to me.

33. For example, see "Cognitive" (3).

34. While I share Tremain's sense that it is "politically naïve to suggest that the term 'impairment' is value-neutral," I nonetheless hope to show that it is possible to cite impairment categories without merely reinforcing normalizing discourses (SI, 34).

35. This characterization is consistent with the overall thrust of Tremain's argument. In "On the Subject of Impairment" (2002), Tremain touches briefly on Foucault's concept of discursive reversibility, noting that the "disciplinary apparatus of the state . . . brings into discourse the very conditions for subverting that apparatus" (44). She maintains, however, that by "articulating our lived experiences" in ways that "continue to animate the regulatory fictions of 'impairment,'" disabled people risk merely augmenting normalizing and homogenizing social processes (44; 45). Similarly, in one paragraph of her introduction to *Foucault and the Government of Disability* (2005), Tremain notes Foucault's interest in the "strategic reversibility" engendered by hegemonic discourses but nonetheless reiterates the central claims of her earlier essay.

36. I strongly concur with Tremain's argument for a disability theory that will "expose the disciplinary character of . . . identity," rather than "ground[ing] its claims to entitlement in that identity" (SI, 44; FG, 10). In fact, Tremain's criticisms of identity-based movements parallel arguments I make in my essay, "Disability Studies and Identity Politics: A Critique of Recent Theory." I share Tremain's view that identity politics risks reifying identity categories that might better be contested, is almost inevitably exclusionary and productive of hierarchies, and impedes alliances with other political minorities. Indeed, I am trying to make these problems apparent in my discussion of the ways in which entrenched ideas within disability studies exclude experiences such as Danquah describes in her memoir. But I am also attempting to demonstrate that Danquah utilizes her self-definition as a "depressive" in ways that do not replicate these dynamics of identity politics movements (18).

37. This discrepancy again exemplifies the limitations of analogies between different forms of oppression. Butler asks, "When and how does a term like 'queer' become subject to an affirmative resignification for some when a term like 'nigger,' despite some recent efforts at reclamation, appears capable of only reinscribing its pain?" (223). For Danquah, such reinscription is also the inevitable effect of hearing this word repeated. She remembers the first time she was called a 'nigger' to her face, by a high school boy she had asked to dance: "Even now when I hear that word—*nigger*—whether it is spoken by a black person or a white person, it is the simple tone and disgust of that boy's voice that I hear" (43).

38. Boyd also observes that it can be difficult to reconcile "beliefs about being strong Black women" with "having an illness that we've long associated with weakness of the lowest kind" (CI, 5). Similarly, Angela Mitchell observes that "one reason Black women don't get treated for depression is that we often expect to feel sad, tired, and unable to think straight" (47). She reminds her readers that "Black women do not have to be depressed. It is not our lot in life" (47). The perception that depression is a form of weakness that Black women cannot "afford" is addressed on numerous web sites about Black women and depression (Marano, 2). See Rouse, 6.

39. Mitchell also connects the "mammy stereotype," which is "rooted in the history of slavery," to Black women's depression, arguing that this stereotype creates an imperative for Black women to prioritize other others' needs over their own (53; 56).

40. Similarly, bell hooks has asserted that "to be strong in the face of oppression is not the same as overcoming oppression . . . endurance is not be confused with transformation" (qtd. in Mitchell, 69). Mitchell makes this point as well: Black women's endurance of "suffering and hardship," she argues, should not be confused with "strength" (69).

41. Wilson and Beresford describe the damaging repercussions of constructions of mental illness that "leave the holder of the diagnosis feeling utterly hopeless" and create a social expectation that those who have been diagnosed with mental illness "can never fully recover" (150). In addition, numerous African American feminists, activists, and critical race theorists have argued for the importance of hope and optimism, on both an individual and a collective level. Alex Mercedes, an African American woman who is a subject of Collins's documentary, argues that "it's important to focus on the individual . . . because the revolution will not happen overnight . . . so in the meantime, I, as an individual, must walk through this sexist, patriarchal hell." Harris criticizes white feminism for its focus on "victimization and misery" and insists upon women's ability to "shape their own lives" (613). Warning against the danger of a "capitulation to a sense of inevitable doom," Patricia Williams expresses an "optimistic conviction" of the possibility of both "institutional power to make change" and "the individual will to change" (64; 65; 68). And in the introduction to *The Black Women's Health Book*, White is hopeful about Black women's power to "address and overcome the numerous issues that have damaged" their health, in part through individual "resilience and stalwart determination" (xiv; xvi).

WORKS CITED

Ackernecht, Erwin M. *Medicine at the Paris Hospital 1794–1848*. Baltimore: Johns Hopkins University Press, 1976.

Barnes, Colin, and Geof Mercer, eds. *Implementing the Social Model of Disability: Theory and Research*. Leeds, UK: The Disability Press, 2004. Cited within the text as IS.

——. *Disability*. Cambridge, UK: Blackwell, 2003.

Boyd, Julia A. *Can I Get a Witness?: Black Women and Depression*. New York: Penguin, 1999. Cited within the text as CI.

——. "Ethnic and Cultural Diversity in Feminist Therapy: Keys to Power." In *The Black Women's Health Book: Speaking for Ourselves*, edited by Evelyn

C. White, 226–34. Seattle, Washington: Seal Press, 1990. Cited within the text as "Ethnic."

Breggin, Peter R., M.D. *Toxic Psychiatry: Why Therapy, Empathy, and Love Must Replace the Drugs, Electroshock, and Biochemical Theories of the "New Psychiatry."* New York: St. Martin's Press, 1991. Cited within the text as TP.

Breggin, Peter R., M.D., and Ginger Ross Breggin. *The War against Children.* New York: St. Martin's Press, 1994. Cited within the text as WA.

Brisenden, Simon. "Independent Living and the Medical Model." In *The Disability Reader: Social Science Perspectives*, edited by Tom Shakespeare, 20–7. London and New York: Cassell, 1998.

Brown, Steven. "Freedom of Movement: Independent Living History and Philosophy." Independent Living Research Utilization. Available online at http://www.ilru.org/html/publications/bookshelf/freedom_movement.html (1–20).

Bulhan, Hussein Abdilahi. *Frantz Fanon and the Psychology of Oppression.* New York and London: Plenum Press, 1985.

Clare, Eli. *Exile and Pride: Disability, Queerness, and Liberation.* Cambridge, Massachusetts: South End Press, 1999.

Collins, Patricia Hill. *Black Feminist Thought: Knowledge, Consciousness, and the Politics of Empowerment.* New York and London: Routledge, 1991.

Collins, Rhonda, dir. *We Don't Live under Normal Conditions.* Videocassette. Boston, Massachusetts: Fanlight Productions, 2000.

"Cognitive Therapy for Depression." Available online at *Psychology Information Online* http://www.psychologyinfo.com/depression/cognitive.htm#lifeexperiences (1–7). Cited within the text as "Cognitive."

Crow, Liz. "Including All of Our Lives: Renewing the Social Model of Disability." In *Exploring the Divide: Illness and Disability*, edited by Colin Barnes and Geof Mercer, 55–73. Leeds, UK: The Disability Press, 1996.

Danquah, Meri Nana-Ama. *Willow Weep for Me: A Black Woman's Journey Through Depression.* New York: Ballantine, 1998.

Davis, Lennard J.. *Enforcing Normalcy: Disability, Deafness, and the Body.* London and New York: Verso, 1995. Cited within the text as EN.

——. *Bending Over Backwards: Disability, Dismodernism and Other Difficult Positions.* Foreword Michael Bérubé. New York: New York University Press, 2002. Cited within the text as BOB.

——. "Why 'Million Dollar Baby' infuriates the disabled." *The Chicago Tribune.* February 2, 2005. Available online at http://metromix.chicagotribune.com/movies/mmx-0502020017feb02,0,6865906.story (1–3). Cited within the text as "Why."

Drake, Stephen and Mary Johnson. "Movies about disabled keep myths alive." *Chicago Sun-Times.* February 12, 2005. Available online at http://www.suntimes.com/output/otherviews/cst-edt-ref12.html (1–2).

Foucault, Michel. *The Birth of the Clinic: An Archeology of Medical Perception.* Translated by A. M. Sheridan Smith. New York: Random House, 1973. Cited within the text as BC.

——. *The History of Sexuality.* Volume I: An Introduction. Translated by Robert Hurley. New York: Random House, 1978. Cited within the text as HS.

——. "Two Lectures." *Power/Knowledge: Selected Interviews and Other Writings, 1972–1977.* Pantheon Books, 1980. Cited within the text as TL.

Garland-Thomson, Rosemarie. *Extraordinary Bodies: Figuring Physical Disability in American Culture in Literature.* New York: Columbia University Press, 1997.

Grillo, Trina and Stephanie M. Wildman. "Obscuring the Importance of Race: The Implications of Making Comparisons between Racism and Sexism (or Other Isms)." In *Critical White Studies: Looking Behind the Mirror*, edited by Richard Delgado and Jean Stefancic, 619–626. Philadelphia: Temple University Press, 1997.

Grobe, Jeanine, ed. *Beyond Bedlam: Contemporary Women Psychiatric Survivors Speak Out.* Chicago: Third Side Press, 1995.

"Guidelines for Disability Studies: Highlights of a 2004 SDS Listserv Discussion." *Disability Studies Quarterly* 24.4 (Fall 2004). Available online at http://www.dsq-sds.org/_articles_html/2004/fall/dsq_fall04_listserv.asp (1–14). Cited within the text as "Guidelines."

Hahn, Harlan. "Advertising the Acceptably Employable Image: Disability and Capitalism." In *The Disability Studies Reader*, edited by. Lennard J. Davis, 172–86. New York: Routledge, 1997. Cited within the text as "Advertising."

Halley, Janet E. "'Like Race' Arguments." In *What's Left of Theory?: New Work on the Politics of Literary Theory*, edited by Judith Butler, John Guillory, and Kendall Thomas, 40–74. New York: Routledge, 2000.

Halperin, David M. *Saint Foucault: Towards a Gay Hagiography.* New York and Oxford: Oxford UP, 1995.

Harris, Angela P. "Race and Essentialism in Feminist Legal Theory." *Stanford Law Review* 42.3 (February, 1990): 581–616.

Hughes, Bill, and Kevin Paterson. "The Social Model of Disability and the Disappearing Body: Towards a Sociology of Impairment." *Disability & Society* 12.3 (1997): 325–40.

Jackson, Grace E., M.D. "The Right to Refuse Treatment." Available online at http://psychrights.org/Articles/rightorefuse.htm

Jakobsen, Janet R. "Queers Are like Jews, Aren't They? Analogy and Alliance Politics." In *Queer Theory and the Jewish Question*, edited by Daniel Boyarin, Daniel Itzkovitz, and Ann Pellegrini, 64–89. New York: Columbia University Press, 2003.

Jamison, Kay Redfield. *An Unquiet Mind: A Memoir of Moods and Madness*. New York: Random House, 1995.

Jewson, N. D. "The Disappearance of the Sick-Man from Medical Cosmology, 1770–1870." *Sociology*. 10.2 (May 1976): 225–244.

Linton, Simi. *Claiming Disability: Knowledge and Identity*. Foreword Michael Bérubé. New York: New York University Press, 1998.

Marano, Hara Estroff. "Race and the Blues." *Psychology Today*. Available online at http://cms.psychologytoday.com/articles/pto-20030930-000001.html

"Massie: exclusion 'more profound' for disabled people." *Ouch!* BBC.co.uk. June 16, 2005. Available online at http://www.bbc.co.uk/ouch/news/btn/massie_exclusion.shtml. Cited within the text as "Massie."

McRuer, Robert and Abby Wilkerson, eds. *GLQ: A Journal of Lesbian and Gay Studies. Desiring Disability: Queer Theory Meets Disability Studies*. 9.1–2 (2003).

"Mental Health: Culture, Race, and Ethnicity Supplement." U.S. Department of Health and Human Services, Office of the Surgeon General. Available online at http://www.mentalhealth.org/cre/execsummary-2.asp (1–4). Cited within the text as "Mental."

Mitchell, Angela. *What the Blues Is All About: Black Women Overcoming Stress and Depression*. With Kennise Herring, Ph.D. New York: Penguin, 1998.

Mitchell, David T. and Sharon L. Snyder, Eds. *The Body and Physical Difference: Discourses of Disability*. Foreword James I. Porter. Ann Arbor: The University of Michigan Press, 1997.

Mollow, Anna. "Disability Studies and Identity Politics: A Critique of Recent Theory." *Michigan Quarterly Review* 43.2 (Spring 2004): 269–96.

"New Report on Women and Depression: Latest Research Findings and Recommendations." Press Release. American Psychological Association. March 15, 2002. Available online at http://www.apa.org/releases/depressionreport.html (1–5). Cited within the text as "New."

Oliver, Michael. *The Politics of Disablement*. London: Macmillan, 1990. Cited within the text as PD.

——. *Understanding Disabilty: From Theory to Practice*. Houndmills, UK: Palgrave, 1996. Cited within the text as UD.

——. "The Social Model in Action: If I Had a Hammer." *Implementing the Social Model of Disability:* *Theory and Research*. Ed Colin Barnes and Geof Mercer. Leeds, UK: The Disability Press, 2004. 18–31. Cited within the text as "Social."

Pfeiffer, David. "The ICIDH and the Need for Its Revision." *Disability & Society* 13.4 (September 1998): 503–23.

Phillips, Jane. *The Magic Daughter: A Memoir of Living with Multiple Personality Disorder*. New York: Penguin, 1995.

Porter, Roy. *The Greatest Benefit to Mankind: A Medical History of Humanity*. New York: W. W. Norton & Company, 1997.

Reiser, Stanley Joel. *Medicine and the Reign of Technology*. Cambridge: Cambridge University Press, 1978.

Rouse, Deborah L. "Lives of Women of Color Create Risk for Depression." *Women's ENews*. http://www.womensenews.org/article.cfm/dyn/aid/666, October 1, 2001. 1–6 (web pagination).

Samuels, Ellen. "My Body, My Closet: Invisible Disability and the Limits of Coming-Out Discourse." *GLQ: A Journal of Lesbian and Gay Studies* 9.1–2 (2003): 233–55.

Silvers, Anita. "Formal Justice." In *Disability, Difference, and Discrimination: Perspectives on Justice in Bioethics and Public Policy*, edited by Anita Silvers, David Wasserman, and Mary B. Mahowald, 13–146. Lanham, MD: Rowan & Littlefield, 1998.

Smith, Barbara. "Notes for Yet Another Paper on Black Feminism, or Will the Real Enemy Please Stand Up?" *Conditions* 5 (1979): 123–142.

Smith, Bonnie G., and Beth Hutchinson, Eds. *Gendering Disability*. New Brunswick, New Jersey, and London: Rutgers University Press, 2004.

Solomon, Andrew. *The Noonday Demon: An Atlas of Depression*. New York: Simon & Schuster, 2001.

Spelman, Elizabeth V. *Inessential Woman: Problems of Exclusion in Feminist Thought*. Boston: Beacon Press, 1988.

Styron, William. *Darkness Visible: A Memoir of Madness*. New York: Random House, 1990.

Tremain, Shelley. "On the Subject of Impairment." *Disability/Postmodernity*. Ed. Mairian Corker and Tom Shakespeare. London: Continuum, 2002. 1–24. Cited within the text as SI.

——. "Foucault, Governmentality, and Critical Disability Theory: An Introduction." In *Foucault and the Government of Disability*, edited by Shelley Tremain. Ann Arbor: University of Michigan Press, 2005. Cited within the text as FG.

Unequal Treatment: Confronting Racial and Ethnic Disparities in Health Care. Ed. Brian D. Smedley, Adrienne Y. Stith, and Alan R. Nelson. Committee on Understanding and Ending Racial and Ethnic Disparities in Health Care. Board on the Health Science Policy. Institute of Medicine of the National

Academy. Washington, DC: The National Academy Press, 2003. Cited within the text as UT.

UPIAS. *Fundamental Principles of Disability.* London: Union of Physically Impaired against Segregation, 1976. Available online at http://www.leeds.ac.uk/disability-studies/archiveuk/UPIAS/fundamental%20principles.pdf

Wendell, Susan. "Unhealthy Disabled: Treating Chronic Illnesses as Disabilities." *Hypatia* 16.4 (2001) 17–33.

White, Evelyn C., ed. *The Black Women's Health Book: Speaking for Ourselves*, 226–34. Seattle, Washington: Seal Press, 1990.

Williams, Patricia J. *Seeing a Color-Blind Future: The Paradox of Race.* The 1997 BBC Reith Lectures. New York: Farrar, Straus and Giroux, 1997.

Wilson, Anne and Peter Beresford. "Madness, Distress and Postmodernity: Putting the Record Straight." In *Disability/Postmodernity*, edited by Mairian Corker and Tom Shakespeare, 143–58. London: Continuum, 2002.

Winick, Bruce J. *The Right to Refuse Mental Health Treatment.* Washington, DC: American Psychological Association, 1997.

Wurtzel, Elizabeth. *Prozac Nation: Young and Depressed in America.* Second edition. New York: Riverhead Books, 1995.

CHAPTER 37

The Enfreakment of Photography

David Hevey

Before reading this chapter, I feel I must contextualise what lies ahead for the reader. In many ways, charity advertising as oppressive imagery appears to be the *bête noire* of disabled people. Unfortunately, oppressive as it is, it represents colours of a social order tied to a specific mast. Those colours and constructions also exist in other areas of photographic representation. This is demonstrated in this chapter. I ask the reader to join me on a journey into oppressive disability imagery. At times, particularly in the examination of the work of Diane Arbus, it can be depressing. However this chapter is here because I feel we have to take the fight against constructed oppression (whether by non-access or by representation) into the camp of the oppressors.

Apart from charity advertising, when did you last see a picture of a disabled person? It almost certainly wasn't in commercial advertising since disabled people are not thought to constitute a body of consumers and therefore do not generally warrant inclusion. It might have been within an "in-house" health service magazine, in which disabled people are positioned to enflesh the theories of their oppressors. The stories might range from the successes of a toxic drugs company to the latest body armour for people with cerebral palsy, and some

person with proverbial "disease" will be shown illustrating the solution and its usefulness. It might have been in an educational magazine, in which a non-disabled "facilitator" will regale in words and text the latest prototype "image-workshop," using disabled people as guinea pigs while developing their "educational" ideas. The text brags about the colonization of disabled people's bodies and identities, while the images show how much "the disabled" enjoyed it. Passive and still and "done to," the images bear a bizarre resemblance to colonial pictures where "the blacks" stand frozen and curious, while "whitey" lounges confident and sure. Whitey knows the purpose of this image, the black people appear not to (or at least, perhaps as employees, have no right to record visual dissent).

The "positive" side of their ultra-minority inclusion, then, is that disabled people are there to demonstrate the successes of their administrators.[1] Apart from the above areas, however, disabled people are almost entirely absent from photographic genres or discussion because they are read as socially dead and as not having a role to play. But although the absence is near absolute, the non-representation of disabled people is not quite total. Taking the structured absence as given, I wanted to discover the terms on which disabled people *were* admitted into photographic representation. As Mary Daly once wrote of feminism, the job entails being a full-time, low-paid researcher of your own destiny.[2]

I visited one of the largest photographic bookshops in London and leafed through the publications. Generally disabled people were absent, but there was a sort of presence. Disabled people are represented but almost exclusively as symbols of "otherness" placed within equations which have no engagement to them and which take their non-integration as a natural by-product of their impairment.

I picked books at random. *The Family of Man; Another Way of Telling; diane arbus; Figments from the Real World*. There were obviously lateral associations but only one, *diane arbus*, I knew to include images of disabled people. In the research for this book, I had begun to uncover sometimes hidden, sometimes open, but always continuous constructions of disabled people as outsiders admitted into culture as symbols of fear or pity. This was particularly true in literature[3] but I wanted to see if it held true in photography, so I picked the books at random. They may have been connected in styles or schools but, as far as I knew, had no connection whatsoever on disability representation. Only Arbus was infamous for having centred disabled people in her work but I felt an uneasy faith that all of them would "use" disabled people somewhere.

The first book examined was entitled *The Family of Man*.[4] The Family of Man exhibition at the Museum of Modern Art, New York, in 1955 is considered the seminal exhibition for humanist-realist photography. It was the photographic height of postwar idealism. It showed the great "positive image" of an unproblematised and noble world—a world from which pain was banished. Where there are images of "working folk," their muscles and their sweat appear to be a part of the great spiritual order of things. Where there are images of black people, the images show poverty; some show harmony, but all are visually poetic. Black life has been harmonised through aesthetics.

However, throughout the catalogue of the show, which contained 503 images show from 68 countries by 273 male and female photographers, there is only one photograph of someone identifiably disabled. This is more than an oversight. Put together ten years after the Second World War, *The Family of Man* was about "positively" forgetting the past and all its misery. Forward into glory, backward into pain! Although this publication and exhibition heralded a brave new world of postwar hope and harmony, on reading it it becomes clear that the inclusion of disabled people—even disabled people tidied up like black people and working people—was not a part of the postwar visual nirvana. Why was this?

The one image of a disabled person appears on the penultimate page of the 192-page publication. It is mixed in among six other images on that page and is part of the final section of the book, which covers children. Children are shown laughing, playing, dancing, crying and so on. Of the thirty-eight images in this section, three buck this trend. The three are all on this penultimate page. In the final section, after five pages of innocent joy, you encounter on the sixth page three that remind you it is not like that always. At the top of these three is a disabled boy who appears to be a below-the-knee amputee. He is racing along the beach with a crutch under his right arm. He is playing and chasing a football. His body tilts to our right as he approaches the ball, while his crutch tilts to our left, to form a shape like an open and upright compass. The ball is situated in the triangle which his left leg and his right-side crutch make on the sand. The triangle shape is completed by a shadow which the boy casts from his right leg to the crutch (and beyond). The ball enters this triangle focusing point but his right leg does not. Its absence is accentuated and impairment here is read as loss. The game he plays is his personal effort to overcome his loss.

The photograph creates a flowing but awkward symmetry and our reading of its flow is continually interrupted by the fact that the triangle's neatness is dependent on the absence of a limb. Two readings occur simultaneously: it is tragic but he is brave. In a book of hope, the disabled person is the symbol of loss. The disabled boy is a reminder that all is not necessarily well in the world but *he* is doing *his* best to sort it out. The image is "positive" in that he is "positively" adjusting to his loss. Because he is "positively" adjusting to his loss, the image is allowed into the exhibition and the catalogue. The image of his disablement has been used not for him but against him. The image's symbolic value is that disability is an issue for the person with an impairment, not an issue for a world being (inaccessibly) reconstructed. In *The Family of Man*, disabled people were almost entirely absented because harmony was seen to rest in the full operation of an idealised working body. The exhibition and catalogue did not admit disabled people (bar one) because it did not see a position for disabled people within the new model army of postwar production or consumption.

Photographically speaking, the decline of this high ground of postwar hope in the "one world, one voice, one leader" humanity was heralded (in historical photographic terms) by an equally influential but far more subversive exhibition, again at the Museum of Modern Art, New York, which was held in 1967. This exhibition was called New Documents and brought into a wide public consciousness reportage portraiture showing the human race as an alienated species bewildered by its existence. New Documents featured the work of Gary Winogrand, Lee Friedlander and Diane Arbus. The importance of these three photographers (and others like Robert Frank) is that their work heralded the breakdown of the universal humanism of *The Family of Man* into a more fragmented, psychic or surrealistic realism. The appalling reverse of the coin is that they anchored the new forms of a fragmented universe (to a greater or lesser extent) in new, even more oppressive images of disabled people.

What is particularly crucial in terms of the representation of disabled people in this photojournalism is a clear (yet still uncritical) emergence of the portrayal of disabled people as the *symbol* of this new (dis)order. Whereas the tucked-away disabled person in *The Family of Man* had been a hidden blemish on the body of humanity, in a world of the Cold War, the Cuban Missile Crisis and Vietnam, disabled people were represented as the inconcealable birthmark of fear and chaos. Diane Arbus was the second photographer whose work I looked at. The monograph that I had pulled from the shelf is from her posthumous retrospective, held at the Museum of Modern Art, New York, in 1972 and entitled *diane arbus*.[5]

Of all photographers who have included or excluded disabled people, Diane Arbus is the most notorious. She was born into an *arriviste* family of immigrants, whose money was made in the fur trade. She became a photographer through her husband, Allan Arbus, and worked with him in fashion photography. She moved away from that (and him) into work which still dealt with the body and its surrounding hyperbole but from a very different angle. It was on her own and in her own work that she became known, unwittingly according to her, as "the photographer of freaks." Whether she liked it or not, there can be no doubt that this is how her work has been received. The monograph contains 81 black-and-white images, of which eleven are of disabled people. These eleven can be divided into three quite critical periods of her work. The first is demonstrated in two portraits of "dwarfs"; the second with the portrait of the "Jewish giant"; and the third with the imagery shot just before her death, that of the "retardees" (her term for people with Down Syndrome).

In any of the material on Arbus, including this monograph, Patricia Bosworth's biography of her entitled *Diane Arbus, A Biography*, and Susan Sontag's discussion of her work in *On Photography*, the stages of her oppressive representations of disabled people are never discussed. Moreover, the "factual" recording of disabled people as freaks is accepted totally without question by major critics like Sontag, who says, "Her work shows people who are pathetic, pitiable, as well as repulsive, but it does not arouse any compassionate feelings."[6] Later, she rhetorically adds, "Do they see themselves, the viewer wonders, like *that*? Do they know how grotesque they are?" (her italics). Sontag brings to the disability imagery of Arbus a complete faith in Arbus's images as unproblematic truthtellers. Bosworth also colludes by patronising disabled people, telling us of Arbus's "gentle and patient" way with "them." Neither of these critics, it goes without saying, considered asking the observed what *they* felt about the images in which they figured. Once again, the entire discourse has absented the voice of those at its center—disabled people.

Since there is only one other book on Arbus's work, and that deals with her magazine work,[7] it is safe to say that Bosworth and Sontag represent key parts of the Arbus industry. In their validations of Arbus's work, they both miss a central point. Although she was profoundly misguided (as I demonstrate further on), there can be no doubt that her work paradoxically had the effect of problematising, or opening up, the issue of the representation of disabled people. Her critics and defenders have built a wall around her work (and any discussion of disability in her work) by "naturalising" the content. In this, the images of disabled people have been lumped into one label, that of "freaks." Perhaps this has been done because her work appears to buck the contradictory trend of "compassion" in the portrayal of disabled "victims" practised by other photographers. Although Arbus's work can never be "reclaimed," it has to be noted that her work, and the use of "enfreakment" as message and metaphor, is far more complicated than either her defenders or critics acknowledge. The process of analysis is not to rehabilitate her or her work but to break it down once and for all.

She was a part of the "snapshot aesthetic" which grew up beyond the New Documents exhibition and exhibitors. This form attempted to overturn the sophisticated and high-technique processes of the Hollywood fantasy portrait, as well as rejecting the beautiful toning of much of *The Family of Man*. However, more than any of her peers, she took this aesthetic nearer to its roots in the family photograph or album (indeed she intended to shoot a project entitled Family Album).[8] Arbus had experienced, in her own family, the emotional and psychological cost of wealth in terms of the painful subjectivity and isolation of the individual hidden and silenced within the outward signs of bourgeois upward mobility and success. In terms of disability, however, Arbus read the bodily impairment of her disabled subject as a sign of disorder, even chaos; that is, as a physical manifestation of *her* chaos, *her* horror. Despite her relationships with disabled people (often lasting a decade or more) she viewed these not as social and equal relationships but as encounters with souls from an underworld.

There was nothing new in this pattern of "reading" the visual site of a disabled person away from a personal value into a symbolic value which then seals the representational fate of the disabled person. However, at least in the first period of her disability work, Arbus deviated from the Richard III syndrome by reading this "disorder" as the manifestation of a psychic disorder not in the subject but in society. There is no question of Arbus using her subjects "positively"—it is clear that she always intended them and their relationships to themselves and others to symbolise something other than themselves. She saw herself and her "freaks" as fellow travellers into a living oblivion, a social death. There is a perverse sense in which she was right—disabled people are expected to inhabit a living death—but the crucial thing is that she considered her projection to be more important than their reality. She "normalised" subjects like Morales, *The Mexican Dwarf*,[9] or *The Russian Midget Friends*[10] by specifically placing them in that great site of bourgeois culture and consumption, the home. The "horror" of Arbus's work is not that she has created Frankenstein but that she moved him in next door! What is more, the freak had brought his family! The "shock" for the hundreds of thousands of non-disabled viewers was that these portraits revealed a hinter-land existing in spite of the segregationist non-disabled world view.

For Arbus, the family—her own family—represented an abyss. She saw in the bourgeois promise to the immigrant family, her own family, a Faustian contract. Her Mephistopheles, her threat to the bourgeois privilege, was to move a non-disabled fear that dare not speak its name into the family snap. In a sense, this first period of her work (a period not of time but of understanding) is her least oppressive and in some ways complete. The sitters acknowledge her presence and her camera. They stare out from the picture at the viewer. Far from making apologies for their presence, they are distinctly proud, they are committed to

their identity. Although the disabled people portrayed existed within subcultures (such as the circus), they were clearly not segregated and it is this which shocked the public who flocked to her posthumous retrospective at the Museum of Modern Art in 1972. It is the *conscious dialogue* between Arbus and the subjects which "horrified" and yet fascinated people more used to compassionate victim images of disabled people obligingly subhuman and obligingly institutionalized as "tragic but brave." Morales, the Mexican "dwarf" in *diane arbus*, is pictured naked but for a towel over his crutch. He wears a trilby at a rakish angle and his elbow leans casually on to the sideboard, resting just in front of a bottle of liquor. It is not clear quite what went on between Arbus and Morales (though Arbus had previously "spent the night" with another disabled subject, Moondance, as part of his agreement to be photographed) but the eroticism of the image cannot be denied. Not only is the so-called "dwarf" distinctly unfreaky in his three-quarters nakedness, he is positively virile! A constant theme of Arbus's work, not just of her disability work, is the relationship between people's bodies and their paraphernalia. While the attire is crisp and clear, the flesh of the subject has been "zombified." This, however, is not the case with her first pictures of "dwarfs." Morales's body is very much alive.

Arbus had attempted to trace the psychic disorder of consumer society back to a primal state of terror within everyday life. That she believed disabled people to be the visual witness of this primal state is clear. That is, she accepted at the level of "common sense" the non-integration of disabled people. However, much of "the Horror, the Horror"[11] with which Arbus's work has been received is in her location of this disabled terror within non-disabled normality. The disabled subjects themselves, at least in this early "freak" work, are treated reverentially. The camera is close. The camera is engaged. The subject has agreed to the session (but agreed in isolation?). The "horror" of the process for non-disabled society is in her placing a disabled normality within a non-disabled normality. The horror is in how she could even think them equivalent. The horror, I repeat, was in Arbus's recording in her constructions of disabled people a double bind of segregation/non-segregation. The "non-segregation," however (and this is where Arbus's crime really lay) did not lead towards integration—the "Russian midgets" were not living down the road as part of an independent living scheme—but towards transgression. It was a spectacle, not a political dialectic (the disability paradox) that Arbus wanted to ensnare. For this she accepted, indeed depended, on the given segregation of disabled people as "common sense."

Things began to disintegrate for Arbus in the second part of her disability work. This is illustrated in the monograph by the image entitled *A Jewish Giant at Home with his Parents in the Bronx, N.Y. 1970*. Again, we see a cosy family setting of a front room with two comfy chairs and a sofa, two elderly and self-respecting pensioners, a lamp by the drawn curtains, a reproduction classic painting in a tasteful frame, and a giant. The "giant" is not given a name in the title but his name was Eddie Carmel.[12] Again, Arbus did not sneak in and sneak out in this shot but got to know and photograph Eddie Carmel over a period of ten years before printing this one which she considered to work. This image of *A Jewish Giant* with its glaring flash-lit room, its portrayal of "the beast" from the womb of the mother, shows less harmony, even a deliberate asymmetry from that of her "dwarf" images. In *A Jewish Giant* she had created an image which took her beyond the reverence in both form and content of her "dwarf" images. Unlike them, Eddie the Jewish "giant" directs his attention away from the presence of the camera, his only acknowledgement that an image is being made is by being on his feet like his parents. His body language appears unclear and unsettled. The flash has cast black halos round the bodies of the subjects and they begin to resemble a Weegee as a found specimen of urban horror. The image of the "giant" as he crouches towards his more formal parents is that of a father over two children. The classic family portrait of parents and child is completely reversed by her use of their size relationship. The body language of the "Jewish giant" is more "out of control" (that is, it diverges more from non-disabled body language signs) than that of the "dwarf." It is all the more "threatening" to the non-disabled family snap because his body is situated with that of his "normal" parents. A clash or a confrontation between styles and discourses is occurring. The alchemy, confrontation and visual disorder of the image bring Arbus closer to avenging the control and repression in her own family. This is the key to her use and manipulation of isolated disabled people. During the ten years of their knowing each other, Eddie Carmel told Arbus about his ambitions, about his job selling insurance, about his acting hopes (and his despair at only being offered "monster" roles), and so on. Arbus dismissed this in her representations. She clearly found his actual day-to-day life irrelevant. Indeed, she appears to have disbelieved him, preferring her own projection of a metaphysical decline. His real tragedy is that he trusted Arbus, and she abused that trust outside of their relationship in an area within her total control, that is, photography.

The visual dialogue within the image between herself and the subject in the "dwarf" works, although decreasing in the imagery of Eddie the "giant," was still prevalent and was important precisely because it created a snapshot family album currency within the imagery. The commonness of this form was a part of its communicative power. As a structure it spoke to millions, while its content, Arbus's enfreakment of disabled people,[13] spoke to the able-bodied fear of millions. Were the subject to disengage, to reject the apparent co-conspiracy (in reality a coercion) or contract between themselves and Arbus, the images would move from the genre of family album currency and understanding of millions, to a reportage subgenre position of one specialist photographer. Arbus's work would then be that of an outsider constructing outsiders which need not be internalised by the viewer. The enfreakment in her disability images was internalised by the non-disabled viewers because the disabled subjects, while chosen for their apparent difference, manifested body language and identity traits recognisable to everyone. Arbus was concerned to show the dichotomy, even the pain, between how people projected themselves and how she thought they "really" were. The projection of this "imagined self" by the subject was through the direct gaze to camera (and therefore direct gaze to viewer). The image of *A Jewish Giant*, to Arbus, suggested a higher level of fear and chaos than the "dwarf" work. This higher level of discrepancy between order (the setting is still the family at home) and chaos (Eddie outgrowing that which contained him), than that manifested in the "dwarf" work, is also highlighted by the fact that, although the "giant" is on his feet posing with his parents, his dialogue is as much between him and his parents as between him and Arbus/the viewer.

Arbus was reported to have told a journalist at the *New Yorker* of her excitement over this image, the first one that had worked for her in the ten years of photographing Eddie. "You know how every mother has nightmares when she's pregnant that her baby will be born a monster? I think I got that in the mother's face as she glares up at Eddie, thinking, 'OH MY GOD, NO!'"[14] You could be forgiven for imagining that the mother recoils from her Eddie

much like Fay Ray recoiled from the horror of King Kong, but this is not the case. Arbus betrayed in her excited phone call to the journalist what she wished the image to say, rather than what it actual does say (though, of course, meanings shift). Arbus's comment about "every mother's nightmare" speaks of her nightmare relationship with her own body, which I believe she viewed as the sole site of her power. It was this loss of control of the body which she saw disability/impairment as meaning. Arbus once quoted a person who defined horror as the relationship between sex and death. She also claimed that she never refused a person who asked her to sleep with them. Furthermore, Bosworth hints that Arbus may have been confused about her bi-sexuality. In any event, the clues suggest that while she viewed her body and sexuality as key points of her power, her sexuality was not clear to her, and sex itself probably failed to resolve her feelings of aloneness and fragmentation. She sought the answer to this dilemma in locating bodily chaos in all her subjects (to varying degrees) and felt she'd found it in its perfect form in disabled people. (That major institutions of American representation, like the Museum of Modern Art, promoted her work shows their willingness to cooperate with this oppressive construction of disabled people.)

The "OH MY GOD, NO!" which she attributes to the mother in *A Jewish Giant* is in reality an "OH MY GOD, YES!" victory call that Arbus herself felt. She had made her psychic vision physical, or so she felt. Diane Arbus's daughter, Doon Arbus, has written that her mother wanted to photograph not what was evil but what was *forbidden*.[15] She believed she had pictured a return of the forbidden and repressed within her own remembered family. In her construction, the awkwardness of *A Jewish Giant* hints at the unwieldiness of her vision as a long-term solution to her own needs and begins to hint at this vision's ultimate destructiveness—not only, and obviously, to disabled people, but to the psychic well-being of Arbus herself.

It is here that the third period in her work on disabled people begins. She starts to photograph "retardees" (as she labels people with Down Syndrome). She moves from observing her subjects at home to observing them in a home; that is, an institution. These images of people with Down Syndrome were practically the last she shot before killing herself. They are clustered, six of them, at the end of the book. In the previous work with "dwarfs" and *A Jewish Giant* Arbus had maintained that she did not photograph anybody who did not agree to be photographed. This was undoubtedly so (although coercion is probably truer than agreement), but the images show a decline in conscious frontal participation of the subject. This decline was also mirrored in the growing discordance on the technical side of her work. The beautiful tones of Morales, the "dwarf," give way to a harsh flashlight in the "Jewish giant." There is no doubt that Arbus, as an ex-fashion photographer, knew what she was doing in using technical disharmony as an underwriting of the narrative disharmony. When we come into the third period, her work on "retardees," Arbus continues to pursue technical discordance. She still uses flash-and-daylight to pick up the figures from their landscape, but the focus is clearly weaker than that of the previous work. The subjects are now barely engaged with Arbus/the viewer *as themselves*.

Arbus finds them not in a position to conspire with her projection. The visual dialogue collapses. The dialectic between body and attire which Arbus had pursued is broken. The chaos of their paper and blanket costumes appears, to her, not to challenge their bodies but to match them. Arbus's order-chaos paradoxical projection has not happened. Instead, Arbus sees zombies in another world. To her they project no illusions of being neighbours to normality. These people are not at home but in a home. The institution of the family give sway to the institution of segregation (in this case, a New Jersey "home" for "retardees"). The people with Down Syndrome are set in a backdrop of large open fields showing only distant woods. For Arbus, their consciousness and activity is arbitrary. She does not know how to make them perform to her psycho-ventriloquist needs. In her career-long attempt to pull the psychic underworld into the physical overworld by manipulating the bodies of disabled people, she has come to the borders in these images. She had met "the limits of her imagination"; she had not found in these images the catharsis necessary for her to continue. Arbus first loved then hated this last work. She entered a crisis of identity because these segregated people with Down Syndrome would not perform as an echo of her despair. Because of this, her despair deepened. In the final image of this series and the final image of her monograph, nine disabled people pass across the view of the camera. Of the nine, only one turns towards the camera. His gaze misses the camera; consequently the possibilities that might have been opened up by a direct gaze are, for Arbus, lost. He joins the rest of this crowd who come into the frame for no purpose. Arbus's camera became irrelevant not only for disabled people, but for Arbus herself. This was her last work before she killed herself.

The next book I looked at was Gary Winogrand's *Figments from the Real World*.[16] Of the 179 black-and-white plates in *Figments from the Real World*, six included the portrayal of disabled people on one level or another. Like Arbus, the inclusion of disabled people, regardless of their role, was that of a significant minority with their oppression unquestioned and constructed as intact. Unlike Arbus's work, however, Winogrand did not produce any images (at least not for public consumption) whose central character was the disabled person or disablement. He did produce bodies of work on women, for example, but where a disabled person appears in the work, it is as a secondary character to the women. Nevertheless, within the "underrepresentation" in *Figments from the Real World*, it becomes clear that, like Arbus and the others from my ersatz list, "the disabled" had a role to play. Nevertheless, Winogrand consciously or otherwise included disabled people with the specific intention of enfreaking disability in order to make available to his visual repertoire a key *destabilising* factor.

With regard to the representation of women by Winogrand, Victor Burgin has critiqued Winogrand's work and has explored the reading of meaning within his imagery and the relationship of this meaning to the wider social and political discourses of his time.[17] Burgin describes and discusses an image of Winogrand from an exhibition in 1976. The image is of four women advancing towards the camera down a city street. The group of women, who are varying degrees of middle age, is the most prominent feature in the right-hand half of the image; equally prominent is a group of huge plastic bags stuffed full of garbage. The introduction to the catalogue of the exhibition makes it clear that this "joke" is intended. The reading of middle-aged women as "old bags" is unavoidable.

Despite the protestations by John Szarkowski in the introduction of *Figments from the Real World* that Winogrand celebrated women (he called the book of this phase of his work, *Women are Beautiful*), it is clear that his construction of women singly or in groups advancing towards the camera from all directions displays an unease, a fear, of what the results of his desire for them might be. Their faces frown by his camera, their eyes bow down to avoid his gaze. Burgin highlighted the dynamics of his "old bag" image. Winogrand's fear at what he reads as a loss of (female) beauty in ageing is registered by his "old bag" image. It is no coincidence that one of the six disability images (and the only one of two showing a wheelchair user) in *Figments from the Real World* involves an almost identical dynamic to that of the "old bags".

The center of the image is three young women. They are lit by a sun behind them and their sharp shadows converge towards the camera. They dominate the center third of the image and they are walking along a ray of light towards the lends. They are dressed in the fashion of the moment. In their movement is recorded an affecting, perhaps transitional beauty. Their symmetry is, however, broken by the gaze of the woman on the right. The symmetry is further challenged by this woman being a step ahead of the other two as she stares down at the presence, in the shadows, of a crouched wheelchair user. The other two women slightly move their heads towards the wheelchair. All of their eyes are tightened and all of their facial expressions "interpret" the presence of the wheelchair user with degrees of controlled horror.

Unlike Winogrand's dumping of middle-aged women into "old bags," he confronts these young women with a warning. He observes them as beautiful but warns them that their beauty and all its "paraphernalia" is all that separates them from the "grotesque" form they are witnessing. Beauty is warned of the beast. Clearly, Winogrand could not assuage his desire for women, whom he spent years photographically accosting on the street. His work harbours a resentment that they do not respond to his aggressive desire and so he implants warnings. The asymmetry of the imagery is anchored in the non-disabled reading (in this instant, Winogrand's) of disabled people as sites of asymmetrical disharmony. The women's body harmony (as Winogrand desires it) is set against the wheelchair user's disharmony (as Winogrand sees it).

Winogrand's use of the disabled person, again enfreaked, is to bring out of the underworld and into the shadows a symbol of asymmetry *as fear and decay* which challenges the three women's right to walk "beautifully" down the street.

Like Arbus, Winogrand's use of disability is to warn the "normal" world that their assumptions are fragile. This he does by the use of differentness of many disabled people's bodies as a symbol of the profound asymmetry of consumer society, particularly in the United States. Despite the fact that the American President Roosevelt had been disabled, the enfreakment of disabled people in these new practices became the symbol of the alienation of humanity which these new photographers were trying to record.

The Family of Man exhibition had all but excluded disabled people because they did not represent hope in the new order, so the post New Documents practitioners *included* disabled people for precisely the same reasons. The Family of Man and the New Documents exhibitions, constructed within photographic theories as radically separate, are inextricably linked, in that the inclusion of disabled people does not mean progress, but regression. Disabled people increased their presence in the new reportage of these photographers not as a sign of enlightenment and integration, but as a sign of bedlam.

The fourth book picked at random, I realized afterwards, takes us to a European setting. In *Another Way of Telling*,[18] the inevitable inclusion of a disabled subject comes almost at the very beginning. This book deals heavily with photographs of the countryside and the peasantry of various countries and the first photo-text piece sets this agenda. This is a story of Jean Mohr taking photographs of some cows, while the cow owner jokingly chastises him for taking pictures with permission and without payment. This first part very much sets the geographic and political agenda for the whole book, which explores the three-way relationship between the photographer, the photographed and the different meanings and readings taken from the photographs.

In every image or image-sequence, excluding the second one in the book (that of a blind girl in India) the images are more or less openly problematical. That is, the relationship between the image and its apparent informative or communicative value is put to the test. "Only occasionally is an image self-sufficient," says Jean Mohr. From this assertion, Mohr and Berger explore the image-making processes and what can be taken on or used within the process of photography that might work for both the photographer and the subject. The genesis of the book is to question meaning and use-value of imagery from all points, not just that of the photographer.

In Mohr's eighty-page first part, he illuminates different contexts of his own image-making, from shooting running children from a passing train, to shooting and reshooting working people and directing his work according to their expressed wishes. The theme which pervades the whole book is that of the working process. Moreover, the working process that they have chosen to explore visually is that of people working on the land and their lives and communities. The image-sequences, whether of cow-herders or of wood-cutters, begin with labour and its dignity. Clearly, unlike many "concerned" social realist photographers, Mohr is attempting to inhabit the process from the inside, not just to observe it externally. His method is through the voice, feedback and acknowledgement of the person photographed in their work. Their work is the anchor, the base, from which the story unfolds.

At one point and in one sequence, Mohr turns the camera on himself. He puts himself in the picture. He talks about the fear, the anxiety, even the panic which assails many people when they are the subject of the camera. Am I too fat? Am I too skinny? Is my nose too large? He tells us that he finds the process of putting himself in the picture difficult and talks about how he attempts to lose his image through technical disguises, like deliberately moving the camera during an exposure so as to blur the image, and so on. He anchors this process of putting himself in the picture on the quite valid and narcissistic idea that he used to imagine that he looked like Samuel Beckett. After bringing the story home by saying that he was finally forced to view his own image by being the subject matter of *other* people's lens, rather than his own, he finally finishes it by telling us that a student who photographed him felt that he did indeed resemble Beckett.

His work on other people's images and stories and his work on his own image and self are linked because, in grappling with the process of representation of his self or of others, he tells us and attempts to show us that the meaning of images is rooted in the process and context in which they were made. This is an important assertion but not unique. This book was published in 1982 and came at a time when other photographers and theorists, like Victor Burgin, Allan Sekula, Photography Workshop (Jo Spence/Terry Dennett) *et al.*, were questioning and problematising and naturalist truth-telling assumptions underpinning the left's use of social realist photography. *Another Way of Telling*, then, was a part of this "movement."

However, *Another Way of Telling*, and Jean Mohr's opening piece in particular, is clearly anchored in finding another way of using naturalist reportage, not abandoning it altogether. Mohr explains the use-value of the naturalist image to the subject. He tells stories of how this or that peasant wanted the image to show the whole body—of the person, of the cow, of the tree-cutting

process—rather than be "unnaturally" cropped. Naturalism, then, to him, has a purpose *in context*.

Here, we begin to get close to the *purpose* of the blind girl pictures within Jean Mohr's piece and the book as a whole. The realist (time/place) agenda is set in the first image, that of the cowman, but the *underlying agenda of "simple" naturalism* (that is to say, Mohr and Berger's belief in its ability to tell a simple story) is anchored in the hypersimplicity of the blind girl's pleasure. These pictures of a disabled person—a blind Asian girl—form the apex of the book's naturalist thesis that the value of naturalism is in its portrayal of unconscious innocence.

The story is called "The Stranger who Imitated Animals." The "stranger" in question is Jean Mohr. In the 250-odd words which accompany the five images, he tells us of visiting his sister in the university town of Aligarh in India and of his sister's "warning" of the blind girl who comes round and likes to know what is happening. He awakes the next morning unclear of where he is when.

> The young blind girl said Good Morning. The sun had been up for hours. Without reasoning why I replied to her by yapping like a dog. Her face froze for a moment. Then I imitated a cat caterwauling. And the expression on her face behind the netting changed to one of recognition and complicity in my play-acting. I went on to a peacock's cry, a horse whinnying, a large animal growling—like a circus. With each act and according to our mood, her expression changed. Her face was so beautiful that, without stopping our game, I picked up my camera and took some pictures of her. She will never see these photographs. For her I shall simply remain the invisible stranger who imitated animals.[19]

Clearly, despite his simplification of his response ("without reasoning why"), he responded with impersonations precisely because he had observed that she was blind. He objectified her, his first impulse on waking up to see a blind person was to play games with the blindness. Underlying this was the assumption that blind people (whatever the level of visual impairment) have no idea of quantifiable physical reality and would, of course, think that the sound really was of a yapping dog waking up in bed. His joke reveals his disability (un-)consciousness, not hers.

But she responds to this with laughter, she joins in. So, he further objectifies her by again distancing himself. While she laughs along with his imitations, he secretly photographs her, because her laughing but blind face was "so beautiful." Clearly, because she is laughing in his pictures, he presumably continued his imitations while he photographed her. The game for two turned into manipulation by one. The pictures show her leaning against the dark wooden surround of the door. She is framed by this and leans into this frame by pressing her ears to his mimicry. She is kept at a distance and keeps her responses on that surface of the mosquito net which fits into the wooden frame. This framing of her by the door is copied in his framing of her in the camera. Out of the five pictures in the sequence, four clearly show her eyes. Technically, these have been deliberately whitened in the printing to highlight the blindness.

As labour is the anchor in the other series, and as narcissism is the anchor in his self-image series, shooting the whites of her eyes is the anchor in this series. Her blindness is the symbol of innocence and nobility. Her blindness is the anchor of her simplicity. Her blindness is the object of his voyeurism. He has taken and symbolised this disabled person's image, which he says "she will never see" (he obviously didn't consider aural description), as the anchor and beauty of naturalism. The text which accompanies this series of images doesn't quite have the once-upon-a-time-ness of some of the other photo-essays, but it still

serves to push the imagery into the magical or metaphysical. The always-to-be natural images of the blind girl are the only set that have no significant time element to them. His work with the cowman spans days, his work with the wood-cutter is over a period of time (enough for the wood-cutter to give an opinion of the finished prints), but the work with the blind girl of beauty and innocence needs saying once, because it is forever. Again, like *The Family of Man*, like Arbus and Winogrand, Mohr has chosen to absent both the three-dimensional disabled person and their social story because it is incongruous to their own disability (un) consciousness. Their images tell us nothing about the actual lives of disabled people, but they add to the history of oppressive representation.

I have just analysed a random selection of four major photographic books, only one of which I knew to have been involved in disability representation. In the event, all four were. In the final analysis, these books which include disabled people in their field of photographic reference do so on the condition that disabled people are, to use Sontag's term for Diane Arbus's work, "borderline" cases. Sontag meant this term in its common reference to psychic or spiritual disorder. However, disabled people in the representations which I have discussed in this and the previous chapters share a commonality in that they live in different camps beyond the border. Whether beauty or the beast, they are outsiders. The basis for this border in society is real. It is physical and it is called segregation. The social absence of disabled people creates a vacuum in which the visual meanings attributable (symbolically, metaphorically, psychically, etc.) to impairment and disablement appear free-floating and devoid of any actual people. In the absence of disabled people, the meaning in the disabled person and their body is made by those who survey. They attempt to shift the disablement on to the impairment, and the impairment into a flaw. The very absence of disabled people in positions of power and representation deepens the use of this "flaw" in their images. The repression of disabled people makes it more likely that the symbolic use of disablement by non-disabled people is a sinister or mythologist one. Disablement re-enters the social world through photographic representation, but in the re-entry its meaning is tied not by the observed, disabled people, but by the non-disabled observers.

It is here that all the work, picked at random, is linked. Disabled people, in these photographic representations, are positioned either as meaningful or meaningless bodies. They are meaningful only as polarised anchors of naturalist humility or psychic terror. Brave but tragic: two sides of the segregated coin? Disabled people are taken into the themes pursued by Arbus, Winogrand, Mohr, and so on, to illustrate the truth of their respective grand narratives. The role of the body of the disabled person is to enflesh the thesis or theme of the photographer's work, despite the fact that most of the photographers had taken no conscious decision to work "on" disability. It is as if the spirit of the photographer's mission can be summed up in their manipulation of a disabled person's image. "The disabled" emerge, like a lost tribe, to fulfil a role for these photographers but not for themselves.

Disabled people appeared either as one image at a time per book or one role per book. The use of disabled people is the anchor of the weird, that is, the fear within. They are used as the symbol of enfreakment or the surrealism of all society. "Reactionary" users of this notion hunt the "crips" down to validate chaos within their own environment (Arbus); "progressive" users of this notion hunt them down within their own environment to find an essential romantic humanity in their own lives (but no question of access). The US "crip" sym-

bol denotes alienation. The impaired body is the site and symbol of all alienation. It is psychic alienation made physical. The "contorted" body is the final process and statement of a painful mind.

While this symbol functions as a "property" of disabled people as viewed by these photographers, it does not function as *the* property of those disabled people observed. Its purpose was not as a role model, or as references for observed people, but as the voyeuristic property of the non-disabled gaze. Moreover, the impairment of the disabled person became the mark, the target for a disavowal, a ridding, of the existential fears and fantasies of non-disabled people. This "symbolic" use of disablement knows no classic political lines, indeed it may be said to become more oppressive the further left you move.[20] The point is clear. If the disability paradox, the disability dialectic, is between impaired people and disabling social conditions, then the photographers we have just examined represent the construction of an "official" history of blame from the disabling society towards disabled people.

The works were selected at random and I fear their randomness proves my point. Wherever I drilled, I would have found the same substance. Were I to continue through modern photographic publications, I have no doubt that the pattern I am describing would continue; the only variation being that some would use disabled people for the purposes described, while others would absent disabled people altogether. A cursory widening of the list, to glance at photographers who have come after those named above, people like Joel-Peter Witkin,[21] Gene Lambert,[22] Bernard F. Stehle,[23] Nicholas Nixon,[24] and others who have all "dealt with" disablement, shows photographers who continued a manipulation of the disability/impairment image but have done so in a manner which depressingly makes the work by, say, Arbus and Mohr (I don't suppose they ever felt they'd be mentioned in the same breath!) seem positively timid! The work of many of the "post New Documentaries" has shifted the ground on the representation of disabled people by making "them" an even more separate category. While the volume of representation is higher, the categorisation, control and manipulation have become deeper. In this sense, the photographic observation of disablement has increasingly become the art of categorisation and surveillance. Also, from a psychological viewpoint, those that appear to have transgressed this commodification of disabled people have only transgressed their own fears of their constructions. The oppression remains the same. The segregated are not being integrated, they are being broken into! The photographic construction of disabled people continues through the use of disabled people in imagery as the site of fear, loss or pity. Those who are prevented by their liberal instincts from "coming out" in their cripple-as-freak, freak-as-warning-of-chaos, circumvent it by attempting to tell the unreconstructed "natural" story of oblivion. Either way, it is a no-win victim position for disabled people within those forms of representation. My intention in this essay is to suggest new forms.

A final note of hope. Diane Arbus was "extremely upset" when she received a reply from "The Little People's Convention" to her request to photograph them. They wrote that, "We have our own little person to photograph us."[25] In terms of disabled people's empowerment, this is the single most important statement in all of the work considered.

NOTES

1. Vic Finkelstein has argued that the "administrative model" of disablement has replaced the "medical model" to the extent that it is now the dominant oppressive one. This model, according to Finkelstein, suggests that the move away from the large "phase-two" institutions (which mirrored heavy industrial production) towards the dispersal of "care in the community" has meant that disablement has shifted from a predominantly cure-or-care issue to an administrative one. There is no doubt in my mind that this shift is being echoed in the production of "positive" images within the UK local authorities. They are similar to the functionalist images of the charities third-stage imagery in their portrayal of the administration of service provision to (grinning) disabled people.

2. *GYN/ecology* (1981), by Mary Daly, London: Women's Press.

3. *Images of the Disabled, Disabling Images* (1987), ed. Alan Gartner and Tom Joe, New York: Praeger.

4. *The Family of Man*, exhibition and publication by the Museum of Modern Art, New York, 1955. (Reprinted 1983.)

5. *diane arbus* (1990), London: Bloomsbury Press.

6. *On Photography* (1979), by Susan Sontag, London: Penguin.

7. "Arbus revisited: a review of the monograph," by Paul Wombell, *Portfolio* magazine, no. 10, Spring 1991.

8. Ibid., p. 33.

9. *diane arbus*, op. cit., p. 23. The full title of the photograph is *Mexican Dwarf in his Hotel Room in N.Y.C. 1970.*

10. *diane arbus*, op. cit., p. 16. The full title for this photograph is: *Russian Midget Friends in a Living Room on 100th St. N.Y.C. 1963.*

11. The death cry of Kurtz on discovering the unpronounceable, in Conrad's *Heart of Darkness*.

12. *Diane Arbus: A Biography* (1984), by Patricia Bosworth, New York: Avon Books, p. 226.

13. It is important to remember that the ability of naturalist photographic practice to "enfreak" its subject is not peculiar to the oppressive portrayal of disabled people. For example, the same process of fragmenting and reconstructing oppressed people into the projection of the photographer is particularly marked in the projection of the working classes. See *British Photography from the Thatcher Years* (book and exhibition) by Susan Kismaric, Museum of Modern Art, New York, 1990.

14. *Diane Arbus: A Biography*, op. cit., p. 227.

15. Ibid., p. 153.

16. Gary Winogrand (1988), *Figments from the Real World*, ed. John Szarkowski, New York: Museum of Modern Art.

17. *The End of Art Theory: Criticism and Post-Modernity* (1986), by Victor Burgin, London: Macmillan, p. 63.

18. *Another Way of Telling* (1982), by John Berger and Jean Mohr, London: Writers and Readers.

19. Ibid., p. 11.

20. For the "left" use of disability/impairment as the site of a defense of the welfare state, see "Bath time at St. Lawrence" by Raissa Page in *Ten-8*, nos. 7/8, 1982. Alternatively, for a cross-section of the inclusion of disability imagery within magazines servicing the welfare state, see the King's Fund Centre reference library, London. Finally, see the impairment charity house journals and read the photo credits, i.e., the Spastics Society's *Disability Now*. Network, Format, Report and other left photo agencies regularly supply uncritical impairment imagery.

21. *Masterpieces of Medical Photography: Selections from the Burns Archive* (1987), ed. Joel-Peter Witkin, California: Twelve-tree Press.

22. *Work from a Darkroom* (1985), by Gene Lambert (exhibition and publication), Dublin: Douglas Hyde Gallery.

23. *Incurably Romantic* (1985), by Bernard F. Stehle, Philadelphia: Temple University Press.

24. *Pictures of People* (1988), by Nicholas Nixon, New York: Museum of Modern Art.

25. *Diane Arbus: A Biography* (1984), by Patricia Bosworth, New York: Avon Books, p. 365.

CHAPTER 38

Blindness and Visual Culture:
An Eyewitness Account

Georgina Kleege

In April 2004, I was invited to speak at a conference on visual culture at the University of California, Berkeley. Speakers were asked to respond to an essay by W. J. T. Mitchell titled, "Showing Seeing: A Critique of Visual Culture," which offers a series of definitions of the emergent field of visual studies, distinguishing it from the more established disciplines of art history, aesthetics and media studies. As an admitted outsider to the field of visual studies, I chose to comment on the following statement: "Visual culture entails a meditation on blindness, the invisible, the unseen, the unseeable, and the overlooked" (Mitchell 2002, 170). In my last book, *Sight Unseen*, I attempted to show blindness through my own experience, and a survey of representations of blindness in literature and film. At the same time, I wanted to show seeing, to sketch my understanding of vision, drawn from a lifetime of living among the sighted in this visual culture we share. I started from the premise that the average blind person knows more about what it means to be sighted than the average sighted person knows about what it means to be blind. The blind grow up, attend school, and lead adult lives among sighted people. The language we speak, the literature we read, the architecture we inhabit, were all designed by and for the sighted.

If visual studies entails a meditation on blindness, it is my hope that it will avoid some of the missteps of similar meditations of the past. Specifically, I hope that visual studies can abandon one of the stock characters of the western philosophical tradition—"the Hypothetical Blind Man" (Gitter 2001, 58). The Hypothetical Blind Man—or the Hypothetical as I will call him for the sake of brevity—has long played a useful, though thankless role, as a prop for theories of consciousness. He is the patient subject of endless thought experiments where the experience of the world through four senses can be compared to the experience of the world through five. He is asked to describe his understanding of specific visual phenomena—perspective, reflection, refraction, color, form recognition—as well as visual aids and enhancements—mirrors, lenses, telescopes, microscopes. He is understood to lead a hermit-like existence, so far at the margins of his society, that he has never heard this visual terminology before the philosophers bring it up. Part of the emotional baggage he hauls around with him comes from other cultural representations of blindness, such as Oedipus and the many Biblical figures whose sight is withdrawn by the wrathful God of the Old Testament or restored by the redeemer of the New. His primary function is to highlight the importance of sight and to elicit a frisson of awe and pity which promotes gratitude among the sighted theorists for the vision they possess.

I will not attempt to survey every appearance of the Hypothetical throughout the history of philosophy. It is enough to cite a few of his more memorable performances, and then to suggest what happens when he is brought face-to-face with actual blind people through their own first-hand, eye-witness accounts. Professor Mitchell alludes to the passages in Descartes' *La Dioptrique* where he compares vision to the Hypothetical's use of sticks to grope his way through space. Descartes's references to the Hypothetical are confusing and are often conflated by his readers. In one instance, he compares the way the Hypothetical's stick detects the density and resistance of objects in his path, to the way light acts on objects the eye looks at. In a later passage, Descartes performs a thought experiment, giving the Hypothetical a second stick which he could use to judge the distance between two objects by calculating the angle formed when he touches each object with one of the sticks. Descartes does not explain how the Hypothetical is supposed to make this calculation or how he can avoid running into things while doing so. I doubt that Descartes actually believed that any blind person ever used two sticks in this way. In fact, the image that illustrates his discussion shows the Hypothetical's dog sound asleep on the ground, indicating that the Hypothetical is going nowhere. Even so, Descartes' description of the way a blind person uses one stick reflects a basic misunderstanding. He imagines that the blind use the stick to construct a mental image, or its equivalent, of their surroundings, mapping the location of specifically identified objects. In fact, then as now, a stick or cane is a poor tool for this kind of mental imaging. The stick serves merely to announce the presence of an obstacle,

not to determine if it is a rock or a tree root, though there are sound cues—a tap versus a thud—that might help make this distinction. In many situations, the cane is more of an auditory than a tactile tool. It seems that in Descartes' desire to describe vision as an extension of or hypersensitive form of touch, he recreates the blind man in his own image, where the eye must correspond to the hand extended by one or perhaps two sticks.

The most detailed depiction of the Hypothetical came about in 1693, when William Molyneux wrote his famous letter to John Locke. He proposed a thought experiment where a blind man who had learned to recognize geometric forms such as a cube and a sphere by touch, would have his sight restored through an operation. Would he be able to distinguish the two forms merely by looking at them? The Molyneux question continues to be debated today, even though the history of medicine is full of case studies of actual blind people who have had their sight restored by actual operations. Apparently, Molyneux was married to a blind woman, which has always led me to wonder why he did not pose his hypothetical question about her. Perhaps he knew that others would object that marriage to a philosopher might contaminate the experimental data. There was a risk that the philosopher might prime her answers or otherwise rig the results. Certainly in commentary on actual cases of restored sight, debaters of the Molyneux question are quick to disqualify those who were allowed to cast their eyes upon, for instance the faces of loved ones, before directing their gaze at the sphere and the cube.

Denis Diderot's 1749 "Letter on the Blind for the Use of Those Who See" is generally credited with urging a more enlightened, and humane attitude toward the blind. His blind man of Puiseaux and Nicholas Saunderson, the English mathematician, were both real rather than hypothetical blind men. As he introduces the man from Puiseaux, Diderot is at pains to supply details of his family history and early life to persuade his reader that this is a real person. Significantly, the man from Puiseaux is first encountered helping his young son with his studies, demonstrating both that he is a loving family man, and capable of intellectual activity. But the questions Diderot poses generally fall under the pervu of the Hypothetical. Certainly, many of his remarks help support Descartes' theory relating vision to touch:

> One of our company thought to ask our blind man if he would like to have eyes. "If it were not for curiosity," he replied, "I would just as soon have long arms: it seems to me my hands would tell me more of what goes on in the moon than your eyes or your telescopes."
> (Diderot 1999, 153)

Diderot praises the blind man's ability to make philosophical surmises about vision, but does not have a high opinion of blind people's capacity for empathy:

> As of all the external signs which raise our pity and ideas of pain the blind are affected only by cries, I have in general no high thought of their humanity. What difference is there to a blind man between a man making water and one bleeding in silence?
> (Diderot 1999, 156)

The phrasing of the question here suggests an afterthought. I imagine Diderot, at his table, conjuring up two men, one pissing, one bleeding. While his visual imagination is practiced in making these sorts of mental images, he is less adept at tuning his mind's ear. He recognizes that for the blood to be spilt at a rate sufficient to create the same sound as the flowing urine, the bleeding man would normally cry out in pain. So he imagines, in effect, a bleeding mute. But he fails to take into account the relative viscosity, not to mention the different odors,

of the two fluids. But Diderot cannot think of everything.

Now I imagine a blind man wandering onto the scene. My blind man is not quite the one Diderot imagines. For one thing he is a bit preoccupied; the philosophers have dropped by again. They talk at him and over his head, bandying about names that are now familiar to him: Locke, Molyneux, Descartes. They question him about his ability to conceptualize various things: windows, mirrors, telescopes—and he responds with the quaint and winsome answers he knows they have come for. Anything to get rid of them. Distracted as he is, the sound of the bleeding mute's plashing blood registers on his consciousness. Lacking Diderot's imagination, however, the thought does not occur to him that this sound emanates from a bleeding mute. His reason opts instead for the explanation that the sound comes from some man relieving his bladder—a far more commonplace phenomenon, especially in the means streets where the blind man resides. It is not that the blind man has no fellow feeling for the mute. Come to think of it, the mute would make a good companion. He could act as a guide and keep an eye out for marauding philosophers, while the blind man could do all the talking. But the blind man does not have enough information to recognize the mute's dilemma. The only hope for the bleeding mute is to find some way to attract the blind man's attention, perhaps by throwing something. But surely, such a massive loss of blood must have affected his aim. While the blind man, living as he does at the margins of his society, is accustomed to being spurned by local homeowners and merchants who find his presence unsightly, and so might flee the bleeding mute's missiles without suspecting that his aid is being solicited.

The blind man quickens his pace as best he can. The mute succumbs at last to his mortal wound. And the philosopher shifts to another topic.

I am wrong to make fun of Diderot, since his treatment of blindness was at once far more complex and far more compassionate than that of other philosophers. And it is not as if his low opinion of the blind's ability to empathize with others' pain has ceased to contribute to attitudes about blindness. Consider this anecdote from recent history. Some weeks after September 11, 2001, the blind musician Ray Charles was interviewed about his rendition of "America the Beautiful," which received a good deal of air time during the period of heightened patriotism that followed that event. The interviewer, Jim Gray, commented that Charles should consider himself lucky that his blindness prevented him from viewing the images of the World Trade Center's collapse, and the Pentagon in flames: "Was this maybe one time in your life where not having the ability to see was a relief?" Like Diderot, the interviewer assumed that true horror can only be evinced through the eyes. Many eyewitness accounts of the event however, were strikingly nonvisual. Many people who were in the vicinity of Ground Zero during and soon after the disaster found it hard to put what they saw into words, in part because visibility in the area was obscured by smoke and ash, and in part because what they were seeing did not correspond to any visual experience for which they had language. People described instead the sound of falling bodies hitting the ground, the smell of the burning jet fuel, and the particular texture of the ankle deep dust that filled the streets. But for the majority of television viewers, eyewitnesses from a distance, those events are recalled as images, indelible, powerful, and eloquent. To many, like the reporter interviewing Ray Charles, it is the images rather than the mere fact of the events that produce the emotional response. The assumption seems to be that because the blind are immune to images they must also be immune to the significance of the events, and

therefore must be somehow detached from or indifferent to the nation's collective horror and grief.

It is fortunate for anyone interested in dismantling the image of blindness fostered by the Hypothetical Blind Man that we have today a great many first-hand accounts of blindness. In recent decades, memoirs, essays and other texts by actual blind people attempt to loosen the grip the Hypothetical still seems to hold on the sighted imagination. Thanks to work by disability historians, we are also beginning to have older accounts of blindness drawn from archives of institutions and schools for the blind around the world. One such account is a text written in 1825, by a twenty-two-year-old blind French woman named Thérèse-Adèle Husson. Born in Nancy into a petit bourgeois household, Husson became blind at nine months following a bout of smallpox. Her case attracted the attention of the local gentry who sponsored a convent education for her, and encouraged her to cultivate her interests in literature and music. At the age of twenty she left home for Paris where she hoped to pursue a literary career. Her first text, "Reflections on the Moral and Physical Condition of the Blind" seems to have been written as a part of her petition for aid from the Hôpital des Quinze-Vingts, an institution that provided shelter and financial support to the indigent blind of Paris. For the most part, her text follows the example of comportment and educational manuals of the time, offering advice to parents and caretakers on the correct way to raise a blind child, and to young blind people themselves on their role in society. It is by turns, formulaically obsequious and radically assertive, since she writes from the premise—revolutionary for the time—that her first-hand experience of blindness gives her a level of expertise that equals or surpasses that of the institution's sighted administrators. While it is unlikely that Husson's convent education would have exposed her to the work of Descartes or Diderot, she considers some of the same questions previously posed to the Hypothetical. It is possible that the provincial aristocrats, who took up her education, may have engaged in amateurish philosophizing in her presence. For instance, like Diderot's blind man of Puiseaux, she prefers her sense of touch to the sight she lacks. She recounts how, at the time of her first communion, her mother promised her a dress made of chiffon, then, either as a joke or in an attempt to economize, purchased cheaper percale instead. When the young Husson easily detected the difference through touch, her mother persisted in her deception, and even brought in neighbor women to corroborate. Whether playing along with the joke, or as a genuine rebuke of her mother's attempt to deceive her, Husson retorted:

> I prefer my touch to your eyes, because it allows me to appreciate things for what they really are, whereas it seems to me that your sight fools you now and then, for this is percale and not chiffon.
>
> (Husson 2001, 25)

In a later discussion of her ability to recognize household objects through touch, her impatience seems out of proportion, unless we imagine that she frequently found herself the object of philosophical speculation by literal-minded practitioners:

> We know full well that a chest of drawers is square, but more long than tall. Again I hear my readers ask what is a square object! I am accommodating enough to satisfy all their questions. Therefore, I would say to them that it is easy enough to know the difference between objects by touching them, for not all of them have the same shape. For example, a dinner plate, a dish, a glass can't begin to be compared with a chest of drawers, for the first two are round, while the other is hollow; but people will probably point out that

it is only after having heard the names of the articles that I designate that it became possible for me to acquire the certainty that they were hollow, round, square. I will admit that they are right, but tell me, you with the eyes of Argus, if you had never heard objects described, would you be in any better position to speak of them than I?

(Husson 2001, 41)

Her emphasis on square versus round objects as well as her tone and her taunt, "You with the eyes of Argus," suggests an irritation that may come from hearing the Molyneux question one too many times. She is also arguing against the notion that such words as "square" and "round" designate solely visual phenomena, to which the blind have no access and therefore no right to use these words.

Almost a century later, Helen Keller gives vent to a similar irritation at literal-minded readers. In her 1908 book, *The World I Live In*, she gives a detailed phenomenological account of her daily experience of deaf-blindness. Early on, she footnotes her use of the verb "see" in the phrase, "I was taken to see a woman":

> The excellent proof-reader has put a query to my use of the word "see." If I had said "visit," he would have asked no questions, yet what does "visit" mean but "see" (*visitare*)? Later I will try to defend myself for using as much of the English language as I have succeeded in learning.
>
> (Keller 2003, 19)

Keller makes good use of her Radcliffe education to show that the more one knows about language the harder it is to find vocabulary that does not have some root in sighted or hearing experience. But, she argues, to deny her the use of seeing-hearing vocabulary would be to deny her the ability to communicate at all.

In their 1995 book, *On Blindness*, two philosophers, one sighted and one blind, conduct an epistolary debate that might seem to put to rest all the old hypothetical questions. Unfortunately, Martin Milligan, the blind philosopher, died before the discussion was fully underway. If he had lived, we can assume not only that he and his sighted colleague, Bryan Magee, would have gotten further with their debate, but also that they would have edited some testy quibbles about which terms to use and which translation of Aristotle is more accurate. Milligan, who worked primarily in moral and political philosophy, and was an activist in blind causes in the United Kingdom, forthrightly resists the impulse to allow the discussion to stray far from the practical and social conditions that affect the lives of real blind people. For instance, he cites an incident from his early life, before he found an academic post, when he was turned down for a job as a telephone typist on a newspaper because the employer assumed that he would not be able to negotiate the stairs in the building. He identifies this as one of thousands of examples of the exaggerated value sighted people place on vision. Any thinking person has to recognize that sight is not required to climb or descend stairs. He asserts that the value of sight would be that it would allow him to move around unfamiliar places with greater ease. He concedes that vision might afford him some aesthetic pleasure while viewing a landscape or painting, but insists that he can know what he wants to know about the visible world from verbal descriptions, and that this knowledge is adequate for his needs, and only minimally different from the knowledge of sighted people. He accuses Magee of voicing "visionist"—or what I might call "sightist"—attitudes that the differences between the sighted and the blind must be almost incomprehensibly vast, and that vision is a fundamental aspect of human existence. Milligan says that these statements seem

to express the passion, the zeal of a missionary preaching to the heathen in outer darkness. Only, of course, your "gospel" isn't "good" news to us heathens, for the message seems to be that ours is a "darkness" from which we can never come in—not the darkness of course that sighted people can know, but the darkness of never being able to know *that* darkness, or of bridging the vast gulf that separates us from those who do.

(Magee and Milligan 1995, 46)

This prompts Magee to cite his own early work on race and homosexuality, as proof of his credentials as a liberal humanist. He also speculates, somewhat sulkily, about whether the first eighteen months of Milligan's life when his vision was presumed to be normal, might disqualify him as a spokesman for the blind, since he might retain some vestige of a visual memory from that period. Later, Magee consults with a neurologist who assures him that the loss of sight at such an early age would make Milligan's brain indistinguishable from that of a person born blind. And so the discussion continues.

Along the way, Magee makes some claims about sight that seem to me to be far from universal. For instance, he states:

By the sighted, seeing is felt as a *need*. And it is the feeding of this almost ungovernable craving that constitutes the ongoing pleasure of sight. It is as if we were desperately hungry all the time, in such a way that only if we were eating all the time could we be content—so we eat all the time.

(Magee and Milligan 1995, 104)

Magee asserts that when sighted people are obliged to keep their eyes closed even for a short time, it induces a kind of panic. To illustrate his point, he notes that a common method of mistreating prisoners is to keep them blindfolded, and this mistreatment can lead them to feel anxious and disoriented. I suspect that his example is influenced by traditional metaphors that equate blindness with a tomb-like imprisonment. Surely a blind prisoner, accustomed to the privation of sight, might still have similar feelings of anxiety and disorientation, due to the threat, whether stated or implied, of pending bodily harm.

To his credit, Magee does allow that some blind experiences are shared by the sighted. Milligan describes how many blind people negotiate new environments, and can feel the presence of large objects even without touching them as "atmosphere-thickening occupants of space." Magee reports that when he

> was a small child I had a vivid nonvisual awareness of the nearness of material objects. I would walk confidently along a pitch black corridor in a strange house and stop dead a few inches short of a closed door, and then put out my hand to grope for the knob. If I woke up in the dark in a strange bedroom and wanted to get to a light-switch on the opposite side of the room I could usually circumnavigate the furniture in between, because I could "feel" where the larger objects in the room were. I might knock small things over, but would almost invariably "feel" the big ones. I say "feel" because the sensation, which I can clearly recall, was as of a feeling-in-the-air with my whole bodily self. Your phrase "atmosphere-thickening occupants of space" describes the apprehension exactly. I suddenly "felt" a certain thickness in the air at a certain point relative to myself in the blackness surrounding me. . . . This illustrates your point that the blind develop potentialities that the sighted have also been endowed with but do not develop because they have less need of them.
>
> (Magee and Milligan 1995, 97–98)

Here, and in a few other places in the correspondence, Magee and Milligan seem to be moving in a new direction. It is not merely that they discover a shared perceptual experience, but one that is not easy to categorize as belonging to one of the five traditional senses. Here, a "feeling" is not the experience of texture or form through physical contact, but an apprehension, of an atmospheric change, experienced kinesthetically, and by the body as a whole. This seems to point toward a need for a theory of multiple senses where each of the traditional five could be subdivided into a number of discrete sensory activities, which function sometimes in concert with and sometimes in counterpoint to others. Helen Keller identified at least three different aspects of touch that she found meaningful: texture, temperature, and vibration. In fact, she understands sound as vibrations that the hearing feel in their ears while the deaf can feel them through other parts of their bodies. Thus she could feel thunder by pressing the palm of her hand against a windowpane, or someone's footsteps by pressing the soles of her feet against floorboards.

What these blind authors have in common is an urgent desire to represent their experiences of blindness as something besides the absence of sight. Unlike the Hypothetical, they do not feel themselves to be deficient or partial—sighted people minus sight—but whole human beings who have learned to attend to their nonvisual senses in different ways. I have deliberately chosen to limit my discussion here to works by people who became blind very early in life. One of the most striking features of the Hypothetical Blind Man is that he is always assumed to be both totally and congenitally blind. Real blindness, today as in the past, rarely fits this profile. Only about 10–20 percent of people designated as legally blind, in countries where there is such a designation, are without any visual perception at all. It is hard to come by statistics on people who are born totally blind, in part because it only becomes an issue when the child, or her parents, seek services for the blind, which tends to occur only when the child reaches school age. We can assume that more infants were born blind in the past, since some of the most prevalent causes of infantile blindness have been eliminated by medical innovations in the nineteenth and twentieth centuries. Nevertheless, in the past, as now, the leading causes of blindness occur later in life, and often leave some residual vision. Some may retain the ability to distinguish light from darkness, while others may continue to perceive light, color, form, and movement to some degree. Some people may retain the acuity to read print or facial expressions, while lacking the peripheral vision that facilitates free movement through space. And regardless of the degree or quality of residual vision, blind people differ widely in the ways they attend to, use or value these perceptions.

Although the situation of the Hypothetical is rare, his defenders are quick to discount anyone with any residual sight or with even the remotest possibility of a visual memory. In traditional discussions of blindness, only total, congenital blindness will do. In a review of my book *Sight Unseen*, Arthur Danto asserted that I had too much sight to claim to be blind (Danto 1999, 35). He quoted a totally blind graduate student he once knew who said that he could not conceptualize a window, and that he was surprised when he learned that when a person's face is said to glow, it does not in fact emit light like an incandescent light bulb. Danto does not tell us what became of this student or even give his name, using him only as a modern-day version of the Hypothetical. He then goes on to relate the history of the Molyneux question.

If only the totally blind can speak of blindness with authority, should we make the same restriction on those who talk about vision? Is there such a thing as total vision? We know that a visual acuity of 20/20 is merely average vision. There are individuals whose acuity measures better than 20/20, 20/15, or even 20/10. Such individuals can read every line of the familiar

Snellan eye chart, or, as in the case of Ted Williams, can read the print on a baseball whizzing toward their bat at a speed close to ninety miles per hour. How many scholars of visual culture, I wonder but won't ask, can claim such a level of visual acuity?

What visual studies can bring to these discussions is an interrogation of the binary opposition between blindness and sight. It is clearly more useful to think in terms of a spectrum of variation in visual acuity, as well as a spectrum of variation in terms of visual awareness or skill. The visual studies scholar, highly skilled in understanding images, who loses some or even all her sight, will not lose the ability to analyze images and to communicate her observations. In his essay, "Showing Seeing," W. J. T. Mitchell describes a classroom exercise in which students display or perform some feature of visual culture as if to an audience that has no experience of visual culture. The exercise assumes that some students will be better at the task, while others might improve their performance with practice, and in all cases their aptitude would have little, if anything, to do with their visual acuity. The skill, as I understand it, is in the telling as much as it is in the seeing—the ability to translate images in all their complexity and resonance into words.

And as we move beyond the simple blindness versus sight binary, I hope we can also abandon the clichés that use the word "blindness" as a synonym for inattention, ignorance, or prejudice. If the goal is for others to see what we mean, it helps to say what we mean. Using the word in this way seems a vestigial homage to the Hypothetical, meant to stir the same uncanny frisson of awe and pity. It contributes on some level to the perception of blindness as a tragedy too dire to contemplate, which contributes in turn to lowered expectations among those who educate and employ the blind. It also contributes to the perception among the newly blind themselves that the only response to their new condition is to retire from view.

I will leave you with a futuristic image of blindness. In Deborah Kendrick's story, "20/20 with a Twist," Mary Seymour, chief administrator of the department of visual equality, looks back on her life from the year 2020. In this blind Utopia, the major handicaps of blindness have been eliminated; private automobiles were phased out a decade earlier and technologies to convert print to Braille or voice had become ubiquitous and transparent. Of course, Mary reflects, it was not always like this. Back in the dark ages of the 1980s and '90s, Braille proficiency had ceased to be a requirement for teachers of blind children, Braille production facilities and radio reading services were shut down, and blind children were no longer being educated at all. Mary and other blind people who had grown up in an earlier, slightly more enlightened period, banded together to lead a nonviolent, visionary rebellion to bring down the oppressive regime. They tampered with the power supply—since darkness is no impediment to blind activity—scrambled computer transmissions and disrupted television broadcasts. All across the country, television screens went blank while the audio continued, interrupted periodically by the revolutionary message: "You, too, can function without pictures."

The rebel leaders were captured, however, and forced to undergo implantation of optic sensors, which, the captors reasoned, would transform them into sighted people who would see the error of their ways and abandon the cause. But the rebels persisted. The power supply was shut down completely. The government fell, and the captured leaders were liberated in triumph.

Significantly, the optic sensors did not transform the revolutionary leaders into sighted people. Rather, each acquired only a facet of visual experience. One gained the ability to perceive color. Another developed a sort of telepathic vision, allowing him to form images of places at great distances. Mary's sensor gave her a kind of literal hindsight, making her able to create a detailed mental picture of a room, only after she had left it. These bits and pieces of vision serve as a badge of the former rebels' heroic past, and allow them to perform entertaining parlor tricks, but are otherwise easy to disregard.

This is a far cry from the Hypothetical. In Deborah Kendrick's image of the future, blindness is a simple physical characteristic rather than an ominous mark of otherness. If the Hypothetical Blind Man once helped thinkers form ideas about human consciousness surely his day is done. He does too much damage hanging around. It is time to let him go. Rest in peace.

REFERENCES

Charles, Ray. Interview. *The Today Show*. NBC Television, October 4, 2001.

Danto, Arthur. 1999. "Blindness and Sight." *The New Republic* 220 (16): 34–36.

Diderot, Denis. 1999. *Thoughts on the Interpretation of Nature and Other Philosophical Works*. Ed. David Adams. Manchester: Clinaman Press.

Gitter, Elisabeth. 2001. *The Imprisoned Guest: Samuel Howe and Laura Bridgman, the Original Deafblind Girl*. New York: Farrar, Straus and Giroux.

Husson, Thérèse-Adèle. 2001. *Reflections: The Life and Writing of a Young Blind Woman in Post-revolutionary France*. Eds. Catherine J. Kudlick and Zina Weygand. New York and London: New York University Press.

Keller, Helen. 2003. *The World I Live In*. Ed. Roger Shattuck. New York: New York Review Books.

Kendrick, Deborah. 1987. 20/20 with a Twist. In *With Wings: An Anthology of Literature by and about Women with Disabilities*, eds. Marsha Saxton and Florence Howe New York: Feminist Press at the City University of New York.

Magee, Bryan and Milligan, Martin. 1995. *On Blindness*. Oxford and New York: Oxford University Press.

Mitchell, W. J. T. 2002. "Showing Seeing: A Critique of Visual Culture." *Journal of Visual Culture* 1 (2):165–181.

CHAPTER 39

Disability, Life Narrative, and Representation

G. Thomas Couser

Disability is an inescapable element of human existence and experience. Although it is as fundamental an aspect of human diversity as race, ethnicity, gender, and sexuality, it is rarely acknowledged as such. This is odd, because in practice disability often trumps other minority statuses. That is, for people who differ from the hegemonic identity in more than one way, certain impairments—such as blindness or deafness—may function as their primary defining characteristic, their "master status." In this sense, disability may be *more* fundamental than racial, ethnic, and gender distinctions. Yet until the recent advent of Disability Studies, it escaped the critical scrutiny, theoretical analysis, and recognition accorded other forms of human variation.

At the same time, disability has had a remarkably high profile in both high and popular culture, both of which are pervaded with images of disability. Unlike other marginalized groups, then, disabled people have been *hyper*-represented in mainstream culture; they have not been disregarded so much as they have been subjected to objectifying notice in the form of mediated staring. To use an economic metaphor that is a literal truth, disability has been an extremely valuable cultural commodity for thousands of years. The cultural representation of disability has functioned at the expense of disabled people, in part because they have rarely controlled their own images. In the last several decades, however, this situation has begun to change, most notably in life writing, especially autobiography: in late twentieth century life writing, disabled people have initiated and controlled their own narratives in unprecedented ways and to an extraordinary degree.

Indeed, one of the most significant developments—if not *the* most significant development—in life writing in North America over the last three decades has been the proliferation of book-length accounts (from both first- and third-person points of view) of living with illness and disability. Whereas in the 1970s it was difficult to find *any* representation of most disabling conditions in life writing, today one can find *multiple* representations of many conditions. Equally significant, and more remarkable, one can find *autobiographical* accounts of conditions that would seem to preclude first-person testimony altogether—for example, autism, locked-in syndrome, and early Alzheimer's disease.

A comprehensive history of disability life writing has yet to be written, but it is safe to say that there was not much in the way of published autobiographical literature before World War II. War both produces and valorizes certain forms of disability; not surprisingly, then, disabled veterans produced a substantial number of narratives after the war. Polio generated even more narratives; indeed, polio may be the first disability to have engendered its own substantial autobiographical literature (Wilson). In the 1980s and 1990s, HIV/AIDS and breast cancer provoked significant numbers of narratives; many of these challenge cultural scripts of the conditions (such as that AIDS is an automatic death sentence or that breast cancer negates a woman's sexuality [Couser 1997]). A dramatic example of the generation of autobiographical literature devoted to a particular condition is the advent of autobiographies by people with autism (sometimes referred to as "autiebiographies"). Before 1985 these were virtually nonexistent; since 1985, nearly one hundred have been produced. (This number does not include the many narratives written by parents of autistic children.) Thus, one major post-World War II cultural phenomenon was the generation of large numbers of narratives about a small number of conditions.

A complementary phenomenon has been the production of small numbers of narratives about a large number of conditions, some quite rare and some only recently recognized. Among these conditions are ALS (also known as Lou Gehrig's disease), Alzheimer's, aphasia, Asperger's syndrome, asthma, cerebral palsy, chronic fatigue syndrome, cystic fibrosis, diabetes, disfigurement, Down syndrome, epilepsy, locked-in syndrome, multiple sclerosis, obesity, obsessive-compulsive disorder, stuttering, stroke, and Tourette syndrome. As the twentieth century drew to a close, then, many disabilities came out of the closet into the living room of life writing.

Like life writing by other marginalized groups—women, African Americans, and gays and lesbian—life writing by disabled people is a cultural manifestation of a human rights movement; significantly, the rise in personal narratives of disability has roughly coincided with the disability rights movement, whose major legal manifestation in the United States is the Americans with Disabilities Act, which was passed in 1990 (but which, some would argue, has never been fully implemented). The first flowering of disability autobiography is also part of a disability renaissance involving other arts and media. Disability autobiography should be seen, then, not as spontaneous "self-expression" but as a response—indeed a retort—to the traditional misrepresentation of disability in Western culture generally.

This rich body of narrative can be approached in a number of ways. One way of getting at the relation between somatic variation and life narrative is through an everyday phenomenon: the way deviations from bodily norms often provoke a demand for explanatory narrative in everyday life. Whereas the unmarked case—the "normal" body—can pass without narration, the marked case—the scar, the limp, the missing limb, or the obvious prosthesis—calls for a story. Entering new situations, or re-entering familiar ones, people with anomalous bodies are often called upon to account for them, sometimes quite explicitly: they may be asked, "What happened to *you*"? Or, worse, they may be addressed as if their stories are already known. Evidence of this is necessarily anecdotal. Let one compelling example suffice. Harriet McBryde Johnson, a Charleston lawyer and disability rights advocate who has a congenital muscle-wasting disease, reports remarks made by strangers she encounters on the street as she drives her power chair to the office:

> "I admire you for being out: most people would give up."
> "God bless you! I'll pray for you."

"You don't let the pain hold you back, do you?"

"If I had to live like you, I think I'd kill myself." (2)

One of the social burdens of disability, then, is that it exposes affected individuals to inspection, interrogation, interpretation, and violation of privacy.

In effect, people with extraordinary bodies are held responsible for them, in two senses. First, they are required to account for them, often to complete strangers; second, the expectation is that their accounts will serve to relieve their auditors' discomfort. The elicited narrative is expected to conform to, and thus confirm, a cultural script. For example, people diagnosed with lung cancer or HIV/AIDS are expected to admit to behaviors that have induced the condition in question—to acknowledge having brought it upon themselves. Thus, one fundamental connection between life narrative and somatic anomaly is that to have certain conditions is to have one's life written *for* one. For people with many disabilities, culture inscribes narratives *on* their bodies, willy nilly.

Disability autobiographers typically begin from a position of marginalization, belatedness, and pre-inscription. Yet one can see why autobiography is a particularly important form of life writing about disability: written from inside the experience in question, it involves *self*-representation by definition and thus offers the best-case scenario for revaluation of that condition. Long the objects of others' classification and examination, disabled people have only recently assumed the initiative in representing themselves; in disability autobiography particularly, disabled people counter their historical subjection by occupying the subject position. In approaching this literature, then, one should attend to the politics and ethics of representation, for the "representation" of disability in such

narratives is a political as well as a mimetic act—a matter of speaking *for* as well as speaking *about*.

With particularly severe or debilitating conditions, particularly those affecting the mind or the ability to communicate, the very existence of first-person narratives makes its own point: that people with condition "X" are capable of self-representation. The autobiographical act models the agency and self-determination that the disability rights movement has fought for, even or especially when the text is collaboratively produced. One notable example is *Count Us In: Growing Up with Down Syndrome*, a collaborative narrative by two young men with the syndrome in question. Not only is the title cast in the imperative mood—"count us in"—the subtitle puns on "up" and "down," a bit of verbal play that challenges conventional ideas about mental retardation, such as that those with it never really mature. Autobiography, then, can be an especially powerful medium in which disabled people can demonstrate that they have lives, in defiance of others' common sense perceptions of them. Indeed, disability autobiography is often in effect a post-colonial, indeed an anti-colonial, phenomenon, a form of autoethnography, as Mary Louise Pratt has defined it: "instances in which colonized subjects undertake to represent themselves in ways that engage with [read: contest] the colonizer's own terms" (7).

People with disabilities have become increasingly visible in public spaces and open about their disabilities. But their physical presence in public life represents only a rather limited kind of access. Properly conceived and carried out (admittedly, a large qualifier), life narrative can provide the public with controlled access to lives that might otherwise remain opaque or exotic to them. Further, much disability life writing can be approached as "quality-of-life" writing because it addresses questions discussed under that rubric in philosophy, ethics, and especially biomedical ethics. It should be required reading, then, for citizens in a world with enormous technological capability to sustain life and repair bodies in the case of acute illness and injury but with very little commitment to accommodate and support chronic disability. Because disability life narratives can counter the too often moralizing, objectifying, pathologizing, and marginalizing representations of disability in contemporary culture, they offer an important, if not unique, entree for inquiry into one of the fundamental aspects of human diversity.

WORKS CITED

Couser, G. Thomas. *Recovering Bodies: Illness, Disability, and Life Writing*. Madison: U of Wisconsin P, 1997.

Johnson, Harriet McBryde. *Too Late to Die Young: Nearly True Tales from a Life*. New York: Henry Holt, 2005.

Kingsley, Jason and Mitchell Levitz. *Count Us In: Growing Up with Down Syndrome*. New York: Harcourt, 1994.

Pratt, Mary Louise. *Imperial Eyes: Travel Writing and Transculturation*. New York: Routledge, 1992.

Wilson, Daniel J. "Covenants of Work and Grace: Themes of Recovery and Redemption in Polio Narratives." *Literature and Medicine* 13, 1 (Spring 1994): 22–41.

CHAPTER 40

Autism as Culture

Joseph N. Straus

AUTISM AS CULTURE

The Originary Moment

In 1943, Leo Kanner, a child psychiatrist working at Johns Hopkins University, published an article titled, "Autistic Disturbances of Affective Contact." (Kanner 1943). In it, he identified a group of children who shared certain traits: "All of the children's activities and utterances are governed rigidly and consistently by the powerful desire for aloneness and sameness" (249). The children shared an "*inability to relate themselves* in the ordinary way to people and situations" and an "*anxiously excessive desire for the maintenance of sameness*," and displayed "an *extreme autistic aloneness* that, whenever possible, disregards, ignores, shuts out anything that comes to the child from the outside" (242, 245, italics in original).

At virtually the same moment, separated by an ocean and a world war, the Viennese psychologist, Hans Asperger, published a study of a group of children with remarkably similar characteristics: "The children I will describe all have in common a fundamental disturbance [that] results in severe and characteristic difficulties of social integration. In many cases, the social problems are so profound that they overshadow everything else" (Asperger 1944/1991, 37). Like Kanner, Asperger chose the term "autism," to refer to what he called "a fundamental disturbance of contact" (38):

> Human beings normally live in constant interaction with their environment, and react to it continually. However, " autists" have severely disturbed and considerably limited interaction. The autist is only himself (cf. the Greek word *autos*) and is not an active member of a greater organism which he is influenced by and which he influences constantly (38).[1]

Presumably there have always been people who had the sorts of neurology and behaviors we now label as autistic, but insofar as they were remarked at all, they were parceled out to different categories (most notably various forms of madness, especially schizophrenia, or "feeblemindedness").[2] By creating the new classification of autism, Kanner and Asperger participate in the endless reshaping of the map of psychological disorders, which rise and fall historically, as much in response to cultural and social pressures as to any neutral, scientific observation.[3] Today, autism may appear a secure, natural category, but it is as historically and culturally contingent as neurasthenia, hysteria, and fugue—science-based and neutral medical categories of a previous era—and may someday share their fate (Hacking 1998; Porter 2002; Davis 2008).

The Rise of Autism

In the decades following Kanner and Asperger's discoveries (or creations), autism remained a small, marginal phenomenon within psychiatry and virtually invisible to the general public. During the 1960s and 1970s, the only mention of autism in the DSM (Diagnostic and Statistical Manual: the official diagnostic guidelines of the American Psychiatric Association) lumped it among the criteria for Childhood Schizophrenia. Autism did not enter the DSM on its own until its third edition, in 1980, and the diagnostic criteria were then significantly expanded and loosened in the fourth edition in 1994, when Asperger's Syndrome was also added to the mix as one of several Autism Spectrum Disorders.[4] As a medical diagnosis, then, autism went from being unknown before 1943, to a marginal phenomenon before 1980, to a remarkably common diagnosis today, with some sources claiming that as many as 1% of all children are or should be classified as somewhere on the autism spectrum (Fombonne 2005).[5]

The rise in diagnosis and classification has fueled a dramatic increase in public awareness, which has in turn encouraged additional diagnosis and classification. As one barometer, articles in the *New York Times* mention autism for the first time in 1960, and contain the word in the title only seventeen times before 1990, when a sharp upward trend begins. In 2008 alone, the *New York Times* ran 169 articles on autism, roughly one every other day, and this degree of attention is indicative of what has been happening in all of the popular media, including the Web. Autism has become a major presence in the culture of early twenty-first century America.

Psychiatric disorders are often a pathologically excessive version of some trait that, in its cultural context, is considered socially desirable (anorexia is excessive thinness, neurasthenia is excessive female passivity, fugue is excessive travel, ADHD is excessive energy and activity, obsession is excessive focus and concentration). In this sense, autism might be understood as excessive individuality, autonomy, and self-reliance, normally understood as highly desirable traits. Autism might be understood to represent a pathological excess of what the Western world most prizes—autonomous individuality, with its promise of liberty and freedom—reconfigured as what it most fears—painful solitude, isolation, and loss of community. Autism has thus become an emblematic psychiatric condition of the late twentieth and early twenty-first centuries, simultaneously a medical diagnosis and a cultural force.

THE CONSTRUCTION OF AUTISM: THE MEDICAL AND SOCIAL MODELS

At present, autism is generally conceived within one of two conceptual models and embedded within one of two sorts of cultures: the medical model and the culture of medical science versus the social model and the culture of the social group. The difference centers on a single question: is autism a medical condition (syndrome, disorder, pathology) or is it a social group (an identity, a shared culture)? Although it is common to imagine culture and science as representing opposing principles (objective versus subjective, part of the natural world, and therefore real, or imagined and created), the work that scientists and doctors do is also creative and imaginative, is also historically contingent, is also expressive of the values of a particular time, place, and worldview.

Medical culture—what has been described and vigorously critiqued within Disability Studies as the *medical model*—has certain defining attributes. First, medical culture treats disability as pathology, either a deficit or an excess with respect to some normative standard. Second, the pathology resides inside the individual body in a determinate, concrete location. Third, the goals of the enterprise are diagnosis and cure. If the pathology cannot be cured—if the abnormal condition cannot be normalized—then the defective body should be sequestered lest it contaminate or degrade the larger community. In this, medical culture is an aspect of what Garland-Thomson (2004) calls "the cultural logic of euthanasia": disabled bodies should either be rehabilitated (normalized) or eliminated (either by being sequestered from sight in homes or institutions or by being allowed or encouraged to die).[6]

Since 1943, when the medicalized construction of autism began, the ways of diagnosing autism, the associated medical interventions or cures, and the conception of autism itself have undergone significant changes. In that sense, it might be better to talk about multiple medical models of autism, including Freudian psychotherapy, cognitive psychology, brain science, and genetics (Nadeson 2005). The shift from model to model comes in part in response to observations and discoveries (the scientific method) and in part in response to changes in fashion: medical science is, in part, a cultural phenomenon with its own history. As that history has unfolded, the medical construction of autism has changed and evolved.

A second way of constructing autism involves the social model of disability as it has been described within Disability Studies. In the social model, disability is understood as socially constructed rather than biologically given: the nature of disability, the kinds of conditions that are considered disabling, and the meanings attached to disability all vary with time, place, and context. For the most part, Disability Studies has concerned itself with physical impairments, especially blindness, deafness, and mobility impairments, tracing their histories and systems of signification in art, culture, and society. Disability Studies, and its social model of disability, have been notably less concerned and successful with cognitive impairments and developmental disabilities, like autism. This has had to do in part with the problem of narration: the member of the minoritized social group should be able to resist medicalized discourse by speaking for him or herself, but people with autism communicate in non-standard ways and may lack the ability to narrate their own experiences.[7] A second issue has been the problem of community: a group of people who have problems with communication and social relatedness may find it difficult to forge a social group, and may thus be difficult to constitute as a self-aware community within a social model of disability.

In recent years, however, thanks to the rapid expansion of the autistic community from the handful of children known to Kanner and Asperger to the vast numbers who now are understood, and understand themselves, to inhabit a broad "autism spectrum," and thanks to the profusion of writing, art, and music by people with autism, and thanks to the Internet which permits reclusive people to find meaningful social contact, it has become possible to conceive people with autism as a social group with a distinctive, shared culture. In what follows, I will critique various medical models of autism, and then argue for a social model of autism—one grounded in Disability Studies—in which we see self-aware people claiming autism as a valued political and social identity and celebrating a shared culture of art and everyday life.[8]

AUTISM AND THE CULTURE OF MEDICINE

Locating Autism in the Psyche: Freudian Psychotherapy

Under the medical model, autism—understood as a sort of illness or disease—has been located in many different places within the defective body, and correspondingly many cures or remedies have been proposed. In the years following the Second World War, amid the ascendancy of Freudian psychoanalysis, autism was located *in the psyche* and conceived as a problem of ego differentiation. For Bruno Bettelheim, the preeminent proponent of the psychoanalytical approach to autism, the condition resulted from a child's deliberate if unconscious choice to withdraw from a hostile, rejecting mother. Like a concentration camp inmate—this analogy was specifically proposed by Bettelheim—the child tries to protect itself from a murderous environment by erecting defenses and retreating into the "empty fortress" of autism. The autism is located within the child, but caused by the "refrigerator mother," whose own pathology prevents the child from developing normally. The proposed cure involves removing the child from the mother's care and providing psychoanalytical treatment.[9] While the psychodynamic approach to autism has largely been abandoned in the US, it persists in other countries (especially France) and in the seemingly ineradicable belief that, when it comes to poor outcomes for children, the mother is always to blame (Ladd-Taylor and Umanski 1998; Landsman 1998).

Locating Autism in the Mind: Cognitive Psychology (Central Coherence, Theory of Mind, and Executive Function)

Approaches to autism that emerge from cognitive psychology locate it *in the mind*. The mind is conceived as a kind of information-processing device, like a computer, and autism results from damage to certain of its "modules." There are three widely discussed theories of autism that identify deficits in *central coherence, theory of mind*, and *executive function*.[10] In the first of these theories, autism is a disorder characterized by "weak central coherence"—an atypically weak tendency to bind local details into global percepts.[11] In this view, the deficits in social relatedness (Kanner's "aloneness"), as well as other intellectual deficits associated with autism, are manifestations of an underlying inability to create larger meanings from discrete elements, or larger social patterns from discrete individuals.[12]

A second prevalent theory of autism based on cognitive psychology contends that the central deficit is a lack of "theory of mind": people with autism are deficient in the ability to attribute intentions, knowledge, and feelings to other people.[13] As a result, people with autism have difficulties both with social relatedness and with communication. Limitations in social relatedness and communication create the impression of isolation, as though the person with autism were living in a separate, self-enclosed world.[14] That notion underpins the label "autism" itself and resonates with both Kanner's "aloneness" and Asperger's "fundamental disturbance of contact."

A third prevalent theory of autism relates autistic behavior to deficiencies in the brain's "executive function." According to this theory, the obsessive routines and inflexibility associated with autism (Kanner's "sameness") result from difficulties in planning strategies for achieving goals and in modulating mental focus or shifting attention easily from task to task.[15]

A Triad of Impairments (Social Interaction, Communication and Imagination, Repetitive Behavior)

The Diagnostic and Statistical Manual of Mental Disorders (DSM) is the authoritative source for a medicalized understanding of autism and other "mental illnesses." The most recent fourth edition of the DSM defines "autistic disorder" as involving three sorts of abnormalities, often referred to as a "triad of impairments: 1) "qualitative impairment in social interaction; 2) "qualitative impairments in communication," which may include "abnormal functioning" in "symbolic and imaginative play"; and 3) "restricted, repetitive, and stereotyped patterns of behavior, interests, and activities." Asperger's Disorder or Asperger Syndrome, which didn't enter the DSM until 1994, is generally understood as a less severe form of autism, along what is commonly referred to as "the autism spectrum."[16]

Locating autism in the psyche or the mind presents a challenge for the medical model, committed as it is to diagnosis and cure. There can be no direct observation of the psyche or the mind—all we can do is observe behaviors and make inferences about the sorts of interior processes that might produce them. In the absence of direct observation, Freudian psychoanalysis and cognitive psychology have to rely on analogy and metaphor. As Susan Sontag (1978) observed, the profusion of metaphors is correlated with the poverty of the science—the metaphors rush into areas of ignorance. The murky causality and ineffectual treatments associated with autism lead directly to metaphorical constructs like "mindblindness," "executive function," and "central coherence," not to mention the "ego." The metaphors are needed to bridge the gap between the behaviors we can observe and their hidden source in the mind.[17] Cognitive scientists generally lack the literary flair of Bettelheim, Kanner, and Asperger, but their language is also necessarily figurative, as they attempt to describe what can only be inferred. The figurative nature of their language enhances a sense that autism is, at least in part, an imaginative

creation of those who describe it, a product of culture as much as science.

Locating Autism in the Brain or the Genes

The most recent science-based studies of autism locate it in the brain or the genes, still inside the individual body, but now in locations that are, at least in principle, available to direct observation. Studies of the brain have focused on its chemistry (Anderson 2005) as well as its structure, development, and function, often using structural and functional imaging studies (MRI and fMRI) (Minshew 2005 and Schultz 2005). Genetic studies have attempted to identify a set of "susceptibility genes" that shape the brain (Rutter 2005).[18]

For the most part, research in both of these areas has been slow to show significant results.[19] That slow progress is certainly due in part to the inherent complexity of the processes being studied. But it is due also to the heterogeneity of the population being studied. Our sense of who is autistic has broadened and diversified remarkably since the originary moment of Kanner and Asperger. For Kanner in particular, autism was an extremely rare disorder affecting children (his term was "infantile autism"), characterized above all by extreme aloneness. In more recent years, autism has been extended to people of all ages who fall anywhere on the autism spectrum (have an "autism spectrum disorder") and even to those who show signs of belonging to a "broader phenotype" of autism (Dawson 2002; Pickles 2000). The definition of autism has not only broadened, but has also changed in fundamental ways: Kanner's "extreme autistic aloneness" is no longer even part of the DSM definition, and in fact does not describe what most people now understand as comprised by autism (people with autism are not "alone"—they mostly want social contact, but they seek it in unusual ways). Medical research is thus directed toward a rapidly expanding and constantly shifting target. I suggested earlier that, due to its lack of secure biological basis, autism might eventually follow the path of neurasthenia and hysteria into quaintness and irrelevance.[20] Now I would like to suggest that this process may be hastened by the increasing incoherence of the category. Eventually, perhaps, what we now think of as autism will collapse from its internal contradictions, its contents redistributed to a variety of new categories and classifications. What holds it together at the moment is not so much science, where we find a striking heterogeneity of possible causes, as culture.

Searching for a Cure

So far I have talked mostly about diagnosis, but the medical model places on equal emphasis on cure. If autism is understood as an illness or disease, and one that is particularly complex in nature and therefore hard to diagnose, it comes as no surprise that proposed cures have sprung up like perennials each spring, and just about as often. People with autism can be induced to function better (i.e. more normally) with behavioral approaches: tasks are broken down into discrete steps, which are rehearsed, and successful completion of them is rewarded.[21] The ineffective cures that have been proposed in recent years include psychotherapy, various forms of play therapy, auditory and sensory integration training, numerous nutritional and dietary regimes, hormone and vitamin treatments, holding therapy, animal therapy, chelation, avoidance of vaccines, and facilitated communication. A small number of drugs may help in moderating some of the behaviors associated with autism, but do nothing to address autism directly. Even the much more promising work going on in neuroscience and genetics may

ultimately prove disappointing—we are much more likely to end up with an at best intermittently reliable genetic screening test that will present prospective parents with a reproductive choice than with a way of curing or significantly remediating autism.[22] Another likely outcome is that genetic research will contribute to the splitting of autism into several different categories—it may turn out that we should be speaking of autisms, rather than autism.[23]

Despite sustained effort, medical science has found little to offer by way of cure, or even significant remediation. This sorry record may have to do simply with the medical, neurological, and genetic complexities of autism. But I suspect it may have also to do with a bad fit between autism and the prevailing culture of science-based medicine: in short, there will never be a cure for autism any more than there were cures for fugue or hysteria because these are not diseases. Rather, they are clusters of behaviors, abilities, and attitudes that, under the right cultural conditions, get grouped together and provided with a label. The label appears to confer coherence on the category, but this is a fiction, or rather, a contingent cultural construction.[24]

Critique of the Medical Model

Instead of thinking of autism as a disease, with apprehensible cause, a determinate diagnosis, and a possible cure, it might be more productive to think of it as a "disease entity," which, according to Davis 2008, "allows us to move away from the positivist kind of descriptive categories of disease and to think of diseases not as discrete objects but as ranges of bodily differences and reaction" (22).[25] Along similar lines, we might begin to think of autism in light of what Morris 1998 calls a *biocultural* model, one that discusses illness and disease as emerging from a complex interaction of biology and culture.[26] In this view, diseases and illnesses of all kinds, including psychiatric conditions like autism, are simultaneously fully real, grounded in biology, and also cultural artifacts.

The medical model requires that we locate autism (like any pathology) in the body of the affected individuals—it is their personal problem and it resides inside them. But autism is intrinsically a relational phenomenon, a function of the interaction between people. In that sense, autism is a social/cultural phenomenon, not located within individuals but rather in the connections among individuals in a community. This may appear ironic in light of Kanner's claim that "aloneness" is the essential feature of autism. But that aloneness is not something individuals can achieve on their own, rather it is something constructed in relation to other people. To talk about it meaningfully, then, we have to consider it within the ambient culture and, more specifically, within the distinctive culture that autistic people have begun to construct.

AUTISM CULTURE

As its central project, Disability Studies has proposed supplanting the medical model of disability with a variety of models that shift our attention from biology to culture.[27] As Rosemarie Garland-Thomson has argued, "The meanings attributed to extraordinary bodies reside not in inherent physical flaws, but in social relationships in which one group is legitimated by possessing valued physical characteristics and maintains its ascendancy and its self-identity by systematically imposing the role of cultural or corporeal inferiority on others."[28] Disability has an evident biological basis in relation to which human societies and cultures create elaborate interpretive networks that give it meaning. The naturally occurring variations in human shape, ability, and behavior are configured and reconfigured to maintain a shifting, culturally contingent distinction between the unremarked, normally abled and the stigmatized disabled. Disability is simultaneously real, tangible, measurable, physical and an imaginative creation designed to make sense of the diversity of human morphology, capability, and behavior. In a related minority-group model, people with disabilities are understood to share a distinctive social, cultural, and political identity, conferred by, among other things, a shared experience of oppression.[29]

To bring the discussion back to autism, we might imagine that it is a social construction rather than a medical pathology, and that people labeled as autistic comprise a definable minority group. But if autism is constructed, who does the constructing? And if people with autism comprise a minority group, what gives the group cohesion and identity other than shared medical symptoms? In answer, I would like to shift attention from autism as an abstract category to people who have been identified, or who might plausibly be identified, or who have identified themselves as autistic and to study the culture that these people have communally begun to create. Within a medical model, autism is constructed by professionals—psychiatrists, psychologists, educators—in their articles, books, and clinical practices. Within a social model, autism is constructed by autistic people themselves through the culture they produce (including writing, art, and music), and its shared features give it cohesion and a distinctive identity.[30]

As an identity group, autism is somewhat amorphous, inclusive, and heterogenous (although no more so than other strategically deployed political groups, such as women, gay, or Hispanic). In current thinking, autism lies along a spectrum, a neat linear progression from "low functioning" to "high functioning." Given the increasing size and diversity of the population classified as autistic, however, it might be better to think of it as an agglomeration, a network of overlapping subgroups, and with the group as a whole defined by boundaries that are notably permeable and porous. As with other "minority groups," one can become autistic in a variety of ways, including medical diagnosis, personal choice and self-identification, and even casual classification by outsiders. I don't think it would be appropriate to impose a litmus test or to require a doctor's note. Instead, I intend the designation "autistic" to be an inclusive one, especially for those who self-identify as autistic, that is, who claim autism.

Using the concept of "neurodiversity" as a point of departure—a belief that autism is not a defect or pathology, but rather an aspect of naturally occurring and inherently desirable human variability—I will explore features of a distinctively autistic cognitive style and creative imagination. I will seek to understand autism as a way of being in the world, a world-view enshrined in a culture: to echo a familiar rallying cry from the disability rights movement, autism is a difference, not a deficit.

The medical model of autism provides a point of departure for a discussion of autistic culture, but in that model, the autistic style and creative imagination are stigmatized as symptoms of a defective body and mind. Aloneness, sameness, deficits in executive function, lack of theory of mind, inadequate drive toward central coherence, impairments in social and communication skills, abnormal functioning in imagination, stereotyped patterns of behavior—all the symptoms of "autistic disorder"—can be reinterpreted and recast as differences rather than deficits. The term *autism* is a medical term with a strongly stigmatizing impact. In what follows, and in keeping with the current impulse to embrace neurological difference, I will attempt to reclaim autism as a term of cultural identification and pride, analogous in this way to *queer* and *crip* (McRuer 2006). My goal is to have autism suggest not a defect but a distinctive and valuable style of thinking and imagining—a vibrant and interesting way of being in the world.[31] In what follows, I suggest three characteristics of the autistic vision, each related to diagnostic categories proposed by clinicians, and then I explore the ways in which this vision is expressed in writing, music, and art by autists. I focus on high autistic culture—writing, music, and art—because here the distinctive autistic sensibility is distilled and presented in the form of durable, public objects. The same traits, however, can be found operating in less sensational ways in the daily lives of people with autism, what I think of as the culture of everyday.

Local Coherence

People with autism are often richly attentive to minute details, sometimes at the expense of the big picture. They have an unusual and distinctive ability to attend to details on their own terms, not subsumed into a larger totality—a propensity to perceive the world in parts rather than as a connected whole. Objects are apprehended in their full discrete and concrete individuality rather than as members or representatives of a larger subsuming abstract category. Autistic cognition involves "detail-focused processing" (Happé 2005, 640); it is based on *local coherence*.[32]

Writing as an insider, a person with autism, Temple Grandin confirms this sense of details perceived in their full individuality without regard to a subsuming context or category:

Unlike those of most people, my thoughts move from video-like, specific images to generalization and concepts. For example, my concept of dogs is inextricably linked to every dog I've ever known. It's as if I have a card catalogue of dogs I have seen, complete with pictures, which continually grows as I add more examples to my video library.... My memories usually appear in my imagination in strict chronological order, and the images I visualize are always specific. There is no generic, generalized Great Dane.

(Grandin 1995, 27–28)

Similarly, Kamran Nazeer, also self-identified as autistic, observes:

Echolalia, or the constant, disconnected use of a particular word or phrase, is one example of rhythmic or repetitive behavior, a trait common among autistic people and often described as the desire for local coherence. This is the preference that autistic people frequently demonstrate for a limited, though immediate, form of order as protection against complexity or confusion.

(Nazeer 2006, 3–4)

One aspect of local coherence is a refusal to subsume perceptions into a hierarchy—individual events are full and complete in themselves, not operating the service of a higher totality (Headlam 2006). As Gunilla Gerland observes,

There was something special about the way I saw things. My vision was rather flat, two-dimensional in a way, and this was somehow important to the way I viewed space and people. I seemed to have to fetch visual impressions from my eyes. Visual impressions did not come to *me*. Nor did my vision provide me with any automatic priority in what I saw—everything seemed to appear just as clearly and with the same sharpness of image. The world looked like a photograph.

(Gerland 1997, 65–66)

Fixity of Focus

In talking about local coherence, Nazeer refers to another characteristic of the autistic cognitive style, namely a preference for repetition.[33] People with autism often have a preference for orderliness, system, and ritual. As Daniel Tammet, self-identified with Asperger Syndrome, says, "I have an almost obsessive need for order and routine which affects virtually every aspect of my life" (Tammet 2006, 1–2). Of course obsession and single-mindedness can be highly desirable traits—human achievement often depends on them—and people with autism often have these traits in a high degree:

In between episodes of compulsive behavior, I yearn for calmness and constancy. When things stay the same it's easier to feel safe, to understand what is expected and to gain a sense of connection.

(Lawson 2000, 2)

Autistic children don't like anything that looks out of place—a thread hanging on a piece of furniture, a wrinkled rug, books that are crooked on the bookshelf. Sometimes they will straighten out the books and other times they will be afraid.... When I became interested in something, I rode the subject to death. I would talk about the same thing over and over again. It was like playing a favorite song over and over on the stereo. Teenagers do this all the time, and nobody thinks that it is odd. But autism exaggerates normal behavior to a point that is beyond most people's capacity for understanding.

(Grandin 1995, 146, 102)

Autistic fixity of focus is a quality that enables another characteristic of autistic cognition, what Oliver Sacks refers to as a "gift for mimesis" (Sacks 1995, 241). People with autism, especially those with so-called "savant skills," often have prodigious rote memories.[34] The autistic cognitive and artistic style often involves doing one single thing with great intensity, again and again.

Private Meanings

Autistic thinking is based on locally coherent networks of private associations.[35]

Like poetry, especially modernist poetry, autistic language often involves unusual, idiosyncratic combinations of elements and images, with as much pleasure associated with the sounds of the words as with their meaning. In Kristina Chew's words, "Autistic language is a fractioned idiom, its vocabulary created from contextual and seemingly arbitrary associations of word and thing, and peculiar to its sole speaker alone . . . Autistic language users think metonymically, connecting and ordering concepts according to seemingly chance and arbitrary occurrences in an 'autistic idiolect'" (Chew 2008, 142, 133). More broadly, a search for privacy—a space safe and secure from the incessant demands of what Julia Rodas calls "compulsory sociality"—is a persistent theme in autism narratives (Rodas 2004 and 2008). Temple Grandin expresses the same notion in personal terms:

> One of my students remarked that horses don't think, they must make associations. If making associations is not considered thought, then I would have to conclude that I am unable to think. Thinking in visual pictures and making associations is simply a different form of thinking from verbal-based linear thought. There are advantages and disadvantages to both kinds of thinking. Ask any artist or accountant.[36]

Autistic expression is often introverted, directed inward rather than outward. Instead of a chain of logical inference, one often finds rich networks of associations, often private in nature. Often these networks consist of richly observed specific details: autistic thinking tends to be concrete rather than abstract.

In its search for private meaning, the autistic imagination often ends up not so much defying conventions as simply ignoring them. People with autism are generally not particularly eager to please, which frees them not only to ignore the social niceties. In speech and in writing, the autistic style is often direct to the point of rudeness, unconstrained by social conventions. As Gerland observes of her own behavior, "This apparent disregard for the conventions contributed to my appearing to be brave. In fact, I had absolutely no idea that there *were* such things as conventions" (Gerland 1997, 90). In autistic writing, music, and art, one often finds a striking originality with its roots in drive toward private meaning with relatively little concern for normal social conventions and normal communication styles.

Autistic Writing

Recent years have witnessed an explosion of writing, both in print and on the Web, by people who identify themselves as autistic. While there has been a small amount of poetry and fiction, the dominant genre by far is that of autobiography or personal memoir.[37] For some critics, the authorship of these narratives is inherently problematic: if people are really autistic, with the difficulties in communication that entails, then they will be unable to write, and if they are able to write, that means they are not really autistic. Autism autobiographies, like those by people with other sorts of cognitive or developmental disabilities, have often required some degree of mediation (from co-authors or editors) and, at least in the early years, often came with forewords from certified autism experts to vouch for their authenticity.[38] It is true that autistic discourse has sometimes had to be mediated to some degree to make it comprehensible to a mainstream (neurotypical) audience, and it is possible that this might, in some sense, compromise a pure, authentically autistic vision. Nazeer (2006), writing as a person with autism, observes,

> There may be something distinctive about autistic minds, but at least some of that

autism has to be removed, or eased, before autistic people can communicate meaningfully, even with one another, and set their minds upon the world. While there's no autistic equivalent of sign language, some level of intervention is necessary (227).

Despite the necessity, in at least some cases, for "some level of intervention," the sheer number of autism memoirs now available, and the qualities they almost universally share, make it possible to treat them both as a coherent body of literature and as one that expresses a reliably authentic autistic world view.[39] In these memoirs, and allowing for considerable individual variation, the features of autistic consciousness discussed above—local coherence, fixity of focus, and private meanings—strongly shape the style of writing. Mark Osteen's comment about Williams 1992 applies to a broad range of autism memoirs: "Williams's voice and viewpoint—blunt, headlong, self-obsessed but curiously unreflective—bespeaks an *autistic* consciousness that rarely generalizes or condenses, shows little comprehension of or interest in how others think, and possesses a weak grasp of narrative connection" (Osteen 2008a, 27). These memoirs generally share a narrow emotional range, often with an appearance of distance between the observer and the events experienced and narrated. They often lack narrative cohesion, preferring to string together brief episodes. They often feel literal-minded and concrete, with little in the way of humor or irony. The fixed, repetitive interests that are described are mirrored in a repetitive, bland style of writing.

As for overall narrative shape, autistic memoirs occasionally appear to conform to the standard ways of narrating disability, namely as a story of overcoming (cure, or the triumph of the human spirit over adversity) or a story of conversion (lessons learned by the passage through a terrible experience).[40] Certainly these are the narratives adopted by within the even larger genre of autism memoirs by parents. But the memoirs by autists themselves generally deviate from the standard script (see Waltz 2005). The title of Grandin 1986 (*Emergence*), is somewhat misleading: the emergence she describes is at best equivocal. Rather than celebrating a triumphant cure, she learns to get along in the normal world, but without changing herself in fundamental ways. Williams 1992 is something closer to a traditional "narrative of normalization" (Osteen 2008b, 28), but even here, the ending is hardly triumphant. More recent memoirs depart even farther from the usual narratives: these authors tell more of self-discovery, of finding and insisting on their essential autistic selves, than they do of overcoming or conversion. They are more like what Frank 1995 calls "chaos stories" in their defiance of traditional narrative order and their resistance to what Osteen 2008b calls "the tyranny of the comic plot" (16).

This difference in narrative shape is reflected also in the metaphors that the authors use to describe autism. In narratives of autism by parents and professionals, the most common images are those of a wall or the alien. The first of these suggests that the person with autism is concealed or imprisoned, inaccessible to the outside world, which is implicitly invited to tear the wall down. The best-known uses of this metaphor are those of Bettelheim (*The Empty Fortress*) and Park (*The Siege*), but there are many others as well. The second of these suggests that the person with autism is a foreigner, a visitor from a different land, or perhaps even a different planet. This metaphor engages the mythical, archetypal figures of the alien, the changeling, the child bewitched (Sacks 1995, 190), and is related to the Romantic notion that cognitive difference, like blindness, may both exemplify and confer a deeper, more spiritual vision. It is related also to the familiar idea of "compensatory faculties":

people with disabilities are often assumed to have gifts that compensate for and may result from their deficiencies—certainly that is the way that autistic "savant" skills are often described.

Clinicians seem particularly prone to these romanticizing notions: Asperger describes one of the children he studied as looking like he had "just fallen from the sky" (Asperger 1944/1991, 60) and Uta Frith refers to their "haunting and somehow otherworldly beauty" (Frith 2003, 1). In a similar but more prosaic vein, Grinker imagines autism as an exotic country whose inhabitants need to be better studied by anthropologists.[41] Grandin neatly turns this image around by imagining herself as an anthropologist trying to make sense of normate culture, which to her is exotic (Sacks 1995). Similarly, Miller 2003, a compilation of memoirs and conversations by autistic women, answers its title question, "Women from Another Planet?" with a resounding no:

> We are *not* from another planet. We tricked you. We made you look. We are from right here, Planet Earth. We are an integral part of this earth's ecosystems, its intricately inter-dependent network of niches and potentialities . . . We are the first wave of a new liberation movement. . . . We are part of the groundswell of what I want to call Neurological Liberation (xii).

The metaphors used in autistic memoirs rarely have to do with walls and aliens. Much more commonly, we find a metaphors of doors (Grandin 1995) and glass (Dawn Prince-Hughes 2004; Wendy Lawson 2000). Both involve an idea of separation—the autistic world and the normate world are distinct—but the boundary between them permits people on both sides to see through (it's not an impermeable wall), and possibly to move through as well. Autism culture is distinct, but it's still a human culture.

Autistic Art

Jessica Park, and Stephen Wiltshire are autistic painters who have had some degree of public attention and commercial success. Jessica Park came to public attention at an early age through one of the first and most important personal narratives of autism by her mother, Clara Park. A later book by Clara Park brought the story up through 2001, and encompassed Jessica Park's burgeoning career as a painter.[42] At an earlier stage of her career, Jessica Park painted mostly heaters, radio dials or mileage gauges, while now she devotes herself almost exclusively to individual architectural structures, mostly houses, painted against an astronomically correct starry sky. Throughout, her work is characterized by vivid sharp lines, geometrical shapes, and bright colors, and imbued with private codes and associations.[43] Each element is separate and distinct—no smudging or blurring—and rendered in astonishing detail. Here is Clara Park's description of the paintings, together with her interpretation of them as expressive of autism:

> There is no vagueness in her painting, no clashing brushwork, no atmospheric washes. It's hard-edge stuff . . . Her art is autistic in other ways too. Autistic literalism has its visual equivalent; Jessy's eye acts like a camera . . . Cameras do not ponder, they record. And there is the lack of shading . . . Most of her colors remain flat. Indeed, that unsettling tension between the prevailing flatness and the few bits of round is part of what makes her realism surreal. No shading. No nuance. If Jessy's painting bespeaks her handicap, it is a handicap not surmounted but transmuted into something rich and strange. Here is autism in its core characteristics, literal, repetitive, obsessively exact—yet beautiful. In her paintings, reality has been transfigured.
>
> (Park 2001, 130–31)

Jessica Park's work, in all of its rich individuality, resonates with the three features of autistic imagination discussed above: local coherence, fixity of focus, and private meanings. I think it is a mistake, however, to overemphasize the camera-like, literal quality of these paintings. While they are meticulously observed and rendered, they are also richly imaginative and interpretive, vibrating with energy and life and, in their incongruous juxtapositions of brilliant colors, and of brightly sunlit houses against a nighttime sky, even humor.

Some of the same issues arise in the work of Stephen Wiltshire which has been extravagantly admired, some would say "enfreaked," for its astonishing, camera-like literalism. Wiltshire draws and paints cityscapes, and he is best known for panoramic views of major cities (including London, Rome, Tokyo, Frankfurt, Madrid, and Jerusalem), often produced after shockingly brief exposure to the sights he depicts in such naturalistic and accurate detail.[44] The ubiquitous Oliver Sacks, who has championed and written about both Wiltshire and Jessica Park, has questioned the extent to which Wiltshire's art can be considered truly creative, given its literal fidelity to his subjects: perhaps his art is too purely imitative to be taken seriously as creative art.[45] I think that underestimates the individual and interpretive aspects of Wiltshire's artistic vision: even a camera offers a particular view, not an unmediated glimpse of reality. Wiltshire's art unfolds within a distinctive culture of autistic perception and cognition, including local coherence (it would be hard to imagine an art richer in detail), fixity of focus (Sacks's "gift for mimesis"), and private meanings (the work vibrates with networks of visual associations), but betrays also a distinctively individual way of seeing the world.

Autistic Music

The autistic style can be felt both in the way autistic people perceive music and they way they make music, as composers and performers. In the domain of pitch perception, I note that Absolute Pitch (AP) is significantly more prevalent among people with autism than in the general population. As a non-relational strategy of pitch perception, one based on the internal qualities of a tone without respect to other tones, AP would seem to epitomize an autistic cognition of music, based on local rather than central coherence.[46] More generally, we might speculate that, if normal, non-autistic listening emphasizes contextualization and patterning, autistic listening emphasizes the integrity of the discrete event, an orientation toward the part rather then the whole.

Autistic listeners may be more attuned to private, idiosyncratic associations than larger shared meanings. Autistic hearing is both private and "fractionated." If normal hearing involves the creation of hierarchies, autistic hearing involves the creation of associative networks.[47] Individual events are not so much clumped together to create larger patterns as they are appreciated both for their own sake and for the associations they may suggest with other individual events. Autistic listeners may have a preference for repetition and the cognitive capacity for recalling extended musical passages in full detail. Like absolute pitch, prodigious rote memory epitomizes autistic hearing.

In the portrait I have painted here, an autistic listener is someone who attends to the discrete musical event in all of its concrete detail (local coherence); who prefers the part to the whole; who is adept at creating associative networks (often involving private or idiosyncratic meanings); and who may have absolute pitch and a prodigious rote memory. In each of these respects, autistic hearing challenges normal hearing, which is presumed to be oriented toward global coherence, the synthesis of wholes from parts, the creation of relationships among discrete events, the subsuming context, and the creation of conceptual hierarchies, particularly in the domain of pitch.

In many ways, the legendary Canadian pianist, Glenn Gould, epitomizes autistic perception of music in his extraordinary performances. In his lifetime, Gould was as famous for his personal eccentricities as for the shocking originality of his musical interpretations, and I would argue that both have a common source in his autism.[48] He disliked the spontaneous give and take, the socially interactive nature of live performance and, fairly early in his career, abandoned the concert stage for the privacy and isolation of the recording studio. His profound social disengagement isolated him not only from the live concert audience but also from the community of past and present pianists—this may thus have contributed to the astonishing originality of his musical interpretations.

Specific aspects of Gould's playing may also be related to his autism, including his preference for extreme isolation of individual tones through persistent staccato articulation. One of the distinctive hallmarks of Gould's playing is separation and detachment: he separates the lines within a polyphonic texture and within each line he separates the notes from each other.[49] The detachment of lines from other lines, and notes from other notes is a striking musical affirmation of an autistic preference for local coherence. In this sense, Gould's autism provides a way of understanding his life and his art in an integrated way. Instead of seeing his famous "eccentricities" as distracting, inessential personal mannerisms, we can see them as part of an autistic worldview.

Although I have emphasized autistic high culture—writing, art, and music— there is also a much broader autistic culture of everyday life, encompassing the sorts of things that autistic people do in their daily lives to express and represent themselves. I am thinking of activities like calendar calculation, puzzle solving, mathematical manipulation, and engagement with and possible memorization of favorite television shows or movies. These do not result in works of art, but they do express the same autistic values of local coherence, private meaning, and fixity of focus that also characterize autistic high art. Autism, like other disabilities, can be thought of, at least in part as a kind of performance: not something you are, but something you do.[50] By performing autistically, gifted writers, artists, and musicians, along with just-average autistics, participate in the construction of autism and in building a community of autistic people.

CLAIMING AUTISM

We are living in a period in which a culture of autism, constructed not by medical professionals but by people with autism, has begun to emerge. Like other cultures in our multicultural landscape, autism culture has involved a search for historical roots. Where were the people we now think of as autistic before the category was created in 1943? Are there historical figures who might be claimed as progenitors, who might be held up as a source of communal pride and identification? The identification of prehistoric (i.e. pre-1943) figures with autism has become a small cottage industry, and many names have been proposed, including the Wild Boy of Aveyron and other "wild boys," Kaspar Hauser, Hugh Blair, John Howard (Frith 2003); Isaac Newton, Alfred Einstein, Andy Warhol (Collins 2004); Wolfgang Mozart, Ludwig van Beethoven, Herman Melville, Ludwig Wittgenstein, Lewis Carroll, Charles Darwin, Vincent van Gogh, Béla Bartók, W. B. Yeats (Fitzgerald 2004).[51]

Historical genealogies of this kind are extremely problematic. First, there is the lack of direct observation—for many of these figures it is hard to know reliably many significant personal details, much less if they met the elaborate and changing criteria for a condition that did not even have a name until 1943. Second, there is the problem of feedback—what Hacking 1999 calls "biolooping." When people are identified with a particular condition, like autism, they may receive certain treatments (both in the sense of medical interventions and responsive behaviors from others), and these may in turn alter the condition. Whatever their underlying neurology, people who live with autism today are behaviorally and cognitively different from earlier generations precisely because of the consequences of being classified as autistic. Third, and most important, to the extent that autism is a social and cultural phenomenon rather than (or in addition to) a medical diagnosis—the central contention of this essay—it simply did not exist or, at best, existed in an entirely different form.[52] Until very recently, people born with the characteristic neurology of autism would have been abandoned or placed in institutions for the insane or feebleminded. In a few cases, if they had remarkable skills, they might have been tolerated as eccentrics, but their eccentricities would not have coalesced into anything very much like autism as it appears today. In my view, the search for ancestors must either be abandoned or pursued in an appropriately tentative way. We will have to content ourselves with the emergence of a community that is new, tracing its roots back only to 1943, but one that is now coalescing and burgeoning.

As autism culture takes shape, with its distinctive cognitive style and worldview, it is becoming a source of identity and pride within a rapidly growing community. More and more, just as self-aware people with disabilities have learned to claim disability (Linton 1998), autists are claiming autism:

I believe autism can be a beautiful way of seeing the world. I believe that within autism there is not only the group—the label—but the individual as well; there is strength in it, and there is terror in its power. When I speak of emerging from the darkness of autism, I do not mean that I offer a success story neatly wrapped and finished with a "cure." I and the others who are autistic do not want to be cured. What I mean when I say "emergence" is that my soul was lifted from the context of my earlier autism and became autistic in another context, one filled with wonder and discovery and full of the feelings that so poetically inform each human life. . . . Much like the deaf community, we autistics are building an emergent culture. We individuals, with our cultures of one, are building a culture of many.

(Prince-Hughes 2004, 2–3, 7)

I totally agree with the need for those with an Autism Spectrum Condition (ASC not ASD [i.e. condition, not disorder]) to be recognized as a minority whose rights and needs need to be acknowledged and respected by the majority. But on the basis that they have a shared information processing difference to the majority of the population. . . . who often fail to provide forms of education, communication, social activities/networks, occupation, and employment most appropriate to this form of information processing.

(Williams 2006, 206)

While it is important for people with autism to maintain our own identities as a culture and a way of being, it is also important to learn how to interface with the vast majority of people who are not on the autism spectrum.

(Shore 2006, 201)

If I could snap my fingers and be nonautistic, I would not—because then I wouldn't be me. Autism is part of who I am . . . As I have said, it has only been recently that I realized the magnitude of the difference between me and most other people. During the past three years I have become fully aware that my visualization skills exceed those of most other people. I would never want to become so normal that I would lose these skills.

(Grandin 1995 60, 180)

We are women, living our ordinary lives, with joys and sorrows as our circumstances dictate/allow, doing many of the things non-autistic women do, feeling many of the same feelings, yet we are, in all of this, profoundly, astonishingly, and perfectly different.

(Miller 2003, xxiii)

Previously, we discussed the social and cultural conditions that made it possible for autism to be conceived as a psychiatric diagnosis, and for that diagnosis to proliferate. Now we are a position to summarize the social and cultural conditions that have made it possible for autism to emerge and flourish as a distinctive human culture with a shared worldview and cognitive style. First, there are the sheer numbers of people who are now either classified as autistic or who self-identify as autistic. Second, there is the recent addition to the ranks of the autistic of large numbers of people with relatively good linguistic, communication, and intellectual skills. These are among the first generation of people with autism to be able to represent themselves effectively in all of the artistic and popular media. Third, there is the Internet with its vast capacity for the formation of social networks, crucial for a group that has, by its very nature, difficulties with conventional social relatedness and communication. Finally, there is the emergence of the disability rights movement, the field of Disability Studies, and the new movement for "neurodiversity" that draws so extensively on both. Autism may remain as a serious psychiatric condition, and it may continue to seem to require medical intervention directed toward normalization and possible cure. But for a new generation of people with autism, it is not about what they can do despite autism (not about overcoming), but about what autism enables them to do, what they do through and with autism (Grandin 1995 describes herself as "a person whose disability has provided me with certain abilities" (204)). In that spirit, they have begun to forge a thriving community of like-minded people, committed to celebrating their shared difference.

NOTES

1. Both Kanner and Asperger took the term "autism" from a Eugen Bleuler, a Swiss psychiatrist of an earlier generation, who had coined it in 1908 with reference to the tendency of his patients with schizophrenia to withdraw from the external world into fantasy. Bleuler also coined the term "schizophrenia."

2. As Kanner (1943) observes: "It is quite possible that some such children have been viewed as feebleminded or schizophrenic. In fact, several children of our group were introduced to us as idiots or imbeciles, one still resides in a state school for the feebleminded, and two had been previously considered as schizophrenic" (242). Of the eleven children in Kanner's original study, only two achieved any degree of independence or self-sufficiency (Kanner 1971). The rest spent their lives in large institutions, with the extremely poor outcomes typical for people with autism in this era: "One cannot help but gain the impression that State Hospital admission was tantamount to a life sentence, with evanescence of the astounding facts of rote memory, abandonment of the earlier pathological yet active struggle for the maintenance of sameness, and loss of the interest in objects added to the basically poor relation to people—in other words, a total retreat to near-nothingness. These children were entered in institutions in which they were herded together with severely retarded coevals or kept in places in which they were housed with psychotic adults; two were eventually transferred from the former to the latter because of their advancing age" (Kanner 1971, 144). For a cultural history of "feeblemindedness" and "mental retardation," see Trent 1994.

3. Similar problems and contingencies of classification affect the natural sciences, too. Biologists, for example, grapple with what they call "the species problem," their ongoing and contentious attempts to carve the world of biological organisms into meaningful groups. See Mayr 1988, Hull 1989, and Ghiselin 1992.

4. This history of autism diagnoses is traced in

Grinker 2007. For vigorous critique of the DSM as more a pragmatic, social document than a scientific one—it functions primarily to provide stable, consistently identifiable populations for researchers to study, drug companies to medicate, and insurance companies to reimburse—see Kutchins and Kirk 1997 and Lewis 2006.

5. The remarkable growth of the autism population—often described as an "epidemic"—can be explained entirely by the equally remarkable relaxation and expansion of diagnostic criteria, together with increased public awareness of autism through the popular media and more vigorous case finding by educational and mental health professionals (Gernsbacher 2005; Grinker 2007).

6. Garland-Thomson 2004, 779–80: "This logic has produced conflicting, yet complementary, sets of practices and ideologies that American culture directs at what we think of broadly as disability. Such thinking draws a sharp distinction between disabled bodies imagined as redeemable and others considered disposable. One approach would rehabilitate disabled bodies; the other would eliminate them. I am positing the cultural logic of euthanasia broadly, not simply as ending a life for reasons of "mercy" or eliminating a group targeted as inferior or flawed—such as people with spina bifida or "mental retardation"—but as an umbrella concept, a mode of thought manifest in particular notions of choice, control, happiness, and suffering that underpin a wide range of practices and perceptions. Our culture encodes the logic of euthanasia in its celebration of concepts such as curing, repairing, or improving disabled bodies through procedures as diverse as reconstructive and aesthetic surgery, medication, technology, gene therapy, and faith healing. At the same time, this logic supports eradicating disabled bodies through practices directed at individuals—such as assisted suicide, mercy killing, and withholding nourishment—and those directed at certain groups deemed inferior—such as selective abortion, sterilization, euthanasia, eugenics, and institutionalization."

7. In an assessment of the state of Disability Studies in 2005, Lennard Davis observes, "The area of cognitive and affective disabilities is only just beginning to see the light of day. . . . The fact that academics are high-functioning people without, for the most part, serious cognitive disabilities has presented a kind of barrier to the construction of an autonomous subjecthood for people with cognitive disabilities. Furthermore, there is a pecking order for affective disorders, so that obsessive-compulsive disorder, depression,

and anxiety disorders are more likely to be represented positively than schizophrenia (so-called), other psychoses, and mental retardation. (Davis 2005, 530–31). On cognitive disability and problem of narration, see Bérubé 2005. On narratives of autism generally, see Murray 2008.

8. Three important recent studies both epitomize and encourage a shift from thinking about autism as a psychiatric illness to thinking about it as a social and cultural phenomenon: Nadeson 2005, Osteen 2008a, and Murray 2008.

9. Bettelheim was an influential public intellectual of his time, speaking and writing widely on the subject of autism, on which he was the universally acknowledged expert. His best-known publication, Bettelheim 1967, describes his experiences with children he treated at his "Orthogenic School" at the University of Chicago. The falsehood of Bettelheim's claims about his life and his work have been widely documented—see Severson 2008 and Schreibman 2005. Bettelheim borrowed the term "refrigerator mother" from Kanner, who related autism to "emotional frigidity in the typical autistic family" and "almost total absence of emotional warmth in child rearing" (Eisenberg and Kanner 1958, 8, 9), attributed autism to a "genuine lack of maternal warmth" (Kanner 1949), and described the mothers of autistic children as "just happening to defrost enough to produce a child" (quoted in *Time Magazine* 25 July 1960). He later repudiated this notion in a speech in 1969 to the newly formed National Society for Autistic Children (now the Autism Society of America): "Herewith I especially acquit you people as parents" (quoted in Park 2001, 11).

10. For summary and critique of all three, see Nadeson 2005, 114–34.

11. See Frith and Happé 1999, Frith 2003, and Happé 2005. Like the "theory of mind" and "executive function" theories discussed below, the "weak central coherence" theory remains controversial due to its lack of demonstrable neurological or biological basis (see Schreibman 2005).

12. According to Uta Frith, the principal proponent of this theory, "We have now enough evidence to formulate a hypothesis about the nature of the intellectual dysfunction in autism. In the normal cognitive system there is a built-in property to form coherence over as wide a range of stimuli as possible, and to generalize over as wide a range of contexts as possible. It is this drive that results in grand systems of thought, and it is this capacity for coherence that is diminished in children with autism. As a result, their information-processing systems, like their very beings, are characterized

by detachment. Detachment, as a technical term, refers to a quality of thought. It could be due either to a lack of global coherence or to a resistance to such coherence" (Frith 2003, 160).

13. Frith 2003, Baron-Cohen 1993, 1997, 2001a, 2001b, 2004. The offensive term "mindblindness" is sometimes used to name this cognitive deficit. "Theory of mind" has encountered significant resistance in the literature. On its absence of biological basis, see Schreibman 2005. On its refutation by the presence of numerous first-person accounts by autistic authors, replete with representations of their own mental states and the mental states of others, see McGeer 2004. For a critique from within the autism community, see Nazeer 2006, esp. 68–75.

14. According to Simon Baron-Cohen, the principal proponent of this theory, "A theory of mind remains one of the quintessential abilities that makes us human. By theory of mind we mean being able to infer the full range of mental states (beliefs, desires, intentions, imagination, emotions, etc.) that cause action. In brief, having a theory of mind is to be able to reflect on the contents of one's own and other's minds. Difficulty in understanding other minds is a core cognitive feature of autism spectrum conditions. The theory of mind difficulties seem to be universal among such individuals" (Baron-Cohen 2001b, 3). Baron-Cohen's clear implication is that the lack of a theory of mind renders people with autism less than fully human.

15. According to Ozonoff 1991, "Executive function is defined as the ability to maintain an appropriate problem-solving set for attainment of a future goal; it includes behaviors such as planning, impulse control, inhibition of prepotent but irrelevant responses, set maintenance, organized search, and flexibility of thought and action. Some features of autism are reminiscent of executive function deficits. The behavior of autistic people often appears rigid and inflexible: many autistic children become extremely distressed over trivial changes in the environment and insist on following routines in precise detail. They are often perseverative, focusing on one narrow interest or repetitively engaging in one stereotyped behavior. Their cognition often seems to lack executive functions; autistic individuals do not appear future-oriented, do not anticipate long-term consequences of behavior well, and have great difficulty self-reflecting and self-monitoring. They frequently appear impulsive, as if unable to delay or inhibit responses (1083). . . . The universality of executive function deficits in the present sample [including subjects

with both "classic high-functioning autism" and Asperger syndrome] and suggests that it might be a primary deficit of autism" (1099). See also Ozonoff 2005 and the essays in Russell 1997.

16. "Asperger syndrome is a severe and chronic developmental disorder closely related to autistic disorder and pervasive developmental disorder not otherwise specified, and, together, these disorders comprise a continuum referred to as the *autism spectrum disorders*. Having autism as the paradigmatic and anchoring disorder in this diagnostic category, the ASDs more generally are characterized by marked and enduring impairments within the domains of social interaction, communication, play and imagination, and a restricted range of behaviors or interests" (Klin 2005, 88).

17. The metaphors around autism comprise what Roy Porter calls an "analogy-based explanatory system." He is speaking of the humors (blood, choler, phlegm, and melancholy), among the earliest medicalized attempts to understand madness, but his observation extends to current theories of autism as well: "Analogy-based explanatory systems of this kind were not just plausible but indispensable so long as science had little direct access to what went on beneath the skin or in the head" (Porter 2002, 40).

18. "The real potential value of genetic research in autism lies in the probability that it will provide invaluable leads for biological studies that will succeed eventually in identifying the neural basis of autism. Identification of the susceptibility genes will not, of course, do that on its own. Genes code for proteins and not for psychiatric disorders or behaviors. Many areas of science will be needed in delineating the indirect pathways leading from susceptibility genes through effects on proteins and protein products, through physiological and neurochemical processes, and ultimately to the proximal pathway that leads to the syndrome of autism" (Rutter 2005, 443).

19. Anderson 2005, 464: "On surveying the field of neurochemical research in autism, it is notable how few replicated differences have been found between autistic and normal subjects." Rutter 2005, 443–44: "At present, the clinical payoff from genetic research has been quite modest and it remains to be seen just what it will deliver."

20. Hacking 1998 identifies a group of what he calls "transient mental illnesses," by which he refers to "an illness that appears in a time, in a place, and later fades away" (1). He adduces hysteria as one such transient illness and devotes much of the book to "fugue" as another. See also Hacking 1999, which identifies transient mental illnesses,

including hysteria and anorexia, as ones that "show up only at some times and some places, for reasons which we can only suppose are connected with the culture of those times and places" (100). It's not that real people don't live, and possibly suffer, with real symptoms; rather, that these disease entities are provisional and contingent ways of grouping and labeling them.

21. Volkmar 2005, 6: "Today there is broad agreement that autism and associated disorders represent the behavioral manifestations of underlying disfunctions in the functioning of the central nervous system, and that sustained educational and behavioral interventions are useful and constitute the core of treatment." Schreibman 2005, 133: "Few people would argue with the statement that today the treatment of choice is that based on the behavioral model. In fact, behavioral treatment is the only treatment that has been empirically demonstrated to be effective for children with autism."

22. For a discussion of genetic testing from a Disability Studies point of view, see Wilson 2006, Hubbard 2006, Saxton 2006, and Garland-Thomson 2004.

23. Geneticists are already eying psychiatric diagnoses for the possibility of significant reconfiguration of the categories on a genetic basis. "One area that might benefit from genetic disease classification is psychiatry. Because of the difficulty of measuring the brain, psychiatric diagnoses are still mainly based on symptoms. The Diagnostic and Statistical Manual of Mental Disorders contains descriptions of conditions as diverse as acute stress disorder and voyeurism. Scientists have found that certain genes appear to be associated with both schizophrenia and bipolar disorder. Those links, and the fact that some drugs work for both diseases, have prompted a debate over whether they are truly distinct disorders. 'The way we categorize these into two separate entities is almost certainly not correct,' said Dr. Wade H. Berretini, a professor of psychiatry at the University of Pennsylvania" (Andrew Pollack, "Redefining Disease, Genes and All," *New York Times* May 6, 2008).

24. This conclusion—that autism may be productively thought of as a cultural phenomenon rather than a medical pathology—tracks that of Nadeson 2008, which is worth quoting at some length. "This genealogy questions whether autism is a homogeneous, pathological condition that can be exhaustively known—or transparently represented—by scientists and their representational technologies (e.g., MRIs). Although I deconstruct the idea of autism as a uniform, biological essence shared by all people labeled as "autistic," I do *not* reject the idea that biological phenomena contribute to the expression of "autistic" symptoms. I believe we need to explore how various institutional relationships, expert authorities, and bodies of knowledge have sought to represent, divide, understand, and act on biologically based, but socially shaped and expressed, behavioral and cognitive differences such as autism. . . . In our everyday thinking and communication, most of us visualize disease as either caused by a scientifically discernable agent such as a virus or bacterium (e.g., AIDS or meningitis) or as emanating from a detectable, localized bodily dysfunction (e.g., heart disease or diabetes). The disease-causing agent or diseased bodily system is seen as objective, available to visual representation (through a microscope, electromagnetic scan, or scientific diagram), and ultimately treatable (even if a "cure" eludes current medical understanding). In effect, disease is represented in our everyday understanding as available to empirical identification, interpretation, and intervention. . . . But autism is probably a heterogeneous condition that is more properly called a syndrome than a disease. Moreover, the causal pathways engendering autistic symptoms are most likely multiple and contingent on level upon level of loosely coupled, synergistic, biological and social systems" (79–80).

25. Similarly, see Hacking 1998 and 1999.

26. "The long-dominant biomedical model provides [a] comprehensive and dubious grand narrative: a theory that reduces every illness to a biological mechanism of cause and effect. By contrast, my argument—that postmodern illness is defined by an awareness of the elaborate interconnections between biology and culture—does not aspire to the status of a grand narrative. It does not seek to explain every affliction on the planet, but rather to describe a new, transitional, and unfinished understanding of illness that typifies numerous industrial societies during the second half of the twentieth century" (Morris 1998, 11). Similarly, see Nadeson 2008: "In short, disease, disability, and bodily difference are at once material and symbolic, both socially constructed and materially inscribed. . . . The biological and the cultural [are] mutually constitutive, inseparable in their constitution of personhood" (81).

27. Linton 1998, 11–12: "The medicalization of disability casts human variation as deviance from the norm, as pathological condition, as deficit, and, significantly, as an individual burden and personal tragedy. Society, in agreeing to assign medical meaning to disability, colludes to keep

the issue within the purview of the medical establishment, to keep it a personal matter and 'treat' the condition and the person with the condition rather than 'treating' the social processes and policies that construct disabled people's lives. The disability studies' and disability rights movement's position is critical of the domination of the medical definition and views it as a major stumbling block to the reinterpretation of disability as a political category and to the social changes that could follow such a shift." Similarly, see Longmore and Umansky 2001.

28. Garland-Thomson 1997, 7. Similarly, see Longmore 2003.

29. Siebers 2008, 3–4: "While seen historically as a matter for medical intervention, disability has been described more recently in disability studies as a minority identity that must be addressed not as personal misfortune or individual defect but as the product of a disabling social and built environment. Tired of discrimination and claiming disability as a positive identity, people with disabilities insist on the pertinence of disability to the human condition, on the value of disability as a form of diversity, and on the power of disability as a critical concept for thinking about human identity in general."

30. Similarly, see Biklen 2005, 65: "I argue that autism is best understood as a social and cultural construction, that the particular aspects of autism's construction are complex and multilayered, and that people classified autistic as well as those around them, including the autism field, have choices to make concerning which constructions to privilege. Autism is not a given condition or set of realities—at least, it is not 'given' or 'real' *on its own*. Rather, autism is and will be, in part, what any of us make it."

31. In order to deflect any charge of essentialism, I want to make clear that I am not suggesting that all autistic people approach the world in the ways I describe, or that anyone who approaches the world in these ways must be autistic. People with autism comprise a diverse community—there are many ways to be autistic—and the qualities that I am describing as autistic are also present, in varying degrees, in the neurotypical population as well. The notion of an autistic cognitive style functions somewhat in the manner of a notion like "Jewish humor"—a provisional point of departure for inquiry and, possibly, a useful tool in establishing a group identity for strategic political purposes.

32. For more on the recasting of the deficit of "weak central coherence" as the difference of "local coherence," see Mills 2008 and Belmonte 2008.

33. This preference involves recasting Kanner's "sameness," deficiencies in "executive function," and the emphasis in the DSM-IV on "restricted, repetitive, and stereotyped patterns of behavior, interests, and activities."

34. There is an extensive literature on autistic savants, formerly known as "idiot savants." While the offensiveness of the first word in that earlier label is clear enough, even the term "savant" itself is problematic. First, it entails an invidious comparison between the narrow ability (the "splinter skill") and the larger disability—it might be better to see the variety of skills possessed by an individual person in the same way we see the variety of skills possessed by groups of people: aspects of naturally occurring and desirable diversity. Second, it carries an impulse toward "enfreakment": the special skill provokes amazement and wonder, and also a sense of irreducible otherness (the skill seems almost inhuman). Third, the "autistic savant" comes to play the same role with respect to the population of autistic people that the "supercrip" does with respect to disabled people: it minimizes the challenges that most people with disabilities face and implies an additional burden, possibly a moral burden, of failing to measure up to an unrealistic standard.

35. The idea of "private meaning" resonates with Kanner's "aloneness," with deficiencies in "theory of mind," and with the deficits in social interaction and communication described in the DSM.

36. Grandin 1995, 173.

37. A very partial list would include Grandin 1986 and Williams 1992 (these are the first two published autistic memoirs), as well as Gerland 1997, Willey 1999, Lawson 2000, Miller 2003, Shore 2003, Prince-Hughes 2004, Ariel 2006, Tammet 2006, Nazeer 2006, and Robison 2007. For a general discussion of autism memoirs, see Cumberland 2008.

38. Bérubé 2000. Grandin 1986 has a co-author (Margaret M. Scariano) and a foreword from Bernard Rimland, at the time a leading figure in autism research—he also wrote the authenticating foreword for Williams 1992. Grandin 1995 has a foreword from Oliver Sacks. Publishers of more recent autistic autobiographies have been more willing to allow their autistic authors to stand on their own.

39. Rose 2008, 47: "I contend, therefore, that the collection of texts that comprise the corpus of autistic life narratives is now such that it enacts a community response to the individuation

of impairment, as each text enacts Couser's antipathological impulse to write back against the more restrictive discursive limits of being diagnosed as autistic." The reference is to Couser 1997.

40. Couser 1997. See also Frank 1995 and Hawkins 1999. On conversion narratives and autism, see Fisher 2008. On autism narratives generally, see Murray 2008.

41. Grinker 2007, 13: "The process of understanding autism itself parallels the work that anthropologists do, since the minds of people with autism are sometimes as hard to understand as foreign cultures."

42. Park 1982 and Park 2001.

43. On the network of private meanings that permeate Jessica Park's life and artistic work, see Park 2001. See also Chew 2008.

44. Wiltshire's paintings can be seen on the Web and in four books: Wiltshire 1987, 1989, 1991, and 1993.

45. Sacks 1995. See discussion in Osteen 2008b, 12–14.

46. Absolute pitch is the ability to name a pitch or produce a pitch identified by name without using an external source. For a survey of work on absolute pitch (AP), including the autism connection, see Ward 1999. Mottron et al. 1999 suggests "a causal relationship between AP and autism," which they relate to an "atypical tendency to focus on the stimulus rather than its context" (486). See also Brown et al. 2003: "Reports of a relatively high prevalence of absolute pitch (AP) in autistic disorder suggest that AP is associated with some of the distinctive cognitive and social characteristics seen in autism spectrum disorders. . . . Piecemeal information processing, of which AP is an extreme and rare example, is characteristic of autism and may be associated as well with subclinical variants in language and behavior. We speculate that the gene or genes that underlie AP may be among the genes that contribute to autism. . . . Inasmuch as AP possessors can identify the individual pitches in a melody, AP is an extreme example of piecemeal information processing. . . . The link between autism and AP points to other neuropsychological processes that might underlie AP. A number of the special abilities found in autistic savants—prodigious memory and AP among them—can be characterized as high-fidelity information processing. . . ." (166).

47. Headlam 2006 makes a similar argument.

48. Maloney 2006 persuasively places Gould on the autism spectrum through careful study of the extensive written and video archive: "Autism is the solution to the perplexing riddle of [Glenn] Gould's existence and is therefore arguably the fundamental story of his life. It leads us to a coherent understanding of both the man and the musician. Not only does it gather all his strange behavioral and lifestyle eccentricities into a unified *gestalt*, it also furnishes intriguing insights into important aspects of his music-making" (134). Autism remains a controversial issue in Gould studies. Ostwald 1997 is a psychobiography that raises but does not pursue the issue of autism. Bazzana 2004 discounts autism, preferring instead a mixed account based on anxiety, depression, hypochondria, and "a variety of obsessional, schizoid, and narcissistic traits" (370).

49. According to Bazzana 1997, "As a general rule, Gould preferred articulation that can best be described as non-legato or detaché . . . His desire for clarity, so basic to his musical personality, extended to his rendering of phrases and even individual notes . . . Detaché was the norm for Gould regardless of tempo" (215–16).

50. Sandahl and Auslander 2005: "Part of sociology's legacy to performance studies is the idea that we do not just live our "real life" identities, we *perform* them . . . Goffman argues that who we are socially is bound up with who we are perceived to be by those around us (our audience) and that we behave as actors in order to control the impressions we make on others. This understanding of everyday behavior emphasizes that identity does not simply reside in individuals but is the product of social interactions among individuals. This perspective is congruent with the view of disability as something that is not an intrinsic characteristic of certain bodies but a construct produced through the interaction of those bodies with socially based norms that frame the way those bodies are generally perceived" (215).

51. A similar list of fictional characters from the pre-autism era who have been placed on the autism spectrum would include Bartelby (Garland-Thomson 2004 and Murray 2008); Jane Eyre (Rodas 2008); Sherlock Holmes (Fitzgerald 2004); and Barnaby Rudge (Grove 1987 and Murray 2008).

52. McDonagh 2008: "My resistance to reading historical figures or literary characters as autistic or aspergian is based on one of the fundamental precepts of this paper: that autism, should it turn out to be a single pathology with an organic cause and thus 'real,' is also perceived within a social dynamic, and our recognition and understanding of autism takes form within this

dynamic. If the social circumstances allowing us to perceive autism did not exist before some point relatively early in the twentieth century, and if the perception and articulation of autism is an important part of its being, then to what extent can we say the condition existed previously?. . . . The biological component of autism, the "indifferent" element [the reference is to Hacking 1999], may have a long history upon which biomedical and neurological research might one day shed some light, but autism as a diagnostic category has also, since its creation, been engaged in a dynamic social exchange that is as crucial as its indifferent element. Thus, although a pre-twentieth-century autism is possible in terms of simple pathology, it seems to be something of a conceptual anachronism" (100).

WORKS CITED

Anderson, George M. and Yoshihiko Hoshino. 2005. "Neurochemical Studies of Autism." In *Handbook of Autism and Pervasive Developmental Disorders*, third edition, ed. Fred R. Volkmar, Rhea Paul, Ami Klin, and Donald Cohen, 435–472. Hoboken, NJ: John Wiley & Sons.

Ariel, Cindy N. and Naseef, Robert A. eds. 2006. *Voices from the Spectrum: Parents, Grandparents, Siblings, People with Autism, and Professionals Share Their Wisdom*. London: Jessica Kingsley.

Asperger, Hans. 1944/1991. "'Autistic Psychopathy' in Childhood," trans. Uta Frith. In Uta Frith, *Autism and Asperger Syndrome*, 37–92. Cambridge: Cambridge University Press.

Baron-Cohen, Simon, ed. 1993. *Understanding Other Minds: Perspectives from Autis*m. Oxford: Oxford University Press.

Baron-Cohen, Simon. 1997. *Mindblindness: An Essay on Autism and Theory of Mind*. Cambridge, MA: MIT Press.

Baron-Cohen, Simon. 2001a. "Theory of Mind and Autism: A Review." Special Issue of *The International Review of Mental Retardation* 23 (2001): 169–184.

Baron-Cohen, Simon. 2001b. "Theory of Mind in Normal Development and Autism." *Prisme 34, 174–183*.

Baron-Cohen, Simon. 2004. *The Essential Difference*. London: Penguin.

Bazzana, Kevin. 1997. *Glenn Gould, The Performer in the Work: A Study in Performance Practice*. Oxford: Clarendon Press.

Bazzana, Kevin. 2004. *Wondrous Strange: The Life and Art of Glenn Gould*. Oxford: Oxford University Press.

Belmonte, Matthew K. 2008. "Human, but More So: what the Autistic Brain Tells Us about the Process of Narrative." In Mark Osteen, ed. *Autism and Representation*, 166–180. New York: Routledge.

Bérubé, Michael. 2000. "Autobiography as Performative Utterance." *American Quarterly* 52: 339–343.

Bérubé, Michael. 2005. "Disability and Narrative." *PMLA* 120/2: 568–576.

Bettelheim, Bruno. 1967. *The Empty Fortress: Infantile Autism and the Birth of the Self*. New York: Free Press.

Biklen, Douglas. 2005. *Autism and the Myth of the Person Alone*. New York: New York University Press.

Brown, Walter A., Cammuso, Karen, Sachs, Henry, et al. 2003. "Autism-Related Language, Personality, and Cognition in People with Absolute Pitch: Results of a Preliminary Study." *Journal of Autism and Developmental Disorders* 33/2: 163–167.

Chew, Kristina. 2008. "Fractioned Idiom: Metonymy and the Language of Autism." In Mark Osteen, ed. *Autism and Representation*, 133–144. New York: Routledge.

Collins, Paul. 2004. *Not Even Wrong: Adventures in Autism*. New York and London: Bloomsbury.

Couser, G. Thomas. 1997. *Recovering Bodies: Illness, Disability and Life Writing*. Madison and London: University of Wisconsin Press.

Cumberland, Debra L. 2008. "Crossing Over: Writing the Autistic Memoir." In Mark Osteen, ed. *Autism and Representation*, 183–196. New York: Routledge.

Dawson, Geraldine, Sara Webb, Gerard D. Schellenberg, Stephen Dager, Seth Friedman, Elizabeth Aylward, and Todd Richards. 2002. "Defining the Broader Phenotype of Autism: Genetic, Brain, and Behavioral Perspectives." *Development and Psychopathology* 14: 581–611.

Davis, Lennard. 2005. "Disability: The Next Wave or Twilight of the Gods?" PMLA 120/2: 527–532.

Davis, Lennard. 2008. *Obsession: A History*. Chicago: University of Chicago Press.

Eisenberg, Leon and Leo Kanner. 1958. "Early Infantile Autism, 1933–1955." In *Psychopathology*, ed. Charles Reed, Irving Alexander, and Sylvan Tomkins, 3–14. Cambridge, MA: Harvard University Press.

Fisher, James T. 2008. "No Search, No Subject? Autism and the American Conversion Narrative." In Mark Osteen, ed. *Autism and Representation*, 51–64. New York: Routledge.

Fitzgerald, Michael 2004. *Autism and Creativity: Is there a Link between Autism in Men and Exceptional Creativity?* New York: Routledge.

Fombonne, Eric. 2005. "Epidemiological Studies of Pervasive Developmental Disorders." In *Handbook* of Autism and Pervasive Developmental Disorders, third edition, ed. Fred R. Volkmar, Rhea Paul, Ami Klin, and Donald Cohen, 42–69. Hoboken, NJ: John Wiley & Sons.

Frank, Arthur W. Frank. 1995. *The Wounded Storyteller: Body, Illness, and Ethics.* Chicago: University of Chicago Press.

Frith, Uta. 2003. *Autism: Explaining the Enigma,* 2nd ed. Oxford: Blackwell.

Frith, Uta and Happé, Francesca. 1999. "Theory of Mind and Self-Consciousness: What is it Like to be Autistic?" *Mind and Language* 14/1: 1–22.

Garland-Thomson, Rosemarie. 1997. *Extraordinary Bodies: Figuring Physical Disability in American Culture and Literature.* New York: Columbia University Press.

Garland-Thomson, Rosemarie. 2004. "The Cultural Logic of Euthanasia: 'Sad Fancyings' in Herman Melville's 'Bartelby.'" *American Literature* 76/4 (2004): 777–806.

Gerland, Gunilla. 1997. *A Real Person: Life on the Outside,* trans. Joan Tate. London: Souvenir Press.

Gernsbacher, Morton Ann, Michelle Dawson, and H. Hill Goldsmith. 2005 "Three Reasons Not to Believe in an Autism Epidemic." *Current Directions in Psychological Science* 14/2: 55–58.

Ghiselin, Michael. 1992. "A Radical Solution to the Species Problem." In Marc Ereshefsky (ed.), *The Units of Evolution: Essays on the Nature of Species,* 279–292. Cambridge, MA: The MIT Press.

Grandin, Temple. 1995. *Thinking in Pictures and Other Reports from My Life with Autism.* New York: Doubleday Books.

Grandin, Temple and Margaret M. Scariano. 1986. *Emergence: Labeled Autistic.* New York: Warner Books.

Grinker, Roy. 2007. *Unstrange Minds: Remapping the World of Autism.* New York: Basic Books.

Grove, Thelma. 1987. "Barnaby Rudge: A Case Study in Autism." *Dickensian* 83: 139–148.

Hacking, Ian. 1998. *Mad Travelers: Reflections on the Reality of Transient Mental Illnesses.* Cambridge, MA: Harvard University Press.

Hacking, Ian. 1999. *The Social Construction of What?* Cambridge, MA: Harvard University Press.

Happé, Francesca. 2005. "The Weak Central Coherence Account of Autism." In *Handbook of Autism and Pervasive Developmental Disorders,* third edition, ed. Fred R. Volkmar, Rhea Paul, Ami Klin, and Donald Cohen, 640–49. Hoboken, NJ: John Wiley & Sons.

Hawkins, Anne Hunsaker. 1999. *Reconstructing Illness: Studies in Pathography,* 2nd ed. West Lafayette, IN: Purdue University Press.

Headlam, Dave. 2006. "Learning to Hear Autistically." In *Sounding Off: Theorizing Disability in Music,* ed.

Neil Lerner and Joseph N. Straus, 109–120. New York: Routledge.

Hubbard, Ruth. 2006. "Abortion and Disability: Who Should and Who Should Not Inhabit the World?" In *The Disability Studies Reader,* 2nd ed., ed. Lennard Davis, 93–104. New York: Routledge.

Hull, David. 1989. *The Metaphysics of Evolution.* Albany, NY: State University of New York Press.

Kanner, Leo. 1943. "Autistic Disturbances of Affective Contact." *The Nervous Child* 2: 217–250.

Kanner, Leo. 1949. "Problems of Nosology and Psychodynamics in Early Childhood Autism." *American Journal of Orthopsychiatry* 19: 416–426.

Kanner, Leo. 1971. "Follow-up Study of Eleven Autistic Children Originally Reported in 1943." *Journal of Autism and Developmental Disorders* 1/2: 119–145.

Klin, Ami, James McPartland, and Fred Volkmar. 2005. "Asperger Syndrome." In *Handbook of Autism and Pervasive Developmental Disorders,* third edition, ed. Fred R. Volkmar, Rhea Paul, Ami Klin, and Donald Cohen, 88–125. Hoboken, NJ: John Wiley & Sons.

Kutchins, Herb and Stuart A. Kirk. 1997. *Making us Crazy: DSM: The Psychiatric Bible and the Creation of Mental Disorders.* New York: The Free Press.

Ladd-Taylor, Molly and Lauri Umanski. 1998. *"Bad" Mothers: The Politics of Blame in Twentieth-Century America.* New York: NYU Press.

Landsman, Gail. 1998. "Reconstructing Motherhood in the Age of 'Perfect' Babies: Mothers of Infants and Toddlers with Disabilities." *Signs: Journal of Women in Culture and Society* 24: 69–99.

Lawson, Wendy. 2000. *Life Behind Glass: A Personal Account of Autism Spectrum Disorder.* London: Jessica Kingsley.

Lewis, Bradley. 2006. *Moving Beyond Prozac, DSM, and the New Psychiatry: The Birth of Postpsychiatry.* Ann Arbor: University of Michigan Press.

Linton, Simi. 1998. *Claiming Disability: Knowledge and Identity.* New York: New York University Press.

Longmore, Paul. 2003. "Introduction." In *Why I Burned My Book and Other Essays on Disability,* 1–18. Philadelphia: Temple University Press, 2003.

Longmore, Paul and Lauri Umansky. 2001. "Introduction: Disability History: From the Margins to the Mainstream." In *The New Disability History: American Perspectives,* ed. Paul Longmore and Lauri Umansky, 1–32. New York: New York University Press.

Maloney, Timothy. 2006. "Glenn Gould, Autistic Savant." In *Sounding Off: Theorizing Disability in Music,* ed. Neil Lerner and Joseph N. Straus, 121–136. New York: Routledge.

Mayr, Ernst. 1988. *Toward a New Philosophy of Biology: Observations of an Evolutionist.* Cambridge, MA: Harvard University Press.

McDonagh, Patrick. 2008. "Autism and Modernism: A Genealogical Exploration." In Mark Osteen, ed. *Autism and Representation*, 99–116. New York: Routledge.

McGeer, Victoria. 2004. "Autistic Self-Awareness." *Philosophy, Psychiatry, & Psychology* 11/3: 235–251.

McRuer, Robert. 2006. *Crip Theory: Cultural Signs of Queerness and Disability*. New York: New York University Press.

Miller, Jean Kearns. 2003. *Women from Another Planet? Our Lives in the Universe of Autism*. Bloomington, IN: First Books.

Mills, Bruce. 2008. "Autism and the Imagination." In Mark Osteen, ed. *Autism and Representation*, 117–132. New York: Routledge.

Minshew, Nancy J, John A. Sweeney, Margaret L. Bauman, and Sara Jane Webb. 2005. "Neurologic Aspects of Autism." In *Handbook of Autism and Pervasive Developmental Disorders*, third edition, ed. Fred R. Volkmar, Rhea Paul, Ami Klin, and Donald Cohen, 473–514. Hoboken, NJ: John Wiley & Sons.

Morris, David. 1998. *Illness and Culture in the Postmodern Age*. Berkeley: University of California Press.

Mottron, L., Peretz, I., Belleville, S. and Rouleau, N. 1999. "Absolute Pitch in Autism: A Case-study." *Neurocase* 5: 485–501.

Murray, Stuart. 2008. *Representing Autism: Culture, Narrative, Fascination*. Liverpool: Liverpool University Press.

Nadeson, Majia Holmer. 2005. *Constructing Autism: Unraveling the "Truth" and Understanding the Social*. New York: Routledge.

Nadeson, Majia Holmer. 2008. "Constructing Autism: A Brief Genealogy." In Mark Osteen, ed. *Autism and Representation*, 78–96. New York: Routledge.

Nazeer, Kamran. 2006. *Send in the Idiots: Stories from the Other Side of Autism*. New York and London: Bloomsbury.

Osteen, Mark, ed. 2008a. *Autism and Representation*. New York: Routledge.

Osteen, Mark. 2008b. "Autism and Representation: A Comprehensive Introduction." In Mark Osteen, ed. *Autism and Representation*, 1–48. New York: Routledge.

Ostwald, Peter. 1997. *Glenn Gould: The Ecstasy and Tragedy of Genius*. New York: Norton.

Ozonoff, Sally, B. F. Pennington, and S. J. Rogers. 1991. "Executive Function Deficits in High-Functioning Autistic Individuals: Relationship to Theory of Mind." *Journal of Child Psychology and Psychiatry and Allied Disciplines* 32: 1081–1105.

Ozonoff, Sally, Mikle South, and Sherri Provencal. 2005. "Executive Functions." In *Handbook of Autism and Pervasive Developmental Disorders*, third edition, ed. Fred R. Volkmar, Rhea Paul, Ami Klin, and Donald Cohen, 606–627. Hoboken, NJ: John Wiley & Sons.

Park, Clara Claiborne. 1982. *The Siege: A Family's Journey Into the World of an Autistic Child*. Boston: Back Bay Books.

Park, Clara Claiborne. 2001. *Exiting Nirvana: A Daughter's Life with Autism*. Boston: Little, Brown and Company.

Pickles, A., E. Starr, S. Kazak, P. Bolton, K. Papanikolaou, A. Bailey, R. Goodman and M. Rutter. 2000. "Variable Expression of the Autism Broader Phenotype: Findings from Extended Pedigrees." *The Journal of Child Psychology and Psychiatry and Allied* Disciplines 41: 491–502.

Porter. Roy. 2002. *Madness: A Brief History*. Oxford: Oxford University Press.

Prince-Hughes, Dawn. 2004. *Songs of the Gorilla Nation: My Journey Through Autism*. New York: Harmony.

Robison, John Elder. 2007. *Look Me In The Eye: My Life with Asperger's*. New York: Crown Publishers.

Rodas, Julia Miele. 2004. "Tiny Tim, Blind Bertha, and the Resistance of Miss Mowcher: Charles Dickens and the Uses of Disability." *Dickens Studies Annual* 34: 51–97.

Rodas, Julia Miele. 2008. "'On the Spectrum': Rereading Contact and Affect in *Jane Eyre*." Nineteenth-Century Gender Studies 4/2.

Rose, Irene. 2008. "Autistic Biography or Autistic Life Narrative?" *Journal of Literary Disability* 2/1: 44–54.

Russel, James, ed. 1997. *Autism as an Executive Disorder*. Oxford: Oxford University Press.

Rutter, Michael. 2005. "Genetic Influences and Autism." In *Handbook of Autism and Pervasive Developmental Disorders*, third edition, ed. Fred R. Volkmar, Rhea Paul, Ami Klin, and Donald Cohen, 425–452. Hoboken, NJ: John Wiley & Sons.

Sacks, Oliver. 1995. *An Anthropologist on Mars: Seven Paradoxical Tales*. New York: Knopf.

Sandahl, Carrie and Philip Auslander, ed. 2005. *Bodies in Commotion: Disability and Performance*. Ann Arbor: University of Michigan Press.

Saxton, Marsha. 2006. "Disability Rights and Selective Abortion." In *The Disability Studies Reader*, 2nd ed., ed. Lennard Davis, 105–116. New York: Routledge.

Schreibman, Laura. 2005. *The Science and Fiction of Autism*. Cambridge, MA: Harvard University Press.

Schultz, Robert T. and Diana L. Robins. 2005. "Functional Neuroimaging Studies of Autism Spectrum Disorders." In *Handbook of Autism and Pervasive Developmental Disorders*, third edition, ed. Fred R. Volkmar, Rhea Paul, Ami Klin, and Donald Cohen, 515–533. Hoboken, NJ: John Wiley & Sons.

Severson, Katherine DeMaria, James Arnt Aune, and Denise Jodlowski. 2008. "Bruno Bettelheim, Autism, and the Rhetoric of Scientific Authority." In Mark Osteen, ed. *Autism and Representation*, 65–77. New York: Routledge.

Shore, Stephen. 2003. *Beyond the Wall: Personal Experiences with Autism and Asperger Syndrome*. Shawnee Mission, KS: Autism Asperger Publishing Co.

Shore, Stephen. 2006. "The Importance of Parents in the Success of People with Autism." In *Voices from the Spectrum: Parents, Grandparents, Siblings, People with Autism, and Professionals Share Their Wisdom*, ed. Cindy N. Ariel and Robert A. Naseef, 199–203. London: Jessica Kingsley Publishers.

Siebers, Tobin. 2008. *Disability Theory*. Ann Arbor: University of Michigan Press.

Sontag, Susan. 1978. *Illness as Metaphor*. New York: Farrar, Straus, and Giroux.

Tammet, Daniel. 2006. *Born on a Blue Day*. New York: Free Press.

Trent, James W. *Inventing the Feeble Mind: A History of Mental Retardation in the United States*. Berkeley: University of California Press, 1994.

Volkmar, Fred R and Ami Klin. 2005. "Issues in the Classification of Autism and Related Conditions." In *Handbook of Autism and Pervasive Developmental Disorders*, third edition, ed. Fred R. Volkmar, Rhea Paul, Ami Klin, and Donald Cohen, 5–41. Hoboken, NJ: John Wiley & Sons.

Waltz, Mitzi. 2005. "Reading Case Studies of People with Autistic Spectrum Disorders: a cultural stud-ies approach to issues of disability representation." *Disability & Society* 20/4: 421–435.

Ward, W. Dixon. 1999. "Absolute Pitch." In *The Psychology of Music*, 2nd ed., ed. Diana Deutsch, 265–298. San Diego: Academic Press.

Willey, Liane Holliday. 1999. *Pretending to be Normal: Living with Asperger's Syndrome*. London: Jessica Kingsley.

Williams, Donna. 1992. *Nobody, Nowhere: The Extraordinary Autobiography of an Autistic*. New York: Harper Collins.

Williams, Donna. 2006. "Culture, Conditions, and Personhood: A Response to the Cure Debate on Autism." In *Voices from the Spectrum: Parents, Grandparents, Siblings, People with Autism, and Professionals Share Their Wisdom*, ed. Cindy N. Ariel and Robert A. Naseef, 204–208. London: Jessica Kingsley Publishers.

Wilson, James C. 2006. "(Re)Writing the Genetic Body-Text: Disability, Textuality, and the Human Genome Project." In *The Disability Studies Reader*, 2nd ed., ed. Lennard Davis, 67–78. New York: Routledge.

Wiltshire, Stephen. 1987. *Drawings*. London: J.M. Dent & Sons.

Wiltshire, Stephen. 1989. *Cities*. London: J.M. Dent & Sons.

Wiltshire, Stephen. 1991. *Floating Cities: Venice, Amsterdam, Leningrad, and Moscow*. New York: Summit Books.

Wiltshire, Stephen. 1993. *American Dream*. London: Michael Joseph Ltd.

PART VII

*F*iction, Memoir, and Poetry

CHAPTER 41

Stones in My Pockets, Stones in My Heart

Eli Clare

Gender reaches into disability; disability wraps around class; class strains against abuse; abuse snarls into sexuality; sexuality folds on top of race . . . everything finally piling into a single human body. To write about any aspect of identity, any aspect of the body, means writing about this entire maze. This I know, and yet the question remains: where to start? Maybe with my white skin, stubbly red hair, left ear pierced, shoulders set slightly off center, left riding higher than right, hands tremoring, traced with veins, legs well-muscled. Or with me in the mirror, dressing to go out, knotting my tie, slipping into my blazer, curve of hip and breast vanishing beneath my clothes. Or possibly with the memory of how my body felt swimming in the river, chinook fingerlings nibbling at my toes. There are a million ways to start, but how do I reach beneath the skin?

* * *

Age 13, hair curling down around my ears, glasses threatening to slide off my nose, I work with my father every weekend building a big wooden barn of a house. I wear overalls, my favorite flannel shirt, sleeves rolled up over a long-john top, and well-worn work boots. Over the years, my mother and I have fought about my hair. I want to cut the curls off; she thinks they're pretty. All morning I have sawed 2 × 12 girders to length, helped my father pound them into place. I come home from the building site to pick up a crowbar and eat lunch. A hammer hangs from my hammer loop; a utility knife rides in my bib pocket. I ask my mother, "Am I feminine?" My memory stops here. I do not remember what possessed me to ask that question, what I wanted to know, what my mother answered.

* * *

Feminine. Female. Girl. I watched my younger sister spend hours in the bathroom with a curling iron, my mother with her nail file and eyebrow tweezers. I watched and listened to the girls in my school talk about boys, go behind the equipment shed to kiss them, later whisper in algebra class about fucking them. I watched from the other side of a stone wall, a wall that was part self-preservation, part bones and blood of aloneness, part the impossible assumptions I could not shape my body around.

Dresses. Make-up. High heels. Perfume. I tried wearing the skirts my mother sewed for me. She urged me into Girl Scouts, slumber parties, the 4-H knitting and sewing clubs. I failed, not wanting any part of these activities. I loved my work boots and overalls long after all the other girls had discovered pantyhose and mini-skirts. But failing left a hole in my heart; I wanted to belong somewhere.

Am I feminine? Maybe I meant: "What am I, a girl, a boy, something else entirely?" Maybe I meant: "Can I be a girl *like this*?" Or maybe I was simply trying to say: "Mama, I don't understand." What did I want her to say? At 13, I didn't have a clue what it meant to be feminine or, for that matter, masculine. Those words were empty signifiers, important only because I knew I was supposed to have an attachment to femininity. At 13, my most sustaining relations were not in the human world. I collected stones—red, green, gray, rust, white speckled with black, black streaked with silver—and kept them in my pockets, their hard surfaces warming slowly to my body heat. Spent long days at the river learning what I could from the salmon, frogs, and salamanders. Roamed the beaches at high tide and low, starfish, mussels, barnacles clinging to the rocks. Wandered in the hills thick with moss, fern, liverwort, bramble, tree. Only here did I have a sense of body. Those stones warm in my pockets, I knew them to be the steadiest, only inviolate parts of myself. I wanted to be a hermit, to live alone with my stones and trees, neither a boy nor a girl. And now 20 years later, how do I reach beneath the skin to write, not about the stones, but the body that warmed them, the heat itself?

* * *

I could start with the ways my body has been stolen from me. Start slowly, reluctantly, with my parents. My father who raised me, his eldest daughter, as an almost son. My father who started raping me so young I can't remember when he first forced his penis into me. My mother who tells me she didn't know about his violence. I believe her because I know how her spirit

vacated the premises, leaving only her body as a marker. My mother who closed her eyes and turned her back, who said to my father, "She's yours to raise as you see fit." My mother who was shaped entirely by absence and my father who taught me the hills and woods: they were the first thieves.

But tell me, if I start here by placing the issues of violence and neglect on the table alongside my queerness, what will happen next? Will my words be used against me, twisted to bolster the belief that sexual abuse causes homosexuality, contorted to provide evidence that transgressive gender identity is linked directly to neglect? Most feminist and queer activists reject these linkages and for good reason. Conservatives often use them to discredit lesbian, gay, bi, and trans identities and to argue for our conversion rather than our liberation. But this strategy of denial, rejecting any possibility of connection between abuse and gender identity, abuse and sexuality, slams a door on the messy reality of how our bodies are stolen.

* * *

I question my mother about that day when I asked, "Am I feminine?" I hope she will remember my question and her answer and offer me some clues about what I wanted to know. She has no memory of that day, but reminds me of something else. One year during the long rainy season we called winter, the Lions Club held a carnival in the old, falling-down junior high gymnasium. I wasted money on "the man-eating fish," only to see Tiny Lawrence eating tuna from a can, laughed at the boys throwing wet sponges at the volunteer firemen, then stood watching a woman draw quick cartoon-like portraits, each signed "Betsy Hammond" with a flourish. She was new to town, and I, curious, eventually paid my dollar to sit down in front of her easel. I recognized myself in the resulting drawing, liked the hard lines that defined my face, the angle of my jaw, the toughness in my mouth.

Weeks later in the grocery store, my mother introduced herself to Betsy. They started talking about husbands and children, and soon my mother mentioned me, her eldest daughter, and the portrait I had brought home from the carnival. Betsy didn't know what my mother was talking about. Finally after much confusion, she asked, "Didn't I draw your son?" I remember the complete joy I felt when my mother came home with this story. I looked again and again at the portrait, thinking, "Right here, right now, I am a boy." It made me smile secretly for weeks, reach down into my pockets to squeeze a stone tight in each fist. I felt as if I were looking in a mirror and finally seeing myself, rather than some distorted fun-house image.

* * *

How do I write not about the stones, but the heat itself? I could start by asking some hard, risky questions. Really, I'd rather hang out with my ten-year-old self and share in her moment of glee as she looked in the mirror. But truly, those questions feel inevitable, and my boyhood pleasure turns cold when I dip into the messy reality of how my body was stolen. So, whatever the risk, let me ask.

How did my father's violence, his brutal taking of me over and over again, help shape and damage my body, my sexuality, my gender identity? How did his gendered abuse—and in this culture vaginal rape is certainly gendered—reinforce my sense of not being a girl? How did his non-abusive treatment of me as an almost son interact with the ways in which his fists and penis and knives told me in no uncertain terms that I was a girl? How did watching him sexually abuse other children—both boys and girls—complicate what I knew of being girl, being boy? How did my mother's willful ignorance of the hurt he inflicted on me influence what I absorbed about femininity and masculinity?

* * *

Little did I know back then as I carried that carnival caricature home with me that the experience of being called sir, assumed to be a young man, would become a regular occurrence. This gender ambiguity, being seen as a woman at one turn and a teenage boy at the next, marks to a large extent my queerness. When people stumble over their pronouns, stammer, blush, or apologize in embarrassment, I often think of Riki Anne Wilchins' description of her friend Holly Boswell:

> Holly is a delicate Southern belle of long acquaintance. . . . S/he has tender features, long, wavy blonde hair, a soft Carolina accent, a delicate feminine bosom, and no interest in surgery. Holly lives as an open transgendered mother of two in Ashville, North Carolina. Her comforting advice to confused citizens struggling with whether to use Sir or Madam is, "Don't give it a second thought. You don't have a pronoun yet for me."[1]

Sometimes when I'm read as a woman, I actively miss hearing "sir," "ma'am" sounding foreign, distant, unfamiliar, even wrong to me. Usually I feel safer, somewhat buffered from men's violence against women, walking the streets after dark, knowing my night-time outline and stride are frequently read as male. But mostly, I feel matter-of-fact: "Oh yeah, this is happening again."

Many dykes feel angered, irritated, dismayed, shamed by the experience of being read as male, feel the need to assert their womanhood. And in the same vein, I hear all the time about gay men who pump up their masculinity. To defend and strengthen one's authentic gender identity is important. But all too often I hear defensiveness in the argument that butch dykes don't mimic men but carve out new ways of being women; in the gay male personals that dismiss femmes and drag queens out of hand. Is this our one and only response to a heterosexist world that refuses to recognize feminine males and masculine females, that challenges our very queerness?

In the past decade, the burgeoning transgender/transsexual movement has questioned and started to wage a struggle against the binary gender system that automatically links female-bodied people to femininity to womanhood and male-bodied people to masculinity to manhood. Even the binary of female-bodied and male-bodied appears more and more to be a social construction as intersexed people—people who for any number of reasons are born with or develop ambiguous genitals, reproductive organs, and/or secondary sex characteristics—begin to speak publicly of their lives and the medical intrusion they've faced. How natural are the rigid, mutually exclusive definitions of male and female if they have to be defended by genital surgery performed on intersexed people? The trans movement suggests a world full of gender and sex variation, a world much more complex than one divided into female-bodied women and male-bodied men. Many trans activists argue for an end, not to the genders of woman and man, but to the socially constructed binary.

Within this context, to answer the homophobes becomes easy, those folks who want to dehumanize, erase, make invisible the lives of butch dykes and nellie fags. We shrug. We laugh. We tell them: your definitions of woman and man suck. We tell them: your binary stinks. We say: here we are in all our glory—male, female, intersexed, trans, butch, nellie, studly, femme, king, androgynous, queen, some of us carving out new ways of being women, others of us new ways of being men, and still others new ways of being something else entirely. *You don't have pronouns yet for us.*

*   *   *

How do I write not about the stones, but the heat itself? I could start with the brutal, intimate details of my father's thievery, of his hands clamping around my neck, tearing into me, claiming my body as his own. The brutal, intimate details, but listen: I get afraid that the homophobes are right, that maybe in truth I live as a transgendered butch because he raped me, my mother neglected me. I lose the bigger picture, forget that woven through and around the private and intimate is always the public and political.

We live in a time of epidemic child abuse, in a world where sexual and physical violence against children isn't only a personal tragedy and a symptom of power run amok, but also a form of social control. When a father rapes his daughter, a mother beats her son, a white schoolteacher sexually fondles a Black student, a middle-class man uses a working-class boy to make child pornography, a nondisabled caregiver leaves a disabled kid to sit in her/his urine for hours, these adults teach children bodily lessons about power and hierarchy, about being boys, being girls, being children, being Black, being working-class, being disabled.

What better way to maintain a power structure—white supremacy, male supremacy, capitalism, a binary and rigid gender system—than to drill the lessons of who is dominant and who is subordinate into the bodies of children. No, not every individual perpetrator thinks, "This kid has stepped too far outside. I need to beat/rape her back into line." But certainly the power imbalances out of which child abuse arises are larger than any individual perpetrator's conscious intentions. Social control happens exactly at the junctures where the existing power structure is—consciously or not—maintained and strengthened.

And here is the answer to my fear. Child abuse is not the cause of but rather a response to—among other things—transgressive gender identity and/or sexuality. The theory I'm trying to shape is not as simple as "My father abused me because I was a queer child who—by the time I had any awareness of gender—was not at all sure of my girlness," although some genderqueer kids do get raped specifically because of their queerness. Rather I want to say, "My father raped me for many reasons, and inside his acts of violence I learned about what it meant to be female, to be a child, to live in my particular body, and those lessons served the larger power structure and hierarchy well."

*   *   *

At the same time, our bodies are not merely blank slates upon which the powers-that-be write their lessons. We cannot ignore the body itself: the sensory, mostly non-verbal experience of our hearts and lungs, muscles and tendons, telling us and the world who we are. My childhood sense of being neither girl nor boy arose in part from the external lessons of abuse and neglect, from the confusing messages about masculinity and femininity that I could not comprehend; I would be a fool to claim otherwise. But just as certainly, there was a knowing that resided in my bones, in the stretch of my legs and arch of my back, in the stones lying against my skin, a knowing that whispered, "not girl, not boy."

Butch, nellie, studly, femme, king, androgynous, queen: how have we negotiated the lies and thievery, the ways gender is influenced by divisions of labor, by images of masculinity and femininity, by racism, sexism, classism, ableism, by the notions of "real" men and "real" women? And how, at the same time, have we listened to our own bodies? For me the answer is not simple.

I think about my disabled body. For too long, I hated my trembling hands, my precarious balance, my spastic muscles so repeatedly overtaken by tension and tremor, tried to hide them at all costs. More than once I wished to amputate my right arm so it wouldn't shake. Self-mutilation is shame of the baldest kind. All the lies contained in the words *retard, monkey, defect*; in the gawking, the pats on my head, and the tears cried on my shoulder; in the moments where I became someone's supercrip or tragedy: all those lies became my second skin.

I think about my disabled body, how as a teenager I escaped the endless pressure to have a boyfriend, to shave my legs, to wear make-up. The same lies that cast me as genderless, asexual, and undesirable also framed a space in which I was left alone to be my quiet, bookish, tomboy self, neither girl nor boy. Even then, I was grateful. But listen, if I had wanted to date boys, wear lipstick and mascara, play with feminine clothes—the silk skirt and pumps, the low-cut blouse, the outrageous prom dress—I would have had to struggle much longer and harder than my nondisabled counterparts. The sheer physical acts of shaving my legs and putting on make-up would have been hard enough. Harder still would have been the relentless arguing with my parents, resisting their image of me as asexual or vulnerable to assault, persuading them that I could in truth take care of myself at the movies with Brent Miller or Dave Wilson.[2] But in truth I didn't want to date Brent or wear the low-cut blouse. I shuddered at the thought. How would I have reacted to the gendered pressures my younger, nondisabled sister faced? For her the path of least resistance pointed in the direction of femininity; for me it led toward not-girl-not-boy. But to cast my abiding sense of gendered self simply as a reaction to ableism is to ignore my body and what it had to tell me. When I look around me in disability community, I see an amazing range of gender expression, running the gamut from feminine to androgynous to masculine, mixed and swirled in many patterns. Clearly we respond in a myriad of ways to the ableist construction of gender.

How do we negotiate the lies and listen to our bodies? I think about my disabled body, my queer butch body read as a teenage boy. The markers of masculinity—my shaved head and broad stance, direct gaze and muscled arms—are unmistakable. And so are the markers of disability—my heavy-heeled gait; my halting, uneven speech; the tremors in my hands, arms, and shoulders. They all twine together to shape me in the ableist world as either genderless or a teenage boy. The first is all too familiar to disabled people. The second arises from the gender binary, where if I am not recognized as a woman, then I am presumed to be a man or more likely, given my lack of height and facial hair, a teenage boy. These external perceptions match in large part my internal sense of gender, my bodily comfort with gender ambiguity. But if the external and internal didn't match, what then?

Once I sat in a writing workshop with straight, feminine, disabled women, and we talked for an entire afternoon about gender identity, precisely because of the damage inflicted when the external ableist perceptions don't match the internal sense of self. All too often, the thieves plant their lies, and our bodies absorb them as the only truth. Is it any surprise that sometimes my heart fills with small gray stones, which never warm to my body heat?

*   *   *

The work of thieves: certainly external perception, stereotypes, lies, false images, and oppression hold a tremendous amount of power. They define and create who we are, how we think of our bodies, our gendered selves. How do I write not about the stones, but the body that warms them, the heat itself? That question haunts me because I lived by splitting body from mind, body from consciousness, body from physical sensation, body from emotion as the bullies threw rocks and called *retard,* as my father and his buddies tied me down, pulled out their knives. My body became an empty house, one to which I seldom returned. I lived in exile; the stones rattling in my heart, resting in my pockets, were my one and only true body.

But just as the stolen body exists, so does the reclaimed body. I think of disabled people challenging the conception of a "perfect" body/mind. Ed Roberts sits out front of his house talking about crip liberation. Ellen Stohl shapes herself into a sex symbol for the disability community. I think of queer people pushing upon the dominant culture's containment of gender, pleasure, and sex. Drag queens and kings work the stage. Dykes take to the streets. Gay men defend public sex. Trans people of all varieties say, "This is how we can be men, women, how we can inhabit all the spaces in between." Radical faeries swirl in their pagan finery. Bisexual people resist a neat compartmentalizing of sexuality. I think of people of color, poor people, working-class people all thumbing their noses at the notion of assimilation. Over and over again, we take the lies and crumble them into dust.

But how do I write about *my* body reclaimed, full of pride and pleasure? It is easy to say that abuse and ableism and homophobia stole my body away, broke my desire, removed me from my pleasure in the stones warm against my skin, the damp sponginess of moss growing on a rotten log, the taste of spring water dripping out of rock. Harder to express how that break becomes healed, a bone once fractured, now whole, but different from the bone never broken. And harder still to follow the path between the two. How do I mark this place where my body is no longer an empty house, desire whistling lonely through the cracks, but not yet a house fully lived in? For me the path from stolen body to reclaimed body started with my coming out as a dyke.

* * *

I was 18 and had just moved to the city. I didn't want to be a girl, nor was I a boy. I hid my body, tried as much as possible to ignore it. During my first week of college, I started meeting dykes. In three weeks I began asking, "Am I a lesbian?" Once before, I had faced this question and known the answer. The summer I was 12, two women, friends of my parents, came visiting from Arkansas. I adored Suzanne and Susan, showed them my favorite spots, the best blackberry brambles, where the muskrat built her den. I wanted them to stay with me in my river valley. They came out to my parents, and later I overheard my father say that Suzanne was gay, his face growing tight and silent. Somehow I knew what that word meant, even though I barely understood *homosexual* and had only heard *lesbian* as a taunt. It made me smile. The image of Suzanne and Susan holding hands as we walked Battle Rock Beach stuck with me for weeks. I knew somewhere deep inside me, rising up to press against my sternum, that I was like them. This I knew, but by the time I turned 13, it had vanished.

Now at the age of 18, I picked the question up again. I had never kissed a boy, never had a boyfriend or girlfriend. I knew nothing about sexual desire. For me sex was bound together with abuse. I had learned the details from my father just as I had learned how to mix a wheelbarrow of concrete, frame a stud wall. Sex meant rape—that simple, that complicated. The only thing I knew about desire was the raw, split-openness that rampaged through me after he was done, how those feelings could overtake my body again late at night in my own bed, mounting up uncontainably. I was not in love with a woman; I didn't even have a crush. And yet the question "Am I a lesbian?" hung with me.

I went to dyke events, read dyke books, listened to dyke music, hung out at my first dyke bar, went to my first dyke dance. I adored watching those women talk, laugh, hold hands, dance, kiss. Those soft butch women who would never have claimed their butchness then, during the lesbian-feminist androgyny of the '70s and early '80s. Those women with buzzed hair and well-defined biceps, jeans faded and soft. Those women who looked me in the eye. Watching them was like polishing my favorite stone to its brightest glint. I knew I could be *this* kind of woman and so slowly over the course of that year came to know myself as a dyke. I waited another four years to kiss a woman.

My coming out wasn't as much about discovering sexual desire and knowledge as it was about dealing with gender identity. Simply put, the disabled, mixed-class tomboy who asked her mother, "Am I feminine?" didn't discover a sexuality among dykes, but rather a definition of woman large enough to be comfortable for many years. And if that definition hadn't been large enough, what then? Would I have sought out hormones and/or surgery? If I had been born a hundred years ago when a specifically lesbian definition didn't exist, would I have been a "passing woman"? If I live long enough to see the world break free of the gender binary, will I find home not as a butch dyke, a woman by default, but as some third, fourth, fifth gender? Some gender that seems more possible since trans people have started to organize, build community, speak out about our lives. Some gender that I have already started reaching toward.

* * *

In queer community, I found a place to belong and abandoned my desire to be a hermit. Among crips, I learned how to embrace my strong, spastic body. Through feminist work around sexual violence—political activism, theoretical analysis, emotional recovery—I came to terms with the sexual abuse and physical torture done to me. And somewhere along the line, I pulled desire to the surface, gave it room to breathe. Let me write not about the stones, but the heat itself.

I think of the first woman I dated. She and I spent many nights eating pizza, watching movies, and talking halfway until dawn. I fell in love but never even kissed her, too afraid to even say, "This is what I want," much less to lean over and put my lips to hers. It made sense only years later when my memories of rape came flooding back. I think of the butch woman, once my lover, now a good friend. One night as we lay in bed, she told me, "I like when your hands tremble over my body. It feels good, like extra touching." Her words pushed against the lies. But all too often, sex was a bodiless, mechanical act for me as I repeatedly fled my body. We decided we'd be happier as friends. I think of the woman who called me her dream butchy *shiksa* and made me smile. I took so long to realize what had flared between us she almost gave up waiting. With her, desire traced my body, vivid and unmistakable, returning me to the taste of spring water, the texture of tree bark as I climbed toward sky. With her, I understood finally what it meant to want my hand on a lover's skin, the weight of a lover's body against mine. A bone long fractured, now mending.

I turn my pockets and heart inside out, set the stones—quartz, obsidian, shale, agate, scoria, granite—along the scoured top of the wall I once lived behind, the wall I still use for refuge. They shine in the sun, some translucent to the light, others dense, solid, opaque. I lean my body into the big unbreakable expanse, tracing which stones need to melt, which will crack wide, geode to crystal, and which are content just as they are.

* * *

But before I make it too simple, let me tell another story about coming to queer community, queer identity. Five or six years after I came out, I lived in Oakland, California, still learning the habits and manners of urban dykes. I remember a weekend when 20 of us, mostly dykes, helped move a friend from north Oakland to west Berkeley. The apartment filled with laughter as we carried endless boxes to the moving van, flexed our muscles over the couch, teased the lovers who sneaked a kiss in the empty closet. That mix of friends, lovers, and ex-lovers, butch dykes, femme dykes, androgynous dykes: we elbowed and jostled and gossiped. Leslie and I hauled a table to the van. On our way back, she off-handedly said how she was glad to be wearing her steel-toed boots, but that her feet were beginning to hurt. I wanted to get to know Leslie better. She was butch and knew it. I liked watching her from across the room, feeling something less than attraction but more than curiosity. I hadn't yet named myself butch but knew I had much in common with Leslie's butchness. So when she mentioned her steel-toed boots, I asked where she worked, assuming she'd have a story about forklifts or hi-los, a warehouse, bailer, mill, factory, or mine. I thought about the summer I was 15 working in the woods. I was the only girl who started the summer with work boots already broken in. The other girls envied me for weeks as they nursed their blistered feet. Leslie said, "I just bought them as a fashion state-ment." I felt as if I'd been exposed as a hick yet again, caught assuming she was some-one I might have grown up with. *A fashion statement.* What did I have in common with Leslie? I felt the stones in my heart grind deep.

Today, more than decade after watching Leslie from across the room, I have settled into a certain butch identity. Often I don't feel drawn to the urban markers of being butch—the leather jacket, the steel-toed boots, the black-on-black look, the arc of chain from wallet to belt loop—but I do understand how certain clothes make me feel inside my body. I learned to dress by watching the loggers and fishermen I grew up around, learned to love t-shirts and torn jeans, dusty work boots and faded flannel shirts from them. The girls with whom I went to school also wore their share of flannel and denim, but when it came time to learn how to dress like "women," they turned to *Vogue* and *Glamour.* To emulate the dress of their working-class moth-ers was somehow shameful. They wanted their lessons to come from the middle- and upper-class beauty mags. The boys on the other hand never thought to dress like anyone except the working-class men around them. For me, *Vogue* and *Glamour* held none of the appeal that Walt Maya did, dressed in his checked shirt, cowboy boots, and wide-brimmed hat. I joined the boys in their emulation.

I knew early on the feel of boots and denim, knew I would never learn to walk in a skirt. I loved how my body felt as I swung an ax, how my mind felt as I worked through the last and hardest algebra problem in Mr. Johnson's advanced math class, the most elusive metaphor in Mr. Beckman's poetry class. I knew I never wanted a child or a husband. I knew these things but could never have put words to them, knew them in spite of all that stole me away from my body.

How did I "know" I never wanted a hus-band, would never learn to walk in a skirt? What does it mean when I write that I "felt" like neither a girl nor a boy? The words *know* and *feel* are slippery in their vague-ness. I pull out an old photo of myself from the night of my high school graduation. I stand outside on our front deck; behind me are the deep greens of western Oregon in May. I wear a white dress, flowers embroi-dered on the front panel, the plainest, sim-plest dress my mother would let me buy. I look painfully uncomfortable, as if I have no idea what to do with my body, hands clasped awkwardly behind me, shoulders caved inward, immobilized, almost fearful beneath my smile. I am in clumsy, uncon-senting drag. This is one of the last times I wore a dress. This is my body's definition of *know* and *feel.*

And yet those things I knew and felt were also deeply shaped and colored by the rural, white, working-class culture of Port Orford. They were cradled not so much by an unconscious baby butch sensibility, but in a working-class town where at weddings and funerals everyone looked as if they had been stuffed into their dress clothes. They were nurtured in the small town hardware store and lumber yard, where, even though George always asked if I could handle the 50-pound bags of cement, I was Bob's eccentric, "handicapped" kid and was never told to stop. They were underlined by my parents' desperate upward scramble toward the middle class and their corre-sponding passion for formal education. They were molded by the common knowl-edge that most of the girls in town would catch their lives on too many kids, most of the boys on alcohol and guns, and only a few of us would leave the county for good.

* * *

The stolen body, the reclaimed body, the body that knows itself and the world, the stone and the heat which warms it: my body has never been singular. Disability snarls into gender. Class wraps around race. Sexuality strains against abuse. *This* is how to reach beneath the skin.

Friday nights I go to the local queer bar, nurse a single Corona, hang out with my dyke friends. Mostly I go to watch one of the wait staff, a woman with long brown hair, sharp nose, and ready smile. She flirts with everyone, moving table to table, making eye contact, hunkering down to have a quiet word or laugh amidst the noise. She flirts with me too, catching me in her wide smile, appreciative gaze. I am under no illusion: this is simply how she works her job. But after a lifetime of numbness I adore her attention, adore tipping back my chair, spreading my legs wide, and watching her from across the room.

I want to take the stone between my tremoring hands—trembling with CP, with desire, with the last remnants of fear, trembling because this is how my body moves—and warm it gentle, but not, as I have always done before, ride roughshod over it. I want to enter as a not-girl-not-boy transgendered butch—gendered differently than when I first came out, thinking simply, "*This* is how I'll be a woman," never imagining there might be a day when the word *woman* was too small; differently from the tomboy who wanted to be a hermit; but still connected to both. Enter with my pockets and heart half-full of stone. Enter knowing that the muscled grip of desire is a wild, half-grown horse, ready to bolt but too curious to stay away.

* * *

In the end, I will sit on the wide, flat top of my wall, legs dangling over those big, uncrackable stones, weathered smooth and clean. Sit with butch women, femme dykes, nellie men, studly fags, radical faeries, drag queens and kings, transsexual people who want nothing more than to be women and men, intersexed people, hermaphrodites with attitudes, transgendered, pangendered, bigendered, polygendered, ungendered, androgynous people of many varieties and trade stories long into the night. Laugh and cry and tell stories. Sad stories about bodies stolen, bodies no longer here. Enraging stories about false images, devastating lies, untold violence. Bold, brash stories about reclaiming our bodies and changing the world.

NOTES

1. Wilchins, Riki Anne, *Read My Lips* (Ithaca, New York: Firebrand Books, 1997), p. 118.
2. I now recognize the disturbing irony of this, given the ways in which my father was sexually using me.

CHAPTER 42

Unspeakable Conversations

Harriet McBryde Johnson

He insists he doesn't want to kill me. He simply thinks it would have been better, all things considered, to have given my parents the option of killing the baby I once was, and to let other parents kill similar babies as they come along and thereby avoid the suffering that comes with lives like mine and satisfy the reasonable preferences of parents for a different kind of child. It has nothing to do with me. I should not feel threatened.

Whenever I try to wrap my head around his tight string of syllogisms, my brain gets so fried it's . . . almost fun. Mercy! It's like "Alice in Wonderland."

It is a chilly Monday in late March, just less than a year ago. I am at Princeton University. My host is Prof. Peter Singer, often called—and not just by his book publicist—the most influential philosopher of our time. He is the man who wants me dead. No, that's not at all fair. He wants to legalize the killing of certain babies who might come to be like me if allowed to live. He also says he believes that it should be lawful under some circumstances to kill, at any age, individuals with cognitive impairments so severe that he doesn't consider them "persons." What does it take to be a person? Awareness of your own existence in time. The capacity to harbor preferences as to the future, including the preference for continuing to live.

At this stage of my life, he says, I am a person. However, as an infant, I wasn't. I, like all humans, was born without self-awareness. And eventually, assuming my brain finally gets so fried that I fall into that wonderland where self and other and present and past and future blur into one boundless, formless all or nothing, then I'll lose my personhood and therefore my right to life. Then, he says, my family and doctors might put me out of my misery, or out of my bliss or oblivion, and no one count it murder.

I have agreed to two speaking engagements. In the morning, I talk to 150 undergraduates on selective infanticide. In the evening, it is a convivial discussion, over dinner, of assisted suicide. I am the token cripple with an opposing view.

I had several reasons for accepting Singer's invitation, some grounded in my involvement in the disability rights movement, others entirely personal. For the movement, it seemed an unusual opportunity to experiment with modes of discourse that might work with very tough audiences and bridge the divide between our perceptions and theirs. I didn't expect to straighten out Singer's head, but maybe I could reach a student or two. Among the personal reasons: I was sure it would make a great story, first for telling and then for writing down.

By now I've told it to family and friends and colleagues, over lunches and dinners, on long car trips, in scads of e-mail messages and a couple of formal speeches. But it seems to be a story that just won't settle down. After all these tellings, it still lacks a coherent structure; I'm miles away from a rational argument. I keep getting interrupted by questions—like these:

Q: Was he totally grossed out by your physical appearance?

A: He gave no sign of it. None whatsoever.

Q: How did he handle having to interact with someone like you?

A: He behaved in every way appropriately, treated me as a respected professional acquaintance and was a gracious and accommodating host.

Q: Was it emotionally difficult for you to take part in a public discussion of whether your life should have happened?

A: It was very difficult. And horribly easy.

Q: Did he get that job at Princeton because they like his ideas on killing disabled babies?

A: It apparently didn't hurt, but he's most famous for animal rights. He's the author of "Animal Liberation."

Q: How can he put so much value on animal life and so little value on human life?

That last question is the only one I avoid. I used to say I don't know; it doesn't make sense. But now I've read some of Singer's writing, and I admit it does make sense—within the conceptual world of Peter Singer. But I don't want to go there. Or at least not for long.

So I will start from those other questions and see where the story goes this time.

That first question, about my physical appearance, needs some explaining.

It's not that I'm ugly. It's more that most people don't know how to look at me. The sight of me is routinely discombobulating. The power wheelchair is enough to inspire gawking, but that's the least of it. Much more impressive is the impact on my body of more than four decades of a muscle-wasting disease. At this stage of my life, I'm Karen Carpenter thin, flesh mostly vanished, a jumble of bones in a floppy bag of skin. When, in childhood, my muscles got too weak to hold up my spine, I tried a brace for a while, but fortunately a skittish anesthesiologist said no to fusion, plates and pins—all the apparatus that might have kept me straight. At 15, I threw away the back brace and let my spine reshape itself into a deep twisty S-curve. Now my right side is two deep canyons. To keep myself upright, I lean forward, rest my rib cage on my lap, plant my elbows beside my knees. Since my backbone found its own natural shape, I've been entirely comfortable in my skin.

I am in the first generation to survive to such decrepitude. Because antibiotics were available, we didn't die from the childhood pneumonias that often come with weakened respiratory systems. I guess it is natural enough that most people don't know what to make of us.

Two or three times in my life—I recall particularly one largely crip, largely lesbian cookout halfway across the continent—I have been looked at as a rare kind of beauty. There is also the bizarre fact that where I live, Charleston, S.C., some people call me Good Luck Lady: they consider it propitious to cross my path when a hurricane is coming and to kiss my head just before voting day. But most often the reactions are decidedly negative. Strangers on the street are moved to comment:

I admire you for being out; most people would give up.

God bless you! I'll pray for you.

You don't let the pain hold you back, do you?

If I had to live like you, I think I'd kill myself.

I used to try to explain that in fact I enjoy my life, that it's a great sensual pleasure to zoom by power chair on these delicious muggy streets, that I have no more reason to kill myself than most people. But it gets tedious. God didn't put me on this street to provide disability awareness training to the likes of them. In fact, no god put anyone anywhere for any reason, if you want to know.

But they don't want to know. They think they know everything there is to know, just by looking at me. That's how stereotypes work. They don't know that they're confused, that they're really expressing the discombobulation that comes in my wake.

So. What stands out when I recall first meeting Peter Singer in the spring of 2001 is his apparent immunity to my looks, his apparent lack of discombobulation, his immediate ability to deal with me as a person with a particular point of view.

Then, 2001. Singer has been invited to the College of Charleston, not two blocks from my house. He is to lecture on "Rethinking Life and Death." I have been dispatched by Not Dead Yet, the national organization leading the disability-rights opposition to legalized assisted suicide and disability-based killing. I am to put out a leaflet and do something during the Q. and A.

On arriving almost an hour early to reconnoiter, I find the scene almost entirely peaceful; even the boisterous display of South Carolina spring is muted by gray wisps of Spanish moss and mottled oak bark.

I roll around the corner of the building and am confronted with the unnerving sight of two people I know sitting on a park bench eating veggie pitas with Singer. Sharon is a veteran activist for human rights. Herb is South Carolina's most famous atheist. Good people, I've always thought—now sharing veggie pitas and conversation with a proponent of genocide. I try to beat a retreat, but Herb and Sharon have seen me. Sharon tosses her trash and comes over. After we exchange the usual courtesies, she asks, "Would you like to meet Professor Singer?"

She doesn't have a clue. She probably likes his book on animal rights. "I'll just talk to him in the Q. and A."

But Herb, with Singer at his side, is fast approaching. They are looking at me, and Herb is talking, no doubt saying nice things about me. He'll be saying that I'm a disability rights lawyer and that I gave a talk against assisted suicide at his secular humanist group a while back. He didn't agree with everything I said, he'll say, but I was brilliant. Singer appears interested, engaged. I sit where I'm parked. Herb makes an introduction. Singer extends his hand.

I hesitate. I shouldn't shake hands with the Evil One. But he is Herb's guest, and I simply can't snub Herb's guest at the college where Herb teaches. Hereabouts, the rule is that if you're not prepared to shoot on sight, you have to be prepared to shake hands. I give Singer the three fingers on my right hand that still work. "Good afternoon, Mr. Singer. I'm here for Not Dead Yet." I want to think he flinches just a little. Not Dead Yet did everything possible to disrupt his first week at Princeton. I sent a check to the fund for the 14 arrestees, who included comrades in power chairs. But if Singer flinches, he instantly recovers. He answers my questions about the lecture format. When he says he looks forward to an interesting exchange, he seems entirely sincere.

It is an interesting exchange. In the lecture hall that afternoon, Singer lays it all out. The "illogic" of allowing abortion but not infanticide, of allowing withdrawal of life support but not active killing. Applying the basic assumptions of preference utilitarianism, he spins out his bone-chilling argument for letting parents kill disabled babies and replace them with nondisabled babies who have a greater chance at happiness. It is all about allowing as many individuals as possible to fulfill as many of their preferences as possible.

As soon as he's done, I get the microphone and say I'd like to discuss selective infanticide. As a lawyer, I disagree with his jurisprudential assumptions. Logical inconsistency is not a sufficient reason to change the law. As an atheist, I object to his using religious terms ("the doctrine of the sanctity of human life") to characterize his critics. Singer takes a note pad out of his pocket and jots down my points, apparently eager to take them on, and I proceed to the heart of my argument: that the presence or absence of a disability doesn't predict quality of life. I question his replacement-baby theory, with its assumption of "other things equal," arguing that people are not fungible. I draw out a comparison of myself and my nondisabled brother Mac (the next-born after me), each of us with a combination of gifts and flaws so peculiar that we can't be measured on the same scale.

He responds to each point with clear and lucid counterarguments. He proceeds with the assumption that I am one of the people who might rightly have been killed at birth. He sticks to his guns, conceding just enough to show himself open-minded and flexible. We go back and forth for 10 long minutes. Even as I am horrified by what he says, and by the fact that I have been sucked into a civil discussion of whether I ought to exist, I can't help being dazzled by his verbal facility. He is so respectful, so free of condescension, so focused on the argument, that by the time the show is over, I'm not exactly angry with him. Yes, I am shaking, furious, enraged—but it's for the big room, 200 of my fellow Charlestonians who have listened with polite interest, when in decency they should have run him out of town on a rail.

My encounter with Peter Singer merits a mention in my annual canned letter that December. I decide to send Singer a copy. In response, he sends me the nicest possible e-mail message. Dear Harriet (if he may) . . . Just back from Australia, where he's from. Agrees with my comments on the world situation. Supports my work against institutionalization. And then some pointed questions to clarify my views on selective infanticide.

I reply. Fine, call me Harriet, and I'll reciprocate in the interest of equality, though I'm accustomed to more formality. Skipping agreeable preambles, I answer his questions on disability-based infanticide and pose some of my own. Answers and more questions come back. Back and forth over several weeks it proceeds, an engaging discussion of baby killing, disability prejudice and related points of law and philosophy. Dear Harriet. Dear Peter.

Singer seems curious to learn how someone who is as good an atheist as he is could disagree with his entirely reasonable views. At the same time, I am trying to plumb his theories. What has him so convinced it would be best to allow parents to kill babies with severe disabilities, and not other kinds of babies, if no infant is a "person" with a right to life? I learn it is partly that both biological and adoptive parents prefer healthy babies. But I have trouble with basing life-and-death decisions on market considerations when the market is structured by prejudice. I offer a hypothetical comparison: "What about mixed-race babies, especially when the combination is entirely nonwhite, who I believe are just about as unadoptable as babies with disabilities?" Wouldn't a law allowing the killing of these undervalued babies validate race prejudice? Singer agrees there is a problem. "It would be horrible," he says, "to see mixed-race babies being killed because they can't be adopted, whereas white ones could be." What's the difference? Preferences based on race are unreasonable. Preferences based on ability are not. Why? To Singer, it's pretty simple: disability makes a person "worse off."

Are we "worse off"? I don't think so. Not in any meaningful sense. There are too many variables. For those of us with congenital conditions, disability shapes all we are. Those disabled later in life adapt. We take constraints that no one would choose and build rich and satisfying lives within them. We enjoy pleasures other people enjoy, and pleasures peculiarly our own. We have something the world needs.

Pressing me to admit a negative correlation between disability and happiness, Singer presents a situation: imagine a disabled child on the beach, watching the other children play.

It's right out of the telethon. I expected something more sophisticated from a professional thinker. I respond: "As a little girl playing on the beach, I was already aware that some people felt sorry for me, that I wasn't frolicking with the same level of frenzy as other children. This annoyed me, and still does." I take the time to write a detailed description of how I, in fact, had fun playing on the beach, without the need of standing, walking or running. But, really, I've had enough. I suggest to Singer that we have exhausted our topic, and I'll be back in touch when I get around to writing about him.

He responds by inviting me to Princeton. I fire off an immediate maybe.

Of course I'm flattered. Mama will be impressed.

But there are things to consider. Not Dead Yet says—and I completely agree—that we should not legitimate Singer's views by giving them a forum. We should not make disabled lives subject to debate. Moreover, any spokesman chosen by the opposition is by definition a token. But even if I'm a token, I won't have to act like one. And anyway, I'm kind of stuck. If I decline, Singer can make some hay: "I offered them a platform, but they refuse rational discussion." It's an old trick, and I've laid myself wide open.

My invitation is to have an exchange of views with Singer during his undergraduate course. He also proposes a second "exchange," open to the whole university, later in the day. This sounds a lot like debating my life—and on my opponent's turf, with my opponent moderating, to boot. I offer a counterproposal, to which Singer proves amenable. I will open the class with some comments on infanticide and related issues and then let Singer grill me as hard as he likes before we open it up for the students. Later in the day, I might take part in a discussion of some other disability issue in a neutral forum. Singer suggests a faculty-student discussion group sponsored by his department but with cross-departmental membership. The topic I select is "Assisted Suicide, Disability Discrimination and the Illusion of Choice: A Disability Rights Perspective." I inform a few movement colleagues of this turn of events, and advice starts rolling in. I decide to go with the advisers who counsel me to do the gig, lie low and get out of Dodge.

I ask Singer to refer me to the person who arranges travel at Princeton. I imagine some capable and unflappable woman like my sister, Beth, whose varied job description at a North Carolina university includes handling visiting artists. Singer refers me to his own assistant, who certainly seems capable and unflappable enough. However, almost immediately Singer jumps back in via e-mail. It seems the nearest hotel has only one wheelchair-accessible suite, available with two rooms for $600 per night. What to do? I know I shouldn't be so accommodating, but I say I can make do with an inaccessible room if it has certain features. Other logistical issues come up. We go back and forth. Questions and answers. Do I really need a lift-equipped vehicle at the airport? Can't my assistant assist me into a conventional car? How wide is my wheelchair?

By the time we're done, Singer knows that I am 28 inches wide. I have trouble controlling my wheelchair if my hand gets cold. I am accustomed to driving on rough, irregular surfaces, but I get nervous turning on steep slopes. Even one step is too many. I can swallow purées, soft bread and grapes. I use a bedpan, not a toilet. None of this is a secret; none of it cause for angst. But I do wonder whether Singer is jotting down my specs in his little note pad as evidence of how "bad off" people like me really are.

I realize I must put one more issue on the table: etiquette. I was criticized within the movement when I confessed to shaking Singer's hand in Charleston, and some are appalled that I have agreed to break bread with him in Princeton. I think they have a very good point, but, again, I'm stuck. I'm engaged for a day of discussion, not a picket line. It is not in my power to marginalize Singer at Princeton; nothing would be accomplished by displays of personal disrespect. However, chumminess is clearly inappropriate. I tell Singer that in the lecture hall it can't be Harriet and Peter; it must be Ms. Johnson and Mr. Singer.

He seems genuinely nettled. Shouldn't it be Ms. Johnson and Professor Singer, if I want to be formal? To counter, I invoke the ceremonial low-country usage, Attorney Johnson and Professor Singer, but point out that Mr./Ms. is the custom in American political debates and might seem more normal in New Jersey. All right, he says. Ms./Mr. it will be.

I describe this awkward social situation to the lawyer in my office who has served as my default lunch partner for the past 14 years. He gives forth a full-body shudder.

"That poor, sorry son of a bitch! He has no idea what he's in for."

Being a disability rights lawyer lecturing at Princeton does confer some cachet at the Newark airport. I need all the cachet I can get. Delta Airlines has torn up my power chair. It is a fairly frequent occurrence for any air traveler on wheels.

When they inform me of the damage in Atlanta, I throw a monumental fit and tell them to have a repair person meet me in Newark with new batteries to replace the ones inexplicably destroyed. Then I am told no new batteries can be had until the morning. It's Sunday night. On arrival in Newark, I'm told of a plan to put me up there for the night and get me repaired and driven to Princeton by 10 a.m.

"That won't work. I'm lecturing at 10. I need to get there tonight, go to sleep and be in my right mind tomorrow."

"What? You're lecturing? They told us it was a conference. We need to get you fixed tonight!"

Carla, the gate agent, relieves me of the need to throw any further fits by undertaking on my behalf the fit of all fits.

Carmen, the personal assistant with whom I'm traveling, pushes me in my disabled chair around the airport in search of a place to use the bedpan. However, instead of diaper-changing tables, which are functional though far from private, we find a flip-down plastic shelf that doesn't look like it would hold my 70 pounds of body weight. It's no big deal; I've restricted my fluids. But Carmen is a little freaked. It is her first adventure in power-chair air travel. I thought I prepared her for the trip, but I guess I neglected to warn her about the probability of wheelchair destruction. I keep forgetting that even people who know me well don't know much about my world.

We reach the hotel at 10:15 p.m., four hours late.

I wake up tired. I slept better than I would have slept in Newark with an unrepaired chair, but any hotel bed is a near guarantee of morning crankiness. I tell Carmen to leave the TV off. I don't want to hear the temperature.

I do the morning stretch. Medical people call it passive movement, but it's not really passive. Carmen's hands move my limbs, following my precise instructions, her strength giving effect to my will. Carmen knows the routine, so it is in near silence that we begin easing slowly into the day. I let myself be propped up to eat oatmeal and drink tea. Then there's the bedpan and then bathing and dressing, still in bed. As the caffeine kicks in, silence gives way to conversation about practical things. Carmen lifts me into my chair and straps a rolled towel under my ribs for comfort and stability. She tugs at my clothes to remove wrinkles that could cause pressure sores. She switches on my motors and gives me the means of moving without anyone's help. They don't call it a power chair for nothing.

I drive to the mirror. I do my hair in one long braid. Even this primal hairdo requires, at this stage of my life, joint effort. I undo yesterday's braid, fix the part and comb the hair in front. Carmen combs where I can't reach. I divide the mass into three long hanks and start the braid just behind my left ear. Section by section, I hand it over to her, and her unimpaired young fingers pull tight, crisscross, until the braid is fully formed.

A big polyester scarf completes my costume. Carmen lays it over my back. I tie it the way I want it, but Carmen starts fussing with it, trying to tuck it down in the back. I tell her that it's fine, and she stops.

On top of the scarf, she wraps the two big shawls that I hope will substitute for an overcoat. I don't own any real winter clothes. I just stay out of the cold, such cold as we get in Charleston.

We review her instructions for the day. Keep me in view and earshot. Be instantly available but not intrusive. Be polite, but don't answer any questions about me. I am glad that she has agreed to come. She's strong, smart, adaptable and very loyal. But now she is digging under the shawls, fussing with that scarf again.

"Carmen. What are you doing?"

"I thought I could hide this furry thing you sit on."

"Leave it. Singer knows lots of people eat meat. Now he'll know some crips sit on sheepskin."

The walk is cold but mercifully short. The hotel is just across the street from Princeton's wrought-iron gate and a few short blocks from the building where Singer's assistant shows us to the elevator. The elevator doubles as the janitor's closet— the cart with the big trash can and all the accouterments is rolled aside so I can get in. Evidently there aren't a lot of wheelchair people using this building.

We ride the broom closet down to the basement and are led down a long passageway to a big lecture hall. As the students drift in, I engage in light badinage with the sound technician. He is squeamish about touching me, but I insist that the cordless lavaliere is my mike of choice. I invite him to clip it to the big polyester scarf.

The students enter from the rear door, way up at ground level, and walk down stairs to their seats. I feel like an animal in the zoo. I hadn't reckoned on the architecture, those tiers of steps that separate me from a human wall of apparent physical and mental perfection, that keep me confined down here in my pit.

It is 5 before 10. Singer is loping down the stairs. I feel like signaling to Carmen to open the door, summon the broom closet and get me out of here. But Singer greets me pleasantly and hands me Princeton's check for $500, the fee he offered with apologies for its inadequacy.

So. On with the show.

My talk to the students is pretty Southern. I've decided to pound them with heart, hammer them with narrative and say "y'all" and "folks." I play with the emotional tone, giving them little peaks and valleys, modulating three times in one 45-second patch. I talk about justice. Even beauty and love. I figure they haven't been getting much of that from Singer.

Of course, I give them some argument too. I mean to honor my contractual obligations. I lead with the hypothetical about mixed-race, nonwhite babies and build the ending around the question of who should have the burden of proof as to the quality of disabled lives. And woven throughout the talk is the presentation of myself as a representative of a minority group that has been rendered invisible by prejudice and oppression, a participant in a discussion that would not occur in a just world.

I let it go a little longer than I should. Their faces show they're going where I'm leading, and I don't look forward to letting them go. But the clock on the wall reminds me of promises I mean to keep, and I stop talking and submit myself to examination and inquiry.

Singer's response is surprisingly soft. Maybe after hearing that this discussion is insulting and painful to me, he doesn't want to exacerbate my discomfort. His reframing of the issues is almost pro forma, abstract, entirely impersonal. Likewise, the students' inquiries are abstract and fairly predictable: anencephaly, permanent unconsciousness, eugenic abortion. I respond to some of them with stories, but mostly I give answers I could have e-mailed in.

I call on a young man near the top of the room.

"Do you eat meat?"

"Yes, I do."

"Then how do you justify—"

"I haven't made any study of animal rights, so anything I could say on the subject wouldn't be worth everyone's time."

The next student wants to work the comparison of disability and race, and Singer joins the discussion until he elicits a comment from me that he can characterize as racist. He scores a point, but that's all right. I've never claimed to be free of prejudice, just struggling with it.

Singer proposes taking me on a walk around campus, unless I think it would be too cold. What the hell? "It's probably warmed up some. Let's go out and see how I do."

He doesn't know how to get out of the building without using the stairs, so this time it is my assistant leading the way. Carmen has learned of another elevator, which arrives empty. When we get out of the building, she falls behind a couple of paces, like a respectful chaperone.

In the classroom there was a question about keeping alive the unconscious. In response, I told a story about a family I knew as a child, which took loving care of a nonresponsive teenage girl, acting out their unconditional commitment to each other, making all the other children, and me as their visitor, feel safe. This doesn't satisfy Singer. "Let's assume we can prove, absolutely, that the individual is totally unconscious and that we can know, absolutely, that the individual will never regain consciousness."

I see no need to state an objection, with no stenographer present to record it; I'll play the game and let him continue.

"Assuming all that," he says, "don't you think continuing to take care of that individual would be a bit—weird?"

"No. Done right, it could be profoundly beautiful."

"But what about the caregiver, a woman typically, who is forced to provide all this service to a family member, unable to work, unable to have a life of her own?"

"That's not the way it should be. Not the way it has to be. As a society, we should pay workers to provide that care, in the home. In some places, it's been done that way for years. That woman shouldn't be forced to do it, any more than my family should be forced to do my care."

Singer takes me around the architectural smorgasbord that is Princeton University by a route that includes not one step, unramped curb or turn on a slope. Within the strange limits of this strange assignment, it seems Singer is doing all he can to make me comfortable.

He asks what I thought of the students' questions.

"They were fine, about what I expected. I was a little surprised by the question about meat eating."

"I apologize for that. That was out of left field. But—I think what he wanted to know is how you can have such high respect for human life and so little respect for animal life."

"People have lately been asking me the converse, how you can have so much respect for animal life and so little respect for human life."

"And what do you answer?"

"I say I don't know. It doesn't make a lot of sense to me."

"Well, in my view—"

"Look. I have lived in blissful ignorance all these years, and I'm not prepared to give that up today."

"Fair enough," he says and proceeds to recount bits of Princeton history. He stops. "This will be of particular interest to you, I think. This is where your colleagues with Not Dead Yet set up their blockade." I'm grateful for the reminder. My brothers and sisters were here before me and behaved far more appropriately than I am doing.

A van delivers Carmen and me early for the evening forum. Singer says he hopes I had a pleasant afternoon.

Yes, indeed. I report a pleasant lunch and a very pleasant nap, and I tell him about the Christopher Reeve Suite in the hotel, which has been remodeled to accommodate Reeve, who has family in the area.

"Do you suppose that's the $600 accessible suite they told me about?"

"Without doubt. And if I'd known it was the Christopher Reeve Suite, I would have held out for it."

"Of course you would have!" Singer laughs. "And we'd have had no choice, would we?"

We talk about the disability rights critique of Reeve and various other topics. Singer is easy to talk to, good company. Too bad he sees lives like mine as avoidable mistakes.

I'm looking forward to the soft vegetarian meal that has been arranged; I'm hungry. Assisted suicide, as difficult as it is, doesn't cause the kind of agony I felt discussing disability-based infanticide. In this one, I understand, and to some degree can sympathize with, the opposing point of view—misguided though it is.

My opening sticks to the five-minute time limit. I introduce the issue as framed by academic articles Not Dead Yet recommended for my use. Andrew Batavia argues for assisted suicide based on autonomy, a principle generally held high in the disability rights movement. In general, he says, the movement fights for our right to control our own lives; when we need assistance to effect our choices, assistance should be available to us as a matter of right. If the choice is to end our lives, he says, we should have assistance then as well. But Carol Gill says that it is differential treatment—disability discrimination—to try to prevent most suicides while facilitating the suicides of ill and disabled people. The social-science literature suggests that the public in general, and physicians in particular, tend to underestimate the quality of life of disabled people, compared with our own assessments of our lives. The case for assisted suicide rests on stereotypes that our lives are inherently so bad that it is entirely rational if we want to die.

I side with Gill. What worries me most about the proposals for legalized assisted suicide is their veneer of beneficence—the medical determination that, for a given individual, suicide is reasonable or right. It is not about autonomy but about nondisabled people telling us what's good for us.

In the discussion that follows, I argue that choice is illusory in a context of pervasive inequality. Choices are structured by oppression. We shouldn't offer assistance with suicide until we all have the assistance we need to get out of bed in the morning and live a good life. Common causes of suicidality—dependence, institutional confinement, being a burden—are entirely curable. Singer, seated on my right, participates in the discussion but doesn't dominate it. During the meal, I occasionally ask him to put things within my reach, and he competently complies.

I feel as if I'm getting to a few of them, when a student asks me a question. The words are all familiar, but they're strung together in a way so meaningless that I can't even retain them—it's like a long sentence in Tagalog. I can only admit my limitations. "That question's too abstract for me to deal with. Can you rephrase it?"

He indicates that it is as clear as he can make it, so I move on.

A little while later, my right elbow slips out from under me. This is awkward. Normally I get whoever is on my right to do this sort of thing. Why not now? I gesture to Singer. He leans over, and I whisper, "Grasp this wrist and pull forward one inch, without lifting." He follows my instructions to the letter. He sees that now I can again reach my food with my fork. And he may now understand what I was saying a minute ago, that most of the assistance disabled people need does not demand medical training.

A philosophy professor says, "It appears that your objections to assisted suicide are essentially tactical."

"Excuse me?"

"By that I mean they are grounded in current conditions of political, social and economic inequality. What if we assume that such conditions do not exist?"

"Why would we want to do that?"

"I want to get to the real basis for the position you take."

I feel as if I'm losing caste. It is suddenly very clear that I'm not a philosopher. I'm like one of those old practitioners who used to visit my law school, full of bluster about life in the real world. Such a bore! A once-sharp mind gone muddy! And I'm only 44—not all that old.

The forum is ended, and I've been able to eat very little of my puréed food. I ask Carmen to find the caterer and get me a container. Singer jumps up to take care of it. He returns with a box and obligingly packs my food to go.

When I get home, people are clamoring for the story. The lawyers want the blow-by-blow of my forensic triumph over the formidable foe; when I tell them it wasn't like that, they insist that it was. Within the disability rights community, there is less confidence. It is generally assumed that I handled the substantive discussion well, but people worry that my civility may have given Singer a new kind of legitimacy. I hear from Laura, a beloved movement sister. She is appalled that I let Singer provide even minor physical assistance at the dinner. "Where was your assistant?" she wants to know. How could I put myself in a relationship with Singer that made him appear so human, even kind?

I struggle to explain. I didn't feel disempowered; quite the contrary, it seemed a good thing to make him do some useful work. And then, the hard part: I've come to believe that Singer actually is human, even kind in his way. There ensues a discussion of good and evil and personal assistance and power and philosophy and tactics for which I'm profoundly grateful.

I e-mail Laura again. This time I inform her that I've changed my will. She will inherit a book that Singer gave me, a collection of his writings with a weirdly appropriate inscription: "To Harriet Johnson, So that you will have a better answer to questions about animals. And thanks for coming to Princeton. Peter Singer. March 25, 2002." She responds that she is changing her will, too. I'll get the autographed photo of Jerry Lewis she received as an M.D.A. poster child. We joke that each of us has given the other a "reason to live."

I have had a nice e-mail message from Singer, hoping Carmen and I and the chair got home without injury, relaying positive feedback from my audiences—and taking me to task for a statement that isn't supported by a relevant legal authority, which he looked up. I report that we got home exhausted but unharmed and concede that he has caught me in a generalization that should have been qualified. It's clear that the conversation will continue.

I am soon sucked into the daily demands of law practice, family, community and politics. In the closing days of the state legislative session, I help get a bill passed that I hope will move us one small step toward a world in which killing won't be such an appealing solution to the "problem" of disability. It is good to focus on this kind of work. But the conversations with and about Singer continue. Unable to muster the appropriate moral judgments, I ask myself a tough question: am I in fact a silly little lady whose head is easily turned by a man who gives her a kind of attention she enjoys? I hope not, but I confess that I've never been able to sustain righteous anger for more than about 30 minutes at a time. My view of life tends more toward tragedy.

The tragic view comes closest to describing how I now look at Peter Singer. He is a man of unusual gifts, reaching for the heights. He writes that he is trying to cre-ate a system of ethics derived from fact and reason, that largely throws off the perspectives of religion, place, family, tribe, community and maybe even species—to "take the point of view of the universe." His is a grand, heroic undertaking.

But like the protagonist in a classical drama, Singer has his flaw. It is his unexamined assumption that disabled people are inherently "worse off," that we "suffer," that we have lesser "prospects of a happy life." Because of this all-too-common prejudice, and his rare courage in taking it to its logical conclusion, catastrophe looms. Here in the midpoint of the play, I can't look at him without fellow-feeling.

I am regularly confronted by people who tell me that Singer doesn't deserve my human sympathy. I should make him an object of implacable wrath, to be cut off, silenced, destroyed absolutely. And I find myself lacking a logical argument to the contrary.

I am talking to my sister Beth on the phone. "You kind of like the monster, don't you?" she says.

I find myself unable to evade, certainly unwilling to lie. "Yeah, in a way. And he's not exactly a monster."

"You know, Harriet, there were some very pleasant Nazis. They say the SS guards went home and played on the floor with their children every night."

She can tell that I'm chastened; she changes the topic, lets me off the hook. Her harshness has come as a surprise. She isn't inclined to moralizing; in our family, I'm the one who sets people straight.

When I put the phone down, my argumentative nature feels frustrated. In my mind, I replay the conversation, but this time defend my position.

"He's not exactly a monster. He just has some strange ways of looking at things."

"He's advocating genocide."

"That's the thing. In his mind, he isn't. He's only giving parents a choice. He thinks the humans he is talking about aren't people, aren't 'persons.'"

"But that's the way it always works, isn't it? They're always animals or vermin or chattel goods. Objects, not persons. He's repackaging some old ideas. Making them acceptable."

"I think his ideas are new, in a way. It's not old-fashioned hate. It's a twisted, mis-informed, warped kind of beneficence. His motive is to do good."

"What do you care about motives?" she asks. "Doesn't this beneficent killing make disabled brothers and sisters just as dead?"

"But he isn't killing anyone. It's just talk."

"Just talk? It's talk with an agenda, talk aimed at forming policy. Talk that's get-ting a receptive audience. You of all people know the power of that kind of talk."

"Well, sure, but—"

"If talk didn't matter, would you make it your life's work?"

"But," I say, "his talk won't matter in the end. He won't succeed in reinventing morality. He stirs the pot, brings things out into the open. But ultimately we'll make a world that's fit to live in, a society that has room for all its flawed creatures. History will remember Singer as a curious example of the bizarre things that can happen when paradigms collide."

"What if you're wrong? What if he con-vinces people that there's no morally sig-nificant difference between a fetus and a newborn, and just as disabled fetuses are routinely aborted now, so disabled babies are routinely killed? Might some future generation take it further than Singer wants to go? Might some say there's no morally significant line between a newborn and a 3-year-old?"

"Sure. Singer concedes that a bright line cannot be drawn. But he doesn't propose killing anyone who prefers to live."

"That overarching respect for the indi-vidual's preference for life—might some

say it's a fiction, a fetish, a quasi-religious belief?"

"Yes," I say. "That's pretty close to what I think. As an atheist, I think all preferences are moot once you kill someone. The injury is entirely to the surviving community."

"So what if that view wins out, but you can't break disability prejudice? What if you wind up in a world where the disabled person's 'irrational' preference to live must yield to society's 'rational' interest in reduc-ing the incidence of disability? Doesn't horror kick in somewhere? Maybe as you watch the door close behind whoever has wheeled you into the gas chamber?"

"That's not going to happen."

"Do you have empirical evidence?" she asks. "A logical argument?"

"Of course not. And I know it's hap-pened before, in what was considered the most progressive medical community in the world. But it won't happen. I have to believe that."

Belief. Is that what it comes down to? Am I a person of faith after all? Or am I clinging to foolish hope that the tragic protagonist, this one time, will shift course before it's too late?

I don't think so. It's less about belief, less about hope, than about a practical need for definitions I can live with.

If I define Singer's kind of disability prejudice as an ultimate evil, and him as a monster, then I must so define all who believe disabled lives are inherently worse off or that a life without a certain kind of consciousness lacks value. That definition would make monsters of many of the peo-ple with whom I move on the sidewalks, do business, break bread, swap stories and share the grunt work of local politics. It would reach some of my family and most of my nondisabled friends, people who show me personal kindness and who sometimes manage to love me through their ignorance. I can't live with a definition of ultimate evil that encompasses all of them. I can't refuse the monster-majority basic respect and human sympathy. It's not in my heart to deny every single one of them, categorically, my affection and my love.

The peculiar drama of my life has placed me in a world that by and large thinks it would be better if people like me did not exist. My fight has been for accommodation, the world to me and me to the world.

As a disability pariah, I must struggle for a place, for kinship, for community, for connection. Because I am still seeking acceptance of my humanity, Singer's call to get past species seems a luxury way beyond my reach. My goal isn't to shed the perspective that comes from my particular experience, but to give voice to it. I want to be engaged in the tribal fury that rages when opposing perspectives are let loose.

As a shield from the terrible purity of Singer's vision, I'll look to the corruption that comes from interconnectedness. To justify my hopes that Singer's theoretical world—and its entirely logical extensions—won't become real, I'll invoke the muck and mess and undeniable reality of disabled lives well lived. That's the best I can do.

CHAPTER 43

Helen and Frida

Anne Finger

I'm lying on the couch downstairs in the TV room in the house where I grew up, a farmhouse with sloping floors in upstate New York. I'm nine years old. I've had surgery, and I'm home, my leg in a plaster cast. Everyone else is off at work or school. My mother recovered this couch by hemming a piece of fabric that she bought from a bin at the Woolworth's in Utica ("Bargains! Bargains! Bargains! Remnants Priced as Marked") and laying it over the torn upholstery. Autumn leaves—carrot, jaundice, brick—drift sluggishly across a liver-brown background. I'm watching *The Million Dollar Movie* on our black-and-white television: today it's *Singing in the Rain*. These movies always make me think of the world that my mother lived in before I was born, a world where women wore hats and gloves and had cinched-waist suits with padded shoulders as if they were in the army. My mother told me that in *The Little Colonel*, Shirley Temple had pointed her finger and said, "As red as those roses over there," and then the roses had turned red and everything in the movie was in color after that. I thought that was how it had been when I was born, everything in the world becoming both more vivid and more ordinary, and the black-and-white world, the world of magic and shadows, disappearing forever in my wake.

Now it's the scene where the men in blue-jean coveralls are wheeling props and sweeping the stage, carpenters shouldering boards, moving behind Gene Kelly as Don Lockwood and Donald O'Connor as Cosmo. Cosmo is about to pull his hat down over his forehead and sing, "Make 'em laugh . . ." and hoof across the stage, pulling open doors that open onto brick walls, careening up what appears to be a lengthy marble-floored corridor but is in fact a painted backdrop.

Suddenly, all the color drains from the room: not just from the mottled sofa I'm lying on, but also from the orange wallpaper that looked so good on the shelf at Streeter's (and was only $1.29 a roll), the chipped blue-willow plate: everything's black and silver now. I'm on a movie set, sitting in the director's chair. I'm grown-up suddenly, eighteen or thirty-five.

Places, please!

Quiet on the set!

Speed, the soundman calls, and I point my index finger at the camera, the clapper claps the board and I see that the movie we are making is called "Helen and Frida." I slice my finger quickly through the air, and the camera rolls slowly forward towards Helen Keller and Frida Kahlo, standing on a veranda, with balustrades that appear to be made of carved stone, but are in fact made of plaster.

The part of Helen Keller isn't played by Patty Duke this time; there's no *Miracle Worker* wild child to spunky rebel in under 100 minutes, no grainy film stock, none of that Alabama sun that bleaches out every soft shadow, leaving only harshness, glare. This time Helen is played by Jean Harlow.

Don't laugh: set pictures of the two of them side by side and you'll see that it's all there, the fair hair lying in looping curls against both faces, the same broad-cheeked bone structure. Imagine that Helen's eyebrows are plucked into a thin arch and penciled, lashes mascared top and bottom, lips cloisonned vermillion. Put Helen in pale peach mousseline-de-soie, hand her a white gardenia, bleach her hair from its original honey blonde to platinum, like Harlow's was, recline her on a *Bombshell* chaise with a white swan gliding in front, a palm fan being waved overhead, while an ardent lover presses sweet nothings into her hand.

I play the part of Frida Kahlo.

It isn't so hard to imagine that the two of them might meet. They moved after all, in not so different circles, fashionable and radical: Helen Keller meeting Charlie Chaplin and Mary Pickford, joining the Wobblies, writing in the *New York Times*, "I love the red flag . . . and if I could I should gladly march it past the offices of the *Times* and let all the reporters and photographers make the most of the spectacle . . ."; Frida, friend of Henry Ford and Sergei Eisenstein, painting a hammer and sickle on her body cast, leaving her bed in 1954, a few weeks before her death, to march in her wheelchair with a babushka tied under her chin, protesting the overthrow of the Arbenz regime in Guatemala.

Of course, the years are all wrong. But that's the thing about *The Million Dollar Movie*. During Frank Sinatra Week, on Monday Frank would be young and

handsome in *It Happened in Brooklyn*, on Tuesday he'd have grey temples and crow's feet, be older than my father, on Wednesday, be even younger than he had been on Monday. You could pour the different decades in a bowl together and give them a single quick fold with the smooth edge of a spatula, the way my mother did when she made black and white marble cake from two Betty Crocker mixes. It would be 1912, and Big Bill Haywood would be waving the check Helen had sent over his head at a rally for the Little Falls strikers, and you, Frida, would be in the crowd, not as a five-year-old child, before the polio, before the bus accident, but as a grown woman, cheering along with the strikers. Half an inch away, it would be August 31, 1932, and both of you would be standing on the roof of the Detroit Institute of the Arts, along with Diego, Frida looking up through smoked glass at the eclipse of the sun, Helen's face turned upwards to feel the chill of night descending, to hear the birds greeting the midday dusk.

Let's get one thing straight right away. This isn't going to be one of those movies where they put their words into our mouths. This isn't *Magnificent Obsession*, blind Jane Wyman isn't going to blink back a tear when the doctors tell her they can't cure her after all, saying, "and I thought I was going to be able to get rid of these," gesturing with her ridiculous rhinestone-studded, catseye dark glasses (and we think, "*Really*, Jane,"); she's not going to tell Rock Hudson she can't marry him: "I won't have you pitied because of me. I love you too much," and "I could only be a burden," and then disappear until the last scene when, lingering on the border between death and cure (the only two acceptable states), Rock saves her life and her sight and they live happily ever after. It's not going to be *A Patch of Blue*: when the sterling young Negro hands us the dark glasses and, in answer to our question: "But what are they for?" says "Never mind, put them on," we're not going to grab them, hide our stone Medusa gaze, grateful for the magic that's made us a pretty girl. This isn't *Johnny Belinda*, we're not sweetly mute, surrounded by an aura of silence. No, in this movie the blind women have milky eyes that make the sighted uncomfortable. The deaf women drag metal against metal, oblivious to the jarring sound, make odd cries of delight at the sight of the ocean, squawk when we are angry.

So now the two female icons of disability have met: Helen, who is nothing but, who swells to fill up the category, sweet Helen with her drooping dresses covering drooping bosom, who is Blind and Deaf, her vocation; and Frida, who lifts her skirt to reveal the gaping, cunt-like wound on her leg, who rips her body open to reveal her back, a broken column, her back corset with its white canvas straps framing her beautiful breasts, her body stuck with nails: but she can't be Disabled, she's Sexual.

Here stands Frida, who this afternoon, in the midst of a row with Diego, cropped off her jet-black hair ("Now see what you've made me do!"), and has schlepped herself to the ball in one of his suits. Nothing Dietrichish and coy about this drag: Diego won't get to parade his beautiful wife. Now she's snatched up Helen and walked with her out here onto the veranda.

In the other room, drunken Diego lurches, his body rolling forward before his feet manage to shuffle themselves ahead on the marble floor, giving himself more than ever the appearance of being one of those children's toys, bottom-weighted with sand, that when punched, roll back and then forward, an eternal red grin painted on their rubber faces. His huge belly shakes with laughter, his laughter a gale that blows above the smoke curling up towards the distant, gilded ceiling, gusting above the knots of men in tuxedos and women with marcelled hair, the black of their satin dresses setting off the glitter of their diamonds.

But the noises of the party, Diego's drunken roar, will be added later by the Foley artists.

Helen's thirty-six. She's just come back from Montgomery. Her mother had dragged her down there after she and Peter Fagan took out a marriage license, and the Boston papers got hold of the story. For so many years, men had been telling her that she was beautiful, that they worshipped her, that when Peter declared himself in the parlor at Wrentham, she had at first thought this was just more palaver about his pure love for her soul. But no, this was the real thing: carnal and thrilling and forbidden. How could you, her mother said. How people will laugh at you! The shame, the shame. Her mother whisked her off to Montgomery, Peter trailing after the two of them. There her brother-in-law chased Peter off the porch with a good old Southern shotgun. Helen's written her poem:

What earthly consolation is there for one like me
Whom fate has denied a husband and the joy of motherhood?. . .
I shall have confidence as always,
That my unfilled longings will be gloriously satisfied
In a world where eyes never grow dim, nor ears dull.
Poor Helen, waiting, waiting to get fucked in heaven.

But not Frida. She's so narcissistic. What a relief to Helen! None of those interrogations passing for conversation she usually has to endure. (After the standard pile of praise is heaped upon her—I've read your book five, ten, twenty times, I've admired you ever since . . . come the questions: Do you mind if I ask you: Is everything black? Is Mrs. Macy always with you?): no, Frida launches right into the tale of Diego's betrayal ". . . of course, I have my fun, too, but one doesn't want to have one's nose rubbed in the shit . . ." she signs into Helen's hand.

Helen is delighted and shocked. In her circles, Free Love is believed in, spoken of solemnly, dutifully. Her ardent young circle of socialists want to do away with the sordid marketplace of prostitution, bourgeois marriage, where women barter their hymens and throw in their souls to sweeten the deal; Helen has read Emma, she has read Isadora; she believes in a holy, golden monogamy, an unfettered, eternal meeting of two souls-in-flesh. And here Frida speaks of the act so casually that Helen, like a timid schoolgirl, stutters,

"You really? I mean, the both of you, you . . .?"

Frida throws her magnificent head back and laughs.

"Yes, really," Frida strokes gently into her hand. "He fucks other women and I fuck other men—and other women."

"F–U–C–K?" Helen asks. "What is this word?"

Frida explains it to her. "Now I've shocked you," Frida says.

"Yes, you have . . . I suppose it's your Latin nature . . ."

I'm not in the director's chair anymore. I'm sitting in the audience of the Castro Theatre in San Francisco watching this unfold. I'm twenty-seven. When I was a kid, I thought being grown up would be like living in the movies, that I'd be Rosalind Russell in *Sister Kenny*, riding a horse through the Australian outback or that I'd dance every night in a sleek satin gown under paper palms at the Coconut Grove. Now I go out to the movies, two, three, four times a week.

The film cuts from the two figures on the balcony to the night sky. It's technicolor: the pale gold stars against midnight blue. We're close to the equator now: there's the Southern Cross, and the Clouds of Magellan, and you feel the press of the stars, the mocking closeness of the heavens as you can only feel it in the tropics. The veranda on which we are now standing is part of a colonial Spanish palace, built in a clearing in a jungle that daily spreads its roots and tendrils closer, closer. A macaw perches atop a broken Mayan statue and calls, "I am queen/I am queen/I am queen." A few yards into the jungle, a spider monkey shits on the face of a dead god.

Wait a minute. What's going on? Is that someone out in the lobby talking? But it's so loud—

Dolores del Rio strides into the film, shouting, "Latin nature! Who wrote this shit?" She's wearing black silk pants and a white linen blouse; she plants her fists on her hips and demands: "Huh? Who wrote this shit?"

I look to my left, my right, shrug, stand up in the audience and say, "I guess I did."

"Latin nature! And a white woman? Playing Frida? *I* should be playing Frida."

"You?"

"Listen, honey." She's striding down the aisle towards me now. "I know I filmed that Hollywood crap. Six movies in one year: crook reformation romance, romantic Klondike melodrama, California romance, costume bedroom farce, passion in a jungle camp among chicle workers, romantic drama of the Russian revolution. I know David Selznick said: 'I don't care what story you use so long as we call it *Bird of Paradise* and Del Rio jumps into a flaming volcano at the finish.' They couldn't tell a Hawaiian from a Mexican from a lesbian. But I loved Frida and she loved me. She painted 'What the Water Gave Me' for me. At the end of her life, we were fighting, and she threatened to send me her amputated leg on a silver tray. If that's not love, I don't know what is—"

I'm still twenty-seven, but now it's the year 2015. The Castro's still there, the organ still rises up out of the floor with the organist playing "San Francisco, open your Golden Gate. . . ." In the lobby now, alongside the photos of the original opening of the Castro in 1927, are photos in black and white of lounging hustlers and leather

queens, circa 1979, a photographic reproduction of the door of the women's room
a few years later ("If they can send men to
the moon, why don't they?") Underneath,
in Braille, Spanish, and English: "In the
1960s, the development of the felt-tip pen,
combined with a growing philosophy of
personal expression caused an explosion
of graffiti . . . sadly unappreciated in its day,
this portion of a bathroom stall, believed
by many experts to have originated in the
women's room right here at the Castro
Theater, sold recently at Sotheby's for $5
million. . . ."

Of course, the Castro's now totally accessible, not just integrated wheelchair seat-
ing, but every film captioned, a voice loop
that interprets the action for blind people,
over which now come the words: "As Dolores del Rio argues with the actress playing
Frida, Helen Keller waits patiently—"

A woman in the audience stands up and
shouts, "Patiently! What the fuck are you
talking about, patiently? You can't tell the
difference between patience and powerlessness. She's being *ignored*." The stage
is stormed by angry women, one of whom
leaps into the screen and begins signing
to Helen, "Dolores del Rio's just come out
and—"

"Enough already!" someone in the audience shouts. "Can't we please just get on
with the story!"

Now that Frida is played by Dolores,
she's long-haired again, wearing one of her
white Tehuana skirts with a deep red shawl.
She takes Helen's hand in hers, that hand
that has been cradled by so many great
men and great women.

"Latin nature?" Frida says, and laughs. "I
think perhaps it is rather your cold Yankee
nature that causes your reaction. . . ." And
before Helen can object to being called a
Yankee, Frida says, "But enough about Diego. . . ."

It's the hand that fascinates Frida, in its
infinite, unpassive receptivity: she prattles

on. When she makes the letters "z" and "j"
in sign, she gets to stroke the shape of the
letter into Helen's palm. She so likes the
sensation that she keeps trying to work
words with those letters in them into the
conversation. The camera moves in close
to Helen's hand as Frida says, "Here on
the edge of the Yucatan jungle, one sometimes see jaguars, although never jackals. I
understand jackals are sometimes seen in
Zanzibar. I have never been there, nor have
I been to Zagreb nor Japan nor the Zermatt,
nor Java. I have seen the Oaxacan mountain Zempoaltepec. Once in a zoo in Zur-
ich I saw a zebu and a zebra. Afterwards, we
sat in a small cafe and ate cherries jubilee
and zabaglione, washed down with glasses
of zinfandel. Or perhaps my memory is
confused: perhaps that day we ate jam on
ziewback crusts and drank a juniper tea,
while an old Jew played a zither. . . ."

"Oh," says Helen.

Frida falls silent. Frida, you painted
those endless self-portraits, but you always
looked at yourself level, straight on, in full
light. This is different: this time your face is
tilted, played over by shadows. In all those
self-portraits, you are simultaneously artist
and subject, lover and beloved, the bride of
yourself. Now, here, in the movies, it's different: the camera stands in for the eye of
the lover. But you're caught in the unforgiv-
ing blank stare of a blind woman.

And now, we cut from that face to the face
of Helen. Here I don't put in any soothing
music, nothing low and sweet with violins,
to make the audience more comfortable
as the camera moves in for its close-up.
You understand why early audiences were
frightened by these looming heads. In all
the movies with blind women in them—or,
let's be real, sighted women playing the
role of blind woman—Jane Wyman and
Merle Oberon in the different versions of
Magnificent Obsession, Audrey Hepburn in
Wait Until Dark, Uma Thurman in *Jennifer
8*, we've never seen a blind woman shot this

way before: never seen the camera come in and linger lovingly on her face the way it does here. We gaze at their faces only when bracketed by others, or in moments of terror when beautiful young blind women are being stalked. We've never seen before this frightening blank inward turning of passion, a face that has never seen itself in the mirror, that does not arrange itself for consumption.

Lack = inferiority? Try it right now. Finish reading this paragraph and then close your eyes, push the flaps of your ears shut, and sit. Not just for a minute: give it five or ten. Not in that meditative state, designed to take you out of your mind, your body. Just the opposite. Feel the press of hand crossed over hand: without any distraction, you feel your body with the same distinctness as a lover's touch makes you feel yourself. You fold into yourself, you know the rhythm of your breathing, the beating of your heart, the odd independent twitch of a muscle: now in a shoulder, now in a thigh. Your cunt, in all its patient hunger.

We cut back to Frida in close up. But now Helen's fingers enter the frame, travel across that face, stroking the downy moustache above Frida's upper lip, the fleshy nose, the thick-lobed ears.

Now, it's Frida's turn to be shocked: shocked at the hunger of these hands, at the almost-feral sniff, at the freedom with which Helen blurs the line between knowing and needing.

"May I kiss you?" Helen asks.

"Yes," Frida says.

Helen's hands cup themselves around Frida's face.

I'm not at the Castro anymore. I'm back home on the fold-out sofa in the slapped-together TV room, watching grainy images flickering on the tiny screen set in the wooden console. I'm nine years old again, used to Hays-office kisses, two mouths with teeth clenched, lips held rigid, pressing stonily against each other. I'm not ready for the way that Helen's tongue probes into Frida's mouth, the tongue that seems to be not so much interested in giving pleasure as in finding an answer in the emptiness of her mouth.

I shout, "Cut," but the two of them keep right on. Now we see Helen's face, her wide-open eyes that stare at nothing revealing a passion blank and insatiable, a void into which you could plunge and never, never, never touch bottom. Now she begins to make noises, animal mewlings and cries.

I will the screen to turn to snow, the sound to static. I do not want to watch this, hear this. My leg is in a thick plaster cast, inside of which scars are growing like mushrooms, thick and white in the dark damp. I think that I must be a lesbian, a word I have read once in a book, because I know I am not like the women on television, with their high heels and shapely calves and their firm asses swaying inside of satin dresses waiting, waiting for a man, nor am I like the women I know, the mothers with milky breasts, and what else can there be?

I look at the screen and they are merging into each other, Frida and Helen, the dark-haired and the light, the one who will be disabled and nothing more, the other who will be everything but. I can't yet imagine a world where these two might meet: the face that does not live under the reign of its own reflection with the face that has spent its life looking in the mirror; the woman who turns her rapt face up towards others and the woman who exhibits her scars as talismans, the one who is only, only and the one who is everything but. I will the screen to turn to snow.

CHAPTER 44

"I Am Not One of the" and "Cripple Lullaby"

Cheryl Marie Wade

I AM NOT ONE OF THE

I am not one of the physically
    challenged—

I'm a sock in the eye with a gnarled fist
I'm a French kiss with cleft tongue
I'm orthopedic shoes sewn on a last of
    your fears

I am not one of the differently abled—

I'm an epitaph [tombstone] for a million imperfect
    babies left untreated
I'm an ikon carved from bones in a mass
    grave in Tiergarten, Germany—
I'm withered legs hidden with a blanket

I am not one of the able disabled—

I'm a black panther with green eyes and
    scars like a picket fence
I'm pink lace panties teasing a stub of milk
    white thigh
I'm the Evil Eye

I'm the first cell divided
I'm mud that talks   [Hindu goddess of empowerment]
I'm Eve   I'm Kali
I'm The Mountain That Never Moves
I've been forever   I'll be here forever
I'm the Gimp
I'm the Cripple
I'm the Crazy Lady
I'm The Woman With Juice

CRIPPLE LULLABY

I'm trickster coyote in a gnarly-bone suit
I'm a fate worse than death in
    shit-kickin' boots

I'm the nightmare booga you flirt with in
    dreams
'Cause I emphatically demonstrate: It ain't
    what it seems

I'm a whisper, I'm a heartbeat, I'm "that
    accident," and goodbye
One thing I am not is a reason to die.

I'm homeless in the driveway of your
    manicured street
I'm Evening Magazine's SuperCrip of the
    Week

I'm the girl in the doorway with no
    illusions to spare
I'm a kid dosed on chemo, so who said life
    is fair

I'm a whisper, I'm a heartbeat, I'm "let's
    call it suicide," and a sigh
One thing I am not is a reason to die
I'm the poster child with doom-dipped
    eyes
I'm the ancient remnant set adrift on ice

I'm that Valley girl, you know, dying
    of thin
I'm all that is left of the Cheshire
    Cat's grin

I'm the Wheelchair Athlete, I'm every dead
    Baby Doe
I'm Earth's last volcano, and I am ready to
    blow

I'm a whisper, I'm a heartbeat, I'm a geno-
    cide survivor, and Why?
One thing I am not is a reason to die.

I am not a reason to die.

CHAPTER 45

"Beauty and Variations"

Kenny Fries

1.

What is it like to be so beautiful? I dip
my hands inside you, come up with—
    what?

Beauty, at birth applied, does not
    transfer
to my hands. But every night, your hands

touch my scars, raise my twisted limbs to
graze against your lips. Lips that never

form the words—*you are beautiful*—
    transform
my deformed bones into—*what?*—if not
    beauty.

Can only one of us be beautiful? Is this
    your
plan? Are your sculpted thighs more
    powerful

driving into mine? Your hands find their
    way
inside me, scrape against my heart. Look

at your hands. Pieces of my skin trail
    from
your fingers. What do you make of this?

Your hands that know my scars, that lift
    me to your
lips, now drip my blood. Can blood be
    beautiful?

2.

I want to break your bones. Make them so
they look like mine. Force you to walk on

twisted legs. Then, will your lips still
    beg
for mine? Or will that disturb the
    balance

of our desire? Even as it inspires, your
    body
terrifies. And once again I find your hands

inside me. Why do you touch my scars?
    You
can't make them beautiful any more than
    I can

tear your skin apart. Beneath my scars,
between my twisted bones, hides my
    heart.

Why don't you let me leave my mark? With
    no
flaws on your skin—how can I find your
    heart?

3.

How much beauty can a person bear? Your
    smooth
skin is no relief from the danger of your
    eyes.

My hands would leave you scarred. Knead
the muscles
of your thighs. I want to tear your skin,
reach

inside you—your secrets tightly held.
Breathe
deep. Release them. Let them fall into my
palms.

My secrets are on my skin. Could this be
why
each night I let you deep inside? Is that

where my beauty lies? Your eyes, without
secrets,
would be two scars. I want to seal your
eyes,

they know my every flaw. Your smooth
skin, love's
wounds ignore. My skin won't mend, is
calloused, raw.

4.

Who can mend my bones? At night, your
hands press
into my skin. My feet against your chest,
you mold

my twisted bones. What attracts you to my
legs? Not
sex. What brings your fingers to my scars
is beyond

desire. Why do you persist? Why do you
touch me
as if my skin were yours? Seal your lips. No
kiss

can heal these wounds. No words
unbend my bones.
Beauty is a two-faced god. As your fingers
soothe

my scars, they scrape against my heart.
Was this

birth's plan—to tie desire to my pain, to
stain

love's touch with blood? If my skin won't
heal, how
can I escape? My scars are in the shape of
my love.

5.

How else can I quench this thirst? My
lips
travel down your spine, drink the smooth-
ness

of your skin. I am searching for the core:
What is beautiful? Who decides? Can the
laws

of nature be defied? Your body tells me:
come
close. But beauty distances even as it
draws

me near. What does my body want from
yours?
My twisted legs around your neck. You
bend

me back. Even though you can't give the
bones
at birth I wasn't given, I let you deep
inside.

You give me—*what*? Peeling back my skin,
you
expose my missing bones. And my heart,
long

before you came, just as broken. I don't
know who
to blame. So each night, naked on the bed,
my body

doesn't want repair, but longs for innocence. If
innocent, despite the flaws I wear, I am
beautiful.

CHAPTER 46

Selections from *Cripple Poetics*

Petra Kuppers and Neil Marcus

THE METAPHOR OF WIND IN CRIPPLE POETICS

How can I speak of cripple and not
     mention the wind.
How can I speak of crippled and not
     mention the heart.
Heart, wind, song, flower, space, time,
     love. To leave these absent is to leave
     cripple in stark terms.
As if we were made of medical parts and
     not flesh and bone.
There is always wind in my cripple
Off shore breezes.
Scented nightflowering vines.
Wild salsa dances that run past
     midnight
Cripple is not extraordinary or ordinary.
Cripple is a full plate
A blown about newspaper
An ox in a rice field, ploughing earth

oh petra,

how fragile the heart is
tho i try hard to make mine not
thats why i dont fall easily
or expect too much
but i can say i am kind and giving
and dont want to hurt you at all . . .
....
a gentle spank tho neil

How about a heart as wide and mobile as an
     octopus?
Arms reach out through breasts and spines,
caress, twist, touch fire and all elements:
pulled in, pulled out, pulsing
uncoil this somersault
this cycle of embrace
and find some space:
salty waters moisten thin membranes
salty tissues reach and swell
salty tears leave rivers on the skin
pathways where eels swim.
All swim, I swim, forward and out, loop the loop
to the coral reefs and the blue ocean.

neilmarcus (11:34:55 AM): my pain sup-
     port group yesterday
neilmarcus (11:35:09 AM): fantastic me
pk (11:36:18 AM): ?
neilmarcus (11:37:52 AM): being a revolu-
     tionary talking about sort of deaf presi-
     dent now politics sex and cripdom.
     pain authority control focault
pk (11:38:30 AM): yes, oh yes. I see that.
neilmarcus (11:38:46 AM): and they lit up.i
     set the room ablaze
pk (11:38:50 AM): sex-positive politics
pk (11:39:08 AM): the caped crusader,
     indeed
neilmarcus (11:39:33 AM): in our group
     needed saying . . . with pain too
neilmarcus (11:40:04 AM): many tongues
     yes

neilmarcus (11:40:35 AM): alternate tongues

pk (11:40:54 AM): that would be something for poetry: pain and eros, not self-induced pain, but how there's something about the experience of pain in another body that is so intimate, links people so closely . . . I am aware of your pain when we make love, somewhat . . . and my own.

pk (11:41:37 AM): tongues—in what language?

neilmarcus (11:41:38 AM): its only a little

pk (11:41:57 AM): well, there are different pains?

neilmarcus (11:42:51 AM): the other mother tongue a book on gay history i saw her speak

pk (11:44:06 AM): ok, ok. I love the connection, and to gay history, too.

neilmarcus (11:44:15 AM): yes pain of speech loss

pk (11:44:30 AM): yes

pk (11:44:38 AM): pain of disconnect

neilmarcus (11:44:47 AM): movement loss

neilmarcus (11:45:11 AM): fear/pain

pk (11:45:13 AM): pain of invisibility, non-fitting, anchorless

pk (11:45:37 AM): pain of loneliness

neilmarcus (11:45:37 AM): gender pain

neilmarcus (11:46:16 AM): separateness pain

pk (11:47:10 AM): pain of sadness

neilmarcus (11:47:51 AM): ok poem of pain? yes and joy

pk (11:48:42 AM): yes, poems out of pain are about connect, love, joy, fullness, being heard, reaching towards understanding

neilmarcus (11:49:03 AM): i love you

pk (11:49:22 AM): I love you

NIGHT ICE

Storm roared joints carol
snow angels in my bed
move my bones
into the white whirl

midnight ball bearing
off to the sleep pillow
to the maw
    night lion's claws

sing over the window
into the white whirl
path clad in crystal armor
lances into the door
at knee fall

to the fingertip
song drift
whiter in the ice air

tonight it is ten degrees outside
in the mirror, I hold a blue pill
one, two, maybe three and I lay down
out on my porch
go to sleep
blue princess
veins like ice flowers

slow crunch of the ice lion
mumbling to his pride
in the thaw of the moon
rock this marble heart

if I hold a cat in each hand,
will I fly?

AT THE GYNECOLOGIST'S

There are qualities in the material world that are seldom experienced; only necessity makes them apparent . . . d drake

Who are we but Atoms
Partly visible. Partly invisible.
Particles of love
Radiating poetry. Art. Philosophy.
I see myself through you and around you
As the world turns
You hold me in and about you
My curves fold on you
We meet turning into
We touch
Our Matter

You might not want children because
issues in his family
gene dance
she said, our chirpy gynecologist,
looking straight at me, slant at my lover
instruments out

What can be seen
What can be talked about
What is love
What is form
What is dance

Love him, but not children like him?
White coat atoms settle into their dance:
dream plane, wish bone, Galton's
    galvanized knowledge
eugenic technology that flies off our bod-
    ies' awkward edges
erasure of the spastic tender
touch, deliberate, the vaginal
    membrane

The air in this place is heavy . . . like water
We glide and float
outer space
For our otter bodies
Playground
You and I twirl in this ether of darkness and light.

The gynecologist motions him to come
    closer,
to look upon the universe
cervix's eye into the inner coil
behold this scene
biological biopsy punches its hole into the
    donut of infinity:
Schroedinger's cat is alive inside me
black box theatre
cage

I do, in part, rely on the kindness of
    strangers
Often it hurts me for people to be
    generous
I need to be clear on what care is.
You go first.
No. after you.
Crash. An accident.
Wasn't that how the bomb was discovered
    . . . by accident ?

we go to the hot springs
and are greeted at the entry gate by an
    older man with scruffy hair and long
    beard
he tells us we are the adventurous
    sort
because we travel with two wheelchairs
    and no 'helper'
he says his name is Basil, which means
    kingly.
He says I remind him of steven
    hawkings
Whom he admires tremendously.
I look away and roll my eyes.
I forgive him anyway.
The king and I.
Hot springs all over the world are
    connected volcanically.

Petra asks the nurse in the drs office how
it is to be working on Christmas eve. Its
awful. I hate you she says.

I hate you

Just kidding she says. Im really ok.
No matter   No matter

CHAPTER 47

Selections from *The Cry of the Gull*

Emmanuelle Laborit

CRY OF THE SEAGULL

I let out screams, lots of them, real ones. Not because I was hungry or thirsty, afraid, or in pain, but because I was beginning to want to talk. I wanted to hear myself, but the sounds I was making weren't rebounding back to me.

I could feel the vibrations. I knew I was screaming but the sounds didn't mean a thing to my mother and father. To them, they were like the piercing cries of a sea bird, like a gull gliding over the ocean. So they nick-named me Mouette, which means *seagull* in French.

The little seagull shrieked above an ocean of noises she couldn't hear, and no one understood her cries.

"You were a very beautiful baby," my mother recalls. "It was an easy birth. You weighed 7 pounds 11 ounces. You cried when you were hungry. You laughed and babbled like other babies. You were happy. We didn't realize right away. We just thought you were well-behaved because, on evenings when we had friends over, you'd sleep soundly even with the music blaring in the living room, which was next to the room where you were sleeping. We were proud to have such a good baby. We thought you were 'normal' because you'd turn your head whenever a door slammed.

We didn't know it was because you could feel the vibrations and drafts on the floor where you were playing. And when your father put on a record, you'd dance in your playpen, swaying back and forth, swinging your arms and legs."

I was at the age when babies crawl around on all fours and start trying to say "mama" and "dada." But I wasn't saying anything. I sensed vibrations on the floor. I felt them from the music and would join in with my seagull-like sounds. At least that's what I've been told.

I was a perceptive little seagull. I had a secret. A world all to myself.

I come from a seafaring family. My mother's father, grandfather, and brother were among the last of the Cape Horn sailors. That's another reason why they called me their little seagull. But the French words for "seagull" and "mute" look and sound practically the same: *mouette/muette*. So which was I? Today, that strange phonetic similarity makes me smile.

Uncle Fifou, my father's older brother, was the first to say, "Emmanuelle makes shrieking sounds because she can't hear herself." My father claims it was my uncle who "was the first to arouse our suspicions." "The scene is frozen in my mind," says my mother.

My parents didn't want to believe it. To

such an extent, in fact, that it was only much later that I found out my paternal grandparents had been married in the chapel of the National Institute for the Deaf in Bordeaux. What's more, the institute's director was my grandmother's stepfather. In an attempt to hide their concern, perhaps, or avoid facing the truth, my parents had forgotten about all that! Basically, they were proud of not having a little brat who would wake them up in the wee hours of the morning. So they got into the habit of jokingly referring to me as their little seagull. It was their way of not admitting they were worried because I was different.

Some people say we end up yelling out what we really want kept silent. In my case, I had to yell to try to hear the difference between my screams and silence, to compensate for the absence of all the words I saw moving on my mother's and father's lips and whose meaning escaped me. And since my parents silenced their anguish, maybe I had to scream for them as well. Who knows?

"The pediatrician thought I was crazy," my mother says. "He didn't believe it either because you seemed to react normally to sounds, but it was the same old story—you were really just feeling vibrations. Yet when we clapped our hands next to you or behind you, you didn't turn your head in the direction of the noise. You didn't respond when you were called. And I could tell it wasn't normal. When I used to walk up to you, you seemed so surprised you would practically jump, as though you had become aware of my presence only a split second before. I started thinking I had psychological problems, especially since the pediatrician still didn't want to believe me even though he saw you for checkups once a month.

"I set up yet another appointment with him to discuss my concerns. That's when he bluntly told me, "Madam, I strongly suggest you get counseling!' Then, he slammed the door on purpose and since you just happened to turn around, maybe because you had felt the vibrations or simply because you found his behavior strange, he said, 'You can clearly see the idea's absurd!'

"I'm angry at him, and at myself for having believed him. After that office visit, your father and I went through a period of real anguish. We observed you constantly. We whistled, called you, slammed doors, watched you clap your hands and sway as though you were dancing to the music. One minute we believed you could hear, the next minute we thought you couldn't. We were totally confused.

"When you were nine months old, I took you to a specialist. He lost no time in telling me you had been born profoundly deaf. It was a tremendous shock. I couldn't accept it and neither could your father. We kept telling ourselves, 'It's a misdiagnosis. There's no way.' We went to see another specialist. I was so hoping he'd grin, reassure us, and send us home.

"Then we went to Trousseau Hospital with your father. During the examination, they made you listen to sounds so loud they practically pierced my eardrums. But you were totally unresponsive to them. You were sitting on my lap and that's when I realized it was true. I asked the specialist three questions.

'Will she talk?'
'Yes but it'll take a long time.'
'What should we do?'
'Have her fitted with a hearing aid and get her into speech therapy as soon as possible. Avoid sign language at all costs.'
'Is there any way I could meet some deaf adults?'
'That wouldn't be a good idea. They belong to a generation that didn't have early training. You'd be disappointed and discouraged.'

"Your father was completely overcome. I cried. Where had this 'curse' come from? Was it genetic? Had it been caused by an illness during pregnancy? I felt guilty and so did your father. We tried, to no avail, to find out who might have been deaf on one side of the family or the other."

I can understand the shock my parents suffered from all that. Parents of deaf children always want to assign guilt. They're always looking for the guilty party. But blaming one parent or the other for a child's deafness is horrible for the child. It shouldn't happen. They still don't know why I'm deaf and never will and it's probably better that way.

My mother says she didn't know what to do with me. She would look at me but couldn't come up with any activities to create a bond between us. Sometimes she couldn't even bring herself to play with me. She stopped talking to me. What was going through her head was, "I can't even tell her I love her any more because she can't hear."

She was in a state of shock, stunned. She couldn't think rationally.

I have strange memories of my early childhood. It's just chaos in my head, a series of completely unrelated images, like film sequences edited together with long strips of blank film, giant lost spaces.

My life up to age seven is full of gaps. I only have visual memories, like flashbacks, images whose time-frame I can't place. I believe there was no sense whatsoever of time progression in my mind during that period. Past, future, everything was on the same time-space line. Mother would say *yesterday*, but I didn't understand where or what *yesterday* was. *Tomorrow* had no meaning either. And I couldn't ask what they meant. I was helpless, completely unaware of time passing. There was daylight and the darkness of night, and that was it.

I still can't assign dates to things during the period from my birth to age seven, or arrange what I did in chronological order. Time was in a holding pattern. I just experienced things as they happened. Maybe

there are memories buried in my head, but I don't know in what order they happened or how old I was. I can't place them. As for events—or I should say situations or scenes because everything was visual—I lived each as an isolated experience, in the present. That's why, in trying to reassemble the puzzle of my early childhood so I could write about it, I found only fragments of images.

Other perceptions dwell in a turmoil that is out of memory's reach. They're locked in that period of solitude, behind that wall of silence, when words were mysterious and language was absent. And yet I was able to manage. I don't know how, but I did.

"Sitting up in your bed," my mother tells me, "you'd see me disappear and come back, to your amazement. You didn't know where I'd gone. To the kitchen, perhaps. I was two distinct images, Mommy disappearing and Mommy coming back. And there was no link between the two."

DOLLS DON'T TALK

I started learning how to communicate with a speech therapist, using the Borel-Maisonny method. She was an extraordinary woman who was receptive to my mother's tale of woe and put up with her anger and tears. She played dolls and water games with me, and we had tea parties. She showed my mother it was possible to have a relationship with me, to make me laugh, so I could go on living as I had before she knew about my deafness.

I learned to pronounce the letters of the alphabet. They taught me the letters using mouth movements and hand gestures.

My mother sat in on the sessions, which ultimately became a way for her to assume her maternal role. By identifying with the therapist, my mother learned to talk to me again. Our way of communicating was instinctive, animal-like. What I call "umbilical." It revolved around simple things like eating, drinking, and sleeping. My mother didn't stop me from gesturing. She didn't have the heart to, even though that's what they recommended. We also had signs that were our very own, completely made up.

"You tried everything under the sun to communicate with me," my mother remembers, "and it made me laugh so hard it brought tears to my eyes! I'd turn your face towards mine so you could try to make out simple words, and you'd imitate me as I went along. It was so cute."

I don't know how many times she drew my face close to hers in a mother-child encounter that was both fascinating and terrifying, and that functioned as our language.

From that moment on, there was hardly any room left for my father. It was even harder when he came home from work. I wasn't spending much time with him and we didn't have an "umbilical" code. I would utter a few words but he almost never understood. It hurt him to see my mother communicating with me in a language whose intimacy was beyond his reach. He felt excluded. And naturally he was, because it wasn't a language that could be shared by all three of us, or with anyone else. He wanted to communicate directly with me and being excluded bothered him. When he came home in the evening, we had nothing to say to each other. I often went up to my mother and pulled on her arm for her to tell me what he was saying. I wanted so much to "talk" with him and know more about him.

I started saying a few words. Like all deaf children, I wore a hearing aid and more or less put up with it. It channeled noises into my head but they were all the same. It was impossible to differentiate between them or use them in any way. It was more tiring than anything else. But the therapists said I had to wear it! I don't know how many times the ear piece fell into my soup. My mother

says the family would find consolation in trite statements like:

"She may be deaf but she's so cute!"
"She'll just be that much smarter!"

Flashback:

I have a fabulous doll collection. I'm not sure how many, but dolls I have! How old am I? I don't know, but I'm at the doll age. It's my doll phase. When it's time to go to sleep, I have to arrange them so they're all lined up in a row. I tuck them in. Their hands have to be outside the covers. Then I close their eyes. I spend a long time arranging them before I go to bed. I probably talk to them. I'm sure I do, using the same code as with my mother, making the sign for sleep. Once all the doll people are in bed, I can go to bed, too.

It's strange that I arranged my dolls so methodically while everything in my head was completely muddled, vague, and mixed-up. I'm still trying to figure out why I used to do it, why I spent an eternity arranging my dolls. My parents always hurried me along so they could put me to bed. It got on my father's nerves. It got on everybody's nerves. But I couldn't sleep if my dolls weren't all in place. They had to be perfectly lined up, eyes closed, the blanket pulled up exactly to where it should be with their arms on top. It all had to be fiendishly precise even though everything in my head was disorganized. Maybe it was my way of putting all the mixed-up experiences I'd had during the day in order before going to sleep. Maybe I was going through the motions of tidying up the day's disorder. During the day, my life was total disorder. At night, I slept neatly tucked away like my dolls, in complete quiet. Dolls don't talk.

I lived in silence because I wasn't communicating. I guess that's what real silence must be like—the total darkness of what can't be communicated. Everyone was dark silence for me except my parents, especially my mother.

Silence therefore had a special meaning for me—the absence of communication. But from another perspective, I've never lived in complete silence. I have my own noises that are inexplicable to hearing people. I have my imagination and it has its noises in image form. I imagine sounds in terms of colors. My own personal silence has colors. It's never black and white.

I perceive hearing people's noises in images too, as sensations. The tranquil waves that gently roll up on the beach evoke a sensation of serenity and calm. Waves that bristle and gallop while arching their backs evoke anger. The wind means my hair floating in the air, freshness and softness on my skin.

Light was important. I liked the day, not the night.

I used to sleep on a sofa in the living room of my parents' tiny apartment. My father was a medical student and my mother, a school teacher. She took time off from her studies to raise me. We weren't very rich, and the apartment was small. I was unaware of all that since I had no idea at the time how society and the hearing world were structured. At night, I slept alone on the sofa. I can still see that yellow and orange sofa. I see a brown wooden table. I see the dining room table with its white frame. The sounds I imagined were always linked to colors, but I couldn't say that a specific sound was blue, green, or red. It's that colors and light played a part in the way I imagined sounds and perceived every situation.

In the light, I could monitor everything with my eyes. Darkness was synonymous with non-communication and, therefore, silence. Absence of light meant panic. Later on, I didn't mind turning out the light before going to sleep.

I have a memory about the darkness of night and how it affected me when I was little: I'm in the living room, lying on my bed, and I see the reflection of headlights shining through the window onto the wall. All those lights that keep coming and going frighten me. I still see them in my mind. There's no wall between the living room and my parents' room. It's a big open space with no door. There's an armchair, a bed, and the large cushion-covered sofa where I sleep. I see myself there as a child, but I don't know how old I am. I'm scared. I was always scared of the cars' headlights at night, those images that came and went on the wall.

Sometimes my parents would tell me they were going out. But did I actually understand what "going out" meant? I thought I was being abandoned, deserted. My perception was that my parents disappeared and then reappeared. Were they going to reappear, though? And when? The notion of "when" was unknown to me. I didn't have the words to express my apprehension to them. I didn't have a language. I couldn't tell them. It was horrible.

I think I could probably guess from their nervous behavior that they were going to "disappear," but their departure always ended up taking me by surprise because I became conscious of it at night. They fed me dinner, put me to bed, and waited till I was sound asleep. They thought they could leave and I wouldn't know. But I would wake up all alone. Maybe I'd wake up because they had left. And I was afraid of the ghostly headlights on the wall.

I was incapable of expressing or explaining that fear. My parents must have thought that nothing could wake me up since I was deaf! But the lights were strange, scary night sounds to me and they alarmed me tremendously. If I had been able to make myself understood, my parents wouldn't have left me all alone. A deaf child has to have somebody there at night. Has to.

I can recall a nightmare I had, too: I'm in the backseat of a car and my mother is driving. I call out to her. I want to ask her something. I want her to answer me. I call her but she doesn't turn around. I keep on calling, and when she finally turns to answer me, we have an accident. The car ends up in a ravine and then in the ocean. I see water all around me. It's horrible. Unbearable. The accident is my fault and I wake up in a state of complete anxiety.

I used to call out to my mother all day long so we could talk. I always wanted to know what was going on, to be in on things. It was a genuine need. She was the only one who truly understood me because of the language we had invented together—that animal-like, "umbilical" language, our special, instinctive code, comprised of mime and gestures. I needed her all the time because there were so many things all mixed-up in my head, so many questions. My great apprehension at that age was crystallized in that nightmare where she didn't turn to look at me.

It's different for children who learn sign language when they're very young or who have deaf parents. They make remarkable strides. I'm astounded by their development. I was really behind because I only learned to sign at seven. Before then I must have been a little like a "retard" or a wild animal.

Now that I look back, I find it incredible. How did I manage before I knew how to sign? I didn't have a language. How could I develop as an individual? How did I understand things? Get people's attention? Ask for things? I remember gesturing a lot.

Was I capable of thinking? Of course, but what did I think about? About my inexhaustible desire to truly communicate. About the sensation I had of being locked behind a huge door that I couldn't open to make people understand me.

I tugged at my mother's sleeve or dress.

I pointed to objects, tons of things. She would understand and answer me.

I was slowly making headway and starting to imitate words. *Water,* for example, was the first word I learned to pronounce. I copied what I saw on my mother's lips. I couldn't hear myself, but I rounded my lips to make the sound. The vibrations I felt in my throat created a distinct sound for my mother. And so these words became special for her and me, words that no one else could understand. Mother wanted me to force myself to speak, and I tried for her sake, but what I really wanted to do was point and show. When I had to go to the bathroom, I would point in that direction. To eat, I pointed to the food I wanted and then put my hand to my mouth.

Before I was seven, there were no words, no sentences in my head. Only images. When I tugged at my mother to tell her something, I didn't want her to look away, but rather at me. She should be looking at my face and nothing else. I remember that. That means I was capable of thinking; I was "thinking" communication. And I wanted it.

I remember some unusual situations. Family get-togethers, for example, when there were loads of people around. Their mouths moved a lot and it all bored me. I would go into another room and look at objects, things. I'd pick them up to really look at them. Then I'd go back to the room full of people and tug at my mother. Tugging at her was my way of calling her so she'd look at me and pay attention to me. It was hard when there were people around. I lost contact with her. I was alone on my planet and I wanted her to come back. She was my only link with the world. My father would look at us. He still didn't understand a thing.

I can remember seeing him very angry, with a particular expression on his face. I imitated his anger as if to ask, "Is something wrong?"

Then he would say, "No, no. It's okay!"

Sometimes I used to go tug at my mother so she could translate because I wanted to know more. I wanted to know what was going on. Why, why had I seen anger on my father's face? But she couldn't translate all the time. When she couldn't, I was left in dark silence.

When there were people around, I stared at their faces. I observed all their facial tics and quirks. Some people didn't look at the person they were talking to at the dinner table. They played with their place setting or ran their fingers through their hair. They just looked like images doing things. I couldn't say what I felt. But I could see. I saw if they were happy or not. I saw if they were irritated or if they weren't listening. I had my eyes for listening, but that was not enough. I could see they were using their mouths to communicate with each other. "That must be how I'm different. They make noise with their mouths," I thought. I didn't know what noise was, or silence for that matter. The two words didn't have any meaning.

But it wasn't really silent inside me. I could hear very high-pitched whistling sounds. I used to think they were coming from somewhere else, from outside me. But no. They were my noises. I was the only one who heard them. Was I noise on the inside and silence on the outside?

They must have fitted me with a hearing aid at nine months. Little deaf children often have hearing aids with two earphones connected by a cord in the shape of a **Y** and a microphone on their stomach. It's a monophonic device. I don't remember hearing things with it. Noises maybe. But they were noises that I heard anyway, like vibrations from cars going by or music. The device made them unbearably loud. But could I hear the sounds children hear? No, my toys were mute.

The noises were too loud. They had no meaning. They brought me nothing and just tired me out. I used to take my hearing aid off to sleep because the noise made me nervous. Loud, nameless, disconnected noises were stressful.

"The speech therapist told us not to worry," my mother remembers. "They said you would eventually be able to speak. They gave us hope. With speech therapy and hearing aids you'd become 'hearing.' Of course you'd be behind for your age, but you'd manage. Although it was completely illogical, we hoped that you would end up actually being able to hear someday, as if by magic. It was so hard to accept the fact that you had been born into a world that was different from ours."

STOMACHS AND MUSIC

After they fitted me with a hearing aid, I began to make the distinction between hearing and deaf people (but I'm not sure exactly when). Hearing people simply didn't wear hearing aids. There were those with and those without. It was a simple distinction.

I wanted to say things, lots of things, but that wall was still there. And it saddened me. I could see that my mother and father were sad, too. I really felt sadness, but wanted my parents to smile and be cheerful. I wanted to make them happy. But I didn't know how. I asked myself, "What's wrong with me? Why do I make them sad?" I still hadn't understood that I was deaf. I only knew I was different.

My first recollection? I have no first or last childhood memory because of the disorganization of my mind at that time. There were only sensations, and eyes and a body to take in those sensations.

I remember stomachs.

Flashback:

My mother is pregnant with my little sister and I feel the vibrations very strongly. I sense that something's happening. With my face buried in my mother's belly, I can "hear" life. I have trouble imagining there's a baby in Mommy's tummy. That seems impossible to me. I see a person. And there's supposed to be another person inside of that same person? I say it isn't true. It's a joke. But I like my mother's belly and the sound of life inside it.

I also like my father's stomach, in the evening when he's discussing things with friends or my mother. When I'm tired, I lie down beside him with my head on his stomach, and I can feel his voice. It goes through his stomach and I can feel the vibrations. It soothes and reassures me. It's like a lullaby. I fall asleep to the vibrations, like a nursery rhyme in my head.

My perception of conflict was physical, too, but it was different: My mother is giving me a spanking. She goes away afterwards. Her hands are sore and so is my behind. Both of us are crying. I can still remember that spanking. I must have understood why she was spanking me, but I don't remember now. My parents never hit me, so I think she was really mad. But I don't know why. That's my only recollection of being punished.

Conflicts with my mother could get complicated. For example, when I didn't want to eat something, Mother would say, "You have to finish your plate."

"I don't want to."

So she plays airplane with the tiny spoon. A spoonful for Daddy, one for Grandma . . . I see what her game is . . . a spoonful for me. I open my mouth and swallow. But sometimes I don't want to eat. Period. I tell Mommy off. The little seagull is angry. And when I'm tired of it all, I leave the table. They all think I'm joking, but I'm not. I'm really mad and want to leave. I pack my suitcase with my dolls.

It's a doll's suitcase, so I don't put my coat in it. I put the doll's coats in along with the dolls. I don't know why. Maybe because the dolls are me and I want to show that I'm the one leaving. I go out to the street. My mother panics and comes after me. That's what I do when we argue and I'm really mad. I'm a person, too. I can't always obey. I'm always supposed to agree with my mother, but I want to be independent. Emmanuelle is different. Mommy and I are different from each other.

My father and I used to play together. We had fun and laughed a lot, but I don't know if we were really communicating. Neither did he at the time. And he felt bad about that. As soon as he found out I was deaf, the first thing he wondered was how I would ever hear music. When I was very little, he took me to concerts as a way of passing his love of music on to me. Or maybe he was refusing to face the fact that I was deaf. Anyway, I thought it was fantastic. And it's still fantastic that he didn't put up a barrier between music and me. I was happy to be with him. And I'm convinced I perceived the music intensely. Not with my ears, but with my body. For a long time my father harbored the hope that I would one day wake up, as if from a long sleep. Like Sleeping Beauty. He was sure that music would work that magic. Since he was wild about all kinds of music—classical, jazz, the Beatles—and since I'd always sway to the beat, my father took me to concerts. I grew up believing I could share everything with him.

One evening, my Uncle Fifou, who was a musician, was playing the guitar. I can see him now. The image is clear in my mind. The whole family is listening. He wants to make me experience the guitar, so he tells me to bite the neck of the instrument. As I do, he begins to play. I keep on biting for hours. I can feel every vibration in my body, both high and low notes. The music enters my body and takes up residence there. It begins to play inside me. Mother looks at me completely astounded. She tries to do the same thing but doesn't like it. She says it echoes in her head. To this day my uncle's guitar still bears my teeth marks.

I was lucky to have music when I was a child. Some parents of deaf children think it's pointless, so they deprive their children of music. And some deaf children make fun of music. I love it. I feel its vibrations. The visual spectacle of the concert has an impact on me, too. The people in the concert hall, the lighting effects, the atmosphere are all part of the vibrations. I can sense that everybody's gathered together at the concert for the same thing. It's fantastic: the sparkling golden saxophone, the trumpet players with their cheeks puffed out, the basses. I feel with my feet, or my whole body if I'm stretched out on the floor. And I can imagine the sounds. I've always imagined them. I perceive music through my body, with my bare feet on the floor, latching onto the vibrations. The piano, electric guitar, African drums, percussion instruments, all have colors and I sway along with them. That's how I see it, in color. But the difference between the guitar and the violin is hard for me to recognize. I can't get the violin. I can't feel it with my feet. The violin flies away. It must be high-pitched, like a bird. Like a bird's song, it's uncatchable. Its music is upward, reaching for the sky, not down towards the earth. Sounds in the air must be high; sounds at earth level, low-pitched. The tom-tom makes music that comes up from the earth. I just love African music. I feel it with my feet, my head, my whole body. But I have trouble with classical music. It's so high in the air I can't catch it.

Music is a rainbow of vibrant colors. It's a language beyond words. It's universal. The most beautiful form of art that exists. It's capable of making the human body physically vibrate. Suppose I came from another planet and ran into humans all speaking different languages. I'm sure I would be able to understand them because I'd sense what they were feeling. That's what happens with music. Notes begin to dance inside my body like flames in a fireplace. The fire sets the rhythm: small, big, small, faster, slower—vibrations, emotions, and colors swirl to a magical beat. The field of music is very wide. It's immense and I often get lost in it.

The sound of singing voices remains a mystery to me. Just once, the mystery was broken. I don't know how old I was, but I was still living only in the present.

Flashback:

Maria Callas is on TV. My parents are watching and I'm sitting with them in front of the set. I see a powerful-looking woman. She seems to have a strong personality. Suddenly, there's a close-up and at that moment I feel her voice. As I stare at her intently, I realize what her voice must be like. I get the impression that the song she's singing isn't a very happy one. I see that her voice is coming from deep within, from far away, that she's singing from her stomach, from her guts. It has a tremendous effect on me.

Did I really hear her voice? I have no idea. But I truly felt emotion. Nothing like that ever happened, before or after. Maria callas had touched me. That's the only time in my life that I felt or imagined a voice singing.

Other singers leave me cold. When I watch video clips of them on TV, I sense a lot of violence, lots of images, one after the other. It's impossible to understand anything. They're all so fast, I can't even begin to imagine the music that goes along with them. But the words of some singers like Carole Laure, Jacques Brel, and Jean-Jacques Goldman really move me.

And then there's Michael Jackson! When I see him dance, it looks like he has an electric body. The beat is electrifying. I associate it with an electric image. I feel the electricity.

Dance is something that permeates your body. When I was a teenager, I used to like to go to nightclubs with my deaf friends. It was the only place where the music could be blaring full-blast and not bother anybody. I danced all night with my body pressed against the wall, swaying to the rhythm. The others (the hearing people there) looked at me in astonishment. They must have thought I was crazy.

WHITE CAT, BLACK CAT

My father used to take me to kindergarten. I liked going with him, but when I got there I would always end up alone in a corner, drawing. In the evening, my mother and I would draw some more. I loved it when she drew a picture and I was supposed to add an eye or a nose. There were drawings everywhere. We used to play a game called Battle, too. Each player had a special color.

I also remember a room with a strange revolving disc. We would put a piece of paper on it, then my mother and I would spurt different colors of paint onto the paper. The colors spread out randomly with the speed of the disc. I didn't know how it worked but it was beautiful.

Another thing we did was watch cartoons on TV or at the movies. After fifteen minutes of Tweety and Sylvester, I was crying, sniveling, and gasping so much my mother got worried. I saw the other kids laughing at Sylvester's blunders, but couldn't figure out why they thought it was funny. It was cruel and it made me feel bad. It wasn't fair that Sylvester always got caught and flattened up against a wall. That's how I saw it. Maybe I was too sensitive. Besides, I really liked cats.

I had a white cat. As far as I knew, it didn't have a name but I was so glad to have it. I used to make it jump in the air and play airplane with it. I'd play helicopter with it and pull it by the tail. I'm sure it was hell for the cat, but it loved me just the same. I did nothing but badger it and it still loved me!

One day, we found the cat with its stomach split open. I don't know how or when it happened. We were in the country. My father was a medical student at the time and tried to save it by sewing its stomach back up. But the operation failed and the cat died. I asked what had happened and my father said, "It's over." For me that meant the cat had disappeared. It was gone. I wouldn't see it any more.

I didn't know the meaning of death. For days I asked where the cat was. They kept explaining that it was over and that I'd never ever see it again. I didn't understand *never*, or *dead*. All I understood was that *dead* meant it was over, *finished*. I thought big people were immortal. They went away and came back. Therefore, they would never be finished.

But it wasn't the same for me. I was going to "go away" like the cat. I couldn't see myself growing up. I thought I'd always be little, all my life. I thought I was limited to my present state. And above all, I thought I was unique, the only one like me in the world. Emmanuelle is deaf and no one else is. Emmanuelle is different. Emmanuelle will never grow up.

Since I couldn't communicate like other people, I couldn't be like them, like grownups who can hear. So I was going to be "finished." Sometimes it was impossible to communicate with people. I couldn't ask about all the things I wanted to know and understand. Or people just didn't answer me. That's when I thought about death. I was afraid, and now I know why: I had never seen a deaf adult. I had only seen deaf children in the special education class at my kindergarten. So, in my mind, deaf children never grew up. We were all going to die as little children. I even think I was unaware that hearing people had once been children! There was no possible point of reference for me.

When I saw that the cat wasn't around any more, that it had "gone away," I tried with all my might to understand what had happened. I really wanted to see the cat again, to understand. I wanted to see it because I could only understand things with my eyes. My parents didn't show me the dead cat so I was left with the idea of "gone away." It was all too confusing.

When my little sister was born, we got another cat. A black one this time. His name was Bobbin. My father chose the name, in deference to Freud's *Fort-Da*,* he said. The cat always used to play with bobbins of thread. He knew I was deaf, and I knew he knew. It was obvious. When Bobbin was hungry, he would follow my mother around and meow at her. He'd run circles around her. Naturally, she could hear him even though she couldn't see him. When we first got him, he tried that with me but soon realized I wasn't reacting and that ticked him off. So he'd plunk himself down right in front of my head and meow in my face. It was obvious: he knew that to be "heard" he had to stare with his beautiful green eyes deep into mine. Sometimes when I was lying on my bed, he would grab at my feet to play. I wanted to communicate with him and let him know he was being a pain. I tried using gestures to tell him, "Stop it, you're bugging me." But he didn't get the message. I knew when he was angry because he didn't respond. He turned into a sort of cat statue.

When I saw Tweety and Sylvester, and all the violence heaped on that poor cat, I hated Tweety. He teased Sylvester and never got flustered. The poor kitty didn't have a clue about what was going on and always took a beating. He may have been naive, but that Tweety was really rotten!

I was striving for a difficult kind of independence in a difficult world. I even had trouble pronouncing the word difficult. I used to say, "It's tifikul."

It was "tifikul" to say "tifikul."

It was "tifikul" for me to have an existence independent of my mother. I tried doing things without the help of my "umbilical cord." All alone, for a change of pace, as an adventure. I remember one instance in particular. How old was I? Was it before or after the cat died? I don't know, but I said, "I'm going to go to the bathroom by myself."

I didn't actually say that to my mother. I only said the words in my mind. Usually, when I had to go, I'd call my mother. But that time, we were at some friends' house and she was busy chatting. She wasn't paying attention to me, so I decided I was going to manage all alone.

I went into the bathroom and locked the door like a big person. But then I couldn't get out! I must have jammed the lock or done something to it. I began screaming and screaming and banging on the door. Being locked inside and not being able to get out was torture. My mother was on the other side of the door and could hear the banging. But of course I didn't know that. Suddenly all communication was cut off. There was literally a wall between my mother and me. It was frightening.

I'm sure my mother tried to reassure me. She probably said, "Don't worry, stay calm." But at the time, I couldn't hear her, since I couldn't see her. I thought she was still talking with her friend and that I was all alone. I was terrified. I thought I'd spend the rest of my life in that little room screaming in silence!

Finally I saw a piece of paper being slipped under the door. My mother had made a drawing, because I didn't know how to read yet. It was a picture of a child crying that had been crossed out. Next to it was a picture of a child laughing. I realized that she was on the other side of the door telling me to smile and that everything would be okay. But she didn't make a drawing to show that she would open the door. She was just telling me to laugh, and not cry. So

I was still panic-stricken. I could feel myself screaming. I felt my vocal chords vibrating. When I let out high-pitched sounds, my vocal chords don't vibrate at all. But if I make low-pitched sounds, if I yell, I feel the vibrations. That day, I made my vocal chords vibrate till I was out of breath.

I must have cried a long time, like an angry seagull in a storm, before a locksmith came and opened the door, that wall separating me from my mother.

IT'S "TIFIKUL"

Everything was difficult. What would have been the simplest of things for a hearing child was hard for me.

They put me in a mainstream kindergarten class for deaf children, and I started making friends with the other kids. That's actually where my social life began.

The speech therapist was able to get me to pronounce a few audible words. In the beginning, I expressed myself with my own particular blend of speech and gesture. "Up to the age of two," my mother says, "you went to a speech therapy center upstairs from a venereal disease clinic. That got me mad. Was deafness a disease to be ashamed of? Then we put you in the neighborhood kindergarten. One day when I came to get you, the teacher was telling the children stories to develop their language skills. You were sitting all by yourself, drawing at a table in a corner, completely oblivious to what was going on. You didn't look very happy."

I don't remember much about that phase of my life. I do remember, though, that I drew a lot. Drawings were important to me. They replaced communication. Through them, I could express part of the unanswered questions that filled my head. But as for that kindergarten with its so-called mainstream class, I've forgotten about it. Or rather, I'd like to forget about it. All those kids sitting in a circle around a teacher telling stories—is that really mainstreaming?

What was I doing there all alone sitting in front of my drawings or jumping rope on the playground? What were they teaching me? Nothing, as far as I'm concerned. What was the point? Who was benefiting from it?

I have a few mental images from that period of my life. One in particular stands out. My father came to get me when I was in the middle of washing my hands at the playground faucet. "Hurry up. We're leaving," he said.

I don't know how he said that or what he did to communicate the fact that I had to hurry so we could leave, but I felt it. He must have prodded me a bit. He probably looked rushed and anxious. Anyway, I got the message from his behavior: "We don't have much time." But I wanted to make him understand another message: "I haven't finished washing my hands." Then, all of a sudden, he wasn't there any more and I started crying my eyes out. There had been a misunderstanding. We hadn't understood each other. He was gone. He had vanished. And there I was all alone, crying. Was I crying about our misunderstanding or because I was alone? Or was it because he had disappeared? I think it was probably about the misunderstanding.

That scene is symbolic of the almost constant breakdown in communication between them and us, the hearing and the deaf. The only way I can understand a piece of information is by visualizing it. I think of it as a scene where I mix physical sensations with a sharpness of observation typical of a mime artist. If something is expressed quickly, it's hard for me to be sure I've understood. But I try to respond at the same pace. That day, when I was washing my hands at the faucet, my father hadn't understood what I wanted to say. Or maybe I was the one who hadn't understood him.

And the penalty for that misunderstanding was that he left!

Naturally he came back to get me after a while. I have no idea how long it was, but I remember I was lonely and desperate. I couldn't explain the reason for my tears to him because everything used to get so complicated when there was a misunderstanding like that. Another situation would always ensue that was even harder to understand than the first.

I don't know if the strange scene I just described is a real memory or if I imagined it. In any case, it's strikingly symbolic of the difficulty I had communicating with my father at that time.

Tifikul is a child's word born of that difficulty. One day, when I must have been older, he and I were home alone. He was cooking steaks and wanted to know if I wanted mine well-done or rare. I could see he was trying to show me the difference between raw and cooked. He used the radiator to explain hot and cold. I understood hot and cold, but not raw and cooked. It went on for a long time, till finally he got mad and cooked both steaks the same.

Another time, he was watching a movie on TV. The name of one of the characters was Laborie, like ours except with an *e*. He kept trying to show me the difference between the *t* in our name and the *e* in the character's name on bits of paper. I just couldn't get it, and I kept telling him over and over, "It's tifikul. It's tifikul."

He didn't understand what I was trying to say. We were both exhausted, so we gave up and waited till my mother got home. He asked her what I meant and she burst out laughing, "It's difficult!"

But it was as "tifikul" for him as it was for me, and that was tough on him. Actually, it was tough on me, too. Deaf children are even more vulnerable and sensitive than others. I know I often used to swing back and forth between anger and laughter.

Anger, for example, would set in when nobody could be bothered to talk to me at mealtime. I would pound on the table furiously. I wanted to "talk," to understand what people were saying. I was sick and tired of being held prisoner of a silence they made no attempt to break. I was always trying hard, but they weren't doing enough. Hearing people didn't make much of an effort and I begrudged them that.

I remember one question that stuck in my mind: How did they understand each other with their backs turned? It was "tifikul" for me to realize that people could talk to each other even if they weren't face to face. I could only understand someone if we were both looking at each other. The only way I could get people's attention was by tugging at them—on a sleeve, the hem of a skirt, or a pant leg. That meant, "Look at me. Show me your face, your eyes, so I can understand you."

Seeing. If I couldn't see, I was lost. I needed the help of facial expressions and mouth movements.

I used my voice, too. I would call out to my father when he played the piano. I yelled "Daddy, Daddy" till he finally looked at me. But what did I want to tell him? I really don't know.

And I banged on things. I poked my mother and took her head in my hands to force her to look right at me.

When the doctor came, he would hunt for the spot where I hurt by poking me till I screamed. As a child, that was my way of talking to doctors when I was sick.

I did a lot of things on the sly. Basically, they were my little experiments.

I loved cough syrup. I secretly polished off every bottle I could find and then, of course, got sick. Nobody had told me cough syrup was bad. How could I know that? It was sweet. It tasted good. And it was supposed to make you better because the doctor prescribed it.

I loved "talami," too. That was my word

for dried salami. It was like candy to me when I was little. I would steal it and hide it in the closet between piles of clothes or anywhere I could. But the smell of well-chewed bits always tipped my mother off.

When I was around five or six, I was going to school with deaf children and didn't feel isolated any more. The teacher knew I was deaf. I learned how to count with dominoes, and I learned the alphabet and how to paint. Now, going to school was fun.

I had a little deaf friend who came to my house to play. They would put us in a room together. Communicating was easier between us because we had our own signs and gestures.

We played with fire and candles because we weren't supposed to. I loved experimenting with whatever was off limits.

We watched *Goldorak* cartoons and then acted them out. We played with dolls, fought, and jumped around.

I spent a lot of time watching my parents and when I played, I tried recreating what I had seen. I was the mother in charge of the house, tea parties, and cooking. My little friend's job was to look after the children—the dolls. We pretended he was just coming home from work and then we playacted:

"Okay, you do this. I'll do that."

"No. I'll do it."

Then we would argue some more, and that's how the game went.

Understanding the difference between a man and a woman was also "tifikul." I could clearly see that my mother had breasts and my father didn't. My parents dressed differently. One was Mommy and one was Daddy. But besides that? I wanted to know the difference between my little friend and me, too.

Once, when we were on vacation in the south of France, he and I were playing in the water together. Since we were little, we weren't wearing bathing suits so the difference between him and me was apparent. I

thought it was funny, and so simple. I understood. We were both deaf children, but we weren't completely identical.

I was like my mother, except that she could hear and I couldn't. She was a big person, but I would never get big. My little friend and I would soon be "finished." That was the period of my life when we still hadn't seen any deaf adults yet and so we couldn't imagine that you could grow up and be deaf, too. There was no point of reference or comparison to make us see that. So we were going to "leave" soon, be "finished"; in other words, die.

And I thought that when I died, my soul would pass into the body of another baby. But this time, the baby would be hearing. I can't explain that strange transformation. How did I know I had a soul? And, at that age, what did I mean by a soul?

I figured it out in my own way after watching a cartoon on TV. It was a story about a little girl. You didn't see her parents for a long time. So to me, that meant they had gone, just like the white cat. To leave was the same as to die. So I thought they were dead. Then the little girl found her parents again. Naturally, they were the same people as at the beginning of the story. It was just that she had been separated from them. But I concocted another story from it: Her parents had come back from the dead and entered other bodies. That's what I called a soul, "leaving and coming back." A soul was something you had or were, and that would leave and come back. In trying to understand death, I must have combined my white cat's disappearance and the cartoon.

At five or six, it's difficult enough for a hearing child to learn concepts. For me, the process was entirely dependent on visual images. The consequence was that I thought that when I was "finished," when it was my turn to leave along with my little friend, our souls would come back in the bodies of other babies. But those babies would be hearing. Maybe I thought the child who was going to take my place would be able to hear because being deaf made life hard for me. Because I didn't have a language to liberate me yet.

It's "tifikul" to understand the world, but you deal with it as best you can. I don't think asking my little friend to show me his private parts at the beach so I could tell the difference between mommies and daddies was much different from what hearing children do.

I believe the major distinguishing characteristic of the way I perceived things before I knew sign language hinged on two things: the absolute necessity of seeing something to be able to understand it, and, having seen it, the momentary impossibility of seeing it differently. That two possible situations might arise out of a single visual element was hard to fathom. For example, I love my maternal grandparents. Conversing with them wasn't easy, but they took care of me a lot when I was kindergarten age. And when I try to recall a visual memory of them, the first thing I see is a dog!

That's because the dog is linked to a situation that I associate with my grandparents and with having to understand a concept for which hearing people had two definitions but, in my mind, was wordless.

First situation: The dog is with his master. It's a big, friendly Doberman type, and they let me pet him.

Second situation: The dog's master is off at work and the dog is alone in a car. I walk up to the car and open the door. The dog barks in my face and bears his teeth at me. I'm terrified. Before, he let me pet him. Now he wants to bite me! I can't imagine two different types of behavior from the same animal image. In the first situation, no one explained the concepts of "friendly" and "vicious" as they related to dogs.

I sense danger. I run away and the dog darts after me. He bites me on the shoulder and I fall. My father comes running and the dog dashes off.

My father wants to give me a shot, but I don't want one. Needles terrify me. My mother realizes that I'm afraid of needles and does her best to comfort me. There they are, the two of them gesticulating above my head, one trying to give me a shot, the other reassuring me. The only thing I can gather from their discussion is the threat of that horrible needle. I want to run to my grandparents' house. They represent total protection, a refuge I love. And I want to go there. But I get the shot instead.

I always had that reflex to run away when people tried to force something on me or when I didn't understand. Whether it was finishing my soup, getting a shot, or submitting to any kind of constraint, I reacted the only way I could because I was unable to talk. Action was a substitute for discourse. In all truthfulness, I should say that my instinct to flee meshed with my personal character when it came to taking orders. I'm by nature independent, determined, and stubborn. Maybe the loneliness of silence accentuated those traits. It's "tifikul" to say.

MY NAME IS "I"

They taught me how to say my name at school. Emmanuelle. But Emmanuelle was a little like someone detached from me, a double. When I referred to myself, I would say,

"Emmanuelle can't hear you . . ."

"Emmanuelle did this or that . . ."

I carried within me a deaf girl named Emmanuelle, and I would try to speak for her, as though we were two separate people.

I knew how to say other words. I could pronounce some of them fairly well and others, not so well. The speech therapy method involved placing my hand on the therapist's throat to feel the vibrations as the therapist vocalized. We learned the letter *r*. It vibrated like "ra." Then we learned *f* and *sh* sounds. *Sh* was a problem for me. It never came out right. We went from consonants to vowels (with more emphasis on consonants), and then on to entire words. We repeated the same word for hours. I would imitate what I saw on the therapist's lips, with my hand on her neck, copying her like a little monkey.

Each time we pronounced a word, a sound frequency would register on the screen of a machine. Little green lines, like the ones on an electrocardiogram in hospitals, danced before my eyes. You were supposed to follow the little lines that would rise and fall, level out, jump up, and dip back down.

What was a word on that screen to me? It was the amount of energy I had to put out so that my little green line would go as high as the therapist's. It was tiring and I repeated word after word without understanding what they meant. It was nothing but a throat exercise, a kind of parroting.

Deaf people can't all learn to speak and it's a lie to say otherwise. Even for those who do, their capacity for oral expression remains limited.

I was going to be seven years old at the beginning of the next school year, and I was still at the kindergarten level. But my life and the confined universe in which I was evolving, mostly in silence, were both about to change dramatically.

My father heard something on the radio. That something was a miracle in the making. I couldn't even have begun to imagine it. I considered the radio a mysterious object that talked to hearing people. I didn't pay much attention to it. But that day my father said a deaf person was talking on the program *France-Culture!* It was Alfredo Corrado, an actor and director. My father explained to my mother that he was speaking silently through sign language. It was a real language based on movements of the hands and body, and facial expressions, too! An interpreter, American like Corrado, was translating orally into French for the listeners.

Corrado said he had founded the International Visual Theater (IVT), the deaf theater in Vincennes, in 1976. He worked in the United States. There was a university in Washington, D.C., called Gallaudet University that had been created for the deaf, and he had studied there.

My father was stunned. Deaf people capable of going to college! Here in France, they could barely get through the sixth grade!

He was both ecstatic and angered.

He was angered because, as a doctor, he had trusted his colleagues. The pediatricians, ear-nose-throat specialists, speech therapists, and educators had all told him the only way to help get me out of my isolation was to have me learn spoken language. But no one had given him any information about sign language. It was the first time he had heard of it, and what's more, he heard it from a deaf person!

He was ecstatic because in Vincennes, just outside Paris, maybe there was—surely there was—a solution for me! He wanted to take me there. He was ready to give it a try because he suffered so much from not being able to talk with me.

Mother said she didn't want to go with him. She was afraid of being traumatized and maybe disappointed, too. Since she was about to give birth, she decided to let my father take me to Vincennes. She sensed that the baby she was carrying wasn't deaf. She could tell the difference between the child still nestled in her womb and me. That baby moved around and reacted to exterior noises. I, on the other hand, had slept all too quietly, sheltered from the racket. For the time being, her first concern was the arrival of the family's second child, almost seven years after me. She needed peace and quiet, time for herself. I can understand how the emotions sparked by this new ray of hope might have been too overwhelming for her. She was afraid of being disappointed again. And besides, we had our own system of communicating, what I call the "umbilical" method. We had gotten used to it. But my father had nothing. He realized I was a natural for communicating with others. It was something I was always trying to do. So he was excited by the new prospect that had miraculously come his way via the radio.

I think that when he gave me the priceless gift of sign language, it was the first time he truly accepted my deafness. It was a gift to himself too, since he wanted desperately to be able to talk to me.

Of course I didn't understand a thing and had no idea what was going on. My father looked perplexed. That's the only memory I have of that day that was so very moving for him and so incredibly fantastic for me: the radio and his face. The next day, he took me to Vincennes.

I can still see some of the visual imprints of that day: We're going up some stairs. We enter a large room. My father is talking to two hearing people—two adults who aren't wearing hearing aids. Therefore, I assume they aren't deaf. At this stage of my life, I recognize deaf people only because of their hearing aids. But, as it turns out, one is deaf and the other isn't. One is Alfredo Corrado and the other Bill Moody, a hearing sign language interpreter.

I see Alfredo and Bill signing to each other. I see that my father can understand Bill because Bill is speaking. But the signs mean nothing to me. They're quick, strange, complicated. I've never seen anything like it before. The simplistic code I invented with my mother was based on mime and a few orally pronounced words. I look at the two men in amazement. Their hands and fingers are moving, their bodies too, and they're making facial expressions. It's beautiful and mesmerizing.

Who's deaf and who's hearing? There's no way to tell. Then I realize, "Hey, that's a hearing person talking with his hands!"

Alfredo Corrado is a tall, handsome, Italian-looking man—thin with very dark hair. He has a mustache and rather sharp features. Bill has straight, medium-length hair, blue eyes, and a cheerful face. He's friendly and open. They both seem around the same age as my father.

Jean Gremion, the founder and head of the deaf social and cultural center, is there, too. He greets us.

Alfredo comes up to me and says, "I'm deaf, like you, and I sign. That's my language."

I mime my response, "Why aren't you wearing a hearing aid?"

He smiles. It's obvious that he thinks deaf people don't need hearing aids. But for me, hearing aids are a visible point of reference.

So Alfredo is deaf, but doesn't wear a hearing aid. What's more, he's an adult. I think it took me awhile to grasp that threefold oddity.

What I did realize right away, however, was that I wasn't alone in the world. It was a startling revelation. And a bewildering one because, up till then, I had thought, as do so many deaf children, that I was unique and predestined to die as a child. I discovered that I could have a future since Alfredo was a deaf adult!

That cruel logic about early death persists as long as deaf children haven't encountered a deaf adult. They need to be able to identify with an adult. It's crucial. Parents of deaf children should be made aware of the importance of having their children come in contact with deaf adults as soon as possible, right after birth. The two worlds need to blend—the world of sound and the world of silence. A deaf child's psychological development will be quicker and much better, and the child will grow up free of the pain of being alone in the world with no constructed thought patterns and no future.

Imagine that you had a kitten and never showed it a full-grown cat. It might spend its entire life thinking it was a kitten. Or imagine that the little cat only lived with dogs. It would think it was the only cat in the world and wear itself out trying to communicate in dog language. The cat might succeed at getting a few basic things across to the dogs through motions—eating, drinking, fear, affection, submission or aggressiveness. But it would be so much happier and more well-balanced among its own kind, young and old, speaking cat!

With the oral technique that had been imposed on my parents from the beginning, I had no chance of meeting deaf adults who could serve as role models for me because my parents had been advised against it. I only had contact with hearing people.

I don't have a precise recollection of that first, stupefying visit to Vincennes when I watched in awe as all those hands whirled about. I don't know what my father and the two men said to each other. I just remember my astonishment at seeing my father understand what Alfredo's hands and Bill's mouth were saying. At the time, I still didn't know that because of those men I was going to acquire a language. What stuck in my mind, though, was the stupendous revelation that Emmanuelle would be able to grow up! That was something I had seen now with my very own eyes.

The following week, my father took me back to Vincennes. They were having a parent-child communication workshop. There were lots of parents. Alfredo had the children gather in a circle around him and began working with them. He demonstrated some signs. The parents watched so they could learn, too. They were simple signs, I remember, like "house," "eat," "drink," "sleep," "table."

He drew a house on a flipboard and showed us the corresponding sign. Then he drew a picture of an adult and said, "This is your daddy. You are your daddy's daughter. This is your mommy. You are your mommy's daughter."

He also showed us someone looking for something, first through mime, next using sign. Then he asked, "Where's Mommy?"

I signed, "Mommy is somewhere else."

Then he corrected me.

"Where's Mommy? Mommy is at home. Make the sign for 'Mommy' and 'house.'"

A complete sentence: "Mommy is at home." Finally at the age of seven, I was signing with both hands to identify my mother and designate where she was!

Elated, with my eyes fixed on Alfredo's, I used both hands to repeat, "Mommy is at home."

The first few times I was there, I learned everyday words and then people's names. He was Alfredo, I was Emmanuelle. A sign for him and a sign for me.

Emmanuelle: "Sun-Coming-from-the-Heart." "Emmanuelle" was my name to hearing people, "Sun-Coming-from-the-Heart" was my name to deaf people.

That was the first time I realized you could give people names. That, too, was fantastic. Except for Mommy and Daddy, I didn't know that people in our family had names. I used to meet people, friends of my parents or members of the family, but, in my mind, they didn't have names. There was no way to define them. I was so surprised to learn that his name was Alfredo and the other man was Bill. And me, especially me, Emmanuelle. I finally understood that I had an identity. I, Emmanuelle.

Until then, when I talked about myself, it was like talking about somebody else. Somebody who wasn't "I." People would always say, "Emmanuelle is deaf." It was always "She can't hear you, she can't hear you." There was no "I." I was "she."

People who have had their name in their head practically from birth, a name that Mommy and Daddy repeated, might find that hard to understand. They're used to turning their head when their name is called. Their identity is given to them at birth. They don't have to think about it or ask themselves questions about who they are. They're "I" or "me." It's natural and effortless. They know who they are. They can identify themselves, introduce themselves to people with a symbol that stands for them. But the deaf Emmanuelle didn't know that she was "I," that she was "me." She discovered it with sign language, and now she knew. Emmanuelle could say, "My name is Emmanuelle."

It was a joy to make that discovery. Emmanuelle was no longer that double whose needs, desires, dislikes, and woes I had to painfully explain. I had discovered the world around me and myself in the midst of it.

It was also at that time, when I started seeing deaf adults on a regular basis, that I stopped being afraid of dying. I never thought about it again. And I had my father to thank for that.

It was like being born again. My life was just beginning. The first barrier had fallen. There were still others around me, but an initial opening had been made in my prison wall. I was going to understand the world with my eyes and hands. I could already sense it and I was so eager!

There before me stood the marvelous man who was teaching me about the world, and the names of people and things. There was a sign for Bill, one for Alfredo, one for Jacques (my father), one for my mother, my sister, the house, the table, the cat . . . I was going to live! And I had so many questions to ask. So many! I was voracious, starved for answers because now people could answer me!

In the beginning, I mixed up all the different communication methods: signs and mime and words that came out orally. I was a bit unsettled, confused. Sign language had happened so suddenly. I was seven years old and had to get things straight in my mind, sort out all the information I was taking in. And there was a good deal of it. You really become a communicating individual, capable of developing, when, for example, you're finally able to use correctly constructed language to say things like, "My name is Emmanuelle. I'm hungry. Mommy is at home, Daddy is with me. My friend's name is Jules, my cat's name is Bobbin."

I didn't learn everything all at once, of course. At home, I continued using a little of the code my mother and I had made up, but started mixing in some sign. I remember they understood me, but I don't recall my first complete signed sentence that they comprehended.

Little by little, I straightened things out in my head and began to construct ideas and organize thoughts. Most importantly, I started communicating with my father.

Then my mother joined us in Vincennes. She, too, was about to emerge from the tunnel of erroneous information and false hopes my parents had been trapped in ever since I was born. She was totally surprised to see that there was a meeting place for the deaf. It was a vibrant, creative place, where they were being taught. It was a place to get to know parents trying to cope with the same problems, to meet professionals specializing in deafness who were rethinking the practices of the medical profession and the information it was disseminating. They had made the decision to teach a language. Sign language. Not a code or jargon, but a real language.

"I was terribly frightened," says my mother in recalling her first visit to Vincennes. "I was face to face with reality. It was like a second diagnosis. Everyone was friendly, but as I listened to the deaf people tell of their suffering as children, of the horrible isolation they had lived in before, of their problems as adults and their ongoing struggle, I was sick. I had been wrong. I had been misled by people who had told me, 'With speech therapy and a hearing aid, she'll be able to speak.' "

"After you were born," my father says, "I could practically hear them say, or at least I wanted to hear them say, 'One day, she WILL HEAR.' "

Vincennes was another world, the real deaf world, devoid of needless patronizing. But it was also a world of hope for the deaf. Sure, deaf people manage to talk, more or less, yet for many of us who are profoundly deaf, it's never more than partially effective. Now, with sign language, plus speech, and my all-consuming desire to communicate, I was going to make tremendous strides.

After seven years of existence, I had just taken a huge step forward. My name is "I."

MARIE, MARIE

When my little sister was born, I asked what her name was. Marie.

Marie, Marie. I had trouble remembering it. I decided to write it down on paper, over and over, like practicing words at school. I kept going back to my mother to ask her what my little sister's name was. I wanted to be sure. And I would repeat it: "Ma-rie, Ma-rie, Ma-rie . . ."

I'm Emmanuelle. She's Marie.

Marie, Marie, Marie . . .

"What's her name again?"

I wrote it more than a hundred times, letter by letter, to be able to remember it visually. But it was still too hard to pronounce. I had to really work at saying her name.

My father took me to the hospital to see my little sister. I hated hospitals. When Mother was pregnant, I saw her having blood samples taken. I was so afraid, I hid under the bed. Even today, I can't stand the sight of blood. I loathe needles. *Hospital* means needles and blood. *Hospital* means threatening place.

My sister was in an incubator. She wasn't premature, but since the hospital wasn't heated, they put her in there with a few other babies to keep warm.

I don't know if I was happy when I saw her. What I saw mystified me—the incubator and a tiny little thing inside. It was hard to imagine anything about her, there behind the plastic. I can't really remember, but my feelings at that moment weren't very clear. I wondered to myself, "Are both of us the same?"

CHAPTER 48

Selections from *Planet of the Blind*

Steve Kuusisto

I believe that in every blind person's imagination there are landscapes. The world is gray and marine blue, then a clump of brown shingled houses stands revealed by rays of sun, appearing now as bison— shaggy and still. These are the places learned by rote, their multiple effects of color made stranger by fast-moving clouds. The unknown is worse, an epic terrain that, in the mind's eye, could prevent a blind person from leaving home.

Since I know the miniature world of Geneva, New York, I decide to attend college there. On campus, though, there are sudden skateboards. I wish for a magic necklace to ward them away. The quadrangle is a world of predatory watching, and so I begin affecting a scowl. I look serious, as if my corpuscles have turned into hot pearls. I'm the angriest-looking boy on earth.

The dean's office knows about my eyes. I have a first-floor room in the dorm in case of fire. The theory is that with a vision impairment, I might not make it down the fire escape. This is the extent of the campus's support service for disabled students in 1973. The unreadable print in books, the dark dormitory room, the inaccessible library books—all these are things left to my dissemblings.

In the classroom I gravitate toward literature. The prevailing pedagogy is still centered on the New Criticism, a method of reading and analysis born in the years after World War II. This is a lucky break for me: the stress here is on the close reading of texts.

One simply has to read a poem to death.

The professor chain-smokes and takes the class line by line through turgid Victorian prosody. We crawl in the nicotine haze through the comma splices of Thomas Hardy.

I listen, hunched in my chair as the machinery of poets is dissected. We are eighteenth-century clock makers: nothing is too small for our rational little universe.

In the dim library I move through the stacks, pressing my nose to the spines. In my pocket I carry a letter from the eye doctor addressed "To Whom It May Concern"—it avows that too much reading is dangerous for me. "The scanning motions inherent in reading make retinal tearing more likely. Therefore Mr. Kuusisto should read in moderation."

Like all true talismans, this letter is frightening. It's designed to protect me from professors who may demand too much from me. But in my pocket it feels like a letter bomb.

Reading is hazardous!

And to me the words of poetry are

onions, garlic, fennel, basil; the book itself an earthenware vessel.

Reading alone with a magnifying glass, nothing on earth makes more sense to me than Wallace Stevens's poem "The Pleasures of Merely Circulating": "The angel flew round in the garden/the garden flew round with the clouds,/and the clouds flew around, and the clouds flew around,/and the clouds flew around with the clouds."

My spastic eye takes in every word like a red star seen on a winter night. Every syllable is acquired with pain. But poetry furnishes me with a lyric anger, and suddenly poems are wholly necessary. Robert Bly's book *The Light Around the Body*, for example, expresses an almost mystical combination of wonder and rage about "the Great Society." He depicts a world gone so awry that the very pine stumps start speaking of Goethe and Jesus, the insects dance, there are murdered kings in the light bulbs outside movie theaters. All of it is glorious, and like my boyhood discovery of Caruso in the attic, Bly's voice, among others—Breton, Nerval, Lorca—follows me in the dark.

*   *   *

I move in a solitude fueled by secrecy. O Lord, let me never be seen with the white cane. Let me roll through the heavy oceans like the beluga whale, filled with dark seeds, always coursing forward. Let no one find me out! This is my lacerating tune. Leaning over my private page, I shake with effort.

Weakness and *lack of affect* are the synonyms for the word *blind*. In Roget's Thesaurus one finds also: *ignorant, oblivious, obtuse, unaware, blocked, concealed, obstructed, hidden, illiterate, backward, crude, uneducated,* and worst of all, *unversed.*

At twilight I walk in the botanical gardens, the night smells richly of lilac. I've read that Immanuel Kant could not bear to visit his friends in sickness; after they died,

he would repress all memories of them. There are limits to cognition and reason. What would he think in the mad purple twilight where I live. Would he visit himself?

I hear radios and TV sets from the open windows on campus.

Under the violet streetlights my glasses, thick as dishes, fill with aberrations at the edges of their thick curves.

College is brutally difficult for me. One poem must take the place of the bulky novel I cannot read, or at least not read in a week. I often go home from the library with the few words I've been able to see and absorb still vivid in my imagination. Alone, I take the words apart and rearrange them like Marcel Duchamp playing chess with his own private rules. Still, I need extra time for every assignment. But exploring what words can do when placed side by side, I'm starting to build the instrument that will turn my blindness into a manner of seeing.

Still, walking around, feigning sight, I step in the rain-washed gutter, brush the street sign, and make a hundred slapstick gestures. In a flash I'm Stan Laurel, the angel of nutty innocence. This can happen without warning. It might be the telephone that does it. A friend calls, saying she'll meet me downstairs in half an hour. She drives a red Chrysler.

I walk down to the street and approach the car. I reach for the door on the passenger's side and give it a tug, but it's locked. I rap on the window, but my friend doesn't seem to hear. I rap again, tug on the door, rap and tug. Then I walk around to her side of the car. Is she in some Wagnerian trance, Brünnhilde at the wheel? When I lean down to her window, I see at last the face of a genuinely terrified Chinese woman. I motion to her to roll down her window. She won't. I try to explain my mistake in sign language—pointing to my eyes, telling her loudly that I've mistaken her car for that of a friend. I begin backing away from her into the street like an ungainly kid on roller skates.

My embarrassments are legion. I know the white cane has become a necessity for the maintenance of my psychological health. I enter bathrooms marked "Ladies," and entering restaurants, I trip down short flights of steps. I appear misty eyed and drunk and walk about in circles looking for exits and entrances.

Without the cane, who will understand me? But it will be another eighteen years before I receive proper Orientation and Mobility training. Before I will accept it.

* * *

In one of my last trips without a cane I visit the great Prado museum in Madrid, where I find I cannot see the famous paintings of Velázquez and Goya because they are hanging behind ropes that prohibit the vandals from drawing too close. Since I can't draw near, I see oceans of mud in vast gilded frames instead of the ceremonial world of court or the sprawl of lusty peasants.

I've waited years to get to the Prado, and now I'm wandering through its broad hallways thwarted by guards and ropes. Of course I should be carrying a white cane. But of course I'm carrying nothing except my sense of not-quite-belonging, which I'm fighting like a man swatting hornets.

At a souvenir counter I buy a museum guide—I'll read about the paintings I can't see—but the print is microscopic. Instead of a book, I find I'm holding a little cup full of sand.

The light in the Prado is alternately prismatic, then dark as a jail. I stand in the sunbeams under the oval skylights and watch the world break up into rainbows, then turn a corner into a great vaulted darkness, where an important painting hangs behind a veil, black as an abandoned lighthouse.

But I've traveled so far to see the paintings, and I hate to be circumscribed by tricks of the light, so I fall in with a group of American tourists. They are dutifully following a Spanish woman tour-guide who is describing paintings in the gallery at which I've arrived. But she spots me as an impostor, a freeloading listener, and as I strain to see the fetlock of a painted horse, she points me out to the group.

"This man is not in our tour," she says. "Sir, you will have to leave."

And I walk from the museum, a flapping windmill of a man, and find myself doing a muddy umbrella-dance in the icy wet park. Two students approach and ask if I'll buy a comic book to help disabled schoolchildren. I give them some money and think that some kid will get a break.

* * *

Dusk is the hour when I'm most likely to misjudge the speed and flow of traffic. It's rush hour—people hurrying home in the autumn rush hour, some on foot, some in cars. In such moments I often feel prematurely aged: I want some help in crossing the street. I want to reach for someone's arm.

Ironically, though, as things visual are in doubt, they grow in unconventional beauty. Dear Jackson Pollock, I've entered your *Autumn Rhythm.* The irregular or sometimes certain flight of color and shape is a wild skein, a tassel of sudden blue here, a wash of red. The very air has turned to hand-blown glass with its imperfect bubbles of amethyst or hazel blue. I stand on the ordinary street corner as if I've awakened at the bottom of a stemware vase. The glassblower's molten rose has landed in my eyes.

I shift my glasses—a slow moon rises on my path, things appear and disappear, and the days are like Zen-autumn.

* * *

A benevolent shakespeare professor finds me a reader. Enter Ramona, a classics major who comes in the afternoons three days a week.

We sit in a sunbeam in a steep room somewhere toward the rear of the library. It's a storage space, old encyclopedias line the shelves. The librarian thinks no one will hear Ramona reading to me in this spot. He's given us two wooden chairs. We stack our books on them and sit on the floor. Soon we have a blanket, which we assiduously roll up and store each night in a closet.

Ramona is a tremendous reader, the shadowy forms of things, ideas, gestalt, whatever, they move as she talks. Together we cross the ancient hot plateaus where words are as mighty as numbers. She reads Gilgamesh, the poems of the Cid. And flat on my back in that tall room, I never fall asleep. What stranger miracles are there? Sometimes she stops, and I learn not to interrupt her silence: she's performing a calculation. It's a lesson for me in absorption. My own nervousness tends to exclude such moments.

Oddly enough, eros, syllables, and alchemy are facts, particularly in the lives of young people. Beside Ramona, listening, my habitual shyness around women begins to fall away. Outside the library, I find myself conversing with my female classmates with ease. For the first time, I discover how conversations between men and women can be like warm soap dissolving in a bath.

In the old student pub—a dark cellar, I meet a strange new girl named Bettina. We talk and drink German beer. Bettina is a polymath, angry, rebelling against her father, who is an executive at a television network.

"The bastard, he'd have been comfortable during the Crusades!" she says, and stubs her cigarette out in an ashtray on the bar.

With this altogether irreverent young woman, I experience puppy love. She's an Irish country girl with long, thrilling, unkempt red hair. Red leaning back toward gold.

Bettina cooks spaghetti over a gas ring in a basement. (She never has an apartment of her own, instead she occupies other people's places without self-consciousness. She knows everyone.) I accept a glass of wine, I'm wrapped in earth tones and sparks. My hands stink of Gauloises cigarettes, my fingers spasm from the nicotine.

She squeezes the juice of a lemon into the salad. Puts Tabasco in the pasta sauce. She throws raw carrot chunks in there too.

"Why are you putting carrots in the tomato sauce? That's disgusting!"

"Oh, shut up, if you'd eaten more carrots, your eyes would be better."

"I ate lots of carrots! My eyes went bad from masturbation!"

"Well, maybe you don't need to do that anymore."

I can't speak, because she's kissing me. It's a potent kiss, her tongue is wet and vital in my mouth.

She draws me to the floor, pulls down my pants, guides me inside her. I can't believe how quickly she does it, my brain is still stuck on the word *carrot*.

She's on top, loosening buttons down the front of her black dress. As her breasts touch my outstretched hands, I come with every ounce of my viscera. I come the way all virgin-boys should—with surrender and reverence. I'm trying to say something.

"It's okay," she whispers. "I'm wearing a diaphragm."

I start to rise on my elbows.

"I'm sorry, I—"

"Shhhhh!"

Her face closes in, her red hair falls over my eyes, tickles, smells faintly of shampoo. She guides my fingers gently to her clitoris. She's an open meadow! A birch tree at midsummer, the sunlight seeming to be above and inside her.

Like all virgins, I'm a narcissist: surely no one has ever experienced this abundant wet circle of girl before? Not like this!

I'm on a rug in a spot of lamplight. The sauce simmers behind us. There's a clatter of water pipes, there are apartments above. Dishes rattle somewhere. Bettina is astride me, and leaning, she kisses me forcefully, filling my mouth with her sip of cabernet.

For the first time the vast silence that follows sex expands in my chest.

"I love you!" I say it. "I love you!"

I begin to cry. I who cannot see a woman's face, who can't look someone in the eye, I, I, who, what, never thought this could happen. I'm crying in earnest, copious sparkles.

"Shhhhh!"

She arches her back, I slip from her, a little fish, laughing and weeping.

Bettina refastens her dress, retrieves a tortoiseshell hair clasp, arranges it, sings very softly some lines from Yeats: "'Ah penny, brown penny, I am looped in the loops of her hair.'"

* * *

Nights. november. books. Smoke. Pierre Reverdy. Emily Dickinson. The windows open, a sweet smell of fallen leaves. I stroke Bettina's neck as she reads from Rexroth's Chinese poems: "'The same clear glory extends for ten thousand miles. The twilit trees are full of crows.'"

I'm unimaginably blessed. The crystallography of sharpened syntax, image, her voice behind it, wash of water on stones.

"'My soul wandered, happy, sad, unending.'" (Neruda)

"'The branches are dying of love.'" (Lorca)

"'Show me, dear Christ, thy spouse, so bright and clear.'" (Donne)

"'Here is the shadow of truth, for only the shadow is true.'" (Warren)

* * *

In the library Bettina finds a box of discarded records. These are Caedmon recordings of Yeats, an actor reading Baudelaire, poems by Carl Sandburg, John Crowe Ransom. The recordings are in miserable condition. And there at the bottom of the pile is a recorded bird-watching disk. A British narrator talks the listener through encounters with dozens of different birds. The birds sing on command, precise, silver, optimistic.

"Listen to the plover!" says the voice. "He's stirring on a spring morning!"

The plover obeys, lets loose its porous notes.

"Now the nightingale. Bird of poetry!"

The nightingale sounds brighter and better rested than the plover. Clearly it is a happy bird.

"The blackbird."

"The oriole."

In some places the needle sticks. The oriole hiccups over and over.

Here come the wild swans.

I'm completely jazzed: all my life I've been a stranger in this neighborhood. I've never seen a bird. Now, hearing them has made a place in my imagination. The birds! The damned birds! I've been missing out on something huge. But where are they?

Someone tells me about the ornithology collection in the biology building. I go there alone on a Saturday, when I know that the building will be deserted. The birds are arranged in display cases on both sides of the first-floor corridor. I press my nose to the glass specimen case and try not to breathe, for breathing fogs the glass. I see cocoon shapes, brown as cordovan shoes. These are the taxidermied and long-fallen members of the parliament, as strange to me as Roman coins and nails.

The labs are empty, the lights off. There is a hum of large refrigerators, a percolating sound. I tap the glass case with my forefinger, and it swings open as if by magic! Perhaps some student assistant has forgotten to lock the case!

Imagine never having seen a bird. And now your hands are free to explore the vagaries of the bird-tomb. How weightless they are, light as dinner rolls! But the feathers are stiff, almost lacquered, like the tiny ribs of a corset I once held in an antique shop. This can't be what a live bird's plumage would feel like. These birds are stiff, Victorian, spent.

But what a miracle of pipe stems and ligatures, the legs and wings joined with such supple delicacy.

I lift a large thing from its perch, hold it to my face, just barely making out its predatory look. A hawk? It's large as a basketball, light as a throwaway newspaper.

Here I am, twentysomething, standing in a deserted corridor, fondling birds. I feel like a frotteurist: a person who has orgasms from casual touch with strangers. I'm some kind of pervert, alone with these dead birds, running my hands over their heads, tracing their beaks with my fingernails. What if a security guard were to appear and ask me what I'm doing?

"I'm blind, sir, and this is my first experience with birds!"

"My name is Kid Geronimo, and I live in the elevator!"

"Have you ever touched a plover, sir?"

"My name is Wigglesworth, I'm searching for insects."

This is a lifelong habit, imaginary conversations with authority figures, usually when I'm touching something, when I'm on the verge of an understanding.

All the birds smell like vintage hats. As I run my hands over their prickly backs, I put names to them, since I have no idea what they are.

"Leather-breasted barnacle chomper."

"Blue-throated Javanese son of Zero."

Outside I sit under a tree and listen to the living catbirds, a thrush, the chickadee. What I wish for is to see a live bird. So one afternoon shortly thereafter, I convince my friend and teacher Jim Crenner to go bird-watching with me. Jim is a poet, a student of anything that possesses color. He is a mosaic man with a Peterson's guide and at least two pairs of binoculars.

We walk into a meadow, talking of poets, Leopardi, Rumi, Eliot.

Jim knows I can't see well but figures he can point me to colors, fix me on a glittering stone from Ravenna, a goldfinch on a fencepost.

"Hold still, right there is a fat finch big as a Spanish gold piece!" he says, whispering through his mustache, as if he were reading aloud in one of his classes.

"There's a red-winged blackbird."

"A vireo."

"A scarlet tanager."

How toothsome they all sound! How thrilling it must be to spy them on their April branches, blond chaff from the skies, afterthoughts of a blue atmosphere.

When I look through binoculars, I see a coral blue/green bubble, perhaps my own eye, but nothing like a bird. I can't quite bring myself to tell this to Jim, who is in a rapture of color and evolutionary wonder.

"To think these things evolved from primal mud without a god!" he says, alert to the sheer improbability of our planet. But by now I realize I am looking at the blue dish of self. My field glasses are trained on my own optic nerves.

I have a major bird thirst, something untranslatable, I can't share it, can't cry aloud at my frustration. Instead I pretend.

"Can you see him? He's right on that post, fat and horny," says Jim, and I look into my own dish of thickened green and say, "Look at him jump!" At the moment I say it, I mean it. I can see that bird hopping up and down, that goldfinch jumping like a penny on a railroad track.

I agree with everything Jim sees, adding my own intensifier and adjectives. I don't want to tell him I can't see the damned things, fearing it will make him self-conscious, for then our outing will become an exercise in description. He'll have to tell me what they look like. And I will have to appreciate them all the more. By pretending to see, I'm sparing us an ordeal. Sure I'm faking it with the binoculars, gloating over imaginary bluejays, but I'm alone with my own imagination, listening casually to an enthusiastic friend, my blindness locked away for the time.

I think Jim imagines I've seen some birds, and maybe I have.

List of Contributors

Michael Adams has served as Treasurer for People First Tameside and was a member of the Learning Disability Partnership Board.

Andrew Barber has served as Chairperson of People First Tameside and was on the European People First Committee.

Colin Barnes is a disabled writer and activist and Professor of Disability Studies in the Centre for Disability Studies, School of Sociology and Social Policy, University of Leeds, England.

Cynthia Barounis is a PhD candidate in English at the University of Illinois at Chicago where she is writing a dissertation on the representational intersections of queerness and disability in twentieth-century American literature and culture. Her work has appeared in *The Journal of Visual Culture* and the *Journal of Medical Humanities*.

Douglas Baynton teaches history and American Sign Language at the University of Iowa. He is the author of *Forbidden Signs: American Culture and the Campaign Against Sign Language* (Chicago, 1996), and co-author, with Jack Gannon and Jean Bergey, of *Through Deaf Eyes: A Photographic History of an American Community* (Gallaudet UP, 2007).

The late **Chris Bell** was a Postdoctoral Research Fellow in the Center on Human Policy, Law, and Disability Studies at Syracuse University. His chief research and teaching interest was the constructed nature of disability studies; who is represented in the discipline, who is not, and how privileges and exclusions operate within the discipline.

Kathy Boxall has worked at Manchester University. She now works at Sheffield University.

Brenda Brueggemann is a Professor of English & Disability Studies at Ohio State University. She is the author of 3 books: *Lend Me Your Ear: Rhetorical Constructions of Deafness; Rhetorical Visions: Reading and Writing in a Visual Culture* (with Wendy Hesford); *Deaf Subjects: Between Identities and Places*. She has also edited or co-edited 5 different book collections featuring work in disability studies and/or deaf studies.

James Charlton is a longtime political activist. He helped found Access Living, one of the country's leading centers for independent living in 1979. He has taught social theory and political economy classes for graduate students in Disability Studies at the University of Illinois since 2000.

His most recent book *Nothing About Us Without Us: Disability, Oppression and Empowerment* (University of California Press) was published in 1998.

Writer and activist, **Eli Clare** has a B.A. in Women's Studies, a M.F.A. in Creative Writing, and most importantly a penchant for rabble-rousing. Among other pursuits, he has walked across the United States for peace, coordinated a rape prevention program, and helped organize the first ever Queerness and Disability Conference. He has spoken all over the United States at conferences, community events, and colleges about disability, queer and trans identities, and social justice. Eli is the author of a book of essays *Exile and Pride: Disability, Queerness, and Liberation* (South End Press, 1999, 2009) and a collection of poetry *The Marrow's Telling: Words in Motion* (Homofactus Press, 2007) and has been published in many periodicals and anthologies.

Lerita M. Coleman Brown is Ayse I. Carden Distinguished Professor of Psychology and Director of the GEMS (Generating Excellence in Science and Math) program at Agnes Scott College in Decatur, Georgia. Professor Brown's early studies centered on nonverbal behavior (particularly communicated toward stigmatized individuals) but other research ranges from women, work and aging to stigma, identity and self-concept. Her recently published essay entitled, "Advising a Diverse Student Body: Lessons I've Learned from Trading Places" appears in the journal, *Liberal Education*.

David Corbett has been a member of the Steering Group for the BA Learning Disability Studies at Manchester University.

G. Thomas Couser is a professor of English and founding director of the Disability Studies program at Hofstra University. He is the author of *American Autobiography: The Prophetic Mode* (Massachusetts, 1979), *Altered Egos: Authority in American Autobiography* (Oxford, 1989), *Recovering Bodies: Illness, Disability, and Life Writing* (Wisconsin, 1997), *Vulnerable Subjects: Ethics and Life Writing* (Cornell, 2004), and *Signifying Bodies: Disability in Contemporary Life Writing* (Michigan, 2009), as well as about fifty articles or book chapters. He is currently writing a book about contemporary American "patriography" (memoirs of fathers by sons and daughters) and a memoir of his own father.

Michael Davidson is Professor of Literature at the University of California, San Diego. He has written extensively on disability issues, most recently "Hearing Things: The Scandal of Speech in Deaf Performance," in *Disability Studies: Enabling the Humanities*, Ed. Sharon Snyder, et al. (Modern Language Association, 2002), "Phantom Limbs: Film Noir and the Disabled Body," *GLQ* 9:1–2 (2003), and "Strange Blood: Hemophobia and the Unexplored Boundaries of Queer Nation," in *Beyond the Boundary: Reconstructing Cultural Identity in a Multicultural Context*, edited by Timothy Powell (Rutgers UP, 1999). His latest book is *Concerto for the Left Hand: Disability and the Defamiliar Body* (U of Michigan, 2008).

Lennard J. Davis is Distinguished Professor of Disability and Human Development, English, and Medical Education at the University of Illinois at Chicago. He is the author of among other works *Enforcing Normalcy: Disability, Deafness, and the Body* (Verso 1995*)*; *Bending Over Backwards: Disability, Dismodernism, and Other Difficult Positions* (New York UP); *My Sense of Silence: Memoirs of a Childhood with Deafness*; *Obsession: A History* (U of Chicago); and *Go Ask Your Father: One Man's Obsession With*

Finding His Origins Though DNA Testing (Bantam). He edited *Shall I Say A Kiss: The Courtship Letters of a Deaf Couple, 1936–1938* and he is currently writing a book on the relationship between the sciences and the humanities.

Daniel Docherty co-founded the Steering Group for the BA Learning Disability Studies at Manchester University and has contributed to Steering Group meetings for the last nine years. He has also co-authored several publications with lecturers at Manchester University.

R. A. R. Edwards is an associate professor of history at the Rochester Institute of Technology. She is the author of numerous essays on Deaf history. Her forthcoming book, Words Made Flesh: Deafness, Disability, and Education (New York UP), explores the rise of Deaf culture in the United States in the nineteenth century. She is currently at work on a project exploring the lives of the Deaf baseball players, William Hoy and Luther Taylor.

Anne Finger has taught creative writing at Wayne State University in Detroit and at the University of Texas at Austin. She is the author of several books, including the memoir *Elegy for a Disease: A Personal and Cultural History of Polio*; *Bone Truth: A Novel*; and *Basic Skills: A Short Story Collection*.

Kenny Fries is the author of *The History of My Shoes and the Evolution of Darwin's Theory*, which received the 2007 Outstanding Book Award from the Gustavus Myers Center for the Study of Bigotry and Human Rights, and *Body, Remember: A Memoir*. He is the editor of *Staring Back: The Disability Experience from the Inside Out*. His books of poems include *Anesthesia* and *Desert Walking*. He has been a Creative Arts Fellow of the Japan/US Friendship Commission and the National Endowment for the Arts, a Fulbright Scholar to Japan, and is a 2009 grantee for innovative literature from the Creative Capital Foundation. He teaches in the MFA in Creative Writing Program at Goddard College.

Rosemarie Garland-Thomson is Professor of Women's Studies at Emory University in Atlanta, Georgia. Her fields of study are feminist theory, American literature, and disability studies. She is the author *of Extraordinary Bodies: Figuring Physical Disability in American Literature and Culture* (Columbia UP), editor of *Freakery: Cultural Spectacles of the Extraordinary Body* (New York UP), and co-editor of *Disability Studies: Enabling the Humanities* (MLA Press). Her most recent book is *Staring: How We Look* (Oxford UP, 2009).

Faye Ginsburg is David B. Kriser Professor of Anthropology at New York University. She has co-edited several books including, *Media Worlds: Anthropology on New Terrain* (2002), *9/11 and After, A Virtual Case Book* (2002), *Conceiving the New World Order: The Global Politics of Reproduction* (1995), and *Uncertain Terms: Negotiating Gender in American Culture* (1990). She is the author of *Contested Lives: The Abortion Debate in an American Community* (1989) as well as the forthcoming book *Mediating Culture: Indigenous Identity in a Digital Age* (Duke UP).

Ruth Hubbard is Professor Emerita of Biology at Harvard University. Her work in the fields of biology, biochemistry and photochemistry has focused on the relationship between biology and women and the relevant issues of disability. She is the author of *The Politics of Women's Biology* (Rutgers UP) and co-author with Elijah Wald of *Exploding the Gene Myth: How*

Genetic Information is Produced and Manipulated by Scientists, Physicians, Employers, Insurance Companies, Educators, and Law Enforcers (Beacon Press).

Richard Hughes has been a member of Manchester People First since 1992. For the last nine years he has been on the Steering Group for the BA Learning Disability Studies at Manchester University.

Tom Humphries is Associate Director and Associate Professor of Education Studies and Associate Professor in the Department of Communication at the University of California, San Diego.

Shayma Izzidien has worked at Manchester University. She now works at the Institute of Education, University of London.

Ian Kaplan has worked at Manchester University. He now works at Leeds Metropolitan University.

Eunjung Kim is Assistant Professor in the Department of Gender and Women's Studies, Department of Rehabilitation Psychology and Special Education at the University of Wisconsin at Madison. Initiative at Emory University. Her main interest is in disabled women's issues in Korea and their experiences of marginalization, the politics of cultural representations, and inter-minority political conflicts and activism. She published essays on the topics of Korean disabled women's movement history, Hansen's Disease and gender, minority politics, asexuality and co-published on postcolonial transactions of disability and sexuality in film.

Georgina Kleege teaches disability studies and creative writing at the University of California, Berkeley. Her recent books include: *Sight Unseen* and *Blind Rage, Letters to Helen Keller.*

Petra Kuppers is a disability culture activist, a community artist, and Associate Professor in the English Department at the University of Michigan. She is also the Artistic Director of The Olimpias (www.olimpias.org). Her books include *Disability and Contemporary Performance: Bodies on Edge* (Routledge, 2003), *The Scar of Visibility: Medical Performances and Contemporary Arts* (Minnesota UP, 2007), and *Community Performance: An Introduction* (Routledge, 2007). Together with Neil Marcus and photographer Lisa Steichmann, she published *Cripple Poetics: A Love Story* (Homofactus Press, 2008).

Steve Kuusisto teaches in the graduate creative nonfiction program at the University of Iowa. He writes daily on disability and public policy on his blog: www.planet-of-the-blind.com

Emmanuelle Laborit, the author of *The Cry of the Gull* (Gallaudet UP), is the recipient of the Moliere award for best actress in *Beyond Silence.*

Harlan Lane is the author of numerous articles in professional journals concerning speech, language, and Deaf history and culture. Among his books are *The Wild Boy of Aveyron: Foundations of Special Education* (Harvard UP); *When the Mind Hears: A History of the Deaf* (Random House); *The Mask of Benevolence: Disabling the Deaf Community* (Alfred Knopf); *A Journey into the Deaf-World* (with R. Hoffmeister & B. Bahan; Dawn Sign Press); and *A Deaf Artist in Early America: The Worlds of John Brewster Jr.* (Beacon Press). His honorary awards include the International Social Merit Award of the World Federation of the Deaf; the John D. and Catherine T. MacArthur Foundation

Fellowship, the Distinguished Service and Literary Achievement Awards of the National Association of the Deaf, and the Order of Academic Palms from the French government. He is currently Distinguished University Professor at Northeastern University.

Bradley Lewis, MD, PhD is associate professor at NYU's Gallatin School of Individualized Study with affiliated appointments in the Department of Social and Cultural Analysis and the Department of Psychiatry. He has dual training in humanities and medicine (with a psychiatric specialty), and he writes and teaches at the interface of medicine, humanities, cultural studies, and disability studies. Lewis is the author of *Moving Beyond Prozac, DSM, and the New Psychiatry: Birth of Postpsychiatry* and an associate editor for the *Journal of Medical Humanities.*

Simi Linton is the President of Disability/ Arts and the author of My Body Politic, Claiming Disability: Knowledge and Identity, as well as numerous articles on disability studies, and disability and the arts. She is Co-director of the University Seminar in Disability Studies at Columbia University.

Neil Marcus: actor. poet. writer. butoh dancer. contact improvisational lover. Berkeley citizen who works with this key idea: disability is not a brave struggle or courage in the face of adversity, disability is an art. Neil performed his show Storm Reading over 300 times across the world, and has acted in many other productions, including an episode of ER. Together with Petra Kuppers and photographer Lisa Steichmann, he published *Cripple Poetics: A Love Story* (Homofactus Press, 2008).

Harriet McBryde Johnson was a lawyer, writer, and disability activist. Her writing on disability has appeared in numer-

ous publications including *New Mobility, South Carolina Lawyer, Review of Public Personnel Administration,* and the *New York Times.* She is the author of the memoir *Too Late to Die Young: Nearly True Tales from a Life* (2005) and the novel *Accidents of Nature* (2006).

Robert McRuer is Professor of English at The George Washington University in Washington, DC, where he teaches critical theory, queer studies, and disability studies. He is the author of *Crip Theory: Cultural Signs of Queerness and Disability* (New York UP, 2006), which won the Alan Bray Memorial Book Award; and *The Queer Renaissance: Contemporary American Literature and the Reinvention of Lesbian and Gay Identity* (New York UP, 1997). With Abby L. Wilkerson, he co-edited *Desiring Disability: Queer Theory Meets Disability Studies* (Duke UP, 2003), which appeared as a special issue of *GLQ: A Journal of Lesbian and Gay Studies* (and was named Best Special Issue by the Council of Editors of Learned Journals). He is also co-editor, with Anna Mollow, of the forthcoming volume *Sex and Disability.* His articles have appeared in *Radical History Review, PMLA, Genders,* the *Journal of Medical Humanities* and numerous other locations.

Ann Millett-Gallant is a lecturer for the University of North Carolina at Greensboro, where she teaches art history and liberal studies courses. Her research, like her teaching, crosses the disciplines of art history and disability studies. She has published a number of journal articles on the work of disabled artists and on the representation of disability in visual culture, as well as several art and film reviews. She is also an amateur artist who enjoys painting, drawing, and performance art.

David Mitchell is the executive director of the Institute on Disabilities at Temple

University in the College of Education. To date, he has edited three books on disability culture and history including *The Body and Physical Difference* (1997). He has also co-written two books including *Narrative Prosthesis* (2000). He is co-editor of *Encyclopedia of Disability* (2006). He has served as president of the Society of Disability Studies and was a founding member of both the Committee on Disability and the Disability Studies Discussion Group for the Modern Language Association.

Anna Mollow is a Ph.D. candidate in English at the University of California, Berkeley, where she is writing a dissertation on literature and medicine. Her work in disability studies has appeared in *MELUS* and *Michigan Quarterly Review*.

Carol Padden is professor in the Department of Communication at UC, San Diego. In addition to *Inside Deaf Culture*, she and Tom Humphries are also the authors of *Deaf in America: Voices from a Culture*.

Patricia Phillips has been a member of Manchester People First and was on the Steering Group for the BA Learning Disability Studies at Manchester University.

Catherine Prendergast is Professor of English, University Scholar, and Director of First Year Rhetoric at the University of Illinois at Urbana-Champaign. A member of the editorial board of the *Journal of Literary and Cultural Disability Studies*, she has published articles related to disability in *American Literary History*, *South Atlantic Quarterly*, *JLCDS*, and *College English*. Her books include *Buying into English: Language and Investment in the New Capitalist World* (Pittsburgh, 2008), and *Literacy and Racial Justice: The Politics of Learning after Brown v.*

Board of Education (Southern Illinois, 2003).

Ato Quayson is Professor of English and Director of the Centre for Diaspora and Transnational Studies at the University of Toronto, where he has been since August 2005. He is the author of *Strategic Transformations in Nigerian Writing* (2000), *Postcolonialism: Theory, Practice or Process?* (2002), *Calibrations: Reading for the Social* (2003), and, most recently, *Aesthetic Nervousness: Disability and the Crisis of Representation* (2007)

Rayna Rapp is a professor of anthropology at New York University. She is the author of *Testing Women, Testing the Fetus: The Social Impact of Amniocentesis in America* (1999) and co-editor of *Conceiving the New World Order: The Global Politics of Reproduction* (1995).

Brendan Regan has been a member of Bury People First and was on the Steering Group for the BA Learning Disability Studies at Manchester University.

Marsha Saxton, Ph.D. teaches Disability Studies at the University of California, Berkeley. She is Director of Research and Training at the World Institute on Disability, in Oakland, CA. She has published extensively about disability rights, women's health, health care disparities, abuse and violence prevention and genetic screening issues. She has been a board member of the Our Bodies, Ourselves Collective and the National Institutes of Health (NIH) Ethical, Legal Social Implications (ELSI) Working Group of the Human Genome Initiative. Her new book is *Sticks and Stones: Disabled People's Stories of Abuse, Defiance and Resilience*, www.wid.org/cape.

Tom Shakespeare is principal research associate in sociology, University of

Newcastle. His books include *The Sexual Politics of Disability*, *Genetic Politics: from Eugenics to Genome* and *Disability Rights and Wrongs*. He writes and broadcasts widely on disability and genetics and he is a member of the Arts Council of England.

Mark Sherry is an Assistant Professor of Sociology at The University of Toledo. He has published three books and is currently working on a fourth book on disability hate crimes.

Tobin Siebers is V. L. Parrington Collegiate Professor, Professor of English and Art and Design at the University of Michigan. He has been a fellow of the Michigan Society of Fellows and the John Simon Memorial Guggenheim Foundation and a Visiting Scholar at the Ecole Polytechnique in Paris. His major publications include *The Mirror of Medusa* (California 1983), *The Romantic Fantastic* (Cornell 1984), *The Ethics of Criticism* (Cornell 1988), *Morals and Stories* (Columbia 1992), *Cold War Criticism and the Politics of Skepticism* (Oxford 1993), *The Subject and Other Subjects: On Ethical, Aesthetic, and Political Identity* (Michigan 1998), *Among Men* (Nebraska 1999), *Disability Theory* (Michigan 2008), *Zerbrochene Schönheit* (Transcript 2008) and *Disability Aesthetics* (Michigan, forthcoming 2010). He is also the editor of *Religion and the Authority of the Past* (Michigan 1993), (Michigan 1994), and *The Body Aesthetic: From Fine Art to Body Modification* (Michigan 2000). His recent work on disability studies has been published in *American Literary History*, *Cultural Critique*, *Literature and Medicine*, *Journal for Cultural and Religious Theory*, *Michigan Quarterly Review*, *PMLA*, and the MLA volume on disability studies. He is currently at work on a book about disability in the history of art.

Marquard Smith is Director of the Institute for Modern and Contemporary Culture at University of Westminster, London, and Founder and Editor-in-Chief of Journal of Visual Culture. Marq publishes widely on the visual and cultural study of bodies, technologies, and sexualities in Modernity. Editor and co-editor of over twenty collections and themed issues of journals on subjects such as disability-visuality, prosthesis, and the performance artist Stelarc, he has monographs forthcoming from Yale UP (on eroticism and hetero-sexuality) and Reaktion Books (on bio art).

Sharon Snyder is the co-author of two books including *Cultural Locations of Disability* (2005), and co-editor of three collections including *Eugenics in America* (2005) and *Disability Studies: Enabling the Humanities* (2003) and *Encyclopedia of Disability* (2006). As founder of the independent production company, Brace Yourselves Productions, she is also an award-winning documentary filmmaker whose work includes *Self-Preservation: The Art of Riva Lehrer* (2004), *Disability Takes on the Arts* (2005), *A World Without Bodies* (2002), and *Vital Signs: Crip Culture Strikes Back* (1996).

Susan Sontag was the author of four novels, five books of essays, and several plays, among them *On Photography* (Picador), *Against Interpretation: And Other Essays* (Picador), and *Illness as Metaphor* (Vintage).

Joseph N. Straus is Distinguished Professor of Music at the Graduate Center, City University of New York. He is the author of numerous books and articles on music since 1900 and is a former president of the Society for Music Theory. His most recent publications, including the co-edited collection *Sounding Off: Theorizing Disability in Music* (Routledge, 2006), are among the first to bring the insights of disability studies to music. He is currently completing a book on music and disability.

Cheryl Marie Wade is a poet, playwright, videomaker, and performer. She is the editor of *Gnarlybone News*, a free online "cut and paste" disability culture newsletter. Her performance video "Body Talk" received an Award of Achievement from Superfest XXI. She is the recipient of the 1994 National Endowment of the Arts Solo Theater Artist's Fellowship and the CeCe Robinson Award for disability writing and performing.

Susan Wendell is Professor Emerita of Women's Studies at Simon Fraser University. She is author of *The Rejected Body: Feminist Philosophical Reflections on Disability* (Routledge) and is currently writing a book on the value of suffering and the ethics of disability.

Edward Wheatley is the Edward L. Surtz, S. J. Professor of Medieval Literature at Loyola University, Chicago. His most recent book, *Stumbling Blocks Before the Blind: Medieval Constructions of a Disability*, is part of the University of Michigan Press series "Corporealities: Discourses of Disability." He is a member of the editorial board of *Disability Studies Quarterly* and participates in programming for CripSlam Sundays, part of Chicago's Access Project, which involves people with disabilities in all aspects of theater, both on and off the stage.

James C. Wilson is professor of English at the University of Cincinnati. His recent books include *Weather Reports from the Autism Front: A Father's Memoir of His Autistic Son* (McFarland, 2008) and *Embodied Rhetorics: Disability in Language and Culture* (Southern Illinois UP, 2001), which he co-edited with Cynthia Lewiecki-Wilson. He has disability related essays in *Cultural Critique*, *DSQ*, and *Disability Studies: Enabling the Humanities* (Modern Language Association, 2002).

Credit Lines

Index

University Readers™
Reading Materials Evolved.

Introducing the

SOCIAL ISSUES COLLECTION

A Routledge/University Readers Custom Library for Teaching

Customizing course material for innovative and excellent teaching in sociology has never been easier or more effective!

Choose from a collection of more than 300 readings from Routledge, Taylor & Francis, and other publishers to make a custom anthology that suits the needs of your social problems/ social inequality, and social issues courses.

All readings have been aptly chosen by academic editors and our authors and organized by topic and author.

Online tool makes it easy for busy instructors:

1. Simply select your favorite Routledge and Taylor & Francis readings, and add any other required course material, including your own.

2. Choose the order of the readings, pick a binding, and customize a cover.

3. One click will post your materials for students to buy. They can purchase print or digital packs, and we ship direct to their door within two weeks of ordering!

More information at www.socialissuescollection.com

Contact information: Call your Routledge sales rep, or
Becky Smith at University Readers, 800-200-3908 ext. 18, bsmith@universityreaders.com
Steve Rutter at Routledge, 207-434-2102, Steve.Rutter@taylorandfrancis.com.

Routledge
Taylor & Francis Group
an **informa** business